The Political Map of Britain

The Political
Map of Britain

Simon Henig and Lewis Baston

First published in Great Britain 2002
by Politico's Publishing
8 Artillery Row
London
SW1P 1RZ
www.politicos.co.uk/publishing

Printed and bound in Great Britain by Bell & Bain Ltd., Glasgow

Contents

Preface

The purpose of this book is to provide an analysis of Britain's electoral and political geography following the 2001 general election; although mainly narrative the aim is to describe *The Political Map of Britain* in all its detail across the many component nations, regions and counties of the United Kingdom. We were inspired by the example of Henry Pelling's informative and well-researched journey through the politics of Britain at the turn of the last century in his *Social Geography of British Elections 1885-1910*. Pelling's book illustrated, through text, tables and maps, the distinctive features of each constituency while presenting an overview of national electoral trends. We hope that this book does the same at the dawn of a new millennium.

Pelling's study covered a period when the two major parties were the Liberals and Conservatives, with an upstart infant called the Labour Party beginning to challenge in a few areas. Since that time, Labour have grown into a national party of government and the Liberals have waned (and started to rise again), though it is striking how many features of Britain's political map have persisted over the last hundred years. Aside from the comparatively recent emergence of nationalist parties in Wales and Scotland, no new party has broken the 'mould' of British politics for three-quarters of a century, and many areas which were strongly Conservative in 1900 remained so in 2001. These and other patterns are picked out and analysed in the chapters which follow and we hope that the reader finds what follows informative and on occasion even entertaining. This volume also provides a welcome opportunity to detail the composition of the many county, district and unitary councils up and down the country, an often neglected but nevertheless crucial part of our political map. Another feature which we hope the reader finds useful are our tables of constituency election results over the last three general elections, which allow an analysis of change in Britain's political map over the period in which 'New Labour' was created and rose to government. In our county summaries we have taken this data back to 1983 when Labour were at their lowest ebb and Margaret Thatcher's Conservatives at their most dominant.

Sadly, readers will be struck in the constituency tables by the precipitous decline in voter turnout from 1992, which has averaged nearly twenty percentage points across the UK. Like most others, the authors hope this is a temporary phenomenon, while fearing that it may be a rather more permanent feature of the political terrain. If so it is incumbent on all those engaged in the political process to try to make politics and elections more interesting and if this book contributes in any way to that cause then it will have proved a worthwhile project.

Simon Henig
Lewis Baston
May 2002

Notes on authors
and contributors

Simon Henig is a lecturer in Politics at the University of Sunderland. He was co-author with Lewis Baston of *Politico's Guide to the General Election* (Politico's Publishing, 2000) and with Ruth Henig of *Women and Political Power: Europe since 1945* (Routledge, 2000). He has also written on constituency campaigning in the 1997 general election and 1994 European election campaigns, while his (unpublished) D.Phil thesis at Nuffield College, Oxford, covered regional variations in voting behaviour across Great Britain from 1955 to 1992. This book has allowed him to combine at least two of his three great interests, politics and maps, though as a Leicester City supporter he has wisely kept references to his third - the great game of football - to a minimum.

Lewis Baston is senior research fellow at CUSP (Centre for the Understanding of Society and Politics) at Kingston University. As well as co-authoring *Politico's Guide to the General Election*, he is author of *Sleaze*, co-author (with Brian Brivati) of the forthcoming T*he Future Labour Offered You* and associate author (under Anthony Seldon) of *Major: A Political Life*. He has also written chapters in academic books on several aspects of Labour Party history and is currently writing a life of Reginald Maudling. Also a devotee of politics and maps, he has enjoyed the opportunity to travel around Britain in the interests of research. While he hopes to return to some places at leisure to appreciate architecture, second hand bookshops and rural beauty, he intends never again to set foot in several towns whose identities should be clearly identifiable from the text.

Roger Mortimore (Regional Trends – the Opinion Polls) is MORI's Senior Political Analyst, concentrating on political and constitutional research as well as on opinion polling methodology. He was extensively involved with MORI's election opinion polling in 1997 and 2001, in particular with the Independent Television News (ITN) exit polls. Prior to joining MORI in 1993, he was researching the British electoral system at University College, Oxford, where he was awarded a D.Phil; he also worked as research assistant to David Butler for the Nuffield College study of the British General Election of 1992. He was co-author with Robert M Worcester of *Explaining Labour's Landslide* (Politico's Publishing, 1999), and of *Explaining Labour's Second Landslide* (Politico's Publishing, 2001) and with Dick Leonard of *Elections in Britain – A Voter's Guide* (Palgrave, 2001).

Russell Deacon (Wales) is a senior lecturer in Government and Politics at the University of Wales Institute Cardiff. He has also worked as a researcher in the National Assembly for Wales, and has on occasion been an electoral adviser to BBC Wales, HTV and ITN. Dr Deacon has written widely on issues concerning Welsh government, politics and elections, most recently *Devolved Great Britain* (with

Peter Lynch and Dylan Griffiths) and *The Governance of Wales: The Welsh Office and the Policy Process 1964-1999*. He is currently researching the history of the Welsh Liberal Party.

Mark Stuart (Scotland) is a graduate of Aberdeen University. Since 1994 he has worked as a researcher for three of Britain's leading political scientists: Lord Norton of Louth (Hull), Professor David Denver (Lancaster) and Philip Cowley (Hull). In 1998 he published *The Public Servant*, an authorised biography of Douglas Hurd. He is currently researching parliamentary voting behaviour in the first two Labour governments, 1924 and 1929-31.

Sydney Elliott (Northern Ireland) is a senior lecturer at the School of Politics, Queen's University Belfast. He is author of *Northern Ireland: A Political Directory 1968-97* and co-author of *Northern Ireland: The District Council Elections of 1989* and a similar volume for 1993.

Acknowledgements

The authors owe a debt of gratitude to many people (probably running into the hundreds) who provided information or anecdotes for this huge project, from Members of Parliament and full time party staff to candidates, journalists, people who gave tours and those with no political connections but a genuine interest in their local area. Although we feel we cannot individually name all those people who assisted us, we would like to give particular thanks to Colin Rallings and Michael Thrasher, whose meticulous compilations of national and local election results provide great assistance not only to this, but many other studies of British electoral behaviour. We would also like to praise the many local authority web sites (particularly those with ward maps and archived election results) which made our task much more straightforward. We would like to acknowledge the *Independent* their constituency map, MORI for the reproduction of opinion poll data and Iain Dale and John Berry at Politico's for coming up with the idea of this volume and helping us see it through to its conclusion.

The research and production of this book took a great deal of time and effort and led to a number of missed or delayed meetings and appointments (not to mention harassed or obsessive behaviour from the authors when they did finally turn up), and we would like to thank the forbearance of our friends and colleagues for putting up with us over this period. This applies most of all to our partners, Katherine and Hannah, to whom we dedicate this book.

General elections 1945-2001

5 July 1945

		MPs	Vote (%)
Conservative	Winston Churchill	213	39.8
Labour	Clement Attlee	393	47.8
Liberal	Archibald Sinclair	12	9.0
Others		22	
Turnout			72.7

Labour majority 146

Before 1997, Labour always looked to 1945 as being an all-time peak. The election followed the dissolution of the wartime coalition which Churchill had led since 1940 and the Conservatives hoped that their leader's prestige would carry the party to victory. Electoral studies were in their infancy, so the record of gains by left wing Independents during the war, and the findings of Gallup's opinion polls also suggesting a Labour victory, were ignored by most observers. When the votes were counted Labour had won their first ever outright majority, by a massive margin on a very large swing since the previous election in 1935.

Labour's gains came all over the country. Some of the most dramatic swings were in the former Conservative stronghold of Birmingham and the party also surged to victory in seats across inner London (Hackney for instance) where Labour had never won before and were never to lose again. Labour won a succession of victories in agricultural areas in eastern England, winning four out of five rural seats in Norfolk for instance. However, the Conservative heartlands of the London suburbs and rural areas in the midlands and south tended to stay with the Tories, as did almost all the seaside resorts and the most affluent urban areas like Bristol West and Manchester Withington. Most of Labour's postwar generation of leaders were first elected in this election, including Hugh Gaitskell (Leeds South), Harold Wilson (Ormskirk), Jim Callaghan (Cardiff South), Michael Foot (Plymouth Devonport) and George Brown (Belper).

23 February 1950

		MPs	Vote (%)
Conservative	Winston Churchill	298	43.5
Labour	Clement Attlee	315	46.1
Liberal	Clement Davies	9	9.1
Others		3	
Turnout			84.0

Labour majority 5

Labour approached the 1950 election with some confidence because of its record in government since 1945, but the Conservatives were also ready for battle after several years of organisational and ideological renewal. Turnout in 1950 was the highest under a universal franchise. The Liberals attempted to fight on a wide front but they were squeezed out and lost 319 deposits out of 478 contests. The result was something of a disappointment to all parties, and Labour formed a second term government with a precarious parliamentary position.

Labour's position in 1945 had been inflated by victories in small depopulated urban constituencies such as those in London's East End, but by 1950 a radical boundary review had merged them into fewer seats. The Tories' loss of the special university seats did not offset this much. Labour were also unlucky in that the swing to the Conservatives was concentrated where it could do most damage – in the middle class suburbs which Labour had won only narrowly in 1945. Several of these Conservative gains provided the leadership of the party for the next quarter century – Edward Heath won Bexley, Reggie Maudling won Barnet and Iain Macleod won Enfield West. Enoch Powell won Wolverhampton South West. By contrast, Labour's support in working class areas was hardly changed since 1945 and enormous majorities were racked up in some mining seats – over 30,000 in six seats including an astonishing 37,680 lead in Hemsworth. Labour suffered from the electoral system in 1950 because votes were piled up in such strongholds. After the 1945 landslide there were few opportunities for notable Labour entrants, although Tony Crosland won Gloucestershire South.

25 October 1951

		MPs	Vote (%)
Conservative	Winston Churchill	321	48.0
Labour	Clement Attlee	295	48.8
Liberal	Clement Davies	6	2.5
Others		3	
Turnout			82.5

Conservative majority 17

The Labour government carried on for eighteen months with its tiny majority before Attlee, rather unnecessarily as a courtesy to the dying King, called a general election. It was a repeat of the 1950 battle in seeing a close contest between the two main parties which aroused massive participation by the electorate, but the Liberals could not find anyone to insure them against lost deposits because of the experience of the previous election. They only stood in 109 seats, and their withdrawal helped the Conservatives to gain just enough seats for a workable overall majority. Local electoral pacts were formed between Liberals and Tories in Bolton and Huddersfield.

The electoral system was again biased against Labour, who polled more votes than the Tories because of monolithic support in working class areas. Labour hung on better than expected in the marginal seats, and even made a couple of gains from the Liberals in Wales (radical Liberal voters disliked the party's increasingly pro-Tory stand), but it was not enough. The overall movement between the parties was very small – the smallest at any election since 1910 – and nationally quite uniform. A footnote to the 1951 election is that it was the first occasion on which the parties made televised party election broadcasts. The very small 'class of 1951' included Cledwyn Hughes (Lab, Anglesey), Tony Barber (Con, Doncaster) and Ted Short (Lab, Newcastle Central).

26 May 1955

		MPs	Vote (%)
Conservative	Anthony Eden	344	49.7
Labour	Clement Attlee	277	46.4
Liberal	Clement Davies	6	2.7
Others		3	
Turnout			76.7

Conservative majority 58

After the excitement and mass interest of the 1950 and 1951 elections, the 1955 campaign was a boring and predictable affair; arousing interest was not helped by a press strike that closed down Fleet Street for much of the election period. Turnout fell significantly and the new Conservative Prime Minister Anthony Eden won an increased majority. Labour's vote, however, held relatively solid and their national share of 46.4 per cent has only been exceeded on one occasion since. The Tories achieved as near to an overall majority of the vote as any party has managed since before the war. An observer at the time called the 1955 election 'just a national census to see who's Labour and who's Conservative.' The movement from Labour to Conservative was relatively uniform nationally. Many of the marginals Labour clung onto in 1951, such as Watford, now fell to the Tories, although there were slight deviations to Labour in agricultural areas and to the Tories in the most modern industrial areas like Coventry and Middlesbrough. There were few notable changes to the membership of the House, although Willie Whitelaw (Penrith and the Border) and Richard Body (Billericay) joined the Conservative benches.

8 October 1959

		MPs	Vote (%)
Conservative	Harold Macmillan	365	49.4
Labour	Hugh Gaitskell	258	43.8
Liberal	Jo Grimond	6	5.9
Others		1	
Turnout			78.8

Conservative majority 100

The 1959 election was a more exciting competition than 1955 – Labour's campaign was reinvigorated by Hugh Gaitskell and Tony Benn, who oversaw the party's modernised election campaigning. The Conservatives were initially wrong-footed but plugged away on their best issue of prosperity ('most of our people have never had it so good' as Macmillan said in 1957) and counterattacked on the cost of Labour's promises. 1959 was the first election at which there was substantial television news coverage of the campaign and the results.

When the votes were counted, the Conservative majority edged up into three figures. The swing was less uniform than in 1955 but still pretty consistent by more recent standards despite regional variations. The Conservatives did particularly well in the midlands, including Birmingham and Leicester. They gained several seats in 1959 which they have never come close to winning since, such as Birmingham Sparkbrook, Hartlepool and Newcastle East (all coincidentally the seats of prominent Labour personalities in recent years). The Tories also did surprisingly well in the seats swollen by New Town development such as Epping (Harlow) and Billericay (Basildon). Labour, however, increased their support against the national tide in Scotland and the Manchester area, gaining several seats. The Liberals started to revive from their 1950s nadir, with Jeremy Thorpe's gain in North Devon and an increase in their vote nationally. This election also saw the entry to parliament of Margaret Thatcher (Finchley), plus soulmates Nicholas Ridley (Cirencester & Tewkesbury) and Teddy Taylor (Glasgow Cathcart).

15 October 1964

		MPs	Vote (%)
Conservative	Alec Douglas-Home	304	43.4
Labour	Harold Wilson	317	44.1
Liberal	Jo Grimond	9	11.2
Others		0	
Turnout			77.1

Labour majority 4

The 1964 election was a close battle between Labour and the Conservatives. Labour were more united and effective under Harold Wilson, while the Conservatives seemed tired and out of touch and were tarred with the Profumo scandal. A second front had opened against them with the revival of the Liberals. However, the Tories put up a strong fight based on Britain's prosperity and their experience in foreign affairs, and the result was a very near thing.

The 1964 election saw more uneven results than 1959. Labour surged in the Liverpool area, gaining four seats on above-average swings as Protestant voters deserted the Conservatives; the Liverpool Conservative vote collapsed with amazing rapidity in the elections that followed. Labour did well for similar reasons in Glasgow. However, the politics of race played a part for the first time in a British general election in the West Midlands in particular, and the Conservatives managed several gains against the tide, including – notoriously – Smethwick. The midlands in general proved difficult ground for Labour in 1964, as did rural areas. Turnout fell in safe Labour areas, which had the effect of removing the electoral system's bias against Labour; the party's lead in votes was smaller in 1964 than it had been in 1951, when they lost. The Liberal revival after their March 1962 Orpington by-election win followed through into a general rise in support with particular strong points in the Highlands of Scotland where they gained three seats from the Tories, and in the south west of England. The Liberals had shaken off their crypto-Tory identity and were back in business on the centre-left. Some of those elected for the first time in 1964 were Roy Hattersley (Lab, Birmingham Sparkbrook), Geoffrey Howe (Con, Bebington), Brian Walden (Lab, Birmingham All Saints), Shirley Williams (Lab, Hitchin) and Eric Heffer (Lab, Liverpool Walton). Sir Winston Churchill, first elected for Oldham in 1900, stood down as Conservative MP for Woodford.

31 March 1966

		MPs	Vote (%)
Conservative	Edward Heath	253	41.9
Labour	Harold Wilson	363	47.9
Liberal	Jo Grimond	12	8.5
Others		2	
Turnout			75.8

Labour majority 96

Harold Wilson timed the 1966 election to perfection and Labour cruised to a relatively easy victory against the Conservatives who had not really transcended the legacy of 1951-64; it was in this election, rather than in 1964, that the phrase 'Thirteen Wasted Years' was heard most. The economy was doing well and earnings were rising sharply. The 1966 swing was, in contrast to the previous two elections, pretty uniform: 'a disturbingly neat and tidy affair, a veritable psephologist's dream' according to Gallup. The main pro-Labour variation was in the West Midlands, including Birmingham, which partly compensated for its below-average performance in 1959 and 1964. Labour also did quite well in some middle class urban and suburban constituencies and intellectual areas – the party won Hampstead, Oxford, Exeter and Lancaster for the first time. The Conservatives held off the Labour challenge in some rural areas, but could hardly claim any great patches of success; they did not gain any seats and Labour only lost one (Colne Valley, to the Liberals). The 1966 election was an interruption to the downward trend in Labour support from the peak of 1951 to the trough of 1983; it was the only occasion in the period when Labour's support as a proportion of the total electorate rose. In its appeal, of moderation, governmental competence and dynamism – as well as its electoral constituency – Wilson's Labour of 1966 anticipated aspects of New Labour. First-time winners included Donald Dewar (Lab, Aberdeen South), Gwyneth Dunwoody (Lab, Exeter), Michael Heseltine (Con, Tavistock) and David Owen (Lab, Plymouth Devonport).

18 June 1970

		MPs	Vote (%)
Conservative	Edward Heath	330	46.4
Labour	Harold Wilson	287	43.0
Liberal	Jeremy Thorpe	6	7.5
Nationalists		1	1.7
Others		6	
Turnout			72.0

Conservative majority 30

The Labour government of 1966–70 was a severe disappointment to many of its supporters; it underwent some of the most severe unpopularity any post war government has suffered (with the exception of the Conservatives in 1992–97) in 1967–69. Economic crises, devaluation and broken promises alienated many electors, but when things started to go right in early 1970 support seemed to be returning and Wilson called an election. Even on election day Labour were widely expected to win and had the lead in all but one opinion poll, but the Tories pulled off a surprise victory, helped by adverse trade figures and deflated national optimism in England after the football team were knocked out of the World Cup. It was actually the only time in the period since 1880 when a government with a secure majority was replaced by a government with a secure majority from the other party. Disillusion with Labour was expressed in Tory voting but also in the rise of voting for the Scottish and Welsh Nationalists and, particularly, abstention – it was the worst turnout in a post-war election before 1997. Labour lost substantial ground among working class voters in 1970.

The swing to the Conservatives was large and fairly uniform across the country, although the cumulative effect of social change pushed several seats into the Conservative column which had been continuously Labour since 1945 – Rossendale, Norfolk North and Dartford among them, but the most famous were two which felled senior Labour figures George Brown (Belper) and Jennie Lee (Cannock). Enoch Powell's views on race and immigration generated a large swing to the Conservatives in the white areas of the West Midlands but ensured that ethnic minority voters lined up behind Labour and cast votes in greater numbers than before. Notable winners in this election included John Smith (Lab, Ayrshire North) and Kenneth Clarke (Con, Rushcliffe) but also Norman Tebbit (Con, Epping), Neil Kinnock (Lab, Bedwellty), Ian Paisley (Unionist, Antrim North), John Prescott (Lab, Hull East) and Dennis Skinner (Lab, Bolsover) – signs of the ideological politics that was to prevail over the next two decades.

28 February 1974

		MPs	Vote (%)
Conservative	Edward Heath	297	37.9
Labour	Harold Wilson	301	37.1
Liberal	Jeremy Thorpe	14	19.3
Nationalists		9	2.6
Others (GB)		2	–
Others (NI)		12	–
Turnout			78.7

No overall majority

The Heath government was dogged by economic and industrial relations trouble from the start, and the February 1974 election was called against the background of a miners' strike and the inflationary consequences of the oil crisis. The Conservatives asked 'Who Governs?' and wanted a vote of confidence for resisting the miners. Labour had endured a divided and unsuccessful period of opposition and had a radical left programme, but Wilson astutely fought a negative campaign. Labour made highly sophisti-cated use of opinion polls conducted for them by MORI. The Liberals, having done well in by-elections in 1972-73, gained support during the campaign. Despite all this, a Conservative victory was expected right to the end.

The results of the February 1974 election were complex. Labour had more seats, despite polling fewer votes than the Conservatives. The Liberal vote surged to a higher level than any other post-war election except 1983 and 1987 but they were poorly rewarded in seats. The rise in the vote for the Scottish Nationalists was more apparent in constituency victories because their vote was more concentrated. In Northern Ireland the alliance between the Unionists and the Conservatives was broken as a Unionist front opposing the Sunningdale power-sharing agreement won 11 of the 12 seats. Two independent Labour candidates won against official party opposition, in Lincoln and Blyth.

The swing in the Black Country was again particularly notable, with many following Enoch Powell's advice to vote Labour because they offered a referendum on Britain's continuing membership of the EEC. Other urban areas tended to Labour, although less markedly – Labour gained Liverpool Garston for the first time. The class conflict of 1974 caused a rallying of working class voters to Labour, and several mining seats produced results reminiscent of 1950 in their massive Labour votes. On the other hand, Labour support plummeted in rural and some suburban areas as the Liberals surged. The Conservatives, however, did badly in rural Scotland where the SNP scored several surprise gains. Notable entrants were Douglas Hurd (Con, Oxfordshire Mid), Nigel Lawson (Con, Blaby), Robin Cook (Lab, Edinburgh Central) and Michael Ancram (Con, Berwick & East Lothian).

10 October 1974

		MPs	Vote (%)
Conservative	Edward Heath	277	35.8
Labour	Harold Wilson	319	39.2
Liberal	Jeremy Thorpe	13	18.3
Nationalists		14	3.5
Others (GB)		0	–
Others (NI)		12	–
Turnout			72.8

Labour majority 3

The October 1974 election was called in an attempt to repeat the 'Wilson two-step' to a comfortable election victory that had worked in 1964-66, but it was less successful. Labour's rather complacent campaign aroused suspicions that the whole story was not being told, while the unorthodox Conservative proposal for a government of national unity attracted some support. Projections of a large Labour majority proved to be inaccurate and the result was the smallest overall majority in parliamentary history – although in practice it sufficed for a full term because the smaller parties would not unite against the government.

Labour again did better in the cities than elsewhere, and won a first-time victory in Birmingham Selly Oak, but the Conservatives managed to retain a string of marginal seats (such as Upminster and Northampton South) against the odds, an impressive achievement under the circumstances. They even gained a couple of seats from the Liberals. The only major shift in political geography in the October election came in Scotland, where the SNP surged again and did lasting damage to the Conservatives' prospects north of the border. There were relatively few new MPs elected, although mention should be made of Margaret Beckett (Lab, Lincoln), Ann Taylor (Lab, Bolton West) and Conservative Nicholas Fairbairn who replaced Sir Alec Douglas-Home (Kinross & West Perthshire).

3 May 1979

		MPs	Vote (%)
Conservative	Margaret Thatcher	339	43.9
Labour	Jim Callaghan	269	36.9
Liberal	David Steel	11	13.8
Nationalists		4	2.0
Others (GB)		0	–
Others (NI)		12	–
Turnout			76.0

Conservative majority 43

Labour Prime Minister Jim Callaghan contemplated calling an election for October 1978, when the party had a small lead in the polls and could claim to have restored stability after the 1974 crisis. The decision to postpone over the winter was a gamble that failed – the government's pay policy broke down in a spate of strikes (the 'winter of discontent'). The election was forced by a one-vote defeat in a March 1979 confidence vote. Labour made up some ground during the campaign, but started too far behind to have a realistic chance of winning.

The Conservative lead of 7 points was the largest either party had enjoyed since 1945 and ushered in a new phase of more lopsided election results – every subsequent winner has had a larger margin of victory in the popular vote. It was epoch-making in that it elected Britain's first woman Prime Minister and started a major shift in policy.

The 1979 election showed a clear gap opening up between the north and south of Britain. Labour did particularly well in Scotland, emerging three seats up on their October 1974 performance, and also polled strongly in the north west of England where they managed to hold seats such as Bury & Radcliffe where the Tories had been ahead even in February 1974. The Conservatives, on the other hand, did extremely well in the south and midlands of England and rural Wales, gaining seats such as Birmingham Northfield and Loughborough which it had not represented since 1945 and some others, like Montgomery, which had not returned a Tory MP for a century. The swing in working class areas north and east of London was particularly enormous – the Tories gained Basildon on an 11 per cent swing

The 1979 election saw the start of the parliamentary careers of a generation of Conservative politicians, including John Major (Huntingdon), David Mellor (Putney), Chris Patten (Bath) and Stephen Dorrell (Loughborough). The Labour class of 1979 included Jack Straw (Blackburn), Frank Field (Birkenhead) and Speaker Michael Martin (Glasgow Springburn).

9 June 1983

		MPs	Vote (%)
Conservative	Margaret Thatcher	397	42.4
Labour	Michael Foot	209	27.6
Lib-SDP Alliance	Roy Jenkins/ David Steel	23	25.4
Nationalists		4	1.4
Others (GB)		0	–
Others (NI)		17	–
Turnout			72.7

Conservative majority 144

The 1979–83 period was exceptionally turbulent. The economy slumped in 1979–81; unemployment climbed inexorably towards three million and riots broke out in British cities; but Britain also won the war in the Falklands in 1982. The Labour Party was wracked by bitter divisions which led to the breakaway of the SDP in 1981, and adopted a left wing programme. The 1983 election was an easy win for the Conservatives; economic recovery had started and Thatcher benefited from the 'Falklands Factor'. The opposition was divided and, in the case of Labour, ran a completely inept campaign.

The votes of both main parties fell because of the appeal of the Alliance, but while Conservative losses were minor Labour suffered a catastrophic slump. It was the party's worst result in votes since 1918 and its worst in seats since 1935; they were in serious danger of coming third in the overall vote. The Conservatives won some unlikely victories, including all three seats in Nottingham and most of the English New Towns; they even returned 14 MPs from Wales. Labour effectively ceased to exist in much of southern England. Its only good results were in the areas worst hit by the recession, such as Liverpool and other big cities. While the Alliance polled the strongest third party vote since 1923, it was too evenly spread to win many seats (a fact which led to increasing demands for proportional representation, and the start of a tactical voting campaign) and nearly all the Labour MPs who had defected to the SDP in 1981–82 were defeated.

The surprise of the 1983 intake in retrospect is the quality of the small Labour contingent – Tony Blair (Sedgefield), Gordon Brown (Dunfermline East) and Clare Short (Birmingham Ladywood) were among them. The large delegation of new Conservative MPs contained some hard-right Thatcherites like Neil Hamilton (Tatton) and Eric Forth (Worcestershire Mid) but others such as Edwina Currie (Derbyshire South) and future senior figures like Peter Lilley (St. Albans) and Francis Maude (Warwickshire North). The Alliance acquired two future leaders, Paddy Ashdown (Yeovil) and Charles Kennedy (Ross, Cromarty & Skye), and Gerry Adams was elected for Sinn Fein in Belfast West.

11 June 1987

		MPs	Vote (%)
Conservative	Margaret Thatcher	376	42.3
Labour	Neil Kinnock	229	30.8
Lib-SDP Alliance	David Steel/ David Owen	22	22.5
Nationalists		6	1.6
Others (GB)		0	–
Others (NI)		17	–
Turnout			75.3

Conservative majority 102

Labour under Neil Kinnock (with the assistance of Peter Mandelson) ran a professional campaign after the shambles of 1983 – it was the first general election in which the red rose made an appearance. Despite this, and divisions at the top of the Conservative campaign, the Tories sailed serenely on with surprisingly few losses. Labour at least could claim to have seen off the Alliance threat to their position as the principal opposition, and some said at the time that the 1987 campaign would in retrospect be seen to have saved the Labour Party from extinction.

The 1987 results were extremely polarised between some reasonably strong Labour improvements in Scotland, Wales and much of the north of England and a continuing trend to the Conservatives in London and parts of southern England. This intensified the areas of relative support for both parties. The Conservatives managed to gain several seats against the tide such as gentrifying Battersea and the Essex heartland of Thurrock, but Labour did well even in middle class areas in the north and Scotland, gaining Manchester Withington and Edinburgh South for the first time ever. The Tories suffered a slump in Scotland as tactical voting bit deep – they lost 11 of their 21 seats.

Several future Labour Cabinet members were elected for the first time in 1987, including David Blunkett (Sheffield Brightside), Alastair Darling (Edinburgh Central), and Mo Mowlam (Redcar); there was also the backbench star Bernie Grant (Tottenham). On the Conservative side was Ann Widdecombe (Maidstone), who won after two unsuccessful runs, and Gillian Shephard (Norfolk South West). The smaller parties welcomed Alex Salmond (SNP, Banff & Buchan) and Menzies Campbell (Liberal, Fife North East).

9 April 1992

		MPs	Vote (%)
Conservative	John Major	336	41.9
Labour	Neil Kinnock	271	34.4
Liberal Democrat	Paddy Ashdown	20	17.8
Nationalists		7	2.4
Others (GB)		0	–
Others (NI)		17	–
Turnout			77.7

Conservative majority 21

The 1992 election took place after considerable change in British politics, including the end of the Cold War, the imposition of the poll tax, the ousting of Thatcher and the signature of the Maastricht Treaty; it took place while the economy was still in recession. The problems of the Conservatives, and Labour's Policy Review which moved the party back to the centre of the political spectrum, led many to expect a Labour win or a hung parliament, but John Major's Tories won a victory that surprised pollsters and commentators.

Although Basildon was the most famous Conservative hold of a marginal seat, the party was successful in the north of England in holding on to a string of very marginal seats either side of the Pennines – the other 'B's – Bolton, Bury, Batley – were even more significant than the Essex New Town. The results partly compensated for the regional divergence of 1987, as the Conservatives did relatively well in Scotland while Labour picked up in London. Labour recovered a lot of ground in several seats where the SDP had drawn off support in the 1980s, most notably Plymouth Devonport where David Owen stepped down.

The Conservative leader Iain Duncan Smith (Chingford) took over from Norman Tebbit and duly inherited the party in 2001, taking up the mantle of Margaret Thatcher (another famous name to stand down in 1992). Duncan Smith overtook two other strong Conservative figures, Liam Fox (Woodspring) and David Willetts (Havant), also elected in 1992. The Labour Party added future Cabinet ministers Stephen Byers (Wallsend), Alan Milburn (Darlington), Geoff Hoon (Ashfield) and Estelle Morris (Birmingham Yardley) – not to forget Peter Mandelson (Hartlepool). Michael Foot, last of the 1945 intake, stood down at Blaenau Gwent.

1 May 1997

		MPs	Vote (%)
Conservative	John Major	165	30.7
Labour	Tony Blair	419	43.2
Liberal Democrat	Paddy Ashdown	46	16.8
Nationalists		10	2.5
Others (GB)		1	–
Others (NI)		18	–
Turnout			71.5

Labour majority 179

The 1997 election was decided on 'Black Wednesday' in September 1992 – the ejection of sterling from the Exchange Rate Mechanism. The Conservatives never recovered from this humiliating devaluation and other events such as pit closures and VAT on fuel created a sustained climate of hostility that was deeper even than the anti-Wilson feeling in 1967-69. Their problems got worse with the accession of Tony Blair to the leadership of the Labour Party in July 1994 and the launch of 'New Labour'. The Conservatives wilted in the six-week campaign in 1997 and Labour won an expected victory – although the size of the landslide was astonishing. The swing, 10 per cent, was easily the biggest since 1945 and the majority the largest since 1935.

The swing to Labour was strong across the country, but it was particularly intense in suburban London where swings of 14 per cent were standard fare. Another unprecedented component of the New Labour electoral coalition was a group of seaside resort constituencies – all three Brighton seats, but also surprise gains in places like Hastings & Rye, Harwich and Morecambe & Lunesdale. Labour also reasserted its dominance in the New Towns, but also managed to add more middle class southern towns such as St. Albans. The Conservatives were wiped out in Scotland and Wales, and nearly so in the urban north of England – they were left with only 2 seats out of 95 in the northern metropolitan counties. The Liberal Democrats were also in at the kill, with their best haul of seats since 1929 and strong representation from south west England and suburban south London.

The stars of the 1997 intake are not yet apparent, although Stephen Twigg (Enfield Southgate) made a splash on day one by unseating Michael Portillo. Patricia Hewitt (Leicester West) and Charles Clarke (Norwich South) had already made the Cabinet by 2001 after prior service in Neil Kinnock's staff. Others with national reputations already include Julie Kirkbride (Con, Bromsgrove), Lembit Öpik (LD, Montgomery) and what Number 10 might regard as the terrible twins of Sussex, Norman Baker (LD, Lewes) and Andrew Tyrie (Con, Chichester).

7 June 2001

		MPs	Vote (%)
Conservative	William Hague	166	31.7
Labour	Tony Blair	412	40.7
Liberal Democrat	Charles Kennedy	52	18.3
Nationalists		9	2.5
Others (GB)		2	–
Others (NI)		18	–
Turnout			59.4

Labour majority 165

Labour in government had an unprecedented easy ride with public opinion – while governments in 1945-55 had also managed not to lose any seats in by-elections, they had been behind in the polls for more than two weeks in their terms. After initial soul-searching, the Conservatives under William Hague adopted populist tactics and focused on hostility to the Euro. When the election campaign came – a month late, delayed by foot and mouth – it was a predictable walkover for a government which had a good economic record against an opposition few took seriously as an alternative. The campaign was dull and the result was predictable, which contributed to the collapse in turnout.

The results of the 2001 election are addressed in the chapters on the parties, and of course the counties, but in summary the main trend was Labour's ability to hold its amazing 1997 gains, sometimes with increased majorities. Labour gained some more ground among the most affluent educated professionals while losing working class voters to abstention. The linkage between class and voting behaviour was at its weakest for a century in 2001, which makes an exercise like the current volume more interesting than when political allegiances could be more easily read off from the class composition of a constituency. Conservative populism was rewarded only with a few good results in south Essex and rural areas.

The 2001 intake was rather small because of the lack of electoral change, and it is far too soon to tell which of its members will achieve eminence. Andrew Rosindell (Con, Romford) was the poster boy for Tory success immediately after the poll, while Boris Johnson (Con, Henley) has made a distinctive contribution. More immediate ministerial prospects beckon for David Miliband (Lab, South Shields) and James Purnell (Lab, Stalybridge & Hyde), recent graduates of the Downing Street policy unit.

The House of Commons lost its last two veterans of the Attlee years as Edward Heath and Tony Benn both stood down. In this, if nothing else, the 2001 election marked the end of an era.

The parties after the 2001 general election

In this section we examine in turn the current position of the various political parties in the light of the results of the 2001 general election, drawing attention to the elements both of continuity and change in their electoral performances. For British political parties currently represented at Westminster we have drawn up 'at risk' tables of seats which are vulnerable to attack from other parties, and 'target' tables of potential gains. The balance is different for each party – while it is pointless to produce a long list of potential gains for Labour, the Tories need to recover a massive amount of territory if they are to challenge again for government. For the nationalist parties in Scotland and Wales we also list the seats at issue in the devolved elections in 2003.

The British political scene has become increasingly fragmented, with minor parties establishing a foothold in popular support and gaining representation in some national-level legislative bodies (Greens and Scottish Socialists at the Scottish Parliament, Greens and UKIP at the European Parliament). As well as the major parties (Conservative, Labour, Liberal Democrat, SNP, Plaid Cymru) we deal with the three minor parties represented at Scottish or European level thanks to proportional representation systems (Greens, UKIP, Socialists). We also discuss a few others which stood candidates in 2001 (BNP, Liberals, Mebyon Kernow; last – and probably least – come the Legalise Cannabis Alliance). However, this chapter does not deal with the completely different range of parties which contest elections in Northern Ireland; for information about politics in Northern Ireland the reader should consult the section of the book devoted to the province.

We do not have separate sections for the range of Independent and single-issue groups which are now making their presence felt on the electoral battlefield. It is a matter for conjecture as to whether the victories of Martin Bell in Tatton (1997) and Richard Taylor in Wyre Forest (2001) are isolated exceptions or the shape of things to come. Prior to these recent events no Independent had been elected to parliament since 1945 (discounting dissident candidates formerly affiliated to a major party). At local government level, also, Independent parties have been undergoing a revival in recent years, sharing control of several local authorities at different times (for example Wyre Forest, Lancaster and Elmbridge). These are a different breed from the traditional Independent candidates (often described unkindly as 'Con-dependent') still found in some rural areas, who have been a declining force for decades. There are various reasons for the rise of the new Independents, including local public services (Wyre Forest), localised interests within merged post-1974 district councils (Morecambe Bay Independents in Lancaster), general disgruntlement (Stoke-on-Trent) and the increasing control over local Labour Party selections through panels. Ethnic politics is a factor in some areas, including Birmingham (where 'Justice for Kashmir' have won seats on the city council) and may lie under the surface in other places. Unlike previous sorts of Independent, the new variety are often organised into local political parties. It may be that the next few sets of local elections will see further groups of Independents gaining ground – and it is difficult to predict where such trends will take shape.

Conservatives

The 2001 election was an appalling defeat for the Conservatives. They made a net gain of only one seat, increasing their parliamentary party to 166. They polled 31.7 per cent of the vote, the party's second worst showing in a general election under a mass franchise. Looking beyond the actual figures, it was arguably an even worse fiasco than 1997 as many, including Conservative MP Andrew Tyrie, have claimed. 1997 came after a period of stale and unpopular Conservative government, when the party was bedevilled by sleaze and division. By 2001 the Labour government was starting to look a bit shop-worn and the Conservatives could have expected to pick up some of the support they had forfeited in 1997. Instead, their vote as a share of the electorate fell even further. William Hague and his team had totally failed to provide an attractive alternative to Labour. As the table demonstrates, it was easily the worst Conservative performance after a full term of Labour government.

Period of Lab gov't	Share of vote (%)			Seats		
	Before	After	Change	Before	After	Change
1923–24	38.1	48.3	+10.2	258	419	+161
1929–31*	38.2	60.5	+22.3	260	521	+261
1945–50	39.8	43.5	+3.7	213	298	+85**
1966–70	41.9	46.4	+4.5	253	330	+77
1974–79	35.8	43.9	+8.1	277	339	+62
1997–01	30.7	31.7	+1.0	165	166	+1

*1931 figures include 'National Liberal' and 'National Labour'

**Affected by redistribution of seats

In the past, a term of Labour government has seen anti-Labour voters flocking to the Conservatives, but in 2001 this failed to happen. The Tories face formidable problems now because of effective and resilient competition from the Liberal Democrats, who have loyal support of their own and offer an attractive alternative refuge for disgruntled Labour voters. The Conservatives face the same sort of situation as Labour did in the 1980s – a low core level of support and the fact that they cannot automatically benefit from the troubles of the government because of the strength of other parties. They need a similar transformation in their basic level of support to that wrought by New Labour in the 1990s.

As Labour did in the 1980s, the Conservatives have retreated into their heartlands. Nearly two-thirds of their parliamentary strength now comes from southern England outside London (and over half from just the south east and East Anglia), compared to 42 per cent in their 1983 high tide. The Conservatives have collapsed in London, the North, Scotland and Wales.

Seats won in...	1983	(%)	1992	(%)	2001	(%)
Greater London	56	14.1	48	14.3	13	7.8
South	168	42.3	161	47.9	107	64.5
Midlands	70	17.6	57	17.0	28	16.9
North	68	17.1	53	15.8	17	10.2
Scotland	21	5.3	11	3.3	1	0.6
Wales	14	3.5	6	1.8	0	0
Conservative MPs	397		336		166	

The Tories are particularly weak in the big cities. This is the culmination of a long-term trend which has seen them eliminated from Glasgow (1982), Liverpool (1983), Manchester, Leicester and Newcastle (1987), Birmingham proper, Cardiff, Sheffield, Leeds, Bristol, Brighton & Hove and Edinburgh (1997) – all places where they have a long tradition of urban parliamentary representation. In most of these, plus the formerly marginal areas of inner London such as Streatham, Hampstead and Lewisham, they continued to deteriorate in 2001. There are also only scraps left of once uniformly Conservative suburban areas around London and the big cities. In 1992 the 'leafy' suburban areas around Nottingham, Bristol, Liverpool and Manchester between them produced 14 Conservative MPs – it is now down to only 3. In London the losses were even more dramatic. There are a couple of cities – Leicester and Hull – which retain a band of Tory suburbia, but these are now the minority. After 2001, the only urban areas presenting an attractive picture for the Tories were Bournemouth-Poole (although even there they lost a suburban seat) and Southend-Castle Point.

The remaining Conservative areas are, as the foregoing might suggest, mostly rural constituencies in southern England, plus some affluent commuter suburbs such as those blanketing Surrey. Although the Tories still draw their main strength from the south, they are not as dominant here as they once were – in 1987 Labour's Andrew Smith was the sole opposition MP in the south east outside London. They have only lost the south east region once, in 1906, and have tended to bounce back quickly after other parties have made inroads. This pattern too was defied in 2001, as Labour and the Lib Dems increased their majorities in many seats in the region – dramatically so in some cases such as Reading West and Lewes. The erosion of Conservative hegemony in southern England is illustrated by the decline in the number of counties with all-Conservative representation. There were 21 in 1987, 13 in 1992 and 2 (Dorset and Surrey) as recently as 1997. In 2001 the Conservatives lost seats in both these counties, and they can now only boast the Isle of Wight, a rather peculiar case. Just as Labour in the 1980s were an unsuccessful working class party, the Conservatives now are an unsuccessful southern rural party.

Andrew Tyrie warned that the Conservatives might be 'on the ledge of an even deeper pit' if they failed to heed the warnings of 2001. It is possible that they could lose some seats they won in 2001, and the table indicates those vulnerable to a 2.5 per cent swing. While one or two might go, particularly to the Lib Dems, it would be a major upset if more than that were to be lost. There are also some seats further out that are in some danger, either through opposition momentum (e.g. Maidenhead, Gosport) or because the Tories won them with a relatively low share of the vote in 2001 that would be vulnerable to tactical voting (e.g. New Forest East, Brentwood & Ongar).

Conservative at risk list

	Constituency	See chapter . . .	Second party	Lead %
1	Galloway & Upper Nithsdale	South of Scotland	SNP	0.2
2	Taunton	Somerset	LD	0.4
3	Orpington	London – Outer South East	LD	0.5
4	Boston & Skegness	Lincolnshire	Lab	1.3
5	Beverley & Holderness	Humberside	Lab	1.7
6	Surrey South West	Surrey	LD	1.7
7	Bedfordshire South West	Bedfordshire	Lab	1.8
8	Basingstoke	Hampshire	Lab	1.8
9	Castle Point	Essex	Lab	2.5
10	Dorset West	Dorset	LD	2.9
11	Upminster	London – East	Lab	3.7
12	Haltemprice & Howden	Humberside	LD	4.3
13	Isle of Wight	Isle of Wight	LD	4.5
14	Canterbury	Kent	Lab	4.6
15	Eastbourne	East Sussex	LD	4.8
16	Bury St. Edmunds	Suffolk	Lab	5.0

The Conservatives could draw extremely limited comfort from some results in the 2001 election. The most dramatic improvement in their performance since 1997 was in a swathe of south Essex, starting in the eastern boroughs of London and extending outwards to Southend – three of their five gains from Labour were in this area. Here, at least, the Hague campaign's emphasis on keeping the pound and toughness over law and order and asylum went down well (in contrast to Kent, where anti-asylum policies were expected to resonate best with voters). It remains to be seen whether this is a reassertion of the area's 1980s trend to the right, or a one-off gain in 2001 which might be compensated for by a relatively weak Tory showing in the next election.

Another set of strong Conservative performances were in some of the most rural constituencies in Britain, where they increased their vote by more than the national average. They did not manage to gain more than a couple seats (Norfolk North West and possibly Taunton) from the rural factor, as most of the affected seats were either already Tory or the movement was damped by new incumbency in seats like Stroud and Dumfries. They also lost deeply rural Ludlow to the Lib Dems. The factor helped them to increase their majorities in rural seats such as those in Norfolk and Suffolk where Labour had run them close in 1997. The rural factor was not exclusively about foot and mouth, for it was poorly correlated with the incidence of culls, but seems more to reflect a complex of 'countryside' issues including hunting, farm incomes and fuel taxes. Its relatively slight impact is testament to what an insignificant part of the rural economy hunting and farming amount to; much of the countryside is in fact 'urban' in the sense that its residents are increasingly drawn from the affluent middle classes who live outside but depend upon urban areas.

The Conservatives again polled humiliatingly badly in Scotland in 2001. Their vote fell by 1.9 percentage points to a meagre 15.6 per cent and they were pushed into fourth place, behind Labour, the SNP and now the Liberal Democrats. They fell even further behind in most of the constituencies they used to hold, coming third in seven seats they represented until 1987 or even later, and fourth in another (Strathkelvin & Bearsden). Other low lights were dismal results in the target seat of Eastwood and foot-and-mouth devastated Dumfries. A little pride was salvaged by relatively good showings by battling former MPs Sir Malcolm Rifkind (Edinburgh Pentlands) and Phil Gallie (Ayr), and above all by the 74-vote victory of Peter Duncan in Galloway & Upper Nithsdale thanks to a collapse in the SNP vote. There was talk before the election of the secession of the Scottish Tories from the UK-wide party, on the model perhaps of the Ulster Unionists in 1974, but nothing has come of this yet. Their prospects for the 2003 Holyrood elections are not encouraging.

It is a little different in Wales, where although they won no seats the Tories managed a 1.5 per cent increase in their vote share to 21 per cent. They came quite close to regaining Monmouth (a seat they represent in the Welsh Assembly) and fell not too far short in Brecon & Radnorshire. There were reasonably healthy swings to the party in Preseli Pembrokeshire in particular, but also in Vale of Clwyd and more distantly Gower. Despite this minor improvement the Conservatives remain on the fringes of Welsh politics as they have been for many years. Even in 1931 they were in a minority, and they are unlikely to add much to their current representation at the Assembly elections in 2003. As in Scotland, they are consigned to permanent opposition by the constellation of party politics.

The number of local authorities under Conservative control plunged in the mid 1990s to a nadir that was only just in double figures. Their long spell in government saw their support in local elections erode year after year and with the extreme unpopularity of the Major government they could hardly win anywhere in the whole four year cycle of elections from 1993 to 1996. Recovery began in 1997, when they regained control of some county councils they should never have lost (such as Surrey), and some others where the main urban areas had been hived off into unitary authorities (such as Bedfordshire). They hauled back a lot of ground in the May 1999 all-out elections for many of the less urban English districts and did well enough to deprive Labour of outright control of many areas in May 2000. The Tories are back in power in many of their traditional strongholds and one of the smaller metropolitan authorities (Solihull), Plymouth and Southend are their only large provincial towns. They must hope to make more progress in and 2003 and 2004. The Tories are the largest party in local government if one takes just the English counties and districts, but they remain weak in urban areas and metropolitan authorities. After the 2002 elections they remained without representation in Newcastle, Manchester, Liverpool or Oxford.

The table below lists in order of majority the seats that would be gained by the Conservatives on a swing of up to 10 per cent – a similar turnaround to the swing to Labour between 1992 and 1997. This swing would put them eleven points in the lead, about what they enjoyed in their 1987 landslide. The electoral landscape has shifted against them to such an extent that in contrast to their 101-strong majority in 1987 they would have a bare majority of 9 seats if they managed to gain every one of these 168 constituencies.

- To aid navigation in such a vast table, each constituency has been given a target number, in order of the size of percentage majority the Conservatives will need to overcome. Some other benchmarks are:
- To win 200 seats, the Conservatives must gain everything up to Rugby & Kenilworth (target number 34, 2.7 per cent swing);
- To equal their 1945 showing of 213 seats, they need to get to Dartford (target number 47, 3.7 per cent swing);
- To equal their 1966 landslide defeat of 253 seats, they need to win the seats up to Gravesham (target number 87, 5.6 per cent swing);
- To equal Labour's losing performance in 1992 of 271 seats, a realistic platform for 'one more heave' to win in 2010, they need everything up to Cheltenham (target number 105, 6.3 per cent swing);
- To be the largest single party in a hung parliament, with 307 seats to Labour's 305, the Conservatives need to win all the seats up to Carlisle (target number 141, 8.2 per cent swing);
- For an overall majority of 1 seat (330 to 329 others), the Tory target is Plymouth Sutton (target number 164, 9.7 per cent swing).

The Conservatives have a huge mountain to climb. Other than Labour in 1997 and 1945, the biggest pick-up since the war was the Conservative recovery in 1950 aided by an extensive redistribution that abolished many Labour seats (net increase of 85 since 1945). On a comparable basis the best Tory recovery was 1970 (77 gains since 1966). The Conservatives are so badly off now that they need 87 gains just to equal their 1966 landslide defeat, when Harold Wilson dominated British politics and people began to talk of Labour as the natural party of government.

The Conservative targets are to be found in all parts of Britain, although many of the apparently easiest are the southern marginals Labour or the Lib Dems won so surprisingly in 1997 and held in 2001. Further down the table are the traditional marginal battlegrounds of the Pennine marginals in West Yorkshire, Lancashire and Greater Manchester, and the Black Country. Also a long way down the table are several London suburban seats which were reliably Conservative until 1997, such as Enfield Southgate and Harrow West. Off the list altogether are some previously reliable Tory seats like Reading West (Labour majority 21.1 per cent) and Blackpool South (Labour majority 21.3 per cent) and seats normally thought of as classic marginals such as Southampton Test (Labour majority 27.0 per cent) and York (Labour majority 28.7 per cent). The working class London seats that went Tory in the 1980s such Feltham & Heston (Labour majority 35.0 per cent) and Hayes & Harlington (Labour majority 41.6 per cent) are now surely beyond the wildest Tory dreams. On the other hand, a Conservative government would have representatives from some previously barren areas. Copeland, a constituency they have not won since 1931, could fall to them even if Labour remain the largest single party. They failed to win Carlisle even in 1983, and Wakefield was Tory only for a few months after 1931. But the oddest presence in the target list is Gower in South Wales (providing an overall majority of 7), which has never elected a Conservative MP under a mass franchise, even in 1895, 1931 and 1983.

Conservative target list

	Constituency	See chapter . . .	Party	Lead %
1	Cheadle	Greater Manchester	LD	0.1
2	Perth	Mid Scotland and Fife	SNP	0.1
3	Dorset South	Dorset	Lab	0.3
4	Braintree	Essex	Lab	0.7
5	Weston-super-Mare	Avon	LD	0.7
6	Norfolk North	Norfolk	LD	0.9
7	Monmouth	South Wales East	Lab	0.9
8	Dorset Mid & Poole North	Dorset	LD	0.9
9	Lancaster & Wyre	Lancashire	Lab	0.9
10	Guildford	Surrey	LD	1.1
11	Kettering	Northamptonshire	Lab	1.2
12	Somerton & Frome	Somerset	LD	1.3
13	Northampton South	Northamptonshire	Lab	1.7
14	Brecon & Radnorshire	Mid and West Wales	LD	2.0
15	Devon West & Torridge	Devon	LD	2.1
16	Hereford	Hereford and Worcester	LD	2.2
17	Welwyn Hatfield	Hertfordshire	Lab	2.8
18	Shipley	West Yorkshire	Lab	3.1
19	Clwyd West	North Wales	Lab	3.2
20	Bexleyheath & Crayford	London – Outer South East	Lab	3.6
21	Ludlow	Shropshire	LD	3.8
22	Milton Keynes North East	Buckinghamshire	Lab	3.9
23	Hornchurch	London – East	Lab	4.2
24	Selby	North Yorkshire	Lab	4.3
25	Edinburgh Pentlands	Lothians	Lab	4.5
26	Hammersmith & Fulham	London – West	Lab	4.5
27	Thanet South	Kent	Lab	4.5
28	Forest of Dean	Gloucestershire	Lab	4.6
29	Wellingborough	Northamptonshire	Lab	4.6
30	Newbury	Berkshire	LD	4.8
31	Romsey	Hampshire	LD	4.9
32	Teignbridge	Devon	LD	5.1

	Constituency	See chapter . . .	Party	Lead %
33	Ilford North	London – East	Lab	5.3
34	Rugby & Kenilworth	Warwickshire	Lab	5.3
35	Gillingham	Kent	Lab	5.4
36	Harwich	Essex	Lab	5.4
37	Enfield North	London – North	Lab	6.0
38	Devon North	Devon	LD	6.1
39	Eastleigh	Hampshire	LD	6.4
40	Calder Valley	West Yorkshire	Lab	6.5
41	Ayr	South of Scotland	Lab	6.6
42	Redditch	Hereford and Worcester	Lab	6.7
43	Peterborough	Cambridgeshire	Lab	7.2
44	Shrewsbury & Atcham	Shropshire	Lab	7.2
45	Moray*	North East Scotland	SNP	7.2
46	Southport	Merseyside	LD	7.3
47	Dartford	Kent	Lab	7.4
48	Scarborough & Whitby	North Yorkshire	Lab	7.5
49	Hove	East Sussex	Lab	7.6
50	Preseli Pembrokeshire	Mid and West Wales	Lab	8.0
51	Bristol West*	Avon	Lab	8.0
52	Gloucester	Gloucestershire	Lab	8.0
53	Putney	London – Inner South	Lab	8.1
54	Hemel Hempstead	Hertfordshire	Lab	8.2
55	Yeovil	Somerset	LD	8.2
56	South Ribble	Lancashire	Lab	8.2
57	Finchley & Golders Green	London – North	Lab	8.5
58	Tayside North	Mid Scotland and Fife	SNP	8.5
59	Wolverhampton South West	West Midlands – Black Country	Lab	8.5
60	The Wrekin	Shropshire	Lab	8.6
61	Croydon Central	London – Outer South	Lab	8.7
62	Elmet	West Yorkshire	Lab	9.1
63	Argyll & Bute*	Highlands and Islands	LD	9.1
64	Wimbledon	London – Outer South	Lab	9.1
65	Stroud	Gloucestershire	Lab	9.1
66	Keighley	West Yorkshire	Lab	9.2
67	Sittingbourne & Sheppey	Kent	Lab	9.3
68	High Peak	Derbyshire	Lab	9.3
69	Stourbridge	West Midlands – Black Country	Lab	9.5
70	Brigg & Goole	Humberside	Lab	9.6
71	Falmouth & Camborne	Cornwall	Lab	9.7
72	Medway	Kent	Lab	9.8
73	Colne Valley	West Yorkshire	Lab	9.9

	Constituency	See chapter . . .	Party	Lead %
74	Wirral West	Merseyside	Lab	10.0
75	Richmond Park	London – Outer South	LD	10.1
76	St. Albans	Hertfordshire	Lab	10.2
77	Angus	North East Scotland	SNP	10.3
78	Cornwall South East	Cornwall	LD	10.4
79	Vale of Glamorgan	South Wales Central	Lab	10.4
80	Burton	Staffordshire	Lab	10.4
81	Hastings & Rye	East Sussex	Lab	10.5
82	Pendle	Lancashire	Lab	10.8
83	Sutton & Cheam	London – Outer South	LD	10.8
84	Bradford West	West Yorkshire	Lab	10.9
85	Chatham & Aylesford	Kent	Lab	10.9
86	Warwick & Leamington	Warwickshire	Lab	11.1
87	Gravesham	Kent	Lab	11.1
88	Carshalton & Wallington	London – Outer South	LD	11.2
89	Great Yarmouth	Norfolk	Lab	11.3
90	Wansdyke	Avon	Lab	11.3
91	Stafford	Staffordshire	Lab	11.3
92	Tamworth	Staffordshire	Lab	11.4
93	Dover	Kent	Lab	11.6
94	Rossendale & Darwen	Lancashire	Lab	11.9
95	Watford	Hertfordshire	Lab	12.0
96	Broxtowe	Nottinghamshire	Lab	12.0
97	Corby	Northamptonshire	Lab	12.1
98	Morecambe & Lunesdale	Lancashire	Lab	12.2
99	Carmarthen W & P'shire S	Mid and West Wales	Lab	12.3
100	Leeds North West	West Yorkshire	Lab	12.3
101	Birmingham Edgbaston	West Midlands – Birmingham	Lab	12.4
102	Pudsey	West Yorkshire	Lab	12.5
103	Ynys Mon*	North Wales	Lab	12.5
104	Brighton Kemptown	East Sussex	Lab	12.6
105	Cheltenham	Gloucestershire	LD	12.6
106	Wirral South	Merseyside	Lab	12.7
107	Colchester	Essex	LD	12.7
108	Aberdeenshire West & Kincardine	North East Scotland	LD	12.7
109	Gedling	Nottinghamshire	Lab	12.8
110	Reading East	Berkshire	Lab	12.8
111	Norwich North	Norfolk	Lab	12.9
112	Harlow	Essex	Lab	13.0
113	Worcester	Hereford and Worcester	Lab	13.0
114	Batley & Spen	West Yorkshire	Lab	13.1

	Constituency	See chapter . . .	Party	Lead %
115	Harrow West	London – West	Lab	13.2
116	Enfield Southgate	London – North	Lab	13.2
117	Cleethorpes	Humberside	Lab	13.2
118	Bolton West	Greater Manchester	Lab	13.4
119	Blackpool North & Fleetwood	Lancashire	Lab	13.4
120	Staffordshire Moorlands	Staffordshire	Lab	13.7
121	Battersea	London – Inner South	Lab	13.7
122	Portsmouth North	Hampshire	Lab	13.9
123	Torbay	Devon	LD	14.1
124	Cardiff North	South Wales Central	Lab	14.3
125	Erewash	Derbyshire	Lab	14.3
126	Copeland	Cumbria	Lab	14.3
127	Loughborough	Leicestershire	Lab	14.4
128	Bury North	Greater Manchester	Lab	14.6
129	Derbyshire South	Derbyshire	Lab	15.1
130	Bedford	Bedfordshire	Lab	15.2
131	Halifax	West Yorkshire	Lab	15.2
132	Twickenham	London – Outer South	LD	15.3
133	City of Chester	Cheshire	Lab	15.4
134	Milton Keynes South West	Buckinghamshire	Lab	15.4
135	Portsmouth South	Hampshire	LD	15.5
136	Derby North	Derbyshire	Lab	15.8
137	Truro & St. Austell	Cornwall	LD	16.0
138	Amber Valley	Derbyshire	Lab	16.2
139	Warrington South	Cheshire	Lab	16.3
140	Winchester	Hampshire	LD	16.3
141	Carlisle	Cumbria	Lab	16.3
142	Swindon South	Wiltshire	Lab	16.9
143	Crawley	West Sussex	Lab	17.1
144	Nuneaton	Warwickshire	Lab	17.4
145	Stirling	Mid Scotland and Fife	Lab	17.5
146	Chorley	Lancashire	Lab	17.6
147	Dudley North	West Midlands – Black Country	Lab	17.6
148	Northavon	Avon	LD	17.7
149	Vale of Clwyd	North Wales	Lab	17.8
150	Oxford West & Abingdon	Oxfordshire	LD	17.8
151	Leeds North East	West Yorkshire	Lab	17.8
152	Conwy	North Wales	Lab	18.1
153	Leicestershire North West	Leicestershire	Lab	18.1
154	Waveney	Suffolk	Lab	18.1
155	Hendon	London – North	Lab	18.2

	Constituency	See chapter . . .	Party	Lead %
156	Cornwall North	Cornwall	LD	18.2
157	Halesowen & Rowley Regis	West Midlands – Black Country	Lab	18.7
158	Dudley South	West Midlands – Black Country	Lab	18.8
159	Ceredigion*	Mid and West Wales	PC	18.8
160	Eastwood	West of Scotland	Lab	18.9
161	Basildon	Essex	Lab	18.9
162	Northampton North	Northamptonshire	Lab	19.0
163	Swindon North	Wiltshire	Lab	19.1
164	Plymouth Sutton	Devon	Lab	19.2
165	Wakefield	West Yorkshire	Lab	19.3
166	Tynemouth	Tyne and Wear	Lab	19.8
167	Gower	South Wales West	Lab	19.8
168	Edinburgh West*	Lothians	LD	19.8

* Conservatives in third place in 2001.

Labour

The 2001 general election was trumpeted by the Labour leadership as the first occasion on which the British electorate had granted them a full second term of office. In fact this is not quite true – Labour won a narrow majority in 1950 to follow the landslide of 1945, but Prime Minister Clement Attlee was to call a further election just 20 months later (despite still having a majority) which the party went on to lose. Nevertheless it is unquestionably the case that Labour have never before won two successive elections so resoundingly, and what cannot be disputed is that a third election win for the party really would be unprecedented.

Leaving aside for one moment the causes of Labour's newly found popularity, they have been helped by a number of factors concerning the operation of the electoral system. For example, the 1945-50 government had to face a comprehensive set of boundary changes which cost them a large number of seats, while this was not true in 2001 (the next review will probably not even be implemented in time for the next election in 2005/6). Second, it is regularly pointed out that the electoral system at present is as 'biased' to Labour as it has ever been to any party, with the result that they could have won the 2001 election with a majority of over seventy seats even if they had been behind the Conservatives in votes cast. By comparison the Tories would have required a double-figure percentage lead over Labour to have enjoyed an overall majority of one. A major reason for this distortion has been Labour's success in marginal constituencies compared with elsewhere (particularly safe Labour seats) over the last three elections – in short they are continuing to attract support where they really need it.

A further factor, though one which may well be related to the character of 'New Labour' itself (specifically its tendency not to frighten middle class voters) is that opposition voters failed to unite behind the Conservative cause in 2001 as happened after at least four previous periods of Labour government: 1924, 1951, 1970 and 1979. Indeed the Liberal Democrat share of the vote increased (see next section) and they continued to gain votes and seats (such as Guildford, Ludlow and Teignbridge) from the Conservatives. Evidence in 2001 suggests that in Labour-Conservative marginals, many Lib Dem supporters continued to vote tactically for Labour, removing any possibility of a serious opposition challenge.

The overall effect of these factors, together with a fourth – that many Labour MPs first elected in 1997 appeared to attract significant 'first time' incumbency votes in 2001 – explains how the 1997-2001 government lost a similar degree of support to its predecessors, but without losing anything like the same number of parliamentary seats. The table below, showing the four 'full Labour terms' in government, graphically illustrates this pattern:

Period of Lab gov't	Share of vote (%)			Seats		
	Before	After	Change	Before	After	Change
1945-50	47.8	46.1	– 1.7	393	315	– 78
1966-70	47.9	43.0	– 4.9	363	287	– 76
1974-79	39.2	36.9	– 2.3	319	269	– 50
1997-01	43.2	40.7	– 2.5	419	412	– 7

It is particularly noteworthy that the Conservatives increased their vote share by four, five and eight percentage points after the first three full Labour governments, but by only a single point in 2001. Although the Liberal Democrats vote increased, this had little adverse effect on Labour because there are very few Labour-Lib Dem marginals.

Labour's vote share may have fallen back in 2001, but it remains in excess of the 40 per cent mark, a figure which seemed a long way off during the 1979-1992 period and one which has proved sufficient to ensure two landslide victories. So how does the geography of 'New Labour's' support differ from the wilderness years of the 1980s and early 1990s? Undoubtedly the party is now much more successful in the South of England – in 2001 there were 58 Labour MPs elected from this area, compared with only 10 in 1992, which accounts for about a third of the party's gains across the country over this period. Only three Labour MPs were elected in the south outside London in both 1983 (Bristol South, Ipswich and Thurrock) and 1987 (Bristol South, Norwich South and Oxford East), out of a total of one hundred and seventy, which was the key factor in the party's poor national showings in those elections. Most of the constituencies gained in 1997 fall into one of three groups. First were the 'New Town' constituencies (Basildon, Harlow, Stevenage and so on), whose socio-economic characteristics suggest they should never have been won by the Conservatives in the first place, but which were particularly attracted by features of Thatcherism such as the 'right to buy' policy, where council tenants could buy their homes at knock-down prices. The second group of gained seats were in the traditional urban centres (Southampton, Bristol, Plymouth, Swindon) of the sort that would have long since been Labour had they been further north. Finally, Labour picked up a large number of coastal seats on enormous swings in 1997 which had hitherto always been Conservative-held. Some of the most unexpected gains of all were in the south (Harwich, Hastings, Hove) though this group included seats from many regions (for example Crosby, Scarborough & Whitby, Morecambe, Clwyd West). Although it has been one of the most clear-cut changes in Britain's electoral geography over the past decade, little research has been conducted to explain why this group of seats has shifted allegiance from Tory (even in previous land-slides like 1945 and 1966) to Labour, though one obvious possibility is that it is linked with the severe economic decline which has blighted many of these places.

The other area of above-average swings to Labour in 1997 was Greater London, particularly a band of northern suburbs, where in many cases the shift away from the Conservatives continued in 2001. London was the scene of some of Labour's worst performances in the country in the 1970s and 1980s (particularly when social class composition is taken into account), with them losing even usually safe seats like Edmonton and Hayes & Harlington, but by 2001 this had reversed completely. Electors in seats like Enfield Southgate and Harrow West now find themselves being represented by Labour MPs and getting used to the idea, a prospect which would have been viewed with some incredulity in the 1980s or even early 1990s. There is some evidence that political attitudes in London are different from the rest of the country, for example more pro-European (see opinion polls chapter) and this seems to have benefited Labour and damaged the Tories in the last two general elections. Whether this becomes a fixed pattern remains to be seen, but there are already slight indications that the greater tendency to 'liberal' viewpoints in the capital is starting to work against Labour as well, to the benefit of the Liberal Democrats in general elections, and also Greens and Socialists in European and local polls.

Another significant cluster of Labour's gains in 1997, almost all of which were held in 2001, came in small towns and suburbs in the Midlands. Some of these towns had swung a long way to the right since the 1970s despite retaining a working class core; classic examples were Wellingborough, Corby and Loughborough, all of which were finally regained in 1997. Many of the suburbs had never been previously won by Labour, notably Birmingham Edgbaston, which was the first marginal gained in front of the television cameras in 1997 and thus assumed totemic status, as Basildon had for the Conservatives in 1987 and 1992. Further north, Labour had managed to hold onto a large number of seats at their 1983 nadir, which saved them from total meltdown, but there were still over thirty marginals gained in 1997, particularly in Lancashire, West Yorkshire and some of the towns around Manchester. It has tended to be former mining areas such as South Yorkshire and large parts of the North East (to which one could add areas of Scotland and South Wales) which have traditionally been the most staunch Labour heart-lands, with few seats left to gain in 1997. Although most of the constituencies in such areas remain very safe, there were signs of an above-average swing away from Labour in 2001. This was particularly true of South Wales, where Labour did badly in the 1999 Assembly elections; in Scotland Labour's vote scarcely dropped in 2001.

The totals of Labour seats won in the main areas of the country at the elections of 1983, 1992 and 2001 are shown below. As can be seen, the northern regions, Wales and Scotland provided over 70 per cent of Labour seats in 1983, a proportion which fell to approximately 55 per cent in 1997 and 2001. As the proportional weight of Labour's northern groups has fallen, it has increased in the south of England and London, making up 27.4 per cent of the total in 2001, compared with just 13.9 per cent in 1983. Indeed the unpromising territory of the south outside London now returns more Labour MPs than Scotland, and a continuation of this pattern will be vital for Labour's long term prospects given that the number of Scottish MPs is to be reduced at the next boundary review.

Seats won in...	1983	(%)	1992	(%)	2001	(%)
Greater London	26	12.4	35	12.9	55	13.3
South	3	1.4	10	3.7	58	14.1
Midlands	30	14.4	43	15.9	71	17.2
North	89	42.6	107	39.5	139	33.7
Scotland	41	19.6	49	18.1	55	13.3
Wales	20	9.6	27	10.0	34	8.3
Labour MPs	209		271		412	

It seems unlikely that Labour will add any more seats at the next general election to their overall total of 412, but precedent suggests the odd constituency can be picked up against the tide (examples include Colne Valley in 1970 and Walthamstow for the Conservatives in 1987) and a repeat should not be ruled out in 2005/6. In particular, Labour (locally if not nationally) will have their eyes on Basingstoke, a southern town which shares the characteristics of many already gained, and which requires a repeat of the very small pro-Labour swing achieved in 2001 to fall. Two rural Scottish seats have now come within feasible range for the first time, with big advances made in both Argyll & Bute (Lib Dem held) and Moray (SNP held) in 2001, though new incumbents may be able to build their majorities back up to comfortable levels.

Labour target list

	Constituency	See chapter...	Party	Lead %
1	Boston & Skegness	Lincolnshire	Con	1.3
2	Beverley & Holderness	Humberside	Con	1.7
3	Bedfordshire South West	Bedfordshire	Con	1.8
4	Basingstoke	Hampshire	Con	1.8
5	Castle Point	Essex	Con	2.5
6	Upminster	London – East	Con	3.7
7	Canterbury	Kent	Con	4.6
8	Bury St Edmunds	Suffolk	Con	5.0
9	Bosworth	Leicestershire	Con	5.1
10	Moray	Highlands & Islands	SNP	5.2
11	Argyll & Bute	Highlands & Islands	LD	5.3
12	Chesterfield	Derbyshire	LD	5.8

The main focus for Labour in the run-up to the next general election will be on retaining their marginal seats (most of which were originally gained in 1997), though they will also undoubtedly come under pressure in many local authorities in 2002, 2003 and 2004. By the start of the1990s, Labour were easily the largest party in local government, but much of this was a reaction to the mid-term unpopularity of successive Conservative administrations, which led to a gradual, but severe, fall in the number of Tory councillors. Labour will hope that the same fate does not befall them; they suffered remarkably few losses in 1999 and 2000 compared with the wipe-outs of the late 1960s and late 1970s, but the chances are that Labour will lose control of a number of other councils to follow the likes of Sheffield, Hartlepool and Oldham in the last parliament. One interesting question is exactly who will provide the main opposition challenge to Labour – in many northern cities, the Conservatives produced no recovery at all in local elections between 1997 and 2001 and it was the Liberal Democrats who were the main (or only) opposition. Although in the short term this may suit Labour as it prevents the Conservatives gaining local momentum in many of the parliamentary seats they must win, in the long term it stores up problems if the Lib Dems start to make significant breakthroughs among Labour's natural electorate.

In Scotland and Wales, Labour will look to strengthen their position at the next set of elections in 2003, but with an 'additional member' system in operation in each case, an overall majority (for Labour or anyone else) is much more difficult to secure than under the 'first past the post' electoral system. In 1999, Labour won very few of the regional list seats on offer because of the proportional way in which they are allocated, with the result that Labour were some way short of a majority at Holyrood despite winning 53 of the 73 constituency seats (only three fewer than at the 1997 and 2001 general elections). In addition the devolutionist-separatist dynamic unleashed by the elections helped the nationalist parties to generate increased support both at constituency and regional level; this was most apparent in South Wales where Plaid Cymru stormed the Labour citadels of Islwyn and Rhondda. Labour attempted a minority administration in Wales, but this was to end in tears, and it seems probable that there will be a continuation of the Labour-Liberal Democrat coalitions at both Cardiff and Edinburgh. This will provide an interesting contrast with the likely growing gap between the two parties at Westminster, and laws passed in Scotland (for example on student finance, long term care for the elderly and foxhunting) have already added to the pressure on Labour nationally to adopt more radical policies.

When it comes to the next general election, the battleground will be much the same as 2001. The list of Labour's 83 most marginal seats (their majority disappears if all are lost) is scattered across the country, with the largest clusters in London (8), Kent (8), West Yorkshire (7) and Lancashire (5). Many of the seats have a high proportion of middle class professionals and as in 2001 the outcome may well depend on the state of the national economy, as well as the extent of any Conservative recovery. There are still comparatively few seats on the 'at risk' list which include significant working class or 'Labour heartland' areas and a tiny number where it is the Liberal Democrats or nationalist parties rather than the Conservatives who are the main challengers. Only just over half of them (46) have a current Labour lead below their national 9 per cent advantage, and to lose the lot (and thus change the government) would take a swing exceeding 6 per cent, which is greater than that achieved by Margaret Thatcher in 1979. All this simply emphasises the comfortable electoral position in which Labour currently find themselves.

Labour at risk list

	Constituency	See chapter ...	Second party	Lead %
1	Dorset South	Dorset	Con	0.3
2	Braintree	Essex	Con	0.7
3	Monmouth	South Wales East	Con	0.9
4	Lancaster & Wyre	Lancashire	Con	0.9
5	Kettering	Northamptonshire	Con	1.2
6	Northampton South	Northamptonshire	Con	1.7
7	Cardiff Central	South Wales Central	LD	1.9
8	Ynys Mon	North Wales	PC	2.4
9	Welwyn Hatfield	Hertfordshire	Con	2.8
10	Shipley	West Yorkshire	Con	3.1
11	Clwyd West	North Wales	Con	3.2
12	Bexleyheath & Crayford	London – Outer South East	Con	3.6
13	Milton Keynes North East	Buckinghamshire	Con	3.9
14	Hornchurch	Essex	Con	4.2
15	Selby	North Yorkshire	Con	4.3
16	Edinburgh Pentlands	Lothians	Con	4.5
17	Hammersmith & Fulham	London – West	Con	4.5
18	Thanet South	Kent	Con	4.5
19	Forest of Dean	Gloucestershire	Con	4.6
20	Wellingborough	Northamptonshire	Con	4.6
21	Ilford North	London – East	Con	5.3
22	Rugby & Kenilworth	Warwickshire	Con	5.3
23	Gillingham	Kent	Con	5.4
24	Harwich	Essex	Con	5.4
25	Enfield North	London – North	Con	6.0
26	Oldham East & Saddleworth	Greater Manchester	LD	6.0
27	Calder Valley	West Yorkshire	Con	6.5
28	Ayr	South of Scotland	Con	6.6
29	Redditch	Hereford & Worcester	Con	6.7
30	Peterborough	Cambridgeshire	Con	7.2
31	Shrewsbury & Atcham*	Shropshire	Con	7.2
32	Dartford	Kent	Con	7.4
33	Scarborough & Whitby	North Yorkshire	Con	7.5
34	Hove	East Sussex	Con	7.6
35	Bristol West	Avon	(2) LD	8.0
			(3) Con	8.1
36	Preseli Pembrokeshire	Mid and West Wales	Con	8.0
37	Gloucester	Gloucestershire	Con	8.0
38	Putney	London – Inner South	Con	8.1
39	Hemel Hempstead	Hertfordshire	Con	8.2

	Constituency	See chapter . . .	Second party	Lead %
40	Western Isles	Highlands and Islands	SNP	8.2
41	South Ribble	Lancashire	Con	8.2
42	Finchley & Golders Green	London – North	Con	8.5
43	Wolverhampton South West	West Midlands – Black Country	Con	8.5
44	Birmingham Yardley	West Midlands – Birmingham	LD	8.6
45	The Wrekin	Shropshire	Con	8.6
46	Croydon Central	London – Outer South	Con	8.7
47	Elmet	West Yorkshire	Con	9.1
48	Wimbledon	London – Outer South	Con	9.1
49	Stroud	Gloucestershire	Con	9.1
50	Keighley	West Yorkshire	Con	9.2
51	Sittingbourne & Sheppey	Kent	Con	9.3
52	High Peak	Derbyshire	Con	9.3
53	Stourbridge	West Midlands – Black Country	Con	9.5
54	Brigg & Goole	Humberside	Con	9.6
55	Falmouth & Camborne	Cornwall	Con	9.7
56	Medway	Kent	Con	9.8
57	Colne Valley	West Yorkshire	Con	9.9
58	Wirral West	Merseyside	Con	10.0
59	St Albans	Hertfordshire	Con	10.2
60	Vale of Glamorgan	South Wales Central	Con	10.4
61	Burton	Staffordshire	Con	10.4
62	Hastings & Rye	East Sussex	Con	10.5
63	Pendle	Lancashire	Con	10.8
64	Bradford West	West Yorkshire	Con	10.9
65	Chatham & Aylesford	Kent	Con	10.9
66	Inverness East, Nairn & Lochaber	Highlands & Islands	SNP	11.1
67	Warwick & Leamington	Warwickshire	Con	11.1
68	Gravesham	Kent	Con	11.1
69	Great Yarmouth	Norfolk	Con	11.3
70	Wansdyke	Avon	Con	11.3
71	Stafford	Staffordshire	Con	11.3
72	Tamworth	Staffordshire	Con	11.4
73	Dover	Kent	Con	11.6
74	Aberdeen South	North East Scotland	LD	11.9
75	Rossendale & Darwen	Lancashire	Con	11.9
76	Watford	Hertfordshire	Con	12.0
77	Broxtowe	Nottinghamshire	Con	12.0
78	Corby	Northamptonshire	Con	12.1
79	Morecambe & Lunesdale	Lancashire	Con	12.2
80	Carmarthen W & P'shire S	Mid and West Wales	Con	12.3

	Constituency	See chapter . . .	Second party	Lead %
81	Leeds North West	West Yorkshire	Con	12.3
82	Birmingham Edgbaston	West Midlands – Birmingham	Con	12.4
83	Pudsey	West Yorkshire	Con	12.5

*sitting MP in Shrewsbury & Atcham has defected to the Liberal Democrats.

Liberal Democrats

After three successive elections in which their share of the vote fell, the Liberal Democrats managed an increase from 16.8 per cent in 1997 to 18.3 per cent in 2001. Their haul of seats increased from 46 to 52, with two losses to the Conservatives compensated with seven gains from that source and one from Labour. They fell just short of their 1929 showing (59). Doubts about the leadership of Charles Kennedy were decisively quashed by the election results.

The Liberal Democrats' performance in 2001 was heartening for them in all sorts of ways. In the past, periods of Labour government have been very bad for the party's vote and parliamentary representation. 2001 is the first time they have ever prospered in seats or votes under a Labour government

	Share of vote (%)		Seats	
	Pre Lab gov't	Post Lab gov't	Pre Lab gov't	Post Lab gov'
1923–24	29.6	17.6	159	40
1929–31*	23.4	7.0	59	37
1945–51	9.1	2.5	12	6
1964–70	11.2	7.5	9	6
1974–79	19.3	13.8	14	11
1997–01	16.8	18.3	46	52

*1931 figures include Lloyd George independent Liberals but not pro-Tory 'National Liberals'.

In contrast with the past pattern there was no rallying of the anti-Labour vote behind the Conservatives after a period of Labour government. The New Labour administration's ability to reassure middle class voters and get through a term without an economic crisis meant that there was no 'fear factor' operating of the sort that had carried the Conservatives to victory in 1931 and 1979 in particular. The Conservative image in 2001 was particularly offputting to voters who had inclined to the Liberal Democrats, and as with the result nationally the 2001 results reaffirmed the decision of 1997 in nearly all the Lib Dem seats.

Another promising feature of the result for Lib Dems was that their performance bore little relation to their dire mid-term results in the European elections of June 1999 in particular, when they came third or even fourth in many of the seats that had elected Lib Dem MPs in 1997. The picture in the south west in particular was very bleak in 1999, but they held on everywhere except Taunton and gained an extra seat at Teignbridge in 2001. Another pattern they defied was their past inability to hand seats on when incumbents retired. Prior to the last two elections there had only been Rochdale (1992), Orkney & Shetland (1983) and Montgomery (1962) since 1945. Now Montgomery and Tweeddale (in 1997) and Orkney & Shetland, Yeovil, Brecon & Radnorshire, Argyll & Bute and Southport (in 2001) have also survived the transfer and no seats were lost for this reason in 2001.

The Lib Dems were also relieved in Scotland, where it was feared that participation in the administration at Holyrood might work against them. As it happened, their vote rose by 3.4 percentage points and they pushed the Conservatives into fourth place.

The 2001 results continued the change in the basis of Liberal Democrat representation away from the 'Celtic fringe' – rural areas of Wales, Scotland and the far south west of England – which had enabled the survival of the Liberals in the 1950s. The proportion of Liberal MPs from the fringe was usually above 60 per cent in the half century after 1945, peaking at 8 out of 9 in 1964 and still being 65 per cent in 1992. They were weak in south east England; the non-fringe Liberal seats tended to be in northern England. In 1997 the 'Celtic fringe' contribution fell to 41 per cent and that from London and the south east rose to 30 per cent (from 5 per cent in 1992); in 2001 the gap was even narrower, with 38 per cent 'fringe' and 29 per cent London and south east. The Liberal Democrats are emphatically not the same sort of party as the old Liberals – they have started to compete with the Conservatives in their traditional heartland. This was brought home in 2001 with their gain of Guildford and their landslide win in Kingston & Surbiton. Their dream of winning the suburbs, which had faded away after their failure to consolidate their by-election win in Orpington in 1962, has started to become a bit more real. Although they fell just short of winning Orpington in 2001, they did manage to reclaim their other 1960s suburban gain of Cheadle.

After the 2001 election the Liberal Democrats proclaimed their ambition to displace the Conservatives as the 'effective opposition' and perhaps eventually as the official opposition. 'Effective' is a value judgement, although Norman Baker of Lewes has probably done more than any Tory to discomfit the Labour government, but in electoral terms the Conservatives are still the main enemy the Lib Dems are fighting. There are 19 seats where the Lib Dems were within 10 percentage points of victory in 2001; 15 Conservative and 4 Labour. Only one of them (Totnes) is in what can be called the Celtic fringe, and six are in the London suburbs or the south east. But it is likely that if they are making gains there will be some from outside this list, on the model of the surprise win in Ludlow in 2001.

Liberal Democrat target list

	Constituency	See chapter...	Party	Lead %
1	Taunton	Somerset	Con	0.4
2	Orpington	London – Outer South East	Con	0.5
3	Surrey South West	Surrey	Con	1.7
4	Cardiff Central	South Wales Central	Lab	1.9
5	Dorset West	Dorset	Con	2.9
6	Haltemprice & Howden	Humberside	Con	4.3

	Constituency	See chapter...	Party	Lead %
7	Isle of Wight	Isle of Wight	Con	4.5
8	Eastbourne	East Sussex	Con	4.8
9	Wells	Somerset	Con	5.4
10	Oldham East & Saddleworth	Greater Manchester	Lab	6.0
11	Westmorland & Lonsdale	Cumbria	Con	6.6
12	Totnes	Devon	Con	7.3
13	Wiltshire North	Wiltshire	Con	7.3
14	Maidenhead	Berkshire	Con	7.6
15	Dorset North	Dorset	Con	7.9
16	Bristol West	Avon	Lab	8.0
17	Birmingham Yardley	West Midlands – Birmingham	Lab	8.6
18	New Forest East	Hampshire	Con	9.1
19	Bournemouth East	Dorset	Con	9.6

The Liberal Democrats are also likely to pose a threat to Conservative seats in by-elections in the current parliament. They had one realistic chance of a gain in a by-election during the 1997–2001 parliament, and they took it. Their achievement in Romsey in May 2000 was remarkable as it took place at a time when the Conservatives were doing relatively well in local elections. Any vacancy in a seat with the Lib Dems in second place (or even a narrow third) and the Conservative share of the vote below 50 per cent in 2001 would present an opportunity.

Looking forward to the devolved elections in 2003, the Liberal Democrats have grounds for renewed confidence. The Scottish Parliament and Welsh Assembly are particularly important for the party because they have, for the first time since the grand coalition of 1940-45, wielded executive power in Britain through those bodies. In Scotland, Jim Wallace even deputised as First Minister on two occasions. The constellation of Scottish politics makes it likely that the Lib Dems will stay in coalition with Labour at Holyrood. Things are less clear-cut in Wales, where Labour can realistically aspire to win overall control, although if Labour fall short as they did in 1999 the Lib Dems might well also continue in coalition there. The 2001 election results showed that the party's coalitions with Labour in the devolved bodies did not interfere with their ability to mount an effective appeal for votes at a Westminster level and, in the case of Cardiff Central, almost win a seat from Labour.

The main problem the Lib Dems face is how to break into the Labour Party's heartlands. Even in optimum conditions in 1983, with a nationwide collapse in the Labour vote and a group of former Labour MPs standing under SDP colours, they could not win many constituencies from Labour. SDP MPs held Woolwich, Plymouth Devonport, Caithness & Sutherland and Stockton South but most of their parliamentary colleagues were defeated. The only entirely new gain from Labour in 1983 ironically went to the Liberals in Leeds West, and their success was short-lived as Labour regained the seat in 1987.

Their gain of Chesterfield in 2001, the first from Labour in a general election since Leeds West, came after 17 years of campaigning and gradually building their vote, and the Benn factor: it thus involved a formula that cannot be readily replicated. Chesterfield is probably an isolated curiosity rather than a harbinger of the future, having previously been a safe Labour seat which has succumbed to Lib Dem activism.

There are one or two other constituencies where they pose an immediate threat to Labour: Cardiff

Central, where they won the Welsh Assembly seat in 1999 is the most serious, with Oldham East & Saddleworth and Birmingham Yardley behind, then Bristol West, Cambridge, Aberdeen South and Colne Valley. None of these is what could be described as a Labour heartland – all were Conservative in 1987 except Aberdeen South, which went Tory against the trend in 1992. The potential Lib Dem gains from Labour are mostly in constituencies where there is an educated, liberal electorate where Labour did particularly well in 1992 and 1997. New Labour's illiberalism and policies such as higher education tuition fees, as well as its failure to meet unrealistic expectations, have caused quite a rapid decline in support from these voters.   There are some more, rather similar, seats further behind these few where the Lib Dems did quite well in 2001: Edinburgh South, Oxford East, Norwich South, and – spectacularly – Hornsey & Wood Green. The Lib Dem/ Labour targets are, broadly, seats full of *Guardian* readers rather than horny-handed sons of toil.

In local elections it is a rather different story. As Labour declined from their peak performance of 1995 the Liberal Democrats picked up rapidly in some traditionally monolithic Labour areas where they had been working for some time. They gained Liverpool in 1998, Sheffield in 1999 and Oldham in 2000 and particularly in Liverpool can deliver local election landslides. It is likely that the trend will continue in the 2001-5/6 parliament, with gains made in 2002 in the London boroughs (notably Islington, LD-controlled since a 1999 by-election) and other long-established Labour cities (Norwich and Hull). Despite the spectacular scale of Lib Dem victories in local elections in some northern metropolitan areas, it did not translate at all into general election voting in 2001, with a particularly weak showing in Sheffield (except ex-Tory Hallam) and no threat to any of Labour's Liverpool seats. This phenomenon was first noted in February 1974, where despite their breakthrough in local elections in 1973 the Liberals did particularly poorly in Liverpool. It owes a certain amount to differential turnout, but more to genuine ticket-splitting. There was a contrast in 2001 between these areas, where a local government breakthrough had already taken place, and some working class areas in the north east where locally active Lib Dems have not yet won control of the council – Blaydon for example. There is a possibility of a Ludlow-style surprise attack in some of these areas, and if there is great disillusionment with Labour at the time of the 2005/6 election the Lib Dems could pick up some of these and perhaps even make good their promise in Liverpool or Sheffield. There is a limited record of centre party gains from Labour in by-elections in Rochdale (1972), Lincoln (1973), Liverpool Edge Hill (1979), Bermondsey (1983) and Greenwich (1987). However, all of these except the first two (in which unusual local factors played a part) took place at moments of exceptional Labour weakness. If the Labour government endures severe unpopularity, as precedent suggests it will, during its second term it is not difficult to imagine the Lib Dems adding to this if the right sort of seat comes up. It would require some record of local activity and a squeezable Conservative vote. Several seats in Merseyside, Sheffield, inner London and the Black Country fit the bill. Amid the generally optimistic picture for the Lib Dems, there are some recent cases of things going badly wrong for them. In the 1980s and early 1990s Chelmsford and Southend West were top targets, and Adur (Shoreham in West Sussex) was a showpiece for them in local government. They slipped to third place in 2001 in all three areas, and while they still have a local government base in Chelmsford they are a greatly diminished force in the other two at all levels. (Even in Liverpool and Sheffield, the two most prized gains in Labour heartlands, they fell back in 2002.) A political life-cycle appears to be at work. In these areas local activism based on *Focus* newsletters gathered a core of support which was augmented by the collapse of the Labour vote in these areas in the 1970s and early 1980s as that party's policies became unpalatable and its organisation declined. In Chelmsford in particular there were close parliamentary battles between Liberal and Conservative, with the Tories surviving in Chelmsford in 1983 by only 378 votes.

When Labour started reviving as a national party the Alliance could initially keep most of the vote it had gathered by appealing to tactical voting arguments. However, without breakthroughs in 1987 or 1992 the latent Labour vote became tired of unproductive tactical voting and the appeal of New Labour was too strong to resist. A lot of this ex-tactical vote slid back to Labour in 1997 (enough for outright Labour victory in some seats like Hastings & Rye and St. Albans) and another chunk followed in 2001. A similar phenomenon can be detected in seats such as Canterbury, Gosport, Folkestone & Hythe and Bridgwater, and across rural Lincolnshire. Another stage of the process followed in Southend, where the Conservatives fought back at pavement politics level and beat the Lib Dems at their own game – what happened there in 2000 and 2001 will be of great interest to the Conservative Party's new anti-Lib Dem unit. Although there are very few Lib Dem v Labour seats, there is even an example of the process taking place in reverse in Sheffield (Hillsborough) where the Lib Dem general election vote has stagnated and fallen back. Perhaps in several seats – Birmingham Yardley, Totnes, maybe Orpington – the same 'win or bust' option faces the Lib Dems at the next general election.

There are 19 seats where the Lib Dems won by 10 percentage points or less and are at risk of losing in the next election, particularly if there is a Conservative revival because the Tories are second in 17 of them. A smaller proportion of Lib Dem seats are vulnerable to small swings than at any time since the party was forming national governments a century ago, and the trend in 2001 was for increased majorities in most of them. The party is quite well insulated against falling back to a number of seats in the low 20s where it was marooned in 1983-97.

However, if the Lib Dems do suffer losses it is unlikely to be in a neat arithmetical pattern. Most of the vulnerable seats (11 out of the 19 below) had new incumbents in 2001, either because they were gains or because a new candidate was replacing an old stager (as in Southport and Yeovil), and should be less at risk than the raw figures indicate. The Conservatives will also have their sights trained on seats with larger majorities, such as Winchester and Torbay, where they did surprisingly badly in 2001. The Lib Dems are an unpredictable element on the electoral scene.

Liberal Democrat at risk list

	Constituency	See chapter...	Second party	Lead %
1	Cheadle	Greater Manchester	Con	0.1
2	Weston-super-Mare	Avon	Con	0.7
3	Norfolk North	Norfolk	Con	0.9
4	Dorset Mid & Poole North	Dorset	Con	0.9
5	Guildford	Surrey	Con	1.1
6	Somerton & Frome	Somerset	Con	1.3
7	Brecon & Radnorshire	Mid and West Wales	Con	2.0
8	Devon West & Torridge	Devon	Con	2.1

Constituency		See chapter...	Second party	Lead %
9	Hereford	Hereford and Worcester	Con	2.2
10	Ludlow	Shropshire	Con	3.8
11	Newbury	Berkshire	Con	4.8
12	Romsey	Hampshire	Con	4.9
13	Teignbridge	Devon	Con	5.1
14	Argyll & Bute	Highlands & Islands	(2) Lab	5.3
			(3) Con	9.1
			(4) SNP	9.1
15	Chesterfield	Derbyshire	Lab	5.8
16	Devon North	Devon	Con	6.1
17	Eastleigh	Hampshire	Con	6.4
18	Southport	Merseyside	Con	7.3
19	Yeovil	Somerset	Con	8.2

Scottish National Party (SNP)

The last general election was not a good one for the SNP. After becoming the main opposition in the Scottish Parliament following the devolved elections of 1999, with a constituency vote of almost 29 per cent, they fell back significantly when it came to the 2001 contest. Not only did they fail to gain any of their target seats, but Labour increased their majorities in what should have been close contests; constituencies like Glasgow Govan, Kilmarnock & Loudoun and Inverness East, Nairn & Lochaber, the SNP's single 1999 gain. Even worse, they lost one of the six seats they had won in the 1997 general election (Galloway & Upper Nithsdale) to the Conservatives, holding on to a second (Perth) by just 48 votes. Their overall share of the vote was nowhere near the level achieved in 1999, even falling two points from the 22 per cent achieved in 1997.

The very real problem for the SNP at the last general election (and probably the next one as well) was how to persuade their supporters that Westminster elections still matter, given that Scotland now has its own parliament at Holyrood. During the 2001 campaign, opinion polls suggested that a proportion of voters would have been prepared to vote SNP in a Scottish, but not a general election, and this was not helped by most of the party's MPs standing down to concentrate on matters at home. Another consequence of this was the loss of any incumbency vote for Margaret Ewing in Moray, Andrew Welsh in Angus, Roseanna Cunningham in Perth, John Swinney in Tayside North and Alasdair Morgan in Galloway. The SNP vote in each of these constituencies fell by a far greater proportion (over ten percentage points in three cases) than in Banff and Buchan, where Alex Salmond had taken the opposite step of concentrating solely on the Westminster political scene. Although only one seat was lost, others (even Moray) will now be considered genuine marginals at the next general election.

Before then, the priority for the SNP will undoubtedly be the 2003 Scottish elections. In 1999, Labour leads were cut in a swathe of constituencies and although the SNP only gained one extra seat, they will be looking to add to their total. Currently, the party have 35 seats out of 129 at Holyrood, of which 28 are regional top-up places (out of 56 elected in this way). Because of the way the proportional system operates, the overall number of SNP MSP's is unlikely to increase by a great amount whatever happens in 2003, because for each constituency seat gained, the potential for proportional top-up seats falls. As a result, even if they make breakthroughs in places like Govan, Ochil and Dundee West, or indeed if they go that next step, regularly threatened, of breaking into Labour's central heartland, the most likely outcome is a continuation of the present situation where the SNP provide the main opposition to a Labour-Liberal Democrat coalition.

SNP target list: 2003 Scottish Parliament elections

	Constituency	See chapter...	Party	Lead %
1	Dundee West	North East Scotland	Lab	0.4
2	Aberdeen North	North East Scotland	Lab	1.4
3	Ochil	Mid Scotland & Fife	Lab	3.5
4	Argyll & Bute	Highlands & Islands	LD	6.4
5	Glasgow Govan	Glasgow	Lab	6.7
6	Kilmarnock & Loudoun	Central Scotland	Lab	7.0
7	Renfrewshire West	West of Scotland	Lab	8.5
8	Linlithgow	Lothians	Lab	8.7
9	Dundee East	North East Scotland	Lab	9.0
10	Clydesdale	South of Scotland	Lab	10.0
11	Aberdeen Central	North East Scotland	Lab	10.2
12	Livingston	Lothians	Lab	10.7

At the next general election, the task facing the party will be much harder. The margins needed to topple Labour are now far greater than in the above list, and a resurgent Conservative party could also provide a threat, though it may be that the new MPs elected in 2001 can at least build up some sort of incumbency factor to protect themselves against this possibility. In all, there are only three constituencies where the SNP are within 10 per cent of the incumbents (compared with ten Scottish parliamentary seats) and a further five where they are 10-20 per cent behind, compared to about thirty for the devolved parliament. All this again goes to show that although the constituencies may be the same, the electoral battleground for the SNP is very different for Holyrood and Westminster contests.

SNP target list: general election

	Constituency	See chapter...	Party	Lead %
1	Galloway & Upper Nithsdale	South of Scotland	Con	0.2
2	Western Isles	Highlands & Islands	Lab	8.2
3	Argyll & Bute*	Highlands & Islands	LD	9.1

	Constituency	See chapter...	Party	Lead %
4	Inverness E, Nairn & Lochaber	Highlands & Islands	Lab	11.1
5	Dundee East	North East Scotland	Lab	13.8
6	Aberdeen North	North East Scotland	Lab	14.7
7	Ochil	Mid Scotland & Fife	Lab	15.2
8	C'ness, S'and & Easter Ross**	Highlands & Islands	LD	15.2

*SNP in fourth place in 2001, ** SNP in third place in 2001.*

Plaid Cymru (PC)

Plaid Cymru have traditionally seen their support limited to those areas where a majority of the population speak Welsh – the rural west and north of Wales. Before 1999, they found it almost impossible to make any sort of advance in Labour's south Wales heartlands, recording vote shares below 5 per cent (and thus losing their deposit) in many constituencies in this area in general elections up to and including 1997. The constituencies in which they have been successful are the large rural seats up the west coast: Ceredigion (Cardigan), Meirionnydd (Merioneth), Caernarfon (Carnarvon) and Ynys Mon (Anglesey), all of which have majority Welsh-speaking populations. These former Labour or Liberal seats were all gained by Plaid Cymru between 1974 and 1992. Ynys Mon has the unique distinction of being held by all four parties in recent memory, with no party managing to hold it after the incumbent MP stood down since 1929, so it was perhaps not too surprising that after Ieuan Wyn Jones opted to concentrate on the Welsh Assembly, the Westminster seat was lost to Labour in 2001. This was at least compensated by the gain of long-time target, Carmarthen East. A 1966 by-election had seen Carmarthen become the first parliamentary seat ever won by Plaid Cymru, and it was also held between 1974 and 1979. Although Labour then regained it, their hold was often precarious, and their long term prospects were not helped by the 1990s boundary changes. A swing exceeding seven per cent gave the nationalists a decisive 2,500 majority in Carmarthen East & Dinefwr in 2001 to keep their parliamentary delegation at four, while they also made advances in the neighbouring seats of Llanelli and Carmarthen West & South Pembrokeshire. Overall, Plaid Cymru recorded their best ever Westminster vote in 2001 (14 per cent), but the geography of their support means that there are still only four seats which they have realistic prospectsof making a gain at the next general election.

Plaid Cymru target list: general election

	Constituency	See chapter...	Party	Lead %
1	Ynys Mon	North Wales	Lab	2.4
2	Llanelli	Mid and West Wales	Lab	17.7
3	Carmarthen W and S P'shire*	Mid and West Wales	Lab	22.9
4	Conwy**	North Wales	Lab	25.3

*Plaid Cymru in third place in 2001.** Plaid Cymru in fourth place in 2001.*

Plaid Cymru are much more competitive when it comes to the Welsh Assembly, which was established following the extremely tight referendum vote in 1997. Prior to the elections of 1999, they added the suffix 'The Party of Wales' to their title, a clever move given the devolutionist dynamic which was unleashed by the contest (it was those electors who felt most 'Welsh' who were more likely to vote). In the event, not only did Plaid hold all their Welsh-speaking seats, but they finally broke into Labour's heartlands as well. The most spectacular of their gains were the Labour citadels of Islwyn and Rhondda (from 6 and 13 per cent of the vote respectively polled in 1997), though they also won Conwy, Llanelli and Carmarthen East, the only one of the five gains to be repeated at the 2001 general election. In addition, Plaid picked up eight of the twenty regional top-up seats in 1999, giving them 17 AM's out of a total of 60. The question is whether this represented the summit for the party or a staging post to greater things in the future. The result of the 2002 Ogmore by-election (when their vote was lower than in 1999) suggests the former, and one should not forget the background to the 1999 contest, particularly the hostile media treatment Labour were receiving after the resignation of Ron Davies and his replacement by the Blair-backed Alun Michael rather than Rhodri Morgan. Labour may well recover in 2003, and if so we should be as mindful of Plaid Cymru's 'at risk' list (four seats where their majority is below 10 per cent) as much as the slightly larger target list.

Plaid Cymru target list: 2003 Welsh Assembly elections

	Constituency	See chapter...	Party	Lead %
1	Cynon Valley	South Wales Central	Lab	3.1
2	Clwyd West*	North Wales	Lab	3.7
2	Carmarthen W & S P'shire	Mid and West Wales	Lab	5.3
4	Pontypridd	South Wales Central	Lab	5.4
5	Swansea West	South Wales West	Lab	8.1
6	Preseli Pembrokeshire	Mid and West Wales	Lab	9.4
7	Neath	South Wales West	Lab	9.7
8	Caerphilly	South Wales East	Lab	10.0

Plaid Cymru in third place in 1999.

Plaid Cymru at risk list: 2003 Welsh Assembly elections

	Constituency	See chapter...	Second party	Lead %
1	Conwy	North Wales	Lab	0.4
2	Llanelli	Mid and West Wales	Lab	2.4
2	Islwyn	South Wales East	Lab	2.5
4	Rhondda	South Wales Central	Lab	8.2

Green Party

The Green Party probably has the best claim to be Britain's largest minor party. It is represented in the European Parliament (Caroline Lucas for the South East, and Jean Lambert for London), the Scottish Assembly (Robin Harper, Lothians) and the Greater London Assembly (Darren Johnson, Victor Anderson and Jenny Jones), as well as on several local authorities. The party was known until 1985 as the Ecology Party and ecology is at the heart of its thinking. As well as its stand on environmental issues, it is strongly anti-war, feminist, libertarian on social issues and anti-globalisation.

The 2001 election was the Green Party's best ever general election, with its 145 candidates averaging 2.8 per cent support. Their vote had been suppressed in 1997 by tactical voting for Labour and the enthusiasm among the left of the electorate for kicking out the Conservatives. Disappointment with New Labour released these voters for the Greens in mid term elections and the 2001 general election, with interesting results.

The best constituencies for the Greens in the general election were in radically-inclined urban areas with large numbers of students, young people and educated professionals. Brighton Pavilion topped the list, with 9.3 per cent voting Green. This followed up the 1999 Euro election, when it was also the Greens' best constituency with 19 per cent of the (smaller) poll. In May 1999 the Greens won the three seats of the ward of St. Peter's in the constituency, and it is certainly an area that offers them potential. Brighton, as it sometimes is, is more metropolitan than London on this measure; the best Green constituency in London was Hackney North & Stoke Newington (7.4 per cent), where they had also had Euro and local election success in 1998-99. The Greens also did well in a swathe of inner north London and a couple of patches in other areas of inner London. But it would be inaccurate to describe the Greens as only a presence in southern trendy areas; while its fourth best seat, Bradford West (7.0 per cent), has a university, its second strongest is working class Leeds West (8.0 per cent). The Greens are largely an urban movement – their best 25 seats are all in cities - although they do have some areas where activism in rural seats has started to produce votes. They reached double figures in the 1999 Euro elections in Stroud and Leominster, although in 2001 they only managed 3.5 per cent and 3.6 per cent respectively.

The Greens have considerable potential for growth in local elections. They are hampered by the first past the post electoral system – it should be noted that their victories in elections for the GLA, the European Parliament and the Scottish Parliament have all been in regional constituencies under PR systems. This factor is offset to some extent by the tendency for Green voters to concentrate in particular student and trendy inner city districts which enables them to win wards in London boroughs and some provincial areas. Much also depends on organisation and pavement politics work to bring the latent Green vote to the polls; their achievement in building a seven-strong group on Oxford city council, with a stake in the administration until the 2002 elections, was down to solid work in a few carefully chosen target wards. They have also been an expanding force in Lancaster, where the city area now has a very high proportion of students. There are scattered other wards where organisation, and attention to local issues, have paid off: the Newsome ward in Huddersfield, and Shipley West in Bradford borough are examples, as is the ward in Braintree where Greens won in 1999 after opposing an incinerator. Green candidates, buoyed by supportive words from Ken Livingstone, won 11.1 per cent in the 2000 GLA elections, and they were disappointed not to make significant electoral inroads into the London boroughs in May 2002. The Greens' scale of operations and their ability to speak for a section of the electorate make them a national force, albeit one which manifests itself rather inconsistently.

The effect of first-past-the-post militates against a strong Green challenge at Westminster level in any of its better seats. Beyond their small core of support, the Greens are competing for the same sorts of voter as the Liberal Democrats, and they are often overshadowed by the larger party. Even in London and Brighton, parliamentary constituencies are too large a unit to offer a sufficient concentration of young, radical voters in order for the Greens to achieve even 10 per cent of the vote in 2001. It is certainly possible that this barrier will be broken in the next general election, particularly if it continues the trends noticeable in 2001 of alienation from the major parties and left-wing disillusion with Labour. The only MP to have been affiliated with the Greens was Ceredigion & Pembroke North's Cynog Dafis, who won his seat under a combined Plaid Cymru-Green ticket in 1992, but that alliance lapsed and latterly Dafis was solely a Plaid Cymru member. To gain any further members the Green Party will have to make similar alliances, receive defectors – or hope for a change in the electoral system for Westminster.

UK Independence Party (UKIP)

The United Kingdom Independence Party (UKIP) was founded in August 1993, although precursor organisations such as the Anti-Federalist League were active at the time of the 1992 general election. Its emblem of a pound sign symbolises the European issue of most contemporary importance – whether to join the Euro – but it is more radical than just saying no to the Euro. Its central policy is British withdrawal from the European Union, or at the very least a referendum putting this question to the British people. It has other policies, mostly of a traditional but not reactionary nature (for instance, UKIP penal policy favours non-custodial sentencing where possible), but these are rather secondary to the EU issue, and the party has to maintain its guard to repel boarders from the extreme right.

The UKIP was rather obscured in 1997 by James Goldsmith's Referendum Party which ran many more candidates and had more money and publicity. The Referendum Party was wound up after the election, giving UKIP a monopoly on the anti-EU vote thereafter. Its best electoral performance was in the June 1999 European elections, when it won 7.0 per cent of the vote, particularly heavily concentrated in the south west of England and coastal areas of the south east. It has never had much support in Scotland or Wales; the idea of 'UK Independence' is a more complex and troubled one from either national perspective. Its vote entitled it to three seats in the European Parliament, from South East (Nigel Farage), Eastern (Jeffrey Titford) and South West (Michael Holmes, until his resignation). UKIP ran second in several seats in the south west, doing particularly well in Devon West & Torridge (19.2 per cent). As with the Greens in 1989, a low-turnout election whose result did not seem to matter all that much was used as a protest vehicle by many voters.

In the 2001 general election UKIP ran 428 candidates (up from 194 in 1997) and saved six deposits. Party leader Nigel Farage did best, gaining 7.8 per cent in Bexhill & Battle in East Sussex, where the Conservatives were divided. Three of the saved deposits were in Devon (Totnes, Devon East and Devon North), one was Harwich in Essex, where the Referendum Party had done exceptionally well in 1997, and one was Stafford. Most of the constituencies where UKIP did best were in the same sorts of areas as the party had polled well in 1999 and the combined anti-EU parties were strong in 1997. These constituencies tend to have above-average proportions of retired people. There were variations in the extent to which the anti-EU vote subsided between 1997 and 2001, with the Conservatives apparently succeeding in squeezing it down for example in Norfolk and Dorset but not in Devon or Surrey.

UKIP stands occasionally in local elections, but the activities of local councils are not central to its concerns. Only in Stafford did it stand a full slate of local candidates in 2001, and they polled a similar share of the vote to its parliamentary candidate.

UKIP has established itself as a persistent minor party, aided ironically by its representatives elected to Strasbourg. Its vote generates anguished debates within the Conservative Party, whose own Eurosceptics see it – probably erroneously – as a pool of basically Tory voters who would come back as long as Conservative policy was sufficiently anti-European. But the party has shown a lack of internal cohesion, with farcical splits wracking it after its 1999 Euro election success, and is a long way from winning except in the context of a low-turnout European election under PR.

The Socialists and far left

There have always been a large number of groups beyond the Labour party competing for the small space that is found on the left fringe of British politics. In electoral terms, the most successful party in the past were the Communists, though their isolated triumphs (one MP elected at three inter-war general elections and two elected together in 1945) were far less substantial than those achieved by sister parties in countries such as France and Italy. The Communists continued to put up a handful of candidates until the party was wound up after the fall of the Berlin Wall, though by that time they were achieving derisory vote totals, as were others who attempted a 'democratic path to socialism' such as the Workers Revolutionary Party (WRP). In recent years however, there are at last some signs that support has now grown from the very small fractions of the past, and some deposits are even being retained, notably in parliamentary by-elections – socialist candidates polled more than 5 per cent at Hamilton South, Tottenham, Glasgow Anniesland, Preston and Falkirk West in the last parliament, and at Ogmore in the second by-election of the current parliament.

The most successful of the current batch of left-wing groups is the Scottish Socialist Party (SSP), who have been built up by Tommy Sheridan, presently an MSP at Holyrood. Sheridan came to public attention as President of the Scottish Anti-Poll Tax Federation, particularly after he was jailed after attempting to prevent a warrant sale. He was elected to Glasgow council from his prison cell in 1992, after polling in excess of 6,000 votes (and finishing in second place) in the Glasgow Pollok constituency as a Scottish Militant Labour candidate at that year's general election. In 1999, Sheridan was elected to the Scottish Parliament as a regional list MSP from Glasgow, and in the following month's European elections, the SSP polled over ten per cent in five of Glasgow's constituencies. In 2001, they retained their deposit in nine of the ten seats in the city, though they only repeated this achievement in one other seat (Coatbridge & Chryston). Their next aim must be to increase their support outside of Scotland's largest city, and with Sheridan's continued high profile – he writes several regular newspaper columns – this possibility should not be ruled out.

South of the border, there are two Socialist parties in the electoral field, and in true left wing style they spend as much time attacking each other as they do the 'true enemy'. Marginally the more successful is the Socialist Alliance (SA), who are supported by various other groups who do not contest elections, such as the Socialist Workers Party. The Alliance talks of 'striving for maximum unity' on the left, though its stated opposition to 'bureaucratic control from above' is as much to do with attacking their rival, Arthur Scargill's Socialist Labour Party (SLP), as it is an attack on the powers of the state. The SLP were formed in May 1996 after Scargill and others left the Labour party, and are at their strongest (though this is a relative concept) in the urban north. They talk of themselves as the natural home for Socialists and 'the millions of people throughout England, Scotland and Wales who feel disenfranchised or dispossessed' but have come nowhere near attracting this sort of support, retaining just one deposit (Warley) out of twenty-eight at the 2001 general election, a particularly dismal share of the vote (2.4 per cent) recorded by Scargill in Hartlepool. The SA did only slightly better in 2001, retaining two deposits. The first of these was in Coventry North East, where their candidate was former MP Dave Nellist, and the second was in St Helens South, where Labour's candidate was Shaun Woodward. Elsewhere they typically recorded 2-4 per cent, slightly higher than the SLP. In several northern constituencies, both parties stood candidates, with the SA tending to come out on top in these 'real' battles.

British National Party (BNP)

The BNP is the leading party on the far right in Britain at the moment, although there are fragments trading under names such as 'National Democrats' and 'National Front'. Its core appeal is its hostility to 'immigration' and 'asylum seekers' and its wish to see the reduction of Britain's ethnic minority population through what it terms 'voluntary repatriation'. It has traditionalist policies on law and order, wishes to withdraw from the EU and fend off globalisation through protectionism, and has used community politics tactics in order to gain support on local issues. In recent years its chairman Nick Griffin has attempted to present a moderate and acceptable face to the rest of the world, in contrast to the ageing stormtroopers who previously represented the party. However, some of the party's leading activists have convictions for violent racist offences and a record in Hitler-worshipping splinter groups. Investigations by the BBC and *Searchlight* magazine have shown that the BNP has not put race hatred and Nazi ideology behind it despite the change in image.

The main area of activity by the BNP in the 2001 election was Oldham, a town which experienced race riots during the election campaign. The Lancashire ex-textile towns have segregated neighbourhoods, which have proved a breeding ground for fear and resentment, in contrast to the easier mixture in London and to a lesser extent the West Midlands. Griffin polled 16.4 per cent in Oldham West & Royton and his running mate managed 11.2 per cent in the other Oldham seat. The second best BNP showing was actually in Burnley, a rather similar place, with 11.3 per cent, and the party also did relatively well in Pendle (5.0 per cent). Its Yorkshire centres were Bradford North (4.6 per cent) and Dewsbury (4.5 per cent). Given the concentration of white voters in certain wards, the BNP had high hopes in the run-up to the 2002 local elections of winning representation and these were realised in Burnley, where they won three council seats. It is notable that a previous far right party, the National Party, won two seats in nearby Blackburn in 1976.

East London is a traditional area of strength for the extreme and racist right, from 'anti-alien' agitation in the early 20th century through Mosley's blackshirts of the 1930s to the present day. True to form, it produced two of the BNP's five saved deposits, with 6.4 per cent in Barking and 5.1 per cent in Poplar & Canning Town, and a very near miss in Dagenham (4.99 per cent). However, the BNP vote slipped back from the levels it had reached in 1997 in both Poplar & Canning Town and Bethnal Green & Bow. The BNP's electoral tide seems to have receded somewhat here since the 1990s; it was in the Tower Hamlets ward of Millwall that it elected its first councillor in a 1993 by-election. The BNP also has some support in the West Midlands, particularly around the Tipton area in West Bromwich West and in central Dudley, but nowhere was it broad enough to save a deposit in 2001. It is quite weak in Leicester, despite that city's past as a hotbed of National Front activity in the 1970s.

The concentrated nature of BNP support in the Lancashire towns gives the party a chance of building an electoral and local government base. However, its potential for growth is surely limited by the unattractive features of violence and Nazism, which the party tries hard to hide, as well as its publicly proclaimed philosophy based around race. It is a localised threat and it is difficult to imagine the BNP doing much better in a general election than it did in Oldham in 2001, when the mood in the town was much disturbed by the recent riots.

Liberal Party

The Liberal Party in its current form was founded in 1988 by the minority of Liberals who refused to accept merger with the SDP on the grounds that it would dilute Liberal principles. There are significant differences in philosophy and policy between them and the Lib Dems, who they tend to call 'Social Democrats': the Liberals are highly libertarian, ecological, completely opposed to nuclear weapons and would pull out of the EU. They aspire to a world government.

The Liberals are only significant in a few areas. The party lists 'areas of activity' as

> Cornwall, Devon, Somerset, Slough, London, Brentwood, Peterborough, Wolverhampton, Wyre Forest, Liverpool, Manchester, Leeds, Sheffield, Sunderland, Gateshead, Edinburgh, Nuneaton.

By far the most successful Liberal candidate in the 2001 election was Steve Radford, a Liverpool councillor standing in that city's West Derby constituency who polled 14.9 per cent of the vote and came second to Labour. Their next best performance was in Exeter (4.9 per cent) where there is a significant group elected to the city council and two Devon county councillors, led by David Morrish. Their other 12 candidates polled much lower shares, with a particularly disappointing 1.4 per cent in Leeds West, the former constituency of their President Michael Meadowcroft. Their presence in Wyre Forest, where Mike and Fran Oborski have been community politics activists for years, is also significant. They have provided the leadership of the borough council, and are allied to Kidderminster Hospital and Health Concern (KHHC) who won the parliamentary seat in 2001. They have scattered wards in other places, mostly with the benefit of a free run from the Liberal Democrats although sometimes not (as in Exeter);

Haymill in Slough is one, and – to the delight of those who recall a Liberal scandal of the 1970s – Dogsthorpe in Peterborough is another. The Liberals are a very long way from winning any constituency.

Mebyon Kernow – The Party of Cornwall

Interest in Cornwall's distinct history and culture has been increasing in recent decades, an echo of the nationalist movements in Scotland and Wales. The Cornish language has undergone a small revival, and the devolution of power to Scotland and Wales in 1999 has stimulated campaigning for a Cornish assembly. The campaign for a Cornish Assembly has attracted 50,000 signatures to its petition.

Mebyon Kernow ('The Sons of Cornwall' in the Cornish language) was founded as a pressure group for Cornish cultural and linguistic campaigning, historical research and self-government in 1951. Its statute described its political aim as 'to further the acceptance of the Celtic character of Cornwall and its right to self-government in domestic affairs in a Federated United Kingdom.' MK describes itself as 'based on four important cornerstones; it is Cornish, Green, Left-of-centre and Decentralist.' The party has campaigned for a Cornish university, separate treatment from the rest of the South West region, EU Objective One status and several Green and internationalist issues.

MK has stood candidates in local and national elections since the 1970s, and its best ever showing was in the 1979 Euro election when its candidate attracted about 10 per cent of the Cornish vote in the Cornwall and Plymouth seat. MK has councillors on four of the six Cornish districts, and was represented on the county council until 2001. It averaged 13 per cent of the poll in the seats where it stood in the county elections, and obtained 2.3 per cent in two seats in the General Election in 2001. Its growth has been hindered by the way in which the established parties, particularly the Liberal Democrats, have adopted some of its causes. It is a long way from being the equivalent of the SNP or Plaid Cymru, but it is a serious and committed presence on the Cornish scene with potential for growth.

Legalise Cannabis Alliance

The LCA was founded as a single-issue party to promote the legalisation of cannabis and make cannabis an important issue in British politics. As well as running its own candidates it lends support to candidates of any party who make their support for legalisation a prominent part of their campaign. It has the support of Howard Marks, the celebrated former cannabis smuggler. The LCA contests local and general elections in several areas including Essex, Norwich and Cumbria. Its best results come in constituencies where the Green Party, which also favours cannabis legalisation, fails to put up candidates, and it can occasionally beat other minor parties such as the Socialist Alliance or the UK Independence Party. Its best result in 2001 was 2.5 per cent in Workington, and two other Cumbrian constituencies (Penrith & The Border and Carlisle) were also in its top five; it's probably those long dark winter evenings.

Since the election the LCA's cause has made surprising headway, with Peter Lilley's libertarian thoughts on the subject, a Home Affairs Select Committee inquiry, David Blunkett's decision to demote cannabis to Class C and above all the police experiment in making it non-arrestable in Lambeth. Despite its insignificance, the LCA might soon be able to claim success, wind itself up and disappear in a puff of aromatic smoke.

Regional trends: the opinion polls

by Roger Mortimore, MORI

In most respects the similarities in attitudes between Britain's regions are far more striking than the differences. Although there are, of course, long-standing distinctions in political party strength, most of these are related to the most obvious socio-demographic differences between different areas of the country and, furthermore, changes in attitudes have tended to be more uniform than not across the country.

Similarly, when one looks at attitudes to political issues in a broad sense, regional differences are muted and, where they exist, the reasons are for the most part obvious. MORI's monthly question in which respondents are asked to name (without being shown a list of options or any other prompting) the 'most important issues facing Britain today', should be a sensitive barometer for detecting any distinctive regional characteristics, yet the general pattern of answers is remarkably similar across the country, as the table (drawing on the combined responses from five monthly surveys following the 2001 election) shows. There is no obvious and dramatic 'north-south divide' or any other broad pattern.

	All %	Sc %	NE %	NW %	ME %	YH %	EM %	WM %	WA %	SW %	EA %	GL %	SE %
n=	5130	498	170	578	111	511	284	418	305	486	503	562	704
NHS/Hospitals	50	44	44	48	45	40	55	50	54	53	55	48	55
Education/schools	32	28	25	28	28	30	32	33	32	32	36	35	35
Defence/foreign	31	31	44	36	31	35	37	31	29	31	33	21	28
Crime/law & order	21	14	16	23	24	20	23	20	23	19	20	25	22
Race /immigration	19	14	16	20	16	19	18	19	18	16	19	19	23
EU/ Single Currency	15	9	15	14	6	15	14	13	9	19	19	12	20
Economy	12	13	10	13	9	13	13	9	13	13	13	14	10
Unemployment	12	20	21	11	17	10	13	14	15	7	7	13	6
Pensions/social security	9	8	6	9	15	5	14	8	11	9	8	6	10
Transport/pub. transport	8	3	*	5	4	7	8	6	6	11	11	12	10
Housing	5	6	2	5	*	2	6	4	3	5	6	10	6
Foot and mouth outbreak/agriculture	4	4	7	6	3	4	2	3	4	11	3	3	3

(Responses below 10 per cent in all regions omitted), Source: MORI/The Times, Base: 5,130 adults aged 18+, July–November 2001

KEY: SC - Scotland, NE - North East, NW - North West, ME - Merseyside, YH - Yorkshire & Humber, EM - East Midlands, WM - West Midlands, WA - Wales, SW - South West, EA - Eastern, GL - Greater London, SE - South East.

The National Health Service is the most frequently named concern in every single region. Education and defence/foreign affairs were two of the next three in every case. (The high rating of defence/foreign affairs, usually very low on the list, is entirely attributable to the terrorist attacks on the USA on 11 September 2001, halfway through the period covered by the surveys, and the subsequent war in Afghanistan.) Of the most prominent regional differences, unemployment is more on the minds of people in Scotland and the North East, where unemployment is highest, Foot and Mouth Disease in the South West and North East, where the outbreak had hit hardest and lingered longest, and housing was a disproportionate issue of concern in London, where house prices were highest and the market most crowded.

Indeed, some differences are far smaller than might be supposed. For example, although concern about public transport is highest in London, the figure is only marginally greater than in the other three regions of southern England, despite the capital's traffic problems and the political furore over the future of the London Underground. Similarly, concern about race relations and immigration was at similar levels in all regions, notwithstanding the considerable variation between regions in the size of the ethnic minority communities.

This broad uniformity of attitudes reflects a broad uniformity of influences and information. Academic studies of the 'important issues' question and similar measures of the public's 'top of the mind' concerns have shown very close correlations with media coverage of the issues of the day – greater concentration upon an issue by television and the newspapers generates greater public awareness. In Britain, far more so than in many countries, experience of news coverage is uniform across the country. Most of the public regard television as their main source of information about news and current affairs, and the vast majority rely on the lunchtime or evening bulletins of the two main national stations. Second to television comes the press, and two-thirds of the adult population regularly read one of a dozen London-based daily titles. Regional newspapers have much lower readership, and regional TV and radio are reporters only of local, not national and international, news.

Scotland is a partial exception to this, with its own newspapers and separately produced broadcast news bulletins. With the launch of the Scottish Parliament there is a separate news agenda, especially on political matters, which can be clearly seen by comparison of the Scottish broadsheets, the Scotsman and the Herald, with their London counterparts. Yet the Scottish public's concerns are much the same as those south of the Border.

This was even true during the 2001 general election: there was remarkably little difference between Scotland and England in the issues that electors said would determine how they would vote. Even though the issues that most concerned English voters, the NHS and education, now come under the control of Holyrood and should not, in theory, be affected by who is sent to Westminster, these were also the issues that were very important to Scots in deciding how to vote. The same was true in Wales.

Q. At this General Election, which, if any, of these issues do you think will be very important to you in helping you decide which party to vote for?

	England%	Scotland%	Wales%	London%
Health care	73	73	67	69
Education	63	63	60	68
Law and order	50	49	50	46
Pensions	39	45	42	29
Taxation	38	38	29	33
Unemployment	30	35	30	32
Managing the economy	30	30	22	30
Public transport	31	27	25	43
Asylum seekers	30	25	18	30
Protecting the natural environment	25	22	21	25
Europe	26	21	15	28
Housing	20	21	17	32
Animal welfare	12	13	7	8
Defence	11	12	8	7
Constitution/devolution	6	8	7	7
Trade Unions	6	8	3	9
Northern Ireland	7	6	4	8
Other	3	2	3	3

Source: MORI/The Times

Base: 2,088 British 18+ (166 in Scotland, 104 in Wales, 244 in London), 5 June 2001

This is not because Scots are unaware of the Scottish Parliament or unable to distinguish between Holyrood politics and Westminster politics. It has been very clear since 1999 that many voters make a clear distinction in their party preferences between the two Parliaments. (The monthly System Three polls for the *Herald* regularly ask the same sample of Scots how they would vote for Westminster and how for Holyrood; invariably, Labour perform better and the SNP worse for Westminster; the difference is usually at least five points, and has touched double figures.) It is simply that they don't necessarily accept that devolution has removed Westminster's influence over devolved policy areas such as education and the NHS – which, since Westminster retains ultimate control over funding, is a reasonable position.

Regional identity and devolution

Regional devolution for England remains on the agenda, if no longer quite so urgent as it seemed when it was briefly seen as the best political answer to the 'West Lothian question'. (The 'West Lothian question' - named in honour of Tam Dalyell, who was MP for West Lothian when he first raised it during the devolution debates of the 1970s – asked how it could be legitimate after the inauguration of a Scottish Parliament that MPs for Scottish seats at Westminster could still speak and vote on matters purely concerning England, while English MPs would be barred from interfering with the same matters in Scotland. Regional devolution, giving similar reserved powers to local assemblies in England as those exercised by the Scottish Parliament, would solve the problem by putting all Westminster MPs on the same footing; but in practice few advocates of regional devolution suggest that the powers to be devolved should be remotely as extensive as those exercised by Holyrood.)

In any case, while there was always strong support in Scotland for a Parliament, attitudes to devolution in England were more ambivalent. London, of course, was a special case in that the introduction of a regional tier of government was merely the restoration of a previously existing level of local government, albeit in a different administrative form. (The old Greater London Council, in effect a county council, had covered the same area as the new Greater London authority.) Elsewhere, regional government would represent a new departure. A MORI survey for the *Economist* in 1999 found that outside London only in the North East, the most compact of the English regions, was there a clear majority in favour of an elected regional assembly, although there was also plurality support in the South West. This was the case even though in a number of the regions where support for a regional assembly was lacking, there was nevertheless backing for the more general proposition of 'greater powers of government to regions in England'; intriguingly the lowest figure for support was recorded in London. Perhaps decentralisation in general terms seems attractive, especially in the regions that feel themselves on the periphery, yet the somewhat artificial administrative regions are not seen as the best level at which to devolve it. It may be, for instance, that some parts of the North West (the region with the biggest gap between support of the general principle and specific proposal) are happy enough to take power away from Westminster, but not for the purpose of giving it to Manchester instead.

Q. As you may know, there will be elections to a Scottish Parliament and a Welsh Assembly next May. Do you support or oppose giving greater powers of government to regions in England?

| | NE | NW | YH | EM | WM | EA | SE | GL | SW |
	%	%	%	%	%	%	%	%	%
Support	51	55	52	49	49	48	48	47	53
Oppose	23	29	23	17	27	34	34	25	26
Don't know	26	17	25	35	24	18	19	28	22
Net support	28	26	29	32	22	14	14	22	27

Source: MORI/Economist

Base: 1,810 aged 15+ across England, 5-8 March 1999

Q. Would you support or oppose your region of England, the .... region, getting its own elected assembly?

	NE %	NW %	YH %	EM %	WM %	EA %	SE %	GL %	SW %
Support	51	42	42	40	46	43	37	60	47
Oppose	29	44	42	35	37	42	47	21	39
Don't know	20	14	16	24	17	15	16	19	13

Source: MORI/Economist

Base: 1,810 aged 15+ across England, 5-8 March 1999

The analysis is based on the administrative government office regions, which are the most likely basis for any devolved structure. It is clear that some of these regions are artificial, and bear little resemblance to the instinctive local identities of their citizens. The MORI /*Economist* survey tested public awareness of the administrative divisions shortly before the European Parliament elections of 1999 (when the same boundaries were used to define the electoral regions that served as constituencies under the list PR electoral system). In the Eastern region, which combines East Anglia with a swathe of territory traditionally considered part of the South East, almost half the respondents were unable even to pick out their region correctly when shown a list; but a third were also incorrect in London (perhaps mistakenly assuming London was not regarded as a separate region) and a quarter in Yorkshire and Humberside.

Q. England is divided into several regions for the purposes of administration of government services. Can you tell me which region you think you are in? (Question asked with showcard list of regions)

	NE %	NW %	YH %	EM %	WM %	EA %	SE %	GL %	SW %
Correct	89	97	66	79	91	52	88	60	86
Incorrect	10	3	26	16	8	46	5	34	11
Don't know	1	0	8	8	1	2	7	6	3

The Euro

Notwithstanding the general uniformity of opinions, there are a few political issues where marked regional differences in attitudes are present to an extent that cannot easily be explained by demographic differences, by obvious local circumstances or indeed by variations in support for the political parties.

Perhaps the most politically significant of these is Europe, both the specific question of joining the

Single Currency and more general attitudes to the European Union. London is, and has been consistently, markedly less hostile to Britain joining the single European currency than is the rest of the country – far more so than can be explained by low Conservative support in London though, indeed, it may be that Conservative opposition to the Euro has been a contributory factor in the disproportionate fall in Conservative support in the capital. (London was the only English region where the Conservative share of the vote fell between the 1997 and 2001 elections.)

In a MORI survey for *The Times* conducted during the 2001 general election, 43 per cent of the British public said that if there were a referendum on whether to stay in or get out of the EU, they would vote to stay in, while 41 per cent would vote to leave, a very slim plurality in favour of the EU; but in London, 57 per cent would stay in and only 28 per cent would leave, a two-to-one majority. Similarly, while nationally only 23 per cent said they would vote to join the Euro in an immediate referendum and 60 per cent would vote against, in London 36 per cent were in favour and 51 per cent against.

The War in Afghanistan

The views of Londoners also proved distinctive in their reactions to the government's handling of the September 11 terrorist attacks on the USA and the military action in Afghanistan that followed. Approval of President Bush's and of Tony Blair's handling of the crisis were persistently lower in London than elsewhere in Britain.

Q Do you approve or disapprove of the way George W Bush is handling the American response to the terrorist attacks on September 11?

	All GB			London		
	Sep	Oct	Nov	Sep	Oct	Nov
	%	%	%	%	%	%
Approve	63	64	66	48	52	52
Disapprove	24	27	24	34	37	31
Don't know	12	9	10	17	11	17

Q Do you approve or disapprove of the way Tony Blair is handling the British response to the terrorist attacks on September 11?

	All GB			*London*		
	Sep	*Oct*	*Nov*	*Sep*	*Oct*	*Nov*
	%	%	%	%	%	%
Approve	72	68	71	60	59	56
Disapprove	19	25	23	23	28	34
Don't know	9	7	6	17	13	10

Source: MORI/The Times

This is not a reflection of antipathy in the capital to Tony Blair – indeed, in November his score on the more general 'satisfaction with the Prime Minister' question, not mentioning the terrorist issue or the war, was slightly higher in London than nationally.

These two findings, on the Euro and the reaction to September 11, might seem to suggest that London takes a distinctive attitude to foreign affairs, perhaps more European and more suspicious of America. Yet this does not seem to be the case. In a MORI survey for the *Economist* in September 1999, respondents were asked whether they thought Europe, America or the Commonwealth would be Britain's most reliable political ally in a crisis: across Britain 59 per cent picked America, only 16 per cent Europe and 15 per cent the Commonwealth; but in London 65 per cent picked America, 16 per cent Europe and only 11 per cent the Commonwealth. No signs of anti-Americanism there. When asked which they most identified with – local community, region, country, Europe, the Commonwealth or the global community – Londoners were only slightly more likely to identify with Europe than were citizens in the rest of England, and, defying expectations that the cosmopolitan nature of the capital might encourage a more global outlook, 'the global community' scored no higher in London than elsewhere, either. But Londoners were less likely than average to identify with a local community.

Q. Which two or three of these, if any, would you say you most identify with?

	London	*Rest of England*	*Scotland*	*Wales*
	%	%	%	%
This local community	33	44	39	32
This region	43	49	62	50
England/Scotland/Wales*	42	41	72	81
Britain	50	42	18	27
Europe	21	16	11	16
The Commonwealth	13	9	5	3
The global community	8	9	5	2

	London	Rest of England	Scotland	Wales
None of these	*	0	0	0
Don't know	1	2	1	0

*Asked as appropriate

Source: MORI/The Economist

Base: 923 British adults 18+, 24-27 September 1999

It is worth noting, as other similar surveys have also found, that while the English are as likely to think of themselves as British, the same is certainly not true in Scotland and Wales. Uniform in many of its attitudes Britain may be, but it by no means has any unanimous sense of its collective identity.

Notes on the county summaries and constituency tables

Most of the chapters which follow are based on the county areas which were established in the 1970s (though note the comments in the local government section below). The exceptions in England are Greater London, which is divided into six smaller areas, and the West Midlands, which is divided into three. Scotland and Wales are both divided into the 'new' European regions, which were used in 1999 for allocating top-up seats for the Welsh Assembly and Scottish Parliament elections. Northern Ireland is dealt with in a single section.

County statistics

The tables at the head of each county, sub-county or region summarise the constituency data in that section. They include vote shares and seats won[1] at the 2001, 1997 and 1992 general elections, and also the 1987 and 1983 general elections for the English sections only (the Liberal Democrat totals for 1987 and 1983 refer to the SDP-Liberal Alliance vote). The Wales and Scotland sections include the results of the 1999 Assembly / Parliamentary elections, with separate tables showing both the constituency aggregate (labelled 1999C) and second vote (labelled 1999R)[2]. Note that 'Others' in these tables include all non-Conservative, Labour or Liberal Democrat candidates. For Northern Ireland, summary data is provided for the 1998 Assembly elections and 1996 Forum elections, as well as the last three general elections.

Local government

We have tried to provide summaries of the political composition of each local authority, as of May 2002, within the area covered by each chapter[3]. Note that in 1986, the county councils in Greater London and six provincial metropolitan counties (West Midlands, Greater Manchester, Merseyside, South Yorkshire, West Yorkshire and Tyne & Wear) were abolished, and each of these areas was divided into a number of single tier 'metropolitan' authorities. In the mid 1990s, a further review of local government (the Banham review) removed the unpopular 1970s creations of Avon, Cleveland and Humberside, and replaced each of them with four single-tier unitary authorities. The remaining counties in England ended up retaining a two-tier set up of county councils with a number of smaller district councils, but it was not as straightforward as this, since the Banham review recommended that a number of areas 'opt out' of their counties and become unitary authorities. This tended to apply, with little apparent overall logic, to larger towns and cities, but also some smaller areas, notably the former county of Rutland and, for some reason, all the authorities in Berkshire. As a result of these changes, forty or so unitary councils were created in England in the 1990s, which essentially form a fourth type of local authority (in addition to metropolitan, county and district councils). If this sounds messy and a recipe for confusion, then it undoubtedly is.

To avoid a multiplicity of county sections in England, we have included the areas covered by the unitary authorities within their old 'parent' county (for example Luton and Bedfordshire are covered in the same section). We have retained chapters for the abolished counties and also Berkshire and Hereford & Worcester, which were officially separated again in the last local government review. Wales and Scotland also moved to a new local government map in the 1990s (entirely made up of single-tier authorities), which meant the abolition of some large areas created in the 1970s such as Dyfed and Strathclyde, and the restoration of several smaller counties abolished twenty-odd years previously. There are too many authorities (about twenty in each case) for a separate section on each, and we have used the larger new regional boundaries instead. These were used in the 1999 elections for the purpose of allocating top-up seats; each of our sections in Wales and Scotland states the local authorities (whose boundaries do not always match the regions) which are included.

Different local authorities have different electoral cycles, most falling into one of two broad categories (all councillors have fixed four-year terms and have elections on the first Thursday in May[4]). The first model is where a third of council seats are contested each year, which is usually referred to (somewhat inaccurately, as one year out of four has no elections) as 'annual elections'. This pattern can be found in all the English metropolitan councils and some of its district and unitary authorities. The second model is found where the whole authority is contested in one 'big bang' or all-out election, which tends to be the case with the smaller English district councils, all remaining English county councils and the London boroughs, and all elections in Wales and Scotland. The majority of all-out elections in District councils (which tend to include a number of two or three member wards) were last held in 1999, and are due again in 2003. County elections in the English 'shire' counties have been held on the same day as general elections in 1997 and 2001, and are next due in 2005. London borough elections are timetabled for 2002 and again in 2006, while the Greater London Assembly elections will take place in 2004. Elections for the Welsh Assembly and Scottish Parliament take place in 2003, with Scottish local government elections also held in 2003 and Welsh councils electing a year later in 2004. To simplify this profusion of election dates, a timetable is given below of the main groups of elections which are due each year:

Election timetable 2003–6

(all seats to be contested unless stated otherwise)

2003   Elections in English district councils and most unitary authorities (one third of seats in some cases)
           English metropolitan council elections (one third of seats)
           Scottish local government elections

Scottish Parliament elections
Welsh Assembly elections
Northern Ireland Assembly elections

2004   Greater London Assembly elections
Welsh local government elections
English metropolitan council elections (one third of seats)
Some district and unitary council elections (one third of seats)
European elections

2005   County council elections in England
Unitary council elections in some areas (mix of all out and one third of seats)
Northern Ireland local government elections

2006   London borough elections
English metropolitan council elections (one third of seats)
Some district and unitary council elections (one third of seats)

In addition, all-out elections for some English metropolitan, unitary and district councils take place when ward boundaries have been changed; there are usually several of these each year.

Boundary review

Reviews of parliamentary boundaries have taken place regularly since the end of the second world war, and have left very few constituencies unaltered. After an emergency review in 1945 (when several very large seats were divided), comprehensive reviews have taken place prior to general elections in 1950, 1974, 1983 and 1997 and a more minor review before 1955. The basic aim of each review and the boundary commission which carries them out is to equalise constituency electorates, and although there are several other rules such as preserving local ties and taking into account 'special geographical factors', the first aim usually overrides the others.

Each review divides the country up into a number of units, though the separate commissions for Wales, Scotland and Northern Ireland conduct reviews at which all constituencies in their area are considered at the same time. In England, the basic unit is the county, with approximately 50 separate reviews due to take place in the present cycle[5]. In each area, the total electorate at the qualifying date (2000 in the present review) is divided by the national electoral quota (69,934) to produce a theoretical entitlement to a number of constituencies, which is then rounded down or up to a whole number. This may be different from the existing total number of seats - in England the general pattern has been for urban areas (notably the metropolitan counties) to gradually lose constituencies while the shire counties (particularly in the midlands and south) gain them. One might think that this would automatically benefit the Conservatives as it is Labour seats which tend to be abolished, new seats often strongly Tory. In the 1990s review, however, it was not as straightforward as this, since new seats often took a disproportionate number of Conservative voters out of existing constituencies, making them easier for Labour to gain in 1997.

Whatever happens in the current review, the major parties now spend a great deal of time and resources attempting to secure the best possible outcome for themselves. This can extend to hiring professional counsel at local inquiries, which take place following publication of the commission's provisional recommendations and receipt of a certain number of objections. Whatever effort is expended by the parties, or indeed members of the public who also have the opportunity to support or object to proposals, the final decisions for each area rests with the commission. Following the inquiry, they will publish revised recommendations (which may or may not differ from the original) and then, after another chance to object, final recommendations, though in practice it is unusual for further changes to be made at this stage. All recommendations across the country (including those for Wales, Scotland and Northern Ireland) will then be put before the Secretary of State when completed, but even this stage can be politically contentious, notably its timing. In 1969 for example, the Labour government delayed the imposition of boundary changes until after the 1970 general election, believing them to be loaded against the party. In the event they lost the election, and ironically returned to power in 1974 after the changes had gone through.

There has been some debate on whether the current review can be completed by the next general election in 2005/6 - at first it seemed possible or even probable that it would be, but recent publications appear to rule out this possibility. Even though proposals may not be implemented until 2011 (an absurd time lag given that the first proposals and local inquiries took place before the 2001 election), we have included a short section at the end of each county introduction (or general introduction for Scotland and Wales) outlining the recommendations made for each area and their possible political consequences. Where recommendations have not yet been published (see timetable below) we have calculated whether the total constituency entitlement is likely to remain as it is, increase or decrease.

Current boundary review timetable *(as of May 2002)*

Final recommendations already announced
South London boroughs
Former Avon area
Cumbria
Hertfordshire
Isle of Wight
Lincolnshire
Northamptonshire
Northumberland
Somerset
Surrey
Swindon

Awaiting final recommendations
North London boroughs

Warwickshire
Wiltshire (not including Swindon)

Provisional recommendations made
Hampshire, Portsmouth and Southampton
Nottinghamshire and Nottingham
Staffordshire and Stoke-on-Trent
Scotland

Derbyshire and Derby
Durham and Darlington
North Yorkshire and York

Provisional recommendations due 2002-2005 (in expected order)
Former Humberside area
Gloucestershire
Oxfordshire
Suffolk

Buckinghamshire and Milton Keynes
Cheshire, Halton and Warrington
East Sussex, Brighton & Hove

Bedfordshire and Luton
Essex, Southend-on-Sea and Thurrock
Shropshire, Telford & Wrekin

Devon, Plymouth and Torbay
Kent and Medway
Lancashire, Blackburn with Darwen and Blackpool

Berkshire
Former Cleveland area
Dorset, Bournemouth and Poole

Cambridgeshire and Peterborough
Cornwall
West Sussex
Herefordshire
Worcestershire
Leicestershire, Leicester and Rutland
Norfolk

Merseyside
Tyne & Wear
West Midlands

Greater Manchester
South Yorkshire
West Yorkshire

Wales
Northern Ireland

Constituency tables

The basic table for all 659 constituencies includes results of the general elections of 2001 and 1997, and also estimated or 'notional' 1992 results on the present boundaries (actual results from 1992 are provided where there was no change in boundaries)[6]. We have shown the number of votes cast and the percentage share of the vote for all the major parties: Conservative, Labour, Liberal Democrat, Scottish National Party in Scotland and Plaid Cymru in Wales (and the main parties for constituencies in Northern Ireland). In addition we have provided vote totals for 'anti EU' parties[7] (though not in Scotland, where their vote was frequently below 1 per cent) and significant 'Others', whose vote exceeded 5 per cent - the level at which candidates retain their deposits - at one of the three general elections in the table[8]. The votes for all other candidates have been aggregated, the number in brackets after the 'Others' vote indicating the number of candidates whose votes have been combined in this way. We have also indicated the name of the Member of Parliament elected after each election together with their party (in brackets) and majority. Where a sitting MP went on to take another party's whip during the parliament, this has been noted. For notional 1992 results we have given the estimated majority on the present boundaries, but have included the name of the MP elected in the constituency which most closely approximated the present seat in 1992[9]. In a few cases, the winning party in the actual and notional 1992 election was different; where this is so it has been noted in the text.

Constituency results of parliamentary by-elections since 1997, the Scottish Parliament and Welsh Assembly elections which took place in 1999, and the Northern Ireland Assembly elections of 1998, are provided below the main table[10]. The constituency sections in Wales include separate paragraphs for Assembly elections, since the results in 1999 were markedly different from recent general elections, with Plaid Cymru in general performing much better and Labour much worse.

Finally, although the tables have been provided in a form which allows comparison of changes in vote from 1992 to 2001, a couple of health warnings need to be given. First, one or two of the estimated 1992 results appear to the authors to be a little suspect - where this is the case we have stuck with the 'official' figures but noted our suspicion in the text. Second, the electorate figures for different elections have been calculated in slightly different ways, particularly the 1992 estimates which tended to inflate the figures somewhat[11]. For this reason, turnout figures should be regarded as approximations, though this should not hide the general (and worrying) downward trend over recent elections.

Party abbreviations

Con	Conservative
Lab	Labour
LD	Liberal Democrat
PC	Plaid Cymru
SNP	Scottish National Party
SSP	Scottish Socialist Party
BNP	British National Party
KHHC	Kidderminster Hospital and Health Concern
MK	Mebyon Kernow
NF	National Front
PJP	People's Justice Party (Justice for Kashmir)

Northern Ireland parties

UUP	Ulster Unionist Party
DUP	Democratic Unionist Party
PUP	Progressive Unionist Party
UDP	Ulster Democratic Party
UKUP	United Kingdom Unionist Party
UPUP	Ulster Popular Unionist Party
SDLP	Social Democratic and Labour Party
SF	Sinn Fein
Alliance	Alliance Party of Northern Ireland
NIWC	Northern Ireland Women's Coalition

Notes

1   The total number of seats in a county or region sometimes changed before the 1997 general election, following the extensive review of parliamentary boundaries. In one case, Buckinghamshire, the number increased by one prior to the 1992 election.

2   The second or 'regional top-up' vote was designed to achieve a proportional outcome overall, by taking into account constituency seats already won. Because parties are only entitled to top-up seats if they have won few or no individual constituencies, the number in the 'seats' column tends to be markedly different from the constituency vote or indeed other elections.

3   This does not include parish or town councils, which in any case are not usually contested along party lines. Political control of local authorities can change rapidly as a result of annual elections, but also local by-elections and transfers of allegiance, which are more frequent at this than the national level. Control on hung councils is particularly susceptible to change.

4   Exceptionally, this rule was departed from in 2001 because of the foot and mouth crisis, with all elections delayed from May to June. In addition, current local government terms in Wales have been extended from four to five years, to de-align the cycle from that for the Assembly and local government boundary reviews are usually followed by all-out elections, foreshortening the terms of recently-elected councillors.

5   Where counties have been 'abolished', metropolitan or unitary authorities are used as a starting point. Metropolitan authorities (for example the London boroughs) are now frequently 'paired' when boundary reviews are conducted, and many unitary authorities have been paired with their former county in the present exercise, though unitaries can also be dealt with in a separate review if the number of seats to which they are entitled is close to a whole number.

6   The sources used for the constituency tables are listed in a separate section, but are the 'official' set of results for each general election - the Britain Votes series and more recently the Electoral Commission publication for 2001. Estimates of the 1992 results on new boundaries were published in a single volume compiled and edited by Colin Rallings and Michael Thrasher of the University of Plymouth.

7   Anti-EU parties are defined as those whose programme was dominated by the issue of Europe, notably the Referendum Party (1997), UK Independence Party and one or two Independent candidates. Although their policies differed in some respects, the aggregation of the votes of these parties and candidates on a constituency level provides a useful guide to the strength of anti-EU feeling in different parts of the country.

8   We have combined the vote of Socialist candidates where more than one party fielded a candidate in the same constituency, in the same way (and for similar reasons) as for the anti-EU parties. The exception to this is Scotland, where the SSP vote is given separately, and incorporates the vote for its forerunners: the Scottish Socialist Alliance in 1997 and Scottish Militant Labour in 1992. In some instances we have specified 'Others' whose vote was between 3 and 5 per cent, particularly where this may have had an effect on the vote of one of the major parties.

Note that we have used the shorthand 'Ind Labour' or 'Ind Conservative' for dissident candidates who, in reality, have had a variety of descriptions (Real Labour, New Labour, Loyal Conservative). The 1999 Registration of Political Parties Act effectively prohibited all such descriptions in any case, limiting candidates to officially registered parties or the alternatives of an 'Independent' or completely blank label.

9   Where the name of the constituency changed, we have indicated the old name below that of the MP. A few seats have no MP included for 1992; those which were newly created by the boundary review (which for obvious reasons had no MP before 1997) and a handful where the present constituency is the result of a merger of two previous seats - here we have stated 'two seats merge' with names of MPs omitted.

10 Results of by-elections between 1992 and 1997 are not provided in full as they were contested under the old boundaries.

11 The notional electorates for 1992 are slightly higher than they would have been at the April general election of that year as the estimated figures included all attainers (those who reach the age of 18 at some point during the year). The electorates for all 'actual' elections before 2001 were calculated with the help of a formula to remove the proportion of attainers on the register who had not yet reached 18 years of age by the time of the election. This causes a discrepancy between 'actual' and 'notional' 1992 results which is usually a few hundred electors per constituency and the consequence is that the notional turnout figures for 1992 are slightly lower than if calculated in the standard way.

The official 2001 electorate figures were more accurate than those for previous elections as the introduction of 'rolling registration' allowed returning officers to add and delete names as appropriate throughout the year, rather than at the enumeration date alone. It should also be noted that some of the non-official published sources of constituency data from general elections vary widely in the figures given for electorate and turnout.

Sources for election and other data

D.Butler & G.Butler *Twentieth Century British Political Facts 1900-2000* (Macmillan 2000)

Electoral Commission *Election 2001: The Official Results* (Politico's Publishing 2001)

C.Rallings & M.Thrasher *Britain Votes 6: British Parliamentary Election Results 1997* (Ashgate / Parliamentary Research Services 1998)

C.Rallings & M.Thrasher *Media Guide to the New Parliamentary Constituencies* (Local Government Chronicle Elections Centre / BBC, ITN, PA News, Sky 1995)

C.Rallings & M.Thrasher *Britain Votes 5: British Parliamentary Election Results 1988-1992* (Dartmouth / Parliamentary Research Services 1993)

F.W.S. Craig *Britain Votes 4: British Parliamentary Election Results 1983-1987* (Gower / Parliamentary Research Services 1988)

F.W.S. Craig British *Parliamentary Election Results volumes for 1974-1983, 1950-1973, 1918-1949, 1885-1918, 1832-1885* (Parliamentary Research Services)

H. Pelling *Social Geography of British Elections 1885-1910* (Macmillan 1967)

D. Butler & D. Kavanagh *The British General Election of 2001* (Palgrave 2001)

C. Rallings & M. Thrasher *Patterns of Voting in Parliamentary Constituencies 1990-2000* (Local Government Chronicle Elections Centre 2001)

C.Rallings & M.Thrasher *Local Government Handbooks 1995-2000* (Local Government Chronicle Elections Centre)

London Research Centre *London Borough Election Results May 1998* and predecessor volumes (LRC / GLA 1998)

London Research Centre *London Assembly Constituencies* (LRC / GLA 2000)

C. Phillips *Birmingham Votes 1911–2000* (Birmingham Library Service 2001)

Scottish Parliament Research Paper 99/1 *Scottish Parliament Election Results 6 May 1999*

Scottish Parliament Research Papers 00-19 & 01-61 *By Election Results*

The Western Mail *Assembly Handbook 1999* (Western Mail / The Stationery Office 1999)

House of Commons Library Research Paper 99/64 *Elections to the European Parliament - June 1999* (House of Commons Library 21 June 1999)

House of Commons Library Research Paper 01/71 *The Local Elections of 7 June 2001* (House of Commons Library 29 September 2001)

House of Commons Library Research Paper 00/53 *The Local Elections and Elections for a London Mayor and Assembly: 4 May 2000* (House of Commons Library 23 May 2000)

House of Commons Library Research Paper 01/113 *Unemployment by Constituency, November 2001* (House of Commons Library 12 December 2001)

Department of the Environment, Transport and the Regions *Indices of Deprivation at ward level 2000* (DETR/DTLR 2000)

Office of National Statistics *Census 1991 Monitor (parliamentary constituencies)* (The Stationery Office 1993–1996)

Opinion poll data courtesy of MORI

London – North

	Conservative		Labour		Liberal Democrat		Others	
	Share of vote	Seats	Share of vote	Seats	Share of vote	Seats	Share of vote	Seats
2001	28.9	1	52.9	11	15.1	0	3.1	0
1997	29.9	1	56.8	11	11.9	0	1.4	0
1992	43.7	7	41.5	6	13.0	0	1.8	0
1987	45.1	9	34.4	4	19.4	0	1.1	0
1983	42.9	9	32.3	4	22.9	0	1.8	0

This chapter covers the boroughs of Barnet, Camden, Enfield, Haringey and Islington; the area stretches from the central London districts of Bloomsbury and Clerkenwell up to some patches of open country on the edge of Greater London. Several lines of the London underground stretch from the centre out to the edge of the metropolitan area – the Northern Line to Hendon, Edgware and Barnet; the Piccadilly Line to Southgate, and the Victoria Line passes through Tottenham. These lines, and a lot of social and ethnic history, link the inner areas to the outer suburbs, and in recent years there has been a clear political trend rippling outwards as well.

To deal with the inner areas first, the three inner boroughs of Camden, Islington and Haringey contain most of the landmarks, people and attributes associated with north London. Many cities have a small 'lentil belt' of trendily progressive areas sporting organic cafes, marijuana accessory shops, futon retailers, pubs with jazz bands and so on, and most of London's super-sized lentil belt is in the inner north: Camden Town, Islington, Highbury, Kentish Town. The media and the arts are well represented in the area leading to its frequent appearance in satire – from Marc Boxer's *Life and Times in NW1* to Knife and Packer's *It's Grim Up North London*, and that's just the cartoons. The Georgian terraces of Islington and Camden Town attracted discerning buyers in the late 1960s and have now become exclusive, and the delightful hill villages of Hampstead and Highgate, with clean air and green spaces, have always been attractive. North London's gentrifying appeal has spread into other less distinctive terraced areas such as Crouch End and West Hampstead.

Inner north London has other elements too, of course. There are some very poor council estates in Islington – Holloway Road remains a poor and polluted district - Camden Town, Tottenham and Kilburn in particular, although there is a council housing presence throughout the area. There are also some distinctive ethnic areas like the Turkish and Cypriot main drag of Green Lanes, Irish Kilburn and black Tottenham. Haringey council estimates that 193 different languages are spoken in the borough. North London's population is drawn from the liberal elements of the top of the social ladder and people who aspire to that status, plus a considerable population at the bottom of the ladder and not a great deal in between. It is a chaotic, very metropolitan mixture of races, classes and lifestyles and therefore a disaster area for the Conservatives in recent times. The Conservatives were once competitive in the inner seats, winning the middle class seats of Hornsey and Hampstead in every election until 1992 (except for a Labour gain in Hampstead in 1966), but the collapse since then has been rapid and they came third in four of the six seats in 2001.

However, inner north London was a little-noticed patch where Labour did extremely badly in 2001, with an 8.7 per cent drop in share of the vote mostly to the benefit of the Liberal Democrats (up 7 per cent). After providing Labour with results that beat the national swing in 1992 and 1997, the inner area showed signs in 2001 of having lost patience with Labour government. While the national constituency for those who are disillusioned with the lack of radicalism of Blair's government is a relatively small one, and mostly expressed through abstention, inner north London contains an appreciable number of people who deserted Labour in 2001 because it was not radical enough. The Liberal Democrats did best at capturing this vote, but the Greens also did very well, gaining between 4.7 per cent and 6.2 per cent in the five constituencies they fought (the adjacent seats on either side of this band, at Brent East and Hackney North & Stoke Newington, were also Green strong points). The Socialist Alliance, the main leftist party in London (its profile is trendier than Scargill's Socialist Labour, whose best results tended to be in the north of England) polled worse than the Greens, but it still picked up 2-3 per cent where it stood.

The suburbs further out, the boroughs of Barnet and Enfield, have followed the London pattern of being affected by outward ripples of people and social trends originating in the inner areas close to them. Edmonton and the east side of Enfield have always been a bit different from the other outer north London seats, a continuation of the working class Tottenham area outwards along the Lea Valley. The valley is dominated by reservoirs, heavy industry and transport and has never been considered a particularly desirable suburban area. However, inland a little the ethnic make-up of Edmonton and Southgate has been altered recently by an influx of Cypriot and Indian residents who have traded up from Tottenham or Hackney and moved to the suburbs. Finchley has also become a more ethnically mixed, principally Indian, area in the last two decades. Ethnicity is only the most visible change. High housing costs in inner London have pushed young, liberal professionals further out to areas like Finchley and Southgate; the sort of people who would have bought around Hampstead or Highgate twenty years ago now end up out here, bringing their political inclinations with them.

North London suburbia has been distinctive for a long time as a Jewish area. Some inner areas, particularly around Hampstead, are also areas of Jewish settlement It is difficult to be precise about numbers, but the Board of Deputies estimate that about a third of Britain's 330,000 Jews live in north London suburbs; the Jewish population of Barnet is about 55,000 or 17 per cent. There was a mass migration from the East End in the middle part of the 20th century. The Jewish vote tended to Labour in the post-war period, but middle class Jews shifted in 1979 and after to support Thatcher's Conservatives, only to swing to Labour quite strongly in 1997. Jews seemed to react against Conservative rhetoric on asylum and anti-European nationalism in 1997-2001, and Jewish areas gave the Tories some of their worst results in the local, European and general elections. All the parties in north London local elections are sensitive to Jewish concerns; there was controversy in the 1990s about the establishment of an orthodox eruv in Barnet to allow greater activity on the Sabbath.

Suburban north London was until recently a Conservative stronghold, whose representatives were powerful figures in the party and in the land. Most famous among these was Margaret Thatcher, who represented Finchley from 1959 until 1992, but there was also Reggie Maudling (Chipping Barnet 1950–79) and of course Michael Portillo (Enfield Southgate 1984–97). Most of these seats were considered safe for the Tories for most of the time since 1950 – only Edmonton and Enfield East (North after 1974) voted Labour in the fifty years between 1947 and 1997. The world was turned upside down in 1997 when Labour suddenly became, for the first time, the dominant force here. The politics of the London suburbs changed, and unlike in the Essex fringes of London there was no sign that Labour's new dominance was weakening in 2001, with the suburban result a virtual replica (on lower turnout) of the 1997 picture. The move from Labour to Lib Dem in the inner area accounts for practically all of the change in the overall figures in the table at the head of this chapter.

Local government
Islington is the most interesting local authority in the area. The 1998 borough elections left Labour and Liberal Democrats tied at 26 seats each, with Labour running the administration on a mayoral casting vote. This ended with a Lib Dem by-election gain from Labour in December 1999. The Lib Dems took control for the first time since mass defections produced an SDP-controlled council for a few months in the lead-up to the May 1982 elections. The Liberal Democrats consolidated their majority in 2002 with 38 councillors to Labour's 10.

Camden has been Labour controlled since 1971, although it is not monolithically Labour voting. There are some Conservative voting areas such as Belsize in the hinterlands of Hampstead, and the Liberal Democrats win in West Hampstead. There are sometimes locally based tenant and resident candidates in local elections and some Green strength around Camden Town. Labour face tests on several fronts but to lose control would be a fiasco for the party – after 2002 they had 35 out of 54 councillors. Haringey is solidly Labour, with only a small opposition presence after the 1994 and 1998 elections. Labour maintained control in 2002, although Lib Dem activity spread out from Muswell Hill and gained them some more wards. The Conservatives regained Enfield council in 2002 after eight years of Labour control. A large swing gave them a 39–24 lead – there are few Lib Dem voters. Barnet also returned to Tory control, albeit more narrowly. It was previously run by a Labour–Liberal Democrat coalition.

On the Greater London authority, the Barnet and Camden seat was perhaps the most surprising Conservative win on the constituency section, with a 1,553 (33-32) majority over Labour for Brian Coleman, and Labour must hope to gain the seat in 2004 unless the government is very unpopular. Enfield and Haringey was a fairly narrow win for Labour's Nicky Gavron, with 32 per cent of the vote to 29 per cent Conservative and 25 per cent for Green and left wing candidates. Islington is in the North East division represented by Meg Hillier. North East gave Ken Livingstone his highest proportion of first preference votes (48 per cent) in the Mayoral election.

Boundary review
All the seats in Barnet are approximately the right size and only minor alterations will take place to align the constituencies with new ward boundaries. The commission's recommendations treat Islington and Haringey similarly, although some seats are rather small; the Conservatives argued at the inquiry for a

cross-border seat between Islington and Hackney. A proposal by Labour to link Camden with a part of Brent was successful; a Hampstead and Kilburn constituency should be a safe Labour seat. Highgate is set to join Holborn & St Pancras. Finally, ther will be small but significant changes in Enfield. Conservative Party proposals to move the Labour Ponders End ward from Enfield North to Edmonton, Palmers Green from Edmonton to Enfield Southgate and the very Tory Highlands from Southgate to Enfield North were accepted. This will tilt Enfield North to the Conservatives but at the expense of strengthening Labour's hold on Southgate.

CHIPPING BARNET

	2001		1997		1992 notional	
Electorate and turnout	70,239	60.4	69,088	71.7	69,176	77.3
Conservative	19,702	46.4	21,317	43.0	30,241	56.6
Labour	17,001	40.0	20,282	40.9	14,028	26.2
Lib Dem	5,753	13.6	6,121	12.3	8,594	16.1
Anti–EU	–	–	1,190	2.4	–	–
Others	–		655 (3)		604	
MP	Sydney Chapman (Con)		Sydney Chapman (Con)		Sydney Chapman (Con)	
Majority	2,701	6.4	1,035	2.1	16,213	30.3

Chipping Barnet was one of the few suburban seats in north London to resist the Labour tide in 1997. Labour narrowly won Barnet (a larger area) in 1945, but it proved a safe berth for Tory high-flier Reginald Maudling in 1950-79 and from then until 1997 for his successor Sydney Chapman. Chapman has lived dangerously in the last couple of elections but has managed to hold on. The swing in 1997, at 14.1 per cent, was massive but a bit lower than in neighbouring seats such as Hendon and Enfield Southgate, which saved Chipping Barnet for the Conservatives. In 2001 Chapman's survival with an increased majority was part of a pattern: across the country, vulnerable Conservative incumbents tended to be able to see off Labour challenges.

Chipping Barnet consists of some rather uniform suburban territory at the edge of London, with no particularly poor areas and a small extremely wealthy area at Totteridge village. Before 1965 parts were in Hertfordshire and parts in Middlesex. Underhill ward is most Labour, Totteridge most Conservative, but there are no real strongholds for either party and in a good Labour year like 1994 or 1998 all wards are close fought. Friern Barnet, a marginally Conservative area, used to be known for a large mental hospital which has now been redeveloped.

Chipping means 'market', and Barnet's market fair has been immortalised in Cockney rhyming slang. It may have been a hairsbreadth win for them in 1997, but the Conservatives remain narrowly on top.

EDMONTON

	2001		1997		1992 actual	
Electorate and turnout	61,788	56.3	63,793	70.3	63,053	75.7
Conservative	10,709	30.8	13,557	30.2	22,076	46.3
Labour	20,481	58.9	27,029	60.3	21,483	45.0
Lib Dem	2,438	7.0	2,847	6.3	3,940	8.3
Anti–EU	406	1.2	968 (2)	2.2	–	–
Others	740 (3)		437		207	
MP	Andy Love (Lab)		Andy Love (Lab)		Ian Twinn (Con)	
Majority	9,772	28.1	13,472	30.0	593	1.3

Edmonton was one of the key battlegrounds of the 1997 election. It is a working class north London marginal, the product of development in the late 19th and early 20th centuries, although with some 1960s estates including the striking tower block estate at Lower Edmonton. Southern Edmonton borders on Tottenham and shares many of its characteristics of ethnic diversity (particularly the black and Cypriot communities), relative deprivation and ironclad Labour voting habits. The south eastern corner, an industrial area down by the River Lea, is the strongest Labour area. Edmonton becomes more and more middle class as one moves north and east, and in the far corner had one ward (Village) that stayed Conservative in 1994 and 1998 and this area is as affluent as much of the Southgate constituency.

The Conservatives performed particularly well among the white working class in outer London and the south east in the 1980s, and this strength pushed Edmonton into their column from 1983 to 1997 – it had been Labour continuously since 1935. But many of these voters deserted the Tories in 1997 and, with Edmonton's shifting ethnic composition, Labour enjoyed a massive win. There was little outside interest in the seat in 2001; overnight, it had become a safe seat once again. It is difficult to imagine Labour losing it again.

ENFIELD NORTH

	2001		1997		1992 actual	
Electorate and turnout	67,204	57.0	67,748	70.4	67,422	77.9
Conservative	15,597	40.7	17,326	36.3	27,789	52.9
Labour	17,888	46.7	24,148	50.7	18,359	34.9
Lib Dem	3,355	8.8	4,264	8.9	5,817	11.1
Anti–EU	427	1.1	1,341 (2)	2.8	–	–
Others	1,056 (3)		590		565	
MP	Joan Ryan (Lab)		Joan Ryan (Lab)		Tim Eggar (Con)	
Majority	2,291	6.0	6,822	14.3	9,430	18.0

Enfield is as far north as you can get and still be in Greater London. The northern seat of Enfield is a rather peculiar and volatile marginal seat, which has so far during its existence been won by the party that formed the government. When the Conservatives held it during the 1980s it seemed to be becoming a safe seat, but Labour dealt a knockout blow in 1997 with a 16 per cent swing. The relatively large swing back to the Conservatives in 2001 in Enfield North was unusual for north London, and requires some explanation. Much of this is to be found in the social composition of the seat.

Enfield North was created by a merger of Labour Enfield East and the bulk of Tory Enfield West, and the join still shows. Up by the old town centre and further west Enfield is very middle class and even rural in the Chase ward; these wards are quite strongly Conservative. East Enfield, down by the Lea river and various parallel canals, highways and railway lines, is an industrial area and the wards down here – Enfield Lock, Enfield Wash and Ponders End have voted Labour, but they sit just across the river Lea from Chingford and Epping Forest and adjoin Broxbourne, a low-status but strongly Tory area. There is a distinct whiff of Essex in the air; Norman Tebbit, it should be remembered, was born in Ponders End. Enfield North was probably influenced by the Tory trend in the south Essex subregion, and is one of the shakier working class outer London seats Labour currently holds. In 2002, all its wards elected Conservative councillors, apart from Ponders End – but that is little consolaton to Labour as boundary commission proposals look set to transfer the ward to Edmonton.

ENFIELD SOUTHGATE

	2001		1997		1992 notional	
Electorate and turnout	65,957	63.5	65,887	70.6	65,109	75.3
Conservative	16,181	38.6	19,137	41.1	28,390	57.9
Labour	21,727	51.8	20,570	44.2	12,845	26.2
Lib Dem	2,935	7.0	4,966	10.7	7,072	14.4
Anti–EU	298	0.7	1,342	2.9	–	–
Others	767 (2)		518 (2)		695	
MP	Stephen Twigg (Lab)		Stephen Twigg (Lab)		Michael Portillo (Con)	
Majority	5,546	13.2	1,433	3.1	15,545	31.7

Enfield Southgate's ejection of Michael Portillo in 1997 was one of the most celebrated moments of the election; Brian Cathcart's book about election night 1997 was called *Were You Still Up for Portillo?* One journalist suggested that Were You Still Up for Mullin? might make an appropriate title for a book about election night 2001, but Enfield Southgate still had something interesting to say. It produced a further large swing to Labour and gave Stephen Twigg an almost comfortable majority – actually larger than that in the traditionally marginal Enfield North constituency. Future boundary changes look like reinforcing this new geography.

Southgate's Labour Party is well-organised, with a high membership, and Stephen Twigg has been a popular, attentive MP who has been energetic in communicating with his constituents. His continuing appeal to liberal-minded electors for his stand on constitutional reform is apparent from the reduction in the Lib Dem vote to such a low level. Southgate was used as a model for training sessions in campaigning at the 2001 Labour conference.

The constituency consists of a slice of suburbia stretching from just south of the North Circular Road to the edge of greater London – Arnos Grove, Palmers Green, Southgate and Winchmore Hill. It is a mix of London N postcodes and suburban Enfield EN codes. Most wards were true-blue until the late 1980s, when Labour started winning the southern wards. Like other London suburbs it has become more and more racially mixed, with a growing population of Indian origin and upwardly mobile Cypriots moving up from Tottenham and Edmonton. It is rather dependent on public transport, particularly the Piccadilly Line and overland commuter services. Southgate's former member, Michael Portillo, rethought his political approach after his defeat here, but the Conservative campaign in 2001, nationally and locally, had a tin ear for this sort of place and they paid the penalty in the result.

FINCHLEY and GOLDERS GREEN

	2001		1997		1992 notional	
Electorate and turnout	76,178	57.3	72,357	69.5	71,081	73.6
Conservative	16,489	37.8	19,991	39.7	28,623	54.8
Labour	20,205	46.3	23,180	46.1	16,149	30.9
Lib Dem	5,266	12.1	5,670	11.3	6,690	12.8
Anti–EU	330	0.8	889 (2)	1.8	–	–
Green	1,385	3.2	576	1.1	–	–
Others	–		–		821	1.6
MP	Rudi Vis (Lab)		Rudi Vis (Lab)		Hartley Booth (Con) Finchley	
Majority	3,716	8.5	3,189	6.3	12,474	23.9

This seat had a special place in the 1997 roll of honour for Labour as the former stronghold of Margaret Thatcher. It is mostly a product of inter-war growth and depends heavily on the Northern Line of the London underground. East Finchley is an increasingly Indian area, and the seat as a whole is 21.2 per cent non-white, but the most prominent local minority is the Jewish community – particularly in the Golders Green area. Many residents commute into central London but there are large local employers, including McDonalds' UK headquarters. Finchley and Golders Green is an affluent area in the top ten seats in the country for professional and non-manual workers, and has some of the intellectual sheen of neighbouring Hampstead and Highgate which has gradually become a safe Labour seat. Hampstead Garden Suburb, indeed, is wholly within this constituency.

Labour MP Rudi Vis was famously unprepared for his surprise victory in 1997; he had to find someone to teach his economics classes at the University of East London at short notice after winning. Labour's second win was less of a shock, because it had been anticipated in good mid-term results for Labour in the Barnet borough elections in May 1998 and even the European elections in June 1999 when Labour lagged only one point behind the Tories. In the end, the rather modest pro-Labour swing in 2001 was perhaps less than might have been expected, and certainly less than Labour managed in Hendon and Southgate. The demographic and political shifts in outer London have transformed places like this from safe reservoirs of Tory support to the new front line of the major party battle. In the long term it may even follow other middle London seats like Streatham and Hornsey and become a reliable Labour seat, but for now it is still vulnerable to any national Tory recovery.

HAMPSTEAD and HIGHGATE

	2001		1997		1992 notional	
Electorate and turnout	65,195	54.3	64,889	67.9	62,954	72.4
Conservative	8,725	24.6	11,991	27.2	18,582	40.8
Labour	16,601	46.9	25,275	57.4	21,059	46.2
Lib Dem	7,273	20.5	5,481	12.4	5,028	11.0
Anti–EU	316	0.9	790 (2)	1.8	–	–
Green	1,654	4.7	–	–	876	1.9
Others	838 (4)		494 (4)		24	
MP	Glenda Jackson (Lab)		Glenda Jackson (Lab)		Glenda Jackson (Lab)	
Majority	7,876	22.2	13,284	30.2	2,477	5.4

Hampstead is an inner London suburb with a distinct image – it has rather set the tone for perceptions of north London more generally. It is certainly true that Hampstead has attracted the more liberal, educated element of the metropolitan middle class, but it has become a target for easy tabloid sneers, echoed now even by Labour politicians, about 'Hampstead issues' – i.e. ideas like freedom of information and civil liberties. It is hardly surprising that Hampstead no longer feels as keen on Labour as once it did, despite as distinguished and artistic a local representative as Glenda Jackson. There was a 9per cent swing from Labour to Liberal Democrat in the 2001 election in Hampstead & Highgate.

Hampstead & Highgate (the latter village the other side of the Heath contributes only a small share of the seat's electorate, and half of it is in another constituency) does take liberal values quite seriously. It has thriving community activities and a well-regarded local newspaper, the Ham and High, which has a middle class readership who take an active interest in local affairs. The first ever Conservative defeat in the constituency, in 1966, was attributed to Henry Brooke's illiberal attitudes. The last – probably ever – Conservative MP for the seat Geoffrey Finsberg was an established local figure with a personal vote, and when he stepped down in 1992 Glenda Jackson reclaimed it for Labour.

It is quite a diverse constituency. There are some Conservative areas to the south and west of Hampstead town, at least in local elections, and marginal territory at Swiss Cottage and Belsize Park. The constituency extends westwards to half of Kilburn, which is strongly Labour with some alienating and ugly housing estates such as the Priory estate, and eastwards to the Labour-voting Gospel Oak area. Highgate, which includes the tomb of Karl Marx, has also tended to favour Labour. The Liberal Democrats poll well in the centre of Hampstead itself (the least deprived part of the borough) and the northern parts of West Hampstead along West End Lane.

Labour probably need to watch the growing Liberal Democrat base more than the fading Conservatives, who were lucky to avoid third place in 2001. The Tories will probably remain competitive in their better areas in local elections because Labour Camden is not well-loved for its hard line on parking and its eagerness to redevelop parts of the borough. Labour will probably continue to dominate in general elections because of a split opposition.

HENDON

	2001		1997		1992 notional	
Electorate and turnout	78,213	52.2	76,264	65.6	72,591	74.3
Conservative	14,015	34.3	18,528	37.0	28,916	53.6
Labour	21,432	52.5	24,683	49.3	18,068	33.5
Lib Dem	4,724	11.6	5,427	10.8	6,289	11.7
Anti–EU	409	1.0	1,245 (2)	2.5	–	–
Others	271 (2)		153		645	
MP	Andrew Dismore (Lab)		Andrew Dismore (Lab)		John Gorst (Con) Hendon North	
Majority	7,417	18.2	6,155	12.3	10,848	20.1

Hendon is the first part of London to greet people arriving from the north on the M1; an untidy tangle of flyovers and the Brent Cross Shopping Centre, a revolutionary development when it opened in 1976. Hendon is a creation of the 20th Century; most of the private housing sprang up during the interwar period and is crisscrossed by arterial roads. It also has quite a high proportion of council housing. There is a large old-fashioned estate at Watling (Burnt Oak) and on the site of the old airfield the large, confusing and rather slummy 1970s Grahame Park estate. Some of Hendon, particularly at Mill Hill, is quietly prosperous and enjoys a pleasant environment with trees and parks. Like the other Barnet seats, Hendon has a prominent Jewish community. The politics of Hendon is also mixed. The estates vote Labour, when they can be bothered. Mill Hill has seen Lib Dem local activity, and Labour have made inroads into the prosperous suburb of Hale; only Edgware still voted Conservative in the 1998 local elections, though it was joined by Hendon Ward in 2002.

Hendon previously seemed a rather resistant constituency as far as Labour were concerned – even in 1966 Tory MP Ian Orr-Ewing held on by a whisker in Hendon North, and Labour's 1945 victory stood alone. Hendon's massive swing to Labour in 1997, and the continued movement in 2001, actually now make this one of Labour's more reliable seats – there are 130 with smaller majorities and Labour could hold it even if the party lost its overall majority.

HOLBORN and ST. PANCRAS

	2001		1997		1992 notional	
Electorate and turnout	62,722	49.6	63,037	60.3	60,803	61.8
Conservative	5,258	16.9	6,804	17.9	10,590	28.2
Labour	16,770	53.9	24,707	65.0	20,377	54.3
Lib Dem	5,595	18.0	4,758	12.5	5,213	13.9
Anti–EU	301	1.0	790	2.1	–	–
Green	1,875	6.0	–	–	896	2.4
Socialist	1,330 (2)	4.3	–	–	163	0.4
Others			946 (6)		321	
MP	Frank Dobson (Lab)		Frank Dobson (Lab)		Frank Dobson (Lab)	
Majority	11,175	35.9	17,903	47.1	9,787	26.1

Holborn and St. Pancras is the seat of Frank Dobson, Labour's unsuccessful candidate for Mayor of London in 2000. He had no problems with re-election as MP in 2001, although his share of the vote slumped and his majority fell in line with the local trend for Lib Dems to profit at the expense of Labour.

This constituency stretches a long way into central London, containing part of the legal district at Lincoln's Inn and Grays Inn, the British Museum and the three large railway termini of Euston, Kings Cross and St. Pancras. The central districts tend to vote Labour in local and national elections; there are several council estates tucked away, and many of the mansion blocks here are not particularly grand. Even so, the old Holborn & St Pancras South seat was Conservative in their 1959 landslide. Further north, there are some poor and troubled areas among the railway lines, and then some partially gentrified inner city districts around Camden Town and Kentish Town. This area formed the bulk of the solidly Labour St Pancras North constituency, where John Major cut his electoral teeth in 1974. The constituencies were merged in 1983. All the wards of Holborn & St Pancras have voted Labour in local elections between 1986 and 1998, although there is Lib Dem and even Green potential in some of them. The left wing parties, split as they often were between Socialist Alliance and Socialist Labour, plus the Greens, polled over 10 per cent, indicating a substantial radical element in Dobson's constituency.

HORNSEY and WOOD GREEN

	2001		1997		1992 actual	
Electorate and turnout	75,974	58.0	74,537	69.1	73,668	75.7
Conservative	6,921	15.7	11,293	21.9	21,843	39.2
Labour	21,967	49.9	31,792	61.7	27,020	48.5
Lib Dem	11,353	25.8	5,794	11.3	5,547	10.0
Anti–EU	–	–	808	1.6	–	–
Green	2,228	5.1	1,214	2.4	1,051	1.9
Socialist	1,400 (2)	3.2	586	1.1	89	0.2
Others	194		–		197	
MP	Barbara Roche (Lab)		Barbara Roche (Lab)		Barbara Roche (Lab)	
Majority	10,614	24.1	20,499	39.8	5,177	9.3

Hornsey and Wood Green is the western half of the London Borough of Haringey, and for a long time a Conservative seat. Labour won Hornsey for the first time in 1992 aided by demographic change, as houses were broken up into flats and the ethnic minority vote increased. Some of the seat is very pleasant, wooded territory inhabited by north London intellectual families, including the more upmarket half of Highgate plus Muswell Hill and Fortis Green. It extends downhill to some relatively trendy areas like Crouch End, and the more down at heel Hornsey area proper. Wood Green is a major shopping centre. All the wards of the seat voted Labour in 1994, with the exception of Tory Highgate, and Labour enjoyed a crushing win in 1997. Things went sour on Labour in 2001 after this run of success, and there was an extremely large (13.2 per cent) swing to the Liberal Democrats. Why?

Inner north London as a whole was a bad area for Labour, with swings of around 8 per cent to the Lib Dems in neighbouring constituencies of a similar kind, but there were obviously special factors in Hornsey. Part of the reason was the government role of Labour MP Barbara Roche, who was Minister of State at the Home Office for asylum and immigration matters and found herself arguing the case for restrictions and vouchers. This offended some liberal consciences in her constituency and attracted a high-profile challenge from Louise Christian for the Socialist Alliance. Despite her credentials as a human rights lawyer and previous Labour candidate (Hendon South, 1987) she made little headway. The Greens mopped up more left wing dissatisfaction, saving their deposit with 5.1 per cent, but the main winner was Lynne Featherstone of the Liberal Democrats. She and her colleagues had come from third place to win Muswell Hill ward in 1998 from Labour (who had ousted the Tories there in 1994) and she was able to achieve credibility across the seat in 2001. The Liberal Democrats made big gains in 2002. The Tory vote having fallen apart, this seat looks like an outside possibility of a Lib Dem gain from Labour in 2005/6. However, their strength here depends on an image as a radical alternative to Labour, which does not necessarily help in their more traditional small town strongholds.

ISLINGTON NORTH

	2001		1997		1992 actual	
Electorate and turnout	61,970	48.8	57,385	62.5	56,814	66.6
Conservative	3,249	10.8	4,631	12.9	8,958	23.7
Labour	18,699	61.9	24,834	69.3	21,742	57.4
Lib Dem	5,741	19.0	4,879	13.6	5,732	15.1
Green	1,876	6.2	1,516	4.2	1,420	3.8
Others	651 (2)		–		–	
MP	Jeremy Corbyn (Lab)		Jeremy Corbyn (Lab)		Jeremy Corbyn (Lab)	
Majority	12,958	42.9	19,955	55.6	12,784	33.8

Islington North is the traditional heartland of working class, immigrant and Irish Islington, packed into flats and low terraces either side of the Holloway Road and stretching up past the Arsenal stadium almost to Finsbury Park. Although Highbury Fields and the streets around it have become colonised by middle-class home owners, Islington North in general remains more ethnically mixed, poor and privately-renting than the stereotypical image of Islington. It is a safe Labour constituency in general elections. Its MP is Jeremy Corbyn, a left-wing supporter of Irish unity and participant in nearly all significant backbench rebellions; if Millbank's writ did run in Islington he would have been deselected years ago, but he remains an independent, awkward voice. Labour dominance of this seat has produced bouts of ugly infighting at several times in the past, with accusations of Tammany Hall machine politics being bandied about particularly during the reign of Michael O'Halloran (1969-83) as MP.

Labour might have to focus on fighting off external threats in the future. The Liberal Democrats did not make much of an impression even in the 1998 local elections, but in 1999 they gained Hillrise (Lower Holloway, near Archway) on a huge swing in the by-election. Having won nearly all the wards in the other Islington constituency the Lib Dems consolidated their majority in 2002 by picking off wards in the north of the borough. Local elections are more interesting than national ones in Islington. Also, Islington North produces consistently good results for the Green Party, with the party's sixth best showing in 2001 and an impressive second place with 17.9 per cent in the 1999 Euro election.

ISLINGTON SOUTH and FINSBURY

	2001		1997		1992 notional	
Electorate and turnout	59,516	47.4	55,468	63.7	54,443	73.1
Conservative	3,860	13.7	4,587	13.0	9,818	24.7
Labour	15,217	53.9	22,079	62.5	20,369	51.2
Lib Dem	7,937	28.1	7,516	21.3	9,232	23.2
Anti–EU	–	–	741	2.1	–	–
Socialist	817	2.9	–	–	–	–
Others	384 (2)		393 (3)		369 (3)	
MP	Chris Smith (Lab)		Chris Smith (Lab)		Chris Smith (Lab)	
Majority	7,280	25.8	14,563	41.2	10,551	26.5

Islington South and Finsbury is a very divided constituency. It has a high proportion of council housing, including some model estates and some much less attractive areas. It also has the most gentrified areas of Islington, including Barnsbury and Canonbury, and therefore two landmarks of new Labour history – the Blairs' house and the Granita restaurant where the deal between Blair and Brown was (or, according to who you believe, wasn't) hatched in 1994. At the south end there is Clerkenwell, an area with many conversions from industrial to residential use, and Finsbury itself. Curiously, despite the social divisions the wards of the seat tend to vote alike. In 1997 this was for Labour, but only a year later the Liberal Democrats came out ahead right across the seat with a 55-32 lead over Labour in the borough elections and won 24 councillors to only 2 Labour.

The 2001 general election was therefore a relative disappointment to the Liberal Democrats, who made pretty much the same progress here as they did in neighbouring Holborn & St Pancras where they have no councillors and no history of activism. Their local strength in Islington started in the days of the SDP, when they briefly took control of the council and gained the adherence of Labour MP George Cunningham. Cunningham was narrowly defeated twice by Chris Smith before the centre vote collapsed in Labour's favour in 1992. The 2001 general election, despite the local election landslides, did not mark a return to close competitive elections in the Islington South and Finsbury parliamentary constituency.

Former cabinet ministers sometimes leave the commons for other important jobs. If Smith accepts a post in the arts or media. Labour could face a very sticky by-election in the supposed birthplace of Blairism.

TOTTENHAM

	2001		1997		1992 actual	
Electorate and turnout	65,568	48.2	66,251	56.9	68,404	65.5
Conservative	4,401	13.9	5,921	15.7	13,341	29.8
Labour	21,317	67.5	26,121	69.3	25,309	56.5
Lib Dem	3,008	9.5	4,064	10.8	5,120	11.4
Green	1,443	4.6	1,059	2.8	903	2.0
Socialist	1,162	3.7	–	–	–	–
Others	270		539 (3)		150	
MP	David Lammy (Lab)		Bernie Grant (Lab)		Bernie Grant (Lab)	
Majority	16,916	53.5	20,200	53.6	11,968	26.7

Parliamentary by-election 22 June 2000: Labour 8,785 (53.5) Lib Dem 3,139 (19.1), Conservative 2,634 (16.0), Socialist 885 (5.4), Green 606 (3.7), Anti EU 136 (0.8), 2 Others 232 Electorate 64,554, Turnout 25.4. MP: David Lammy (Lab), Majority 5,646 (34.4).

Tottenham, in contrast to the other five inner north London seats, bears hardly a trace of upward mobility. It is predominantly working class and the home to a large number of black residents, particularly in the Bruce Grove area although the entire seat is a multicultural area. It is an acutely deprived, poor area; seven of its eleven wards (pre 2002) were among the 10 per cent most deprived in England. Its most famous landmark is White Hart Lane football ground.

Tottenham is a super-safe Labour seat with fewer than 20 Labour seats having a larger percentage majority. It elected Bernie Grant rather narrowly in 1987 despite a tabloid onslaught, and returned him with increasing majorities until he died during the 1997 parliament. Grant, according to his successor, 'walked a tightrope between street heroism and government office.' David Lammy won the seat in a by-election in 2000 and is an impressive presence on Labour's benches. He quickly chose government office, and joined the lowest rung of the government as PPS to Estelle Morris after the general election. In May 2002 he became a junior health minister. Lammy could well go a long way in politics – he is still the youngest MP in the House and Tottenham is an exceptionally secure base.

London – East

	Conservative		Labour		Liberal Democrat		Others	
	Share of vote	Seats	Share of vote	Seats	Share of vote	Seats	Share of vote	Seats
2001	28.6	3	54.6	13	11.6	0	5.3	0
1997	26.9	1	56.0	15	10.4	0	6.7	0
1992	40.5	6	43.2	12	14.6	0	1.7	0
1987	41.4	8	36.4	10	21.7	0	0.6	0
1983	37.6	7	35.7	11	23.6	0	3.1	0

East London, for our purposes, consists of the East End plus all the parts of Essex that became part of the Greater London area in 1964. It stretches out as far as Chingford, Harold Hill and Rainham at the edge of the London built-up area. This metropolitan area divides into several distinct parts. Innermost is the East End, the traditional working class and immigrant part of London, comprising Tower Hamlets, Hackney and Newham. Outward to the north are Ilford and Walthamstow and their suburban hinterlands in the boroughs of Waltham Forest and Redbridge, which are very much parts of London.

Further east, there are Barking & Dagenham and Havering boroughs, which are to be distinguished from the rest of this sub-region because of their continued affinity with Essex. They have little of modern London's social and ethnic diversity, being nearly all-white, skilled working class and lower middle class areas which sprang up primarily in the interwar period and continued to add suburbs and estates after 1945. Despite the District Line, striking out from the City eastward through the East End to Barking and Upminster, the two eastern boroughs see themselves as distinct from 'London'. There are political differences too, as we shall see.

The heart of London's East End, where the story of the whole area begins is the borough of Tower Hamlets, hard by the City of London, plus the neighbouring cockney areas of south Hackney and West Ham. The East End considers itself the heartland of working class London but it is also subtly set apart from the rest of the metropolis by its unique culture and history. It developed as a working class, industrial adjunct to the City of London servicing its most menial trades, with more than its share of bad-neighbour industries like brewing and tanning, and providing a workforce for the London docks. Development reached further out in the Victorian period, with enormous gasworks in West Ham and more reputable suburbs forming in East Ham north Hackney and Walthamstow. Meanwhile the inner East End became a sink of crime and squalor, nationally publicised by the Jack the Ripper murders in 1888 and Arthur Morrison's novel *A Child of the Jago*. Shortly after Morrison's book was published the Old Nichol slum area in Shoreditch was levelled and replaced by one of Britain's very first public housing projects, the still-extant Boundary Estate, a little over a hundred years ago.

The East End has been an area in constant flux. The electorate in the three inner boroughs has fallen by over half, from a peak of 776,893 in 1931 to 386,543 in 1992, although it has stabilised and slightly recovered in the last ten years. Until 1950, there were 18 MPs from the area, compared to six now. Bombing destroyed a lot of the old slums in 1940-45 and when the East End was rebuilt it was by the local authorities, to a lower density, although the concrete estates of Poplar and Hackney have worn badly. Thirty years ago Tower Hamlets was more or less entirely council estates – upwards of 85 per cent of households – and although this has dropped these are still council estate constituencies. The economy has changed too; the docks, mainstay of the local economy, were run down from the 1950s until they closed finally in 1981. There is still textile production and small scale industry, including printing, car repair and light engineering, but no more big employers outside the public sector.

The decline in population of the East End is mirrored by growth in outer East London and south Essex. There has been a steady outward trend in population as people have become better off. The first phase of movement was to inner suburbs like East Ham and Walthamstow; in the 1920s an enormous council estate was constructed east of Barking at Dagenham-Becontree, swelling the electorate of the Romford constituency to well over 100,000 by the 1935 election. Heavy industrial jobs followed, but are now disappearing. After the war, the New Towns of Basildon and Harlow absorbed planned overspill from the East End, but there was also a continuous drift among the better-off to privately built suburbs. Outer East London, such as Hornchurch and Romford, and the south Essex towns such as Brentwood and Canvey Island, are full of expatriate white East Enders.

The remaining East End's population is one of the most ethnically mixed in Britain, if not the world. The Tower Hamlets area has a tradition of absorbing waves of immigrants, from the Huguenots onwards. There are large black communities in the northern part of Newham and throughout Hackney, and areas of Tower Hamlets are so strongly Bengali that one new ward has 'Bangla Town' as part of its name. In 1991 23% of the population of Tower Hamlets was of Bangladeshi origin and 64% were white. In Newham there were 14% black, 23% from the Indian subcontinent and 58% white; in Hackney it split 22% black, 66% white. In the first half of the 20th Century the East End was a concentrated area of Jewish settlement, although this population has largely dispersed to the suburbs of north Ilford and beyond except for an ultra-orthodox redoubt in north Hackney. Asians have also tended to move upwards and outwards, to Ilford and Leyton. In recent years there have been waves of immigration – Bengalis since the 1970s and more recently Somalis, Sudanese and Afghans – to Tower Hamlets, and no doubt the process of immigration and outward movement will repeat itself in future.

Many images of the East End are enduring despite all the change. It is reputed to be a place where there are close knit communities, perhaps somewhat insular and over-tolerant of gangsters who are nice to their dear old mums; a premium is put on a sentimental vision of family life. Its inhabitants are reputed to be quick-witted and entrepreneurial, perhaps a legacy – like Liverpool – of a long history of casual employment in the docks and the necessity to make a living from ducking and diving. The modern image of the East End comes largely from the BBC soap opera *EastEnders*. If the London Borough of Walford (from Walthamstow and Stratford) existed, it would be in this area. On the special tube maps produced for the BBC Walford East lies between Bow Road and West Ham, near the border between Tower Hamlets and Newham. Its residents would probably have voted for Labour's Oona King (or stayed at home) in 2001 despite the entrepreneurial activities that seem to flourish in Walford. However, the visitor will not find Albert Square here – it exists physically as a set in Elstree studios in the Hertfordshire constituency of Hertsmere. The crime-ridden streets of Sun Hill, home of ITV's *The*

Bill, lie a little to the west of Walford somewhere around Bethnal Green. Alf Garnett is probably buried somewhere in his beloved West Ham (Warren Mitchell, a Jewish socialist in the real world, is alive and well in Highgate and White Hart Lane).

The inner East End has the poorest areas of London. Ordnance ward in Canning Town, Newham, is the most deprived area in London, and 35th most deprived in England, followed by a number of Tower Hamlets wards – 5 feature in the top 100 in the country. In Hackney the poverty is unrelieved by any significant pockets of wealth or advantage – the least deprived ward in Hackney is still among the 10 per cent worst-off areas in England. Newham and Tower Hamlets are hardly any better off, although the Docklands development has created a relatively affluent element to the population of southern Tower Hamlets. Further out, the estates of Dagenham are fairly uniform, without great extremes of poverty, but there are still some areas of acute deprivation in old Barking and Leyton. There are some affluent suburbs in the Woodford and Cranham areas, but there are no elite areas of the sort found on the other sides of London. The imprint of the East End's labouring origins is still apparent.

The inner East End may seem the very model of a traditional Labour stronghold, but it has always been more complicated than that. At various times fascists, communists and Liberals have challenged Labour's dominant local role in Tower Hamlets, and it contains one of the only two seats in Britain where the Conservatives obtained a swing in their favour in the 1997 election. Other than the old docks, there used to be few large-scale unionised employers in Tower Hamlets and a lot of small trades, which inhibited Labour traditions from forming. Further east, in Newham, there were such large industries in the gasworks, railways and sugar refining as well as more modern docks, that West Ham was one of the very first Labour areas. Keir Hardie was elected for West Ham South in 1892 and the area has not lapsed from Labour representation since gasworkers' union leader Will Thorne regained it in 1906. Hackney and to a lesser extent East Ham were more respectable and Conservative suburbs before the war.

Labour have not lost a parliamentary election in the inner East End since 1945 (when a Communist won Mile End), and have not suffered any particularly close calls in any of the seats; trends to other parties in parts of the area have never actually followed through to victory. Other parties' representation has come about through defections (Reg Prentice of Newham North East to the Conservatives in 1977-79, and Ron Brown of Hackney South and Shoreditch to the SDP in 1981-83). The Conservatives looked set to win Newham South in the late 1980s, and the Alliance did quite well in the Tower Hamlets seats at the same time, but boundary changes and a Labour recovery seem to have removed these possibilities. Labour polled 62 per cent in the inner three boroughs in 1997 and 63 per cent in 2001, against splintered opposition.

The minor parties have traditionally done fairly well in the East End, and got over 10 per cent of the vote in 1997. In the 1930s Mosley's British Union of Fascists found local anti-semitism made it fertile territory, and the far right (NF in the 1970s, BNP now) has attracted appreciable support in recent years. The BNP won a seat on Tower Hamlets council in 1993 but lost it in 1994, and there is fascist potential in several wards of the area. Other minor parties have some support – independent Liberals, Greens and socialists, although the Communist Party's one-time strength in the area vanished even before the CP did. The party system, and Labour's dominance, seem built on shakier ground in the East End than in the heartlands of the north. East End politics is also noted for extremely low turnout. The only election in the last 40 years in which Labour voters have outnumbered abstainers is February 1974. Turnout in 2001 was a dismal 48.6 per cent in the area as a whole, although this represented a below-average fall in electoral interest and was not so dreadfully below that in the October 1974 election (53.8 per cent).

Further out, the boroughs of Waltham Forest and Redbridge follow a recognisable London political trend, with Labour inner areas and Conservative outer suburbs (Woodford sent Winston Churchill to parliament until 1964) and their parliamentary constituencies swinging with the rest of London – to the Conservatives in 1987 and Labour in 2001. The Conservative leader Iain Duncan Smith represents a suburban part of this area, but Labour tend to predominate. The southern part of each borough bears some relation to the traditional East End in ethnic diversity and strong economic links to central London and the City in particular. It is now hard to imagine Labour losing Leyton (although the Tories won it in a 1965 by-election), Walthamstow (although the Tories won it in 1987) or Ilford South (once a crucial marginal). Only Ilford North, a stray piece of Middlesex commuter Metroland which has wandered over to the east retains its old status as a marginal seat Labour needs to do well to win.

The eastern two boroughs were once, on balance, decisively Labour. Barking and Dagenham both produced massive majorities, Dagenham churning out 20,000+ leads election after election. The Romford seat was continuously Labour from 1955 until 1974 (on different boundaries to those that exist now) and only Hornchurch was really marginal. There was a revolution in the politics of the area in 1979 and afterwards. Council house sales, share ownership, the nationalist, *Sun* reading Essex culture and material prosperity – plus a certain amount of white working class misgivings about Labour's association with ethnic minorities and gays – won the area for Thatcher. The Conservatives won 31% in October 1974, but surged to 43.6% in 1979, inched up to 43.8% in 1983 and surged again to 48% in 1987 and 48.2% in 1992. The Havering seats seemed safe, while Labour trembled on the brink of losing Dagenham in 1987. Labour recovered at the expense of the Alliance in 1992, and enjoyed an enormous swing in 1997 which defeated the Conservatives even in Romford and Upminster. In 2001, however, it was one of the most receptive areas for William Hague's anti-EU, anti-asylum populism and provided the Tories with 2 of their 5 gains from Labour anywhere in the country. The Conservative vote rose by 7.5 per cent in the two boroughs and Labour fell 6 per cent, making it their best area in Britain and the hot-spot of their generally strong showing in south Essex.

Local government

East London boroughs come in a wide variety of political configurations. Newham (a 1965 merger of West Ham and East Ham) is the least interesting. Labour have either had a complete monopoly, or only been one or two seats short, on the council for many years now. The borough's administration is fairly uncontroversial, providing relatively good services and focusing on education improvement, the redevelopment of the Stratford area, the docks and the impact of the Channel Tunnel Rail Link on the area. In 2002 Robin Wales (a veteran Labour politician) was elected as mayor. Tower Hamlets is a different story. Until the late 1970s Labour often ran unopposed in its council wards, or racked up over 80 per cent of the vote, but Liberal community activism brushed the rotten and flimsy Labour machine aside and the Liberals seized control of the council in 1986. A curious episode in local politics followed. The Tower Hamlets Liberals indulged in campaign tactics that were rough and dirty even by the standards of inner city politics, even pandering to racism, and national attention was drawn to their failings in 1993 after the British National Party won the Millwall seat in a local by-election. Labour swept the Liberal Democrats out in 1994 and have held the council since. Hackney has probably been the most incompetent local authority in the country in recent years. Labour ran several inept administrations, followed by a period of no overall control and rule by consensus after 1998, when the borough's finances went out of control to the point that in October 2001 the government ordered Hackney to prepare a strategy to get on top of its finances. There is a prospect of Hackney being relieved of control of local services, but the new administration has hopes of following Lambeth out of the mire. Labour regained control in 2001 after by-election wins and consolidated their hold in 2002. The other parties were embarrassed when it was proved in court that a Lib Dem and a Tory councillor had been guilty of electoral fraud by putting fake names on the register. The parties could be forgiven for competing not to take over Hackney in future borough elections.

The four outer boroughs prove that the local politics of the suburbs can be less alarming and intriguing than the inner city, but still have some variety. Labour have an overwhelming majority in Barking & Dagenham and have run the London borough since its creation in 1964; even Labour's meltdown in the local elections in 1968 was a mere ripple here. Rival parties fail to offer complete slates of candidates in borough elections. Waltham Forest has a peculiar local political alignment. The Conservatives send a solid delegation from the Chingford area but do not show anywhere else. In a good Liberal Democrat year the party can win enough seats in Leyton and Walthamstow to deprive Labour of overall control. Labour gained the borough in 1998 but lost it in 2002, every set of local elections is a challenge. Redbridge is usually Tory but from 1994 to 2002 was a Labour-led hung council. The Conservatives will have been pleased to regain it because of its marginal status and the fact that their new leader, Iain Duncan Smith, represents part of the borough. Havering Council has been hung since 1986, with Labour falling just short of a majority in 1994 and 1998. Following the general election gains of Romford and Upminster, it was not surprising when the Conservatives made big gains in 2002 – but it is still under no overall control.

On the Greater London Authority the City & East division which includes Tower Hamlets, Newham and Barking is represented by John Biggs; Hackney and Waltham Forest are part of the North East division represented by Meg Hillier. Both these GLA constituencies are very safe Labour, although in 2000 the Greens polled particularly well in North East (16%) and the BNP did quite well in City & East (7%). Havering & Redbridge voted for the Conservative candidate Jeremy Evans in May 2000, with 38% to 30% for Labour, 13% for the Lib Dems and 12% for the Havering Residents. The Conservatives must be hopeful of holding it given the 2002 local election results.

Boundary review
The options here are not as entangled as in west London. The boundary commission have proposed that the Waltham Forest and Redbridge seats should be minimally altered and the pairing of the boroughs retained, which found favour with Labour. The pairing of Tower Hamlets and Newham has been broken but this makes little difference politically. Hackney is somewhat fortunate to retain two seats. The only definite loss of a seat is to the east, where Barking & Dagenham and Havering have been paired, with five seats reduced to four. The Conservatives proposals were accepted after a public inquiry – essentially Hornchurch is to be abolished and a new Dagenham and Rainham constituency created, where the Tories would have an outside chance in a good year.

BARKING

	2001		1997		1992 *notional*	
Electorate and turnout	55,229	45.5	53,458	61.7	*56,574*	*69.1*
Conservative	5,768	23.0	5,802	17.6	*13,229*	*33.9*
Labour	15,302	60.9	21,698	65.8	*20,409*	*52.2*
Lib Dem	2,450	9.8	3,128	9.5	*5,436*	*13.9*
Anti–EU	–	–	1,283	3.9	–	–
BNP	1,606	6.4	894	2.7	–	–
Others	–		159		–	
MP	Margaret Hodge (Lab)		Margaret Hodge (Lab)		Jo Richardson (Lab)*	
Majority	9,534	37.9	15,896	48.2	*7,180*	*18.4*

* Margaret Hodge (Lab) elected at June 1994 by–election.

Barking lies across a creek from East Ham; although not much of a physical barrier the creek is an important political and psychological divide. People in Barking talk of 'going up to London', and consider themselves part of Essex. The landscape of Barking is industrial in employment and municipal in housing – apart from some central terraces it is composed largely of council-built estates. Unlike Dagenham, however, Barking is an old town with the ruins of an important abbey and a tradition, until the Thames became too polluted, as a fishing port supplying London.

Barking formed part of a reliable Labour seat for decades after 1935, but in the three Thatcher elections the Labour vote sagged and the Conservatives came within sniffing distance of an astounding victory. Labour's revival in 1992, however, saw the party pull more comfortably ahead, and the June 1994 by-election produced an enormous Labour majority which has been repeated twice since. However, the Conservatives made some inroads and turnout slumped in 2001 to the extent that Labour polled hardly better than in 1983. There is certainly potential for Barking to worry Labour again, although the local Conservatives are not well organised and fail to put up candidates in many wards.

Barking is an undersized constituency and in the boundary changes it is likely to expand to take in some of the estates in Dagenham.

BETHNAL GREEN and BOW

	2001		1997		1992 notional	
Electorate and turnout	76,556	50.2	74,146	60.3	65,485	68.1
Conservative	9,323	24.3	9,412	21.1	7,316	16.4
Labour	19,380	50.5	20,697	46.3	23,863	53.5
Lib Dem	5,946	15.5	5,361	12.0	11,498	25.8
Anti–EU	–	–	557	1.2	–	–
Green	1,666	4.3	812	1.8	152	0.3
BNP	1,211	3.2	3,350	7.5	1,578	3.5
Liberal	–	–	2,963	6.6	–	–
Others	888		1,530 (2)		188	
MP	Oona King (Lab)		Oona King (Lab)		Peter Shore (Lab)	
					Bethnal Green & Stepney	
Majority	10,057	26.2	11,285	25.3	12,365	27.7

Bethnal Green and Bow is Tower Hamlets North, although it dips down to the river in the west at St Katharine's and Wapping. It is the constituency containing most of the landmarks, real and fictional, of the traditional East End, although not much of the parallel world that calls itself Docklands.

The Conservatives ran relatively close to Labour in St. Katharine's, the ward most close to the City and most influenced by it, in 1998 and it is not impossible that the Tories could win there. The Liberal Democrats have a much diminished local stronghold at the other end of the borough around Bow, the least redeveloped and concreted part of Tower Hamlets and probably the closest approximation to the old East End, but this vote does not transfer fully to general elections. In 2002 the Lib Dems gained several wards in Bethnal Green, but Spitalfields remained solidly Labour.

Labour's general election vote has run below what might be expected in recent elections. Part of the reason is Liberal 'community politics', part the demographic change that has brought a few Conservatives to the area, and part has been to do with candidates. Conservative candidate Kabir Choudhury did well to achieve one of only two swings to the Tories in 1997, and some ex-Labour voters seem to have gone to the BNP in 1997 rather than vote for Oona King, who is of black and Jewish origin. The 'rag tag and bobtail' candidates did particularly well here in 1997 but slipped back in 2001 with all the major parties – Oona King most of all – benefiting. Bethnal Green and Bow is a fascinating mix of people and cultures and it is certainly capable of producing thrills and spills in elections.

CHINGFORD and WOODFORD GREEN

	2001		1997		1992 notional	
Electorate and turnout	63,252	58.5	62,904	70.7	63,606	77.2
Conservative	17,834	48.2	21,109	47.5	30,656	61.4
Labour	12,347	33.4	15,395	34.6	10,455	21.0
Lib Dem	5,739	15.5	6,885	15.5	7,154	14.3
BNP	1,062	2.9	1,059	2.4	–	–
Others	–		–		1,636 (3)	
MP	Iain Duncan Smith (Con)		Iain Duncan Smith (Con)		Iain Duncan Smith (Con)	
					Chingford	
Majority	5,487	14.8	5,714	12.9	20,201	40.5

Chingford was famous for sending Norman Tebbit to parliament from 1974 until 1992, and Tebbit's hard-line politics clearly struck a chord with Chingford electors. Chingford is the middle class north end of the borough of Waltham Forest; it is not particularly glamorous or affluent but it is mainly white, car-driving and socially conservative. Only one ward, Valley, deviated from the Conservative trend and elected a Labour councillor in 1998 – it returned to the Tories in 2002. Chingford has drifted to the right over the decades; in 1964 the area provided a majority of Labour councillors and was formerly split between two marginal seats, Walthamstow East and Epping, both of which voted Labour in 1966.

The 1997 boundary changes added two wards from the abolished Wanstead and Woodford seat, but this hardly affected the political leanings of the seat. One ward, Church End, votes Lib Dem in local elections. If anything, the Woodford Green section is more established, comfortable and liberal middle class than Chingford, although its influence is slight compared to the right-wing inclinations of Chingford.

The constituency of a party leader can have a subtle effect on the attitude and image of a political party. The estates of Harold Wilson's Huyton were a 1960s study in modernity, while Thatcher represented comfortable and rather Jewish suburbia in Finchley, and Michael Foot's Ebbw Vale was a place of warm, sentimental communities amid industrial dereliction. Iain Duncan Smith's constituency is individualistic, patriotic and proud to have made it good, but does not go in particularly for higher education or liberal values. It remains to be seen whether what works in Chingford – and Romford – can work in the rest of Britain.

DAGENHAM

	2001		1997		1992 notional	
Electorate and turnout	59,340	46.5	58,232	62.1	62,395	69.8
Conservative	7,091	25.7	6,705	18.5	16,052	36.9
Labour	15,784	57.2	23,759	65.7	22,499	51.7
Lib Dem	2,820	10.2	2,704	7.5	4,992	11.5
Anti–EU	–	–	1,411	3.9	–	–
BNP	1,378	5.0	900	2.5	–	–
Others	507 (2)		684 (3)		–	
MP	Jon Cruddas (Lab)		Judith Church (Lab)		Bryan Gould (Lab)*	
Majority	8,693	31.5	17,054	47.2	6,447	14.8

* Judith Church (Lab) elected at June 1994 by–election.

Dagenham is the product of municipal enterprise between the wars, a vast council estate sprawling east of Barking big enough to support an entire constituency. Dagenham's estates, though, are not blocks of flats or concrete monstrosities but acre upon acre of curving roads full of semi-detached houses amid parks and playing fields. It is a working class, state-sponsored version of the middle class utopias that were springing up around Hendon and Harrow at the same time. Rather than underground trains to central London, Dagenham's economy was powered by heavy industry, most notably the Ford motor manufacturing complex that opened by the Thames in 1931. Car production ceased at Ford Dagenham in early 2002, contrary to a 1997 assurance from the company, but the plant will not close because Ford have other concerns there such as a diesel engine plant. Jobs at the motor works have been shed gradually for years – as recently as the 1980s it was the largest private sector employer in London – so the 1,900 losses, although painful, will not cause the area to go into a slump.

From the outset Dagenham was a Labour stronghold producing massive majorities, but during the Thatcher years it responded favourably to the Conservatives. The right to buy was a particularly popular cause here, giving tenants the opportunity to invest in some well-built family housing. Dagenham, a nearly all-white and rather traditionalist area, also felt alienated by the concerns of London Labour in the 1980s. As in Barking, a Labour recovery in 1992 was followed by massive victories in 1994 and 1997 and then a partial Conservative comeback in 2001. Dagenham provided the sixth largest swing to the Conservatives from Labour at the 2001 general election, and a low turnout. The general south Essex factor may have been heightened by the loss of a second Labour MP of whom much was expected in seven years. There was also a substantial increase in support for the BNP, which saved its deposit.

Dagenham will be seriously altered in the boundary changes. Already undersized, it must donate some territory to Barking. In exchange it takes some territory to the east from Hornchurch to form a Dagenham and Rainham seat.

EAST HAM

	2001		1997		1992 notional	
Electorate and turnout	71,255	52.3	66,111	60.3	69,761	61.7
Conservative	6,209	16.7	6,421	16.1	13,751	32.0
Labour	27,241	73.1	25,779	64.6	23,212	54.0
Lib Dem	2,600	7.0	2,599	6.5	6,049	14.1
Anti–EU	444	1.2	845	2.1	–	–
Socialist	783	2.1	2,697	6.8	–	–
BNP	–	–	1,258	3.2	–	–
Others	–		290		–	
MP	Stephen Timms (Lab)		Stephen Timms (Lab)		Ron Leighton (Lab)* Newham North East	
Majority	21,032	56.4	19,358	48.5	9,461	22.0

* Stephen Timms (Lab) elected at June 1994 by–election.

East Ham has done Labour proud in recent elections, with above-average swings in 1997 and, quite spectacularly, 2001 – it was extremely unusual for an inner city seat in producing a higher Labour total vote in 2001 than 1997 and seeing the Socialist Labour Party fall back so badly. In 1994 Labour's appeal was so powerful that the Lib Dem candidate defected to the party during the by-election campaign.

Most of East Ham consists of rather monotonous terraced housing stretching flat and straight either side of the District Line of the London underground as it heads out towards Barking; East Ham itself, Little Ilford and Manor Park being the best known. There is a very large and increasing ethnic minority population, both black and Asian, but a particularly strong Indian community which spans the borough boundary with Ilford South in Redbridge. There is little racism in East Ham – as one resident put it to the authors in 1994, 'if you were a racist you wouldn't live round here.'

The East Ham wards are mostly overwhelmingly Labour at all levels of election, although one (Greatfield) had the temerity to elect two Conservatives in 1990 for single terms. North Woolwich and the new Beckton estates at the far end of Docklands are more unpredictable than the other wards. The Docklands area is somewhat out of step with a resolutely 'East End' constituency, but it poses no threat to Labour in this colossally safe seat. There are only eleven safer Labour seats in the land.

HACKNEY NORTH and STOKE NEWINGTON

	2001		1997		1992 actual	
Electorate and turnout	60,444	49.0	62,308	52.0	56,768	61.2
Conservative	4,430	15.0	5,483	16.9	9,356	26.9
Labour	18,081	61.0	21,110	65.2	20,083	57.8
Lib Dem	4,170	14.1	3,306	10.2	3,996	11.5
Anti–EU	–	–	544	1.7	–	–
Green	2,184	7.4	1,395	4.3	1,111	3.2
Socialist	756	2.6	–	–	–	–
Others	–		544 (2)		178	
MP	Diane Abbott (Lab)		Diane Abbott (Lab)		Diane Abbott (Lab)	
Majority	13,651	46.1	15,627	48.3	10,727	30.9

Hackney North and Stoke Newington is an eclectic mixture of people and areas. North Hackney was established as a middle class suburb, but it has slid down the social scale continuously since the war to the point where it is primarily an area of acute inner city deprivation. It suffers from crime, including violence generated by drug dealing gangs. There is a lot of poverty and high unemployment, concentrated among the black community. The problems with Hackney were amply demonstrated by several thousand electors 'disappearing' to avoid the poll tax in the early 1990s – for this reason the figure given for the electorate in 1992 should be treated with caution. (The estimated figure for Hackney South, which takes this factor into account may be more accurate).

There are a couple of areas that are somewhat distinct from the rest of the constituency. Stamford Hill is home to a substantial ultra-Orthodox Jewish population, who have tended to vote Conservative in recent local elections in the Springfield and neighbouring wards. Springfield's Joe Lobenstein was once Hackney's only Tory councillor; he completed his fourth mayoral term in 2001 and has seen the Hackney Conservatives become a fairly serious force in local elections. Stoke Newington was formerly a small independent borough but was absorbed into Hackney in 1965. It has a north London postcode – N16 – and is therefore to be distinguished from the massed E postcodes of the rest of the East End. 'Stokey' is influenced by progressive and radical young professionals and students; in the 1998 elections two Greens were elected from its wards. It seems a slightly misplaced part of Islington or Camden.

The May 1998 local elections in the area were very bad for Labour, but the party still led against divided opposition and it cannot be regarded as anything other than a safe Labour seat. Diane Abbott was the first black woman elected to Parliament when she won in 1987, and has continued to be an effective, awkward backbencher. The Greens and Socialists took 10 per cent of the vote in 2001, and the Greens had 16.5 per cent in Euro 99, indicators that this is a self-consciously radical constituency.

HACKNEY SOUTH and SHOREDITCH

	2001		1997		1992 notional	
Electorate and turnout	63,990	47.4	62,000	54.5	67,545	54.7
Conservative	4,180	13.8	4,494	13.3	10,699	29.0
Labour	19,471	64.2	20,048	59.4	19,702	53.4
Lib Dem	4,422	14.6	5,058	15.0	5,525	15.0
Anti–EU	–	–	613	1.8	–	–
Ind Lab	–	–	2,436	7.2	–	–
Socialist	1,401	4.6	–	–	–	–
Others	873 (3)		1,113 (4)		997	
MP	Brian Sedgemore (Lab)		Brian Sedgemore (Lab)		Brian Sedgemore (Lab)	
Majority	15,049	49.6	14,990	44.4	9,003	24.4

The southern part of the borough of Hackney has become increasingly fashionable among artists and people who like living somewhere arty, and estate agents have tried to draw the boundaries of 'Hoxton' ever further outward. Parts of southern Hackney also shade into Georgian Islington at De Beauvoir. However, the artistic and gentrified areas are a minimal contribution to the demographics of this parliamentary constituency. Hackney South and Shoreditch starts very near to Liverpool Street station at the tip of the borough, and slides eastwards parallel to the neighbouring seat of Bethnal Green and Bow. For the most part it is an impoverished, ethnically diverse and working class part of East London. It shares some East London myth and history, including the Kray family home in Vallance Road.

Like its southern neighbour, it is less overwhelmingly Labour than it might be. Part of the explanation is the chaotic local government politics of Hackney, in which Labour have not given a good account of themselves, but part is also down to tradition. In the early 1920s south Hackney elected the jingoistic fraudster Horatio Bottomley before he was imprisoned. Like Tower Hamlets, fascism has reared its head in this area – it was an NF area in the 1970s – and there has also been, putting it politely, a nativist, insular form of Liberal community politics in the past. In 1998, the artistic influx coincided with a Conservative win in the Moorfields ward on the edge of the City. More respectable Lib Dem activism has spread north into the Dalston area and the north side of Victoria Park, winning some surprising gains in 1998, but in 2002 Labour hit back and won all wards in the constituency.

In general elections there is no threat to Labour MP Brian Sedgemore. His vote was depressed in 1997 by the high share going to a rebel councillor described as 'New Labour' (Labour have frequently split in Hackney) but bounced back in 2001. Local elections may continue to spring surprises, but general elections produce predictable Labour wins.

HORNCHURCH

	2001		1997		1992 actual	
Electorate and turnout	61,008	58.3	60,392	72.8	60,484	79.8
Conservative	15,032	42.3	16,386	37.3	25,817	53.5
Labour	16,514	46.4	22,066	50.2	16,652	34.5
Lib Dem	2,928	8.2	3,446	7.8	5,366	11.1
Anti–EU	893	2.5	1,595	3.6	–	–
Others	190		448 (2)		453	
MP	John Cryer (Lab)		John Cryer (Lab)		Robin Squire (Con)	
Majority	1,482	4.2	5,680	12.9	9,165	19.0

A lot of London's population is drawn from the top and bottom of the social and income scale, and a large range of cultures, but there are areas that are resolutely ordinary places, inhabited mainly by skilled manual and lower middle class white people. One such is Hornchurch, north and east of the (now much downsized) Ford motor production plant at Dagenham and home to many of its workers. Most of its wards are mixed and marginal. Labour do better in the flat industrial area by the Thames, including the detached area of Rainham, set amid marshes. The Conservatives, although not so much in local elections, do better in the northern wards. The old village of Hornchurch is not far south of Romford town centre, and the seat covers the territory between Romford and the river.

Hornchurch has long been a critical marginal, prone to large swings, and was duly a Labour gain on a 16 per cent swing in 1997. John Cryer is the son of the late Bob Cryer MP and Ann Cryer, another new MP of 1997 (Keighley). He is well to the left of the 1997 intake and a participant in most of the major rebellions in this parliament, and also an assiduous worker on behalf of his constituency. He suffered a swing of more than 4 per cent against him in 2001, another dramatic Hornchurch result, but the swing was lower and the Labour majority bigger than in Romford or Upminster, so Cryer held on against his predecessor Robin Squire.

The Conservatives will no doubt look to extend their Havering successes into Hornchurch at the next general election, but John Cryer is tough opposition and the voters of south Essex can react in unexpected ways. Whatever the course of politics in the next few years, Hornchurch is a constituency to watch at the general election, though it may be its last, as the Boundary Commission have proposed its effective abolition (the name will be retained in the Hornchurch and Upminster seat).

ILFORD NORTH

	2001		1997		1992 notional	
Electorate and turnout	68,893	58.4	67,151	72.7	67,904	74.0
Conservative	16,313	40.5	19,911	40.8	29,076	57.8
Labour	18,428	45.8	23,135	47.4	15,027	29.9
Lib Dem	4,717	11.7	5,049	10.3	6,174	12.3
Anti–EU	776	1.9	–	–	–	–
BNP	–	–	755	1.5	–	–
MP	Linda Perham (Lab)		Linda Perham (Lab)		Vivian Bendall (Con)	
Majority	2,115	5.3	3,224	6.6	14,049	27.9

Linda Perham is one of Labour's unsung heroines of their two election triumphs. She held on well in Ilford North while the seats to her north and east saw swings to the Conservatives which would have unseated her, and did in fact topple her colleagues Eileen Gordon and Keith Darvill.

Ilford North is a pretty uniform stretch of suburban London strung out along the A12 and the further reaches of the Central Line. There is one large council-built estate at Hainault but a lot of it has been sold under the right to buy and the gap between it and 1930s semi-detached suburbia at Fullwell and Barkingside is not so great. Many of the wards are marginal, with representation from Aldborough and Fairlop both being split between the parties in 1998. A lot of Ilford North is an Essex equivalent of the Metroland that sprawled over Middlesex in the 1930s (see London – West). Its main local peculiarity is the high number of London cabbies who live in the area, although it is also known as the most Jewish constituency in the eastern suburbs of London. Although taxi drivers are reputed to have right wing Conservative opinions, a lot of them have a re-elected Labour MP.

The Ilford North seat now extends up to Woodford Bridge after the abolition of the Wanstead and Woodford constituency, long famous for sending Winston Churchill to parliament; the largest part of that seat has been absorbed into Ilford North. The Woodford part is not as Tory as once it was – Labour have some votes at Woodford Bridge, and the Lib Dems won the Roding ward in the last three local elections. A previous Ilford North was Labour in 1945 and October 1974, but did not contain the Conservative areas from Woodford which are now included; this seat is probably best regarded as another extraordinary suburban Labour gain like Harrow West or Wimbledon. The standstill result in 2001 reflected two forces tugging Ilford North in opposite directions – the influence of south Essex pulling it to the Tories, and the influence of middle class 1930s London suburbia pulling it to Labour.

Ilford North will remain a difficult seat for Labour to win in future, but Linda Perham has managed it twice against the odds and it is in seats like this one that Labour's two landslide majorities have been built.

ILFORD SOUTH

	2001		1997		1992 notional	
Electorate and turnout	76,025	54.3	71,202	70.2	68,665	74.0
Conservative	10,622	25.7	15,073	30.1	24,677	46.9
Labour	24,619	59.6	29,273	58.5	22,147	42.1
Lib Dem	4,647	11.3	3,152	6.3	5,493	10.5
Anti–EU	1,407	3.4	1,073	2.1	–	–
Others	–		1,448 (2)		269	
MP	Mike Gapes (Lab)		Mike Gapes (Lab)		Mike Gapes (Lab)	
Majority	13,997	33.9	14,200	28.4	2,530*	4.8*

* Estimated Conservative majority allowing for boundary changes.

Ilford South is now a pretty safe Labour seat, which is a break from its previous marginal status which had swung it back and forth between Labour and the Conservatives for decades. Labour MP Mike Gapes won it in 1992 with a big swing for that election of 5.9 per cent, and had to win it all over again when a Tory-inclined ward was added in 1997. He had no trouble, and won two massive majorities in 1997 and 2001 as the Tory vote crumbled.

Part of the reason why Ilford South is no longer marginal is its ethnic composition – its southern wards are increasingly populated by people of Asian origin who tend to be loyal supporters of Labour. It has increasingly come to be closer in spirit to East Ham, just across the borough boundary, than Romford or Woodford, and this was apparent in the large drop in the Conservative vote in 2001. The Conservative vote has also fallen apart in local elections during the 1990s with former marginals becoming Labour strongholds. There are only 139 safer Labour seats, which means that Ilford South should stay Labour even if the party crashed to a worse defeat than 1983.

LEYTON and WANSTEAD

	2001		1997		1992 notional	
Electorate and turnout	61,549	54.8	62,176	63.2	65,812	68.9
Conservative	6,654	19.7	8,736	22.2	14,006	30.9
Labour	19,558	58.0	23,922	60.8	20,775	45.8
Lib Dem	5,389	16.0	5,920	15.1	9,300	20.5
Anti–EU	378	1.1	–	–	–	–
Others	1,739 (2)		744 (2)		1,275	
MP	Harry Cohen (Lab)		Harry Cohen (Lab)		Harry Cohen (Lab)	
					Leyton	
Majority	12,904	38.3	15,186	38.6	6,769	14.9

Leyton, in the borough of Waltham Forest, is a drab area between Stratford and Walthamstow; still essentially part of the East End but without its peculiar social and political history. Leyton was a creation of the first outward surge of East Enders across the empty flats of south Essex in the 19th century, and remains an area of Victorian terraces interspersed with modern estates. Leytonstone is similar. It is still working class, quite poor and ethnically mixed, and little affected by gentrification - The Land that Yuppies Forgot. Leyton has a solid Labour tradition, except for two lapses – the Conservatives won the seat in a 1965 by-election, engineered in a failed attempt to return Labour's Foreign Secretary Patrick Gordon Walker to the Commons, and in the early 1980s Labour MP Bryan Magee joined the SDP. In both cases Labour resumed command after the next general election.

Wanstead contributes 15,000 voters to this seat; it is a suburban area in the borough of Redbridge and was previously part of a solid Tory seat. It has been most famous in recent years for the environmental protests over the construction of the M11 road link. Wanstead and Snaresbrook have been continuously Tory except in 1998, when Labour gained a foothold in both wards. The most concentrated opposition to Labour in this seat is actually a Liberal Democrat area in Leyton itself and Cann Hall in the far south of Leyton, but there are still enough Tories in Wanstead to keep the party in second place. A substantial Lib Dem vote in local elections seems not to cross over to general elections.

POPLAR and CANNING TOWN

	2001		1997		1992 notional	
Electorate and turnout	76,009	44.9	68,068	57.7	62,190	65.7
Conservative	6,758	19.8	5,892	15.0	10,517	25.7
Labour	20,866	61.2	24,807	63.2	20,935	51.2
Lib Dem	3,795	11.1	4,072	10.4	7,986	19.6
Anti–EU	–	–	1,091	2.8	–	–
BNP	1,733	5.1	2,849	7.3	831	2.0
Others	950		557		586	
MP	Jim Fitzpatrick (Lab)		Jim Fitzpatrick (Lab)		Mildred Gordon (Lab) Bow & Poplar	
Majority	14,108	41.4	18,915	48.2	10,418	25.5

Poplar and Canning Town is the 'Docklands' seat of inner East London, a strip of territory along the north bank of the river Thames including the loop of the Isle of Dogs, and eastward to the London City Airport and part of Beckton. Its landscape has been transformed in the past 20 years, most dramatically at Canary Wharf. This former derelict dock has become a major office centre, with two new towers rising to accompany the original tower, and expensive restaurants serving the workers in the financial and journalism complexes of the Wharf. Luxury flats have appeared at Canary Wharf and along the Thames loop, and more ordinary suburbia in the Beckton area. The Docklands development has been the major reason for the enormous increase in the electorate in this seat since 1992.

Middle class Docklands is grafted uneasily onto the working class and immigrant East End. Shadwell, Poplar and Canning Town are all dominated by council estates, and the Isle of Dogs still has its estates alongside the new developments. The racial tensions between white and Asian inhabitants of the area have given an unpleasant dimension to local politics with the success in 1993 of the British National Party in Millwall (Isle of Dogs) and BNP saved deposits in the last two general elections. Canning Town has a reputation as an inward looking white community, and the neighbouring ward of Ordnance is the most deprived area in the whole of London.

Poplar and Canning Town has produced two massive Labour wins, reflecting the long Labour traditions in the area. The southern end of Newham – Silvertown and Plaistow – has the longest continuous period (nearly 100 years) of Labour representation of anywhere in Britain, but it looked as if it was coming to an end in the late 1980s. In 1987 and 1992 the Conservatives challenged strongly, drawing strength from the new Essex-style private estates of the outer Docklands development at Beckton and the mainly white ethnic composition of Newham South. Boundary changes destroyed the Tory hopes, but there is still a potential for them in this constituency if they can mount an effective national campaign and get organised locally. Many of the new inhabitants do not vote (something they share with the other residents – turnout was dismal in 2001) and have little interest in local affairs. But for now, Labour have a dominant position in this divided constituency.

ROMFORD

	2001		1997		1992 *notional*	
Electorate and turnout	59,893	59.6	59,276	71.1	*60,903*	*77.6*
Conservative	18,931	53.0	17,538	41.6	*27,462*	*58.1*
Labour	12,954	36.3	18,187	43.2	*13,398*	*28.3*
Lib Dem	2,869	8.0	3,341	7.9	*5,865*	*12.4*
Anti–EU	533	1.5	1,431	3.4	–	–
Others	414		1,622 (2)		*546*	
MP	Andrew Rosindell (Con)		Eileen Gordon (Lab)		Michael Neubert (Con)	
Majority	5,977	16.7	649	1.5	*14,064*	*29.8*

Romford is the heartland of metropolitan Essex – a traditional brewing town, a town centre of decent shopping and notoriously unsophisticated nightlife surrounded by virtually all-white lower middle class suburbs such as Rise Park and Ardleigh Green. It was a surprise Labour gain of 1997 and one of the rare Tory gains of 2001, and on their best swing of the night: 9.1 per cent. Although south Essex and metro-politan Essex was one of the best areas for the Tories, Romford was an exceptional result. The Conservatives won a higher share of the vote in Romford than they did in strongholds such as Beaconsfield and Surrey East and only did better in ten seats in the whole country.

Part of the reason for Tory success was the personality of Andrew Rosindell, a flamboyant campaigner who gained his Chase Cross ward from the Lib Dems in 1990 and built up the largest Conservative share in any ward in London by 1998. His idiosyncrasies – like the union flag-wearing dog Spike which recently expired after accompanying him canvassing – were not buffoonery but a clever means of getting himself noticed and appealing to the peculiar local culture. Rosindell made great play of the Labour-led Havering council failing to fly the flag, outmanoeuvred a diffident Labour MP, and credited a visit by Margaret Thatcher for sealing his victory. The national Conservative campaign in 2001, although it went down badly in many places, also appealed strongly to the patriotic, recently-made good voters of Romford and south Essex, as is apparent from the results in neighbouring constituencies like Upminster. The Conservatives won every ward in Romford in the 2002 local elections.

There are ironic echoes of 1983. Just as Rosindell won by being more Thatcherite and more populist even than Hague, Labour's best results in 1983 were in Liverpool – particularly the Militant stronghold of Broadgreen – where the electorate were offered a more hard-line and uncompromising version of socialism than was on offer from Michael Foot. Both Liverpool and south Essex are very culturally distinctive sub-regions of England and what works with them may not work elsewhere. Labour ignored the siren voices of Merseyside socialism – will the Tories avoid falling into the trap of drawing too many lessons from Rosindell's success?

UPMINSTER

	2001		1997		1992 notional	
Electorate and turnout	56,829	59.6	56,793	72.8	58,553	79.2
Conservative	15,410	45.5	16,315	39.5	25,121	54.2
Labour	14,169	41.9	19,085	46.2	13,964	30.1
Lib Dem	3,183	9.4	3,919	9.5	7,300	15.7
Anti–EU	1,089	3.2	2,000	4.8	–	–
MP	Angela Watkinson (Con)		Keith Darvill (Lab)		Nicholas Bonsor (Con)	
Majority	1,241	3.7	2,770	6.7	11,157	24.1

Upminster was the most difficult gain the Conservatives managed to achieve from Labour in the 2001 general election – it was fiftieth in their target list and if they had done as well everywhere William Hague would be leader of a somewhat revitalised opposition, with a parliamentary party of similar number to Neil Kinnock's troops in 1987. Upminster is the eastern seat of the outer borough of Havering, which provided their Romford gain as well and was at the centre of a band of territory from Barking to Southend where the Tories did well.

Most Londoners have heard of Upminster, but few have been there. It is at the far east end of the District Line and is a familiar sight on destination boards. The constituency is a variegated collection of suburbs, stretching from Harold Hill in the north (a big council built estate which saw the first large scale sale of council houses in the early 1970s), through the wealthy areas of Cranham and Emerson Park to Upminster itself. Harold Hill produces two safe Labour wards, and Harold Wood has some Labour elements, but the party enjoys little support in the other half of the seat. In local elections the Upminster and Cranham areas vote overwhelmingly for the Havering Residents Association, but these affluent areas provide much of the Tory vote in general elections. The whole constituency has a low proportion of non-white residents, and has a lot in common with Romford. The Conservative message went down relatively well in areas like this, and the Labour vote sagged in Harold Hill and areas like it as turnout fell. When Upminster was first created in 1974, its two disparate elements made it a tightly fought marginal, and after years as a Tory stronghold it has reverted to this tradition.

A proposal to split Upminster's two halves was reversed at the boundary inquiry. Instead, it will gain some territory (and a longer name) at the expense of Hornchurch, probably helping the Conservatives.

WALTHAMSTOW

	2001		1997		1992 notional	
Electorate and turnout	64,403	53.5	63,818	62.8	66,412	71.4
Conservative	6,221	18.1	8,138	20.3	17,650	37.2
Labour	21,402	62.2	25,287	63.1	21,001	44.3
Lib Dem	5,024	14.6	5,491	13.7	7,489	15.8
Anti–EU	298	0.9	1,139	2.8	–	–
Others	1,484 (3)		–		1,285	
MP	Neil Gerrard (Lab)		Neil Gerrard (Lab)		Neil Gerrard (Lab)	
Majority	15,181	44.1	17,149	42.8	3,351	7.1

Walthamstow was Britain's first working class suburb, a Victorian settlement which sprang up because of the Great Eastern Railway's cheap fares for working men. It was an early example of the outward tendency that has characterised movement from the East End; Walthamstow was succeeded in turn by the estates of Dagenham, the suburbs of Upminster and Romford, and Essex towns such as Brentwood, Basildon and Chelmsford as the destination for outward movement.

Most of Walthamstow consists of acres of terraced housing, and like many such areas in London it has a large ethnic minority population. It proudly boasts the longest street market in Europe. Before 1974 Walthamstow was split into two seats – safe Labour – except in a 1967 by-election – West, and marginal East and the distinction between the two sides of Walthamstow is still present. To the south and west, Walthamstow shades into Leyton and the East End, but to the north and east it has some suburban avenues in areas such as Chapel End. Since the opening of the London underground's Victoria Line in the 1960s it has become much more accessible to the West End and has a sprinkling of gentrification and professional first-time buyers. Walthamstow's most famous resident in the past was William Morris (now commemorated in the name of a ward), whose print patterns no doubt adorn many of the area's walls.

The Conservatives are now very weak in Walthamstow and risk losing second place to the Liberal Democrats, who are active in local elections in several wards of the seat. Walthamstow, it is now difficult to recall, was a Conservative seat between 1987 and 1992. Like several other working class outer London seats (see also Hayes & Harlington) it has returned to Labour with a vengeance in 1997 and 2001 and is now so safe that if Labour were reduced to 70 seats Walthamstow would probably be one of them.

WEST HAM

	2001		1997		1992 notional	
Electorate and turnout	59,828	48.9	57,589	58.5	64,245	58.4
Conservative	4,804	16.4	5,037	15.0	11,229	30.0
Labour	20,449	69.9	24,531	72.9	21,717	57.9
Lib Dem	2,166	7.4	2,479	7.4	3,602	9.6
Anti–EU	657	2.2	–	–	–	–
Green	1,197	4.1	–	–	587	1.6
BNP	–	–	1,198	3.6	–	–
Others	–	–	416 (2)		352 (2)	
MP	Tony Banks (Lab)		Tony Banks (Lab)		Tony Banks (Lab)	
					Newham North West	
Majority	15,645	53.4	19,494	57.9	10,488	28.0

West Ham is the inner constituency of Newham. It is an old heavy industrial town that was absorbed into London's built up area in the 19th century and has a particularly strong tradition of trade unionism and Labour voting. It suffered severe depopulation in the middle of the 20th century, West Ham being reduced from four constituencies to one plus a part of the Poplar and Canning Town seat. There are some council estates but for the most part West Ham is made up of Victorian terraces in areas like Plaistow, Upton and Forest Gate. Cheap terraced housing was attractive to immigrants in the 1950s and 1960s and West Ham now has a large population from both major ethnic minorities. Stratford, in the north west of the seat, is a town centre for a swathe of inner east London and the council have great things planned for its facilities and already strong transport connections. The Jubilee Line extension ends here, but in the future it is anticipated that fast trains from the Channel Tunnel will call here and unleash Euro-prosperity in West Ham.

West Ham is known for its football club, which attracted the fanatical adherence of Alf Garnett, the bigoted central character of Johnny Speight's *Till Death Us Do Part*. Alf's views decisively lost the battle in Britain in general and West Ham in particular, which has never deviated from its Labour identity since 1945. All the component wards consistently vote Labour, although in the very southern wards there is occasional BNP activity. West Ham fans sing about forever blowing bubbles, but West Ham is forever voting Labour.

London – Inner South

	Conservative		Labour		Liberal Democrat		Others	
	Share of vote	Seats	Share of vote	Seats	Share of vote	Seats	Share of vote	Seats
2001	21.5	0	54.0	10	19.2	1	5.3	0
1997	23.6	0	57.9	10	14.3	1	4.2	0
1992	37.3	2	47.2	9	13.9	1	1.6	0
1987	38.4	6	42.8	5	17.8	1	1.0	0
1983	36.0	5	40.6	6	21.7	1	1.7	0

This sub-region contains the area most people mean when they say South (or even Sarf) London; its reputation in popular culture is of loveable dodgy geezers Del and Rodney from *Only Fools and Horses*, and to crime fiction fans the mean streets patrolled by Nick Sharman. There is some reality to both unfavourable portraits, but neither comes close to an accurate portrait even of Peckham, let alone all four boroughs (Lewisham, Southwark, Lambeth and Wandsworth) covered in this chapter.

Although rather small in area, south London covers a huge variety of urban environments, radiating outwards like rings on a tree trunk. Leisure, transport and office facilities line the south bank of the Thames, giving way further east to redeveloped dockland at Tower Bridge and Canada Water. The docks were once a dominant local employer in Southwark but have been replaced by service employment. In 1951 90 per cent of the workforce had manual occupations; in 1991 this was down to 30 per cent, with 55 per cent working in the public sector or financial services. To the west along the river lie the desirable areas of riverside Battersea (including the new Richard Rogers complex, Montevetro), where calling it 'South Chelsea' is not such a joke anymore, and suburban Putney. Just inland to the south is a band stretching from Stockwell in Lambeth across to Deptford in Lewisham, where you will find the real mean streets and concrete jungles. Some of the estates here are bywords for bad planning and violent crime, from Stockwell Park to North Peckham via the enormous Aylesbury estate. There is considerable poverty and deprivation in south London.

A little further out again, there is acre upon acre of Victorian terraces, often rented or bought by young professionals, students and the nurses and junior doctors of the several vast hospital complexes in the area (Guy's, St. Thomas's, St. George's, Kings College Hospital…): Battersea, Tooting, Clapham, Brixton, Herne Hill, East Dulwich, Brockley, Ladywell… Particularly in the Clapham and Battersea areas some of these buildings have been reconverted from flats back into family houses for the older and better-off members of the professional classes. Clapham, according to the London Property Guide, is no longer 'up and coming' but 'up and come' and the same applies to parts of Battersea. These areas have enormous mobility of population, with thousands of people moving in and out each year. Finally, there are some areas of suburban villas stretching through Putney, Streatham,

Dulwich and Sydenham, and the odd large council estate such as Roehampton in the west and Downham in the east.

The London underground makes only feeble efforts to penetrate south London, the Northern Line striking out boldly to Morden, the District Line making its way to Wimbledon via Putney and the Jubilee and Bakerloo only scraping the inner part of the area. The East London Line extensions south of New Cross Gate, to Wimbledon via Peckham and Streatham, and Croydon and Crystal Palace via Forest Hill, will open more of south London up from 2006. For the moment, most residents are dependent on a complex network of overland trains and overcrowded buses to get to central London, where many of them work. Transport is possibly an even bigger political issue here than elsewhere in London.

In many areas of Britain Asians outnumber blacks as the main ethnic minority, but in south London Afro-Caribbeans and Africans are the largest minority. In Lambeth, for instance, 25 per cent of the population is black and 9 per cent from other ethnic minorities. Brixton is the most famous multiracial centre, first for its 1981 riots and latterly as an edgy, but increasingly bustling and trendy part of town, but there is a substantial black population throughout south London, including Peckham, Camberwell and Lewisham. Black Africans are the largest ethnic minority in Southwark, with 9.2 per cent of the population to 8.9 per cent for Afro-Caribbeans and 2.8 per cent for other black minorities according to 1996 estimates.

With the exception of Wandsworth, at the west of the area, most of this diverse area has recently been united by hostility to the Conservative Party. Even in 1964 Streatham, Norwood and two Lewisham seats stayed Conservative, although all these areas are now heavily Labour in general elections. The Conservatives had never been wiped out in this area before 1997, but now they are serious contenders in only two seats, Putney and Battersea and produced dismal showings in other areas. Part of the reason is social change – the growing black vote, although turnout is low, is very loyal to the Labour Party – 85 per cent support is not an uncommon finding for black Labour support in opinion polls. This has been a long term benefit to Labour in this area.

Political change is not just about demographics, it is also about politics. Simon Hughes's victory in the February 1983 Bermondsey by-election started a chapter of Alliance and Liberal Democrat success in the northern part of the borough of Southwark, which has spilled over into central Southwark and Lambeth. In the 2001 general election the Liberal Democrats moved into second in Camberwell & Peckham and Streatham, reflecting a modest level of local activism and the collapse of the Conservatives. There is a potential threat to Labour's hegemony here, as in Vauxhall, but one has the feeling that it would probably take a by-election to crystallise. Labour's vote slipped quite badly in several inner seats in 2001, a victim of low turnout and disappointment among radically-minded voters about the government's record; the Green Party did well in Deptford and Dulwich.

Local government

Conservative interest is concentrated in Wandsworth. The influx of young professionals into Battersea and Putney has been of a slightly different character from other areas of inner south London; more money, and old money in particular, and looking to Chelsea rather than Soho or Covent Garden. Conservatism is also strengthened by the positive image of their ruling group on Wandsworth borough.

Wandsworth has been run by the Conservatives since 1978 and their control has been unassailable since they won a landslide against the trend in 1990. Wandsworth council was among the first to contract out its services, and it still prides itself on providing the basic services well at a low cost. For a while, after interim reforms to the poll tax in 1991, its residents paid no local taxes at all, and council tax levels are still low. Wandsworth has aggressively sold off much of its housing stock, while more traditional housing in Putney and Between the Commons has been reconverted from flats into family housing for the upper middle class. Demographic change, assisted by social engineering, has helped the Tories here despite London's general trend to the left.

In Lambeth, by contrast, local government has been a byword for chaos and political embarrassment. In the 1980s it was run by assorted left wing factions who indulged in gesture politics while services crumbled despite exorbitant local taxes. Labour lost control of the council in 1994 and an all-party agreement led to cuts and managerial reforms. Labour won control back in 1998, and despite an improved image, lost control again in 2002. In Lewisham a popular Labour regime has run the council for years and in the 1990s nearly monopolised council representation. Residents voted narrowly in 2001 to establish an elected mayoralty in Lewisham, with Steve Bullock winning the election for Labour in May 2002. Southwark has been Labour since its creation in 1964, under traditionalist, left wing and New Labour leadership in turn, although the party's overall majority vanished thanks to defections in 2000. Liberal Democrats were hoping to gain outright control of the council in 2002 but fell two seats short. A proposal for an elected mayor was resoundingly defeated.

Lambeth and Southwark together form a single Greater London Authority constituency, which is a Labour stronghold with Lib Dems second and is currently represented by Valerie Shawcross. Lewisham is grouped with Greenwich to create another safe Labour seat for Len Duvall. Wandsworth and suburban Merton form a GLA constituency which the Conservative candidate Elizabeth Howlett won well (40-28 per cent) in 2000.

Boundary review

After radical change in 1997, the broad pattern of seats in the area will remain unchanged, with some adjustment of wards to improve the electorate in the small Camberwell & Peckham seat. The exception is Lewisham, where the Commission proposed to cross the boundary with Bromley (see London: Outer South East) because its seats are undersized. The new Lewisham West and Penge seat is less safely Labour than the current Lewisham West, but would still have seen comfortable Labour wins in 1997 and 2001.

BATTERSEA

	2001		1997		1992 notional	
Electorate and turnout	67,495	54.5	66,895	70.9	67,426	77.8
Conservative	13,445	36.5	18,687	39.4	26,411	50.4
Labour	18,498	50.3	24,047	50.7	21,630	41.3
Lib Dem	4,450	12.1	3,482	7.3	3,700	7.1
Anti–EU	–	–	1,054 (2)	2.2	–	–
Others	411		127		686	
MP	Martin Linton (Lab)		Martin Linton (Lab)		John Bowis (Con)	
Majority	5,053	13.7	5,360	11.3	4,781	9.1

Battersea has famously been the scene of successful social engineering by the Conservative controlled Wandsworth council, aided by its proximity to Chelsea and the West End which has attracted many upwardly mobile professionals. The riverside and Battersea Park areas deserve their reputation as 'south Chelsea', while the area near Clapham Junction station (Northcote) has also moved up in the world since the days of *Up the Junction*. 'Between the Commons' is one of the first places ever described as 'gentrifying'. The constituency stretches down as far as Balham, also an increasingly expensive but hardly fashionable corner. Interspersed with the upwardly mobile terraces and avenues are some grim council estates where Wandsworth's right to buy policies have been less enthusiastically taken up. The Doddington Estate is notorious for the corrupt methods by which it was built in the 1960s; the council leader responsible, Sidney Sporle, was jailed for taking bribes. Social change pushed Battersea over to the Conservatives in 1987 and it was a surprise when they lost it ten years later.

John O'Farrell's *Things Can Only Get Better* is a grimly hilarious account of Labour's string of defeats in Battersea, culminating in the loss of the seat in 1987 and humiliation in the council elections of 1990. Things did get better for Labour in Battersea, although it has not been an uncomplicated story. Since 1997, the voters of Battersea have divided their favours. They are willing to vote Tory in local elections for Wandsworth council and even the Greater London Authority, but choose Labour when national issues are at stake in general elections, and even in the 1999 European election the Tories were only a whisker ahead here despite their strong national showing.

The electorate in much of Battersea, as in most of inner London, is very changeable – over half the people on the register in the constituency at the time of the 1997 election were no longer there in 2001, replaced by 37,000 new names. This poses a formidable task for the parties in identifying their supporters and running an election machine, and also makes election results sensitive to subtle changes in social trends. House prices doubled again during the 1997 parliament, but this had the effect of encouraging houses to be divided into flats again and, as one observer put it, made the number of doorbells increase rather than the average income. Labour MP Martin Linton did extremely well to gain a slight swing in his favour in 2001, helped by Labour's increasing strength among the professional middle class, but Battersea will still be a top Conservative target.

Wandsworth's Toryism is the Toryism of winners rather than losers; the confidence of successful and aspirational voters rather than the sullen defensiveness of those whom change is leaving behind. The paradox of such a seat voting overwhelmingly for Tories in local elections but supporting New Labour nationally is not so difficult to resolve. Battersea does remain a marginal seat with Conservative potential, but in the last couple of general elections Labour's economic policies and the Conservatives' unpopular populism have given Labour the advantage.

CAMBERWELL and PECKHAM

	2001		1997		1992 notional	
Electorate and turnout	53,687	46.8	51,313	55.3	64,229	51.3
Conservative	2,740	10.9	3,283	11.6	7,841	23.8
Labour	17,473	69.6	19,734	69.5	19,891	60.4
Lib Dem	3,350	13.3	3,198	11.3	4,974	15.1
Anti–EU	–	–	692	2.4	–	–
Others	1,541 (4)		1,467 (4)		244	
MP	Harriet Harman (Lab)		Harriet Harman (Lab)		Harriet Harman (Lab) Peckham	
Majority	14,123	56.3	16,451	58.0	12,050	36.6

The middle part of the London Borough of Southwark is a place with a wretched reputation. It is known best for the grim North Peckham estate, a concrete wasteland where Damilola Taylor was murdered in 2000. The estate is now being pulled down; similar modern slum clearances accounted for some of the very large drop in electorate between 1992 and 1997. Camberwell Green is an uneasy juxtaposition of some unpopular but less notorious council estates and some pleasant gentrifying streets. It is near the large medical complex at Kings College Hospital and the Maudsley. Peckham does have a future. It has a large African community which gives it a distinct flavour as an area, it has a fine new library and the tube will – eventually –arrive here.

Politically, this is a monolithically Labour seat with consistently low turnout in general elections. In local elections there is some carefully targeted Liberal Democrat activity intended to add sufficient councillors to their existing Bermondsey stronghold to take power in Southwark, something that Labour's popularity narrowly denied them in 1994 and 1998, but no sign that any of this has had an impact on national voting trends. The left also mounts a feeble and divided challenge in such a troubled area, with three left wing candidates in each of the last two elections. There are only 11 safer Labour seats in the country.

DULWICH and WEST NORWOOD

	2001		1997		1992 notional	
Electorate and turnout	71,621	53.4	70,203	65.0	75,179	67.7
Conservative	8,689	22.7	11,038	24.2	21,779	42.8
Labour	20,999	54.9	27,807	61.0	23,582	46.3
Lib Dem	5,805	15.2	4,916	10.8	4,998	9.8
Green	1,914	5.0	–	–	454	0.9
Anti–EU	–	–	1,056 (2)	2.3	–	–
Others	839		798 (3)		77	
MP	Tessa Jowell (Lab)		Tessa Jowell (Lab)		Tessa Jowell (Lab)	
					Dulwich	
Majority	12,310	32.2	16,769	36.8	1,803	3.5

This seat was purportedly a marginal when it was first created in 1997, but it has never known a close contest and is unlikely to be marginal in the future. Labour have enjoyed two thumping majorities in 1997 and 2001.

Dulwich village is a smaller-scale, south of the river, Hampstead. There are large houses, attractive commons and a public school, but the village (which does vote Tory in local elections) is only a small part of the constituency. East Dulwich is a perfectly ordinary inner London suburb, and in the north the Dulwich area fades gradually into Peckham around Rye Lane. On the West Norwood side there are several wards of broadly similar character such as Gipsy Hill. Most of this area consistently votes Labour. It is not surprising that, as in similar seats such as Lewisham West or Streatham, the Conservative challenge has faded. This sort of seat, heavily dependent on public transport, ethnically diverse, full of young, educated people, has been terra incognita for the Conservative Party for some time. There are signs, as in inner north London, that the electoral life cycle of these seats is slowly entering a new phase with a fall in the Labour vote in favour of the 'more radical' Liberal Democrats and Greens.

LEWISHAM DEPTFORD

	2001		1997		1992 notional	
Electorate and turnout	60,275	48.3	58,141	57.9	57,583	65.4
Conservative	3,622	12.4	4,949	14.7	10,395	27.6
Labour	18,915	65.0	23,827	70.8	22,816	60.6
Lib Dem	3,409	11.7	3,004	8.9	4,432	11.8
Anti–EU	–	–	868	2.6	–	–
Green	1,901	6.5	–	–	–	–
Others	1,260		996		–	
MP	Joan Ruddock (Lab)		Joan Ruddock (Lab)		Joan Ruddock (Lab)	
Majority	15,293	52.5	18,878	56.1	12,421	33.0

Deptford itself is a run-down inner city area close to the river; although a historic part of London's dockland it is mostly high-density council housing. Christopher Marlowe, killed in a pub in the area in 1593, used to be commemorated in the name of one of Lewisham's wards. The Deptford constituency stretches away from the Thames, up the gradient to New Cross and then to the Brockley and Crofton Park area which is popular with first time buyers and young professionals. However, the dominant tone of the area is set by the council tenants, African and Afro-Caribbean residents of Deptford and New Cross. Every ward of the seat was strongly Labour at the 1998 local elections, although since then there have been two Socialist by-election victories in the now abolished Pepys ward. The Greens and Socialist Alliance together polled nearly 11 per cent of the vote in 2001; both the Greeens and Socialists are now represented on the council and it would not be impossible for a left wing candidate to come a distant second to Labour in the constituency as a whole, so weak are the Conservatives here. It is the 25th safest Labour seat.

LEWISHAM EAST

	2001		1997		1992 notional	
Electorate and turnout	56,657	53.1	56,333	66.4	58,328	74.2
Conservative	7,157	23.8	9,694	25.9	18,510	42.8
Labour	16,160	53.7	21,821	58.3	19,633	45.4
Lib Dem	4,937	16.4	4,178	11.2	4,935	11.4
Anti–EU	361	1.2	910	2.4	–	–
Others	1,469 (2)		805 (3)		196	
MP	Bridget Prentice (Lab)		Bridget Prentice (Lab)		Bridget Prentice (Lab)	
Majority	9,003	29.9	12,127	32.4	1,123	2.6

Lewisham East and Lewisham West have been marginal seats which have moved in tandem in recent years – both Conservative gains in 1983 and Labour gains in 1992, and large Labour victories in 1997 and 2001. East is now a bit weaker for Labour than West, a reversal of the pattern before 1983 when it was perceived as the more Labour-inclined of the two seats.

Lewisham East is mainly composed of middle-London suburbs such as Grove Park, Hither Green and half of Blackheath. Many of these wards were competitive between Labour and Conservative in the 1980s but Labour have had the whip hand lately. In 2002 Labour kept the middle class, villagey Blackheath ward but the Conservatives gained representation in the less favoured Grove Park area. To the south of the constituency is the large council-built Downham estate which sends Lib Dems to the council chamber. Despite this, there is little prospect of Labour losing the seat – Colin Moynihan's spell as MP for Conservative Lewisham East in 1983-92 seems to have been an aberration.

LEWISHAM WEST

	2001		1997		1992 actual	
Electorate and turnout	59,176	52.1	58,659	64.0	59,372	73.0
Conservative	6,896	22.4	8,956	23.8	18,569	42.8
Labour	18,816	61.1	23,273	62.0	20,378	47.0
Lib Dem	4,146	13.5	3,672	9.8	4,295	9.9
Anti–EU	485	1.6	1,098	2.9	125	0.3
Others	472		565 (2)		–	
MP	Jim Dowd (Lab)		Jim Dowd (Lab)		Jim Dowd (Lab)	
Majority	11,920	38.7	14,317	38.1	1,809	4.2

Lewisham West used to be the traditional marginal seat in Lewisham, changing hands in 1992, 1983, 1974, 1970, 1966, 1950 and 1945, but its marginal days seem over. It is now safer for Labour than Barking. Unlike the other two Lewisham seats, the swing to Labour continued in 2001.

Lewisham West is a more completely suburban constituency than East, centring around Forest Hill, Catford and Sydenham. There are council-built estates interspersed throughout these suburbs. It is still quite an average part of London, with many social indicators being close to the norm for the capital. A local peculiarity is that residents are dependent on rail travel to a greater extent than anywhere else in the country; a large proportion of the electorate work in central London and commute in via the several railway lines in the borough.

The Conservatives used to have some strength in the Catford area but anti-Labour political forces in this area seem to have, at least temporarily, collapsed, and the party is dominant in all areas of the seat. Labour had a monopoly of councillors from this constituency in May 2002, in contrast to East and even Deptford. The boundary commission proposes to breach the borough boundary with Bromley and form a combined Lewisham West and Penge constituency. This might reduce Labour's majority a little but poses no threat to the party's hold on the seat as long as they remain ahead nationally.

PUTNEY

	2001		1997		1992 actual	
Electorate and turnout	60,643	56.5	60,015	73.3	61,915	77.9
Conservative	13,140	38.4	17,108	38.9	25,188	52.2
Labour	15,911	46.5	20,084	45.7	17,662	36.6
Lib Dem	4,671	13.6	4,739	10.8	4,636	9.6
Anti–EU	347	1.0	1,751 (2)	4.0	–	–
Others	185		313 (5)		757 (2)	
MP	Tony Colman (Lab)		Tony Colman (Lab)		David Mellor (Con)	
Majority	2,771	8.1	2,976	6.8	7,526	15.6

Putney has tended to move in line with broad social trends. It was Conservative from 1918 to 1964, as most suburban districts were, but Labour held it from 1964 to 1979 because of the construction of large council estates in the area. The Conservatives did well from 1979 to 1997, helped by right-to-buy sales in the council estates and an influx of young, affluent professionals. However, social change cannot explain Labour's recent hold on the seat. This has happened because Labour have managed to cut into the professional middle class vote in general elections while holding on to their shrinking working class base in this seat.

Putney is a surprising Labour seat. It had the unique distinction in 2001 of being the only Labour seat with no local Labour councillors. The only part of Putney that looks like a Labour stronghold is Roehampton, a massive modernist estate built by the London County Council in the 1950s next to Richmond Park and Wimbledon Common. Even Roehampton, however, elected a full slate of Conservative councillors in 1998 including their 2001 parliamentary candidate Michael Simpson. There are some other estates on the other side of Wimbledon Common, at Parkside and Southfields, but many of these flats and houses have been sold off. The rest of Putney, including the district by the river commonly referred to by that name, is affluent, rather intellectual suburbia. The inner part resembles Fulham, the outer part shades into Richmond. Although all these areas vote Tory in elections for Wandsworth council, there is some Labour presence everywhere.

The failure in 2001 to regain Putney, or even dent Labour's majority, was shocking for the Conservatives who felt that a strong candidate, good local campaign and demographic change were all working in their favour. The national campaign had, it seems, put off the affluent, confident voters of Putney who are happy enough with Labour in Whitehall and the Tories in the Town Hall. Putney will remain a hard fought marginal seat for the foreseeable future.

SOUTHWARK NORTH and BERMONDSEY

	2001		1997		1992 notional	
Electorate and turnout	73,529	50.1	67,546	60.4	69,011	62.5
Conservative	2,800	7.6	2,835	6.9	5,170	12.0
Labour	11,359	30.8	16,444	40.3	14,889	34.5
Lib Dem	20,991	56.9	19,831	48.6	22,158	51.4
Anti–EU	271	0.7	543	1.3	–	–
Others	1,441 (3)		(4) 1,140		909	
MP	Simon Hughes (LD)		Simon Hughes (LD)		Simon Hughes (LD) Southwark & Bermondsey	
Majority	9,632	26.1	3,387	8.3	7,269	16.9

Southwark North and Bermondsey is an anomaly – a safe Liberal Democrat seat in the inner city. The constituency comprises a stretch of the south bank of the Thames, opposite Canary Wharf, the City and Temple, and territory inland to the border of Camberwell and Peckham. Redevelopment has produced some very attractive residential areas by the river, particularly in the old dockland warehouses near Tower Bridge, and some more ordinary semi-suburban private estates at Canada Water and Surrey Quays. The collapse of manufacturing industry in the area has created inland areas of surplus land which are gradually being developed. Southwark also has a large number of obsolete office blocks now being converted to residential use, most notably the 400-flat 'Metro Central Heights', previously the head-quarters of the Department of Health and Social Security overlooking the Elephant and Castle round-about and shopping centre. Interspersed with the redeveloped areas, and providing a majority of the population, are some very deprived council estates such as the gargantuan Aylesbury estate the other side of the Elephant. Demographically, it should be a safe Labour seat, and that is what it was until a disastrous by-election in February 1983 when it was seized by Simon Hughes.

Since the initial debacle Labour have tried various approaches to win the seat back – an established MP dispossessed by boundary changes in June 1983, a Militant in 1987, long-time Euro MP and local politician Richard Balfe in 1992, council leader Jeremy Fraser in 1997, and black Merton councillor Kingsley Abrams in 2001. Nothing has worked and the Liberal Democrats have also virtually monopo-lised the area's council representation in 1990s local elections, winning in deprived estates, trendy riverside and quiet parts of Rotherhithe alike. Simon Hughes probably has as long as he wants repre-senting the seat, and the only circumstances in which the Lib Dem local stranglehold looks like being broken is paradoxically if they take over Southwark council and have to make some hard decisions. In the boundary review this constituency gets yet another new name as Bermondsey and Old Southwark.

STREATHAM

	2001		1997		1992 notional	
Electorate and turnout	76,021	49.1	74,583	60.2	71,008	70.1
Conservative	6,639	17.8	9,758	21.7	19,114	38.4
Labour	21,401	57.3	28,181	62.8	24,585	49.4
Lib Dem	6,771	18.1	6,082	13.6	4,966	10.0
Anti–EU	–	–	864	1.9	–	–
Green	1,641	4.4	–	–	673	1.4
Others	906		–		434	
MP	Keith Hill (Lab)		Keith Hill (Lab)		Keith Hill (Lab)	
Majority	14,630	39.2	18,423	41.0	5,471	11.0

Although mainly suburban, Streatham includes some inner areas such as the southern part of Brixton, including Lambeth's Town Hall at the corner of Acre Lane, Railton Road and the tough estates of Tulse Hill, and the more up-market Clapham Park area sometimes known to estate agents as Abbeville village. South of Brixton, Streatham lies either side of the busy A23 as it splutters and coughs its way southwards from London to Croydon and Brighton. Streatham was once a rather staid, comfortable suburb, but it has changed even more than most halfway out areas of London. It has drifted down the social scale; the shopping facilities of Streatham High Road are a shadow of what they once were. Streatham, in the London property market, has become a refuge for poorer middle class workers in flats, and some families in the larger houses that exist in the area. Streatham's black population has risen steadily, in the flats of estates and mansion blocks and the houses of suburbia alike.

Streatham was continuously Tory from 1918 until 1992, but since then the Conservative vote in Streatham has fallen apart. All the local Conservative councillors lost their seats in 1998 and the party was relegated to third place in 2001. Their former strongholds in the south of Streatham fell to the Liberal Democrats, who are locally active in both the Streatham and Vauxhall constituencies and have long had a base in Streatham Hill. As befits a rather trendy area, the Greens and Socialist Alliance between them achieved 6.9 per cent of the vote in 2001 and there was a degree of deliberate abstention. Labour seem completely dominant in general elections for the foreseeable future.

TOOTING

	2001		1997		1992 actual	
Electorate and turnout	68,447	54.9	66,536	69.3	68,307	74.8
Conservative	9,932	26.4	12,505	27.1	20,494	40.1
Labour	20,332	54.1	27,516	59.7	24,601	48.2
Lib Dem	5,583	14.9	4,320	9.4	3,776	7.4
Anti–EU	–	–	829	1.8	–	–
Green	1,744	4.6	527	1.1	694	1.4
Others	–		408 (4)		1,523 (3)	
MP	Tom Cox (Lab)		Tom Cox (Lab)		Tom Cox (Lab)	
Majority	10,400	27.7	15,011	32.6	4,107	8.0

Tooting is the southern seat of the borough of Wandsworth, and has been less affected by social change than Battersea or Putney. It is quite like the neighbouring areas of Streatham and Mitcham & Morden, composed for the most part of acre upon acre of terraces interspersed by large parks and the occasional council estate. Tooting is more ethnically mixed than Battersea, and loyalty from ethnic minority and working class owner occupier voters means that three wards –Tooting, Graveney and Furzedown – have tended to Labour even in most recent local elections. In retrospect, the Conservative near-miss in 1987 owed more to Labour's weak position across London than social change in Tooting. Earlsfield, by the railway line, is semi-marginal. There are some more solid Conservative areas, particularly at the end of the constituency near Wandsworth Common. Labour MP Tom Cox, having served quietly since 1970, is now a veteran member (born 1930); if Cox steps down there will be stiff competition for the Labour nomination. The forces of revolutionary socialism have a virtual history in Tooting, thanks to *Citizen Smith*'s popular front in the 1970s comedy, but its current voting behaviour is orthodox enough.

VAUXHALL

	2001		1997		1992 notional	
Electorate and turnout	74,474	44.8	70,424	55.5	67,961	63.7
Conservative	4,489	13.4	5,942	15.2	11,517	26.6
Labour	19,738	59.1	24,920	63.8	24,278	56.1
Lib Dem	6,720	20.1	6,260	16.0	6,247	14.4
Green	1,485	4.4	864	2.2	898	2.1
Others	960 (2)		1,080 (2)		338 (2)	
MP	Kate Hoey (Lab)		Kate Hoey (Lab)		Kate Hoey (Lab)	
Majority	13,018	39.0	18,660	47.8	12,761	29.5

Vauxhall is a rather generic name for a collection of distinct neighbourhoods in the north of the borough of Lambeth. In the far north is Lambeth's share of the South Bank, including attractions such as the London Eye and the National Theatre and the transport hub of Waterloo. Kennington and Vauxhall proper have some fine Georgian houses, increasingly gentrified and the home to many politicians, including former Lib Dem leader Paddy Ashdown. Further south lie the less desirable Stockwell and Angell areas and the northern halves of Clapham and Brixton. The Lib Dems did well in these areas in the 2002 local elections. Ferndale ward, in north west Brixton, is the area where John Major won his first election (in 1968) but there are few Conservatives around here now. A lot of Vauxhall constituency is a mixture of increasingly trendy and desirable streets and some of the most unpleasant concrete estates south London has to offer; it is an edgy, exciting urban mix which is an exaggerated caricature of the diversity of London. The registered electorate has been rising strongly in recent years. Although Labour win large majorities, the turnout is very low (the 15th worst in the country, and the second worst in London, in 2001) and the Lib Dems can entertain long-term ambitions in the area.

London – Outer South East

(Greenwich and former Kent)

	Conservative		Labour		Liberal Democrat		Others	
	Share of vote	Seats	Share of vote	Seats	Share of vote	Seats	Share of vote	Seats
2001	38.9	4	38.6	4	18.9	0	3.6	0
1997	36.1	4	40.1	4	18.2	0	5.6	0
1992	48.9	8	27.9	2	21.8	0	1.4	0
1987	49.4	8	22.4	0	28.2	2	1.0	0
1983	49.6	8	20.5	1	29.3	1	0.8	0

This grouping is based on the suburbs which were transferred from Kent to London in the reorganisation in 1963-65 (Bexley and Bromley), plus the borough of Greenwich which has been part of London since the Victorian period although always with a slightly separate feel about it. Greenwich is tacked onto the Kent suburbs because it has been paired with the outer borough of Bexley for parliamentary purposes since 1997. Bromley, to the south, is the largest borough in London in terms of area, and even includes some areas of open country in its southern reaches although most of it is composed of very low density residential areas. This part of London, except for central Greenwich, is perhaps the least familiar to the visitor. In the three boroughs there is only one tube station, the white elephant North Greenwich station built to serve the Millennium Dome, and this is one more than the area had in mid 1999. Residents who commute into central London, a considerable proportion of the working population, use overland rail services provided by the much criticised Connex franchise.

Greenwich has been for centuries London's maritime centre, with a strong influence from the former Royal Naval College. Woolwich, further downriver, was a military town dependent on the Royal Arsenal which was a massive employer. The Arsenal's land extended into the town centre and over a large swathe of what is now the Erith & Thamesmead constituency. Strong trade union and co-operative movements made Woolwich a cradle of the Labour movement in Britain, with the first Labour victory coming in a by-election in 1903 for Will Crooks. Labour's record here is not unbroken by any means, particularly as the two previous Labour MPs defected to the Liberals (Christopher Mayhew, 1974) and SDP (John Cartwright, 1981), but labourism still flourishes in the town.

There was hardly any settlement in the suburban area before the railways came in the mid 19th century, except for the market town of Bromley. Most of the suburban area is the product of interwar development of the same kind that fuelled the growth of Metroland to the north west of London – suburbs formed around stations to convey white-collar workers into London and around the new arterial roads out of the city. Thirties bungalows, a commonplace of English townscapes, are rare in most of

London but are found in relatively large numbers out here. Unlike the suburbs in other directions, the south eastern area has not been greatly affected by trends with their origins in inner London. The boroughs of Bromley and Bexley are 95 per cent and 93 per cent white respectively, dependence on public transport is relatively low for London and there is little of the liberal professional colonisation that has so changed places like Finchley and Wimbledon. Bromley and Bexley are still inhabited by professional and managerial workers in large detached houses with big gardens, and by more lower middle class residents in semis and bungalows. Bromley and Bickley have a certain amount of that outer London wide-boy-made-good feel in common with Sutton and Romford. There is the odd patch of working class London overspill, but these are very traditional suburbs.

The voting behaviour of the suburbs is also quite traditional – the Conservatives have sagged rather less here than on the other edges of London in 1997 and 2001. The anti-EU vote in 1997 was relatively high (4.1 per cent) and the Tories recouped some ground in 2001. Extensive boundary changes over the years make comparisons difficult, but Orpington, Chislehurst and a large Bexley seat have been Liberal or Labour in the past but stuck by the Conservatives in the last two elections (albeit not by much in Orpington). Bexleyheath and Crayford is a very marginal Labour seat. Eltham, half way out, is still just about marginal, and has a long marginal tradition. The traditional picture is not quite completed by Greenwich and Woolwich, which abandoned their Labour allegiances in the 1980s because of an SDP defection (Woolwich) and a by-election (Greenwich) but both have reverted completely to supporting Labour since 1992.

Local government
Labour control Greenwich borough, and have done so continuously since the first elections for the present borough in 1964, except for a lapse in 1968-71. Despite the SDP's strength at parliamentary level in the 1980s it made relatively minor inroads locally, and Labour are unlikely to lose control in the future. Bexley was Labour's only gain of a London borough in 2002 – a result that surprised many observers as the party only had control once previously. Usually it has been Conservative run. Bromley could have been purpose-built as a secure Conservative council, but the Tories managed to lose control – for the first time – in 1998 and were replaced by a Lib Dem administration supported by Labour. The Conservatives regained outright control in July 2001 thanks to by-election gains and consolidated their grip in 2002. The most controversial issue in local politics is the proposed redevelopment of Crystal Palace park, which both administrations of Bromley supported despite serious environmental protests until the scheme collapsed in May 2001.

On the Greater London Authority Greenwich and Lewisham provide a safe seat for Labour's Len Duvall. The other two boroughs provide the safest Conservative seat on the GLA, which the party would even have held in 1997 and their candidate Robert Neill won 47 per cent of the vote in 2000 (to 22 per cent each for Labour and Lib Dem). It was one of only two districts where Steve Norris led Ken Livingstone in the Mayoral election.

Boundary review
There were radical revisions before the 1997 election, in which the area lost two seats. The next review will rearrange things less dramatically, with the pairing of Greenwich and Bexley being kept up.

However, the currently oversized Bromley seats will be cut down to size through a pairing with Lewisham; the new cross-border seat Lewisham West & Penge will be Labour but the knock-on effects will strengthen the Conservatives in the three all-Bromley seats.

BECKENHAM

	2001		1997		1992 notional	
Electorate and turnout	72,772	62.6	73,126	74.3	75,388	77.4
Conservative	20,618	45.3	23,084	42.5	35,154	60.2
Labour	15,659	34.4	18,131	33.4	12,341	21.1
Lib Dem	7,308	16.0	9,858	18.1	9,765	16.7
Anti–EU	782	1.7	2,169 (2)	4.0	–	–
Other	1,195 (2)		1,108 (2)		1,153	
MP	Jacqui Lait (Con)		Piers Merchant (Con)		Piers Merchant (Con)	
Majority	4,959	10.9	4,953	9.1	22,813	39.1

Parliamentary by-election 20 November 1997: Conservative 13,162 (41.2), Labour 11,935 (37.4), Lib Dem 5,864 (18.4), 5 Others 947 Electorate 73,232, Turnout 43.6%. MP: Jacqui Lait (Con), Majority 1,227 (3.8).

Beckenham is the innermost of the Bromley seats, but it is hardly what might be described as an inner city seat. For the most part it is comfortable suburban domesticity, with broad avenues in Eden Park and Shortlands making up wards with very few social problems. A few parts of the seat, such as Coper's Cope, have seen family houses replaced by blocks of flats, but these tend to be privately owned and provide a younger, but not particularly differently inclined, portion of the electorate. There is some rather different territory in Anerley and Penge, near Crystal Palace, with Bromley's only substantial ethnic minority communities and some rather densely packed terraces.

Beckenham should be safely Conservative, but Labour came very close in the November 1997 by-election. This was not entirely because of Labour's strong performance across the London suburbs, but also because the by-election was called for an embarrassing reason – the Conservative MP Piers Merchant, who had been given the benefit of the doubt in May, had been spotted behaving foolishly again with a Soho nightclub hostess in October 1997 and resigned. But having failed to gain the seat then, and a near repetition of the May 1997 result in 2001, Labour's best chance seems to have passed and Jacqui Lait should now hold on.

The boundary changes will further strengthen the Conservative position. The Labour voting inner wards are to be moved into a seat based on Lewisham West, and in exchange some more outer wards join the seat; Beckenham becomes a nearly undiluted constituency of prosperous suburbia.

BEXLEYHEATH and CRAYFORD

	2001		1997		1992 notional	
Electorate and turnout	63,580	63.5	63,373	76.1	64,601	81.1
Conservative	16,121	39.9	18,527	38.4	28,380	54.2
Labour	17,593	43.6	21,942	45.5	16,377	31.3
Lib Dem	4,476	11.1	5,391	11.2	7,515	14.4
Anti–EU	780	1.9	1,934 (2)	4.0	–	–
BNP	1,408	3.5	429	0.9	–	–
Others	–		–		115	
MP	Nigel Beard (Lab)		Nigel Beard (Lab)		Cyril Townsend (Con)	
					Bexleyheath	
Majority	1,472	3.6	3,415	7.1	12,003	22.9

Bexleyheath is a very suburban area, with many commuters travelling on the rather poor trains into central London. It lies either side of the A2 as it gradually shakes London off. It is mainly of inter-war vintage, with few extremes of wealth or poverty in the area. Its wards are mostly quite mixed politically. Crayford, added in 1997, tends to be Labour althought the others see tight contests between Labour and Conservative.

The Conservatives benefited from a trend in their favour in this area over the years since Edward Heath first seized Bexley by 133 votes, thanks to a Communist, in 1950. Labour came within 2,000 votes in Bexleyheath in October 1974 – it was thought to be marginal when it was redrawn that year and Heath stood for the safer southern part designated as Sidcup. The Tory majority built up for Heath-supporting Cyril Townsend until major boundary revisions gave part of the seat to the Sidcup seat and added a large section of the abolished Erith & Crayford seat to the rest in 1997. Labour surprised most observers by defeating David Evennett, who had won the Tory selection battle for the new seat, and again by holding on in 2001. Nigel Beard's majority on the latter occasion was reduced and there are only nine Labour seats more vulnerable to a Conservative recovery. It would be catastrophic for Iain Duncan Smith if the Conservatives fail for a third time here.

BROMLEY and CHISLEHURST

	2001		1997		1992 notional	
Electorate and turnout	67,183	64.3	71,210	74.1	73,653	79.0
Conservative	21,412	49.5	24,428	46.3	36,028	62.0
Labour	12,375	28.6	13,310	25.2	10,027	17.2
Lib Dem	8,180	18.9	12,530	23.8	10,370	17.8
Anti–EU	1,264	2.9	1,176	2.2	–	–
Others	–		1,294 (3)		1,725	
MP	Eric Forth (Con)		Eric Forth (Con)		TWO SEATS MERGE	
Majority	9,037	20.9	11,118	21.1	25,658	44.1

Bromley is the easternmost of the market towns swallowed up by greater London in its great 1919-39 expansion. It has a town centre, with an old high street and a modern enclosed centre, smaller than Croydon but comparable to Sutton, and some small outlying suburbs of its own such as the Sundridge Park area (whose woods are inhabited by stray birds of paradise – Bromley is that kind of place). Chislehurst, set amid green commons, is quieter and even classier, and was where French Emperor Napoleon III retired after he was overthrown in 1871. It is still a very affluent, comfortable place with an environment well worth preserving. Chislehurst, amazingly, has twice voted Labour in the past (1945, 1966) but it then extended eastwards to the Cray Valley and other less exalted areas. Paired with central Bromley and points south, it is an extremely safe Conservative seat with only occasional Lib Dem and Labour (in the overspill Mottingham estate) activity.

Bromley's Tories have tended to the left of the party – Harold Macmillan from 1945 to 1964, and more recently two liberal-minded but less famous figures Roger Sims (Chislehurst) and John Hunt (Ravensbourne, i.e. Bromley centre). In 1997 the merged seat took a big step to the right with combative Eric Forth, from Scotland via Worcestershire. Forth, when it was suggested that he was a Philistine, responded that his questioner 'probably believes that there are quite a few Philistines out there. Does he not think that they deserve representation in this place?' Bromley and Chislehurst will continue to be represented by a Conservative, Philistine or not.

ELTHAM

	2001		1997		1992 notional	
Electorate and turnout	57,554	58.7	57,358	75.7	60,650	76.5
Conservative	10,859	32.1	13,528	31.2	20,384	43.9
Labour	17,855	52.8	23,710	54.6	18,604	40.1
Lib Dem	4,121	12.2	3,701	8.5	7,213	15.6
Anti–EU	706	2.1	1,414	3.3	–	–
Others	251		1,075 (2)		198	
MP	Clive Efford (Lab)		Clive Efford (Lab)		Peter Bottomley (Con)	
Majority	6,996	20.7	10,182	23.4	1,780	3.8

Eltham is a collection of middle London suburbs on the hills south and west of Woolwich town centre: Eltham itself and Plumstead are the best known. Eltham's wards are a mixture of small council and ex-council estates and private developments. Its south eastern end, around Eltham Park and Palace, is the most Conservative area. Labour score strongly in the Plumstead area near Woolwich town, and the parts of Kidbrooke in the seat. However, the political colours of Eltham vary patch by patch on a small scale, and the constituency is fought out street by street in close elections. Under the name of Woolwich West it was the first by-election gain the Conservatives made under Thatcher, in 1975.

Eltham is peculiar for a halfway-out London seat in not having changed much demographically; it is still mainly skilled working class and lower middle class, and it is the least ethnically mixed seat in inner London. It has also not changed into a Labour stronghold like Hornsey or Streatham and remains marginal. In the past it was one of the largest constituency Labour Parties in the country, based on strong Co-op and union movements in the area.

Eltham has a bad reputation as one of the most racist areas of London. Stephen Lawrence was murdered on its streets in 1993 and there have been other attacks; Brian Cathcart in his study of the murder said of Eltham then that 'by London's standards it was a place with a distinctly ugly streak.' The seat was highly marginal in 1992 and the incumbent Tory MP Peter Bottomley left it for Worthing. Clive Efford, a taxi driver and Labour councillor for Well Hall ward, gained the seat by a wide margin in 1997. Labour led in all the mid term elections here, a sign that Eltham for the moment has put aside its marginal traditions. It is Labour's 151st most marginal seat, which means that Labour would now have to do slightly worse than in 1992 in order to lose it.

ERITH and THAMESMEAD

	2001		1997		1992 notional	
Electorate and turnout	66,371	50.2	63,417	65.6	66,600	74.2
Conservative	8,602	25.8	8,388	20.2	15,615	31.6
Labour	19,769	59.3	25,812	62.1	21,245	43.0
Lib Dem	3,800	11.4	5,001	12.0	12,555	25.4
Anti–EU	–	–	1,668(2)	4.0	–	–
Socialist	1,180	3.5	–	–	–	–
Others	–		718			
MP	John Austin (Lab)		John Austin-Walker (Lab)		TWO SEATS MERGE	
Majority	11,167	33.5	17,424	41.9	5.630	11.4

Erith and Thamesmead is composed partly of territory from the borough of Greenwich – technically in inner London – and partly from the suburban borough of Bexley. It is a roughly equal merger of the pre-1997 Woolwich and Erith & Crayford seats. However, the constituency makes sense as it unites the GLC-created 'New Town' of Thamesmead in one seat. Thamesmead has never really taken off; its setting is a rather bleak and flat bend in the river, some of the early architecture is alienating (Kubrick's *A Clockwork Orange* was filmed there), and it seems more a collection of estates than a town in its own right. Its population, projected for 100,000, has only reached 30,000. Newer developments, however, are more pleasant. The constituency also includes a couple of older areas of Woolwich, around the east side of Plumstead and Abbey Wood. The whole area was formerly the hinterland of the Woolwich Arsenal, a marshy testing ground for weapons.

East of Thamesmead is the Erith part of the constituency, very much a minority partner in the seat. Erith is an older settlement but quite industrial and working class, although it is accompanied by a couple of suburbs. Surprisingly, in 1983 and 1987 neither part of this seat was represented by a Labour MP. The Conservatives did very well to win Erith & Crayford three times – a white working class outer seat like Hayes & Harlington – and the SDP's John Cartwright won Woolwich twice under those colours until he lost to Labour in 1992. Since the collapse of the SDP the Thamesmead wards have produced mighty Labour majorities, with the exception of Abbey Wood where the SDP has enjoyed a curious life after death, winning the council elections in 1994 (Labour won in 1998). Erith is less monolithic, but still Labour voting, and the whole now adds up to a safe Labour seat (though the swing in 2001 was more typical of Essex than Kent). The only reason leading Conservatives have had to visit the area lately has been the new Belmarsh prison, where Archer and Aitken have both been guests.

GREENWICH and WOOLWICH

	2001		1997		1992 notional	
Electorate and turnout	60,114	54.1	61,352	65.9	66,051	71.1
Conservative	6,258	19.2	7,502	18.6	8,565	18.2
Labour	19,691	60.5	25,630	63.4	20,951	44.6
Lib Dem	5,082	15.6	5,049	12.5	16,478	35.1
Anti–EU	672	2.1	1,670	4.1	–	–
Others	833 (2)		552 (2)		990	
MP	Nick Raynsford (Lab)		Nick Raynsford (Lab)		Nick Raynsford (Lab)	
					Greenwich	
Majority	13,433	41.3	18,128	44.9	4,473	9.5

Greenwich is the place where London's naval heritage is most apparent; the market and old town near the Cutty Sark are a magnet for tourists. There are some charming streets in Greenwich, and some more across the park and heath at the middle class metropolitan village of Blackheath, but this constituency bears little resemblance to Richmond or Hampstead. The upmarket part of Greenwich is surrounded by some rather typical inner London council-built estates, most notably the large and intimidating Ferrier estate.

The Greenwich and Woolwich constituency is more Greenwich than Woolwich; although the town centre of the latter place is in this seat, its eastern parts are in Erith & Thamesmead and its southern area in Eltham. The central Woolwich area bears the shabby, depressed appearance of a northern town marooned on the south bank of the Thames. Between the two towns, on the Greenwich peninsula, is the empty Millennium Dome and a large site with somewhat vague development plans.

All the component wards of this seat are Labour in most years, often massively so, with the exception of Blackheath. Labour's majority in 1992 was abnormally low because the centre vote then included the vote for SDP incumbents Rosie Barnes and John Cartwright. 1987 is the only election since the war when Greenwich has failed to vote Labour, and that was in exceptional circumstances a few months after a by-election.

OLD BEXLEY and SIDCUP

	2001		1997		1992 notional	
Electorate and turnout	67,841	62.1	68,079	75.5	68,877	80.8
Conservative	19,130	45.4	21,608	42.0	31,340	56.3
Labour	15,785	37.5	18,039	35.1	11,768	21.1
Lib Dem	5,792	13.7	8,284	16.1	11,642	20.9
Anti–EU	1,426	3.4	2,946 (2)	5.7	–	–
Others	–		514 (2)		936	
MP	Derek Conway (Con)		Edward Heath (Con)		Edward Heath (Con)	
Majority	3,345	7.9	3,569	6.9	19,572	35.2

Old Bexley and Sidcup is the southernmost seat in Bexley, bordering on the Chislehurst area of Bromley. Most of it is interwar suburbia, with the occasional postwar privately developed area and the anomalous presence of the more working class North Cray area. Sidcup is the most affluent and Conservative element of the constituency, a reliable fortress even in local elections, although some of the rest of the seat has shown Lib Dem or even Labour tendencies in local elections.

This seat is indissolubly linked with Edward Heath, who first won the larger seat of Bexley from Labour in 1950 and took over this part as Prime Minister when the seat was rearranged in 1974. Heath seemed an appropriate voice for London-Kent Conservatism – modern, not wedded to tradition, rather egalitarian and lower middle class, managerial rather than professional, and the seat gradually became safer during his term. New Labour's appropriation of some of his style of politics, though, was accompanied by a big swing in 1997 which made the seat seem marginal.

Labour had outside hopes of a gain in this seat in 2001. It seemed possible that there were a fair few electors of this constituency who cast their votes for Ted Heath as the most effective way of irritating the contemporary leadership of the Conservative Party, but this theory was disproved when Heath retired in 2001 and was replaced by former whip Derek Conway as Conservative candidate. On the other hand, a relatively high anti-EU vote also persisted in 2001, showing that Heath's pro-European views had not put off all that many right wing Tories. Old Bexley and Sidcup will probably continue to be a bit beyond Labour's reach, although politics can be unpredictable. Conway, after all, was previously MP for Shrewsbury & Atcham, and developments in that constituency in recent years have been somewhat strange.

ORPINGTON

	2001		1997		1992 notional	
Electorate and turnout	78,853	64.6	78,831	76.3	82,032	81.1
Conservative	22,334	43.9	24,417	40.6	36,770	55.3
Labour	5,517	10.8	10,753	17.9	9,837	14.8
Lib Dem	22,065	43.3	21,465	35.7	18,840	28.3
Anti–EU	996	2.0	2,842 (2)	4.7	–	–
Others	–		685 (2)		1,085	
MP	John Horam (Con)		John Horam (Con)		John Horam (Con)	
Majority	269	0.5	2,952	4.9	17,930	27.0

Orpington is famed in Liberal Democrat history as the scene of a by-election triumph in 1962, which destabilised the Macmillan government and seemed to open the way to a realignment of British politics. However, Orpington was only followed into the Liberal column by one other suburb (Manchester's Cheadle) and it lapsed back to the Conservatives in 1970. More recently, it is associated with disappointment of Lib Dem hopes, most cruelly in 2001 when the Conservative MP John Horam (a prized target because he defected first from Labour to SDP and then to the Tories) clung on after recounts by 269 votes. The Lib Dems poured workers and resources into the seat, which nearly disappeared under yellow posters, but it was not quite enough.

Orpington is very much commuter country, and its tone is straightforwardly middle class rather than ultra-affluent for the most part. Starter homes sprouted across the area in the 1950s, filling in gaps between existing suburbs. To the north, however, are the Cray twins – St. Paul's Cray and St. Mary Cray – which are overspill estates. In 1997 it was extended (as it had been before 1983) into open country on the southern edge of the borough of Bromley at Biggin Hill; it has a substantial proportion of the very few farms in London. The pattern of voting in local elections rather depends on Lib Dem *Focus* activity – they do well in the more densely populated central Orpington wards plus downmarket St. Paul's Cray and even in the rich village of Biggin Hill, but the Conservatives fight back in the rest of the seat.

Each of the last three elections has been a fight between Tory John Horam and Lib Dem Chris Maines, with Maines edging ever closer. Perhaps appropriately for a seat where Darwin lived, elections here are survival of the fittest and Labour has faded away. Orpington will be a key battleground, and must surely fall if the Lib Dems are serious about being 'the effective Opposition'. It was originally proposed that Orpington should lose the rural and Biggin Hill area in the boundary review, but after a public inquiry it was reinstated and the new Cray Valley West ward is lost instead. This will make the Lib Dem task slightly – but perhaps importantly – harder when the review is implemented.

London – Outer South
(former Surrey)

	Conservative		Labour		Liberal Democrat		Others	
	Share of vote	Seats	Share of vote	Seats	Share of vote	Seats	Share of vote	Seats
2001	34.4	1	30.2	4	32.2	5	3.2	0
1997	36.6	1	32.1	4	27.4	5	3.9	0
1992	52.5	11	22.5	1	24.6	0	0.4	0
1987	54.3	12	18.6	0	26.9	0	0.2	0
1983	52.1	12	15.9	0	31.6	0	0.4	0

This chapter includes the boroughs of Croydon, Kingston, Merton, Richmond and Sutton. The area contains many of the most stereotyped parts of comfortable suburbia – Surbiton, Carshalton Beeches, East Cheam and the purlieus of Coulsdon and Purley. Its seats sound like a roll-call of suburban railway stops from a Seventies sitcom.

Much of the physical appearance of the area dates from the 1930s, when London's built up area exploded with suburban development and semi-detached and detached housing sprouted rapidly around the capital. The curving Kingston by-pass on the A3 was one of the first dual carriageway arterial roads in Britain. The march of suburbia across north Surrey was particularly quick and complete, submerging previous land uses such as the lavender fields of Mitcham and Carshalton (in recent years there has been a small revival in lavender growing on surplus land). Several parts of this built-up, metropolitan part of Surrey were important towns before they were absorbed into greater London. Croydon and Kingston in particular are major service, shopping and administrative centres not only for the suburban areas but also for communities still in the administrative county of Surrey. Sutton and Richmond serve similar functions on a smaller scale.

A lot of the housing stock is rather undifferentiated owner-occupied family housing, although there are patches of older terraces in Merton and the main towns, and occasional blocks of flats and council estates, the largest of which is the St. Helier estate spanning the border between Sutton and Merton. There are also a few highly select areas, around the metropolitan villages in Wimbledon and Richmond Hill. Richmond is a liberal, very middle class borough. One of its peculiarities is that it has a local newspaper read mostly by social groups A and B, rather than C2 and D as elsewhere, and it has two or three large letters pages so that its articulate residents can let off steam. Awareness of local issues, tactical voting and the personalities of MPs and council candidates is very high, as is – traditionally – turnout in all sorts of election. There are some less chic but still extremely affluent suburban areas like south Cheam, Coombe Hill and Coulsdon. There is a high concentration of professional and managerial workers in Richmond and on the southern fringe of the area, but in general the social profile is in the middle of the large British middle class.

The influence of the social change inner London has experienced has rippled outward. The most strongly affected are the Morden and lower Wimbledon districts, which are served by the London underground, and the ethnically mixed northern side of Croydon which has become a Labour stronghold in the last decade. Districts further out, such as Kingston, Sutton and Twickenham are desirable areas where London's young professionals settle down and start having families, thanks to the pleasant environment and the excellent state schools in the outer boroughs.

There has been something of a revolution in the politics of the suburbs in recent years. The ex-Surrey suburbs produced a preponderance of Conservative MPs for over a century. There was only one Liberal victory in any of the seats covering part of the area (Reigate, 1906) in any of the general elections between 1885 and 1918; except for a rebel Tory in Richmond in 1922 and a freak Labour win in the 1923 Mitcham by-election, Conservatives had a clean sweep until 1945. Mitcham, Croydon Central (then called South), Wimbledon and Spelthorne (which included part of Twickenham) fell to Labour in 1945, but this success was short lived and the Tories had 100 per cent representation again from 1950 until a narrow Labour win in Croydon South in 1966. Boundary changes created a better Labour prospect in Mitcham & Morden in 1974, but that seat too went Tory in a 1982 by-election. The collapse of the Conservatives in 1997 was therefore a radical reversal of the area's political history and their continued decline in 2001 reinforces the impression that the change has been lasting and profound.

The new suburban hostility to Conservatism has several contributing factors. Owner-occupation is very high, and many residents have to juggle several criteria – space, environment, proximity to central London, affordability – and spend a large proportion of their income on housing. High mortgage rates in the early 1990s, and low rates under Labour in 1997-2001, were influential. New Labour's image broke with Labour's traditional image as being the party of the unionised working class, a movement with which the clerical and service sector workers of the suburbs could not identify. Additionally, many of the suburb dwellers are not rich enough to opt out of state provision of health and education, and commuters depend on public transport, so the state of public services is important to these voters. They also have some of London's social liberalism about race, asylum and minorities (despite the *Daily Mail* reading habits of the traditional suburban woman) and some of its diversity; the voters of Kingston & Surbiton delivered a devastating defeat to right wing populism in the 2001 election. The western part of the sub-region has also seen one of the most concentrated patches of Liberal Democrat community politics activism over decades, which has detached even more Tory voters.

There are still some Tories in the suburbs. The last couple of general elections in this area must make the Conservatives wonder whether PR is not such a good idea after all. Despite having slightly more votes, they have been crushed in terms of seats by a pincer movement of Labour and the Liberal Democrats. In 1997, indeed, share of the vote was inversely related to number of seats! More than any other region, this area of London shows the damage that anti-Conservative tactical voting has inflicted on the party, and the pattern only intensified in 2001. There was a local website, www.stophague.com, which promoted tactical voting for the Lib Dems in Kingston & Surbiton and Labour in Wimbledon. All this said, if the Conservatives are able to mount a national recovery all the seats look potential targets with the exception of Croydon North, Mitcham & Morden and probably Kingston & Surbiton.

Local government

The Conservatives used to run all the local authorities in the area, even in good Labour years like 1971, but lost Richmond in 1982, Sutton and Kingston in 1986, Merton in 1989 and Croydon in 1994. Labour have become the dominant force in the boroughs of Croydon and Merton, while the Liberal Democrats are in control of Kingston and Sutton and formerly Richmond. In 2002, Labour held the Tory target of Croydon, despite (as in 1994 and 1998) polling fewer votes than the Conservatives. Nearly two decades of power saw the gloss come off the Liberal Democrat administration in Richmond-upon-Thames, with increasing criticism of the council over the standard of services and planning decisions such as the proposed Twickenham riverside development. The ruling party lost seats in each round of council elections since its 1986 landslide, and were swept aside by the Conservatives in 2002. In Kingston-upon-Thames, on the other hand, the Lib Dems gained overall control. They had a majority in the 1994 elections but lost it in 1998. A minority Conservative administration had been in control, although the group suffered from a wave of defections in 2001 after their general election meltdown in the borough.

The Liberal Democrat strength in the area was apparent in the 2000 Greater London elections. They nearly won the South West seat (including Kingston, Richmond and also Hounslow) – Conservative member Tony Arbour led only 35-30 and also suffered only a 1 per cent swing against them since 1997 in Croydon & Sutton. Andrew Pelling won the seat for the Conservatives with 41 per cent, to 26 Lib Dem and 25 Labour.

Boundary review

The boundary review here was uncontentious and only minor adjustments are proposed to the current constituencies. The area lost two seats in the 1997 changes.

CARSHALTON and WALLINGTON

	2001		1997		1992 actual	
Electorate and turnout	67,337	60.3	66,064	73.3	65,209	80.9
Conservative	13,742	33.8	16,223	33.5	26,243	49.7
Labour	7,466	18.4	11,565	23.9	9,333	17.7
Lib Dem	18,289	45.0	18,490	38.2	16,300	30.9
Anti–EU	501	1.2	1,507 (2)	3.1	–	–
Others	614		638 (2)		880 (2)	
MP	Tom Brake (LD)		Tom Brake (LD)		Nigel Forman (Con)	
Majority	4,547	11.2	2,267	4.7	9,943	18.8

While Sutton and Cheam is uniformly middle class, this other half of the London Borough of Sutton is more varied. In the north it contains the borough's part of the large St. Helier estate, which elects Labour councillors, and industrial areas around Beddington and the Wandle valley. Carshalton and Wallington themselves are middle class suburbs between Sutton and Croydon. To the south are the wealthy Carshalton Beeches and Woodcote areas. There is a pocket of poverty and social exclusion in the Roundshaw estate on the site of the old Croydon airfield, which is benefiting from a vast regeneration project.

Demographically, it could be a Tory-Labour marginal, and Labour won the seat in the 1973 GLC elections, but local politics has produced Liberal Democrat ascendancy in all parts of the constituency – even inroads into St. Helier. This was translated from local to national politics in 1997 with the victory of Lib Dem Tom Brake, which was consolidated by another strong showing in the local elections in 1998 and even the 2000 GLA election, and then by a convincing Lib Dem victory in 2001. Brake, like his colleague Paul Burstow in the Sutton seat, is a very attentive constituency MP and local activist. Even if there is a Conservative recovery in the next election, the Lib Dems have dug in well in this constituency and should be able to hang on.

CROYDON CENTRAL

	2001		1997		1992 notional	
Electorate and turnout	77,568	59.1	80,152	69.6	81,757	74.8
Conservative	17,659	38.5	21,535	38.6	33,940	55.5
Labour	21,643	47.2	25,432	45.6	19,279	31.5
Lib Dem	5,156	11.2	6,061	10.9	7,934	13.0
Anti–EU	545	1.2	2,176 (2)	3.9	–	–
Others	857 (2)		595		–	
MP	Geraint Davies (Lab)		Geraint Davies (Lab)		Paul Beresford (Con)	
Majority	3,984	8.7	3,897	7.0	14,661	24.0

This constituency occupies a middle band of the London Borough of Croydon, from the town centre eastwards (Croydon East might be a better name). The centre of Croydon has a striking skyline of office towers and flyovers, and boasts a large shopping centre that serves a wide area of south London, Surrey and even Sussex – but there are few voters here. Croydon's new tramlines weave through the constituency, uniting its disparate parts. Furthest is New Addington, a massive council estate housing 14,000 electors on a hill overlooking London, surrounded by fields and even farms. It was the council base of the Labour MP Geraint Davies. On the way to New Addington the tram meanders through the Conservative Fairfield and Heathfield wards, with northern branches to the more mixed areas of Addiscombe and Woodside. It is a large seat, and despite its name 46 per cent of the voters come from the abolished Croydon NE seat, not the old Central. The new territory is more marginal than the polarised wards of the old seat.

The Conservatives led in the mid term elections in 1997-2001, although always by a relatively modest margin, and Croydon Central looked the sort of seat they might find it difficult to win if Labour were still in a strong position at the general election. As it happened, Labour probably picked up enough extra support from the strongly middle class wards and the ex-North East portion in the Addiscombe area to compensate for the fall in turnout in New Addington and Geraint Davies won another term. This seat is one of only two in the area with any kind of Labour tradition (the party won a similar seat in 1945 and 1966) but it is still a crucial marginal.

CROYDON NORTH

	2001		1997		1992 notional	
Electorate and turnout	78,675	53.2	77,063	68.2	80,076	72.3
Conservative	9,752	23.3	14,274	27.2	25,865	44.7
Labour	26,610	63.5	32,672	62.2	25,705	44.4
Lib Dem	4,375	10.4	4,066	7.7	6,340	11.0
Anti–EU	606	1.4	1,551 (2)	3.0	–	–
Others	539		–		–	
MP	Malcolm Wicks (Lab)		Malcolm Wicks (Lab)		Malcolm Wicks (Lab) Croydon North West	
Majority	16,858	40.3	18,398	35.0	160*	0.3*

* Estimated Conservative majority allowing for boundary changes.

The north side of Croydon shades into the southern fringe of Lambeth, and has been subject to the same social trends. There is not much separating Thornton Heath from Streatham, both desirable areas for black families able to afford owner-occupation and eager to move out of the inner city. Norwood spans the boundary between Croydon and Lambeth.

North Croydon has been swinging strongly to Labour for some time. The party failed to win it in 1945 or 1966, but edged closer during the 1970s. The trend was interrupted by a Liberal Alliance by-election win in 1981, but the Tories had only nine more years after they regained Croydon North West in 1983. Malcolm Wicks gained the seat on a high swing in 1992.

The pattern carried over into local elections. Formerly safe Conservative suburbs started falling to Labour in local elections in 1990 and 1994, such as Beulah, Norbury and the Norwood wards, and Labour consolidated the advantage in the 1998 local elections. The Croydon North seat dips further south, into the inner urban core of Croydon itself at Broad Green, a source of Labour support, but all parts of the constituency have given Labour a lead of some sort in recent general elections. Although nominally a Conservative seat in 1992 (on the estimated effect of the boundary review) it turned in huge Labour victories in 1997 and 2001.

Croydon North continued to move towards Labour in 2001, with the result that there are fewer than 100 safer Labour seats starting from the 2001 result. Social change has produced a heartland Labour seat in the ex-Surrey suburbs.

CROYDON SOUTH

	2001		1997		1992 notional	
Electorate and turnout	73,372	61.4	73,787	73.5	74,777	78.0
Conservative	22,169	49.2	25,649	47.3	35,937	61.7
Labour	13,472	29.9	13,719	25.3	9,513	16.3
Lib Dem	8,226	18.3	11,441	21.1	12,599	21.6
Anti–EU	998	2.2	2,940 (2)	5.5	–	–
Others	195		450 (2)		242	
MP	Richard Ottaway (Con)		Richard Ottaway (Con)		Richard Ottaway (Con)	
Majority	8,697	19.3	11,930	22.0	23,338	40.1

Croydon South is a uniform tract of suburbia – Purley and Coulsdon are the largest areas in the seat, although it also includes Sanderstead and Selsdon (of 'Selsdon Man' fame in 1970). The latter two wards are the most tree-lined and affluent areas, with Selsdon being in the top 100 wards in England (out of 8,414) for lack of social deprivation. Purley is associated with suburban comfort, particularly since the long-running 1970s sitcom *Terry and June*.

Since 1997 Croydon South has stretched a little further northward, into the Waddon area to the west of Croydon town centre. It has traditionally been extremely Conservative, and is still the sole Tory seat in this sub-region although the days when over 30,000 Tory voters would flood out from the avenues of semi-detached houses on polling day seem to be over. There is a respectable sprinkling of Labour – perhaps particularly New Labour – support in the best areas of the seat, and the traditionally marginal ward of Waddon. The Liberal Democrats have some local strength in Coulsdon, but neither they nor Labour can threaten the Tory hold on Croydon South.

KINGSTON and SURBITON

	2001		1997		1992 notional	
Electorate and turnout	72,687	67.5	73,836	75.4	70,238	79.6
Conservative	13,866	28.2	20,355	36.6	29,674	53.1
Labour	4,302	8.8	12,811	23.0	10,991	19.7
Lib Dem	29,542	60.2	20,411	36.7	14,510	25.9
Anti–EU	438	0.9	1,888 (2)	3.4	–	–
Others	945 (3)		200 (2)		762	
MP	Edward Davey (LD)		Edward Davey (LD)		Richard Tracey (Con)	
					Surbiton	
Majority	15,676	31.9	56	0.1	15,164	27.1

The smashing Liberal Democrat victory in Kingston & Surbiton was one of the most startling results of election night 2001. A majority of 56 was transformed into one of well over 15,000 and MP Ed Davey achieved the highest Liberal Democrat share of the vote anywhere in the country. What explained the result?

In an election like 2001, when there was little sense that it was 'about' anything, it was possible for some constituencies to become like by-elections and offer a verdict on particular local issues or personalities. While in Wyre Forest it was about a local issue, in this seat it was about personalities. Davey was undoubtedly an extremely good candidate. Since his surprise win in 1997 he had hardly been out of the local papers, conducted eight times as many surgeries as his Tory predecessors and put in appearances at innumerable local events. He is intelligent, energetic and likeable and some have even started to talk of him as a future leader of the party.

This was in contrast to David Shaw, the Conservative candidate, who had been MP for Dover from 1987 to 1997. Although articulate, he was gratingly partisan and right-wing and his anti-asylum rhetoric struck the wrong note for a rather cosmopolitan and liberal area. The Liberal Democrats hammered Shaw on his past record, quoting newspaper articles calling him a 'thug' and 'the vilest MP in Britain'. Even his own colleagues had harsh words for him – one told the *Evening Standard* diary that Shaw was 'a w***er' – and the word in question was not 'winner'. The Labour vote switched almost en bloc to Davey to keep Shaw out, and the party leadership was not displeased that Shaw was humiliated.

Kingston and Surbiton sounds like a very suburban district, and so it is for the most part. Kingston is one of the largest shopping centres in southern England and has a flourishing university, but outside the central area it gets suburban pretty quickly. Surbiton sprang up as a result of the main line railway (Victorian Kingston refused to have the main line put through their town), and other settlements like Tolworth hug the Kingston Bypass. There are pockets of Labour support in Tolworth and Norbiton in particular but for the most part in local elections the battle is between Lib Dems and Tories. Ed Davey is surely safe for a third term in parliament.

MITCHAM and MORDEN

	2001		1997		1992 actual	
Electorate and turnout	65,671	57.8	65,402	73.3	63,752	80.3
Conservative	9,151	24.1	14,243	29.7	23,789	46.5
Labour	22,936	60.4	27,984	58.4	22,055	43.1
Lib Dem	3,820	10.1	3,632	7.6	4,687	9.2
Anti–EU	486	1.3	927 (2)	1.9	–	–
Others	1,568 (2)		1,160 (4)		655	
MP	Siobhan McDonagh (Lab)		Siobhan McDonagh (Lab)		Angela Rumbold (Con)	
Majority	13,785	36.3	13,741	28.7	1,734	3.4

Morden is at the far southern end of the London Underground and is a 1930s-style suburban sprawl, identifying quite closely with London. North of Morden is Colliers Wood, which borders onto the southern end of Tooting and shares many of its characteristics. Mitcham is somewhat different, a Surrey town once sitting among lavender fields now overrun by down at heel development and actually rather difficult to get to and from by public transport. Mitcham town centre is fringed on two sides by large council estates, the older avenues of St. Helier and the troubled 1960s/1970s Phipps Bridge estate. Affluent Lower Morden is the only reliably Conservative element of the seat; otherwise the constituency sends a preponderance of Labour councillors to Merton town hall from terraces and estates alike.

Mitcham & Morden, like many parts of London that are neither outer suburbs nor inner city, has swung with great force to Labour over the 1990s – there has been a swing here of nearly 25 per cent to Labour since 1987, including a substantial 3.8 per cent swing since 1997. From a 1982 by-election until 1997 it was the seat of Angela Rumbold, for a time vice-chairman of the Conservative Party. The local Conservatives seemed surprised by their defeat in 1997, although hardly anyone else was as the seat was an easy target for Labour and the local Labour Party are very well-organised. Labour MP Siobhan McDonagh (sister of the party's former general secretary Margaret) is now sitting on a comfortable majority.

RICHMOND PARK

	2001		1997		1992 notional	
Electorate and turnout	72,251	68.0	71,951	79.0	69,091	85.5
Conservative	18,480	37.6	22,442	39.5	30,609	51.8
Labour	5,541	11.3	7,172	12.6	5,211	8.8
Lib Dem	23,444	47.7	25,393	44.7	22,225	37.6
Anti–EU	348	0.7	1,467	2.6	–	–
Others	1,338 (2)		379 (3)		1,008	
MP	Jenny Tonge (LD)		Jenny Tonge (LD)		Jeremy Hanley (Con)	
					Richmond & Barnes	
Majority	4,964	10.1	2,951	5.2	8,384	14.2

Richmond Park is an outer London seat comprising, as its name might suggest, a series of districts bordering on the largest of the London Royal Parks. The main centre of the seat is Richmond, a pleasant and prosperous town – it is ungenerous to call it a suburb - by the Thames. North lies Kew and the highly favoured residential suburbs of Palewell and Barnes, which are surprisingly close to central London. The new accessions to the seat in 1997 consisted of the northern half of the abolished Kingston seat, comprising the wealthy Tudor Drive, Kingston Hill and New Malden areas part of central Kingston. The seat has two Millionaire's Rows, at Richmond Hill and Coombe, and other than the small Ham estate little of it is shabby. It is the fifth most 'professional/ managerial' seat in the country.

That Richmond Park was lost by the Conservatives in 1997 may seem bizarre, but many observers were surprised that Jeremy Hanley, the jovial Tory MP for Richmond and Barnes 1983-97, held on for so long. The Lib Dems have been practising pavement politics in Richmond for a quarter of a century now and ran the borough council from 1984 to 2002. The wards transplanted from Kingston were supposed to have made the seat safer for the Tories, but in 1997 they were swamped.

The 2001 campaign here was interesting. Conservative candidate Tom Harris ran an energetic effort, playing the Lib Dems at their own game of local issues such as park traffic, aircraft noise and the failings of the borough council. Harris also managed to persuade his supporters to put up posters and boards, giving the impression to locals and visitors that the Tories were fighting back. He did well enough to cause some Lib Dem jitters and a strong response from dozens of their activists, and the failure of the national Conservative campaign worked against him. Hague's rhetoric against the supposed liberal elite was not going to win any support in places like Richmond, where the liberal elite actually live and vote (Jeremy Paxman, Andrew Marr, Trevor MacDonald and the Dimblebys are locals, as are many top civil servants).

SUTTON and CHEAM

	2001		1997		1992 actual	
Electorate and turnout	63,648	62.4	62,824	75.0	60,995	82.3
Conservative	15,078	38.0	17,822	37.8	27,710	55.2
Labour	5,263	13.2	7,280	15.5	4,980	9.9
Lib Dem	19,382	48.8	19,919	42.3	16,954	33.8
Anti–EU	–	–	1,975 (2)	4.2	–	–
Others	–		96		577 (2)	
MP	Paul Burstow (LD)		Paul Burstow (LD)		Olga Maitland (Con)	
Majority	4,304	10.8	2,097	4.5	10,756	21.4

The Liberals (and Liberal Democrats) have been working hard in the Sutton area for decades, ever since the victory of Graham (now Lord) Tope in a 1972 by-election. Despite losing the seat in February 1974, their activism continued and they took control of the borough council in 1986. Much of the Sutton & Cheam constituency is composed of 1930s vintage outer London suburbs, with some nuances of demographic difference between its wards. Cheam, with its scattered Tudor buildings, is posher than Sutton's 1960s town centre despite its association with Tony Hancock's ménage. Both areas have large numbers of commuters. Sutton in particular is something of a south London version of Romford, a destination for the affluent lower middle class. But it has little in common with Romford politically. Nearly all the wards are Liberal Democrat in local elections, except the southern, most affluent, part of Cheam. The central Sutton town wards return massive Lib Dem leads. There are no reservoirs of Labour support; it had three of the five weakest Labour wards in London in 1998.

The two most recent MPs for Sutton have had contrasting political styles. Paul Burstow for the Lib Dems is a grassroots politician with long council experience and a near obsessive concern for local issues. Olga Maitland, Conservative MP 1992-97 and candidate in 2001, is an ex-gossip columnist and a flamboyant campaigner for assorted right wing causes. Burstow's 2001 victory has probably seen Maitland off, but the Conservatives will throw a lot of effort into this seat in the next general election.

TWICKENHAM

	2001		1997		1992 notional	
Electorate and turnout	75,225	66.4	73,569	79.0	71,805	83.3
Conservative	16,689	33.4	21,956	37.8	29,652	49.6
Labour	6,903	13.8	9,065	15.6	6,194	10.4
Lib Dem	24,344	48.7	26,237	45.1	23,531	39.3
Anti–EU	579	1.2	589	1.0	–	–
Others	1,423		297 (2)		434	
MP	Vincent Cable (LD)		Vincent Cable (LD)		Toby Jessel (Con)	
Majority	7,655	15.3	4,281	7.4	6,121	10.2

While Richmond has some glamour and intellectualism, Twickenham is known mostly for rugby. The stadium is surrounded by suburbs which have sprawled in the gaps between the older towns and villages of Teddington, Hampton and Hampton Wick – they are quite obscure places, such as Fulwell, Whitton and Strawberry Hill. The most pleasant parts of Twickenham lie by the Thames as it loops its way around the eastern and southern edges of the constituency. All wards, except the middling Heathfield ward, rank very low on the index of deprivation.

Twickenham was a Conservative stronghold from its creation in 1918, although Labour ran them fairly close in a 1929 by-election and 1945. During the 1970s and 1980s the Liberals and the Alliance campaigned strongly on local issues, building a powerful pavement politics machine which won every Twickenham ward in 1986. They also edged closer to winning the parliamentary seat, which fell in the 1997 rout of the Conservatives and produced an even larger win in 2001. Vincent Cable's result in 2001 was undoubtedly impressive, with a significant drop in the Tory vote rather than a squeeze on Labour being the main contribution to his increased majority. Success at parliamentary level has coincided with the turning of the tide in local elections, as the Conservatives gained ground in 1998 and swept to victory in 2002.

Labour's vote here is depressed for political and tactical reasons. In demographic terms Twickenham is not so very different from seats Labour can win such as Wimbledon or Enfield Southgate but there is a long history of Liberal activism dating back to the early 1970s. In elections under PR, such as the Euro election of 1999, Labour's vote bounces back somewhat. It now seems a strong seat for the Lib Dems for national, rather than local, political reasons. Like Richmond Park, its residents show their interest in the political process by producing high turnouts at all elections.

WIMBLEDON

	2001		1997		1992 actual	
Electorate and turnout	63,930	64.3	64,113	75.4	61,966	80.2
Conservative	15,062	36.6	17,684	36.6	26,331	53.0
Labour	18,806	45.7	20,674	42.8	11,570	23.3
Lib Dem	5,341	13.0	8,014	16.6	10,569	21.3
Anti–EU	414	1.0	993	2.1	–	–
Others	1,486 (2)		979 (4)		1,211 (3)	
MP	Roger Casale (Lab)		Roger Casale (Lab)		Charles Goodson-Wickes (Con)	
Majority	3,744	9.1	2,990	6.2	14,761	29.7

There are few better examples of Labour's astonishing strength in suburban London in the last two general elections than Wimbledon. Although Labour narrowly won a seat called Wimbledon in 1945 it then included parts of what is now Mitcham and Morden, so in a real sense Labour's gain on a swing of over 17 per cent in 1997 was unprecedented. Modern Wimbledon includes some affluent metropolitan areas like Wimbledon village, home of the tennis tournament, and the commuter suburb of Raynes Park. There are a few dowdier areas east of the main railway line down towards the South Wimbledon tube station.

The London borough of Merton, half of which is Wimbledon, has been one of Labour's growth areas in the 1990s, but even so nobody expected Roger Casale to win in 1997. Having got used to the idea of Labour Wimbledon, it was less of a shock when he held on with an increased majority in 2001. Wimbledon will remain a Conservative target, but the educated, professional voters of the constituency reacted badly to the national Tory campaign and were attracted instead by Labour's much vaunted economic stability and Roger Casale's record as a hard-working constituency MP. There is a slight sense that the Tories are running up a down escalator in trying to regain Wimbledon, as the demographic and political trends of inner London move outwards and the place becomes more ethnically mixed, populated by young people and socially liberal; they might manage it, but Wimbledon is unlikely ever to revert to being a safe Tory seat.

London – West

	Conservative		Labour		Liberal Democrat		Others	
	Share of vote	Seats	Share of vote	Seats	Share of vote	Seats	Share of vote	Seats
2001	31.8	4	50.5	13	12.6	0	5.1	0
1997	34.4	4	51.8	13	10.1	0	3.7	0
1992	49.0	14	37.2	5	11.5	0	2.3	0
1987	50.2	15	31.6	4	17.4	0	0.8	0
1983	46.3	15	30.6	4	21.9	0	1.2	0

This chapter covers the central part of London, the main tourist districts of Westminster and the central residential areas of Marylebone, Kensington and Chelsea. It spills out west (via Hammersmith, Ealing and Hounslow) and north west (via Brent, Harrow and Hillingdon) to the edge of Greater London, forming a triangular wedge of the city. As the table suggests, it has areas of strength for both main parties but has proved stony ground for the Alliance and Liberal Democrats. Labour achieved very good results in 1997 and 2001, but in some ways the most extraordinary result in recent history was in 1987, when Labour's local government troubles and the boom in the economy caused a surge in the Conservative vote.

Westminster is, as its slogan proclaims, the heart of London. It contains the political centre of Britain, in the area around the Palace of Westminster and Buckingham Palace, and many of the commercial and tourist areas of central London. 565,000 people work in Westminster, making it the country's largest concentration of employment and a centre for people commuting from all over London and beyond. Westminster has some non-commercial areas and the resident population is 245,000. The City, the longer-established bit of central London, is of course known for finance as well as its long history; although only 5,000 people live there about 250,000 come in to work. The central London ambience spills over into residential Kensington and Chelsea as well. These central areas are some of the most loyally Conservative parts of the entire country, rare remnants of thoroughly urban areas still dominated by the Tories. Fifty years ago the wealthy west ends of most cities were Conservative enclaves, but now only these exclusive areas remain. There have been no non-Conservative victories in general elections in the central zone since 1906 (but the inner city northern parts of Kensington and Westminster can produce Labour seats).

Further west from Kensington, there are fast-gentrifying terraces in Fulham and Hammersmith, and to some extent also in Chiswick and Ealing. As well as accessibility, these areas offer relatively pleasant surroundings with parks and the river, although it helps if you like aeroplanes as well. The large BBC complexes at Shepherd's Bush and the flotilla of independent TV production companies bobbing in its wake give this area something of a media vibe; the Ealing studios where the comedies were produced in the 1950s are now leased to independents. Much of this territory is traditionally marginal, particularly around Hammersmith and Chiswick, and party fortunes have tended to ebb and flow with the national tides (although in Fulham the Conservatives have gained steadily from social change).

West London is not all Sloanes and media luvvies. It has a large patch of urban blight which bears comparison with those in other parts of London, although this area lacks a single name to describe it or a single borough to administer it. It starts with Kilburn (itself an area split between Brent, Camden and Westminster), stretches into north Kensington and the troubled Harlesden area and takes in some derelict industrial and railway lands in the far north of Hammersmith, Brent and Ealing. There are ambitious redevelopment projects for some of these areas, the most advanced being the new W12 centre – with new tube and overland stations – on derelict land in the north of Shepherd's Bush. Proximity to London's affluent areas, and good transport links, have eroded the edges of the area (gentrification has gradually crept northward into north Kensington and Queen's Park, and westwards into Shepherd's Bush and Acton), but there is still much to be done. This slice of London is overwhelmingly Labour, particularly in Brent South, when it can be bothered to turn out.

The western inner city is ethnically mixed. Southern Brent is heavily black, particularly in the Harlesden and Stonebridge area. Some of the black residents here are the original community who founded the Notting Hill Carnival and have been displaced to the north. Brent's politics has at times been vicious and confrontational because of ethnic conflicts, but at present it is fairly harmonious. Ealing was one-third non-white in 1991 and although much of this was at suburban Southall, there are many black and Asian residents in Acton. There are still substantial numbers of Irish people in the inner west, particularly at Kilburn but also in Shepherd's Bush and Acton.

Further out, west London is mostly inter-war suburbia. The county of Middlesex (basically the outer boroughs in this chapter plus Hendon, Enfield, Twickenham and Staines) was almost entirely built over by 1939, although a few scraps of countryside survive such as Horsenden Hill in Ealing. The north western suburbs of Wembley (Brent North), Harrow and the Northwood area of Pinner are the inner part of John Betjeman's 'Metroland', suburbia which sprawled across Middlesex during the 1920s and 1930s, mushrooming outward from the stations of the London underground that were planted speculatively in open fields. The housing is mainly family-sized semi-detached dwellings, organised into quiet avenues and closes with local services focused on the areas near some of the underground stations. There is not a great deal to attract the casual visitor to much of the area, except for the Wembley complex – once and future (supposedly) site of the national stadium, with outlying buildings such as the Arena serving as concert and conference venues. Like the Heathrow area it has a substantial Asian population, drawn from those who came from East Africa in the late 1960s and early 1970s and from people who have done well and traded up from the more run-down streets of Southall. Wembley and Harrow are London's premier Asian residential areas; the ethnic minority population of Brent and Harrow taken together was 43 per cent in 1999. Central Ealing, Uxbridge, Ruislip and Northwood have larger white populations. The Asian suburbs were as Conservative as white ones for many years, but swung extraordinarily to Labour in 1997 and have continued in that direction since. Harrow West, for instance, was a seat Labour never dreamed of winning before 1997, but which now has a 6,000 majority for young MP Gareth Thomas. The whiter suburbs have stayed more loyal to the Conservatives, including Uxbridge – a rare seat which Labour failed to win in 1997 but which has been Labour in a previous recent election (1966).

There is considerable industrial and commercial activity in the outer part of west London. Although London's manufacturing industry has been in severe decline for decades, there is still some productive industrial land in west London, including the Park Royal estate (mostly in Ealing), a 1930s development whose dominating figure is a huge Guinness plant overlooking the North Circular Road and the A40. Ealing North, Southall, Hayes and Feltham are industrial areas. Harrow, too, has industry; the largest private sector employer in the borough is Kodak. Except for Southall, much of this area despite its composition cast off its Labour traditions and voted Conservative in the 1980s and took until 1997 for this effect to completely wear off. Labour did even better in much of this territory in 2001 than it did in 1997.

Heathrow airport is a dominant presence in the outer west of London – planes are ever-present in the skies and its economic impact is enormous. It is the world's busiest international airport with over 62 million passengers annually – and has created jobs in the airport itself (68,000 work there), plus distribution and airline-related industries such as single-serving catering (another 108,000 in total). Strongly represented in all these working class and routine non-manual jobs are the local Asian community centred around Southall but with a strong influence across Hounslow, Hayes and out to Slough in Berkshire. The uncertainty in the airline industry after September 2001 has already been felt in some job losses, although the construction of the mammoth Terminal 5 will – or so its backers claim – create more jobs. Heathrow is best regarded as a medium-sized city, where around 200,000 people a day pass through and a similar number depend fairly directly upon it for their livelihood. The Heathrow seats produced some unlikely victories for the Conservatives in Hayes and Feltham in the 1980s, but have now swung massively to Labour.

Local government

The City of London council is an anomaly. Elections take place, though without parties and often without contest, for representatives from the 25 wards to the Court of Common Council. Uniquely, businesses have the vote and dominate local government. Changes to the system are currently underway, but New Labour are extending the business franchise rather than abolishing it – now corporations as well as partnerships and sole traders will have votes.

The central residential district produces two safely Conservative councils, a rarity in London or in fact anywhere during the 1990s. Westminster is the more controversial, thanks to the legacy of Shirley Porter, its leader during the 1980s. The Conservatives had a close shave in the 1986 borough elections, when their majority fell to 4, and pulled out all the stops to win the next elections. Part of this strategy was what is generally known as 'homes for votes', which was ruled as a politically corrupt scheme in 2001 by the Law Lords. They were also helped by a generous grant settlement from the government which enabled a low poll tax in 1990 and low council taxes ever since. Porter's successors have been less abrasive, but it is still a right wing authority. The Conservatives gained ground in 1998 and were advantaged by the new ward boundaries in 2002. Neighbouring Kensington & Chelsea is the most politically static authority in the country, with 39 Conservatives and 15 Labour at every council election between 1982 and 1998 inclusive (new ward boundaries reduced Labour to 12 in 2002). K & C practices a more patrician style of Conservatism than Westminster.

Working outward, Hammersmith & Fulham has been a marginal and hard-fought authority for years, although Labour have tended to prevail (the Tories have only run it in 1968-71 and also 1982-86 in coalition with the Liberals). The Conservatives have gained steadily from demographic change in Fulham and regarded the council as a top target for the 2002 local elections but were held off by Labour. Hounslow has been unusually loyal to Labour for a suburban authority, lapsing only in 1968-71, practising steady and unexciting local government throughout the wild times of the 1980s. Ealing, traditionally marginal, was a particularly controversial 'loony left' Labour authority in 1986-90, contributing to bad general election results locally in 1987 and being defeated against the trend in 1990. Neil Kinnock, a local resident, was not amused. Labour regained Ealing in 1994 and held it well in 1998 and 2002. Hillingdon, on the far edge of London, is a peculiar authority. Before it was fashionable it had a left wing council until it was defeated in a local landslide in 1978; wild swings have taken place at local elections here since 1986, not always in an anticipated direction (i.e. to the Tories in 1990 and 1998 but not 2002) and the administration has changed hands frequently. The volatile wards are concentrated in Uxbridge and Ruislip (Labour have a strong grip in Hayes and Harlington); it is currently under no overall control.

Now looking north west, Brent was notorious in the 1980s and early 1990s for political eccentricity. A hard-left Labour regime took over in 1986 and made itself immensely unpopular with some peculiar policies on race. Labour lost control of the borough in 1990, and the Conservatives constructed a shaky regime with the assistance of two African nationalist defectors from Labour until 1994 and then a mayoral casting vote (which disappeared when the Tories were ambushed during the mayor-making vote in 1996). The follies came to an end in 1998 and the borough returned to political normality with a large swing to Labour. Four years of relatively quiet and competent local government, plus the general election results, were followed by Labour retaining control in 2002. Harrow council was a surprise gain for Labour in 1998, following up on the party's general election triumphs in 1997. This was the first time Labour had ever won a majority in the borough, and was all the more stunning as the Conservatives had a good majority in 1990 and the Liberal Democrats fell not far short of control in 1994. Labour's one-seat majority disappeared in 2002; the council is now hung. The 2002 elections were notable for most Lib Dem candidates being disqualified from standing after a blunder over their nomination papers. Harrow voted against an elected Mayor in 2001.

On the Greater London authority, the Ealing and Hillingdon seat was a surprise defeat for Labour in 2000 when Richard Barnes was elected for the Tories with 37 per cent to 32 per cent for Labour's Gurcharan Singh (Labour actually led in the party list vote 33-31). It must be a top target for Labour in 2004. The Brent and Harrow seat was held, as anticipated, by Labour's Toby Harris, although his lead over the Tories was only 38-33 per cent. Hounslow is grouped with Kingston and Richmond in South West, represented by Tony Arbour for the Conservatives. Westminster, Kensington and Hammersmith & Fulham are in Angie Bray's Conservative seat of West Central (44-27 per cent in 2000); Labour had a lead in the area in 1997 and by a whisker 2001 but it is a hard nut to crack in a low turnout local election. For the City, see London – East as it is grouped with East End boroughs.

Boundary review

The north west London boundary review was one of the most contentious in the country; the public inquiry in autumn 2001 heard weeks of evidence in several different hearings across the area because of the complex interactions between boroughs. Brent, for instance, was provisionally paired with

Westminster, while Labour wanted it paired with Camden, the Conservatives with Harrow, and Brent politicians favoured keeping three separate seats. Each option had knock-on effects elsewhere. The only point which was not at issue was that Ealing was now big enough for three seats of its own, requiring the dissolution of the Ealing, Acton and Shepherd's Bush seat. Boundary reviews are important here because so many neighbouring areas have different political complexions – depending on how it is drawn, the northern half of Westminster can be the basis of a safe Labour seat or a Tory-inclined marginal. There was a lot at stake.

Revised recommendations were published in May 2002. Brent and Camden were linked in the form of a new Hampstead & Kilburn seat, while Westminster and the City were restored to the pre 1997 position of two seats of their own. Two safe inner-city Tory constituencies appear, anmely Chealsea and Fulham and Kensington, while Labour can breathe easily in the new Hammersmith seat.

Further out, there is less good news for the Conservatives. Their Ruislip Northwood stronghold takes the best Tory areas from both Harrow West and Uxbridge; Labour look secure in both amended Harow seats and are still in with a chance at Uxbridge. In Ealing, the revised Acton should be Labour.

BRENT EAST

	2001		1997		1992 notional	
Electorate and turnout	55,891	51.9	53,548	65.9	56,812	64.3
Conservative	5,278	18.2	7,866	22.3	13,365	36.6
Labour	18,325	63.2	23,748	67.3	19,314	52.8
Lib Dem	3,065	10.6	2,751	7.8	3,237	8.9
Anti–EU	188	0.6	–	–	–	–
Green	1,361	4.7	–	–	546	1.5
Others	775 (2)		907 (4)		96	
MP	Paul Daisley (Lab)		Ken Livingstone (Lab) (Ind)		Ken Livingstone (Lab)	
Majority	13,047	45.0	15,882	45.0	5,949	16.3

Brent East is a slice of urban London, stretching north in radial fashion along the long, straight Edgware Road and a portion of the Jubilee Line from Kilburn to *Private Eye*'s favourite suburb of Neasden. The south east corner is quite close to central London, and while Queens Park is increasingly gentrified, most of Kilburn is shabby and the aristocratic-sounding Carlton area is composed of bleak and menacing concrete estates. Further north is inner suburbia, a patchwork of gracious avenues (Brondesbury Park), row upon row of modest terraces, bedsit-land and the odd council estate. It is ethnically as well as socially mixed: Kilburn and Cricklewood are long-standing Irish areas and the influence is still apparent; there is a somewhat diminished Jewish community at Willesden Green; and there are also a large number of black and Asian residents.

All this should add up to a safe Labour seat, and that is what Brent East basically is. It had a wobble in 1987, when Ken Livingstone deselected incumbent MP Reg Freeson and the Labour council was at its most outrageous and unpopular, but even then an effective Tory campaign could not topple Labour. For the next couple of borough elections many of East's wards disappointed Labour, but things swung round in 1998. A predecessor seat, Willesden East, was Conservative in 1959, but Labour should now be safe – there are only 57 safer Labour seats. Paul Daisley, the new MP, led Brent council back to sanity after 1996.

BRENT NORTH

	2001		1997		1992 *notional*	
Electorate and turnout	58,789	57.7	54,149	70.5	*55,433*	*68.0*
Conservative	9,944	29.3	15,324	40.1	*21,660*	*57.4*
Labour	20,149	59.4	19,343	50.7	*11,430*	*30.3*
Lib Dem	3,846	11.3	3,104	8.1	*3,999*	*10.6*
Others	–		403 (2)		*624 (2)*	
MP	Barry Gardiner (Lab)		Barry Gardiner (Lab)		Rhodes Boyson (Con)	
Majority	10,205	30.1	4,019	10.5	*10,230*	*27.1*

Brent North recorded the nation's largest swing to Labour in 2001 (9.8 per cent), a feat that is all the more remarkable given that it also had this honour in 1997 with a mammoth swing of 18.8 per cent (a post-war record). The quiet suburbs of Wembley – including Sudbury, Queensbury, Kenton and Roe Green – are now more solidly Labour than ex-mining seats such as Normanton.

Ethnic politics plays a large part in Brent North's recent electoral behaviour. Prosperous London Asians have tended to settle in Wembley and Harrow, and the area attracted the middle class Asians expelled from Uganda in 1972. Wembley provides high quality 1930s family housing and a pleasant environment, while still being close to facilities like the Temple at Neasden and the traditional Indian area of Southall. By 1991 the non-white population was 41.3 per cent in Brent North – it is considerably higher now – but the seat was still safely Conservative, reflecting its very middle class composition, until like much of suburban London it threw its Tory MP out in 1997. Labour MP Barry Gardiner has worked very hard to build support as an incumbent, and taken an interest in Indian affairs as the founder of Labour Friends of India, and his personal standing helped to generate the second record swing in 2001. He was also helped by the Conservative rhetoric on asylum, which seemed to these voters a long way from the decency Robert Carr had shown many of them as Tory Home Secretary in 1972.

Brent North was the only one of Labour's surprise gains of 1997 to stick with the party in the 1999 European elections, and the party also made gains in the 1998 borough elections. Given the continuing demographic trend, Labour's breakthrough among suburban voters and Gardiner's affinity with India, the Labour Party is in a commanding position in Brent North.

BRENT SOUTH

	2001		1997		1992 notional	
Electorate and turnout	55,891	51.2	53,505	64.5	59,070	63.4
Conservative	3,604	12.6	5,489	15.9	11,651	31.1
Labour	20,984	73.3	25,180	73.0	21,568	57.6
Lib Dem	3,098	10.8	2,670	7.7	3,551	9.5
Anti–EU	–	–	497	1.4	–	–
Others	951 (2)		662 (3)		655 (2)	
MP	Paul Boateng (Lab)		Paul Boateng (Lab)		Paul Boateng (Lab)	
Majority	17,380	60.7	19,691	57.1	9,917	26.5

Brent South includes some of London's most deprived and troubled areas. It is a straggling strip of territory either side of Harlesden – stretching in one direction to Wembley town centre and the other to Kensal Rise at the top of Ladbroke Grove. Stonebridge Park is a notorious estate, now being redeveloped, although Kensal Rise is becoming a northern extension of Notting Hill. The main fact about Brent South is its ethnic composition – it had the lowest proportion of white residents of any constituency in 1991 and almost certainly still does. Black residents are concentrated around Harlesden town centre and are the largest minority, although there are also many Asians, particularly around Wembley centre. Harlesden was dubbed the gun crime capital of London, but since the start of 2001 a campaign by the Metropolitan Police and Brent Council has reduced gun crime by around a quarter.

Not surprisingly, Brent South is an extremely safe Labour seat. It sends Paul Boateng to parliament with massive majorities, and although the turnout is quite low it is really not too bad for an inner city seat. All its component wards are Labour-inclined, although the Lib Dems win the outer ward of Alperton in local elections. However, Brent South is likely to be dissolved in the boundary review because of its long, thin shape and small electorate. This will pose a problem for Boateng, a senior Labour politician who won the seat ('Today Brent South, tomorrow Soweto') in 1987 and became Britain's first black Cabinet minister in May 2002.

BRENTFORD and ISLEWORTH

	2001		1997		1992 notional	
Electorate and turnout	82,878	53.7	80,722	69.5	79,763	74.2
Conservative	12,957	29.1	17,825	31.8	26,994	45.6
Labour	23,275	52.3	32,249	57.4	25,319	42.8
Lib Dem	5,994	13.5	4,613	8.2	5,962	10.1
Anti–EU	412	0.9	614	1.1	–	–
Green	1,324	3.0	687	1.2	904	1.5
Others	552 (2)		147		–	
MP	Ann Keen (Lab)		Ann Keen (Lab)		Nirj Deva (Con)	
Majority	10,318	23.2	14,424	25.7	1,675	2.8

Brentford and Isleworth constituency is the inner seat of the borough of Hounslow – unlike many boroughs the inner seat is the more attractive residential area while the outer one (Feltham and Heston) is more industrial and working class. Brentford & Isleworth consists of several districts along and in from the north bank of the Thames from Chiswick and Stamford Brook, which are just across the borough boundary from Hammersmith, out to the eastern side of Hounslow town centre. Chiswick is a part of sophisticated inner west London, but most of the seat is suburban post-Middlesex sprawl of varying vintages and compositions. Gunnersbury, with its aging estates, lies under the elevated M4; Isleworth further out is quieter and more suburban. Labour have some strong wards in Hounslow town (thanks partly to the Asian vote), but much of the rest is quite marginal territory in local and national elections. Both main parties are quite well-organised with high memberships. The constituency as a whole voted Conservative – though very narrowly – in its first two elections in 1974, then more comfortably Tory in 1979-97, and now twice for Labour's Ann Keen. As a footnote, the Conservative MP in 1992-97, Nirj Deva, was the first Asian MP to sit for the Conservatives in a century; he is now an MEP. The large Labour majority in his old seat is a sign of quite how far the Conservatives have fallen behind in London rather than indicating any great demographic shift here.

   In the boundary review, only minor shuffling in the Hounslow town area was proposed for this oversized seat by the commission, and although both main parties had ideas for this seat (Labour wanted to cut off Chiswick and add a bit of Hounslow town, making this a safer seat; the Conservatives proposed taking some of Hounslow away, making it easier for them to win back) the original proposals stand.

CITIES of LONDON and WESTMINSTER

	2001		1997		1992 notional	
Electorate and turnout	71,935	47.2	74,035	54.2	65.613	65.5
Conservative	15,737	46.3	18,981	47.3	25,512	59.3
Labour	11,238	33.1	14,100	35.1	10,368	24.1
Lib Dem	5,218	15.4	4,933	12.3	6,077	14.1
Anti–EU	464	1.4	1,376 (2)	3.4	–	–
Others	1,318		765 (5)		1,051	
MP	Mark Field (Con)		Peter Brooke (Con)		Peter Brooke (Con) City of London & W'minster S'	
Majority	4,499	13.2	4,881	12.2	15,144	35.2

This central London constituency unites a large number of the landmarks associated with London to the visitor – Big Ben, Westminster Abbey and Buckingham Palace in the smaller area generally known as Westminster, but also Soho, Fleet Street, the Bank of England, Piccadilly, Temple, Oxford Street, Marble Arch, Hyde Park… It has 32 underground stations, including the main line stations of Victoria, Charing Cross, Liverpool Street and Paddington. It is the bustling, noisy core of London.

Amid the busyness, there are some residential areas. Pimlico in the south was once of dubious repute, but has gone increasingly upmarket; Marylebone, Mayfair and the areas bordering on Hyde Park have always been respectable, and the permanent inhabitants of the bewilderingly cosmopolitan Bayswater-Lancaster Gate area are rather similar to the people of neighbouring Notting Hill. Some people choose to live permanently right in the centre of things around Soho and Charing Cross, but there are also a large number of corporately owned flats and weekday pied-a-terre residences.

The turnover of population gives this constituency a typically low turnout for an inner city area, but its voting behaviour is distinctively Conservative – hardly surprising in an area of such great wealth. Belgravia and Bryanston, for instance, vote 70 per cent plus Conservative. It is more of a question where the Labour voters come from; there are some council-built estates beneath the watchful gaze of Millbank Tower and the distinguished 1950s Churchill Gardens estate, and Bayswater, but the Conservatives have predominated here too in recent local elections. There was some speculation in the press that Labour might just manage to win here in 2001, but it was wide of the mark and the Tories should be safe enough. This constituency holds the English record in 2001 for the place where the winner scored the lowest share of the entire electorate – a mere 21.9 per cent.

EALING ACTON and SHEPHERD'S BUSH

	2001		1997		1992 notional	
Electorate and turnout	70,697	52.6	72,078	66.7	68,324	72.7
Conservative	9,355	25.1	12,402	25.8	19,553	39.4
Labour	20,144	54.1	28,052	58.4	23,024	46.4
Lib Dem	6,171	16.6	5,163	10.7	5,998	12.1
Anti–EU	476	1.3	1,022 (2)	2.1	–	–
Others	1,055 (3)		1,422 (5)		1,087	
MP	Clive Soley (Lab)		Clive Soley (Lab)		George Young (Con)	
					Ealing Acton	
Majority	10,789	29.0	15,650	32.6	3,471*	7.0*

* Estimated Labour majority allowing for boundary changes.

This multi-titled seat is an inner city constituency in the west of London, covering the far east end of the borough of Ealing and the north end of the borough of Hammersmith & Fulham. The Shepherd's Bush portion is the most strongly Labour part of the latter borough, comprising council estates such as White City, the ethnically mixed terraces off Uxbridge Road in Coningham and Wormholt and some more upwardly mobile terraced areas around Shepherd's Bush Green. The BBC influence and the proximity of Notting Hill have attracted some famous residents; this is where Patsy and Edina of *Absolutely Fabulous* live, much as they pretend it is really Holland Park. The Acton part is the completely unglamorous although undoubtedly convenient inner suburb of that name, dissected by railway lines and major roads, but the constituency stretches far enough west to the suburban Ealing Broadway and Hanger Lane areas which offer the only Conservative strong point in the constituency.

Acton is one of the areas of London whose political allegiance depends very much on where the boundaries are drawn. The Acton area itself was a Labour seat from 1945 to 1974 (except for a Tory interregnum after a by-election in 1968), but it was a small seat. In 1974 the Conservative seat of Ealing South was abolished, and the quiet, affluent suburbs that it donated to Ealing Acton were enough to tip the seat over to the Tories even when Labour won the 1974 elections nationally. In 1997 the middle class area was removed again, and Acton was paired with Shepherd's Bush in a relatively reliable Labour seat which has given Clive Soley two five figure majorities.

The next set of boundary changes will dissolve this seat, because Ealing is the right size again for three independent seats. The Ealing Acton seat will be revived. This was Conservative when it existed between 1974 and 1997, but Labour would certainly have won it in 1997 and 2001, given the favourable trend to Labour in London recently and slightly different boundaries. Labour would start favourites in the restored Acton despite its history. The Shepherd's Bush portion left over will go into a large Hammersmith seat which should be reliably Labour.

EALING NORTH

	2001		1997		1992 notional	
Electorate and turnout	77,524	58.0	78,144	71.3	75,908	76.7
Conservative	13,185	29.3	20,744	37.2	29,917	51.4
Labour	25,022	55.7	29,904	53.7	20,842	35.8
Lib Dem	5,043	11.2	3,887	7.0	6,266	10.8
Anti–EU	668	1.5	689	1.2	–	–
Green	1,039	2.3	502	0.9	651	1.1
Others	–		–		524	
MP	Stephen Pound (Lab)		Stephen Pound (Lab)		Harry Greenway (Con)	
Majority	11,837	26.3	9,160	16.4	9,075	15.6

Ealing North has been a hard-fought marginal seat since its creation in 1950, and it was a key target for Labour in 1997 which fell on a typically large London swing. It is a rather unpretentious working class place, although it has the wealthy district of Pitshanger in the east which had previously helped keep the Ealing Acton seat so Conservative. It lies on both sides of the A40 main road out of London towards Oxford. Many of the wards are quite marginal and prone to high swings in local elections. Its Labour MP Stephen Pound, in a witty maiden speech in 1997, described it as 'a mixture of hamlets, towns, villages and communities, bound together by many things – but most of all by the Boundary Commissioner' and rather devoid of interesting landmarks and local history, except for a curious incident in 1889 when a circus elephant, with its last breath, staggered out of the seat into Acton rather than die in Ealing North. The electors of Ealing North voted to 'Keep the Pound' in 2001, but not in the way William Hague would have wanted.

London has little manufacturing industry left, but there is still an industrial tone to Ealing North, particularly in the areas around Park Royal and Northolt. Ealing North has the largest Polish population in Britain, because of the Polish Air Force presence at Northolt during the war. Ealing North also boasts a large open space, spared from the developers in the 1930s, around Horsenden Hill.

After veering off to the Conservatives in the 1987 general and 1990 local elections, Ealing North has swung as violently back to Labour since. Labour's performance in Ealing North has beaten the national swing by 5.5 points (1992) 6 points (1997) and 7 points (2001) in the last three elections, making it appear almost safe now. Labour have not done quite as well in local elections since 1990, but had recovered from most of the damage caused by the unpopular Labour administration of 1986-90 by 1998.

EALING SOUTHALL

	2001		1997		1992 notional	
Electorate and turnout	82,373	56.8	81,704	66.9	75,444	74.3
Conservative	8,556	18.3	11,368	20.8	20,340	36.3
Labour	22,239	47.5	32,791	60.0	25,371	45.3
Lib Dem	4,680	10.0	5,687	10.4	4,567	8.2
Anti–EU	–	–	1,282 (2)	2.3	–	–
Ind Sunrise	5,764	12.3	–	–	–	–
Green	2,119	4.5	934	1.7	1,044	1.9
Socialist	921	2.0	2,107	3.9	–	–
Ind Lab	–	–	–	–	4,660	8.3
Others	2,549 (3)		473		49	
MP	Piara Khabra (Lab)		Piara Khabra (Lab)		Piara Khabra (Lab)	
Majority	13,683	29.2	21,423	39.2	5,031	9.0

The Ealing Southall constituency is centred on Southall, a working class industrial area west of Ealing's centre. Since the 1950s Southall has become one of the most concentrated areas of settlement by people from the Indian subcontinent and their descendants, and some of its wards such as Broadway and Green are 90 per cent Asian. The 'little India' feel of Southall has brightened up a drab Victorian town. The Southall wards vote nearly unanimously for Labour in local and most general elections. The constituency extends to the north, at the suburb of Dormer's Wells, and east to the affluent suburbia of Ealing Common.

Southall is, as might be expected, a Labour seat with a large majority, but it is not politically simple. The currently defined Southall seat gained an infusion of Conservative voters when the Acton constituency was moved eastwards and the southern side of suburban Ealing became part of the Southall constituency instead. This Conservative vote seems to have dispersed, as in other London suburbs. In 1992 Labour also suffered from the continued candidacy of deselected MP Sydney Bidwell, standing as True Labour. In 1997 there were only Socialist Labour and Greens drawing off left wing votes, and Piara Khabra won with a massive majority.

In 2001 Labour's majority was down again, thanks to inroads from the Greens and a more unusual candidacy. Avtar Lit, Chief Executive of London's Sunrise Radio (a station with a mainly Asian audience) stood as an Independent and polled the third highest Independent share after Richard Taylor and Martin Bell. Sunrise was fined £10,000 by the Radio Authority for lack of balance in its election coverage, but Lit's strong showing is food for thought for Labour in Southall.

FELTHAM and HESTON

	2001		1997		1992 notional	
Electorate and turnout	73,458	49.2	71,868	64.9	73,296	72.8
Conservative	8,749	24.2	12,563	26.9	22,894	42.9
Labour	21,406	59.2	27,836	59.7	24,294	45.5
Lib Dem	4,998	13.8	4,264	9.1	6,189	11.6
Anti–EU	–	–	1,099	2.4	–	–
Others	1,024 (3)		859 (2)			
MP	Alan Keen (Lab)		Alan Keen (Lab)		Alan Keen (Lab)	
Majority	12,657	35.0	15,273	32.8	1,400	2.6

Feltham and Heston lacks glamour – even its name seems to unite a young offenders' institution and a motorway service area. Planes fly low over the constituency on their final approach to Heathrow airport, a major local employer as well as an environmental consideration for residents. Feltham is a down at heel place on the western fringe of the borough of Hounslow and of London. Its component wards are nearly all solidly Labour, although the Liberal Democrats can challenge intermittently. Heston, on the other hand, is relatively pleasant suburbia which suffers somewhat from its proximity to the airport and the M4 motorway. Heston has become an increasingly Asian area – it is very close to Southall – and this has caused a noticeable trend to Labour in its wards. The constituency also includes the western side of Hounslow town.

All this sounds like a recipe for a safe Labour seat, and that is what Feltham and Heston is now. But in the elections of 1983 and 1987, when Labour were doing abnormally badly in working class areas in outer London and the south east, the Conservatives managed to win the seat despite continuing Labour dominance in local elections for Hounslow borough. Political and demographic changes have surely put paid to any chance of the Tories reviving their 1980s glory days here.

HAMMERSMITH and FULHAM

	2001		1997		1992 notional	
Electorate and turnout	79,303	56.4	78,637	68.7	72,731	75.9
Conservative	17,786	39.8	21,420	39.6	28,487	51.6
Labour	19,801	44.3	25,262	46.8	21,313	38.6
Lib Dem	5,294	11.8	4,728	8.8	4,553	8.3
Anti–EU	375	0.8	1,206 (2)	2.2	–	–
Green	1,444	3.2	562	1.0	679	1.2
Others	–		848 (3)		141	
MP	Iain Coleman (Lab)		Iain Coleman (Lab)		Matthew Carrington (Con)	
					Fulham	
Majority	2,015	4.5	3,842	7.1	7,174	13.0

This seat has seen its share of titanic electoral confrontations; Fulham East in 1933, Hammersmith South in 1949 and Fulham in 1986 in by-elections; and the repeated 'Battles of Barons Court' in the 1950s and 1960s in general elections. It is still a close fight. Labour council leader Iain Coleman beat Matthew Carrington, previously the Tory MP for Fulham, in 1997 and 2001 but by rather slender majorities. Much of the political geography of London has shifted, but Hammersmith and Fulham has stuck by its traditions of providing nail-biting two-way fights between the main parties, both of which are well-organised in this area.

Fulham has been climbing the social ladder for decades and now has the reputation of being London's most overpriced residential area. The steady advance of Conservatism in the area is concentrated in a group of wards south of Fulham Broadway, which have swung relentlessly to the right. Sulivan, for instance, saw its Tory lead stretch, against the trend, from 5 points in 1986 to 34 points in 1998. Chelsea has exported its Conservative tendencies as well as some of its wannabe residents.

The northern wards around Hammersmith Broadway have, by contrast, followed the London trend towards Labour. Ravenscourt Park and Brook Green are both sought-after areas; the latter had several million-pound house sales in the most recent boom. There are some council estate areas which tend to Labour, among which appropriately enough is the Clem Attlee estate, now modernised to include a lower-rise John Smith Close.

The constituency remains a top target for the Conservatives in local and general elections and it looks set to maintain its marginal tradition at least until the boundary review. The commission's recommendations unsportingly propose to pair Fulham with Chelsea in a safe Conservative seat, while throwing Hammersmith back in with Shepherd's Bush in a safe Labour seat, thereby ending the excitement. Labour unsuccessfully challenged the plan at the public inquiry.

HARROW EAST

	2001		1997		1992 notional	
Electorate and turnout	82,269	58.4	79,981	71.2	77,203	77.4
Conservative	15,466	32.2	20,189	35.4	31,624	52.9
Labour	26,590	55.3	29,923	52.5	20,219	33.9
Lib Dem	6,021	12.5	4,697	8.2	6,471	10.8
Anti–EU	–	–	2,001 (2)	3.5	49	0.1
Others	–		171		1,375	
MP	Tony McNulty (Lab)		Tony McNulty (Lab)		Hugh Dykes (Con)	
Majority	11,124	23.1	9,734	17.1	11,405	19.1

Labour won Harrow East in the landslides of 1945 and 1966, so it was not a complete surprise when it fell to Tony McNulty in 1997. What was a surprise was the crushing margin of his victory, with a swing of 18.1 per cent, which made it look like a relatively safe seat. At the time this was attributed to a local issue, the Conservative government's treatment of Edgware Hospital, but Labour's continuing improvement despite the disappointment of some of the Edgware Hospital hopes shows that the change here is more deep-seated. Even in the 1999 European elections Labour were still 4.5 per cent ahead, and by election day 2001 it was no surprise that Labour won with a comfortably increased majority.

Harrow East is less exclusive and wealthy than West, although it is largely devoid of council estates. It includes the Wealdstone district of Harrow, stretches up to the Barnet border at Stanmore and adjoins Brent North at Kenton. It is about a third non-white, mostly Asian, and rather similar to Brent North. In local elections there is some Liberal Democrat activity in Harrow Weald in particular, although the party was knocked back severely by Labour's local election win in 1998. Labour did particularly well in the Kenton and central Harrow wards, while the Conservatives have some strength in the north east of the seat at Stanmore Park and Canons. Harrow East is now a safer Labour seat than Blackburn – 166 Labour seats have smaller majorities and Tony McNulty would have a chance of survival even if the Conservatives gain an overall majority.

Under the boundary commission recommendations, this constituency will shift slightly eastwards away from central Harrow; the Conservatives argued unsuccessfully at the inquiry for a new cross-border seat with Brent including Kenton and Queensbury.

HARROW WEST

	2001		1997		1992 notional	
Electorate and turnout	74,083	63.0	72,146	72.8	70,781	77.4
Conservative	16,986	36.4	20,571	39.2	30,227	55.2
Labour	23,142	49.6	21,811	41.5	12,337	22.5
Lib Dem	5,995	12.9	8,127	15.5	11,045	20.2
Anti–EU	525	1.1	1,997	3.8	–	–
Others	–		–		1,151	
MP	Gareth Thomas (Lab)		Gareth Thomas (Lab)		Robert Hughes (Con)	
Majority	6,156	13.2	1,240	2.4	17,890	32.7

Until 1997 the idea of Labour representing the lush suburbs of Harrow West was preposterous. West is composed almost entirely of very affluent suburbia with low levels of deprivation. Gareth Thomas's victory was, to those who know Pinner and Harrow-on-the-Hill, one of the most unbelievable results of the evening. The seat also includes tracts of suburbia around Headstone Lane and Rayner's Lane. Labour had never won, and failed to come within 9,000 votes of the Conservatives even in 1945. Unlike East, it has no Labour history and until recently no Labour wards.

There is still a reasonably solid bloc of Conservative wards in the north of the constituency, at Hatch End and Pinner, but the southern part around central Harrow voted Labour in the 1998 local elections as well as the general elections. The Liberal Democrats were formerly quite strong in each part, but have been caught in a pincer movement and had a strong grip only on the Rayner's Lane ward in 1998 (which they lost in 2002 after messing up their nomination papers). However, Gareth Thomas did well across the seat in 2001 with a swing of over 5 per cent in his favour against senior Conservative policy adviser Danny Finkelstein. Harrow West is still a seat the Conservatives should aspire to win, but they have to contend with Labour's formidable recent strength in the borough of Harrow and the personal following of Gareth Thomas.

The boundary changes will help Thomas even more, as they propose to chip off the safest Conservative area at Hatch End and Pinner to a seat based on Northwood and move Harrow West slightly to the east. The Conservatives objected but to no avail.

HAYES and HARLINGTON

	2001		1997		1992 notional	
Electorate and turnout	57,561	56.3	56,783	72.4	58,665	74.1
Conservative	7,813	24.1	11,167	27.2	19,511	44.9
Labour	21,279	65.7	25,458	62.0	19,467	44.8
Lib Dem	1,958	6.0	3,049	7.4	4,477	10.3
Anti–EU	–	–	778	1.9	–	–
Others	1,353 (2)		639 (2)		–	
MP	John McDonnell (Lab)		John McDonnell (Lab)		Terry Dicks (Con)	
Majority	13,466	41.6	14,291	34.8	44	0.1

Hayes and Harlington has produced such thumping Labour victories in 1997 and 2001 (there are now only 82 safer Labour seats in the country) that it is difficult to imagine it ever having been a Tory seat, still less a place where a Tory MP could achieve a majority of nearly 6,000 as Terry Dicks did in 1987.

Hayes and Harlington is the area immediately north of Heathrow, and the constituency nominally includes a large part of the airport's land. The airport provides work, but airport noise and congestion, plus the pros and cons of the new Terminal 5, are also important issues here. The constituency is working class, but not particularly poor, and mostly the product of 1930s development when new industries were booming in west London and out to Slough. Although it was formerly quite a council estate seat, much of the housing has been bought up by tenants. Hayes has some of the attributes of a New Town planned community, historically and socially, and this spilled over into its political outlook. Like the proper New Towns, it revolted against Labour in 1979-87, with white working class voters swinging behind the Tories either directly or after a halfway house in the SDP. The local Labour Party in the constituency is traditionally one of the most left wing in London, and voters seemed to prefer Thatcherism and its local representative, the rather crude populist Terry Dicks. But in 1997, after Black Wednesday and the rise of Blair, the voters of Hayes were more receptive to Labour and swung over en bloc to left winger John McDonnell. It is a constituency of extreme likes and dislikes – even the SDP candidate here in 1987, Sue Slipman, had joined the party straight from the Communists.

In the boundary changes, West Drayton joins the constituency from Uxbridge to little partisan effect. The Conservatives proposed instead linking it with part of Heston, across the airport, and creating an MP for Heathrow, but this idea attracted minimal support.

KENSINGTON and CHELSEA

	2001		1997		1992 notional	
Electorate and turnout	64,707	43.3	67,786	54.7	64,046	66.4
Conservative	15,270	54.5	19,887	53.6	28,979	68.2
Labour	6,499	23.2	10,368	28.0	7,080	16.7
Lib Dem	4,416	15.8	5,668	15.3	5,590	13.2
Anti–EU	416	1.5	540	1.5	–	–
Others	1,437 (3)		625 (5)		855	
MP	Michael Portillo (Con)		Alan Clark (Con)		Nicholas Scott (Con)	
						Chelsea
Majority	8,771	31.3	9,519	25.7	21,899	51.5

Parliamentary by-election 25 November 1999: Conservative 11,004 (56.4), Labour 4,298 (22.0), Lib Dem 1,831 (9.4), Anti EU 450 (2.3), 14 Others 1,873 Electorate 65,806, Turnout 29.7. MP: Michael Portillo (Con), Majority 6,706 (34.4).

Kensington and Chelsea is the safest Conservative seat in London, and the third safest in the whole country. It has the highest-status demographics in Britain, with the largest proportion of employers and managers and a large number of very wealthy people. K & C is probably the only constituency where the upper class, as opposed to the working and middle classes, carries significant electoral weight.

Chelsea was famous for its contribution to youth culture in the 1960s and 1970s, but its residents are now very staid and respectable for the most part, particularly those who make it onto the electoral register and cast votes. Chelsea Football Club plays in Fulham, draws most of its support from south of the river and most of its players from the other side of the Channel. What is left is the territory of the Sloane Ranger – first designated by Peter York in the late 1970s, there is presumably a second generation of Sloanes here now. Kensington has a less distinct image, but its grand terraces are cosmopolitan, artistic and cultured, and it has a concentration of fine museums north of South Kensington underground station. Further north is Kensington High Street, Holland Park and Notting Hill Gate, with similarly comfortable and fashionable residential areas.

The Conservatives, even in their worst borough elections in recent times, can rely on around 70 per cent of the vote in much of Chelsea and South Kensington in wards such as Hans Town (near Harrods), Queen's Gate and Royal Hospital. The area around Earls Court is a bit more competitive, with both Labour and Liberal Democrats active in several wards, and there is a Labour voting estate at World's End, at the far end of the King's Road. In the far north, the Conservative share falls to around 50 per cent. The extremely rapid population mobility, and the utter safety of the seat, keeps the turnout very low – it was the ninth worst in Britain in 2001 and one of only two Conservative seats in the worst 100 (the other was neighbouring Cities of London and Westminster). Its recent Conservative MPs have been a characterful lot – Nicholas Scott, Alan Clark and Michael Portillo. The local selectorate clearly tends to take an indulgent view of human foibles and frailties.

REGENT'S PARK and KENSINGTON NORTH

	2001		*1997*		*1992 notional*	
Electorate and turnout	75,886	48.8	69,261	68.4	*69,959*	*74.9*
Conservative	9,981	26.9	13,710	29.0	*21,503*	*41.1*
Labour	20,247	54.6	28,367	59.9	*25,317*	*48.3*
Lib Dem	4,669	12.6	4,041	8.5	*4,163*	*8.0*
Anti–EU	354	1.0	867	1.8	–	–
Green	1,268	3.4	–	–	*1,055*	*2.0*
Others	533 (2)		359 (2)		*330*	
MP	Karen Buck (Lab)		Karen Buck (Lab)		John Wheeler (Con)	
					Westminster North	
Majority	10,266	27.7	14,657	31.0	*3,814**	*7.3**

* Estimated Labour majority allowing for boundary changes.

This cumbersomely named constituency links the northern parts of Kensington & Chelsea and Westminster, each of which is an inner city area out on a limb in those wealthy, bustling central London boroughs. North Kensington has some acutely deprived areas, particularly Golborne at the north end of Portobello Road, a lot of social housing and a multiracial population. North Kensington is the main centre for the Notting Hill Carnival, a late summer explosion of exuberant Caribbean culture which attracts a million visitors to the area's narrow streets. Colville ward is the heart of Notting Hill, around the Portobello market; in the 1999 film Hugh Grant's character's flat with the blue door and the bookshop where he worked were both in Colville. The North Kensington wards, despite an astonishing escalation in house prices, have been solidly Labour in every borough election since 1982.

Most of the seat is north Westminster. In the west this is very like North Kensington, with social housing and deprivation in the wards by the tatty Harrow Road and Labour voting habits in all elections. Like North Kensington, many asylum seekers have ended up here. Maida Vale and Little Venice are mixtures, with grand avenues and wealthy mansion blocks and the occasional council estate. They have voted Conservative in council elections since 1990, but probably returned Labour majorities in the 2001 general election. Church Street ward is a Labour voting area with many council tenants, but it is an island in the staid suburban grandeur of St. John's Wood. The former seat of Westminster North (to be revived by the boundary changes) was a disappointment to Labour as the Conservatives held on, latterly with the assistance of Shirley Porter's gerrymandering. But the new RPKN was a gift for Labour, and Karen Buck has won large majorities in her two elections (the first with the assistance of Bridget Jones, who recorded excitedly voting Buck! in her diary) despite the nation's worst drop in turnout in the 2001 election. The fall in turnout was due to the fact that it was no longer a marginal (Labour had given it target treatment in 1997)and its young, mobile population.

RUISLIP NORTHWOOD

	2001		1997		1992 notional	
Electorate and turnout	60,788	61.1	60,393	74.2	61,393	78.1
Conservative	18,115	48.8	22,526	50.2	30,130	62.9
Labour	10,578	28.5	14,732	32.9	9,521	19.9
Lib Dem	7,177	19.3	7,279	16.2	7,981	16.7
Others	1,271 (2)		296		294	
MP	John Wilkinson (Con)		John Wilkinson (Con)		John Wilkinson (Con)	
Majority	7,537	20.3	7,794	17.4	20,609	43.0

West London has two rare examples of safe Conservative inner London constituencies; in London, truly safe Conservative suburbs are also something of a rarity. They are now only four in number within the GLA area – Chingford & Woodford Green, Bromley & Chislehurst, Croydon South – and Ruislip Northwood. This constituency is definitely part of Metroland, with the Metropolitan Line's branches serving most areas of the seat as well as the further reaches of the Central Line at Ruislip.

In 1998 all but two of the ten wards were Conservative, some with large majorities. Ruislip proper, Northwood and Eastcote are affluent, very quiet and uniform suburbs, reminiscent of the commuter country in Buckinghamshire or Hertfordshire South West. South Ruislip, however, is rather a distinct area and has some social housing – Labour occasionally show here and in the built-up village of Harefield in the west of the constituency. But for the most part the gradations between the wards are between 50 per cent Conservative and 70 per cent Conservative in local elections. Eurosceptic MP John Wilkinson has a very safe seat.

The proposed boundary changes, in which the boroughs of Harrow and Hillingdon are paired, creates a cross-borough seat of Ruislip, Northwood and Pinner based on this seat and if anything even more Conservative. South Ruislip will join Uxbridge. The Conservatives objected to this plan at the public inquiry; (it concentrated a lot of their strongest areas in one constituency) but they failed to reverse the proposals.

UXBRIDGE

	2001		1997		1992 notional	
Electorate and turnout	58,068	57.5	57,414	72.4	59,528	75.9
Conservative	15,751	47.1	18,095	43.6	25,467	56.4
Labour	13,653	40.9	17,371	41.8	13,099	29.0
Lib Dem	3,426	10.3	4,528	10.9	5,663	12.5
Anti–EU	588	1.8	1,153	2.8	–	–
Others	–		398		928	
MP	John Randall (Con)		Michael Shersby (Con)		Michael Shersby (Con)	
Majority	2,098	6.3	724	1.7	12,368	27.4

Parliamentary by-election 31 July 1997: Conservative 16,288 (51.1), Labour 12,522 (39.3), Lib Dem 1,792 (5.6), Anti EU 39 (0.1), 7 Others 1,226 Electorate 57,446, Turnout 55.5%. MP: John Randall (Con), Majority 3,766 (11.8).

Uxbridge is the main centre in the outer London Borough of Hillingdon. While it is administratively part of London and is served by the tube, Uxbridge has its own telephone code and a certain sense of independence from the metropolis. As well as Uxbridge town, the seat contains the straggling suburb of Hillingdon proper on the A40 and stretches down the Colne valley (not to be confused with the one in Yorkshire) to the towns of Yiewsley, Cowley and West Drayton. Most of this territory is marginal in local and national elections, although the suburb of Ickenham to the north of Uxbridge town is the strongest Tory area in Hillingdon borough. Labour used to be strong enough in Uxbridge to hold the seat even in Tory years such as 1951 and 1955, but since then have only won it in 1966 – despite by-elections in favourable circumstances for the party in 1972 and 1997. Uxbridge is well located near Heathrow and by a tangle of motorways and has become increasingly well off, taking on some of the social and political attributes of neighbouring Buckinghamshire.

The 1997 by-election was the first since 1989 where the Conservative was elected – the last by-election winner William Hague had just become party leader. Despite taking place at a time when Labour had a 33-point lead in the polls the Tories held on quite well. Labour suffered for Millbank's imposition of a new candidate and Tory John Randall's local credentials, and a feeling that it was a bit greedy to ask for an even bigger parliamentary majority. The Conservatives then did surprisingly well in the 1998 borough elections. A Labour gain was anticipated also in 2001, but it failed to materialise. Uxbridge is the Verdun of the modern Conservative Party – perilously besieged, but never taken.

Avon (former county of)

	Conservative		Labour		Liberal Democrat		Others	
	Share of vote	Seats	Share of vote	Seats	Share of vote	Seats	Share of vote	Seats
2001	31.5	1	36.8	6	27.8	3	4.0	0
1997	32.7	1	36.5	6	26.3	3	4.5	0
1992	44.5	6	27.5	3	26.5	1	1.5	0
1987	47.9	9	24.0	1	27.0	0	1.1	0
1983	47.3	9	24.3	1	27.6	0	0.8	0

Avon was one of the most unpopular creations of the local government review of the early 1970s, and it was abolished in the smaller review in the mid 1990s. It was broken into four unitary authorities, namely the City of Bristol plus the councils of North Somerset, Bath & North East Somerset and South Gloucestershire (three entities with scarcely more local identity than Avon had). But CUBA ('the County that Used to Be Avon') is still a useful unit for some purposes, including political geography. It is quite well-defined as being the Bristol city-region plus Bath and its hinterland. The west country is often thought of by outsiders as being concerned primarily with tourism and agriculture, but Avon is mainly urban with considerable industrial and commercial employment. Labour currently lead in Avon, but the county is hard fought by all three main parties. Bristol West is the only constituency in this position, but each party has areas of strong support in parts of the county. Labour dominate working class south, and most of east, Bristol plus Kingswood and the former Somerset coalfield. The Liberal Democrats are a presence in much of Avon. Their three seats reflect strength in three different sorts of area. Bath is a sophisticated, educated urban electorate where long years of campaigning came good; Weston is a west country holiday resort; Northavon is an ultra-modern landscape of detached suburbs which provided a surprise gain in 1997 and a triumph in 2001. The party is also active in Bristol, where it has strong representation from the refined west end and a presence in the working class east of the city, but has slipped back in the safe Tory area of Woodspring. The Conservatives can only really rely on Woodspring and scattered wards in other areas, but seemed completely dominant as recently as 15 years ago.

Avon seems to be an area that rewards governments for economic performance. In 1987 the Conservatives did better, particularly in Bristol, than in their 1983 landslide and in 2001 Labour managed to improve on another landslide. In each case the Bristol region was doing well economically and its mainly white, skilled working class electorate swung behind the government. However, in the recession election of 1992 it was one of the areas that punished the Conservatives most severely, with the loss of Bristol East, Bath and Kingswood and the disappearance of a healthy majority in Bristol NW. Labour have to keep on delivering if the voters of the Avon seats are to keep faith.

Local government

The city of Bristol has been under Labour control since 1986. Oddly, the Conservative Party as such has not had control of the city for a century. Until the 1970s the right was represented in local politics by the Citizens Party, which started as a Conservative-Liberal alliance but became indistinguishable from the Tories. During the 1990s the Tories were reduced to a rump, and they have shown few signs of recovery (their deputy leader resigned after scathing local press comment about his decision to adopt a golliwog as the group's mascot in 2001). The Liberal Democrats are the main opposition to Labour, with strength in the intellectual west end and industrial east Bristol. Local political observers felt that Labour's good city election results in 2001 reflected extra Labour voters brought to the polls by the general election rather than the council's popularity and consider that Labour would be lucky to maintain control throughout the 2001–5 parliament. Their majority was cut to 2 in 2002.

South Gloucestershire is under majority Liberal Democrat control, thanks to sweeping victories in Northavon and scattered success in the rest of the district. Their majority is only four, so it will be a stern test for the party in 2003. Bath and North East Somerset (abbreviated, unattractively, to BANES or even B-NES) is hung, with the Lib Dems the largest party thanks to their dominance in Bath. The Conservatives gained North Somerset council in 1999 from a minority Lib Dem administration, but with a majority of only three and relatively poor Tory showings in the general election this looks vulnerable.

Boundary review

Avon is about to gain an eleventh seat, called Filton & Bradley Stoke, to the immediate north of Bristol. There are other significant alterations because the Boundary Commission decided not to cross the boundaries of the unitary local authorities in the area. The main impact of the changes is to make Bristol West a relatively safe Labour seat (while Bristol NW becomes a three-way marginal) and create an entirely new three way marginal at Filton & Bradley Stoke. South and east, the marginal Labour seat of Wansdyke will become North East Somerset, probably a Tory seat, and Kingswood becomes a little less safe.

BATH

	2001		1997		1992 notional	
Electorate and turnout	71,372	64.9	70,975	76.1	70,277	82.8
Conservative	13,478	29.1	16,850	31.2	25,289	43.4
Labour	7,269	15.7	8,828	16.4	4,761	8.2
Lib Dem	23,372	50.5	26,169	48.5	27,298	46.9
Anti–EU	708	1.5	1,507 (2)	2.8	127	0.2
Green	1,469	3.2	580	1.1	433	0.8
Others	–		55		314 (2)	
MP	Don Foster (LD)		Don Foster (LD)		Don Foster (LD)	
Majority	9,894	21.4	9,319	17.3	2,009	3.5

Since the 1960s Bath has changed from being a centre for rural Somerset to an affluent and metropolitan area – Hampstead–on–Avon – helped by the arrival of the university and fast trains to London. It is an attractive and historic city, and an increasingly cultured and intellectual one. Much of it comprises beautiful Georgian terraces made of pleasing stone, spilling over the ridges and hills surrounding the city centre. There are a few less favoured parts of the city, such as the Twerton area in the south west.

Bath has tended to be a Conservative city; in the century before 1992 it failed to vote Tory on only two occasions, the Liberal landslide of 1906 and the 1923 general election when the Liberals managed one-off gains in quite a few traditionally Tory areas. Labour came quite close in 1945, and were only 800 votes short in 1966, but have never won. Since 1974 Bath has been a key target for the Liberals and successors, who edged closer and closer as the Labour vote fell until the constituency provided one of the bigger shocks of election night 1992 with the defeat of Chris Patten, then Chairman of the Conservative Party.

Don Foster, the Lib Dem MP who defeated Patten, has won increasingly large majorities in Bath since then. The Liberal Democrats are dominant in nearly all the wards of Bath, and Labour hardly show now even in the estates. The Conservatives can eke out victories in the hilly north of the city at Lansdown ward and Bathwick to the east, but this is about it in a normal year. The council is only hung because the Lib Dems are very weak in the Wansdyke portion. In the boundary review Bath loses some territory around Bathavon, outside the old city, which it only acquired in 1997. This should make it even easier for the Liberal Democrats to hold.

BRISTOL EAST

	2001		1997		1992 notional	
Electorate and turnout	70,279	57.4	69,118	69.7	69,428	78.5
Conservative	8,788	21.8	11,259	23.4	20,472	37.6
Labour	22,180	55.0	27,418	56.9	25,754	47.3
Lib Dem	6,915	17.1	7,121	14.8	8,025	14.7
Anti–EU	572	1.4	1,479	3.1	–	–
Green	1,110	2.8	–	–	–	–
Others	769 (2)		924 (2)		251	
MP	Jean Corston (Lab)		Jean Corston (Lab)		Jean Corston (Lab)	
Majority	13,392	33.2	16,159	33.5	5,282	9.7

Labour's Jean Corston gained Bristol East in 1992, after a nine-year period of Conservative representation following the defeat of Tony Benn in 1983, and in 1997 and 2001 there was no serious threat to Labour. Most of the explanation was in the national swing, but boundary changes also helped. Bristol East is the part of the city which travellers see as trains approach Temple Meads station from east or north. It is a mainly working class area of the city, although areas of it such as Brislington are quite affluent. The tower block estates of Lawrence Hill are a bit of an anomaly – Bristol East is not generally a council estate seat.

There has been Liberal Democrat activity in several wards of the seat, particularly Eastville and Easton, and in local elections they run second (with 31.3 per cent to 39.7 per cent for Labour in 1999), but they are a long way off from converting their slowly growing support into a serious parliamentary challenge to Labour. Boundary changes will remove Lawrence Hill and Easton, the heartland of working class north east Bristol, to the urbane Bristol West constituency, and add two wards formerly in Kingswood, but this will have little impact on Labour's dominant position.

BRISTOL NORTH WEST

	2001		1997		1992 notional	
Electorate and turnout	76,903	60.4	73,133	75.5	73,542	81.2
Conservative	13,349	28.7	16,193	29.3	23,148	38.8
Labour	24,236	52.1	27,575	49.9	27,019	45.2
Lib Dem	7,387	15.9	7,263	13.1	8,849	14.8
Anti–EU	1,140	2.5	1,609	2.9	–	–
Ind Lab	–	–	1,718	3.1	–	–
Others	371		887 (3)		703	
MP	Doug Naysmith (Lab)		Doug Naysmith (Lab)		Michael Stern (Con)	
Majority	10,887	23.4	11,382	20.6	3,871*	6.5*

* Estimated Labour majority allowing for boundary changes

Bristol North West is the classic marginal seat of the city, having frequently changed hands between the Conservatives and Labour. The northern fringe of the city contains some troubled council estates such as Southmead, the traditional working class dockland of Avonmouth, and mixed suburbs like Henbury and Horfield which voted Labour in 2001. The constituency also spills out of the city into South Gloucestershire, covering the exurbs of Filton, Patchway and Stoke Gifford near the M4 and Bristol Parkway station. These are not Tory strongholds, Filton in particular being a centre of the aircraft industry, but they are not Labour's strongest area in the seat. For now this seat seems a safe bet for Labour, but there are clouds on the horizon. Bristol NW has shown itself capable of producing large swings when the gloss comes off a government (as in 1992) and the Lib Dems have been eroding Labour strength in Lockleaze ward in particular. The biggest cloud is, however, the boundary review. Bristol NW is severely affected. It loses the South Gloucestershire portion to a new seat called Filton and Bradley Stoke (see Northavon) and gains some areas that strike fear into Bristol Labour supporters – the Tory fortresses of Stoke Bishop and Westbury-on-Trym, plus the Lib Dem v Tory Henleaze ward. Adding the 2001 local election results in the new Bristol NW gives Labour 35 per cent, Conservative 33 per cent and Lib Dem 29 per cent, although this understates Labour support as some voters in the ex-Bristol West area clearly voted for Lib Dem councillors and for Labour MP Valerie Davey. While Labour would have won it in 2001, and won a similarly constituted seat in October 1974, there is not much of a margin to cushion any Labour loss of popularity. While the current Bristol NW is a bellwether two-party marginal, its successor could be something altogether more unpredictable and strange.

BRISTOL SOUTH

	2001		1997		1992 notional	
Electorate and turnout	72,490	56.5	72,493	68.8	75,860	76.0
Conservative	9,118	22.3	10,562	21.2	19,144	33.2
Labour	23,299	56.9	29,890	59.9	27,259	47.3
Lib Dem	6,078	14.8	6,691	13.4	10,361	18.0
Anti–EU	496	1.2	1,486	3.0	–	–
Green	1,233	3.0	722	1.4	756	1.3
Others	746 (2)		508 (2)		155	
MP	Dawn Primarolo (Lab)		Dawn Primarolo (Lab)		Dawn Primarolo (Lab)	
Majority	14,181	34.6	19,328	38.8	8,115	14.1

Bristol South is the working class heartland of the city. Inner city Windmill Hill climbs from the Avon south of Temple Meads station, its tumbling terraces providing a solid Labour vote; Bedminster to the west is also a Labour-voting inner ward. However, much of Bristol South consists of housing estates tucked amid the downs. Knowle is a mixed, suburban area, but Filwood, Hartcliffe, Southville and Whitchurch Park are council estates of varying vintages and accessibility to the city centre. Filwood in particular is extremely deprived, ranking 221st on the government's index of multiple deprivation. All these wards are safely Labour. The two non-Labour wards in Bristol South are Hengrove, a suburban three way marginal, and Bishopsworth. Bishopsworth is a working class, rather deprived ward in the south west of Bristol which the Conservatives won by a large majority in 1999 despite its previously marginal status. There is some Green and left wing opinion in Windmill Hill in particular. These slight elements of political variety do not make Bristol South anything other than a very safe Labour seat which has voted for the party at every general election since 1935. Labour's most dangerous moment here was 1987, when their majority fell to only 1,404 following the deselection of Michael Cocks as MP; he had fought off Tony Benn in 1983 when parts of Benn's old Bristol South East were added to the constituency, but fell in 1987. Since her shaky first election, Dawn Primarolo has built up a healthy majority and reasserted South's Labour tradition.

BRISTOL WEST

	2001		1997		1992 notional	
Electorate and turnout	84,821	65.6	85,275	73.5	77,906	76.3
Conservative	16,040	28.8	20,575	32.8	26,850	45.1
Labour	20,505	36.8	22,068	35.2	13,900	23.4
Lib Dem	16,079	28.9	17,551	28.0	17,356	29.2
Anti–EU	490	0.9	1,304	2.1	–	–
Green	1,961	3.5	852	1.4	906	1.5
Others	590		291 (2)		465 (4)	
MP	Valerie Davey (Lab)		Valerie Davey (Lab)		William Waldegrave (Con)	
Majority	4,426	8.0	1,493	2.4	9,494	16.0

The Conservatives' third place in Bristol West in 2001 was a dramatic illustration of the decline of the Tories as a party of the professional middle class. The seat contains many of the most attractive areas of Bristol including Clifton and Stoke Bishop, plus the suburban heartland of Westbury-on-Trym. The Clifton area is strongly influenced by the university and as a whole the constituency has one of Britain's most educated and intellectual electorates. The Conservatives held the seat, usually with a big majority, at every election from its creation in 1885 until Cabinet Minister William Waldegrave was defeated thanks to a Labour surge from third place in 1997.

Labour are by no means secure in Bristol West. In local elections the Liberal Democrats tend to outpoll the other parties in the constituency, with a particularly strong base in the Clifton area (they led comfortably in the local elections in Bristol West on the same day as the 2001 general election). They pose a strong potential challenge if they can either attract disillusioned intellectual Labour voters or Conservative tactical support. The Conservatives are far from down and out either, and the Labour vote has been eroded at the fringe by the Green Party (who polled 3.5 per cent in 2001), so Bristol West has the making of a fascinating battle to come – although perhaps for only one more election.

Bristol West, currently oversized, will be radically altered in the boundary changes. It loses three extremely middle class outer western suburbs (where there are few Labour voters) to Bristol North West and gains in recompense a very different area from Bristol East: the wards of Easton and Lawrence Hill (where there are virtually no Conservatives). Its centre of gravity shifts definitively to Bristol's city centre. The partisan effect of this will eliminate the Conservatives from contention here and make Bristol West a moderately safe Labour seat with a Liberal Democrat presence.

KINGSWOOD

	2001		1997		1992 notional	
Electorate and turnout	81,602	64.6	77,221	77.6	76,320	84
Conservative	14,941	28.4	17,928	29.9	29,562	45.8
Labour	28,903	54.9	32,181	53.7	26,222	40.6
Lib Dem	7,747	14.7	7,672	12.8	8,771	13.6
Anti–EU	1,085	2.1	1,463	2.4	–	–
Others	–		643 (3)		–	
MP	Roger Berry (Lab)		Roger Berry (Lab)		Roger Berry (Lab)	
Majority	13,962	26.5	14,253	23.8	3,340*	5.2*

* Estimated Conservative majority allowing for boundary changes

Kingswood is the urban sprawl to the east of Bristol: the industrial area of Mangotsfield, residential Oldland, Downend and Hanham and a desultory shopping centre at Staple Hill. It also extends into Bristol's eastern fringe at Frome Vale and Hillfields, which is pretty indistinguishable from the rest of the seat. Its lack of distinct identity is reflected in the regularity with which bits of it are swapped and shifted to and from other constituencies at boundary reviews. It is home to a large number of skilled workers in engineering and other trades – a classic 'C2' seat in the jargon used in the 1980s before we had heard of Essex Man and Worcester Woman.

Labour's Roger Berry gained the seat (on different boundaries, naturally) in 1992 and held it with a large swing in his favour in 1997 and another improved showing in 2001. It is possible that Kingswood might swing back a long way if Labour disappoint badly – it has swung 22 per cent to Labour since 1987 compared to 10 per cent for the nation as a whole, without major demographic change. It is clearly a volatile area.

The next set of boundary changes will carve up Kingswood all over again. It loses all its Bristol city territory to Bristol East and its northern end to the new seat of Filton & Bradley Stoke, and in recompense dips further to the south by taking some suburbs (Bitton and Hanham Abbotts) from Wansdyke. This area has Liberal Democrat tendencies in local elections but supported Labour in the general election. This does not affect Kingswood's allegiances much but makes the successor to the current Wansdyke seat much harder for Labour.

NORTHAVON

	2001		1997		1992 notional	
Electorate and turnout	78,840	70.7	79,011	79.1	74,496	84.7
Conservative	19,340	34.7	24,363	39.0	32,700	51.8
Labour	6,450	11.6	9,767	15.6	7,625	12.1
Lib Dem	29,217	52.4	26,500	42.4	21,759	34.5
Anti–EU	751	1.3	1,900	3.0	–	–
Others					1,049 (2)	
MP	Steve Webb (LD)		Steve Webb (LD)		John Cope (Con)	
Majority	9,877	17.7	2,137		10,941	17.3

Northavon has been a boom area in recent years, with only 1.0 per cent unemployment at the time of the 2001 election. It is less like a British New Town than it is like an American suburb, with a young population and high levels of car ownership. The main employers, excepting the NHS, are modern ones – Hewlett Packard, Ministry of Defence and BAe. The Lib Dems have been astute in realising the potential of community politics in an area like this, of high mobility and fluid political allegiances, and there is a cascade of *Focus* newsletters through Northavon's letterboxes.

Yate is essentially a small New Town adjacent to the older village of Chipping Sodbury, and is the most working class area of the seat. It now votes solidly Liberal Democrat. Thornbury is more middle class and Tory, but it too has succumbed to Lib Dem activism, and the satellite town of Bradley Stoke has been an area of rapid growth since the 1980s. The Liberal Democrats nearly monopolised local election representation in the area in the 1999 elections for South Gloucestershire. Yate carried the seat for the Lib Dems in 1997, but all areas (except rural fringes by the Severn and at Badminton) fell into line in 2001. Steve Webb's second victory was remarkably comfortable, a textbook example of how to win an election as an incumbent. Lib Dem material hammered home the same messages, promoting Webb's personal vote, attacking the Tories as a backward-looking force and encouraging Labour tactical votes. The Conservatives put up a reasonably good fight, and had a strong if somewhat divisive candidate in Carrie Ruxton, but were still trounced.

Northavon is a rather oversized seat, and with Bristol NW and Kingswood giving up their northern-most wards there is enough electorate to produce two seats in this area. The core of Northavon will become Thornbury & Yate, whose electoral prospects will be similar to the old seat. The joker in the pack is the entirely new seat of Filton & Bradley Stoke, which closely follows the M4 corridor from Downend and Staple Hill over to the Severn Bridges. The Lib Dems are strong in the ex-Northavon portions, Labour lead in the ex-Kingswood part and the ex-Bristol NW part, although Tories are present throughout. In the 1999 local elections, when Labour had a narrow national lead, Labour led in this seat but only with 33.4 per cent of the vote to 32.2 per cent Lib Dems and 31.3 per cent Conservatives. The Boundary Commission have produced a fascinating potential three-way contest and a headache for all party strategists.

WANSDYKE

	2001		1997		1992 notional	
Electorate and turnout	70,850	69.9	69,270	79.0	68,742	85.8
Conservative	17,593	35.5	19,318	35.3	27,852	47.2
Labour	23,206	46.8	24,117	44.1	16,082	27.3
Lib Dem	7,135	14.4	9,205	16.8	13,921	23.6
Anti–EU	655	1.3	1,765 (2)	3.2	–	–
Others	958		317 (2)		1,150	
MP	Dan Norris (Lab)		Dan Norris (Lab)		Jack Aspinwall (Con)	
Majority	5,613	11.3	4,799	8.8	11,770	19.9

Wansdyke is a mixture of rural, suburban and small town elements, of a kind that normally produces a Conservative outcome in southern England. The suburbs are normal enough – Keynsham is a politically mixed town set between Bath and Bristol which supplies commuters to both and has a strongly Labour estate on the south side of town, while Saltford is a Conservative stronghold. Wansdyke also includes suburbs such as Bitton and Hanham which are marginal. Some of the north Somerset countryside is Conservative – the Chew Valley area in the west of the seat and the villages around Bath in the east – but much of it is quite working class and Labour voting, thanks to the heritage of the long worked-out Somerset coalfield. Rural areas like Clutton, Timsbury, Publow and Whitchurch voted Labour in 1999 while the party was competitive in other bucolic areas such as Farmborough and High Littleton. Labour's advantage stacks up in the old mining towns of Radstock and Midsomer Norton – tough little places – and their outlying villages like Paulton and Peasedown St. John.

Despite its characteristics Labour had only won the north Somerset coalfield constituency three times – as Frome in 1923, 1929 and 1945 – before Dan Norris won in 1997 and held his seat with an increased majority in 2001. Norris was one of the most outspokenly anti-hunting MPs in the 1997 parliament and his victory was a major defeat for the hunting lobby. Rural voters, as results like this constituency and Labour wins in Stroud, South Dorset and other areas demonstrate, are not a uniform bloc influenced by 'countryside' issues.

Wansdyke loses the Bitton and Hanham area back to Kingswood in the boundary changes, and gains some affluent little villages from the Bath seat. This has the effect of making the revised seat (to be renamed North East Somerset) more rural and more favourable to the Conservatives with the loss of those volatile suburbs. Dan Norris's remarkable run of success may extend to a third victory, but seems likely to be terminated when the new boundaries come into effect.

WESTON-SUPER-MARE

	2001		1997		1992 notional	
Electorate and turnout	74,322	62.8	72,555	73.6	70,851	79.5
Conservative	18,086	38.7	20,133	37.7	27,063	48.1
Labour	9,235	19.8	9,557	17.9	6,420	11.4
Lib Dem	18,424	39.5	21,407	40.1	21,691	38.5
Anti–EU	650	1.4	2,280	4.3	–	–
Others	285 (2)		–		1,131	
MP	Brian Cotter (LD)		Brian Cotter (LD)		Jerry Wiggin (Con)	
Majority	338	0.7	1,274	2.4	5,372	9.6

Weston-super-Mare gave Jeffrey Archer and John Cleese to the world – Archer's family, strangely, took over a flat from the Cleese family. Archer wears the town's name with pride in his peerage, although whether Weston is so proud of the connection is another matter. For the most part Archer's Conservatism has prevailed, but in 1997 Weston came into line with the Cleese tradition by voting for the Liberal Democrats. It was yet another Conservative defeat in a seaside resort constituency. Weston is quite close to Bristol and has been able to counteract the decline of the English holiday resort and its own dubious charms in this respect (cynics call it Weston-super-Mud) by developing as a commuting and day trip centre.

The portents for the 2001 election suggested a Conservative gain, with very poor Liberal Democrat performances in the local and European elections in 1999, but Brian Cotter kept the swing below 1 per cent and squeaked home with the second smallest majority among the 52-strong body of Liberal Democrats. Losing the council, as the Torbay result demonstrated even more, can be a blessing in disguise for a Lib Dem MP. The closeness of the 2001 result may also help the Lib Dems here to squeeze the Labour vote as they have not succeeded in doing up until now. It could be tougher for the Tories than it looks on paper; and the fact that the most prominent Tory associated with the town is currently in prison cannot help.

WOODSPRING

	2001		1997		*1992 notional*	
Electorate and turnout	71,018	68.7	70,069	78.4	*68,755*	*80.5*
Conservative	21,297	43.7	24,425	44.4	*29,529*	*53.3*
Labour	12,499	25.6	11,377	20.7	*6,863*	*12.4*
Lib Dem	11,816	24.2	16,691	30.4	*17,523*	*31.7*
Anti–EU	452	0.9	1,641	3.0	*–*	*–*
Green	1,282	2.6	667	1.2	*749*	*1.3*
Independent	1,412	2.9	–	–	*–*	*–*
Others	–		153 (2)		*696 (2)*	
MP	Liam Fox (Con)		Liam Fox (Con)		Liam Fox (Con)	
Majority	8,798	18.0	7,734	14.1	*12,006*	*21.7*

Woodspring is the last Tory seat in Avon. It is a mixture of plush Bristol suburbs just across the Clifton suspension bridge and several smaller towns. Seaside Clevedon is the largest, with 23,000 population; Nailsea is a part of the former Somerset coalfield and has – with the neighbouring area of Backwell – 25,000 people. Portishead, near the modernised Royal Portbury Dock, is a bit smaller with 12,500 although it has been designated an area of future growth. Economically, there is substantial commuting as well as local employment in branches of large companies. The Conservatives are strong in all its component parts. In the early 1990s it looked like a Liberal Democrat long shot similar to Northavon, and they achieved a lead in the votes cast in the 1995 local elections, but their prospects have deteriorated here and in 2001 they ceded second place to Labour.

Labour candidate Chanel Stevens, a businessman, achieved a very good result for the party in 2001. Stevens was elected a district councillor in Clevedon in 1999, a reflection of Labour's growth in the area in recent years which has been concentrated in Clevedon. Liam Fox is a young, rightwing Shadow Cabinet member although his position as the star of the 1992 intake has faded compared to Iain Duncan Smith. The boundary changes in this area are minimal but the seat is renamed North Somerset. Under whatever guise this constituency is safely Conservative.

Bedfordshire including Luton

	Conservative		Labour		Liberal Democrat		Others	
	Share of vote	Seats	Share of vote	Seats	Share of vote	Seats	Share of vote	Seats
2001	39.4	3	42.8	3	14.8	0	3.1	0
1997	38.6	3	44.0	3	12.8	0	4.6	0
1992	53.2	5	30.3	0	14.8	0	1.7	0
1987	54.2	5	24.2	0	21.1	0	0.5	0
1983	51.0	5	22.6	0	26.3	0	0.1	0

Bedfordshire is a small county, particularly after the excision of Luton from its administrative boundaries, but it has considerable internal variety. It has a long history as a transitional zone, with Bedford marking the southern edge of the Danelaw and in more recent times the influence of London being strong in the south and fading towards the north of the county. Bedford itself is more of an East Midlands town than a London satellite; parts in the west of the county are at the bleak north end of the Chilterns, or look to Milton Keynes, and an area of the east is influenced by Cambridge. The south of the county, around Luton and Dunstable, is heavily industrialised, the middle has a number of slightly odd industries such as brick making and cereal bar manufacture, plus comfortable villages, and the north, other than Bedford, is primarily fertile flatlands where market gardening and arable farming take place. Across the county distribution and transport are important employers, reflecting its strategic location.

Bedfordshire's political history is quite unusual. Before 1945 Labour hardly featured, but in that year the party suddenly gained two of the three seats (Luton and Bedford, then incorporating rural hinterlands). The Conservatives reasserted their strength in 1950, winning Luton and Bedford back, and in 1951 Labour lost South Bedfordshire which had been created in 1950. Since 1945 Luton has been a bellwether marginal, only getting one election 'wrong' (1950, when Charles Hill won under the odd description 'Conservative and Liberal'), even when the seat has been divided in two since 1974. Labour won Bedford and South Beds in 1966, but lost them both in 1970 and in the case of South Beds did not recover it even in 1997 (although the old seat contained some Labour-voting areas of Luton which would have tipped the balance). Bedfordshire, like other eastern counties, has seen a long term movement to the Conservatives in its rural areas which the 1997 election did not completely reverse.

Luton, on the other hand, seems more loyal to Labour than it used to be, after a serious flirtation with Thatcherism in the 1980s. It bears a strong resemblance socially and politically to places like Slough and Reading. Luton has a very young population (24.4 per cent of Lutonians are aged under 16 and 13.5 per cent are of pension age, compared to 20.4 per cent and 18.1 per cent in the UK in 1998), a significant Asian community (a tiny but noisy number of Islamic extremists among them), industry, an airport, and relatively low levels of deprivation. The town is light on history and local identity, although the borough council is currently active in encouraging the arts and the university has added status to Luton. It is an aspirant for recognition as a city. The other large town, Bedford, is also Labour inclined and the borough (which includes rural territory) was 10 per cent non-white in 1991. The rural areas are mostly very Conservative, with not much Liberal Democrat strength of the sort found in counties to the south and west in local elections. The 1997 boundary changes separated Bedford and Luton from their hinterlands and made them relatively safe for Labour, while creating two very solid Tory rural seats. The only close marginal now, Beds South West, is made up mostly of two smaller urban areas, Dunstable and Leighton Buzzard.

Local government

Bedfordshire county council is currently Conservative controlled with a majority of 3 following the 2001 county elections. From 1997 to 2001 the Tories ran it with a majority of one seat, which had been won by 2 votes in the county elections; from 1981 until 1997 it had been a hung council, although it then included Luton. Bedfordshire is very marginal.

Luton became a unitary authority in 1997. It currently has a strong Labour majority dating from all-out elections in 1999; Labour have run the borough since 1991 and seem highly likely to retain the town in the next round of local elections. The Conservatives ran the town in the 1980s but in 1995 and 1999 were reduced to only one ward, the Lib Dems providing the main opposition to Labour.

There is nothing particularly striking about the politics of the Bedfordshire district councils. Bedford borough elects annually and is perennially hung, with Labour and Liberal Democrats strong in the town and the Conservatives dominating the rural hinterland. South Bedfordshire, also electing annually, sees large swings in votes and representation and is currently Conservative led. There were all-out elections on new ward boundaries in 2002 for both councils which did not produce change in control in either case, though the Conservatives will hope to gain Bedford next time. Mid Bedfordshire elects every four years and has had a strong Conservative majority since 1999, although Labour polled well in 1995.

Boundary review

Bedfordshire with Luton remains entitled to six seats and boundary changes are likely to be minor following the major changes in 1997. Luton's unitary status may mean that the small rural area in Luton South is transferred to Beds SW with a possible ripple effect to Beds Mid.

BEDFORD

	2001		1997		1992 notional	
Electorate and turnout	67,762	59.9	66,560	73.5	65,764	76.5
Conservative	13,297	32.8	16,474	33.7	22,863	45.4
Labour	19,454	47.9	24,774	50.6	18,318	36.4
Lib Dem	6,425	15.8	6,044	12.3	8,263	16.4
Anti–EU	430	1.1	1,503	3.1	–	–
Others	973		149		881	
MP	Patrick Hall (Lab)		Patrick Hall (Lab)		Trevor Skeet (Con) Bedfordshire North	
Majority	6,157	15.2	8,300	17.0	4,545	9.0

Bedford has only been a Labour seat at times of national landslide – 1945, 1966, 1997 and 2001. In the first two, the wins were by microscopic margins (288 votes and 378 votes respectively), but in the most recent elections Labour have had comfortable victories. Even in bad elections nationally for Labour, such as Euro 1999 and the 2000 local elections, Labour have still done quite well in Bedford.

Part of the reason is that the current Bedford seat is tightly drawn around the town, without the substantial rural element that helped the Conservatives stay in the lead in the past. Bedford is a gritty, multicultural town with prominent Irish, black, Italian, Asian and Greek communities, a mix of industries and also rather good cultural and educational facilities. It is less of a regional centre than it might be, perhaps lacking a substantial university to make the town complete. It lies on the frontiers of the south east and the east Midlands and bears some comparison with towns to its north like Wellingborough and Kettering.

The inner urban wards of Bedford, where there are most Asian and black residents living in Victorian terraces and blocks of flats, are Labour strongholds – Cauldwell, Queen's Park and Harpur. The Liberal Democrats, at least in local elections, are strong in the northern suburban wards such as Brickhill, De Parys and Goldington (though the Conservatives made gains here in 2002), and have received 29 per cent in local elections in 1997 and 2001 across the constituency. Kempston, across the Ouse from Bedford proper and never sure whether it is really part of Bedford or a separate little town, is marginally Labour. In the 2001 county elections none of the Bedford wards voted Conservative, although in a reasonable year (such as 2002) they can win Castle and suburban Newnham.

In 1997 more than half of the local Lib Dem vote failed to transfer across to the party's general election candidate on the same day; Labour benefited from a 9 per cent boost in share of the vote while the Tories were only 4.5 per cent better off. Rather fewer Lib Dems voted tactically in 2001, but Labour still gained 6 per cent and the Conservatives 3 per cent in the general election compared to the local elections. Tactical voting is yet another handicap for the Tories in Bedford.

BEDFORDSHIRE MID

	2001		1997		1992 notional	
Electorate and turnout	70,794	65.9	66,521	78.9	60,723	83.3
Conservative	22,109	47.4	24,176	46.0	31,561	62.4
Labour	14,043	30.1	17,086	32.5	10,016	19.8
Lib Dem	9,205	19.7	8,823	16.8	7,973	15.8
Anti–EU	1,281	2.7	2,257	4.3	–	–
Others	–		174		1,022	
MP	Jonathan Sayeed (Con)		Jonathan Sayeed (Con)		NEW SEAT	
Majority	8,066	17.3	7,090	13.5	21,545	42.6

Like most constituencies with 'Mid' in their title this seat is a bit of a ragbag. The two principal towns are Ampthill and Flitwick although it covers a large acreage of the county between Bedford and Luton. Most of it is in the Mid Bedfordshire district, but it also includes a few wards of South Bedfordshire around Barton-le-Clay and a rural part of Bedford borough at Wootton. It contains the main campus of the business-oriented Cranfield University, which unusually has its own small airport. The constituency was radically altered from the previous version in the 1990s boundary changes.

Parts of Mid Beds are convenient for commuting into London along the Thameslink line, and the southern end around Harlington looks to St. Albans. Mid Beds is uniformly middle class and affluent (with low deprivation scores) if not particularly prestigious or beautiful – parts of it look lunar because of quarrying and brickworks around Maulden and Stewartby. One unlikely boast of Mid Bedfordshire is that it has the biggest hole in the ground in Europe.

Mid Beds is an extremely safe Conservative seat, although the chill winds of competition blew in the mid 1990s with a strong Labour showing in the meltdown local elections of 1995 and a drastically reduced majority in 1997. However, all the county council wards in the constituency except Barton voted Conservative in 2001 and it is a safe haven for Jonathan Sayeed, displaced from Bristol East in 1992.

BEDFORDSHIRE NORTH EAST

	2001		1997		1992 notional	
Electorate and turnout	69,877	64.8	65,308	77.2	62,068	84.4
Conservative	22,586	49.9	22,311	44.3	31,081	59.3
Labour	14,009	31.0	16,428	32.6	10,478	20.0
Lib Dem	7,409	16.4	7,179	14.2	9,706	18.5
Anti–EU	1,242	2.7	2,490	4.9	–	–
Ind. Con.	–	–	1,842	3.7	–	–
Others	–		138		1,127	
MP	Alistair Burt (Con)		Nicholas Lyell (Con)		Nicholas Lyell (Con)	
					Bedfordshire Mid	
Majority	8,577	19.0	5,883	11.7	20,603	39.3

Bedfordshire North East is a mainly rural seat around Bedford, including the northern tip of the county near Milton Keynes. The main urban settlements are the small towns of Sandy and Biggleswade, bypassed by the A1 in the east of the county, and a few fringe areas around Bedford.

There is substantial arable farming and market gardening in the north of Bedfordshire, and the agricultural influence pervades the towns; Biggleswade is a dusty agro–industrial town where cereal bar manufacture is a major concern. Sandy is more famous as the headquarters of the Royal Society for the Protection of Birds; there are a few London commuters using the Great Northern line into King's Cross from these towns and Arlesey, and some influence from Cambridge. The farming areas are safely Conservative in politics, but the towns are marginal. The Bedford fringes, Clapham and Bromham, are also Conservative strongholds, and further out at Harrold is huntin' and shootin' territory, adding up to a safe Tory seat where it is surprising that Labour got as close as they did in 1997.

Alistair Burt was previously the MP for Bury North, which he held from 1983 to 1997 with the aid of a significant personal vote. He achieved a good result in Beds NE in 2001, albeit with the help of the disappearance of an Independent Conservative who polled 3.7 per cent in 1997. This is a very safe Conservative constituency.

BEDFORDSHIRE SOUTH WEST

	2001		1997		1992 *notional*	
Electorate and turnout	70,666	62.1	69,781	75.8	*69,727*	*82.0*
Conservative	18,477	42.1	21,534	40.7	*32,000*	*56.2*
Labour	17,701	40.4	21,402	40.5	*14,660*	*25.7*
Lib Dem	6,473	14.8	7,559	14.3	*9,475*	*16.6*
Anti–EU	1,203	2.7	2,207 (2)	4.2	–	–
Others	–		162		*818*	
MP	Andrew Selous (Con)		David Madel (Con)		David Madel (Con)	
Majority	776	1.8	132	0.2	*17,340*	*30.5*

Bedfordshire South West was a near miss for Labour in both 1997 and 2001. In the former it was a pleasant surprise for them to get so close, while in 2001 it was a frustrating defeat. Labour had not managed, despite the replacement of long-serving moderate MP David Madel with right wing newcomer Andrew Selous, to overcome a slender Tory lead; it seems possible that the contrast between this seat and Dorset South, where Labour overcame greater odds to win, is down to party organisation. Beds SW is a seat which seems prone to exaggerate national trends, swinging wildly to the Conservatives in the 1980s only for Labour to surge back in 1997. This tendency applies also to local elections – Labour did particularly well here in 1995 and very badly in 2000.

Beds SW is rather a strange seat. It is based around two urban centres, Dunstable and Leighton Buzzard, with only a small rural population in between the two towns. Dunstable is an ugly place, sprawling along the A5 and part of a continuous built up area with Luton. Its population is drawn mostly from the skilled working class, who are employed mainly in local distribution and manufacturing or else in Luton, but despite its social base it is a Tory town in all but the very best Labour years – the Tories led 46-39 in its wards in the 2001 local elections. Dunstable's northern satellite, the largely poor and council-built Houghton Regis, is the only area in the seat where the Conservatives do poorly, and taken together Dunstable and Houghton produced a Labour lead of 173 votes and half the votes cast in the seat.

About a third of the votes cast in Beds SW are in Leighton Buzzard, including Linslade. Leighton-Linslade is close to the Buckinghamshire border and its centre, with its wide High Street, resembles Thame or Buckingham. Its outskirts are a mixture of scrubby estates and some plush new-build executive housing for the commuters using the rail services into London or Milton Keynes. The votes in Leighton-Linslade in 2001 went 37 per cent Conservative, 32 per cent Labour and 29 per cent Lib Dem in the local elections. Labour polled about 5 per cent better across the constituency in the general election than the local elections, while the Conservatives did less than 1 per cent better; some might have been tactical voting in Leighton-Linslade for Labour's Andrew Date, a local man. It was not quite enough, however, for Date to win. The remainder of the constituency, the rural element around Eaton Bray and Stanbridge, is heavily Conservative and in the last couple of general elections has tipped the balance in this complex and hard fought seat.

LUTON NORTH

	2001		1997		1992 notional	
Electorate and turnout	67,554	57.9	64,618	73.2	64,559	81.2
Conservative	12,210	31.2	16,234	34.3	26,853	51.2
Labour	22,187	56.7	25,860	54.6	19,496	37.2
Lib Dem	3,795	9.7	4,299	9.1	5,311	10.1
Anti–EU	934	2.4	689	1.5	–	–
Others	–		250		750	
MP	Kelvin Hopkins (Lab)		Kelvin Hopkins (Lab)		John Carlisle (Con)	
Majority	9,977	25.5	9,626	20.3	7,357	14.0

Both Luton seats returned large Labour majorities in the last two general elections, reflecting the national swing and the traditional marginality of the town. Glamorous Luton is not, but it is a productive place with a modern economic base. As early as the 1960s it was a test-bed for social research about the apparently 'instrumental' attitudes and voting behaviour of skilled workers. It has been won by the winning party in the general election in every election since 1951, and since it was divided in 1974 both seats have moved in tandem.

North is a rather more polarised place than South; it contains both the high class residential area of Icknield (the only Conservative ward in the town) and the estates of Leagrave and Sundon Park. It was previously the seat of John Carlisle, one of the most right wing Conservative MPs in the House, but has now switched to the relatively left wing Kelvin Hopkins, who rebelled several times in the 1997 parliament. Luton's trend to Labour has continued since the 1997 election. Labour did well in Luton in the borough elections of May 1999, winning seven out of eight wards in North (no change since 1995), then kept ahead in the 1999 Euro election and held the seat with an increased majority in 2001. Although Luton now seems a solid Labour town, a word of caution is in order. The Conservatives wiped out what seemed comfortable Labour majorities in 1979 and by 1987 seemed to have a lock on the town, with control of the council and increased majorities in both seats – only for that power base to crumble away. Luton is a volatile place.

LUTON SOUTH

	2001		1997		1992 notional	
Electorate and tutnout	71,439	55.1	68,395	70.4	66,027	78.4
Conservative	11,586	29.4	15,109	31.4	22,928	44.3
Labour	21,719	55.2	26,428	54.8	22,396	43.2
Lib Dem	4,292	10.9	4,610	9.6	5,795	11.2
Anti–EU	578	1.5	1,595 (2)	3.3	–	–
Others	1,176 (3)		442 (2)		676	
MP	Margaret Moran (Lab)		Margaret Moran (Lab)		Graham Bright (Con)	
Majority	10,133	25.8	11,319	23.5	532	1.0

The southern side of Luton contains the rapidly developing airport, where 7,000 people work. The airport is something of a success story, having been given a facelift in 1999 and nearly trebled passenger numbers in five years. However, the other major employer, Vauxhall Motors, closed in March 2002 after 97 years of car production, a major problem for the town as over 2,000 jobs will disappear; although losses will affect areas across south Bedfordshire and north Hertfordshire, Luton South will bear the brunt. However, suppliers to Vauxhall will stay in business supplying GM's Cheshire plant, and the East of England Development Agency (EEDA) is investing in retraining, with the large site likely to be redeveloped.

The seat also contains the town centre, dominated by an outsize Arndale Centre, and most of the Asian population of the town in Dallow and Biscot wards. Dallow also houses Luton Town football club. South is a working and lower middle class area, but some more rural leavening is provided by two South Bedfordshire wards in a strip of territory between Luton and Harpenden.

The Conservatives had a tenacious hold on Luton South in the 1980s, hanging on narrowly in 1992, but Labour's Margaret Moran swept to a massive majority in 1997, and Luton has been loyal to Labour since in all elections. There were no Labour losses in Luton in the 1999 local elections, and even in the Euro election Labour were 7.6 per cent ahead, a precursor of the Labour hold with a favourable swing in 2001. In general elections Luton South is a two-party fight but in local elections the Liberal Democrats have tightened their hold on three eastern suburban wards, including Crawley (site of the airport and Vauxhall works) and Stopsley, and run second to Labour across the constituency.

Berkshire (former county of)

	Conservative		Labour		Liberal Democrat		Others	
	Share of vote	Seats	Share of vote	Seats	Share of vote	Seats	Share of vote	Seats
2001	40.2	4	30.7	3	26.0	1	3.1	0
1997	42.2	4	28.5	3	24.6	1	4.7	0
1992	55.3	7	19.8	0	23.5	0	1.4	0
1987	56.7	7	17.3	0	25.0	0	1.0	0
1983	54.7	7	16.0	0	28.1	0	1.2	0

The county of Berkshire stretches west of Greater London along the Thames valley corridor; the M4 and the Great Western railway line being the principal transport arteries. London's influence is strong, particularly in the east of Berkshire. Slough is effectively an extension of west London areas like Hayes and Southall, with their large Asian population, industrial base and proximity to Heathrow airport. Further out there is Berkshire's commuterland: Maidenhead and the pleasant riverside villages like Cookham and Wargrave, plus Windsor and its hinterland, although in practice people commute from as far as the villages west of Newbury.

Berkshire's main town of Reading was formerly reliant on three industries – bulbs (Sutton seeds), beer and most famously Huntly & Palmer biscuits, but all these industries closed in the 1970s and have been replaced by new business. Economic modernity is a common feature of Berkshire towns like Newbury, Wokingham, Reading, Maidenhead and Bracknell. Only Cambridgeshire is a serious rival to it as the high-tech centre of southern England, with all sorts of computer, mobile phone and internet related information technologies being represented in locally-generated employment by firms such as Oracle, Vodafone and Microsoft. Some analysts referred to this area as the 'dot.com corridor' in 1999–2000, but the bursting of the dot.com bubble leaves one looking for a new label for the area – 'Silicon Valley' is the local favourite. Financial services and corporate headquarters also line the M4. Berkshire's population is young and well-educated; in 1998 the pension-age population was only 14.6 per cent, compared to 18.1 per cent in the UK as a whole, with particularly young populations in Bracknell Forest (12.6 per cent) and Slough (13.2 per cent). In Bracknell Forest and Wokingham in particular there has been strong recent population growth. Reading has also invested in itself as a shopping centre and upgraded itself into Britain's thirteenth most significant shopping venue. Unsurprisingly, it is a serious aspirant for city status.

In the far west of Berkshire there is some genuinely rural agricultural territory, although much of Berkshire's countryside is appreciated for its aesthetic appeal rather than used for farming. The whole of the county has low levels of deprivation, with none of its wards scoring in the most deprived thousand wards and over thirty numbering among the thousand most fortunate wards. Even peripheral council estates, like

Whitley in Reading, are comparatively not that badly off, and Windsor & Maidenhead, Bracknell Forest and Wokingham council areas in particular have some concentrated districts of wealth and privilege.

Berkshire is traditionally Conservative. Labour have a strong history in 1930s-built Slough, only losing the seat in 1964, 1983, 1987 and very narrowly 1992, but Slough was a part of Buckinghamshire until 1974. Depending on where the boundaries are drawn in Reading, that town has proved capable of voting Labour even in close elections like 1923, 1929, 1950 and 1955. However, since 1974 Labour's task has been made more difficult because Reading has been split into two seats both of which draw in suburban and rural territory. Labour overcame this problem, and then some, in 1997 and 2001. Berkshire was the county with the highest swing to Labour in 2001, a tribute to particular political factors in Reading but also the association of New Labour with prosperity and stability. It was a frightening result for the Conservatives to slip even further back in such a modern, prosperous, booming county, where previously such growth would have tended to cement their position. Maidenhead now looks quite vulnerable, and even Bracknell is possibly endangered by Labour's strength and potential boundary changes.

Local government
Berkshire was the only traditional county council to be abolished in the 1990s local government review; the other victims were all new and unloved creations (Avon, Cleveland, Hereford & Worcester, Humberside). County council functions were dispersed to Berkshire's previous district councils, all of which became unitary authorities. The Conservatives did so badly in the final elections for the county in 1993 that they had fewer councillors either than Labour or the Liberal Democrats, which cannot have endeared the place to the then government.

Labour's enormous majority on Reading borough council is a tribute to years of work by Reading's strong and active Labour Party. At the time of writing, Labour had not lost a seat on the council since 1983, and the council prides itself on its standard of services (including the nation's most generous pensioner bus pass system, which keeps this group – who turn out and vote – happy) and the new investment in the town. Slough is also overwhelmingly Labour in local politics, although in some wards the continuing Liberal Party is a significant presence.

Bracknell Forest (as the council is now known) was Labour in 1995 but the Conservatives regained it in the 1997 unitary elections and have run it since. In the 1980s it was 100 per cent Conservative, but there now seems a well-established minority Labour group. West Berkshire (Newbury and around), Windsor & Maidenhead and Wokingham councils are closely contested between Conservatives and Liberal Democrats with Labour hardly featuring. The Conservatives regained outright control of Wokingham in 2002.

Boundary review
Berkshire is entitled to 8.3 seats, which means that it should retain its current allocation of 8 seats although each will be rather large. Bracknell is the largest seat and will need to be reduced a little; Labour will want to chip off as many strong Conservative wards to the Windsor and Wokingham constituencies as possible. Although all its authorities are unitary, the old county is still the statutory unit of account for the parliamentary boundary review.

BRACKNELL

	2001		1997		1992 notional	
Electorate and turnout	81,118	60.7	79,292	74.5	69,433	85.6
Conservative	22,962	46.6	27,983	47.4	35,916	60.4
Labour	16,249	33.0	17,596	29.8	12,036	20.2
Lib Dem	8,428	17.1	9,122	15.4	11,511	19.4
Anti–EU	1,266	2.6	2,205 (2)	3.7	–	–
Ind Lab	–	–	1,909	3.2	–	–
Others	324		276		–	
MP	Andrew MacKay (Con)		Andrew MacKay (Con)		Andrew MacKay (Con)	
					Berkshire East	
Majority	6,713	13.6	10,387	17.6	23,880	40.2

Bracknell is the only New Town seat the Conservatives held in the general elections of 1997 and 2001. This exceptionalism reflects the fact that most of Bracknell was built later and more by private development than, say, Basildon and Harlow. While those were predominantly working class New Towns, Bracknell has more middle class characteristics, with 42 per cent of its population in professional or managerial social groups compared to 28 per cent in Harlow and 35 per cent in marginal Hemel Hempstead.

The Bracknell seat also contains an area to the south west of the town based around Crowthorne and Sandhurst, which rather resembles brash, affluent Surrey Heath just across the border. As one would expect there is military influence around Sandhurst; Crowthorne is home to Wellington School (the one Jeffrey Archer did not attend). Broadmoor secure hospital makes up a trio of institutions. The territory outside Bracknell is extremely Conservative.

Labour virtually ceased to exist in the area in the 1980s but Bracknell clearly warmed to New Labour. Labour ran the borough council from 1995 to 1997, and the party has edged closer to contention in the 2001 election in the absence of a splinter candidate as in 1997. Bracknell is an oversized seat and it is likely that the areas to be removed in a subsequent boundary review will be among the Tories' best – the wards from Wokingham. Bracknell is still hardly a marginal seat, but the Conservatives may have to look over their shoulder here in future elections.

MAIDENHEAD

	2001		1997		1992 notional	
Electorate and turnout	69,837	62.0	67,302	75.6	66,059	83.5
Conservative	19,506	45.0	25,344	49.8	33,958	61.6
Labour	6,577	15.2	9,205	18.1	4,741	8.6
Lib Dem	16,222	37.4	13,363	26.3	16,462	29.8
Anti–EU	741	1.7	1,915 (2)	3.8	–	–
Others	272		1,062 (2)		–	
MP	Theresa May (Con)		Theresa May (Con)		Michael Trend (Con) Windsor & Maidenhead	
Majority	3,284	7.6	11,981	23.5	17,496	31.7

Maidenhead produced a most ominous result for the Conservatives in the June 2001 general election. It had still looked a very safe seat even in 1997, but in 2001 the Liberal Democrats surged to within sniffing distance of unseating Shadow Cabinet member Theresa May. Since 1992 it has declined from being the 75th safest Tory seat in the land to the twelfth most vulnerable Tory seat to the Lib Dems.

Maidenhead itself is a prosperous commuter town in the Thames Valley between Reading and Slough – although most Maidenhead people have little to do with that industrial town, as they work in office and technological employment in Maidenhead itself, London or Reading. Maidenhead town tends to vote Liberal Democrat in local elections, as does Twyford (the next town along the main rail line to Reading), but the remainder of the constituency is more rural and Conservative in places such as Hurst and Wargrave. Maidenhead is the highest-status and most affluent constituency in Berkshire, and it is a sign of the Conservative Party's devastatingly weak showing among the professional and educated classes in June 2001 that it is now a marginal. Labour's candidate in 2001 was writer John O'Farrell, who wrote entertainingly about trying to persuade millionaires to support the minimum wage. His comment on the Lib Dem surge was:

> "good luck to them". The rise in tactical voting across the country is an expression of the electorate's exasperation with the current system and we have to find a way to make people's votes really count. Otherwise the frustration and anger of the voters will finally boil over in places like Maidenhead. They'll tut and look skywards.

NEWBURY

	2001		1997		1992 notional	
Electorate and turnout	75,487	67.3	74,046	76.3	71,100	82.8
Conservative	22,092	43.5	21,370	37.8	32,898	55.9
Labour	3,523	6.9	3,107	5.5	3,584	6.1
Lib Dem	24,507	48.2	29,887	52.9	21,841	37.1
Anti–EU	685	1.3	1,294 (2)	2.3	–	–
Others	–		818 (2)		539	
MP	David Rendel (LD)		David Rendel (LD)		Judith Chaplin (Con)*	
Majority	2,415	4.8	8,517	15.1	11,057	18.8

* David Rendell (LD) elected at May 1993 by-election.

David Rendel's stunning 22,000-vote Liberal Democrat victory in the by-election here did not come out of the blue. They had run the Tories close in 1974 and taken over the council in 1991, and the tactical position was clear because Labour have never amounted to much in Newbury. Since 1997, the Conservatives have clawed their way back from their humiliation in 1993. Although the Lib Dems control the council, West Berkshire, the Conservatives gained several wards in the 2000 local elections and outpolled the Liberal Democrats by about three points in the Newbury constituency. In the 2001 general election they gave the Lib Dems a fright, with a significant swing in their favour. Richard Benyon, standing for the Tories a second time, is a well-established local figure who ran a strong campaign and rallied Tory support in this fairly rural constituency.

Newbury town is strong in high-tech industry and services, and has become so prosperous that there is nearly no unemployment and wages, even for very menial jobs, are high. Newbury is also close enough to London to house some metropolitan commuters and the west Berkshire countryside is an attractive part of the world; the constituency extends over a sparsely populated hinterland to the horsy downs around Lambourn. Newbury's problems are the envy of other towns – how to reconcile massive demand for new housing and employment with the pleasant local environment, and how to continue to attract business to a high-wage economy. The town, and its neighbour Thatcham, tend to support the Liberal Democrats but the rural areas, particularly to the west, are Conservative again. Newbury must be very high on the Conservative list of priorities.

READING EAST

	2001		1997		1992 notional	
Electorate and turnout	74,637	58.4	71,586	70.2	69,817	74.9
Conservative	13,943	32.0	17,666	35.2	25,699	49.1
Labour	19,538	44.8	21,461	42.7	15,115	28.9
Lib Dem	8,078	18.5	9,307	18.5	10,684	20.4
Anti–EU	525	1.2	1,294 (2)	2.6	–	–
Others	1,541 (3)		492 (2)		814	
MP	Jane Griffiths (Lab)		Jane Griffiths (Lab)		Gerard Vaughan (Con)	
Majority	5,595	12.8	3,795	7.6	10,584	20.2

A lot has been written about the decline in party activism, but it is alive and well in Reading and has made a great difference to election results. Labour's machine in Reading uses techniques developed by the Liberal Democrats to communicate with the electorate and build up loyalty. There are year-round deliveries of material including a borough wide paper the *Labour Banner*. Labour councillors distribute ward newsletters about every quarter, and the party engages in a lot of direct mailing. The Labour council in Reading has been popular, providing relatively generous services and presiding over redevelopments including the Oracle centre and the new football stadium; the council and the government benefit from the sense of progress and optimism in the area. The parliamentary seats both went Labour in 1997 and gave the party increased majorities in 2001.

The East constituency reaches into the town centre of Reading, including the inner wards of Katesgrove and Abbey. It adds the affluent areas north of the river Thames, the wards of Caversham, Peppard and Thames. All were once safely Conservative, but Labour are now the leading party in Caversham, the Lib Dems are ahead in Peppard and Thames has been the solitary Conservative ward in Reading even in local elections like 2000 when the Tories have done well nationally. Reading East extends out of the town to the south east, taking in 17,000 electors from the suburban township of Woodley, which is a logical enough fit with a Reading town seat but belongs in Wokingham for local government purposes. In the local elections in June 2001 Woodley voted 29 per cent Conservative, 27 per cent Labour and 45 per cent Lib Dem, but it seems likely that even in Woodley Labour ran a bit ahead of the Tories in general election voting in 2001.

Jane Griffiths is a less prominent and outspoken local figure than her western colleague Martin Salter, and there was some dispute over her renomination in 2001, but she too has benefited from the Reading effect and should be difficult to dislodge.

READING WEST

	2001		1997		1992 notional	
Electorate and turnout	71,089	59.1	69,073	70.1	68,848	77.3
Conservative	13,451	32.0	18,844	38.9	27,888	52.4
Labour	22,300	53.1	21,841	45.1	15,256	28.7
Lib Dem	5,387	12.8	6,153	12.7	9,461	17.8
Anti–EU	848	2.0	1,231 (2)	2.5	–	–
Others	–		320		638	
MP	Martin Salter (Lab)		Martin Salter (Lab)		Tony Durant (Con)	
Majority	8,849	21.1	2,997	6.2	12,632	23.7

'The Best MP in Britain?' wondered the Reading *Evening Post* on the day after the 2001 election. Martin Salter, elected for the first time in 1997, had stormed to a massive victory in Reading West. From being a long shot chance for Labour, Reading West has been converted into a seat that Labour would hold even if the overall parliamentary position reverted to what it was in 1992.

This was a personal triumph for Martin Salter. His personal profile, as a generally loyal Labour MP who would speak out when constituency or personal reasons dictated a different line, was appealing to voters who wanted Labour in again but disliked the control freak tendency. He has also been extraordinarily energetic with casework, actively seeking direct contact with voters and their concerns, and very skilled at generating publicity. The 2001 slogan 'Stick with Salter' fell on fertile ground.

Salter's efforts were helped by Labour's strong base in Reading. There were signs during the 1997 parliament that Reading West was going well for Labour; they were only a whisker behind in the 1999 Euro election, and actually led slightly in the 2000 council elections. Reading West was always going to be the sort of place to respond warmly to New Labour (see also St. Albans). These factors, combined with an energetic Labour campaign in 2001 and an uninspired Conservative effort, produced the Salter landslide.

There is considerable internal variety in Reading West. Most of the town centre of Reading is in the East constituency; this seat is a collection of outlying residential districts, varying from the council estates such as Whitley along the Southampton road which have long been Labour wards to the smarter areas on the A4 west of the town like Kentwood. The seven wards of the Reading borough in West have voted 6 Labour and 1 Lib Dem (Tilehurst) at all recent opportunities. The West constituency spills over into parts of the West Berkshire district, including some suburbs indistinguishable from the town (Theale and west Tilehurst) and the plush commuter villages up the Thames as far as Pangbourne, areas where Labour are traditionally weak. Labour made a particular effort to scrape up votes in the West Berkshire portion in 2001, with Martin Salter moving house to Theale. It seemed to work, with Labour's vote nearly levelling up in the Theale area in particular.

As the 1997 election proved in some Conservative seats, personal votes can be swept away in a strong enough national tide, and Salter is a bit more vulnerable than the raw figures might suggest. However, he is well established and will be extremely difficult for any Conservative to shift even if the national party can manage to reconnect with this sort of area.

SLOUGH

	2001		1997		1992 notional	
Electorate and turnout	73,008	53.4	70,283	67.9	69,450	77.0
Conservative	10,210	26.2	13,958	29.2	23,544	44.1
Labour	22,718	58.3	27,029	56.6	23,580	44.1
Lib Dem	4,109	10.5	3,509	7.4	3,841	7.2
Anti–EU	738	1.9	1,124	2.4	–	–
Others	1,223 (2)		2,112 (2)		2,500 (5)	
MP	Fiona MacTaggart (Lab)		Fiona MacTaggart (Lab)		John Watts (Con)	
Majority	12,508	32.1	13,071	27.4	36*	0.1*

* Estimated Labour majority allowing for boundary changes

Slough is a working class industrial town, which marks it out as an anomaly in the Thames valley. It is not a New Town but it grew around private sector light industrial development starting in the 1930s. Most Slough residents can trace their ancestry back out of the town within a couple of generations – the 1930s migrants into the town came mostly from Wales during the depression. It is not renowned for its beauty and culture – John Betjeman invited friendly bombs to fall on the place in a poem that has dogged Slough's reputation since. Its town centre has been made over but it still has the ugliest bus station in England. Slough's most noted employer is Mars confectionery, and the aroma of chocolate sometimes pervades the town.

Since the 1950s Slough has also seen large scale immigration from the Indian subcontinent and is intimately linked with Southall and Heathrow. A previous Conservative interlude, in 1964–66 when it narrowly elected Anthony Meyer against the tide, was attributed at the time to racial tension but things are more harmonious now. As well as the industry of most of Slough there are also less grimy residential areas at either end of the town in Burnham, Cippenham, Upton and Langley. However, with its solidly Labour council and its Asian, industrial character it is more surprising that the Tories managed to hold the Slough seat from 1983 to 1997 than that Labour MP Fiona MacTaggart currently has a large majority. It is now the safest Labour seat in the south east outside London.

WINDSOR

	2001		1997		1992 notional	
Electorate and turnout	73,854	57.0	69,132	73.5	67,545	79.3
Conservative	19,900	47.3	24,476	48.2	30,138	56.3
Labour	10,137	24.1	9,287	18.3	6,645	12.4
Lib Dem	11,011	26.1	14,559	28.7	15,587	29.1
Anti–EU	1,062	2.5	1,978(2)	3.9	–	–
Others	–		481(2)		1,184	
MP	Michael Trend (Con)		Michael Trend (Con)		NEW SEAT	
Majority	8,889	21.1	9,917	19.5	14,551	27.2

Windsor is the safest Conservative seat in Berkshire, less of an honour than once it was. It unites several bastions of the establishment. Principal among them, of course, is the royal fortress of Windsor Castle with its associated landmarks such as the Great Park. Across the river is Eton, a village wholly dependent on its public school. Ascot needs no introduction as a racing and society centre, and Sunningdale houses the civil service college. As might be expected, Windsor votes for the classic party of the establishment and its Conservative MP, Michael Trend, is even the son of a former Cabinet Secretary.

The voting habits of these places offer some surprises. The Castle ward of Windsor votes Liberal Democrat; Eton West, incongruously, elects the only Labour councillor on the borough council. The rural parts and Sunningdale are massively Conservative. Windsor constituency also includes a marginally Labour-inclined Slough ward, Foxborough, but Windsor as a whole offers no real foothold to either Liberal Democrats or Labour.

WOKINGHAM

	2001		1997		1992 notional	
Electorate and turnout	68,430	64.1	66,781	75.0	66,150	80.0
Conservative	20,216	46.1	25,086	50.1	32,692	61.7
Labour	7,633	17.4	8,424	16.8	5,987	11.3
Lib Dem	14,222	32.4	15,721	31.4	13,575	25.6
Anti–EU	897	2.0	–	–	–	–
Others	880		877		701 (2)	
MP	John Redwood (Con)		John Redwood (Con)		John Redwood (Con)	
Majority	5,994	13.7	9,365	18.7	19,117	36.1

John Redwood's constituency comprises several areas that are within the orbit of Reading. Wokingham itself is quite a small town, with well-off commuters working in Reading or London, and a certain amount of modern locally generated employment. The constituency also includes the suburb of Winnersh, closer in to Reading, and a tail of rural territory to the south of Reading as far as Burghfield (not far from Aldermaston). Most of the Wokingham constituency is extremely comfortable, but this does not automatically produce Tory votes. Emmbrook is the 6th least deprived ward in England, but the Tories still lost the seat to the Liberal Democrats in the 2000 local elections.

Labour are not in contention in any of the wards making up the Wokingham constituency, most of which are closely fought between Lib Dems and Conservatives (there are a couple of Tory strongholds such as Shinfield). The balance of local politics in Wokingham is so fine that the council was tied, 27-27, between Lib Dems and Conservatives from 2000 to 2002, when it fell to the Conservatives. The Liberal Democrats seem unlikely to gain the parliamentary seat, particularly as Maidenhead seems a better Lib Dem target and even on the same day in 1997 Wokingham produced a neck and neck result in the local elections while comfortably returning John Redwood. The Conservatives are safe enough here. Labour's candidate here as in Maidenhead was a celebrity. Matthew Syed is a table tennis champion, but even his skills at spin could not do much for Labour in Wokingham. A curious footnote is that Wokingham produced the Monster Raving Loony Party's best result nationally in 2001 (2.0 per cent). Despite what his detractors say, John Redwood's political views are obviously too sensible for an element among his constituents.

Buckinghamshire

including Milton Keynes

	Conservative		Labour		Liberal Democrat		Others	
	Share of vote	Seats	Share of vote	Seats	Share of vote	Seats	Share of vote	Seats
2001	45.5	5	30.7	2	19.8	0	4.0	0
1997	43.7	5	30.6	2	21.2	0	4.5	0
1992	57.0	7	19.2	0	22.1	0	1.7	0
1987	57.0	6	15.5	0	27.0	0	0.5	0
1983	56.8	6	14.4	0	28.5	0	0.3	0

Buckinghamshire is the archetypal Home County; it is an arc of territory to the north west of London from the Thames Valley around to the fringes of the East Midlands near Milton Keynes. The county's social composition is strongly affected by London's influence, with the M40 corridor, the commuter rail lines and the far end of the London Underground ferrying commuters in and out every day. Much of the landscape of the county is wooded, Chiltern country and it offers a retreat for London's most affluent who want clean air, pleasant surroundings and a general atmosphere of comfort and security. Small towns in the centre and south of the county are generally pleasant dormitories, as are its villages; there is more agriculture in the sparsely populated north. Its charms are well known to the political class – Chequers is here, as is Cliveden. The larger towns, on the other hand, are surprisingly industrial and working class – High Wycombe traditionally so and Aylesbury through London overspill development. Buckinghamshire is generally settled, stable commuterland; the population of the administrative county only grew 7.7 per cent between 1981 and 1998, and there is a lower proportion of pensioners than the national average.

In contrast to the rest of Buckinghamshire, the north eastern end of the county has been an area of massive recent growth. The Milton Keynes area's population grew by 61.3 per cent between 1981 and 1998 and it is still rising. Parliamentary boundaries in the area tell the story – it was part of a Buckingham seat before 1983, then a seat on its own until it was divided in a most unusual interim boundary review before the 1992 election. The New City was designated in 1967, the last entirely new town of the post war programme. It is home to another Wilson-era legacy, the Open University. Contrary to popular belief, the name owes nothing to two antithetical economists (or even a poet and an economist) – there was a small village called Milton Keynes in the area before the new city. 'MK' evolved in the 1970s and 1980s into a quasi-American city built around a grid of wide roads. It boasts the first multiplex cinema and the first drive-through fast food outlet in Britain. Unlike the other New Towns, MK's growth has taken place mainly since the end of large scale public housing, so that except for the early estates it is mostly privately developed and owner-occupied. Its economic base is small firms – 80 per cent of the work force work in firms employing fewer than 10 people, although it does have some larger employers in distribution, reflecting its good transport links to London, the West Midlands and the North. Despite these economic and social differences, its demographics resemble other New Towns. It was very stony ground for the radical, union-based Labour Party of the 1970s and 1980s but is archetypal New Labour territory.

Buckinghamshire was the only county to remain under Conservative control after the local elections of 1993, a sign of its complete commitment to the party. However, it has a surprisingly interesting electoral history which contrasts with other south eastern counties. It has become more Conservative in recent decades, while previously solid Tory counties such as East Sussex and Surrey have become less so. In 1945 Labour, astonishingly, polled slightly more votes than the Conservatives in Buckinghamshire and won 3 out of the county's four seats (including Slough, which is now in Berkshire, plus Wycombe and Buckingham). The party could win the Buckingham seat, which was based on the old towns of Wolverton and Bletchley but included a large rural area, even in closely fought elections like 1950 and 1964.

However, in Labour's recent high tides the Conservatives have remained comfortably ahead in the county as a whole. Parts of it have become so Tory that four of the remaining depleted band of safe Conservative seats are here, including three of their best thirteen constituencies. Labour interest is concentrated in Milton Keynes, but other than High Wycombe there is little for them in the rest of the county. The Lib Dems have performed well in local elections in Aylesbury and the north eastern part of Milton Keynes but have not managed to mount a serious parliamentary challenge in either area. The two constituencies of greatest interest in the area are Milton Keynes NE, a very marginal Labour seat in the last two elections, and Wycombe where the Conservatives have held on. If the Tories are doing really well they can think about gaining Milton Keynes SW which they won in its first election in 1992.

Local government

Buckinghamshire was the only county council in Britain to survive the rout of the Conservatives in the May 1993 elections, a sign of its utter safety. It is even safer since Milton Keynes became an independent unitary authority in April 1997 and in 2001 it elected 40 Conservatives, to 9 Liberal Democrats (five from Aylesbury town, two from Chesham plus Ivinghoe and Marlow South) and 5 Labour (all from High Wycombe). Milton Keynes, by contrast, is politically competitive; Labour had control for most of the 1990s but the Lib Dems won an overall majority in all-out elections in 2002. Normally MK has annual local elections, but not in every ward. It was the first local authority in recent years to hold a referendum on levels of local tax and services.

Of the four district councils of Buckinghamshire, only Aylesbury Vale is not currently Conservative controlled. This authority blends the very Tory countryside of the Buckingham area with the Lib Dem town of Aylesbury and was left a closely balanced hung council by the 1999 elections. The Conservatives did very well in the elections for Wycombe in 1999, taking a large overall majority, and even in their worst ever year, 1995, they were still the largest single party. The Conservatives also managed to lose Chiltern (Amersham and around) and South Buckinghamshire (Beaconsfield and around) in 1995 but they both came back to their habitual Tory loyalty in 1999. The Lib Dems have a substantial group in Chiltern (and were largest single party in 1995), while politics in South Bucks district is between Conservatives and Independents. Neither council has any Labour members.

Boundary review

Buckinghamshire, including Milton Keynes, will keep its current allocation of seven seats. There are likely, though, to be some boundary alterations to reduce the size of the Aylesbury seat and equalise electorates – Buckingham, though growing, is still a bit small. There are several permutations as to how this might be done, but they are unlikely to have great bearing on the political balance, thought there will be changes between the two Milton Keynes seats as the much-changed local wards no longer align with constituency boundaries.

AYLESBURY

	2001		1997		1992 notional	
Electorate and turnout	80,002	61.4	79,047	72.8	76,093	80.2
Conservative	23,230	47.3	25,426	44.2	34,983	57.3
Labour	11,388	23.2	12,759	22.2	8,205	13.4
Lib Dem	13,221	26.9	17,007	29.5	16,943	27.8
Anti–EU	1,248	2.5	2,196	3.8	–	–
Others	–		166		904	
MP	David Lidington (Con)		David Lidington (Con)		David Lidington (Con)	
Majority	10,009	20.4	8,419	14.6	18,040	29.6

Aylesbury, the county town of Buckinghamshire, is far from being a wealthy enclave. It has suffered some insensitive development and received some overspill estates such as Southcourt; to the motorist it is a bewildering collection of roundabouts. There are no particularly strongly Conservative areas in the town, which voted 39 per cent Lib Dem, 32 per cent Conservative and 26 per cent Labour in the 2001 county elections.

The town provides around 42,000 electors, so the constituency also includes some rural commuter areas in the Chiltern Hills including Wendover, Great Missenden (and Chequers), Princes Risborough and Stokenchurch set on its ridge overlooking the Oxfordshire plain. This chalky countryside, drawn in mostly from the Wycombe and Chiltern districts, is the source of the Conservative majority in Aylesbury; its wards nearly all voted over 50 per cent Conservative in 2001. In the late 19th century there was a rather feudal tone to politics in the area – the Rothschild family had bought up estates around Aylesbury, sent a member of the family to Parliament from 1885 to 1923 and took the area's loyalty with them from Liberal to Liberal Unionist (later Tory) in 1886.

The Liberal Democrats are a powerful force in Aylesbury in local elections, but they have not been able to translate their strength into general election voting. They led, although by less than one percentage point, in the area in the 1999 local elections but this represented a strong Conservative revival from their low point in 1995. In 2001 both Labour and the Tories profited from the fall in Lib Dem voting and the Tory majority crept over 10,000. There are only 42 Conservative constituencies safer than Aylesbury – three of them surrounding the seat in the same county! Boundary changes might remove some of the outlying area, tilting the seat slightly away from the Conservatives, but on current perform-ance even a new Aylesbury would remain a pretty safe Conservative seat.

BEACONSFIELD

	2001		1997		1992 notional	
Electorate and turnout	69,342	60.8	68,959	72.8	68,755	78.3
Conservative	22,233	52.8	24,709	49.2	34,316	63.7
Labour	9,168	21.8	10,063	20.0	7,371	13.7
Lib Dem	9,117	21.6	10,722	21.4	10,452	19.4
Anti–EU	1,626	3.9	4,082 (3)	8.1	–	–
Others	–		625 (3)		1,697 (3)	
MP	Dominic Grieve (Con)		Dominic Grieve (Con)		Tim Smith (Con)	
Majority	13,065	31.0	13,987	27.9	23,864	44.3

Beaconsfield is a rather small town; the constituency includes a number of other small towns which are also primarily commuter dormitories housing some of London's most wealthy and senior executives. Gerrards Cross and Denham lie between Beaconsfield itself and the London border at Uxbridge, and are rather similar. To the west the constituency includes a couple of prosperous oversized villages from the Wycombe district at Bourne End (the 28th least deprived ward in the country) and Loudwater. South of the town and the M40 is a small stretch of Chiltern countryside around Burnham Beeches and Hedgerley. The removal of Slough from Buckinghamshire means that this constituency has two little tails of territory either side of that industrial town, at Taplow and Iver. Iver, by the M25 near Heathrow, is as downscale as Beaconsfield gets and produces some Lib Dem voting, the only element of political diversity here.

The constituency is the fourth safest Conservative seat in the country, after two large rural seats in the north and urban Kensington & Chelsea. The other political parties are hardly present as organisations in the area. Tony Blair's first electoral outing was here, in a 1982 by-election, but Beaconsfield is indissolubly linked with Conservatism – when Disraeli was elevated to the House of Lords as Prime Minister in 1876 he took the title Lord Beaconsfield. Labour won both the seats covering the area in 1945 but since a south Buckinghamshire seat was created in 1950 it has never failed to produce a five-figure Conservative majority, even in 1997 when the incumbent MP had to stand down during the campaign for taking cash in brown envelopes from Mohamed Fayed.

BUCKINGHAM

	2001		1997		1992 notional	
Electorate and turnout	65,270	69.4	62,945	78.5	59,535	83.7
Conservative	24,296	53.7	24,594	49.8	31,045	62.3
Labour	10,971	24.2	12,208	24.7	7,999	16.1
Lib Dem	9,037	20.0	12,175	24.6	10,401	20.9
Anti–EU	968	2.1	–	–	–	–
Other	–		421		391	
MP	John Bercow (Con)		John Bercow (Con)		George Walden (Con)	
Majority	13,325	29.4	12,386	25.1	20,644	41.4

Buckingham is the most sparsely populated seat in the south east, a large tract of rural England sprawling across the north and centre of the county. Buckingham is the only town of any size, and it is a small and sleepy place with no rail station. The rest of the constituency is made up of villages, some rather remote and agricultural and some such as Haddenham and Winslow more convenient for commuters. Most of the constituency is a quiet backwater; according to its former MP George Walden 'today even the local historians admit that the story of Buckingham over the last 1,000 years has been one of relative decline.'

There was once a constituency called Buckingham that Labour could win (they held it in 1945-51 and, with Robert Maxwell as MP, in 1964-70) but that reached north east and incorporated all of the towns now part of Milton Keynes. The present seat reaches south, consisting entirely of territory within the Aylesbury Vale district council area. There are a couple of Lib Dem outposts around Ivinghoe and Wing near the Bedfordshire border, but the Conservatives poll over 50 per cent in nearly every county ward in Buckingham even in an election like 2001. Buckingham is the eighth safest Conservative seat in the country and is a secure base for its MP John Bercow, a right winger drifting very gradually towards the centre.

CHESHAM and AMERSHAM

	2001		1997		1992 notional	
Electorate and turnout	70,021	64.7	70,029	74.5	68,602	81.0
Conservative	22,867	50.5	26,298	50.4	35,207	63.4
Labour	8,497	18.8	10,240	19.6	5,758	10.4
Lib Dem	10,985	24.3	12,439	23.8	13,606	24.5
Anti–EU	1,367	3.0	3,146 (2)	6.0	–	–
Others	1,567 (2)		74		982	
MP	Cheryl Gillan (Con)		Cheryl Gillan (Con)		Cheryl Gillan (Con)	
Majority	11,882	26.2	13,859	26.6	21,601	38.9

Chesham and Amersham are the two Buckinghamshire commuter towns at the far end of the furthest bucolic branches of the London Underground's Metropolitan Line. The line branches at Chalfont & Latimer, which are also luxurious commuter settlements. The constituency is one of the greatest concentrations of wealthy and comfortable families in the country, and the greatest in the south east (in terms of the proportion of the population in households with earnings over £25,000 in 1997 only Cheadle scored higher). While mainly urban, Chesham and Amersham does not look or feel densely populated because it is made up of small towns and most of the population of those towns live amid trees, avenues and gardens.

Chesham is the most politically mixed component of the seat, voting 38 per cent Conservative, 35 per cent Lib Dem and 22 per cent Labour in the 2001 county elections, but the Conservative allegiance is heavily reinforced by the other elements. Amersham is 52 per cent Conservative, the Chalfonts (a pain in the anatomy for anyone challenging the Tories here) were 57 per cent Conservative and Hazlemere, brought in from the Wycombe district, even more so. The constituency includes Asheridge, where Nye Bevan and Jennie Lee had their farm. The forces of socialism in Chesham and Amersham have an honoured history, but not much by way of a present or a future. It is the 13th safest Conservative seat in the country.

MILTON KEYNES NORTH EAST

	2001		1997		1992 notional	
Electorate and turnout	72,909	64.6	70,395	72.8	61,057	81.0
Conservative	17,932	38.1	19,961	39.0	26,212	51.6
Labour	19,761	42.0	20,201	39.4	12,036	23.7
Lib Dem	8,375	17.8	8,907	17.4	11,693	23.0
Anti–EU	1,026	2.2	1,492	2.9	–	–
Others	–		675 (2)		857	
MP	Brian White (Lab)		Brian White (Lab)		Peter Butler (Con)	
Majority	1,829	3.9	240	0.5	14,176	27.9

Milton Keynes North East was the southernmost of a group of four contiguous seats which were left precariously marginal after the 1997 election. With Northampton South, Wellingborough and Kettering, Labour led the Conservatives by a total of 1,370 votes, but won all four seats in the psephological equivalent of picking four aces in a row. The story of the 2001 election is told in the fact that Labour held each of these seats with an increased majority.

North East is the more sparsely settled half of the new city. It includes the older towns of Newport Pagnell (by the M1 motorway) and Olney at the northern tip of the former county of Buckinghamshire, but most of the electorate is in the enormous new housing estates that marched across the landscape during the 1980s in the new city neighbourhoods such as Linford, Willen and Pineham.

Labour's victory in 1997 was surprising not only because it required a huge 14 per cent swing from the Tories, but also because the Liberal Democrats have a very strong base in local government here. They attract nearly 70 per cent of the vote in the Newport Pagnell area and can outpoll the other parties in most of the wards in the seat, even in the 2000 borough elections. If local elections translated straight across into national ones, it would be a safe seat for the Lib Dems. Their third place in 1992 was a bad blow, as it stopped them from making the case for tactical voting. Once Labour had won, holding on was easier, with the benefit of incumbency (Brian White played the local card strongly against Conservative candidate Marion Rix) and the reassuring ability of the party to get through a parliamentary term without an economic crisis. MKNE remains a tough seat for Labour to hold, although it has slid from third most vulnerable to the relative comfort of 13th. The party needs to keep delivering the economic goods and keep attracting anti-Tory tactical votes from people who vote Lib Dem locally.

MILTON KEYNES SOUTH WEST

	2001		1997		1992 actual	
Electorate and turnout	72,823	62.3	71,070	71.4	67,365	76.0
Conservative	15,506	34.2	17,006	33.5	23,840	46.6
Labour	22,484	49.5	27,298	53.8	19,153	37.4
Lib Dem	4,828	10.6	6,065	11.9	7,429	14.5
Anti–EU	848	1.9	–	–	–	–
Others	1,718 (3)		389		727 (2)	
MP	Phyllis Starkey (Lab)		Phyllis Starkey (Lab)		Barry Legg (Con)	
Majority	6,978	15.4	10,292	20.3	4,687	9.2

The division of Milton Keynes in an unusual interim boundary review before the 1992 election created a seat where Labour always thought they were in with a chance and were disappointed not to pick up in 1992. In 1997 Milton Keynes South West came good, with a swing not far short of 15 per cent.

The reason for Labour's confidence was the presence in this seat of their strongest areas of Milton Keynes without any rural element hindering their chances. Additionally, South West is the half of the city which most closely resembles the Hertfordshire New Towns, contrasting with the 1980s sprawl of the North East seat. The old towns, now woven into the new city, of Bletchley and Wolverton grew up by the railway and provided a Labour vote strong enough to carry the old Buckingham seat in 1945, 1950, 1964 and 1966 (on the latter two occasions for Robert Maxwell). Bletchley and Wolverton still provided Labour's strongest areas even in the 2002 elections. The new town estates such as Woughton, are also relatively good for the party – they include some of the more experimental architectural efforts in the city. The Tories can win a couple of these areas in their better years like 2000, but they still lagged behind Labour then and in the 1999 Euro election.

Labour held South West comfortably in 2001, but suffered an adverse swing a little greater than the national average, which was not a very good result for a southern marginal. Labour could lose MKSW and still be the largest party in a hung parliament – it is their 114th most vulnerable seat. It is still a marginal, in the sense that if the parties were to be neck and neck nationally it would be close.

WYCOMBE

	2001		1997		1992 notional	
Electorate and turnout	74,297	60.5	73,589	71.1	72,794	77.5
Conservative	19,064	42.4	20,890	39.9	30,040	53.3
Labour	15,896	35.3	18,520	35.4	12,096	21.4
Lib Dem	7,658	17.0	9,678	18.5	12,982	23.0
Anti–EU	1,059	2.4	2,394	4.6	–	–
Green	1,057	2.4	716	1.4	685	1.2
Other	240		121		610 (2)	
MP	Paul Goodman (Con)		Ray Whitney (Con)		Ray Whitney (Con)	
Majority	3,168	7.0	2,370	4.5	17,058	30.2

High Wycombe sits in a bowl of hills in the middle of the Chilterns, its suburbs sloping up the hillsides. It was traditionally a furniture making town, with radical sympathies among its working population – there were riots in 1885 after the narrow victory of a Conservative candidate. Narrow Tory wins in 1997 and 2001 were received with more equanimity. High Wycombe is still quite industrial and working class, with a well-established Asian population that was around 15 per cent in the town in 1991, concentrated in the terraced areas near the town centre. Like Buckinghamshire's other large town, Aylesbury, Wycombe's centre is a bustling area but it is overrun with crass development. West Wycombe is more attractive, with its most peculiar caves and hilltop church put there by Francis Dashwood, 18th Century hellraiser and possibly Britain's worst ever Chancellor. High Wycombe looks as if should be a Labour stronghold, but as in other bits of Buckinghamshire the Conservatives do comparatively well. In the 2001 county elections the town wards (including West Wycombe) voted Labour, but only by 43 per cent to 37 for the Tories.

High Wycombe's electorate is just under 50,000, so the constituency extends across a short stretch of country by the M40 to Marlow, sitting by the Thames at the end of a branch line from Maidenhead. Marlow is a pleasant little commuter town where incomes are high – Labour won only 14 per cent of the local vote here in June 2001. Marlow, and the small rural element, cast a decisive vote in 1997 and almost certainly 2001 as well. Labour's victories in 1945 and 1950 in Wycombe seem destined not to be repeated. It is the Conservative seat 16th most vulnerable to any further Labour advance and it would be a dire result for the party if they were to lose it.

Cambridgeshire including Peterborough

	Conservative		Labour		Liberal Democrat		Others	
	Share of vote	Seats	Share of vote	Seats	Share of vote	Seats	Share of vote	Seats
2001	42.8	5	32.3	2	21.2	0	3.7	0
1997	42.0	5	34.5	2	17.9	0	5.6	0
1992	54.5	5	23.3	1	19.7	0	2.5	0
1987	53.1	6	18.5	0	27.9	0	0.6	0
1983	51.0	5	17.0	0	31.6	1	0.4	0

Cambridgeshire has existed in its current form since 1974, when Cambridge City, Huntingdonshire and the Soke of Peterborough joined Cambridgeshire County and the Isle of Ely under one administration. Despite this diversity, the county makes eminent sense as a social and administrative unit and the merger of these elements was one of the more sensible recent reforms to the local government map.

Most of the county looks to Cambridge as its centre, although there is a corner that centres on Peterborough. The rural areas have a long agricultural history as flat, fertile arable farming country, in the north produced by marsh drainage in previous centuries. The cities, however, are much more than market centres for the surrounding rural areas. Cambridge needs no introduction as an ancient university which has been conspicuously successful at fostering scientific and technological progress. The university influence pervades the city, and has powered the boom in computer technology, software and high tech creativity that has given the area the inevitable name 'Silicon Fen'. Peterborough lacks the academic infrastructure and has a more traditional economic base, around distribution and light industry. It was designated a New Town in 1968, although these later cut-price New Towns built on existing large towns.

In the rural areas the farm workers' vote, aided by rural nonconformist traditions, used to be a source of Liberal and Labour voting – all the seats in the current county voted Liberal in 1906 and in the 1920s Huntingdon and Isle of Ely were still favouring the Liberals. The seat of Cambridgeshire, comprising the current South and SE seats, voted Labour in 1945, but the rural areas have become increasingly Tory since, as farming involved fewer unskilled labourers and the villages became populated by the middle classes. This trend has taken place across East Anglia. However, the individualistic Liberal MP Clement Freud did manage to hold Isle of Ely between a 1973 by-election and 1987.

The two large cities of Cambridgeshire have remained marginal. Peterborough has a long tradition as a marginal since Labour first won in 1929, and its sprawling growth since the late 1960s has done little to tip the balance one way or the other between the parties. Cambridge is also traditionally marginal, but used to be quite a difficult constituency for Labour, succumbing only in the 1945 and 1966 landslides. The two pre-1950 Cambridge University seats were always dominated by orthodox Conservatives, rather than Independents as in some other university seats. A Labour victory here in 1992 was a sign of the long term weakening of the Conservatives in academic, intellectual circles, confirmed dramatically in 2001 when the Tories crashed to third place.

The 1980s and 1990s saw an inrush of population into Cambridgeshire, building on the previous two decades of gradual increase. Its population grew 23.8 per cent between 1981 and 1998, the fastest growth of any county. Even the city of Cambridge grew by nearly 20 per cent. The new growth has been predominantly in small firms, often of a high-tech nature, and dispersed throughout many villages and small towns rather than producing a new urban settlement. Every village around Cambridge seems to have added new private housing developments at various stages since the 1960s. This dispersal has resulted in the addition of more people than live in a New Town like Stevenage to south Cambridgeshire, without the creation of a big new urban settlement. While people like the feeling of living in the country, this pattern does put pressure on Cambridge which is particularly apparent on its congested roads. A small new town, of about 6-14,000 houses, is currently planned for a few miles outside the city (the location is yet to be decided).

The incomers to Cambridgeshire have tended, therefore, to be people who prefer country to town and they tend to be absorbed into existing social structures in the villages. This has been a recipe for a strong adherence to Conservatism in recent years, intensified by the presence of one of the county's MPs in Number 10 from 1990 to 1997. The Conservative Party is still a formidable organisation in the county, in Huntingdon in particular. Rural and small town Cambridgeshire, that is the whole of the county excluding Cambridge and Peterborough, is made up of five pretty safe Conservative seats. The Conservatives can aspire to regain Peterborough, which they lost in 1997, but have been reduced to third in Cambridge which they lost in 1992.

Local government

Cambridgeshire county council lost control only over the Peterborough unitary authority in the 1990s local government review – Cambridge is still within its bailiwick. The Conservatives control the authority and have done so since 1997, with 34 councillors to 16 Lib Dems and 9 Labour in 2001. Labour and Lib Dem dominate the city, the Lib Dems are strong in the south eastern county wards, and the Conservatives have the rest. Peterborough is usually under no overall control – Labour often seem to fall just short even in good years for them, and only briefly gained control in 1996. The continuing Liberal Party has representation on the council. The Conservatives won an outright majority in 2002.

The Liberal Democrats gained control of Cambridge city, a long cherished ambition of the party, in May 2000. During the 1980s Labour seemed to do better in local than parliamentary elections in Cambridge, while the Lib Dems saved their main challenge for parliament; now it is the other way round. The Conservatives are only barely a presence on the council now. Control of the council in the past has oscillated between Labour and hung, and it will be interesting to see if the Lib Dems can take a firmer grip. The Lib Dems gained East Cambridgeshire from Independents in all-out elections in May 1999, a sign of the decline of non-party local politics in rural areas. The process is not complete in South Cambridgeshire, currently hung with the Conservatives the largest party ahead of Lib Dems and Independents – it may be a battleground in future between Tories and Lib Dems.

Huntingdonshire is massively Conservative, and did not embarrass John Major by falling from their control in the 1990s. Labour have fallen upon hard times – wards the party used to be able to win in the

1980s and early 1990s have been lost and the party is now unrepresented. **Fenland** council (in the north east) is another matter. It was Conservative from its establishment in 1973 until Labour managed a stunning victory in the 1995 local elections. This was a one-off, and Fenland reverted to a comfortable Tory majority in 1999.

Boundary review

This time, Cambridgeshire is unlikely to get another seat at the boundary review. While some of the seats are too large, it does not have quite enough electors to create an eighth seat. There may be some reshuffling of wards as Peterborough is a bit small and Huntingdon, Cambridgeshire South East and Cambridgeshire North East are all too large. The way in which this is done could have significant partisan implications; Labour would prefer to bring southern Peterborough back into the seat while the Conservatives would like to transfer some of their strong rural territory from NE or NW to the city.

CAMBRIDGE

	2001		1997		1992 actual	
Electorate and turnout	70,665	60.6	71,812	71.5	69,011	73.2
Conservative	9,829	22.9	13,299	25.9	19,459	38.5
Labour	19,316	45.1	27,436	53.4	20,039	39.7
Lib Dem	10,737	25.1	8,287	16.1	10,037	19.9
Anti–EU	532	1.2	1,262	2.5	–	–
Green	1,413	3.3	654	1.3	720	1.4
Others	1,009 (3)		401 (3)		258 (2)	
MP	Anne Campbell (Lab)		Anne Campbell (Lab)		Anne Campbell (Lab)	
Majority	8,579	20.0	14,137	27.5	580	1.2

The city of Cambridge is more completely under the influence of its university than Oxford, parts of which have a working class identity centred on the Cowley car plant. As in Oxford, the university has directly and indirectly spawned other concerns, with research and science parks on the edge of the city and large public sector employers such as Addenbrooke's Hospital (the biggest single employer in the county, with 5,400 workers). Cambridge is also the centre of what is in effect a considerable metropolitan area, dispersed here and there in small towns and villages in the south of the county. Even the headquarters of the South Cambridgeshire District Council are in the city rather than the area it governs.

Academic discontent with the Conservatives, and the retirement of the city's last Conservative MP Robert Rhodes James, who was well-regarded as a moderate man and himself an academic, led to a Labour gain from third place in 1992. It had previously been a target for the SDP, whose candidate in 1987 was Shirley Williams, but Labour's revival under Neil Kinnock attracted many centre-left voters and the centre parties faded. Cambridge's enthusiasm for Labour increased in 1997, but none of the major parties can be very happy with the latest Cambridge result.

For the Conservatives, 2001 was simply abysmal as they slipped into third place with a pathetic share of the vote in a seat they had lost only narrowly before 1997, even in good Labour years like 1966. Cambridge, as an academic city with a large public sector, is hostile territory at the moment. There may also have been differential migration – incomers to the county who prefer living in the city rather than the villages will probably have more liberal, urban values than the new villagers. Labour saw its thumping majority of 1997 cut down to size; the volatile student vote was not impressed by tuition fees, public sector workers were disappointed; the Greens and the left polled 5 per cent between them. The Lib Dems had some reason for cheer, but did not manage to replicate their strong showing in local elections which has given them control of the city council. In local elections they do well in the most collegiate wards, such as Market and West Chesterton, while Labour fight back in the eastern and northern suburbs. In the 2001 county elections Labour's lead was only 291 votes – the Lib Dems polled 4,000 fewer votes in the general election and Labour 3,000 extra. Cambridge is now a long-shot target for the Lib Dems, in their new capacity as radical opposition rather than the centrist party of the 1980s.

CAMBRIDGESHIRE NORTH EAST

	2001		1997		1992 notional	
Electorate and turnout	79,891	60.1	76,353	72.6	73,005	79.8
Conservative	23,132	48.1	23,855	43.0	31,168	53.5
Labour	16,759	34.9	18,754	33.8	7,928	13.6
Lib Dem	6,733	14.0	9,070	16.4	18,007	30.9
Anti–EU	1,189	2.5	2,636	4.8	–	–
Others	238		1,110 (2)		1,136	
MP	Malcolm Moss (Con)		Malcolm Moss (Con)		Malcolm Moss (Con)	
Majority	6,373	13.3	5,101	9.2	13,161	22.6

Cambridgeshire North East is a far-flung part of England. It is the most traditional seat in the county, relatively unaffected by the surge in population and economic activity in the south of the county until recently. It has the highest proportion of pensioners of any seat in the county. It is the constituency most completely made up of fens – the main district council indeed bears the name of Fenland. The towns and villages seem like islands in a flat, endless sea of marshland and prairie farms. In contrast to the other rural Cambridgeshire seats, NE is based around towns rather than expanded villages – Wisbech is the largest (20,000 population) and oldest but there is also the railway town of March (19,000) and the fenland towns of Whittlesey (16,000) and Chatteris. To the east are Littleport and Downham Market, on a faster rail line to Cambridge and London and most subject to change. Neither town nor country are particularly affluent – the north side of Wisbech is among the most deprived 10 per cent of wards in England and there are no plush areas of the kind found further south. Some villages around Wisbech are also poor and isolated places with considerable social problems.

Before 1983 the seat included Ely and was known poetically as the Isle of Ely. The seat has a tradition of being won when the Liberals have stood a famous, independent-minded candidate. James de Rothschild held it between the wars; before 1918 a Liberal could win in the area, according to Henry Pelling, if the candidate was 'of a special type – wealthy and interested in racing.' From 1973 until 1987 it sent the multi-talented Clement Freud to parliament in the Liberal interest. The increasingly normal, businesslike image of the Liberal Democrats has seen them slide to a poor third here and it is now a fairly safe Conservative seat. The Liberal Democrats poll poorly in local elections too, except in Littleport, and the Conservatives have a surprisingly strong hold nearly everywhere, despite the seat's relative poverty. Labour managed to poll the most votes in their best local election year, 1995, but are too far behind in general elections to pose a real threat.

CAMBRIDGESHIRE NORTH WEST

	2001		1997		1992 *notional*	
Electorate and turnout	71,247	61.7	65,791	74.2	*65,640*	*78.6*
Conservative	21,895	49.8	23,488	48.1	*32,170*	*62.4*
Labour	13,794	31.4	15,734	32.2	*13,361*	*25.9*
Lib Dem	6,957	15.8	7,388	15.1	*4,503*	*8.7*
Anti–EU	881	2.0	2,208 (2)	4.5	–	–
Others	429		–		*1,559*	
MP	Brian Mawhinney (Con)		Brian Mawhinney (Con)		NEW SEAT	
Majority	8,101	18.4	7,754	15.9	*18,809*	*36.5*

Cambridgeshire North West for the most part looks to Peterborough as its major urban centre. It extends deep into the Peterborough built-up area in the south of the city, including the two Orton wards (Longuevillle and Waterville) and Fletton. Most of the Labour minority in this constituency is from this section. The other areas close to Peterborough are very different – some rural areas (rapidly becoming suburban) to the west of the city such as Glinton and Barnack which produce consistently enormous Conservative shares of the poll.

The other element of this new seat is the northern part of Huntingdonshire, including some fenland around Ramsey (with an 8,000 population the constituency's largest settlement excluding the Peterborough wards), and Sawtry and Stilton (the cheese is made in Leicestershire but has historically been sold here) just off the A1. This area has deep blue veins in its political preferences as well, partly through the influence of its former member John Major.

The new seat's complete safety freed Brian Mawhinney, whose Peterborough seat had previously been marginal, to concentrate on the national Conservative campaign in 1997. Even that disaster left him with a comfortable majority here which edged up a bit in 2001. It is the 58th safest Conservative seat.

CAMBRIDGESHIRE SOUTH

	2001		*1997*		*1992 notional*	
Electorate and turnout	72,095	67.1	70,557	76.1	*68,550*	*82.1*
Conservative	21,387	44.2	22,572	42.0	*32,914*	*58.5*
Labour	11,737	24.3	13,485	25.1	*8,624*	*15.3*
Lib Dem	12,984	26.9	13,860	25.8	*13,976*	*24.9*
Anti–EU	875	1.8	3,598 (2)	6.7	*–*	*–*
Others	1,358 (2)		466 (2)		*718*	
MP	Andrew Lansley (Con)		Andrew Lansley (Con)		Anthony Grant (Con)	
					Cambridgeshire SW	
Majority	8,403	17.4	8,712	16.2	*18,938*	*33.7*

Southern Cambridgeshire lacks towns, a peculiarity which has not stopped population growth here since 1945 on a scale that is comparable with the establishment of a New Town in the locality. Instead, lots of villages have each taken some share of the growth and it has preserved some of its traditional character as the economic base has shifted from agriculture to commuting. The two railway lines from Cambridge to London both run through the constituency and have encouraged growth in villages such as Whittlesford. Other small towns included are Bassingbourn and Sawston, but the latter place with a bit over 7,000 population is the biggest settlement. This seat includes two wards from the city of Cambridge, namely Queen Edith's and Trumpington, former Conservative areas which now tend to vote Lib Dem, and some areas northwest of the city such as collegiate Girton and the new suburb of Bar Hill.

South Cambridgeshire is by far the most affluent and upper middle class constituency in Cambridgeshire and it bears demographic comparison with Tory fortresses like Rayleigh and Bracknell. It should probably be more Tory than it has been in the last couple of elections; it had the smallest Tory share of the vote of any of the rural Cambridgeshire seats in 1997 and avoided this distinction by less than 0.1 per cent in 2001. The Conservative lead in the 2001 county elections was only 4 or 5 per cent compared to 17 in the general election; about 10 per cent voted Lib Dem in the locals but split 6-3 to Labour in the general. Some Cambridge liberalism has probably affected the seat. It also bears comparison, ominously for the Conservatives, to Romsey in Hampshire and there is certainly a latent Liberal Democrat threat to its senior Conservative MP Andrew Lansley.

CAMBRIDGESHIRE SOUTH EAST

	2001		1997		1992 notional	
Electorate and turnout	81,663	63.5	76,393	74.4	71,672	80.2
Conservative	22,927	44.2	24,397	42.9	33,080	57.5
Labour	13,714	26.4	15,048	26.5	11,105	19.5
Lib Dem	13,937	26.9	14,246	25.1	12,217	21.2
Anti–EU	1,308	2.5	2,838	5.0	–	–
Others	–		278 (2)		1,050	
MP	James Paice (Con)		James Paice (Con)		James Paice (Con)	
Majority	8,990	17.3	9,349	16.5	20,863	36.3

Cambridgeshire South East stretches flatly to the east of Cambridge. It comprises some territory which is part of the South Cambridgeshire district, in small but rapidly growing towns such as Linton and Cottenham, and the Histon area just outside the city. The constituency also includes a large part of the East Cambridgeshire district based around the little cathedral city of Ely (13,700 population) and the sprawling overgrown village of Soham.

The countryside to the east includes the hinterland of Newmarket (the town, curiously, is in Suffolk but is surrounded on three sides by Cambridgeshire), and is therefore strongly influenced by the horse racing interest. In the north, towards Ely, there is a bleak stretch of fenland between Haddenham and Isleham. While lacking towns of any size, it is still not traditionally rural.

SE is therefore a blend of the old Liberal territory of NE and the new potential for the party in the Cambridge exurbs. There is recent Liberal Democrat activity in the East Cambridgeshire area which has given them control of the district council and most county council seats – they led here in the 1999 local elections and came within a percentage point or two in the 2001 county elections. Labour's best area is Fulbourn while Linton and Waterbeach are Lib Dem; the Conservatives strike back in Willingham, the area nearest Huntingdon. This seat is likely to remain Tory and even in 2001 they had a commanding lead over divided opposition, but there is some potential for a challenge and it is the sort of seat the Lib Dems must aspire to win if they are to succeed in displacing the Tories.

HUNTINGDON

	2001		1997		1992 notional	
Electorate and turnout	80,335	61.1	76,094	74.9	71,409	79.6
Conservative	24,507	49.9	31,501	55.3	34,124	60.0
Labour	11,211	22.8	13,361	23.5	8,234	14.5
Lib Dem	11,715	23.9	8,390	14.7	12,153	21.4
Anti–EU	1,656	3.4	3,445 (2)	6.0	–	–
Others	–		266 (2)		2,342 (7)	
MP	Jonathan Djanogly (Con)		John Major (Con)		John Major (Con)	
Majority	12,792	26.1	18,140	31.8	21,971	38.6

Huntingdon lies north west of Cambridge and south, along the A1, from Peterborough. The constituency extends to the neighbouring towns of St. Ives and St. Neots – the latter is in fact the largest urban centre in the seat and the largest town in Cambridgeshire with 27,000 residents. St. Neots, a composite town of Eynesbury, Eaton Socon and Eaton Ford, received north London overspill in the 1960s and what Labour support is left in the seat is to be found there.

Huntingdon itself is a small town, with links to London which have been growing stronger over the last few decades. It is within commuting distance, and there is also a large and quite rough London overspill estate in the north of the town at Oxmoor. St. Ives, Hemingford Grey and the rural areas are the most affluent parts of the constituency, but other than Oxmoor and small parts of St. Neots there are hardly any seriously deprived areas. The seat has a young, growing population.

The Huntingdon constituency is predictably Conservative, but it is more strongly so than similar – even a bit more upscale – seats in the same areas such as the two rural Bedfordshire constituencies. The answer owes much to politics – it did not behave particularly differently until the late 1980s. Huntingdon's recent history has been strongly influenced by its member from 1979 to 2001, John Major. Major was strongly endorsed by his constituents in 1992 and suffered a very small fall in his vote in 1997 compared to his Conservative colleagues elsewhere; his well-attested charm evidently convinced many Huntingdon voters that he deserved a personal vote, and to some extent this spilled over into support for the Tories more generally. The Conservative Party is still a formidable organisation in Huntingdon, with a large membership and a network of activists throughout its towns and villages. The Tories maintained control of the council even through their worst years in the 1990s and the party is still a big factor in local society as it is in few other places.

The loss of Major's personal vote explains most of the rather large drop in the Conservative share of the vote in 2001. It seems that voters who would otherwise have voted Lib Dem supported Major, but felt no allegiance to the Tories once right winger Jonathan Djanogly took his place in 2001. The Lib Dems also made a couple of local election gains, including John Major's home county council ward of Brampton. Huntingdon is still the 16th safest Tory seat in Britain and would elect a Tory MP in any imaginable circumstances.

PETERBOROUGH

	2001		1997		1992 notional	
Electorate and turnout	64,874	61.4	66,506	72.8	71,804	74.5
Conservative	15,121	38.0	17,042	35.2	26,455	49.5
Labour	17,975	45.1	24,365	50.3	20,201	37.8
Lib Dem	5,761	14.5	5,170	10.7	4,973	9.3
Anti–EU	955	2.4	1,241 (2)	2.6	–	–
Others	–		609 (2)		1,839	
MP	Helen Brinton (Lab)		Helen Brinton (Lab)		Brian Mawhinney (Con)	
Majority	2,854	7.2	7,323	15.1	6,254	11.7

Peterborough is a frontier town between the south east, East Anglia and the midlands. As such it has exploited its transport links well and jobs have been created in distributive trades such as Freeman's catalogues and the Post Office. It was designated a New Town in 1968 although it is also a very old town – a Roman centre with a fine mediaeval cathedral. The new estates ring the town to the north, east and south-west (although the south of Peterborough is in the Cambridgeshire NW constituency). The first were predominantly public sector but newer growth has been privately built and quite Conservative inclined. Recent growth has tended to be in strongly Conservative areas such as the suburb of Werrington. The Peterborough constituency as currently defined takes in the centre, north and western areas of the city and is now quite a compact seat. In previous decades it encompassed part of east Northamptonshire.

Peterborough has an extraordinary history of marginality. Conservative MP Harmar Nicholls started his years of living dangerously when he gained the seat in 1950 by 144 votes; next year he won by only 373; in 1966 he held on by 3 votes and in February 1974 by 22. The axe fell in October 1974, but Labour only held it until 1979. Since then it has produced larger majorities, first for the Conservatives and in 1997 for Labour.

Labour did quite badly in Peterborough in 2001, a performance presaged by a very good Conservative showing in the 2000 local elections. Labour MP Helen Brinton had attracted unfavourable publicity in her first term and the Tory candidate Stewart Jackson mounted a strong campaign. The demographics of this seat are also changing a bit, with more Tory voters coming to the west of Peterborough. It is now quite exposed to any further Conservative advance, being 27th on their target list from Labour, and could quite easily see even more recounts in future.

Cheshire including Halton and Warrington

	Conservative		Labour		Liberal Democrat		Others	
	Share of vote	Seats	Share of vote	Seats	Share of vote	Seats	Share of vote	Seats
2001	35.6	4	46.3	7	15.6	0	2.5	0
1997	33.4	3	46.5	7	12.3	0	7.8	1
1992	44.7	5	39.1	5	15.3	0	0.9	0
1987	44.8	7	34.4	3	20.6	0	0.3	0
1983	45.6	7	29.7	3	24.4	0	0.2	0

Cheshire is a socially mixed county situated to the south of Merseyside and Greater Manchester. It was reduced in size by the 1973 county revisions, particularly in terms of population, when it had its western and eastern arms chopped off. In the west, the Wirral peninsula was transferred to Merseyside while in the east, the many towns to the south and east of Manchester including Altrincham, Stockport, Hyde and Stalybridge went to Greater Manchester. These losses were slightly compensated by the gain of Widnes and Warrington from Lancashire, though in the more recent local government reorganisation, they were to become unitary authorities, taking Runcorn, now part of Halton borough, with them.

Although Cheshire is officially part of the heavily industrialised north west region, much of what remains in the county, particularly in its eastern and western areas, is semi-rural. Such areas provide a handy countryside retreat for those who can afford it, while still being within easy commuting distance of the main cities. Cheshire contains more than its fair share of Britain's richest neighbourhoods, particularly to the south of Manchester. Here, an area roughly bordered to the north by Knutsford and Wilmslow and to the south by Holmes Chapel and Macclesfield takes in three of the country's forty least deprived wards as well as a concentration of wealthy footballers and more established social elites. But Cheshire is not all a leafy rural idyll. Despite the loss of the most heavily urbanised areas, towns like Ellesmere Port as well as Runcorn, Widnes and Warrington are heavily industrialised and would not seem out of place in one of the neighbouring metropolitan counties. Each of these towns contains poorer areas of terraced streets or council estates, as indeed do the smaller centres of Crewe, Northwich and Winsford further to the south. Even the city of Chester has its problem areas, though it is ringed on three sides by prosperous suburbs and surrounded by another belt of affluent commuter villages.

Politically, the area included in this chapter was extremely stable over a long period. At each election from 1955 until 1979, the Conservatives always won six seats and Labour three, even though this period covered four changes of government. In the blue corner could be found Chester, Knutsford, Macclesfield, Northwich, Nantwich and Runcorn, the first four of which had been Tory since the end of the first world war, never mind the second. Labour always won the railway town of Crewe and the former Lancashire towns of Widnes and Warrington from 1945 onwards, without looking particularly likely to win any other seats. Then in a big shake-up in 1983 Nantwich and Runcorn were abolished, and new constituencies created at Ellesmere Port, Congleton and Warrington. Politically, the effect was still only slight, with the Tories, who won both of the old seats, winning all the new ones as well in both 1983 and 1987. Indeed they almost gained the new Crewe and Nantwich, which would have completely wiped Labour out in the 'historic Cheshire' constituencies still in the county.

Fortunes began to change in 1992, when Labour narrowly gained Ellesmere Port & Neston and Warrington South, failing to add Chester to this tally by the slim margin of 1,101 votes. Boundary changes then handed Labour a sixth seat, the new Weaver Vale, and although the effect of this change should have placed Warrington South back in the Tory column, the landslide conditions of 1997 meant that Labour continued to win here as well. The greater drama however could be found in three seats which had always elected Conservatives since 1918. The city of Chester was finally gained by Labour for the first time, and even Eddisbury (similar to the old Northwich) almost surrendered to the advancing red hordes. More extraordinarily, the Tory fortress of Tatton (formerly Knutsford) which had hitherto appeared impregnable, did fall after allegations of sleaze, the appearance of a man in a white suit and the tactical withdrawal of Labour and Liberal Democrat candidates.

As a result of these changes, it was the Conservatives who were now reduced to three seats as against Labour's seven, not to mention Martin Bell, the first out-and-out Independent elected to parliament since 1945. There was to be a slight recovery by the Tories in 2001, but that was always on the cards as Bell had pledged to sit for a single term, and in the relatively normal circumstances which followed, Tatton was easily regained. There would be no immediate comeback in Chester or Warrington South, and the size of the Labour majorities recorded suggest that these seats will not be automatically regained next time either. Elsewhere, Eddisbury does at least now look secure again, and the Lib Dem challenge in Congleton (their only serious prospect in the county) has waned. Cheshire may have begun the slow retreat to electoral normality, though it does at least retain the distinction (shared with Cardiff and the London borough of Hounslow) of a husband and wife sitting for next-door constituencies, to which one could add a healthy overall quota (5 out of 11) of women MPs.

Local government
The local government map of Cheshire pretty much mirrors the pattern of parliamentary seats, though this could change fairly rapidly, as most of the councils (unusually for a shire county) elect annually. In the urban north, Ellesmere Port and the now unitary authority of Halton have always been controlled by Labour, with a formerly strong Conservative group declining in the former and the Lib Dems growing in the latter. The other council to go unitary, Warrington, was formerly controlled by the Tories from 1973 until 1979, but has been Labour since 1983, heavily so since 1991. As in Halton it is the Lib Dems who now form the only real opposition. Vale Royal has been Labour controlled since 1991, with the Tories the biggest group on a hung council before this. Crewe and Nantwich is evenly divided between Labour and Conservative. Chester was controlled by the Conservatives from 1973 until 1986, but they have lost ground since and the council is these days typically balanced, with at the time of writing (early 2002) almost equally sized groups representing each of the three main parties. The Conservatives remain in charge of Macclesfield with a healthy overall majority, the Lib Dems forming the main opposition group. Congleton was previously Lib Dem controlled but they lost ground recently and the Conservatives are now the largest group on a hung council. Given the overall mixed pattern, it

should come as no surprise that the **county council** is perennially hung, though in 2001 the Conservatives performed rather better than in the same day's parliamentary contests by regaining control, largely because of the absence of Warrington and Halton as well as a slight increase in their vote.

Boundary review

As in other cases, exactly what happens when the boundary review considers the area will depend on the treatment of the unitary authorities. Warrington will retain two seats in any event, but Halton is only really entitled to a single seat and Cheshire seven, making ten in total. If however Halton and the remaining parts of Cheshire were put together, their joint entitlement rises to 8.75, and thus the old county area would retain eleven in total. In that case the average constituency size will be 68,000, and there may be few alterations to existing boundaries.

CITY of CHESTER

	2001		1997		1992 notional	
Electorate and turnout	70,382	63.8	71,730	78.4	68,557	83.6
Conservative	14,866	33.1	19,253	34.2	25,641	44.7
Labour	21,760	48.5	29,806	53.0	23,281	40.6
Lib Dem	6,589	14.7	5,353	9.5	7,808	13.6
Anti–EU	899	2.0	1,487	2.6	–	–
Others	763		358 (2)		593 (2)	
MP	Christine Russell (Lab)		Christine Russell (Lab)		Gyles Brandreth (Con)	
Majority	6,894	15.4	10,553	18.8	2,360	4.1

The historic city of Chester was won by the Conservatives at all general elections from January 1910 until 1992, a total of 23 contests plus two by-election victories thrown in for good measure. Then, like many of England's other ancient cities (Gloucester, Lancaster, Worcester, Exeter) it fell to New Labour in 1997. Christine Russell's sweeping majority of 10,500 was larger than the Tories had managed since 1955.

Chester itself is very mixed politically. Labour are strong in the centre and the wards towards and in Blacon (a peripheral council estate which is one of the most deprived 300 wards nationally), but the Conservatives hit back in rural wards such as Christleton and Mollington, and the Liberal Democrats have been doing well in the wards east of the city centre. Labour were about 9 per cent ahead overall in the 1999 local elections, the 2000 contest producing a three-way split, reflecting the composition of the council. Russell's majority in 2001 was barely reduced in percentage terms from the high 1997 figure, and indeed the Conservative vote actually fell further, suggesting an incumbency vote in 1997 for the celebrity Gyles Brandreth. They will have their work cut out to win this seat back next time - there are now a hundred Labour constituencies which will be numerically easier to regain.

CONGLETON

	2001		1997		1992 notional	
Electorate and turnout	71,941	62.7	68,873	77.6	66,069	84.3
Conservative	20,872	46.3	22,012	41.2	27,007	48.5
Labour	13,738	30.5	14,713	27.5	10,684	19.2
Lib Dem	9,719	21.6	15,882	29.7	17,657	31.7
Anti–EU	754	1.7	811	1.5	–	–
Others	–		–		373	
MP	Ann Winterton (Con)		Ann Winterton (Con)		Ann Winterton (Con)	
Majority	7,134	15.8	6,130	11.5	9,350	16.8

Cheshire contains some extremely wealthy small towns and villages as well as some very poor areas in its major towns. Congleton, a new seat created in 1983, is decisively made up of territory in the first category. Holmes Chapel, near the M6 motorway, was ranked the 18th least deprived ward nationally in 1998, while the larger settlements of Alsager (population 11,000), Sandbach (15,000) and Congleton itself (24,000) are hardly in the image of gritty, industrial northern towns either. Unsurprisingly, the seat has been won from the start by Ann Winterton for the Conservatives, and is now their 80th safest in Britain, though all has not been totally plain sailing.

The reason for occasional Conservative discomfort here has been the threat posed by the Liberals and now Liberal Democrats. The majority in the inaugural 1983 contest was only 8,400, and though this then increased, the figure fell back to a less than comfortable 6,000 in 1997. The Lib Dems also became the largest party on the council in 1987, gaining outright control in the 1990s and at one time holding over two-thirds of the seats. By 2002, however, the Lib Dems had collapsed in spectacular fashion both in local and national elections. A damaging local row caused a split in the party, which ended their control of the council (the Conservatives became the largest party in 2002). In 2001, Labour advanced to take second place in a general election for the first time as the Lib Dem vote fell to its lowest level since the constituency was created. Given her minority vote, and the now common pattern of tactical voting elsewhere, Ann Winterton probably has cause to be thankful for the waning of the Lib Dem challenge here.

CREWE and NANTWICH

	2001		1997		1992 notional	
Electorate and turnout	69,040	60.2	68,472	73.9	68,307	81.9
Conservative	12,650	30.4	13,662	27.0	21,751	38.9
Labour	22,556	54.3	29,460	58.2	26,622	47.6
Lib Dem	5,595	13.5	5,940	11.7	6,991	12.5
Anti–EU	746	1.8	1,543	3.0	–	–
Others	–		–		579	
MP	Gwyneth Dunwoody (Lab)		Gwyneth Dunwoody (Lab)		Gwyneth Dunwoody (Lab)	
Majority	9,906	23.8	15,798	31.2	4,871	8.7

The famous railway town of Crewe has been represented by Labour MPs since 1945, but the boundary changes of the early 1980s appeared to threaten that record as Nantwich was always a Tory seat from its creation in 1955 until abolition after 1979. Gwyneth Dunwoody (first elected in February 1974) won the inaugural contest in the new mixed constituency by just 290 votes, steadily increasing the margin to just over 1,000 in 1987 and 2,700 in 1992. The boundary changes of the 1990s this time helped her position by removing some of the most Tory villages, and then the national landslide conditions of 1997 resulted in an unprecedented majority here of over 15,000, substantially more than that achieved in 1945.

Crewe remains by far the best part of the constituency for Labour – they polled 13,000 votes against 4,300 for the Tories to win its four county council wards in 2001, while their best share of the vote in the wards outside the town was only 38 per cent. Most of those other wards were won by the Conservatives, though they narrowly lost Nantwich to an Independent. The local council results of 2000 also revealed big Tory leads in places like Haslington and Willaston, but for the moment this is not enough for them to seriously challenge for the parliamentary seat.

EDDISBURY

	2001		1997		1992 notional	
Electorate and turnout	69,181	64.2	65,394	75.6	62,352	81.5
Conservative	20,556	46.3	21,027	42.5	26,794	52.7
Labour	15,988	36.0	19,842	40.1	15,798	31.1
Lib Dem	6,975	15.7	6,540	13.2	7,553	14.9
Anti–EU	868	2.0	2,041	4.1	–	–
Others	–		–		699 (2)	
MP	Stephen O'Brien (Con)		Alastair Goodlad (Con)		Alastair Goodlad (Con)	
Majority	4,568	10.3	1,185	2.4	10,996	21.6

Parliamentary by-election 22 July 1999: Conservative 15,465 (44.8), Labour 13,859 (40.2), Lib Dem 4,757 (13.8), 3 Others 416. Electorate 67,086, Turnout 51.4%. MP: Stephen O'Brien (Con), Majority 1,606 (4.7)

Eddisbury covers an extensive area of west Cheshire, with several mainly rural wards from three local districts: Chester, Crewe & Nantwich and Vale Royal, included in the seat. Despite this, Labour came very close to pulling off a stunning victory in both the 1997 general election and the by-election which took place in the middle of Labour's first term. This can be mainly explained by the presence of Winsford (population 30,000), a fairly drab industrial town with its fair share of poor areas, which generally votes Labour. In the 2001 county council poll they won both its wards easily with 6,500 votes as against 2,600 for the Tories and a similar number for the Liberal Democrats. Clearly if that was all there was to the parliamentary seat, it would be solidly Labour, but the extensive surrounding rural areas are far more prosperous and very Conservative. This is true of wards from all three districts. Tarporley in Vale Royal is one of the 100 least deprived wards in Britain, where Labour were third in the 1999 local elections. The rural Crewe wards in the south of the constituency such as Audlem and Wrenbury gave their Conservative candidates about 80 per cent of the vote in the 2000 locals, while not to be left out, the Chester wards of Malpas and Tarvin notched up over 70 per cent.

Unsurprisingly then, the Eddisbury seat has been won by the Conservatives at all contests since its creation in 1983. Alastair Goodlad's majority reached almost 16,000 in 1987 when the opposition was almost perfectly split into two, but Labour surged into second place in 1992 and almost into the lead five years later. Gaining the seat in the by-election would have been quite extraordinary for a party in government, and though this was not quite achieved, the margin remained close after an occasionally rowdy contest (Tony Blair was jostled on a campaign visit). Labour opted to highlight the hunting controversy in the by-election, proving that mainly rural seats are as divided on the issue as anywhere else. In the more normal circumstances of 2001, Conservative Stephen O'Brien boosted his majority to an almost comfortable 4,500.

ELLESMERE PORT and NESTON

	2001		1997		1992 notional	
Electorate and turnout	68,147	60.9	67,573	77.8	67,037	83.7
Conservative	12,103	29.1	15,275	29.1	23,603	42.1
Labour	22,964	55.3	31,310	59.6	26,836	47.8
Lib Dem	4,828	11.6	4,673	8.9	5,012	8.9
Anti–EU	824	2.0	1,305	2.5	–	–
Others	809		–		648 (2)	
MP	Andrew Miller (Lab)		Andrew Miller (Lab)		Andrew Miller (Lab)	
Majority	10,861	26.2	16,035	30.5	3,233	5.8

Ellesmere Port is an industrial town on the banks of the Mersey, dominated by the huge Shell refinery at Stanlow, which is practically a town in its own right and was also the starting point of the September 2000 fuel protests. To the north can be found the large Vauxhall car plant, which has proved less troubled than its former Luton counterpart. Despite this unusual concentration of heavy industry, the constituency of which it is a part was, until 1992, usually represented by Conservative MPs. This came about because the town (population about 65,000) has never quite been large enough to form its own seat. Until 1974 it was part of the large and strongly Tory Wirral constituency, then it was paired with the middle class suburbs of Bebington in what was a closely fought marginal, and since 1983 it has been joined with the affluent little town of Neston as well as the Chester ward of Elton. Even in this latest configuration, the constituency was won in 1983 and 1987 by the Conservatives, Andrew Miller finally gaining it for Labour in 1992 by 2,000 votes. The national swing has since provided him with rather more comfortable majorities, but the seat is still just about vulnerable to a Tory recovery.

Most of Ellesmere Port itself remains strongly Labour: they polled around 80 per cent in the Central, Grange and Stanlow & Wolverham wards in 2000. To the west however, villages like Willaston & Thornton, Burton & Ness and Parkgate, a delightful spot on the edge of the Dee Estuary facing North Wales, continue to heavily back the Tories. Although these wards are a minority of the constituency (even Neston itself votes Labour), they do provide the Conservatives with a base should the national recovery ever arrive.

HALTON

	2001		1997		1992 *notional*	
Electorate and turnout	63,742	54.1	65,058	68.3	*66,187*	*76.9*
Conservative	6,413	18.6	7,847	17.7	*15,426*	*30.3*
Labour	23,841	69.2	31,497	70.9	*30,363*	*59.6*
Lib Dem	4,216	12.2	3,263	7.3	*4,499*	*8.8*
Anti–EU	–	–	1,036	2.3	–	–
Others	–		796 (2)		*637 (2)*	
MP	Derek Twigg (Lab)		Derek Twigg (Lab)		Gordon Oakes (Lab)	
Majority	17,428	50.6	23,650	53.2	*14,937*	*29.3*

The parliamentary seat and unitary borough of Halton combines the two equally sized towns of Widnes and Runcorn, which are on opposite banks of the Mersey and were previously in neighbouring counties. The character of the two places is very different. Widnes, a rugby league town, is mainly made up of terraced housing and council estates and still has the feel of central Lancashire of which it was once part. Runcorn is mainly made up of newer estates, though includes a fair amount of ugly industry (mainly chemicals based) on its western edge. The two are connected by a graceful bridge, which featured in the political drama, *GBH*, when Michael Palin could not make himself drive over it. The journey has been successfully made, however, by Runcorn's non-league football club, who moved to Widnes in 2001 and incorporated 'Halton' as part of their name.

The present parliamentary constituency was only created in 1983, before which both towns formed the basis of their own seats. Labour won Widnes at all elections from 1945 onwards (the majority exceeding 10,000 in 1979), but Runcorn was always Conservative-held, the size of their majority never falling below 5,000. Labour won the newly combined seat by 7,000 in 1983, doubling their lead in 1987, a result very much in line with those in nearby Merseyside. Since then, they have piled up huge majorities and after 2001 this was one of 35 constituencies where Labour were more than 50 percentage points ahead of their nearest challenger. The Widnes wards in particular remain heavily Labour: in 2001 their share of the vote in elections to the unitary council was 76 per cent in Appleton, about the same in Hough Green and almost 80 per cent in Ditton. Although they do well in many parts of Runcorn as well, the Lib Dems were able to win Heath and Beechwood wards to the south of the centre, though this vote may not have been repeated when it came to the general election ballot papers. The Tories attract some votes in the more residential northern parts of Widnes, but overall Halton is set to remain a very safe Labour seat for present incumbent Derek Twigg.

MACCLESFIELD

	2001		1997		1992 notional	
Electorate and turnout	73,123	62.3	72,049	75.2	70,834	81.5
Conservative	22,284	48.9	26,888	49.6	32,332	56.0
Labour	15,084	33.1	18,234	33.6	13,202	22.9
Lib Dem	8,217	18.0	9,075	16.7	11,958	20.7
Others	–		–		246	
MP	Nicholas Winterton (Con)		Nicholas Winterton (Con)		Nicholas Winterton (Con)	
Majority	7,200	15.8	8,654	16.0	19,130	33.1

Macclesfield has been a Conservative stronghold since 1918 when they won it off the Liberals. Unlike other places in Cheshire which could boast a similar record (Chester and Wallasey for example), the Tories have not lost it in the last ten years, or for that matter come remotely close to losing. Much of the reason is that the area is favoured by the more prosperous (and downright rich) from Manchester, who have steadily been moving further and further away from the city itself. The district can boast as many as eight wards in the least deprived 5 per cent nationally, a very different pattern from most places in the north. Admittedly some of these wards are in next-door Tatton, but the list of desirable settlements in this constituency includes Poynton, Bollington and Prestbury, where the Conservatives polled 85.6 per cent in the 2000 local council elections.

   Although there is a social cachet to some parts of the seat, long-serving local MP, Nicholas Winterton (first elected at a 1971 by-election in the closest post-war contest here) has undoubtedly done well to maintain a decent majority in Macclesfield. Labour continue to attract support in the town itself, ahead in two county council wards in 2001, and the Liberal Democrats generally win a smattering of district council seats as well. But the Tories have performed well here in recent general elections, slightly increasing their vote in 1992 and only losing half as much as the national average five years later. As a result, Winterton's majority in 1997 was significantly greater than that of his predecessor in Labour's two previous landslide years of 1945 and 1966. Indeed, in the half-century since 1955 there has only been a miniscule 2 per cent swing away from the Conservatives here compared with 6 per cent nationally and far higher figures in most other parts of the north west.

TATTON

	2001		1997		1992 notional	
Electorate and turnout	64,954	63.5	64,099	76.1	63,700	81.4
Conservative	19,860	48.1	18,277	37.5	32,235	62.2
Labour	11,249	27.3	–	–	9,870	19.0
Lib Dem	7,685	18.6	–	–	9,387	18.1
Anti–EU	769	1.9	–	–	–	–
Ind Bell	–	–	29,354	60.2	–	–
Others	1,715 (4)		1,161 (8)		350	
MP	George Osborne (Con)		Martin Bell (Ind)		Neil Hamilton (Con)	
Majority	8,611	20.9	11,077	22.7	22,365	43.1

Tatton was the scene of the remarkable 1997 contest when former Conservative minister, Neil Hamilton, linked with allegations of sleaze and cash in brown envelopes, was routed by the white-suited Independent challenger and former BBC journalist, Martin Bell, the margin over 11,000 votes. This one result more than any other encapsulated the ending of the Conservative era after eighteen years in power. It was extraordinary for many reasons. An outright Independent (as opposed to one previously connected with a major party) had not won a seat in a British general election since 1945. Then again, a major party had not withdrawn their candidate in favour of a better-placed challenger since the isolated Conservative-Liberal deals in Huddersfield and Bolton in the 1950s. Tatton was hardly the sort of place where one would expect such events; a blue-chip Tory stronghold which was their fifth safest seat in the land, having been held by the party on a continual basis (until 1983 as Knutsford) since 1910. Even in 1945 the majority here was nearly 20,000 votes, and that lead had never fallen below 10,000 in all the contests since.

The glare of the national media allied to the withdrawal of Labour and Liberal Democrat candidates were undoubtedly major factors behind Bell's success, and when normal conditions resumed in 2001, George Osborne was easily able to regain the seat for the Conservatives. Tatton has fallen slightly down the pecking order since 1992 (now their 42nd safest seat), but other than that, the 1997 contest appears to have had very little lasting effect. Neither Labour nor the Lib Dems have significantly improved their position or even given themselves any hope for future contests. Perhaps this is unsurprising as Alderley Edge, Knutsford and Wilmslow remain overwhelmingly upmarket, Tory places where almost half of the population are in the top social groups. They are hardly the sorts of places which are likely to elect Labour or even Liberal representatives, but then the wonder is that the Conservatives could ever have lost here in the first place.

WARRINGTON NORTH

	2001		1997		1992 notional	
Electorate and turnout	72,445	53.7	72,815	70.4	72,455	76.9
Conservative	8,870	22.8	12,300	24.0	19,420	34.9
Labour	24,026	61.7	31,827	62.1	29,626	53.2
Lib Dem	5,232	13.4	5,308	10.4	6,307	11.3
Anti–EU	782	2.0	1,816	3.5	–	–
Others	–		–		366	
MP	Helen Jones (Lab)		Helen Jones (Lab)		Doug Hoyle (Lab)	
Majority	15,156	39.0	19,527	38.1	10,206	18.3

Warrington is a very mixed town straddling the Manchester Ship Canal and River Mersey at the point where it becomes straightforward to cross (in fact there is a bridge to the west linking Runcorn and Widnes - see Halton - but it is relatively recent). While many of the more favoured residential areas to the south and west of the town centre are contained in the South seat, Warrington North (essentially the successor to the old Warrington) contains its fair share of terraced streets as well as industrial units off the A49. This area also includes one of Britain's earliest IKEA stores, attracted by the town's geographical location and motorway links, which make it within an hour's travel of practically the entire north west. The constituency extends north of the M62 to Burtonwood and east of the M6 to Birchwood, but this barely affects its political composition and the only serious Tory vote can be found in Culcheth, a few miles to the north.

The only occasion on which Labour have come to losing the seat was in a 1981 by-election. It was the first to be contested by the newly formed SDP, with one of the founding 'gang of four' Roy Jenkins attempting to re-enter Parliament. In the event, he added more than 30 per cent to the 1979 Liberal vote, a sign of victories to come, but not enough to win Warrington with Labour's Doug Hoyle holding on by 1,700 votes. Contests became rather more straightforward thereafter, and by the time Hoyle opted to enter the House of Lords shortly before the 1997 election, the majority was already in five-figures. His replacement was one of two Helen's who now represent Warrington seats, Helen Jones.

WARRINGTON SOUTH

	2001		1997		1992 notional	
Electorate and turnout	74,283	61.2	72,461	76.0	69,324	81.1
Conservative	15,022	33.0	17,914	32.5	25,698	45.7
Labour	22,419	49.3	28,721	52.1	22,945	40.8
Lib Dem	7,419	16.3	7,199	13.1	7,316	13.0
Anti–EU	637	1.4	1,082	2.0	–	–
Others	–		166		290	
MP	Helen Southworth (Lab)		Helen Southworth (Lab)		Mike Hall (Lab)	
Majority	7,397	16.3	10,807	19.6	2,753*	4.9*

* Estimated Conservative majority allowing for boundary changes.

Warrington South has had a short history, formed as recently as 1983 following the growth in population around the town and break-up of the Runcorn seat. The first two contests were won by the Conservatives, but this was always a key Labour target, and Mike Hall initially won the seat in 1992 with a tight majority of just 191 votes. Further boundary changes appeared to undo Hall's good work, and he opted to follow a minority of his electors into the newly created and much safer Weaver Vale constituency before 1997. His replacement here, Helen Southworth, has had few problems however, Labour 'gaining' the seat for a second successive election in 1997, this time by the huge margin of almost 11,000. Four years on, there was only a very small swing back to the Tories percentage-wise, with the majority remaining in excess of 7,000.

The constituency takes in not only those areas of Warrington south of the Mersey, but also the town centre itself as well as areas to the west (north of the river) such as the closely-fought Great Sankey and Labour-inclined Penketh. It is the streets between the river and ship canal (an area which includes Labour's regional headquarters) which provide the strongest Labour vote, particularly Westy. Further south can be found the best Conservative areas such as Appleton, while they also do well in Lymm on the other side of the M6 motorway. However, in local contests it is the Liberal Democrats who win these wards, and in both 2000 and 2002 they won several others as well to lead by a mile across the constituency. This appeared to have very little effect in the general election of 2001, when several thousand local Lib Dem voters must have backed the two main parties, particularly Labour, and they remained in a poor third place.

WEAVER VALE

	2001		1997		1992 notional	
Electorate and turnout	68,236	57.6	66,125	73.0	65,447	79.2
Conservative	10,974	27.9	13,796	28.6	18,515	35.7
Labour	20,611	52.5	27,244	56.4	25,265	48.8
Lib Dem	5,643	14.4	5,949	12.3	7,506	14.5
Anti–EU	559	1.4	1,312	2.7	–	–
Others	1,484		–		537	
MP	Mike Hall (Lab)		Mike Hall (Lab)		NEW SEAT	
Majority	9,637	24.5	13,448	27.8	6,750	13.0

The name Weaver Vale evokes images of a rural idyll in deepest Cheshire, and given that the constituency is based on the equally grandiose sounding Vale Royal district council, one might expect it to be held by the Conservatives. But in reality this is a reasonably safe Labour seat, to such an extent that MP Mike Hall could abandon Warrington South for its security in 1997.

Although the constituency does run along the River Weaver, its electorate is concentrated in and around the former salt-mining town of Northwich, the smaller settlements of Frodsham and Helsby which adjoin the M62 motorway to the west, and also the eastern part of Runcorn. There are very few wards which can be described as rural (outside these main towns the electorate is just 15,000) as the most sparsely populated parts of Vale Royal district can be found in Eddisbury and Tatton. Northwich is strongly Labour, with the party also competitive in some of its smaller neighbours such as Weaverham, though the more upmarket Hartford & Whitegate is the one large ward won by the Tories. Frodsham and Helsby are very marginal between Labour and Conservative, but it is the Runcorn part of the seat which proves politically decisive. For example in the 2001 unitary council elections, Castlefields ward produced a 68 per cent share of the vote for Labour as against less than 10 per cent for the Tories, Murdishaw an even greater lead of 75-10. The Conservatives would need to build up a very large vote elsewhere in the seat to make up for this sort of handicap, and for the moment this looks unlikely.

Cleveland (former county of)

	Conservative		Labour		Liberal Democrat		Others	
	Share of vote	Seats	Share of vote	Seats	Share of vote	Seats	Share of vote	Seats
2001	26.2	0	59.3	6	12.4	0	2.1	0
1997	25.2	0	62.4	6	9.8	0	2.6	0
1992	37.1	2	50.0	4	12.8	0	0.2	0
1987	33.8	2	44.7	4	20.9	0	0.6	0
1983	35.8	1	37.9	4	26.2	1	0.1	0

Cleveland, which for most administrative purposes has now been abolished, was based on industrial Teesside, including Middlesbrough and Redcar (until 1973 part of the North Riding of Yorkshire), Stockton-on-Tees and Hartlepool (both historically part of County Durham). Though the south and east of this area, around the Cleveland Hills, is picturesque, for the most part this is harsh industrialised landscape, the vista of oil refineries and towers said to be the inspiration for the bleak opening scenes of the film *Blade Runner*. As one might expect from such territory, Labour have generally won a majority of parliamentary seats here, and in the last two elections, all of them. But this corner of England is not as tribal in its ties with Labour as, say, County Durham or South Yorkshire. As recently as the early 1960s the Conservatives held three seats to Labour's two and the party still entertains hopes of regaining Stockton South and Middlesbrough South & East Cleveland (formerly Langbaurgh) which were both lost in 1997.

Labour's strongest seat in the area has always been Middlesbrough, but because the town has never quite been large enough to support two whole constituencies of its own, some of its middle class segments have always formed the basis of a second, more politically interesting, seat. Until 1979, this was Middlesbrough West, which included Thornaby-on-Tees, and was known as Thornaby from 1974 onwards. Following the extensive boundary changes of 1983, this seat was abolished (somewhat confusingly, most moved into Stockton South) but the seat of Langbaurgh was then created, linking the southern suburbs of Middlesbrough with the small towns of the Cleveland Hills. All these constituencies have been important marginals: Middlesbrough West/Thornaby changed hands in 1945, 1951, 1962, 1970 and February 1974, Stockton South has already been held by all three main parties despite existing for fewer than twenty years, and Langbaurgh and its successor changed hands in 1991, 1992 and 1997.

Elsewhere, the industrial constituency of Redcar has been rock solid for Labour since its creation in 1974, Stockton/Stockton North has been won by Labour at all post-war general elections, though was notionally lost by the party when sitting MP Bill Rodgers helped establish the Social Democrats, and Hartlepool has been Labour since 1945 with the exception of 1959-64. But this area has been no one-party state: the Conservatives won the constituency known as Cleveland (linked with Whitby after 1970) in 1959, 1974 and 1979, while the Liberals have a history here as well, holding both this seat and Middlesbrough West before the war. Thus there can be little doubt that this has been a politically volatile area in the past, and this characteristic still survives, as demonstrated by the fact that the twenty-one point increase in Labour's vote since 1983 has been their largest advance in any county (or former county) in England over that period.

Over the last few years, the Cleveland area has attracted its fair share of nationally known politicians, with both Mo Mowlam (Redcar) and Peter Mandelson (Hartlepool) representing constituencies here. Mowlam stood down from both government and parliament in 2001, but Mandelson famously fought on despite twice losing his place in the government. Personalities of a very different kind were coming to the fore in 2002, when Ray Mallon, the Middlesbrough police chief who became known for 'zero tolerance' policing, resigned from the force to contest the mayoral election in the town. The likelihood of Mallon standing was a major reason for the unprecedented support (84 per cent) for the mayoralty in a referendum, and it was no surprise when he was elected overwhelmingly in May 2002. The combination of Mallon as mayor with a heavily Labour council (see below) will surely test the whole concept of elected mayors to the limit.

Local government
Cleveland is now divided into four unitary authorities after the county council was abolished by the local government reforms of the 1990s. Labour have always been dominant in Middlesbrough, winning 41 seats in 1999 as against just 12 for all the other parties combined. In Stockton-on-Tees, the Conservatives are stronger, but still only have 12 councillors (and the Lib Dems 5) as against Labour's 38 at the time of going to press. Redcar and Cleveland, which takes in an extremely diverse area from working-class Eston on the fringes of Middlesbrough to seaside resorts like Saltburn and the town of Guisborough in the hills, saw a significant Tory advance in 1999, Labour's 17 losses reducing their overall majority to single figures. The following year, things were even worse in Hartlepool (the only one of the four councils to hold annual elections), with Labour losing control of the council for the first time since the 1970s after some dramatic defeats, though this outcome was assisted by the Liberal Democrats and Conservatives not opposing each other in seven of the nine wards which Labour lost. Like Middlesbrough, Hartlepool also held elections for a mayor in 2002, alongside its normal local elections. The result of the mayoral contest was anything but 'normal' however, as the Hartlepool United Football Club mascot 'H'angus the Monkey' (otherwise known as Stuart Drummond) was elected. Even thought he immediately promised to dispense with the costume, the nest few years could be as interesting in Hartlepool as down the road in Middlesbrough.

Boundary review
When the Boundary Commission get around to making their proposals for Cleveland, they are likely to recommend few, if any, changes. Hartlepool is exactly the right size for a parliamentary seat, Stockton the right size for two. The other boroughs are entitled to one-and-a-half seats each, and will likely be paired (as they are now) to form three seats. Ultimately a 'no change' situation is on the cards.

HARTLEPOOL

	2001		1997		1992 actual	
Electorate and turnout	68,164	55.8	67,712	65.6	67,969	76.1
Conservative	7,935	20.9	9,489	21.3	18,034	34.9
Labour	22,506	59.1	26,997	60.7	26,816	51.9
Lib Dem	5,717	15.0	6,248	14.1	6,860	13.3
Anti–EU	–	–	1,718	3.9	–	–
Socialist	912	2.4	–	–	–	–
Others	981 (2)		–		–	
MP	Peter Mandelson (Lab)		Peter Mandelson (Lab)		Peter Mandelson (Lab)	
Majority	14,571	38.3	17,508	39.4	8,782	17.0

Following the events of the previous twelve months (not to mention those of May 2002), the 2001 general election result in Hartlepool marked something of a triumph for the Labour Party in general and Peter Mandelson in particular. In May 2000, Labour had lost overall control of the council for the first time in 22 years after losing no fewer than nine council wards, some regarded as strongholds, to Liberal Democrats and Conservatives, who appeared to be operating a thinly veiled coalition designed to oust Labour from power. This performance was already enough to have Labour worried about Hartlepool, but six months later came another bombshell with the resignation from the government, for a second time, of Peter Mandelson over the Hinduja 'passport affair'.

Mandelson's decision to continue as Hartlepool's Member of Parliament led to a wave of speculation about possible high-profile opponents and a shock result to match Tatton's in 1997. Many seemed taken in by the hype, notably Mandelson's colourful Conservative opponent Gus Robinson and Socialist Labour Party boss Arthur Scargill, who sensed the chance to defeat one of the main architects of 'New Labour' in a traditional setting. In the event, such optimism was completely misplaced as Hartlepool's voters demonstrated that general elections are won and lost on national issues. Not only did Mandelson romp home with a comfortable 14,500 majority (which surprised even himself), but the swing away from Labour was smaller than in neighbouring constituencies. Scargill limped home with fewer than 1,000 votes, demonstrating that electors were just as unlikely to vote for a left-wing alternative as they were for the traditional right.

Yet Hartlepool has not always been safe for Labour. As up the coast in Sunderland, there is something of a working-class Tory tradition here, the Conservatives holding the parliamentary seat between 1959 and 1964. As recently as 1983 they only lost by about 3,000 votes, and given that they gained four council wards from Labour in 2000, one might have expected a better showing in 2001. That this did not materialise is a tribute to Mandelson, though it also underlines the extent of the swing from Tory to Labour that has taken place in northern towns like Hartlepool over recent decades.

MIDDLESBROUGH

	2001		1997		1992 notional	
Electorate and turnout	67,662	49.8	70,931	65.0	74,097	74.1
Conservative	6,453	19.1	7,907	17.2	16,424	29.9
Labour	22,783	67.6	32,925	71.4	33,543	61.1
Lib Dem	3,512	10.4	3,934	8.5	4,925	9.0
Anti–EU	–	–	1,331	2.9	–	–
Others	969 (2)		–		–	
MP	Stuart Bell (Lab)		Stuart Bell (Lab)		Stuart Bell (Lab)	
Majority	16,330	48.4	25,018	54.3	17,119	31.2

The constituency of Middlesbrough takes in most of this large town, including the centre, and was one of Labour's fifty safest seats in Britain after both the elections of 1997 and 2001. The constituency, which is more or less the same as the old Middlesbrough East division, was won as long ago as 1892 by an Independent Labour candidate and had a volatile history before and after the first world war. It was held by the Liberals on several occasions and even by the Conservatives in 1900 and 1922, then gained by Labour's Ellen Wilkinson in 1924 before the Liberals won it for the last time in 1931. Labour regained it narrowly in 1935 and have held on ever since, the incumbent since 1983 being first past the post campaigner, church commissioner, and occasional author, Stuart Bell.

Middlesbrough includes no fewer than 12 wards out of 18 where Labour took more than 70 per cent of the vote in the most recent local elections (1999). Support reaches a peak in St Hilda's, which includes the shady docks area and famous Transporter Bridge, and the council estate wards of Pallister and Thorntree, with all three of these council divisions featuring in the top ten most deprived (out of over 8,000) in England. Perhaps unsurprisingly in view of this, Conservative candidates for the council in 1999 received the princely totals of 41 and 22 votes in Pallister and less than 100 in the other two wards. The opposition parties attract slightly more support in the more affluent southern suburbs such as Acklam and Kader, but this sustains only a handful of councillors and a barely respectable vote in general elections. It took the Independent candidacy of Ray Mallon in the 2002 mayoral election for Labour to be defeated in Middlesbrough – whether this will lead to an enduring shift in political alignments remains to be seen.

MIDDLESBROUGH SOUTH and EAST CLEVELAND

	2001		1997		1992 *notional*	
Electorateand turnout	72,104	61.0	70,481	76.0	*69,836*	*80.7*
Conservative	14,970	34.0	18,712	34.9	*25,802*	*45.8*
Labour	24,321	55.3	29,319	54.7	*24,401*	*43.3*
Lib Dem	4,700	10.7	4,004	7.5	*6,163*	*10.9*
Anti–EU	–	–	1,552	2.9	–	–
MP	Ashok Kumar (Lab)		Ashok Kumar (Lab)		Michael Bates (Con) Langbaurgh	
Majority	9,351	21.3	10,607	19.8	*1,401*	*2.5*

The seat formerly known as Langbaurgh must be one of the most politically interesting and diverse in Britain. Current incumbent Ashok Kumar originally gained it by 2,000 votes in a by-election in late 1991, only to lose it again just five months later to his by-election opponent, Michael Bates. Five years on, Kumar won round three with a knock-out majority of over 10,000 and there was even room for a slight further swing to Labour in 2001.

The current name of the constituency suggests there are two parts to this seat, but in reality there are at least four. The small towns to the south east of the Teesside conurbation such as Guisborough and Skelton are politically mixed and can see close battles between Labour and Conservatives. The seaside resort of Saltburn-by-the-Sea was traditionally Tory but like many similar towns around the country is now marginal. The more rural ward of Hutton is currently held by the Liberal Democrats, and is one of Labour's weakest in the constituency: they polled less than 20 per cent here in 1999. Meanwhile the seven Middlesbrough wards included in the seat divide into two very distinct parts: rock-solid Labour areas (Easterside and Park End) where the most frequent decision is between voting Labour or not voting at all, and affluent suburbs (Nunthorpe and (Coulby) Newham) which produce a large vote in council elections for the Conservatives and Lib Dems, though one suspects a surprisingly high vote for Labour in the last two general elections.

All in all there is something for everyone here, and perhaps the only safe assessment is that the various and diverse parts of the seat make any predictions for the future, such as a local newspaper's wildly inaccurate poll predicting a Conservative victory in 2001, a very risky business.

REDCAR

	2001		1997		1992 notional	
Electorate and turnout	67,798	56.3	68,965	71.0	73,753	79.0
Conservative	9,583	25.1	11,308	23.1	19,823	34.0
Labour	23,026	60.3	32,975	67.3	31,237	53.6
Lib Dem	4,817	12.6	4,679	9.6	7,241	12.4
Others	772		–		–	
MP	Vera Baird (Lab)		Mo Mowlam (Lab)		Mo Mowlam (Lab)	
Majority	13,443	35.2	21,667	44.3	11,414	19.6

The constituency of Redcar, created as recently as 1974, is associated with the name of Mo Mowlam, who in just three terms as Member of Parliament rose to cabinet rank as well as becoming one of the most popular ministers in Labour's 1997-2001 government. Mowlam inherited and bequeathed a very safe Labour seat, as despite its sometime seaside resort status and racecourse, Redcar's political geography owes far more to the sprawling presence of ICI Wilton and adjacent steelworks. This industrial complex separates the town from the other part of the parliamentary seat, working-class Grangetown, Eston and South Bank. It is these wards which are Labour's strongest, for example, a 77 per cent share of the vote in South Bank in the 1999 local elections and 73 per cent in Grangetown, which ranks as the 9th most deprived local government ward in the country. In the same election, the Redcar ward was actually gained by the Conservatives, while the Liberal Democrats confirmed that they too are a growing force in council elections, with all 11 seats won in the borough of Redcar & Cleveland in 1999 included in this parliamentary constituency. Despite this, Mowlam's successor Vera Baird, one of a very small number of women who won selection battles in safe seats in 2001, retained a substantial majority of over 13,000 in the most recent general election.

STOCKTON NORTH

	2001		1997		1992 notional	
Electorate and turnout	64,629	54.8	64,472	69.0	66,795	75.8
Conservative	7,823	22.1	8,369	18.8	16,666	32.9
Labour	22,470	63.4	29,726	66.8	27,332	54.0
Lib Dem	4,208	11.9	4,816	10.8	6,060	12.0
Anti–EU	–	–	1,563	3.5	–	–
Others	926		–		550	
MP	Frank Cook (Lab)		Frank Cook (Lab)		Frank Cook (Lab)	
Majority	14,647	41.3	21,357	48.0	10,666	21.1

Stockton North includes not only the northernmost wards of Stockton-on-Tees itself but also industrial Billingham on the other side of the A19. The constituency, which is similar to the Stockton division which existed before 1983, has a strong working-class character, and throughout the post-war era has returned Labour MPs. However, one of those members, Bill Rodgers, was part of the 'gang of four' (his memoirs are modestly entitled *Fourth Among Equals*) who established the Social Democratic Party in 1981 in response to Labour's lurch to the left. Like all but one of the MPs who crossed the floor of the Commons to join the new party, Rodgers continued to sit as SDP member for Stockton until 1983, when he was duly defeated by present incumbent Frank Cook. Rodgers finished in third place, though he did attract nearly 30 per cent of the vote and in so-doing almost handed victory to the Conservatives, who trailed Labour by less than 1,900. Indeed both new Stockton seats saw exciting three-cornered contests in 1983, though in North, general elections since then have been a touch more predictable, Cook increasing his majority in subsequent contests to over 20,000 by 1997. Such results are not surprising given that Labour currently holds 26 of the 30 council seats in the constituency, and that the Conservatives polled fewer than 150 votes in no fewer than nine wards in the most recent (1999) council elections. Indeed, it is nowadays difficult to comprehend that future Conservative Prime Minister Harold Macmillan was Stockton's MP in the inter-war period before he sought a safer southern refuge after 1945.

STOCKTON SOUTH

	2001		1997		1992 notional	
Electorate and turnout	70,337	62.9	68,585	76.0	65,354	79.3
Conservative	14,328	32.4	17,205	33.0	23,331	45.0
Labour	23,414	53.0	28,790	55.2	18,435	35.6
Lib Dem	6,012	13.6	4,721	9.1	10,080	19.4
Anti–EU	–	–	1,400	2.7	–	–
Others	455		–		–	
MP	Dari Taylor (Lab)		Dari Taylor (Lab)		Tim Devlin (Con)	
Majority	9,086	20.6	11,585	22.2	4,896	9.4

Stockton's second seat was only created by the boundary commissioners prior to the 1983 general election, but has always been viewed as a marginal and has already been held by all three main parties. On its creation, it was held by sitting SDP member, Ian Wrigglesworth (MP for the abolished Thornaby seat from 1974 until 1983), who unlike Bill Rodgers was successfully re-elected in his new colours, though his vote was just 100 ahead of, perhaps surprisingly, the Conservatives. Labour finished in third place in both 1983 and 1987, that second contest seeing Wrigglesworth defeated by Tim Devlin, the margin this time a slightly larger 774. Five years later, Stockton South produced easily the best Tory performance in the country, Devlin adding an eye-catching 7,500 votes to his total as the third party vote collapsed, though the cloud on the horizon was that Labour had finally secured second place and were likely to challenge strongly next time around. In the event, the landslide conditions of 1997 rendered the outcome here a foregone conclusion, though Labour's advance of almost 20 per cent was their sixth best performance anywhere in the country, Dari Taylor winning by an enormous margin (for a gained constituency) exceeding 11,500. This result certainly maintained the seat's reputation for extreme electoral volatility, a feature inherited from its predecessor Thornaby/Middlesbrough West, which changed hands five times between 1945 and 1974.

Local election results in Stockton South give a few pointers to the political character of this fascinating constituency. In 1999, Labour won 12 council seats as against 9 for the Conservatives and 4 for the Liberal Democrats, a very different pattern to Stockton North (see above). Labour's strength is concentrated in 'old' working class Thornaby (wards such as Mandale and Victoria) and central Stockton, while the Conservatives poll strongly in the western suburbs of Stockton such as Bishopsgarth, Fairfield and Hartburn. In the south of the constituency (essentially commuter-belt territory), Yarm is politically marginal between all three parties and Independents as well, Egglescliffe is strongly Lib Dem and the expanding suburb of Ingleby Barwick (one of the 400 least deprived wards in England) won by the Conservatives locally but with a surprisingly large Labour vote.

In summary this remains a diverse marginal seat which any party seeking to govern needs to win. Indeed if one combines the history of Stockton South with its previous incarnations, this constituency is one of the more accurate bellwether seats in the country, and certainly the most accurate in the north-east, won by the party who triumphed nationally in no fewer than fourteen of the sixteen post-war general elections.

Cornwall including Isles of Scilly

	Conservative		Labour		Liberal Democrat		Others	
	Share of vote	Seats	Share of vote	Seats	Share of vote	Seats	Share of vote	Seats
2001	32.6	0	17.3	1	44.8	4	5.2	0
1997	30.4	0	17.1	1	43.9	4	8.6	0
1992	42.7	3	13.9	0	41.7	2	1.7	0
1987	47.3	4	12.6	0	40.0	1	0.1	0
1983	49.3	4	8.9	0	40.8	1	1.0	0

Cornwall is a very distinctive part of England; some of its inhabitants would attempt to deny that it is really part of 'England' at all. It is Celtic rather than Anglo–Saxon, replete with mysterious stone circles and with its own myths and legends such as the Arthurian myth surrounding Tintagel. Cornwall has its own language, although fewer than a thousand speak it, and its own small nationalist movement Mebyon Kernow (see the chapter on the political parties). It is distant from London in every sense, including geographically – Penzance is as far from the capital as Carlisle, and transport links are rather poorer. A petition for a Cornish assembly has attracted 50,000 signatures, including local political leaders.

Cornwall has hit severe economic problems in the last couple of decades. Its remoteness makes it an unattractive location for inward investment and its own economic base is outmoded. Tourism is the principal industry, and although not as badly hit by the decline of the English seaside resort as places like Clacton or Hastings, thanks to Cornwall's warmer climate and better beaches, it has still suffered. Agriculture is important across much of the acreage of the county. Many used to be employed in tin mining, which has now ceased, and mining for other metals and minerals. Cornwall was the most prosperous mining area in the world in the late 18th century, but the decline of mining has hurt towns like Camborne and Redruth. Around St. Austell there are still active china clay (kaolin) mines, which have created a strange lunar landscape. Cornwall lacks a university, or a motorway and has only recently developed a functioning airport at Newquay. It is, however, a popular retirement destination and in 1998, 23 per cent of its population were of retirement age. Caradon, in the south east, and North Cornwall have both gained more than 20 per cent in population between 1981 and 1998, mostly through retirement.

Cornwall's distinctiveness extends to its politics. When the Liberal Party collapsed in most areas it remained a viable force in the county, while Labour struggled to obtain a foothold. As late as 1929 Cornwall returned a full slate of Liberal MPs, and even in its darkest days in the early 1950s it maintained second place in Cornwall North and Bodmin, two of only six English second places the party managed in 1955. Labour have only ever won one constituency in Cornwall, the one based on Falmouth (with Penryn in 1945 and Camborne in 1950-70 and since 1997). The Liberals recovered second place in the county as a whole in 1959 and gained Bodmin in 1964, their first win in the county since 1945, then North in 1966. During Jeremy Thorpe's years as party leader the Liberals consolidated their position and eroded the Labour vote in St. Ives and Truro – in the latter seat to the point that the Liberals gained it in October 1974. Truro alone remained Liberal in 1979-92, through Thorpe's trial and the 1980s when the Conservatives fought off serious challenges across the county and the Alliance added little to Liberal support.

Recent elections in Cornwall have seen Conservative resistance collapse. North Cornwall succumbed to the Liberal Democrats in 1992 and then in 1997 the Tories were wiped out, as the Lib Dems reclaimed Cornwall South East (Bodmin's successor) and won St. Ives, while Labour came from third place to win Falmouth & Camborne.

The presence of so many retired people, its remoteness, and a small but well publicised fishing fleet angry at EU quotas, have generated a strong anti-EU vote in Cornwall. In 1997 the Eurosceptic minor parties polled 6.2 per cent, and in the 1999 Euro election the UKIP polled 15.2 per cent, their best share in any county. It was therefore something of a surprise that the Conservatives did not make up more ground in 2001 with their populist, anti-EU campaign. This was something of a testament to incumbency, and it is notable that the two constituencies where the Tories made appreciable progress were the two (North, Truro) where the Lib Dem MP had been elected before 1997. The Hague campaign fell between two stools – it put off the educated, affluent professionals in London, but it failed to speak with the authentic voice of the alienated periphery.

The Cornish Conservatives could not mop up all of the anti-EU vote; in 2001 3.7 per cent were still voting UKIP. In the next election the Conservatives must hope to do better, although none of the seats look all that attractive for them as their support everywhere was clustered in the low 30s. The Lib Dems also have a larger Labour vote to mine for tactical support in future elections than they did in the 1980s.

Local government

Local politics in large parts of Cornwall is still the preserve of Independent candidates, which makes it difficult to estimate where each party's national support comes from. Cornwall county council is run by an all-party executive with portfolios allocated proportionately among a 35-strong Liberal Democrat group, 25 Independents (plus one Liberal) and 9 councillors each for the Conservatives and Labour, with a clump of three Labour wards in Camborne. The Lib Dems had outright control from 1993 to 1997 but suffered splits after 1997. The Isles of Scilly have a small all-purpose council of their own, where councillors do not have party labels.

The Cornish district councils are also mostly non-partisan, although Liberal Democrat gains in the 1990s ended outright Independent control except in North Cornwall (Bodmin, Bude, Launceston). Kerrier (Camborne, Redruth and Helston) too is Independent-led with Labour narrowly the second largest party and some Lib Dems. Penwith (Penzance and St. Ives) is farthest west, and always hung – currently with Independents and Conservatives being the largest groups. Caradon (south east Cornwall, around Saltash and Liskeard) is dominated by Lib Dems and Independents. Carrick (Truro and Falmouth) is under outright Lib Dem control, with Labour weak despite Falmouth's role in a Labour constituency. Restormel (St. Austell, Newquay and Fowey; the name comes from a castle) was Liberal Democrat from 1991 until 1999, when they lost control although the party is still the largest single element ahead of Conservative and Independent groups.

Boundary review

Cornwall's five seats are all rather large, and the county is narrowly entitled to a sixth seat in the boundary review. All the options for the sixth seat would involve radical disruption to long-established patterns and the creation of unfamiliar hybrids: St. Austell and Bodmin? Truro and Falmouth? Truro and Newquay? Newquay and Camborne? Labour would fight hard against an attempt to dismantle the Falmouth & Camborne pairing which produces its sole chance of a seat in the county. Any new seat would probably be a tussle between Conservatives and Lib Dems, with the latter party starting with the advantage.

CORNWALL NORTH

	2001		1997		1992 actual	
Electorate and turnout	84,662	63.8	80,076	73.0	76,333	82.1
Conservative	18,250	33.8	17,253	29.5	27,775	44.3
Labour	5,257	9.7	5,523	9.4	4,103	6.6
Lib Dem	28,082	52.0	31,100	53.2	29,696	47.4
Anti–EU	2,394	4.4	3,636	6.2	–	–
MK	–	–	645	1.1	–	–
Others	–		338 (2)		1,066 (3)	
MP	Paul Tyler (LD)		Paul Tyler (LD)		Paul Tyler (LD)	
Majority	9,832	18.2	13,847	23.7	1,921	3.1

The Cornwall North constituency covers a swathe of Cornwall's Atlantic coastline from Bude, a town beloved of traditional holidaymakers and limerick writers alike, in the north east, to Newquay in the south west. Newquay has become celebrated in recent years as Britain's best surfing beach; there are also smaller coastal settlements at Padstow and Tintagel where King Arthur's Castle is located. But it is not a strip of holiday resorts, as a lot of the coastline is rugged and unspoilt. Inland the two main towns are the market centre of Launceston, and Bodmin on its bleak moor to the south. The population has been growing steadily over the years through incoming retirees.

Cornwall North is probably the constituency with the weakest Labour traditions in the country – the party was in third place even in the elections of the early 1950s when the Liberals had less than 3 per cent of the national vote. Labour's highest ever share was 16.4 per cent in 1951. The party's 7.9 per cent share in the 1999 Euro elections under PR, their only single-figure percentage in the country, indicates that Labour weakness here is not about tactical voting. Labour briefly represented the seat, however, when the sitting Liberal MP Tom Horabin defected in 1947. Curiously, another seat of similarly extreme Labour weakness, Leominster, experienced Labour representation through defection in 1998.

Labour's poor performance has meant that the constituency is a battleground between Lib Dems and Conservatives, changing hands in 1924, 1929, 1950, 1966, 1979 and 1992. In recent years the Liberal Democrats have had the upper hand, gaining majorities in 1997 and 2001 much larger than the area is accustomed to, but in the 1980s the Conservative MP Gerry Neale was a dogged survivor. The Conservatives are hindered by the continuing strength of the UK Independence Party, which polled particularly strongly in the 1999 Euro election (16.9 per cent). The current Lib Dem MP Paul Tyler represented Bodmin between the two 1974 elections but appears much more secure in this seat – although oddly the potential loss of Bodmin in boundary changes might make it less reliable. The electorate of the constituency was grossly oversized in 2001 and it is almost certain to lose a substantial element to a new central Cornish constituency, and Bodmin is a quite Lib Dem inclined town on the edge of the current seat.

CORNWALL SOUTH EAST

	2001		1997		1992 actual	
Electorate and turnout	79,090	65.4	75,825	75.7	73,028	82.1
Conservative	18,381	35.5	20,564	35.8	30,565	51.0
Labour	6,429	12.4	7,358	12.8	5,536	9.2
Lib Dem	23,756	45.9	27,044	47.1	22,861	38.1
Anti–EU	1,978	3.8	1,428	2.5	227	0.4
MK	1,209	2.3	573	1.9	–	–
Others	–		465 (2)		799 (2)	
MP	Colin Breed (LD)		Colin Breed (LD)		Robert Hicks (Con)	
Majority	5,375	10.4	6,480	11.3	7,704	12.8

Cornwall South East is relatively well off for Cornwall. Parts of it, such as Saltash and Torpoint, have become increasingly popular as commuter settlements for Plymouth while others have resisted the decline of the English seaside resort more successfully than most – Looe and Polperro, and the charming double village of Kingsand and Cawsand. Inland is Lostwithiel, an ancient and somewhat austere-looking town which seems more 'ethnically' Cornish than the rest.

As the most 'English' part of Cornwall, South East might be expected to be most Conservative. Not so. The Lib Dem victories since 1997 are not a recent flash in the pan – the seat had switched back and forward between the Liberals (1922-24, 1929-35, 1964-70, Feb-Oct 1974) and Conservatives (1918-22, 1924-29, 1935-64, Oct 1974-97) in its current form and as 'Bodmin' before 1983.

The knockout 12-point swing in 1997, larger than any other in the south west (except by-election influenced Christchurch), must have in part reflected the loss of the personal vote accruing to moderate Conservative Robert Hicks, MP since 1970 except for a brief interlude in 1974. Lib Dem winner Colin Breed (whose campaign team toyed with the idea of using the slogan 'Breed for Cornwall'), as an experienced Saltash local politician, played the local card strongly. In 2001 there was a very similar result to 1997, although a slight increase in the anti-EU vote went against the local trend. Saltash is the strongest Lib Dem area, with over 55 per cent support in the county elections. South East is still the most vulnerable of the four Cornish Lib Dem seats to any Conservative recovery, but it would still take a lot of work to reclaim from a strong incumbent.

FALMOUTH and CAMBORNE

	2001		1997		1992 actual	
Electorate and turnout	72,833	64.3	71,383	75.1	70,712	81.1
Conservative	14,005	29.9	15,463	28.8	21,150	36.9
Labour	18,532	39.6	18,151	33.8	16,732	29.2
Lib Dem	11,453	24.5	13,512	25.2	17,883	31.2
Anti–EU	1,328	2.8	3,889 (2)	7.3	–	–
MK	853	1.8	238	0.4	–	–
Ind Lab	–	–	1,691	3.2	–	–
Others	649		688 (2)		1,579 (4)	
MP	Candy Atherton (Lab)		Candy Atherton (Lab)		Sebastian Coe (Con)	
Majority	4,527	9.7	2,688	5.0	3,267	5.7

Falmouth and Camborne is remote and surprisingly ugly for Cornwall. Camborne is not a town on the tourist circuit; it is surrounded by derelict mining stacks, and has the sullen and dispirited feel of a place that has suffered greatly from unemployment and neglect. The Camborne area, with Redruth and Illogan, has three wards in the worst-off 10 per cent in England. The Camborne School of Mines is an impressive reminder of past glories, but the last tin mine closed during the Major government. Falmouth was once a significant port but now depends more on the tourist trade, where it is at a disadvantage compared to prettier places like St Ives and Looe. Its fishermen form a tiny but vocal minority with some sway over the more sentimental voters, and their resentment at EU fishing policy has undoubtedly fuelled the growth of anti-European feeling in west Cornwall. Ironically, Cornwall is a big net beneficiary of EU funding through its regional development budget.

Falmouth and Camborne is a fascinating seat. It was narrowly held by Labour from its creation in 1950 until the independently minded Conservative David Mudd seized it in 1970. Mudd built up an enormous majority in the elections of the 1970s, but the Conservatives slipped back steadily in the 1980s to the benefit of the Alliance. The Liberal Democrats thought they could take the seat in 1992 when Mudd retired, but Seb Coe came out just ahead in a close three-party race. The Lib Dems were denied again in 1997 when Labour came from third to first, although there was again less than 10 per cent between the first and third parties. 1997 was also a good year for the rag, tag and bobtail candidates, with Lands End entrepreneur Peter de Savary saving his deposit for the Referendum Party, a rebel Labour man polling 3.2 per cent and interventions by old-style Liberals, Cornish Nationalists and Loonies. Labour's gain was therefore on a very low share of the vote and a lot was left uncertain in advance of the 2001 election. In the event, Candy Atherton increased her majority in the absence of the independent Labour candidate with little change in the Tory and Lib Dem shares, despite the efforts of independent-minded Tory radio personality Nick Serpell. The Conservatives must hope that this area's feelings of neglect and distance from the centre will focus in future on the Labour government, but it is far from guaranteed and they still have the Lib Dems as competitors for the disgruntled vote and a proportion of the electorate loyal to the anti-EU parties. It remains an unpredictable constituency.

ST. IVES

	2001		1997		1992 actual	
Electorate and turnout	74,256	66.3	71,680	75.2	71,154	80.3
Conservative	15,360	31.2	16,796	31.2	24,528	42.9
Labour	6,567	13.3	8,184	15.2	9,144	16.0
Lib Dem	25,413	51.6	23,966	44.5	22,883	40.1
Anti–EU	1,926	3.9	4,281 (2)	7.9	–	–
Others	–		674 (3)		577	
MP	Andrew George (LD)		Andrew George (LD)		David Harris (Con)	
Majority	10,053	20.4	7,170	13.3	1,645	2.9

St Ives itself is a small Cornish resort with wide sandy beaches and an artistic community drawn by the clear light and the contrasts of sea, sand and hills; it is also the site of a branch of the Tate Gallery. It is not the largest town in the division; that is Penzance, the end of the Great Western railway line and the commercial capital of west Cornwall. Beyond Penzance is the sinister landscape of Penwith, strewn with mysterious stone circles on dark moors, and the tourist trap of Lands End. The constituency extends out into the sea past Lands End, as it includes the Isles of Scilly, 30 miles offshore with a population of 2,000.

St. Ives now seems the safest Liberal Democrat seat in Cornwall, with the largest percentage majority in the county. This is a powerful tribute to the recent activism of Andrew George, candidate in 1992 and MP since 1997, in a constituency that did not have much of a prior Liberal tradition and had not been won by a Liberal (discounting bogus 'National Liberals') since 1929. Labour's vote has retreated since its recent peak of 17.8 per cent in 1987 as the Lib Dems have been able not only to stop the national rise in Labour's popularity from spilling over locally, but also to erode the core Labour vote. The Conservatives failed to convince voters on the edge of England that the party could be an effective advocate for their interests. Their efforts cannot have been helped when Conservative candidate Joanna Richardson was quoted as saying (according to the *Daily Telegraph*) that Andrew George would never be taken seriously in Parliament because of his 'funny Cornish accent'.

As in other Cornish seats, anti-EU sentiment is strong in St. Ives. The minor anti-EU parties polled nearly 8 per cent in 1997 and 15 per cent in the 1999 Euro elections, with 4 per cent maintaining this allegiance in 2001. But St. Ives is likely to return pro-European Lib Dem Andrew George for some time to come.

TRURO and ST. AUSTELL

	2001		1997		1992 actual	
Electorate and turnout	79,219	63.5	76,634	74.0	75,119	82.3
Conservative	16,231	32.3	15,001	26.4	23,660	38.3
Labour	6,889	13.7	8,697	15.3	6,078	9.8
Lib Dem	24,296	48.3	27,502	48.5	31,230	50.5
Anti–EU	1,664	3.3	4,258 (2)	7.5	–	–
Meb. Kern.	1,137	2.3	450	0.8	–	–
Others	78		839 (3)		885 (3)	
MP	Matthew Taylor (LD)		Matthew Taylor (LD)		Matthew Taylor (LD)	
					Truro	
Majority	8,065	16.0	12,501	22.0	7,570	12.2

Truro and St. Austell is the most easterly of the three Cornish seats with both Channel and Atlantic coastlines. Truro, in the west, is Cornwall's small cathedral city and is the administrative and shopping centre for the county. St. Austell is the larger town, although it did not get a mention in the constituency name until 1997, and it is rather different. It is an industrial town and china clay mining centre. The extremely popular eco-tourism centre at the Eden Project is in a pit just outside St. Austell. The constituency also includes some countryside and beautiful coastline including the peninsular town of St. Mawes, across from Falmouth.

St. Austell once provided quite a large working class Labour vote, and Labour came within 1,608 votes of victory in 1966. This vote disappeared rapidly with the revival of the Liberals in the early 1970s, suggesting that much of it was Liberal at heart, and enough had gone over for Liberal candidate David Penhaligon to win, against the trend, in October 1974. Nearly two thirds of the remaining Labour vote switched en bloc to the Liberals in 1979, also against the trend, and it has been a safe Liberal constituency since. Penhaligon died at a tragically young age and was replaced by Matthew Taylor in a 1987 by-election. Taylor has now served longer and won more elections than Penhaligon did, and one has have to go a long way north (Berwick, the Borders, Orkney and Shetland) to find a seat with a longer continuous third party history.

Truro lost its place as the safest Lib Dem seat in Cornwall to St. Ives in 2001, thanks to a respectable increase in the Conservative vote. It is only a marginal in Conservative dreams at the moment, but the seat could go back if they were to do particularly well in a future election or if Labour were to revive. Sitting as it does in the centre of the county, it is likely to be broken up if Cornwall gets a sixth seat, which could create a difficult choice for Matthew Taylor.

Cumbria

	Conservative		Labour		Liberal Democrat		Others	
	Share of vote	Seats	Share of vote	Seats	Share of vote	Seats	Share of vote	Seats
2001	39.6	2	38.8	4	19.3	0	2.3	0
1997	33.5	2	45.9	4	16.5	0	4.1	0
1992	46.3	2	36.9	4	16.0	0	0.8	0
1987	48.1	3	33.1	3	18.7	0	0.1	0
1983	46.7	3	31.2	3	21.8	0	0.3	0

Cumbria was the scene of some of Labour's worst performances in the 2001 election. Most commentators readily assumed their seven per cent drop in support, alongside a six per cent increase in the Conservative vote, was a direct consequence of the outbreak of foot and mouth disease, which proved more devastating here than anywhere else in the country. It should be noted however that Labour support dropped as much in Copeland and Workington in west Cumbria as in the areas around Carlisle and Penrith most directly affected. Furthermore, Labour had already lost control of both Carlisle and Barrow councils two years previously in 1999.

That no parliamentary seats changed hands in 2001 despite the highest swing from Labour to Tory anywhere in Britain is a consequence of a highly polarised electoral map in the county. Cumbria combines some heavily industrialised landscape, particularly up its west coast, with far-flung rural areas in the Lake District and further east. The Labour vote is heavily concentrated in the urban areas, and is strong enough to ensure victory not only in Barrow and Carlisle but also Copeland and Workington, both of which contain significant areas of Conservative support away from the main towns. In 2001, Labour still polled more than half of the vote in each of these four seats. Indeed Workington, though briefly lost in a 1970s by-election, has been held at every general election since 1918, Copeland since 1935 and Carlisle since 1964, while Barrow has returned to safe Labour status after a blip in the 1980s.

On the Conservative side, the huge Penrith and the Border constituency covers the largest geographical area of any seat in England and has been held comfortably at each general election, though somewhat less comfortably in a 1983 by-election, since its creation in 1950. In the south, Westmorland, until 1973 a county in its own right, has been continually Tory since 1918. However the Liberal Democrats put in their strongest ever challenge here in 2001, cutting the majority to just over 3,000 votes, and will undoubtedly look to make further inroads next time.

Prior to 2001, the main changes that had occurred in the voting habits of Cumbria over the past thirty years or so could be firmly ascribed to the fluctuations in Labour's nuclear and defence policies. During the 1970s all four of the party's strongholds were held comfortably - indeed Barrow even swung to Labour in 1979 despite Margaret Thatcher taking power nationally. But four years later it was a very different story as Labour's commitment to unilateral nuclear disarmament directly led to a collapse of their vote in Barrow, heavily reliant on the nuclear submarine industry. As a result the parliamentary seat was won by the Conservatives for the first time since 1935, the margin almost 5,000 votes. That Copeland, whose largest employer has long since been the Windscale/Sellafield complex, was retained by Labour (albeit by less than 2,000 votes) seemed a personal triumph for Jack Cunningham in the face of an unpopular national policy. The belief that Labour's nuclear policy was directly influencing constituency results in Cumbria was underlined by the next two elections. In 1987, Labour's policy and the electoral pattern remained largely unchanged, but in 1992 after abandoning unilateralism, Barrow was comfortably regained with one of Labour's strongest performances anywhere in the country.

Local government
Local government in Cumbria underlines the extent of polarisation within the county. On the same day as the general election, Labour narrowly lost control of the county council, which is now ruled by a Conservative-Liberal Democrat coalition. The 40 seats won by Labour in the county council election are heavily concentrated in urban areas and surrounded by a sea of blue. There are stretches of Lib Dem yellow in the south of the county, reflecting their strength on the hung South Lakeland council, where they are the largest group. The local elections of 1999 saw Labour comfortably retain District Councils in Allerdale (based on Workington, Maryport and the Solway coast) and Copeland, but Carlisle was lost to the Conservatives, who then strengthened their position in 2000 though fell back in 2002. Meanwhile, Labour were having problems with disaffected councillors in Barrow who created the 'Furness People's Party' prior to the 1999 all-out elections. Their limited success in 1999 and 2000 has cost Labour control of the council. Finally, the largely rural council of Eden in the east of the county is, like neighbouring Teesdale in County Durham, one of the few Independent-controlled councils in England.

Boundary review
Parliamentary boundary changes are set to help the Conservatives when implemented. The final recommendations of the boundary commission which followed a three-day local inquiry will bring the rural Wetheral ward into Carlisle (a change resisted in the last set of changes) and bring Copeland into the heart of the Lake District - the first change to the boundaries of this hitherto undersized parliamentary constituency since 1950. Both alterations will significantly increase the pressure on Labour, who have already seen their majorities in these two seats cut to approximately 5,000, as the rural areas transferring in are heavily pro-Conservative.

BARROW and FURNESS

	2001		1997		1992 actual	
Electorate and turnout	64,746	60.3	67,007	72.0	67,835	82.0
Conservative	11,835	30.3	13,133	27.2	22,990	41.3
Labour	21,724	55.7	27,630	57.3	26,568	47.7
Lib Dem	4,750	12.2	4,264	8.8	6,089	10.9
Anti–EU	711	1.8	1,208	2.5	–	–
Independent	–	–	1,995	4.1	–	–
MP	John Hutton (Lab)		John Hutton (Lab)		John Hutton (Lab)	
Majority	9,889	25.3	14,497	30.1	3,578	6.4

The industrial working-class town of Barrow-in-Furness, which still likes to view itself as part of Lancashire despite a geographical location in the south west of Cumbria, seems a long way from anywhere; certainly whoever named the northernmost tip of Alaska 'Barrow Point' had a sense of humour. The windswept terraced streets here appear an obvious location for a safe Labour seat, a perception underlined by majorities of almost 10,000 in 2001 and 14,500 in 1997. But the main employer in this remote town has long since been Vickers, builders of nuclear submarines, and this fact alone means even Labour is vulnerable if its defence policies appear to threaten the industry's future. Thus a Labour majority of almost 8,000 in 1979, which had actually increased since 1974 despite the failure and ultimate fall of the Labour government, was spectacularly overturned in 1983 at a time when Labour and its MP had committed themselves to a policy of unilateral nuclear disarmament.

There are Conservative voters in the constituency, notably in the smaller Furness towns of Dalton and Ulverston (birthplace of the comedian Stan Laurel), but there are simply not enough of them to win in anything like normal times. It was Labour's difficulties over their defence policy which allowed Manchester councillor Cecil Franks, who had previously represented the Conservatives at a Cumbria boundary inquiry, to pile up a majority of 4,500 in 1983. The Labour vote fell by a far greater margin than the national average, and the overall swing of almost 10 per cent to the Tories (noted as an 'outstanding performance' in the 1983 *Times Guide to the House of Commons*) was almost double the national figure. Four years later, Franks held on comfortably to win again by a similar margin.

Labour were rescued in the late 1980s by their policy review, the unpopular unilateralist policy ditched under the cover of the Gorbachev-Reagan arms reduction talks. Nationally, the defeat and small two per cent swing achieved in the following general election was a disappointing outcome for these efforts, but in Barrow Labour surged to victory after a swing of seven per cent, their policies no longer seeming to threaten the future of the town. By 1997 the constituency had returned to its former status as a secure Labour seat for John Hutton, who suffered only a small adverse swing in 2001 despite results elsewhere in Cumbria. In between times Labour lost overall control of Barrow-in-Furness District Council, though this was largely accounted for by the formation of the 'Furness People's Party', who held the balance of power after 1999.

CARLISLE

	2001		1997		1992 notional	
Electorate and turnout	58,811	59.4	59,917	72.8	61,008	78.5
Conservative	12,154	34.8	12,641	29.0	19,746	41.2
Labour	17,856	51.2	25,031	57.4	21,667	45.3
Lib Dem	4,076	11.7	4,576	10.5	6,232	13.0
Anti–EU	–	–	1,233	2.8	–	–
Others	823 (2)		126		230	
MP	Eric Martlew (Lab)		Eric Martlew (Lab)		Eric Martlew (Lab)	
Majority	5,702	16.3	12,390	28.4	1,921	4.0

The border city of Carlisle has reliably returned Labour MP's since 1964, and like many other urban areas in the north has seen a shift to the left over recent decades. Labour's majority here in 1951 was only 3,000 and in 1955 the Conservatives regained a seat lost ten years previously by the margin of 370 votes. Carlisle returned to Labour in 1964, but the majority was again cut to less than 3,000 in 1970 and just 71 in 1983. From this close shave, the size of the Labour lead has grown significantly, and even after a six per cent swing to the Tories in 2001, the majority remained higher than in 1945.

The constituency of Carlisle contains not only built-up areas but also a growing rural segment, which undoubtedly helps the Conservatives. For example the Tories picked up no less than 77 per cent of the vote in Dalston ward in the 1999 local elections, and 75 per cent in Wetheral, due to move into the constituency when the next boundary changes are implemented. Labour wards include Denton Holme, Harraby and Upperby, all to the south of the centre, but wards such as Botcherby (next to the M6 at the far east of the built-up area) and Belah (north of the centre and River Eden) have seen significant Tory advances in local elections in recent years, and the Lib Dems can also usually pitch in and win a couple of council wards. The result of all this was that the Conservatives took control of the district council in 1999, fully two years before the foot and mouth outbreak, and they will undoubtedly view the parliamentary seat as a serious target. A final point of note is that turnout levels at the last three elections have been a good indicator of national participation rates.

COPELAND

	2001		1997		1992 actual	
Electorate and turnout	53,526	64.9	54,263	76.3	54,911	83.5
Conservative	13,027	37.5	12,081	29.2	19,889	43.4
Labour	17,991	51.8	24,077	58.2	22,328	48.7
Lib Dem	3,732	10.7	3,814	9.2	3,508	7.6
Anti–EU	–	–	1,036	2.5	–	–
Others	–		389		148	
MP	Jack Cunningham (Lab)		Jack Cunningham (Lab)		Jack Cunningham (Lab)	
Majority	4,964	14.3	11,996	29.0	2,439	5.3

To an outsider, the west Cumbrian division of Copeland might appear unpromising territory for Labour. The constituency extends from Whitehaven all the way down the coast through St.Bees with its private school, Egremont, Seascale and Ravenglass and its miniature railway as far as isolated Millom. It also includes the western fringes of the Lake District including Ennerdale and Wasdale, which contain not only some of the most stunning scenery in England but also rural farming areas which are strongly inclined to the Conservatives. Yet in spite of first appearances Copeland has been held by Labour without interruption since 1935 and by present incumbent Jack Cunningham since 1970.

The Labour strength here is based on a number of factors. There is a large Labour vote not only in Whitehaven itself (the name of the seat until 1983), but also the evocatively named small towns which surround it: Cleator Moor, Frizington and Egremont. Some of this support is undoubtedly a tradition from coal-mining days, even though the West Cumbria coalfield has long since disappeared. A further factor however is undoubtedly the presence of the Sellafield nuclear reprocessing plant. By far the area's largest single employer, Sellafield has been strongly supported by local MP Jack Cunningham even when his party appeared hostile. Thus he was able to hold on in 1983, albeit with a majority of less than 2,000, at the same time as the safer Labour seat of Barrow was gained by the Conservatives. Having said all that, the Tories poll strongly from picturesque St Bees (the starting point of the famous 'Coast to Coast walk') all the way down the coast to Millom, which is politically marginal. Labour are extremely weak in many of these areas, and in Bootle ward (far removed from its Merseyide namesake) received a paltry 7.5 per cent of the vote in the 1999 local council elections. Once Keswick and surrounding wards are transferred into the constituency and Cunningham finally stands down, Labour will have their work cut out to maintain their dominance here.

PENRITH and the BORDER

	2001		1997		1992 *notional*	
Electorate and turnout	68,605	64.5	66,496	73.6	*64,311*	*79.5*
Conservative	24,302	54.9	23,300	47.6	*30,030*	*58.7*
Labour	8,177	18.5	10,576	21.6	*5,644*	*11.0*
Lib Dem	9,625	21.8	13,067	26.7	*14,848*	*29.0*
Anti–EU	938	2.1	2,018	4.1	–	–
Others	1,207 (2)		–		*633 (2)*	
MP	David Maclean (Con)		David Maclean (Con)		David Maclean (Con)	
Majority	14,677	33.2	10,233	20.9	*15,182*	*29.7*

Penrith and the Border is a huge constituency stretching from Longtown on the Scottish border, ten miles north of Carlisle, and Bowness-on-Solway (the end of Hadrians Wall) as far south as Appleby, Brough, Tebay and Kirby Stephen which were historically part of the county of Westmorland. It includes the cobbled streets of Alston, surely the most remote market town in England, the beautiful lake of Ullswater and the flooded reservoir of Haweswater. The seat appears to completely surround the urban island of Carlisle, while its own largest town, Penrith, has a population of barely 10,000. Given its predominantly rural nature, it is hardly a surprise that Penrith and the Border has been safely Conservative since its creation in 1950. For almost thirty years it was the secure political base of Willie Whitelaw, though it was his elevation to the Lords shortly after the 1983 election which presented the Tories with their only serious battle here. The resulting by-election saw the Liberals cut the majority to just 552 votes, but having failed to prevent Whitelaw's successor David Maclean from inheriting the seat, the Liberal challenge has gradually faded in more recent contests. In 2001, Maclean could boast a majority of almost 15,000 while the Liberal Democrats barely held onto second place, with their lowest vote since 1979.

As befits its size, the constituency contains parts of three local government districts. To the north west are four wards from Allerdale district including the small, politically mixed town of Wigton. To the north east are several rural wards in Carlisle district; the strength of the Conservatives here can be gauged from the 1999 local elections when they polled almost 70 per cent of the vote in Brampton and the wards which surround it. The remainder of the constituency, centred on Penrith, is made up of the district of Eden which is still dominated by Independents, who are frequently unchallenged in local contests. Although Labour pick up some votes in Penrith itself, this was always hostile territory for the party even before foot and mouth ravaged many of the local farms. After 2001 this was the Conservatives' second safest seat in Britain, behind only William Hague's Richmond. Short of another by-election, it is hard to see them ever being dislodged here.

WESTMORLAND and LONSDALE

	2001		1997		1992 notional	
Electorate and turnout	70,637	67.8	68,563	74.1	67,523	77.5
Conservative	22,486	46.9	21,463	42.3	29,775	56.9
Labour	5,234	10.9	10,452	20.6	7,898	15.1
Lib Dem	19,339	40.4	16,942	33.4	14,381	27.5
Anti–EU	552	1.2	1,924	3.8	–	–
Others	292		–		273	
MP	Tim Collins (Con)		Tim Collins (Con)		Michael Jopling (Con)	
Majority	3,147	6.6	4,521	8.9	15,394	29.4

Westmorland and Lonsdale might seem as safe a bet for the Conservatives as its larger northern neighbour Penrith and the Border. It would seem only natural that genteel retirement locations such as Bowness, Windermere and Grange over Sands should return a Tory MP. Even the largest centre of population in the constituency, Kendal, has regularly been voted the most desirable town in the country in which to live. Given all this it is hardly surprising that the area has been held by the Conservatives since 1918, and that even in 1945 and 1966 over half of voters stuck with the party.

Yet in recent years, all has not been smooth for the Tory machine here. In local politics the Liberal Democrats have been building their strength on South Lakeland district council, on which they are presently the largest party. Now this success is translating to parliamentary contests, with the Lib Dems adding 6 per cent to their vote at each of the last two general elections. Clearly if this trend were to continue, they would be on course to record a famous victory next time and end or at least interrupt the promising career of Tim Collins, who inherited the seat from former Agriculture Minister Michael Jopling in 1997.

Liberal Democrat strength here is well spread. In 1999 they won wards as far apart as Ambleside to the north, Milnthorpe to the south and Broughton in the west, where they recorded a mighty 92 per cent of the vote (a record for the Lib Dems anywhere in Britain?). Both the Lib Dems and Labour regularly win wards in the town of Kendal, leaving the Conservatives to mop up in some of the surrounding villages as well as Kirkby Lonsdale and Sedbergh over in the east of the constituency. There seems little doubt that energetic Lib Dem candidate Tim Farron must have squeezed the Labour vote in Kendal in the 2001 election as he cut Collins' majority to barely 3,000, and although he was re-adopted as prospective candidate for the next general election as early as April 2002 the final few votes required to topple the Tories may prove more difficult.

WORKINGTON

	2001		1997		1992 notional	
Electorate and turnout	65,965	63.4	65,766	75.1	66,865	80.8
Conservative	12,359	29.6	12,061	24.4	19,696	36.5
Labour	23,209	55.5	31,717	64.2	29,296	54.2
Lib Dem	5,214	12.5	3,967	8.0	4,028	7.5
Anti–EU	–	–	1,412	2.9	–	–
Others	1,040		217		1,018 (2)	
MP	Tony Cunningham (Lab)		Dale Campbell-Savours (Lab)		Dale Campbell-Savours (Lab)	
Majority	10,850	25.9	19,656	39.8	9,600	17.8

The west Cumbrian seat of Workington has been won by Labour at all general elections since 1918. It was sensationally lost in a by-election in 1976 following the move to the House of Lords of former minister Fred Peart, but Dale Campbell Savours comfortably regained the constituency in 1979 and assiduously built up Labour's vote in succeeding contests - his retirement in 2001 is likely to have been as much a factor as foot and mouth in the sharp fall in the Labour vote in 2001.

The Labour vote is particularly strong in the towns of Workington, once home to England's most remote Football League club, and Maryport, where most wards were uncontested in the 1999 local council elections. The smaller and more genteel towns of Cockermouth and Keswick are politically mixed, with Cockermouth tending to the Conservatives and Keswick recently seeing some very close local battles between all of the main parties (and for good measure Independents as well). The constituency extends up the coast beyond Aspatria and Silloth, and in the rural areas outside of these towns, both the Liberal Democrats and Conservatives poll heavily. Amongst the strongest Tory areas of all are Derwent Valley and Crummock (87 per cent of the vote in the 1999 local elections), which contain the Lake District beauty spots of Borrowdale and Buttermere, but these areas are sparsely populated and easily outvoted by the west coast towns in general election contests. Tony Cunningham was MEP for Cumbria & North Lancashire between 1994 and 1999; the proportional list system did for his chances in 1999, but he should now be secure representing his home town constituency at Westminster.

Derbyshire including Derby

	Conservative		Labour		Liberal Democrat		Others	
	Share of vote	Seats	Share of vote	Seats	Share of vote	Seats	Share of vote	Seats
2001	31.1	1	50.0	8	17.5	1	1.4	0
1997	29.5	1	53.6	9	13.8	0	3.1	0
1992	41.5	6	43.4	4	14.7	0	0.4	0
1987	43.2	6	36.2	4	20.5	0	0.1	0
1983	41.5	6	34.9	4	22.6	0	1.0	0

Derbyshire may have only ten parliamentary constituencies, but is a highly diverse county extending almost fifty miles from Saddleworth Moor in the north, over the 'High Peak' into a belt of small towns and villages, and beyond Derby to Swadlincote in the south. The north east corner of the county includes part of the large former coalfield which extended from West Yorkshire as far as Nottinghamshire before most of it shut down in the 1980s and 1990s. Small towns are scattered all the way down the east of the county close to the M1 motorway, notably Chesterfield (population 75,000) but also places like Alfreton, Ilkeston and Long Eaton. The biggest urban area, now a unitary authority, is of course Derby itself (220,000), which includes its own university, a number of typical inner-city wards and just about the only significant non-white population.

The western side of Derbyshire is very different. This area is rural and picturesque, including affluent little towns like Ashbourne and Bakewell, close to the grandeur of Chatsworth House. The Peak District area, almost all of which lies within Derbyshire, attracts large numbers of tourists and day-trippers, particularly as it is so close to large urban centres such as Sheffield and Manchester. Indeed the main route between these two cities, the regularly closed (due to snow) 'Snake Pass' is within the county, as are the Edale valley, collapsed road at Mam Tor and caving centre of Castleton. The largest town in this area is Buxton, beyond which we are in the orbit of Greater Manchester. Though still officially within Derbyshire, towns like New Mills and Glossop have a distinct northern feel, and seem slightly detached from the remainder of the county.

Politically, Labour have tended to be strong in the area from the former coalfield constituencies down to Derby, while the Conservatives hit back in the west. From 1950 until 1970 Labour could always count on seven seats in total: two in Derby (they had won a seat here at the party's very first contest in 1900), together with Bolsover, Chesterfield, North East Derbyshire, Ilkeston and Belper. The Conservatives always won West Derbyshire and (except for 1966) High Peak. The tenth constituency, South East Derbyshire (now Erewash), was always marginal and changed hands in 1959, 1964 and 1970. That year also saw Labour's George Brown lose Belper, and started a period which saw a slow swing to the right in the southern part of the county. Labour's disaster year, both nationally and in Derbyshire, was 1983, when they went down in the revamped seat of Amber Valley (the old Ilkeston without the town itself), finally lost Derby North, where they had been clinging on by smaller and smaller margins, and almost Derby South as well. 1987 was in some senses even worse as the Tories consolidated their grip on their two gains, and even in 1992 Labour failed to regain any seats. Then in 1997 the national landslide was enough not only to recapture the seats lost in 1983, but also Erewash, South Derbyshire (the old Belper without the eponymous town) and High Peak, only won on one previous occasion.

In 2001, Labour held on to all their recent gains, but lost the formerly safe seat of Chesterfield to the Liberal Democrats, the first time since the second world war that a Derbyshire constituency had been won by the third party. In fact Labour had been steadily losing their grip on the seat since a by-election in 1984, though it took another four elections to complete the turnaround. The SDP and more recently Lib Dems have often talked about 'replacing' Labour or beating them in their heartlands, but Chesterfield is a very rare example at a general election level (and the first since Bermondsey and Greenwich in the 1980s) of this actually taking place. The Lib Dems have had success in Labour areas at a local council level, taking control of cities like Liverpool and Sheffield, but without ever looking like repeating the trick at national contests. Meanwhile, almost all of their recent general election gains have come in formerly Conservative seats. Chesterfield is at present an almost unique case, but the Lib Dems will hope the first of many.

Further Labour losses at the next general election in 2005/6 are likely to be at the hands of the Conservatives. In particular High Peak looks vulnerable with a majority under 10 per cent, but Amber Valley, Erewash, Derby North and South Derbyshire are all seats that the Tories will need to win if they are to seriously threaten to regain power. This means that the county will again be under the media spotlight, something which does not happen as much as it did when famous names like George Brown, Tony Benn and Edwina Currie had their bases here. Even a young Matthew Parris, now a regular and entertaining political sketch-writer, was briefly MP for West Derbyshire. The county can still boast a cabinet member in Margaret Beckett, but her career seemed to hit a ceiling when temporarily leading the Labour Party after the death of John Smith in 1994, and she has never quite been at the 'New Labour' power centre. On the 'old' Labour side, Dennis Skinner, the 'Beast of Bolsover', seems a lot quieter than in days gone by, and one feels in general that politics here, perhaps reflecting the rest of the country, are not quite what they once were.

Local government

Labour dominate a number of Derbyshire's local authorities, including the county council. Even here, things seem a lot less colourful than they were in the heady days when well-known left wing leader David Bookbinder was in charge. District councils which have been solidly Labour since 1973 include Bolsover, North East Derbyshire and Chesterfield, though in the latter the Liberal Democrats seem to be getting ever closer to taking control. South Derbyshire has always been Labour with the exception of the late 1970s. Amber Valley was also usually Labour, but in all-out elections in 2000, no fewer than twenty seats were lost along with control of the council to the Conservatives. Thus far Labour have retained control of Erewash and High Peak, both of which have seen periods of Tory administration in the past. The unitary authority of Derby, which as a district council was also held by the Tories on a couple of occasions, saw its Labour majority cut to 3 in 2002 and with annual elections this could be whittled away over a few years. The one normally Conservative district is Derbyshire Dales in the west of the county, though even here they lost overall control in the 1990s.

Boundary review

Provisional recommendations for Derby and Derbyshire were announced in May 2002. The area's entitlement is now eleven and a new constituency will appear near Derby. The proposal is for Derby West Seat (the possibilities for confusion with Liverpool's West Derby constituency are obvious) and a Derby North & Heanor seat extending into what is now Amber Valley. The successor to Amber Valley is 'Belper and Ripley'. All these seats will be hard-fought marginals if created – ther is bound to be a public inquiry.

AMBER VALLEY

	2001		1997		1992 notional	
Electorate and turnout	73,798	60.3	72,116	76.0	72,931	83.7
Conservative	15,874	35.7	18,330	33.5	28,360	46.5
Labour	23,101	51.9	29,943	54.7	27,077	44.4
Lib Dem	5,538	12.4	4,219	7.7	5,582	9.2
Anti–EU	–	–	2,283	4.2	–	–
MP	Judy Mallaber (Lab)		Judy Mallaber (Lab)		Phillip Oppenheim (Con)	
Majority	7,227	16.2	11,613	21.2	1,283	2.1

The evocative sounding Amber Valley is based on the rather less glamorous small towns of Ripley (population 20,000), Heanor (15,000) and Alfreton (8,000), all of which lie off the main A38 road a few miles north of Derby. This has always been marginal territory ('middle England' in more than one sense) with the constituency witnessing some particularly dramatic movements between the two main parties over recent years. The Conservatives won the first two contests after the seat was created in 1983, with a particularly strong showing in 1987 when they added nearly 7,000 votes and 10 percentage points to their share. Labour then hit back in 1992, when another huge (in pre-1997 terms) swing of 8 per cent left Philip Oppenheim hanging on by just 712 votes. Despite boundary changes which slightly improved his position, there was no way Oppenheim could survive five years later, and in the event a swing this time only slightly above the national average gave Labour's Judy Mallaber a huge majority exceeding 11,500.

Since those heady days, there has been something of a mixed pattern here. The Conservatives made local advances in 1999 (and led narrowly in the Euro election), before an all-out local election in 2000 resulted in another dramatic outcome with their gain of 20 seats and control of Amber Valley council. On paper this appeared just about the worst Labour result of that year's local elections, but the headline figure exaggerated the change in vote, and in the constituency the Conservatives were only about four points ahead, since some of their gains came in wards in the West Derbyshire constituency. The 2001 election was, for once in Amber Valley, a much less volatile affair, resulting in a slightly reduced, but nevertheless comfortable, Labour lead of 16 per cent. In 2002, Labour staged something of a recovery in the council elections; this remains a highly marginal area – if Labour lost it at the next general election the two main parties would be neck and neck in parliament.

BOLSOVER

	2001		1997		1992 notional	
Electorate and turnout	67,693	56.5	66,547	71.2	67,485	78.1
Conservative	7,472	19.5	7,924	16.7	13,339	25.3
Labour	26,249	68.6	35,073	74.0	34,018	64.5
Lib Dem	4,550	11.9	4,417	9.3	5,374	10.2
MP	Dennis Skinner (Lab)		Dennis Skinner (Lab)		Dennis Skinner (Lab)	
Majority	18,777	49.1	27,149	57.3	20,679	39.2

Most people have an image of Bolsover as some sort of northern Labour bastion dominated by coal mining and heavy industry, a picture which fits with its long-serving (since 1970) leftwing firebrand MP, Dennis Skinner. In fact the seat is in the Midlands, though it does border South Yorkshire to the north. It was in former times very much a mining seat, but as elsewhere the industry has almost vanished here. There is no argument that the constituency is a Labour stronghold, their 38th safest after 2001. It has been held continually since its creation in 1950, and its predecessor Clay Cross was also Labour for 28 years prior to that.

The seat takes in a strip of Derbyshire roughly covering that part of the county east of the M1 motorway (though with an area to its west around South Normanton) from Woodall services just south of Sheffield almost 20 miles down to the junction with the A38. This territory includes a number of small towns and villages, many of which formerly had their own collieries and still provide strong support for Labour; indeed they were unopposed in 14 of Bolsover district's 24 wards in the 1999 local elections. In Bolsover itself (population 11,000), which is still dominated by its hill-top medieval castle, Labour were only challenged in 1999 by a Socialist. In Shirebrook to the east (9,000), not one of the five wards was contested, though in the 2001 Derbyshire county council elections Labour polled 78 per cent here. There was competition in 1999 in South Normanton (8,000), with Labour recording vote shares of 70 and 77 per cent against Conservative opponents. Labour only lost in some of the smaller villages such as Tibshelf next to the new motorway services of the same name, and in Whitwell, Elmton & Creswell which are in the far north east of the constituency towards Worksop. Overall in 1999 (including the four wards in the constituency from North East Derbyshire) Labour won or were returned unopposed in 39 of the 45 council seats, winning all eight county council wards in 2001. The opposition who succeeded in being elected tended to be Independents rather than representing rival political parties, and it is currently difficult to see how Labour might ever lose here.

CHESTERFIELD

	2001		1997		1992 actual	
Electorate and turnout	73,216	60.7	72,472	70.9	71,685	78.1
Conservative	3,613	8.1	4,752	9.2	9,473	16.9
Labour	18,663	42.0	26,105	50.8	26,461	47.3
Lib Dem	21,249	47.8	20,330	39.6	20,047	35.8
Others	916 (3)		202		–	
MP	Paul Holmes (LD)		Tony Benn (Lab)		Tony Benn (Lab)	
Majority	2,586	5.8	5,775	11.2	6,414	11.5

Chesterfield was one of the very few seats which changed hands in 2001, and is the only constituency which Labour have lost to the Liberal Democrats (or their predecessors) in a general election since the 1980s. There are many possible explanations for this, but there is no doubt that recent results here have gone dramatically against the national grain, rather like the town's famous crooked spire. In 1983, former cabinet minister, Eric Varley, easily defeated the Conservatives by 8,000 votes, with the Liberals in third place with less than 20 per cent of the vote. The Labour lead was not only their second biggest in the county, but also the East Midlands region as a whole, larger than neighbouring Derbyshire North East or even the nearby Nottinghamshire constituencies of Ashfield and Bassetlaw. Since then however, their fortunes have gradually declined and the Lib Dems have scored a rare northern victory in a traditionally Labour, rather than Conservative, setting.

The first part of the explanation for what has happened relates to the 1984 by-election, when the Liberals put in a much stronger challenge to finish in second place, though Tony Benn (who had been defeated in Bristol East in 1983) still won comfortably enough by more than 6,000 votes. The momentum from the by-election was enough for the Conservatives to be kept in third place in 1987, since when their vote has steadily been squeezed in classic Liberal style. Thus a sizeable Tory vote in 1983 of 32 per cent was reduced to 25 per cent in 1987, 17 per cent in 1992 and just 9 per cent by 1997. This pattern was repeated in local elections, while the Liberals/Lib Dems have steadily worked at increasing their presence. From no councillors at all in 1983, their group increased to seven in 1987 (becoming the main opposition to Labour), eleven in 1991, a similar number in 1995, and nineteen in 1999. Although Labour still have a majority on the council, one theory is that the Lib Dems are at their most dangerous in elections when on a steady upward trend (and the main opposition), but just before they have actually taken control of anything. Thus in 2001 they were able to win in Chesterfield after their fourth successive improved performance at a general election.

The final part of Labour's difficulties here may well have involved the 'Benn factor'. Although one write-up at the time suggested that Chesterfield Labour Party were 'lucky' to have landed their man in 1984, Benn was very much associated with Labour's lurch to the unelectable left in the early 1980s, and no individual would have been more capable of uniting the opposition in a bid to get rid of him. This was clearly another part of the reason for the steady collapse of the Tory vote, and may explain why in similar circumstances elsewhere (the Lib Dems finishing second to Labour in a by-election) the same has not happened - see Newcastle-under-Lyme in Staffordshire for example. It is ironic that Benn quit while still ahead, but in hindsight this may have been a wise move. His successor Reg Race (MP for Wood Green in London between 1979 and 1983) was on a hiding to nothing in 2001, despite winning a contentious selection contest. He was quite unable to prevent the ultimate triumph of the Liberal Democrats in Chesterfield, but this was just the culmination of a process which had begun in the mid 1980s.

DERBY NORTH

	2001		1997		1992 actual	
Electorate and turnout	76,248	57.8	75,880	74.0	73,177	80.7
Conservative	15,433	35.0	19,229	34.3	28,574	48.4
Labour	22,415	50.9	29,844	53.2	24,121	40.9
Lib Dem	6,206	14.1	5,059	9.0	5,638	9.6
Anti–EU	–	–	1,816	3.2	–	–
Others	–		195		686 (3)	
MP	Bob Laxton (Lab)		Bob Laxton (Lab)		Greg Knight (Con)	
Majority	6,982	15.8	10,615	18.9	4,453	7.6

Derby North has generally been regarded as a key marginal constituency in recent times, and certainly the more vulnerable of the two Derby seats for Labour. Although it was held continuously by Labour from its creation in 1950, the Conservatives came close in 1959, February 1974 and 1979 (when Labour held on by just 214 votes), before Phillip Whitehead, now a regional MEP, was finally defeated by Conservative Greg Knight in 1983. Knight's majority then almost doubled in 1987 – a strong result matched by neighbouring Amber Valley – before Labour started their recovery in 1992. Finally in 1997 the constituency was regained by former Derby council leader Bob Laxton, after an above-average swing of 13 per cent.

The constituency includes strongly Conservative territory in the middle class suburbs of Allestree and Darley off the A6 to the north of the centre, but also Labour areas such as the council estates of Chaddesden to the east and Mackworth to the west. Although the local council is elected annually, not all wards are contested each year, which makes it difficult to detect overall trends; nevertheless Labour were slightly ahead in the wards contested in 1998, 1999 and 2000. In the 2001 general election, there was a small swing from Labour to Conservative, as indeed there was in most parts of Derbyshire, though the majority is still close to 7,000. Derby North is now Labour's 115th most marginal seat nationally.

DERBY SOUTH

	2001		1997		1992 *notional*	
Electorate and turnout	77,082	55.9	76,157	68.0	*75,664*	*75.6*
Conservative	10,455	24.3	13,048	25.2	*23,400*	*40.9*
Labour	24,310	56.4	29,154	56.3	*27,627*	*48.3*
Lib Dem	8,310	19.3	7,438	14.4	*6,195*	*10.8*
Anti–EU	–	–	1,862	3.6	–	–
Others	–		317		–	
MP	Margaret Beckett (Lab)		Margaret Beckett (Lab)		Margaret Beckett (Lab)	
Majority	13,855	32.2	16,106	31.1	*4,227*	*7.4*

Derby has a special place in Labour history, as the town was one of only two places (the other being Merthyr Tydfil in Wales) won by the Labour Representation Committee (original name for the Labour Party) at their first election in 1900. Having said that their candidate, Richard Bell, who was the secretary of the Railway Servants Union, soon became a Liberal MP. Labour regained the seat in 1909 with another railwayman J.H.Thomas, who became a member of the first two Labour cabinets in 1924 and 1929-31. Then however he was to follow Prime Minister Ramsay MacDonald into the National government (as a 'National Labour' MP), and for the second time, Labour officially lost their representation here.

Ever since Derby was divided into two constituencies in 1950, South has been regarded as the more Labour of the two. It takes in the area of dense terraced housing just south of the centre around the famous railway works, which was the original reason behind Labour's success in Derby, as it was estimated at the turn of the last century that 40 per cent of the electorate was employed there. A hundred years on, this area has a significant Asian presence, (the overall non-white proportion of the population in Derby South in 1991 was 18 per cent) and the wards in this part of the seat gave Labour approximately two out of every three votes cast in the 2000 local elections. Further out, the Conservatives' best areas should be the white middle class suburbs of Mickleover and Littleover on either side of the A38 by-pass, though locally these wards are now won by the Liberal Democrats. This showed in the 2001 general election result, when the Lib Dems advanced and the Conservatives again dropped back, leaving a gap of only 5 percentage points between the two. None of this of course troubled cabinet minister Margaret Beckett, who was first elected here by only 421 votes in 1983 but who has since found a rather safer berth than in her previous seat of Lincoln.

DERBYSHIRE NORTH EAST

	2001		*1997*		*1992 actual*	
Electorate and turnout	71,527	58.9	71,653	72.5	*73,320*	*80.6*
Conservative	11,179	26.5	13,104	25.2	*22,590*	*38.2*
Labour	23,437	55.6	31,425	60.5	*28,860*	*48.8*
Lib Dem	7,508	17.8	7,450	14.3	*7,675*	*13.0*
MP	Harry Barnes (Lab)		Harry Barnes (Lab)		Harry Barnes (Lab)	
Majority	12,258	29.1	18,321	35.2	*6,270*	*10.6*

North East Derbyshire more or less surrounds Chesterfield on three sides, but unlike the recent dramatic advance by the Liberal Democrats in the town itself, there has been nothing to match it in the nearby smaller towns and villages. The largest settlement here is Dronfield (population 23,000), which looks across the county boundary to nearby Sheffield as much as Chesterfield, though that is all the more reason why one might anticipate a Lib Dem knock-on effect here. In fact they did win the county council seat in Dronfield South in 1997 and 2001, but it was a tight race and the overall pattern in the town is close to a three-way split. Elsewhere the territory tends to divide into either safe Conservative or safe Labour (mainly former coal mining) areas. Notable in the latter category is Clay Cross in the southern part of the seat (population 9,000), which became a famous political name in the 1970s after its councillors were surcharged for refusing to set a rate, an earlier version of the similar events which took place in Liverpool in the mid 1980s. Labour's other strong area is to the east of Dronfield, particularly Eckington and Killamarsh, which are also just outside the South Yorkshire county boundary and display its political characteristics as well, Labour polling about two thirds of the vote here in the 2001 county council elections.

There are one or two Conservative-supporting villages off the main A61 road, and particularly to the west of Chesterfield on the way to the Peak District National Park. They won the Holymoor and Wingerworth county seat in 1997 and 2001, and have had an enduring minority vote in general election contests, but it is probably too small a base from which to launch an assault on the entire constituency. North East Derbyshire has been a Labour seat since 1935 (represented by left winger Harry Barnes since 1987) and it looks likely to stay that way for the foreseeable future.

DERBYSHIRE SOUTH

	2001		1997		1992 notional	
Electorate and turnout	81,217	64.0	76,672	78.2	74,534	84.8
Conservative	18,487	35.6	18,742	31.3	29,825	47.2
Labour	26,338	50.7	32,709	54.5	27,878	44.1
Lib Dem	5,233	10.1	5,408	9.0	5,235	8.3
Anti–EU	1,074	2.1	3,108 (2)	5.2	–	–
Others	813 (2)		–		291	
MP	Mark Todd (Lab)		Mark Todd (Lab)		Edwina Currie (Con)	
Majority	7,851	15.1	13,967	23.3	1,947	3.1

Derbyshire South includes the two southernmost wards of Derby (Boulton and Chellaston) and then all the remaining territory in the county to the south of Derby itself. The biggest town in this area is the mainly working class Swadlincote (population 25,000), where Labour are very strong, picking up 67 per cent in the 2001 county council elections (and 69 per cent in neighbouring Newhall). The remainder of the constituency consists of small towns and villages, the largest of which is Melbourne (4,500) which is very marginal between the two main parties, both winning seats in the 1999 locals. There are a number of more strongly Conservative villages in the constituency such as Etwall, Hilton and Repton, which is home to a well-known private school. The Tories won the Etwall county ward by nearly 2,000 votes in both 1997 and 2001, but this was nowhere near enough to save them across the constituency. Indeed it appeared from various statements made to the media during the 1997 election campaign that Edwina Currie was one of the few Conservatives who realised the sheer scale of the likely swing away from the government. Given that she had a small (notional) majority of less than 2,000 in Derbyshire South following boundary changes, her own defeat must have seemed inevitable; in the end a 13 per cent swing gave Labour an enormous majority of almost 14,000 and deprived the Commons of one of its more colourful characters.

Currie had won the seat at its inaugural contest in 1983, which followed a big shake-up of constituencies around Derby. There was formerly a marginal seat called South East Derbyshire, but much of that went into the new Erewash division. Most of the present South constituency was previously in Belper (though without the town itself), which was held by George Brown for Labour from 1945 until he was defeated in 1970. Labour regained it in February 1974, but lost it again in 1979; four years later two-thirds of Belper was transferred to the present seat. One can conclude from all this that much of this area is a rather good weather-vane for the prevailing political conditions, having gone the 'right way' at all elections since 1964. In this context the slight swing from Labour to Conservatives in 2001 was only to be expected, and it will again be a key battleground in 2005/6.

DERBYSHIRE WEST

	2001		*1997*		*1992 notional*	
Electorate and turnout	74,651	67.8	72,716	78.2	70,158	84.0
Conservative	24,280	48.0	23,945	42.1	31,944	54.2
Labour	16,910	33.4	19,060	33.5	13,164	22.3
Lib Dem	7,922	15.7	9,940	17.5	13,824	23.5
Anti–EU	672	1.3	2,983 (2)	5.3	–	–
Others	805 (2)		955 (3)		–	
MP	Patrick McLoughlin (Con)		Patrick McLoughlin (Con)		Patrick McLoughlin (Con)	
Majority	7,370	14.6	4,885	8.6	18,120	30.7

The only remaining Conservative seat in Derbyshire can be found in the west of the county. Here, affluent towns like Ashbourne (population 6,000), Bakewell (4,000) and Matlock (10,000) have usually formed the basis of a strong Tory seat. The only time they ever lost it was in the unusual circumstances of the second world war, when by-elections were not supposed to be contested, but the Conservatives were challenged and defeated by an 'Independent' candidate. This was one of several safe Tory seats to be lost at that time (Eddisbury, Skipton and Chelmsford were others) and gave an accurate indication of things to come when the war was over. Sure enough Labour won here in 1945, though the margin was a very tight 156 votes. Thereafter, with one exception, the constituency reverted to its normal status, the Conservatives slowly increasing their vote until majorities reached 15,000 in 1983 and over 18,000 in 1992. During part of this period, its MP was Matthew Parris, probably better known since as a lively political commentator and satirist, but it was his resignation to move to the media in 1986 which caused the latest political flutter here, with replacement Patrick McLoughlin clinging on in the resulting by-election by just 100 votes. A year later the Liberal challenge receded, and they fell back to third place in 1997.

In the 2001 county elections, the Conservatives won all the wards in the 'Derbyshire Dales' part of the constituency with the single exception of Matlock, which was narrowly held by the Liberal Democrats. Ashbourne gave the Tories 60 per cent of the vote, while Labour finished third in two of the six wards, and fourth in Bakewell. Indeed in the 1987 general election, Labour polled less than 12 per cent across the constituency, though they have almost trebled their total since. Labour's strongest area in the parliamentary seat in the most recent elections was in Amber Valley district, the politically marginal town of Belper, which gave its name to a Labour constituency for many years (see Derbyshire South above) before being transferred 'west' in 1983. Some of Belper's neighbours (notably Duffield) are as strongly Conservative as anywhere in the original part of the seat, and overall one has to conclude that if the Tories could hang on here by almost 5,000 votes in 1997, they are unlikely to be dislodged, particularly while Labour are the main challengers.

EREWASH

	2001		1997		1992 *notional*	
Electorate and turnout	78,484	61.9	77,402	78.0	*76,953*	*82.5*
Conservative	16,983	34.9	22,061	36.6	*29,970*	*47.2*
Labour	23,915	49.2	31,196	51.7	*24,247*	*38.2*
Lib Dem	5,586	11.5	5,181	8.6	*8,623*	*13.6*
Anti–EU	692	1.4	1,404	2.3	–	–
Others	1,420 (3)		496		*645*	
MP	Liz Blackman (Lab)		Liz Blackman (Lab)		Angela Knight (Con)	
Majority	6,932	14.3	9,135	15.1	*5,723*	*9.0*

The constituency of Erewash, named after the eponymous canal and river, which forms its eastern boundary (and pronounced 'Erry-wash' rather than 'Ear-wash') is based on the Derbyshire towns of Ilkeston, Sandiacre and Long Eaton, lying either side of the M1 motorway between Derby and Nottingham. This is very much marginal territory, and remarkably Erewash joined no fewer than five bordering constituencies (Derby North, Derbyshire South, Leicestershire North West, Broxtowe and Amber Valley) in being gained by Labour in 1997. Former Sheffield councillor Angela Knight had been elected for the first time in 1992, but lasted just one parliamentary term before losing to another ex-councillor, Liz Blackman. The Labour majority of more than 9,000 in 1997 fell slightly in 2001, but the Tories will need to do much better next time – this is a seat they must win if they are to seriously challenge Labour nationally.

Erewash is based on parts of two old seats, South East Derbyshire, which was always an important marginal constituency, and Ilkeston, which had been solidly Labour since 1935. South East was Labour from 1950 until 1959 and again in the 1960s, electing Conservative MPs in 1959 and after 1970. Politically, Erewash is very much its successor – in the 2001 county poll, the Conservatives won three wards, particularly strong in the area between the two main centres of Long Eaton (population 35,000) and Ilkeston (34,000). For example they led Labour by 800 votes in Sandiacre and about the same margin in Draycott. Long Eaton is marginally Labour (just over 50 per cent of the vote in 2001), but Ilkeston has a very different political character altogether and at the moment tilts the balance across the constituency. In 1999, Labour polled about three-quarters of the vote in its three district council wards and only slightly less in Cotmanhay to the north. The 2001 county results again revealed a big Labour lead over the Conservatives in these wards (and adjoining Kirk Hallam), while elsewhere in the constituency it was almost neck and neck.

HIGH PEAK

	2001		1997		1992 notional	
Electorate and turnout	73,833	65.2	72,448	78.9	71,205	84.1
Conservative	17,941	37.3	20,261	35.5	27,535	46.0
Labour	22,430	46.6	29,052	50.8	22,717	37.9
Lib Dem	7,743	16.1	6,420	11.2	8,860	14.8
Anti–EU	–	–	1,420	2.5	–	–
Green	–	–	–	–	794	–
MP	Tom Levitt (Lab)		Tom Levitt (Lab)		Charles Hendry (Con)	
Majority	4,489	9.3	8,791	15.4	4,818	8.0

The High Peak constituency is one of the most scenic in England, including most of the Peak District National Park and tourist centres like Buxton, Castleton and Edale. It extends all the way from Glossop and New Mills on the fringes of Greater Manchester right across the Snake Pass to the Ladybower reservoir complex and Hathersage. Politically, it has usually been held by the Conservatives, but was won by Labour in 1966 and also saw a respectable vote for the SDP in 1983, when political thinker David Marquand pushed Labour into third place. In 1992, Labour's vote advanced by 9 per cent, and then at his second attempt Tom Levitt won the seat in 1997 with a comfortable majority of 9,000. Following an above-average 3 per cent swing back to the Conservatives in 2001, the majority here is now Labour's 52nd smallest, with High Peak their most vulnerable seat in the Derbyshire-Nottinghamshire area.

A large proportion of the constituency's electorate live in towns which look towards Manchester as their centre, notably Glossop (population 27,000), New Mills (9,000), Chapel-en-le-Frith (9,000), Whaley Bridge (6,000) and Buxton (20,000), which leaves the bulk of this seat somewhat cut-off from the rest of Derbyshire, particularly when the snow falls. Labour's strongest area is Gamesley (near Glossop), but they also attract significant support in parts of Buxton and New Mills. Thus in the 2001 county elections, Labour led the Conservatives in the three Glossop wards by about eight to five thousand, and in Buxton by five to four thousand. The Conservatives' safest areas are on the other side of the Snake Pass in the more upmarket villages of Bradwell and Hathersage, part of the Derbyshire Dales district. Overall, the constituency's 28 district council wards seem unlikely to provide any party with an entirely safe seat and it will again be very hard fought at the next general election. The boundary review may give Labour a small but crucial boost after then; the constituency could lose some very Tory villages to a revised Derbyshire West.

Devon including Plymouth and Torbay

| | Conservative | | Labour | | Liberal Democrat | | Others | |
	Share of vote	Seats	Share of vote	Seats	Share of vote	Seats	Share of vote	Seats
2001	39.0	4	23.6	3	31.9	4	5.5	0
1997	36.8	5	25.9	3	31.3	3	6.1	0
1992	47.5	9	19.3	1	30.4	1	2.9	0
1987	49.5	10	13.1	0	36.6	1	0.9	0
1983	52.8	10	11.1	0	35.4	1	0.7	0

Devon lies in the south west of England, with only Cornwall to its west on the mainland. Devon and Cornwall are grouped together for some purposes, including policing, but the county forms a transitional zone between core England and the Celtic fringe at Cornwall. It shares with Cornwall a commitment to nonconformist religion, small farming and Liberalism, and like Cornwall is heavily dependent now on tourism and retirement. There has never been much industry in Devon outside Plymouth and a little patch around Barnstaple. The coastal areas developed in the 19th century as resort and retirement centres to the extent that it could be said in 1895, as quoted by Henry Pelling, 'The coast is studded with watering places inhabited by a nomadic population of invalids and of retired naval and military officers.' So it remains.

Devon also has considerable agriculture, although it is more prominent in terms of area than economic activity or population. In 1995 it was estimated that only 25,570 were directly employed in farming in the county out of a population a little over 1 million. Devon agriculture is mostly pastoral, based around relatively small farms, and has therefore been badly affected by recent problems in farming. Incomes had fallen badly even before the foot and mouth epidemic of 2001 devastated the county's farms and threatened moorland wild animals. Unlike the other worst-hit county, Cumbria, there was no identifiable political effect.

The area around Exeter (population 107,000) in the north east of the county is rather atypical of Devon. Exeter is a cathedral city and the Anglican church is stronger in this corner than elsewhere – the Exeter diocese had to cover the entire south west peninsula until Truro was given a bishop in 1876, and its neglect fuelled the growth of Wesleyan observance (and Liberalism). Modern Exeter is more cosmopolitan than the rest of Devon, influenced by the university and the relatively good transport connections with London, Bristol and points north. It has the most ethnically diverse population in Devon – although this is not saying much as it is still 98.7 per cent white (the county as a whole is 99.3 per cent white according to the 1991 census). Like other similar cities, it has swung a long way towards Labour in recent years despite its history of Conservatism. Labour won it for the first time in 1966, and then not at all until 1997, but it now looks a relatively safe seat.

The other Devon city, Plymouth, in the south west corner, is its largest city (257,000 population). It has a large naval dockyard and other port functions. Large parts of the city were destroyed in German bombing raids in the Second World War, and Jill Craigie's film of the 1945 Devonport election has eerie images of her soon-to-be-husband Michael Foot electioneering amid the ruins. The centre was rebuilt in high modernist style and peripheral estates sprouted in the north of the city. Plymouth is a remote metropolis, lacking good transport links, and its poorer areas are in just as much need of redevelopment funds as the depressed areas of northern cities. It also lacks the ethnic mix of other major cities, being 99.1 per cent white in 1991.

Plymouth has an interesting political history, and has sent some notable characters to parliament. Between 1885 and 1918 the Devonport constituency voted against the retiring government on every occasion except 1895 largely on issues associated with the Royal Navy. It was Liberal or National Liberal for most of the time between the wars for Leslie Hore-Belisha, whose beacons still adorn British streets, before being won by Michael Foot for Labour in 1945. In 1919 the Sutton division became the first constituency represented in parliament by a woman, Lady Astor. From 1966 to 1992 David Owen was the city's best-known MP, although Alan Clark was also a national figure when he represented Sutton from 1974 to 1992. Plymouth constituencies have kept traditional names – Devonport, Sutton and if there is a third seat Drake – but boundary alterations often mean that the same name has been used to describe very different sorts of territory.

Outside Exeter and Plymouth (including Devon South West as it is based on Plymouth suburbs) Labour ran third in every constituency in 2001 and have done so in every general election since February 1974. The traditional mainsprings of Labour support in the past, trade unions, council houses and manual working class jobs, are all scarce in rural Devon. New Labour has not taken off either, as it did in rural Suffolk in 1997 for instance, as the Liberal Democrats had established a firm presence across the county. Liberalism, nurtured by chapel and Devon's position near the Celtic fringe, never really went away. Its modern revival began in the late 1950s, when the Liberals gained their first post-war by-election win at Torrington in 1958. Although they did not hold it in 1959, Jeremy Thorpe gained North Devon and held it until 1979. Under Thorpe's leadership, although they did not gain any more Devon seats, the Liberals were firmly established as a presence. In the 1980s the Alliance really did seem to be complementary in Devon, with the SDP heartland being Plymouth and the Liberals traditionally strong in the rural areas. Only Exeter was a contested zone, and conflict lingers on as it is one of the remaining areas of strength of the anti-merger Liberals. Since the collapse of the SDP Plymouth has become a very weak area for the Liberal Democrats, who have no councillors there. The representative under the Lib Dem column for 1983 and 1987 in the table above is in fact David Owen – the changing fashions of centre party politics sometimes result in incongruous simplifications. In 1992 the Lib Dems started to pick up again, with the gain of North Devon, and in 1997 they added Torridge & West Devon and – only just – Torbay. Teignbridge followed in 2001, making Devon – equal to Cornwall – the shire county with the largest Lib Dem delegation.

The Conservatives have a difficult job in restoring their parliamentary fortunes, as the Liberal Democrats are all strong incumbents (and Teignbridge will have a new incumbent's bonus in 2005/6). Devon West & Torridge is the most vulnerable, with the Lib Dem majority less than half the size of the UKIP vote. On paper Devon North looks the next easiest, with the combined Conservative and UKIP vote in 2001 only 500 behind Nick Harvey. Torbay, after the 2001 election, looks very difficult for the Tories. The three Labour seats all have quite substantial majorities and Labour would have to be losing the election nationally in order to lose any of them. 2001 showed that local factors were not going to sweep the Conservatives in on local factors in seats where they had done well in local elections like Plymouth Sutton and Torbay. The Tories also risk losing some of their own seats, particularly Totnes, but the danger receded there and in Tiverton & Honiton in 2001.

Euroscepticism is strong in Devon – the UKIP polled extremely well in its rural seats in the 1999 Euro election, and its share of the vote in 2001 (3.8 per cent) was hardly down on the combined Eurosceptic vote in 1997 (4.0 per cent). This is the product of farming and retirement, and also the feeling that Europe is a metropolitan project which has little to offer people here. The presence of this strand of feeling in Devon poses a problem for the Conservatives – whether to move to the right to capture it, or to compete with the pro-European Lib Dems on their territory? How they solve the dilemma, and whether their solution will work, is still to be seen.

Local government

Devon county council is currently hung, as it has been since 1993, with 23 Conservatives, 21 Liberal Democrats, 5 Labour, 3 Independents and 2 old style Liberals. Exeter is out of step with the rest of the county, providing all the Labour and independent Liberal representatives. The executive is formed by a power-sharing agreement and the council has no leader. Plymouth city council is currently Conservative by a large majority (39-21), but this is not the natural condition in what is fundamentally a marginal city. Labour won control of the council in 1991 but accumulated discontents and grievances and were swept out in 2000. The landslide was magnified by the near absence of Liberal Democrats in the city, and the marginality of most wards – Labour had won 55-5 in 1995. The Conservatives won Torbay from the divided local Liberal Democrats in similar circumstances in 2000, but have since lost ground in by-elections and of course in the general election.

There is more partisanship on the Devon district councils than their equivalents in Cornwall. Labour gained Exeter, after years of no overall control, in 1995 and did well in mid term council elections even in 2000, when Labour were resoundingly returned to power. The party has a harder job to maintain control throughout the 2001 parliament in annual elections, but made a promising start in 2002. East Devon (Honiton, Exmouth and Sidmouth) is dominated by the Conservatives to the extent that they had half the seats even in 1995. Mid Devon (Tiverton and around) is under no overall control with Independents the main force and the Liberal Democrats (after controlling the council from 1995 to 1999) the second largest group. Teignbridge (Newton Abbot and around) is divided nearly equally between Conservatives, Independents and Lib Dems but after their parliamentary triumph the Lib Dems must have aspirations to take control in 2003. South Hams (Totnes and Ivybridge) reverted to Conservative control in 1999 after an interlude of no overall control in 1995-99. North Devon (Barnstaple and Ilfracombe) has been under Liberal Democrat control since 1991, with Independents making up most of the rest of the council. Near the Cornish border Independents are stronger, and have controlled Torridge (Okehampton, Bideford and Torrington) since 1973. West Devon (Tavistock and around), traditionally Independent, had a spell of Lib Dem control after 1995 but is now under no overall control.

Boundary review

Devon's population has grown sufficiently for the award of a twelfth seat in the next redistribution. The main population growth has taken place in the area around Exeter, including Teignbridge and Tiverton & Honiton as well as the city, and the extra seat will appear somewhere to the south of Exeter. One controversial prospect, a nightmarish one for Labour, would be to split Exeter and create new seats such as Exeter North and Honiton on one side, and Exeter South and Dawlish on the other. Another possibility would be to chip a ward or two off Exeter, reduce Teignbridge to a coastal strip and create a Mid Devon seat which would be a Conservative/ Lib Dem marginal. It is also probable that Plymouth will be treated separately and will regain its third (probably marginally Conservative over Labour in 2001) seat.

DEVON EAST

	2001		1997		1992 notional	
Electorate and turnout	69,542	68.8	69,146	76.0	68,036	80.8
Conservative	22,681	47.4	22,797	43.4	28,895	52.5
Labour	7,974	16.7	9,292	17.7	6,685	12.2
Lib Dem	14,486	30.3	15,303	29.1	14,902	27.1
Anti–EU	2,696	5.6	3,659 (2)	7.0	–	–
Ind Con	–	–	–	–	1,855	3.4
Loony	–	–	–	–	1,230	2.2
Liberal	–	–	1,363	2.6	857	1.6
Others	–		131		571	
MP	Hugo Swire (Con)		Peter Emery (Con)		Peter Emery (Con)	
					Honiton	
Majority	8,195	17.1	7,494	14.3	13,993	25.4

Devon East is, like a couple of seats in Sussex, completely dominated by retirees. 30 per cent of the East Devon district council's population is of retirement age, and this constituency contains its settlements with the oldest population. Given their greater propensity to vote, it is entirely possible that pensioners cast a majority of the votes in Devon East in 2001. This preponderance has several political effects. First is high turnout – the 18th best in England in 2001. Next is a strong Conservative vote, accompanied by a high vote for the Eurosceptic parties, which was sustained in 2001 with the 3rd best UKIP showing. Another consequence is that the voters of east Devon are set in their ways – there has been remarkably little electoral change here since 1992 despite the dramatic shifts in popularity in most of the rest of the country.

The largest town in the constituency is Exmouth (34,000 population), a seaside town a short hop from Exeter, but it is not typical of the place in its composition or its relatively lukewarm commitment to the Conservatives (40 per cent support in the 2001 local elections). Budleigh Salterton and Sidmouth are the true retirement ghettoes and this area voted over 60 per cent for the Conservatives in 2001. The Conservative county councillor for Sidmouth Rural (69 per cent support) is Stuart Hughes, once a leading light of the Monster Raving Loony Party and elected under that party's peculiar colours in 1993. He has stepped – some would say not very far – into the political mainstream and carried his electors with him. Long-standing MP Peter Emery retired in 2001 and was replaced by Hugo Swire, who is young enough to be the grandson of many of his constituents.

DEVON NORTH

	2001		1997		1992 notional	
Electorate and turnout	72,100	68.3	70,521	77.7	70,051	83.0
Conservative	18,800	38.2	21,643	39.5	26,596	45.7
Labour	4,995	10.1	5,347	9.8	3,406	5.9
Lib Dem	21,784	44.2	27,824	50.8	27,389	47.1
Anti–EU	2,484	5.0	–	–	–	–
Green	1,191	2.4	–	–	657	1.1
Others	–		–		107	
MP	Nick Harvey (LD)		Nick Harvey (LD)		Nick Harvey (LD)	
Majority	2,984	6.1	6,181	11.3	793	1.4

The main town in North Devon is Barnstaple (population 22,000), which has some industry, but North Devon also contains other seaside towns such as Ilfracombe (population 12,000), Lynmouth and Lynton plus some countryside inland. After Torbay, the north Devon coast is the most common destination for tourists in Devon, but the interior is surprisingly remote and deeply rural. Some of it, around the market town of South Molton and Chulmleigh to its south, is strongly agricultural. The majority of the population, however, lives along the coastal strip.

North Devon has been a tough fight between Liberals and Conservatives in most elections for nearly half a century now. Its most celebrated MP was Jeremy Thorpe, who represented the seat from 1959 to 1979 and led the Liberal Party from 1967 to 1976. He lives in the constituency and is an honoured local figure, serving as the President of the local Liberal Democrats. North Devon's Liberalism revived in 1992 with the victory of Nick Harvey.

Thorpe holds the record for a Lib Dem majority in North Devon – 11,072 in February 1974 – but Harvey had a healthy lead in 1997. This fell sharply in 2001 as Devon North produced the 16th largest fall in the Lib Dem share of the vote in the country, and the worst in the south west except for by-election influenced Christchurch. Part of the reason was Europe. In deference to Harvey's Eurosceptic voting record in the 1992-97 parliament, he had faced no opposition from anti-EU minor parties in the 1997 election, but his Euroscepticism was always a rather relative phenomenon and he became more aligned with the rest of his party by 2001. He therefore faced a UKIP opponent, who turned out to be the former Tory MP for Stroud, Roger Knapman, who saved his deposit in a seat where the UKIP won 16 per cent in the 1999 Euro election. There are still a lot of Conservatives in North Devon, but the party faces obstacles in trying to oust a popular incumbent like Harvey. Thorpe's majority bobbed up and down dramatically during his term, and the last time the Conservatives displaced a Liberal incumbent here, it was while criminal charges were hanging over Thorpe. Harvey is unlikely to face this particular handicap.

DEVON SOUTH WEST

	2001		1997		1992 notional	
Electorate and turnout	70,922	66.1	69,293	76.2	65,667	81.4
Conservative	21,970	46.8	22,659	42.9	30,796	57.7
Labour	14,826	31.6	15,262	28.9	8,470	15.9
Lib Dem	8,616	18.4	12,542	23.8	13,666	25.6
Anti–EU	1,492	3.2	2,159 (2)	4.1	–	–
Others	–		159		489	
MP	Gary Streeter (Con)		Gary Streeter (Con)		Gary Streeter (Con)	
					Plymouth Sutton	
Majority	7,144	15.2	7,397	14.0	17,130	32.1

Devon South West is the successor seat to the 1974-97 version of Plymouth Sutton. 60 per cent of its electorate was formerly in the Sutton seat – the communities of Plympton and Plymstock which lie across the river Plym from the main part of the city. These are middle class suburbs, many of whose residents commute over the rather congested bridges to Plymouth city centre. The old seat stretched west across the river into the main built-up part of the city, but Devon SW looks in the other direction and takes in some rural territory instead. There is some development around the A38 at Ivybridge but most of this two-fifths of the seat consists of quiet coastal villages and the southern fringes of Dartmoor around Ugborough. There is a village called Brixton, which is definitely not to be confused with the district of south London.

Labour can win some of the Plymouth city wards in a good year, and won most of them in the party's peak showing in the 1995 local elections. This area produced a respectable Labour vote in the last two general elections, but even here the Conservatives were probably a bit over 1,000 votes ahead. Labour are weak in the rural part of the constituency, polling something like 20 per cent in the local elections in 2001, and Devon South West adds up to a safe Conservative seat. It might, however, be dissolved at the boundary review and something similar to the old Sutton constituency that sent Alan Clark to parliament could be restored. That would have provided a very close fight in the last two general elections.

DEVON WEST and TORRIDGE

	2001		1997		1992 notional	
Electorate and turnout	78,976	70.5	75,919	77.9	74,364	81.2
Conservative	22,280	40.0	22,787	38.5	28,458	47.1
Labour	5,959	10.7	7,319	12.4	5,748	9.5
Lib Dem	23,474	42.2	24,744	41.8	25,187	41.7
Anti–EU	2,674	4.8	3,787 (2)	6.4	–	–
Green	1,297	2.3	–	–	865	1.4
Others	–		508		137	
MP	John Burnett (LD)		John Burnett (LD)		Emma Nicholson (Con) (LD)	
Majority	1,194	2.1	1,957	3.3	3,271	5.4

This constituency always proves a problem in alphabetical listings: does it begin with W, D or T? We have followed the Electoral Commission's practice this time, although it is possible to argue that they categorised it wrongly. Despite this problem its name describes where it is pretty well. It is a large and sparsely populated seat stretching nearly the entire north-south span of Devon. It is one of the two seats (with Tiverton & Honiton) in the south west to rank among the top twenty agricultural seats in Britain. It has no large urban centres, but a scatter of resort and market towns such as Bideford, Great Torrington and, in the south, Tavistock. A lot of the acreage is made up of the lonely reaches of Dartmoor. The Torrington portion was briefly Liberal under Mark Bonham Carter in 1958-59, but for the most part the moderate Conservatism of Tavistock's last MP as a separate seat (1966-74), Michael Heseltine, has prevailed.

The two traditions of the seat converged in December 1995 thanks to the defection of the sitting Conservative MP Emma Nicholson to the Liberal Democrats. Nicholson did not fight the seat under her new colours in 1997 but handed over to John Burnett, a local farmer and solicitor who had fought the seat in 1987. Burnett won a small majority, thanks mainly to a Conservative slide to the anti-Europeans, and his tenure looked even more uncertain when the Lib Dems were beaten by the UKIP, which polled an astonishing 19.2 per cent, as well as the Tories in the 1999 Euro election.

In the light of this, Burnett's performance in 2001 was arguably a more impressive result than 1997 despite the small reduction in his majority. The Greens siphoned off some of his vote, and this constituency's agriculture probably suffered worse than anywhere else in southern England in the foot and mouth epidemic of 2001. Burnett's own local strength and his knowledge of farming must have helped stave off the Conservatives, and there will be another stiff contest in the next election.

EXETER

	2001		1997		1992 notional	
Electorate and turnout	81,946	64.2	79,418	77.9	76,587	81.5
Conservative	14,435	27.4	17,693	28.6	25,693	41.2
Labour	26,194	49.8	29,398	47.5	22,629	36.2
Lib Dem	6,512	12.4	11,148	18.0	12,129	19.4
Anti–EU	1,109	2.1	638	1.0	–	–
Liberal	2,596	4.9	2,062	3.3	1,132	1.8
Green	1,240	2.4	643	1.0	780	1.2
Others	530		282		81	
MP	Ben Bradshaw (Lab)		Ben Bradshaw (Lab)		John Hannam (Con)	
Majority	11,759	22.3	11,705	18.9	3,064	4.9

Exeter is a pleasant city with a civilised air to it. It is the sort of cathedral city that used to be Conservative when the Church of England was the Tory party at prayer (see also Chester, Hereford, Oxford, Worcester – all also Tory in 1945). It has a well regarded university, which affects the political tastes of the electorate by bringing students, and underpaid and overeducated academics, to town; usually to the detriment of the Conservatives and the benefit of Greens, Lib Dems and Labour. The old Liberal Party is still a significant minority force in Exeter as well, at least in local elections.

Labour had only won Exeter once before 1997, and that was in 1966, and came third to a strong SDP challenge in the 1980s. In 1992, however, Labour surged to a close second place and on the retirement of popular Conservative MP John Hannam in 1997 the party was well placed to make a gain. Exeter became one of the most bitter and highly publicised contests in the 1997 election. Labour candidate Ben Bradshaw won the seat comfortably, despite a messy Labour selection procedure and a ferocious campaign against him by right wing moraliser Adrian Rogers for the Conservatives. Bradshaw's success, and that of Stephen Twigg in Enfield Southgate, showed that openly gay candidates could attract votes for the same political reasons as heterosexuals – or, for that matter, celibates (as in Maidstone and the Weald). Conservative candidate Anne Jobson opposed Bradshaw in 2001 with more decorum than Rogers managed but she obtained a similar result.

Bradshaw, who was appointed deputy leader of the Commons, has a relatively safe seat – it is Labour's 162nd most marginal and could survive a defeat almost as bad as 1987. Labour poll well in most of the city, including the central areas and peripheral estates such as Whipton and suburbs across the river like Exwick. In general elections about half the local Lib Dem or Liberal vote seems to vote Labour. If Exeter is cut down to size rather than split in the boundary review, the logical two wards to lose would be Countess Wear and the detached little estuary settlement of Topsham which is strongly Conservative. This would make Exeter even safer for Labour.

PLYMOUTH DEVONPORT

	2001		1997		1992 notional	
Electorate	73,666	56.6	74,483	69.8	75,564	78.4
Conservative	11,289	27.1	12,562	24.2	21,111	35.6
Labour	24,322	58.3	31,629	60.9	27,877	47.0
Lib Dem	4,513	10.8	5,570	10.7	7,830	13.2
Anti–EU	958	2.3	1,964 (2)	3.8	–	–
Ind SDP	–	–	–	–	2,152	3.6
Others	637 (2)		238		293	
MP	David Jamieson (Lab)		David Jamieson (Lab)		David Jamieson (Lab)	
Majority	13,033	31.2	19,067	36.7	6,766	11.4

Devonport is something of a misnomer for this constituency, which comprises the northern edge of Plymouth plus about half the western area generally thought of as Devonport. It is a predominantly working class constituency, with the highest proportion of council tenants in the south west although a very small ethnic minority population – essentially a northern 'heartlands' seat hundreds of miles out on a limb.

Devonport's Labour traditions were obscured by the defection of its MP, David Owen, to the SDP but as soon as Owen vacated the seat in 1992 voters came flooding back to Labour. Plymouth was also tilted a little to the right by its naval tradition, a factor which seems to have disappeared with the end of the Cold War (see also Portsmouth, Gosport and Barrow).

While a safe Labour seat, Devonport still has a capacity to produce surprising results, in mid-term at least. Labour had run Plymouth since 1991 and the council was increasingly unpopular, culminating in a Tory landslide in the elections of May 2000. Previously rock solid Labour wards such as dockland Keyham and the council estate of Southway elected Tory councillors and the overall voting in the constituency was virtually a tie between the two main parties on 43 per cent each. This seemed to be a verdict on the council that did not apply to the Blair government in 2001, but like other heartlands further north Devonport has shown that it cannot be taken for granted.

PLYMOUTH SUTTON

	2001		1997		1992 notional	
Electorate and turnout	68,438	57.1	70,666	67.4	66,738	79.1
Conservative	12,310	31.5	14,441	30.3	22,049	41.8
Labour	19,827	50.7	23,881	50.1	20,989	39.8
Lib Dem	5,605	14.3	6,613	13.9	8,673	16.4
Anti–EU	970	2.5	2,153 (2)	4.5	–	–
Others	361		564 (2)		1,076 (3)	
MP	Linda Gilroy (Lab)		Linda Gilroy (Lab)		Janet Fookes (Con)	
					Plymouth Drake	
Majority	7,517	19.2	9,440	19.8	1,060	2.0

Sutton is a densely populated constituency in the centre of Plymouth. St. Peter and Sutton wards contain the post-war city centre area and surrounding districts, such as the carefully preserved Barbican and the sordid Union Street area. St Peter is one of the poorest wards in Britain (249th on the index of multiple deprivation). North of the city centre, among the hills that give Plymouth its distinctive cityscape, is the comfortable Tory area of Compton; north-west are the terraces of marginal Stoke. Plymouth seats often chop and change at the whim of the Boundary Commission; the current Sutton resembles 'Drake', a marginal Tory seat from 1974 to 1997. Labour's Linda Gilroy won an easy victory in the first contest for the new Sutton in 1997 as Tory MP Janet Fookes retired.

The 2001 election saw a standstill result in Sutton, with all three main parties gaining slightly as the Referendum Party vote subsided. This was something of a surprise, as the Conservatives had done very well in the Euro election of 1999 (5 points ahead) and the local elections of 2000 (10 points ahead) and it seemed possible that Plymouth would swing strongly towards them. As it happened, the 2000 vote seemed like a reaction to local issues, and this mixed seat had no intention of turning Labour out of national government. It is still the sort of seat which the Tories need to win if they are to form a government again.

TEIGNBRIDGE

	2001		1997		1992 notional	
Electorate and turnout	85,533	69.3	82,098	76.7	76,740	82.3
Conservative	23,332	39.3	24,679	39.2	31,740	50.3
Labour	7,366	12.4	11,311	18.0	8,181	13.0
Lib Dem	26,343	44.4	24,398	38.8	22,192	35.1
Anti–EU	2,269	3.8	1,601	2.5	–	–
Others	–		956 (2)		1,047 (2)	
MP	Richard Younger-Ross (LD)		Patrick Nicholls (Con)		Patrick Nicholls (Con)	
Majority	3,011	5.1	281	0.4	9,548	15.1

Teignbridge is in east Devon, between Exeter and Torbay. As its name suggests, it spans the river Teign, from the coast at Teignmouth inland into Dartmoor. It also covers the genteel coastal town of Dawlish, where main line train travellers are carried along a viaduct across the beach, and some Exeter fringe areas such as Kenn valley. The largest town is Newton Abbot (21,000 electors), a market town with some light industry set on a fast road to Exeter.

The Liberal Democrats had hopes for Teignbridge for some time, and had run the Conservatives within a hair's breadth in 1997. Unlike several other narrow Conservative survivals of 1997, Patrick Nicholls did not manage an increased majority in 2001 but fell victim to the Lib Dems. It was a gain much savoured by the Lib Dems, not just because it was the culmination of long-held ambitions but also because Nicholls was a controversial character much disliked by political opponents.

The 2001 victory came after some bad mid-term results for the Lib Dems here. The Conservatives gained several seats from them in the 1999 local elections and the Lib Dems crashed to fourth place in the Euro election, behind the UKIP and Labour as well as the Tories. It was a similar picture to neighbouring Torbay both in mid term and in the general election. New Lib Dem MP Richard Younger-Ross should be difficult to dislodge now he has made it to parliament. Most of the constituency produced a very close result between Lib Dem and Tory, although Newton Abbot is the strongest Lib Dem area.

Teignbridge has too many voters and is likely to be cut down to size at the boundary review, involving the loss either of Dawlish or of the inland territory. The Lib Dems could probably survive either alteration, but their majority would fall if they lost the inland area.

TIVERTON and HONITON

	2001		1997		1992 notional	
Electorate and turnout	80,646	69.2	76,154	77.6	72,796	81.8
Conservative	26,258	47.1	24,438	41.3	30,536	51.3
Labour	6,647	11.9	7,598	12.8	6,524	11.0
Lib Dem	19,974	35.8	22,785	38.5	18,872	31.7
Anti–EU	1,281	2.3	2,952	5.0	–	–
Green	1,030	1.8	485	0.8	952	1.6
Liberal	594	1.1	635	1.1	2,059	3.5
Others			236		611	
MP	Angela Browning (Con)		Angela Browning (Con)		Angela Browning (Con)	
					Tiverton	
Majority	6,284	11.3	1,653	2.8	11,664	19.6

Tiverton and Honiton is a large rural constituency wrapped around the north of Exeter. It is, at least in land usage, mainly agricultural, with several small towns. Tiverton in Mid Devon is the largest of them, a market town with 19,000 population. Honiton in East Devon, logically enough, is next largest with 10,000 population; Ottery St. Mary and Cullompton are the other places of any size at all. The constituency consists mainly of villages. Mid Devon is the area of the county least visited by tourists, who tend to speed through it on their way west.

The Tiverton seat, the predecessor to the current one, has been the object of some Liberal hopes since the early 1960s, but has always remained Conservative. The 1997 election here was a close call for the Tories, but they bounced back well in 2001 as front bencher Angela Browning hoisted her majority back into relative safety. The constituency was badly affected by foot and mouth and Browning's experience in government at the agriculture ministry was on this occasion an asset. Jim Barnard, a strong Lib Dem candidate, was denied again. The Conservatives also did well in the local elections, leading in most wards including the two Tiverton divisions in the county elections of 2001. Labour hardly feature in Tiverton and Honiton, and their vote has formed a stable and apparently irreducible core in the last three elections. Having survived 1997 and 2001 the Conservatives should be able to look to this constituency with renewed confidence, although it could well be radically altered in boundary changes.

TORBAY

	2001		1997		1992 actual	
Electorate and turnout	76,072	62.5	72,258	73.8	71,184	80.6
Conservative	17,307	36.4	21,082	39.5	28,624	49.9
Labour	4,484	9.4	7,923	14.9	5,503	9.6
Lib Dem	24,015	50.5	21,094	39.6	22,837	39.8
Anti–EU	1,512	3.2	1,962	3.7	–	–
Others	251		1,261 (2)		425 (2)	
MP	Adrian Sanders (LD)		Adrian Sanders (LD)		Rupert Allason (Con)	
Majority	6,708	14.1	12	0.02	5,787	10.1

Torbay likes to call itself the English Riviera. True enough, there are sandy beaches and the mild climate of Devon allows palm trees to grow, and it is more sophisticated than most English seaside towns, but it is rather provincial compared to Cannes. Although there are no ultra–affluent areas there is also less concentrated poverty than in other resorts – none of its wards make it into the most deprived 10 per cent in England. The seat includes Torquay and Paignton, but the third Torbay town of Brixham is in the Totnes seat. It is almost entirely urban and residential, with a large (26.2 per cent in the borough) retired population. Hotels, leisure and tourism are the important industries; *Fawlty Towers* was set in, and inspired by, Torquay although this is perhaps not something the tourist authorities are keen to stress.

The Conservative majority in Torbay had gradually been eroding before it fell to the Lib Dems in 1997, by 12 votes. It was not the first close contest in Torbay between Tories and Liberals – from 1885 to 1910 it was a very tight marginal seat, producing majorities between 11 votes (January 1910) and the relatively princely 460 (1906). The 12-vote majority that Adrian Sanders had won in 1997 looked distinctly shaky, as the Liberal Democrats came a bedraggled fourth in the Euro election here and went on to suffer a crushing defeat in the council elections in May 2000. Simon Hughes admitted on election night that 'a year ago we thought it would be almost impossible to hold.'

Torbay was the first result to be declared on election night 2001 that caused any kind of sensation. The Conservatives confidently expected to gain the seat, even on polling day, and were appalled to discover when the votes were counted that their candidate Christian Sweeting had been at the wrong end of a big swing to the Liberal Democrats. 'Sanders of the Riviera' was the tubby, beaming face of Lib Dem success in election 2001. It is still a seat the Conservatives will hope to regain, but it now looks quite difficult and the Tories cannot take too much comfort from any good news in local or European elections.

TOTNES

	2001		1997		1992 notional	
Electorate and turnout	72,548	67.9	70,920	75.8	68,071	83.1
Conservative	21,914	44.5	19,637	36.5	28,736	50.8
Labour	6,005	12.2	8,796	16.4	6,842	12.1
Lib Dem	18,317	37.2	18,760	34.9	20,110	35.6
Anti–EU	3,010	6.1	3,551 (2)	6.6	–	–
Ind Con	–	–	2,369	4.4	–	–
Others	–		656 (2)		853	
MP	Anthony Steen (Con)		Anthony Steen (Con)		Anthony Steen (Con)	
					South Hams	
Majority	3,597	7.3	877	1.6	8,626	15.3

South Devon is a beautiful and peaceful part of England, its coast crinkled with inlets. The Totnes constituency includes the small yachting towns of Salcombe and Kingsbridge to the south, Totnes itself in the centre, and the third Torbay town of Brixham on the coast in the north east. Totnes has become a rather New Age town, and has an unofficial website promoting it as a centre of cannabis culture. The rest of the constituency, however is very traditional with a high proportion of retired residents. From 1983 to 1997 the seat covering most of this was known as South Hams.

The 2001 election in Totnes was an unedifying but interesting spectacle. The Tories had a close call in 1997, largely thanks to a vote of 11 per cent which splintered between two anti-EU candidates and a 'Local Conservative'. The national Conservatives did well in Totnes in the local and European elections of 1999. In the latter election, the Lib Dems nearly came fifth, beating the Greens by only 2.3 per cent. Totnes was a tougher seat for the Lib Dems than it seemed from the 877 Tory majority although it was still a top target for the party. Their candidate Rachel Oliver, unwisely given that Totnes is a retirement area, was quoted in the *Economist* as saying 'the choice here is between a woman in her thirties at the height of her energy, confidence and resources, and a white-haired old man who is burnt out.' Anthony Steen gave as good as he got, with scathing comments about Oliver and having his nomination papers signed by the wife of the 1997 Lib Dem candidate. When the votes were counted Steen had done well and achieved a significant increase in his majority. The Conservatives were strongest at Kingsbridge and Dartmouth, while the Lib Dems may have had a narrow lead in Brixham.

Totnes should continue to be a seat in which the Tories just about hold off the Lib Dems. Rachel Oliver was far from disgraced and polled the highest Liberal share of the vote in living memory in the area, but the Conservatives must look at the rather high UKIP share of the vote as a pool to draw upon in future contests.

Dorset including Bournemouth and Poole

	Conservative		Labour		Liberal Democrat		Others	
	Share of vote	Seats	Share of vote	Seats	Share of vote	Seats	Share of vote	Seats
2001	45.3	6	21.1	1	31.5	1	2.1	0
1997	41.8	8	18.8	0	34.1	0	5.3	0
1992	54.5	7	13.4	0	31.2	0	0.9	0
1987	57.8	7	11.3	0	30.8	0	0.1	0
1983	58.6	7	10.2	0	29.7	0	1.4	0

Dorset has the image of being a rural county, but in fact most of its population live in a quite large built-up area. The two Bournemouth constituencies plus Poole are so urban that they count as borough constituencies, and two other constituencies (Dorset Mid & Poole North and Christchurch) are dominated by areas which are essentially suburbs of the Bournemouth-Poole metropolitan area, accounting for 400,000 residents in total. This puts it on a par with Hull or Stoke-on-Trent in terms of the population of its urban area, although at the moment it lacks many of the facilities that make up a true regional capital.

There was hardly any settlement in Bournemouth other than a small fishing village until the Victorian era, when the town embarked on an astonishing burst of growth and quickly spread over the surrounding sandy heathland. It became a rather refined seaside and retirement resort, a world away from the plebeian seaside towns of Clacton or Margate, or even sinful Brighton. Bournemouth has been 'respectable' since the very beginning and unlike most other resorts has not slid into general seediness and decline.

Bournemouth has traditionally had the image of being a sleepy town full of blue-rinse pensioners snoozing on deck chairs by sandy beaches. This was never the whole story, and it is increasingly inaccurate (although 24.7 per cent of the town's population, compared to 18.1 per cent nationally, were of retirement age in 1998). Bournemouth has also drawn large employers such as Eagle Star insurance, and students through its large university. It was hailed by style magazine Harpers & Queen in summer 2001 as 'the next coolest town in the universe' and claims more bars than Soho although its population is only 160,000. Poole is an older town (population around 140,000), rather more traditional and industrial in parts, although with some resort areas like Canford Cliffs which shade into Bournemouth. Christchurch is a less independent satellite of Bournemouth, despite also being an older town.

The urban area is unusual in not having any particularly good Labour prospects and (until the Liberal Democrats won Dorset Mid & Poole North) having a continuous history of Conservative voting in general elections since 1918. The result of the Christchurch by-election in July 1993, which the Lib Dems gained on an enormous swing, was an indicator of the depths of unpopularity the Major government plumbed at the time rather than a sustained local swing away from the Tories. The Conservatives have not slumped in Bournemouth as they have in most other seaside resorts in recent elections and they have maintained their hold on the core urban seats, perhaps because Bournemouth is still relatively successful as a resort. But its recent trendy status and economic diversification lead one to wonder whether it will always remain a Conservative area. The 2001 results gave a slight glimmer of hope to the other parties that eventually the town will follow Portsmouth into being composed of one Lib Dem seat (East) and one Labour (West). If Bournemouth's new trendy status is more than a flash in the pan it might yet throw off its Tory traditions, but this is still something of a long shot and if the Conservatives mount any sort of national recovery their Bournemouth seats should be in no danger.

The remainder of Dorset, to be fair, is very rural. Unusually, the urban seats are more safely Conservative than the rural areas. Weymouth, the only large town outside the Bournemouth-Poole conurbation, is not large enough to make a whole constituency and with a considerable rural element forms the Dorset South seat. The other two, North and West, consist of small towns and a lot of villages. Dorset's regional identity is a little unclear; it is in on the edge of the south west for most purposes including the standard regions and Euro election constituencies, but it is at the heart of the vaguely defined 'Wessex' region. Wessex was more or less invented in its modern form by the author Thomas Hardy (1840-1928) of Dorchester in West Dorset, who portrayed life in the towns and villages of Dorset and, like Arnold Bennett in Stoke-on-Trent, has scattered the landscape with alternative place names. 'Casterbridge' is Dorchester; 'Shaston' is Shaftesbury. Wessex has official recognition only in the title chosen by Prince Edward and Sophie Rhys-Jones.

Dorset has, despite its increasingly urban nature, been a very Conservative county for many years. It was one of two counties (with Surrey) to retain 100 per cent Conservative representation in the 1997 general election, and had produced only four Tory defeats in eighty years, with single-term Liberal wins in the North constituency (1923 and 1945) and East (1929) and a freak Labour by-election gain in South (1962); in the interwar period Bournemouth was the base of the ferociously right wing Henry Page Croft. One has to look before 1918 to find competitive politics here.

The Conservatives' fifty-year run of success in general elections ended in 2001 with two losses – Dorset South to Labour, and Dorset Mid & North Poole to the Lib Dems. Both these changes took place on very small swings – the constituencies have both produced majorities of under 1,000 in two successive elections – but it was enough for Dorset to have been one of the main areas of change in England in 2001. The Conservatives were also quite exposed in the two mainly rural constituencies but survived determined Lib Dem assaults. The Conservative monopoly in 1997 had stirred up some opposition and calls for a more plural composition to Dorset's parliamentary delegation. The singer Billy Bragg, a resident of Dorset West, advocated tactical voting in his own seat for the Liberal Democrats and in neighbouring Dorset South for Labour. Contrary to the outcome of most calls for tactical voting, it appeared to be most effective in the Labour target seat, which was one of two Labour gains in 2001; Dorset West remained Conservative. The Lib Dems did manage to pick up the suburban marginal of Dorset Mid & Poole North. Had it not been for an effective squeeze by the Tories on the vote for the Eurosceptic minor parties (down from 5.1 per cent in 1997 to 1.9 per cent in 2001) there would possibly have been two more knife-edge marginals in West and maybe North. The Conservatives are completely safe in Christchurch, despite it being the constituency with the most recent pre-2001 history of being won by another party, and nearly so in Poole.

Local government

In contrast to their two general election losses in 2001, the Conservatives did well in the Dorset county council elections on the same day. They made eight gains, replacing Lib Dem casting-vote control with an overall Conservative majority. The Tories have 23 seats with representation from across the county (although particular areas of strength in East Dorset and North Dorset); there are 14 Lib Dems, scattered a bit less thickly across the county (but with a clump of four in West Dorset), four Labour (all from Weymouth & Portland) and one Independent from Portland.

Bournemouth unitary is under no overall control, although after fairly good results in 1999 the Conservatives are in the lead with 27 seats, to 18 for the Lib Dems, 6 for Labour and 6 others. Poole unitary authority had elections in May 1999 and is currently led by a minority Liberal Democrat group with 19 councillors to 17 Conservatives and three Labour. Representation in Poole is polarised between a northern suburban area where the Lib Dems are dominant, and the eastern coastal area, which is Conservative.

The remainder of the county is divided into six district councils, two of which (Weymouth & Portland and Purbeck) elect annually. Weymouth & Portland is the only council in Dorset with a strong Labour element, but except in its inaugural election in 1973 Labour have never won an outright majority. It has been under no overall control since 1980, with Labour narrowly leading the Lib Dems for the position of largest party after the 2002 elections. Purbeck (Swanage and Wareham) is under Conservative control, with a large majority over small Lib Dem and Independent groups; 1999 was the first occasion on which the party won overall control because there was formerly a strong Independent presence.

Independents have been a declining force in Dorset local elections. West Dorset is under no overall control, with the Conservatives the largest group and Lib Dems and Independents also having substantial representation. Dorchester provides a few Labour councillors, and Bridport sends one, the party's only local representatives outside Weymouth and the two unitaries. The Conservatives gained Christchurch in 1999, thanks principally to gains from Independents who were once strong in the area but are now on the way out; even in 1995 two years after the by-election the Lib Dems could not take control. East Dorset (Ferndown, Corfe Mullen and Wimborne) is also a strongly Conservative council since the 1999 elections, although the Lib Dems gained it in 1995 and ran the Tories quite close in 1991. North Dorset is closer, with the Conservatives having half the seats and Lib Dems and Independents the rest; it was Lib Dem controlled from 1991 until 1999, and Independent before that.

Boundary review

After the major changes in the 1990s, Dorset is likely to be pretty much unchanged in the next review as the seats are all about the right size. Bournemouth, as a unitary authority, will keep its two slightly small seats of its own. Poole is too big for one constituency and too small for two, so it will continue to be paired with the rest of the county.

BOURNEMOUTH EAST

	2001		1997		1992 notional	
Electorate and turnout	61,520	58.2	61,858	70.2	63,396	72.7
Conservative	15,501	43.3	17,997	41.4	25,558	55.5
Labour	7,107	19.9	9,181	21.1	5,916	12.8
Lib Dem	12,067	33.7	13,655	31.4	14,315	31.1
Anti–EU	1,124	3.1	2,599 (2)	6.0	–	–
Others	–		–		277	
MP	David Atkinson (Con)		David Atkinson (Con)		David Atkinson (Con)	
Majority	3,434	9.6	4,342	10.0	11,243	24.4

Bournemouth East does not contain the town centre; it consists of the suburbs of Boscombe and Southbourne and surrounding areas. East has Bournemouth's most deprived ward, Boscombe West, which is a deteriorated seaside area ranking 415th on the official index of deprivation, but it also has the best residential and retirement areas of the town at Muscliff. The constituency can also boast a swathe of Bournemouth's famous sandy beach.

East has been a safe Conservative seat since it was separately designated in 1950, although it has known some disputatious Conservative politics. Nigel Nicolson fought against deselection in the 1950s over his views on Suez. His successor John Cordle was a controversial character who was obliged to resign from the House in disgrace in 1977 over his activities on behalf of corrupt architect John Poulson. The current Conservative MP, David Atkinson, held the seat in the ensuing by-election.

However, the Conservatives face the possibility of a challenge in East. The Liberal Democrats did quite well in 2001 without trying particularly hard and this looks a logical target for the party to work on in future; unlike the other two wholly urban seats in the area, the Labour vote fell. Even so, it would take an earthquake for the Conservatives to lose any Bournemouth seat.

BOURNEMOUTH WEST

	2001		1997		1992 notional	
Electorate and turnout	63,196	53.2	62,032	66.2	63,222	73.9
Conservative	14,417	42.8	17,115	41.7	24,532	52.5
Labour	9,699	28.8	10,093	24.6	9,110	19.5
Lib Dem	8,468	25.2	11,405	27.8	12,815	27.4
Anti–EU	1,064	3.2	2,191 (2)	5.3	–	–
Others	–		268 (2)		257	
MP	John Butterfill (Con)		John Butterfill (Con)		John Butterfill (Con)	
Majority	4,718	14.0	5,710	13.9	11,717	25.1

Bournemouth West contains the town centre and districts to its north and west such as Winton and Westbourne; it is this constituency that is most affected by the sudden fashionability of Bournemouth at the turn of the 21st century. It also contains some more working class areas such as Kinson and Wallisdown which produce a respectable Labour vote. Wallisdown is the most deprived ward in West (441st on the official index) and these two wards with their council-built estates are the two best (and often only) Labour wards in Bournemouth. The remainder of the constituency, consisting of the central and seafront areas, is contested between Tories and Liberal Democrats. None of West is particularly affluent, its better wards such as Winton scoring middling results on the index of deprivation, and organisational factors probably count for something in the continued resilience of the Conservative vote here.

Labour overtook the Liberal Democrats for second place in 2001 and enjoyed a swing in their favour from the Conservatives. For some reason Bournemouth West has always had a below-average turnout and the mass apathy of June 2001 was more prevalent here than in working class Stockton North. If Labour could get better organised and ensure that its solid areas turn out, West has the potential to be a seat in which the Conservatives are seriously challenged, but the anti-Tory vote is at present too divided to prevail. Any national pick-up in Tory support should see them increase their majority comfortably here.

CHRISTCHURCH

	2001		1997		1992 notional	
Electorate and turnout	73,447	67.5	71,566	78.5	68,353	80.8
Conservative	27,306	55.1	26,095	46.4	35,237	63.8
Labour	7,506	15.1	3,884	6.9	6,678	12.1
Lib Dem	13,762	27.8	23,930	42.6	12,913	23.4
Anti–EU	993	2.0	2,290 (2)	4.1	–	–
Others	–		–		418 (2)	
MP	Christopher Chope (Con)		Christopher Chope (Con)		Robert Adley (Con)*	
Majority	13,544	27.3	2,165	3.9	22,324	40.4

* Diana Maddock (LD) elected at July 1993 by–election.

The Christchurch constituency lies to the east and north east of Bournemouth. Christchurch is an old town on the coast, but the constituency stretches inland across the airport to a separate residential area lying either side of the A31 main road. Of the places in this East Dorset portion of the constituency Verwood is furthest north, on the edge of rural north Dorset, and Ferndown, West Moors and St. Leonards-St. Ives are bungalow suburbs sitting amid pine woods.

Christchurch has one of the most elderly electorates in Britain, with the coastal area and the inland suburbs both serving as retirement areas for people originating all over the country. The central areas of Christchurch are competitive between Conservatives and Liberal Democrats but further out the Tories enjoy mammoth leads in nearly all elections, with Labour always and everywhere a distant third. The coastal resorts of Mudeford and Highcliffe turn out strong Conservative leads, which are even exceeded by the area around Ferndown (59 per cent Conservative in the 2001 county elections) and St. Leonards & St. Ives (70 per cent Conservative).

Christchurch is basically a very safe Conservative seat, and its voters reasserted this pattern in 2001 after the close result in 1997. The Liberal Democrats came near to victory then because they had an incumbent MP who had been elected in a July 1993 by-election at probably the lowest point of the Major government. VAT on fuel had just been introduced and the Conservative Party was tearing itself to bits in the final stages of ratifying the Maastricht treaty. If Christchurch could fall, the number of Conservative seats that were safe in by-elections was reduced to a handful – after Chelsea, Sutton Coldfield and Huntingdon there seemed to be few others. As memories of the by-election faded, the Conservative tradition revived and the Labour vote bounced back, with young candidate Judith Begg doubling Labour's share in 2001. Christchurch is a mirror image of the safe Tory seat just across the county border in Hampshire, New Forest West; indeed, much of the constituency was only acquired by Dorset from Hampshire in the 1970s local government reorganisation.

DORSET MID and POOLE NORTH

	2001		1997		1992 notional	
Electorate and turnout	66,675	65.6	67,357	75.3	64,833	77.0
Conservative	17,974	41.1	20,632	40.7	24,999	50.1
Labour	6,765	15.5	8,014	15.8	5,959	11.9
Lib Dem	18,358	42.0	19,951	39.3	18,945	38.0
Anti–EU	621	1.4	2,136	4.2	–	–
MP	Annette Brooke (LD)		Christopher Fraser (Con)		NEW SEAT	
Majority	384	0.9	681	1.3	6,054	12.1

This constituency is a rather odd shape, reminiscent of a district drawn in California for partisan purposes whose creator defended it as 'contiguous at low tide'. There is a small neck of territory near Lytchett Minster linking the two areas which give the constituency its cumbersome name. About two-thirds of the electorate are in the northern five wards of the borough of Poole. Parts of Canford Heath, north of Poole, were controversially built upon in the 1980s and 1990s with close after close of private residential development, but development has slowed to a trickle now. Corfe Mullen, from East Dorset district, adjoins it closely and is essentially part of the same north Poole suburban area. The other section, across the join at Lytchett, is 'Mid Dorset', the largest part by area, but contributing a minority of the electorate. This mainly rural area is from Purbeck district and includes Wareham and Bere Regis.

In local elections the north Poole wards are fairly solidly Liberal Democrat, with thirteen Lib Dems and two Conservatives being elected in the 1999 unitary elections. The county remainder is only a little less so, with Corfe Mullen in particular returning strong Lib Dem support (63 per cent in a straight fight) in the 2001 county elections. Despite regularly topping the poll in local elections (41.5 per cent to 35.0 in 1999, for instance, and wider margins in 1995 and 1991) the Lib Dems narrowly failed to win the new seat in 1997 and only just managed in 2001. Local election results can sometimes be an unreliable guide to national voting behaviour and it is quite possible that the 1992 estimate for this constituency, which contains parts of four pre-1997 seats, was in error. The authors must confess that our prognostication in 2000 in a previous book was even more in error.

Having made good on the Lib Dem promise this seat always offered, Annette Brooke now has to hold this suburban seat with rural elements against a Conservative counter-attack. Brooke is an experienced activist and former mayor of Poole, but she needs to continue to work hard to retain and expand her base of support.

DORSET NORTH

	2001		1997		1992 *notional*	
Electorate and turnout	72,140	66.3	68,923	76.3	*64,923*	*81.4*
Conservative	22,314	46.7	23,294	44.3	*29,855*	*56.5*
Labour	5,334	11.2	5,380	10.2	*3,195*	*6.1*
Lib Dem	18,517	38.7	20,548	39.1	*19,784*	*37.5*
Anti–EU	1,019	2.1	3,365 (2)	6.4	–	–
Others	637 (2)		–		–	
MP	Robert Walter (Con)		Robert Walter (Con)		Nicholas Baker (Con)	
Majority	3,797	7.9	2,746	5.2	*10,071*	*19.1*

Dorset North, like West, is a predominantly rural constituency with several towns which serve their immediate hinterland. Wimborne Minster is closest to the Bournemouth–Poole urban area and the most modern part of the constituency, linked not only to the towns to its south but with its own high-tech employer of Cobham aerospace contractors. Blandford Forum in the centre of the constituency is a market town unfortunately famous lately for a particularly unpleasant local horsefly. In the north is Shaftesbury (Hardy's 'Shaston'), a picturesque market town where to the dismay of Yorkshire patriots Hovis advertisements were filmed. There is a lot of Dorset North which could arouse the sort of nostalgic feelings evoked by Hovis's appeal to traditionalism.

Although North has the most recent pre-2001 record of non-Conservative voting in a general election – Liberal Frank Byers was MP for the area from 1945 until a narrow defeat in 1950 – it is now the most Conservative of the three rural constituencies. Labour's share of the vote was at background level in the wards that make up the constituency in 2001. The Liberal Democrats were quite competitive in the North Dorset district council part of the constituency, polling 40 per cent to 48 per cent for the Conservatives in the 2001 county elections, but the Tories did slightly better in the area included from East Dorset district. Cranborne Chase, appropriately enough given its place in one of the titles handed down through the Cecil family, was a particularly Tory area (58 per cent support in 2001). The Liberal Democrats are strong enough to make a real contest of Dorset North, although the Conservatives have recently had the edge even in their disaster years of 1997 and 2001.

DORSET SOUTH

	2001		1997		1992 notional	
Electorate and turnout	69,223	65.5	66,493	74.0	67,747	76.6
Conservative	18,874	41.6	17,755	36.1	26,405	50.9
Labour	19,027	42.0	17,678	35.9	10,805	20.8
Lib Dem	6,531	14.4	9,936	20.2	13,788	26.6
Anti–EU	913	2.0	3,652 (2)	7.4	–	–
Others	–		161		864 (2)	
MP	Jim Knight (Lab)		Ian Bruce (Con)		Ian Bruce (Con)	
Majority	153	0.3	77	0.2	12,617	24.3

The main population centre in Dorset South is Weymouth, at the west end of the constituency, a port with a significant tourism and light industrial base. The peninsula of Portland lies to its south. Portland was formerly the site of a large naval base, and its recent closure caused thousands of job losses which have fortunately been made up by new employment; stone quarrying remains in business.

But Dorset South is far from being just Weymouth and Portland. The constituency stretches a long way east, through countryside as beautiful as any in the west country, to Poole Harbour and Brownsea island, familiar to generations of boy scouts and girl guides. The coast has splendid features such as Lulworth Cove and Durdle Door; this part of the constituency is composed mainly of villages plus the small town of Swanage and accounts for a significant 21,000 of the constituency's electors.

Labour's 77-vote defeat in 1997 served to galvanise the local Labour Party, and preparations for the coming election were meticulous. The candidate who had come so close, Jim Knight, was quickly readopted and promoted throughout the constituency. Its isolated position for Labour, nearly equidistant between Exeter and Southampton and with the nearest marginal with any Labour interest being Wansdyke near Bath, helped the local party to maintain Dorset South's status as a Labour target seat. John Prescott spoke from the constituency during the launch of the 2001 Labour campaign as a symbol of Labour's determination to win more. Labour managed to plaster the constituency with posters. The result was a tiny swing to Labour as both they and the Conservatives squeezed the minor parties, but it sufficed for victory and one of two Labour gains on the night. The local Lib Dem vote seems to have lost nearly equal amounts to Labour and the Conservatives for the national contest. Labour are strongest in Weymouth, naturally, although the party put effort into locating votes in the rural remainder. It ran contrary to expectations that Labour gained two seats, here and Ynys Mon, both of which had substantial rural elements.

Jim Knight is a strong MP, with a new 'double-incumbency', which should protect him somewhat from any anti-Labour movement of opinion in the next election, but Labour's prospects in this seat surely depend on another national landslide. It has moved from Labour's number one target after 1997 to the Conservatives' number one target after 2001.

DORSET WEST

	2001		1997		1992 notional	
Electorate and turnout	71,291	69.5	70,369	76.1	67,278	81.2
Conservative	22,126	44.6	22,036	41.1	27,766	50.9
Labour	6,733	13.6	9,491	17.7	7,082	13.0
Lib Dem	20,712	41.8	20,196	37.7	19,755	36.2
Anti–EU	–	–	1,590	3.0	–	–
Others	–		239		–	
MP	Oliver Letwin (Con)		Oliver Letwin (Con)		James Spicer (Con)	
Majority	1,414	2.9	1,840	3.4	8,011	14.7

Dorset West is the most 'west country' of the Dorset constituencies, lying well clear of the Bournemouth-Poole conurbation and bordering rural areas of Somerset and Devon. The principal town is Dorchester, just north of Weymouth, which serves as the county town. However, the character of the constituency is predominantly rural with market towns serving surrounding villages. There are many places of note in the area, including the resort of Lyme Regis, the trade union place of pilgrimage at Tolpuddle and the Cerne Abbas giant brandishing his weapon on a chalk hillside.

Many of the component wards of Dorset West were quite closely fought between the Conservatives and Liberal Democrats in the 2001 county elections, with the overall share of the vote turning out very similar to the general election result. The Lib Dems were strongest in Dorchester town and the rural area near Sherborne (possibly a spill-over from their activism in south Somerset) and the Conservatives were best off in Sherborne town and around Cerne.

Oliver Letwin spent a lot of the 2001 campaign in his own constituency. This was not just because it was marginal but also because his intervention on the national stage opened up embarrassing questions about the scale of cuts in tax and public services the Conservatives were proposing – was it £7bn, £8bn or £20bn? Letwin was filmed by a *Newsnight* crew as he was addressing a Roman-style election meeting dressed in a toga. Perhaps surprisingly, Letwin survived as he and his Lib Dem rival Simon Green both increased their numerical vote slightly on a rather high turnout. The tactical vote failed to come over in sufficient numbers, despite the prominence of the campaign here, to give Green victory. Since the election Letwin has emerged as one of the most thoughtful members of the Shadow Cabinet. He will have to watch his position in Dorset West and, no doubt, fight off the Lib Dems again if his political career is to advance any further.

POOLE

	2001		1997		1992 notional	
Electorate and turnout	64,644	60.7	65,928	71.0	64,285	78.4
Conservative	17,710	45.1	19,726	42.1	27,768	55.1
Labour	10,544	26.9	10,100	21.6	5,880	11.7
Lib Dem	10,011	25.5	14,428	30.8	14,787	29.4
Anti–EU	968	2.5	2,419 (2)	5.2	–	–
Ind Con	–	–	–	–	1,126	2.6
Others	–		137		824	
MP	Robert Syms (Con)		Robert Syms (Con)		John Ward (Con)	
Majority	7,166	18.3	5,298	11.3	12,981	25.8

Poole is the oldest urban settlement in a built-up area of fairly recent vintage. It is a working and leisure port set on Europe's largest natural harbour and has an attractive old town. As befits its status, Poole is the main arts centre in the area and is the main base for Bournemouth Symphony Orchestra. Its famous pottery, however, has recently moved to North Poole. The Poole constituency covers the old town area by the harbour, plus the Parkstone and Hamworthy areas to each side and Canford Cliffs adjoining Bournemouth West, although a bit over half of the inland suburban area has now been placed in the Dorset Mid and Poole North constituency. Canford Cliffs in particular is a retirement area, with 48 per cent of the electorate aged over 65 and an exclusive enclave on a long spit of land.

The wards of the Poole constituency tend to the Conservatives; in 1999 they elected 15 councillors from the area, to 6 Lib Dems and 3 Labour, and outpolled the Lib Dems 46-30. Even in the meltdown year of 1995 they still had a five-point lead, and they have been ahead by 5,000 or more in every election since a Poole seat was designated in 1950. The Labour share of the vote rose considerably in Poole in 2001, but this was a sign as much as anything of its relatively high-class residential nature, and not a prospect of future dramatic developments. Poole is still a safe Conservative seat – their share of the vote is a bit higher than in Bournemouth and the anti-Tory vote is now split very evenly.

County Durham including Darlington

	Conservative		Labour		Liberal Democrat		Others	
	Share of vote	Seats	Share of vote	Seats	Share of vote	Seats	Share of vote	Seats
2001	20.4	0	62.9	7	14.2	0	2.5	0
1997	17.6	0	68.5	7	9.7	0	4.2	0
1992	28.4	0	57.1	7	14.2	0	0.3	0
1987	28.3	1	52.0	6	19.7	0	0.0	0
1983	30.4	1	45.5	6	23.9	0	0.1	0

County Durham has been a Labour stronghold for almost a hundred years, the key factor unquestionably the growth of coal-mining in the nineteenth century, which transformed a hitherto mainly rural northern outpost into a heavily industrialised area. By 1913, no fewer than 166,000 men were employed in the industry in the county (old boundaries) with 140 pits still in operation upon nationalisation in 1947. The effect of the industry on the life, including politics, of the county over the last century cannot be under-estimated, with miners and their families forming a huge chunk of the population in many constituencies and many MPs over that period themselves former miners. The importance of the industry to the political, social and cultural life of the area is perhaps best appreciated by the annual 'big meeting' or miners gala, which in its heyday attracted vast crowds to the centre of Durham, thousands marching behind their colliery banners watched over by the leaders of the Labour Party and trade union movement. Though this event continues to this day, it has become more a poignant memorial occasion since the Durham coalfield was finally killed off by the Major government of the early 1990s. Alongside the closure of associated industry such as the Consett steelworks, the disappearance of the pits has again radically altered the landscape, though as yet not the political loyalties of voters.

Before the growth of mining, the main towns were based on religious centres, Durham dominated by its cathedral, Bishop Auckland the home of the Bishops of Durham at Auckland Castle, and Darlington known as a Quaker town. From the mid-nineteenth century, the spread of mining led to the growth not only of these towns but also of large numbers of smaller colliery villages dotted around the county. By the 1880s, when the electoral system started to evolve into something we would recognise today (equally sized constituencies and a majority of males entitled to vote), almost all constituencies were dominated by miners, and won by Liberal candidates. For example in 1885 the Conservatives won only one seat of the eight which are still part of the county today, Durham, and that by just 120 votes. The other seven were then all won by Liberals, but from the formation of the Labour Party in 1900, this was to change as the allegiances of working men in general and miners in particular switched. One of the new party's first gains was Barnard Castle in a by-election in 1903, and they soon added Chester-le-Street in 1906, a town which has been represented by Labour MPs ever since. Other constituencies were not gained until after the First World War, but by 1922 it was Labour who won seven of the nine seats (the exceptions were Darlington and oddly enough Barnard Castle, both of which were held by the Conservatives) and the party's period of dominance had begun.

Since 1945, Labour have held all the County Durham seats continuously with the single exception of Darlington, which was held by the Conservatives during their periods of strength in the 1950s and 1980s. Darlington is in fact the county's largest town, but is the least associated with coal-mining, and has always included sizeable middle class neighbourhoods. The leafier parts of the town would almost seem more at home as part of North Yorkshire, and for local government purposes, Darlington has now withdrawn from County Durham to become a unitary authority. Durham City is the home of a prestigious University as well as a dramatic Cathedral, but this is a small enclave of just 25,000, surrounded by a number of large villages, which are almost all a legacy of mining days. As a result, the Durham constituency has become as great a stronghold for Labour as its neighbours. Easington and Chester-le-Street/Durham North and to a lesser extent Durham North West and Bishop Auckland have always been dominated by mining and are very strongly Labour, though the western valleys of Weardale and Teesdale can now produce a significant vote for the Liberal Democrats. The seventh and final constituency is of course Sedgefield, abolished between 1974 and 1983 but won on its re-emergence by a 30 year-old London barrister, Anthony Blair. Eleven years later, he became leader of the Labour Party, and three years after that led the party to its first general election victory since 1974. Blair often states that his 'New Labour project' began in Sedgefield, and considering that the seat is part of Labour's greatest stronghold (the county could boast the highest percentage Labour vote in Britain in 1997 and the joint highest in 2001), such sentiments seem highly appropriate.

Local government

County Durham contains six district councils, one unitary authority and a county council based at the imposing or hideous (depending on one's views on 1960s architecture) County Hall at Aykley Heads, Durham. The council chamber here has always been dominated by row upon row of Labour councillors, with the party currently (as of early 2002) holding as many as 53 of the 61 seats. A similar pattern can be found in Chester-le-Street (30 councillors out of 33), Derwentside, which links Consett with Stanley (47 out of 55), Easington (45 out of 51) and Sedgefield (43 out of 49). Durham City is also Labour controlled, but has a significant Liberal Democrat group of 13 councillors. Wear Valley, which includes Bishop Auckland, Willington, Crook and the more rural and increasing wild valley off to the west, saw a sensational Liberal-Alliance advance in 1991, when they gained 23 seats to take control of the council off Labour. However this lasted just four years before Labour won the council back again in 1995 and the Lib Dems are now down to just 4 councillors compared with Labour's 30. Teesdale is the odd council out, this mainly rural area around Barnard Castle in south-west Durham controlled by Independents with only 10 Labour councillors out of 31. Finally, the unitary authority of Darlington includes just about the only group of Tory councillors one finds anywhere in the county, though their 15 members are still heavily outnumbered by Labour's 35. All councils in the county have all-out elections every four years, the most recent in 1999.

In total, there are just 19 Tory councillors throughout County Durham (none at all on five authorities), which is less than five per cent of the total number. By comparison there are, at the time of going to press, 27 Liberal Democrats, 49 Independents and a remarkable 326 elected councillors representing

Labour, which is over three-quarters of the total and a figure which averages out at 46 per parliamentary constituency. All this may change however, if as expected the North East region opts for a regional assembly – at that stage one tier of local authorities will go.

Boundary review

The provisional recommendations were published in May 2002. The commission proposed hardly any changes to existing constituencies and decided to review Durham and Darlington together. Unusually, a 'no change' plan may prove controversial – Darlington is a unitary authority and if it was considered separately the Conservatives might hope to put some pressure on Alan Milburn thanks to the inclusion of extra rural areas.

BISHOP AUCKLAND

	2001		1997		1992 notional	
Electorate and turnout	67,368	57.2	67,294	68.4	68,591	76.0
Conservative	8,754	22.7	9,295	20.2	17,109	32.8
Labour	22,680	58.8	30,359	65.9	24,825	47.6
Lib Dem	6,073	15.7	4,293	9.3	10,184	19.5
Anti–EU	–	–	2,104	4.6	–	–
Green	1,052	2.7	–	–	–	–
MP	Derek Foster (Lab)		Derek Foster (Lab)		Derek Foster (Lab)	
Majority	13,926	36.1	21,064	45.7	7,716	14.8

Bishop Auckland is quite a diverse constituency, including not only the town and its castle (residency of the Bishops of Durham) but also the nearby towns of Spennymoor and Shildon as well as a large geographical area based on Barnard Castle and rural Teesdale.

It was Barnard Castle which was the scene of one of Labour's earliest triumphs, when Arthur Henderson won a by-election here against both Conservative and Liberal opposition in 1903; the seat then alternated between Labour and the Conservatives before being absorbed into Bishop Auckland in 1950. These days, the influence of factors such as mining and nonconformity, so politically important for Labour's 1903 victory, have largely disappeared. Barnard Castle is a prosperous town on the edge of the moors featuring a dramatic castle and nationally important museum, but it is no longer such a good area for Labour; Teesdale district (of which it is the biggest centre) returns mainly Independent local councillors and Conservative county councillors. This whole area, however, contains fewer than 20,000 electors in total, and despite its narrow Tory lead in 2001, it was massively outvoted by the pro-Labour towns further east.

In West Auckland, Bishop Auckland, Shildon and Spennymoor, the Tory vote was less than 10 per cent in the 2001 county council poll. Although there is a reasonable Liberal Democrat vote here, which can occasionally trouble Labour, it is these built-up areas which form the basis of Labour's dominant position in the constituency. The parliamentary seat has been held continually by the party since 1935, with post-war chancellor Hugh Dalton a famous former MP, while current incumbent Derek Foster is now a veteran having been first elected in 1979. Foster's majority reached the barely believable margin of over 20,000 in 1997, but has now fallen back to a more realistic level just short of 14,000.

CITY of DURHAM

	2001		1997		1992 actual	
Electorate and turnout	69,610	59.6	69,417	70.8	68,166	74.6
Conservative	7,167	17.3	8,598	17.5	12,037	23.7
Labour	23,254	56.1	31,102	63.3	27,095	53.3
Lib Dem	9,813	23.7	7,499	15.3	10,915	21.5
Anti–EU	1,252	3.0	1,723	3.5	–	–
Others	–		213		812	
MP	Gerry Steinberg (Lab)		Gerry Steinberg (Lab)		Gerry Steinberg (Lab)	
Majority	13,441	32.4	22,504	45.8	15,058	29.6

Durham City has been won by Labour at every general election since 1922, with the usual exception of 1931 when it was lost by 270 votes. Labour's record of success here may seem a surprise given that Durham includes a very old University and a number of middle class suburbs, not to mention a dramatic Cathedral voted Britain's best loved building by the BBC's *Today* programme. In fact Durham is firmly in the Labour column because of surrounding villages like Bearpark (86 per cent of the vote in the 1999 local elections), Esh Winning (80 per cent), Brandon (71 per cent), Ushaw Moor (65 per cent) and a number of others which in total actually comprise over half of the constituency's electorate. Most of these settlements grew up around their collieries, and have retained a strong loyalty to Labour which has transcended both the closure of the pits and the subsequent and steady growth of the Liberal Democrats in Durham City itself.

When the county council elections took place on the same day as the general election in June 2001, all four seats won by the Lib Dems across County Durham could be found in the city and its suburbs, where they polled approximately 10,000 votes. The Lib Dems achieved a much better share of the vote in the county election (36 per cent) than the general (24 per cent), though they still pushed the Conservatives into third place in the national contest, reviving memories of their 1983 surge when the SDP cut Labour's majority to less than 2,000. Whether the Lib Dems can go further next time remains to be seen, but they will certainly need to reach beyond a constituency of students and the local professional classes in order to mount a serious challenge to Labour.

DARLINGTON

	2001		1997		1992 actual	
Electorate and turnout	64,354	62.0	65,169	73.9	66,094	83.6
Conservative	12,095	30.3	13,633	28.3	23,758	43.0
Labour	22,479	56.3	29,658	61.6	26,556	48.1
Lib Dem	4,358	10.9	3,483	7.2	4,586	8.3
Anti–EU	–	–	1,399	2.9	–	–
Others	967 (3)		–		355	
MP	Alan Milburn (Lab)		Alan Milburn (Lab)		Alan Milburn (Lab)	
Majority	10,384	26.0	16,025	33.3	2,798	5.1

Darlington is the largest town in County Durham, just about the right size to form its own parliamentary seat, and is very unusual in having had no changes to its boundaries since 1950. The town has however seen plenty of political fluctuations in that time, with the Conservatives able to hold the constituency when strong nationally in the 1950s and 1980s, but Alan Milburn regaining it for Labour following a tight battle in 1992 and holding on rather more comfortably since then. Although Darlington has shifted slightly to the left over the years, it remains far more marginal than the many rock-solid Labour seats to the north, and remains a long shot for the Tories if the Labour government runs into serious problems.

In fact there remains a significant Conservative vote in the more affluent southern and western areas of the town, such as Mowden and Park West, and the total of 15 Tory members on the council after 1999 can be compared with just four in the whole of the rest of County Durham. Darlington does also include its fair share of safe Labour areas, which are generally north of the centre such as Cockerton and Northgate, and as a result both the local council and parliamentary seat have usually been won by Labour over the post-war period. In 1983, Darlington was to prove a totally unreliable guide to national fortunes when Ossie O'Brien famously held the seat for Labour in a March by-election (there was even a slight swing from the Conservatives to Labour) before Labour were routed and Darlington lost in the general election just 77 days later. O'Brien's tenure was even shorter than that of a very colourful earlier representative, one Trebisch Lincoln, who held the seat for the Liberals from January until December 1910. One of the great conmen of his time, Hungarian-born Lincoln managed to persuade the local Liberals to adopt him as their candidate when not even a British citizen, going on to defeat the sitting Tory MP by 29 votes. His short career as MP for Darlington was the prelude to a career of dubious financial dealings and espionage, which saw him do time in Parkhurst Prison and finish up as a Buddhist monk known as 'The Venerable Chao Kung'; needless to say electing him as its Member of Parliament was not one of Darlington's finest hours.

DURHAM NORTH

	2001		1997		1992 notional	
Electorate and turnout	67,755	56.9	68,135	69.2	66,503	76.3
Conservative	7,237	18.8	6,843	14.5	12,610	24.9
Labour	25,920	67.2	33,142	70.3	30,374	59.9
Lib Dem	5,411	14.0	5,225	11.1	7,755	15.3
Anti–EU	–	–	1,958	4.2	–	–
MP	Kevan Jones (Lab)		Giles Radice (Lab)		Giles Radice (Lab)	
Majority	18,683	48.4	26,299	55.8	17,764	35.0

North Durham contains the towns of Chester-le-Street and Stanley as well as a number of smaller settlements, many of which were originally associated with coal-mining. Chester-le-Street, the former name for two-thirds of the constituency, is a market town and site of the new international cricket venue at the Riverside, a remarkable achievement for a town of just 20,000 inhabitants. In fact this part of the constituency happens to be Labour's weakest, with the northern and eastern neighbourhoods of the town electing three of the four non-Labour councillors out of a total of sixty-three across the parliamentary constituency. As this indicates, much of the rest of the seat is almost monolithically Labour, particularly the town of Stanley, which was formerly a part of the Consett division abolished in 1983. The old Stanley urban district council could boast a set of elections in 1961 at which not one of the 33 council seats was contested; similar traditions exist in the ex-mining villages of Sacriston and Pelton.

Labour's only serious problems here came as a result of the local government scandals which engulfed this part of the world in the early 1970s. In 1973, the Liberals polled almost 19,000 votes in a by-election in the Chester-le-Street constituency, though in the days of high turnouts this was not enough to prevent the election of Giles Radice. The size of the Liberal group on Chester-le-Street council also peaked in the 1970s, a highly unusual pattern found in few other places. Nowadays, Labour appear totally dominant, though there has been a big growth in new housing developments in such places as Waldridge Park (in the 10 per cent least deprived wards nationally), Urpeth and Lumley, and the constituency is the base for a substantial number of Gateshead, Newcastle and Sunderland-bound commuters. As yet this has had little effect politically, with the constituency bucking at least one trend by retaining its ranking as the 41st safest Labour seat, despite the retirement of Radice after 28 years as MP and thus the loss of any incumbency factor. Labour's new representative here is a former GMB union organiser and Newcastle councillor, Kevan Jones.

DURHAM NORTH WEST

	2001		1997		1992 notional	
Electorate and turnout	67,062	58.5	67,390	68.7	68,120	74.8
Conservative	8,193	20.9	7,101	15.3	13,930	27.3
Labour	24,526	62.5	31,855	68.8	29,596	58.1
Lib Dem	5,846	14.9	4,991	10.8	7,458	14.6
Anti–EU	–	–	2,372	5.1	–	–
Socialist	661	1.7	–	–	–	–
MP	Hilary Armstrong (Lab)		Hilary Armstrong (Lab)		Hilary Armstrong (Lab)	
Majority	16,333	41.6	24,754	53.4	15,666	30.7

Durham North West is quite a large constituency which takes in the towns of Consett, Crook and Willington as well as smaller places like Lanchester and Tow Law, alongside Wolsingham, Stanhope and the remote Wear Valley to the west. Consett formed its own parliamentary seat until being abolished in 1983, which added insult to injury after the closure of its massive steelworks, in many ways the reason for the town's existence. Most of the site has now been cleared, and the greatest problems faced by local MP Hilary Armstrong in the last election concerned foot and mouth disease and an animal carcass burial site near Tow Law. This was probably the biggest reason for a larger than average swing away from Labour here, though this remains a very safe Labour seat.

Much of the constituency consists of small terraced towns and villages and it is very difficult to see where an opposition challenge might come from, though there are Tory voters in Lanchester and a scattering of Independent councillors along the rural part of the Wear Valley from Wolsingham and Stanhope to St Johns Chapel. The valley becomes increasingly scenic in a rugged sort of way, and the lead mining centre at Killhope near the border with Cumbria, 25 miles west of the A68 and 1,500 feet up must be just about the most remote place in England; it certainly feels that way! Back in the more populated areas, Crook, Willington and Consett all produce a Labour share of the vote around the 65–70 per cent mark, and Hilary Armstrong, whose father Ernest Armstrong was MP here for 23 years before her, has a very secure base.

EASINGTON

	2001		1997		1992 actual	
Electorate and turnout	61,532	53.6	62,518	67.0	65,062	72.5
Conservative	3,411	10.3	3,588	8.6	7,879	16.7
Labour	25,360	76.8	33,600	80.2	34,269	72.7
Lib Dem	3,408	10.3	3,025	7.2	5,001	10.6
Anti–EU	–	–	1,179	2.8	–	–
Socialist	831	2.5	503	1.2	–	–
MP	John Cummings (Lab)		John Cummings (Lab)		John Cummings (Lab)	
Majority	21,949	66.5	30,012	71.6	26,390	56.0

The constituency of Easington runs down the once blackened Durham coast from Seaham (the name of the seat until 1950) past Easington itself to Peterlee Newtown and on to Blackhall Rocks, just to the north of Hartlepool. This is an area traditionally dominated by coal mining; Seaham alone had three pits and as well as Easington colliery, one could add Murton, Shotton, South Hetton, Horden and Blackhall to the long list of mining villages in the constituency. Many of these collieries survived until the 1980s and 1990s, which probably explains why Labour continue to pile up the sort of enormous majorities which have started to erode elsewhere. After 2001 this was the party's safest seat in the North East and third safest in Britain, after Bootle and Sheffield Brightside.

The most famous episode here (before the making of the film *Billy Elliot*) was the titanic 1935 contest between former Labour leader and Prime Minister Ramsay MacDonald, then a representative of the small 'National Labour' grouping, and firebrand Manny Shinwell who hoped to regain the seat for the official Labour Party. MacDonald had been one of Labour's most important figures when the party was being built up in the early years of the century, not to mention his status as Labour's first Prime Minister, but caused great bitterness when he chose to create the National government with the Conservatives and Liberals in 1931. Many Labour supporters now viewed MacDonald as a traitor to the cause, so it was to much rejoicing that Shinwell defeated him in the 1935 'battle of Seaham', going on to hold the seat for another 35 years before moving up the corridor to the House of Lords after 1970. Labour have never been remotely threatened on the East Durham coast since those heady days of the 1930s and seem in little imminent danger now. The incumbent since 1987 has been a former miner, John Cummings.

SEDGEFIELD

	2001		1997		1992 notional	
Electorate and turnout	64,925	62.0	65,181	72.3	66,143	76.3
Conservative	8,397	20.9	8,383	17.8	14,161	28.1
Labour	26,110	64.9	33,526	71.2	31,391	62.2
Lib Dem	3,624	9.0	3,050	6.5	4,897	9.7
Anti–EU	974	2.4	1,683	3.6	–	–
Others	1,153 (3)		474		–	
MP	Tony Blair (Lab)		Tony Blair (Lab)		Tony Blair (Lab)	
Majority	17,713	44.0	25,143	53.4	17,230	34.2

The constituency of Sedgefield, recreated by the boundary commission in 1983 after a ten-year absence, is based on a number of small towns and villages in the centre of County Durham. These include Ferryhill, the Trimdons (Colliery, Grange, Station and Village), Newton Aycliffe and the eponymous town itself, though the parliamentary seat also curls around the town of Darlington in a strange way to take in a few much more up-market villages like Hurworth and Middleton St. George which face North Yorkshire across the River Tees. The name of the constituency is also rather strange and inappropriate in political terms, since the small and somewhat prim town of Sedgefield with its racecourse contains just about the only serious Conservative vote one will find in mid Durham, while Labour's base is up the road in Trimdon and the largest centre of population is in Newton Aycliffe, to the west of the A1.

For nearly twenty years now, Sedgefield has been associated with the name of Tony Blair. The future leader of the Labour Party was elected in the constituency's inaugural contest after its rebirth in 1983, and indeed the lack of an incumbent Labour candidate or MP was vital for a then 30 year-old London barrister to win the selection contest in the first place. Blair could hardly have hoped for a safer base as he began his climb to the top of the political ladder; even in Labour's disastrous year of 1983, he had a majority of 8,000, and this figure subsequently increased to 13,000 in 1987, 15,000 in 1992 (prior to the boundary changes) and 25,000 in 1997, when Sedgefield was the party's 51st safest seat. The slight shift away from Labour in 2001 was similar to the pattern in nearby Bishop Auckland and North West Durham, though in any case still leaves a very healthy majority for Britain's sitting Prime Minister.

Essex including Southend and Thurrock

	Conservative		Labour		Liberal Democrat		Others	
	Share of vote	Seats	Share of vote	Seats	Share of vote	Seats	Share of vote	Seats
2001	42.8	11	34.7	5	16.7	1	5.8	0
1997	40.3	10	36.5	6	18.2	1	5.0	0
1992	53.9	15	23.5	1	21.7	0	1.0	0
1987	54.1	16	18.9	0	26.6	0	0.3	0
1983	51.9	15	17.8	1	29.8	0	0.6	0

Essex is a large and varied county, stretching from metropolitan Epping, with its tube line, to East Anglian Harwich, nearly 80 miles away. The important dividing line is between south Essex and north Essex, running roughly from Harlow to Shoeburyness east of Southend. The landscape, as well as the culture and politics, is very different either side of the line and the classic stereotypes of Essex only really have validity in the south of the county. South Essex is an extraordinary part of England. From Barking, inside the Greater London boundary, to Southend it comprises a metropolitan area that if it had a single centre would be England's third largest city. It is structured rather like an American suburb. The towns have spread together and are rather undifferentiated; the main roads have rows of small shops every now and then and there are sporadic new complexes of out of town superstores and multiplexes. Just as many American suburbs are the creations of outwardly and upwardly mobile blue-collar white families, south Essex is full of expatriate and second and third generation white East Enders. The A13 is Britain's Route 66 – shorter and less glamorous but still an emblem of freedom, affluence and what Margaret Thatcher called 'the great car economy'. South Essex is also, to mix international metaphors, England's Bavaria, without Munich and without the mountains; while believing itself the most loyal and characteristic part of England its excesses are regarded with amusement or embarrassment by most of the rest of the country.

The politics of south Essex swung a long way to the right during the 1980s. The displacement of people from the East End, particularly in the planned New Towns of Basildon and Harlow, had created a large potential Labour vote but it was clear as early as the election of 1959 that political allegiances did not carry over automatically. In elections where the Conservatives defeated Labour governments in 1970 and 1979 there could be very large swings, and the surprise was that these continued in 1983 and 1987 and were hardly offset by small pro-Labour swings in 1992. Thatcherism had a particularly strong appeal here among white skilled working and lower middle class voters – it was receptive territory for an appeal to self-reliance, material prosperity and entrepreneurial values, not to mention council and New Town corporation house sales. Thatcher's outspoken nationalism also struck a chord with populist *Sun*-reading voters, while Labour's 1980s interest in minorities went down badly. South Essex has never had much time for the compromises and consensus of the Liberals and successors. Thurrock, Labour's last seat, went Tory in 1987 and was only narrowly regained in 1992.

Northern Essex is a different world, being that crucial few miles further out from London, and shares much with Suffolk. The countryside is beautiful, with gentle hills, pleasant valleys and picturesque Constable landscapes inland, and a coastline of peaceful wetlands and yachting havens. The northern part of the coast, around Harwich, is a retirement area with 29.2 per cent of the population of the Tendring council area being of retirement age. Colchester is a large, historic town and Chelmsford has a cathedral, although the middle part of the county around Chelmsford has seen the fastest population growth in recent years. The Conservatism has tended to be of a milder variety than the populism of the south, although still Eurosceptic for the most part, and the Liberal Democrats have long-established political bases in Chelmsford and Colchester. The north lacks the south's traditional volatility; the Conservatives had a monopoly on its representation between their gain of Maldon from Labour in 1955 and the 1997 landslide.

In 1997, the components of Essex marched more or less in step with enormous swings of 15.2 per cent (the four easternmost London boroughs), 14.0 per cent (south Essex) and 12.4 per cent (north Essex). The different parts of Essex reacted very differently in the general election of 2001. The south, plus the metropolitan area, gave the Conservatives one of their few patches of success, with a 3.3 per cent swing from Labour and the gain of the Castle Point constituency in the south. In the four outer eastern London boroughs there was a 2.8 per cent swing and two gains. North Essex, by contrast, rewarded the Tories with a puny swing of 0.7 per cent and the party failed to regain two extremely vulnerable Labour seats, Braintree and Harwich. David Amess, the Conservative MP for Southend West, invited Tories despondent about their 2001 performance to come to Essex to cheer themselves up, but this would only work as long as they didn't venture too far north. The Hague formula was – relatively – successful in south Essex, but that only emphasises quite how unusual the place is.

The Conservatives must hope to regain Braintree and Harwich next time if they are to be plausible as a party of government any time before 2015. The southern seats could swing a long way back to the Conservatives if Labour become really unpopular, but they would be doing well to gain Harlow – or, even more, Basildon – at the next election.

Liberal Democrat interest in Essex at parliamentary level is concentrated on Colchester, which they gained on its reassembly as an urban seat in 1997 and held with an increased majority in 2001. Under certain circumstances, Saffron Walden seems the sort of place that might fall their way, but it is a very long shot; in 2001 their vote in Brentwood was depressed by Martin Bell's intervention. Essex has two examples of the interesting phenomenon of *Focus* burnout, where the Liberal Democrats came close to victory in previous years but have declined more recently, in Chelmsford and even more dramatically in Southend West. Labour were reduced to below 10 per cent in both seats in 1983 but have bounced back to achieve second place in both in 2001. It appears that there is a limit to the number of times people are prepared to vote tactically without success, and that Labour's revival as a national party encouraged people disillusioned with repeated unproductive tactical votes to return to their original colours. Another stage of Focus burnout is what has happened in Southend, where the Conservatives have successfully emulated pavement politics techniques and beaten the Lib Dems at their own game.

Local government

Before the 2001 elections the Conservatives ran Essex county on casting votes, but they obtained a more comfortable majority in 2001 with 49 councillors, to 19 Labour, 10 Lib Dem and one other. Labour's representatives include 5 each from the New Towns of Basildon and Harlow, plus scattered others; 4 of the Lib Dems are from Chelmsford, three from Colchester, two from Epping Forest and one from Brentwood.

The Conservatives swept to a massive victory in Southend in the 2000 local elections, and were still dominant on new boundaries at election time in 2001. The local party has taken pavement politics seriously, taking particular pride in the 'decriminalisation of parking' in 2001, but their 2000 victory also owed something to local ill-feeling about Southend's alleged status as a 'dumping ground' for asylum seekers. Thurrock unitary authority (which includes the Stanford-le-Hope area of the Basildon constituency) is Labour-controlled, with a large majority that would take extraordinary events to overturn.

The Local Government Commission reviewed the ward boundaries for many of the authorities in Essex in 2000-2001, with the result that all-out elections on new boundaries took place in May 2002 in several councils with annual elections (Basildon, Epping Forest, Brentwood, Harlow, Rochford, Colchester). Of the south Essex councils, annual elections for Basildon council (which also covers Billericay) have displayed extraordinary volatility. In May 1992 the Conservatives won every seat and took control, but only two years later they won nothing. Labour regained control in 1996 but lost again in 2000. Also volatile, but less obviously so as it only has elections every four years, is Castle Point; in the 1980s it was 100 per cent Conservative but Labour nearly swept the board in 1995 and held on more narrowly in 1999. In both 1997 and 2001 it voted Conservative in the county elections. The Castle, incidentally, is Hadleigh; it is harder to see the Point of the place, as it were, but it is probably the tip of Canvey Island. Harlow was always Labour controlled, but the council attracted criticism from residents and the Liberal Democrats and Conservatives have been growing in strength in local elections, in different wards. Labour's hold was broken in the 2002 local elections, when Lib Dems and Tories won 12 seats apiece to Labour's paltry 9. Brentwood, in local elections, has seen Liberal Democrat activity – they first gained the council in 1991 and have held it since; the Conservatives did not recover much ground here in the 1997-2001 parliament. Epping Forest has remained under no overall control since the Conservatives lost it in 1994. Rochford (some small towns including Rayleigh north of Southend), to complete the picture, is also an authority which the Conservatives should probably control but lost in 1990 and struggled to reassert control; the Lib Dems even had an overall majority in 1994-98. On the eve of the 2002 elections the Conservatives had nearly accomplished their comeback – they went on to gain it convincingly.

Looking north, Chelmsford council has been a battleground between the Conservatives and the Liberal Democrats/ Alliance for twenty years, with control frequently changing and small majorities in its quadrennial elections; it is currently under no overall control with the Lib Dems the largest single party. Uttlesford is the local authority for the Saffron Walden area; it is currently under no overall control with the Lib Dems the largest single party; the Conservatives lost it after 22 years of control in 1995 and made rather little progress in 1999. Braintree was a Labour gain in 1995 which the party held in 1999 with surprisingly few losses – although the Greens picked up a ward because of a local grievance over an incinerator. Colchester combines the town area, where the Lib Dems do very well and there is some Labour strength, with deeply Conservative north Essex countryside. The Lib Dems gained an outright majority in the mid 1990s but lately they have been only the largest single party. Tendring (Harwich, Clacton and Brightlingsea) is a hung council where Labour forms the largest party – it was, rather surprisingly, under majority Labour control between 1995 and 1999. The Lib Dems were once the leading party but have faded.

Boundary review

Essex is in line to gain another seat in the forthcoming boundary review, but it is not clear where it will appear as most seats in the county are a little large. It seems probable that Southend, now it is unitary, will have two seats of its own once more and a new Tory seat will pop up somewhere in the centre of the county. There may be knock-on effects from one end of the county to the other; there are dozens of permutations available.

BASILDON

	2001		1997		1992 notional	
Electorate and turnout	74,121	55.1	73,714	72.0	76,236	79.4
Conservative	13,813	33.8	16,366	30.8	27,291	45.1
Labour	21,551	52.7	29,646	55.8	24,645	40.7
Lib Dem	3,691	9.0	4,608	8.7	8,599	14.2
Anti–EU	1,397	3.4	2,462	4.6	–	–
Others	423		–		–	
MP	Angela Smith (Lab)		Angela Smith (Lab)		David Amess (Con)	
Majority	7,738	18.9	13,280	25.0	2,646	4.4

Basildon won emblematic status in 1992 when the Conservatives held the seat early on election night with a small adverse swing. It was not the first time the seat had disappointed Labour – its predecessors stayed Tory in 1964 and swung sharply to the right in 1979. Before 1983 the outlying territory around Billericay was cut off, supposedly making the core Basildon seat safe for Labour, but the Tories triumphed again three times. In 1997 there was no Labour disappointment, and the incumbent Conservative who had loudly proclaimed the virtues of Basildon saw the writing on the wall and decamped to Southend. Labour held on in 2001 despite suffering a 3 per cent swing as turnout dropped steeply on the most Labour-inclined estates.

Basildon is the largest of the New Towns, with a population of 100,000, but this seat is not identical to the town. New Town neighbourhoods such as Pitsea and Laindon are in the Billericay seat, and this 'Basildon' seat also includes the eastern reaches of Thurrock borough around Stanford-le-Hope, whose private estates and massive oil refinery nestle in a bend of the Thames. This constituency has the most working class areas of the New Town, including the early New Town neighbourhood of Vange, some system built estates and the well-planned town centre. There are some troubled and deprived areas in Basildon: two of the six wards in the country with the worst educational deprivation are in Basildon. The central Fryerns area and Vange are the most Labour parts of Basildon, although the Stanford-le-Hope area is more Conservative-inclined – particularly semi-rural Orsett. In exceptional elections such as the local elections of 1992, the Tories can win everywhere, but recently Labour have restored their dominance in their best areas.

Labour will always have to beware of Basildon. It is a seat the Conservatives need if they are to become the largest party, and its history of volatility can given them some hope that they can manage a local triumph against the trend at some time in the future. Angela Smith, however, is a strong candidate for Labour, with the local roots – and accent – to prove it, and it would be a major surprise if she was denied a third term.

BILLERICAY

	2001		1997		1992 notional	
Electorate and turnout	78,528	58.1	76,304	72.6	73,644	80.7
Conservative	21,608	47.4	22,033	39.8	34,274	57.6
Labour	16,595	36.4	20,677	37.3	11,914	20.0
Lib Dem	6,323	13.9	8,763	15.8	13,276	22.3
Anti–EU	1,072	2.4	–	–	–	–
Ind Con	–	–	3,377	6.1	–	–
Others	–		570		–	
MP	John Baron (Con)		Teresa Gorman (Con)		Teresa Gorman (Con)	
Majority	5,013	11.0	1,356	2.5	20,998	35.3

Billericay is essentially outer Basildon. The Basildon district is sharply divided between the New Town and the outlying areas grouped in this seat. Billericay and Wickford are commuter towns (commuting to the City, not to Basildon) where Labour polls few votes in local elections and the battle is between Lib Dems and Tories. The Conservatives have predominated lately, with a monopoly on representation from the five wards north of Basildon itself and a very high share of the vote in the 2002 elections. Billericay itself is not particularly grand, despite the olde-worlde high street. The old centre is surrounded by private estates dating from the 1960s and after – some of whose houses seem to be built-on afterthoughts to enormous 'carport' garages. Wickford was described by the *London Commuter Guide* as 'a tumour of Sixties estates built onto the village of Shotgate.'

Since 1997 the constituency has also included the New Town neighbourhoods of Pitsea and Laindon, on the east and west edges of Basildon where Labour have stronger support. Laindon, however, is an area where the Conservatives can poll quite well in an even year. The whole adds up to a seat which should be quite safely Conservative. Labour came close in 1997 partly because a 'Loyal Conservative' candidate stood against Teresa Gorman, whose rebel antics had earned her a spell without the party whip in 1994-95. The Conservative vote reunited in 2001 around John Baron, and with the help of the south Essex effect Billericay was restored to safety.

BRAINTREE

	2001		*1997*		*1992 notional*	
Electorate and turnout	79,157	63.6	73,032	76.1	*68,995*	*84.0*
Conservative	20,765	41.3	22,278	40.1	*29,278*	*50.5*
Labour	21,123	42.0	23,729	42.7	*15,890*	*27.4*
Lib Dem	5,664	11.3	6,418	11.5	*12,039*	*20.8*
Anti–EU	748	1.5	2,165	3.9	*–*	*–*
Green	1,241	2.5	712	1.3	*705*	*1.2*
Others	774		274		*19*	
MP	Alan Hurst (Lab)		Alan Hurst (Lab)		Tony Newton (Con)	
Majority	358	0.7	1,451	2.6	*13,388*	*23.1*

The Braintree constituency sits in the centre of the county of Essex; two towns (Braintree and Witham, comprising about 70 per cent of the electorate) and a swathe of countryside extending northward into the gentle hills as far as Great Bardfield. Coggeshall is the other little town in the seat. To the political historian it is Maldon without the town of Maldon, and will always be associated with flamboyant Labour MP Tom Driberg who represented the seat from 1942 to 1955. Its recent MPs have been less notorious, but generally well regarded. Tony Newton's un-flashy personal charm and good constituency record won him many admirers. Few people thought the Tories were in real trouble here in 1997, but in the event Newton joined the cull of seven Tory cabinet ministers being defeated. His Labour replacement, Alan Hurst combines sceptical loyalty to the government with a special concern for rural interests. Labour are well-organised in the constituency, with a full time agent and weekly constituency surgeries.

The 2001 campaign in Braintree was another exciting close battle between Labour and Conservative. The Tories poured in a lot of effort, but their campaign was not particularly well-targeted (it concentrated on keeping the pound, and a couple of small local issues) and a visit from William Hague shortly before the poll seemed to stir up opposition rather than support. Even so, they came very close to victory, and Labour had to rely on tactical votes to hold the seat.

The main Labour strength is in the town of Witham, particularly its north side, and the Conservatives are strongest in the rural tip of the seat in the north. The county council wards of Braintree and its conjoined twin Bocking are all marginal, and in 2001 despite the parliamentary result the Conservatives gained all three. Braintree is a town much swollen by overspill, although the recent growth of the population around the town has been in higher-class developments such as those around Great Notley. Commuting into London has also recently been increasing. Some of this growth is displaced expansion from Chelmsford, where Labour has been weak, and Braintree Labour constantly need to work for votes among this element.

If the Conservatives make any sort of national recovery in the next election, Braintree should fall quite easily. It is the second most vulnerable Labour seat in the country, after South Dorset.

BRENTWOOD and ONGAR

	2001		1997		1992 notional	
Electorate and turnout	64,693	67.3	66,181	76.6	66,767	83.7
Conservative	16,558	38.0	23,031	45.4	32,187	57.6
Labour	5,505	12.6	11,231	22.1	6,102	10.9
Lib Dem	6,772	15.6	13,341	26.3	17,012	30.5
Anti–EU	611	1.4	3,123	6.2	–	–
Ind Bell	13,737	31.5	–	–	–	–
Others	359 (3)		–		555	
MP	Eric Pickles (Con)		Eric Pickles (Con)		Eric Pickles (Con)	
Majority	2,821	6.5	9,690	19.1	15,175	27.2

Brentwood and Ongar lies on the edge of Greater London, north and east of Romford. Brentwood is a sprawling township bypassed by the A12, which is a dormitory town for the commuters who pour into London every morning from the busy stations of Brentwood and Shenfield (the best area in the constituency). These places started out as villages, and retain some features such as independent shops, but started to balloon with suburban growth in the 1930s and added an entire new neighbourhood, Hutton, in the 1960s. The constituency includes a part of Epping Forest district as well, around Chipping Ongar. Ongar used to be the last station on the Central Line of the underground, and the line to Epping is supposed to be reopening on another basis soon. There is also some countryside north of Ongar to Matching, east of Harlow.

Brentwood and Ongar is a high income constituency, the best-off in Essex and among the top 10 per cent nationally, its inhabitants often working in City, professional or managerial jobs in London. It is effectively a bit of Surrey that has drifted across to Essex. As such, it is traditionally very Conservative, and less volatile than the A13 towns to the south. It also has a Liberal Democrat presence in local elections.

The 2001 election was an unusual business in Brentwood and Ongar. Independent MP Martin Bell had made an impulsive promise to the electors of Tatton that he would only serve one term as their MP, but found that he was attracted to parliamentary life and thought there was more to do. He was approached by dissident Conservatives who asked him to stand in Brentwood (there was apparently much less demand for Bell to come to constituencies with Labour figures facing allegations such as Coventry NW and Leicester E). The grievances in Brentwood were more obscure; it had much to do with the perceived influence of the Pentecostal (and litigious) Peniel Chapel on local Conservative politics. But Bell attracted people who liked the idea of keeping an Independent in parliament. A lot of Martin Bell's vote in the general election seems to have come from people who voted Liberal Democrat in the local elections, plus a chunk of around 6 per cent each voting Conservative or Labour locally and for Bell nationally. If, as in Tatton, Labour and Lib Dem (or probably even only one of them) had stood down for Bell he would have won Brentwood. Eric Pickles, having survived Bell's challenge, should be safer in future elections. However, the Liberal Democrats led in the constituency in the 1999 local elections, so there is still potential for a different kind of challenge to Conservative dominance.

CASTLE POINT

	2001		1997		1992 actual	
Electorate and turnout	68,108	58.4	67,324	72.1	66,229	80.4
Conservative	17,738	44.6	19,462	40.1	29,629	55.6
Labour	16,753	42.1	20,605	42.4	12,799	24.0
Lib Dem	3,116	7.8	4,477	9.2	10,208	19.2
Anti–EU	1,273	3.2	2,700	5.6	–	–
Others	886 (2)		1,301		643	
MP	Robert Spink (Con)		Christine Butler (Lab)		Robert Spink (Con)	
Majority	985	2.5	1,143	2.4	16,830	31.6

Castle Point is perhaps the true heartland of Essex. Unlike Basildon and Harlow it is the product of private development rather than planning and as a result it is among the two or three most completely owner-occupied constituencies in Britain. It consists of Benfleet, a residential town by the A13 bordering on Southend, and Canvey Island. Benfleet is a nearly all-white suburban sprawl – even the Indian restaurants have English names. The Island is an extraordinary, un-English flat landscape enclosed by a Dutch-built sea wall, with a rather half-hearted seaside resort alongside oil refineries, landfill and sprawling private estates. It is home to white boy blues band Doctor Feelgood and an occasionally successful non-league football club. The north of Canvey, and the east of Benfleet near Basildon are the Labour areas, while the Conservatives strike back in the resort area of Canvey and the west of Benfleet where it shades imperceptibly into Southend West.

Castle Point was one of only five Conservative gains from Labour in the 2001 general election, and one of the few seats among their top thirty targets that actually swung their way enough to change hands. However, compared with the neighbouring south Essex seats of Southend, Basildon and Thurrock it was actually a relatively low swing for the area – Christine Butler's incumbency in such a marginal seat seems to have damped down the regional movement. The Tories were also hindered by a split in their ranks, with their former council group leader standing as an independent Conservative and polling 1.7 per cent. The swing in 1997 was so large that even with the swing back in 2001 Castle Point's move to Labour since 1992 is still well above average.

Local election voting behaviour in Castle Point is slightly peculiar. Labour won a landslide in 1995 – more people turned out to vote for the party in the local elections than in the 1992 general election – and held on with a reduced majority in 1999. However, the Conservatives led in the Essex county wards in the borough in 1997 and 2001; perhaps the reason is that the Liberal Democrats hardly stand any candidates in borough elections but feel obliged to for the county, splitting the anti-Tory vote.

Conservative MP Robert Spink resumed his parliamentary career in 2001, but his three figure majority makes him the ninth most vulnerable Tory incumbent. However, with the loss of Butler's incumbency vote Castle Point will be difficult for Labour to take back.

CHELMSFORD WEST

	2001		1997		1992 notional	
Electorate and turnout	78,073	61.7	76,271	76.8	73,616	84.9
Conservative	20,446	42.5	23,781	40.6	34,284	54.8
Labour	14,185	29.5	15,436	26.4	9,443	15.1
Lib Dem	11,197	23.3	17,090	29.2	18,098	29.0
Anti–EU	785	1.6	1,859 (2)	3.2	–	–
Others	1,530 (2)		411		699	
MP	Simon Burns (Con)		Simon Burns (Con)		Simon Burns (Con) Chelmsford	
Majority	6,261	13.0	6,691	11.4	16,186	25.9

Chelmsford was a great Liberal hope in the 1970s and 1980s but they have faded badly in recent general elections. This seat, which contains most of the Essex county town and its sprawling new suburbs of Broomfield and Writtle, plus some rural areas like the cheerily named village of Good Easter, is the successor to the old Chelmsford, although the boundary changes have helped the Conservatives to keep their hold on the seat.

Chelmsford is large enough and old enough to have different sides of town. The north west of the town has some working class Labour areas, and Moulsham to the south is a terraced area which tends to the Liberal Democrats. Springfield, to the north, is not where the Simpsons live but it might be – it is a large suburb. The newer areas of Chelmsford, and the rural areas, gave the Conservatives their lead in 2001 while the town area tended to the Lib Dems in the local elections and Labour in the general election. There is very little social deprivation in Chelmsford. Its economy is boosted by the large number of London commuters – its station has claimed to be the busiest in Britain.

The Labour vote was reduced to a mere 5.1 per cent in 1983, but it has rebounded strongly since then and the party moved into second place in 2001. Chelmsford voters have clearly lost the habit of tactically voting Liberal, but the third party is still strong and led in local elections during the 1997-2001 parliament – even in the 2001 county elections they had a narrow lead. Labour have also gained because of the appeal of Blairism in places such as this – aspirational, well-off, commuting towns in southern England. However, the division of the anti-Tory vote enables sitting MP Simon Burns to survive on a relatively low share of the vote with comfortable majorities and this pattern should continue.

COLCHESTER

	2001		1997		1992 notional	
Electorate and turnout	77,958	56.1	74,743	69.6	73,347	76.8
Conservative	13,074	29.9	16,305	31.4	23,692	42.0
Labour	10,925	25.0	15,891	30.6	13,582	24.1
Lib Dem	18,627	42.6	17,886	34.4	18,424	32.7
Anti–EU	631	1.4	1,776	3.4	–	–
Others	479		148		658	
MP	Bob Russell (LD)		Bob Russell (LD)		Bernard Jenkin (Con) Colchester North	
Majority	5,553	12.7	1,581	3.0	5,268	9.4

Colchester claims to be the oldest town in Britain, having been a Roman settlement sacked by Boudicca – perhaps the original Essex Eurosceptic - and then a Norman centre. Currently it is a rather odd mix of garrison and university town, which can give nights on the town here a bit of an edge. The University of Essex is a centre of electoral studies, and there is now something interesting on the doorstep.

Colchester is an area of Lib Dem activity in local elections, and the reunited town seat created in 1997 gave them a chance to translate this into parliamentary success. They managed – just. It was the closest three-way battle in the country with all three main parties winning just over 30 per cent. Having established incumbency, and with such a large third place Labour vote, the odds were always on the new MP Bob Russell consolidating his hold on the constituency in 2001 despite the other parties' hopes. The surprise was possibly that the Conservative vote fell as well as Labour's, giving the Lib Dems a substantial majority.

All three parties are still viable in Colchester. The Conservatives ran third in the share of the vote in the 1999 local elections, with Lib Dems first; a month later in the Euro election the positions of the two parties were reversed. In the 2001 county elections Labour's share of the vote was considerably higher than in the general election, with the three parties again all polling between 30 and 37 per cent, but some of the local Labour vote (about 6 per cent of voters) went over to the Lib Dems in the general election. All the county wards in the constituency are three-way marginal, although in a good year for the Lib Dems they can win nearly everything. In 2001, however, in contrast to the national picture they lost one each to Labour and Conservative.

Colchester is still a three-way marginal, but after 2001 it has become significantly harder for Labour to win; the rather low Conservative share of the vote suggests that unless there is a surge in support for that party it should remain Lib Dem.

EPPING FOREST

	2001		1997		1992 notional	
Electorate and turnout	72,589	58.4	72,690	72.9	71,990	79.1
Conservative	20,833	49.1	24,117	45.5	34,034	59.8
Labour	12,407	29.3	18,865	35.6	12,851	22.6
Lib Dem	7,884	18.6	7,074	13.3	9,520	16.7
Anti–EU	1,290	3.0	2,208	4.2	–	–
Others	–		743		544	
MP	Eleanor Laing (Con)		Eleanor Laing (Con)		Steve Norris (Con)	
Majority	8,426	19.9	5,252	9.9	21,183	37.2

Epping Forest is the Essex constituency with the closest links to London, thanks to the Central Line branches that serve parts of it. The forest is surrounded by small towns which are effectively residential London suburbs. Grange Hill and Chigwell are closest in, just across the border from Ilford North, and Buckhurst Hill is a northern extension of Woodford. Loughton is the largest town, and has some council-built estates which provide the principal Labour vote in the Epping Forest constituency. At the end of the Central Line (and, unlike most of the seat, outside the M25 ring) lies Epping, and to the west – hard by the Lea Valley and just outside Enfield – is Waltham Abbey.

Epping Forest is where the most successful and rich upwardly mobile East Enders come when they have made it, and its residents include many businessmen and footballers. Epping Forest is also, according to legend, where London villains end up – the successful ones in guarded mansions in places like Chigwell, and the unsuccessful ones in shallow graves in the more remote parts of the forest.

Most of this territory is very prosperous and Conservative, and has become more so over recent decades. When a basically similar seat called Chigwell was created in 1955, the Conservatives only won by 1,875 votes, but it has gradually become a completely safe seat. A five per cent swing to the Conservatives in 2001 made it even more so; the Labour vote slumped, many abstaining but some switching to the Liberal Democrats. The Conservatives do not have it all their own way in local elections, as there are strong wards for Labour, Lib Dem and Resident parties; the sole Lib Dem gain in the Essex county elections was Epping. But in general elections it is a Tory stronghold.

ESSEX NORTH

	2001		1997		1992 notional	
Electorate and turnout	71,605	62.8	68,008	75.3	66,739	81.3
Conservative	21,325	47.4	22,480	43.9	31,309	57.7
Labour	14,139	31.5	17,004	33.2	10,347	19.1
Lib Dem	7,867	17.5	10,028	19.6	12,059	22.2
Anti–EU	1,613	3.6	1,202	2.3	–	–
Others	–		495		544	
MP	Bernard Jenkin (Con)		Bernard Jenkin (Con)		NEW SEAT	
Majority	7,186	16.0	5,476	10.7	19,250	35.5

The North Essex constituency is essentially 'Colchester rural'. It completely surrounds the town and has no substantial settlement to act as an alternative centre of gravity. There are a few towns scattered around the place, but most of them are little known outside their immediate vicinity. Brightlingsea, where animal rights protests took place at the docks in the mid 1990s is on the Tendring peninsula near Clacton. Manningtree and Mistley are villages which have grown together near the Suffolk border, with fast London trains calling at Manningtree and generating a commuting population. Wivenhoe is a detached Colchester suburb next to Essex University; Tiptree is a little town with a Residents' party, and West Mersea sits on an island south of Colchester. As well as having Colchester in common, these areas share a political preference for the Conservative Party. The Tories won all the component county wards fairly easily in 2001, with their strongest ward being Constable (the ward name being an appropriate honour for the painter who immortalised the scenery of north Essex). The fairly substantial Labour vote in this comfortable rural constituency is spread quite evenly, although Brightlingsea was their best area in the 2001 county elections. Conservative MP Bernard Jenkin secured a fairly good swing in 2001 and has a secure majority.

HARLOW

	2001		1997		1992 notional	
Electorate and turnout	67,196	59.7	64,314	74.3	65,004	82.2
Conservative	13,941	34.8	15,347	32.1	24,568	46.0
Labour	19,169	47.8	25,861	54.1	22,881	42.8
Lib Dem	5,381	13.4	4,523	9.5	6,002	11.2
Anti–EU	1,223	3.0	1,762 (2)	3.7	–	–
Others	401		319			
MP	Bill Rammell (Lab)		Bill Rammell (Lab)		Jerry Hayes (Con)	
Majority	5,228	13.0	10,514	22.0	1,687	3.2

Harlow, the constituency centred around the New Town in Essex, was one of the seats in which Conservatism proved popular in the 1980s; in the 1987 election it looked almost safe for moderate MP Jerry Hayes, Tory support having doubled since 1974 (although Harlow had a prehistory of electing Norman Tebbit when it was the dominant part of the Epping seat in 1970). As in many of the other southern new and expanded town seats Labour took Harlow on a massive swing in 1997 and MP Bill Rammell won with a five-figure majority.

The New Town is showing its age. Harlow has flourishing manufacturing industry but little in the way of high paying employment or advanced education; it seems like an idealistic past's vision of the future rather than a modern place. Parts of the town seem as run down as the streets their residents left in north London 45 years ago. Labour ruled the councils for forty years, remaining dominant throughout the 1980s, but complaints piled up about the council's stewardship and Labour lost seats heavily to the Conservatives and Lib Dems in 2002, finishing third on the new council.

Harlow does not only contain the New Town. There are several pretty villages included, some woven into the New Town fabric at Old Harlow and some outside the town such as Roydon and Sheering. This staunch Tory minority in the seat has been joined since 1997 by the enormous Church Langley private development, on an empty quarter between the New Town and the M11 motorway. It has added around 4,000 (mostly Conservative) voters to the seat so far and is still growing.

In 2001, the Labour vote fell 6.3 percentage points in the general election, with Conservative candidate Robert Halfon picking up a bit and the Lib Dems bouncing back after a poor showing in 1997. The local elections saw the Lib Dems and Tories gaining even more. Harlow is now a better Tory target than Harrow West and a potentially dangerous area for Labour in future elections.

HARWICH

	2001		1997		1992 notional	
Electorate and turnout	77,509	62.1	75,927	70.5	74,676	76.1
Conservative	19,355	40.2	19,524	36.5	29,372	51.7
Labour	21,951	45.6	20,740	38.8	14,047	24.7
Lib Dem	4,099	8.5	7,037	13.1	13,187	23.2
Anti–EU	2,463	5.1	4,923	9.2	–	–
Others	247		1,290		256	
MP	Ivan Henderson (Lab)		Ivan Henderson (Lab)		Iain Sproat (Con)	
Majority	2,596	5.4	1,216	2.3	15,325	27.0

Against some stiff competition, Harwich can probably claim the title of the most surprising Labour hold of 2001. Labour's first victory in the seat in 1997 was widely if incorrectly written off as a freak result caused by the highest Referendum Party vote in the country.

Harwich is a working trading and ferry port, with links primarily to Holland and Scandinavia. It is a rather charming town, little visited because it is so far off the beaten track. The constituency also includes a strip of coast including the seaside towns of Walton on the Naze and genteel Frinton (which resisted chip shops and pubs for decades), stretching down to Clacton-on-Sea, the largest town in the constituency (25,000 electorate). Clacton is a tired, dowdy seaside resort. The Clacton-Frinton-Walton area is a major retirement district and a high proportion of the population are retired. Labour won most of the wards in Harwich and Clacton towns in the May 1999 local elections (and led 44–33 in the Clacton wards in June 2001) but had little support in the smaller centres; Frinton and Walton together were 56 per cent Conservative in the June 2001 county elections.

Harwich was safely Conservative from 1931 until 1997, when it suddenly fell to Labour on a swing of over 14 per cent while Referendum Party candidate Jeffrey Titford polled 9.2 per cent. It was the strongest UKIP seat in the Eastern Region in the 1999 Euro election as well, with 14.8 per cent; Titford was elected an MEP. Harwich has a curiously divided attitude to Europe, relying on trade but with massive fortifications outside the town reflecting fears of invasion in 1802-15, 1914-18 and 1939-45. The UKIP saved its deposit in 2001 as well, with its strongest area reputedly being traditionalist Frinton.

Ivan Henderson has been a very successful member of parliament. Before he was elected he was a Harwich dock worker and since he won he has been active and prominent in every part of the seat, and a regular contributor to the local media. In the circumstances of 2001, Henderson was rewarded for his efforts with an increased total vote (a rare honour) at the expense of the Lib Dems. He won an increased majority over Iain Sproat, the former junior minister whose trail of electoral tears started when he left Aberdeen to lose Roxburgh in 1983, and continued as he saw a 15,000 majority vanish under his feet in Harwich in 1997. If and when the Tories ever mount a plausible challenge for government, Harwich should be extremely vulnerable despite the high regard in which its residents hold Ivan Henderson. There is also a possibility that boundary changes might break the link between Harwich and Clacton, which would be bad news for Labour.

MALDON and CHELMSFORD EAST

	2001		1997		1992 notional	
Electorate and turnout	70,252	62.8	64,680	77.9	64,712	79.7
Conservative	21,719	49.2	24,524	48.7	32,944	63.9
Labour	13,257	30.1	14,485	28.7	6,592	12.8
Lib Dem	7,002	15.9	9,758	19.4	11,359	22.0
Anti–EU	1,135	2.6	935	1.9	–	–
Others	987		685		696	
MP	John Whittingdale (Con)		John Whittingdale (Con)		John Whittingdale (Con)	
					Colchester South & Maldon	
Majority	8,462	19.2	10,039	19.9	21,585	41.8

The little town of Maldon, a yachting haven where the best-regarded sea salt in Britain is produced, is a tenacious presence in constituency names despite being paired with different areas in successive boundary reviews. Until 1974 it gave its name to a division based on Braintree; then it looked southward to territory that now finds itself in Rayleigh until 1983; then north to Colchester until 1997, and now west to Chelmsford. The next review could do something different again. When it was linked with Braintree Labour could win, even in 1951, but when it looks in any other direction it produces a safe Conservative seat. The countryside around Maldon has significant hunting activity.

This constituency stretches west from Maldon through villages such as Danbury to the eastern fringes of Chelmsford, around the A12 bypass at Great Baddow and Galleywood, where new estates and bungalows abound. There is some Lib Dem strength at local elections in this part of Chelmsford, but little in the villages. It is quite hard to discern where the Labour vote in this constituency comes from – the party has scattered councillors in Maldon, Southminster and Burnham-on-Crouch, but no areas of great strength. With Rayleigh and Chelmsford West, this constituency provides a band of constituencies with pro-Labour swings in 2001 marking out a boundary between south Essex and the rest of the county. It is the 52nd safest Conservative seat.

RAYLEIGH

	2001		1997		1992 notional	
Electorate and turnout	70,653	60.5	69,040	74.3	67,206	80.5
Conservative	21,434	50.1	25,516	49.7	33,065	61.1
Labour	13,144	30.7	14,832	28.9	8,032	14.8
Lib Dem	6,614	15.5	10,137	19.8	11,868	21.9
Anti–EU	1,581	3.7	–	–	–	–
Others	–		829	–	1,152	
MP	Mark Francois (Con)		Michael Clark (Con)		Michael Clark (Con) Rochford	
Majority	8,290	19.4	10,684	20.8	21,197	39.2

Rayleigh is basically the old Rochford seat, less the town of Rochford. The Rayleigh constituency contains some of the most up-market areas of south Essex; it is to Benfleet and Southend what Billericay is to Basildon. Rayleigh itself is an old market town, much swollen since the 1930s by residential development. Neighbouring Hockley is of newer vintage, a suburban sprawl which has developed around the smaller village of Hockwell. It also includes smaller settlements such as Hullbridge and a few villages in the Rochford district.

Across the river Crouch lies a portion of the seat which belongs to Chelmsford borough. South Woodham Ferrers is a small privately developed new town where construction began in 1976. It was intended to be a cut above most south Essex sprawl, with strict building control including in the 1990s regulations banning satellite dishes – a wise precaution in Essex. It has grown rapidly in the last twenty years and is very comfortable and safe, with a strong evangelical church.

Rayleigh and South Woodham are the most Conservative elements of the seat; Hullbridge has some Labour voters and there is Lib Dem activity in parts of the seat in local elections, but overall it is a Conservative stronghold. Rayleigh, however, produced a relatively poor result for the Conservatives in 2001, given the south Essex context, although incumbency was a factor with the retirement of Michael Clark. This probably had something to do with its high-class demographics, and the proximity of parts of the seat to Chelmsford rather than Southend. It is the fiftieth safest Conservative seat.

ROCHFORD and SOUTHEND EAST

	2001		1997		1992 notional	
Electorate and turnout	71,005	52.7	73,075	63.7	67,171	75.9
Conservative	20,058	53.6	22,683	48.7	30,096	59.0
Labour	13,024	34.8	18,458	39.6	14,019	27.5
Lib Dem	2,780	7.4	4,387	9.4	6,011	11.8
Others	1,590 (2)		1,007		861	
MP	Teddy Taylor (Con)		Teddy Taylor (Con)		Teddy Taylor (Con) Southend East	
Majority	7,034	18.8	4,225	9.1	16,077	31.5

Despite the name, the dominant element of this seat is the eastern part of the seaside resort of Southend. The tacky splendour of Southend's town centre, with its one and a third mile long pier, kiss-me-quick hats, sweet shops and amusement arcades is in this constituency, in the marginal Milton ward. The Labour vote is strongest in the other central ward, the exotically named Kursaal, the Victoria area just north of the town centre and the ward beyond it, St. Luke's, which is based on a council estate next to the main London highway. The Conservatives, however, have a larger lead in the three wards further along to the east, covering Southchurch, Thorpe Bay and West Shoebury; furthest to the east Shoeburyness is marginal. The Rochford wards in the seat, including Great Wakering and the town of Rochford, are not overwhelmingly Conservative. Had the Heath government's project for a new airport at Maplin sands, accompanied by a deep water port and a New Town, come to fruition there would probably be a separate constituency or two here by now. As it is, the marshes of Foulness and Potton islands are nearly uninhabited military land.

Southend East was for a while a seat Labour could aspire to win in a very good year. The Conservative majority was reduced to 517 in 1966, and a perilous 430 in a by-election in March 1980. It was the 13th most vulnerable seat to further Labour advance from 1966, when the party had a majority of nearly 100, but there are now only 56 safer Tory seats on the 2001 figures. A lot of the drift to the right in Southend has been for political rather than demographic reasons. Teddy Taylor is a popular MP; even those who disapprove of his strongly Eurosceptic views acknowledge that he is an affable man who works hard for his constituents. There are also a substantial number who agree, and even when the UKIP stood candidates against some anti-EU Tories in 2001 Taylor was exempt. In addition, the Conservatives surged in 2000 and sustained a strong vote in 2001 across Southend. Labour have never been organised enough in Southend to capitalise on the potential the place has to offer, and their performance has lagged behind other seaside resorts such as Brighton, or even Clacton.

SAFFRON WALDEN

	2001		1997		1992 notional	
Electorate and turnout	76,724	65.2	74,184	76.9	70,475	83.7
Conservative	24,485	48.9	25,871	45.3	33,378	56.6
Labour	11,305	22.6	12,275	21.5	8,468	14.4
Lib Dem	12,481	24.9	15,298	26.8	16,885	28.6
Anti–EU	1,769	3.5	2,966 (2)	5.2	–	–
Others	–		640 (2)		246	
MP	Alan Haselhurst (Con)		Alan Haselhurst (Con)		Alan Haselhurst (Con)	
Majority	12,004	24.0	10,573	18.5	16,493	28.0

Saffron Walden itself is a pleasant market town in the north east of Essex, with a population a little under 15,000. Cambridge is much the closest city, and people in Saffron Walden take the Cambridge evening papers. Labour can win a couple of council seats in the town area, which is competitive between the three parties, but Saffron Walden is a small element of the seat that bears its name. It extends over a wide area of rural north Essex around Saffron Walden itself, plus another chunk of countryside around the small town of Halstead, the other urban centre in the constituency. To the south it includes Stansted airport and the nearby town of Stansted Mountfitchet. The Conservatives poll well in the towns and dominate the villages that make up the bulk of the seat. The population has the highest proportion of professional and managerial workers in Essex. Their natural advantage is compounded by a party organisation which has activists in most settlements in the constituency.

In contrast to southern Essex, Saffron Walden prefers a liberal version of Conservatism typified by its long term MP (1929-65) Rab Butler. The current incumbent Alan Haselhurst is a well-liked liberal Tory, and a relatively non-partisan figure as Deputy Speaker. He has the safest Tory seat in Essex and the 22nd safest overall, and should be safe as long as he wishes to stay on. If the Conservatives were to choose a strident right winger for this seat, however, it could swing a long way to the Liberal Democrats, who have a foothold on the local council and a base in the Stansted area.

SOUTHEND WEST

	2001		1997		1992 actual	
Electorate and turnout	64,461	58.0	66,539	69.9	64,199	77.8
Conservative	17,313	46.3	18,029	38.8	27,319	54.7
Labour	9,372	25.1	10,600	22.8	6,139	12.3
Lib Dem	9,319	24.9	15,414	33.1	15,417	30.9
Anti–EU	1,371	3.7	2,370 (2)	5.1	–	–
Others	–		101		1,073 (3)	
MP	David Amess (Con)		David Amess (Con)		Paul Channon (Con)	
Majority	7,941	21.2	2,615	5.6	11,902	23.8

Southend West is part of the chain of suburbia stretching from London to the coast; it is hardly to be distinguished on the ground from Castle Point and Southend East on each side, but it is politically unusual. It was for decades a pocket borough for the Guinness family in the Conservative interest, but the last of that line was former Cabinet minister Paul Channon who stood down in 1997. The local Conservative office is still called Iveagh House.

The Liberals regarded it as a target seat in the elections of the 1980s and were once very strong in local elections of Southend, but after coming reasonably close in 1997 they suffered a disaster in 2001. In the general election they slumped to third, and in the local elections they were reduced to a shaky lead in only two wards, Leigh-on-Sea and Blenheim Park inland from Leigh, and a minority stake in Labour-inclined Westborough near the town centre. Leigh-on-Sea is the most distinctive part of the seat, a fishing village turned suburb. The Conservatives have come back powerfully in the middle class outer Southend wards of Prittlewell and Chalkwell by adopting Lib Dem pavement politics tactics, with councillors stressing local issues and distributing *Focus*-style leaflets.

The Conservatives have mounted a powerful recovery in Southend in local and national elections and now look very difficult to dislodge. At the moment Southend West is their 38th safest seat, although the size of their majority depends on an almost even division of the anti-Tory vote – which may well be sustained in future elections. The increase in the Tory vote in 2001 was impressive; it seems unlikely that Southend West is ever going to lapse from its newly reinforced status as a stronghold for the party.

THURROCK

	2001		1997		1992 actual	
Electorate and turnout	76,180	49.0	71,763	65.8	69,211	78.1
Conservative	11,124	29.8	12,640	26.8	23,619	43.7
Labour	21,121	56.5	29,896	63.3	24,791	45.9
Lib Dem	3,846	10.3	3,843	8.1	5,145	9.5
Anti–EU	1,271	3.4	833	1.8	117	0.2
Others	–		–		391	
MP	Andrew McKinlay (Lab)		Andrew McKinlay (Lab)		Andrew McKinlay (Lab)	
Majority	9,997	26.8	17,256	36.6	1,172	2.2

Thurrock lies just across the border from London, and is in many ways a continuation of the Barking-Dagenham-Hornchurch industrial sprawl. Down by the Thames, below the bridge carrying traffic from the M25 over to Kent, there is a stark industrial landscape and the largest working remnant of London's docks is located at Tilbury. Towns such as Tilbury and Purfleet are bleak little places, overwhelmingly working class, surrounded by heavy industry and marshland. It is very hard to believe that Thurrock elected a Conservative MP in 1987.

It was hard to believe even when it happened; it was at the height of Thatcherism's appeal to working class white southerners, but without the Essex local culture of strident nationalism it would not have fallen to right-wing Tory Tim Janman. Thurrock's five Tory years were an aberration, but Labour's gain in 1992 was still by a surprisingly narrow margin.

There is another side to Thurrock from the heavy industrial riverside. Not all its towns are as run down as Tilbury; Grays has some developments which have attracted lower middle class London commuters, and East Tilbury has a 1930s model estate built by the Bata shoe company. Physically, parts of the inland area resemble any other part of the south Essex sprawl like Benfleet or Southend West. In recent years Thurrock has attracted large amounts of money because of the Lakeside shopping centre just off the M25, which so dominates local affairs that it has a local newspaper named after it.

The swing in Thurrock ibn 2001, nearly 5 per cent, was a good result for the Conservatives even in the context of their strong patch in south Essex. Part of the reason was the appeal of William Hague's campaign; part is also demographic. Population growth since 1992 has been in the Chafford Hundred area, a small new town adjoining the Lakeside mall with its own new railway station. Chafford Hundred is by a long way the most affluent ward in Thurrock and is home to white working class families made (modestly) good. It is full of high density mock Tudor boxes of the crassest sort. In 2001 it gave Labour a one-vote majority in the local elections.

Labour start from a position of advantage and can probably hold Thurrock despite demographic change and its volatile political temperament, unless there is a Conservative landslide.

Gloucestershire

	Conservative		Labour		Liberal Democrat		Others	
	Share of vote	Seats	Share of vote	Seats	Share of vote	Seats	Share of vote	Seats
2001	40.9	2	33.7	3	21.9	1	3.5	0
1997	39.5	2	34.0	3	22.6	1	4.0	0
1992	47.4	4	23.1	0	28.3	1	1.2	0
1987	50.4	5	18.2	0	31.4	0	0.0	0
1983	50.7	5	16.7	0	32.1	0	0.5	0

Gloucestershire is a surprisingly diverse county, given its image as a rural idyll. True, tourism is a major industry in Gloucestershire, particularly in the Cotswolds and the resort town of Cheltenham, and there is considerable agriculture, but not far short of half the population live in the urban agglomeration around Gloucester and Cheltenham. Gloucester is an industrial city, while Cheltenham is a service centre, and the urban area as a whole is a modern, relatively prosperous place.

The county is unusual in southern England in having rural areas with recent radical traditions. In Stroud and the Forest of Dean there are small industrial towns set in beautiful countryside which have solid traditions of Labour voting, and in Stroud the Green Party has tapped into the independent-minded, environmentally conscious vote in local elections. There are also more traditional country areas in the north and east of the county with a stronger agricultural presence, some aristocratic estates and a correspondingly stronger Conservative vote.

Gloucestershire as a whole produced a standstill result in 2001, but this masks different trends in the component constituencies. The Conservatives managed respectable increases in their vote in the rural seats of Forest of Dean and Cotswold, and – for different reasons – in urban Gloucester. Stroud, however, was a rural triumph for Labour, and there was also a slight swing to the party in the mixed Tewkesbury seat and in Cheltenham.

Gloucestershire has generally been a Tory county except in the best Labour years and all the non-Conservative seats are vulnerable to a Tory recovery. The safest of these is the Lib Dem seat of Cheltenham, despite the Conservatives' success in turning the tide in local elections, while Labour must fight hard to keep its hold on Forest of Dean, Gloucester and Stroud in future elections. Forest of Dean must be a particular worry for the party, because of relatively poor results in 1997 and 2001, and the long term demographic trend in a seat the Tories had never won before 1979 but only narrowly failed to recover in 2001.

Local government
Gloucestershire county council has been a hung council since 1981 and no party is close to a majority.

Each of the three main parties has strongholds that can resist national tides – Labour in Gloucester and the Forest of Dean, the Liberal Democrats in Cheltenham and nearby suburbs, and the Conservatives in the rural fastness of Cotswold. The Tories and Independent allies account for 27 councillors, to 19 Labour, 16 Lib Dem and a single non-aligned independent. The administration is formed from a Lib-Lab coalition.

Labour had a narrow majority in Gloucester before 2002, but polled poorly and the council is closely balanced between the three parties. There was a dramatic change in Cheltenham, too, as the Lib Dems reasserted control after a three year Tory interlude. The Conservatives gained Stroud from no overall control, a strong recovery since the mid 1990s. Labour's majority in Forest of Dean is tested in 2003. The Conservatives are the largest group in hung Tewkesbury, although Labour have a significant group on the council. There are still substantial numbers of Independent councillors in Tewkesbury, Forest of Dean and Cotswold districts, in the last-named case only just short of an overall majority.

Boundary review

At the time of writing no official information was available. However, Gloucestershire is entitled to 6.2 seats so its current allocation of six seats will be unchanged. There may be some reshuffling of wards to equalise electorates, perhaps involving Tewkesbury donating wards to Cheltenham and Forest of Dean in exchange for a bit of Gloucester, and further south a transfer from Stroud to Cotswold. This should help the Tories in Cheltenham and the Forest, while weakening them in Stroud. All the seats except Cheltenham have increasing electorates.

CHELTENHAM

	2001		1997		1992 notional	
Electorate and turnout	67,563	61.9	67,950	74.0	69,121	81.4
Conservative	14,715	35.2	18,232	36.2	24,861	44.2
Labour	5,041	12.0	5,100	10.1	3,769	6.7
Lib Dem	19,970	47.7	24,877	49.5	26,808	47.6
Anti–EU	482	1.2	1,367 (2)	2.7	573	1.0
Others	1,627 (4)		727 (3)		285 (2)	
MP	Nigel Jones (LD)		Nigel Jones (LD)		Nigel Jones (LD)	
Majority	5,255	12.6	6,645	13.2	1,947	3.5

Cheltenham enjoys a pleasing townscape of floral parks, wide avenues and gracious Georgian streets, the product of thoughtful planning and affluence fed by its attractions as a spa and retirement area. The town is also a centre for service sector employment in education and private business, particularly insurance, and the massive government GCHQ intelligence establishment is a major influence. Like other spa towns (see also Bath and Harrogate) the Lib Dems are strong and Labour weak. The Lib Dems used to win local election landslides, but the Conservatives became competitive again and deprived the Lib Dems of control of the council from 1999 to 2002. Most wards are closely fought, although the Lib Dems have a couple of strongholds, in the centre of the town and the estate of Hesters Way. Labour's solitary outpost is Oakley.

Nigel Jones first won Cheltenham in 1992 against John Taylor (now Lord Taylor of Warwick) and Cheltenham has since laboured unfairly under the image of being a racist town. The retiring MP in 1992, Charles Irving, had a measurable personal vote and Cheltenham has a tendency to vote for locals against outsiders, regardless of whether they are black and from Birmingham or white and from Gloucester. Taylor did relatively well, as is apparent from the bigger majorities Jones has won against Tory candidates with strong local credentials – John Todman in 1997 and Robert Garnham in 2001. The Cheltenham Conservatives must hope for a national recovery in their party's fortunes if they are to make any headway.

COTSWOLD

	2001		1997		1992 notional	
Electorate and turnout	68,140	67.5	67,590	75.6	63,555	82.4
Conservative	23,133	50.3	23,698	46.4	28,496	54.4
Labour	10,383	22.6	11,608	22.7	5,697	10.9
Lib Dem	11,150	24.2	11,733	23.0	17,479	33.4
Anti–EU	1,315	2.9	3,393	6.6	–	–
Others	–		689 (2)		722	
MP	Geoffrey Clifton-Brown (Con)		Geoffrey Clifton-Brown (Con)		Geoffrey Clifton-Brown (Con)	
					Cirencester & Tewkesbury	
Majority	11,983	26.1	11,965	23.4	11,017	21.0

Cotswold is the name for the seat covering the entire eastern edge of Gloucestershire from Chipping Campden down to Wotton-under-Edge. The largest town in the constituency is Cirencester; other towns are Tetbury, Stow-on-the-Wold and Moreton-in-Marsh. Most of the countryside is very attractive, and the towns are pleasant little places built of Cotswold stone, full of teashops and craft centres. Cirencester is the home of the Royal Agricultural College and the dependence of even the towns on tourism and agriculture makes for a thoroughly Conservative tone to the area in parliamentary elections, although in local elections there is a sizeable Independent presence.

Labour left most of the county council wards uncontested in the 2001 local elections, which makes the task of finding where the rather substantial 23 per cent Labour vote comes from even harder. Tetbury provides a rare Labour councillor on Cotswold District, while Cirencester was Liberal Democrat in the 2001 county elections without Labour opposition. Cotswold is an extremely safe Conservative seat – there are only fourteen where their percentage majority was greater.

FOREST of DEAN

	2001		1997		1992 notional	
Electorate and turnout	66,240	67.3	63,732	78.7	62,882	83.1
Conservative	17,301	38.8	17,860	35.6	21,444	41.0
Labour	19,350	43.4	24,203	48.2	22,176	42.4
Lib Dem	5,762	12.9	6,165	12.3	8,422	16.1
Anti–EU	661	1.5	1,624	3.2	–	–
Green	1,254	2.8	–	–	–	–
Others	279		332 (3)		204	
MP	Diana Organ (Lab)		Diana Organ (Lab)		Paul Marland (Con)	
					Gloucestershire West	
Majority	2,049	4.6	6,343	12.6	732*	1.4*

* Estimated Labour majority allowing for boundary changes.

The Forest of Dean is a weird place. Dennis Potter, playwright and son of the Forest, described it as 'rather ugly villages in beautiful landscape, a heart shaped place between two rivers, somehow slightly cut off from the rest of England.' It is the part of England between the Severn and the Welsh border at the river Wye. Its woods are dense and somewhat spooky, and littered with the remains of a proud industrial past. There are still a few 'freeminers' with the right to dig for coal more or less where they feel like it, but all the pits have now closed. Most of the towns are not twee, hunting and cream teas places, but rather forbidding, with roads looping through bleak estates – see for example Cinderford and Coleford. Other parts are very pretty, particularly along the Wye opposite Tintern Abbey. Some of the Forest in the north has become commuter country for Gloucester and Cheltenham, and long term demographic change has gradually pushed it into the Conservative column. As early as 1962 Potter described 'The Changing Forest' in which old working class loyalties were blurring, and Paul Marland's capture of the seat for the Tories in 1979 seemed to close a chapter. But, helped by boundary changes, Diana Organ recaptured the Forest for Labour in 1997 although apparently on a low swing.

In the county elections of 2001 the Liberal Democrats did rather well in the Forest, scoring nearly 30 per cent (to 30 per cent Labour and 32 per cent Conservative), but this does not translate into general election voting. Labour were strongest in Cinderford, Brooksdean and Lydney, and the Conservatives led in Newent and Tidenham.

Forest of Dean produced a bad result for Labour in 2001, but rather than a continuation of a long term trend it may well have been a reaction to foot and mouth disease, which had a severe impact on the grazing commons of Dean. Parts of the constituency were virtually impassable because of the epidemic, and there was genuine rural discontent here. It remains a seat the Conservatives will have high hopes of gaining at the next election; it is the 19th most vulnerable Labour seat and seems likely to change hands unless there is yet another national Labour landslide.

GLOUCESTER

	2001		1997		1992 *notional*	
Electorate and turnout	81,207	59.4	78,852	73.4	*76,487*	*81.2*
Conservative	18,187	37.7	20,684	35.7	*28,274*	*45.5*
Labour	22,067	45.8	28,943	50.0	*22,867*	*36.8*
Lib Dem	6,875	14.3	6,069	10.5	*10,961*	*17.7*
Anti–EU	822	1.7	1,937 (2)	3.3	*–*	*–*
Others	272		281		*–*	
MP	Parmjit Dhanda (Lab)		Tess Kingham (Lab)		Douglas French (Con)	
Majority	3,880	8.0	8,259	14.3	*5,407*	*8.7*

Gloucester is a crossing point of the wide River Severn, and this position has kept a town here, from Roman Glevum to the current manufacturing centre and cathedral city. It also makes it prone to traffic jams and ugly road schemes. There are few strongly Conservative wards – their vote is dispersed throughout the city. Labour kept control of Gloucester in the local elections of 2000 by one seat, but this did not survive the next election in 2002. Gloucester is a traditional marginal which seems to allow parties a long lease on its representation. Labour had the seat from 1945 to 1970, and the Conservatives then held it from 1970 until 1997. If the past is a guide, Labour should be all right until the first election of the 2020s.

The circumstances of the 2001 election were unusual in Gloucester. Tess Kingham, elected in 1997, stood down in frustration at the unsociable hours and boys' club atmosphere of parliament which had changed disappointingly little during the 1997 parliament. Her successor as Labour candidate was Parmjit Dhanda, who was welcomed to the city by an article in the local paper saying that Gloucester was not ready to be represented by a 'foreigner'. This aroused considerable protest and the paper backed off. Dhanda won the seat, although with a halved majority.

In local elections the Liberal Democrats poll quite well in Gloucester, particularly in the eastern suburbs like Hucclecote. On the same day they received 14.3 per cent in the general election they polled 26.5 per cent in the locals. This difference went only slightly towards Labour's general election majority – a net addition of 300 rather than the 5,000 boost David Drew received in Stroud. This is probably mostly about incumbency, although it is arguable that there was more racist voting behaviour in Gloucester in 2001 than in Cheltenham in 1992. In 2005 Dhanda, elected at the age of 29, will be in the unusual position of being a new Labour incumbent defending a marginal seat and can expect to do better than the national trend – and perhaps hold on until the 2020s.

STROUD

	2001		1997		1992 notional	
Electorate and turnout	78,818	70.0	77,856	78.8	75,249	83.4
Conservative	20,646	37.4	23,260	37.9	29,032	46.2
Labour	25,685	46.6	26,170	42.7	18,451	29.4
Lib Dem	6,036	10.9	9,502	15.5	13,582	21.6
Anti–EU	895	1.6	–	–	–	–
Green	1,913	3.5	2,415	3.9	1,718	2.7
MP	David Drew (Lab)		David Drew (Lab)		Roger Knapman (Con)	
Majority	5,039	9.1	2,910	4.7	10,581	16.9

Stroud is a town where five valleys meet amid beautiful countryside. Stroud town itself, and the smaller towns of Dursley and Cam, have rather fierce socialist traditions and some industrial history. During poll tax protests in Bath in 1990, Chris Patten is supposed to have complained that the demonstrators were 'bussed in from radical places like Stroud'. Stroud was the first local authority to elect a significant Green group. The radical tradition, however, is not the dominant one. There are Conservatives in the towns, and the towns are also surrounded by some Conservative countryside, but Labour have come out on top in 1997 and 2001.

Labour MP David Drew, unusually, managed to squeeze the Liberal Democrat and Green votes further in 2001, which was the main source of the swing in his favour. Drew polled over 5,000 more votes than his running mates in the county council elections, most of which was drawn from people who voted Lib Dem in the local elections. Drew is a good example of how Labour benefited from incumbency in 2001, as his personal standing was very high. He has concentrated on rural, agricultural and environmental issues and whatever rural interests thought about the Blair government Drew could not be accused of ignoring the countryside.

Stroud has the unaccustomed position of producing the largest Labour majority in Gloucestershire, although Conservative runner-up Neil Carmichael had the dubious honour of being among the select band of candidates to poll over 20,000 votes in 2001 and still lose. Stroud is still a highly marginal seat and if an election comes at a time when there is real discontent with Labour the Conservatives should be able to overcome Drew's personal vote.

TEWKESBURY

	2001		1997		1992 notional	
Electorate and turnout	70,930	63.7	68,453	76.2	64,159	82.0
Conservative	20,830	46.1	23,859	45.8	28,300	53.8
Labour	12,167	26.9	13,665	26.2	5,297	10.1
Lib Dem	11,863	26.2	14,625	28.0	18,503	35.2
Others	335		–		488	
MP	Laurence Robertson (Con)		Laurence Robertson (Con)		NEW SEAT	
Majority	8,663	19.2	9,234	17.7	9,797	18.6

Tewkesbury is a historic town, but it gives its name to what is essentially a suburban constituency. A finger of territory pokes down between Gloucester and Cheltenham along the M5, where there has been considerable housing, industrial and retail development in places such as Churchdown, Brockworth and Hucclecote which are part of the Gloucester built-up area. Some western suburbs of Cheltenham are also included, such as Prestbury and Up Hatherley, plus the Cheltenham satellite town of Bishop's Cleeve.

Politically, Tewkesbury does have some elements of pluralism. Labour district councillors are elected from some Gloucester suburbs – their 2001 candidate Keir Dhillon represents part of Churchdown – and bits of Tewkesbury and the neighbouring area of Ashchurch. Bishop's Cleeve and much of Churchdown is Lib Dem, but the Conservatives poll a respectable vote everywhere and can rely on solid support from the rural parts of northern Gloucestershire. Labour edged up into second place in 2001 but there is no real threat to right wing Tory MP Laurence Robertson, who associated himself with the ravings of John Townend.

Greater Manchester

	Conservative		Labour		LiberalDemocrat		Others	
	Share of vote	Seats	Share of vote	Seats	Share of vote	Seats	Share of vote	Seats
2001	24.3	1	53.7	25	18.3	2	3.7	0
1997	24.1	2	56.3	25	16.0	1	3.5	0
1992	35.5	9	47.3	20	15.7	1	1.6	0
1987	35.9	10	44.0	19	19.9	1	0.1	0
1983	36.2	11	39.7	18	23.6	1	0.5	0

Greater Manchester includes not only the city itself, but a large number of towns which surround it on all sides, such as Bolton, Bury, Oldham, Rochdale, Stockport and Wigan. Thus there are as many as ten metropolitan boroughs covering the area - six are based on the aforementioned towns, while the others are Manchester itself (which covers a surprisingly small part of the conurbation), Tameside (covering Ashton-under-Lyne, Hyde and Stalybridge), Trafford (which includes Stretford, Altrincham and Sale) and Salford, which lies just to the west of Manchester's centre, though the boundary is hardly discernible. Most of the new metropolitan county was previously (before 1973) included in Lancashire, though the southern and part of its eastern segments were in Cheshire.

The whole Manchester area became industrialised from a very early date – it is sometimes claimed that the Industrial Revolution began here – and Manchester with its satellite towns expanded enormously with the cotton industry during the nineteenth century. Although such sudden industrial and urban growth created a large amount of wealth for some (there has always been a belt of upmarket properties on the fringes of the built-up areas), many more suffered miserable living and working conditions. Although protest by the poor and repression by the state have both been rare in Britain, a location near the old Free Trade Hall witnessed the 'Peterloo massacre' in 1819, when mounted soldiers charged at an 80,000 strong crowd demonstrating against the Corn Laws, killing eleven and injuring several hundred. From that date on, Manchester became associated with campaign for social reform; even Karl Marx's sidekick Friedrich Engels worked in the cotton mills here as he pondered the condition of the English working classes. Many of the city's constituencies and those of surrounding towns voted Liberal as soon as they could, and the area was one of the first to see major Labour breakthroughs after the party's formation at the start of the twentieth century. Even today, there are two museums in the area dedicated to the history of the Labour / Trade Union movement, while evidence of the area's industrial past in the shape of large, often decaying, cotton mills abounds.

Despite its industrial and population decline in recent decades (and permanently miserable weather), Manchester retains a certain vibrancy, and is in many ways the capital of the north west. Its airport is Britain's largest outside London, its football clubs (or at least one of them) has a greater support base and greater success than any other and it also claims the largest number of university students of any city in the UK. In 2002 Manchester was due to host the Commonwealth Games, centred on a new stadium built in the run-down east end of the city. Other new developments have included the Lowry Centre in neighbouring Salford (the famous artist was born here and reproduced many of its industrial scenes), while a more long-standing attraction is the Granada TV studios, specifically the set of *Coronation Street* which is filmed and based here. The idealised close-knit communities of the Street more accurately reflect life in the 1950s than today - both Manchester and Salford suffer appalling levels of deprivation, with Manchester providing no fewer than 10 of the nation's 75 most deprived wards. Periodically there are clearance schemes aimed at improving the social environment, and this is one reason for the fall in population, which has resulted in a cut in the number of parliamentary constituencies in the city from ten before the second world war down to just five today.

Politically, Labour won seven of its thirty seats in the area at the 1906 election, the first to be seriously contested by the new party. Three of the gains were in Manchester itself, but it was to take until 1945 for the party to establish genuine dominance here. In 1918 the Conservatives could win eight of the city's ten seats, and in 1931 they won all of them, though Labour did hang on in that greatest ever landslide election in the Lancashire coalfield seats to the west, which have proved (along with parts of Durham, South Yorkshire and South Wales) the most loyal areas to Labour in the country. Even in the post-second world war period, the Conservatives retained a large number of constituencies in the towns around Manchester, and it is only very recently that they have come close to being wiped out. In their good years in the 1950s the Tories could count on about ten seats in the area, and although reduced to just a couple in 1966 (both in Manchester itself) they built back up to double figures in the 1980s. By that time some of the names of constituencies had changed, but the geography was almost identical to that in the 1950s. Conservative-held seats in the Thatcher years included two in each of Bolton and Bury, three in Stockport, two in Tameside (Altrincham and Davyhulme), Littleborough & Saddleworth and only one seat in Manchester, Withington.

In both the 1987 and 1992 elections, Labour were to gain just a single seat as the other marginals proved frustratingly difficult to win. In 1987 it was Withington, the Conservatives' last seat in Manchester itself, which fell after a huge (in those days) swing exceeding seven per cent, and five years later Stockport followed suit. But the Conservatives crucially held on in seats like Bury North and South, and it was to take the national landslide conditions of 1997 for Labour to finally break through. The Liberal Democrats also played their part by finally winning Hazel Grove, though they were also to lose Rochdale (held since a 1972 by-election) and Oldham East (held since 1995) back to Labour. The Conservatives were again reduced to just two seats, but this time they did not bounce back four years later, even managing to lose one of them (Cheadle) in 2001. This left just Altrincham & Sale, a Tory seat since 1924, as their last surviving refuge in Greater Manchester.

Next time the Conservatives will have to start making inroads as part of any national recovery, but it may not be straightforward. Numerically the easiest seat to regain will be Cheadle, but the Liberal Democrats have proved that they can dig themselves in after narrow initial wins (see Kingston) and the possibility of an increased majority should not be dismissed. Neighbouring Hazel Grove now seems beyond the reach of the Conservatives, and they will probably instead concentrate on two seats at the opposite corner of the conurbation, notably Bolton West and Bury North, which are just about within range, needing swings of seven per cent or thereabouts. Further gains seem unlikely; former Tory seats now held by Labour like Bury South, Stockport, Stretford & Urmston and Withington all have majorities exceeding 30 per cent (Stalybridge & Hyde is now more marginal than any of them). Only Bolton North East represents another serious prospect, though even this requires a swing of almost 11 per cent. The electoral arithmetic here shows just how big a hole the Conservatives are currently in – even a recovery to four or five seats would be something of a triumph, but that would leave them with only half as many seats as 1992, when the overall Tory majority was about as low as it could get while still remaining workable.

Local government

As in many parts of the country, the last twenty years have seen a dramatic collapse in the number of Conservative councillors, with the Liberal Democrats now often forming the opposition to Labour. Overall on the ten metropolitan authorities in the area, the Conservatives have declined from 370 councillors in 1978 to just 58 by 1999, with just about their only remaining significant group to be found in Trafford borough, though they started to recover in Bolton and Bury in the 2000 elections. Over the same period, Labour have increased from 251 to 460, while the Lib Dems have gone from a tiny group of 21 up to 118. Such changes have implications for national politics, as the Conservatives' grass-roots strength has withered in an area where until recently they could win ten parliamentary constituencies. Their replacement by the Lib Dems in many middle class council wards has provided the stimulus for changes in general election voting patterns as well, which makes it all the more difficult for the Tories to recover, though with annual elections in all authorities, changes in political composition can take place quite quickly.

Manchester city council has seen the Conservatives completely wiped out, even though they had 46 of its 99 councillors in the late 1970s. After 2002, Labour had a 75-strong group with the Lib Dems on 22. The council has always been run by Labour since the 1973 re-organisation, and usually before that as well. The Conservatives previously had majorities on Bolton (1975-80) and Bury (1975-86), but Labour took control of both in the 1980s and remain in control, though Bolton in particular (which has a reasonable Lib Dem group as well as a Tory one) could be vulnerable during the current parliament. Wigan has always been almost monolithically Labour, with 65 councillors out of 72 after 2002, and two other metropolitan councils which are strongly Labour are Salford and Tameside, though the latter was briefly Tory-run in the late 1970s.

The jewel in the Conservative crown used to be Trafford (54 councillors out of 63 in 1978) but their majority was slowly whittled away in the 1980s and 1990s and they finally lost control in 1995. Labour continued to strengthen in the late 1990s to take an overall majority, which they retained after 2000 and 2002, though this may come under severe pressure; the regain of this authority would be the first step back on the road to electoral respectability for the Conservatives. Stockport was also Conservative from 1975-83 (a year in which they won three of its parliamentary seats) but it is the Liberal Democrats who have shown most recent growth, currently enjoying an overall majority. In 1999 there were only two Tory councillors left here, and although that number subsequently increased, it will be a long recovery process. Finally, Labour have generally been the largest party on Rochdale council, though with a significant Lib Dem group, and Oldham was gained by the Liberal Democrats from Labour in 2000, to add to their similar recent triumphs in Sheffield and Liverpool. However, as in those cities, they lost ground here in 2002 to lose overall control of the council.

Boundary review

Greater Manchester will almost certainly lose another constituency when the commissioners consider the area near the end of the current review. Which one is more difficult to predict as most boroughs have seen a slight decline in their constituency entitlement rather than any dramatic population changes. There are already a number of seats which cross borough boundaries, and it may be that they are more vulnerable than most, particularly Denton & Reddish (which links Stockport and Tameside), since most other seats in these boroughs are a little too small at present. Needless to say, any changes will be hotly contested – all three parties have a strong interest in the Stockport borough in particular.

ALTRINCHAM and SALE WEST

	2001		1997		1992 notional	
Electorate and turnout	72,288	60.3	70,625	73.3	71,031	78.4
Conservative	20,113	46.2	22,348	43.2	30,343	54.5
Labour	17,172	39.4	20,843	40.3	14,727	26.4
Lib Dem	6,283	14.4	6,535	12.6	10,261	18.4
Anti–EU	–	–	1,618 (2)	3.1	–	–
Others	–		438 (2)		366	
MP	Graham Brady (Con)		Graham Brady (Con)		Fergus Montgomery (Con)	
					Altrincham and Sale	
Majority	2,941	6.8	1,505	2.9	15,616	28.1

Following the loss of Cheadle in 2001, Altrincham and Sale now boasts the distinction of being the only Conservative-held seat out of a total of 95 in the former metropolitan counties in the north of England (Greater Manchester, Merseyside, West Yorkshire, South Yorkshire, and Tyne and Wear). Such a statistic graphically illustrates the problems facing the Tories at the start of the twenty-first century, and it could have been even worse had Labour scraped together another 1,500 votes in 1997. The above-average swing then achieved by Trafford councillor Jane Baugh was not quite enough to cause a sensation, and in 2001 a rematch saw Graham Brady double his majority.

There is no doubt that this should be a safe Tory constituency. The previous seat of Altrincham and Sale had been Conservative since 1945, while neighbouring Davyhulme (which provided 18,500 new electors after its abolition after 1992) was also a relatively safe berth for Winston Churchill, grandson of his more famous namesake. The present constituency includes some of Greater Manchester's most desirable residential neighbourhoods, notably in Hale where tree-lined avenues almost drip with wealth; hardly surprisingly the Conservatives picked up 75 per cent of the vote here in the 2000 local elections and Labour just 12 per cent. There are Labour areas to the north and west of Altrincham itself, but nevertheless it is difficult to see how Labour could possibly have accumulated 20,000 votes in the constituency in 1997. Although there has been a significant long-term swing away from the Tories across the borough of Trafford (as in nearby Cheadle and Hazel Grove), one would expect the Conservatives to start rebuilding their majority here in future contests.

ASHTON-UNDER-LYNE

	2001		1997		1992 notional	
Electorate and turnout	72,820	49.1	72,308	65.4	74,551	73.3
Conservative	6,822	19.1	8,954	18.9	15,706	28.8
Labour	22,340	62.5	31,919	67.5	31,138	57.0
Lib Dem	4,237	11.8	4,603	9.7	6,519	11.9
Anti-EU	-	-	1,346	2.8	-	-
BNP	1,617	4.5	-	-	-	-
Others	748		458		1,271 (2)	
MP	David Heyes (Lab)		Robert Sheldon (Lab)		Robert Sheldon (Lab)	
Majority	15,518	43.4	22,965	48.6	15,432	28.2

Labour have held Ashton-under-Lyne since 1935, though also won it seven years earlier after the sitting Tory MP was adjudicated a bankrupt and disqualified from office. When Labour lost here in a 1931 by-election, they blamed it on the intervention of Oswald Mosley's (pre-fascist) 'New Party', their angry reaction said to have pushed Mosley further to the right. Another point to note is that the level of voter turnout in the inter-war period was in excess of 80 per cent, and at election times, fireworks in the winning party's colours would be set off from the town hall roof. All this indicates a certain enthusiasm for elections which a sub-50 per cent turnout in 2001 suggests is no longer apparent.

Although the seat has been Labour for almost seventy years, their majority was reduced to less than a thousand votes in 1950, but they have steadily increased their majority since then, retaining a healthy lead of 7,500 even in 1983 and trebling this figure by 1997. A slight swing away from the party in 2001 was probably only to be expected after its MP of 37 years, Robert Sheldon, well known as chairman of the Public Accounts Committee, stood down.

The old textile town of Ashton is one of several which makes up the metropolitan borough of Tameside, to the east of Manchester. The parliamentary constituency also includes Droylsden on the other side of the newly completed M60 motorway and three wards from the southern part of Oldham borough. Two of these, Failsworth East and Hollinwood, have fallen (like so many in Oldham) to the Liberal Democrats - in the former, Labour's vote collapsed from 76 per cent in 1995 down to 23 per cent in 2000, as calamitous a performance as anywhere in the country. The Ashton wards (and even more so those in Droylsden) remain rather better for Labour locally, though there is a minority Conservative vote in wards like Hurst off the Mossley Road. In 2001, Sheldon's successor David Heyes (a former councillor for nearby Chadderton ward in Oldham) won easily, with no apparent knock-on effect from the Lib Dem council success in the Oldham segment of the constituency, though a slight echo of the BNP's performance up the road.

BOLTON NORTH EAST

	2001		1997		1992 notional	
Electorate and turnout	69,514	56.0	67,996	72.4	69,722	80.1
Conservative	12,744	32.7	14,952	30.4	23,477	42.1
Labour	21,166	54.3	27,621	56.1	26,494	47.5
Lib Dem	4,004	10.3	4,862	9.9	5,638	10.1
Anti-EU	-	-	1,096	2.2	-	-
Others	1,036 (2)		676		213	
MP	David Crausby (Lab)		David Crausby (Lab)		Peter Thurnham (Con) (LD)	
Majority	8,422	21.6	12,669	25.7	3,017*	5.4*

* Estimated Labour majority allowing for boundary changes.

Bolton North East was a hyper-marginal for three general elections after its creation in 1983, with Peter Thurnham defeating Labour's Ann Taylor in 1983 and then holding on by just over 800 votes in 1987 and less than 200 in 1992, before boundary changes improved Labour's prospects. Five years later, by which time Thurnham had defected to the Liberal Democrats, the national swing produced a Labour lead in five figures. Despite the large majorities recorded in 1997 and 2001, it remains a constituency that the Conservatives need to keep in their thoughts if they are to form a majority government in the future - after all, together with its predecessor constituency (Bolton East) this seat has only once gone against the national tide since 1950.

The centre of the town, with its significant Asian population, forms part of the constituency, but it extends out as far as Jumbles Reservoir on the edge of the moors to the north. Although usually perceived and portrayed as a working class town, a number of Bolton's outlying suburbs contain residential areas of real prosperity, and as one might expect this produces a very polarised pattern electorally. Thus in the 2000 local elections, the Conservatives won three wards, Astley Bridge, Bradshaw and Bromley Cross, polling sixty per cent of the vote and leading Labour by nearly 4,000 votes in this section of the seat. The wards comprising mainly terraced housing further in, like Halliwell and Tonge, remained strongly Labour, and clearly held sway in both 1997 and 2001, though one suspects that 'New Labour' must have attracted a greater proportion of the vote out in the suburbs as well when it came to the two most recent general elections. For now, David Crausby appears reasonably safe, but he will be mindful of the seat's past record, particularly if the Conservatives produce a national recovery.

BOLTON SOUTH EAST

	2001		1997		1992 notional	
Electorate and turnout	68,140	50.1	66,542	65.1	66,566	74.3
Conservative	8,258	24.2	8,545	19.7	14,192	28.7
Labour	21,129	61.9	29,856	68.9	26,863	54.3
Lib Dem	3,941	11.5	3,805	8.8	5,236	10.6
Anti-EU	–	–	973	2.2	–	–
Ind Labour	–	–	–	–	2,891	5.8
Others	826		170		290	
MP	Brian Iddon (Lab)		Brian Iddon (Lab)		David Young (Lab)	
Majority	12,871	37.7	21,311	49.2	12,671	25.6

Bolton South East was another new constituency created in 1983, though it is much safer than North East (or West) for Labour. It most closely resembles the old Farnworth seat, which was broken up in the 1980s boundary review after being held by Labour since 1935, though its sitting MP, John Roper, had defected to the SDP in 1981. South East's inaugural contest produced the town's only Labour victory of that year, David Young (MP for Bolton East since 1974) elected by almost 9,000 votes, and the seat has more or less retained its ranking as approximately Labour's one hundredth safest ever since, though it was a little higher after 1997 and a bit lower after 2001.

The territory to the south and east of the town centre is dominated by rows of terraced housing, and this remains a very traditional, northern working class seat, with the 51st highest proportion of skilled manual workers of any constituency (and the 44th lowest number of professionals) according to the 1991 census. Of the seven individual wards, Labour won them all relatively easily in the mid 1990s (with over eighty per cent of the vote in one ward and over seventy per cent in another three) but they narrowly lost Kearsley to the Liberal Democrats in 1999. Worse was to follow in 2000 when not only did the Lib Dems stretch their lead here, but the Conservatives gained Derby ward, having polled just 16 per cent the year before. This sudden turnaround in fortunes may not have been unconnected with the Tories opting to select an Asian candidate in a ward which contains a large (possibly now majority) non-white population, something which has also started to happen across the Pennines in Bradford. The repeat of this tactic in the 2001 general election led to a significant above-average swing from Labour to the Conservatives, though former councillor and organic chemistry lecturer Brian Iddon remains safe enough.

BOLTON WEST

	2001		1997		1992 notional	
Electorate and turnout	66,033	62.4	63,607	77.3	63,070	82.5
Conservative	13,863	33.6	17,270	35.1	24,619	47.3
Labour	19,381	47.0	24,342	49.5	20,338	39.1
Lib Dem	7,573	18.4	5,309	10.8	6,862	13.2
Anti-EU	–	–	865	1.8	–	–
Others	397		1,374		208	
MP	Ruth Kelly (Lab)		Ruth Kelly (Lab)		Tom Sackville (Con)	
Majority	5,518	13.4	7,072	14.4	4,281	8.2

The third Bolton seat is another important marginal. West is a very mixed constituency on both sides of the M61 motorway, centred on the new 'Reebok Stadium' which serves as home to Bolton Wanderers FC. The seat includes strong areas of Labour support in the working-class towns of Blackrod and Westhoughton (itself a Labour seat from 1906 to 1983), but also areas inclined to the Conservatives such as Deane-cum-Heaton, on the western fringes of Bolton itself.

Bolton West has an interesting history, having been held by all parties since its creation in 1950 – it was Labour from 1950-51, 1964-70 and 1974-83, Liberal from 1951-64 and Conservative from 1970-74 and after 1983. For a period, the Conservatives did not put up candidates here, even though they had finished second to Labour in the seat's inaugural contest in 1950. The year after, their withdrawal allowed a Liberal to gain the seat, the compliment returned in Bolton East where the Liberals withdrew and the Conservatives won. This unusual pact continued for two further elections, keeping Labour out of the town until 1964, when there was a full slate of candidates again and Labour duly regained both constituencies.

In recent years, results here have remained very close, the seat swapping sides in 1970, October 1974 and 1983. Labour narrowly failed to win it back in 1987 and 1992, but succeeded at the third attempt in 1997, when 28 year old Ruth Kelly defeated Tom Sackville with a swing of 11 per cent. Last time there was only a very slight movement back to the Conservatives, despite local council elections in May 2000 at which Labour had won no wards at all. On that occasion, it was the Liberal Democrats who polled most votes, proving that third party traditions persist here, and though this support is no longer always repeated in general elections, they did add an impressive eight percentage points to their tally in 2001.

BURY NORTH

	2001		1997		1992 actual	
Electorate and turnout	71,108	63.0	70,717	77.8	69,531	84.8
Conservative	16,413	36.6	20,657	37.5	29,266	49.7
Labour	22,945	51.2	28,523	51.8	24,502	41.6
Lib Dem	5,430	12.1	4,536	8.2	5,010	8.5
Anti-EU	–	–	1,337	2.4	–	–
Others	–		–		163	
MP	David Chaytor (Lab)		David Chaytor (Lab)		Alistair Burt (Con)	
Majority	6,532	14.6	7,866	14.3	4,764	8.1

Bury is another of the many former cotton towns to be found to the north of Manchester, but traditionally it has voted Conservative, even in 1945. The town's single seat only went Labour for the first time in 1964, the Tories regaining it in 1970 before Labour notched up further victories in October 1974 and 1979 by the tight margins of 442 and 38 votes respectively. In 1983 the town divided into two constituencies, and both were duly gained by the Conservatives and held (to Labour's great frustration) until the national landslide of 1997.

Bury North was slightly safer for the Tories than South, as it comprises not only most of Bury itself, but also Ramsbottom and Tottington towards the Lancashire moors – an area which has always had large numbers of instinctive Conservative voters. The latter ward even resisted the Labour tide in local elections in the mid 1990s, but it was alone in this behaviour as the other seven wards in the constituency were all won by Labour, Bury East and Redvales both giving the party over 80 per cent of the vote. North's MP, Alistair Burt, had actually seen his numerical vote increase twice since his initial victory in 1983, but his run of success was to come to an end in 1997, a swing of 11 per cent fairly close to both the national and regional average.

Burt's popularity was shown by the fact that the Conservative vote dropped further in 2001, despite them leading by almost 10 per cent (and winning five wards) in the 2000 local council elections. 1997 winner David Chaytor was returned with an almost unchanged percentage majority, a telling indicator of the complete failure of the opposition last time, even in the traditional Tory areas at which their campaign was apparently aimed. Bury North, however, remains a crucial marginal and will undoubtedly be targeted again (possibly with better results) next time.

BURY SOUTH

	2001		1997		1992 notional	
Electorate and turnout	67,276	58.8	66,797	75.4	66,391	81.6
Conservative	10,634	26.9	16,277	32.3	24,925	46.0
Labour	23,406	59.2	28,658	56.9	24,197	44.6
Lib Dem	5,499	13.9	4,227	8.4	4,853	9.0
Anti-EU	-	-	1,216	2.4	-	-
Others	-		-		229	
MP	Ivan Lewis (Lab)		Ivan Lewis (Lab)		David Sumberg (Con)	
Majority	12,772	32.3	12,381	24.6	728	1.3

After narrowly spurning them in 1992, Bury South was almost at the top of Labour's target list in 1997, and duly fell with a swing of 13 per cent, slightly above the national and regional average, and enough for Labour to win with a huge majority exceeding 12,000. The constituency itself is not really based on the town of Bury (which lies within Bury North), but rather the working-class town of Radcliffe together with more prosperous Manchester commuter territory to the north and south of the M60 motorway, including Whitefield, Prestwich and Sedgley Park. Many of these wards were formerly part of the Middleton and Prestwich seat, which was usually Conservative, though narrowly Labour after 1974.

This was one of the very few of Labour's 'gain seats' of 1997 which Labour held in both the 1999 Euro elections and 2000 local elections, when they still led the Conservatives by 11 percentage points. The result in 2001 therefore, although eye-catching, was not really a surprise and predicted in certain quarters. A major factor may well have been the large number of Jewish voters in the constituency (almost certainly the highest proportion outside North London), who were particularly alienated by the rhetoric of the Hague-led campaign. The result was another substantial fall in the Tory vote and a big increase in the percentage majority of the constituency's local Jewish MP, Ivan Lewis. Even though it was a Conservative seat just a few short years ago, Bury South is now safer for Labour than traditional industrial constituencies like Bridgend and Falkirk East, and it seems hard to classify it as a marginal any more.

CHEADLE

	2001		1997		1992 notional	
Electorate and turnout	69,001	63.2	67,853	77.3	68,789	82.7
Conservative	18,444	42.3	22,944	43.7	32,804	57.7
Labour	6,086	14.0	8,253	15.7	7,080	12.4
Lib Dem	18,477	42.4	19,755	37.7	16,828	29.6
Anti-EU	599	1.4	1,511	2.9	-	-
Others	-		-		183	
MP	Patsy Calton (LD)		Steven Day (Con)		Steven Day (Con)	
Majority	33	0.1	3,189	6.1	15,976	28.1

Cheadle lies to the south of Stockport, a leafy suburban constituency in which Labour were reduced to third place as long ago as 1959. According to the 1991 census, almost half of its population are in the professional or managerial classes, just about the highest proportion one finds anywhere north of Watford. Cheadle Hulme itself has long since been the sort of place where the prosperous middle classes have aspired to move to; unsurprisingly it is included in the ten per cent least deprived wards in the country, though Bramhall (the next suburb out and also included in the seat) comes even higher up that exclusive list.

Despite all this, there has not been an uninterrupted period of Conservative dominance here. The first political shock took place in 1966, when the parliamentary seat was gained by the Liberal Dr Michael Winstanley, the margin after a huge swing 655 votes. He was to last only a single term, and by 1979 the Conservatives had built their lead back up to an apparently impregnable 30 per cent. By this time, Cheadle had spawned neighbouring Hazel Grove (a new seat created in 1974), which was to attract the bulk of Liberal campaigning efforts in the Greater Manchester area, though after winning its initial contest they were to be frustrated there on several occasions before finally making the breakthrough (by a huge majority) in 1997. Having achieved one victory, the Liberal Democrats will have fancied their chances of a second next door, particularly after they reduced Steven Day's majority to just 3,000 in 1997. In the event, Stockport borough councillor Patsy Calton was able to further increase her party's share of the vote in 2001 by just enough to scrape home by 33 votes, the smallest majority in the country last time. It will be fascinating to see whether she can last longer than Winstanley did; it will undoubtedly be a tough test as the constituency stands as the Conservatives' number one target seat in the country.

DENTON and REDDISH

	2001		1997		1992 notional	
Electorate and turnout	69,236	48.5	68,866	66.9	70,758	75.1
Conservative	6,583	19.6	9,826	21.3	18,010	33.9
Labour	21,913	65.2	30,137	65.4	28,164	53.0
Lib Dem	4,152	12.4	6,121	13.3	5,298	10.0
Anti-EU	945	2.8	–	–	–	–
Others	–		–		1,699 (2)	
MP	Andrew Bennett (Lab)		Andrew Bennett (Lab)		Andrew Bennett (Lab)	
Majority	15,330	45.6	20,311	44.1	10,154	19.1

The constituency of Denton and Reddish is very much part of the Manchester conurbation, but actually links the boroughs of Stockport and Tameside. Reddish lies to the north of the centre of Stockport, on the other side of the M60 motorway. Its two wards are typically won by Labour with enormous majorities, though their vote has declined slightly from the 82.8 per cent share recorded in a three-way contest in Reddish North in 1995. The Tameside segment of the seat lies to the north east, including not only Denton, but also Audenshaw and Dukinfield. In the 1999 local elections, all these wards were won by Labour, but the following year the Liberal Democrats captured Audenshaw.

In parliamentary elections, the seat has been very safe for its MP Andrew Bennett ever since its creation in 1983. Prior to that, much of the constituency was included in the old Stockport North, a key marginal which was often held by the Conservatives and which changed hands in 1964, 1970 and 1974. Bennett was first elected in February 1974, holding on by just 333 votes in 1979. Then the boundary commissioners made his life a lot less stressful with a major review of boundaries in the area and in 1983 he was able to win the newly configured seat by 5,000 votes, though the flip side was the Tory win in the new single Stockport division. After another good Labour performance here in 2001, Denton and Reddish rose to their 57th safest seat.

ECCLES

	2001		1997		1992 notional	
Electorate and turnout	68,764	48.3	69,645	65.6	72,247	74.4
Conservative	6,867	20.7	8,552	18.7	16,730	31.1
Labour	21,395	64.5	30,468	66.7	30,960	57.6
Lib Dem	4,920	14.8	4,905	10.7	5,186	9.7
Anti-EU	-	-	1,765	3.9	-	-
Others	-		-		867 (2)	
MP	Ian Stewart (Lab)		Ian Stewart (Lab)		Joan Lestor (Lab)	
Majority	14,528	43.8	21,916	48.0	14,230	26.5

Eccles, which lies on the western side of Greater Manchester along the M602 motorway and nearby ship canal, is these days part of Salford metropolitan borough, but has had a parliamentary constituency (not to mention being able to boast its own distinctive cakes) since 1885. Before the first world war it was won by the Liberals, but after 1918 was generally Conservative, though Labour could win in 1922, 1923 and 1929. After the second world war it firmly passed into the Labour column and has remained there ever since.

The constituency includes Swinton to the north as well as Irlam and Cadishead, which are half way to Warrington on the north bank of the ship canal to the south west. Almost all of these areas are traditionally very loyal to the Labour Party, and in the 1995 local elections, they chalked up vote shares exceeding 80 per cent in six of the seat's eight wards (and did not do all that much worse in the other two). In 1997, former TGWU regional officer Ian Stewart significantly increased Joan Lestor's majority to almost 22,000 votes to inherit the seat.

In the mid-term local elections which followed, something of a Conservative vote re-emerged across the constituency, and they even gained council seats in Cadishead and Swinton South in 2000, coming within striking distance in two other wards, Eccles and Irlam. Not much of this seemed to feed through into the 2001 general election, and Stewart was comfortably re-elected by 14,500 votes.

HAZEL GROVE

	2001		1997		1992 actual	
Electorate and turnout	65,105	59.1	63,863	77.3	64,300	85.0
Conservative	11,585	30.1	15,069	30.5	24,479	44.8
Labour	6,230	16.2	5,882	11.9	6,390	11.7
Lib Dem	20,020	52.0	26,883	54.5	23,550	43.1
Anti-EU	643	1.7	1,323 (2)	2.6	–	–
Others	–		183		204	
MP	Andrew Stunell (LD)		Andrew Stunell (LD)		Tom Arnold (Con)	
Majority	8,435	21.9	11,814	23.9	929	1.7

Hazel Grove was a new division created in the boundary review of the 1970s. The suburban seat to the south east of Stockport immediately offered an enticing prospect to the Liberals, who in 1966 had won its parent constituency of Cheadle. Former MP Michael Winstanley (who lost Cheadle in 1970) stood and won the new seat at its inaugural contest in February 1974, but this success was to prove even less enduring than on the previous occasion, and just eight months later Winstanley was defeated by Conservative Tom Arnold.

In 1979 Arnold's majority increased to more than 15,000, but the revival of the centre vote which was prompted by the newly created SDP-Liberal Alliance produced a 14-point increase in Liberal support in Hazel Grove in 1983 and the Tory majority was cut to just over 2,000. From then on it became a top Liberal/Liberal Democrat target, but they failed to make the breakthrough on two further occasions as Arnold (who had an influential role in the selection of Conservative candidates across the country) doggedly held on. Finally in 1997 the writing was on the wall. Arnold wisely stood down and Andrew Stunell gained the seat with a stunning majority of almost 12,000, which after years of near misses suddenly transformed the seat into the party's safest in England and third safest in the UK.

This affluent residential constituency comprises not only Hazel Grove itself, but also Bredbury, Romiley and Marple to the north, which are all railway stations on the Manchester to Sheffield line. Locally, the Lib Dems win everything, with the once reasonable Labour vote in Bredbury and Romiley disappearing, though the Conservatives are not too far behind in South Marple. In 2001, Stunell held on easily (despite his party transferring their attention to neighbouring Cheadle) and Hazel Grove will be a very difficult constituency for the Conservatives to regain.

HEYWOOD and MIDDLETON

	2001		1997		1992 notional	
Electorate and turnout	73,005	53.1	73,898	68.4	74,759	74.5
Conservative	10,707	27.6	11,637	23.0	17,591	31.6
Labour	22,377	57.7	29,179	57.7	25,885	46.5
Lib Dem	4,329	11.2	7,908	15.6	11,119	20.0
Anti-EU	–	–	1,076	2.1	–	–
Others	1,366 (2)		750		1,093 (2)	
MP	Jim Dobbin (Lab)		Jim Dobbin (Lab)		Jim Callaghan (Lab)	
Majority	11,670	30.1	17,542	34.7	8,294	14.9

Heywood and Middleton takes in the southern part of the borough of Rochdale, its component parts previously included in several different seats. Middleton formed a large section of the normally Conservative Middleton & Prestwich division, which once produced a vote of 98.7 per cent for the Conservatives, though it should be noted that this was in a 1940 by-election, with the only opposition coming from the British Union of Fascists. In fact the seat had been narrowly held by Labour since February 1974, its MP Jim Callaghan (the lesser known one) elected for the new constituency in 1983. Heywood, on the other side of the M62 motorway, had been linked with Radcliffe before 1950, then Royton until 1983. This latter combination was the constituency of Joel Barnett, Chief Secretary to the Treasury in the 1970s, who is nowadays famous for apparently unwittingly 'inventing' the Barnett formula on regional funding, which has become so controversial more than twenty years later.

Most of the component wards of the constituency vote Labour, but the strong exception is the rural Norden & Bamford ward, which extends around the west of Rochdale into the Lancashire moors. Most of its electorate live in the more residential western fringes of Rochdale, and Labour finish third in local elections with the Conservatives in first, a pattern true even of the mid-1990s. Both Heywood and Middleton themselves return an almost full slate of Labour councillors, though the Liberal Democrats usually win Castleton and the Conservatives can win Middleton South. Despite this internal variety, Labour continue to win the constituency in general elections with some degree of comfort; Callaghan's successor Jim Dobbin enjoyed five-figure majorities in 1997 and 2001.

LEIGH

	2001		1997		1992 notional	
Electorate and turnout	71,054	49.7	69,908	65.7	70,188	74.9
Conservative	6,421	18.2	7,156	15.6	14,341	27.3
Labour	22,783	64.5	31,652	68.9	31,196	59.3
Lib Dem	4,524	12.8	5,163	11.2	6,539	12.4
Anti-EU	750	2.1	1,949	4.2	–	–
Others	820		–		525	
MP	Andy Burnham (Lab)		Lawrence Cunliffe (Lab)		Lawrence Cunliffe (Lab)	
Majority	16,362	46.4	24,496	53.3	16,855	32.1

Leigh has been a Labour seat on a continual basis since 1922, and has never elected a Conservative MP, having been won by the Liberals from 1885 until then. The constituency is at the centre of a staunchly Labour area (nowadays roughly bordered by the M6, M61 and M62 motorways) which mirrors the defunct Lancashire coalfield - other seats here include Makerfield and Wigan, which have been held by the party since 1906 and 1918 respectively. The smallest Labour majority in Leigh was 2,000 in 1931 (when they lost almost everywhere else) and from 1945 onwards the margin has always been in five figures.

The constituency includes not only the rugby-league town of Leigh itself but also its smaller neighbours of Atherton and Hindley. This makes little difference politically - all wards voted Labour in 1999 and 2000, though vote shares have fallen slightly since the mid 1990s when over 80 per cent was recorded in Hindley Green and Lightshaw wards and two others went uncontested. The only serious challenges to the party are those which occasionally come from rebel Labour candidates, and the replacement of the ailing Lawrence Cunliffe with 31-year old Andy Burnham in 2001 was never likely to prove problematic once the selection process was completed. A small adverse swing, combined with a rather larger decline in turnout (to below 50 per cent), did reduce the numerical majority here by a third, but Burnham should have few worries in a seat just outside Labour's safest fifty.

MAKERFIELD

	2001		*1997*		*1992 notional*	
Electorate and turnout	68,457	50.9	67,358	66.8	68,557	75.5
Conservative	6,129	17.6	6,942	15.4	12,640	24.4
Labour	23,879	68.5	33,119	73.6	32,787	63.3
Lib Dem	3,990	11.4	3,743	8.3	4,751	9.2
Anti-EU	-	-	1,210	2.7	-	-
Others	858		-		1,582 (2)	
MP	Ian McCartney (Lab)		Ian McCartney (Lab)		Ian McCartney (Lab)	
Majority	17,750	50.9	26,177	58.2	20,147	38.9

Another strong Labour seat, Makerfield includes the small towns to the south and west of Wigan such as Abram, Ashton-in-Makerfield and Orrell. Its predecessor seat (Ince) went Labour as soon as they first started to seriously contest general elections, the new party polling 70 per cent of the vote in 1906. That figure rose to an even more impressive 87 per cent in 1918 and even in the national meltdown year of 1931 they attracted 63 per cent. They have had little trouble since and this was Labour's 25th safest seat in the country in 1997, despite Ian McCartney spending most of the campaign overseeing the rather more crucial campaign in the region's many marginals. The modest swing to the Conservatives in 2001 was standard for an ex-mining seat, and Makerfield's Labour majority dropped only slightly to their 31st largest.

In local council elections, Labour polled almost 91 per cent of the vote in Abram in 1995 and 90 per cent in Worsley Mesnes, just south of the centre of Wigan. Those figures had fallen by 2000, and one ward, Orrell, was narrowly lost to the Conservatives. In fact the character of this small part of the seat (on the western side of the M6) differs from much of the rest, even preferring Rugby Union to League, which in the north is a sure sign of a middle class area. Results here are unlikely to worry McCartney too much, who has been in the government since 1997 and whose various prominent roles have included signing up to the European social charter soon after Labour's initial victory, helping ensure the success of the Manchester commonwealth games in 2002 and overseeing the development of Labour's new policy-making processes.

MANCHESTER BLACKLEY

	2001		1997		1992 notional	
Electorate and turnout	59,111	44.9	62,474	57.2	65,317	66.4
Conservative	3,821	14.4	5,454	15.3	11,285	26.0
Labour	18,285	68.9	25,042	70.0	26,977	62.2
Lib Dem	3,015	11.4	3,937	11.0	4,786	11.0
Anti-EU	-	-	1,323	3.7	-	-
Others	1,402 (3)		-		342	
MP	Graham Stringer (Lab)		Graham Stringer (Lab)		Ken Eastham (Lab)	
Majority	14,464	54.5	19,588	54.8	15,692	36.2

Manchester Blackley provides a graphic illustration of the decline of the Conservatives in the city. Blackley was usually a Conservative seat before 1945, recaptured in 1951 and held again until 1964. Even in February 1974, Labour's majority was only 5,500, but that figure has remorselessly increased from 1983 onwards, and it is now their 17th safest seat in the country. Meanwhile, the Conservatives did not even bother contesting four of the seven wards in the 2000 local elections.

The constituency covers the northern wards of Manchester, which extend as far out as the large open spaces of Heaton Park and the M60 motorway and as far in as Cheetham, previously a Jewish area (and the name of a former constituency until 1974) which is now populated largely by Asians. There is something of a local Liberal Democrat vote in wards like Charlestown, Moston and Blackley itself, but nothing as yet to trouble Labour, who still won all wards in the seat in 2000. Their strongest ward in the constituency that year was Crumpsall, where Manchester city council leader Richard Leese has his seat; this is highly appropriate since the MP for Blackley is Graham Stringer, who was leader of the council between 1984 and 1996. Stringer, one of a significant number of Labour MPs who have previously led councils, was made a government whip in June 2001.

MANCHESTER CENTRAL

	2001		1997		1992 notional	
Electorate and turnout	66,268	39.1	64,823	51.7	66,475	58.8
Conservative	2,328	9.0	3,964	11.8	7,581	19.4
Labour	17,812	68.7	23,803	71.0	27,009	69.1
Lib Dem	4,070	15.7	4,121	12.3	4,105	10.5
Anti-EU	–	–	742	2.2	–	–
Green	1,018	3.9	–	–	–	–
Others	700 (2)		907 (2)		370 (2)	
MP	Tony Lloyd (Lab)		Tony Lloyd (Lab)		Bob Litherland (Lab)	
Majority	13,742	53.0	19,682	58.7	19,428	49.7

Manchester Central suffered the second lowest turnout of any seat in the 2001 general election; as in Liverpool Riverside fewer than four out of ten bothered to vote. This should certainly knock on the head any idea that such apathy is a symptom of an affluent 'post-materialist' culture, as this is undoubtedly one of the poorest constituencies in the country. Six of its eight wards are in the bottom 75 in England for multiple deprivation, and as of November 2001 the unemployment rate here was the sixth highest in the UK. One could point to similarly depressing data in other seats with appalling levels of turnout such as Riverside, Leeds Central and Glasgow Shettleston.

As in those other cities, the paradox is that enormous amounts of wealth are being generated in the constituency, but not shared with its permanent residents. City centre Manchester boasts perhaps the second largest shopping area in the country, the Arndale Centre now rebuilt after the IRA bomb, not to mention a large number of other financial and commercial firms. But these businesses serve commuters and shoppers who travel into the centre by car or rail from miles around, rather than locals who live in the immediate surroundings. It is a pattern very familiar in the United States and one which now seems commonplace in most of Britain's provincial cities.

Politically, those who do still bother to vote in Central tend to back Labour. To the south of the centre, the party polled 76 per cent in Ardwick and 75 per cent in Moss Side in the 2000 locals. However, some of the very poorest wards are now turning to the Liberal Democrats in council elections, with the party winning the Bradford ward (the 22nd most deprived in the country) in 1999 and Beswick & Clayton (17th) on several occasions recently (though not 2002). Interestingly, these are the very wards to the east of the centre where the Commonwealth games were due to be held, and all parties will hope that the re-developments which have taken place lead to a sustained improvement in the quality of life and levels of civic engagement here.

MANCHESTER GORTON

	2001		1997		1992 notional	
Electorate and turnout	63,834	42.7	65,352	55.6	62,673	60.6
Conservative	2,705	9.9	4,249	11.7	7,388	19.5
Labour	17,099	62.8	23,704	65.3	23,658	62.3
Lib Dem	5,795	21.3	6,362	17.5	5,324	14.0
Anti-EU	462	1.7	812	2.2	-	-
Green	835	3.1	683	1.9	595	1.6
Others	333		501		988 (4)	
MP	Gerald Kaufman (Lab)		Gerald Kaufman (Lab)		Gerald Kaufman (Lab)	
Majority	11,304	41.5	17,342	47.8	16,270	42.9

Gorton was one of Labour's gains of 1906, and the constituency bearing this name has been held by the party ever since, with the single exception of 1931. In fact the post-1983 Gorton most resembles the former Ardwick seat, which was broken up in that year having been held by Labour (again with the usual 1931-35 exception) since 1922. Ardwick's MP from 1970 (replacing Leslie Lever) was Gerald Kaufman, who transferred to the new seat in 1983 and is now one of the most senior back-bench Labour MPs. Well known as chairman of the Culture, Media and Sport select committee, he also wrote a book popular among apparatchiks in and around New Labour's first administration called *How to be a Minister*.

The constituency takes in areas to the south of the city centre from Fallowfield and Rusholme in the west (near Manchester City's football ground and the city's prestigious Grammar School) past Belle Vue and its famous dog track to Gorton itself and the Tameside boundary at Debdale Park. Rusholme is best known for its neon-lit strip known as the Curry (or Golden) mile, full of Indian restaurants and Asian jewellers along the Wilmslow Road, an area which is also populated by a large number of students – Manchester University is close by. The ward went Liberal Democrat in 2000, following the Gorton wards and Levenshulme, which have been won at a city council level by the Lib Dems for a while now. Labour are still strong locally in Fallowfield and Longsight, which also has a large Asian population, while the Conservatives barely exist any more at any level (they recorded just 4.2 per cent in Rusholme in 2000 and 3.5 per cent in Gorton South). In general elections, many local Lib Dem voters must be supporting Labour, though they have also climbed into a clear second place, with the Tory vote dropping below 10 per cent in 2001.

MANCHESTER WITHINGTON

	2001		1997		1992 notional	
Electorate and turnout	67,480	51.9	66,894	65.8	63,987	70.9
Conservative	5,349	15.3	8,522	19.4	14,193	31.3
Labour	19,239	54.9	27,103	61.6	23,907	52.7
Lib Dem	7,715	22.0	6,000	13.6	6,442	14.2
Anti-EU	-	-	1,079	2.5	-	-
Green	1,539	4.4	-	-	723	1.6
Others	1,208		1,323 (4)		128	
MP	Keith Bradley (Lab)		Keith Bradley (Lab)		Keith Bradley (Lab)	
Majority	11,524	32.9	18,581	42.2	9,714	21.4

Manchester Withington is another of those urban seats in the north of England which have swung dramatically from Conservative to Labour over the post-war period. The constituency was won by the Tories at all elections from 1931 until 1983 (the Liberals twice gained it in the 1920s), with a majority which exceeded 8,000 in 1945. It was lost in 1987 after a spectacular advance by Labour and following further falls in their vote in the 1990s, the Conservatives were reduced to a poor third place in 2001. Even though it was one of only two seats held by the party in Greater Manchester in 1966, it seems unlikely that Withington will ever be regained now.

Part of the explanation for the political change here has been the sort of long term change in social composition which has taken place in many cities, with the affluent middle classes moving further and further away from the places where they work. Didsbury was at one time viewed as the number one prized location for the prosperous, but many professionals rich enough now move out to Cheadle Hulme, Wilmslow, or the villages out into Cheshire. A large proportion of those who do remain here are the public sector middle class, a group who have exhibited a marked shift to the left over the 1980s and 1990s. The result has been a safe Conservative seat becoming a safe Labour one.

In local elections, the Liberal Democrats have now taken over as the main 'opposition' party to Labour, winning wards like Didsbury and Barlow Moor which in previous times offered good prospects for the Conservatives (who have now fallen to third in Didsbury). Labour win Chorlton and the more downmarket Burnage and Old Moat wards in council elections, but must win just about everything in national contests for their majorities to reach the large five-figure margins recorded in 1997 and 2001. Keith Bradley is the first Labour MP to have ever represented Withington, having gained the seat for the party for the first time in 1987, but the former Deputy Chief Whip and now Home Office minister will surely not be the last.

OLDHAM EAST and SADDLEWORTH

	2001		1997		1992 notional	
Electorate and turnout	74,511	61.0	73,189	73.9	74,061	77.3
Conservative	7,304	16.1	10,666	19.7	20,271	35.4
Labour	17,537	38.6	22,546	41.7	17,300	30.2
Lib Dem	14,811	32.6	19,157	35.4	19,712	34.4
Anti-EU	677	1.5	1,116	2.1	-	-
BNP	5,091	11.2	-	-	-	-
Others	-		616 (2)		-	
MP	Phil Woolas (Lab)		Phil Woolas (Lab)		Geoffrey Dickens (Con)*	
					Littleborough and Saddleworth	
Majority	2,726	6.0	3,389	6.3	559	1.0

* Chris Davies (LD) elected at July 1995 by-election.

Labour's triumph in 1997 did not arrive purely at the expense of the Conservatives; in the Greater Manchester area, the party gained two seats from the Liberal Democrats. In the case of Oldham East and Saddleworth, the gain was notionally made from the Conservatives, but the constituency is largely based on the former Littleborough and Saddleworth division (minus the town of Littleborough itself), which was won by Liberal Democrat Chris Davies in a hard-fought by-election contest in 1995.

This is marginal territory, with little of the seat being in Oldham itself. Most of the villages to the east in the Saddleworth portion were formerly in the Yorkshire marginal of Colne Valley (before the boundaries changed). These are scenic places where people aspire to retire to, notably Uppermill and Delph, and local government wards here were won by the Lib Dems from an early stage. The Lib Dems have also won Shaw, just north of Oldham for a long time - in 1995 they polled almost 70 per cent in a three-way contest. Labour have traditionally done better in the more built up wards towards Oldham, and they also do reasonably in the one ward left from Rochdale, Milnrow (next to the M62 motorway) though there is deeply ingrained Lib Dem support here as well.

Davies must have been disappointed to lose to his adversary Phil Woolas in 1997, but he then moved on to the European Parliament, heading the Liberal Democrats' North West regional list in 1999. His candidature probably accounted for his party polling the most votes here in the Euro elections; remarkably this was one of only three constituencies they 'won' in the whole country. In council elections, the Lib Dems also continued to make gains, taking fully 60 per cent of the vote in the constituency in the May 2000 local elections. Despite all this, the 2001 general election battle saw almost no change between the three main parties. The gainers however were the far right British National Party, who as in Oldham West came from nowhere to record a substantial share of the vote, following riots in the town just prior to the election. All this somewhat overshadowed Woolas' achievement in again holding off the Lib Dems in their top target in the area.

OLDHAM WEST and ROYTON

	2001		1997		1992 notional	
Electorate and turnout	69,409	57.6	69,203	66.1	70,300	75.0
Conservative	7,076	17.7	10,693	23.4	20,093	38.1
Labour	20,441	51.2	26,894	58.8	25,887	49.1
Lib Dem	4,975	12.4	5,434	11.9	6,031	11.4
Anti-EU	-	-	1,157	2.5	-	-
BNP	6,552	16.4	-	-	-	-
Others	918		1,560 (2)		722	
MP	Michael Meacher (Lab)		Michael Meacher (Lab)		TWO SEATS MERGE	
Majority	13,365	33.4	16,201	35.4	5,794	11.0

Unlike the marginal Oldham East which has been held by all three parties in recent years, Oldham West has been solidly Labour at all general elections since its creation in 1950. Michael Meacher became its MP in 1970, regaining the seat after he had lost it in a 1968 by-election, which was held during the most unpopular period of Wilson's government. In the 1990s boundary changes, some of West (Failsworth) was transferred to Ashton-under-Lyne, and over 30,000 voters were transferred in from Oldham Central, a seat which had only existed since 1983. The estimate was that this would have significantly reduced Labour's 1992 majority, but the changed boundaries have scarcely mattered in the favourable national circumstances of 1997 and 2001.

This constituency includes most of the town, along with neighbouring Chadderton (to the west) and Royton (to the north). Both of these two satellites are usually good areas for Labour, though there is something of a minority Conservative vote in both local and general elections. The 2001 contest, however, was notable mainly for the dramatic vote polled by the leader of the British National Party, Nick Griffin, who attracted 6,500 votes and almost finished in second place. This was surely not unrelated to the riots here just days earlier, which had a significant racial dimension. As in many other northern towns, wards in Oldham have become quite segregated between different communities, to which one could add significant levels of deprivation which affect them all (three Oldham West wards are in the most deprived 80 in the country). This heady mix did not require much to set it alight, and the BNP were the party who benefited in electoral terms (mainly at the expense of the Conservatives). In 2002, the BNP continued to poll strongly in local elections, though without gaining any council seats as they did in Burnley.

ROCHDALE

	2001		1997		1992 notional	
Electorate and turnout	69,506	56.7	68,723	70.0	69,019	77.2
Conservative	5,274	13.4	4,237	8.8	12,378	23.2
Labour	19,406	49.2	23,758	49.4	20,076	37.7
Lib Dem	13,751	34.9	19,213	40.0	20,204	37.9
Anti-EU	-	-	-	-	-	-
Others	981 (2)		874 (2)		629 (2)	
MP	Lorna Fitzsimons (Lab)		Lorna Fitzsimons (Lab)		Liz Lynne (LD)	
Majority	5,655	14.3	4,545	9.5	128	0.2

Although first won by Labour as long ago as 1922, Rochdale has never been a safe Labour seat. The Liberals were strong before and after the first world war, and from 1951-58 the Conservatives won here. Then, after fourteen years as a Labour seat from 1958 to 1972, the town fell to the Liberals in a by-election. This was not a total shock; on top of their early successes, the Liberals had finished second in all but one of the previous four contests.

Larger-than-life MP Cyril Smith proceeded to hold Rochdale from 1972 until 1992, though Labour remained in a close second, and in retrospect it is perhaps surprising that Liz Lynne managed to hold on (by about 1,800 votes) in 1992, especially given that Smith's final majority was less than 3,000. However there was to be no repeat five years later when Labour challenger and former NUS president Lorna Fitzsimons triumphed in a sometimes bitter contest with a majority exceeding 4,500.

In local council elections, Labour remained only 7 per cent behind the Liberal Democrats in 2000, a far narrower margin than in neighbouring Oldham East & Saddleworth, and one which suggested that they would hold on in the next general election rather more comfortably here. Sure enough, in 2001, Fitzsimons increased her majority, as the Lib Dem vote dropped by another five percentage points, mainly to the benefit of the Conservatives, whose vote recovered after years of being squeezed by the Liberals. Although they can never take it for granted, Labour should now be able to retain Rochdale with a reasonable degree of comfort in future contests.

SALFORD

	2001		1997		1992 notional	
Electorate and turnout	54,152	41.6	58,851	56.3	61,048	65.2
Conservative	3,446	15.3	5,779	17.4	10,545	26.5
Labour	14,649	65.1	22,848	69.0	23,532	59.1
Lib Dem	3,637	16.2	3,407	10.3	5,017	12.6
Anti-EU	-	-	926	2.8	-	-
Others	782 (3)		162		711 (2)	
MP	Hazel Blears (Lab)		Hazel Blears (Lab)		Stan Orme (Lab)	
					Salford East	
Majority	11,012	48.9	17,069	51.5	12,987	32.6

Immediately to the west of Manchester lies the borough of Salford, though as the built-up area has long since been continuous, it is almost impossible to see the join. In fact there is no commercial 'centre' to Salford as such, as it is so close to that of its larger neighbour; the focus is perhaps provided by the University buildings and nearby Lowry Centre off the main A6 road, just a mile from Manchester Victoria station.

Salford, particularly the wards in this parliamentary constituency (the borough also takes in Eccles and most of Worsley) is one of the poorest areas in the country, featuring on a *Newsnight* investigation into deprived areas prior to the 2001 election. The terraced streets are now a long way from the idealized community scenes in *Coronation Street* or *East is East*, with the usual inner-city problems of unemployment and crime. Some of the older areas were pulled down in the 1970s and 1980s to make way for high-rise flats, but this has proved no solution either. To be fair, not all of the constituency meets the stereotype image; areas in the north of the constituency around Kersal and Higher Broughton include middle class residential neighbourhoods as well as Manchester United's training ground at The Cliff.

The fact that Salford had three parliamentary seats bearing its name until 1950, and two from then until 1983, indicates a rapid population decline, as well as making long-term political trends difficult to pin down. Salford East (which this seat was called until 1997) was always Labour, held by Frank Allaun from 1950 until 1983, though he was the unlucky MP squeezed out in that year as his neighbour Stan Orme (MP for West since 1964) moved across to represent the newly configured seat. In 1997 Orme was replaced by the energetic Hazel Blears, who has taken a leading role in the modernization of Labour's structures and who became a health minister after 2001. She should have few problems continuing to win Salford (it was Labour's 39th safest seat after 2001), though a couple of wards have been picked up by Liberal Democrats in recent council elections.

STALYBRIDGE and HYDE

	2001		1997		1992 notional	
Electorate and turnout	66,265	48.4	65,589	65.7	67,303	73.2
Conservative	8,922	27.8	10,557	24.5	17,708	35.9
Labour	17,781	55.5	25,363	58.9	25,435	51.6
Lib Dem	4,327	13.5	5,169	12.0	4,443	9.0
Anti-EU	1,016	3.2	1,992	4.6	-	-
Others	-		-		1,693 (3)	
MP	James Purnell (Lab)		Tom Pendry (Lab)		Tom Pendry (Lab)	
Majority	8,859	27.6	14,806	34.4	7,727	15.7

Stalybridge and Hyde lies within the borough of Tameside on the eastern edge of the Greater Manchester conurbation. As well as the two towns in the title, the seat also includes their smaller neighbour of Mossley and also Longdendale on the border with Derbyshire. Most of these areas formerly made up the thin north eastern sleeve of Cheshire, and were known, not untypically in these parts, for cotton and engineering, though these days little industry remains.

Labour have held the parliamentary seat since 1945, but it has not always been plain sailing here. The seat was generally Conservative during the inter-war period (Labour did briefly hold it from 1929-31) and in 1951 and 1955 they could still get within a few hundred votes of victory. From 1970 until 1997 the seat was represented by Tom Pendry, who steadily built the majority up, though on his departure the figure dropped down to less than 9,000 votes, which makes this Labour's fourth most vulnerable seat to the Conservatives in Greater Manchester. Pendry's successor is James Purnell, a former member of the 10 Downing Street Policy Unit.

Locally, Labour still win most wards in council elections, though a substantial Conservative vote remains in Hyde Werneth and also Stalybridge South, where there are some prosperous neighbourhoods up the hill overlooking the town's football ground. The Liberal Democrats have not done much in local elections and here at least it is still a straight fight between Labour and the Conservatives, with Labour ahead in all but a really disastrous year.

STOCKPORT

	2001		1997		1992 notional	
Electorate and turnout	66,395	53.3	65,437	71.3	67,141	80.1
Conservative	9,162	25.9	10,426	22.3	20,384	37.9
Labour	20,731	58.6	29,338	62.9	25,852	48.0
Lib Dem	5,490	15.5	4,951	10.6	6,894	12.8
Anti-EU	–	–	1,280	2.7	–	–
Others	–		674 (3)		678 (2)	
MP	Ann Coffey (Lab)		Ann Coffey (Lab)		Ann Coffey (Lab)	
Majority	11,569	32.7	18,912	40.5	5,468	10.2

Stockport could previously boast a couple of marginal seats, with North changing hands in 1964, 1970 and 1974 and South gained by Labour off the Conservatives in 1964 and notionally going SDP when sitting MP Tom McNally defected to the new party in 1981. Then there was a big shake-up in boundaries, with the creation of a safe Labour seat (Denton & Reddish) and this one, which at the time appeared inclined to the Conservatives. Tony Favell was able to win the inaugural contest in the pared-down Stockport constituency by nearly 6,000 votes, with McNally's continued presence for the SDP splitting the opposition almost down the middle. Even without McNally however, Favell retained the seat by 2,850 in 1987, before it was gained by Labour's Ann Coffey on quite a big swing in 1992. Five years later, the constituency suddenly looked like a Labour stronghold after another 15 per cent swing, and the majority after 2001 still looks very healthy.

Stockport is a centre in its own right to the south of Manchester, though a significant chunk of the electorate is based in Heaton towards its large neighbour. In fact this area borders the Withington constituency, which has seen a dramatic switch from right to left over recent decades, and something similar seems to have taken place here, though (unlike in Withington) the Conservatives can still win local council elections here. South of the centre, there is also a decent Tory vote in Davenport, though Edgeley (around the football ground) is a Labour stronghold, as is Brinnington, an isolated council estate ward (the most deprived in Stockport) on the other side of the M60 from the centre. To complete the picture, the Lib Dems can also win the Manor ward, although their strength in the constituency is (as yet) nothing like that in neighbouring Cheadle and Hazel Grove. For now, this constituency seems set to remain Labour, with the Conservatives posing more of a threat than they do in several of the other nearby seats which they have lost in recent years.

STRETFORD and URMSTON

	2001		1997		1992 notional	
Electorate and turnout	71,222	54.8	69,913	69.7	73,507	74.8
Conservative	10,565	27.1	14,840	30.5	22,443	40.8
Labour	23,836	61.1	28,480	58.5	26,925	48.9
Lib Dem	3,891	10.0	3,978	8.2	5,084	9.2
Anti-EU	-	-	1,397	2.9	-	-
Others	713		-		567	
MP	Beverley Hughes (Lab)		Beverley Hughes (Lab)		TWO SEATS MERGE	
Majority	13,271	34.0	13,640	28.0	4,482	8.1

This constituency comprises the northern part of Trafford borough, which includes upmarket, politically marginal territory in Urmston, Davyhulme and Flixton to the west of the M60 motorway, and more solidly working-class areas in Stretford itself, where two wards, Bucklow and Clifford, are in the most deprived five per cent in the country. The north eastern boundary of the seat merges seamlessly into the City of Manchester, reaching to within a mile of the city centre and underlining the total illogicality of present borough boundaries. Indeed it is this seat that contains many of Manchester's most famous landmarks: the football and cricket grounds at Old Trafford, the huge industrial estate of Trafford Park and the much newer Trafford Centre shopping mall.

Politically, this area has been shifting to the left for many years. The former Stretford seat was held by the Tories at all elections between 1950 and 1983 with the single exception of 1966. Davyhulme, almost two thirds of which was transferred into this seat in the boundary changes of the 1990s, was also Conservative throughout its brief 1983-1997 existence.

That this is now difficult to believe simply underlines the scale of the political transformation here, with former Trafford council leader Beverley Hughes amassing huge majorities in both 1997 and 2001, when there was a further three-point swing from Conservative to Labour. Although in council elections the Conservatives still win the two Davyhulme wards and Flixton, in general elections Stretford and Urmston now appears as safe a Labour seat as those 'officially' in Manchester itself. Even the candidature of the model 'Jordan' in 2001 failed to halt the decline in turnout, with Katie Price (her real name) attracting barely 700 votes and rather less interest than is afforded her in the tabloid press.

WIGAN

	2001		1997		1992 notional	
Electorate and turnout	64,040	52.5	64,689	67.7	65,629	75.5
Conservative	6,996	20.8	7,400	16.9	12,538	25.3
Labour	20,739	61.7	30,043	68.6	30,028	60.6
Lib Dem	4,970	14.8	4,390	10.0	5,787	11.7
Anti-EU	-	-	1,450	3.3	-	-
Others	886		536 (2)		1,173 (2)	
MP	Neil Turner (Lab)		Roger Stott (Lab)		Roger Stott (Lab)	
Majority	13,743	40.9	22,643	51.7	17,490	35.3

Parliamentary by-election 23 September 1999: Labour 9,641 (59.6), Conservative 2,912 (18.0), Lib Dem 2,148 (13.3), Anti-EU 834 (5.2), 5 Others 652. Electorate 64,775, Turnout 25.0%. MP: Neil Turner (Lab), Majority 6,729 (41.6).

Wigan has been a Labour stronghold for many years, first won by the party in January 1910 and then rather more permanently from 1918. Like its neighbours, Ince (now Makerfield) and Leigh, it was retained even in 1931, when the party won only fifty-two seats nationally. Although coal mining (which provided the initial stimulus for Labour support) has long since disappeared, the town still retains an industrial air, taking in the large Heinz factory as well as the redeveloped Wigan Pier, once the title of a famous George Orwell book on the English working class, but now like so much else just a tourist attraction.

All the wards in the town vote Labour in both local and national elections, and although there is a strong Conservative vote in Swinley to the north of the centre, Labour continued to win all wards in the 2000 council elections. Even the 1999 by-election which followed the death of Roger Stott (MP here since 1983 and for Westhoughton for ten years before that) did not really present Labour with much of a test, the Conservatives advancing by just one per cent and the Liberal Democrats failing to attract the extra votes they usually do in such circumstances. The biggest problem for Labour is apathy; only one in four came out to vote in the by-election, and though that figure recovered in 2001, there was still a fifteen-point drop in turnout since 1997. The job of re-invigorating Wigan's electorate passes to Neil Turner, a former Wigan councillor who became MP in 1999.

WORSLEY

	2001		1997		1992 notional	
Electorate and turnout	69,300	51.0	68,978	67.8	69,186	76.0
Conservative	8,406	23.8	11,342	24.2	16,888	32.1
Labour	20,193	57.1	29,083	62.2	28,291	53.8
Lib Dem	6,188	17.5	6,356	13.6	6,661	12.7
Anti-EU	-	-	-	-	-	-
Others	576		-		731 (2)	
MP	Terry Lewis (Lab)		Terry Lewis (Lab)		Terry Lewis (Lab)	
Majority	11,787	33.3	17,741	37.9	11,403	21.7

Worsley is a constituency which takes in bits of both Wigan and Salford metropolitan boroughs. It is more or less bordered on two sides by the M60 and M61 motorways, taking in the small towns of Worsley itself, Walkden and Tyldsley. The seat was only created in 1983, taking in a large part of the former Farnworth constituency (Labour from 1935 onwards), whose MP John Roper had defected to the SDP and who stood here in 1983. Roper was to finish in third place, well behind Labour's new standard bearer Terry Lewis, who won the new seat by 4,000 votes from the Conservatives.

In fact there are still Tory voters here, particularly in the middle class Worsley & Boothstown ward, which includes Worsley Old Hall and several desirable areas such as Boothstown itself, just off the A580 East Lancs Road. Labour were third here with just 13 per cent of the vote in the 2000 local elections, though until their victory of that year the Conservatives had tended to lose recent contests to the Liberal Democrats. Elsewhere in the constituency, the territory is much more typical for Greater Manchester, with Labour very strong in Walkden (83 per cent in its northern ward in 1999) and Tyldsley East. The Lib Dems win the ward of Hindsford, which lies between Tyldsley and Atherton, in council elections, but overall this is yet another safe Labour seat with a comfortable five-figure majority for Lewis, even after a slight fall in support in 2001.

WYTHENSHAWE and SALE EAST

	2001		1997		1992 notional	
Electorate and turnout	72,127	48.6	72,086	63.2	75,738	71.8
Conservative	8,424	24.0	11,429	25.1	18,977	34.9
Labour	21,032	60.0	26,448	58.1	26,935	49.5
Lib Dem	4,320	12.3	5,639	12.4	7,869	14.5
Anti-EU	-	-	1,060	2.3	-	-
Others	1,279 (2)		957	2.1	600 (2)	
MP	Paul Goggins (Lab)		Paul Goggins (Lab)		Alf Morris (Lab) Manch'r Wythenshawe	
Majority	12,608	36.0	15,019	33.0	7,958	14.6

Wythenshawe and Sale East takes in the southern extremity of the City of Manchester (which reaches as far out as the airport) and in recent elections three wards from Trafford borough. Virtually all the constituency lies on the outside of Manchester's orbital motorway (the M60), but despite its geographical location, the character of Wythenshawe differs sharply from adjoining suburbs. Here, endless red-brick council estates have provided the basis of a safe Labour seat since 1964; though there are small patches of new housing, this has remained very strong Labour territory through even the barren 1980s, with five-figure majorities achieved by Alf Morris in 1983 and 1987. This is also a very poor area; according to neighbourhood statistics, one ward (Benchill) is the most deprived out of 8,414 in England; another (Woodhouse Park) ranks 64th.

By the 1990s the electorate of Wythenshawe had declined to about 20,000 voters below average, and rather than abolish the seat (as originally proposed), the boundary commission agreed to a scheme which brought in 23,000 voters from nearby Sale in the borough of Trafford, even though they had very little in common with their neighbours. Illogical maybe, but at least this might have been expected to make general election contests a little more interesting (the estimate was that Labour's 1992 majority would be reduced from 12,000 to 8,000). In the event, the politically mixed voters of Sale have failed to deny Labour their five-figure majorities. Having fallen heavily in 1997, the Tory vote continued to slide in 2001 (as in neighbouring seats), and one is left to wonder how they could possibly have held Wythenshawe between 1950 and 1964.

Hampshire
including Southampton and Portsmouth

	Conservative		Labour		Liberal Democrat		Others	
	Share of vote	Seats	Share of vote	Seats	Share of vote	Seats	Share of vote	Seats
2001	41.5	10	27.6	3	27.8	4	3.1	0
1997	41.2	11	28.3	3	25.3	3	5.1	0
1992	54.2	14	18.6	1	26.0	0	1.2	0
1987	55.3	15	14.5	0	30.0	0	0.2	0
1983	55.1	15	14.7	0	29.9	0	0.2	0

Hampshire and Essex vie for the title of England's largest county in terms of population, with both currently being allocated seventeen parliamentary seats including the unitary authorities recently floated off. Such a large county naturally has considerable variety within its borders. The north east of Hampshire is effectively part of the Home Counties, strongly under the influence of London and sharing a good many characteristics with Surrey in reliance on commuting, high incomes and a military presence. Aldershot and Farnborough, tucked in a little corner next to Surrey, are the centre of a conurbation with a strong defence sector (but little sense of common identity) stretching into Surrey and Berkshire, but they are a little anomalous. More typical are the growing commuter settlements, and expensive villages, around the M3 and the main railway line; while agriculture does exist in north Hampshire most of the countryside is woodland, preserved in order to stop the towns sprawling together. There are two larger towns – Basingstoke is the biggest town, a virtual New Town of estates, roundabouts and booming business. It claims to have the tallest office block between London and New York. Pictures of the town fifty years ago, before the overspill estates were built and the development process kicked off, are unrecognisable. Andover is smaller and quieter, but also accepted London overspill. The population in several districts in the north of the county is rather young by national comparison. The northern territory is solid Conservative territory in parliamentary elections, having returned an all-blue delegation at every opportunity since 1924, although Basingstoke's growth has created an opportunity for Labour which has not quite come off yet.

London's influence is still apparent in the centre and south of the county, particularly in the wealthy little city of Winchester which is about an hour out of Waterloo on the fast trains. Its educated electorate has shown increasing favour to the Liberal Democrats over the years, and the party is also quite strong in some rural areas around it. Coincidental factors have created a bloc of Lib Dem seats in this area – Eastleigh was first, in 1994, and was joined by Winchester in 1997 and Romsey in 2000; none of them is safe from a Conservative revival and the area will no doubt be a battleground in future elections. These areas are a northern hinterland of Southampton, traditionally a port city. The cruise and container ports are still operating, but it has become a rather post-industrial service centre with the biggest employers being local government, the NHS and the university; there is still substantial manufacturing at the Ford motor works and a cigarette factory. Its position near the average in most demographic indicators has made it fiercely contested between the parties for much of the last eighty years, with both main parties tending to be well-organised. The Conservatives, however, have crumbled somewhat recently; they have felt an inexorable tide coming in against them just as much as King Canute (proclaimed King here in 1014) famously did. Labour have won both traditionally marginal seats with landslide majorities twice in succession, and would have even won them on current boundaries in 1992. Southampton influence extends into the New Forest, particularly the East constituency – surely a potential candidate to expand the yellow patch in the centre of the county – but the west of the Forest is a timeless, traditional place as befits a 1,000 year old royal hunting ground.

Southampton's great rival is Portsmouth, 20 miles to its east along the coast; there is very little open countryside between them now. While Southampton was a merchant city, Portsmouth is traditionally associated with the Royal Navy and its tourist trade centres around the historic ships Victory and Mary Rose. It is a flat, densely populated city on an island, a key point in Britain's southern defences for centuries. Despite its reputation as a naval town it has the full, expected range of employment including a large IBM plant in the north of the city. While more working class and earthy than Southampton, Portsmouth (and its satellite of Gosport even more so) has proved difficult territory for Labour because the defence influence has skewed it to the right. This factor seems to be coming to an end; the Conservatives have lost massive amounts of ground here since their 1980s heyday and slipped further in both the city's seats in 2001 while seeing Gosport reduced to a marginal. The outlying middle class areas of Fareham and Havant remain more secure, although in the latter case this has much to do with a split anti-Tory vote.

Overall, Hampshire is what it always has been – a Conservative county. Even in the last two elections they returned a majority of its parliamentary delegation, and will probably always do so. However, there is lively party competition now, not only in the cities but also in some areas – Basingstoke and Romsey – where the Tories were not seriously challenged in living memory before 1997.

Local government

Hampshire county council is relatively safely under Conservative control. Their cause was greatly helped after 1997 by the exclusion of the cities of Southampton and Portsmouth, which were and are areas of considerable Tory weakness. In the 2001 local elections the Conservatives won 46 county councillors, to 9 Labour and 19 Liberal Democrats. The Labour representatives are from Basingstoke (3), Gosport (2), Havant (2), Aldershot (1) and Eastleigh (1); the Liberal Democrats have a power base in Eastleigh (5) and Winchester (4) and other more scattered holdings. The Conservatives dominate the New Forest and the rural parts of the north of the county.

Labour lost overall control of both Southampton and Portsmouth in the 2000 local elections (but ran them with minority administrations), and future local elections will follow the inconclusive all-out elections on new boundaries in May 2002. Labour would be doing very well to recapture either of them, although no other party seems a plausible challenger for outright control. The history of each city is rather different; Southampton has been a marginal swinging back and forth with the national tide between the main parties for decades, although as in other provincial cities Labour have gained formerly reliable Tory wards while losing their own backyards to the Lib Dems. Portsmouth was Conservative, except for a year-long interlude of Labour control in 1964-65, for forty years before 1990 and Labour's period of control in 1995-2000 was its first sustained rule of the city.

The district councils of Hampshire are for the most part unremarkable. Basingstoke and Deane is run by a Lib-Lab administration with a small majority after years of Conservative administration; the Liberal Democrats have a rather firmer grip on Eastleigh and Winchester (which covers a rural area as well as the city) councils. The Conservatives have regained control of many of the other districts since 1997, including New Forest and East Hampshire (both Lib Dem in 1991 and 1995), plus Test Valley (Romsey and Andover) which was a 22-22 tie between Tories and Lib Dems in 1995. Fareham which was a Lib Dem led hung council at the Conservative nadir has also reverted (though the Tory majority was only 3 after 2002), and in Havant the Tories have also returned to control. Gosport was controlled by the Lib Dems until the late 1990s. Since then, Labour's rise has made it an almost even split between the three main parties. Hart (the fleet area) is strongly Conservative. The people of the borough of Rushmoor – while returning to Conservative control after a late 1990s hung interlude - voted in May 2000 to keep its name, despite its obscurity – probably because there was no agreement on whether to rename it 'Aldershot and Farnborough' or 'Farnborough and Aldershot'.

Boundary review

Hampshire is entitled to an extra, 18th, parliamentary seat in the boundary review even after the award of two new seats as of the 1997 general election. The provisional recommendations published in February 2002 include the creation of a new constituency in the south east of the county called Meon Valley made up of Horndean and Cowplain from the current Hampshire East plus a rural section of the current Winchester including Wickham and Bishop's Waltham. It will be a Conservative seat with a few Lib Dems and next to no Labour presence. There will be a ripple effect in the north of the county, with Aldershot and Basingstoke both reduced to urban cores and in the latter case made a real Labour prospect. In the centre of Hampshire there will be a game of musical chairs, with Romsey losing Chandler's Ford and Hiltingbury to Eastleigh and gaining a smaller area in northern Southampton; Winchester will pick up Fair Oak and Bishopstoke from Eastleigh. Although it is difficult to know, this will probably make Romsey and Winchester easier for the Lib Dems to hold but Eastleigh significantly harder. There is bound to be a public inquiry.

ALDERSHOT

	2001		1997		1992 notional	
Electorate and turnout	78,255	57.9	76,499	70.8	75,321	78.3
Conservative	19,106	42.2	23,119	42.7	34,300	58.1
Labour	11,394	25.2	13,057	24.1	8,154	13.8
Lib Dem	12,512	27.6	16,498	30.5	15,584	26.4
Anti–EU	797	1.8	794	1.5	–	–
Others	1,479 (3)		683 (2)		956	
MP	Gerald Howarth (Con)		Gerald Howarth (Con)		Julian Critchley (Con)	
Majority	6,594	14.6	6,621	12.2	18,716	31.7

The Aldershot constituency is based around the small, highly urbanised borough of Rushmoor, which comprises the adjoining towns of Aldershot and Farnborough. The constituency also spills over into the Hart district, including the Yateley area. It is a compact constituency tucked into the north eastern corner of Hampshire, just across the border from Surrey Heath and Bracknell constituencies.

Aldershot will always be associated with the British Army, and it certainly has a strong presence in the area. There are large camps, barracks and open spaces used for military training around Aldershot, and a considerable transient population of squaddies, few of whom cast their votes. The Queens ward of central Aldershot has long been notorious for low turnout because of the military vote. Senior officers tend to have firmer local attachments, and cast a higher proportion of their votes.

Farnborough is known for military aviation, and also has a defence industry flavour. But both towns, Farnborough in particular, have more to them; they are within commuting distance of London and Farnborough has some service industries too and a stratum of very affluent, retired residents. The combination produces a Conservative seat, but not without internal variation. The two Aldershot county council wards are close fought between Labour and Conservative, as is Farnborough North, but the other two Farnborough wards are Tory (with some Lib Dem presence). Yateley, to complete the picture, is a Lib Dem stronghold. The Conservatives prevail by the traditional technique of divide and conquer.

BASINGSTOKE

	2001		1997		1992 notional	
Electorate and turnout	79,113	60.7	77,063	74.1	75,307	83.6
Conservative	20,490	42.7	24,751	43.3	33,695	53.5
Labour	19,610	40.9	22,354	39.1	15,809	25.1
Lib Dem	6,693	13.9	9,714	17.0	12,819	20.4
Anti–EU	1,202	2.5	–	–	–	–
Others	–		310		653	
MP	Andrew Hunter (Con)		Andrew Hunter (Con)		Andrew Hunter (Con)	
Majority	880	1.8	2,397	4.2	17,886	28.4

Basingstoke was a tantalising near miss for Labour in the 2001 election. At the start of the campaign the Tory MP thought he might well lose, and Labour candidate Jon Hartley fought a spirited campaign with the assistance of a very well-produced website. But when the votes were counted not quite enough of the Labour vote had turned out and the Conservatives held the seat with a reduced majority. Basingstoke is now the Conservative seat fourth most vulnerable to Labour.

Basingstoke is a sprawling town in north Hampshire, sitting by the M3 and at a major railway junction. It is a popular site for new industries of all kinds, including high-tech concerns, financial services, publishing and distribution. Since the 1960s, housing and industrial estates have marched relentlessly north and west from the old town. Only 27 constituencies had lower unemployment (0.9 per cent) in May 2001, so it is a flourishing although hardly beautiful or charming place. Labour's position is strongest in the north and west of the town (the North ward in the county election was 59 per cent Labour in 2001) where the Expanded Town character of Basingstoke is most concentrated. The Conservatives lead against a divided opposition in the east and south, around the older parts of town, and have a strong position in the rural wards still included in the constituency north and south of the town. Their rural strength was critical in holding Basingstoke in 2001 as Labour certainly had a lead in the town.

Every boundary review lately has lopped off more rural territory as the town has grown, and the next will continue the pattern if the provisional recommendations are upheld. The latest proposed changes would have been enough, just about, to tip Basingstoke into the Labour column in 2001, and the town has surely not seen its last close contest.

EASTLEIGH

	2001		1997		1992 notional	
Electorate and turnout	74,603	63.8	72,405	76.6	67,556	83.3
Conservative	16,302	34.3	18,699	33.7	28,620	50.9
Labour	10,426	21.9	14,883	26.8	10,947	19.5
Lib Dem	19,360	40.7	19,453	35.1	16,708	29.7
Anti–EU	849	1.8	2,459 (2)	4.4	–	–
Others	636		–		–	
MP	David Chidgey (LD)		David Chidgey (LD)		Stephen Milligan (Con)*	
Majority	3,058	6.4	754	1.4	11,912	21.2

* David Chigley (LD) elected at June 1994 by-election

Eastleigh was one of many bad results for the Conservatives in the 2001 election. It looked a promising seat on paper, with a small Lib Dem majority in 1997 in a result that was affected by a dramatic 1994 by-election. The Tories were confident that their candidate, young Southampton councillor Conor Burns, was on his way to Westminster, but it was not to be.

Eastleigh is a suburban area wrapped around the north and east of Southampton. Its main town, from which it draws its name, was once a working class town centred on a major railway junction and engineering works, but it has become a commuting centre, looking south to Southampton and north to London. The M27 motorway links the town to the rest of the constituency; Hedge End is an expanding, recently built satellite town of Southampton, and further south lie the old villages of Bursledon, Botley and Hamble and the little town of Netley on Southampton Water. Labour support appears patchily and inconsistently in different parts of the seat, but for the most part, the battle is between the Liberal Democrats, who control the council, and Conservatives in local elections. Even in May 2000 the Lib Dems were comfortably ahead of the Tories. Results in the 2001 county elections were relatively uniform, except in working class south Eastleigh which is Labour's remaining stronghold. In the 2001 general election the Lib Dems managed to squeeze the Labour vote back a little, which they had not done in 1997, and if they can continue the pattern they should put up strong resistance even to a more impressive Tory recovery than the party mounted in 2001.

FAREHAM

	2001		1997		1992 notional	
Electorate and turnout	71,526	63.5	68,787	75.9	66,082	81.3
Conservative	21,389	47.1	24,436	46.8	32,588	60.6
Labour	14,380	31.6	14,078	27.0	7,980	14.9
Lib Dem	8,503	18.7	10,234	19.6	12,489	23.2
Anti–EU	1,175	2.6	2,914	5.6	–	–
Others	–		515		679	
MP	Mark Hoban (Con)		Peter Lloyd (Con)		Peter Lloyd (Con)	
Majority	7,009	15.4	10,358	19.9	20,099	37.4

Fareham lies between Southampton and Portsmouth, a link in the sprawling urban area sometimes called Solent City. Fareham town was once surrounded by strawberry fields but it now sits among super-stores and office parks by the M27.

The Fareham constituency stretches beyond the town on either side. East, towards Portsmouth and rather in that city's orbit, is Portchester. It has an old castle overlooking Portsmouth Harbour, some pleasant old houses and a mixture of commuter and overspill developments. To the west towards Southampton are some straggling villages including Titchfield and Swanwick, the latter the home of the troubled new privatised national air traffic control system, and huge amounts of recently built infill development. The main growth around Fareham has taken place to the west of the town, in the sprawling private suburbia of Locks Heath. The county electoral division of Fareham Western Wards, which covers this area, has an electorate approaching 26,000 compared to around 11,000 in most other Hampshire county wards, reflecting massive growth since the last review of ward boundaries, including 4,000 since 1997. This territory is the least deprived part of a generally highly prosperous and secure constituency.

Most component wards of Fareham are Conservative in anything but a disaster year for them – even in 2001, only Lib Dem Portchester did not support them in the local elections as they gained two seats from the Lib Dems. The Conservatives even 'held' the constituency on the basis of the 1995 local elections. Labour support in Fareham was minimal in the 1980s (just over 7 per cent in 1983) but it climbed, astonishingly, to over 30 per cent in 2001 despite a lack of a local government base. Labour's general election vote was about 9 point higher than in the simultaneous county elections, while the Lib Dems were 11 point lower. Fareham's slight tilt to Labour in 2001 probably reflects new support from people who had not voted for the party in 1997 for fear of economic crisis. However, it remains too substantial a Conservative fortress for Labour to think about winning.

GOSPORT

	2001		1997		1992 actual	
Electorate and turnout	69,626	57.1	68,830	70.3	69,817	76.6
Conservative	17,364	43.6	21,085	43.6	31,094	58.1
Labour	14,743	37.1	14,827	30.7	7,275	13.6
Lib Dem	6,011	15.1	9,479	19.6	14,776	27.6
Anti–EU	1,162	2.9	2,538	5.2	–	–
Others	509		426		332	
MP	Peter Viggers (Con)		Peter Viggers (Con)		Peter Viggers (Con)	
Majority	2,621	6.6	6,258	12.9	16,318	30.5

Gosport, like Fareham, used to be a complete desert for the Labour Party (9 per cent of the vote in 1983) but here the growth in Labour strength has been even more remarkable. It is now Labour's target number 13 vis-à-vis the Conservatives, and although still a long shot a previously unthinkable Labour victory here cannot be totally ruled out.

Gosport was long considered the most working class safe Conservative seat; it is a tough little naval town sitting just across Portsmouth Harbour from the city centre of Portsmouth and shares a lot of the larger city's characteristics – densely populated, owner-occupied, defence industry related. It was once a walled military town and the precursor of the RAF was founded here. As in other military towns, the end of the cold war and four years of power seemed to unlock previously unattainable working class Labour support in the defence sector.

For parliamentary purposes Gosport includes Hill Head and Stubbington, a quiet, detached part of Fareham down by the Solent shoreline. The Conservative votes provided by this area saved Gosport from being an ultra-marginal seat in 2001. The town itself has some areas which are now strongly Labour, such as Rowner, although the Tories still won the Town and Lee county wards. As late as 1997 the Liberal Democrats were very active, and had control of the borough council (and led in the constituency in 1995), but Labour have made local election gains and the council is now hung.

Remnants of the Lib Dem vote are apparent in local elections (there were about 4,000 more people voting Lib Dem locally than nationally) but it is now clear that Gosport is a two-party fight between Labour and Conservative. Labour candidate Richard Williams achieved the 15th best increase in the Labour vote in the country in 2001. Of the top fourteen, eleven were achieved by Labour incumbents first elected in 1997 and the other three were by-products of previous incumbency votes for non-Labour MPs; Labour in Gosport can take particular pride – and hope – from their 2001 result.

HAMPSHIRE EAST

	2001		1997		1992 notional	
Electorate and turnout	78,229	64.3	76,890	75.6	73,748	80.4
Conservative	23,950	47.6	27,927	48.0	35,960	60.6
Labour	9,866	19.6	9,945	17.1	5,605	9.5
Lib Dem	15,060	29.9	16,337	28.1	16,303	27.5
Anti–EU	1,413	2.8	3,270 (2)	5.6	–	–
Others	–		649		1,451	
MP	Michael Mates (Con)		Michael Mates (Con)		NEW SEAT	
Majority	8,890	17.7	11,590	19.9	19,657	33.1

The three main settlements of Hampshire East are Alton, a county town in mid Hampshire, Petersfield, and a built up suburban area including Catherington, Horndean and Cowplain in the far south. Alton is a rather detached element of the seat, but the other centres fit well together as they are by the A3 north of Portsmouth and tend to look to that city.

The Liberal Democrats have a narrow lead over the Conservatives in Alton, but the position is reversed in Petersfield, Horndean and Cowplain. The Conservative advantage is stronger in the other areas that make up the balance of the constituency between Alton and Petersfield, such as Four Marks and Medstead. East Hampshire District Council is currently Conservative controlled, albeit by a relatively narrow margin over the Liberal Democrats.

There is not a great deal of agriculture; the seat is mainly small town and suburban. It saw a further slight movement away from the Conservatives in 2001, as did several such areas, but should be safe enough for Michael Mates. It has been growing in population and the Boundary Commission's provisional scheme removes the southern end of the constituency around Horndean to a new 'Mean Valley' seat which will offer good Tory prospects.

HAMPSHIRE NORTH EAST

	2001		1997		1992 notional	
Electorate and turnout	71,304	61.6	69,437	73.6	65,880	80.1
Conservative	23,379	53.2	26,017	50.9	33,782	64.0
Labour	8,744	19.9	8,203	16.0	4,854	9.2
Lib Dem	10,122	23.0	11,619	22.7	13,242	25.1
Anti–EU	1,702	3.9	2,872 (2)	5.6	–	
Others	–		2,400		907	
MP	James Arbuthnot (Con)		James Arbuthnot (Con)		Michael Mates (Con) Hampshire East	
Majority	13,257	30.2	14,398	28.2	20,540	38.9

Hampshire North East is a true Conservative stronghold. It is the fifth safest Tory seat in the land, a far more reliable chunk of Hampshire than East (65th safest) or even North West (19th safest). All its component county council wards are also formidable Tory bastions.

The seat is based on the Hart district council area, with Fleet being the largest town. Fleet is a wealthy commuter settlement, a Hampshire extension of the Surrey stockbroker belt. The town is surrounded by some even more plush residential areas: Hook and Winchfield by the railway, and Crondall, described by its former MP Julian Critchley as being full of retired senior military men and their wives. The military flavour extends to the East Hampshire district countryside, with a camp at Bordon, although some comprises deep, comfortable civilian woodlands around Selborne. The Liberal Democrats used to be able to do well in local elections in Hart, and even controlled the council for a while in the 1980s, but the Conservatives have washed them away. Even in 1995 the Tories led by seven points (40-33) and in 1999 extended their lead to 59-25. Like Hampshire NW, this constituency was a refuge for a London Conservative MP whose seat had been effectively abolished in the pre-1997 boundary changes; in this case James Arbuthnot of Wanstead & Woodford.

HAMPSHIRE NORTH WEST

	2001		1997		1992 notional	
Electorate and turnout	78,044	62.3	73,663	74.2	70,905	80.5
Conservative	24,374	50.1	24,730	45.2	33,154	58.1
Labour	12,365	25.4	12,900	23.6	7,175	12.6
Lib Dem	10,329	21.2	13,179	24.1	15,990	28.0
Anti–EU	1,563	3.2	2,916 (2)	5.3	–	–
Others	–		942 (3)		768	
MP	George Young (Con)		George Young (Con)		David Mitchell (Con)	
Majority	12,009	24.7	11,551	21.1	17,164	30.1

The main town of Hampshire North West is Andover, with its precinct and overspill estates a smaller and less successful version of Basingstoke. There are a few Labour votes on the north side of Andover town, but the party has no district or county councillors in the seat and its constituency organisation was defunct for a while.

Hampshire North West covers the rural territory around Andover, plus an area of Basingstoke & Deane council between Andover and the town of Basingstoke, containing the towns of Whitchurch, Kingsclere and Tadley. The Whitchurch area elects a Lib Dem county councillor, but the rest is very Tory with shares of the vote around 55-60 per cent in the 2001 county elections. Labour did well to get a quarter of the vote and come second in the 2001 general election, while the Lib Dems have never challenged strongly here (except in the 1995 local elections when they had a narrow lead). Hampshire NW amounts to a very safe Conservative seat and offered a home to Sir George Young, a moderate Cabinet minister displaced from his Acton seat in boundary changes in 1997.

HAVANT

	2001		1997		1992 notional	
Electorate and turnout	70,246	57.6	68,625	70.4	68,530	77.2
Conservative	17,769	43.9	19,204	39.7	27,981	52.9
Labour	13,562	33.5	15,475	32.0	10,465	19.8
Lib Dem	7,508	18.6	10,806	22.4	13,812	26.1
Anti–EU	561	1.4	2,395	5.0	–	–
Others	1,037 (2)		442		678	
MP	David Willetts (Con)		David Willetts (Con)		David Willetts (Con)	
Majority	4,207	10.4	3,729	7.7	14,169	26.8

Parts of Havant do not look like a Conservative seat capable of surviving two landslide defeats. Just off the A3 motorway lie the large council-built estates of Leigh Park, Battins, Bondfields and Barncroft. One of these wards, Warren Park, is a severely deprived area (one of the 4 per cent worst off in England, and worse than anywhere in the London borough of Lambeth). These Portsmouth overspill areas vote Labour by considerable margins, but the turnout is very low – only 42 per cent in one ward in the 2001 general election.

However, half of Havant is more prosperous suburbia, such as Stakes, Bedhampton and Havant itself, and the remainder comprises the little town of Emsworth and the seaside dormitory of Hayling Island, both very Conservative areas. The Liberal Democrats are a presence in some suburbs, losing Bedhampton narrowly in 2001, but their strength here has eroded and they are third on the borough council (the Conservatives gained control in 2002). In the Conservative disaster year of 1995 it was they who were narrowly third behind the Lib Dems, who led, and Labour.

In 2001 Labour polled respectably in the suburbs but must have been disappointed by the turnout in the estates. David Willetts, the Conservative MP since 1992, wrote that modern Conservatives should be equally happy to drink in either of the nearby pubs called the Richard Cobden and the Prince of Wales, symbolising belief both in free markets and in tradition. Havant Tories have kept out of the Last Chance Saloon and Willetts should be safe enough.

NEW FOREST EAST

	2001		1997		1992 notional	
Electorate and turnout	66,723	63.2	65,736	74.6	64,361	81.9
Conservative	17,902	42.4	21,053	42.9	27,980	53.1
Labour	9,141	21.7	12,161	24.8	6,704	12.7
Lib Dem	14,073	33.4	15,838	32.3	17,632	33.4
Anti–EU	1,062	2.5	–	–	–	–
Others	–		–		423	
MP	Julian Lewis (Con)		Julian Lewis (Con)		Michael Colvin (Con)	
					Romsey & Waterside	
Majority	3,829	9.1	5,215	10.6	10,348	19.6

The New Forest is a very traditional forest, of dense woods and bleak heaths, hunting and small rural communities. In its woods lurk several unusual species, including New Forest ponies, adders and Tory voters. New Forest East contains the largest area of the Forest, although most of its electorate is in an urbanised strip along Southampton Water: Totton and Hythe are the largest towns, although the most striking feature is the vast oil refinery at Fawley. These areas are strongly influenced by Southampton. Inland, amid the forest, are the little towns of Lyndhurst and Brockenhurst, very traditional hunting territory.

A sizeable Labour vote appeared from nowhere in the 1997 election – there are no Labour council-lors in the seat. It probably came mostly from Totton, the only area where Labour are at all competitive in local elections. The Liberal Democrat heartland is Dibden and Hythe, where the 2001 candidate Brian Dash won 57 per cent in the local elections, although they also have some local strength in Fawley and Totton. The Conservatives are strongest at Brockenhurst. The division of the anti-Tory vote helped vitriolic right winger Julian Lewis win a healthy-looking majority on a rather low share of the vote. The Liberal Democrats led by miles in the 1995 local elections but even in 1999 when the Conservatives recovered the Lib Dems still had a small overall lead. Their vote has stayed fairly strong and if they could attract a more convincing tactical vote it would be possible to unseat Lewis, but this scenario remains a long shot.

NEW FOREST WEST

	2001		1997		1992 notional	
Electorate and turnout	67,725	65.1	66,599	74.7	63,917	79.8
Conservative	24,575	55.7	25,149	50.6	30,982	60.7
Labour	6,481	14.7	7,092	14.3	4,179	8.2
Lib Dem	11,384	25.8	13,817	27.8	15,583	30.5
Anti–EU	1,647	3.7	3,692 (2)	7.4	–	–
Others	–		–		293	
MP	Desmond Swayne (Con)		Desmond Swayne (Con)		Patrick McNair-Wilson (Con) New Forest	
Majority	13,191	29.9	11,332	22.8	15,399	30.2

New Forest West is a bit of a ragbag of towns and villages, lacking focus since the Forest was split into two seats. There are villages and several country towns scattered around the forest, including Fordingbridge in the north, Ringwood at the centre of the forest and the boating town of Lymington in the south. West of Lymington there are some coastal retirement areas such as Milford-on-Sea. The Milford area, with Barton and New Milton, borders closely on Christchurch and the Bournemouth conurbation and provides about a third of the electorate.

Desmond Swayne, like his colleague in New Forest East, is an eccentric right-winger, but unlike Julian Lewis he is utterly safe. West is the sixth safest Tory seat in the land, while East is 127th. The difference is that West is old England, a place of agriculture and retirement, while part of East is suburban and even industrial. All the county wards of the constituency were Conservative in 2001, several with massive majorities, and even in the 1995 local elections the Tories were ahead with 49 per cent of the vote.

Election results here have shown remarkable stability in recent general elections. News of the collapse of the Conservative Party's electoral base has not reached New Forest West. Labour support has risen gently, apparently at the expense of both Conservatives and Liberal Democrats. However even in local elections the Conservatives dominate, although there is some patchy and intermittent Lib Dem strength in Fordingbridge and Lymington.

PORTSMOUTH NORTH

	2001		1997		1992 notional	
Electorate and turnout	64,256	57.4	64,539	70.1	65,614	76.2
Conservative	13,542	36.7	17,016	37.6	25,368	50.7
Labour	18,676	50.7	21,339	47.1	16,610	33.2
Lib Dem	3,795	10.3	4,788	10.6	7,529	15.1
Anti–EU	559	1.5	2,055 (2)	4.5	–	–
Others	294		72		511	
MP	Syd Rapson (Lab)		Syd Rapson (Lab)		Peter Griffiths (Con)	
Majority	5,134	13.9	4,323	9.5	8,758	17.5

Portsmouth North is one of several seats which is regularly among the first to be announced on election night. In 1997, Labour's gain on a 14 per cent swing was a portent of what would happen in many southern marginals. In 2001, Labour MP Syd Rapson looked lugubrious, almost defeated, on the platform but this masked his delight at winning a second term with an increased majority.

Portsmouth North is, to coin a phrase, exactly what it says on the tin – the northern half of the city of Portsmouth, straddling the channel between the mainland and Portsea Island. It is low-lying and flat, except for a ridge in the far north from which forts have long guarded the city. The housing is composed mostly of densely packed terraces on the island, with council estates and varying sorts of suburb on the mainland. The safest Labour ward in Portsmouth North is the deprived estate of Paulsgrove, which anti-paedophile riots made notorious in summer 2000. Syd Rapson himself lives in Paulsgrove and tried to speak up for its residents. Most of North is less troubled territory, such as marginal Cosham and the safely Conservative residential suburb of Drayton & Farlington. The core Labour vote in Portsmouth North is difficult to motivate, and its apathy gave the Conservatives some ground for hope in the 1997-2001 midterm, but enough came out in the general election to give Labour a comfortable win.

Like several other constituencies with a defence flavour to them, Labour did particularly badly in the 1980s but recovered well after the end of the Cold War and the policy review and continued to gain ground in 2001. Portsmouth North, however, is a seat with a record of volatility and cannot be taken for granted. Tory MP Peter Griffiths gained the seat in 1979, led Labour by over 21,000 in 1987 but was still defeated in 1997.

PORTSMOUTH SOUTH

	2001		1997		1992 actual	
Electorate and turnout	77,095	50.9	81,014	63.8	77,648	69.1
Conservative	11,397	29.1	16,094	31.1	22,798	42.5
Labour	9,361	23.9	13,086	25.3	7,857	14.6
Lib Dem	17,490	44.6	20,421	39.5	22,556	42.0
Anti–EU	321	0.8	1,770 (2)	3.4	–	–
Others	647		324 (2)		440 (2)	
MP	Mike Hancock (LD)		Mike Hancock (LD)		David Martin (Con)	
Majority	6,093	15.5	4,327	8.4	242	0.5

Portsmouth South is an interesting and unusual seat. After two elections when the Conservatives defeated Mike Hancock by hairsbreadth majorities (202 in 1987, 242 in 1992), we have had two elections when Hancock has had the satisfaction of inflicting two defeats on the Conservatives, by much larger margins. This was not because he squeezed the Labour vote – it was in fact a big swing from Tory to Labour that let him in at the 1997 election. Perhaps, had Hancock not won a by-election here in 1984, the seat would have gone Labour by now. Labour are still a significant force in Portsmouth South, winning council seats and sustaining a reasonable vote in general elections, and might yet convert the constituency into a genuine three-way marginal.

About half of the Portsmouth South constituency thinks of itself as Southsea, a patchily elegant but not totally successful Hampshire version of Brighton's Regency grandeur. The rest is decidedly Portsmouth, with the working class central ward of Charles Dickens, the university area and the tightly packed terraces of Fratton near the football ground of Portsmouth FC. Fratton is the political base of Lib Dem MP Mike Hancock, who still sits for the ward on the city council. The Conservatives do best in the Southsea area and Lib Dems and Labour often fight it out in the rest, reflecting the SDP origins of centre activity here. The constituency is densely populated, with a tradition of low turnout in some Southsea wards as well as the navy-influenced wards dragging the overall turnout to barely over 50 per cent in 2001 – a dismal outcome in such a crucial seat. Even if a lot of its own electors seem to disagree, there is always something interesting going on in Portsmouth South's politics.

ROMSEY

	2001		1997		1992 *notional*	
Electorate and turnout	72,128	67.2	67,866	76.4	*65,546*	*82.6*
Conservative	20,386	42.1	23,834	46.0	*34,218*	*63.2*
Labour	3,986	8.2	9,623	18.6	*6,982*	*12.9*
Lib Dem	22,756	47.0	15,249	29.4	*12,496*	*23.1*
Anti–EU	730	1.5	3,115 (2)	6.0	–	–
Others	601		–		*420*	
MP	Sandra Gidley (LD)		Michael Colvin (Con)		NEW SEAT	
Majority	2,370	4.9	8,585	16.6	*21,722*	*40.1*

Parliamentary by-election 4 May 2000: Lib Dem 19,571 (50.6), Conservative 16,260 (42.0), Labour 1,451 (3.7), Anti EU 901 (2.3), 2 Others 526 Electorate 69,701, Turnout 55.5%. MP: Sandra Gidley (LD), Majority 3,311 (8.6).

The Romsey constituency has had a dramatic history since its formation in 1997. When created, it seemed to be a very safe Conservative seat (it was number 273 on the Lib Dem target list based on 1992 figures). It is a rather ill-assorted seat. About half the population comes from the generally affluent though rather straggling northern suburbs of Southampton: Chandler's Ford, Hiltingbury, Chilworth and North Baddesley; and the only reliably Tory ward of the city, namely Bassett. Hiltingbury is a particularly high-class area. Romsey itself is a growing historic town a few miles outside Southampton. The seat also includes some villages up the river Test towards the downs to the east of Salisbury Plain. Labour has not elected a district councillor anywhere in the seat for many years, and although the Lib Dems had some local strength in Romsey town and a foothold in Chandler's Ford, the Conservatives dominated all areas.

In 1997 there was a relatively large (12 per cent) swing to the Lib Dems, but that still left the Conservatives ahead in all the component parts of the constituency and it would surely have remained safe had a by-election not been called in May 2000. The Liberal Democrats mounted an effective squeeze on the Labour vote and swept to a surprise victory. Romsey was the only seat to change hands in a by-election in the 1997-2001 parliament (other than the nominal transfer of West Bromwich West from Speaker to Labour). The victorious Lib Dem, Sandra Gidley, repeated her triumph the following year in the general election – if anything an even more stunning victory. Late-term by-election winners have a poor survival rate, as the short terms served by Nicol Stephen (1991), Elizabeth Shields (1986) and David Austick (1973) demonstrate.

The Romsey by-election, and the fact that the 2001 general election replicated its voting patterns, should be a terrifying intimation of electoral mortality to the Conservatives. A lot of their remaining seats are places rather like Romsey. If Romsey could fall at a time when they were doing relatively well nationally, then there are not many safe seats for the Tories in by-elections.

SOUTHAMPTON ITCHEN

	2001		1997		1992 notional	
Electorate and turnout	76,557	54.0	76,910	70.0	73,697	77.5
Conservative	11,330	27.4	15,269	28.4	24,065	42.1
Labour	22,553	54.5	29,498	54.8	25,118	44.0
Lib Dem	6,195	15.0	6,289	11.7	7,924	13.9
Anti–EU	829	2.0	1,832 (2)	3.4	–	–
Others	466 (2)		950 (4)		–	
MP	John Denham (Lab)		John Denham (Lab)		John Denham (Lab)	
Majority	11,223	27.1	14,229	26.4	1,053	1.8

The river Itchen flows through the east of Southampton and gives its name to one of the city's two constituencies. Southampton is a middling city, socially and politically, with a nearly average distribution of classes and ethnic groups. Itchen includes the city centre Bargate ward, a solid Labour ward, plus several working class and lower middle class wards east of the river. Other than Bargate, and the peripheral Thornhill estate in the Bitterne ward, they are rather undifferentiated mixtures of council and privately built suburbs built at various times from the late Victorian period to the 1930s and 1960s. In local elections the Lib Dems can pick off the wards nearest the river, and in a good year for them the Conservatives can win the rather middle class Harefield ward on the edge of the city, but Labour has probably led in all the wards in the last two general elections.

In general elections the Conservatives could only win Itchen in 1983 and 1987, when the traditional Labour vote was split after the defection of Bob Mitchell MP to the SDP. With the demise of the SDP, Labour's John Denham recaptured the seat on a large swing in 1992 and won big majorities in 1997 and 2001. In theory, Itchen might be vulnerable again in future – the Liberal Democrats were ahead in the constituency in the May 2000 local elections and there are still some Tories out there – but it would take an electoral fiasco for Labour to lose it again. Despite their different natures, Itchen and Test have produced nearly identical election results since 1987.

The new ward boundaries create a ward, Swaythling, which has what Southampton officials believe is a unique distinction. Parts of this ward are in three different constituencies – Romsey, Southampton Itchen and Southampton Test – and will remain so until the boundary review realigns the constituency and ward boundaries.

SOUTHAMPTON TEST

	2001		1997		1992 notional	
Electorate and turnout	73,840	56.3	73,087	71.8	71,957	75.1
Conservative	10,617	25.5	14,712	28.1	21,843	40.4
Labour	21,824	52.5	28,396	54.1	24,565	45.5
Lib Dem	7,522	18.1	7,171	13.7	7,087	13.1
Anti–EU	792	1.9	1,616 (2)	3.1	–	–
Others	820 (2)		546 (3)		537	
MP	Alan Whitehead (Lab)		Alan Whitehead (Lab)		James Hill (Con)	
Majority	11,207	27.0	13,684	26.1	2,722*	5.0*

* Estimated Labour majority allowing for boundary changes.

Test is the name of the larger of the two rivers of the city of Southampton, and of its western constituency. The river itself is cut off from the constituency by the newer part of the docks, but any poetry in constituency names is to be welcomed, and the name is good for headline writers. Test is less socially uniform than Itchen, containing some of the best and worst areas of Southampton. In the far west is the sprawling 1930s council estate that makes up the safe Labour Redbridge ward, a mini-Dagenham that forms the most deprived area of the city. To its north are the 1970s Lordshill and Coxford peripheral estates. Closer in lies Shirley, an attractive and quiet residential area on the west side of Southampton Common which was formerly a Conservative stronghold but now a marginal thet Labour can win in all but the best Tory years. There are a couple of terraced areas north of the new docks, at Freemantle (Conservative continuously until 1988 but Labour from then until 2002) and Millbrook. To complete the picture is the Portswood area, increasingly student dominated as it lies near Southampton University, and inner city, multiracial St. Luke's (now called Bevois ward). Test combines a lot of different varieties of urban England.

The Liberal Democrats, oddly in a traditional two party marginal, have a strong local government presence which has spread out from Portswood (solidly theirs since 1984) to the other wards – as in Itchen, they were a little ahead in the constituency in May 2000. Test has a rather overdone reputation for being a bellwether seat won by the national winner since it was established in 1950. In fact, Labour held it against the tide in 1951, while the Conservatives held on despite narrow national Labour victories in 1964 and February 1974. On current boundaries, Labour would have won in 1992 as the 1990s changes brought in an inner city area and took out the only solid Tory area of the city, Bassett. Test is rather a poor predictor of the national result. The Conservatives can now aspire to winning Test only in their wildest dreams – an election that reproduced their 1983 landslide would not quite suffice to topple the seat because it is Labour's 205th safest seat.

WINCHESTER

	2001		1997		1992 notional	
Electorate and turnout	81,801	72.3	79,272	78.3	75,123	83.9
Conservative	22,648	38.3	26,098	42.1	32,604	51.7
Labour	3,498	5.9	6,528	10.5	4,734	7.5
Lib Dem	32,282	54.6	26,100	42.1	23,286	36.9
Anti–EU	664	1.1	2,381 (3)	3.8	2,334	3.7
Others	66		947 (2)		134	
MP	Mark Oaten (LD)		Mark Oaten (LD)		Gerry Malone (Con)	
Majority	9,634	16.3	2	0.00	9,318	14.8

* John Browne, Conservative MP for Winchester 1979–92, contested the seat in 1992 as an Independent Conservative and in 1997 as an Independent Anti Federal Europe candidate. His 1992 vote is listed under anti–EU.

Parliamentary by-election 20 November 1997: Lib Dem 37,006 (68.0), Conservative 15,450 (28.4), Labour 944 (1.7), Anti EU 521 (1.0), 4 Others 463 Electorate 79,116, Turnout 68.7%. MP: Mark Oaten (LD), Majority 21,556 (39.6).

Winchester produced the highest turnout, but the lowest Labour share of the vote, in any constituency in Britain in 2001. The reason for these extreme results goes back to the general election of 1997 and its peculiar sequel. Winchester produced the closest margin seen in a parliamentary election since 1931, but the 2-vote majority was disputed and the election was re-run in November 1997. Voters in Winchester had a clearer demonstration than most of the value of an individual vote, which seems to still influence their willingness to turn out. The Labour vote fell away nearly to nothing in the November by-election, perceived as a straight fight between Lib Dem and Tory, and a majority of Labour supporters in Winchester were still voting tactically in 2001.

The local elections on the same day produced a Liberal Democrat lead of nearly 2,000 (compared to nearly 10,000 in the general election). The main difference between local and national voting was that Labour polled more than twice as many votes in the local elections as it did for the parliamentary seat. In local elections, the city of Winchester itself has a respectable Labour vote based on council-built estates. There can be few clearer demonstrations of tactical voting than this vote's en bloc transfer to the Lib Dems for the general election. The Conservatives also underpolled their local strength, presumably reflecting some personal votes for Mark Oaten on the one side and Tory councillors on the other. The strident Euroscepticism of the Tory campaign in Winchester cannot have helped.

The constituency is coterminous with the City of Winchester district, which extends over rural territory east of the city proper including Bishop's Waltham and New Alresford. Much of the rural area produces a strong Liberal Democrat vote as well, although the Meon Valley is the remaining Conservative stronghold. The Conservatives will be looking to regain the seat once memories of 1997 have faded, but Mark Oaten is a formidable opponent and an attentive local member.

Hereford and Worcester

(former county of)

	Conservative		Labour		Liberal Democrat		Others	
	Share of vote	Seats	Share of vote	Seats	Share of vote	Seats	Share of vote	Seats
2001	41.1	4	27.4	2	19.4	1	12.1	1
1997	41.0	4	32.6	3	21.9	1	4.5	0
1992	50.8	7	24.6	0	23.1	0	1.5	0
1987	51.8	7	17.9	0	29.7	0	0.6	0
1983	52.3	7	15.3	0	31.4	0	1.0	0

This chapter should probably start with an apology to the people of Herefordshire and Worcestershire for continuing to lump their counties together. This follows on from the fact that the defunct county of Hereford and Worcester was in existence when the parliamentary boundary commission conducted their last review. The 1970s merger of the two counties was not regarded as a great success and the combined county was disbanded in the 1990s local government review; its demise was little lamented.

Herefordshire is a mainly rural, sparsely populated county which, with Shropshire to its north, forms the Marches, English border territory adjoining Wales. It is best known for cattle and cider, appropriately bucolic products given the nature of the county. Hereford, the only urban settlement of any great size, sits in the centre of the county and serves as its principal centre; Ross-on-Wye, Leominster and Ledbury are all much smaller places. Most of the population lives in villages or isolated farms and hamlets. In terms of population, Herefordshire is one of the smallest of the English counties.

Like Shropshire to the north the border county of Herefordshire has had a strong tradition of Conservatism, although here the Labour Party has been even weaker. The Liberals lost both their seats here in January 1910 and, other than a short-lived victory in Hereford in 1929 the Conservatives then won everything until the Lib Dems gained Hereford in 1997 and the remaining Conservative MP Peter Temple-Morris defected to Labour in 1998. In 2001 the Conservatives predictably reasserted their control in Leominster, but less expected was their good result in Hereford which trimmed the Lib Dem majority below 1,000 and left the seat a key target for the next election.

Worcestershire's differences from Herefordshire are obvious, which made it an odd idea to merge them. It has several fairly large urban centres, with Worcester being big enough for a constituency in its own right and Redditch and Kidderminster requiring fairly small additional elements to make up constituencies. Worcestershire is much more part of the English mainstream, being served by the M5 and fast rail lines running north-south through the county and especially in the north strong links with Birmingham. It even has a New Town, albeit quite a backwater among New Towns, in Redditch. It perhaps deserves the oft-claimed title of being the heart of England (although in outline on a map, the county looks curiously like France); its hills and fields have inspired artists and, famously, the composer Edward Elgar. Its stolid English virtues were reflected politically in the persona of Stanley Baldwin, who represented Bewdley and served three times as Prime Minister between 1923 and 1937. Worcestershire has a fair amount of agriculture, particularly fruit growing, in the fertile Vale of Evesham between the Malvern and Cotswold hills. But despite this, rural life is not central to its identity as it is in Herefordshire and fewer than 1 per cent of the county's work force are employed in agriculture.

However, BBC radio's long-running rural soap opera *The Archers* is set in rural Worcestershire. 'Ambridge' is a composite of Inkberrow (the only rural Wychavon district ward in the Redditch constituency), where a pub called The Old Bull is put to service as a setting for publicity material, and Hanbury (in Worcestershire Mid) where the parish church is the setting for Ambridge weddings. It is incongruous, but there is an arguable case that the archetypal English village has a Labour MP.

Worcestershire's constituencies are quite an interesting lot. There are two safe Conservative seats, the outer Birmingham suburban seat of Bromsgrove and the rural acres of Worcestershire Mid, but all the others are a bit unpredictable. Worcestershire West is Conservative, although the Liberal Democrats surged in 1997 and can still regard it as a target despite a slippage in their vote in 2001. The Conservatives gained Worcester against the tide in 1923 from a Liberal, and held it continuously despite a latter erosion of their majority until Labour gained it in 1997. Redditch is a precariously Labour New Town, and the Conservatives must hope to win it at the next election. Wyre Forest was another middle-ranking Labour/ Conservative marginal until a local protest party scored an astonishing victory in the 2001 general election; politics in the area is in a very uncertain state. There is no sign yet that the instability in Wyre Forest has affected anywhere else in Worcestershire, although the proximate cause of it – downgrading of the facilities at Kidderminster hospital – was also a factor in the election in Ludlow in Shropshire.

Local government

The unitary county of Herefordshire is under no overall control. The Conservatives are the largest party with 22 seats, followed by 17 Lib Dems, 15 Independents, 5 Labour and one non-aligned. Labour are absent outside Hereford except for a single outpost in Leominster town; the Liberal Democrats draw their main support from Hereford, Ledbury and Ross, while the Conservatives and Independents have some urban representation but basically share out the country areas between them. The creation of the unitary authority threatened the survival of Hereford's centuries-old mayoralty and city traditions, an unanticipated consequence of restoring the old county.

Worcestershire county is also under no overall control, as it has been since its revival and as the combined county was ever since a controversial Conservative administration lost it against the tide in 1989. The Tories are the largest single party with 26 seats, being particularly strong in the rural centre and the Bromsgrove commuter belt. Labour come next with 14, nearly all from Worcester and Redditch; the party won no seats in its previously strong area of Wyre Forest, which is now dominated by 'others': six from the Kidderminster hospital party (KHHC) plus two independent Liberals. The Lib Dems have eight, in Malvern and a few elsewhere, and there is one Independent. A Conservative minority administration forms the cabinet and rules by consensus.

Wyre Forest borough council has annual elections and has been near permanently hung, except for a Conservative interlude in 1976-79 and a period of Labour control lasting from 1996 to 1999 when Kidderminster Hospital and Health Concern (KHHC) started sweeping all before them. In 2002, KHHC (which claims a comprehensive set of policies rather than just a single issue focus) gained overall control of the council. Labour lost Worcester, another authority with annual elections, more straight-forwardly because of Conservative and Independent gains in May 2000 after fourteen years in power. The Conservatives had half the seats after the 2002 elections and can aspire to control. Labour lost Redditch, another council with annual elections, in May 2002 after 19 years of control. The others elect all-out every four years. Labour managed to win Bromsgrove at the party's 1995 high water mark, but in 1999 the Conservatives (who are on something of a roll in the area) regained control resoundingly. The Tories also bounced back strongly in Wychavon (Evesham, Droitwich and Pershore) in 1999 having lapsed from control in 1995. The other district council, Malvern Hills, formerly contained areas of Herefordshire but it was truncated after the counties were divorced. The Liberal Democrats led in 1991 and 1995 without a majority, but another strong showing saw the Conservatives fall just short in 1999.

Boundary review

The main task of the boundary review here is to complete the work of disentangling the two mismatched counties by removing bits of Worcestershire from the Leominster constituency (a small area in Wyre Forest and a somewhat larger bit around Tenbury Wells). The knock-on effects of this might ripple over to Redditch, which may well acquire a few thousand more rural voters and make the revised seat a knife-edge marginal.

BROMSGROVE

	2001		1997		1992 *notional*	
Electorate and turnout	68,081	67.1	67,744	77.1	*71,079*	*82.7*
Conservative	23,640	51.7	24,620	47.1	*31,773*	*54.1*
Labour	15,502	33.9	19,775	37.8	*18,021*	*30.7*
Lib Dem	5,430	11.9	6,200	11.9	*8,118*	*13.8*
Anti–EU	1,112	2.4	1,662 (2)	3.2	*–*	*–*
Others	–		–		*858*	
MP	Julie Kirkbride (Con)		Julie Kirkbride (Con)		Roy Thomason (Con)	
Majority	8,138	17.8	4,845	9.3	*13,752*	*23.4*

Part of the Bromsgrove constituency is composed of the fringe of Birmingham and has similar characteristics to its neighbours across the metropolitan border – in the west the Tory town of Hagley is south of the posh part of Stourbridge; Rubery adjoins the south edge of Northfield and is marginal, while the rest is deeply Conservative commuterland resembling the better-off parts of Solihull. It lost a more working class component with the transfer of 9,000 residents at Frankley into Birmingham in 1998. Barnt Green is a commuter suburb in the top 5 percent of wards in England for its low scores on the index of multiple deprivation and there are similar communities along both railway lines into Birmingham. Geographically and socially, the Bromsgrove constituency, plus Solihull and part of Meriden, form Birmingham's miniature version of Surrey.

Bromsgrove town is less elite, being a former nail-making town which now seems like a particularly somnolent Birmingham dormitory, although it too is quite well off. Its 26,000 electors provide the main Labour strength in the constituency although even here the Conservatives were a couple of hundred votes ahead in the 2001 local elections thanks to the strong support they received in the south of the town. After a relatively low swing to Labour in 1997, and a strong Conservative bounce-back in 2001, it has climbed the charts of the safest Conservative seats from 190th in 1992 to 62nd in 2001. Labour have never won Bromsgrove in a general election – although they did manage to win a seat of that name which included Redditch in a 1971 by-election – and look unlikely to do so now. Julie Kirkbride now has a safer seat than her husband, Andrew MacKay of Bracknell.

HEREFORD

	2001		1997		1992 notional	
Electorate and turnout	68,468	65.2	69,864	75.2	69,057	80.8
Conservative	17,276	38.7	18,550	35.3	26,217	47.0
Labour	6,739	15.1	6,596	12.6	5,910	10.6
Lib Dem	18,244	40.9	25,198	47.9	23,063	41.4
Anti–EU	1,184	2.7	2,209	4.2	–	–
Green	1,181	2.6	–	–	587	1.1
MP	Paul Keetch (LD)		Paul Keetch (LD)		Colin Shepherd (Con)	
Majority	968	2.2	6,648	12.7	3,154	5.7

The cathedral city of Hereford comprises about half the electorate of the constituency. While it has some council estates, industry and distribution as well as its functions as a commercial and administrative centre, Hereford is more bound up with its rural hinterland than many cities of its size. It has a famous cattle market, although Hereford beef production was badly affected first by the BSE export ban and then by foot and mouth restrictions. The second largest private employer in the county is Hereford cider production, and from apples to bottling it is a prominent local industry. The other town in the Hereford constituency is Ross-on-Wye, down at the south eastern end of the seat where Wales and Gloucestershire also meet near Symond's Yat in the steeply wooded Wye valley.

Hereford was a long term Liberal hope which came good in 1997 but nearly repeated its behaviour after the last Liberal win in 1929 when it reverted to the Conservatives after a single term. Despite strong candidates in the 1950s in Frank Owen (journalist and 1929-31 MP for the seat) and Robin Day it eluded them, and continued to do so in the 1970s and 1980s as Conservative MP Colin Shepherd won a series of small majorities. A straw in the wind in 1997 was the ecstatic reception Paddy Ashdown received on a campaign visit, and it was no surprise when the Lib Dems swept to victory a few days later. However, like many seats across the regional boundary in the south west, the Lib Dems did very badly in the Euro elections in 1999, coming third. In 2001 the constituency was a rare excellent Conservative performance against the Lib Dems, with Virginia Taylor's energetic campaign and a rallying of rural voters being stymied by the failure of the national Conservative campaign to lift the base level of Tory support. The Lib Dem majority depends on getting their vote, concentrated in Hereford city, to the polls.

LEOMINSTER

	2001		1997		1992 notional	
Electorate and turnout	67,317	69.4	65,993	76.6	63,182	81.0
Conservative	22,879	49.0	22,888	45.3	28,837	56.4
Labour	7,872	16.8	8,831	17.5	6,294	12.3
Lib Dem	12,512	26.8	14,053	27.8	14,236	27.8
Anti–EU	1,590	3.4	3,403 (2)	6.9	530	1.0
Green	1,690	3.6	1,086	2.1	1,281	2.5
Others	186		292		–	
MP	Bill Wiggin (Con)		Peter Temple-Morris (Con) (Ind)(Lab)		Peter Temple-Morris (Con)	
Majority	10,367	22.2	8,835	17.5	14,601	28.5

Leominster is a sparsely populated, extremely rural constituency covering the northern part of Herefordshire. Leominster is the main town, sitting in a central spot in the constituency, but does not exert a strong influence; much of it really looks to Hereford. The smaller towns of Bromyard and Ledbury in the east and Kington in the west near the Welsh border are the only other urban locations in the constituency, although this is stretching the limits of 'urban' to breaking point.

As with some other deeply rural seats Leominster's voting patterns have changed relatively little in recent elections. It was at one time a great Liberal hope but they have gone backwards since they came within 574 votes of victory in October 1974. Leominster has never warmed to Labour – the party did not bother to put up candidates until 1950 and peaked in a straight fight in 1955; as soon as the Liberals stood a candidate again in 1959 Labour returned to third. The defection of Europhile Tory MP Peter Temple-Morris to Labour in 1998 gave the party an improbable, brief hold on the seat before it predictably returned to the Tories in 2001.

Leominster has one of the most active Green party groups of any rural seat. Most constituencies where the Greens have appreciable support are the trendier parts of inner cities and areas of heavy student settlement; Leominster and Stroud rather stand out as the exceptions to this rule. The Greens polled 13.5 per cent here in the 1999 Euro elections, missing out by a whisker on coming second (an honour that would have found Leominster in the company of three inner London seats). The seat might be a unique case where politics has gone from a pre-Labour model to post-Labour without a period of Labour support in the middle – Peter Temple-Morris was, one can say with near certainty, Leominster's first and last Labour MP.

REDDITCH

	2001		1997		1992 notional	
Electorate and turnout	62,565	59.2	60,924	73.4	60,193	80.9
Conservative	14,415	38.9	16,155	36.1	22,930	47.1
Labour	16,899	45.6	22,280	49.8	19,643	40.4
Lib Dem	3,808	10.3	4,935	11.0	5,716	11.7
Anti–EU	1,259	3.4	1,151	2.6	–	–
Others	651		227		384	
MP	Jacqui Smith (Lab)		Jacqui Smith (Lab)		Eric Forth (Con) Worcestershire Mid	
Majority	2,484	6.7	6,125	13.7	3,287	6.8

Redditch is a New Town, designated in 1964 in the north east of Worcestershire and the recipient of displaced population from Birmingham since then. In a similar way to Crawley in West Sussex, it has created a rather working class, Labour voting island in an otherwise very Conservative part of the country; again, like Crawley, it took a combination of being reduced to a nearly all-urban core and the national swing for it to go Labour for the first time in a general election in 1997. Redditch, however, was the main element of Labour's one-off gain of Bromsgrove in a 1971 by-election.

The New Town was built around an existing small town which specialised in making needles; a National Needle Museum has been established in the town, and the town still has a substantial presence in making needles and fish hooks. There are also many employers who do not produce sharp bits of metal, and some Birmingham commuting. It is a quiet, wooded town. There is a range of neighbour-hoods, from working class Batchley to the prosperous west side and the village of Feckenham. The constituency has a single ward of the Wychavon district, Inkberrow (see the note on Ambridge in the county introduction). Support for the parties in most of the New Town districts is quite evenly distrib-uted, although Labour has emerged on top in every contest lately; the west and rural parts, however, have few Labour votes. The seat adds up to a marginal. Like most of the southern New Towns Redditch had an above-average swing to the Conservatives in 2001 thanks to a slump in turnout on Labour's best estates, reducing it to the party's 29th most vulnerable seat. Labour could lose it on a uniform swing and still be doing better than in 1966. Labour in Redditch must hope that turnout in its better areas recovers at the next election, or else the seat will be in serious danger.

WORCESTER

	2001		1997		1992 notional	
Electorate and turnout	71,255	62.0	69,234	74.6	63,622	82.8
Conservative	15,712	35.5	18,423	35.7	23,960	45.5
Labour	21,478	48.6	25,848	50.1	21,013	39.9
Lib Dem	5,578	12.6	6,462	12.5	6,890	13.1
Anti–EU	1,442	3.3	886	1.7	–	–
Others	–		–		823 (2)	
MP	Michael Foster (Lab)		Michael Foster (Lab)		Peter Luff (Con)	
Majority	5,766	13.0	7,425	14.4	2,947	5.6

Worcester was one of many seats Labour gained for the first time in 1997, but unlike a lot of them this was not much of a surprise. The 1990s boundary changes had trimmed off some rural areas, and Labour had made considerable progress in 1992, so it was a target marginal the party needed to become the largest single party in a hung parliament. Its defiance of the national trend in 1945 was only by four votes, and as in several other cathedral cities the forces of conservatism have been weakening over the last few decades (see also Exeter and Chester). Worcester lacks a full-scale university of its own, which has probably kept the Conservatives in contention. Parts of Worcester are industrial and working class; brown sauce is not the only thing to be manufactured here.

Worcester has a variety of wards within its boundaries, six out of nine named in proper ecclesiastical fashion after saints. Labour's strongest area is the eastern inner city around Shrub Hill railway station; St. Barnabas was over 70 per cent for the party in 2001. Labour won the other eastern wards, Nunnery and the growing area of St. Martin, and two wards in the west across the Severn (St. John and St. Clement). The Conservative areas of Worcester are to the north and south of the city centre in the residential areas of St. Stephen and Claines to the north and Bedwardine and St. Peter to the south. Unusually, Worcester's city centre is split between two wards which have usually been Conservative.

'Worcester Woman' was much discussed in the run-up to the 1997 election; media shorthand for the suburban woman with aspirations as well as children, concerned about public services but focused on economic competence and mortgage rates. This sort of voter was not found in especially high concentration in Worcester – it was probably the marginal constituency that made the alliteration work best. Worcester Woman, and Man, voted for Labour in 1997 and again slightly less enthusiastically in 2001. Michael Foster attracted the odium of the pro-hunting campaign for his 1997 bill to ban the sport, but this made next to no difference to the result in urban Worcester. If Labour lose Worcester, it will be because enough people have turned against the government on a broad front to overturn the party's national majority.

WORCESTERSHIRE MID

	2001		1997		1992 notional	
Electorate and turnout	72,055	62.3	68,407	74.3	63,596	78.8
Conservative	22,937	51.1	24,092	47.4	27,535	55.0
Labour	12,310	27.4	14,680	28.9	8,832	17.6
Lib Dem	8,420	18.8	9,458	18.6	13,081	26.1
Anti–EU	1,230	2.7	2,426 (2)	4.8	–	–
Others	–		163		663	
MP	Peter Luff (Con)		Peter Luff (Con)		NEW SEAT	
Majority	10,627	23.7	9,412	18.5	14,454	28.9

The Worcestershire Mid constituency is based around Evesham in the south east and Droitwich in the north west (the seat of the same name before 1997 was based on Redditch). It covers most of the fertile Vale of Evesham and is the core of agricultural Worcestershire. Droitwich is an old spa town sitting near the M5 and within easy reach of Worcester and Birmingham, with a famously often repaired radio transmitter, while Evesham is deeper in the countryside. At a stretch, parts of the Cotswold end of the seat are commutable to London, but in general people who move into the area from Birmingham or London are retiring or downsizing to part time work, or seeking employment in local concerns. It is a prosperous area without any particular pockets of extreme wealth or any islands of poverty.

The political allegiance of the constituency is steadily, solidly Conservative – 40 per cent is as low a share of the vote as they received in the 2001 county elections, even in the towns. In rural areas such as Bowbrook and around Broadway the Tory share approached 60 per cent. The Lib Dems have some local support scattered in the countryside, and Labour won a narrow victory in the Droitwich Town ward, but there is not much of a base to challenge the Conservative hold. It is their safest seat in the West Midlands, and their 26th safest nationally.

WORCESTERSHIRE WEST

	2001		1997		1992 notional	
Electorate and turnout	66,769	67.1	64,712	76.3	63,144	80.0
Conservative	20,597	46.0	22,223	45.0	27,654	54.8
Labour	6,275	14.0	7,738	15.7	6,967	13.8
Lib Dem	15,223	34.0	18,377	37.2	14,785	29.3
Anti–EU	1,574	3.5	–	–	114	0.2
Green	1,138	2.5	1,006	2.0	990	2.0
MP	Michael Spicer (Con)		Michael Spicer (Con)		Michael Spicer (Con)	
					Worcestershire South	
Majority	5,374	12.0	3,846	7.8	12,869	25.5

Worcestershire West's largest urban area is Malvern, including Great Malvern and Malvern Link. Great Malvern is a quiet, staid spa town sitting on the steep slopes of the Malvern Hills. The rest of the town has some unusual industries such as hand-built Morgan cars and the large Defence Evaluation and Research Agency (DERA) which forms the core of a small complex of high-tech industry and invention – semiconductors and sophisticated optics equipment are devised in this apparently traditional part of England. The Worcestershire West constituency extends northwards into the rural areas north and west of Worcester, and south to Upton-upon-Severn. There is also a rather detached blob, from the Wychavon district rather than the Malvern Hills district which forms the majority of the seat, at Pershore to the east.

The Liberal Democrats did extremely well in 1997, but were disappointed not to continue their improvement in 2001 as Worcestershire West seemed a much more plausible Lib Dem gain than Ludlow. Despite a new challenge from the UKIP, Eurosceptic Tory Michael Spicer increased his majority. The Lib Dem centre in the constituency is Malvern town which supplies 30,000 electors, they led the Tories here 48-40 in the 2001 county elections, and in the plain below the Malvern hills at Powick. The Conservatives, however, had a longer lead in rural areas such as Bredon, Hallow and Croome. Labour hardly feature in this seat. The Liberal Democrats will no doubt be trying again in the next election, taking comfort from their Ludlow triumph and hoping to repeat the performance here.

WYRE FOREST

	2001		1997		1992 notional	
Electorate and turnout	72,152	68.0	73,083	75.3	71,767	82.2
Conservative	9,350	19.1	19,897	36.1	27,999	47.5
Labour	10,857	22.1	26,843	48.8	18,414	31.2
Lib Dem	–	–	4,377	8.0	12,551	21.3
KHHC	28,487	58.1	–	–	–	–
Anti–EU	368	0.8	2,268 (2)	4.1	–	–
Liberal	–	–	1,670	3.0	–	
MP	Richard Taylor (KHHC)		David Lock (Lab)		Anthony Coombs (Con)	
Majority	17,630	35.9	6,946	12.6	9,585	16.3

Wyre Forest is the constituency based on the town of Kidderminster, although it also includes the two smaller towns of Stourport-on-Severn and Bewdley, and some villages in the area. Despite its sylvan name the electorate of the Wyre Forest constituency is mostly urban. Kidderminster, unlike many West Midland towns, has retained its traditional trade of carpet-making and the industry is an important employer in the area. The Labour vote in Wyre Forest, concentrated in the Puxton and Blakebrook areas in the north of Kidderminster and in Stourport, has not however been strong enough to win the constituency before 1997 except in 1945.

The 2001 election campaign in Wyre Forest was truly extraordinary, but it had its roots in a decision taken several years before to downgrade accident and emergency provision at Kidderminster hospital. The Labour government's decision to approve the change led to the foundation of a local political party, Independent Kidderminster Hospital and Health Concern (KHHC) which started fighting local elections in 1999 and had instant success. The party won seven seats out of eleven in 1999 and swept eleven out of thirteen in 2000 after attracting some Labour defectors – KHHC won 45 per cent of the vote to 23 per cent for the Conservatives and 22 for Labour and was nearly in control of the council. It won in traditional Tory Bewdley and Rock as well as normally Labour areas. The Liberal Party, still active in the area with three councillors, nailed its colours to the same mast by dubbing itself 'Liberal Focus Save Our Hospital'.

Haplessly but sincerely, Labour MP David Lock argued that the hospital decision was the right one but he was in a minority against a massive movement in local opinion. KHHC put up a strong candidate, hospital consultant Richard Taylor in the general election and the Lib Dems withdrew in his favour. Taylor's manifesto, though focused on the hospital, covered other issues and took a generally middle-of-the-road line on other issues (backing Gordon Brown, sounding sceptical but not anti the Euro, lower fuel taxes, nationalising Railtrack, supporting Clause 28 but arguing for 'impartial' information on homosexuality, criticising 'spin'). Taylor swept all before him on a high turnout, leading in every area. In the local elections the vote split four ways, with Conservatives, Labour, KHHC and combined Liberal and Lib Dem all winning between 21 and 27 per cent (although counting the Liberals with KHHC gave them a lead over the others.)

The local question about the future of Wyre Forest is whether the pitch of activity and feeling can be maintained, and if electing Taylor fails to bring A&E back to Kidderminster the movement might deflate in disillusion and return to politics as usual. Wyre Forest has seen dramatic gyrations in other recent elections – Labour added 12 points in 1992 and 17 in 1997 before collapsing in 2001 – and is a volatile place. On the other hand, KHHC is well organised and funded (it has a money-raising lottery) and continued making gains to win outright control of the council in 2002.

Recent elections have been a lightning-strike on the party system as we know it. At the very least governments will think twice in future before closing smaller A&E departments; but Wyre Forest has shown the fragility of the hold the party system exercises over popular feeling in Britain and may be the first breakthrough of a new sort of politics.

Hertfordshire

	Conservative		Labour		Liberal Democrat		Others	
	Share of vote	Seats	Share of vote	Seats	Share of vote	Seats	Share of vote	Seats
2001	41.8	6	38.9	5	16.9	0	2.5	0
1997	40.6	6	39.7	5	16.0	0	3.7	0
1992	53.0	10	25.8	0	20.2	0	1.0	0
1987	52.0	10	19.8	0	27.8	0	0.4	0
1983	50.3	10	19.0	0	30.2	0	0.5	0

Hertfordsgire is a prosperous county, middle class in the American sense of the term, and there are few pockets of poverty within its boundaries. It has advanced industry and high-tech employment in IT, pharmaceuticals and armaments as well as a range of service sector employers. A number of its medium-sized towns have extremely low levels of poverty and deprivation, with Berkhamsted, Bishop's Stortford and Harpenden being three of the most uniformly affluent towns in England. There are one or two estates suffering from social exclusion in Stevenage, Hatfield and Letchworth but in general even the unfavoured parts of Hertfordshire towns have deprivation statistics that would be the envy of many parts of England. Overall, its weekly average earnings in 2000 were £462, below only London (£530), former Berkshire (£503) and Surrey (£487) on a comparable basis.

The county is fairly urbanised, with most of the population living in towns to the south and along the transport routes out of London. The Euston rail line goes up via Watford and Hemel Hempstead; the St. Pancras line links Borehamwood, St. Albans and Harpenden; the Kings Cross line thunders northward through Hatfield, Welwyn, Stevenage and Hitchin; Broxbourne, Hertford and Bishop's Stortford are served by the lines into Liverpool Street. The rural areas in the north and east, where transport to London is less convenient, are sparsely populated.

A curiosity is that none of Hertfordshire's towns is quite large enough for a constituency of its own, a fact which has caused the county more than its share of disruption from boundary reviews and created some rather oddly-shaped constituencies. Harpenden, for instance, has been paired with three different towns in three successive reviews – Hemel Hempstead before 1983, St. Albans from 1983 to 1997 and now Hitchin. A lot of the towns are quite close together in the south and centre of the county and planning policy has to be strict to stop them sprawling together in one big conurbation.

Hertfordshire was formerly very Conservative, with only the one-off Liberal victories in Watford and Hitchin in 1906, and Hemel Hempstead in 1923, plus a peculiar independent in 1918, marking non-Tory victories in all the general elections between 1885 and 1945. Labour, however, broke through in 1945 with wins in Hitchin, Watford, St. Albans and the new seat of Barnet, although the Conservatives had regained all the seats by 1955.

Before 1945 the county only had five constituencies, and it covered a larger area than it does now. The fact that it is now entitled to 11 shows that its population has massively increased – from 375,000 in 1931 to 563,000 in 1951 and a million now. This influx of people has had an interesting effect on the politics of the county.

A considerable proportion of the growth has been in traditional suburbs, for instance up the Lea valley at Cheshunt and in the south west of the county around Rickmansworth and Watford. These areas, and growing suburban towns like Harpenden and Potters Bar have, over time, produced safe new Conservative seats such as Broxbourne and Hitchin & Harpenden. However, much growth has also arisen from the foundation of the New Towns by the Attlee government, of which there are four in Hertfordshire – Stevenage, Hatfield, Welwyn Garden City and Hemel Hempstead. The New Towns caused an influx of skilled working class voters into Hertfordshire in the post-war decades, and as they grew the Labour influence in the county gradually increased. Stevenage tipped the Hitchin seat over to Labour in 1964. Hemel Hempstead went Labour, for the first time ever, in October 1974, and was joined by the new seat of Welwyn & Hatfield. With Watford voting Labour in all the post-war elections except 1955 and 1959, the Conservative tradition in Hertfordshire looked like being submerged.

But the Conservatives were not built out of Hertfordshire and it was Labour that suffered a disaster in Hertfordshire during the 1980s. All the party's seats were lost to the Conservatives in the 1979 election, and Labour came third in every single seat in the county in 1983 and remained locked out of parliamentary representation until 1997. Labour did poorly in general elections in all the New Towns of the south east, and this had a decisive effect on the politics of Hertfordshire. The Conservatives increased their vote in the New Towns, and the county as a whole, both in 1987 and in 1992. Some voters who had deserted Labour for the SDP in 1983 – the new party polled well in the New Towns then – drifted over to the Conservatives in 1987 and 1992. For example, the Tory vote in West Hertfordshire, the Hemel Hempstead seat, increased from 46.7 per cent in 1983 to 49.7 per cent in 1987 and 51.5 per cent in 1992. Tory support in the county as a whole rose steadily in the elections after 1983 until it plunged in 1997. Labour could take solace only in local elections, where Stevenage remained loyal despite placing the party third in parliamentary elections in 1983 and 1987.

Labour recovered somewhat in the 1992 election, reclaiming second place in the New Town seats, but their gains were mostly at the expense of the defunct Alliance rather than the Tories and no seats fell. This all changed in 1997, when there was an enormous swing of over 13 per cent and five seats fell to Labour. The party made the expected gain in Stevenage, picked up others like Welwyn Hatfield, Watford and Hemel Hempstead and managed an unexpected triumph in St. Albans. Labour held all these constituencies in 2001. The latter four seats are still marginal, particularly Welwyn Hatfield where the Conservatives did relatively well in 2001 and only need a 1.4 per cent further swing to win. Some of the Conservative seats left in the county looked vulnerable on the eve of the 2001 election, notably Hertsmere and Herts NE, but in the end the Conservatives improved their majorities in both cases. There is no significant Liberal Democrat threat in any constituency; they ran third everywhere in 1997 and 2001, although their strength in local elections in Watford and Herts SW make them a latent presence.

Local government

Hertfordshire county council is marginally Conservative held, with a majority of 3 after the 2001 county elections. It had previously been run by a Labour–Lib Dem coalition until the Tories overturned its one-seat majority in a 1999 by-election.

Broxbourne borough in the east is a safe Conservative council, one of only a handful of local authorities to survive the 1990s under uninterrupted Conservative control. Stevenage, by contrast, has been solidly under Labour control for decades. Rural East Hertfordshire, around Hertford and Bishop's Stortford, has a large Tory majority, but many of the other councils are important battlegrounds. Dacorum, the strangely named local authority for Hemel Hempstead and towns to its west, is under tenuous Conservative control having been Labour in 1995–99 and will be hard-fought in the all-out elections in 2003. The name, Dacorum council explains, is a mediaeval Latin rendition of an Anglo-Saxon word for Danish, which was how the western edge of Hertfordshire was known. North Hertfordshire (Hitchin, Letchworth and Royston) is currently Conservative controlled, as is Hertsmere (Potters Bar and Borehamwood) in the far south, although both these councils fell briefly to Labour at their peak strength in local elections in the late 1990s. Three Rivers (Chorleywood and Watford suburbs) has long-standing Liberal Democrat local activism which currently produces a small overall majority on the council despite the Conservatism of the Hertfordshire SW seat. St. Albans city (which includes Harpenden and outlying villages) is hung, with 20 Lib Dems, 21 Conservatives, 15 Labour and 1 other councillor in 2002; the Cabinet is formed from an all-party coalition. Prior to 2002 Watford was run by a minority Labour administration, but an elected mayor was approved in a referendum in July 2001 and the mayoral poll was easily won by the Liberal Democrat candidate, Dorothy Thornhill. Welwyn Hatfield, on the other hand, is fiercely competitive between Labour and Conservative, frequently changing control – Labour, oddly, wrested control from the Tories in May 2000 – although in previous decades it was usually Labour, and in 2002 it returned to the Conservatives.

Boundary review

The boundary commission recommendations for Hertfordshire are for the constituencies to be adjusted to fit new ward boundaries; there will be minimal effects on any of Hertfordshire's 11 constituencies.

BROXBOURNE

	2001		1997		1992 notional	
Electorate and turnout	67,987	55.7	66,817	70.3	66,062	79.0
Conservative	20,487	54.1	22,952	48.9	32,518	62.3
Labour	11,494	30.4	16,299	34.7	11,168	21.4
Lib Dem	4,158	11.0	5,310	11.3	8,353	16.0
Anti-EU	858	2.3	1,633	3.5	–	–
Others	848		782 (2)		181	
MP	Marion Roe (Con)		Marion Roe (Con)		Marion Roe (Con)	
Majority	8,993	23.8	6,653	14.2	21,350	40.9

Broxbourne is the borough, and constituency, in the far south eastern corner of Hertfordshire, just across the border from Enfield North. It comprises several towns in the Lea Valley bypassed by the A10 – Waltham Cross, Cheshunt, Flamstead End, Wormley, Broxbourne and Hoddesdon. The constituency extends to a single ward outside the borough, the highly Conservative Northaw ward, from Welwyn-Hatfield borough to the west. Most of Broxbourne, though, is not particularly high-status and it is not as affluent and professional as suburbs like Enfield Southgate or south eastern towns like Reading. It consists mostly of sprawling privately built suburbs.

However, Broxbourne is more faithfully Tory than any of these other places in its white, lower middle-class sort of way: all its component county council wards were more than 50 per cent Conservative in 2001. Labour have only really done well in their peak year 1995, and have some points of relative strength scattered in the area such as Waltham Cross and Rye Park. More usually these are submerged by the strong Conservative tendencies of the seat which have given the party continuous control of the council since it was formed in 1973. Broxbourne seems spiritually part of south Essex and the large swing to the Tories in the general election certainly followed the pattern of that unusual sub-region. From its physical appearance and social statistics, it does not look the part of the 25th safest Conservative seat in the land.

HEMEL HEMPSTEAD

	2001		1997		1992 notional	
Electorate and turnout	73,602	62.3	71,924	76.6	71,471	81.8
Conservative	17,647	38.5	21,539	39.1	29,248	49.9
Labour	21,389	46.6	25,175	45.7	19,090	32.6
Lib Dem	5,877	12.8	6,789	12.3	9,005	15.4
Anti-EU	970	2.1	1,327	2.4	–	–
Others	–		262		1,313 (3)	
MP	Tony McWalter (Lab)		Tony McWalter (Lab)		Robert Jones (Con)	
					Hertfordshire West	
Majority	3,742	8.2	3,636	6.6	10,158	17.3

Hemel Hempstead has an unusual electoral history. It was a fortress of Conservatism for many years, deviating only in a freak Liberal gain in 1923, until October 1974 when Labour won for the first time. The reason for the trend to the left over such a long time was the growth of the New Town at Hemel Hempstead itself, which caused an influx of working class voters and council tenants. These were people displaced mainly from north west London, around Acton and Willesden. The new town development raised the Labour vote in the town, and raised the electorate in the seat so that boundary reviews gradually cut off more and more outlying Tory territory. Although there was a low swing in 1979, Labour did extremely badly in 1983 and 1987; the Conservatives and the SDP invaded previously solid Labour areas of the New Town. In 1997 there were no other significant elements in the constituency, and a big recovery in Labour support in the New Towns of southern England, which was a recipe for the second Labour victory in Hemel Hempstead.

Hemel Hempstead is fairly middle class for a New Town and has some quite differentiated neighbourhoods. The old town and Boxmoor, near the railway station, tend to the Conservatives, while Labour strike back in the estates such as Gadebridge, Bennetts End and Adeyfield. The Conservatives have remained a viable, competitive force in the area, taking a narrow majority on Dacorum council in 1999 (although their power base lies in the parts of Dacorum in the Herts SW constituency), and looked to the 2001 election with some optimism. This optimism was ill-founded as Labour's Tony McWalter returned with an increased majority, making this yet another prosperous southern seat where Labour did very well in 2001. The Conservatives will regroup and try again to restore their dominant position in Hemel Hempstead.

HERTFORD and STORTFORD

	2001		1997		1992 notional	
Electorate and turnout	75,794	62.2	72,259	75.5	70,578	80.1
Conservative	21,074	44.7	24,027	44.0	31,942	56.5
Labour	15,471	32.8	17,142	31.4	9,529	16.9
Lib Dem	9,388	19.9	9,679	17.7	14,408	25.5
Anti-EU	1,243	2.6	3,338 (2)	6.2	–	–
Others	–		385 (2)		660	
MP	Mark Prisk (Con)		Bowen Wells (Con)		Bowen Wells (Con)	
Majority	5,603	11.9	6,885	12.6	17,534	31.0

The railway line from Liverpool Street to Cambridge meanders back and forward across the boundary between Hertfordshire and Essex, from Broxbourne over to Harlow and then back over the border to run through this seat. Bishop's Stortford is a prosperous market and commuting town very close to Stansted Airport. It is the largest town in the constituency and has sprouted large private estates in recent years, particularly around Thorley in the south west. East Hertfordshire has been the fastest growing district in Hertfordshire in recent years, its population up 16 per cent between 1981 and 1998, and much of this has been in the Bishop's Stortford area. Sawbridgeworth is a similar little town just to the south.

There is a stretch of open country in this constituency to the west as far as the Lea valley at Ware, which almost runs into the county town of Hertford, which is a relatively small town. Hertford and Stortford is a primarily urban seat, although none of the towns are particularly large. Their voting habits are all somewhat similar and support for the parties was distributed relatively evenly across the constituency in 2001. In the local elections Labour and Lib Dems polled 20-30 per cent each in most wards, but the Conservatives prevailed against divided opposition. Labour did rather better in the general election than the locals, and may have led in Hertford. The Conservatives did poorly in 2001, probably in part because the MP since 1979 was stepping down.

HERTFORDSHIRE NORTH EAST

	2001		1997		1992 notional	
Electorate and turnout	68,718	65.0	67,469	77.1	65,875	84.9
Conservative	19,695	44.1	21,712	41.8	28,911	51.7
Labour	16,251	36.4	18,624	35.8	11,908	21.3
Lib Dem	7,686	17.2	9,493	18.3	14,775	26.4
Anti-EU	1,013	2.3	2,166	4.2	–	–
Others	–		–		355	
MP	Oliver Heald (Con)		Oliver Heald (Con)		Oliver Heald (Con) Hertfordshire North	
Majority	3,444	7.7	3,088	5.9	14,136	25.3

Letchworth, the largest town in this constituency, has a distinctive place in the history of town planning. It was the first Garden City, laid out according to the plans of Ebenezer Howard in 1903 to combine the civilised facilities of a town with the environmental benefits of living in the countryside. Letchworth Garden City is composed of pleasant avenues and greens – though few pubs – and has flourishing community activities and craft fairs. Its population is earnest, liberal and middle class and it has the air of a rather refined commune. There is, however, another side to Letchworth, of industrial estates and council housing such as the shabby Jackmans estate in the south east. Letchworth's east side runs together with the neighbouring town of Baldock. Letchworth votes Labour, but by a smaller margin than might be imagined – with Baldock, by a little over 1,000 in the 2001 county elections. Tactical voting by Lib Dems probably boosted this in the general election.

The rest of the seat is inclined to the Conservatives. Royston is a small market town which forms a little Hertfordshire salient surrounded by Cambridgeshire, and there is a swathe of rural territory sweeping around the east side of the Stevenage seat reaching down nearly as far as Hertford, including the rural hinterland of Bishop's Stortford. It is the most rural seat in the county. Although the Liberal Democrats can poll well in the north of the rural area, most of it is true blue and despite Letchworth the seat is a little beyond Labour's grasp even in elections like 1997 and 2001.

HERTFORDSHIRE SOUTH WEST

	2001		*1997*		*1992 notional*	
Electorate and turnout	73,247	64.5	72,276	76.7	*68,566*	*84.2*
Conservative	20,933	44.3	25,462	46.0	*34,189*	*59.2*
Labour	12,752	27.0	15,441	27.9	*10,062*	*17.4*
Lib Dem	12,431	26.3	12,381	22.3	*13,034*	*22.6*
Anti-EU	847	1.8	1,853	3.3	–	–
Others	306		274		*462*	
MP	Richard Page (Con)		Richard Page (Con)		Richard Page (Con)	
Majority	8,181	17.3	10,021	18.1	*21,155*	*36.6*

Hertfordshire South West is a thin, 22-mile long strip of territory on the edge of the county, consisting of the hinterlands of Watford in the south and Hemel Hempstead in the north with rather few links between the two bits. SW is Hertfordshire's part of the Chiltern hills. It is the most upscale constituency in Hertfordshire in its social composition but not the safest Conservative seat any more.

Most of the population of the constituency is in the south, in the Three Rivers district council area centred around Chorleywood and Rickmansworth. These towns are on the Metropolitan Line of the London underground and house a high proportion of London commuters. Chorleywood was a centre of utopian communism during the English Civil War, but it is now tightly contested between Liberal Democrats and Conservatives with Labour – or the Socialist Alliance – nowhere. Rickmansworth is more mixed, the Conservatives predominating. Moor Park lies further in, just across the county boundary from Northwood. There are a couple of outlying suburbs of Watford, too; Croxley to the west is a Lib Dem area and the constituency encompasses a small corridor to the south of Watford, including the Labour-voting but apathetic South Oxhey estate. Turnout in South Oxhey was only 52 per cent in 2001, compared to 69 per cent in Croxley and 73 per cent in Chorleywood.

The northern minority of the seat comes from Dacorum (Hemel Hempstead) borough, consisting of the towns of Tring and Berkhamsted and some Chiltern country areas around them. The towns are quite closely contested between Tories and Lib Dems, but the country is strongly Conservative. If people voted the same way in general elections as they do locally, the seat would be vulnerable to the Lib Dems, but about a fifth of their local voters choose Labour or the Conservatives nationally. Herts SW resembles Buckinghamshire just across the boundary in its political preferences as well as social and geographical make-up, the whole making a safe Conservative seat in anything other than by-election conditions.

HERTSMERE

	2001		1997		1992 notional	
Electorate and turnout	68,853	60.3	68,093	73.9	66,079	79.6
Conservative	19,855	47.8	22,305	44.3	30,439	57.8
Labour	14,953	36.0	19,230	38.2	11,473	21.8
Lib Dem	6,300	15.2	6,466	12.8	10,364	19.7
Anti-EU	–	–	2,156 (2)	4.3	–	–
Others	397		191		347	
MP	James Clappison (Con)		James Clappison (Con)		James Clappison (Con)	
Majority	4,902	11.8	3,075	6.1	18,966	36.0

Hertsmere lies just outside the boundary of Greater London. The constituency was assembled in 1974 out of spare bits, left across the county boundary, from the former seats of Barnet and Enfield West. Hertsmere is composed of suburbia of varying types.

It has some of the most affluent and comfortable outer suburbia in the country, around Potters Bar. Aldenham East has the distinction of being the least deprived ward in England, and Hertsmere has two other wards in the top 100– Heath South and Potters Bar North. Potters Bar is a suburban commuter town. As well as this elite territory, Hertsmere also includes the large council-built estates, amounting to a small new town, at Borehamwood. Borehamwood runs into Elstree, noted for being one of the important centres of the film industry in Britain. Bushey, just south of Watford, is a more traditional outer suburb, with a significant Jewish population. While Borehamwood is Labour but prone to low turnout, and Bushey is Lib Dem at least in local elections, a lot of the rest is normally very Tory. Labour, astonishingly, had overall control of Hertsmere council in the mid 1990s and came quite close to winning the parliamentary seat in 1997, but fell back in 2001 as Borehamwood failed to come out to vote. The Conservatives have the edge in Hertsmere.

HITCHIN and HARPENDEN

	2001		*1997*		*1992 notional*	
Electorate and turnout	67,196	66.9	67,219	78.0	*66,883*	*81.3*
Conservative	21,271	47.3	24,038	45.9	*33,402*	*61.4*
Labour	14,608	32.5	17,367	33.1	*9,711*	*17.9*
Lib Dem	8,076	18.0	10,515	20.1	*10,766*	*19.8*
Anti-EU	606	1.3	–	–	–	–
Others	363		507 (2)		*498*	
MP	Peter Lilley (Con)		Peter Lilley (Con)		NEW SEAT	
Majority	6,663	14.8	6,671	12.7	*22,636*	*41.6*

Hitchin and Harpenden is an odd new seat created in 1997, combining two towns that have relatively little to do with each other. Its residents would not thank the authors for noting that their main common feature amounts to links with Luton. Peter Lilley wisely followed the Harpenden portion of his old seat, St. Albans, when the new seat was created and saved himself from joining seven of his Cabinet colleagues in losing his seat.

Harpenden is an extremely middle class commuter town set between St. Albans and Luton; all of its four wards are among the least deprived 5 per cent of England but the West Common is the best area even of this select town. Harpenden was recently revealed as housing Britain's greatest concentration of millionaires. It has 21,000 electors, who voted 51 per cent Conservative and 30 per cent Lib Dem in the 2001 county elections. The town brings with it a Conservative stretch of countryside north of St. Albans, including the large, plush villages of Wheathampstead and Redbourn where there are few Labour voters. The market and commuter town of Hitchin has 29,000 electors. The town is on the main rail line in the north of Hertfordshire, to the east of Luton, and is less of a single-class township. Hitchin is the principal source of Labour strength in this constituency. Even so, the Conservatives still led 42-38 in its three county wards in 2001.

This is a very safe Conservative seat, which withstood an enormous swing to Labour in 1997 (15 per cent if the boundary estimate for 1992 was correct) and still left Peter Lilley with a relatively comfortable majority. Lilley slightly improved his position in 2001 against Alan Amos, formerly the Conservative MP for Hexham, who fought this seat for Labour.

ST. ALBANS

	2001		1997		1992 notional	
Electorate and turnout	66,040	66.3	65,560	77.5	64,771	79.8
Conservative	15,423	35.2	16,879	33.2	23,586	45.7
Labour	19,889	45.4	21,338	42.0	12,932	25.0
Lib Dem	7,847	17.9	10,692	21.0	14,452	28.0
Anti-EU	602	1.4	1,619	3.2	–	–
Others	–		277 (2)		690	
MP	Kerry Pollard (Lab)		Kerry Pollard (Lab)		Peter Lilley (Con)	
Majority	4,466	10.2	4,459	8.8	9,134	17.7

St. Albans is a very affluent, prosperous place, a traditional city in a very modern county. It is a historic place, with the ruins of Roman Verulam and a fine cathedral, and its fast rail links into the City make it a favoured location for the discerning commuter as well as a centre in its own right. Its demographics and place in relation to London are quite similar to Guildford. This makes it sound a rather Conservative town, probably with a Liberal Democrat presence, and this is what it seemed until 1997 when Labour pulled off a stunning victory, surging from a bad third to a clear first.

St. Albans includes some solid Labour areas such as Ashley and Sopwell on the edge of the city, and the large council-built estate of London Colney. Sopwell in the south of the city is the most deprived ward in St. Albans, but it still belongs in the least deprived 50 per cent of England. The central wards are hard fought between Labour and the Lib Dems, who dominate even well-off parts of the city, but St. Stephen's to the south west is fought between Lib Dems and Tories. The Conservative Party is surprisingly feeble in this high-class little city even in local elections when they do well elsewhere, as in May 2000, a sign that they have a real problem in St. Albans and might not be able to rely on any national swing to recover the constituency. Labour has now won two successive elections here with fairly comfortable majorities, proving that the party's appeal is definitely no longer dependent on poverty and disadvantage. It was the Labour constituency with the lowest unemployment in May 2001 (0.8 per cent).

STEVENAGE

	2001		1997		1992 notional	
Electorate and turnout	69,897	60.7	67,086	76.6	67,015	81.8
Conservative	13,459	31.7	16,858	32.8	24,078	43.9
Labour	22,025	51.9	28,440	55.3	21,159	38.6
Lib Dem	6,027	14.2	4,588	8.9	9,379	17.1
Anti-EU	-	-	1,194	2.3	–	–
Others	942 (3)		306 (2)		220	
MP	Barbara Follett (Lab)		Barbara Follett (Lab)		Tim Wood (Con)	
Majority	8,566	20.2	11,582	22.5	2,919	5.3

Stevenage was the first post war New Town and it is generally regarded as one of the most successful. It lies in mid Hertfordshire, up the A1 and King's Cross main line from London, and as well as having its own industries has become an acceptable refuge for people priced out of London property. The modern town centre is ringed by residential neighbourhoods on three sides and to the west, by the A1M, is a long strip of industrial and commercial territory. Engineering, pharmaceuticals, armaments and chemicals are represented here – Stevenage has large Du Pont and Glaxo Wellcome facilities. The north of the town, around Old Stevenage, is the smartest area. Plans have frequently been drawn up to extend the town to the west, and if approved this time round about 4,000 new houses will appear.

Stevenage has a volatile history, providing a (Labour) political base for Shirley Williams from 1964 until her surprising defeat in 1979 at the hands of the Conservatives. In the 1980s Stevenage was one of the few places where the SDP had a strong appeal without much of a prior Liberal tradition – the new party almost won the seat in 1983 and polled well in 1987. However, Labour stayed in control of the borough in local elections and re-emerged as the main challenger to the Tories in 1992 before their massive victory in 1997 with a swing of nearly 14 per cent. Labour had no trouble holding support in the 1997-2001 parliament, still leading well in the 1999 Euro election and the 2000 locals. However, Labour's victory in 2001 was a little less emphatic, with a big drop in turnout and the return to the Lib Dems of people who had cast tactical votes for Labour in 1997.

In local elections the only Tory ward is Woodfield, on the far north of the town, and the Lib Dems win Manor, in the east. All the rest are Labour, sometimes overwhelmingly, and the other parties did not offer full slates of candidates in May 2000. Stevenage, with 60,000 electors, is not quite big enough for its own parliamentary seat and extends out to a few villages in the surrounding area such as Walkern and Knebworth, where the Conservatives lead Labour by better than two to one, but there are only 10,000 electors in this section of the seat.

Stevenage was notable in the 2001 general election for the scale of postal voting which took place – a third of the votes were cast by post, and 40 per cent of the borough electorate have registered for permanent postal votes. It is estimated that turnout among those receiving postal votes was 74 per cent, while turnout among the remainder was a little over 50 per cent.

WATFORD

	2001		1997		1992 notional	
Electorate and turnout	75,872	61.1	74,015	74.6	72,192	81.1
Conservative	15,437	33.3	19,227	34.8	28,159	48.1
Labour	20,992	45.3	25,019	45.3	19,896	34.0
Lib Dem	8,088	17.4	9,272	16.8	9,807	16.8
Anti-EU	535	1.2	1,484	2.7	–	–
Others	1,320 (2)		234		673	
MP	Claire Ward (Lab)		Claire Ward (Lab)		Tristan Garel-Jones (Con)	
Majority	5,555	12.0	5,792	10.5	8,263	14.1

Watford, lying within the M25 London orbital motorway, is hardly to be distinguished from outer London towns like Kingston and Romford, but the county boundary puts it into Hertfordshire. It has a railway history, but its most famous industries lately have been betting – the Camelot group which runs the National Lottery is based in Watford and residents were pleased that it retained the franchise – competitor Richard Branson runs the unpopular West Coast train service that runs through Watford. Ladbrokes UK are also based here.

Politically, the seat has a history of being a crucial marginal with something of a tradition of disappointing the Conservatives – it voted Labour in 1951 when a Conservative gain was expected, and stayed Labour in 1970 as well. From 1979 to 1997 it was the base of Tristan Garel-Jones, a clever player of the Westminster game with a colourful turn of phrase, and on his retirement swung decisively with the tide and elected Labour's Claire Ward. Ward, elected at the age of 24, was just finishing a term as Mayor of the town of Elstree and Boreham Wood having already served on Labour's NEC – a very early start to a political career.

Watford borough has 60,000 electors, rather too small to have a constituency of its own. The parliamentary seat includes a few wards from Three Rivers council to make up numbers. These inclusions are Abbots Langley and Leavesden to the north and Carpenders Park and Oxhey Hall to the south; they are all sensible additions as they are suburbs with strong links to Watford. The borough area is marginally Labour, but the party runs third in the Three Rivers wards. There is a strong Liberal Democrat vote in local elections which fails to come across in general elections; in 2001 this increment split two to one in Labour's favour.

Watford is a rather average seat, with many indicators being close to the national level; this attracted some Labour focus group research in 1997. It is a mixed town, with down-at-heel Victorian terraces in the town centre, Thirties suburbia all around it, and a high-class residential area in the west of town around Cassiobury Park. Watford has the only substantial element of non-white population in Hertfordshire. Except in 1951 and 1970 it has gone with the national trend since 1931. The Watford result was fairly close to the national result in 2001, although Labour's vote was rather higher than in the country at large. The Conservatives need to be back in contention in Watford if they are to be nationally competitive again.

WELWYN HATFIELD

	2001		1997		1992 notional	
Electorate and turnout	67,004	63.9	67,395	78.6	68,502	83.3
Conservative	17,288	40.4	19,341	36.5	27,139	47.5
Labour	18,484	43.2	24,936	47.1	20,556	36.0
Lib Dem	6,021	14.1	7,161	13.5	9,147	16.0
Anti-EU	798	1.9	–	–	–	–
Others	230		1,530 (2)		247	
MP	Melanie Johnson (Lab)		Melanie Johnson (Lab)		David Evans (Con)	
Majority	1,196	2.8	5,595	10.6	6,583	11.5

Welwyn Hatfield has been a complex and volatile constituency since it was created in 1974; it has changed hands in October 1974, 1979 and 1997, and Labour sank into third place in 1983 and 1987. As the name suggests, it is made up of several distinct parts.

Hatfield is smaller and shabbier than the other London area New Towns; south Hatfield feels more like an overspill estate than a community in its own right. In the past an aviation centre, Hatfield now depends on education (the University of Hertfordshire) and shopping (the vast American style Galleria mall). Hatfield also contains an attractive district, Old Hatfield, nestling in feudal fashion below Hatfield House. Lord Salisbury would often run the country from Hatfield House when Prime Minister, and Hatfield's connection with aristocratic Toryism continues through Lord Cranborne. Hatfield New Town's ordinary voters, however, are mainly Labour.

Welwyn has more liberal ideological roots. It is in three parts; an old village, the early 20th Century Garden City and the post war New Town. The Garden City was the dream of social reformer Ebenezer Howard, who is commemorated in the form of a large shopping centre next to the rail station. Howard laid out a town centre of surprising beauty, and the Garden City is full of cottages and tree-lined avenues. Politically, the old village in the north is very Tory, the Garden City to the west of the railway line rather less so, and the New Town to the east mainly Labour. There is considerable industry tucked away, including major ICI and Roche pharmaceutical facilities. The seat also includes outlying Tory areas such as the commuter town of Brookmans Park. As a whole, Welwyn Hatfield is more middle class than Stevenage.

Welwyn Hatfield is a reproach to simplistic demographic theories about political change. The Conservative victories were despite council tenants making up the majority of the population at the time of the 1981 census; much has now been sold off but Labour's vote has increased during that process. It is a volatile seat of skilled working and middle-middle class white people, and can never be taken for granted. It recently displayed its tendency to go its own way by, uniquely, changing over to Labour control in the May 2000 local elections. Despite this, it was one of the better results in 2001 for the Conservatives with a swing of 3.9 per cent in their favour that made it extremely marginal (they also regained the council in 2002). It is the Labour seat 7th most vulnerable to the Conservatives, and Melanie Johnson is currently the minister with the shakiest individual majority.

Humberside   (former county of)

	Conservative		Labour		Liberal Democrat		Others	
	Share of vote	Seats	Share of vote	Seats	Share of vote	Seats	Share of vote	Seats
2001	32.8	3	46.7	7	17.1	0	3.4	0
1997	30.4	3	50.4	7	15.8	0	3.3	0
1992	41.7	4	40.3	5	17.4	0	0.6	0
1987	41.9	4	34.8	5	23.1	0	0.2	0
1983	43.9	5	29.2	4	26.8	0	0.2	0

Humberside was arguably the most unpopular of all of the 1970s creations, and the last local government review finally put it out of its misery by dividing it into four unitary authorities, effectively reviving the old division along the Humber. The two segments of Humberside never had that much in common apart from the graceful white elephant that is the Humber Bridge, and the speed with which the new unitary councils renamed themselves after their original (pre-1973) areas was an indication of the strong feelings of local identity which have persisted. To the north there is now a unitary council for the city of Hull, surrounded by the 'East Riding of Yorkshire', which is in fact a little smaller than the original (the eastern area of Selby and the southern fringes of Ryedale having been assimilated into North Yorkshire). To the south, the two new authorities named themselves 'North Lincolnshire' and 'North East Lincolnshire' respectively, something made even more confusing by the fact that their slimmed-down mother county to the south survived the 1990s reforms intact.

This is very much an isolated and unknown part of the country. At the end of the M62 motorway, Hull (it is rarely referred to by its complete 'Kingston-upon-Hull' name) is a large city of almost 300,000 inhabitants, which is a major port and ferry terminal as well as containing a reasonably successful university and remarkably unsuccessful football team; Hull is the largest city in England never to have hosted football in the top division. The city can boast a certain distinctiveness, perhaps resulting from its geographical isolation; it has a separate telephone system from the rest of the country and its old-style phone boxes are white rather than red, it has two competing rugby league teams and the football ground even has six floodlight pylons rather than the regulation four. Hull undoubtedly has its problems – no fewer than ten of its twenty wards are in the bottom 10 per cent for multiple deprivation and unemployment remains relatively high. Turnout rates in elections can be dire, though when people do come out to vote, it tends to be for Labour, who have held all the parliamentary seats since 1964.

East Riding is a very different sort of area. Just outside of Hull's boundaries can be found expanding middle class suburbs such as Hessle and Cottingham, while a few miles north is the charming town of Beverley, dominated by its Minster; its town square and intimate streets resembling a miniature version of York. The rest of the area, as even the council publicity admits, is a secret to most. Flat landscapes are the home to a generally agricultural area, with the occasional small town such as Driffield relieving the monotony. The east coast feels like an awfully long way from anywhere, with old-fashioned towns like Bridlington, Hornsea and Withernsea having higher than average retired populations, a few beaches and the odd caravan park. This part of the coast is bordered by the equally dramatic cliffs of Flamborough Head in the north and several-mile long sandy spit of Spurn Head to the south, which guards the entrance to the still busy Humber estuary.

Politically, East Riding is a solid area of blue in most elections, forming the start of the chain of Conservative seats which extends right across the country to the west coast, but here at least this hides a great deal of diversity. Labour slashed the Tory majority in Beverley and Holderness to 1,200 in 1997, even reducing this further in 2001, while David Davis also saw his majority in Haltemprice and Howden cut to 2,000 in 2001, this time by the Liberal Democrats. Assuming a national recovery, those figures should rise somewhat next time, though Davis remains vulnerable to a further Lib Dem squeeze of Labour voters. The third seat, Yorkshire East, is the safest, though even this was in the news during the 2001 campaign because of the views of its retiring MP John Townend and the issue of whether or not he would be disciplined by his party leadership for holding them.

South of the Humber, the largish industrial towns of Grimsby and Scunthorpe are strongly Labour. At the end of the forty-mile long M180 motorway and A180 dual carriageway, Grimsby is a major fishing port, with a large nearby refinery at Immingham, but like Hull it has higher than average unemployment and pockets of serious deprivation. Scunthorpe has been reliant on its steelworks for many years, but is closer to the larger population and alternative employment over the border in Yorkshire and is thus better placed if this were to shut down completely. Both of these towns have been Labour since 1945, with the short interlude of 1979-87 in Scunthorpe, and should remain that way. Less expected were the 1997 Labour gains of Cleethorpes and particularly Brigg & Goole, which cover much of the land area of North East and North Lincolnshire. Cleethorpes is a classic fading English seaside resort; a larger version of Mablethorpe, Ingoldmells and Skegness down the coast. As with many such places it traditionally voted Conservative, then swung to Labour somewhat dramatically in the 1990s, and so far has not swung back. Brigg and Goole is a patchwork of a constituency, linking a large rural chunk of North East Lincs with the town of Goole, a small port just beyond the point at which the Humber divides into Trent and Ouse. Goole is actually in East Riding, and though previously in the Conservative Boothferry seat, is a Labour town - but this was an unanticipated gain in 1997 and remains vulnerable to a Tory recovery. It is the most obvious marginal within the Humberside, or as it now seems to be called 'Humber' area and will again be under the spotlight in 2005/6.

Local government

It was all change in 1995, with four all-purpose unitary authorities replacing the old county council and a number of small districts. East Riding of Yorkshire took in the territory of all of the northern districts except Hull, namely Holderness, 'East Yorkshire' (which was previously known as East Wolds), Beverley and Boothferry. Although Holderness was previously Independent-controlled, the other districts were generally Conservative, so it was a bit of a surprise that the new council was well and truly hung, with all three main parties boasting reasonably strong groups. This remained the case in 1999, and although Labour dropped to 12 councillors, the Liberal Democrats have only five fewer than the Tories. Hull was solidly Labour for a long time and after 1999, Labour could still boast over fifty of the sixty representatives in the city, though this was to drop the following year after a number of wards were gained by the Lib Dems. However this was but a minor tremor compared witht he electoral earthquake of 2002, when in all-out elections Labour lost about 20 seats along with control of the city. South of the Humber, both of the two new unitaries had slim Labour majorities in 1999. North Lincolnshire, based on Scunthorpe and the surrounding rural areas, is a straight urban Labour versus rural Conservative contest - the former Scunthorpe council was always Labour and its six wards elected a full complement of 18 Labour councillors in 1999. The surrounding areas, much of which was previously part of Glanford, are almost as strong for the Tories, with 19 elected in 1999, though critically Labour also scraped five seats, giving them control of the council. North East Lincolnshire is made up of the former boroughs of Great Grimsby and Cleethorpes (including a couple of surrounding rural wards), and is a little more diverse, with a handful of Lib Dems and Independents elected in 1999, fewer Conservatives and an equally precarious Labour majority.

Boundary review

Somewhat oddly, the boundary commission failed to follow public sentiment by announcing a timetable which continued to deal with the two parts of Humberside together, rather than taking the 'three Lincolnshires' at the same time. As a result of this decision, recommendations for parliamentary boundaries in Lincolnshire (the slimmed down 1970s version) have already been finalised, while North and North East will not even be considered until 2003. Because these areas are only entitled to 3.4 seats, they will still need to be paired with East Riding (entitled to 3.5), and as a result Brigg and Goole, which straddles the two areas, looks set to survive. The alternative would be a reduction to three parliamentary seats south of the Humber and six to the north; this would create larger constituencies and be bad news for Labour, as not only would they lose a seat, but Scunthorpe would be significantly weakened. The likelier scenario is the first, with only minor changes to equalise electorates.

BEVERLEY and HOLDERNESS

	2001		1997		1992 notional	
Electorate and turnout	74,741	62.0	72,049	72.9	69,161	79.1
Conservative	19,168	41.3	21,629	41.2	29,800	54.5
Labour	18,387	39.6	20,418	38.9	10,981	20.1
Lib Dem	7,356	15.9	9,689	18.4	13,843	25.3
Anti–EU	1,464	3.2	695	1.3	–	–
Others	–		111		62	
MP	James Cran (Con)		James Cran (Con)		NEW SEAT	
Majority	781	1.7	1,211	2.3	15,957	29.2

Beverley and Holderness was created in 1997, linking the Minster town just outside Hull with a swathe of surrounding territory as far as the east coast, running from Hornsea in the north to the long sandy spit of Spurn Head in the south. Prior to 1997, there had been a separate Beverley seat, which extended from the town westwards, while Holderness was included in Bridlington. Both of these constituencies were overwhelmingly Conservative; their majorities exceeded 16,000 in each in 1992, with Labour in third place. As a result, it was assumed that the new seat would be safely Tory as well, but in the event a huge 19 per cent advance by Labour left them just over 1,200 behind James Cran, a margin which was then reduced further in 2001. Part of this may have been a coastal seat effect – Holderness includes the seaside resorts of Hornsea and Withernsea - and the 1997 swing here was very much in line with that up the coast in Scarborough and Whitby and indeed many other seaside constituencies up and down the country. Another part of the huge swing however must have occurred in Beverley itself, which is ringed by new housing estates of the sort where the 'New Labour' (as opposed to old Labour) appeal seems to be at its greatest.

The whole constituency now finds itself part of the re-invented East Riding of Yorkshire unitary authority, and in 1999 there was surprising diversity to its council election outcomes. Between them, the two large southern Holderness wards (east of Hull) returned two Conservatives, two Liberal Democrats, one Labour and one Independent councillor, which marked an improvement for the Tories since 1995. Mid Holderness is held by the Lib Dems, while North Holderness is a strong Tory area, as is the rural area around Beverley. Labour hit back in Beverley Minster (the town itself), where they picked up over half of the vote in 1999, while the neighbouring St Mary's ward is marginal between everyone, with the Tories slightly ahead.

The very mixed pattern of local council results reinforces the impression that Labour have done extraordinarily well here (and the Tories incredibly badly) for the margin to get as close as it did in the 1997 and 2001 general elections. Although this is currently the Conservatives' 5th most vulnerable seat in Britain, it would be a disaster if they actually managed to lose it.

BRIGG and GOOLE

	2001		1997		1992 notional	
Electorate and turnout	64,647	63.5	64,073	73.0	63,013	81.2
Conservative	16,105	39.2	17,104	36.5	25,499	49.8
Labour	20,066	48.9	23,493	50.2	18,258	35.7
Lib Dem	3,796	9.2	4,692	10.0	7,406	14.5
Anti–EU	688	1.7	1,513	3.2	–	–
Others	399		–		–	
MP	Ian Cawsey (Lab)		Ian Cawsey (Lab)		David Davis (Con) Boothferry	
Majority	3,961	9.6	6,389	13.7	7,241	14.2

Brigg and Goole is a somewhat curious constituency and another to be created at the last boundary review. It is the only seat which straddles the two parts of former Humberside, taking in a chunk of the old constituency and local government borough of Boothferry, centred on the town of Goole itself and now part of the East Riding of Yorkshire unitary authority, but also a large part of what is now North Lincolnshire, reaching as far as Epworth on the other side of the M180 motorway and east to the small town of Brigg. To reach this semi-detached part of the constituency one needs to travel around (or more likely through) the town of Scunthorpe. In fact Brigg had been linked with Scunthorpe for parliamentary purposes in the past, though it was then connected with Cleethorpes before continuing its wanderings into the present constituency.

Labour's victory in 1997 was something of a surprise, although it was one of the most winnable of the many non-targeted seats gained. There are strong Labour areas in Goole (very much a working class town) as well as an unusually strong rural Labour vote in some of the nearby villages. The Conservatives hit back in South Axholme as well as in Brigg, and they were probably just about ahead overall in the 1999 local council elections. In the 2001 general election, the Conservatives were to make little headway, though a modest two per cent swing in their favour did at least slightly reduce Ian Cawsey's majority. This is now one of 57 Labour-held seats where their majority is below 10 per cent, and is bound to again be targeted by the Tories next time around.

CLEETHORPES

	2001		1997		1992 notional	
Electorate and turnout	68,392	62.0	68,763	73.4	68,355	78.0
Conservative	15,412	36.3	16,882	33.4	25,582	48.0
Labour	21,032	49.6	26,058	51.6	19,169	35.9
Lib Dem	5,080	12.0	5,746	11.4	7,833	14.7
Anti–EU	894	2.1	1,787	3.5	–	–
Green	–	–	–	–	751	1.4
MP	Shona McIsaac (Lab)		Shona McIsaac (Lab)		Michael Brown (Con) Brigg & Cleethorpes	
Majority	5,620	13.2	9,176	18.2	6,413	12.0

Cleethorpes was another of the many seaside towns which fell to Labour after a huge swing in 1997, former Wandsworth councillor Shona McIsaac defeating the MP for Brigg and Cleethorpes Michael Brown, now a political journalist, by over 9,000 votes. As in similar constituencies elsewhere in the country, the area had already started to move away from its traditional allegiance in previous elections, with Labour's vote advancing in 1992 by fully 12 per cent, three times the national average.

As well as Cleethorpes itself, the seat takes in Barton-upon-Humber some miles to the north west (the southern entrance to the Humber Bridge) as well as the rather ugly port and refinery of Immingham, before curling around Grimsby to take in a number of more pleasant and affluent villages to the west and south. It is this part of the constituency, the 'Wold Parishes' and Humberston, which see the strongest Conservative vote, while Labour picks up plenty of support in Cleethorpes itself, particularly in the terraced streets around Grimsby Town FC (who technically play in Cleethorpes rather than Grimsby). Overall, Labour led narrowly in the 1999 council elections, and then survived a modest 2.5 per cent swing back to the Tories in 2001. The constituency will undoubtedly see another tough battle next time, as it remains one of Labour's hundred most marginal seats.

GREAT GRIMSBY

	2001		1997		1992 actual	
Electorate and turnout	63,157	52.3	65,216	66.1	67,427	75.3
Conservative	7,634	23.1	9,521	22.1	18,391	36.2
Labour	19,118	57.9	25,765	59.8	25,897	51.0
Lib Dem	6,265	19.0	7,810	18.1	6,475	12.8
MP	Austin Mitchell (Lab)		Austin Mitchell (Lab)		Austin Mitchell (Lab)	
Majority	11,484	34.8	16,244	37.7	7,506	14.8

The town of Grimsby feels like a long way from the rest of the country, but remains a major fishing port and frozen food centre, with a large docks area surrounding a striking 350-foot high Italianate 'fish tower'. Inland, Grimsby is not without its problems – there is still plenty of unemployment and real social deprivation here, and two wards are in the most deprived 300 in the country. This may well have influenced Grimsby's most famous MP, Tony Crosland, who represented the town between 1959 and 1977. His death led to a by-election which, unusually for the time, was actually held by Labour. The winning candidate was former journalist Austin Mitchell, who has been MP ever since and is one of the few Labour members to take a Eurosceptic viewpoint; he is also probably the only MP (of any party) to write a book of Yorkshire jokes.

Labour's majority has steadily increased in Grimsby – they won it for the very first time in 1945, Crosland held it by just 101 votes at his first contest in 1959, and Mitchell's margin in 1983 was 731. These days it looks very safe, with the Liberal Democrats now starting to challenge the Conservatives for second place. The last council elections (1999) saw the Lib Dems win Park ward by miles – also sharing the representation in Yarborough and getting quite close in a couple of others. Labour win their share of wards, but were having problems in 1999 with Independents in the deprived Marsh ward (which covers much of the docks area), and lost Scartho, more or less a separate settlement south of the centre, to the Conservatives. For the moment this has not fed through to their general election performances, with only a very slight percentage movement away from Labour in 2001.

HALTEMPRICE and HOWDEN

	2001		1997		1992 notional	
Electorate and turnout	66,733	65.8	65,685	75.4	64,046	79.2
Conservative	18,994	43.2	21,809	44.0	30,085	59.3
Labour	6,898	15.7	11,701	23.6	7,774	15.3
Lib Dem	17,091	38.9	14,295	28.8	12,772	25.2
Anti–EU	945	2.2	1,671 (2)	3.4	–	–
Others	–		74		110	
MP	David Davis (Con)		David Davis (Con)		James Cran (Con)	
					Beverley	
Majority	1,903	4.3	7,514	15.2	17,313	34.1

David Davis was a surprise contender for the Conservative Party leadership in 2001, but just weeks earlier survived by less than 2,000 votes as the Liberal Democrats dramatically squeezed Labour's vote in his constituency to advance by over 10 percentage points. Haltemprice and Howden is essentially the successor to Beverley (without the town itself), which had been Conservative by 16,500 in 1992 – its reversion to the original name of Haltemprice (which was the fictional location of Alan B'stard's constituency in *The New Statesman*) was not expected to hurt the Tories, if anything the reverse. Then came the 1997 landslide, with the swing away from the Conservatives here even greater than the national average, though masked by a divided opposition. In 2001, the Liberal Democrats clearly persuaded electors that they were the clear challengers, and they will now see this as a real target.

The Lib Dems' 2001 advance came on the back of earlier successes in local government elections. In 1999, they held Howden (the other part of the constituency name) with almost two-thirds of the vote, and they also won four of the five wards in the seat which lie just outside of Hull's boundaries, including Tranby and Wolfreton with about 60 per cent of the vote. This segment of the constituency contains what appears to be only a small slice of its overall area, but in fact around two thirds of the seat's electors – overall the Lib Dems led here by about 7.5 per cent in 1999, with the Labour vote heavily squeezed. The Conservatives do better in the larger rural wards of Dale and Howdenshire to the west, but they will need to regain a greater share of Hull's middle class commuter vote if Davis is to enjoy more comfortable majorities in the future.

HULL EAST

	2001		1997		1992 actual	
Electorate and turnout	66,397	46.5	68,400	59.2	69,078	69.3
Conservative	4,276	13.8	5,552	13.7	11,373	23.8
Labour	19,938	64.6	28,870	71.3	30,096	62.9
Lib Dem	4,613	14.9	3,965	9.8	6,050	12.6
Anti–EU	1,218	3.9	1,788	4.4	–	–
Others	830		311 (2)		323	
MP	John Prescott (Lab)		John Prescott (Lab)		John Prescott (Lab)	
Majority	15,325	49.6	23,318	57.6	18,723	39.1

Labour's Deputy Leader has his parliamentary base in the appropriate location (for a former seaman) of Hull East. This is the most working class of Hull's three seats; it includes industrial areas alongside the docks, while near the centre are rows of terraced streets, and further out can be found several council estates – in 1991, over 40 per cent of homes in the constituency were still rented from the local authority.

Unsurprisingly in view of its character, Hull East has been continually held by Labour since 1935, and by Prescott since 1970. In February 1974 he polled more than 40,000 votes, and although tallies have fallen since, he has come nowhere near losing, with a majority exceeding 10,000 even in 1983. In the mid-1990s, Labour were piling up enormous majorities in local contests: over 80 per cent of the vote in Longhill and Marfleet wards in 1995, a year in which they won all 21 council seats within the constituency, by margins of over 1,000 votes in all but a single case. In 1997 it was Labour's 29th safest seat nationally, but since then they have lost council seats in Drypool ward to the Lib Dems, and their total local election vote fell from about 12,500 (in 1995) down to 6,500 (in 2000), even before the local meltdown of 2002 (though most wards retained in the city that year were in the East). In 2001 Labour lost 9,000 votes and 7 percentage points. Despite this, Hull East remains a very safe seat for the Deputy Prime Minister.

HULL NORTH

	2001		1997		1992 actual	
Electorate and turnout	62,938	45.5	68,091	57.0	71,395	66.7
Conservative	4,902	17.1	5,837	15.0	11,235	23.6
Labour	16,364	57.2	25,542	65.8	26,619	55.9
Lib Dem	5,643	19.7	5,667	14.6	9,504	20.0
Anti–EU	655	2.3	1,533	4.0	–	–
Others	1,069 (3)		215		254	
MP	Kevin McNamara (Lab)		Kevin McNamara (Lab)		Kevin McNamara (Lab)	
Majority	10,721	37.4	19,705	50.8	15,384	32.3

According to recent figures, Hull North actually contains more poor areas than East; two of Britain's 70 most deprived wards can be found here. One of these, the splendidly named council estate ward of Noddle Hill (now renamed Bransholme East), had a turnout of just 11 per cent in the 2000 local elections. When they do bother to vote, these areas have been heavily Labour, but the constituency also includes more up-market areas around the city's pleasant University. With the general leftward drift of academics and students over the last twenty or thirty years, the inclusion of this area has not caused Labour too much damage in general elections – indeed it has probably contributed to what is a significant swing towards them since the 1950s, when Hull North returned Conservative MPs.

In local contests, however, it is now a different matter; in 2002 the Liberal Democrats were able to win six wards, including the confusingly named Beverley (off the Beverley Road rather than in the separate town) and also Avenue and University. There were already indications of what was to follow in 2001, with quite a sharp swing away from Labour, and the Lib Dems taking second place. None of this as yet threatens Kevin McNamara, who has been MP here since a famous by-election in 1966, the campaign arguably leading to the building of the Humber Bridge, and the result almost certainly prompting Harold Wilson to call a general election, which Labour went on to win handsomely.

HULL WEST and HESSLE

	2001		1997		1992 notional	
Electorate and turnout	63,035	45.9	65,349	58.7	66,996	67.3
Conservative	5,929	20.5	6,933	18.1	13,634	30.3
Labour	16,880	58.4	22,520	58.7	23,251	51.6
Lib Dem	4,364	15.1	6,995	18.2	7,837	17.4
Anti–EU	878	3.0	1,596	4.2	–	–
Others	865 (2)		310		335	
MP	Alan Johnson (Lab)		Alan Johnson (Lab)		Stuart Randall (Lab) Hull West	
Majority	10,951	37.9	15,525	40.5	9,617	21.3

Hull West has been Labour since its re-appearance in 1955, and like the other seats in the city is a stronghold for the party, even after the addition of two wards outside the city's boundaries in 1997. The effect of this was estimated to reduce the Labour share by six per cent, but it is difficult to notice now, and the seat has even become a little safer than Hull North after 2001. In fact Hessle, to the west of Hull and now a part of the East Riding of Yorkshire, elects Liberal Democrat councillors, but Labour are ahead of the Conservatives in local elections, and attract many of the Lib Dem voters as well when it comes to national contests. The nearby (but within the city limits) Boothferry ward is of a similar residential character, but beyond the decaying football ground, the territory becomes different. Terraced streets and the odd tower block predominate on the way to Hull 'Paragon' railway station and the city centre – all the wards in this area are usually Labour, and two of them are in the 150 most deprived in the country, though there has been some recent redevelopment at the quayside on the south side of the centre.

Since 1997, the Labour MP here has been Alan Johnson, former leader of the Communication Workers Union, who rose to ministerial rank after June 2001. His result in the most recent general election was markedly better than that in the other two Hull seats, possibly because of the large middle class element in the constituency, or alternatively because of a first-time incumbency effect. Whatever the cause, there is no doubt that Johnson has a safe base from which to launch a ministerial career.

SCUNTHORPE

	2001		1997		1992 notional	
Electorate and turnout	59,367	56.6	60,393	68.8	62,268	76.4
Conservative	9,724	28.9	10,934	26.3	17,467	35.9
Labour	20,096	59.8	25,107	60.4	26,370	54.3
Lib Dem	3,156	9.4	3,497	8.4	3,727	7.7
Anti–EU	–	–	1,637	3.9	–	–
Others	649 (2)		399		1,035	
MP	Elliot Morley (Lab)		Elliot Morley (Lab)		Elliot Morley (Lab)	
					Glanford & Scunthorpe	
Majority	10,372	30.8	14,173	34.1	8,903	18.3

Scunthorpe is a large steel town off the M180 motorway on the way to Grimsby, but its predominantly industrial and working class character has not automatically meant that it has always returned Labour MPs. This was because for many years the town was linked for parliamentary purposes with its smaller neighbour of Brigg, which is in a Conservative-supporting area to the east. The constituency was won for the first time by Labour in 1929, and then again from 1935, but in 1959 the majority was as low as 2,000, and twenty years later it was regained by the Conservatives by the margin of 486 votes. The transfer of Brigg to Cleethorpes in 1983 might have been expected to end Labour's problems (Tory MP Michael Brown even followed a minority of his electors out of the seat), but this was not to be due to the party's general weakness in the early 1980s. The renamed 'Glanford and Scunthorpe' returned another Conservative MP in 1983, the margin this time 637, and even when it was finally regained by Labour in 1987, Elliot Morley's first majority was only just over 500.

Scunthorpe's days as a marginal came to an end in 1992, when a nine per cent advance in Labour's vote saw them pile up a majority exceeding 8,000, which seemed rather more fitting for a place like this. In 1997 that figure increased to over 14,000, and even after a small reversal in 2001, the margin remained in five figures. Locally, the wards of North Lincolnshire council within the town all elect Labour councillors, with Labour polling approximately 65 per cent of the vote in 1999. To the south, Bottesford and the rural Ridge ward are both won by the Conservatives, which does at least give them some sort of local base, though one feels that Labour's Agriculture Minister should remain reasonably secure, even if there is a larger swing away from the government next time.

YORKSHIRE EAST

	2001		1997		1992 notional	
Electorate and turnout	72,052	60.1	69,482	70.5	67,185	75.7
Conservative	19,861	45.9	20,904	42.7	25,759	50.6
Labour	15,179	35.0	17,567	35.9	13,487	26.5
Lib Dem	6,300	14.5	9,070	18.5	11,629	22.9
Anti–EU	1,661	3.8	–	–	–	–
Others	313		1,430 (2)		–	
MP	Greg Knight (Con)		John Townend (Con)		John Townend (Con)	
					Bridlington	
Majority	4,682	10.8	3,337	6.8	12,272	24.1

Yorkshire East takes in the northern part of the East Riding, extending from Pocklington and Market Weighton, past Driffield, to the east coast resort of Bridlington, which is easily its largest town (population 32,000). It is a relatively unknown and quiet corner of England, though gained brief media notoriety with the controversial comments made on race by retiring MP John Townend in the run-up to the 2001 general election. That was to be the main worry for the Conservatives here last time – Townend's successor Greg Knight (MP for Derby North between 1983 and 1997) increased the majority to a relatively comfortable ten per cent, with the Labour vote remaining static from its improved 1997 showing.

The strongest Conservative areas in the seat are in the west; this area resembles neighbouring North Yorkshire and sees Tory victories in local elections. Thus in the grand-sounding wards of Pocklington Provincial, Wolds Weighton, and Driffield & Rural, the Tories led Labour by about 5,000 votes to 2,700 in the 1999 local elections, the Lib Dems finishing third (or fourth) in each case. The Conservatives are also well ahead in the large East Wolds and Coastal ward, but things get a bit more interesting in Bridlington. Although the town gave its name to a safe Conservative seat between 1950 and 1997, it is the home of the only real Labour strength in the area, with the party winning the southern ward and usually 'Old Town' as well. In 1999 however there was continued opposition from a now unusual quarter, with a couple of Social Democrats being elected, a mere nine years after the national Social Democrats were finally wound up. Clearly, things change slowly, if at all, in East Yorkshire, whatever the prevailing national currents. This is probably good news for the Conservatives and Greg Knight, who should not have his parliamentary career interrupted this time.

Isle of Wight

ISLE of WIGHT

	2001		1997		1992 actual	
Electorate and turnout	104,431	60.8	101,680	72.0	99,839	79.8
Conservative	25,223	39.7	24,868	34.0	38,163	47.9
Labour	9,676	15.2	9,646	13.2	4,784	6.0
Lib Dem	22,397	35.3	31,274	42.7	36,336	45.6
Anti–EU	2,106	3.3	5,806 (2)	7.9	–	–
Others	4,080 (4)		1,565 (4)		350	
MP	Andrew Turner (Con)		Peter Brand (LD)		Barry Field (Con)	
Majority	2,826	4.5	6,406	8.8	1,827	2.3

Results of the previous two elections on the Isle of Wight:

1987: Conservative 51.2, Liberal Alliance 43.0, Labour 5.9 turnout 79.6; Barry Field (Con) elected;

1983: Liberal Alliance 51.0, Conservative 46.3, Labour 2.4, 1 Other 0.3 turnout 80.0%; Stephen Ross (Lib) elected.

The Isle of Wight is a diamond shape 23 miles east to west and 13 miles north to south, sheltering Southampton from the Channel and creating that port's double high tides. It is best known for holidays and prisons, although it also boasts a royal palace and a yachting festival. The main towns are Cowes and Newport on the Medina river, and the Ryde to Shanklin resorts of the east coast. Tourism and retirement (25.8 per cent of the population are of pension age) are the staples of the local economy, although there is also a surprising amount of manufacturing industry – hovercraft are built at Ryde. Wight is not a rich area – unemployment is above the national average and wage rates something like 20 per cent below the national average. Commuting is hardly an option. Its economic base is narrow and has tended to deteriorate. Wight's characteristics, and literal insularity, make it, although technically part of the south east region, rather similar to the south west.

The politics of the island is also reminiscent of the south west. It was safely Conservative for many years until the Liberals suddenly surged to victory in the February 1974 general election. Since 1974 the Conservatives and Liberals (or successors) have battled it out in general elections and Labour have been sidelined. The Isle of Wight returned Labour's worst performance ever in a parliamentary general election with 2.4 per cent in 1983 (in the 1993 Newbury by-election Labour only achieved 2.0 per cent, and in Winchester in November 1997 Labour reached its absolute nadir, at 1.7 per cent). In the 1980s it was the most completely two-party constituency in the country, with the combined Conservative and

Liberal vote exceeding 90 per cent in 1979 and the next three elections; the Tories twice polled over 45 per cent (1979 and 1983) and still lost.

South western parallels have continued in recent years. Like that region, the Isle of Wight returns a high anti-European vote and the mid term elections in 1997-2001 saw the Lib Dems poll very poorly; they came third, behind Labour, in the 1999 Euro elections. On the island this was followed through by losing the seat in 2001, while only Taunton on the mainland trod the same path. Comment after the election blamed divisions among the local Lib Dems; it is unlikely that outgoing MP Peter Brand's controversial comments on care for the terminally ill had all that much of an impact. The Conservatives, too, mounted an effective campaign and, unusually, polled more votes than they did in 1997, but the main reason for their victory was the splintering of the once solid Lib Dem bloc.

Labour have had a small scale revival on the island, improving in every election since 1983 and are now able to win several wards in local elections, particularly in Cowes and Newport. Independent councillors represent urban and rural parts of the island and there is sporadic Green activity. Several independents of various shades contested the 2001 general election. From being a duopoly, voting behaviour on the island has become a lot more plural. There is also geographical diversity, with the Lib Dem heartland being Ryde and Bembridge while the Conservatives do well in Freshwater.

The future shape of politics on the island, which has always gone its own way, is unclear. The Lib Dems seem to be fading, the Conservatives have been revitalised by their campaigning before 2001, Labour and the others wait in the wings. Perhaps even the fantasy of Julian Barnes in *England, England*, that the place will declare independence and become a theme park, could come true.

Local government

The Isle of Wight was the first unitary council to be created in the 1990s local government review; its residents had concluded that the division of the island into two district councils, Medina and South Wight, and a county council was pointless. The Lib Dems won a big majority in the first elections for the new body in 1995, building on their success in the elections for the old county council since 1981, but have slipped badly since. The most recent elections for the Island council, in 2001, produced a hung council, with 19 Liberal Democrats forming the largest single party compared to 12 Conservatives, 12 Independents and 5 Labour councillors. The administration is formed from Lib Dems and some Independents, trading as the 'Island First' group.

Boundary review

The Isle of Wight was one of the easiest and earliest decisions of the current review. It remains a constituency on its own despite having the biggest electorate of any seat in Britain. There is little support on the island – and presumably still less on the mainland – for a constituency uniting parts of Wight and parts of a port with connections with it; Southsea & Ryde, or Southampton Central & Cowes, or Lymington & West Wight all seem absurd ideas. The island was actually technically entitled to two small seats of its own this time round but the commission decided to use its discretion to take geographical factors into account and leave it as one. There were only two letters of complaint from islanders, and four in support; people seem happy enough despite their relative under-representation.

Kent including Medway

	Conservative		Labour		Liberal Democrat		Others	
	Share of vote	Seats	Share of vote	Seats	Share of vote	Seats	Share of vote	Seats
2001	43.4	9	37.7	8	15.5	0	3.4	0
1997	40.5	9	37.1	8	17.0	0	5.4	0
1992	53.1	16	24.3	0	21.3	0	1.3	0
1987	54.0	16	19.3	0	26.1	0	0.6	0
1983	53.9	16	18.6	0	26.9	0	0.7	0

Kent lies south east of London and is one of three shire counties (with Hampshire and Essex) to send a delegation of 17 MPs to the House of Commons. Like the other two big shires, it was completely dominated by the Conservatives in the 1980s but has seen their supremacy greatly diminished by the elections of 1997 and 2001.

As a large county, Kent has considerable variety within its borders. Near London, along the Thames estuary, it is suburban and industrial by turn in a rather similar way to south Essex, which is clearly visible across the water, although without that area's distinctive local culture. At this stage in its course, the Thames does not provide sought-after leisure activities and pleasant views but is functional, with docks serving industrial areas in Gravesend in particular. The Medway conurbation amounts to a city the size of Plymouth, and resembles it in its military history, its working class air and its hilliness although not its remoteness.

Further inland Kent resembles neighbouring Surrey in being dominated by affluent managerial and business commuters who have sought, and found, a comfortable semi-rural existence. Further out, Kent retains more genuine agriculture than Surrey and is indeed home to an agricultural college at Wye. A distinctive Kent crop is hops, used in making beer (for London breweries as well as Kent's own such as those in Faversham) and the reason for the appealing little oast houses which dot the landscape and increase the value of residential conversions. Along the coast are seaside resorts in varying stages of decay and ferry ports, most notably Dover, from whose cliffs France can be dimly made out on a clear day.

The county's links with France and the European mainland are an important element in its make-up. Its historic buildings often have royal associations with past kings who have stayed at them on the way to talk peace or wage war with France. Nowadays the tunnel and short sea crossings go from Kent, and the accessibility of France means that a lot of people in Kent travel across quite frequently, particularly for cigarette and alcohol shopping. Tourists and day trippers from across the Channel are a noticeable feature in Dover and Canterbury in particular. Places in Kent will be using the Euro regardless of any UK referendum on the subject. Consciousness of Europe cuts two ways - some Kent residents dislike its effects, and also object to the number of asylum-seekers housed in the county's resorts, while others rely on it for business and feel comfortable with Britain being at the heart of Europe.

Kent has historically been a Conservative county, where the Liberals struggled to make much headway in the late Victorian period (the strength of Anglicanism emanating from Canterbury, the brewing interest and its commuting population made it difficult ground). Other than the Medway conurbation Kent lacks large cities. Labour made sporadic appearances between the wars in Gravesend, Medway and Dartford, although it was not until 1945 that the party could win Dover and have a reliable hold on any of the others. Dartford was Labour at every election between 1945 and 1979 except 1970, Rochester & Chatham lapsed additionally in 1959, and Gravesend has swung with the tide in every election since 1918, excepting only 1929 and 1951. Dover was a more difficult seat, going Labour only in 1945, 1964 and 1966, and Gillingham was a 1945-only seat. The Liberals and successors have never had much of a base in the county – hopes in the last couple of decades in Folkestone & Hythe, Canterbury, Gillingham and Maidstone have come to nothing – so the Conservatives continued their ascendancy. In 1997, however, Labour won in all the seats they had ever won before and expanded to take seaside Thanet South for the first time, and went on to hold all their gains in 2001.

Kent does not divide into different sections quite as neatly as Essex, but there is a clear distinction between the coast and the rest in their composition and recent political behaviour. The Conservatives did best in 2001 along the coast. Folkestone & Hythe and Thanet North looked vulnerable on the basis of the 1997 figures but saw significant Conservative improvement in 2001; Dover had a high swing to the Tories which cut deep into the large Labour majority in the seat. Characteristically, the Tories failed to achieve anything like the same swing in the one vulnerable Labour marginal on the coast, namely Thanet South, and this constituency was an unlikely Labour seat for a second term.

The estuarine and inland parts of Kent produced no net Conservative improvement in 2001, a shockingly bad result for the party which had gambled heavily on anti-asylum and Eurosceptic feeling boosting their performance. The five Labour seats, all of them plausible targets, either swung to Labour (Gravesham, Chatham & Aylesford, Gillingham) or saw tiny pro-Conservative movements (Dartford, Medway). While no Conservative seats fell, their majority in Canterbury was whittled away some more, and they failed to clamber back over 50 per cent in the desirable commuterland around Sevenoaks and Tonbridge. For the future, the Tories must try again in their Labour targets, and must regain at least Thanet South and two or three others to be taken seriously as an aspiring party of government. Canterbury is still a potential Labour gain if they remain strong at the next election, while Lib Dem hopes have receded in their former targets.

Local government

Kent county council is controlled by the Conservatives with a majority of 20; they have 52 councillors to 22 Labour and 10 Lib Dem. The Tories have a solid delegation from Sevenoaks and tend to predominate in most areas while the Lib Dems in particular are now a scattered force. Labour have centres of strength in Dover, here and there in Thanet, and the Thames bank from Dartford along to Sheppey. Medway unitary authority (Rochester, Chatham and Gillingham) has a minority Conservative administration following the 2000 local elections. The Tories have 38 councillors, to 25 Labour, 15 Lib Dem and 2 Independent Lib Dem. Its Labour mayor in 2001/2, Tony Goulden, was formerly a member of 1960s band Vanity Fare. Labour fell just short of a majority in its first elections in 1997.

The two north western urban councils, Gravesham (Gravesend) and Dartford are both Labour-controlled with quite large majorities dating from the 1999 all-out elections, but it was not ever thus. Gravesham was run by the Conservatives for years on a mayoral casting vote (they and Labour were tied 22-22 in two successive elections in 1987 and 1991). Dartford also fell to Labour in 1995 after thirteen years of Conservative control. The other western councils are rather different. Sevenoaks council has been Conservative since its creation in 1973, except for a surprising collapse in support to Lib Dems and Labour in 1995. In 1999 the Conservatives regained it, principally at the expense of the Lib Dems. The pattern in Tonbridge & Malling is very similar, except that the Conservatives fell one seat short of regaining control in 1999. In Tunbridge Wells, which has annual elections, Conservative defeats in 1994 and 1995 symbolised the depths of disillusion with the Major government; it has now reverted to its customary Tory control.

In the centre, the borough council of Swale (Sittingbourne and Faversham) was perennially hung after the Conservatives lost it in 1986. The Conservatives did very badly in local elections here in the mid 1990s, and were reduced to third largest group, but regained control in 2002. Maidstone also has annual elections and a long tradition of no overall control (since 1973, except for a Tory period in 1976-83), with all three main parties having solid representation. Canterbury (including Herne Bay), although it does not have annual elections, is another seemingly permanent hung council now, although the Conservatives ran it until 1991 and the Lib Dems fell only one seat short in 1995. Currently the three parties are quite evenly balanced.

Taking the coastal councils. Shepway (Folkestone and Hythe) was once run by the Lib Dems, but they have faded away. They lost control thanks to Labour gains in 1995, and in 1999 the Conservatives made enough gains for a small overall majority. Dover has always been a Conservative v Labour fight, with Labour losing outright control in 1999 all-out elections and currently having exactly half of the councillors. Thanet (Margate, Ramsgate and around) was Labour for the first time ever with a landslide majority in 1995 and a reduced but still comfortable majority after 1999.

Boundary review

Kent is still entitled to the same 17 seats it was allocated in the last boundary review; Hampshire and Essex pull ahead with 18 each. None of the Kent constituencies is egregiously large or small, although Thanet South could do with picking up some more voters from somewhere, probably Thanet North. The only case in which there would be radical change, as opposed to shuffling of wards, would be if the Medway Towns were treated separately in the review and allocated three seats of their own. The Chatham & Aylesford seat would have to be disbanded, with knock-on consequences across the north and west of the county. It is more likely that the current pairing will be retained.

ASHFORD

	2001		1997		1992 actual	
Electorate and turnout	76,699	62.5	74,512	74.2	71,768	79.2
Conservative	22,739	47.4	22,899	41.4	31,031	54.6
Labour	15,380	32.1	17,544	31.7	11,365	20.0
Lib Dem	7,236	15.1	10,901	19.7	13,672	24.1
Anti–EU	1,229	2.6	3,201	5.8	–	–
Green	1,353	2.8	660	1.2	773	1.4
Others	–		89		–	
MP	Damian Green (Con)		Damian Green (Con)		Keith Speed (Con)	
Majority	7,359	15.4	5,355	9.7	17,359	30.5

The Ashford constituency is geographically the largest in Kent, covering a swathe of the centre of the county around the town of Ashford. The town's station has now been dubbed 'Ashford International' because Eurostar trains stop there, and it hopes to be a key trading point on the axis between London, Paris and Brussels. There has been English and Euro-fuelled growth in the town, with new estates particularly in the south of Ashford around the oddly named Beaver area. Ashford town itself tends to Labour, although not overwhelmingly: it voted 41 per cent Labour, 33 per cent Conservative and 26 per cent Lib Dem in the 2001 local elections.

But the balance in the constituency is tipped by the rural hinterland. The strongest Conservative element is the little town of Tenterden and its surroundings (60 per cent Conservative) although the other rural areas are only a little less supportive of the Tories. Wye has an agricultural college, and Pluckley was the setting for the rural idyll of *The Darling Buds of May*. Given that the town supplies less than half the electorate, it is clear that the constituency is a safe Conservative seat for Damian Green, and has voted Tory at every opportunity since the one-off Liberal gain in 1929. Ashford will have to grow rather more before the boundary commission starts to lop off outlying rural areas to make it even a remote Labour prospect.

CANTERBURY

	2001		1997		1992 notional	
Electorate and turnout	74,144	60.9	74,684	72.5	72,680	77.2
Conservative	18,711	41.5	20,913	38.6	28,290	50.4
Labour	16,642	36.9	16,949	31.3	8,635	15.4
Lib Dem	8,056	17.8	12,854	23.8	18,293	32.6
Anti–EU	803	1.8	2,741(2)	5.0	–	–
Green	920	2.0	588	1.1	716	1.3
Others	–		64		197	
MP	Julian Brazier (Con)		Julian Brazier (Con)		Julian Brazier (Con)	
Majority	2,069	4.6	3,964	7.3	9,997	17.8

Canterbury has one of the longest continuous histories of representation by a single party – the Conservatives have held it uninterruptedly since 1874. The close identification of the Tories with Anglicanism in the late Victorian period makes it unsurprising that Canterbury's status as the capital of 'the Tory Party at prayer' carried over into voting behaviour. It is a small and attractive city, clustered around its cathedral and has some sparsely populated areas even in the centre. Development around the city has been strictly controlled. Since the 1960s it has added the University of Kent, which is part of the reason for its weakening Conservative allegiance. The city has developed a vaguely alternative, green and liberal side to its culture. The discontent within the Church of England at the Thatcher government's policies during the 1980s, the increasing liberalism of church doctrine on many issues (and New Labour's conservatism on some of those on which the church still holds to a restrictive line) have also eroded Tory dominance. Until recently the Conservatives seemed more vulnerable to the Liberal Democrats, but it has been one of Labour's best growth areas in the 1990s and is now a close marginal seat.

The actual city of Canterbury is very competitive between the three political parties, although it sits in more Conservative countryside. Labour gained Canterbury Central from the Lib Dems in the county elections in 2001, and the Tories gained East, in both cases with only a third of the vote. In none of the four county wards of Canterbury, which include some rural areas, did any party poll under 20 per cent. The constituency also stretches up to the north Kent coast at Whitstable, which is 45 per cent Conservative and a weak area for the Lib Dems. There was a significant difference between local and general election voting in Canterbury, with about 7 per cent of those voting choosing Labour in the general election and Lib Dem or Green in local elections. Labour clearly had the better of the argument about tactical voting in 2001, but it was not quite enough to unseat eccentric right winger Julian Brazier. It is hard to imagine the Conservatives slipping further, but Canterbury is a seat they will have to watch.

CHATHAM and AYLESFORD

	2001		1997		1992 notional	
Electorate and turnout	69,759	57.0	69,644	70.6	69,821	78.4
Conservative	14,840	37.3	18,401	37.4	28,056	51.3
Labour	19,180	48.3	21,191	43.1	14,633	26.7
Lib Dem	4,705	11.8	7,389	15.0	11,643	21.3
Anti–EU	1,010	2.5	2,031 (2)	4.1	–	–
Others			149		401	
MP	Jonathan Shaw (Lab)		Jonathan Shaw (Lab)		Andrew Rowe (Con)	
					Kent Mid	
Majority	4,340	10.9	2,790	5.7	13,423	24.5

Rochester and Chatham run together and are interdependent, but they have been parted for parliamentary purposes since 1983. Chatham is now paired with a semi rural tail stretching down south westwards to Aylesford itself, north west of Maidstone. This area has little in common with Chatham but Kent has consistently posed problems for the Boundary Commissioners in creating constituencies that make some sense. Chatham and Aylesford is not the silliest ever result of their deliberations.

Chatham is a quite traditional working class town, sprawling along the steep hills and valleys that punctuate the Medway conurbation. The Labour Luton ward comprises tightly packed terraces and Wayfield is a peripheral estate. Some of the other wards, such as Lordswood and Horsted, were Conservative gains in May 2000, and Walderslade is reliably Tory. Chatham is less Labour than it looks, reflecting the military tradition that lingers on after the closure of the naval yard, although the party has certainly led there in the last two general elections. The 'Aylesford' portion consists of several small towns and overgrown villages from the Tonbridge and Malling borough council area just off the M20 motorway, including Snodland, Larkfield and Aylesford. This area seems to be an emerging suburban town, with superstores, new private estates and some industry including a big newsprint plant and a regional television centre. It was Conservative, but not overwhelmingly so, in the 2001 local elections.

Even though Chatham has not been a navy town for some time, it followed the trend of defence-industry towns in swinging to Labour in 2001 on top of a large swing in 1997, and Labour did well in quite a lot of new growth areas in the 2001 election too. Both components, plus incumbency for an articulate MP, helped Jonathan Shaw to win by a very respectable margin – it is now Labour's 65th most marginal and could in theory survive a cut in Labour's majority to around 40. The swing since 1992, at 17.7 per cent, is extremely high for a seat outside suburban London.

DARTFORD

	2001		1997		1992 notional	
Electorate and turnout	72,241	61.9	69,726	74.6	68,319	82.9
Conservative	18,160	40.6	20,950	40.3	28,796	50.9
Labour	21,466	48.0	25,278	48.6	20,482	36.2
Lib Dem	3,781	8.5	4,872	9.4	6,873	12.1
Anti–EU	989	2.2	–	–	–	–
Others	344		939 (3)		468	
MP	Howard Stoate (Lab)		Howard Stoate (Lab)		Bob Dunn (Con)	
Majority	3,306	7.4	4,328	8.3	8,314	14.7

Dartford is an unpretentious town, very much within London's orbit, its north side almost a mirror image of the industrial landscape across the river in Thurrock and its south side a continuation of suburban Bexley and Sidcup. Dartford lies between two extraordinary monuments to consumerism – Lakeside mall in Thurrock and the even newer Bluewater centre near Greenhithe, east of Dartford in a former gravel pit. The malls have created thousands of jobs – unemployment is low and has been falling relatively fast - and widened opportunities for Dartford people, but created some problems for the town centre. Dartford's most famous son is Mick Jagger, who attended the town's grammar school and is now commemorated in the form of an arts centre bearing his name.

Dartford tends towards Labour, although the Conservatives can put up a reasonable showing everywhere except in north Dartford, the grimy Stone area near the tunnel entrance, and riverside Swanscombe. The Conservative vote gets stronger on the south side of Dartford and is augmented by the two rural wards from Sevenoaks attached to Dartford for parliamentary purposes. The Liberal Democrats are not a presence, running only one candidate and polling a mere 78 votes in the 1999 local elections. The Labour vote was solid enough for the party, unusually in southern England outside London, not to sink into third place in 1983. Labour won the seat back after 18 years represented by Conservative Bob Dunn in 1997 and defeated him again in 2001. Recent local and general elections have been close, hard fought battles between the two main parties, with Labour emerging consistently on top by relatively thin margins. Dartford remains a crucial marginal seat.

DOVER

	2001		1997		1992 notional	
Electorate and turnout	69,024	65.1	68,713	78.9	69,646	82.8
Conservative	16,744	37.2	17,796	32.8	25,443	44.1
Labour	21,943	48.8	29,535	54.5	24,583	42.6
Lib Dem	5,131	11.4	4,302	7.9	6,234	10.8
Anti–EU	1,142	2.5	2,567 (2)	4.7	–	–
Others	–		–		1,422	2.5
MP	Gwyn Prosser (Lab)		Gwyn Prosser (Lab)		David Shaw (Con)	
Majority	5,199	11.6	11,739	21.7	860	1.5

In 1983 Peter Rees won his final term as Dover's Conservative MP against opposition from Mr Love for the Labour Party and Mr Nice for the SDP. There has been little love or niceness in Dover politics since. First came David Shaw as Conservative MP from 1987 until his defeat in 1997, an interval during which he specialised in smear campaigns against Labour and aggressive tactics that alienated some of his own colleagues. It seemed scarcely possible, but in 2001 the Shaw era seemed relatively pleasant. The cause was the divisive politics of asylum.

Dover is Britain's main ferry port, with ships still shuttling back and forward to Calais and the Belgian ports, and although employment in the docks and customs has fallen it is still a significant element of the town. However, Dover's seaside economy has declined and the town's oversupply of hotels and rented accommodation made it a convenient place to locate asylum seekers during the 1990s. Many in the town reacted with resentment and suspicion and racist fringe parties tried to whip up tensions. A local newspaper dubbed the incomers 'human sewage' and there were violent incidents in the town in 1999. Despite this, the eight wards of Dover town are predominantly Labour, with only Castle voting Conservative in the 1999 local elections. Three of the eight are among the 10 per cent most deprived in England.

A similar constituency to this one was formerly known as Dover and Deal, and the smaller town has something of a claim to recognition in the constituency name. Deal is also Labour, although Walmer is the Conservative stronghold in that corner of the seat. A lot of the countryside around Dover is conventionally Conservative but a little further inland are some Labour-voting small town and rural areas around Aylesham and Eythorne which were formerly the location of the Kent coalfield.

Dover is a key marginal seat which went Labour in 1945, 1964 and 1966 and almost in 1992 (it had drifted gently to the left relative to the rest of the south east). The strong swing to the Conservatives in 2001 followed an acrimonious campaign in which Labour MP Gwyn Prosser accused leading Conservatives of playing the asylum card and damaging community relations in the town. This result has reduced it to being Labour's 73rd most marginal; the party could lose it and still have a bare majority in the House. However, the 2001 figures might be a misleading starting point because of the short-term asylum factor and could disguise a rather safer Labour seat.

FAVERSHAM and MID KENT

	2001		1997		1992 notional	
Electorate and turnout	67,995	60.4	67,130	73.9	66,379	81.6
Conservative	18,739	45.6	22,016	44.4	32,047	59.2
Labour	14,556	35.5	17,843	36.0	12,448	23.0
Lib Dem	5,529	13.5	6,138	12.4	9,225	17.0
Anti–EU	828	2.0	2,504 (2)	5.0	–	–
Others	1,399 (2)		1,105 (4)		456	
MP	Hugh Robertson (Con)		Andrew Rowe (Con)		NEW SEAT	
Majority	4,183	10.2	4,173	8.4	19,599	36.2

The mid-Kent element, essentially wards from Maidstone borough council's area, is the centre of gravity of this constituency. Its boundaries extend into the Maidstone built up area to its east side, including the large and slightly detached Shepway estate plus the growing suburb of Bearsted. Parts of Shepway are run-down (its west side is among the 10 per cent most deprived wards of England) and it is strongly Labour, although it only managed 49 per cent turnout in 2001. Bearsted, on the other hand, is Conservative.

The Maidstone borough wards also include a large rural element to the east of the town, including Harrietsham and Lenham along the A20, Leeds with its famous castle, and several plush commuter villages around Headcorn. The Maidstone Rural East ward was over 60 per cent Conservative in the 2001 county elections, and the other rural areas were similarly strongly Tory. At the east end of the seat is the town of Faversham, an old market centre with a prominent brewing industry, which gave the Conservatives a significant lead in the 2001 county elections. It is something of a puzzle as to how Labour have managed to win 36 per cent of the vote in the last couple of elections; the Conservatives should be safe enough here anyway.

FOLKESTONE and HYTHE

	2001		*1997*		*1992 notional*	
Electorate and turnout	71,585	64.1	71,561	72.7	*64,414*	*81.4*
Conservative	20,645	45.0	20,313	39.0	*27,435*	*52.3*
Labour	9,260	20.2	12,939	24.9	*6,347*	*12.1*
Lib Dem	14,738	32.1	13,981	26.9	*18,527*	*35.3*
Anti–EU	1,212	2.6	4,566 (2)	8.8	–	–
Others	–		251 (2)		*123*	
MP	Michael Howard (Con)		Michael Howard (Con)		Michael Howard (Con)	
Majority	5,907	12.9	6,332	12.2	*8,908*	*17.0*

The Liberal Democrats have flattered to deceive in Folkestone and Hythe for several elections; it has been talked up as a gain but they have failed to unseat Michael Howard, the only one of the BBC's election night 'Dicey Dozen' senior Conservatives to survive the 1997 election. Despite more predictions he increased his percentage majority in 2001.

Folkestone is a seaside resort south west along the coast from Dover; it also has a ferry port for the short crossing to France. The Channel Tunnel emerges into the light just north of the town, and has produced a major transport interchange there with consequences for the environment but also fortunately for jobs – central Folkestone has suffered from the decline of seaside resorts and is among the 6 per cent worst off in England. South west of Folkestone are the little towns of New Romney and Hythe, and the expanse of Romney Marsh. North of Folkestone is the Elham valley area, a rural area which grew by nearly 3,000 electors between 1989 and 2001.

In the three wards (electorate 32,500) of Folkestone itself the Liberal Democrats had a lead of 1,600 votes in the 2001 county elections, with percentage votes of 42 per cent Lib Dem, 34 per cent Conservative and 25 per cent Labour. Their problem is the half of the constituency which lies outside the town, which gave around 50 per cent support to the Conservatives in the local elections. There was a slight but interesting variation between the local and general election results. Labour's vote was similar (21 per cent local, 20 per cent general) reflecting the failure of a tactical vote to appear. The Lib Dems polled four points below their local performance, with Michael Howard getting two points more than his running mates despite a UKIP candidate appearing in the general but not the local election. Howard, despite his abrasively partisan approach, obviously attracts support from people who favour the Lib Dems in local elections.

GILLINGHAM

	2001		1997		1992 notional	
Electorate and turnout	70,901	59.5	70,389	72.0	70,789	79.1
Conservative	16,510	39.1	18,207	35.9	29,092	52.0
Labour	18,782	44.5	20,187	39.8	13,332	23.8
Lib Dem	5,755	13.6	9,649	19.0	13,150	23.5
Anti–EU	933	2.2	2,082 (2)	4.1	–	–
Others	232		558 (3)		425	
MP	Paul Clark (Lab)		Paul Clark (Lab)		James Couchman (Con)	
Majority	2,272	5.4	1,980	3.9	15,760	28.1

Gillingham is the easternmost of the Medway towns, and the largest. While fascinating politically, it is itself a relatively dull residential area to the east of Chatham, extending across flatter land than the other two towns to the Labour Twydall estate and the more Conservative suburbs of Rainham and Parkwood. Rainham has its own station and supplies commuters to London as well as the centre of the Medway towns. To the south is the Tory suburb of Hempstead Valley which has become the principal out of town centre around Medway. The Gillingham seat also, anomalously, covers most of the area of the former Chatham naval dockyard, which is now a development area. The recovery of the contaminated land was an enormous undertaking, like the Dome site upriver – it practically glowed in the dark after it was abandoned, but now it is developing into a rather anonymous suburb. Before the closure, works buses carried people from all over the Medway conurbation to the yard – the destinations are still listed on a long wall near the old gates.

Gillingham was Labour in 1945 but after this it seemed pretty thoroughly Conservative despite its rather working class composition. The Cold War factor in politics in military towns skewed it to the right, and the development of suburbs around Rainham confirmed it. In later years the Liberals and Liberal Democrats put down local roots and in 1992 the Tories had a big majority courtesy of an even split in the opposition vote. It was therefore a massive shock when Labour achieved the swing required (over 14 per cent) in 1997, and even more when Paul Clark won a second term in 2001 thanks to a strong squeeze on the Lib Dems. It was another good Labour showing in an ex-military and mainly suburban constituency. Gillingham is still a top Tory target – it is the 23rd most vulnerable Labour seat, and the government could survive its loss with a three-figure overall majority.

GRAVESHAM

	2001		1997		1992 notional	
Electorate and turnout	69,588	62.7	69,288	76.9	70,514	83.0
Conservative	16,911	38.8	20,681	38.8	29,031	49.6
Labour	21,773	49.9	26,460	49.7	23,663	40.4
Lib Dem	4,031	9.2	4,128	7.8	5,207	8.9
Anti–EU	924	2.1	1,441	2.7	–	
Others	–		543 (2)		634 (3)	
MP	Chris Pond (Lab)		Chris Pond (Lab)		Jacques Arnold (Con)	
Majority	4,862	11.1	5,779	10.9	5,368	9.2

The rationale for calling the borough, and hence this constituency 'Gravesham' rather than 'Gravesend' is obscure – even the borough council's website admits that they aren't completely sure. It appears to be a mediaeval name revived with local government reform in the 1970s. North Kent is a functional part of the world, and the Thames estuary here is dominated by industrial development and marshland. The borough also includes Northfleet, a mainly Labour industrial town with some grim-looking but not too badly off estates, and some very Conservative suburbs and villages inland – Shorne voted Conservative by more than three to one in May 1999.

Gravesend has been a key marginal for many years. It is the truest bellwether seat in the country. Since 1918 – not just since 1945 – it has been won by the party which has gone on to form the government – with the exceptions only of 1929 and 1951. Its unusual deviance in these elections is perhaps accounted for by the fact that the national 'winner' in each case was elected with fewer votes than its main opponent. The council was so finely balanced that the Conservatives ran it on successive mayoral casting votes for nearly eight years, but it is now more comfortably Labour. In the last two general elections Labour has been ahead by a margin approximating its national lead. It is the 68th most marginal Labour seat, which means that Labour could retain a small overall majority and still lose Gravesham if swing was uniform. It remains a closely contested two party marginal – the Lib Dems have never had a look-in here.

MAIDSTONE and THE WEALD

	2001		1997		1992 notional	
Electorate and turnout	74,002	61.6	72,735	73.7	71,009	80.2
Conservative	22,621	49.6	23,657	44.1	31,951	56.1
Labour	12,303	27.0	14,054	26.2	7,097	12.5
Lib Dem	9,064	19.9	11,986	22.4	17,237	30.3
Anti–EU	978	2.1	2,337 (2)	4.4	–	–
Others	611		1,574 (3)		693	
MP	Ann Widdecombe (Con)		Ann Widdecombe (Con)		Ann Widdecombe (Con)	
					Maidstone	
Majority	10,318	22.6	9,603	17.9	14,714	25.8

Maidstone is the shopping centre for mid Kent and the administrative centre for the whole county, with the council and the police headquarters in the town. It is a big and bustling centre, and has added neighbourhoods around the Victorian core since the 1960s. The constituency based on the town is highly Conservative, more than might be expected from a significant urban area. There are three main reasons for this.

Maidstone is not a university town, unlike superficially comparable centres such as Guildford and Colchester, which means that it lacks a large student – and academic – liberal-left vote. Its main institutional presence has instead come from a prison and a barracks (now closed) which produce more conservative tendencies.

Despite this, a Maidstone seat consisting solely of the urban core would give Labour or the Liberal Democrats a strong but far from guaranteed chance in good elections like 1997 and 2001. However, the current seat does not include the most Labour-inclined parts of the town (which are hived off into Faversham and Kent Mid) and instead reaches down into 'The Weald' at Cranbrook, Sissinghurst and Benenden. This area offers powerful reinforcement to the Conservatives of Maidstone (the county ward was 57 per cent Tory in 2001) and makes it a very difficult seat for any other party as long as the current boundaries are upheld.

An additional factor locally is the personality of Ann Widdecombe, regarded as a forthright and honest political figure, who attracts some personal support. But the current constituency would probably be safe for any Conservative.

MEDWAY

	2001		1997		1992 actual	
Electorate and turnout	64,934	59.5	61,878	72.3	61,737	80.2
Conservative	15,134	39.2	16,504	36.9	25,924	52.3
Labour	18,914	49.0	21,858	48.9	17,138	34.6
Lib Dem	3,604	9.3	4,555	10.2	4,751	9.6
Anti–EU	958	2.5	1,825 (2)	4.1	–	–
Liberal	–	–	–	–	1,480	3.0
Others	–		–		234	
MP	Robert Marshall-Andrews (Lab)		Robert Marshall-Andrews (Lab)		Peggy Fenner (Con)	
Majority	3,780	9.8	5,354	12.0	8,786	17.7

The Medway constituency is based around the city of Rochester, now subsumed into the Medway Towns unitary authority. Rochester and its southern suburbs are on the east bank of the River Medway. The centre, with a cathedral and a ruined castle and a charming old high street full of independent shops, is an attractive alternative to the department stores which are based in Chatham. A lot of the constituency is on the west bank. Strood is just across the bridge from Rochester and effectively one of its suburbs; to the south are the villages of Cuxton and Halling overshadowed by a cement works, and to the north a peninsula between the Medway and the Thames including the little town of Hoo St. Werburgh and ending at the Isle of Grain. The whole area was immortalised by Charles Dickens, who set *The Mystery of Edwin Drood* in Rochester and began *Great Expectations* in the 'savage' marshes of Cooling, by the Thames.

Rochester, when paired with Chatham, was a seat Labour could win in good years and occasionally in bad years such as 1955. The Medway seat is a bit more difficult, but it was still not really a surprise that it went over to Labour in 1997 and stayed with the party in 2001. A lot of Medway's wards are quite marginal in local elections, with several switching to the Conservatives in 2000. The Conservatives led by 9 points in the 2000 local elections and hoped to translate it into general election victory, but the result was disappointing. Having conducted a successful prosecution in 1997 Bob Marshall-Andrews QC won for the defence in 2001. Marshall-Andrews is an independent-minded, rather left wing Labour backbencher. A Labour government with a majority of less than about 50 would probably not be in a position to command his critical support in parliament.

SEVENOAKS

	2001		1997		1992 notional	
Electorate and turnout	66,648	63.9	66,531	75.4	66,706	80.2
Conservative	21,052	49.4	22,776	45.4	30,847	57.6
Labour	10,898	25.6	12,315	24.6	8,626	16.1
Lib Dem	9,214	21.6	12,086	24.1	13,160	24.6
Anti–EU	1,155	2.7	2,138	4.3	–	–
Others	295		834 (3)		887	
MP	Michael Fallon (Con)		Michael Fallon (Con)		Mark Wolfson (Con)	
Majority	10,154	23.8	10,461	20.9	17,687	33.1

Sevenoaks is a safe Conservative seat. It is the part of Kent which most resembles Surrey, with its uniformly middle class population and a large number of well-off London commuters. In the 2001 local elections, even Sevenoaks Central ward was 55 per cent Conservative, and there are no pools of Labour or Lib Dem support large enough to elect a county councillor. Only at district ward level does any variety emerge.

The constituency also contains the small town of Swanley, which is out of sympathy with Sevenoaks proper in being working class and lower middle class overspill, a difference reflected by its Labour loyalties. The comedian Mark Steel called Swanley a town whose 'purpose was boredom' and the same goes, in a classier way, for Sevenoaks itself. The boredom extends to parliamentary elections, where the Conservatives have enjoyed five-figure majorities in every election since 1950. In the Conservatives' worst ever local election year, 1995, the Liberal Democrats polled rather more votes than the Tories but this was a flash in the pan. It provides a safe refuge for Michael Fallon, who was ejected from Darlington by Alan Milburn in 1992.

SITTINGBOURNE and SHEPPEY

	2001		1997		1992 notional	
Electorate and turnout	65,824	57.5	63,880	72.3	65,141	77.6
Conservative	13,831	36.5	16,794	36.4	24,669	48.8
Labour	17,340	45.8	18,723	40.6	12,106	24.0
Lib Dem	5,353	14.1	8,447	18.3	13,541	26.8
Anti–EU	661	1.7	1,554 (2)	3.4	–	–
Others	673		644		236	
MP	Derek Wyatt (Lab)		Derek Wyatt (Lab)		Roger Moate (Con) Faversham	
Majority	3,509	9.3	1,929	4.2	11,128	22.0

Sittingbourne is an expanding town on the main Victoria to Dover railway line and is the largest single element of the seat. New privately owned estates are springing up around Milton Regis and Kemsley. It is set on what is now the A2, but was Watling Street in Roman times and a pilgrimage route to Canterbury, and has a fine High Street but is for the most part a humdrum but pleasant town. There is also a certain amount of Kent countryside around Newington, and the rather isolated Isle of Sheppey projecting into the bleak Thames estuary opposite Southend. Sheerness is a ferry port; despite an impressive Victorian Gothic Conservative club in its centre it is a Labour town and property is exceptionally cheap. There are also desultory Sheppey seaside resorts and industrial towns. It is flat, marshy countryside that needs strong sea defences.

This seat is basically what used to be called Faversham, less the eponymous town. It was a continual source of frustration to Conservatives as Labour MP Percy Wells held on with hair-raisingly narrow majorities throughout the 1950s thanks to one of the most active constituency Labour Parties in the country. It finally fell in 1970 and the Conservatives built up a large lead which disappeared in 1997 on a 14.5 per cent swing, propelling the rather surprised Derek Wyatt into parliament as a Labour MP.

Wyatt was not given much of a chance of another term by many observers, but defied expectations and won an increased majority in 2001 – as did several other Labour MPs for seats that appeared improbable before May 1997. He owed his victory to a squeeze on the Lib Dem vote and tactical support from local Lib Dem voters. In contrast to the general election result, in the county elections here the Conservatives led by about 37-35, with 27 per cent for the Lib Dems. Of the wards in the constituency, only Swale East is safely Conservative and Sheerness safely Labour; all the others are three way marginals. Labour have to maintain their hold on the tactical vote to keep Sittingbourne and Sheppey.

THANET NORTH

	2001		1997		1992 actual	
Electorate and turnout	71,012	59.0	71,112	68.8	70,977	76.0
Conservative	21,050	50.3	21,586	44.1	30,867	57.2
Labour	14,400	34.4	18,820	38.4	12,657	23.5
Lib Dem	4,603	11.0	5,576	11.4	9,563	17.7
Anti–EU	980	2.3	2,973 (2)	6.1	–	–
Others	835 (2)		–		873	
MP	Roger Gale (Con)		Roger Gale (Con)		Roger Gale (Con)	
Majority	6,650	15.9	2,766	5.7	18,210	33.8

Thanet North consists of a strip of resorts at the east end of the north coast of Kent, the most famous town among them being Margate. Margate is a brash place catering to day-tripping and holidaying working class Londoners, while the lesser known resorts are quieter retirement areas – Cliftonville, Birchington, Westgate and the town of Herne Bay from the Canterbury district. Thanet has the highest proportion of pensioners in the population of Kent – 25.1 per cent in 1998, and many of them live and vote in North.

Margate has suffered from the decline of the seaside holiday trade and has some surprisingly depressed areas; the Pier ward in central Margate is the 77th most deprived in England. Decay and dereliction lie not far beneatht the tcky facade of day tripper pubs and amusement arcades. Margate and Cliftonville make for quite competitive wards in county council elections but Birchington is more strongly Conservative. Herne Bay produces a sizeable Liberal Democrat vote in local elections, but it does not seem to translate into general election voting. Unusually in 2001, Conservative incumbent Roger Gale drew a greater share of the Lib Dem local vote than his Labour opponent did. In Margate the turnout fell by much less than Herne Bay, and the Conservatives did well – in Thanet North at least, more of their vote came out than Labour's.

Thanet North was one of the best Conservative results in the south, the 5.1 per cent swing being more typical of south Essex than north Kent. Roger Gale's populism seems to go down well with the electorate here. The good Conservative result must encourage them to believe that they can deprive Labour of control over Thanet in the next round of local elections in 2003.

THANET SOUTH

	2001		1997		1992 notional	
Electorate and turnout	61,680	63.9	62,792	71.6	63,317	77.0
Conservative	16,210	41.1	17,899	39.8	25,222	51.7
Labour	18,002	45.7	20,777	46.2	13,723	28.2
Lib Dem	3,706	9.4	5,263	11.7	8,936	18.3
Anti–EU	502	1.3	631	1.4	–	–
Others	1,012 (2)		418		870	
MP	Stephen Ladyman (Lab)		Stephen Ladyman (Lab)		Jonathan Aitken (Con)	
Majority	1,792	4.5	2,878	6.4	11,499	23.6

Labour's 1997 gain in Thanet South was a part of its unprecedented success in seaside resorts, but this seat attracted more notice than most because the defeated Tory was Jonathan Aitken. Instead of another term in parliament, Aitken found himself serving a term in prison for perjury. In 2001 the Conservatives were confident of picking up this seat because they had a new candidate, a big swing in the 1999 Euro election, and more significantly because the asylum issue was expected to play well in a down-at-heel seaside constituency adjoining Dover. Their failure in 2001 was perhaps even more surprising than the original loss in 1997.

Thanet South includes the quiet seaside resort of Broadstairs, Edward Heath's place of origin, and the more rough and ready port and resort of Ramsgate, as well as some inland parts of the Isle of Thanet. These are all in Thanet council's area, but the seat extends a little into the Dover district and includes the pleasant little town of Sandwich where there is a large pharmaceutical complex run by Pfizer. Broadstairs and Sandwich are Conservative towns, but not by overwhelming margins. Ramsgate is a different proposition, with strongly Labour areas in the north of the town and at Northwood and Eastcliff and the south of the town being very marginal.

Labour's majority in 2001 was dependent on tactical voting. The county election results were nearly dead level here between Labour and the Conservatives, but it seems clear that a large proportion of the 16 per cent who voted Lib Dem in the local elections cast tactical or personal votes for Stephen Ladyman and against the Conservative line on asylum and Europe. These issues, it should be remembered, cut both ways in Kent. It is still one of Labour's most perilous seats, being the Conservatives' 16th easiest target from Labour – the Tories can win Thanet South and still be worse off than Labour were in 1983.

TONBRIDGE and MALLING

	2001		*1997*		*1992 notional*	
Electorate and turnout	65,979	64.3	64,988	75.8	64,102	80.7
Conservative	20,956	49.4	23,640	48.0	31,462	60.8
Labour	12,706	29.9	13,410	27.2	8,841	17.1
Lib Dem	7,605	17.9	9,467	19.2	10,721	20.7
Anti–EU	1,169	2.8	2,507 (2)	5.1	–	–
Others	–		205		711	
MP	John Stanley (Con)		John Stanley (Con)		John Stanley (Con)	
Majority	8,250	19.4	10,230	20.8	20,741	40.1

Tonbridge is a town by a railway junction in mid Kent, which has been overshadowed since the establishment of Tunbridge Wells to its south. It has commuters, and local employment in the Benn family publishing business. It is quite a small town, particularly if its satellite of Hildenborough is excluded, and the constituency covers a swathe of rural Kent which is mixed between agricultural use and commuter settlements.

West Malling is a charming little town with Tudor and Georgian buildings in its High Street; it is rather closer to and more influenced by Maidstone than Tonbridge although it also has its share of London commuters. Between and around Malling and Tonbridge are many villages and little towns, including such affluent places as East Peckham (which is definitely not to be confused with part of inner city south London). Since 1997 it has also included Edenbridge and its surroundings from the Sevenoaks district. Edenbridge is an odd mixture of a council-built overspill estate labouring under the name of Spittals Cross and some pleasant commuterland; with it comes some more villages.

Tonbridge and Malling is a Conservative stronghold. The two Tonbridge town county council wards gave the Conservatives 46 per cent of the vote to 32 per cent for Labour in 2001; it is the main source of Labour support. The Liberal Democrats can win local elections in some of the rural Malling wards, but neither party is a plausible challenger to Sir John Stanley, who unlike many people in similar circumstances has decided to stay in parliament since losing his ministerial job in 1988.

TUNBRIDGE WELLS

	2001		1997		1992 notional	
Electorate and turnout	64,534	62.3	65,259	74.1	66,280	77.6
Conservative	19,643	48.9	21,853	45.2	28,297	55.0
Labour	9,332	23.2	9,879	20.4	7,563	14.7
Lib Dem	9,913	24.7	14,347	29.7	15,151	29.5
Anti–EU	1,313	3.3	2,122 (2)	4.4	–	–
Others	–		153		433	
MP	Archie Norman (Con)		Archie Norman (Con)		Patrick Mayhew (Con)	
Majority	9,730	24.2	7,506	15.5	13,146	25.6

Tunbridge Wells was established as a new town based around a spa south of Tonbridge when a mineral spring was found in 1606. A century before Brighton, Tunbridge Wells was mildly notorious in London society as the scene for illicit dalliances. Most of its current residents would be a bit scandalised – it is a place which has probably become more conservative since it was first founded.

Modern Royal Tunbridge Wells is accessible for London commuters and is a pleasant residential town with good facilities and a sense of community. It grew somewhat, particularly in the fringe areas around High Brooms and Southborough, in the 1960s and 1970s but has been stable in population recently. Southborough and Pembury are the main non-Conservative areas, although in a bad year for the Tories central wards like Pantiles (where the old spa is still in business) can vote for the Lib Dems.

Tunbridge Wells is an essentially Conservative area, although the party lost control of the council in the mid 1990s. Despite these local troubles, the Conservatives have maintained a strong grip on the politics of the area – their vote has dropped by less than the national average and the Liberal Democrat challenge fell away in 2001, leaving the anti-Tory vote evenly divided. There are only 19 safer Tory parliamentary seats, and businessman Archie Norman can represent the seat for as long as he takes an interest in elected office.

Lancashire

including Blackburn and Blackpool

	Conservative		Labour		Liberal Democrat		Others	
	Share of vote	Seats	Share of vote	Seats	Share of vote	Seats	Share of vote	Seats
2001	36.4	2	46.7	13	13.3	0	3.5	0
1997	34.2	2	49.2	13	12.7	0	3.9	0
1992	45.0	9	38.9	7	15.2	0	0.9	0
1987	46.3	13	34.4	3	18.9	0	0.3	0
1983	48.2	13	29.4	3	21.9	0	0.5	0

The red rose county of Lancashire is much truncated from its traditional shape, its size and population dramatically reduced in 1973 following the creation of Merseyside and Greater Manchester. None of the urban centres which remain in the county are huge, though the industrial towns of Preston (recently made a city), Blackburn and Burnley are all large enough to support their own parliamentary divisions, and the mammoth seaside resort of Blackpool (sometimes said to contain more hotel beds than Portugal) the best part of two. Until 2002 the only city in Lancashire was the former county town of Lancaster in the north, which can boast several historic buildings including a large castle, (the most expensive property on the Lancashire version of Monopoly), which was the location of the trial of the Pendle Witches and more recently the Birmingham Six. Around these centres can be found wild moorland in the east of the county and rolling farmland in the west, with a number of small towns dotted around that can all be described as 'conservative' though their political inclinations vary.

As this suggests, the smaller version of Lancashire remains extremely diverse, and as a consequence, politically interesting. Labour have tended to dominate the major towns, though not Blackpool and Morecambe, which like seaside resorts up and down the country, were formerly associated with strong support for the Conservatives. Over the past twenty years, this loyalty has collapsed rapidly, with such places now an unheralded but important part of the 'new Labour coalition'; results in Blackpool in particular suggest a permanent shift in alignments. Meanwhile the small towns of east Lancashire, a bedrock of the early Labour party, have been swinging slowly to the right, with a growing ethnic dimension apparent in Burnley and to a lesser extent, Pendle. In the south of the county, West Lancashire (and particularly Skelmersdale) is heavily influenced by Merseyside, while there is something of a Manchester influence towards Chorley. Finally the university city of Lancaster has recently entered a post-Labour political phase otherwise found only in the south of England (Brighton, Cambridge, Oxford and parts of inner London), with Labour struggling in the last few years to hold back a major shift to the Greens.

Until the most recent two general elections, the Conservatives could always count on winning at least eight parliamentary seats in the county. As well as the rural seats of Ribble Valley and Fylde to which they are now reduced, the Tories always won the seaside resorts of Blackpool and Morecambe, and usually the less industrial small town constituencies such as Chorley, Lancaster and Ormskirk/West Lancs as well. In the 1980s, they went further by gaining the three small-town east Lancashire seats (Hyndburn, Pendle and Rossendale), which had voted Labour for decades, making a total of 13 Tory seats in the county to only 3 for Labour: Blackburn, Burnley and Preston.

In the ten years since, Labour's advance in Lancashire has been considerable. The party gained four seats in 1992 (West Lancashire together with the recapture of the east Lancs trio) and by the time that six more constituencies were picked up in 1997, there had been dramatic gains in local government as well (see below). Labour have now reached record levels in terms of both representation and popular support, with their near-50 per cent vote in 1997 some five to six points higher than that achieved in the elections which followed the second world war. Over the same fifty-year period the Conservative vote has collapsed - maybe not to the extent that it has in Merseyside or Scotland - but enough to leave what should be a highly marginal battleground between the two main parties looking very one-sided. Meanwhile the Liberal Democrats have huffed and puffed in parts of the east of the county, but failed to hold their only ever post-war win here (the 1991 Ribble Valley by-election) at the following general election and they have also subsided in Pendle. Elsewhere the third party vote is extremely weak in parliamentary contests.

Lancashire remains a crucial battleground, and if they are to make any sort of national recovery, then there is no question that the Conservatives must start regaining seats here. Their complete failure to do so in 2001 does not bode well, and any long-term change in the political behaviour of seaside resorts will hinder a major breakthrough. Lancaster & Wyre really should have been gained in 2001 and that seat will be their top target next time, but the Tories will need to look at places like Chorley and South Ribble as well as East Lancashire if power is to regained. They will be helped by the county's preference (no longer true in local council contests) for supporting the two main parties, which does at least mean that any serious problems for the Labour government should produce an electoral dividend for the Tories.

Local government

The tide has been starting to turn away from Labour since 1997 (though somewhat unevenly), after the previous decade in which the party seemed to be sweeping to power all over the county. By the early-mid 1990s, Labour were in control of almost all town halls in Lancashire, from the county council (based in Preston) where they removed the Conservatives from power as early as 1981, to district councils like neighbouring Lancaster and Wyre, neither of which had ever been Labour since their creation in 1973. Indeed, Wyre district could still boast 43 Conservative councillors out of 56 in 1987, and Lancaster had 37 Tories in 1983, a number which fell to 11 by 1995. Even more spectacular was the Tory collapse in Blackpool, from 32 out of 44 councillors in 1983 down to just 2 by 1995, with Labour seizing and still retaining control of what was traditionally seen as a citadel of the right. Hyndburn and Rossendale were both gained by Labour in the mid-1980s after previous periods of Conservative rule, Chorley, South Ribble and West Lancashire have also seen shifts from Tory to Labour, while Blackburn was gained from no overall control in the early 1980s. Even in Fylde and Ribble Valley, the Conservatives lost overall control, though it was the Liberal Democrats who did the damage in the latter and Independents and Ratepayers who between them outnumber the Tory group in Fylde. Finally Pendle has seen some dramatic twists and turns, all three main parties taking turns at running the council over the last twenty-five years, though the Conservatives are now very much the third party in numbers of councillors. Labour did not have a free hand here in the mid-late 1990s as elsewhere in the county as the Lib Dems briefly took control until 1999.

Since the election of the Labour government in 1997, their local government fortunes in Lancashire have been less good, as one would probably expect with most elections held in mid-term, though Labour here seem to be doing a lot worse locally than in many other areas between 1998 and 2000. First to go in 1999 were the most unexpected gains. Wyre was regained by the Conservatives, Lancaster lost to no overall control, though here it was the Greens (five gains in Lancaster itself) and Independents (thirteen, mainly in Morecambe) who picked-up seats rather than the Conservatives, whose decline continued here. Hyndburn was lost in 1999 and won outright by the Tories in 2000, an outcome repeated that year in neighbouring Rossendale. Some of Labour's most unexpected problems have come in the bigger towns. It was a major shock when Preston was lost to no overall control in 1999, having previously been Labour since 1980, though it had admittedly been noted for major Labour infighting and a rapid succession of council leaders. Burnley saw dramatic recent growth by an Independent grouping, which caused a big fall in the local Labour vote and consequently the loss of outright control on the council in 2000, By 2002, Labour had regained their majority and they held on comfortably in the May elections, though this poll was notable for a substantial portion of the anti-Labour vote switching to the far right BNP, who claimed three council seats as a result. The 2002 elections also saw Labour regain Hyndburn and Rossendale, but the conservatives gain West Lancashire, where Labour had suffered a split in 2001. Labour have so far held on to the new unitary authority of Blackpool despite its Conservative traditions, suggesting (as do the parliamentary results) a long-term political change of allegiances in Britain's largest seaside resort. Labour have also retained Lancashire county council despite the withdrawal of Blackpool and Blackburn to unitary status, though they have undoubtedly been assisted by the county elections corresponding with the national contest in both 1997 and 2001.

Boundary review

The boundary review will only reach Lancashire towards the end of the current cycle, probably 2003 or 2004. Last time around, the reduction of one seat in the county's total allocation, plus the abolition of the safe Tory seat of Wyre caused radical changes in the north of the county including the unpopular division of the historic city of Lancaster into two seats. At the time these changes appeared to favour the Conservatives, but in the event it was Labour who were to benefit, gaining all four most altered seats in this part of the county (two thirds of their 1997 dividend): Morecambe, Lancaster & Wyre, Blackpool South and Blackpool North & Fleetwood. This time, Lancashire's overall electorate (including Blackpool and Blackburn) of 1.1 million should mean the county keeping fifteen seats, with the average electorate about 72,000, though matters are complicated by the two unitary authorities, each of which are entitled to about one and a half seats. Assuming the unitaries are paired with the county, any changes which do occur are likely to be far less extensive than last time, and should be concentrated in the slightly undersized East Lancashire divisions.

BLACKBURN

	2001		1997		1992 actual	
Electorate and turnout	72,611	55.5	73,132	64.9	73,337	75.0
Conservative	12,559	31.2	11,690	24.6	20,606	37.5
Labour	21,808	54.1	26,141	55.0	26,633	48.4
Lib Dem	3,264	8.1	4,990	10.5	6,332	11.5
Anti–EU	1,185	2.9	1,892	4.0	–	–
Socialist	1,091 (2)	2.7	635	1.3	–	–
Green	–	–	608	1.3	878	1.6
Others	377		1,539 (3)		529 (2)	
MP	Jack Straw (Lab)		Jack Straw (Lab)		Jack Straw (Lab)	
Majority	9,249	23.0	14,451	30.4	6,027	11.0

The mill town of Blackburn has always been won by Labour since the single seat was recreated in 1955, its terraced streets and recent Asian influx helping maintain the party's dominance. For over thirty years this was the constituency of Barbara Castle, who became a prominent minister in the Wilson governments before later becoming an MEP and then a member of the House of Lords. Her successor as MP for Blackburn was a young research assistant and former NUS President called Jack Straw, who as things have turned out surpassed even Castle's ministerial record by becoming Home Secretary during Labour's first term of office and Foreign Secretary in the second. Straw's career has been helped by his astute support for Tony Blair's leadership bid in 1994 as well as his tough line on crime, a policy stance that may not have endeared him to *Guardian* readers, but one which was very much shared by the Labour leader.

Back in Blackburn there has always been a strong minority Conservative interest, with wards in the north of the town like Beardwood and Roe Lee producing a large Tory vote in local elections. Labour poll strongly in the wards around the town centre such as Audley, Wensley Fold and Bastwell, where there are large numbers of Asian voters (the number of non-white voters here is higher than in Burnley), as well as Ewood, home of the town's football club, unlikely Premier League champions in 1994. All in all this is not the Labour monolith one might find in a major city or former mining area, but it remains safe enough to provide cabinet ministers with a secure political base.

BLACKPOOL NORTH and FLEETWOOD

	2001		1997		1992 notional	
Electorate and turnout	74,456	57.2	75,097	71.6	74,797	80.2
Conservative	15,889	37.3	19,105	35.5	29,838	49.8
Labour	21,610	50.8	28,051	52.2	22,562	37.6
Lib Dem	4,132	9.7	4,600	8.6	7,167	12.0
Anti–EU	950	2.2	1,704	3.2	–	–
Others	–		288		387 (2)	
MP	Joan Humble (Lab)		Joan Humble (Lab)		Harold Elletson (Con)	
					Blackpool North	
Majority	5,721	13.4	8,946	16.6	7,276	12.1

North was always regarded as the stronger of the two seats in Blackpool for the Conservatives, and like South had been won at all elections in the post-war period, the margin in 1945 comfortably in five figures. Then in the late 1980s the tide started to change dramatically. Labour had achieved just 21 per cent of the vote in Blackpool North in 1983, but added ten percentage points in 1987 and another ten in 1992, at a time when the party nationally advanced by just three per cent each time. Part of the explanation for the above-average swings was put down to the perceived failings of the local Tory council, which they eventually lost control of part way through the 1987-91 period. Labour took full control of the town hall in 1991, and four years later the gathering storm was to wreak its full vengeance on the Conservatives, reducing them to just two councillors in Blackpool, while up the road they managed to lose their bastion of Wyre as well. The general election result in 1997 could be seen as just the culmination of the changed conditions, as despite boundary changes (the addition of over 30,000 electors from Fleetwood and Wyre) which should have strengthened the Conservative position, Joan Humble easily defeated Harold Elletson by nearly 9,000 votes. In 2001 little seemed to have changed, with Labour retaining a comfortable majority despite a sharp fall in turnout.

The constituency starts just to the north of the town centre, taking in some reasonably up-market territory along the North Shore around the Norbreck Castle complex; in the Bispham and Norbreck wards Labour trailed the Conservatives by a distance in the 2000 local elections. The seat continues up the tramlines into the district of Wyre (unlike to the south of Blackpool there is no separating green belt) and includes Cleveleys and the private Rossall School before ending at Fleetwood. The fishing port was previously the most Labour (and just about only Labour) part of the old Wyre constituency, and in 1999 no fewer than 15 of Labour's 19 councillors on Wyre district council were elected here. Despite this, there are still significant numbers of Tory voters in Rossall and the adjoining Bailey ward, and on balance one feels that together with the voters in the northern wards of Blackpool, they really ought to form a majority in this constituency and clearly would have done at any point before the 1990s. Certainly if the Conservatives are to challenge once again for national office this is a seat they will need to regain.

BLACKPOOL SOUTH

	2001		1997		1992 *notional*	
Electorate and turnout	74,311	52.2	75,861	67.7	75,009	78.5
Conservative	12,798	33.0	17,666	34.4	25,957	44.1
Labour	21,060	54.3	29,282	57.0	25,563	43.4
Lib Dem	4,115	10.6	4,392	8.6	7,148	12.1
Anti–EU	819	2.1	–	–	–	–
Others	–		–		233	
MP	Gordon Marsden (Lab)		Gordon Marsden (Lab)		Nick Hawkins (Con)	
Majority	8,262	21.3	11,616	22.6	394	0.7

Like its northern neighbour, Blackpool South had been held continually by the Conservatives since its creation after the war; even in its inaugural contest in 1945, the majority was the mammoth margin of 16,000 votes. The majority was still in five figures as recently as 1983 when Labour almost finished in third place, but as in North, Labour then advanced spectacularly at the next two general elections to put them within touching distance in 1992. Boundary changes then improved Labour's position further with the transfer of the centre of the town into the constituency, and it was not really a great surprise when *History Today* editor Gordon Marsden triumphed in his second attempt here, though the size of his majority (over 11,500) was fairly extraordinary for a town which had never previously elected a Labour MP.

The constituency includes most of the tourist attractions Blackpool has to offer, including the famous Tower in the centre and huge Pleasure Beach complex along the promenade to the south. Politically, Labour currently come out on top in most of the local council wards, with the Tories winning only eight of the constituency's thirty council seats in 2000, their vote now largely restricted to the eastern and southern suburbs towards Stanley Park and Squires Gate airport, though Squires Gate itself is held by the Lib Dems. It seems a long time since the profusion of B&B's in tourist resorts such as this were automatically associated with support for the Conservative party, and for now Labour seem to have found themselves an unlikely safe seat along the Fylde coast.

BURNLEY

	2001		1997		1992 actual	
Electorate and turnout	66,271	55.7	67,582	66.9	69,128	74.2
Conservative	7,697	20.9	9,148	20.2	15,693	30.6
Labour	18,195	49.3	26,210	57.9	27,184	53.0
Lib Dem	5,975	16.2	7,877	17.4	8,414	16.4
Anti–EU	866	2.3	2,010	4.4	–	–
BNP	4,151	11.3	–	–	–	–
MP	Peter Pike (Lab)		Peter Pike (Lab)		Peter Pike (Lab)	
Majority	10,498	28.5	17,062	37.7	11,491	22.4

Burnley has been a Labour seat since 1935, its left wing credentials demonstrated even earlier when the leader of the marxist Social-Democratic Federation, H.M.Hyndman, came within 400 votes of victory in 1906. In more recent times, Labour only seemed in trouble here in their disastrous year of 1983, when new standard-bearer Peter Pike defeated Tory Ian Bruce (who moved on to Dorset South) by just 770 votes. Now, however, Labour seems to have problems here again. Even before the general election of 2001, it was clear that something was amiss: Labour's local election vote had fallen from 60 per cent in 1995 down to 43 per cent in 1999, and it dropped by another six points in 2000, when they lost overall control of the council. It was not the Conservatives or Liberal Democrats who were picking up these deserting Labour votes, rather a new grouping of Independents, some of whom had split away from the ruling Labour group. Opponents suspected that these developments might have a racial element; Burnley has a large Asian community, and there were accusations that the wards in which they were concentrated received an unfair slice of public funding. Then in June 2001 the British National Party picked up fully 11 per cent of the vote after voicing similar sentiments. It was the far right party's second best performance in the country, but unlike in Oldham, their support appeared to come almost entirely from previous Labour voters. The summer riots which briefly dominated the national news agenda gave the town more unwelcome publicity, and the BNP were still able to record nearly 20 per cent of the vote in one of three council by-elections held in late 2001, which was a portent of things to come in the 2002 local poll.

In those elections the BNP claimed their first victories for nearly a decade, winning three council seats despite failing in apparently similar circumstances in nearby Oldham. They were helped in Burnley by the already large Independent vote, some of which seems to be quite happy to switch to the far-right. Equally the failure of the opposition parties (Conservative and Liberal Democrat) to field full slates of candidates enabled the BNP to garner a large slice of the anti-Labour vote.

Whatever the cause, politicians from the mainstream parties will hope that this does not mark the start of a shift to the far-right in British politics as has taken place elsewhere.

CHORLEY

	2001		1997		1992 notional	
Electorate and turnout	77,036	62.2	74,615	77.3	73,536	82.4
Conservative	16,644	34.7	20,737	35.9	27,752	45.8
Labour	25,088	52.3	30,607	53.0	25,228	41.6
Lib Dem	5,372	11.2	4,900	8.5	7,249	12.0
Anti–EU	848	1.8	1,319	2.3	–	–
Others	–		143		373	
MP	Lindsay Hoyle (Lab)		Lindsay Hoyle (Lab)		Den Dover (Con)	
Majority	8,444	17.6	9,870	17.1	2,524	4.2

Chorley has been an important marginal seat for many years. It has changed hands on the previous four occasions on which the governing party in has been defeated: 1970, February 1974, 1979 and 1997. After 1979, boundary changes (the transfer of Leyland to the new South Ribble seat) were thought to make things better for the Tories, but after holding on in 1992, Den Dover's 18 years as MP came to an end in the landslide conditions of 1997.

The constituency is based on the small town itself (population about 35,000) plus a large number of surrounding villages, which provide many of the Tory votes. In the 2000 locals Charnock Richard (near the motorway services of the same name) and Brindle & Hoghton gave their Conservative candidates over 70 per cent of the vote, and they also polled well in some of the outer western suburbs of Chorley. Labour however won most of the wards in the town, and must have had a fair lead here in both 1997 and 2001. They are also strong in Adlington to the south, while other centres of population like Euxton and the new housing estates in Clayton up the M61 towards Preston are more mixed. Lindsay Hoyle (son of former Labour MP for Warrington, Doug, now Lord, Hoyle) actually increased his majority in percentage terms in 2001, and the fact that there are now 122 more vulnerable Labour seats in the country shows just how much work the Conservatives have to do if they are to regain this modern day bellwether.

FYLDE

	2001		1997		1992 notional	
Electorate and turnout	73,460	60.9	71,460	72.9	70,389	75.1
Conservative	23,383	52.3	25,443	48.9	31,849	60.2
Labour	13,773	30.8	16,480	31.7	9,827	18.6
Lib Dem	6,599	14.8	7,609	14.6	10,937	20.7
Anti–EU	982	2.2	2,372	4.6	–	–
Others	–		163		268	
MP	Michael Jack (Con)		Michael Jack (Con)		Michael Jack (Con)	
Majority	9,610	21.5	8,963	17.2	20,912	39.6

Fylde has the distinction of being the only constituency in Lancashire which the Conservatives have not lost over the last 10–15 years. In fact they have held this seat at all general elections since 1918, with the party's share of the vote only dropping below 50 per cent on a single occasion, 1997. Given that even in Labour's landslide year, Michael Jack (a minister in the outgoing government) won by nearly 9,000, it is clear that this is and remains a very safe Tory seat. Indeed under its old name of South Fylde, the constituency produced a majority of more than 32,000 in 1979, the largest in Britain. Such status is probably unsurprising given that the main centre of population here is twee Lytham St Annes (two towns which appear to have seamlessly merged), a few miles down the coast from its much larger and rather vulgar neighbour, Blackpool, though thankfully separated by a clear green space. The seat also includes Warton with its British Aerospace plant and Kirkham a little inland, but none of this hurts the Conservatives much, and Labour usually win only a single local council seat, though this did increase to an unprecedented six (out of 49) in 1995. More successful in local contests are a collection of Independents and Ratepayers, who have denied the Tories outright control of the council, but no-one seems likely to deny them outright victory in the parliamentary seat.

HYNDBURN

	2001		1997		1992 notional	
Electorate and turnout	66,533	57.5	66,931	72.1	66,766	83.2
Conservative	12,681	33.2	15,383	31.9	23,995	43.2
Labour	20,900	54.7	26,831	55.6	26,026	46.9
Lib Dem	3,680	9.6	4,141	8.6	5,314	9.6
Anti–EU	982	2.6	1,627	3.4	–	–
Others	–		290		219	
MP	Greg Pope (Lab)		Greg Pope (Lab)		Greg Pope (Lab)	
Majority	8,219	21.5	11,448	23.7	2,031	3.7

Hyndburn covers the small towns which lie between Blackburn and Burnley, notably Accrington (the name of the seat until 1983) but also Great Harwood, Rishton, Clayton-le-Moors and Oswaldtwistle. It is a traditionally working class constituency which was always won by Labour between 1945 and 1979, but even in those days majorities could be small (600 in 1959 and 1970) and it was not a total shock when the Tories finally gained it in 1983, though the fact that the margin was just 21 votes after five recounts did win a certain amount of headline space. The Conservative Kenneth Hargreaves increased his majority to 2,000 in 1987 before losing by the same margin in 1992, and it now looks as safe a Labour seat as it has ever been. Before 2001, local election results (Labour lost the council in 1999 and the Tories gained outright control in 2000) suggested there might be problems in store for Greg Pope, but an impressive performance in the general election saw only a minimal drop in the Labour vote compared with all the neighbouring constituencies. Whereas the Labour vote fell by 8.6 percentage points in Burnley and Pendle and 5 points in Rossendale & Darwen, and the Tory vote increased by 6 points in Jack Straw's Blackburn, Hyndburn recorded little change and Pope's majority remains over 8,000 votes, a wider margin than Labour ever recorded here between 1945 and 1979. Labour's victories continued with recapture of the council in 2002.

LANCASHIRE WEST

	2001		1997		1992 notional	
Electorate and turnout	73,046	58.8	73,320	74.6	73,013	81.7
Conservative	13,761	32.0	15,903	29.1	25,243	42.3
Labour	23,404	54.5	33,022	60.3	29,470	49.4
Lib Dem	4,966	11.6	3,938	7.2	4,147	7.0
Anti–EU	–	–	1,025	1.9	–	–
Others	840 (2)		841 (2)		792 (2)	
MP	Colin Pickthall (Lab)		Colin Pickthall (Lab)		Colin Pickthall (Lab)	
Majority	9,643	22.4	17,119	31.3	4,227	7.1

Lancashire West (or West Lancs as it is known locally) is centred on the new town of Skelmersdale but also includes its rather more long-standing neighbour of Ormskirk and smaller settlements such as Burscough and Parbold. It is an odd mixture. 'Skem' was always a Merseyside overspill settlement, and seems to have imported its political culture as well: solid Labour voting combined with some rather vicious in-fighting, and local de-selections and reselections were reaching their height in the run-up to the 2001 elections. Shortly afterwards, a group of disaffected Labour councillors broke away to form their own group (West Lancashire First) and as a result Labour lost control of the district council.

The political contours in the more established areas of the constituency are very different. The new town was planted in an area which had traditional Conservative voting habits; Ormskirk was a very safe Tory seat from 1950 until 1970, and Robert Kilroy-Silk (the very same) only won it in 1974 and 1979 because of the brief inclusion of Kirkby. The southern suburbs of Ormskirk still exude an air of affluence. In 1999 the Tories polled well over 70 per cent of the vote in Aughton Park and Aughton Town Green while the rural wards around the town are also strongholds. As a consequence, it was they who won the first two contests after West Lancashire was created in 1983, despite the inclusion of Skelmersdale. Colin Pickthall finally gained the seat for Labour in 1992, and despite a huge majority in 1997, it still cannot be totally secure. If the Conservatives were ever to threaten a national majority again, this is probably somewhere they would consider winnable (they gained outright control of the council in 2002), particularly if the local Labour party continues to inflict damaging blows on itself with such great enthusiasm.

LANCASTER and WYRE

	2001		1997		1992 notional	
Electorate and turnout	79,458	65.9	78,684	74.8	75,314	78.6
Conservative	22,075	42.2	23,878	40.6	30,838	52.1
Labour	22,556	43.1	25,173	42.8	19,554	33.1
Lib Dem	5,383	10.3	6,802	11.6	8,264	14.0
Anti–EU	741	1.4	2,214 (2)	3.8	–	–
Green	1,595	3.0	795	1.4	330	0.4
Others	–		–		180	
MP	Hilton Dawson (Lab)		Hilton Dawson (Lab)		TWO SEATS MERGE	
Majority	481	0.9	1,295	2.2	11,284	19.1

The Conservatives' failure to regain Lancaster and Wyre was one of the party's more dismal results in 2001 – after all, here was a seat that Labour had gained against all expectations in 1997, and even then their rather small majority was exceeded by the Referendum Party vote (1,516). Lancaster had been a Labour seat previously (1966-70), but this new constituency should be far more favourable to the Tories; shorn of Labour-supporting areas in Lancaster north of the River Lune (transferred to Morecambe) it includes a huge swath of Tory-supporting farmland almost as far south as Preston and runs west as far as Poulton-le-Fylde in Wyre district, hardly a bastion of the left either. Although the five Lancaster wards which remain in the constituency were all won by Labour in the 1995 local elections and will have produced a healthy Labour lead in 1997, Hilton Dawson must have gained support in some unlikely places to have collected the 25,000 votes required for victory.

By 2001, the chances of a repeat seemed slim as Labour not only had to fend off the Tories but also had the additional challenge of squeezing the growing Green vote in Lancaster. Boosted by growing numbers of students in the city (now estimated at between 10 and 15,000, almost one in three of the local population), the party won five council seats from Labour in 1999 and were determined to follow-up with a county council seat in 2001. But whereas the Greens successfully polled no fewer than 4,500 votes in the county council election on June 7th, the figure fell to approximately 1,500 in the general election, the assumption being that most of the missing 3,000 voted Labour nationally. With the Tories failing to advance, the outcome was that, against all the odds, Labour won here again. With a majority of under 500 (Labour's 4th most marginal seat) there will undoubtedly be another major battle at the next general election.

MORECAMBE and LUNESDALE

	2001		1997		1992 notional	
Electorate and turnout	68,159	61.1	68,114	72.3	68,375	78.1
Conservative	15,554	37.3	18,096	36.7	26,292	49.2
Labour	20,646	49.6	24,061	48.9	15,720	29.4
Lib Dem	3,817	9.2	5,614	11.4	10,183	19.1
Anti–EU	935	2.2	1,313	2.7	–	–
Others	703		165		1,223 (2)	
MP	Geraldine Smith (Lab)		Geraldine Smith (Lab)		Mark Lennox-Boyd (Con)	
Majority	5,092	12.2	5,965	12.1	10,572	19.8

Prior to 1997, the idea that Morecambe could be represented by a Labour MP seemed absurd. As in many traditional seaside resorts, the Conservatives always won general elections, even though socio-economic statistics showed Labour should have been performing a whole lot better than they did. Many put this discrepancy down to the 'landlady vote' (fierce hoteliers voting Tory), though a rather more encompassing explanation might have been that the myriad of small businesses which have always abounded in seaside resorts made them predisposed to the Tories and instinctively hostile to Labour. All that changed however in the 1990s, possibly because of the perceived economic failures of the Major government. In Morecambe and neighbouring Heysham, this first became apparent in the 1995 local elections when Labour advanced spectacularly to pick up a record haul of council seats. Meanwhile, boundary changes added to the parliamentary seat 10,000 voters in Labour-supporting Skerton, essentially Lancaster north of the Lune. The outcome was that in 1997 Geraldine Smith defeated long-serving MP Mark Lennox-Boyd, the 16 per cent swing well above both the national and regional average. Even though Labour then lost many of its newly won council seats in 1999 (to the 'Morecambe Bay Independents' rather than the Conservatives), they retained an almost unchanged majority in 2001.

Labour strength here is concentrated in two parts of the constituency. Skerton has long been their best part of the city of Lancaster, while the southern ward of Heysham, where the nuclear power stations have lately been the major employer, has been Labour's most frequently held council ward in Morecambe. The centre of Morecambe itself has its fair share of social deprivation, but still seems a rather conservative (if no longer Conservative) kind of place where older voters constantly moan about the type of people attracted by major events while simultaneously decrying the death of tourism in the town. Such attitudes reach a peak in the inappropriately named Bare (where the latest figures suggest 42 per cent are aged 60 or over), and beyond that the seat becomes semi-rural, with the Conservatives continuing to poll strongly aside from the railway town of Carnforth, noted as the scene of the film *Brief Encounter* and still home to a reasonable Labour vote. The rural Lunesdale portion of the seat contains only a few thousand voters, though is noteworthy for an estimate that more than one in four were Conservative members in the 1980s. As in Lancaster and Blackpool North, one feels that the Tories really must win seats like this if they are to form governments in the future.

PENDLE

	2001		1997		1992 actual	
Electorate and turnout	62,870	63.2	63,090	74.6	64,066	82.9
Conservative	13,454	33.9	14,235	30.3	21,384	40.3
Labour	17,729	44.6	25,059	53.3	23,497	44.2
Lib Dem	5,479	13.8	5,460	11.6	7,976	15.0
Anti–EU	1,094	2.8	2,281	4.8	–	–
BNP	1,976	5.0	–	–	–	–
Others	–		–		263	
MP	Gordon Prentice (Lab)		Gordon Prentice (Lab)		Gordon Prentice (Lab)	
Majority	4,275	10.8	10,824	23.0	2,113	4.0

Pendle is the easternmost constituency in Lancashire, named after Pendle Hill (not to mention the Pendle witches) and based on the towns of Nelson and Colne which lie between Burnley and the Yorkshire border, though also including smaller settlements like Earby and Barnoldswick and the surrounding rural areas to the north.

Under its former name of Nelson and Colne, the constituency had been held by Labour almost continually from its formation at the end of the First World War onwards, but following the death of MP Sydney Silverman in 1968, a by-election was won by the Conservatives after a swing of 11 per cent. Although Labour's national ratings were to recover from the depths of the late 1960s, they failed to win the seat back in 1970, and although Doug Hoyle did briefly regain it in October 1974, it was promptly lost again (by just 436 votes) in 1979. The three-term stint of moderate Tory John Lee was brought to an end when he was defeated by sitting incumbent Gordon Prentice in 1992, one of thirteen occasions since 1950 when the majority here has been less than 5,000 votes.

In recent years Pendle has continued to see activity by all three main political parties, and the larger than average swing to the Tories in 2001 seems to have confirmed a return to marginal status. The Conservatives' main areas of strength in the constituency can be found in the more rural areas; they polled nearly 80 per cent in the Reedley ward in the 2000 local elections and almost 90 per cent in Pendleside, also winning Earby and Barrowford. Labour do well in most parts of Nelson, which has a significant non-white population (one in ten of the constituency's electors are Asian), while the Lib Dems can still win council wards, though their local and national vote has retreated somewhat from the peaks of the 1980s. Labour just about retain the upper hand, but after 2001 the seat leapt 90 places from being Labour's 153rd most vulnerable seat up to their 63rd, and it can certainly not be taken for granted.

PRESTON

	2001		1997		1992 *notional*	
Electorate and turnout	73,309	49.2	73,097	65.8	*72,856*	*75.8*
Conservative	8,272	23.0	10,540	21.9	*17,876*	*32.4*
Labour	20,540	57.0	29,220	60.8	*29,342*	*53.1*
Lib Dem	4,746	13.2	7,045	14.7	*7,644*	*13.8*
Anti–EU	–	–	924	1.9	–	–
Green	1,019	2.8	–	–	–	–
Others	1,464 (2)		345		*376*	
MP	Mark Hendrick (Lab)		Audrey Wise (Lab)		Audrey Wise (Lab)	
Majority	12,268	34.0	18,680	38.9	*11,466*	*20.8*

Parliamentary by-election 23 November 2000: Labour 9,765 (45.7), Conservative 5,339 (25.0), Liberal Democrat 3,454 (16.2), Independent Socialist 1,210 (5.7), Anti–EU 458 (2.1), Green 441 (2.1), 3 Others 696. Electorate 72,229, Turnout 29.6%. MP: Mark Hendrick (Lab), Majority 4,426 (20.7).

In the 1970s, Preston could provide two wafer-thin marginal constituencies which regularly oscillated between Labour and the Conservatives. Thus in 1979, Robert Atkins gained Preston North for the Tories by just 29 votes (confusingly defeating Labour's Ronald Atkins), while Labour held Preston South by the slightly more comfortable 621. But in the early 1980s, boundary changes pared the two seats down to an urban core, with suburbs to the north transferred to Ribble Valley, and those to the south linked with Leyland in the new South Ribble constituency. The result was that the single Preston seat became safely Labour, held by left-winger Audrey Wise for 13 years from 1987. Her death sparked a major succession battle within the local Labour party, not unused to internal conflict, between her daughter and former council leader, Valerie Wise, and the moderate former MEP for Lancashire Central, Mark Hendrick. A very hard-fought race was won by Hendrick, who then found the actual by-election contest rather more straightforward, though as ever in inner-city by-elections these days, fewer than one in three bothered to vote. In the general election, Labour's majority returned to five-figures with turnout remaining below 50 per cent.

The seat includes the centre of the town, radiating out to the west and east, but does not include the more prosperous northern suburbs in and around Fulwood, most of which are included in Ribble Valley, or the two affluent north-western wards which are currently part of Lancashire's other Tory seat, Fylde. The Preston wards which are in the constituency largely comprise fairly dense terraced housing, these days mostly filled either by Asians or students, the growth of the latter group a major reason for the sharp recent drop in turnout which has exceeded the national fall. Since the last set of boundary changes the seat has also included the old mill town and Labour stronghold of Bamber Bridge, rather unfairly the cheapest property on the Lancashire version of Monopoly, and Walton-le-Dale which is more mixed. All in all it is difficult to see where a challenge to Labour might come from; the poor performance of both Conservatives and Liberal Democrats even in the exceptional conditions of a by-election hardly suggests a breakthrough is imminent.

RIBBLE VALLEY

	2001		1997		1992 notional	
Electorate and turnout	74,319	66.2	72,920	78.5	71,262	84.4
Conservative	25,308	51.5	26,702	46.7	31,629	52.6
Labour	9,793	19.9	9,013	15.8	5,254	8.7
Lib Dem	14,070	28.6	20,062	35.1	23,000	38.2
Anti–EU	–	–	1,297	2.3	–	–
Others	–		147		282	
MP	Nigel Evans (Con)		Nigel Evans (Con)		Nigel Evans (Con)	
Majority	11,238	22.9	6,640	11.6	8,629	14.3

It now seems extraordinary that the town of Clitheroe presented the new Labour Representation Committee, forerunner of today's Labour Party, with one of their earliest parliamentary gains in 1902. The Ribble Valley, with Clitheroe at its heart, now appears a solid Conservative heartland - part of a chain of seats from Fylde on the west coast to Beverley and Holderness on the east which destroys the popular misconception that the Tories cannot win in the north. Tory majorities here reached almost 20,000 in 1983 and 1987, and defeat at the hands of the Liberal Democrats in the 1991 by-election which followed the move of former Home Secretary, David Waddington to the House of Lords was seen as a disaster for the party.

Yet it was not so long ago that Labour could pose a serious challenge here. Although the Tories regained the seat of Clitheroe in 1922 and held on throughout the inter-war period, Labour made a second short-lived breakthrough in 1945, and continued to record votes of over 40 per cent throughout the 1950s. Only in recent times has this seat (renamed Ribble Valley in 1983) appeared to become safe for the Conservatives, partly a result of the boundary changes which removed a number of small working-class towns around Accrington, Blackburn and Burnley and replaced them with prosperous suburbs to the north of Preston, and partly a result of significant social change which has seen the area become one of the most desirable commuter locations in the north of England. Even though Labour are recovering here from the squeeze of the 1991 by-election, the Lib Dems, for whom Michael Carr has now stood in six consecutive parliamentary elections, are in clear retreat. Conservative MP Nigel Evans, defeated by Carr in 1991 but victorious in the last three contests, appears to now have a secure base.

ROSSENDALE and DARWEN

	2001		1997		1992 notional	
Electorate and turnout	70,884	58.7	70,154	73.0	70,176	82.2
Conservative	15,281	36.7	16,521	32.3	24,995	43.5
Labour	20,251	48.7	27,470	53.6	25,044	43.6
Lib Dem	6,079	14.6	5,435	10.6	6,978	11.8
Anti–EU	–	–	1,108	2.2	–	–
Others	–		674		652 (2)	
MP	Janet Anderson (Lab)		Janet Anderson (Lab)		Janet Anderson (Lab)	
Majority	4,970	11.9	10,949	21.4	49	0.1

Rossendale and Darwen covers the south-eastern portion of the present county of Lancashire, mainly consisting of wild moorland surrounding narrow valleys filled with terraced houses, originally built to service the many mills in the area. Even the names like Bacup and Rawtenstall sound remote, while the two main parts of the seat cannot even be reached by road from each other without travelling through neighbouring seats because of the barrier created by the moors.

The constituency produced one of the closest and most dramatic results of the 1992 election, when Janet Anderson defeated sitting Conservative MP and then government minister, David Trippier, by just 120 votes. The former Rossendale seat had been Labour from 1945 until it was lost in 1970, but thereafter gradually shifted towards the Tories compared with the average pattern across Lancashire. Although it was temporarily regained by Labour in October 1974 by another tiny margin, 203 votes, Trippier won it with a large swing in 1979, and the Conservative position was if anything strengthened by the boundary changes of the early 1980s. These revisions brought in the town of Darwen, part of a constituency which had reliably returned Conservative MPs since the 1930s. Although some of its most Tory segments were distributed to Blackburn, Ribble Valley and Bolton, the transfer of Darwen itself (which produced an almost exact three-way split in the 2000 local elections) certainly did not make Labour's task of winning the seat any easier. In 1983 they lost by fully 9,000 votes, but their narrow victory two elections later has paved the way for two more comfortable wins in 1997 and 2001. The seat cannot be regarded as safe however; Rossendale council was lost to the Conservatives in 2000 and there was a larger swing here in 2001 than the national or county average. It is now Labour's 75th most vulnerable seat nationally – though they will be heartened by the regain of the council in 2002; perhaps the swings to the Tories in 2000–2001 were a short-lived 'Hague effect'.

SOUTH RIBBLE

	2001		1997		1992 notional	
Electorate and turnout	73,794	62.5	71,670	77.1	71,002	83.0
Conservative	17,584	38.1	20,772	37.6	29,366	49.9
Labour	21,386	46.4	25,856	46.8	20,526	34.8
Lib Dem	7,150	15.5	5,879	10.6	8,695	14.8
Anti–EU	–	–	1,475	2.7	–	–
Others	–		1,249 (2)		326	
MP	David Borrow (Lab)		David Borrow (Lab)		Robert Atkins (Con)	
Majority	3,802	8.2	5,084	9.2	8,840	15.0

The constituency of South Ribble is made up of four distinct parts: the southern suburbs of Preston around Penwortham (literally Preston south of the Ribble), newer suburban estates centred on Lostock Hall, the small town of Leyland made famous by its vehicle production and finally some rather more rural areas to the west, off the Preston to Southport road. As this suggests, South Ribble is a very mixed seat where all three main parties win their fair share of local council seats. Labour mop up a large vote in Leyland and parts of Penwortham, the Conservatives are very strong in the small, commuter-belt settlements off the A59 such as Hutton, Longton, Hoole and Tarleton and the Lib Dems are (locally at least) ahead in Farington and parts of Leyland.

From its creation in 1983, South Ribble was held by Robert Atkins for the Conservatives, but this was exactly the kind of place which Labour had to win if they were to get back into power with a reasonable majority, and in 1997 former Preston council leader David Borrow duly gained the seat with a 12 per cent swing. Four years later, Labour held on comfortably after a miniscule advance by the Tories, who will need to do an awful lot better if they are to regain crucial marginal constituencies such as this one. This is now Labour's 41st most marginal seat.

Leicestershire

including Leicester and Rutland

	Conservative		Labour		Liberal Democrat		Others	
	Share of vote	Seats	Share of vote	Seats	Share of vote	Seats	Share of vote	Seats
2001	38.1	5	41.5	5	17.0	0	3.4	0
1997	36.8	5	43.8	5	15.1	0	4.3	0
1992	48.7	6	33.0	3	17.1	0	1.2	0
1987	52.0	6	27.3	3	20.2	0	0.5	0
1983	50.6	8	25.3	1	22.7	0	1.4	0

Leicestershire is just about at the geographical heart of England, a hundred miles north of London and closer to more built-up areas to the west and north. It is a county which is very much divided between its largest urban centre and the generally affluent small towns and villages which surround it. Leicester itself is approximately the tenth largest city in England (depending on how these things are calculated) with a population just under 300,000. That figure has remained remarkably constant in recent years because the outwardly bound middle classes have been replaced with a large Asian population predominantly of Indian and East African origin. Many were initially attracted by jobs in the hosiery and knitwear industries, and estimates of current numbers tend to be around the 80–100,000 mark – indeed a recent report predicted that Leicester would soon become the first majority non-white city in Britain. Neighbourhoods such as those off the Belgrave Road to the north of the city centre are now some of the most flourishing ethnic centres one will find outside of London, and there is no question that this has prompted a political change too (see below).

Outside of Leicester, no single town can boast a population greater than 60,000. The most well-known of the other towns is Loughborough (45,000), which boasts a university well known for its sporting prowess. The second largest settlement in the county is actually Hinckley (58,000), which has grown in size somewhat over recent decades. Smaller towns include Melton Mowbray (25,000), Market Harborough (17,000), Coalville (30,000) and the most exotically named of all, Ashby-de-la-Zouch (12,000). There is also a substantial population of 150,000 or so living in a suburban ring just outside of the Leicester city boundaries, in places like Oadby, Wigston and Blaby. These are the places which have grown most in size since the second world war as certain groups have moved out of Leicester itself. The more affluent have moved even further out, into the band of villages towards Lutterworth and Market Harborough in the south and towards Loughborough in the north. These areas are close enough to the M1 motorway to provide good transport links while retaining their rural character, with parts of the Charnwood Forest in particular seeming about a million miles away from the inner city wards of Leicester.

This section also includes the now restored pocket-sized county of Rutland, which sits between Leicestershire and Lincolnshire. 'Rutlandshire' has a population of just 30,000, presumably the reason for its abolition in 1973, but never came to terms with its absorption into its larger neighbour, and was always a candidate for unitary status in the recent local government review. The county's main town is Oakham (8,700), and it also includes the large man-made reservoir of Rutland Water. It has a couple of private schools, some expensive house prices, and perhaps unsurprisingly in view of all this has been represented by Conservative MPs on a continual basis since 1868 - the last time the Tories lost a general election here was 1841. For parliamentary purposes, Rutland lost its separate representation immediately after the first world war, paired first with Stamford in Lincolnshire from 1918 until 1983, and thereafter with Melton, the easternmost district of Leicestershire.

Most of the other constituencies in this section (with the exception of two relatively recent creations, Blaby and Charnwood) have seen changes in their political complexion in the post-war period. In general, the rural areas seem to have witnessed a gradual swing to the right, while Leicester itself has undoubtedly shifted in the opposite direction. Both Harborough and Bosworth are in the small group of seats won by Labour in 1945 but not in 1997 or 2001, though in the case of Bosworth, this is down to boundary changes, the creation of North West Leicestershire in 1983 taking away most of Labour's better areas. When one adds Melton & Rutland and the two new seats, both of which have always been won by the Conservatives, one is left with a bloc of five Tory seats in Leicestershire, each covering a slice of suburban and rural territory around Leicester. In the north of the county, Labour currently win both Loughborough and North West Leicestershire (a seat largely based on the old coalfield), but these 1997 gains remain marginal and are vulnerable to any national Conservative recovery.

Leicester is different. It was one of the few major cities (along with Bradford, Hull and Stoke) where Labour retained all the seats in 1979, and although they were less fortunate in 1983, the party has again held all three seats ever since 1987. Prior to 1974, the old South East constituency was always won by the Tories, and it was generally assumed that they would be well placed to win the new Leicester South as well. This has not come to pass; apart from a single occasion (Labour's meltdown year of 1983, when they lost the seat by just seven votes) the Conservatives have failed to win here, and at the moment they are battling to hold on to second place. Leicester East was gained by the Conservatives in somewhat fortuitous circumstances in 1983, when sitting member Tom Bradley stood for the SDP, split the Labour vote, and allowed the Tories to win with 39 per cent, but since then it has reverted to type. In 1987, East returned Keith Vaz, Britain's first Asian MP in the post-war period, and since then Labour have not looked in any danger here, despite the adverse publicity generated in 2001. The one seat held by Labour throughout the period since 1983 is Leicester West, the city's old working class constituency, which was represented for many years by Barnett and then Greville Janner, and now by cabinet minister Patricia Hewitt.

Local government

Leicestershire's pattern of local council control follows the colours of the parliamentary map to a large extent, though with far greater Liberal Democrat support. This is particularly true around Leicester: the Lib Dems have controlled the small Oadby & Wigston district to the south of the city since 1991, and currently (early 2002) have over twenty of the twenty-six seats. They are also now the largest opposition group on Leicester unitary authority, though Labour have a narrow overall majority, and were in control of the old city council for most of the 1973-1995 period. The Lib Dems are the largest party on balanced Hinckley & Bosworth, which was run by the Conservatives from 1976 until 1991 and narrowly second on another usually Tory (but now balanced) council, Harborough. Other hung councils are Charnwood (which Labour won for the first time in 1995), Rutland unitary (lots of Independents and Others), and Melton, which has seen perhaps the most remarkable change of all, as Labour have increased their representation from no councillors at all between 1979 and 1991 to the largest group on the council after 1999. Elsewhere, Blaby (only ever lost in 1995) is heavily Conservative, while North West Leicestershire is generally Labour. What remains of Leicestershire county council has tilted (in the absence of Leicester) towards the Conservatives, who were the largest group in a balanced council after 1997 and took overall control after 2001.

Boundary review

At each of the last three reviews, new seats have been created in Leicestershire (Blaby in 1974, North West Leicestershire in 1983 and Charnwood in 1997) but this pattern is unlikely to continue this time. Leicester remains entitled to three parliamentary seats, though there may be minor changes between them as South is slightly too big, East and West too small. The remainder of Leicestershire and Rutland should retain seven seats – again there are some seats slightly over-sized at present (notably Charnwood), but it seems unlikely that any changes will be particularly drastic.

BLABY

	2001		1997		1992 notional	
Electorate and turnout	73,907	64.5	70,471	76.0	67,238	83.5
Conservative	22,104	46.4	24,564	45.8	31,882	56.8
Labour	15,895	33.4	18,090	33.8	12,213	21.8
Lib Dem	8,286	17.4	8,001	14.9	11,261	20.1
Anti–EU	–	–	2,018	3.8	–	–
Others	1,357		920 (2)		781	
MP	Andrew Robathan (Con)		Andrew Robathan (Con)		Andrew Robathan (Con)	
Majority	6,209	13.0	6,474	12.1	19,669	35.0

Like Nottingham, the city of Leicester is surrounded by a ring of seats which take in many of its middle class suburbs. To the north, places like Birstall and Thurmaston are included in Charnwood, to the south east, Oadby and Wigston make up much of the electorate of the Harborough constituency, while in the south west, places like Narborough, Braunstone, Blaby and Whetstone form the core of the Blaby seat. Unlike the Nottingham area, all these constituencies have remained in the Conservative column in the last two general elections. They are helped by the greater geographical area which they cover, reaching out in all cases to take in chunks of rural Leicestershire; Blaby includes Broughton Astley and Lutterworth, which both voted Conservative in the 2001 county council poll, though there is something of a Labour vote in Lutterworth. In fact the Tories are on top in most wards in the constituency, with the strongest Labour area found in Braunstone, and Blaby itself home to a reasonable Liberal Democrat vote.

Blaby was for many years the constituency of Nigel Lawson, Chancellor of the Exchequer between 1983 and 1989. After his resignation from the government, Lawson stood down at the following general election to be replaced by Andrew Robathan. In 1992 he was duly elected by more than 25,000 votes against split opposition, at that time the Tories' 26th largest majority in the country. After 1992, boundary changes made Blaby slightly less safe by transferring 15,000 electors around Leicester Forest East to Charnwood, and the effect of this along with the huge national swing in 1997 was to reduce the majority to just 6,000 over Labour. Very little changed in 2001, though the constituency has now fallen out of the list of the one hundred safest Tory seats.

BOSWORTH

	2001		1997		1992 notional	
Electorate and turnout	69,992	64.4	68,249	76.4	66,420	84.1
Conservative	20,030	44.4	21,189	40.6	28,863	51.7
Labour	17,750	39.4	20,162	38.7	14,732	26.4
Lib Dem	7,326	16.2	9,281	17.8	11,576	20.7
Anti–EU	–	–	1,521	2.9	–	–
Others	–		–		716	
MP	David Tredinnick (Con)		David Tredinnick (Con)		David Tredinnick (Con)	
Majority	2,280	5.1	1,027	2.0	14,131	25.3

It now seems surprising that Bosworth was held continuously by Labour between 1945 and 1970, and even more unlikely that the last Labour MP for the seat was Woodrow Wyatt, before his days as the Thatcherite 'voice of reason'. In fact the current constituency is very different from its earlier incarnation, with significant boundary alterations in the early 1980s removing 26,000 voters in the former Leicestershire coalfield area (around the appropriately named Coalville) to Leicestershire North West. Bosworth is now focused on the town of Hinckley, along with smaller more working-class settlements such as Barwell and Earl Shilton, which provide the bulk of the 'core' Labour vote here.

In 1983 and 1987, Labour finished third in the redrawn Bosworth, behind the Liberals and more than 20,000 votes adrift of the Conservatives. Then in 1992 their vote advanced by nearly 9 percentage points to move into second place, and in 1997 a further swing of 12 per cent left MP David Tredinnick hanging on by just 1,000 votes. The Tories mounted something of a recovery in the 1999 local council elections, though the Liberal Democrats remain the largest party on the hung Hinckley & Bosworth council. Hinckley itself was very marginal between all three parties in the 2001 local (county council) elections, with Market Bosworth and its famous battlefield strongly Tory and Earl Shilton Labour. Interestingly, the Lib Dems were able to poll 11,777 across the constituency in the county election, losing about a third of those when it came to the general election ballot paper. Of these 4,000 or so 'ticket-splitters', Labour gained three votes for every one that went to the Tories, reducing a 4,500 county election deficit, but not by enough to deny Tredinnick victory. His increased majority (since 1997) of 2,280 means his party may now be able to breathe a little more easily here.

CHARNWOOD

	2001		1997		1992 notional	
Electorate and turnout	74,900	64.4	73,034	76.9	71,672	80.9
Conservative	23,283	48.2	26,110	46.5	35,126	60.6
Labour	15,544	32.2	20,210	36.0	12,526	21.6
Lib Dem	7,835	16.2	7,224	12.9	10,345	17.8
Anti–EU	1,603	3.3	2,104	3.7	–	–
Others	–		525		–	
MP	Stephen Dorrell (Con)		Stephen Dorrell (Con)		NEW SEAT	
Majority	7,739	16.0	5,900	10.5	22,600	39.0

Charnwood (named after the forest of the same name) was a new constituency created in 1997. It is made up of middle class suburbs just outside the Leicester city boundaries such as Thurmaston, Birstall and Syston to the north of the city and Leicester Forest East, Kirby Muxloe and Glenfield (home of Leicestershire county council) to the west. The newly created seat was always assumed to be safely Tory, though the 1997 result was a lot closer than anticipated. Part of the reason for this seems to have been that the notional 1992 results over-estimated the Conservative vote in Charnwood by up to 2,000, under-estimating it by a similar figure in Loughborough (these figures are, after all, best guesses based largely on local council results). Stephen Dorrell was still wise to make the switch from the nearby University town, but only won his new base by 6,000 rather than the larger lead predicted. In 2001 the Labour vote subsided somewhat, allowing Dorrell to increase his majority to a more comfortable 7,739.

Though the Conservatives win most wards locally, all parties have areas of support in local elections. The Lib Dems are very strong in Birstall just outside of Leicester, and it may well have been that these voters have been switching to Labour rather than the Conservatives in national elections, resulting in the calculation problem with the 1992 result mentioned above. There is also a large Labour vote in the suburb of Thurmaston, and a significant minority in places like Syston, Mountsorrel and Rothley. Some of the smaller villages to the west of the A6 and close to the M1 are among the most desirable locations in the county, just about commutable to London, and as a result very Conservative. The party could poll 77 per cent in the village of Thurcaston in 1999 and 65 per cent in Kirby Muxloe and Leicester Forest East. Labour are very weak in places like this, attracting just one in six of the vote in the 2001 county council elections in Bradgate, which is notable for a country park still containing the ruins of the home of the sixteenth century nine-day Queen, Lady Jane Grey.

HARBOROUGH

	2001		1997		1992 notional	
Electorate and turnout	73,300	63.3	70,424	75.3	68,122	81.5
Conservative	20,748	44.7	22,170	41.8	29,274	52.7
Labour	9,271	20.0	13,332	25.2	6,828	12.3
Lib Dem	15,496	33.4	15,646	29.5	19,122	34.5
Anti–EU	912	2.0	1,859	3.5	–	–
Others	–		–		290	
MP	Edward Garnier (Con)		Edward Garnier (Con)		Edward Garnier (Con)	
Majority	5,252	11.3	6,524	12.3	10,152	18.3

Harborough is, like Bosworth, one of the select band of seats which were won by Labour in 1945 but not in 1997. Boundary changes are a less important part of the explanation than in Bosworth, with a large part of the difference between the two results here resulting from changes in class composition. Over many decades now Harborough has been a refuge for the richer middle classes, who have swapped Leicester for the affluent avenues of Oadby or the villages on the way to Market Harborough such as Great Glen and the Kibworths. The political effect has been to make this, in normal times, an utterly safe Tory seat, with Labour's vote dropping from 38 per cent in 1951 down to just 12 per cent in 1992. A second main reason for the Conservatives' success here has been a split opposition, with the Liberals moving into second place in 1983 and retaining it ever since, though without squeezing the last drops out of the Labour vote as they have elsewhere.

The parliamentary seat includes the entire pocket-sized district of Oadby & Wigston (population 51,500), which is overwhelmingly controlled by the Liberal Democrats and has been since 1991. In the county council elections held on the same day as the general election in June 2001, the Lib Dems polled 11,000 votes here as against 9,500 for the Tories and 6,000 for Labour. This suggests that the Harborough part of the seat is strongly Tory, but even here the Lib Dems were only just behind in the county poll, winning the ward of Market Harborough (as they do in district council elections). An overall analysis of the results suggests that in two successive elections, two or three thousand electors have voted Lib Dem locally and Conservative nationally (Labour's vote has been about the same). This has been enough to deny a rare third party breakthrough in the Midlands and keep Edward Garnier in Parliament with a just about comfortable majority.

LEICESTER EAST

	2001		1997		1992 actual	
Electorate and turnout	65,526	62.1	64,253	69.1	63,435	78.7
Conservative	9,960	24.5	10,661	24.0	16,807	33.7
Labour	23,402	57.6	29,083	65.5	28,123	56.3
Lib Dem	4,989	12.3	3,105	7.0	4,043	8.1
Anti–EU	–	–	1,015	2.3	–	–
Others	2,310 (3)		538 (2)		947 (3)	
MP	Keith Vaz (Lab)		Keith Vaz (Lab)		Keith Vaz (Lab)	
Majority	13,442	33.1	18,422	41.5	11,316	22.7

It is hard to believe that Leicester East was held by the Conservatives from 1983 until 1987. In 2001 they failed to advance their support from its low base of 24 per cent, despite the adverse publicity which had attached itself to Keith Vaz over the previous few months. Although Labour's vote did drop by more than average, it was the Lib Dems and a collection of 'others' who benefited. In fact the result was less bad for Vaz than that suffered by Shaun Woodward in St Helens South, or indeed than predicted by much of the media. In part this again demonstrates that general elections really are 'national' events, with the record of MPs or individual government ministers something of an irrelevance compared with the record of the government as a whole. There is no doubt however that a part of the reason why Vaz could still build a majority of 13,400 relates to the ethnic composition of his Leicester East constituency. According to the 1991 census, over a third of the population are of south Asian (or East African) origin, and that figure was undoubtedly higher still by 2001. Loyalty to Vaz, the first Asian MP (when first elected) since the 1920s, appeared to withstand attacks from the almost exclusively white media, though whether this will remain the case after his recent (2002) month-long suspension from the House of Commons remains to be seen.

In reality this has always been a fairly safe Labour seat, though it has become extremely polarised in recent contests. In the tightly packed terraced streets off the Belgrave Road and in many other inner-city parts of the seat, the electorate is now almost entirely of Asian origin, which favours Vaz and Labour, not least because they actually turn out and vote. Thus Belgrave ward produced a Labour share of 65 per cent in 1999, Latimer 79 per cent and Charnwood 82 per cent, the average turnout (for local council elections) very healthy at more than four in ten. As a result, the five inner-city wards in the constituency produced a huge Labour lead over the Tories of 9,000 - 1,600, a margin which if anything will have been even wider in 2001. The eastern part of the constituency is very different. Suburbs like Evington and Humberstone are overwhelmingly white, middle class and with an above-average retired population. These wards gave the Conservatives eight councillors out of their ten elected across the city in the 1999 all-out elections, but are usually heavily outvoted by the other part of the seat in general elections.

The exception was in 1983, when Conservative Peter Bruinvels won by 933 votes. This owed much at the time to a divided opposition, sitting MP Tom Bradley (first elected in 1962) defecting and standing for the SDP, thus splitting the Labour vote. After four years of ceaseless publicity (including an offer to be the hangman if capital punishment were to be restored), Bruinvels lost in 1987 after the Labour vote recovered by almost 10 percentage points. That increase was to be repeated in both 1992 and 1997, by which time Leicester East had become far safer than Labour's traditional best seat in the city (West) and indeed was their 116th safest seat nationally. That ranking was to fall by thirty places in 2001, but if anything the most recent contest has revealed just how secure Labour now are here.

LEICESTER SOUTH

	2001		1997		1992 actual	
Electorate and turnout	72,674	58.0	72,583	66.3	71,120	75.1
Conservative	9,715	23.1	11,421	23.7	18,494	34.6
Labour	22,958	54.5	27,914	58.0	27,934	52.3
Lib Dem	7,243	17.2	6,654	13.8	6,271	11.7
Anti–EU	330	0.8	1,184	2.5	–	–
Others	1,893 (2)		941 (2)		708 (2)	
MP	Jim Marshall (Lab)		Jim Marshall (Lab)		Jim Marshall (Lab)	
Majority	13,243	31.4	16,493	34.3	9,440	17.7

Leicester South contains some of the city's most desirable neighbourhoods in places like Stoneygate and Knighton, on either side of the main A6 road as it leaves the city. In spite of this, the constituency has been won since October 1974 by Jim Marshall for Labour, with the sole exception of 1983, when the Conservatives squeaked home by 7 votes. Part of the reason is that the constituency also takes in a number of very inner-city areas such as Crown Hills, Highfields and Spinney Hill, which were about 80 per cent non-white in 1991. Another explanation is that the posh end of the seat includes Leicester University and a growing number of students, whose influence caused a significant swing to the left in the 1980s and 1990s, a pattern similar to that found in other University cities such as Brighton, Cambridge, Lancaster and York.

In local elections here, the non-white inner-city wards remain very strongly Labour, notably Spinney Hill where the party polled over 80 per cent in the 1999 unitary council elections. Labour also win the wards of Castle (which includes the football and rugby grounds) and Wycliffe (which takes in the railway station and much of the city centre), as well as the council estate ward of Eyres Monsell off the ring road on the city's southern boundary. The Conservatives hit back in Aylestone in the south west, while the Lib Dems now win three of the more residential wards including both of the tree-lined Knighton seats (these areas border the Lib Dem controlled district of Oadby and Wigston). Overall in the constituency, the Tories finished in a poor third place in the 1999 unitary elections, polling just 16 per cent of the vote as against 33 per cent for the Lib Dems and 47 per cent for Labour. As in other former urban strongholds (such as Newcastle Central, the southern seats of Liverpool and Sheffield) both their local base and parliamentary vote now appear to have shrivelled, and a serious attempt at regaining the parliamentary seat looks unlikely in the short term.

LEICESTER WEST

	2001		1997		1992 actual	
Electorate and turnout	65,267	50.9	64,878	63.1	65,511	73.7
Conservative	8,375	25.2	9,716	23.7	18,596	38.5
Labour	18,014	54.2	22,580	55.2	22,574	46.8
Lib Dem	5,085	15.3	5,795	14.2	6,402	13.3
Anti–EU	–	–	970	2.4	–	–
Others	1,745 (3)		1,853 (5)		688 (2)	
MP	Patricia Hewitt (Lab)		Patricia Hewitt (Lab)		Greville Janner (Lab)	
Majority	9,639	29.0	12,864	31.4	3,978	8.2

It is ironic that West now has the smallest Labour majority of any of the three seats in Leicester, as it was for many years considered the best Labour seat in the city and was the only constituency held in the entire county in 1983. West is still the most working class of the three divisions, and in 1991 still had over a third of housing rented from the local authority. It also has by far the lowest proportion of non-white residents of the Leicester seats, which must be part of the explanation for its fall in the pecking order from Labour's point of view in recent elections. In fact the 'out of line' results were those recorded in 1987 and 1992, when their vote advanced by just 2 per cent compared with 12 per cent in South and 19 per cent in East. This may have been caused by the appeal of the Conservatives at that time to the skilled, white working class (Leicester West has the 27th highest proportion of skilled manual workers in the country according to the 1991 census). Equally, the constituency does not have much of a public sector middle class, a group who swung to Labour particularly heavily at that time.

The 1992 election was to be the last for Greville Janner, who had succeeded his father Barnett (MP for the similar Leicester North West seat for 25 years) in 1970. In 1997 Patricia Hewitt was elected for the seat (after failing to win Leicester East some fourteen years previously) and soon after being returned with a very slightly reduced majority in 2001, entered the cabinet as Trade and Industry Secretary. She still has what should be a very safe seat, though locally the Lib Dems won five wards to Labour's four in the 1999 council elections, including the council estate ward of North Braunstone, which is listed as the 57th most deprived in the country. Labour's best areas these days are in the terraced areas of Abbey and Westcotes wards, which are similar to the inner wards in the East and South constituencies. The Conservatives do poorly in local contests, recording less than 4 per cent in St Augustine's ward in 1999 and polling fewer votes than the Socialists in North Braunstone. While they remain the main challengers for the parliamentary seat, Labour will probably continue to win comfortably.

LEICESTERSHIRE NORTH WEST

	2001		1997		1992 notional	
Electorate and turnout	68,414	65.8	65,069	80.0	62,949	86.5
Conservative	15,274	33.9	16,113	31.0	24,735	45.4
Labour	23,431	52.1	29,332	56.4	23,869	43.8
Lib Dem	4,651	10.3	4,492	8.6	5,648	10.4
Anti–EU	1,021	2.3	2,088	4.0	–	–
Others	632		–		198	
MP	David Taylor (Lab)		David Taylor (Lab)		David Ashby (Con)	
Majority	8,157	18.1	13,219	25.4	866	1.6

Leicestershire North West was a new constituency created in 1983 from the western part of Loughborough and northern section of Bosworth, both of which had been Labour for many years after 1945. As the new seat covered some of the best parts of these two from Labour's point of view (almost the entire Leicestershire coalfield area), it was naturally assumed that they would win it comfortably. In the event (like Sherwood in Nottinghamshire), the new constituency confounded expectations and was easily won by the Conservatives in its first two contests, David Ashby's majority rising to almost 8,000 in 1987. Labour then advanced by almost 10 per cent to come within 1,000 votes of winning in 1992, but it was to take them until 1997 before finally tasting victory, David Taylor gaining the seat by the huge margin of 13,000 votes.

Labour's strongest areas in the constituency can still be found in the former mining towns like Coalville, Whitwick and Ibstock; overall in these three county council wards they out-polled the Tories by 9,000 votes to 4,500 in 2001. The Conservatives are marginally ahead in the north towards the airport at Castle Donington, while the mixed town of Ashby-de-la-Zouch ('constituency' of New Labour MP Pandora Braithwaite in the latest *Adrian Mole* diaries) is closely fought, though won by Labour in 1997 and 2001. Overall there was a 3.6 per cent swing back to the Tories in 2001, and the seat remains vulnerable to any serious Conservative recovery; indeed it is precisely the sort of seat they will have to regain to form a majority again in the future.

LOUGHBOROUGH

	2001		1997		1992 notional	
Electorate and turnout	70,078	63.1	68,973	75.9	65,156	76.8
Conservative	15,638	35.3	19,736	37.7	23,412	46.8
Labour	22,016	49.7	25,448	48.6	19,920	39.8
Lib Dem	5,667	12.8	6,190	11.8	5,635	11.3
Anti–EU	933	2.1	991	1.9	–	–
Others	–		–		1,081 (2)	
MP	Andy Reed (Lab)		Andy Reed (Lab)		Stephen Dorrell (Con)	
Majority	6,378	14.4	5,712	10.9	3,492	7.0

Loughborough was a Labour seat from 1945 until 1979, but was then lost to the Conservatives and not regained until 1997. Boundary changes have been as important as national swings of opinion in this pattern; in 1983 the seat lost some of its best Labour territory to the new Leicestershire North West, and Stephen Dorrell could pile up majorities of 16,000 in 1983 and 17,500 in 1987. Then after losing by another five-figure margin in 1992, the next boundary review came to Labour's rescue by transferring 20,000 mainly Tory voters into the new Charnwood seat and replacing them with Labour-inclined Shepshed. Dorrell wisely opted to fight the safe Tory bet of Charnwood in 1997, and Andy Reid (who had added 8 per cent to the Labour vote in 1992) duly regained what is again a very important marginal by just under 6,000 votes.

The town of Loughborough itself contains its fair share of terraced housing near the centre of the town as well as a smallish University, and generally provides Labour with a reasonable lead. In 2001 they out-polled the Conservatives in the five county council wards by about 13,500 to 8,800. Shepshed is also Labour (by about 1,000 in the 2001 county election), but the villages to the south such as Barrrow upon Soar and Sileby incline to the Conservatives, though with a reasonable Labour vote as well. The best local council wards for the Tories are Nanpantan and Outwoods to the south west of Loughborough itself, which are rather more affluent and have more in common with the villages now in neighbouring Charnwood. In 2001, Labour were able to slightly increase their majority across the parliamentary seat, which could prove very important in the event of a national Tory recovery in 2005/6. This is currently the 105th most vulnerable Labour seat, an improvement from 72nd after 1997.

RUTLAND and MELTON

	2001		1997		1992 notional	
Electorateand turnout	73,264	64.2	70,239	74.9	67,694	82.1
Conservative	22,621	48.1	24,107	45.8	34,137	61.4
Labour	14,009	29.8	15,271	29.0	8,730	15.7
Lib Dem	8,386	17.8	10,112	19.2	11,556	20.8
Anti–EU	1,223	2.6	3,140 (2)	6.0	–	–
Others	817		–		1,136 (2)	
MP	Alan Duncan (Con)		Alan Duncan (Con)		Alan Duncan (Con)	
Majority	8,612	18.3	8,836	16.8	22,581	40.6

Rutland re-emerged onto the local government map of Britain after the review of the 1990s, its residents having waged a long-running campaign to re-establish its 'independence' after it was subsumed into its larger neighbour Leicestershire in 1973. With a population of just 31,500, it is the smallest unitary authority in England, and for parliamentary purposes will still need to be combined with the east of Leicestershire to which it has been linked since 1983. In fact the parliamentary seat brings together three local authorities: the whole of Rutland, Melton, plus a part of Harborough reaching as far in as the Leicester city limits at Thurnby.

Rutland itself regularly comes near the top on the list of most desirable places in which to live. Its main towns of Oakham and Uppingham are prosperous, if slightly twee, places which both have their private boarding schools, and if anything locations around the Rutland Water reservoir are even more desired by those with the disposable wealth to afford it. Overall, all but two of Rutland's sixteen wards were in the least deprived third in the country in 2000, and fewer than 3 per cent of its inhabitants were recorded as on income support, compared with 10 per cent in nearby Nottingham. The political character of the place is clouded by the fact that many (unopposed) local councillors are Independents, with few contests between the political parties. We can deduce however, particularly from the results of the 2001 county council election elsewhere in the constituency, that the Conservatives must have had a fair lead in the most recent election.

The evidence for this that in the borough of Melton (another very small authority with 45,000 residents), Labour polled as many as 8,500 votes and the Liberal Democrats 3,000 in the county poll. In recent years, the Labour vote has become quite strong in the town of Melton Mowbray, which is best known for its pork pie production, though the Conservatives still do well in the Vale of Belvoir to the north. Meanwhile, the Harborough part of the seat was won locally by the Lib Dems in 2001, their supporters in Scraptoft and Thurnby (which are more or less extensions of Leicester suburbia) outvoting the Conservative villages further east along the A47. All this suggests that it is Rutland which provides the bulk of Alan Duncan's majority, electoral support which has clearly been long-lasting given that the Conservatives have now enjoyed an unbroken period of over 130 years representing England's tiniest county.

Lincolnshire

	Conservative		Labour		Liberal Democrat		Others	
	Share of vote	Seats	Share of vote	Seats	Share of vote	Seats	Share of vote	Seats
2001	46.2	6	35.7	1	16.1	0	1.9	0
1997	42.4	6	36.9	1	17.5	0	3.1	0
1992	53.5	6	25.8	0	19.8	0	0.9	0
1987	53.8	6	18.5	0	27.4	0	0.4	0
1983	53.2	6	15.1	0	31.4	0	0.3	0

Lincolnshire is a very large and rural county in the east of England. It is known for its agriculture as well as for pretty churches, both of which have tended to incline the county to the Conservatives in political terms, since farmers are just about the most loyal Conservative voters of any occupational group, while the Church of England was once described as 'the Tory party at prayer'. We should note however that the far more industrial (and politically different) north Lincolnshire was removed in the county redrawing of the early 1970s, to be linked with Hull in the unpopular creation of Humberside. Although this has now been effectively abolished and the two resulting unitary councils quickly renamed North and North East Lincolnshire respectively, they remain outside the county as far as the boundary commission and other electoral bodies are concerned, and are dealt with in another chapter.

The biggest town in what remains of the county is Lincoln itself (population about 80,000), with nowhere else really meriting an 'urban' label. Lincoln is an attractive city, with streets full of small shops climbing the accurately named Steep Hill to the large and striking cathedral, best known for its 'Lincoln Imp', which provides the local football club with its nickname. The cluster of old buildings on the hilltop includes a large castle and the city attracts its fair share of tourists and day-trippers. As a result of the mainly flat countryside (in fact there are a few low lying hills), the cathedral can be seen from miles around; in a similar manner, the Boston 'Stump' (a tall church tower) in the south east of the county, also provides a striking landmark over surrounding fields. Boston is the third largest town in the county (with a population of 26,500) at the edge of The Wash. It includes the odd dock and a bit of industry on its edges, things which are lacking in most of the rest of the county, though Gainsborough (18,000) at the opposite corner of the county still has warehouses lining the banks of the Trent. Other towns such as Margaret Thatcher's Grantham (32,000), Spalding (20,000), Louth (15,000) Sleaford (10,000) and most of all Stamford (14,000) are genteel places with their fair share of old stone cottages, antique shops and above-average concentrations of retirees. This latter point applies most of all to the seaside resorts of Skegness, Ingoldmells and Mablethorpe, indeed a majority of the population of the Sutton & Trusthorpe ward, next to Mablethorpe, are now retired. These places seem a long way from anywhere, but contain the only real deprivation (aside from the odd ward in Gainsborough) to be found within the present county boundaries. On the index of multiple deprivation, Ingoldmells ranks 242nd in the country, with Mablethorpe only slightly lower at 311th, while Skegness has three wards in the most deprived ten per cent.

Politically, there were large concentrations of Liberalism in Lincolnshire at the start of the twentieth century, but despite a revival by the Alliance in 1983, the third party vote has slowly subsided. Despite its overwhelmingly rural character, the Liberals could win six of the county's eight seats in 1906: Boston, Gainsborough, Lincoln, Louth, Sleaford and Spalding. Some of those were lost four years later as the political importance of religious nonconformity slowly declined, and by 1918 the Conservatives won everything, with the exception of Boston, which went Labour. There was a revival of rural Liberalism (as also in the south west) in the early 1920s, with Gainsborough, Grantham, Horncastle and Louth all returning to the party, but this was to be a very brief 'last hurrah' and by 1924 the Conservatives won all the rural seats once again, including Boston. The electoral pattern of the county thereafter froze, with Lincoln voting Labour (except in 1931 and 1935) until their local difficulties of the 1970s, and all the other seats safely Tory, with only two exceptions. The first was Boston, which was won by the Liberals in 1929, thereafter returning 'National Liberal' and then 'National Liberal and Conservative' MPs until this small group was officially subsumed into the Conservatives in the early 1960s. The second exception was Grantham, which provided one of the spectacular by-election reverses during the second world war, won by an Independent in 1942 and again in 1945. Apart from that, the Conservatives have built up some very safe seats here - they held onto all of them even in 1966, though the majority in Boston fell to 300 and in Grantham, 2,000.

Labour's loss of Lincoln in the 1970s, first as a result of Dick Taverne's resignation from the party, and then more conventionally a Conservative gain in 1979, deprived the party of its only seat in the county. In 1983, Labour finished more than 10,000 votes adrift here, and they were a poor third everywhere else, recording less than ten per cent of the vote (and at that time losing their deposit) in two constituencies. The Liberal-Alliance picked up a reasonable vote without looking like repeating their victories of earlier eras - the closest they got was a 5,000 vote deficit in Gainsborough. Since then, much of the Liberal vote has moved across to Labour, without making much of a difference to the outcome outside of Lincoln, which after a near miss in 1992 was finally regained (with the help of boundary changes) in 1997. For the most part, the rural Conservative MPs have remained safe, though Richard Body's lead in Boston & Skegness was cut to 650 at his last election in 1997, and there was an even slimmer lead for his successor in 2001 after Labour designated it a key seat. Assuming a Conservative recovery here and continued Labour safety in Lincoln, electoral interest in the next election seems likely to be minimal. Perhaps because of the lack of opposition, Lincolnshire remains one of last great redoubts of the old style Tory 'grandee': sitting MPs include Quentin Davies, Douglas Hogg and Sir Peter Tapsell. All these politicians remain rather more respectable than Louth's former representative between 1969 and 1974, one Jeffrey Archer, who later became one of two prominent Conservatives to follow a parliamentary career with one behind bars.

Local government
Although the Conservatives are strong throughout the county in general elections, this has not always translated into local politics because of the large numbers of Independent councillors. There are strong

non-party traditions in the large East Lindsey district (35 Independent councillors out of 60 in 1999), though Independents have now lost control of South Holland (around The Wash), with the Conservatives on the point of taking overall charge. The Conservatives are usually in control of South Kesteven (around Grantham and Stamford) and though they lost their majority in the 1990s, they are on the brink of regaining it. Many of the other rural councils are balanced, each having a good scattering of Independent, Labour, Conservative and Liberal Democrat members - examples are North Kesteven (which includes Sleaford and North Hykeham), West Lindsey (including Gainsborough and rural areas to the north of the county), where the Lib Dems are particularly strong and Boston, where Labour and the Conservatives are the two largest groups. Lincoln, which elects annually, is overwhelmingly Labour and has been since the early 1980s. Lincolnshire county council is controlled by the Conservatives, with 49 councillors out of 77 after 2001. Labour have a reasonably sized opposition group of 21, mainly from Lincoln and Boston, though with three county councillors from Grantham and the odd ward elsewhere. The Lib Dems have a couple of councillors from Gainsborough but few elsewhere, and there are a handful of Independents.

Boundary review

Recommendations for Lincolnshire were finalised early in the current review. There was a two-day public enquiry (which took place prior to the 2001 general election), at which the main arguments concerned the wards which should or should not be included in the Lincoln constituency, given that the borough is slightly too small to form its own seat. As a result of the enquiry and its deliberations, the commission stuck with their original proposal to include two wards from North Kesteven district (the Conservatives wanted five, Labour one), which should not have too great an electoral impact assuming Labour stays in one piece in Lincoln itself. The only other change will be the inclusion of an extra rural ward, Stickney, in Boston and Skegness, which will marginally help the Conservative recovery here.

BOSTON and SKEGNESS

	2001		1997		1992 notional	
Electorate and turnout	69,165	58.3	67,623	68.9	65,577	77.2
Conservative	17,298	42.9	19,750	42.4	25,721	50.8
Labour	16,783	41.6	19,103	41.0	14,299	28.2
Lib Dem	4,994	12.4	7,721	16.6	10,613	21.0
Anti–EU	717	1.8	–	–	–	–
Green	521	1.3	–	–	–	–
MP	Mark Simmonds (Con)		Richard Body (Con)		Richard Body (Con)	
					Holland-with-Boston	
Majority	515	1.3	647	1.4	11,422	22.6

Labour have come extremely close in the last two general elections to winning an unlikely victory in Boston and Skegness, which combines the two towns with a large swathe of rich farming country in between. Boston has been held briefly by Labour before, though one needs to go all the way back to the immediate post-war period (post first world war that is), with the party winning the old Holland-with-Boston seat in 1918 and holding on in 1922 and 1923 before losing in 1924. Unlike many other early gains, they did not re-claim the seat in 1929 or even 1945, and seemed unlikely to do so again, particularly given the loss of small industry and associated social changes in places like this. The replacement of the 'Holland' part of the seat after 1992 with the seaside resort of Skegness, formerly part of the very safe Tory seat of East Lindsey, hardly seemed to improve Labour's prospects. But in 1997 the huge size of the national swing reduced the majority of Euro-rebel Richard Body to a wafer-thin 647, and one can only speculate as to what may have transpired had the Referendum party fielded a candidate and picked up 3,000 votes as in nearby Norfolk North West.

The town of Boston, said to be the fourth wealthiest in provincial England some 650 years ago as a result of its international trading links, still contains docks and some industry as well as its more famous church tower or 'stump', which dominates the utterly flat surrounding area. Politically the town is mixed; Labour were the largest party on the balanced council between 1995 and 1999, and remain strong in wards such as Central, Skirbeck and Staniland, though the Conservatives became the largest party after polling most votes in 1999. There is genuine poverty and Labour voters in the seaside resort of Skegness as well, with five district councillors elected here in 1995, three in 1999 and one county councillor in 2001. However a majority of local representatives in the East Lindsey portion of the constituency remain Independents, whose vote one assumes is swept up by Conservatives in national contests, and indeed this area (as those further north) has returned a Tory to parliament since the 1920s. It would not be surprising if new MP Mark Simmonds is able to rebuild a decent majority here in future contests.

GAINSBOROUGH

	2001		1997		1992 notional	
Electorate and turnout	65,870	64.2	64,106	74.6	62,796	80.3
Conservative	19,555	46.2	20,593	43.1	26,919	53.4
Labour	11,484	27.1	13,767	28.8	10,533	20.9
Lib Dem	11,280	26.7	13,436	28.1	12,993	25.8
MP	Edward Leigh (Con)		Edward Leigh (Con)		Edward Leigh (Con)	
					Gainsborough & Horncastle	
Majority	8,071	19.1	6,826	14.3	13,926	27.6

The town of Gainsborough lies on the River Trent on the western border of the county, but the parliamentary constituency extends a lot further eastwards to take in the whole of the district of West Lindsey as far as the small town of Market Rasen, well known for its racecourse. Gainsborough, which is more working class than most Lincolnshire towns, is best known for its magnificent fifteenth century manor, set incongruously in the middle of a much more modern housing estate. The town votes Liberal Democrat locally, and the Conservatives were actually third (behind Labour as well) in one of its county council wards in 2001. But the town only comprises a third of the constituency's electorate, and elsewhere the seat is predominantly rural and agricultural; as a result it has been safely held by the Conservatives since 1924.

The main challenge formerly came from the Liberals, who held the seat from 1906-18 and again from 1923-4. After a period in which Labour finished a distant second, the Liberals advanced to within 4,000 votes of victory in October 1974, and nine years later the then Liberal-Alliance were 5,000 behind new Conservative standard-bearer Edward Leigh. This did not however lead to a concerted third party attempt on the seat - despite growing numbers of local councillors, their general election vote share declined from over 40 per cent in 1983 to 35 per cent in 1987 and just 26 per cent in 1992. The Labour vote over this period has recovered, and the now equally divided opposition ensured that in 1997, Leigh survived relatively easily despite his own vote falling by ten points. There was continued confusion over how to vote tactically in 2001, and in the absence of a clear challenger it is hard to see the Conservatives being seriously threatened.

GRANTHAM and STAMFORD

	2001		1997		1992 notional	
Electorate and turnout	75,500	61.3	72,310	73.3	67,426	80.1
Conservative	21,329	46.1	22,672	42.8	31,263	57.9
Labour	16,811	36.3	19,980	37.7	14,105	26.1
Lib Dem	6,665	14.4	6,612	12.5	8,663	16.0
Anti–EU	1,484	3.2	3,277 (2)	6.1	–	–
Others	–		429 (2)		–	
MP	Quentin Davies (Con)		Quentin Davies (Con)		Quentin Davies (Con) Stamford & Spalding	
Majority	4,518	9.8	2,692	5.1	17,158	31.8

Grantham is best known as the town where a young Margaret Thatcher grew up, though when she entered parliament and became Prime Minister, it was as the representative of the London seat of Finchley. Thatcher (or Roberts as she was then) was the daughter of a greengrocer, and Grantham has, as a result, become misleadingly viewed as a town of small businessmen. In fact it is a reasonably sized town (the second largest in Lincolnshire) with its fair share of industrial estates just off the A1, and has a strong Labour vote – the party won three county council wards in 2001.

The centre of the town has a number of fine stone buildings, but this is nothing as compared with the second town in the constituency, Stamford, which is almost perfectly preserved with numerous cream-coloured stone cottages and churches, as well as William Cecil's fine Elizabethan mansion, Burghley House. 'England's most attractive town' (according to Betjeman) is otherwise best known as the place where Daniel Lambert, reputedly Britain's fattest man, died, weighing almost 53 stones. Even the combined weight of the Conservative vote here would probably come to less, though in national elections at least this has always been solid Tory territory. Stamford (linked in a constituency with Rutland until the 1970s) has been represented by the party for just about as long as there have been proper elections, while Grantham has been pretty safe since it was regained from an Independent in 1950. Quentin Davies was first elected for the constituency of Stamford and Spalding in 1987. His majority was almost 23,000 in 1987, though boundary changes (notably the inclusion of Grantham) reduced the margin. Labour did well to get as close as they did in 1997, but it is hard to see them going a step further, and this should remain a safe Conservative seat.

LINCOLN

	2001		1997		1992 notional	
Electorate and turnout	66,299	56.0	65,565	71.0	65,087	79.6
Conservative	11,583	31.2	14,433	31.0	22,905	44.2
Labour	20,003	53.9	25,563	54.9	23,869	46.1
Lib Dem	4,703	12.7	5,048	10.8	4,561	8.8
Anti–EU	836	2.3	1,329	2.9	–	–
Others	–		175		500	
MP	Gillian Merron (Lab)		Gillian Merron (Lab)		Kenneth Carlisle (Con)	
Majority	8,420	22.7	11,130	23.9	964*	1.9*

* Estimated Labour majority allowing for boundary changes.

The cathedral city of Lincoln was held by Labour from 1924 until 1931 and then continuously from 1945 until 1973, at which point its MP Dick Taverne resigned from the party and fought the seat in a by-election as a 'Democratic Labour' candidate. Taverne duly won the by-election and narrowly held on in February 1974 against the official Labour party candidate, but then lost by under 1,000 to Margaret Jackson, now Margaret Beckett, in October 1974. However, Labour's troubles were not over as the seat was then promptly lost to the Conservatives in 1979, who were to hold the seat until 1997. The Conservative MP from 1979 was Kenneth Carlisle, who had a majority of over 10,000 in 1983, but just 2,000 by 1992, and even this was whittled away by boundary changes before 1997. Carlisle wisely opted to stand down before the election, when a swing of 11 per cent returned Lincoln to Labour and Gillian Merron to parliament.

Since 1997, Labour have continued to dominate local politics in Lincoln; indeed the Conservatives won just two council seats in 1999. Labour even managed to top the poll in the same year's European elections, a rarity for a seat gained in 1997 and a result which was a precursor to Labour's good perform-ance here in 2001 when they suffered only a very small adverse movement in opinion. This very much suggests that the constituency may have finally returned to its pre-1973 status as a reasonably secure Labour seat surrounded by rural bastions of Conservatism. Labour will be helped in future contests by the boundary commission rebuffing Conservative attempts to add more electors from nearby North Hykeham.

LOUTH and HORNCASTLE

	2001		1997		1992 notional	
Electorate and turnout	71,556	62.1	68,824	72.6	65,996	79.0
Conservative	21,543	48.5	21,699	43.4	27,499	52.7
Labour	13,989	31.5	14,799	29.6	7,122	13.7
Lib Dem	8,928	20.1	12,207	24.4	16,529	31.7
Green	–	–	1,248	2.5	1,018	2.0
MP	Peter Tapsell (Con)		Peter Tapsell (Con)		Peter Tapsell (Con)	
					Lindsey East	
Majority	7,554	17.0	6,900	13.8	10,970	21.0

Louth and Horncastle is a very large constituency which covers the north east of the county (not to be confused with the very different 'North East Lincolnshire' which covers Grimsby and Cleethorpes and used to be in Humberside). The main towns here include those in the title, but both are small, with Louth boasting 15,000 inhabitants and Horncastle just 5,000. Elsewhere, the constituency includes a built-up area around Mablethorpe and Sutton on Sea along the east coast, but the remaining half of the electorate are based in numerous villages and hamlets scattered around the district of East Lindsey. Given this fact, it is not really a great surprise that this is a safe Conservative seat, but it perhaps is that Labour performed so well in 1997, more than doubling their vote and as a result surging into second place.

Back in 1983, Labour could only poll a miserable 8 per cent in the old Lindsey East constituency, and the realistic challengers to Peter Tapsell were assumed to be the Liberals, who cut his lead to 7,500 votes. Their tide was to slowly recede in 1987 and 1992, but even in the landslide conditions of 1997, their fall to third place (particularly given its Liberal traditions - Louth was Liberal before the first world war and from 1920-24) must have been very disappointing. In 2001 their vote dropped further, with Labour managing to add another couple of percentage points. They even gained the Mablethorpe county council ward from the Lib Dems and also won the tongue-twister ward of Louth South, failing to gain Louth North by just 23 votes (as in Mablethorpe the Lib Dems slumped from first to third place). The three rural Louth wards remained safely Conservative, as did Tattershall and its striking castle, while the Tories made another gain from the Lib Dems in Horncastle. Overall it is clear that the Lib Dems are in retreat here, whatever their successes elsewhere, though this will not necessarily worry Peter Tapsell (now one of the longest serving MPs left in the Commons), since it is almost impossible to even consider that Labour might ever win here.

SLEAFORD and NORTH HYKEHAM

	2001		1997		1992 notional	
Electorate and turnout	75,061	64.9	71,637	74.2	66,382	80.4
Conservative	24,190	49.7	23,358	43.9	31,180	58.4
Labour	15,568	32.0	18,235	34.3	11,698	21.9
Lib Dem	7,894	16.2	8,063	15.2	8,873	16.6
Anti–EU	1,067	2.2	2,942	5.5	–	–
Others	–		578		1,603	
MP	Douglas Hogg (Con)		Douglas Hogg (Con)		Douglas Hogg (Con)	
					Grantham	
Majority	8,622	17.7	5,123	9.6	19,482	36.5

Most of the Lincolnshire constituencies were significantly altered as a result of the extra seat given to the county by the boundary commission at the last review. Sleaford and North Hykeham sounds like a new creation, but in fact most of the constituency was in the old Grantham seat; only the town itself shifted into a neighbouring constituency. More important from an electoral viewpoint was the addition of a built-up suburban area extending southwards from the Lincoln city boundaries. This was not good news for the Conservatives, since Labour's position in the Lincoln seat was greatly improved by the removal of the North Hykeham wards. It did, however, provide Douglas Hogg with a very safe seat, which meant that the former Agriculture minister was a cabinet member who actually survived the 1997 cull.

Sleaford is a typical Lincolnshire town of 10,000 souls, and is in fact the largest town of the local government district of North Kesteven. It boasts a fine market place surrounded by well-preserved old buildings, has the ruins of a castle and a working flour mill - undoubtedly this area has something of a timeless character to it. Politically, it should not come as a great surprise that the usual preference is for the Conservatives, though in the town itself 'New Labour' attracts a strong minority vote, which is true also of the 15-20,000 electors of the suburban Lincoln segment. The rural areas remain more heavily Tory, and overall there is little imminent danger to the Conservatives, particularly after they added six per cent to their total in 2001.

SOUTH HOLLAND and THE DEEPINGS

	2001		1997		1992 notional	
Electorate and turnout	74,390	62.1	69,674	71.9	64,244	79.2
Conservative	25,611	55.4	24,691	49.3	29,017	57.0
Labour	14,512	31.4	16,700	33.3	12,254	24.1
Lib Dem	4,761	10.3	7,836	15.6	9,619	18.9
Anti–EU	1,318	2.9	–	–	–	–
Others	–		902		–	
MP	John Hayes (Con)		John Hayes (Con)		NEW SEAT	
Majority	11,099	24.0	7,991	15.9	16,763	32.9

South Holland and the Deepings is essentially the seventh and extra constituency created by the boundary commission in their last review, combining the southern section of the old Holland-with-Boston with the eastern part of the old Stamford and Spalding. On a map it forms the south eastern part of Lincolnshire, a corner of territory bordering the marshy inlet that is The Wash.

Much of the territory of the constituency is taken up by flat agricultural land, an area of fens not unlike those found in neighbouring Cambridgeshire and Norfolk (or indeed Holland, thus the name). The largest town, Spalding (population 20,000) is still best known for its annual flower show, while other towns include Holbeach (8,000), Long Sutton (4,000) and Market Deeping, which is one of a handful of wards in the constituency which are in South Kesteven district. Deeping is nowadays ringed by new housing estates (like a lot of places across the Cambridgeshire border) and is very much part of the Peterborough commuter belt. Elsewhere the villages and towns are more traditional, though seem to have long since lost any political radicalism which they may have had in the early decades of the twentieth century. In 2001, Holbeach county council ward actually returned a Conservative unopposed, while its rural segment was not contested by rival political parties. Spalding also voted Tory but with a significant Labour minority, and Market and West Deeping also remained safely in the Tory camp. Overall the Conservatives added six per cent in 2001 to an already better than average performance in 1997, making this comfortably their strongest seat even in Lincolnshire, and 21st safest nationally.

Merseyside

	Conservative		Labour		Liberal Democrat		Others	
	Share of vote	Seats	Share of vote	Seats	Share of vote	Seats	Share of vote	Seats
2001	20.1	0	58.7	15	17.8	1	3.4	0
1997	19.7	0	61.9	15	14.4	1	3.9	0
1992	29.0	4	51.4	12	16.9	1	2.7	0
1987	28.9	4	47.4	11	23.3	2	0.3	0
1983	35.0	5	39.9	11	23.7	1	1.4	0

Merseyside was a 1973 creation, based on the city of Liverpool and its immediate environs, but taking in a larger area than this in three directions. The boundaries of the new metropolitan county were drawn around the town of St. Helens to the east, the Wirral peninsula, formerly part of Cheshire, to the west, and the genteel resort of Southport to the north, providing a total population well over the million mark. In many ways it is an odd mixture; Liverpool's influence undoubtedly extends to Birkenhead, but the west and south of the Wirral still look to Chester as their natural centre, while Southport would almost certainly have rather remained part of Lancashire. Even St Helens, part of a belt of mid-Lancashire towns split into many parts in the 1970s shake-up, has more affinity with neighbouring towns like Wigan and Widnes which became parts of Greater Manchester and Cheshire respectively.

Merseyside's unloved reputation in some quarters is in many ways unfair. Despite the widely held image, crime here is probably less of a problem than in many parts of London, while the Toxteth riots of the early 1980s were replicated in many other places. What is undeniably true is that whereas Liverpool was booming at the start of the twentieth century, huge ships lining the banks of the Mersey, the city has rapidly declined since then. The population has fallen by a greater margin here than any other English city: from 850,000 in the early 1950s down to just 450,000 today, and it shows in the number of derelict buildings and clearance schemes. Unlike other cities in the north, Liverpool has not had an influx of Asians to replace the outward-bound middle classes, with its own relatively small ethnic minority grouping arriving a hundred years ago through the port. Despite (or perhaps because of) all this, Liverpool remains a fascinating place. It was at the centre of the explosion of popular music in the 1960s, with bands like the Beatles and Gerry and the Pacemakers developing international followings after starting out on the local club scene. Liverpool football club were the dominant force in the land in the 1970s and 1980s, the top side in Europe on several occasions. Many other famous names can call this their home from Cilla Black to Edwina Currie, while television series' set locally such as *Z-Cars* and more recently *Brookside* have also developed wide followings.

Politically, the city has seen some extraordinary changes as its population has declined. It has been reduced from eleven constituencies during the inter-war period to just five today, with the Conservatives falling from ten seats in the city in 1931 to none by 1983. In 1951, the Tories could still poll over 200,000 votes; by 2001 this had fallen to a miserable 14,500. In the meantime Labour have taken a stranglehold on all the remaining parliamentary seats, though they have had far greater problems with the local council. In the 1980s, names like Derek Hatton and Tony Mulhearn became well-known across the land, as Labour were taken over by the Militant grouping, who were unafraid to take on the Thatcher governments. By refusing to set a rate in 1985, Liverpool council set itself on course for an outright battle with the government, but as in the case of Clay Cross in the 1970s, it was the councillors who came out on the losing side. Hatton and Militant were even denounced by their own party leader Neil Kinnock in a famous speech to the Labour Party conference in Bournemouth, which many believe marked the start of the upturn in the party's national fortunes. By the late 1980s, known supporters of Militant were being expelled from the party, including the MP Terry Fields, and the 1991 Walton by-election essentially marked the end of the left wing grouping as they polled just 2,600 votes compared with over 21,000 for the party's official candidate, Peter Kilfoyle. However, Labour's problems were far from over: during the 1990s they lost control of the council to the Liberal Democrats, who have continued to strengthen their position to the extent that they now hold 72 of the 99 council seats. Labour's steady routing at a local level (down to 20 councillors after 2000) has not as yet had any knock-on effect on national election results, but this situation may not continue indefinitely.

The constituencies immediately bordering Liverpool are some of the safest Labour seats to be found anywhere, notably Birkenhead and Bootle (which currently boasts the largest per-cent majority of any UK seat), but also Knowsley North and South (the successor to Harold Wilson's Huyton) and the two St.Helens divisions. Further afield however, the remaining five seats: Crosby, Southport, Wallasey, Wirral South and West, are of a different character altogether, far more middle class in their composition, and all held by the Conservatives in 1983. These were the places to which the Liverpool middle classes had fled over many decades, but somehow the Tories were to lose all of them by 1997, leaving them without a single MP in the county. First to go in 1987 was Southport, a generally affluent place with a large retired population which was gained by the Liberals, who had been strong here since the 1970s. At this time the third party held two seats in Merseyside (very unusual for a metropolitan county), as David Alton won a by-election in Liverpool Edge Hill shortly before the 1979 general election and held this and its successor seat (Mossley Hill) until 1997. They were not so lucky in Southport, which was regained by the Tories in 1992, but the Lib Dems fought back to win again in 1997, retaining the seat in 2001. The other gains were all made by Labour: Wallasey at the northern tip of the Wirral in 1992 and then more impressively Crosby and the two remaining Wirral seats in 1997. None of these four seats had ever been previously lost by the Conservatives in a post-war general election, but in 2001 their vote was to fall further in three of them, and they must now hope that the middle class areas of Merseyside are not following the earlier relentlessly downward trend set in Liverpool.

Local government

Merseyside is divided into five metropolitan boroughs. Liverpool, the largest, elects 99 councillors, and although Labour controlled from 1983 until 1992, has always had a significant non-Labour presence, generally represented by Liberals. The biggest group from 1973 to 1976, it was not a total surprise when they (the Liberal Democrats) re-took control in 1998, though their current total (2002) of 66 seats, based on over half of the popular vote in 1999 and 2000, is extraordinarily high. Labour began to stage a recovery in 2002, but it will be a long road back to power.

There are no such problems for Labour in Knowsley and St Helens, both controlled outright since their creation in 1973. Labour could boast 59 of the 66 councillors in Knowsley in 2002, the only serious opposition coming from the Liberal Democrats. In St Helens the Conservative group contained 20 councillors in the late 1970s, but since the late 1980s it has been the Lib Dems who have grown, though Labour still retain a reasonable majority. Sefton council, based on the mixed bag of Southport, Formby, Maghull, Crosby and Bootle, is these days perennially hung (though it was held by the Tories from 1973 until 1986), with all three parties enjoying areas of strength. Finally, the borough of Wirral has generally been Conservative controlled, though Labour had a brief spell in charge in the early 1990s. Currently the council is hung.

Boundary review

Merseyside should yet again lose one of its constituencies when the boundary review reaches the county towards the end of the current cycle, now entitled to only 15.1 seats rather than 16. However there is a real complication, since the Wirral and Knowsley are each presently over-represented by half a seat, and given that a 'Mersey tunnel' seat would be highly controversial, it is unclear just how the commissioners will proceed. If a seat does disappear on either side of the Mersey, it will leave those surrounding it significantly over-sized and larger on average than those on the opposite bank, creating the sort of disparities in electorate which the commission are supposed to reduce. Politically, the loss of any seat will initially hurt Labour, though may allow them to strengthen one or more of their existing marginals.

BIRKENHEAD

	2001		1997		1992 actual	
Electorate and turnout	60,026	48.3	59,630	65.9	62,673	73.0
Conservative	4,827	16.7	5,982	15.2	11,485	25.1
Labour	20,418	70.5	27,825	70.8	29,098	63.6
Lib Dem	3,722	12.8	3,548	9.0	4,417	9.7
Anti–EU	–	–	800	2.0	–	–
Others	–		1,168		733 (2)	
MP	Frank Field (Lab)		Frank Field (Lab)		Frank Field (Lab)	
Majority	15,591	53.8	21,843	55.5	17,613	38.5

Birkenhead is, like its strange nickname 'the one-eyed town', a difficult place to pin down. A shadow of its close neighbour on the other side of the Mersey, to which it is well connected via rail, tunnel and ferry, Birkenhead has nonetheless been the largest centre on the Wirral peninsula since its sudden development (from shipyard prosperity) in the Victorian era. Then again, as it merges almost seamlessly into more middle-class suburbs to the south and west, it is difficult to define what exactly constitutes the place. Most residents undoubtedly travel over or under the river to Liverpool for many of their services, and even the local football club takes the name of a small neighbourhood rather than that of the town itself, all adding to the lack of clear identity.

Politically, matters are somewhat less complicated. Labour have won all general election contests since 1945, usually with a comfortable majority. Even in 1983 their lead was almost 10,000 votes, and after 2001 this was Labour's 18th safest seat in the country. Locally, Labour win most wards, usually by massive margins in Bidston, Tranmere and Birkenhead itself. The exception is Oxton to the west, which is a more affluent area and elects Liberal Democrats. Otherwise this is in the main a poor, working class seat which has its fair share of problems including a relatively high unemployment rate, not helped by the run down of the Cammell Laird shipyard which was in previous times the major local employer.

The MP here since 1979 has been Frank Field, who survived early left-wing attempts to deselect him. A radical thinker on social policy and welfare reform, he was briefly a government minister after 1997, but rapidly fell out of favour with the Labour leadership. It seems incredible that Field was once described as to the left of his predecessor: Edmund Dell was a finance minister during the Callaghan administration before later joining the SDP.

BOOTLE

	2001		1997		1992 notional	
Electorate and turnout	55,455	49.8	57,284	66.7	60,913	71.3
Conservative	2,194	8.0	3,247	8.5	6,130	14.1
Labour	21,400	77.6	31,668	82.9	33,250	76.5
Lib Dem	2,357	8.5	2,191	5.7	2,812	6.5
Anti–EU	–	–	571	1.5	–	–
Socialist	1,643 (2)	5.9	420	1.1	–	–
Others	–		126		1,248 (2)	
MP	Joe Benton (Lab)		Joe Benton (Lab)		Joe Benton (Lab)	
Majority	19,043	69.0	28,421	74.4	27,120	62.4

Bootle is the safest seat in the land for any party, an honour it has held after both 1997 and 2001. If ever there was a constituency where one could weigh the Labour vote, then this must be it. But it has not ever been thus. It was a Conservative seat for all but two years of the inter-war period, and they were still fewer than 3,000 votes behind as recently as 1959. Since then the working class Tory vote has completely collapsed; their share of the vote over the 1955-2001 period dropping by more than forty percentage points, compared with a national decline of less than half this figure. The reasons are pretty much the same as those in Liverpool, which it borders to the south and east (the dividing line between the two is almost impossible to discern on the ground). Religion has been a major factor (see Liverpool Walton), but equally significant has been the decline of the docks which line the bank of the Mersey at Bootle, once thriving but now largely quiet and empty. Inward and outward trade brought a great deal of wealth to the area in decades gone by, not to mention jobs created by the shipbuilding industry, but now that ships are no longer built here and rarely even drop by, Bootle has become a depressed place. All its seven component wards are in the most deprived 550 nationally, and no-one could claim that this was an easy place to represent.

Such gloom reached its peak in 1990 when two Bootle MPs died young, first Allan Roberts (representative since 1979) and then Mike Carr just six months later. The first by–election was notable for the Monster Raving Loony Party defeating David Owen's rump SDP, which wisely wound itself up soon after. The second contest was won by Joe Benton, who has happily survived in this difficult patch ever since. He has no need to worry politically - even in the all-out council elections of 2000 when not doing so well nationally, Labour recorded huge majorities in all wards, with the only majority of under 500 (Netherton & Orrell) coming against Socialist opposition.

CROSBY

	2001		1997		1992 notional	
Electorate and turnout	56,610	65.1	57,190	77.2	58,877	81.3
Conservative	11,974	32.5	15,367	34.8	23,329	48.7
Labour	20,327	55.1	22,549	51.1	13,738	28.7
Lib Dem	4,084	11.1	5,080	11.5	9,558	20.0
Anti–EU	–	–	813	1.8	–	–
Others	481		332 (2)		1,237 (3)	
MP	Claire Curtis-Thomas (Lab)		Claire Curtis-Tansley (Lab)		Malcolm Thornton (Con)	
Majority	8,353	22.7	7,182	16.3	9,591	20.0

Labour's victory in Crosby in 1997 was one of the more astonishing results of a dramatic election, a swing of 18 per cent not only sweeping the Conservatives out, but providing Labour with a sizeable majority of their own. The result, one of the first to be declared, was the first confirmation of Labour's landslide win, but sadly it was not televised, viewers having to make do with Peter Snow's swingometer going off the end of the scale.

Crosby had seen drama before, with 63 years of unbroken representation by the Conservative Party ending in a famous 1981 by-election, though on that occasion the victors were Shirley Williams and the new SDP. Those were heady days for the new party, their victory by over 5,000 votes a huge advance from the Liberals' third place in 1979, the swing between the two contests exceeding 25 per cent. It did not last, the SDP failing to make the predicted breakthrough in 1983 and Williams losing a second successive general election (for two different parties), with Malcolm Thornton regaining the seat by 3,401 votes. That election saw Labour poll barely one in ten of the vote in Crosby, but in 1987 and 1992 the third party vote slowly subsided, with Labour just edging second place on the latter occasion, though their position was further helped by boundary changes which added a ward from Bootle while removing Maghull. Even so, the constituency retained its most up-market areas up the coast such as Blundellsands and Formby, and Labour's 1997 performance (their first ever win here) was exceptional. Barely believably, they were to further increase their lead in 2001, and as a result, Crosby now almost looks a secure Labour seat, officially safer than Blaydon, Halifax, Hyndburn or indeed 160 others. It is certainly possible that Labour could lose their overall majority while retaining Crosby, a big change since 1945 and 1966 when Labour won big nationally without coming particularly close here.

KNOWSLEY NORTH and SEFTON EAST

	2001		1997		1992 notional	
Electorate and turnout	70,781	53.0	70,918	70.1	74,154	75.1
Conservative	6,108	16.3	8,600	17.3	14,930	26.8
Labour	25,035	66.7	34,747	69.9	30,316	54.4
Lib Dem	5,173	13.8	5,499	11.1	8,670	15.6
Others	1,201 (3)		857		1,805	
MP	George Howarth (Lab)		George Howarth (Lab)		George Howarth (Lab)	
					Knowsley North	
Majority	18,927	50.4	26,147	52.6	15,386	27.6

The estates of Kirkby to the north east of Liverpool are some of the most depressing and depressed parts of Britain. Three wards here are in the national top twenty for multiple deprivation, while a fourth (Cantril Farm) is also in the top forty. Little wonder that the place was the setting for the BBC's *Z-Cars*, though in the thirty-plus intervening years, the problems here have only become worse. Politically, the area is solidly Labour when it can be bothered to turn out and vote - in the 2000 local elections not a single one of the Knowsley wards in the seat achieved even a 20 per cent poll, with barely one in ten voting in one ward (Tower Hill).

George Howarth first contested the seat as an imposed NEC candidate in a 1986 by-election following the departure to the media of Robert Kilroy-Silk, and won fairly comfortably in the face of a strong Liberal challenge. He went on to poll 78 per cent of the vote here when Labour lost nationally in 1992, and at the time Knowsley North was the party's third safest seat in Britain. Since then however, the boundary commissioners have transferred Prescot to Knowsley South and replaced it with Maghull, together with Aintree and its famous racecourse, from the borough of Sefton. This is different territory altogether, with the Lib Dems winning all the council wards by a streak in 2000. This local vote has not yet translated into general election contests, and for now Howarth can still pile up huge majorities, though his seat has now slumped to a lowly 34th place in Labour's list of strongholds.

KNOWSLEY SOUTH

	2001		1997		1992 notional	
Electorateand turnout	70,681	51.8	70,532	67.5	72,282	73.8
Conservative	4,250	11.6	5,987	12.6	10,936	20.5
Labour	26,071	71.3	36,695	77.1	37,071	69.5
Lib Dem	4,755	13.0	3,954	8.3	4,818	9.0
Anti–EU	–	–	954	2.0	–	–
Others	1,514 (2)		–		487	0.9
MP	Eddie O'Hara (Lab)		Eddie O'Hara (Lab)		Eddie O'Hara (Lab)	
Majority	21,316	58.3	30,708	64.5	26,135	49.0

Huyton was famous as the seat of Harold Wilson, who was MP here between 1950 and 1983, leader of the Labour Party for thirteen of those years and Prime Minister for eight. He could always count on a secure base, particularly after 1964 when he enjoyed what was then the huge swing of 9.7 per cent in his favour, and for three elections polled over 40,000 votes. Huyton was reduced in size after 1970 and abolished in 1983, but Knowsley South is essentially its successor, particularly following the inward transfer of Prescot, part of the old Huyton, for the two most recent contests.

In 1997, Eddie O'Hara (first elected in a 1990 by-election with nearly 70 per cent of the vote) racked-up a majority of over 30,000, which was more than Wilson ever achieved, and Labour's 11th best showing nationally. Despite a slight swing to the Lib Dems in 2001, this undoubtedly remains a very safe seat, with Labour particularly strong in Whiston (the southern part of Prescot), Swanside and Princess wards, the latter the 8th most deprived ward in the country where almost one in three of the population are under 16. In local election contests, the Lib Dems are doing well in parts of Prescot and Halewood (which includes the Ford factory once famous for militancy, now churning out shiny Jaguars instead) but as in so many other constituencies they have failed to capitalise in general elections.

LIVERPOOL GARSTON

	2001		1997		1992 notional	
Electorate and turnout	65,094	50.2	66,873	65.0	69,614	70.9
Conservative	5,059	15.5	6,819	15.7	12,340	25.0
Labour	20,043	61.4	26,667	61.3	25,214	51.1
Lib Dem	7,549	23.1	8,250	19.0	10,680	21.7
Anti–EU	–	–	833	1.9	–	–
Others	–		913 (3)		1,104	
MP	Maria Eagle (Lab)		Maria Eagle (Lab)		Eddie Loyden (Lab)	
Majority	12,494	38.3	18,417	42.4	12,874	26.1

Garston is the southernmost and one of the more diverse of Liverpool's five constituencies. It includes the airport, now renamed Liverpool 'John Lennon' after its famous son (the signs predictably lyricize 'above us only sky') and neighbouring council estate at Speke, as well as the nearby former industrial / docks area of Garston itself. The seat also takes in some of the city's remaining middle class neighbourhoods at Allerton, Woolton and Grassendale, the first two wards having the highest retired population in Liverpool.

Only twenty to thirty years ago, hard as it now is to believe, this was a marginal. Indeed the Conservatives held Garston from its creation in 1950 until 1974, achieving a majority of more than 14,000 in 1959. After Eddie Loyden gained the seat for Labour for the first time in February 1974 (by 681 votes) and consolidated in October of the same year, Malcolm Thornton actually regained it for the Conservatives by almost 3,000 in 1979. Then boundary changes, notably the transfer of Aigburth to the then Mossley Hill seat, weakened the Tory position, and a big swing in 1987, when their vote dropped fully 14 percentage points, finished them off altogether. A further small swing to Labour in 1992 and rather larger one for Maria Eagle (twin sister of Wallasey's Angela) in 1997 gave the constituency the safe Labour status of the many surrounding constituencies: after 2001 this was their 107th strongest in the country.

Locally, almost all contests are now won by Liberal Democrats (though Labour started to recover in 2002), In 1999 the Lib Dems actually polled 68 per cent in the council elections across Garston's seven wards, winning middle class wards (74 per cent in Grassendale) and working class (55 per cent in Speke, the 2nd most deprived ward in the country). Labour won just a single ward, Netherley, but they even lost that in 2000 to complete the Lib Dem clean sweep here. The mystery is why, as elsewhere in Liverpool, this seems to influence general election results to such a small degree. Clearly voters are discriminating between different elections, happy for the time being to elect a local Liberal Democrat council and a national Labour government, but the sheer scale of 'split ticket' voting here is unprecedented and a telling sign of the breakdown of firm party loyalties.

LIVERPOOL RIVERSIDE

	2001		1997		1992 notional	
Electorate and turnout	74,827	34.1	73,954	51.6	71,118	59.1
Conservative	2,142	8.4	3,635	9.5	4,572	10.9
Labour	18,201	71.4	26,858	70.4	28,760	68.4
Lib Dem	4,251	16.7	5,059	13.3	7,744	18.4
Anti–EU	–	–	586	1.5	–	–
Socialist	909	3.6	776	2.0	–	–
Others	–		1,221 (4)		949	
MP	Louise Ellman (Lab)		Louise Ellman (Lab)		Robert Parry (Lab)	
Majority	13,950	54.7	21,799	57.2	21,016	50.0

Liverpool Riverside is a constituency of extremes. It covers an area of the city previously divided (immediately after the second world war) into five parliamentary constituencies, it contains three of the ten most deprived wards in Britain, and most notably of all in 2001 it produced the lowest turnout ever recorded in a general election in modern times.

In many ways this is the constituency which includes Liverpool at its best and worst. It covers the centre of the city, with its stunning cathedrals, the grand Pier Head buildings and redeveloped Albert Dock, but also extremely poor areas near the riverfront to the north and south. Of these the best known is probably Toxteth for its riots in the early 1980s, the L8 postcode (immediately south of the city centre) still having a certain notoriety. To the north, wards like Everton and Vauxhall have seen huge drops in population over the last hundred years, the latter ward covering just about the entire original Liverpool Scotland seat, which was an Irish enclave for many years and even returned an Irish Nationalist MP from 1885 until 1929 before becoming Labour's first real foothold in the city.

These days, Labour are dominant in parliamentary contests. They have won the Riverside seat by a canter since its creation in 1983, though turnout has always been low even before nearly two out of three voters stayed at home in 2001. In the local elections of 2000 the participation rate was even lower - just 11 per cent in Abercromby and Smithdown wards - while as elsewhere in the city the Lib Dems won their fair share of wards, including the more residential Aigburth, though Labour did hold most of the northern wards in the seat. For now, Riverside remains a secure base for former leader of Lancashire county council, Louise Ellman, one of three women now representing Liverpool constituencies.

LIVERPOOL WALTON

	2001		1997		1992 actual	
Electorate and turnout	66,237	43.0	67,606	59.5	70,118	67.4
Conservative	1,726	6.1	2,551	6.3	5,915	12.5
Labour	22,143	77.8	31,516	78.4	34,214	72.4
Lib Dem	4,147	14.6	4,478	11.1	5,672	12.0
Anti–EU	442	1.6	620	1.5	–	–
Others	–		1,042 (3)		1,454 (3)	
MP	Peter Kilfoyle (Lab)		Peter Kilfoyle (Lab)		Peter Kilfoyle (Lab)	
Majority	17,996	63.2	27,038	67.2	28,299	59.9

Liverpool Walton, which lies to the north of the centre and takes in both Everton and Liverpool football grounds, has seen perhaps the most extreme long-term swing of any constituency in Britain. It was a Conservative seat during the inter-war years and again from 1950 until 1964, with the party recording over half of the vote in three elections in the 1950s. Since then, and without any contribution from boundary changes, their vote has simply disappeared. The Tory share of the vote has dropped by 46 percentage points since 1955, with Labour's rising by 32, the extent of this swing (39 per cent) even exceeding those in the formerly blue-chip seaside resorts up and down the country which are now in the Labour column.

A major factor behind this dramatic long-term change, and one which has to some extent taken place all over Liverpool as well as in many neighbouring seats, has been religion, or more specifically its declining saliency. Although in national terms the political influence of religious denomination waned around the time of the first world war, in Liverpool the factor persisted for much longer, probably because of the large Irish population in the city. As a rule, Catholics supported Labour and Protestants voted Tory, and as a result the Conservatives could win ten of the eleven seats on offer in 1922 and 1931, and six out of nine as recently as 1959. Then in 1964, this pattern began to break down. Eric Heffer's gain of Walton following a swing of 8 per cent was matched in Toxteth and West Derby, where the pro-Labour shift was even greater. Despite Labour's national problems in the 1970s, there was to be no swing back to the Tories in Liverpool, their remaining vote then collapsing in the 1980s in dramatic fashion. As a result, Heffer could enjoy a majority of over 23,000 when he won his final general election in 1987, attracting support from all communities in Walton. Following his death, the main opposition in the 1991 by-election was provided by the Liberal Democrats and former Militants, Labour's anti-left champion in an extremely bitter contest one Peter Kilfoyle. Walton has continued to back Labour solidly since then, even though Kilfoyle has now fallen out of favour with the party leadership, and is currently their 5th safest seat nationally.

LIVERPOOL WAVERTREE

	2001		1997		1992 notional	
Electorate and turnout	72,555	44.3	73,251	62.7	73,095	70.3
Conservative	3,091	9.6	4,944	10.8	6,422	12.5
Labour	20,155	62.7	29,592	64.4	21,237	41.3
Lib Dem	7,836	24.4	9,891	21.5	17,857	34.7
Anti–EU	348	1.1	576	1.3	–	–
Ind Labour	–	–	–	–	4,762	9.3
Others	708 (2)		915 (3)		1,137 (2)	
MP	Jane Kennedy (Lab)		Jane Kennedy (Lab)		Jane Kennedy (Lab)	
					Liv'pool Broadgreen	
Majority	12,319	38.3	19,701	42.9	3,380	6.6

Wavertree covers much of the east of the city, including up-market suburbs in Childwall as well as terraced streets closer to the centre. The constituency includes the largest chunk of two previous seats: Mossley Hill, which was held by Liberal David Alton in its brief 1983-1997 life, and Broadgreen, which was Labour over this period though held by left-winger Terry Fields, who was ultimately expelled from the party for his support for Militant. Fields stood in Broadgreen as an Independent Labour candidate in 1992, polling almost 6,000 votes, and as a result the projected result for the new seat was always likely to under-estimate the Labour share of the vote. So it proved in 1997, when Jane Kennedy (who had replaced Fields as the official Labour candidate in 1992) increased her vote share by over 23 per cent to win by nearly 20,000, and this now looks a very safe seat.

As elsewhere in Liverpool, the big majorities now piled up by Labour represents a major change from the past. The original Wavertree constituency, abolished in 1983, was won by the Conservatives at every election from 1945 until 1979, and Alton's victories in Edge Hill in 1979 and later Mossley Hill mean that almost all of the present seat has had a non-Labour MP in the past twenty years. Indeed, the Lib Dems can still win all wards in the seat in council elections, polling over 70 per cent of the vote in 2000 and almost as high a share in 2002. They must regret Alton's decision to retire in 1997 rather than battle to keep their flag flying, since he is as yet the only third party candidate in the city who has managed to translate significant support in local elections into general election votes.

LIVERPOOL WEST DERBY

	2001		1997		1992 notional	
Electorate and turnout	67,921	45.5	68,775	61.3	68,613	69.6
Conservative	2,486	8.0	3,656	8.7	6,975	14.6
Labour	20,454	66.2	30,002	71.2	30,830	64.6
Lib Dem	3,366	10.9	3,805	9.0	7,297	15.3
Anti–EU	–	–	657	1.6	–	–
Liberal	4,601	14.9	4,037	9.6	1,263	2.6
Others	–		–		1,374 (2)	
MP	Robert Wareing (Lab)		Robert Wareing (Lab)		Robert Wareing (Lab)	
Majority	15,853	51.3	25,965	61.6	23,533	49.3

West Derby has been less affected by the population declines and boundary changes that have regularly changed the configuration of Liverpool's other constituencies, but it has shared the gradual but severe swing from right to left found in neighbouring seats. Aside from a one-off Liberal victory in 1923, the Conservatives held West Derby from 1918 until 1964, the MP from 1935 to 1954 David Maxwell Fyfe, who played an important role in reshaping the party following the defeat of 1945. Ironically, the reforms which took his name have completely failed to prevent the collapse of the Tory vote here, a 54 per cent share in 1945 falling to just 8 per cent in 2001. As elsewhere in the city the reasons are partly connected with religion, partly socio-economic, with many of the wards here dominated by council estates and the constituency in the bottom 50 nationally for numbers in the professional and managerial groups. There are new estates at Croxteth Park (setting for the gritty soap opera, Brookside) but this scarcely alters the political composition of the place, and Labour's main opposition in general elections now comes from an Independent Liberal, who is a councillor for the Tuebrook ward. MP Robert Wareing briefly lost the Labour whip in the last parliament and appeared to be on his way out, but even though now in his 70s, he was again re-selected by his local party.

ST HELENS NORTH

	2001		*1997*		*1992 actual*	
Electorate and turnout	71,313	52.7	71,416	68.9	71,262	77.4
Conservative	7,076	18.8	8,536	17.3	15,686	28.5
Labour	22,977	61.1	31,953	64.9	31,930	57.9
Lib Dem	6,609	17.6	6,270	12.7	7,224	13.1
Anti–EU	–	–	1,639 (2)	3.3	–	–
Socialist	939	2.5	833	1.7	–	–
Others	–		–		287	
MP	Dave Watts (Lab)		Dave Watts (Lab)		John Evans (Lab)	
Majority	15,901	42.3	23,417	47.6	16,244	29.5

St Helens is an industrial, working class town about 10 miles east of Liverpool along the A580 or M62. It is at the heart of an area which is probably still best described as 'central Lancashire' (despite the 1973 changes which tore it into three parts), which includes neighbouring rugby league strongholds like Wigan, Leigh, Widnes and Warrington. St Helens is most well known for glass (the huge Pilkington glass plant in the centre dominates the skyline) as well as its successful rugby league team, but the northern parliamentary seat, only created in 1983, takes in little of the town itself. Instead it includes smaller surrounding centres such as Newton-le-Willows (which was at the heart of its own constituency until abolished before 1983), Haydock and Billinge, extending as far as Haydock Park race course and the former Parkside colliery, two well-known landmarks (though the latter now demolished) on either side of the M6 motorway.

Local contests in St. Helens North produce a mixed outcome. In the farther flung parts, it is non-Labour representatives who tend to be elected. Newton-le-Willows has been a Liberal Democrat strong-hold for a while now (over 65 per cent of the vote in East in the 2000 elections), while to the north of St Helens itself, Rainford is represented by three of the borough's five Conservative councillors (the others are in neighbouring Windle). Labour win easily in the terraced streets of Haydock and Blackbrook, but overall the 2000 council elections produced a split of 47 per cent for Labour as against 26 per cent each for the Tories and Lib Dems, which was far closer than any general election outcome here. In 2001, former borough council leader Dave Watts suffered a small adverse swing but won easily by over 15,000 votes, and this is likely to remain a very safe Labour seat for the foreseeable future.

ST HELENS SOUTH

	2001		1997		1992 notional	
Electorate and turnout	65,741	51.4	66,554	66.5	68,545	73.1
Conservative	4,675	13.8	6,628	15.0	12,263	24.5
Labour	16,799	49.7	30,367	68.6	30,572	61.0
Lib Dem	7,814	23.1	5,919	13.4	6,961	13.9
Anti–EU	336	1.0	1,165	2.6	–	–
Socialist	3,829 (2)	11.3	–	–	–	–
Others	351 (2)		179		304	
MP	Shaun Woodward (Lab)		Gerry Bermingham (Lab)		Gerry Bermingham (Lab)	
Majority	8,985	26.6	23,739	53.6	18,309	36.5

The late selection of Shaun Woodward for the safe Labour seat of St Helens South gained a great deal of press attention during the 2001 general election campaign, and unlike in Hartlepool and Leicester East (see elsewhere) the adverse publicity did appear to make a difference. Labour's showing (a drop of nineteen percentage points) was their worst in the country apart from Wyre Forest, but it is equally of note that the Conservatives did not benefit at all, clearly regarded as beyond the pale by disaffected Labour supporters. Instead it was the Liberal Democrats (who hold three of the nine local council wards) and two Socialist candidates who mopped up the extra votes, which meant that Woodward could still enjoy a majority of nearly 9,000 on election night.

If anything, South should be slightly the stronger of the two St Helens constituencies for Labour. After 1997 it was one of their safest fifty nationally, despite a swing from 1992-97 which was below average. The seat includes the centre and majority of the town, with Labour achieving vote shares of 80 per cent and 70 per cent respectively in 1999 for Parr & Hardshaw and Queen's Park wards, which lie on either side of the centre. Four other wards to the south west, Grange Park, Thatto Heath, West Sutton and Rainhill are also strongholds, but Labour have recently lost both Sutton & Bold at the southern end of the borough and also Marshalls Cross to the Lib Dems, the latter ward notable for a miserable Conservative vote of 17 in 1999, just 1.0 per cent. The more residential Eccleston ward to the west is also a Lib Dem stronghold, providing a base for them to challenge Labour in the future, though one rather suspects that with plenty of hard work Woodward will increase his majority substantially in 2005/6.

SOUTHPORT

	2001		1997		1992 actual	
Electorateand turnout	70,202	58.6	70,194	72.1	71,444	77.6
Conservative	15,004	36.5	18,186	35.9	26,081	47.0
Labour	6,816	16.6	6,129	12.1	5,637	10.2
Lib Dem	18,011	43.8	24,346	48.1	23,018	41.5
Anti–EU	555	1.3	1,368	2.7	–	–
Other	767		571 (3)		704 (2)	
MP	John.Pugh (LD)		Ronnie Fearn (LD)		Matthew Banks (Con)	
Majority	3,007	7.3	6,160	12.2	3,063	5.5

It may seem unusual to find a Conservative-Liberal Democrat marginal in Merseyside, but then again Southport still likes to consider itself part of Lancashire. It has long been viewed as of the more fashionable of the North West's seaside resorts, with villages to the south such as Ainsdale and Birkdale attracting some extremely wealthy residents to the sands and neighbouring championship golf course. It is probably no surprise that the seat was held by the Conservatives from 1924 until 1983, or that they topped 70 per cent of the vote in 1955, but since then something rather similar has happened here as in other coastal resorts: the Tory vote has collapsed. Unlike in Blackpool or Morecambe it has not been Labour who have benefited - Labour have never even achieved a third of the vote here - but the Liberals, who did after all hold the seat on three occasions before the first world war and again from 1923-24.

After initially losing in 1970 by more than 9,000 votes, Ronnie Fearn cut the Tory majority in February 1974 to under 4,000, and persisted, finally winning in 1987 at his fifth attempt (he skipped a contest in 1983). The Conservatives bounced back in 1992 to reclaim the seat, but then Fearn won again in 1997 to make it two wins in seven attempts over a 27-year period. Despite his retirement, and the failure of the Liberals to ever win two successive elections here previously, successor John Pugh managed to hold the seat in 2001 by an almost comfortable 3,000 votes. Although Southport is now the Liberal Democrats' 18th most vulnerable seat in the country, they will feel they have done the hard part by hanging on with a new candidate (albeit the former leader of Sefton borough council) and will aim to make this a relatively safe seat. In the 2002 local elections they faced opposition from a new source as the 'Southport Party' won three council seats.

WALLASEY

	2001		1997		1992 actual	
Electorate and turnout	64,889	57.6	63,493	73.8	65,670	82.6
Conservative	10,442	28.0	11,190	23.9	22,722	41.9
Labour	22,718	60.8	30,264	64.6	26,531	48.9
Lib Dem	4,186	11.2	3,899	8.3	4,177	7.7
Anti–EU	–	–	1,490	3.2	–	–
Others	–		–		785 (2)	
MP	Angela Eagle (Lab)		Angela Eagle (Lab)		Angela Eagle (Lab)	
Majority	12,276	32.9	19,074	40.7	3,809	7.0

Wallasey was won by the Conservatives in all national contests from 1918 until 1987, only lost to an Independent during a wartime by-election. During the 1950s, the Tories could amass over 30,000 votes here at each election, and it looked a very safe seat indeed. Then Labour got within 600 of victory in 1966, and although they failed to advance further until twenty-six years later, there were signs of a long-term shift in political behaviour. In 1987, a year in which they performed very well across Merseyside, Labour's share of the vote advanced nearly 10 per cent and government minister Lynda Chalker held on by just 279. There would be no repeat in 1992 when a second surge by Labour resulted in a near-4,000 majority for Angela Eagle. A third enormous swing in 1997 produced a majority of almost 20,000, completing an extraordinary turnaround in this northern part of the Wirral peninsula.

Wallasey's changed political landscape (a fall of more than 35 percentage points in the Tory share of the vote since 1955 compared with 18 points nationally) is similar to the fate which has befallen them in other coastal constituencies such as Blackpool South (down 32) and Morecambe (down 33). Part of the explanation is social change, as quite simply these are no longer places where the more affluent choose to retire. A connected factor is economic decline. There is a run-down feel to places like New Brighton, a former seaside resort on the mouth of the Mersey, and Seacombe where there were once thriving docks to the north of Birkenhead. It can surely be no co-incidence that after slowly declining for thirty years, the Conservative vote collapsed completely in the 1980s and 1990s during the years of harsh depression in places like this. Whether they can recover now Labour are in power remains to be seen; they did advance dramatically in the 2000 council elections to regain seats in New Brighton, Liscard and Moreton wards and outpolled Labour again across the constituency by 54–34 per cent. The following year however the Tories were to be disappointed as apart from a slightly larger swing in their favour than the national average, Labour remained well ahead in the general election.

WIRRAL SOUTH

	2001		1997		1992 notional	
Electorate and turnout	60,653	65.6	59,321	81.1	62,103	80.9
Conservative	13,841	34.8	17,495	36.4	25,550	50.8
Labour	18,890	47.4	24,499	50.9	17,382	34.6
Lib Dem	7,087	17.8	5,018	10.4	6,572	13.1
Anti–EU	–	–	768	1.6	–	–
Others	–		315 (2)		765 (2)	
MP	Ben Chapman (Lab)		Ben Chapman (Lab)		Barry Porter (Con)*	
Majority	5,049	12.7	7,004	14.6	8,168	16.3

* Ben Chapman (Lab) elected at February 1997 by–election.

The Wirral South by-election a few weeks before the 1997 general election proved a very good indicator of the landslide to come, Labour's Ben Chapman gaining the seat by 8,000 votes from the Conservatives after a swing of 18 per cent. The result was extremely significant since although a part of Merseyside, Wirral South is largely middle-class commuter territory and the main parties were only too well aware that the many constituencies like this around the country (most in the midlands and south) are crucial in determining national election outcomes. It should therefore not have been too great a shock when Labour not only retained Wirral South in the 'real thing' nine weeks later but also gained a large number of similar suburban seats.

The constituency extends southwards from Birkenhead, through Bebington and the delightful model village of Port Sunlight as far as Bromborough and Eastham. It also takes in Heswall on the western side of the Wirral. Labour's fortunes tend to decline as one moves away from the influence of Birkenhead/Liverpool: they are generally on top in Bebington and Bromborough (though lost both of them in the 2000 council elections) but Eastham at the southern edge of the built-up area is a local Liberal Democrat fiefdom and Heswall, which feels more like the middle of Cheshire, massively pro-Tory. All in all it is extremely marginal and remains Labour's 85th most vulnerable seat despite the poor showing by the Conservatives here in 2001.

WIRRAL WEST

	2001		1997		1992 actual	
Electorate and turnout	62,294	65.0	60,732	77.2	62,471	81.6
Conservative	15,070	37.2	18,297	39.0	26,852	52.7
Labour	19,105	47.2	21,035	44.9	15,788	31.0
Lib Dem	6,300	15.6	5,945	12.7	7,420	14.6
Anti–EU	–	–	1,613	3.4	–	–
Others	–	–	–		888 (2)	
MP	Stephen Hesford (Lab)		Stephen Hesford (Lab)		David Hunt (Con)	
Majority	4,035	10.0	2,738	5.8	11,064	21.7

There can be few more unlikely Labour seats in the land than Wirral West. The feel of the area is more mid-Cheshire than Merseyside, with large mansions gazing across the Dee Estuary to the Welsh coast from places like Caldy Village and the Royal Liverpool Golf Course. Indeed, Liverpool seems a very long way away, with a gentle air of prosperity blowing through towns like Hoylake and West Kirby (which should definitely not be confused with Kirkby in Knowsley North) as well as the newer and more established middle class estates inland. For decades these have been the areas in which the Merseyside professional classes have sought refuge, with the 1991 census data showing the seat to be in the top hundred nationally for numbers of both professional and managerial groups, and the top thirty for owner occupation. Hardly surprisingly the area has long seemed a Tory monolith, a suitable base for cabinet ministers like Selwyn Lloyd (who amassed over 40,000 votes here even in 1945) and David Hunt (who could boast a similar total at his first general election in 1979).

Labour's path to victory here was steep: in 1983 they polled fewer than 10,000 votes and finished in third place. Above-average swings in their favour in 1987 and 1992 put the seat theoretically within range, but it was still one of the biggest upsets on a night of shocks when David Hunt was defeated by Stephen Hesford in the 1997 landslide. Even today it is hard to see how this was achieved: Labour were still in third place across the constituency, some 28 per cent adrift of the Conservatives, in the 2000 locals, picking up just 14 per cent of the vote in Hoylake and less in Royden. Their one strong area is Upton in the centre of the peninsula but they are nowhere near winning any other local council seats. Yet in 2001 Labour's general election majority here actually increased, and according to the list this seat is now safer than 57 others, an indication of just how wide an appeal was enjoyed by 'New Labour' at the start of the new millennium.

Norfolk

	Conservative		Labour		Liberal Democrat		Others	
	Share of vote	Seats	Share of vote	Seats	Share of vote	Seats	Share of vote	Seats
2001	41.6	4	35.5	3	19.6	1	3.3	0
1997	36.7	4	39.9	4	18.2	0	5.1	0
1992	49.2	7	31.2	1	18.6	0	1.0	0
1987	51.0	7	22.9	1	25.8	0	0.2	0
1983	49.8	8	22.0	0	27.9	0	0.3	0

In past centuries Suffolk and Norfolk were rather isolated parts of England, with impenetrable fens to the west and dense forest to the south cutting them off from the rest of England. Norfolk is still a rather traditional and insular place which has been known to go its own way politically.

Norfolk has one major urban area, Norwich, which serves as a centre for most of the county. It was one of the main cities in England in mediaeval times, and although it is still important in the region its national significance has declined over the centuries as industrialisation and the drift to the south east have taken place. It has its problems, but it is one of the most interesting and historic of Britain's larger cities. The smaller towns of Norfolk are less enticing. Great Yarmouth claims, many would feel dubiously, to be Britain's third largest seaside resort but it has a particularly morbid case of the decline of the English seaside combined with industrial dereliction. King's Lynn, another port, has some of the most tragic 1950s/60s redevelopment mistakes but maintains some of its attractions. Smaller than these two are several slow-paced country towns which are market and business centres for the rural areas around them, scattered throughout the county – Dereham, Diss, Aylsham… Fakenham is agro-industrial and a rather incongruous base for Linda McCartney's vegetarian food firm. To complete the picture, the northern coast is a pleasant leisure and retirement area.

Norfolk has a clutch of seats which were Labour in previous elections but did not vote for the party in 1997 when it achieved its biggest ever majority. Norfolk North was Labour in 1922-31 and continuously from 1945 until 1970; Norfolk South was also in 1920, 1923 and in 1945; Norfolk South West voted Labour in 1929 and 1945-64 except for 1951. All were Tory in 1997, although North has now switched to the Lib Dems.

This fact is connected with Norfolk's unusual history of Labour-voting agricultural countryside. Norfolk's farming has tended to be in large farms and arable rather than pastoral (although not exclusively). Harvest time would see large numbers of people employed as unskilled labour. Older Norfolk people can remember grim, backbreaking work in the fields, poverty and bad housing in villages that would feature on no picture postcard. Trade unionism became a strong force, and with it came support for the Labour Party; agricultural workers' union leaders Edwin Gooch and Bert Hazell represented

Norfolk North in 1945-70. Changes in farming, meaning that there are fewer labourers tied to the land, and the gradual doing-up of villages for middle class settlement have eroded this rural Labour vote. It is rather reminiscent of midlands ex-mining areas like Bosworth.

In the 1980s Norfolk's constituencies looked very reliably Conservative except for the liberal-minded Norwich South, but Labour came up strongly in 1992 and drew level in seats – and just ahead in votes – in 1997. Norfolk was one of the very best areas for the Conservatives in 2001, with the 4.6 per cent swing only being exceeded by one other English county, namely Cumbria. Unlike Cumbria, there were hardly any foot and mouth cases in the area, although movement restrictions did interfere with rural life here during 2001. The Conservatives were helped by a more effective squeeze on the Eurosceptic vote than occurred in most counties – the combined anti-EU share fell from 4.1 per cent in 1997 to only 1.7 per cent in 2001 despite the UKIP contesting an extra constituency. There were also concerns over law and order in the rural areas, particularly in the light of the case of west Norfolk farmer Tony Martin who killed a burglar and went to prison.

Local government

The Conservatives, as part of their strong showing in the county, retook Norfolk county council in June 2001 after eight years of no overall control. The Conservatives won 48 seats, to 26 Labour and 10 Lib Dem. There are no Conservative councillors from the sixteen Norwich city wards, but they dominate the representation from the rural areas often because of divided opposition rather than overwhelming voting strength.

Norwich city has a long Labour history – it first voted in a Labour majority in 1933 and the party has only lost control very briefly since. However, the Liberal Democrats have been making progress in annual city elections in recent years and it was one of their top targets. They duly won control on a large swing in 2002. Broadland council, north of Norwich, was regained by the Conservatives in 1999 after a five year period of no overall control. More surprisingly the Conservatives also picked up Great Yarmouth in 2000 after ten years of Labour control, including gains in some very poor neighbourhoods. They should hold both councils for the next few years, although Labour might be able to engineer a recovery in Yarmouth.

The other councils elect only every four years. South Norfolk district council is run by the Liberal Democrats, who first won control in 1995 and held it well in 1999. North Norfolk is split fairly equally between the three main parties and Independents. King's Lynn & West Norfolk was Labour-controlled from 1995 until 1999, after which the party formed a minority administration. The late Moss Evans, former general secretary of the TGWU, retired to the area and enjoyed a spell on the council including a term as mayor.

Boundary review

Norfolk is entitled to an extra seat at the next redistribution, which will appear in the west of the county. There are several permutations of how this might arise, but the centre of gravity of the Norfolk SW seat will probably have to shift to the east and Norfolk NW will probably lose a few rural wards and once again bear the name of King's Lynn, which is good news for Labour's hopes of regaining the seat. The new West Norfolk seat, however it is constituted, should be an additional safe Tory seat in a county which has tended to bring them good news.

GREAT YARMOUTH

	2001		1997		1992 actual	
Electorate and turnout	69,194	58.3	68,525	71.3	68,263	77.9
Conservative	15,780	39.1	17,416	35.6	25,505	47.9
Labour	20,344	50.4	26,084	53.4	20,196	38.0
Lib Dem	3,392	8.4	5,381	11.0	7,225	13.6
Anti–EU	850	2.1	–	–	–	–
Others	–		–		284	
MP	Tony Wright (Lab)		Tony Wright (Lab)		Michael Carttiss (Con)	
Majority	4,564	11.3	8,668	17.7	5,309	10.0

Great Yarmouth is an isolated place, a narrow urban strip separating the Broads from the coast. The seaside resort area is in the north of the town, where there is a promenade and many hotels. On the peninsula to the south there are docklands, a large industrial area, some of which is utterly derelict, and some poverty-stricken neighbourhoods. Great Yarmouth has one unwelcome distinction. Its Regent ward is the most deprived part of southern England – worse than any ward of London, Birmingham or even Sheffield or Hartlepool – and only 18 other places in the whole of England rank worse. Nelson ward is almost as badly off, being as multiply deprived as the depressed Elswick ward of Newcastle or Knowsley's notorious Cantril Farm, and several other parts of the town suffer from great poverty. Unemployment in the constituency was running high throughout the 1990s, and remained at 6.5 per cent in May 2001, worse than deprived areas such as Jarrow or Liverpool Garston.

Great Yarmouth borough and constituency – the two are coterminous – extend beyond the town into a more affluent hinterland. Along the coast are the less crashed-out resorts of Caister and Gorleston (although Gorleston has the large Magdalen estate), and inland there is an area around Burgh Castle. The Conservatives did very well in mid-term elections in the 1997-2001 parliament, taking control of the borough council in May 2000 after two sets of landslide gains. In the general election Labour looked vulnerable in this constituency, which the party had only managed to win previously in 1945 and 1966, but in the end the swing was a little below the Norfolk average. Its isolation and economic decline have made Yarmouth a key test of Labour's ability to combat 'social exclusion' and the next result may depend on whether any progress has been made.

NORFOLK MID

	2001		1997		1992 *notional*	
Electorate and turnout	77,158	68.1	75,311	76.3	*71,208*	*83.6*
Conservative	23,519	44.8	22,739	39.6	*32,481*	*54.6*
Labour	18,957	36.1	21,403	37.3	*15,537*	*26.1*
Lib Dem	7,621	14.5	8,617	15.0	*11,316*	*19.0*
Anti–EU	1,333	2.5	3,229	5.6	–	–
Green	1,118	2.1	1,254	2.2	–	–
Others	–		215	–	*209*	
MP	Keith Simpson (Con)		Keith Simpson (Con)		Richard Ryder (Con)	
Majority	4,562	8.7	1,336	2.3	*16,944*	*28.5*

Norfolk Mid, on the map, is shaped a little like a shapely leg, bent at Norwich and ending at the shoe-shaped Great Yarmouth. It is a quite solidly rural constituency with no particularly large centres within it; most of it looks towards Norwich. The eastern stretch is the outer part of the Broadlands district council's area, including Brundall and Reedham, the larger villages of Wroxham and Acle and a large stretch of peaceful watery countryside around the Norfolk Broads. Aylsham, a market town to the north, is the main town of the Broadland section. To the west there is a wider area of country in the north of the Breckland district at Dereham, another slow-paced central Norfolk market town. The town was known until recently as East Dereham and many residents keep using the 'full' name. The two county wards in the town (17,000 electors) were both narrowly Conservative in the county elections in 2001. The Conservatives were ahead across most of the constituency in the 2001 county elections, although often not by particularly large margins.

As in many seats where the Conservative majority was looking pretty threadbare in 1997, there was a swing in 2001 sufficient to restore it to safe-ish status. Labour candidate Daniel Zeichner worked very hard in the last two general elections, but the Conservative tendencies of this rural area prevailed on both occasions.

NORFOLK NORTH

	2001		1997		1992 actual	
Electorate and turnout	80,061	70.2	77,365	76.0	73,780	81.0
Conservative	23,495	41.8	21,456	36.5	28,810	48.2
Labour	7,490	13.3	14,736	25.1	13,850	23.2
Lib Dem	23,978	42.7	20,163	34.3	16,365	27.4
Anti–EU	608	1.1	2,458	4.2	–	–
Others	649		–		726 (2)	
MP	Norman Lamb (LD)		David Prior (Con)		Ralph Howell (Con)	
Majority	483	0.9	1,293	2.2	12,445	20.8

Cromer is a turn of the (previous) century resort, and its pier boasts the last traditional end-of-the-pier variety show in Britain; Cromer is also noted for crab fishing. It has some of the problems of seaside resorts elsewhere, but not in the extreme form found in Great Yarmouth. The rest of the long coastline consists of small towns such as Sheringham and Wells-next-the-Sea, some villages and miles of quiet, empty beaches. The coast is an attractive feature which has been attracting retirees and weekenders for decades now. Inland, Holt is a charming place but Fakenham and North Walsham are more functional market towns. North Norfolk was once a heavily agricultural area, but in 1991 only 7 per cent were employed in agriculture compared to 18 per cent in manufacturing. The decline of farming employment, and its replacement by incomers, has changed the character of the constituency.

Norfolk North was once a reasonably reliable Labour seat thanks to the votes of farm labourers, who were unionised and fought against squalid and degrading employment conditions in the first half of the 20th century. Labour first won in 1922 and held it until the 1931 wipeout, and then again from 1945 to 1970. The seat gradually slipped away from Labour in the 1960s as more bungalows appeared on the coast and farm employment fell. A residual Labour vote remained even as the Tories built up their majority between 1970 and 1987; the very rural county ward of Erpingham and Melton Constable (inland villages) was Labour-held until very recently, and Labour held on to 19.1 per cent of the vote even in 1983. There are still some pools of rural poverty.

In the 1990s, however, the Liberal Democrats started to build a base here (they are strongest on the coast at Sheringham) and new Conservative MP David Prior was elected on a low share of the vote in 1997. He was undone in 2001 as the traditional, resistant Labour vote plummeted in favour of three-time Lib Dem candidate Norman Lamb. Despite achieving one of the top fifty increases in the Conservative vote, Prior was defeated after one term, although by a very small majority. The Conservative local election candidates in 2001 were ahead, 41-23-33, so this is another seat they lost thanks to tactical voting. The odds are probably that Lamb will be able to consolidate his position in future elections.

NORFOLK NORTH WEST

	2001		1997		1992 actual	
Electorate and turnout	78,707	65.1	77,083	74.7	77,439	80.7
Conservative	24,846	48.5	23,911	41.5	32,554	52.1
Labour	21,361	41.7	25,250	43.8	20,990	33.6
Lib Dem	4,292	8.4	5,513	9.6	8,599	13.8
Anti–EU	704	1.4	2,923	5.1	–	–
Others	–		–		330	
MP	Henry Bellingham (Con)		George Turner (Lab)		Henry Bellingham (Con)	
Majority	3,485	6.8	1,339	2.3	11,564	18.5

The core of Norfolk North West is King's Lynn, which contributes 25,000 electors to the constituency. It has an unusual mix of influences – it is at the end of a fast train line to Cambridge and London, and has received London overspill, but it also has links to the midlands and even the north (local televisions are often tuned to transmitters whose principal audiences are in Yorkshire). Its history as a port has given it links with Holland and Germany apparent in some fine old buildings, and it also serves as a centre for a rural area of Norfolk and the fenlands. Lynn is a working town, a port, manufacturing (formerly steel) and food processing centre. Parts of it are depressingly poor and ugly – Lynn North is 139th (out of 8414) on the official index of multiple deprivation. Lynn voted 52-34 Labour in 2001 in the local elections.

Lynn has villages which have effectively become suburbs, such as Winch and the Woottons, and there are a couple of retirement resorts north of Lynn such as Heacham and Hunstanton. The rest of the seat is rural, although unlike other areas of the country this does not mean Tory domination. Farm workers have provided the basis for Labour victories in local elections in rural wards; the royal palace at Sandringham sits in Labour-voting countryside and in other wards the Liberal Democrats enjoy clear runs against the Tories. The royal connection is perhaps not coincidental – in Victorian times royal estates let workers vote the way they wanted at a time when other rural landowners used pressure and intimidation, and once established, voting traditions can last surprisingly long.

The rural Labour vote is essential for Labour to win the seat, as Lynn is not large enough on its own. Labour used to be able to win King's Lynn in an even year – as in 1950 and 1964 - but this seat now seems vulnerable only in a landslide and even then tends towards the Conservatives. The reason is the long term erosion of the rural Labour vote as in the rest of Norfolk. George Turner said before the election that 'I'm convinced there are enough people who support what we are doing but I'm not convinced they're all going to vote.' It was an acute point.

The forthcoming boundary changes will probably help Labour a little by removing rural wards. If the Conservatives come back strongly nationally then this seat will be a predictable Tory victory, but if Labour are on for another big win then they will hope to regain this hard-fought constituency, particularly under revised boundaries when they are introduced.

NORFOLK SOUTH

	2001		1997		1992 notional	
Electorate and turnout	82,710	67.6	79,239	78.4	76,494	84.1
Conservative	23,589	42.2	24,935	40.2	33,669	52.4
Labour	13,719	24.5	16,188	26.1	11,841	18.4
Lib Dem	16,696	29.9	17,557	28.3	17,305	26.9
Anti–EU	856	1.5	2,933 (2)	4.7	–	–
Others	1,069		484		1,495 (4)	
MP	Richard Bacon (Con)		John MacGregor (Con)		John MacGregor (Con)	
Majority	6,893	12.3	7,378	11.9	16,364	25.4

Norfolk South is a mainly rural constituency to the south of Norwich. None of its towns are particularly large or well known, although Diss, Long Stratton and Wymondham are small centres for the surrounding areas. None of these towns is large enough to have more than one county council ward, and they sit in thoroughly rural surroundings with many small villages. In 2001 Richard Bacon, a public relations writer who lists 'snobbery and racism' as his pet hates, held the seat for the Conservatives against divided opposition but is one of the more vulnerable Conservative MPs despite his quite large majority.

The Lib Dems have been active in local elections in Norfolk South for some years. They led in the wards that make up the seat in the 1999 local elections and control the local authority. Most of the county wards that make up the seat were fairly closely contested in 2001 between Conservatives and Liberal Democrats, with Lib Dems narrowly ahead in Diss and Long Stratton and the Tories returning the favour in the more completely rural wards, except for Loddon where they polled nearly 70 per cent in the county election. Labour's local election share was 18 per cent, thinly and evenly spread, but another 6 per cent supported them in the general election mainly at the expense of the Lib Dems.

The Conservative share of the vote is only a shade above that in Norfolk North, which they lost in 2001, and if the Liberal Democrats could squeeze the Labour vote as efficiently as they have in North the seat would be too close to call. They might be assisted by the clearer tactical position in the constituency after 2001. Norfolk South has the potential to be a very interesting contest.

NORFOLK SOUTH WEST

	2001		1997		1992 notional	
Electorate and turnout	83,903	63.1	80,406	73.1	78,711	79.1
Conservative	27,633	52.2	24,694	42.0	34,098	54.7
Labour	18,267	34.5	22,230	37.8	16,848	27.1
Lib Dem	5,681	10.7	8,178	13.9	11,343	18.2
Anti–EU	1,368	2.6	3,694	6.3	–	–
MP	Gillian Shephard (Con)		Gillian Shephard (Con)		Gillian Shephard (Con)	
Majority	9,366	17.7	2,464	4.2	17,250	27.7

Norfolk SW used to be one of the most famous constituencies in the country for its unusual behaviour at election time between 1929 and 1964, when it was frequently won by small majorities and in defiance of the national trend; Labour gained it in 1955 and lost it in 1964. Since the Conservatives held it despite Labour's national landslide in 1966 it has been safely Tory, except in 1997. It is now, on the rather unusual 2001 result, their 64th safest seat.

Thetford is the principal town in the constituency with 14,000 electors; a market town with added London overspill, bypassed by the A11, which was the birthplace of Thomas Paine, the revolutionary and rationalist. Paine would be pleased that his home town tends to the left, giving Labour a 53-36 majority in the 2001 local elections. The rest of the constituency would be less to his taste. Swaffham and Attleborough are smaller towns, which are rather more Conservative. The farming areas around Thetford were once, like other parts of rural Norfolk, quite Labour-voting and unionised, but the party struggled to get 25-30 per cent in most of it in 2001 while the Tories led comfortably. Thetford is surrounded by the Breckland forest, a low-lying area of heathland and pine woods, and large tracts of military land which are off-limits to the visitor. The current constituency includes a bit of west Norfolk as well, around Downham Market up towards Kings Lynn, which is even more Conservative.

Since 1987 the local MP has been Gillian Shephard, who was elevated to the Cabinet in 1992 by fellow East Anglian John Major. In 2001 she comfortably saw off a Labour challenge which was rather unusually endorsed by the Lib Dem candidate. This endorsement proved counterproductive, as the Labour poll slumped in most of the component wards. Norfolk SW was never a place to take any notice of how it was told it should vote.

NORWICH NORTH

	2001		1997		1992 notional	
Electorate and turnout	77,158	59.1	72,706	75.7	71,785	80.6
Conservative	15,761	34.6	17,876	32.5	25,558	44.2
Labour	21,624	47.4	27,346	49.7	23,288	40.3
Lib Dem	6,750	14.8	6,951	12.6	8,462	14.6
Anti–EU	471	1.0	1,777	3.2	–	–
Others	1,008 (2)		1,107 (3)		543	
MP	Ian Gibson (Lab)		Ian Gibson (Lab)		Patrick Thompson (Con)	
Majority	5,863	12.9	9,470	17.2	2,270	3.9

The purist might object to the name of this seat; only 28,000 of its electors are actually in Norwich City Council's area while nearly 50,000 are within Broadland council's area. However, the Broadland element consists of suburbs which look to Norwich and are for the most part in the city's built-up area. The suburbs are grouped into three townships – Thorpe St. Andrew in the east, and Sprowston and Hellesdon to the north, plus some other adjoining areas.

The Norwich city contribution is mainly composed of working class areas, such as Mile Cross, and has a high proportion of council tenants. It was the core of what was before boundary changes in 1983 the safest Labour seat in East Anglia. All the wards were Labour in 2001, and the party led 53-23 (and 21 for the Lib Dems) in the local elections, although turnout was only 53 per cent. The suburbs are marginal, with all the wards producing reasonably close results in 2001, but they incline to the Conservatives, who can win nearly everything in a good election for them like 2000. In 2001 the Broadland portion voted 40-34 for the Conservatives, and turnout was 63 per cent. The gap in turnout meant that the city had 36 per cent of electors but cast only 32 per cent of the vote, making Labour's task a bit harder.

Very good mid-term results for the Conservatives in the local and European elections led people to expect a close fight, or even an upset Tory win, in 2001. As it happened the swing was only a little more than the national average and Labour held on comfortably. It is their 88th most marginal seat and therefore a key target if the Conservatives are going to deprive Labour of an overall majority in the next election.

NORWICH SOUTH

	2001		1997		1992 notional	
Electorate and turnout	71,276	59.8	70,009	72.6	69,638	79.8
Conservative	10,551	24.8	12,028	23.7	21,196	38.1
Labour	19,367	45.5	26,267	51.7	25,546	46.0
Lib Dem	9,640	22.6	9,457	18.6	7,820	14.1
Anti–EU	473	1.1	1,464	2.9	–	–
Green	1,434	3.4	736	1.4	874	1.6
Others	1,127 (2)		849 (2)		132	
MP	Charles Clarke (Lab)		Charles Clarke (Lab)		John Garrett (Lab)	
Majority	8,816	20.7	14,239	28.0	4,350	7.8

The South constituency contains the city centre as well as the southern suburbs of Norwich. Mediaeval prosperity gave Norwich a large city centre, which according to a local saying has a church for every week of the year and a pub for every day. Norwich is the commercial and administrative centre for Norfolk and its influence as regional capital extends a bit into neighbouring counties. The city has a substantial manufacturing and working class presence, and a large element of council-built housing of generally high standard thanks to housing programmes since the 1930s. In 1963 it added a new university, UEA, to the mix. Norwich South is home to a substantial number of educated middle class professionals, many in the public sector and education, plus most of the student population. This makes it an unusual seat for East Anglia in general and Norfolk in particular.

The politics of Norwich South is not too surprising given its social characteristics. A predecessor seat was a Tory-inclined marginal, but in this seat the Conservatives were lucky to avoid third place in 2001 alongside Cambridge, Oxford East and a lot of inner London. In the local elections on the same day they did come third in every ward except suburban Eaton and the small area from South Norfolk in the seat around Costessey. Labour and the Lib Dems were level in the local election vote in 2001, but 7,000 local Lib Dem voters did not vote for the party's parliamentary candidate, mostly to the benefit of Labour's Charles Clarke. Their local performance itself was much worse than in 2000 when they led by about 20 points in the seat. Although disappointed in 2001, the Lib Dems cruised to victory in the 2002 local elections and hold out rather speculative hopes of inflicting even worse embarrassment on the Labour Party's Chair.

Northamptonshire

	Conservative		Labour		Liberal Democrat		Others	
	Share of vote	Seats	Share of vote	Seats	Share of vote	Seats	Share of vote	Seats
2001	41.2	1	43.8	5	12.6	0	2.5	0
1997	40.4	1	45.0	5	11.1	0	3.4	0
1992	51.8	6	33.5	0	14.3	0	0.4	0
1987	51.7	6	27.1	0	20.8	0	0.4	0
1983	49.0	6	25.5	0	25.3	0	0.3	0

Northamptonshire is the southernmost of the counties which make up the East Midlands. Many of its towns have an unmistakable Midlands character to them, though the short (less than 100 miles) distance from London has also left its mark in terms of growing numbers of affluent commuters, particularly in the more rural areas close to the M1 motorway. There has also been a mushrooming of new housing estates around the largest town, Northampton (officially designated a New Town though it has existed for centuries), with its population growing from 100,000 in the 1950s to about double that figure today. Like much of the county, Northampton was formerly known for making shoes, and its central core is still made up of terraced streets, just as one would find in Leicester or Derby. There is an industrial tradition to all of the main towns in the county; in the past, Kettering and Wellingborough were also known for footwear manufacture, and the new town of Corby for its steelworks. On the other hand there are also large rural areas around the main towns, one segment covering Rockingham Forest and Oundle in the north east of the county, and another to the north of Northampton, which includes Althorp House, home to the Spencer family and burial site of Princess Diana. To the south west of the M1 motorway, the territory becomes even more up-market, resembling Home Counties such as Buckinghamshire over the border; this area (which is commutable to Milton Keynes, Oxford or even London thanks to good motorway links) includes Towcester, Brackley and the Silverstone motor racing circuit. The South Northamptonshire district of which they are part also contains a large number of pretty and pretty affluent villages - overall it is one of the ten least deprived local government districts in the whole country.

The parliamentary constituency to the west of the M1 motorway (at present called Daventry) has always been Conservative, usually with a comfortable majority, but elsewhere the county's seats were dominated by Labour after 1945. Northampton was always won by the party from 1945 until 1974, Kettering (which included Corby) from 1945 to 1983, and Wellingborough from 1945 to 1959 and again for five years in the late 1960s. During the 1970s and 1980s however, there was a marked swing to the right, which was helped by the creation of new constituencies in each of the 1974 and 1983 boundary reviews. The division of Northampton into two initially created a couple of marginals, but the

Conservatives had decisively gained both by 1983, while the creation of a new Corby seat not only made Kettering safe for the Tories, but unexpectedly tipped Corby over to them as well, thanks to Labour's unpopularity in the 1980s. As a result of this, and Wellingborough's slow swing to the Conservatives, Labour were left with no seats at all in the county from 1983 until 1997.

In 1997, this pattern was spectacularly reversed as Northamptonshire proved to be one of the most fertile (and most unexpected) providers of Labour gains in the landslide election. From a starting point of zero, the party gained no fewer than five of the six parliamentary constituencies in the county, which went well beyond the anticipated wins in Corby and Northampton North, both of which had disappointed Labour in 1992. The other three gains of Kettering, Wellingborough and Northampton South had not been targeted and were a big surprise, perhaps as much for the defeated Conservative incumbents as the three newly elected MPs. In each case the margin was less than 1,000, and Labour's efficient spread of votes across the county resulted in an extremely disproportional outcome of votes to seats, though then again a similar argument could have been made about the reverse outcome five years previously. Indeed Northamptonshire is a classic example of the way in which the British electoral system still converts small changes of opinion into bigger changes in representation, thus paving the way for decisive national results. Under a proportional system, probably only a single seat out of six in the county, rather than five out of six, would have changed hands in 1997.

In 2001, the three narrow 1997 gains were Labour's first, second and fifth most marginal seats in the whole country. Most commentators assumed that they would lose all of them, since this required a swing to the Conservatives of less than one percentage point. In the event, not only did Labour hold all three, but their majorities increased - after 2001, Wellingborough is now only Labour's 20th most vulnerable seat with an almost comfortable majority of nearly 2,500. In part this pattern must have been down to incumbency effects - newly elected MPs often pick up a few extra votes at the first election after their initial win, and this effect doubles if (as in all three cases here) the former MP does not seek re-election, thus depriving their party of their old incumbency vote. Another factor in 2001 will have been the national popularity of the government, particularly to mortgage-paying middle class voters, and Labour's fate here next time around will almost certainly depend on whether this continues.

Local government

Labour's recent success at a parliamentary level has been reflected at local council level as well. This was particularly the case in Wellingborough, which was gained by Labour in 1999 from no overall control, after previous periods with a narrow Conservative majority. Labour also control Northampton with a reasonable majority - here too the Tories were in charge until the early 1990s. Kettering saw Labour gain a majority for the first time in 1995, but then narrowly lose it four years later, although they remain the largest group. Corby has always been strongly Labour, with 27 councillors out of 29 elected (or returned unopposed) in 1999. West of the dividing line that is the M1 motorway, the political complexion is very different. South Northamptonshire was Conservative from 1979 until 1995, then balanced, but saw the Tories easily reclaim overall control in 1999. Majorities have often been rather smaller in Daventry, and the council was balanced in the 1990s, but here too the Tories regained an overall majority in 1999 and increased it in 2002. At the opposite end of the county, East Northamptonshire has also tended to be Conservative, though there is Labour support in towns like Rushden and Irthlingborough.

The county council reflects most of these divisions. For example, Labour win everything in Corby, the Conservatives all seats in South Northants. Overall, it has a very small Labour majority, though the Tories made gains in 2001. The Liberal Democrats have only a single solitary county councillor (out of over seventy) and are weak throughout the county. In total they had only twenty councillors on the eight authorities in early 2002, and their only decent-sized group can be found on Northampton borough council.

Boundary review

Final recommendations for Northamptonshire have now been made following a two-day public enquiry held in December 2000. There will be widespread changes, following the creation of a seventh seat in the west of the county. The new seat will be called Northamptonshire South (the original name of the continuing Daventry constituency) and will include some of the expanding southern suburbs of Northampton. It will undoubtedly be a Conservative seat, but its creation is not necessarily good news for the party, because of the effect this will have on Northampton South in particular. In fact the loss of the rural element of this constituency, along with the Nene Valley and Hunsbury wards, should turn it into a safe Labour seat. Elsewhere, Kettering also loses its (Daventry district) rural component, which again will help Labour. In Wellingborough, however, the two wards from the district to be transferred to Daventry are based on Labour supporting Earls Barton; initially the Tory north ward was due to go as well, but the Conservatives successfully argued in favour of its retention at the inquiry.

CORBY

	2001		1997		1992 actual	
Electorate and turnout	72,594	65.0	69,446	77.7	68,334	82.9
Conservative	17,583	37.2	18,028	33.4	25,203	44.5
Labour	23,283	49.3	29,888	55.4	24,861	43.9
Lib Dem	4,751	10.1	4,045	7.5	5,792	10.2
Anti–EU	855	1.8	1,863 (2)	3.4	–	–
Others	750		133		784	
MP	Phil Hope (Lab)		Phil Hope (Lab)		William Powell (Con)	
Majority	5,700	12.1	11,860	22.0	342	0.6

Corby is the nearest one gets to a Scottish colony south of the border, its former steelworks having acted as a magnet drawing Scottish workers to an unlikely home in deepest Northamptonshire. The town's politics have generally followed a Labour tradition; even in 1999 Labour won 27 of the 29 seats on the district council, and of the 13 wards, three were uncontested and Labour polled over 70 per cent of the vote in a further six. Yet the parliamentary constituency has not been so easy for Labour, and indeed was held by the Conservatives from its creation in 1983 until 1997. The largest part of the explanation for this is that the constituency has always included nearly as many electors from the district of East Northamptonshire as voters from the town of Corby itself. The Conservatives are as strong in its villages and public school town of Oundle as Labour are in Corby, and helped by favourable national circumstances, William Powell was able to win the seat for the Tories with a series of small majorities. Powell's luck ran out in the very different political atmosphere of 1997, Labour's Phil Hope amassing a majority of almost 12,000.

The 2001 elections again starkly demonstrated the divided nature of this constituency: in the county council election, Labour polled 16,000 votes in Corby as against 7,000 for the Conservatives, whereas in the East Northamptonshire wards the Tories led by 11,600 to 8,500. This last figure is actually quite impressive for Labour and is as important in their continuing to win the seat as are the votes stacked up in Corby. In 2001 they narrowly won the small towns of Irthlingborough (by 18 votes) and Raunds (by 74) in county elections. Across the constituency however, there was a large five per cent swing back to the Conservatives, which may be linked with slow demographic changes, particularly the influx of a greater number of commuters. Although not enough to threaten Labour in 2001, if such trends continue, there may well be another tight contest next time. This is now Labour's 78th most marginal seat.

DAVENTRY

	2001		1997		1992 notional	
Electorate and turnout	86,510	65.5	80,750	76.5	75,148	82.5
Conservative	27,911	49.2	28,615	46.3	35,842	57.8
Labour	18,262	32.2	21,237	34.4	14,831	23.9
Lib Dem	9,130	16.1	9,233	15.0	10,933	17.6
Anti–EU	1,381	2.4	2,461	4.0	–	–
Others	–		204		422	
MP	Tim Boswell (Con)		Tim Boswell (Con)		Tim Boswell (Con)	
Majority	9,649	17.0	7,378	11.9	21,011	33.9

The Daventry constituency covers the large south western section of Northamptonshire (roughly bordered by the M1 motorway) and its representative Tim Boswell finds himself, since 1997, in the unexpected position of being the only Conservative MP in the county. Unexpected but certainly not unheard of – the same pattern existed in the 1960s for example, though this seat was then known as South Northamptonshire. That name still survives as a local district, and is apparently the eighth least deprived out of 354 in the country. Given this statistic, it is probably not that surprising that in 2001, the Conservatives won all nine county council wards within its boundaries, polling roughly 60 per cent of the vote in the process. Some of this territory is admittedly in the Northampton South constituency, but those places within the Daventry seat such as Brackley, Towcester and Silverstone (next to the famous formula one racetrack) are as heavily Tory as anywhere. The only real pockets of Labour support can be found in Middleton Cheney and King's Sutton near Banbury, and some parts of Daventry itself, which has its own district in the north of the constituency. Even here, villages like Weedon and Flore just off the M1 motorway produce almost monolithic Conservative support, and the overall result is never in much doubt. The constituency has only ever been tightly fought on two previous occasions, Labour coming within 1,200 in 1945 and slightly closer in a 1962 by-election. Apart from that it has been a strong Tory seat, currently the 71st safest in the country.

KETTERING

	2001		1997		1992 notional	
Electorate and turnout	78,946	68.1	75,456	75.5	72,383	80.9
Conservative	23,369	43.5	24,461	42.9	30,884	52.7
Labour	24,034	44.7	24,650	43.3	18,697	31.9
Lib Dem	5,469	10.2	6,098	10.7	9,012	15.4
Anti–EU	880	1.6	1,551	2.7	–	–
Others	–		197		–	
MP	Phil Sawford (Lab)		Phil Sawford (Lab)		Roger Freeman (Con)	
Majority	665	1.2	189	0.3	12,187	20.8

Kettering was the most marginal Labour-held seat in the country after 1997 when Phil Sawford squeezed home by just 189 votes, but remarkably he held on to it with a slightly increased – though still precarious – majority of 665 in 2001. It is one of many medium sized Midlands towns to have fallen to 'New Labour's' charms (Wellingborough, Loughborough, Rugby & Kenilworth, Warwick & Leamington, Stafford, and so on) but remains exactly the sort of place that the Conservatives must regain if they are to make any sort of recovery.

The constituency was actually held continually by Labour from 1945 until 1983, but in those days it was very differently constituted, including the staunchly Labour steel town of Corby. As soon as it was removed to form the basis of its own seat in 1983, the Conservatives were able to win Kettering with majorities of around 10,000, and the Labour vote collapsed to 20 per cent and a poor third place. Despite a fairly dramatic recovery in 1992, when Phil Hope (now MP for Corby) added twelve percentage points to Labour's total, the seat must have still seemed a secure base for Roger Freeman's ministerial ambitions, but alas, Freeman joined some of his higher profile cabinet colleagues (such as Michael Portillo, Malcolm Rifkind and Michael Forsyth) in being defeated at the polls in 1997.

In the 2001 county poll, Labour won the Kettering district (all of whose wards are in the parliamentary seat) by the margin of 19,259 to 17,884, but the smaller number of predominantly Conservative electors to the west around Pitsford Water (part of Daventry district) cut this lead by a half. As is normal these days, the rural areas are easily the Tories' best, as Kettering Rural also heavily backed the Conservatives, while the small towns of Desborough and Rothwell to the north west marginally backed Labour.

NORTHAMPTON NORTH

	2001		*1997*		*1992 notional*	
Electorate and turnout	74,124	56.0	73,757	70.1	*73,395*	*77.3*
Conservative	12,614	30.4	17,247	33.4	*25,972*	*45.8*
Labour	20,507	49.4	27,247	52.7	*21,905*	*38.6*
Lib Dem	7,363	17.7	6,579	12.7	*8,630*	*15.2*
Anti–EU	596	1.4	464	0.9	*–*	*–*
Others	414		161		*232*	
MP	Sally Keeble (Lab)		Sally Keeble (Lab)		Tony Marlow (Con)	
Majority	7,893	19.0	10,000	19.3	*4,067*	*7.2*

Northampton formed a single constituency until 1974, and from 1945 it had been held continuously by Reginald Paget for Labour. Then the growing 'New Town' was divided into two (with some surrounding areas added), and the political effect was to turn one Labour seat into two hyper-marginals. Labour held North in the two 1974 contests by 1,033 and 1,538, but in 1979 the seat was lost to the Conservatives. A rightward swing seemed to be confirmed by majorities of nearly 10,000 for Tony Marlow in 1983 and 1987, but the Labour vote recovered by over 5,000 in 1992, and in 1997 a swing of over 13 per cent was comfortably enough to see off the Euro-rebel MP.

The North seat is compact, including a mix of older housing stock towards the centre and newer estates to the north. Locally the Liberal Democrats have made some headway, winning a number of wards such as Boughton Green and Kingsthorpe, but nationally such areas were always likely to find 'New Labour' attractive, and so it proved with former Southwark council leader, Sally Keeble, amassing a majority of exactly 10,000 at the last general election. Since May 1997, Labour have maintained their strength, leading by approximately 20 per cent over the Conservatives in local council elections in 1999, when the Liberal Democrats also polled more votes than the Tories across the constituency. This clearly had some effect in 2001 when the general election Lib Dem vote increased (albeit from a low base) and the Tory vote dropped further. As a result, Keeble was able to maintain a virtually unaltered 19-point lead despite a slight fall in her own vote.

NORTHAMPTON SOUTH

	2001		1997		1992 notional	
Electorate and turnout	85,668	59.6	79,672	71.7	73,499	80.4
Conservative	20,997	41.1	23,470	41.1	32,898	55.7
Labour	21,882	42.9	24,214	42.4	17,854	30.2
Lib Dem	6,355	12.5	6,316	11.1	8,355	14.1
Anti–EU	1,237	2.4	2,564 (2)	4.5	–	–
Others	558 (2)		541		–	
MP	Tony Clarke (Lab)		Tony Clarke (Lab)		Michael Morris (Con)	
Majority	885	1.7	744	1.3	15,044	25.5

Northampton South always seemed a more unlikely gain for Labour than its northern counterpart, partly due to the sprawling new housing estates to the south and east of the centre, but mainly because the constituency also includes 11,400 rural electors from South Northamptonshire district where the Conservatives remain very strong. On its creation in 1974, the seat was initially won by Michael Morris for the Conservatives by just 179 and 141, but this total then increased to 3,634 in 1979, 15,126 in 1983 and similar figures in 1987 and 1992. It certainly seemed as if this was a secure base for Morris to pursue his career as Deputy Speaker, but even he could not withstand a swing of over 13 per cent in 1997, which was enough to overturn his seemingly impregnable majority and replace it with a rather smaller one for local councillor Tony Clarke.

Even though Labour remained ahead of the Conservatives by 45-34 per cent in the Northampton part of the seat at the 1999 local elections, the Tories were optimistic of a regain in 2001, particularly as this was one of a handful of seats where Labour's 1997 majority was exceeded by the Referendum Party vote. Perhaps for this reason, Northampton was the scene of a high profile visit by Margaret Thatcher during the 2001 campaign. Thatcher visited at least two other seats with the same 1997 arithmetic (Lancaster & Wyre and Romford), and campaigners on the ground suggested her appearances were about the one thing that generated real passion among electors. Unfortunately for the Tories, this was equally true of Labour supporters as Conservatives, and the net result was stalemate. When the voters went out to the polls, the vote shares for the two main parties were almost identical to 1997, and the UK Independence Party even retained a reasonable vote, underlining the failure of the Thatcher strategy. Defeat for the Tories prevented what would have been the election of a rare (indeed unique) non-white Conservative MP, but this seat remains Labour's 6th most vulnerable, and if the boundary changes are not implemented in time to save it, may not withstand a fall in Labour's national popularity ratings next time.

WELLINGBOROUGH

	2001		1997		1992 actual	
Electorate and turnout	79,549	64.1	75,221	74.8	73,876	81.9
Conservative	21,512	42.2	24,667	43.8	32,302	53.4
Labour	23,867	46.8	24,854	44.2	20,486	33.9
Lib Dem	4,763	9.3	5,279	9.4	7,714	12.7
Anti–EU	864	1.7	1,192	2.1	–	–
Others	–		297		–	
MP	Paul Stinchcombe (Lab)		Paul Stinchcombe (Lab)		Peter Fry (Con)	
Majority	2,355	4.6	187	0.3	11,816	19.5

Wellingborough constituency includes the eponymous town itself as well as nearby Rushden (now known for 'Rushden and Diamonds' football club) and Higham Ferrers. The seat was a third unexpected 1997 gain in Northamptonshire to be retained by Labour in 2001, this time with an impressive increase in their majority. In fact the constituency has had thirty years of Labour representation in the past, held from 1918 to 1922, 1923 to 1931, 1945 to 1959 and again from 1964 to 1969. Then, following a by-election victory in 1969, Conservative MP Peter Fry presided over what seemed a long-term swing to the right, increasing his lead to over 14,000 in 1987. This political change occurred over the same period as the loss of industry in the towns of Wellingborough and Rushden, and the days of Labour victories here seemed to be over. But Phil Sawford (now Labour MP for Kettering) increased Labour's vote by 7 per cent in 1992, and five years later a nationally average swing of 10 per cent was enough for Paul Stinchcombe to defeat Fry by less than 200 votes.

Perhaps even more surprising than Labour gaining the parliamentary seat in 1997 was the gain of the local council in 1999, from its previously balanced state. Although most of their gains were made from Independents, Labour's local vote held-up or even slightly increased from 1995 to 1999, a pattern strikingly contrary to that almost everywhere else. Thus their increased general election majority in 2001 should probably not have come as too great a surprise, though it has meant a move up from 2nd most marginal Labour seat to a heady 20th.

Northumberland

	Conservative		Labour		Liberal Democrat		Others	
	Share of vote	Seats	Share of vote	Seats	Share of vote	Seats	Share of vote	Seats
2001	26.1	1	43.2	2	27.9	1	2.8	0
1997	22.7	1	48.7	2	25.0	1	3.7	0
1992	30.8	1	39.9	2	28.2	1	1.0	0
1987	28.6	1	34.7	2	36.4	1	0.4	0
1983	33.5	1	30.0	2	36.3	1	0.2	0

England's third smallest county in terms of population and number of parliamentary seats since the creation of Tyne and Wear removed Newcastle and North Tyneside, Northumberland remains one of the largest in terms of the geographical area it covers. It is also starkly divided, the south east corner as heavily industrialised as anywhere in northern England, but elsewhere the character very much rural, verging on deserted.

Bordering onto Tyne and Wear, traditional working class towns such as Blyth and Ashington provide loyal support for the Labour party and the basis of two safe parliamentary seats, though the colourful history of the Blyth constituency has meant that Labour have not always held both. The growth of new housing estates in the southern part of the county were thought to pose a threat to Labour in the 1980s, but it is unlikely that they have made too much difference recently, and may have even helped Labour achieve such a gigantic swing in Hexham in 1997. Most of the electorate of this third seat is based in the pretty small towns along the Tyne Valley, such as Corbridge, Hexham, Haydon Bridge, and Haltwhistle, which as with rural towns all over England are now a combination of bases serving the rural communities around and dormitories for commuters, in this instance bound for Tyne and Wear.

Much of the large remainder of the county (it is 60 miles from north to south and about 40 from east to west) is extremely rural and can in places seem totally empty, whether along the beaches strung out along the coast or towards the remote Cheviots on the Scottish border. One might have thought from this that the Conservatives would also have two secure parliamentary seats, but this has only rarely been the case and not at any time since 1973. In that year, a by-election saw Liberal candidate Alan Beith recapture Berwick, which had actually been gained by the Conservatives against the tide in the 1945 general election despite them simultaneously losing around 200 other seats. Beith has now built up his majority from just 57 votes to several thousand, surviving far longer than the last Liberal MP, one William Beveridge, by developing the sort of personal following that perhaps only third party MPs can. The Conservatives will almost certainly have to wait for Beith's departure before challenging for Berwick again, but in the meantime their position almost deteriorated further when in 1997, just 222 votes separated them from defeat in Hexham and total wipe out in the county. The foot and mouth crisis (which began at Heddon-on-the-Wall, part of the Hexham constituency) may have contributed to the majority becoming rather more comfortable in 2001, and it seems unlikely that Labour will ever get as close to victory here in future contests.

Local government

Northumberland may have only four parliamentary seats, but it is served by seven local authorities, comprising six small district councils and a county council based at Morpeth (this may change if regional government is linked with a move to unitary authorities). Labour strength is concentrated in the industrial south east corner, though Labour lost control of Blyth Valley council in the 1980s following a Lib Dem surge, and having recovered now seem to be in similar difficulties in neighbouring Wansbeck. In the other more rural parts of the county, there are still large numbers of Independent councillors, and as a result the other four authorities are usually 'balanced' or controlled by coalitions of more than one group. Alnwick falls into this category, though Berwick (where a referendum rejected an elected mayor in 2001) currently has a Liberal Democrat majority. Castle Morpeth consists of several different areas and as a result, all the main parties are represented. Currently (early 2002) Labour have eight councillors, mainly in traditional mining villages towards the coast, the Conservatives have four and the Lib Dems also eight, most in middle-class Ponteland near Newcastle airport. There is even a Green councillor in Morpeth itself, though the largest group consist of eleven Independents, who run the council with the Lib Dems. Tynedale council, which includes a number of small towns along the river west of Newcastle, is almost as divided, though this is the one council in Northumberland where the Conservatives are currently the largest group, a position held by Labour between 1995 and 1999. Wansbeck could boast of being the strongest Labour council in the land between 1995 and 1999, given that there was not a single opposition councillor, but in the election of that year, the party lost 20 seats to the Liberal Democrats and was somewhat fortunate to retain overall control. Blyth Valley remained more comfortably in Labour hands after their earlier problems here, with 34 councillors out of 50 in early 2002, though the Lib Dems remain the main opposition group. All these authorities elect in all-out elections, the next set of contests due in May 2003.

Finally, Northumberland county council reflects the divided electoral geography of the county, with 29 Labour county councillors out of 30 in Blyth and Wansbeck, but a much more divided picture elsewhere. The smattering of Labour representatives from their other strongholds such as Prudhoe and down the coast from Amble are currently enough to provide an overall majority of the 60-odd council members, though the council was balanced for periods in the 1970s and 1980s. There is still a respectable Tory group of seventeen (most from Tynedale) but the number of Lib Dems has fallen to nine, almost all representing wards in Alnwick, Berwick and Castle Morpeth.

Boundary review

For the second successive review, the boundary commission have decided that there will be no changes to the boundaries of Northumberland's parliamentary seats. The commissioners also rejected a proposal to rename the Berwick seat as 'Berwick and Mid Northumberland' which would have been geographically accurate but extremely cumbersome.

BERWICK-UPON-TWEED

	2001		1997		1992 actual	
Electorate and turnout	56,918	63.8	56,878	73.5	54,937	79.1
Conservative	10,193	28.1	10,056	24.1	14,240	32.8
Labour	6,435	17.7	10,965	26.2	9,933	22.9
Lib Dem	18,651	51.4	19,007	45.5	19,283	44.4
Anti–EU	1,029	2.8	1,775 (2)	4.2	–	–
MP	Alan Beith (LD)		Alan Beith (LD)		Alan Beith (LD)	
Majority	8,458	23.3	8,042	19.2	5,043	11.6

Alan Beith gained Berwick in a by-election in 1973 by just 57 votes, but somehow he has held on, initially by the margins of 443 and 73 respectively in February and October 1974, but rather more comfortably in subsequent contests. Indeed it is now difficult to categorise the famous border town as a marginal, such is the size of the Liberal Democrat majority.

This is a very different outcome from that which befell the previous Liberal by-election winner in Berwick. In 1944, Sir William Beveridge succeeded to the seat (wartime by-elections were not contested between the main parties) only to lose to the Conservatives in 1945 just as his post-war blueprint of a welfare state was about to be enacted by the new Labour government. Beveridge's fate was symptomatic of the Liberal party's in elections after 1945 as they were hopelessly squeezed by the two main parties, appearing at one point to be on the road to extinction. However, by the time of the 1973 contest, by-elections had been transformed into opportunities for the third party to collect protest votes and victories over their two larger rivals. Berwick was to be one name in a continuing story of famous gains, though few have been held for nearly as long as England's northernmost constituency.

The town of Berwick is perhaps best known for changing hands between England and Scotland thirteen times before ending up on the southern side of the border, though its football team plays in the Scottish League and accents here retain a distinct Scots edge. However, the parliamentary seat extends nearly fifty miles south of the town with its walls and famous 'border' bridges, taking in the whole of the borough of Alnwick and even several wards from Castle Morpeth. The constituency also includes a large number of sites of interest, including Holy Island, reached only by a causeway at low tide, spectacular castles at Bamburgh, Dunstanburgh, Warkworth and Alnwick and the brooding Cheviot Hills. Politically the territory is somewhat less diverse, with Liberal Democrats and Independents dominating local contests in Berwick and Alnwick, though Labour are strong in the fishing village of Amble and the Castle Morpeth wards of the seat which lie to the south and which include the region's last colliery at Ellington. Conservative councillors are sparse, and although they undoubtedly mop up much of the Independent vote in national contests, this has not been enough to prevent Beith from consolidating his by-election gain for a period of what is now nearly 30 years.

BLYTH VALLEY

	2001		1997		1992 actual	
Electorate and turnout	63,183	54.7	61,761	68.8	60,975	80.7
Conservative	5,484	15.9	5,666	13.3	7,691	15.6
Labour	20,627	59.7	27,276	64.2	24,542	49.9
Lib Dem	8,439	24.4	9,540	22.5	16,498	33.5
Others	–		–		470	1.0
MP	Ronnie Campbell (Lab)		Ronnie Campbell (Lab)		Ronnie Campbell (Lab)	
Majority	12,188	35.3	17,736	41.7	8,044	16.4

The working class town of Blyth with its port, power station and former colliery appears to be the basis for another safe northern Labour seat, but this has not always been so. In 1974, sitting MP Eddie Milne was deselected by his local party, stood against the new official Labour candidate as an Independent, and won. Unlike the telling of the tale in the drama series *Our Friends in the North*, Milne only held on for another eight months before losing by just 78 votes in October 1974, though he did continue to poll more than 18,000 in 1979. However, the drama was not yet over as many of those who had supported Milne switched to the new SDP in the 1980s, cutting Labour's majority to just 853 votes in 1987, a year in which they also lost control of the local council. Since then, Labour's lead has returned to a level one might expect from the territory, even though the mine which once dominated the town has gone (power is now provided by England's first offshore wind turbines) and new housing estates in Cramlington have multiplied. Blyth is Labour's 125th safest seat, and although the Liberal Democrats still poll well in some parts of Cramlington and a couple of wards south of Blyth, Labour appear to have completed their recovery here. The MP since 1987, Ronnie Campbell, is a former miner at the local colliery, though better known as a regular irritant to the Labour leadership.

HEXHAM

	2001		1997		1992 actual	
Electorate and turnout	59,810	70.9	58,914	77.5	57,812	82.4
Conservative	18,917	44.6	17,701	38.8	24,967	52.4
Labour	16,388	38.6	17,479	38.3	11,529	24.2
Lib Dem	6,380	15.0	7,959	17.4	10,344	21.7
Anti–EU	728	1.7	2,532 (2)	5.6	–	–
Others	–		–		781	
MP	Peter Atkinson (Con)		Peter Atkinson (Con)		Peter Atkinson (Con)	
Majority	2,529	6.0	222	0.5	13,438	28.2

The Hexham constituency covers a great deal more than the eponymous town itself, extending from Allendale Town near the borders with Cumbria and County Durham all the way north to the remote Kielder reservoir and forest. The main centres of population principally lie along the Tyne, including the Labour stronghold of Prudhoe, Corbridge and its Roman remains, and the town of Haltwhistle, which claims to be the geographical centre of Britain. The seat also includes approximately 10,000 electors in Ponteland just beyond Newcastle Airport, which is well known in the area for its concentration of millionaires, many of whom live in the tree-lined residential neighbourhood of Darras Hall. Only a small proportion of Hexham's voters live in the huge and largely barren area north of Hadrian's Wall, but nevertheless this is universally regarded as a rural seat; it is also the constituency where the 2001 foot and mouth outbreak first came to the nation's attention, at a farm near Heddon-on-the-Wall just off the A69.

The Conservatives received a mighty shock here in 1997 when their majority was cut to just 222 votes, but despite a big push in 2001 Labour fell further behind and now seem to have missed their big chance here. Hexham has been held continuously by the Tories since it was gained in 1924, though interestingly before that point it was regarded as a Liberal seat, which was ascribed to the presence of lead-mining and methodism. Even though the influence of these factors may have passed, the Liberals continue to record a sizeable vote locally and finished second in the general elections of 1983 and 1987. However, neither they nor Labour would now seem to be in a position to prevent Hexham from returning to its normal post-war status as a safely Conservative rural seat.

WANSBECK

	2001		1997		1992 actual	
Electorate and turnout	63,132	59.3	63,082	71.6	63,502	79.2
Conservative	4,774	12.8	6,299	13.9	11,872	23.6
Labour	21,617	57.8	29,569	65.5	30,046	59.7
Lib Dem	8,516	22.8	7,202	15.9	7,691	15.3
Anti–EU	482	1.3	1,146	2.5	–	–
Green	954	2.5	956	2.1	710	1.4
Others	1,076		–		–	
MP	Denis Murphy (Lab)		Denis Murphy (Lab)		Jack Thompson (Lab)	
Majority	13,101	35.0	22,367	49.5	18,174	36.1

Wansbeck is based on the towns of Morpeth, Ashington and Bedlington, which all lie a few miles outside Tyne and Wear at the northern extremity of the built-up industrial north east. The constituency was formerly known as Morpeth, but only a minority of its electors are drawn from the Castle Morpeth borough, which finds itself split into three seats. In addition, the historic town is also somewhat more leafy and politically out of step with the neighbouring borough of Wansbeck, which provides a majority of electors. Given that Morpeth stands on the River Wansbeck, the new (since 1983) constituency name is probably more geographically accurate than the old, though not as historic and to the uninitiated, somewhat anonymous.

In fact Morpeth, then a separate seat from Wansbeck, was notable for electing the first working class MP in the country (a 'Lib-Lab') as early as 1874. These days, the town tends to elect mainly Independent councillors as well as a Green, whereas Wansbeck is much more traditionally solid for Labour, electing a full slate of 46 Labour councillors out of 46 in 1995. This was to change rather abruptly in 1999 when the Lib Dems gained twenty council seats, with particular success in Newbiggin-by-the-Sea and some parts of Ashington, hitherto best known as the birthplace of football's famous Charlton brothers. Had the Lib Dems been confident enough to field a full slate of candidates in 1999, they would have almost certainly won at least another seven seats and as a result gained control of the council, but one can forgive them for this error given their starting point of zero. Even so, the result here was as dramatic as any in the history of local government elections, and shows just how volatile the electorate can now be, even in an apparently safe Labour area which has loyally supported the party for generations. The events of 1999 clearly had some, though admittedly reduced, impact on the general election result in 2001, with a 7.5 per cent swing to the Lib Dems from Labour, a large drop in the size of the majority and a fall in the pecking order from Labour's 65th safest seat after 1997 to their 127th after 2001.

Nottinghamshire including Nottingham

	Conservative		Labour		Liberal Democrat		Others	
	Share of vote	Seats	Share of vote	Seats	Share of vote	Seats	Share of vote	Seats
2001	34.0	2	50.9	9	13.1	0	2.0	0
1997	30.6	1	54.3	10	10.9	0	4.3	0
1992	42.7	4	44.4	7	12.1	0	0.7	0
1987	46.0	7	34.7	4	18.7	0	0.6	0
1983	45.1	8	32.2	3	21.9	0	0.7	0

Nottinghamshire, the county of such contrasting famous Englishmen as Robin Hood, D.H.Lawrence and Brian Clough, also contains some varied landscapes and townscapes. Its main city, Nottingham (population just under 300,000), is a bustling place with affluent suburbs to the west and south (some of which are in the borough of Rushcliffe) but also a number of peripheral council estates; hard as it is to believe, it is the 12th most deprived local government authority in the country. The other large towns in the county are almost all connected with coalmining, and retain an industrial air despite the end of the mining industry itself. The largest of these places is Mansfield (90,000), though there are also significant towns in Ashfield just to the south (Kirkby and Sutton have a combined population of 70,000); to the north can be found Worksop (40,000) and Retford (21,000). Very different is the town of Newark in the east of the county, a slightly old-fashioned sort of place which, along with the countryside on either side of the A1, would not be out of place in neighbouring Lincolnshire. In the centre of the county can be found the remaining bits of Sherwood Forest, though this area has long been impinged upon by development, most recently by the coalfields which opened up (and closed again) in the twentieth century. There are also one or two pretty villages along the Trent in the south of the county; south of the river can be found a belt of prosperous small towns and villages, with West Bridgford (across the bridge from Nottingham itself) as pleasant and wealthy a suburban area as one will find anywhere in Britain.

Politically, Labour have always held a number of constituencies in the north of the county, which are part of a continuous red belt, matching the historic coalfield area, into north Derbyshire and South Yorkshire. Thus Mansfield has been Labour since 1923, Ashfield (and its predecessor constituency) at all general elections since 1918 and Bassetlaw since 1935. Newark was also Labour from 1945 until 1979, but then had its best Labour areas removed to a new seat of Sherwood. Nottingham itself has tended towards Labour, though the Conservatives won three out of what were then four seats in 1959. Elsewhere, the Conservatives could only count on the seats lapping around the edges of Nottingham: Rushcliffe (except in 1966), Carlton (now renamed Gedling) and (after its creation in 1974) Beeston/Broxtowe. Overall, the Conservatives only had two out of ten seats in the county in 1951, increasing to five in 1959 with gains in Nottingham, before falling back to just one in 1966. The recovery began in the 1970s, the party holding all three suburban seats in 1974 winning a by-election in Ashfield in 1977 and then gaining Newark in 1979, which paved the way for further dramatic gains in the Thatcher period.

Nottinghamshire's tradition for electoral volatility has continued in recent elections. In the 1980s, Labour were reduced to their lowest ebb, swept out of the city of Nottingham in 1983 and under severe pressure in their mining strongholds in the north of the county around the time of the 1984-85 miners strike (Nottinghamshire miners were in the vanguard of opposition to the Scargill-led NUM). It was symptomatic of the party's problems that a new mining seat assumed to be a safe Labour bet, Sherwood, was won by the Conservatives on its creation in 1983 and even the red fortress of Mansfield was almost stormed four years later. Reduced to their three supposedly safe seats in the north of the county in 1983 (Mansfield, Ashfield and Bassetlaw), Labour did at least re-establish a presence in Nottingham in 1987, but a recovery elsewhere did not seem imminent as the decade drew to a close.

The Conservatives' dominant position in the 1980s would however unravel rapidly in the 1990s. At the start of the decade they lost their other two Nottingham seats as urban areas led the shift back to Labour, and in the same election (1992) Labour finally won Sherwood, ironically just as the Nottinghamshire coalfield was facing shutdown. The next stage in the breakthrough came after the election of Tony Blair and the transition to 'New Labour' after 1994, when middle class suburbia followed the inner-city and mining town areas by deserting the Tories. Labour's gains of 1997 were accurately foreseen by the local elections of 1995, when the party gained Broxtowe and Gedling, councils which had always been dominated by the Conservatives since their creation in 1973. The Tories even lost control of Rushcliffe in that calamitous year, though in the 1997 general election, the Labour tide did have the decency to retreat slightly, thus leaving a single Tory outcrop in the large shape of Kenneth Clarke. Four years on, there was a very mixed set of results which saw significant swings back to the Conservatives in many seats, the regain of Newark, but increased Labour majorities in their other marginals. The Conservatives will hope that Newark once again marks the start of a political comeback in the area; history is certainly on their side. Recovery, however, is not inevitable and depends on the party regaining the support of middle class voters who clearly deserted in large numbers in the early 1990s and have, as yet, shown little inclination to return.

Local government

Nottinghamshire county council has been controlled by Labour since 1981, with the party boasting 40 of its 63 members after 2001. There has always been a significant Conservative group (20 at present) and few Liberals or Liberal Democrats. Nottingham unitary authority has a very similar political complexion: after all-out elections in 2000, Labour had 40 councillors, as against 11 Conservatives. The old council was run by the Tories for brief periods in the late 1970s and late 1980s, and another recovery should not be ruled out, particularly as the Lib Dems remain fairly weak, with only 4 councillors at present. In the north of the county, Ashfield, Mansfield and Bassetlaw have always, like their parliamentary seats, been Labour. Ashfield had just a single non-Labour councillor in 1991, and only on Bassetlaw is there a significant Tory group. Historically, the most marginal council is Newark and Sherwood, which has had spells of Labour, Conservative and no overall control since 1973. Labour gained outright control again in the 1990s but lost their majority in 1999 and could well be overtaken by the Tories by the time of the next general election. By the mid 1990s, the Conservatives did not have control of a single authority in the county, managing to lose Broxtowe (Beeston and Stapleford) and Gedling (Nottingham's northern suburbs) to Labour in 1995, and Rushcliffe to no overall control. Rushcliffe was regained by the Tories in 1999, as (rather less comfortably) was Gedling, but Broxtowe was to remain in Labour's hands, despite its continuous Tory rule from 1973-95.

Boundary review

Provisional recommendations for the county were released just before this book went to press in early 2002. The boundary commission has opted to deal with the city and county separately, though in fact this is a continuation of existing arrangements. Nottingham will continue to have three seats of its own, with only minor changes to take account of ward boundary alterations. Nottinghamshire will have more significant changes; it is proposed that Newark takes in the north east part of Rushcliffe (around the town of Bingham) and loses Retford back to Bassetlaw. These changes would undoubtedly turn Newark into a safe Conservative seat, without particularly altering the character of the other constituencies affected, though Sherwood would become a bit safer for Labour with the transfer to Newark of the village of Lowdham (see Sherwood section). Changes proposed elsewhere simply realign parliamentary with ward boundaries, thought the Conservatives may propose adding more rural wards to Gedling.

ASHFIELD

	2001		1997		1992 *notional*	
Electorate and turnout	73,428	53.6	72,299	70.0	*73,276*	*79.5*
Conservative	9,607	24.4	10,251	20.3	*19,015*	*32.6*
Labour	22,875	58.1	32,979	65.2	*31,978*	*54.9*
Lib Dem	4,428	11.3	4,882	9.6	*7,285*	*12.5*
Anti–EU	–	–	1,896	3.7	–	–
Socialist	969 (2)	2.5	–	–	–	–
Others	1,471		595		–	
MP	Geoff Hoon (Lab)		Geoff Hoon (Lab)		Geoff Hoon (Lab)	
Majority	13,268	33.7	22,728	44.9	*12,963*	*22.2*

The industrial towns to the south west of Mansfield have proved fertile territory for the Labour Party for many decades. Both Sutton–in–Ashfield and its smaller southern neighbour, Kirkby–in–Ashfield are working class places which traditionally return an almost full slate of Labour councillors and have (almost) always returned Labour Members of Parliament. The constituency of Ashfield has been won at all general elections since its creation in 1955, and much of its territory was previously included in Broxtowe, which was also continually Labour since the end of the first world war, remaining loyal even when the party was practically wiped out in 1931.

The only blip in eighty-plus years of Labour voting came in 1977, following the resignation of David Marquand after eleven years as MP. The resulting by-election, during what was a very difficult period for the 1970s Labour government, produced an enormous 21 per cent swing to the Conservatives and an unlikely victory for their candidate Tim Smith, by the margin of 264 votes. Normal service was resumed in the following general election, and Defence Secretary Geoff Hoon, first elected as recently as 1992 (though he was a local MEP before that) now enjoys very comfortable majorities: this was one of Labour's 100 safest seats after 1997. The once important mining industry, whose bleak landscapes so depressed author D.H.Lawrence (born in Eastwood, a part of this seat), may have gone, but its political traditions in this part of Nottinghamshire seem set to continue for some time to come.

BASSETLAW

	2001		1997		1992 notional	
Electorate and turnout	68,417	56.8	68,101	70.5	69,415	78.4
Conservative	11,758	30.2	11,950	24.9	19,061	35.0
Labour	21,506	55.3	29,298	61.0	29,056	53.4
Lib Dem	4,942	12.7	4,915	10.2	6,339	11.6
Anti–EU	–	–	1,838	3.8	–	–
Socialist	689	1.8	–	–	–	–
MP	John Mann (Lab)		Joe Ashton (Lab)		Joe Ashton (Lab)	
Majority	9,748	25.1	17,348	36.1	9,995	18.4

The constituency of Bassetlaw comprises the northernmost part of Nottinghamshire, centred on the town of Worksop. This is closer to Sheffield than Nottingham, and the area's political (and indeed football) allegiances seem to follow those of South Yorkshire. Bassetlaw has been a Labour seat continually since 1935, and the council is also comfortably Labour controlled. For 33 years its well-known MP was Joe Ashton, who combined his parliamentary duties with being a director of Sheffield Wednesday, a club supported by many of his constituents.

Ashton was replaced in 2001 by John Mann, who retained a majority of almost 10,000 despite an above-average swing to the Conservatives, though it should be noted that there was a similar movement in all of the Nottinghamshire mining (or former mining) constituencies, and some of the neighbouring South Yorkshire seats as well. In fact there has always been a solid Tory minority in Bassetlaw, both in parliamentary and local contests. The Conservatives were the largest party on the council between 1976 and 1979, and still have a strong group even though Labour are now comfortably in control. The Tory vote is still very strong in some of the villages in the north east of the constituency, which share the character of neighbouring Lincolnshire, such as Clayworth (78 per cent of the vote in the 2000 local elections) and Rampton (81 per cent in 1999). Labour usually win five of the six wards in Worksop (the exception is South) and also Harworth next to the main A1 road, and they should remain safe here.

BROXTOWE

	2001		1997		1992 notional	
Electorate and turnout	73,665	66.5	74,264	78.3	73,754	82.5
Conservative	17,963	36.7	21,768	37.4	31,033	51.0
Labour	23,836	48.6	27,343	47.0	21,162	34.8
Lib Dem	7,205	14.7	6,934	11.9	8,378	13.8
Anti–EU	–	–	2,092	3.6	–	–
Others	–		–		293	
MP	Nick Palmer (Lab)		Nick Palmer (Lab)		Jim Lester (Con)	
Majority	5,873	12.0	5,575	9.6	9,871	16.2

Broxtowe exemplifies the problems in which the Conservatives find themselves at the start of the twenty-first century. This largely suburban middle-class constituency on the western edges of Nottingham could boast a Tory majority of 16,500 in 1987 and almost 10,000 in 1992. The local government borough had also been controlled by the Conservatives from its creation in 1973 until 1995, and its strongest Labour area, Eastwood, is not even included in the parliamentary seat. Yet in 1997, a swing of 13 per cent ended the 23-year parliamentary career of Jim Lester, Labour's Nick Palmer victorious by over 5,000 votes. In 2001 there was a further slight movement to Labour, underlining the complete failure of William Hague's Tories to mount any sort of recovery in middle England.

The constituency is largely based on the towns of Beeston (the name of the seat until 1983) and Stapleford, extending in a narrow strip north to Kimberley, passing the village and motorway service station of Trowell on the way. Labour are strong in Beeston, the Conservatives hit back in some of the villages to the north such as Awsworth & Cossall and Nuthall, and also poll strongly in Attenborough and Toton on the way to Long Eaton. Locally, the Lib Dems also pitch in and win wards in Stapleford, but their vote subsides in general elections, undoubtedly squeezed by the two main parties. This remains a seat which the Tories must win if they are to again challenge for national office, but at the moment there seems no imminent likelihood of them regaining it, Labour sitting pretty in this very typical slice of the East Midlands.

GEDLING

	2001		1997		1992 actual	
Electorate and turnout	68,519	63.9	68,878	75.7	68,954	82.3
Conservative	16,785	38.3	20,588	39.5	30,191	53.2
Labour	22,383	51.1	24,390	46.8	19,554	34.4
Lib Dem	4,648	10.6	5,180	9.9	6,863	12.1
Anti–EU	–	–	2,006	3.8	–	–
Others	–		–		168	
MP	Vernon Coaker (Lab)		Vernon Coaker (Lab)		Andrew Mitchell (Con)	
Majority	5,598	12.8	3,802	7.3	10,637	18.7

Gedling comprises the north eastern suburbs of Nottingham: Arnold, Carlton (the name of the constituency from 1950 until 1983) and Gedling itself as well as the nearby village of Burton Joyce. As in the case of Broxtowe to the west and Rushcliffe to the south, this is very much middle-class suburban Nottingham, even if the city's narrowly drawn official boundaries fail to reflect this reality. All three of the 'outer Nottingham' constituencies really ought to return Conservative MPs, and until recently Carlton/Gedling has behaved as one would expect, a majority of 4,000 achieved even in 1966, increasing to 16,500 by 1987. Then in the 1990s, the advent of 'New Labour' dramatically altered all electoral assumptions in seats like this. First of all in 1995, Gedling council, always dominated by the Tories, was narrowly gained by Labour. Two years later, former Rushcliffe council leader, Vernon Coaker defeated sitting MP Andrew Mitchell by nearly 4,000 votes, even though the constituency was not one of those targeted by his party. In 2001, Coaker did even better, adding almost 2,000 votes to his majority on the same day that Labour lost the nearby seat of Newark and suffered adverse swings throughout the old mining areas immediately to the north.

The 2001 result could be partially explained by a personal incumbency factor, which often seems to reach its peak after a new MP's first term in office; one should also bear in mind that the Conservatives will have also lost any incumbency factor carried by Mitchell in 1997. Second, Labour were undoubtedly better organised here in 2001 than in 1997, the constituency now included on the official key marginal list. The third and perhaps most important reason for Labour's continued success here however was the strength of the economy and associated low interest and mortgage rates, for which the government was clearly given the credit. In the past, these factors have benefited sitting Conservative governments, notably in the mid 1980s, but for the first time they are now helping Labour achieve success in middle class suburbia across the country.

MANSFIELD

	2001		1997		1992 actual	
Electorate and turnout	66,765	55.2	67,093	70.7	66,965	82.2
Conservative	10,012	27.2	10,038	21.2	18,208	33.1
Labour	21,050	57.1	30,556	64.4	29,932	54.4
Lib Dem	5,790	15.7	5,244	11.1	6,925	12.6
Anti–EU	–	–	1,588	3.3	–	–
MP	Alan Meale (Lab)		Alan Meale (Lab)		Alan Meale (Lab)	
Majority	11,038	30.0	20,518	43.3	11,724	21.3

Mansfield has been a Labour-held seat ever since 1923, when it was gained off the Liberals. Labour's vote here, traditionally connected with the coal-mining industry, has tended to generate extremely comfortable majorities even when the party has lost nationally, for example margins of 16,000 in 1959 and again in 1970. The size of Labour's lead was cut to just over 2,000 votes in their national debacle of 1983, but the party was to face its greatest challenge yet some four years later. The 1987 election followed the year-long ultimately unsuccessful miners strike of the mid-1980s, which had seen Arthur Scargill's National Union of Mineworkers challenged by breakaway miners returning to work, particularly in the Nottinghamshire coalfield. Many of these working miners joined the new UDM (Union of Democratic Mineworkers), which was supported by Mansfield's MP at the time, Don Concannon, and the whole atmosphere at the time was extremely bitter and politically charged. Although Neil Kinnock and the Labour leadership tried to keep their distance from the whole dispute, their new candidate in Mansfield, Alan Meale, was perceived as left wing and a supporter of the NUM. The result was that Labour struggled to hold on in the general election, winning by the tiny margin of 56 votes.

Five years later, coal-mining in this part of the world was facing extinction, and the problems faced by Labour and Meale in the 1980s seemed a very long time in the past. Labour's majority in Mansfield returned to a comfortable 10,000-plus after a huge swing of 10 per cent, which could be compared with a national movement of just over 2 per cent. By 1997, the majority almost doubled to 20,000, and this was again one of Labour's safest seats. Despite an above-average swing back in 2001 (which was entirely typical of the old coalfield areas) Labour have now recovered from a difficult period in Mansfield, results both here and in neighbouring Ashfield amply demonstrating that, irrespective of short-term political disturbances, areas tend to return to their traditional political allegiances in the long run.

NEWARK

	2001		1997		1992 actual	
Electorate and turnout	71,061	63.5	69,886	74.4	68,802	82.2
Conservative	20,983	46.5	20,480	39.4	28,494	50.4
Labour	16,910	37.5	23,496	45.2	20,265	35.8
Lib Dem	5,970	13.2	5,960	11.5	7,342	13.0
Anti–EU	–	–	2,035	3.9	–	–
Others	1,284 (2)		–		435	
MP	Patrick Mercer (Con)		Fiona Jones (Lab)		Richard Alexander (Con)	
Majority	4,073	9.0	3,016	5.8	8,229	14.6

Newark was one of only five seats, and the furthest north, lost by Labour to the Conservatives in 2001; the 7.5 per cent swing was the Tories' 16th best performance anywhere in the country and one of Labour's fifty worst. A number of factors contributed to this eye-catching result. First, we should note that the constituency is unlikely Labour territory to start with. Newark lost most of its Labour-voting areas in the former Nottinghamshire coalfield when the seat of Sherwood was created in 1983. What remained was the reasonably affluent town of Newark itself, the small town of Southwell with its Minster and large numbers of rural villages in between, though Labour were given some hope by the transfer from the Bassetlaw constituency of Retford to the north. Unsurprisingly the Tory majority reached 13,500 in 1987, and although the constituency fell to Labour on a nationally average swing in 1997, it was always a little unclear where the 23,500 Labour votes had come from. In the 1999 local elections, Labour were reduced to third place in the constituency, polling just under a quarter of the vote compared with 46 per cent for the Conservatives and even 26 per cent for the Liberal Democrats.

If this spelled trouble, then the headlines surrounding new Member of Parliament Fiona Jones in 1999 seemed unlikely to improve Labour's prospects. Jones was initially disqualified from office after being accused of falsifying election expenses, a surprisingly rare offence in recent times. Even after her acquittal on appeal, some of the mud seems to have stuck, and the local Labour party were far from united in the run-up to 2001. In the event, Labour's vote fell by almost 8 per cent while Patrick Mercer added about the same to the Conservative total, enough for a comfortable winning margin of 4,000. Having regained it, one would assume that Newark will now return to quieter times as a reasonably safe Tory seat.

NOTTINGHAM EAST

	2001		1997		1992 actual	
Electorate and turnout	65,339	45.5	65,644	60.5	67,939	70.1
Conservative	7,210	24.3	9,336	23.5	17,346	36.4
Labour	17,530	59.0	24,755	62.3	25,026	52.6
Lib Dem	3,874	13.0	4,008	10.1	3,695	7.8
Anti–EU	–	–	1,645	4.1	–	–
Others	1,117		–		1,548 (3)	
MP	John Heppell (Lab)		John Heppell (Lab)		John Heppell (Lab)	
Majority	10,320	34.7	15,419	38.8	7,680	16.1

It now seems mildly astonishing that all three Nottingham seats were represented by Conservative MP's during the 1980s. In fact this politically mixed city also went Tory in the 1950s, three of the four divisions then in existence won by the party in 1959. At other times in the post-war period Labour have held sway, though majorities of a few thousand were previously common rather than the five-figure margins recorded in the last two contests. In fact Nottingham (and particularly East) has seen a long term shift to the left in its political preferences, a pattern true of many cities to the north as well as its East Midlands neighbour, Leicester.

The constituency labelled Nottingham East has had a somewhat volatile electoral history, abolished in 1955 after being held by all three parties over the previous 25 years. It was restored in the 1970s and initially won by Labour by 3,000-6,000 votes, but then boundary changes before 1983 appeared to threaten this position. Those changes removed the centre and nearby Meadows estate to the new South, replacing them with what then seemed good suburban Tory areas from the old North. Partly as a result, Michael Knowles gained the seat by 1,500 votes in 1983, holding on four years later by just 456. In 1987, Labour also removed their candidate Sharon Atkin at the last moment, and though this probably made little difference to the result, it did demonstrate the growing influence of the national party on candidate selection. Five years later there was to be no such controversy as John Heppell defeated Knowles by nearly 8,000 after what then seemed a huge swing of 8.5 per cent. An even bigger movement in 1997 gave the seat the unusual appearance of a rock-solid Labour citadel, which a slight shift back to the Tories in 2001 has done little to change.

NOTTINGHAM NORTH

	2001		*1997*		*1992 actual*	
Electorate and turnout	64,281	46.7	65,735	63.0	69,495	75.0
Conservative	7,152	23.8	8,402	20.3	18,309	35.1
Labour	19,362	64.5	27,203	65.7	29,052	55.7
Lib Dem	3,177	10.6	3,301	8.0	4,477	8.6
Anti–EU	–	–	1,858	4.5	–	–
Others	321		637		274	
MP	Graham Allen (Lab)		Graham Allen (Lab)		Graham Allen (Lab)	
Majority	12,240	40.7	18,801	45.4	10,743	20.6

North has always been considered the safest Labour seat of the three Nottingham constituencies; it is currently (after Bolsover) their second most secure in the East Midlands and is also in the top 100 nationally. However, even here, Labour were to lose to the Conservatives in 1983, Richard Ottaway pulling off one of the party's most unlikely victories (of many) in that year by 362 votes.

This is somewhat difficult to believe these days, as North includes a number of very safe Labour wards, and Labour could still boast after the 1999 elections all but one of the constituency's nineteen councillors. The exception was the marginal Portland ward (one Conservative and one Labour), but elsewhere majorities remain very comfortable if not overwhelming. Unlike many other cities (and the odd ward in Nottingham South), Labour have not yet faced a strong challenge from the Liberal Democrats, who tend to finish a very poor third in both council and general elections. Until recently there was a perennial challenge from a Communist-turned Green, John Peck, but even he is no longer on the scene. Meanwhile the Conservatives remain beyond the pale to many voters in areas like Nottingham North, and as a result, election outcomes in the 1990s tended to be foregone conclusions, though this may of course change if the government becomes unpopular.

Graham Allen originally regained the parliamentary seat for Labour in 1987 by 1,665 votes, increased his share by a whopping 11 percentage points in 1992 and another ten in 1997. He now looks very secure. A strong advocate of constitutional reform, Allen has recently written a pamphlet on the powers of the Prime Minister entitled *The British Presidency*.

NOTTINGHAM SOUTH

	2001		1997		1992 actual	
Electorate and turnout	73,049	50.1	72,479	66.9	72,796	74.2
Conservative	9,960	27.2	13,461	27.7	22,590	41.8
Labour	19,949	54.5	26,825	55.3	25,771	47.7
Lib Dem	6,064	16.6	6,265	12.9	5,408	10.0
Anti–EU	632	1.7	1,523	3.1	–	–
Other	–		446		263	
MP	Alan Simpson (Lab)		Alan Simpson (Lab)		Alan Simpson (Lab)	
Majority	9,989	27.3	13,364	27.5	3,181	5.9

Nottingham South has been seen as the best seat in the city for the Conservatives since its (re) creation in 1983, the party winning the inaugural contest by almost 6,000 votes. In 1987 they held on by just over 2,000, before MP Martin Brandon-Bravo was defeated by Labour left winger (and prominent Campaign Group member) Alan Simpson in 1992. Simpson has since built up a decent majority here in a very mixed seat which still contains its share of Tory-inclined neighbourhoods.

In the 2000 unitary elections, the Conservatives easily won three wards, Abbey and Wollaton, on the western fringes of the city around the pleasant University buildings and neighbouring park, and Wilford, which borders Rushcliffe borough on the south bank of the Trent. Labour's strongest areas in local contests are Clifton, which is an almost detached council-estate ward of the city south of the river, and Lenton and Park wards, just west of the city centre. There is one other ward which they really should win, Bridge, which covers the troubled Meadows estate between the centre and Trent Bridge, but this is now held (with a big majority) by the Liberal Democrats in local elections - an echo of voting patterns in larger cities to the north such as Sheffield and Liverpool.

Across all the wards of the constituency in 2000, Labour led the Conservatives 41-37, with 22 per cent for the Lib Dems; clearly Labour did quite a bit better in the following year's general election and the Conservatives substantially worse. Unlike the two other Nottingham seats and the former mining areas further north, there was almost no swing away from Labour in 2001 compared with 1997, possibly because of the influence of the middle class areas of the seat. Although it was only gained in 1992, Nottingham South now looks reasonably safe for Labour, in national contests at least.

RUSHCLIFFE

	2001		1997		1992 actual	
Electorate and turnout	81,847	66.5	78,849	78.8	76,284	83.0
Conservative	25,869	47.5	27,558	44.4	34,448	54.4
Labour	18,512	34.0	22,503	36.2	14,682	23.2
Lib Dem	7,395	13.6	8,851	14.3	12,660	20.0
Anti–EU	1,434	2.6	3,085 (2)	4.9	–	–
Green	1,236	2.3	–	–	775	1.2
Others	–		115		761	
MP	Ken Clarke (Con)		Ken Clarke (Con)		Ken Clarke (Con)	
Majority	7,357	13.5	5,055	8.1	19,766	31.2

Rushcliffe covers the southern part of Nottinghamshire to the south of the River Trent, including the prosperous suburbs of West Bridgford as well as towns and villages like Bingham, Radcliffe and Keyworth. Aside from the former mining village of Cotgrave (which in any case was lost to the Conservatives in 2001), the only red to be found is on the shirts of Nottingham Forest football club, situated next to Trent Bridge cricket ground just over the river from Nottingham itself. Otherwise this suburban belt, one of the least deprived areas of the country according to official figures, is blue-chip Tory territory, and it seems as if it would take a political earthquake to alter its allegiances.

Although Labour did win the constituency called Rushcliffe by 380 votes in 1966 before present incumbent Ken Clarke regained it, the boundaries were radically different to those of today, taking in much of what is now Broxtowe. Since the constituency took on its present form, the Conservatives have piled up huge majorities: 17,500 in February 1974 and over 20,000 in 1983 and 1987. There was a minor sensation locally when the Conservatives lost Rushcliffe borough council, which shares the same boundaries as the parliamentary seat, by the narrowest of margins in 1995; after all they had held 51 out of 54 council seats as recently as 1983. But Clarke was able to resist the landslide of 1997 by the relatively comfortable margin of 5,000 votes, thereby avoiding the grisly fate of cabinet colleagues such as Michael Portillo and William Waldegrave, who lost apparently secure parliamentary seats as well as their government posts.

In 1999, the Conservatives comfortably regained their majority on the council, and then in 2001 their lead in the general election increased to almost 7,500. Clarke, who held ministerial office throughout the 1979-97 period, had rather more difficulty winning the hearts and minds of parliamentary colleagues in 1997 and party members in 2001, when he fought and lost two leadership contests. He seems to be rather more popular with his electors in Rushcliffe, where his pro-European views do not do him as much harm (even the anti-EU vote is not particularly high) and although he may never become party leader, Clarke has a safe seat for as long as he wants it.

SHERWOOD

	2001		1997		1992 actual	
Electorate and turnout	75,558	60.7	74,873	75.5	73,355	85.5
Conservative	15,527	33.8	16,259	28.8	26,878	42.9
Labour	24,900	54.2	33,071	58.5	29,788	47.5
Lib Dem	5,473	11.9	4,889	8.6	6,039	9.6
Anti–EU	–	–	1,882	3.3	–	–
Others	–		432		–	
MP	Paddy Tipping (Lab)		Paddy Tipping (Lab)		Paddy Tipping (Lab)	
Majority	9,373	20.4	16,812	29.7	2,910	4.6

Sherwood is a relatively new constituency created in 1983, bringing together the mining areas of the old Newark seat (which kept it in the Labour column from 1950 until 1979) with the town of Hucknall, previously a part of Ashfield. Both of these segments were viewed as Labour strongholds, and their failure to win the inaugural contest in 1983 was seen as one of the biggest shocks of a calamitous night for the party. The result in Sherwood and elsewhere suggested that the party's left wing manifesto was as unpopular with working class voters as everyone else, but Labour would have to wait another nine years to undo the damage here, since in 1987 the bitterness caused by the miners strike (see Mansfield) contributed to a sharply increased Tory majority. Finally, the constituency fell to Labour in 1992, Paddy Tipping winning by 3,000 votes. A better than national swing enabled him to secure a very healthy-looking position in the 1997 election, but there was a significant shift back to the Conservatives in 2001, as there was in neighbouring seats like Bassetlaw, Mansfield and most decisively, Newark.

It is the former mining areas which remain Labour's strongest in Sherwood - in 1999 they enjoyed reasonable leads in places like Bilsthorpe, Blidworth and Rainworth (all just east of Mansfield) and were very strong in Ollerton. The town of Hucknall (just north of Nottingham) is also a solid Labour ex-mining area. The Conservatives pick up a strong vote in some of the commuting villages in between - for example 70 per cent in Lowdham in 1999. They also do well in the small Gedling portion of the seat, winning the Newstead county council ward (named after the Abbey, the ancestral home of Lord Byron who is buried nearby) in 2001. In an even year, this area is outvoted, but it does provide a solid base of support which is missing in neighbouring constituencies such as Ashfield. Though it looks unlikely from the figures, Sherwood may just about still be vulnerable if the government becomes seriously unpopular - on the list it is the sort of constituency which the Conservatives will need to win if they are to form a government with a workable majority.

Oxfordshire

	Conservative		Labour		Liberal Democrat		Others	
	Share of vote	Seats	Share of vote	Seats	Share of vote	Seats	Share of vote	Seats
2001	37.9	4	29.5	1	27.3	1	5.3	0
1997	38.0	4	31.7	1	24.7	1	5.6	0
1992	51.3	5	23.7	1	23.5	0	1.5	0
1987	52.7	5	20.3	1	26.6	0	0.4	0
1983	51.5	6	18.4	0	29.3	0	0.8	0

Oxfordshire has influences from several regions of England. Strongest is the pull of London in the south and east of the county, which is within quite easy commuting distance by one of several road and rail routes. Oxford itself is home to some London commuters as it is less than an hour from Paddington and the life of its university is linked into metropolitan society. The London influence extends even to the further parts of the county, but it is diluted to the north in towns like Banbury and Bicester which have a distinct Midlands feel, and to the west where the Cotswolds shade into the west of England.

Oxfordshire is a prosperous county, with a strategic location, a skilled workforce and the attractions of the Cotswolds and the city of Oxford. The problem facing planners here is how to regulate expansion and stop the place being choked by congestion and development, rather than how to attract new business. There is a broad, strict green belt around Oxford to prevent the city growing in uncontrolled fashion across its surroundings. Where new building is permitted, as at Bicester, Banbury and in the A34 Abingdon- Wantage - Didcot corridor to the south, the pace of development is spectacular if often not particularly attractive. House prices in the county are extremely high by all but London standards.

These issues and others have generated a strong environmental consciousness in Oxford city in particular. The council was a pioneer of 'park and ride' bus services to reduce congestion in the city centre with all its adverse consequences for the environment and Oxford's unique set of historic buildings. The votes of students, academics and people who enjoy living in a centre of art and learning have created a powerful Green movement in the city which gave them their largest group on any local authority in Britain and until May 2002 a share in running the administration. The student and intellectual vote has created a strong movement away from the Conservatives, initially to Labour but now sometimes towards Lib Dems, and Greens in local elections.

Historically, Oxfordshire has tended to be Conservative, with 100 per cent Tory representation from 1924 until Labour's first victory in Oxford in 1966. Its working class population, except for that generated by the appearance of the car industry in Cowley, east Oxford, between the wars, has always been relatively small. As the most Establishment-minded university, Oxford's fellows and - perhaps even more so - its retinue of college servants produced a solid Conservative vote in most elections. The

Oxford city constituency was the scene of a famous by-election in 1938 in which Lord Hailsham (who died in 2002) held the seat for Chamberlain and the Munich agreement against the independent challenge of A.D. Lindsay who was backed by young political figures such as Denis Healey and Edward Heath. Until the 1950 redistribution the university's graduates had two extra MPs, elected by the single transferable vote, who were always Conservative or Independent.

In 1945 Oxford was the strongest of the county's constituencies for the Tories, with Labour running close in Banbury and Henley (which then included the Cowley area). Tory dominance in Oxford declined during the 1960s and 1970s, and Oxford became easier for Labour to win (for instance, Labour won in October 1974 but not in 1964). Even so the pattern of the county's politics was of increasingly Conservative countryside surrounding a marginal city that Labour could only win when the party was doing well. This was not altered by the 1970s local government reform in which Oxfordshire gained Abingdon, Wantage and the Downs to their west from Berkshire.

Oxfordshire has seen less change in the pattern of parliamentary representation in recent years than most counties. The Conservatives lost Oxford East to Labour in 1987, and then Oxford West & Abingdon to the Lib Dems in 1997, but have not come particularly close to losing their four other seats even in the last two elections (Witney, however, was Labour following the 1999 defection of Shaun Woodward). Only in Wantage is there a realistic chance of the Conservatives losing any more ground, and then only if there is a tactical rallying of forces against them. On the other hand, the Tories have hardly any chance of winning either Oxford seat again. No change seems the most likely pattern in future elections in Oxfordshire – with the proviso that the boundary review may shake things up again by the time of the election due around 2010.

Local government

The Conservatives lost Oxfordshire county council in 1985 and have failed to recover it since – in 1989 thanks to an electoral pact between Labour and Lib Dem and since then because of poor electoral performance and the continued inclusion of the Oxford city area. The Tories had hopes of taking control in 2001 (something they achieved in several other shire counties) but made no net gains, staying on 26 seats. Labour made five gains, rising to 24 seats, while the Lib Dems (18 seats) and Greens (2 seats) fell back. The administration is formed from Tories and Lib Dems.

Oxford city council was Labour from 1973 to 2000, except between 1976 and 1980. The collegiate wards, particularly Carfax and Holywell (successors to the old Central ward), are highly volatile because the bulk of the electorate is replaced for each set of annual local elections. In recent years Liberal Democrats and Greens have predominated. The Lib Dems and Greens also have a firm hold on the ex-Tory northern suburbs, and in 2000 the Lib Dems polled strongly in the normally Labour eastern suburbs too. In 2002, Labour did well to turn the electoral tide and eject the Lib Dem–Green coalition from power.

The other councils are less exotic. Cherwell (Banbury and Bicester) returned to Conservative control with a large majority in 2000, although Labour briefly (1996-98) had control at their local election high tide. It normally has annual elections, although ward boundary revisions meant all-out elections on new wards in 2002. West Oxfordshire (Witney and around) hit the headlines in 1990 when most of its Conservative group resigned from the party over the poll tax, and the Conservatives only recovered majority control in 2000. The two remaining councils have all-out elections every four years. Vale of White Horse (Wantage and Abingdon) has been Lib Dem controlled since 1995 and the Tories made up very little ground in 1999 although they had run it continuously from 1973 to 1995. South Oxfordshire (Henley and Didcot) was one of the very worst Conservative results in 1995, being reduced to third place on a council they had controlled since its creation in 1973. They did recover in 1999 to parity with the Lib Dems in a hung council.

Boundary review

Oxfordshire is just about entitled to a seventh seat at the next boundary review, although it is conceivable that the commission might use its discretion to keep the existing allocation of six. Banbury in particular has grown too large, although all the seats in the west of the county are oversized. It is not obvious where the new seat will appear - perhaps at Abingdon and up to the west of the city of Oxford, or to the north and west of Oxford - and the permutations have different partisan implications. If Abingdon is linked to part of Wantage there could even be two Lib Dem seats. As in Wiltshire the constituency names have tended to be short, a practice the authors wish to commend to the boundary commission for nationwide use.

BANBURY

	2001		1997		1992 notional	
Electorate and turnout	84,371	61.1	77,797	75.1	69,557	81.0
Conservative	23,271	45.2	25,076	42.9	30,886	54.9
Labour	18,052	35.0	20,339	34.8	15,155	26.9
Lib Dem	8,216	15.9	9,761	16.7	10,027	17.8
Anti–EU	695	1.3	2,609 (2)	4.5	–	–
Green	1,281	2.5	530	0.9	–	–
Others	–		131		241	
MP	Tony Baldry (Con)		Tony Baldry (Con)		Tony Baldry (Con)	
Majority	5,219	10.1	4,737	8.1	15,731	27.9

Banbury in north Oxfordshire is in an area where the London influence diminishes mile by mile – it is justifiably described as being in the south Midlands and is reminiscent of other market towns with an industrial presence like Bedford or Wellingborough. Its strategic location (midway between London and Birmingham on the M40 motorway) is well known and its Cross celebrated in a nursery rhyme. It has a population of around 40,000. The constituency also includes the smaller town of Bicester which has become a prime development area in recent years (its fast-growing population has reached 28,000), and some countryside areas such as Bloxham.

Banbury town's five wards returned four Labour and one Conservative county councillor in 2001, although this gives a rather deceptive impression of the balance of opinion as all the wards are quite marginal. Labour's lead in votes was a modest 42-39 per cent in the local elections, although probably more in the general election. There were unusual reports from Bicester on election day in 2001 of queues '40 to 50 deep' outside polling stations. This had little to do with excessive democratic enthusiasm in the town, but rather showed that provision of polling stations had failed to keep pace with recent breakneck population growth. Another manifestation of growth came in the election result in the grossly oversized Bicester North county council ward, which Labour won for the first time ever in 2001. The settled South ward was Tory, making the combined town narrowly Conservative. The rural remainder of the seat contributed almost as many electors as Banbury, and they were, as is customary, heavily Conservative. This element tipped the balance and made the seat a fair bet for the Tories even in 1997 and 2001.

Thanks largely to growth at Bicester, the constituency is now much too large and will have to be reduced at the boundary review. Banbury will be reduced to the town plus a smaller rural area, and will probably lose Bicester; although it would produce a smaller majority, a new Banbury seat would start with the Conservatives ahead.

HENLEY

	2001		1997		1992 notional	
Electorate and turnout	69,081	64.3	66,424	77.6	66,340	79.6
Conservative	20,466	46.1	23,908	46.4	31,651	60.0
Labour	9,367	21.1	11,700	22.7	7,802	14.8
Lib Dem	12,008	27.0	12,741	24.7	12,608	23.9
Anti–EU	1,413	3.2	2,299	4.5	–	–
Green	1,147	2.6	514	1.0	–	–
Others	–		381 (2)		716	
MP	Boris Johnson (Con)		Michael Heseltine (Con)		Michael Heseltine (Con)	
Majority	8,458	19.0	11,167	21.7	19,043	36.1

Henley attracted a lot of media interest in the 2001 election, not because it was a crucial marginal seat – it is a Conservative stronghold – but because it saw one prominent personality taking over from another. Michael Heseltine had represented the division since 1974 and was standing down in favour of *Spectator* editor Boris Johnson. Heseltine's career was long and successful, but he was denied the ultimate prize and had to settle for a term as Deputy Prime Minister in 1995-97; Johnson still combines his editorial duties with his seat in parliament, as weekly editors Iain Macleod and Dick Crossman had done previously.

Henley is a little town on the north bank of the Thames, famous for the annual boating regatta and the upper-class excess that accompanies it. The constituency bearing its name stretches a long way to its north via Watlington, Dorchester and a rural area around Ewelme, wrapping around the eastern edge of the city of Oxford to Wheatley and Forest Hill and up to the market town of Thame near the Buckinghamshire border. A lot of it is very prosperous commuter country, particularly around Goring and Henley itself. In the words of Johnson's maiden speech of 12 July 2001:

> Suppose one is travelling on the M40; just before junction 6, one suddenly comes to that dramatic cutting—the Khyber pass of the Chilterns—where ahead, spread out like a land of dreams, is the plain of south Oxfordshire. That, roughly speaking, is my constituency.

Unusually, the strongest Conservative area is the principal town – Henley at least is politically true to its social reputation, unlike (say) Eton. The Conservatives polled 53 per cent and 60 per cent in its two county wards in 2001. The Liberal Democrats have some reasonable rural areas, won Chalgrove and Wheatley in the county elections (and were narrowly ahead in the constituency at the Tory low point of the 1995 local elections); Labour are very weak. The other parties do not have enough of a base to challenge the Conservatives here and Johnson should be able to enjoy a lengthy parliamentary career representing this slice of Tory England.

OXFORD EAST

	2001		1997		1992 notional	
Electorate and turnout	71,357	55.8	69,952	68.4	68,309	73.0
Conservative	7,446	18.7	10,540	22.0	16,718	33.6
Labour	19,681	49.4	27,205	56.8	25,031	50.2
Lib Dem	9,337	23.4	7,038	14.7	6,971	14.0
Anti–EU	570	1.4	1,625 (2)	3.4	–	–
Green	1,501	3.8	975	2.0	962	1.9
Others	1,313 (4)		494 (3)		150	
MP	Andrew Smith (Lab)		Andrew Smith (Lab)		Andrew Smith (Lab)	
Majority	10,344	26.0	16,665	34.8	8,313	16.7

Oxford East is the successor to the marginal Oxford seat as it existed between 1950 and 1983, despite losing the most distinctive section of the city to the Oxford West & Abingdon seat. The constituency has a number of contrasting elements of town and gown. The inner wards are strongly influenced by the colleges. Many students and academics live out in areas across Magdalen Bridge off the three roads – Iffley Road, Cowley Road and St. Clement's. East also has a large number of students based at Oxford Brookes University in suburban Headington, and massive NHS employment in several hospitals including the John Radcliffe. There are also some traditional working class areas, such as the Blackbird Leys estate on the edge of town where screaming tyres are more familiar than dreaming spires. The car production complex at Cowley, established between the wars by Lord Nuffield, is still very much in business and produces Rover's new Mini; it employs around 2,000 people and provides a solid trade union core to Oxford East's Labour organisation.

Although Steve Norris won the inaugural contest for the Conservatives in 1983, this was always going to be a difficult seat for the Tories and they duly lost it in 1987 – their only loss that year in London or the south east. By 1997 senior Labour politician Andrew Smith had built up an enormous majority. In 2001 his margin of victory slipped quite significantly, but this was not due to any Tory recovery – in fact the party slid even further to a miserable 18.7 per cent of the vote. Labour's share of the vote was also a little below its 1992 level; the cause was an increase in the vote for the Lib Dems and secondarily the Greens and Socialists who polled 6.3 per cent between them. Labour in government had irritated students with tuition fees, and public sector workers in any number of ways; a chunk of Oxford East's left wing vote deserted Labour. This was already apparent in the 2000 local elections, when the Greens did well in the inner city area and the Lib Dems picked off most of the suburban wards.

Labour should be able to hold on to Oxford East, even if the government is relatively unpopular at the next election, because it is doubtful whether all the opposition can unite behind the Lib Dems. Even in the 2000 local elections Labour were ahead, with 35 per cent to 25 per cent for the Lib Dems and 19 per cent each for Conservatives and Greens. It is one of a handful of seats in England that Labour have to defend on their left flank.

OXFORD WEST and ABINGDON

	2001		1997		1992 *notional*	
Electorate and turnout	79,915	64.5	78,425	78.0	77,866	76.7
Conservative	15,485	30.0	19,983	32.7	27,630	46.2
Labour	9,114	17.7	12,361	20.2	9,642	16.1
Lib Dem	24,670	47.8	26,268	42.9	21,408	35.8
Anti–EU	451	0.9	1,516 (2)	2.5	90	0.2
Green	1,423	2.8	691	1.1	712	1.2
Others	425 (2)		377 (3)		267	
MP	Evan Harris (LD)		Evan Harris (LD)		John Patten (Con)	
Majority	9,185	17.8	6,285	10.3	6,222	10.4

This constituency contains the centre of the city of Oxford, and therefore most of the college buildings of the ancient university, in its Central, North and West wards. It also has the rows of North Oxford villas which appeared in the 19th century when restrictions on college fellows having families were relaxed, plus some suburbs further out along the Banbury and Woodstock Roads, and the smaller city houses of Jericho and Osney. Oxford West accounts for about 29,000 electors, so the majority of the constituency is outside the city. To the north lies Kidlington, a dull suburban township of nearly 12,000 electors. Abingdon, which was in Berkshire until the 1970s reorganisation, lies several miles south of Oxford and is a market town augmented by new industrial and housing estates, with a current population of 35,000.

'Oxwab' was one of the easier Liberal Democrat victories in 1997 and a thoroughly predictable hold in 2001. The Lib Dems had been active in all areas of the constituency for several years and the sophisticated Labour electorate concentrated in collegiate Oxford was voting tactically from an early stage. A still-visible piece of graffiti in the city centre, daubed in 1987, urged residents to 'Vote Tactical'. Oxwab's composition suggests why it is increasingly good ground for the Lib Dems. Part of it is an urban, intellectual area where the Conservatives are dying out (the party came fourth in the Oxford West wards in 2001!) and Labour have passed their peak. The rest is basically a high income suburban growth zone of the sort which emphatically rejected the Tories in 1997 and was further alienated in 2001. Depending on how the new boundaries are drawn, Oxwab may even provide the basis for two Lib Dem seats after the next review.

WANTAGE

	2001		1997		1992 actual	
Electorate and turnout	76,129	64.5	71,768	78.1	68,329	82.7
Conservative	19,475	39.6	22,311	39.8	30,575	54.1
Labour	13,875	28.2	16,222	28.9	10,955	19.4
Lib Dem	13,776	28.0	14,862	26.5	14,102	25.0
Anti–EU	941	1.9	2,014 (2)	3.6	–	–
Green	1,062	2.2	640	1.1	867	1.5
MP	Robert Jackson (Con)		Robert Jackson (Con)		Robert Jackson (Con)	
Majority	5,600	11.4	6,089	10.9	16,473	29.2

The Wantage seat in south west Oxfordshire contains some quite contrasting territory. The largest area is covered by sparsely inhabited downlands, including the famous chalk white horse carved on a hillside at Uffington, but most of the population is in the low-lying east of the constituency around the A34 road and the Great Western railway line. Rail travellers in the west of England will be familiar with the junction at Didcot, a town which has expanded rapidly over the last twenty years as looping through roads, shopping centres and privately developed housing estates have appeared. The fast trains make it a reasonable commuting base for London. Wallingford, near Didcot, is a more expensive and attractive town. The other urban area is around Wantage, including Grove. Drayton and Harwell (with its noted scientific research laboratory) lies just off the A34 south of Abingdon.

All three main parties have areas of strength in the Wantage constituency. In the 2001 county elections both Didcot divisions were Labour, while the Wantage area was a Lib Dem centre. The Conservatives do better in the western rural area at Shrivenham (site of the new Royal Military College) and Faringdon, despite a history of radical politics in the local aristocracy. Two successive victories on less than 40 per cent of the vote do not betoken a safe Conservative seat, despite Robert Jackson's respectable percentage majority. The Tories here benefit from the lack of a clear challenger. While Labour squeaked into second in the general election, the Liberal Democrats were clearly second and only about four points behind the Conservatives in the county elections in 2001. If the Lib Dems can remedy their weakness in Didcot, Wantage is one of their most attractive opportunities for a gain in the 2005/6 general election.

WITNEY

	2001		1997		1992 notional	
Electorate and turnout	74,612	65.9	73,520	76.7	69,746	83.7
Conservative	22,153	45.0	24,282	43.1	33,743	57.8
Labour	14,180	28.8	17,254	30.6	10,582	18.1
Lib Dem	10,000	20.3	11,202	19.9	13,150	22.5
Anti–EU	767	1.6	3,027 (2)	5.4	–	–
Green	1,100	2.2	636	1.1	611	1.0
Others	1,003		–		284	
MP	David Cameron (Con)		Shaun Woodward (Con) (Lab)		Douglas Hurd (Con)	
Majority	7,973	16.2	7,028	12.5	20,593	35.3

The Witney constituency lies west of Oxford, covering Oxfordshire's share of Cotswold countryside including Blenheim Palace. Witney is the largest town (population 22,000), traditionally in the blanket trade but also now a commuting and industrial centre, but it does not exercise such a strong influence as, say, Banbury does in its constituency. There is also an armed forces area at Carterton near RAF Brize Norton. More visited are the Cotswold stone towns of Chipping Norton, Charlbury and Woodstock. Perhaps affected by senior Oxford academics with cottages in these parts, the first two of these places returned Labour county councillors in 2001. The countryside around here is a particularly striking illustration of a more general phenomenon, whereby traditional rural and small town activities and attitudes decline and are replaced by people who commute into the cities. This area, however, is unusual in its political allegiance – most of west Oxfordshire is Tory, particularly agricultural Burford not far from the Gloucestershire border.

The voters of Witney seem more loyal to the Tories than their elected representatives. The local Conservative councillors resigned en masse in 1990 over the introduction of the poll tax to become Independents, and in 1999 new MP Shaun Woodward crossed the floor to join Labour because he found the current trend of politics in the Conservative Party extremist and intolerant of diversity. Woodward represented Witney for a year and a half as a Labour MP but there was never any question that the Labour leadership would ask him to fight Witney; a transfer to St. Helens South was arranged shortly before the 2001 election. Woodward therefore has had the unsettling (and probably unique) experience of double-digit swings against him in successive general elections, but should probably not take it personally. David Cameron, who lost Stafford in 1997, regained Witney for the Tories without any trouble in 2001.

Shropshire including Telford & Wrekin

	Conservative		Labour		Liberal Democrat		Others	
	Share of vote	Seats	Share of vote	Seats	Share of vote	Seats	Share of vote	Seats
2001	39.0	1	38.1	3	18.6	1	4.2	0
1997	37.2	2	39.7	3	20.5	0	2.7	0
1992	46.3	3	30.7	1	22.0	0	1.0	0
1987	48.2	3	25.4	1	26.0	0	0.3	0
1983	49.0	4	21.3	0	29.7	0	0.1	0

Shropshire is the core county of the Marches, a rather vague and not officially recognised region of England defined by its proximity to Wales. In centuries past it was a military frontier marked out by Offa's Dyke, an 8th century earthwork built to keep the Welsh out, and many mediaeval castles. The struggle over the allegiance of parts of it in the west of the Ludlow and Shropshire North constituencies is apparent from village names like Nantmawr and Bettws-y-crwyn, not to mention Croesau Bach ('small welcome'). Shrewsbury and Oswestry still both serve as local centres for parts of Wales lying just across the border.

Since England and Wales stopped fighting Shropshire has been rather on the edge of developments, with one important exception. The county is mostly rural and is bordered by rural stretches of other counties (particularly on the Welsh side), so hardly any of it, except a small section around Bridgnorth not too far from the West Midland conurbation, is influenced by large cities. Shrewsbury is the undisputed county town and commercial and administrative capital of the county. The smaller market towns are traditional and quite small places, and other than one or two planning blunders have remained attractive – particularly Ludlow with its fine old buildings and castle. The rural areas are quite agricultural, often pastoral (foot and mouth was a serious threat here); Shropshire's country is celebrated in the poetry of A.E. Housman such as *A Shropshire Lad*. The exception to this traditional English picture is the area around the hill of the Wrekin which is now grouped into Telford. The very beginnings of the industrial revolution took place here in the early 18th Century where coal, iron and fast flowing rivers met and Britain's rise as an industrial power began. Early industrial towns appeared in the district, although the Wrekin was overtaken as an industrial area during the 19th Century by the Black Country thirty miles to the south west. It was renewed as an industrial area in the 1960s when Telford New Town was established and has attracted an influx of population since then sufficient to create a new constituency.

Like many borderland areas, Shropshire has tended to nationalism in its political leanings – in this case a strong allegiance to the Conservatives in contrast to Liberal rural Wales. Shrewsbury, Ludlow, and Oswestry were all Conservative in every general election between 1886 and 1997 (Oswestry goes back to 1835), with Victorian elections in Oswestry particularly polarised on national-religious lines. The constituency based around the industrial towns has always been more inclined to the left, although until 1997 the industrial area shared a constituency with rural elements and produced a close-fought bell-wether marginal.

Labour have advanced somewhat in Shropshire in recent years. The growth of the New Town made The Wrekin Labour in 1987, only the third time in a century it had failed to vote for the national winner, and has created the safe Telford constituency since. Labour's 1997 sweep carried two unexpected seats along too, the redrawn and semi-rural The Wrekin seat and Shrewsbury & Atcham where the party had been running third. It was another surprise when both reaffirmed their Labour support with increased majorities in 2001, although Paul Marsden of Shrewsbury subsequently defected to the Liberal Democrats. As well as failing to recover their 1997 losses, the Conservatives saw Ludlow fall to a well-organised attack from the Lib Dems, reducing the party to an unprecedentedly weak position in the county. Their sole MP Owen Paterson salvaged the party's narrow lead in votes cast by turning in a strong performance in Shropshire North. Shropshire politics is influenced quite strongly by local factors, which receive an airing in the very widely read *Shropshire Star* newspaper – Paterson, Peter Bradley of The Wrekin and Matthew Green of Ludlow have been assiduous in courting local publicity and saw their efforts pay off in 2001. The Conservatives in the centre and south of the county will have to work harder in future, and hope for a national recovery, if they are to regain Ludlow and The Wrekin, but Shrewsbury & Atcham looks easier because of Marsden's defection.

Local government
Shropshire county council provided an unusual instance of the Conservatives being ejected from the administration after the 2001 county elections. Despite events in Shrewsbury, the county is run by a coalition administration formed from Labour (11 seats, mainly from Shrewsbury), Lib Dem (9, four from Ludlow and three from the north) and 'Progressive Independents' (4, from the Oswestry and Ludlow areas). The opposition are the Conservatives (17, from the rural centre, north and east of the county) and three other Independents. The county, incidentally, laboured under the peculiar name of 'Salop' from 1974 to 1980. Telford and Wrekin unitary council took over the most urbanised area of the county in April 1998 comprising Telford and the bulk of the Wrekin constituencies. It is run by a Labour majority (30 councillors) elected in 2000 thanks to strong support in Telford; the opposition divides between 15 Conservatives, four Lib Dems and five Independents and Residents. The next elections are due in May 2003 after a ward boundary review.

The Shropshire district councils, other than Shrewsbury, elect every four years and are not particularly partisan. Bridgnorth, to the south east, has an overall majority of councillors not affiliated to the major parties, with four councillors each from Labour, Conservative and Liberal Democrats. South Shropshire (Ludlow to the Welsh border) has a narrow majority of Independents over Liberal Democrats since Lib Dem gains in 1999, and could surely fall to the party if they tried in 2003. These two districts cover the Ludlow constituency. In the north, Oswestry borough also has a majority of non-party councillors, although this time Labour are next largest. North Shropshire (Wem and Market Drayton) is also Independent, although the Conservatives made several gains in 1999. In these Independent councils political groups can still exercise considerable influence in local affairs and 'control' is not such a hard and fast concept as it is, say, in the London boroughs. Shrewsbury & Atcham borough was a perennial hung council (from 1980 until 2002) with all three main parties having strong points; the Conservatives gained control in May 2002 despite Labour previously having been the strongest party.

Boundary review

Having gained a seat in 1997 Shropshire will retain five seats in the next review. The devil is in the detail, caused by Telford & Wrekin's unitary status. It can either be given two very small seats while the rest of the county has three large seats, or can continue to be paired. If reviewed separately, The Wrekin would lose the Albrighton area and be an improved prospect for Labour; if reviewed together it could end up donating territory to Telford and gaining from Ludlow to the benefit of the Conservatives. There may also be reshuffling in the centre of the county to boost Ludlow's electorate.

LUDLOW

	2001		1997		1992 notional	
Electorate and turnout	63,514	67.9	61,267	75.5	58,316	81.1
Conservative	16,990	39.4	19,633	42.4	24,415	51.6
Labour	5,785	13.4	11,745	25.4	10,134	21.4
Lib Dem	18,620	43.2	13,724	29.7	12,108	25.6
Anti–EU	858	2.0	385	0.8	–	–
Green	871	2.0	798	1.7	643	1.4
MP	Matthew Green (LD)		Christopher Gill (Con)		Christopher Gill (Con)	
Majority	1,630	3.8	5,909	12.8	12,307	26.0

The Ludlow seat in south Shropshire has two significant towns, Ludlow to the south and Bridgnorth to the east, but most of the electorate is in a scatter of villages; about 15 per cent are dispersed in small hamlets and isolated houses in deep countryside. To the west is the Clun forest, whose near total lack of trees is a bit of a surprise to the uninitiated. Ludlow, town and country, is a beautiful and unspoiled part of England.

Ludlow featured on very few commentators' lists of potential surprises in the 2001 election, but it provided a shock Liberal Democrat gain from the Conservatives in their rural heartland. Perhaps the fact that it is such a rural seat, remote from centres of population, discouraged London-based political journalists from finding out about Ludlow. After 2001 there is no excuse; the place has fascinating lessons for the parties. Ludlow was a startling example of what a surprise Liberal Democrat attack can achieve where one of the two bigger parties is complacent. The Conservatives had held the seat since 1886 and a lot of the seat was not particularly used to political activity. This changed as the Lib Dems organised a distribution network that could deliver *Focus* even to some of the most isolated parts of the constituency, and promoted Matthew Green energetically. The Lib Dems also had a significant but soft Labour vote to squeeze, and in the absence of much of a Labour effort they succeeded dramatically in 2001. They were helped at chipping away the Conservative vote by the retirement of Eurosceptic MP Christopher Gill at a relatively late stage and his replacement by a candidate without Green's local credentials. Like Wyre Forest, Ludlow illustrates the perils of allowing a place to feel neglected. About 20,000 electors of the seat in the south east regard Kidderminster as their principal urban centre and were as exercised as people in Wyre Forest about the downgrading of Kidderminster hospital. There was no independent in Ludlow, but the Liberal Democrats had positioned themselves astutely as campaigners for the hospital and in the absence of Gill (who had also joined the campaign) they mopped up the protest vote. There was also a feeling in Ludlow that its neglect would not be addressed if it turned in a boring Tory hold. Green is a young MP, a sharp political operator who can probably put in the effort required to build up his majority. There are a considerable number of constituencies, Tory and Labour, where the Ludlow approach might work and produce a surprise victory for the Lib Dems (or even locally organised political parties). The Lib Dems do not have unlimited resources – surely to the relief of the two bigger parties – but local knowledge of what is going on in all corners of England will be more important than ever in the years running up to the 2005/6 election.

SHREWSBURY and ATCHAM

	2001		1997		1992 actual	
Electorate and turnout	74,964	66.6	73,563	75.2	70,636	82.4
Conservative	18,674	37.4	18,814	34.0	26,681	45.8
Labour	22,253	44.6	20,484	37.0	15,157	26.0
Lib Dem	6,173	12.4	13,838	25.0	15,716	27.0
Anti–EU	1,620	3.2	1,823 (2)	3.3	–	–
Others	1,189 (2)		385 (2)		677	
MP	Paul Marsden (Lab) (LD)		Paul Marsden (Lab)		Derek Conway (Con)	
Majority	3,579	7.2	1,670	3.0	10,965	18.8

Shrewsbury is the largest town in the remainder of Shropshire since the excision of the Telford area. It is the county town with an abbey and winding streets of Tudor buildings. As well as the olde-worlde centre and the commercial and administrative functions, it is quite industrial in places.

Shrewsbury is a Labour inclined town. Some of its wards are strongholds by any comparison – the inner wards of Castlefields & Ditherington and Belle Vue, and Sundorne to the north east, were all over 60 per cent Labour in the 2001 county elections, and Labour had an unopposed run in Belle Vue in the 2000 borough elections. The suburbs to the south west, including Copthorne and Sutton, are more Conservative, but they were run close in 2001. Even in 2000 Labour won six of the town wards, to four Conservatives and two Lib Dems.

Three quarters of the constituency is in Shrewsbury, but the other quarter is a stretch of countryside in central Shropshire which voted around 50 per cent Conservative in the local elections in 2001 (the rural area was formerly the Atcham district which is recognised in the constituency name). This element makes Shrewsbury a current marginal rather than being the sort of pre-1997 marginal seat which is now safely Labour. It was a considerable achievement for Paul Marsden to win the first Labour victory in the seat in 1997 and increase his majority in June 2001. However, Marsden became disaffected with the government over the war in Afghanistan and fell out with the Labour whips; his defection to the Liberal Democrats in December 2001 was no surprise by the time it took place.

Marsden's defection is ironic, as he managed one of the most effective squeezes of the Lib Dem vote in the 2001 election (it was the fourth biggest fall in the Lib Dem vote in the country) in a seat which had a history of a resistant Liberal vote. Liberalism's survival had meant that the Conservatives held the seat in 1945 and 1966 on minority votes. Labour had come third in every election between 1974 and 1997.Unlike many defectors Marsden would be well advised to stay put and try to revive the strong latent Lib Dem vote in Shrewsbury. In the 2001 local elections they polled 19 per cent, despite contesting only 11 of the 16 wards. The next election in the constituency might be a bitter grudge match between Marsden and his spurned Labour activists – not forgetting the Conservatives who are still quite strong and could well come through the middle to reassert control in a constituency which they won on every occasion (except a one-off Liberal win in 1923) between 1885 and 1997.

SHROPSHIRE NORTH

	2001		1997		1992 notional	
Electorate and turnout	73,716	63.1	70,970	72.6	68,301	78.2
Conservative	22,631	48.6	20,730	40.2	27,159	50.8
Labour	16,390	35.2	18,535	36.0	13,978	26.2
Lib Dem	5,945	12.8	10,489	20.4	12,283	23.0
Anti–EU	1,165	2.5	1,764	3.4	–	–
Others	389		–		–	
MP	Owen Paterson (Con)		Owen Paterson (Con)		John Biffen (Con)	
Majority	6,241	13.4	2,195	4.3	13,181	24.7

The Shropshire North constituency consists of a swathe of rural England with a market town at each end – Oswestry in the west, close to the Welsh borders, and Market Drayton in the east not too far from Crewe and Newcastle-under-Lyme. In the centre of the constituency around Ellesmere is a little lake district, and there are some rugged hilly areas. South of Oswestry is the oddly named Ruyton-XI-Towns (there is only one place, and it is a village of 1,360 souls – the name comes from its mediaeval status as main manor of eleven places).

It is hard to tell from county election results what the internal configuration of the constituency is, because Labour, Lib Dem and two Progressive Independent candidates failed to put up candidates against each other in 2001. Labour enjoyed fairly narrow victories in Oswestry East and Market Drayton and a lot of the massive Lib Dem local vote in Wem must have gone Labour in the general election. The largest Conservative majorities were in the rural eastern areas north and south of Market Drayton but in several other places they would have had considerable majorities in the absence of the apparent electoral pact.

Owen Paterson had a hard act to follow in John Biffen, but achieved a good result for the Conservatives in 2001 after Labour did surprisingly well in 1997. He is a relatively right wing MP who has developed a reputation as a hard working constituency member and been good at local publicity. He fought off a determined Labour campaign in 2001 and now has a relatively safe seat. Shropshire North, and Oswestry before it, has been Conservative since 1885 with only a fleeting Liberal victory in a 1904 by-election that reverted to the Tories in 1906 interrupting a continuous flow of Conservative victories ever since 1835.

TELFORD

	2001		1997		1992 *notional*	
Electorate and turnout	59,431	52.0	56,558	65.6	*57,194*	*71.2*
Conservative	8,471	27.4	10,166	27.4	*13,546*	*33.3*
Labour	16,854	54.6	21,456	57.8	*21,473*	*52.8*
Lib Dem	3,983	12.9	4,371	11.8	*5,049*	*12.4*
Anti–EU	1,098	3.6	1,119	3.0	–	–
Others	469		–		*634*	*1.6*
MP	David Wright (Lab)		Bruce Grocott (Lab)		Bruce Grocott (Lab) The Wrekin	
Majority	8,383	27.2	11,290	30.4	*7,927*	*19.5*

Telford is one of only two constituencies in the United Kingdom to be named reasonably directly after a person (Regent's Park and Kensington North is the other, borderline, case; the Milton Keynes seats aren't – see Buckinghamshire for details). It is relatively common practice, though, in Australia. Telford is a New Town (designated in 1963 as Dawley but expanded later in the 1960s) named after the engineer Thomas Telford.

The New Town did not create a settlement out of whole cloth, but instead brought together a scattering of small industrial towns and gave them a focus. The Telford area is where the industrial revolution began, with Abraham Darby first using coke to smelt iron at Coalbrookdale in 1708-09 and the construction of the world's first iron bridge in 1779. The names of the villages and towns bear out their very early industrial and mining history and the area is listed as a UN World Heritage site. By the 1960s, however, the economic base was in need of renewal and the New Town has helped attract new employers. The economy still has several large industrial employers such as the Lilleshall foundry and Aga food services.

Telford was formerly the core of a marginal constituency (see The Wrekin for its odd history) but the current seat was drawn tightly around the centre of the New Town and the traditional industrial area to the south down to Ironbridge. It returned 24 Labour councillors out of 30 in the 2000 elections, giving the party an 18 point lead over the Tories in the opposition's best local elections in recent times, and unless Labour ever return to 1983 levels of support it is a safe seat.

The WREKIN

	2001		1997		1992 notional	
Electorate and turnout	65,781	63.1	60,211	75.2	58,103	83.8
Conservative	15,945	38.4	18,218	40.2	23,259	47.8
Labour	19,532	47.1	21,243	46.9	15,539	31.9
Lib Dem	4,738	11.4	5,807	12.8	9,391	19.3
Anti–EU	1,275	3.1	–	–	–	–
Others	–		–		489	
MP	Peter Bradley (Lab)		Peter Bradley (Lab)		NEW SEAT	
Majority	3,587	8.6	3,025	6.7	7,720	15.9

The Wrekin is a strange, steep hill in the south of this constituency, which has borne its name since 1918. The main centres of population are Wellington, a town which has become part of the Telford New Town, plus Hadley to its east which is notable as the location where all BT's public telephones are built; plus the more traditional market town of Newport to its north east and some rural areas where beef and sugar beet are produced. It extends into Shropshire proper in the Albrighton area to the south east of Telford. The boundaries were much altered in the 1990s review when the Telford constituency was created.

The Wrekin was an unlikely Labour gain in 1997. The party is quite weak in local elections, with support concentrated in the New Town areas fringing the Telford constituency. Even in Wellington the Conservatives and Liberal Democrats won the majority of wards, and Newport is Lib Dem and Independent in local elections. Labour held on in 2001 with a small favourable swing, as in many marginals; the Conservatives motivated rural support but the urban and suburban New Labour support in new private estates such as Leegomery was too strong for them.

The previous The Wrekin seat, including the Telford industrial area, was noted for a most peculiar electoral history. It changed hands thirteen times between 1918 and 1987, surely a record, and voted for the winning party in every general election from 1895 (as Wellington) to 1987 except 1951. Wrekin members, even apart from the electoral fluctuations, tended to have short terms of service. Boundary changes reflecting the growth of Telford tilted it to Labour in 1983 and the party won despite losing nationally in 1987 and 1992. The current seat, however, should be Conservative except in disastrous elections for them (on a uniform swing they could regain it and still be worse off than Labour were in 1983). The Conservative selection committee here displays what can charitably be called interesting judgement; they attempted the political resurrection of volunteer hangman Peter Bruinvels in 1997 and chose Jacob Rees-Mogg, who had fought Fife Central in 1997 with the help of his nanny, for the consideration of the electors in 2001. Both offers were declined in favour of Labour's ex-Westminster councillor Peter Bradley. What will they think of next?

Somerset

	Conservative		Labour		Liberal Democrat		Others	
	Share of vote	Seats	Share of vote	Seats	Share of vote	Seats	Share of vote	Seats
2001	40.9	3	16.5	0	39.6	2	2.9	0
1997	36.5	2	17.4	0	40.6	3	5.4	0
1992	45.3	4	12.9	0	40.2	1	1.5	0
1987	50.2	4	11.8	0	37.9	1	0.0	0
1983	51.2	4	11.7	0	37.0	1	0.1	0

Somerset is at the heart of the west country, a rather traditional place of agriculture, market towns and small seaside towns. There is very little by way of industry. Somerset has no large cities and all five of its constituencies have significant rural elements. To the west, Somerset is quite wild and rugged, particularly at Exmoor and the strange, bleak Somerset levels. Farming here is struggling and the rural areas were not particularly well off even before the damage caused by foot and mouth in 2001. In the east, flatter and more fertile land is conducive to dairy farming. Communications in the east are also better, with fast rail routes calling at Taunton and Castle Cary, and the levels of deprivation much lower. Somerset's short stretch of coastline has attracted retirees. The towns, even Taunton and Yeovil, are relatively small and have a provincial air to them; they are market centres for the surrounding villages rather than industrial or professional centres.

Bath and Bristol, the big urban centres which serve Somerset, became part of the county of Avon in the 1970s and took sections of the north of Somerset with them. For the constituencies of Bath, Wansdyke, Weston-super-Mare and Woodspring, all of which consider themselves really part of Somerset, the reader is advised to turn to 'Avon'. The remainder is to be found here.

Somerset is politically tightly contested between Conservatives and Liberal Democrats – Labour have run third in all its constituencies since 1983. However, this duopoly is only relatively recently established. Unlike Devon and Cornwall the Liberals faded in the county after their wipe-out defeat in 1924 and did not win again until Paddy Ashdown's 1983 victory in Yeovil. Labour did quite well in 1945, winning Taunton, failing by only 174 votes in Yeovil and also gaining Frome (most of which is now in Avon). The Liberals, where they stood, ran third in 1945 and were still doing so as late as 1970. Wells was the first place where they started to gain ground, although ironically they have never followed through to general election success there. Labour disappeared quite rapidly in Somerset in the 1970s and early 1980s; its union-based radicalism went down badly in a traditional part of the country with few large industrial employers. Labour also suffered from the demographic trends which have gradually shifted rural Wiltshire, Cambridgeshire and Norfolk into the Conservative column, but in Somerset there was just enough west country radicalism (and effort from individuals such as Ashdown in Yeovil and Alan Butt Philip in Wells) for the Liberals to rise instead.

The Liberal Democrat vote has changed remarkably little in Somerset since 1983, with the main change being the rise – against the trend – in 1992. This was associated with Paddy Ashdown's first election as leader; it has been noted that leaders of major parties tend to obtain relatively good results in the sub-region associated with their constituency in their first general election. The Ashdown factor vanished in 2001. Labour's vote has also moved within a relatively small band. The Conservatives have been more volatile, with a big slide from 1987 to 1997 and a relatively strong recovery in 2001. The Conservatives campaigned hard on 'countryside' issues in Somerset in the last election. Ian Liddell-Grainger, who held onto Bridgwater, was chairman of the Countryside Alliance in Devon. In Taunton blood sports enthusiasts rallied behind the Conservatives against outspoken Lib Dem MP Jackie Ballard. Hunting and farming issues were important in the west of the county in particular, where foot and mouth was also a particularly important concern. The Tories did better in Somerset than in many other counties in reducing the anti-EU share of the vote, from 4.9 per cent in 1997 to 2.2 per cent in 2001. The county now contains two knife-edge marginals, Taunton for the Conservatives and Somerton & Frome for the Lib Dems and is therefore of considerable interest for the next election as the parties battle it out for title of the effective opposition.

Local government

The Liberal Democrats did badly in the Somerset county council elections in 2001. Their 15-strong majority disappeared and they were left with 29 seats, to 24 Conservatives and 5 Labour county councillors. The Conservatives picked up several rural seats, while Labour gained two seats in Bridgwater town, but despite the parliamentary result the Lib Dem strongholds in Taunton town and Yeovil remained solid, providing blocs of five and four Lib Dems respectively. The rural wards tend to divide on an east-west pattern, with the Tories dominating the west and the Lib Dems stronger in the east.

The 1999 all-out district elections told a sad tale for the Liberal Democrats. They lost Taunton Deane, a council they had run for eight years, to no overall control and also saw Sedgemoor (Bridgwater) revert to Conservative control as their group were reduced from 12 to 3; both Tories and Labour made gains. From being within one seat of control in Mendip (Wells and Frome) they fell back behind the Conservatives in a three-way hung council. Their ray of sunshine was in South Somerset (Yeovil and Somerton), where their large majority survived nearly unscathed.

Boundary review

All Somerset's seats are a little large but not sufficiently so to justify the allocation of a sixth constituency. Taunton will be cut down to size a bit by transferring a small but very Conservative rural area to Bridgwater, with important consequences for highly marginal Taunton. After an inquiry, the names of these two seats were revised: Taunton becomes Taunton Deane, and Bridgwater becomes Bridgwater and West Somerset. Pacifying local objectors has come at the cost of more cumbersome names.

BRIDGWATER

	2001		1997		1992 actual	
Electorate and turnout	74,273	64.4	73,412	74.4	71,575	79.5
Conservative	19,354	40.4	20,174	36.9	26,610	46.8
Labour	12,803	26.8	13,519	24.8	12,365	21.7
Lib Dem	14,367	30.0	18,378	33.6	16,894	29.7
Anti–EU	1,323	2.8	2,551	4.7	–	–
Others	–		–		1,041 (3)	
MP	Ian Liddell-Grainger (Con)		Tom King (Con)		Tom King (Con)	
Majority	4,987	10.4	1,796	3.3	9,716	17.1

Bridgwater is a sleepy backwater of the west country. The town of Bridgwater, which contributes about 25,000 electors, is much less commercial and active than Taunton down the road. It is a quiet industrial port and former brick making centre with a reputation for being slow-moving even by Somerset standards. Bridgwater sits amid the fenland of the Somerset levels and the district council is called Sedgemoor, an old name for this bleak landscape. The constituency extends westward to seaside Minehead and Porlock on the moors. The coast around Minehead and Watchet is the principal retirement area of Somerset; 31.8 per cent of the West Somerset council's population are pensioners, easily the highest proportion in the county.

Bridgwater's reluctance to follow fashion is apparent from the relatively small movements of support between the parties in recent elections. Since 1983 the Alliance and Liberal Democrat share of the vote has been remarkably static; in four out of five elections their vote has been within 0.3 per cent of 30 per cent, and in 1997 it was not much higher. Labour's vote has gradually increased at the expense of the Conservatives since the party's 1983 low point. Bridgwater disappointed Liberal Democrat hopes in 2001. It was a classic scenario for a gain – a substantial Labour vote to squeeze, and a long serving Tory MP retiring – but still they failed.

Unlike many other Lib Dem targets the party does not have much of a base in local government in Bridgwater. They did not manage to elect a single county councillor in the area in 2001 and came third in the 1999 local elections with a weak share of the vote and few councillors. Bridgwater town is a Labour pocket in the wilderness of Somerset (the four wards containing the town voted 44 per cent Labour, 29 per cent Lib Dem and 27 per cent Conservative in the June 2001 county elections) but the minimal Labour vote in the rest of the seat precludes a Labour win. The last time the seat failed to vote Conservative was in 1938 and 1945, when independent progressive Vernon Bartlett stood – on the first occasion without Labour or Liberal opposition. It would probably take another such display of centre left unity for the Conservatives to be toppled.

SOMERTON and FROME

	2001		1997		1992 notional	
Electorate and turnout	75,977	69.3	74,240	77.3	72,545	82.3
Conservative	22,315	42.4	22,554	39.3	28,287	47.4
Labour	6,113	11.6	9,385	16.3	6,217	10.4
Lib Dem	22,983	43.6	22,684	39.5	24,036	40.3
Anti–EU	919	1.7	2,780 (2)	4.9	–	–
Others	354		–		1,132 (2)	
MP	David Heath (LD)		David Heath (LD)		Mark Robinson (Con)	
Majority	668	1.3	130	0.2	4,251	7.1

Somerton and Frome is a constituency of villages and small towns; Frome is the largest town in this constituency (18,000 electors), and it is no metropolis. The seat covers some of the traditional heartland of Somerset; villages with excellent names like Curry Rivel and Huish Episcopi, and the puzzling inland town of Milborne Port. Castle Cary is on the far fringe of possible London commuter territory. There is some light industry in the towns but the tone of the seat is overwhelmingly rural.

Frome is a three-way marginal town, and the source of most of the (admittedly minimal) Labour vote in the constituency (it gave its name to a north Somerset seat which voted Labour in 1923, 1929 and 1945). However, the rest of the constituency is a collection of marginal rural wards where the Tories and Lib Dems were very close in 2001. Elections here really have been photo-finishes in recent years, and turnout has stayed relatively high.

Liberal Democrat David Heath eked out a narrow victory in 1997 and surprisingly held it with a swing in his favour in 2001 while the other Somerset seats were swinging to the Conservatives. With a neat symmetry the Conservative rise was almost identical to the fall in the anti-EU vote, and (net of a small loss to the independent Liberals) the Labour vote fell back by the same amount as the Lib Dems rose. The seat will remain the scene of pitched battles between Liberal Democrats and Conservatives and remains perilously marginal. Any serious Conservative revival should sweep it away.

TAUNTON

	2001		1997		1992 actual	
Electorate and turnout	81,651	67.6	79,783	76.5	78,037	82.3
Conservative	23,033	41.7	23,621	38.7	29,576	46.0
Labour	8,254	14.9	8,248	13.5	8,151	12.7
Lib Dem	22,798	41.3	26,064	42.7	26,240	40.8
Anti–EU	1,140	2.1	2,760	4.5	–	–
Others	–		318		279	
MP	Adrian Flook (Con)		Jackie Ballard (LD)		David Nicholson (Con)	
Majority	235	0.4	2,443	4.0	3,336	5.2

Taunton was one of two Conservative gains from the Lib Dems in 2001, and probably the more surprising one – the Isle of Wight has something of a tradition of going its own way. Taunton is a less than fascinating town, but it is prosperous for Somerset and has had its growth fuelled by rapid access from the M5 and InterCity railways. Like many towns it has spawned a 'Little America' district of office parks, DIY stores and multiplexes by a motorway junction, plus an industrial hinterland with the deceptively bucolic name of 'Norton Fitzwarren' where cider is mass-produced. Taunton has some rather run-down estates, particularly Halcon (Somerset's only ward in the 10 per cent most deprived in England). The town is too small (41,000 electors) for a seat of its own and the constituency extends far out to the west, via Wellington and Wiveliscombe across the wilds of Exmoor to Dulverton inland from Minehead.

Taunton finally went over to the Lib Dems in 1997 after high hopes in 1992 were dashed, although even then there were worrying signs in the relatively low swing and the anti-EU vote exceeding the Lib Dem majority. A series of bad mid-term results followed including the loss of the council and a 27-point Euro election defeat, but in contrast to other south western seats (which they held) this was followed by a narrow parliamentary loss for Jackie Ballard in 2001.

Taunton town was still quite supportive of the Lib Dems in 2001; it gave them five out of six county wards and voted for them 42 per cent to 35 per cent for the Conservatives and 22 per cent for Labour. However, turnout was 62 per cent and was particularly low in the working class parts of Taunton. In contrast, turnout in the Dulverton and Exmoor ward reached 77 per cent, and this ward was over 70 per cent Conservative in the county elections. It is a stag-hunting area and according to Ballard its voters were motivated by a passion and anger unusual in the 2001 election. However, if all else had been going well it would not have mattered.

Taunton will remain a closely-fought battle between the Conservatives and Liberal Democrats, but Ballard will not be standing again, having chosen to study in Tehran. The boundary changes will eventually remove the Dulverton area and tip it back notionally into the Lib Dem column, but new MP Adrian Flook will hope to have built up enough of a power base to survive the loss of this area.

WELLS

	2001		1997		1992 actual	
Electorate and turnout	74,189	69.2	72,426	77.8	69,833	82.7
Conservative	22,462	43.8	22,208	39.4	28,620	49.6
Labour	7,915	15.4	10,204	18.1	6,126	10.6
Lib Dem	19,666	38.3	21,680	38.5	21,971	38.0
Anti–EU	1,104	2.2	2,196	3.9	–	–
Others	167		92		1,042	
MP	David Heathcoat-Amory (Con)		David Heathcoat-Amory (Con)		David Heathcoat-Amory (Con)	
Majority	2,796	5.4	528	0.9	6,649	11.5

The Wells constituency is in the north west of Somerset and borders on Weston-super-Mare, now part of Avon. Wells is a small city, dominated by an impressive cathedral and Bishop's Palace. The constituency also includes most of the Mendip council area except Frome. Among the Mendip hills lies the mysterious town of Glastonbury, which has become a New Age theme park on the basis of a rather fanciful legend about Jesus travelling to the area. Glastonbury Tor has a strange habit of appearing on the skyline at totally unexpected places. Shepton Mallet, a centre for part of rural Somerset, is in the seat too, as is an area of the Levels, stretching flatly to the coast at Burnham and Highbridge. King Alfred, who legendarily burnt some cakes while hiding out anonymously here, is commemorated in the name of a rural county council ward. To complete a particularly attractive part of the English country-side is Cheddar, known for cheese and caves.

Most of the wards of the Wells constituency are marginal between Conservatives and Liberal Democrats, with the Lib Dems just ahead in the towns and the Conservatives just ahead in the rural areas; Labour are not a presence except in Shepton Mallet and won no county wards in the division in 2001.

The Liberals have long set their hearts on winning Wells, but have been repeatedly rebuffed, and Conservative David Heathcoat-Amory, now a senior figure in the party and from a famous west country political family, has had two narrow victories over the Lib Dems in 1997 and 2001. Just as in Bridgwater, the Liberal Democrat vote has flatlined in Wells since 1983, remaining between 37.6 per cent (1987) and 39 per cent (1983) ever since. They have had plausible ambitions of winning the seat for all this time but have always been disappointed and must after 2001 feel that their day will never come.

YEOVIL

	2001		1997		1992 notional	
Electorate and turnout	74,991	64.2	74,383	72.7	72,802	81.4
Conservative	17,338	36.0	14,946	27.7	21,890	36.9
Labour	7,077	14.7	8,053	14.9	5,702	9.6
Lib Dem	21,266	44.2	26,349	48.7	30,634	51.7
Anti–EU	1,135	2.3	3,574	6.6	–	–
Others	1,320 (2)		1,131 (3)		1,045 (3)	
MP	David Laws (LD)		Paddy Ashdown (LD)		Paddy Ashdown (LD)	
Majority	3,928	8.2	11,403	21.1	8,744	14.8

Yeovil (41,000 population) is the main town of south Somerset. It has some industries, most notably Westland helicopters, but it also has a tradition of glove and leather manufacture. It is a market town for the surrounding rural area and has a weekly cattle market (although this was of course suspended for much of 2001). The constituency includes a few other small towns – Chard and Crewkerne – and a rural area. Yeovil town's 28,000 electors are the strongest source of Lib Dem support, voting 47 per cent for them to 31 per cent Conservative and 22 per cent Labour in the 2001 local elections. The other elements of the seat are more closely contested, but the Liberal Democrats were ahead here as well.

The Yeovil constituency tends to be faithful to one party for some time. It was Liberal from 1885 to 1918, then Conservative until 1983 and since then has stuck by the Liberals/ Liberal Democrats. The Liberals in the past have been something of a federation of independents, whose parliamentary representation depended to a great extent on the efforts and personal reputation of the individual candidates. In the 1992 parliament only Liz Lynne (Rochdale) and Matthew Taylor (Truro) had inherited their seats from Liberal predecessors. When Paddy Ashdown first won Yeovil, in 1983, it had been a striking personal triumph and it was a valid question as to whether his vote would transfer to his successor David Laws, particularly as Laws was a London-based economist rather than a local worthy.

The withdrawal of the Ashdown factor did cause a worse result for the Lib Dems in Yeovil even than in the neighbouring Somerset seats, with a 6.5 per cent swing to the Conservative candidate Marco Forgione, but Lib Dem strength was based on more than personal loyalty to Ashdown and Laws was still able to win with a respectable margin. He cannot take its loyalty for granted, but is likely to be able to build on his initial majority.

Staffordshire including Stoke-on-Trent

	Conservative		Labour		Liberal Democrat		Others	
	Share of vote	Seats	Share of vote	Seats	Share of vote	Seats	Share of vote	Seats
2001	35.9	3	48.0	9	12.5	0	3.6	0
1997	33.7	3	51.3	9	10.7	0	4.2	0
1992	44.0	6	41.8	5	13.4	0	0.8	0
1987	44.8	7	33.9	4	21.1	0	0.2	0
1983	44.9	7	32.9	4	22.1	0	0.1	0

Staffordshire is the largest county of the West Midlands, leaving aside the metropolitan boroughs around Birmingham and the Black Country. In the south it is strongly influenced by that conurbation, producing areas such as the South Staffordshire constituency which are effectively commuter belt seats, affecting the character of Lichfield somewhat similarly, and also providing an influx of population to Tamworth. In the centre, either side of Stafford, is a band of countryside with market and industrial towns scattered across it, while in the north there is empty moorland. The main urban area within the county itself is the built up district around Stoke-on-Trent in the north west. Staffordshire's constituencies cover a spectrum, from two safe Conservative seats (South and Stone), a Conservative-held marginal (Lichfield), Labour-held marginals (Burton, Stafford, Tamworth, Moorlands), a safe-ish Labour seat which was Tory in the 1980s (Cannock Chase) and a clutch of truly safe Labour seats around Stoke and Newcastle.

Stoke-on-Trent is the largest city in Staffordshire, with a population of just over a quarter of a million. The urban area grew rapidly from the late 18th century thanks to canals and the presence of raw materials and soon dominated the British (and world) markets for pottery and china of all sorts. Mining, steel and other heavy industry also located here. Several small industrial towns grew together into an agglomeration. The area became known as the Potteries or the Six Towns and in 1910 was fused into the county borough of Stoke-on-Trent, designated a city in 1925. During the first part of the 20th century it was the setting for the novels of Arnold Bennett, who wrote evocatively of ordinary life in an industrial, provincial town. Bennett is an honoured local figure, except perhaps in Fenton (see Stoke South for details). Stoke's growth, being overwhelmingly industrial and working class, made it promising territory for the Labour Party from the early days, and (except in recent local elections) it has been solidly, obstinately loyal to the party in good times and bad. All its seats have been Labour since 1935, the only place of its size to be so loyal. Its MPs have for the most part been unobtrusive backbenchers, although Stoke Central sent Lady Cynthia Mosley to parliament in 1929 and Jack Ashley represented Stoke South for many years. Stoke's influence extends to Newcastle-under-Lyme, a town which guards its independence from the city

Staffordshire's variety means that more or less whatever is going on nationally there will be a seat or two of interest in the county. It is a rare election in the last 35 years (only 1987 and 2001 qualify) when a seat has not changed hands. The Conservatives must concentrate on regaining some of the marginals such as Burton and Stafford currently held by Labour which the party has usually managed to win in past elections. No Tory seat looks vulnerable, and there are no good Lib Dem prospects.

Local government

Staffordshire county council has been Labour controlled since 1981, and was usually Labour before that, and it the southernmost county that can be regarded as reliably Labour (Northamptonshire is currently marginally Labour-run). It was made a lot less safe for the party in 1997, or so it seemed, with the excision of Stoke-on-Trent. Labour can still muster 36 councillors, to 24 Conservatives and 2 Lib Dems, after the 2001 county elections. Labour are strongest in Newcastle-under-Lyme, Cannock, Stafford and Tamworth while the Conservatives do well in the south, rural centre and Lichfield.

Stoke-on-Trent city is now a unitary authority. It had one of the longest histories of Labour control of any large city in the country, with only one year of Conservative control since 1945. Labour's majority, however, dwindled from sixty (100 per cent representation) to a perilously low four at the end of 2001; Labour won only three wards out of twenty in 2000. The Conservatives and Lib Dems have picked up seats but the motive force has been an Independent group which has spread out from the north of the city to win nine seats in 2000 – all the more remarkable as it did not put up candidates in the other eleven wards. The Independent group are primarily Stoke nationalists, speaking against the alleged neglect of the city; voter discontent was fuelled by big cuts in services while prestige projects went ahead. All-out elections in May 2002 saw Labour lose power and tie with the Independents for the position of largest single party. Although humiliating, these results were better for Labour than those in 2000, and they must hope to regain ground from this local revolt in the following years.

There is little that is unexpected about the politics of most of the Staffordshire district councils. South Staffordshire is a Conservative council which even survived the 1995 rout. East Staffordshire, based on Burton, is Labour with a comfortable majority following the 1999 elections, although the rural areas produce an irreducible Conservative core. Cannock Chase, reflecting the peculiarities of the parliamentary constituency, has been Labour since 1973 except for a spell of no overall control in 1982-87. Newcastle-under-Lyme (the borough also includes Kidsgrove and Loggerheads) is also usually Labour and was run by the party between 1979 and 2002, although it has quite a large Liberal Democrat group. Stafford (which includes a large rural area around Stone and Eccleshall) is under no overall control, although a solid showing in the town from Labour kept them the largest party in 1999. Staffordshire Moorlands (a significantly different coverage than the constituency) is under no overall control, with its diverse composition reflected in the four-way split on its council. The Conservatives gained Lichfield in 1999 after a four year Labour period; it is quite a close Lab-Con contest. Tamworth is the joker in the pack, with a large swing to the Conservatives in 2000 (blamed locally on high parking charges) cutting Labour's majority right down – most of its wards are marginal and volatile though Labour performed well in 2002. Cannock Chase and Newcastle normally have annual elections but like Stoke had all-out elections on new boundaries in May 2002.

Boundary review

Staffordshire will remain entitled to its current allocation of 12 seats but the commission propose to shuffle some wards around to reduce the inequalities in the size of the existing seats. Labour benefit slightly from both changes – Burton loses a rural ward, as does Staffordshire Moorlands; the constituencies that gain them (Stoke North and Lichfield) will not be greatly affected. The commission chose to continue to review Stoke and the rest of Staffordshire together.

BURTON

	2001		1997		1992 *notional*	
Electorate and turnout	75,259	61.7	72,638	75.0	*72,244*	*81.7*
Conservative	17,934	38.6	21,480	39.4	*28,454*	*48.2*
Labour	22,783	49.0	27,810	51.0	*24,327*	*41.2*
Lib Dem	4,468	9.6	4,617	8.5	*6,219*	*10.5*
Anti–EU	984	2.1	–	–	–	–
Others	288		604		–	
MP	Janet Dean (Lab)		Janet Dean (Lab)		Ivan Lawrence (Con)	
Majority	4,849	10.4	6,330	11.6	*4,127*	*7.0*

Burton's association with brewing leads to a suspicion that the town's voting behaviour is more Conservative than its working class demographics might suggest. This appears not to have been the case even when the beer interest and the Tory Party were closely allied in the late 19th Century – Burton voted enthusiastically for Sir Arthur Bass in 1885 and returned him unopposed thereafter in the Liberal interest, proving that as long as the candidate was a brewer from the town, party labels did not matter much. In modern times straightforward national party allegiances have determined voting here. The Burton town wards voted 57 per cent for Labour in the 2001 county elections, to 30 per cent Conservative. Labour's strongest areas were in the dense terraces of central Burton, parts of which are surprisingly run down and deprived.

A seat consisting solely of Burton would be a pretty reliable Labour seat, but the town is not really big enough and the constituency extends across some strongly Conservative countryside by the river Dove to the little town of Uttoxeter. Uttoxeter is marginal, but the net effect of the non-Burton element has been to make Burton a constituency Labour have only won in landslide years – 1945, 1997 and 2001. Even in 1966 the Tories held on by 277 votes. Labour have done well enough here in the last couple of elections for it to have become a slightly more difficult seat for the Conservatives – it is the 61st most vulnerable Labour seat and Labour should win it as long as their majority is over 40.

CANNOCK CHASE

	2001		1997		1992 notional	
Electorate and turnout	74,172	55.4	70,784	74.0	70,749	84.4
Conservative	12,345	30.1	14,227	27.2	22,790	38.2
Labour	23,049	56.1	28,705	54.8	29,259	49.0
Lib Dem	5,670	13.8	4,537	8.7	7,283	12.2
Anti–EU	–	–	1,663	3.2	–	–
Ind Lab	–	–	1,615	3.1	–	–
Socialist	–	–	1,120	2.1	–	–
Others	–		499		383	
MP	Tony Wright (Lab)		Tony Wright (Lab)		Tony Wright (Lab)	
					Cannock & Burntwood	
Majority	10,704	26.1	14,478	27.6	6,469	10.8

Cannock Chase is an area of woodland and heath lying just south east of Stafford, and quite close to the west midland metropolitan boroughs of Walsall and Wolverhampton. The population of the constituency comes not from villages for the most part, but from some quite gritty little towns on the eastern edge of the Chase: Cannock itself plus Hednesford and Norton Canes to the south, and Rugeley to the north.

The major settlements of Cannock Chase developed as mining towns and villages, and for many years this was a solid, Labour voting, midlands mining seat. Like other such seats (Belper in south Derbyshire for example, and Bosworth in Leicestershire) it gradually became less of a mining seat in the post war period as pits closed, new industries rose in their place, and new middle class commuter settlements grew up. Cannock fell to the Conservatives in 1970 (as did Belper and Bosworth) but was restored in 1974 when boundary changes took away the most Conservative areas. Its fall in 1983 was another shock for Labour. The very right wing Conservative Gerald Howarth held on until normal service was resumed in 1992. Mining had only another year left in Cannock - the last colliery, at Huntington, closed in 1993. Electricity generation is still there: Rugeley's power station looms by the main line railway, like a checkpoint between the north of England and the south.

Most areas of Cannock Chase have returned Labour majorities in the last couple of elections. Rugeley North is Lib Dem in local elections; Cannock town itself, however, was a Conservative gain in the 2001 county elections – perhaps we have not heard the last of Cannock's ability to spring unwelcome surprises on Labour.

LICHFIELD

	2001		1997		1992 notional	
Electorate and turnout	63,234	65.9	62,753	77.4	61,995	83.6
Conservative	20,480	49.1	20,853	42.9	29,583	57.1
Labour	16,054	38.5	20,615	42.4	18,993	36.6
Lib Dem	4,462	10.7	5,473	11.3	2,970	5.7
Anti–EU	684	1.6	1,652	3.4	–	–
Others	–		–		312	
MP	Michael Fabricant (Con)		Michael Fabricant (Con)		Michael Fabricant (Con) Staffordshire Mid	
Majority	4,426	10.6	238	0.5	10,590	20.4

Lichfield itself is a small city of just under 22,000 electors, an ecclesiastical centre with a fine three-spired cathedral. The city is rather conveniently situated for commuting to Birmingham seventeen miles away. During the 1980s and 1990s it sprouted new private housing estates. It is Conservative inclined, voting 47 per cent for them in the 2001 county elections to 36 per cent for Labour. Lichfield holds the balance between the two other types of territory in the constituency bearing its name.

The other urban element of the constituency is Burntwood, contributing about 20,000 electors. Burntwood is a more working class town, with a mining history and since 1999 a new factory producing Reliant Robin cars. It is the Labour voting section of the constituency with 50 per cent for Labour and 37 per cent for the Conservatives in the 2001 county elections. There are, however, a bit over 20,000 rural electors in villages north and west of Lichfield who have the strong Conservative allegiance typical of such areas – the Tory lead here in 2001 was something like 25 per cent of the poll.

Michael Fabricant did very well in 2001, gaining a swing of 5 per cent in his favour. Lichfield slipped from number four on Labour's target list to 32nd, surely beyond the government's wildest dreams. Lichfield's most famous son, Dr Samuel Johnson, said that 'most schemes of political improvement are very laughable things.' Similar words have often unkindly been said about the hair of Lichfield's current member, but Lichfield seems to retain Johnson's scepticism about European or New Labour schemes of improvement, and votes for pragmatic conservatism.

NEWCASTLE-UNDER-LYME

	2001		1997		1992 actual	
Electorate and turnout	65,739	58.8	66,686	73.7	66,595	80.3
Conservative	10,664	27.6	10,537	21.4	15,813	29.6
Labour	20,650	53.4	27,743	56.5	25,652	47.9
Lib Dem	5,993	15.5	6,858	14.0	11,727	21.9
Anti–EU	594	1.5	1,510	3.1	–	–
Liberal	–	–	1,399	2.8	–	–
Socialist	–	–	1,082	2.2	–	–
Others	773		–		314	
MP	Paul Farrelly (Lab)		Llin Golding (Lab)		Llin Golding (Lab)	
Majority	9,986	25.8	17,206	35.0	9,839	18.4

Newcastle-under-Lyme is a less completely working class town than Stoke-on-Trent, with which the constituency is joined by a continuous built-up area; middle class residential areas have always provided the basis for a substantial non-Labour vote but the constituency has always extended to pottery and mining districts around the town. Keele University has added a student and academic population to the area. Despite its marginal social characteristics Newcastle has been one of Labour's longest established constituencies, and this has much to do with one man.

From 1906 to 1942, Newcastle's MP was Josiah Wedgwood of the famous pottery family. Wedgwood was first elected as a radical Liberal but changed allegiance to Labour in 1919. His popularity was such that other parties often did not oppose him, even in 1931 and 1935. Newcastle therefore has one of the longest continuous histories of Labour representation in the country, whether one starts from 1906 or 1919.

In Chesterfield the 1984 by-election was a starting point for a determined Lib Dem assault on the constituency which gathered force until victory in 2001. A 1986 by-election in Newcastle-under-Lyme saw the Lib Dems cut Labour's majority down to 799, but their vote has faded in general elections since in a more typical fashion than Chesterfield. They are still active in local elections and are the largest non-Labour party but in the county elections of 2001 this translated into several reasonable seconds rather than any seats. They did rather better in 2000, when turnout was lower and Labour more unpopular, and a couple of other seats were picked up by the Conservatives (residential Seabridge) and a local political organisation called the Caring Party (ex-mining Silverdale). However, Labour's baton was safely handed on in the 2001 general election to new MP Paul Farrelly.

STAFFORD

	2001		1997		1992 notional	
Electorate and turnout	67,934	65.3	66,789	77.5	66,380	82.9
Conservative	16,253	36.6	20,292	39.2	26,464	48.1
Labour	21,285	48.0	24,606	47.5	19,229	34.9
Lib Dem	4,205	9.5	5,480	10.6	9,097	16.5
Anti–EU	2,315	5.2	1,146	2.2	–	–
Others	308		248		257	
MP	David Kidney (Lab)		David Kidney (Lab)		Bill Cash (Con)	
Majority	5,032	11.3	4,314	8.3	7,235	13.2

Stafford is just clear enough of the West Midlands conurbation to be a centre in its own right, aided by its status as the county town. It is a commercial and administrative centre, although it has a history as a railway town and a centre of the boot and shoe industry. Stafford town provides 42,000 electors to the constituency and is, unsurprisingly, the Labour power base. In its four county council wards in June 2001 Labour won 51 per cent to 30 per cent for the Conservatives and even gained the South Gate ward which contains Stafford's most middle class suburbs such as Weeping Cross (among the 3 per cent least deprived places in England). Labour's strongest area is the north of the town.

The pre-1997 Stafford constituency contained a tract of countryside and the small town of Stone, most of which is now in the Stone constituency. This element made it very difficult for Labour to win the seat and produced a Conservative majority in excess of 5,000 even in 1966. Now this element has been reduced to a few villages just outside Stafford such as Seighford and replaced by the town of Penkridge and its surrounding countryside from the South Staffs district. This area tends to the Tories, but it was notably unenthusiastic in 2001 and only gave them a 300-vote lead over Labour in the county elections.

One of the reasons the 2001 election was quite as dreadful for the Conservatives in Stafford was the local strength of the UK Independence Party. Its general election candidate was the Earl of Bradford, newly enfranchised by reform of the House of Lords, who saved his deposit. The only other five UKIP saved deposits were in coastal retirement areas. It is tempting to think that deferential voting is alive and well in Stafford, but UKIP also unusually ran a full slate of county council candidates who polled similarly, with a particular strong point in Penkridge.

STAFFORDSHIRE MOORLANDS

	2001		1997		1992 notional	
Electorate and turnout	66,760	63.9	65,742	77.8	67,045	80.2
Conservative	15,066	35.3	16,637	32.5	20,787	38.7
Labour	20,904	49.0	26,686	52.2	21,972	40.9
Lib Dem	5,928	13.9	6,191	12.1	9,381	17.5
Anti–EU	760	1.8	1,603	3.1	–	–
Ind Con	–	–	–	–	1,366	2.5
Others	–		–		263	
MP	Charlotte Atkins (Lab)		Charlotte Atkins (Lab)		David Knox (Con)	
Majority	5,838	13.7	10,049	19.7	1,185*	2.2*

* Estimated Labour majority allowing for boundary changes

The small town of Leek (20,000 population) is the main centre in this constituency and gave its name to the seat until 1983. Leek is on the edge of the Peak District national park and the eastern part of the constituency consists of hilly moors extending as far as Dovedale. Biddulph is a working class little place with traditions of iron and ceramic production, close to Stoke-on-Trent although it is just across the Cheshire county boundary from Congleton. Since 1997 the Moorlands constituency has extended to Kidsgrove, a town which is part of the Potteries built up area and administered by Newcastle-under-Lyme borough.

From 1945 to 1970 Leek was a Labour seat, but the Conservative gain in 1970 was one of a number of breakthroughs the Tories made in that election in somewhat similar seats – rural areas with a town originally firmly working class but changing rapidly – such as Belper, Rossendale and Cannock. Leek has stopped being an isolated textile town, and has Manchester and Stoke commuters and locally based services, including the Britannia Building Society.

Labour did not regain Leek/ Moorlands in 1974 or 1992 after boundary changes, but the boundary inquiry rode to the rescue before 1997 by taking away some rural territory and adding Kidsgrove. Leek is a marginal town even in good local elections for Labour – the party led only 36-31 from the Conservatives in the town wards in the 2001 county elections, and the Conservatives were miles ahead in the rural division surrounding it. The Caverswall area, just outside the Stoke city limit, was marginal. The real Labour strength comes from Kidsgrove which by itself produced a 2,000 vote Labour lead over the Tories in the 2001 local elections, and Biddulph whose town ward added another 1,500 to Labour's margin. The Stoke-Newcastle conurbation provides four safe Labour seats, and enough urban territory to tip the balance in this marginal in all but the better Tory years. It is Labour's 97th most marginal seat, meaning that Labour could lose their overall majority without losing Moorlands.

STAFFORDSHIRE SOUTH

	2001		1997		1992 notional	
Electorate and turnout	69,959	60.3	68,896	74.2	68,716	81.1
Conservative	21,295	50.5	25,568	50.0	32,982	59.2
Labour	14,414	34.2	17,747	34.7	14,367	25.8
Lib Dem	4,891	11.6	5,797	11.3	8,391	15.1
Anti–EU	1,580	3.7	2,002	3.9	–	–
MP	Patrick Cormack (Con)		Patrick Cormack (Con)		Patrick Cormack (Con)	
Majority	6,881	16.3	7,821	15.3	18,615	33.4

Most of Staffordshire lies north of the West Midland conurbation. There is, however, a tail of territory hanging down between rural Shropshire and the built-up areas of Wolverhampton and Dudley. This is the basis for the Staffordshire South constituency, which also includes a strip north of Wolverhampton to Cheslyn Hay and Great Wyrley near and rather similar to Cannock. There are no large towns in the constituency – Codsall and Wombourne are little places that send commuters mainly to Wolverhampton.

Overall, the constituency is affluent, car-driving and white, although it falls short of the levels of prosperity enjoyed in Solihull or Sutton Coldfield in West Midlands county. The local authority, South Staffordshire District Council, is Conservative controlled with a large majority and it is no surprise to note that the popular incumbent, Sir Patrick Cormack, is comfortably returned election after election. It is not completely uniform in its political preferences, however. Labour won the county ward of Great Wyrley and also Essington, also just outside Wolverhampton to the north. On the other hand, the Conservatives polled nearly 60 per cent in rural Kinver in the far south, and not much less in the rest of the suburban and rural majority of the seat. The Tories led even in the 1995 local elections and are completely safe here.

STOKE-ON-TRENT CENTRAL

	2001		1997		1992 actual	
Electorate and turnout	59,750	47.4	64,396	62.5	65,528	68.1
Conservative	5,352	18.9	6,738	16.7	12,477	27.9
Labour	17,170	60.6	26,662	66.2	25,897	58.0
Lib Dem	4,148	14.6	4,809	11.9	6,073	13.6
Anti–EU	–	–	1,071	2.7	–	–
Independent	1,657	5.8	–	–	–	–
Others	–		965 (2)		196	
MP	Mark Fisher (Lab)		Mark Fisher (Lab)		Mark Fisher (Lab)	
Majority	11,818	41.7	19,924	49.5	13,420	30.1

The Six Towns of the Potteries are distributed two apiece to the three Stoke parliamentary constituencies. This one contains Stoke itself (Knype in Arnold Bennett's novels), which is the administrative centre, the site of the main station and still has two large potteries, Spode and Royal Minton. Hanley (Hanbridge to Bennett) is the main commercial and shopping centre and boasts a statue of local hero Stanley Matthews. The majority council estate ward of Brookhouse, in the east of the constituency, is the most impoverished part of Stoke-on-Trent, ranking 113th on the index of multiple deprivation, but the rest of the constituency is not as bleak. Hartshill, to the west, is heavily owner-occupied and the second most well-off ward of the city. South of Hanley centre is Etruria, a district of pottery workers' housing built by Josiah Wedgwood.

Stoke Central is now the safest Labour seat in the Potteries, but it was the last to go Labour originally (1929, for Lady Mosley, while Burslem and Hanley voted Labour in 1918 and 1922 respectively) and until the 1950s was actually slightly less Labour than the others. Like the other Stoke seats, the main recent interest has come from local elections.

In Labour's local election meltdown in 2000 the party was defeated in six out of the seven wards of Central, surviving only in Hartshill. This was because, in contrast to the other wards, anti-Labour voters did not rally strongly behind the best-placed challenger. Independents won three, Lib Dems two and the Conservatives one. There is some potential for the Liberal Democrats in local elections here, but their vote still trailed Labour 33-26 per cent in 2000. In the general election normal service was resumed and Mark Fisher was re-elected with the customary large Labour majority on a low turnout. In 2002 Labour lost control of the council, but actually polled better here than in 2000.

STOKE-ON-TRENT NORTH

	2001		1997		1992 notional	
Electorate and turnout	57,998	51.9	59,165	65.4	*61,250*	*73.6*
Conservative	5,676	18.8	7,798	20.2	*15,189*	*33.7*
Labour	17,460	58.0	25,190	65.1	*24,693*	*54.8*
Lib Dem	3,580	11.9	4,141	10.7	*4,718*	*10.5*
Anti–EU	–	–	1,537	4.0	–	–
Independent	3,399	11.3	–	–	–	–
Others	–		–		*466*	
MP	Joan Walley (Lab)		Joan Walley (Lab)		Joan Walley (Lab)	
Majority	11,784	39.1	17,392	45.0	*9,504*	*21.1*

The North constituency is based around two more of the Six Towns, Burslem (Bennett called it Bursley) and Tunstall (Turnhill), plus the Baddeley area to their east. Burslem, now cleaning off the industrial grime of centuries, is the location of Port Vale football club. The hilly town of Tunstall is perhaps best known now for being where singer Robbie Williams was born in February 1974. The two traditional towns have some of the poorest areas in Stoke-on-Trent, with four of the six city wards being in the worst-off 900 (out of 8,414) in England. The exceptions are the eastern suburbs, which although better off would not be mistaken for places where the rich and famous live. North extends a little beyond the city boundary to include a small area of the Staffordshire Moorlands council's area at Brown Edge and Endon. This is rural territory south of Biddulph and vastly better off than the city portion, but it only contributes a bit over 5,000 electors and poses no threat to the thumping Labour majority generated in the rest of the constituency.

North has generated interesting results in recent local elections. The Independents have done well here, winning three of the six wards in 2000 to Labour's two and one Liberal Democrat, but Labour were still ahead in the total vote with 33 per cent to 27 per cent for the Independents (who admittedly did not contest every ward). The Independent strength carried over into the general election as well, with Tunstall North councillor Lee Wanger (first elected to Stoke council in 1998) gaining an impressive 11.3 per cent of the vote and almost pushing the Lib Dems into fourth. However, in parliamentary terms North remains a very safe Labour seat (fewer than 100 are safer) despite its Independent tendencies. Labour really would have to do *Somethin' Stupid,* to quote the song popularised by Robbie Williams, to lose here.

STOKE-ON-TRENT SOUTH

	2001		1997		1992 actual	
Electorate and turnout	70,032	51.4	70,171	65.9	71,317	74.3
Conservative	8,877	24.6	10,342	22.4	19,471	36.7
Labour	19,366	53.8	28,645	62.0	26,380	49.8
Lib Dem	4,724	13.1	4,710	10.2	6,870	13.0
Anti–EU	–	–	1,103	2.4	–	–
Independent	1,703	4.7	–	–	–	–
BNP/ NF*	1,358	3.8	856 (2)	1.9	–	–
Others	–		580		291	
MP	George Stevenson (Lab)		George Stevenson (Lab)		George Stevenson (Lab)	
Majority	10,489	29.1	18,303	39.6	6,909	13.0

* BNP 2001, BNP and ND 1997

Stoke South is the nearest the city has to a marginal seat, although this status is of fairly recent vintage. It is based, like the other Stoke seats, on two Potteries towns. Longton was the most polluted and chaotic of the Six Towns when it was expanding – its landscape of chimneys, the filthy air and the squalid housing up against the factories led Bennett to compare 'Longshaw' to hell. It is now cleaner and tidier but still industrial and working class. Bennett's Five Towns omitted Fenton; it was a later Victorian sprawl lacking an identifiable centre, and he thought 'Five Towns' had a more euphonious sound to it.

Fenton in particular was strongly influenced by coal mining, and potteries were actually the second industry of the town a hundred years ago. Like other ex-mining areas in the midlands there has been a slow swing to the right in recent decades. South also includes neighbourhoods on the edge of the conurbation. Trentham Park to the south west is the most middle class residential ward in the city, and Meir Park in the south east is a mixture of council and owner-occupied housing. These two wards grew considerably in the 1980s while the population in the rest of the seat was unchanged or falling. The Conservatives edged closer to contention in 1987 but since then national trends have carried the seat away from them.

In a good year for them Labour can win every ward, but their local election performance has been in sharp decline. The Conservatives and Independents won three wards each in 2000, the Lib Dems one and Labour were wiped out; the Tories had a narrow 32-31 lead. Trentham Park went Independent, although it was Tory in 1999, proving the widespread appeal of the Stoke Independents in all sorts of area. In the general election the Labour vote dropped quite sharply, producing a 5 per cent swing to the Conservatives. South is still a safe Labour seat, but if the Conservatives come back strongly to national favour they might convert it into a proper marginal.

STONE

	2001		1997		1992 notional	
Electorate and turnout	68,847	66.3	67,756	78.3	66,426	83.8
Conservative	22,395	49.1	24,859	46.8	31,156	56.0
Labour	16,359	35.8	21,041	39.6	16,077	28.9
Lib Dem	6,888	15.1	6,392	12.0	7,554	13.6
Others	–		782 (2)		854	
MP	Bill Cash (Con)		Bill Cash (Con)		NEW SEAT	
Majority	6,036	13.2	3,818	7.2	15,079	27.1

Stone is a predominantly rural constituency in the centre of Staffordshire, forming a K-shaped tract with the linking part of the constituency being the small town of Stone lying between Stafford and Stoke-on-Trent. Much of the Stone constituency looks to Stafford as its main centre, and indeed the west of the new division was in a Stafford seat before 1997. Stafford's then MP, Bill Cash, wisely followed this portion of his old constituency and has a safe seat.

Stone's creation drew off the most Conservative areas of the former Stafford and Moorlands constituencies, with fatal consequences for the Conservatives defending those seats in 1997. Stone itself is the most Labour element of the seat and the largest town, with 49 per cent of the local vote in 2001, but it contributes only 11,500 electors. Eccleshall, Gnosall and a small rural area from Newcastle borough including the village of Loggerheads (which actually seems in agreement with the rest of the constituency) are all safely Tory components of the west side of Stone. Madeley is closer to Newcastle and more Labour-inclined. To the north east of Stone town is Staffordshire's Cheadle, a country town rather than a suburb, and the countryside around the Alton Towers amusement park. But for electoral thrills and spills Stone is not a constituency to set the heart racing.

TAMWORTH

	2001		1997		1992 notional	
Electorate and turnout	69,596	57.8	67,205	74.2	65,089	81.6
Conservative	15,124	37.6	18,312	36.7	26,209	49.4
Labour	19,722	49.0	25,808	51.8	20,804	39.2
Lib Dem	4,721	11.7	4,025	8.1	5,275	9.9
Anti–EU	683	1.7	1,532 (2)	3.1	–	–
Others	–		177		825	
MP	Brian Jenkins (Lab)		Brian Jenkins (Lab)		David Lightbown (Con)*	
					Staffordshire SE	
Majority	4,598	11.4	7,496	15.0	5,405	10.2

* Brian Jenkins (Lab) elected at April 1996 by–election.

Tamworth is known nationally for two things – pigs and the place where in 1834 Robert Peel announced his 'Tamworth Manifesto' and thereby founded the Conservative Party as it is now. Since 1974 it has formed the main element in three successive marginal seats and has so far always voted for the party with an overall national lead. Labour's gain in a 1996 by-election on an impressive swing was a portent of what was to happen nationally in 1997.

Tamworth began to expand from being a market town in the 1960s when it started to house Birmingham overspill tenants on estates built away from the old town centre. During the 1980s and 1990s growth continued, although this time the developments were privately built. Labour won all the Tamworth borough wards in the Staffordshire county elections in June 2001, which was a considerable turnaround since the May 2000 local elections when the party was badly defeated. Voting behaviour in Tamworth wards is quite uniform, hence a tendency for either Labour or the Conservatives to win everything or nothing. Labour had 51 per cent, to 33 per cent for the Conservatives, in the town – a 5,500 lead – in the 2001 county elections. Despite its recent growth Tamworth is too small to merit a seat all to itself and it takes 13,000 electors from neighbouring parts of the Lichfield district including Fazeley and a very Tory rural area. One ward produced a staggering 91 per cent Conservative vote in the 1999 local elections. The net effect of the additions trimmed back the Labour majority. As the 72nd most marginal Labour seat, the government could lose it and have a bare overall majority, but it is more likely that Tamworth will continue to vote for the national winner whoever that is.

Suffolk

	Conservative		Labour		Liberal Democrat		Others	
	Share of vote	Seats	Share of vote	Seats	Share of vote	Seats	Share of vote	Seats
2001	40.7	5	39.7	2	16.0	0	3.6	0
1997	37.6	5	40.2	2	17.6	0	4.6	0
1992	49.9	5	28.7	1	20.4	0	1.1	0
1987	52.5	6	23.2	0	23.6	0	0.6	0
1983	52.5	5	22.1	1	25.3	0	0.1	0

Suffolk is the southern county of the core of East Anglia; it is rather off the beaten track and even its tourist promotion material calls it 'the undiscovered corner of England'. Its principal town is Ipswich, but much of the acreage of the county is rural and agricultural. Despite this, farming accounts for only 4 per cent of the workforce of the county, less than a quarter the proportion employed in manufacturing. Excluding Ipswich and the other large built-up area around Lowestoft in the north, the agricultural element is larger, but it is still well under 10 per cent.

Suffolk is rather too far from London to be heavily under its influence, and except for Ipswich and – at a stretch – Sudbury and areas accessible to Diss, its transport links are inadequate to serve as much of a commuting base. Ipswich is the centre for most of the county, but parts in the west are quite close to Cambridge and more strongly linked with that city. The country areas in central Suffolk are deep, quiet and rather insular territory, and while the coast is probably its most picturesque area the peaceful river scenes in the south have inspired artists for centuries.

Such a heartland of old England – it was over 97 per cent white in the 1991 census – might be thought of as a Conservative stronghold, but recently Suffolk has been surprisingly marginal. None of the Conservative seats are as safe as the Labour outposts in Ipswich (regained 1992 after a lapse in 1987) and Waveney (gained in 1997 after nearly forty Conservative years). The reasons are partly that agricultural labourers on large farms are perfectly capable of voting for the left, although mechanisation has meant that there are fewer of them than after the war when Sudbury went Labour and Eye voted for a radical Liberal. Small farmers by contrast are overwhelmingly Conservative and always have been. Another reason has been that the towns are quite working class little places – Haverhill and Sudbury in particular have sprouted 'overspill' estates of expatriate Londoners in the postwar era which provide solid – if apathetic – Labour votes. The Conservatives survived a close call in 1997, despite being outpolled in the county: two more Tory seats would have fallen on a 2 per cent bigger swing in 1997, while all four would have gone if there was a 4 per cent bigger swing.

Suffolk did not join Norfolk in its high swing against Labour in 2001; its movement was very close to the national average. However, Labour did sag in the rural seats the party narrowly missed in 1997. Part of the problem was that the Labour vote in some of them, in the overspill areas of Haverhill and Sudbury, is distinctly poor working class 'core vote' which proved difficult to motivate in 2001, while the Suffolk seats are light on the educated, affluent professionals who formed many of Labour's new recruits of 2001. It seems probable that the future parliamentary politics of the county will continue to be Labour towns against Conservative country, although all of the seats have interesting aspects to them.

Local government

Suffolk county council has not returned to Conservative control, partly because it still includes Ipswich but also because the Conservatives did not do as well in the smaller towns as they did in Norfolk. The Tories also faced what looks very much like an electoral pact between Labour and the Liberal Democrats in 2001, which denied them five seats from the Lib Dems and one (maybe more) from Labour. Labour leads an the administration with 35 councillors, to 31 Conservatives, 12 Lib Dems and 2 others. Labour's base is Ipswich, with 14 of their number coming from there, but the party is strong in the other urban areas. The Conservatives and Lib Dems split the rural areas.

Suffolk district councils have some strong contenders for the most strangely named council in Britain. St. Edmundsbury is the counter-intuitive name for the authority covering Bury St. Edmunds and Haverhill; it is Conservative controlled with a fairly small majority, having been Labour-controlled at that party's high tide in 1995. Forest Heath is the anonymously titled council for the north west of the county, around Newmarket and Mildenhall; it is a strongly Conservative council where the Tories currently have 21 out of 25 councillors; they were the largest single party even in 1995. Babergh subtitles itself on signs 'South Suffolk', which is where it is, around Sudbury and Hadleigh; the largest group are Independents although the Liberal Democrats have been gaining and are only just behind.

The more normally named Mid Suffolk, around Stowmarket and providing many of the electors of the Bury St. Edmunds seat, is a hung council where the Conservatives are the largest party but fell well short of an overall majority in 1999. Suffolk Coastal, which includes Felixstowe, is Conservative controlled with a minority Liberal Democrat and Labour presence. All these councils elect every four years, but the urban boroughs elect annually. Waveney (Lowestoft, Beccles and Southwold), unlike its northern neighbour Great Yarmouth, remained loyal to Labour throughout the 1997 parliament though was lost to no overall control in 2002. Ipswich has been Labour, pretty solidly and uncontroversially, since 1979 despite the town's adventures in parliamentary elections.

Boundary review

Having gained a seat in the 1990s, there is no need yet for another although the average electorate of Suffolk's seats is a little high. The commission may wish to switch some wards around to equalise electorates which is unlikely to have much partisan effect – although if Bury St. Edmunds loses much rural territory Labour will benefit a bit.

BURY ST. EDMUNDS

	2001		1997		1992 notional	
Electorate and turnout	76,146	66.0	74,017	75.0	70,181	79.9
Conservative	21,850	43.5	21,290	38.3	25,742	45.9
Labour	19,347	38.5	20,922	37.7	14,565	26.0
Lib Dem	6,998	13.9	10,102	18.2	15,097	26.9
Anti–EU	831	1.7	2,939	5.3	–	–
Others	1,231 (2)		272		666	
MP	David Ruffley (Con)		David Ruffley (Con)		NEW SEAT	
Majority	2,503	5.0	368	0.7	10,645	19.0

'BSE' was good news for the Conservatives in only one sense in 1997 – Bury St. Edmunds stayed Conservative by a perilous margin of 368 votes. Survival in 1997 meant that the Conservatives had a good chance of holding on in 2001 – the trend across the country was for the most marginal incumbents of the main parties to strengthen their position in 2001. David Ruffley's is still the most marginal seat in Suffolk, but he can breathe a little easier now.

There are two main towns in the constituency. 28,000 of the seat's electors are in Bury St Edmunds itself. It is an ecclesiastical, quiet place, with a fine mediaeval centre boasting England's smallest pub. It is reasonably accessible for Cambridge, which boosts house prices. Labour's main vote in the constituency comes from Bury, which produced a 45-32 Labour lead (around 3,000 votes) in the county elections. The other town, Stowmarket, is a market town on the A14 between Bury and Ipswich with around 11,000 electors, and in 2001 it was a little more Conservative, although Labour still had a small lead. The Conservative majority was built up in the rural remainder of the seat in mid Suffolk.

The official Conservatives did well to increase their majority in 2001, particularly considering the independent challenge of Mike Brundle, the former Tory leader on St. Edmundsbury council, who polled 651 votes (1.3 per cent) on a traditionalist platform. Bury St. Edmunds remains a marginal seat, although Labour have now missed two good chances to gain it.

IPSWICH

	2001		*1997*		*1992 notional*	
Electorate and turnout	68,198	57.0	66,947	72.2	*68,148*	*79.0*
Conservative	11,871	30.5	15,048	31.1	*23,288*	*43.3*
Labour	19,952	51.3	25,484	52.7	*23,623*	*43.9*
Lib Dem	5,904	15.2	5,881	12.2	*6,135*	*11.4*
Anti–EU	624	1.6	1,845 (2)	3.8	*–*	*–*
Others	522 (2)		107		*769*	
MP	Jamie Cann (Lab)		Jamie Cann (Lab)		Jamie Cann (Lab)	
Majority	8,081	20.8	10,436	21.6	*335*	*0.6*

Parliamentary by-election 22 November 2001: Labour 11,811 (43.4), Conservative 7,794 (28.4), Lib Dem 6,146 (22.4), Christian People's Alliance 581 (2.1), Anti-EU 276 (1.0), 4 Others 727. Electorate 68,244, Turnout 40.2%. MP: Chris Mole (Lab), Majority 4,087 (14.9).

Ipswich is a large and rather independent town, an aspirant for city status and the centre for a considerable rural hinterland. Its centre is bustling, with handsome market buildings indicating a prosperous history. The town has docks along the river Orwell and manufacturing industry concentrated in the southern area. Labour are strongest in the wards in the south and south west of the town, such as Priory Park, Chantry, Sprites and Bridge, and in the centre. In 2001 the only non-Labour wards in the town were two suburban areas - Conservative Bixley to the east and Lib Dem St. Margarets to the north.

Despite its current Labour strength, Ipswich has had a peculiar marginal history over the last thirty years. Conservative Ernle Money gained it by 13 votes in 1970 and had a swing in his favour in February 1974, but lost to Labour's Ken Weetch in October 1974. Weetch then held the seat well in Labour's disaster years of 1979 and 1983, but lost it to the Tories against the national trend in 1987. Jamie Cann won it back on a small swing in 1992, and held it comfortably in 1997 and 2001. Cann died in October 2001 and Ipswich was the scene of the first by-election of the new parliament. His Labour successor Chris Mole, former leader of Suffolk County Council, had little difficulty in stepping into his shoes. Labour's vote sagged a bit, but disturbingly for the Conservatives, they polled their worst share ever as the Lib Dems came up a bit in this traditionally two-party town. The by-election also disappointed those commentators who would have liked to say that the election attracted fewer voters than the number of spectators who saw Ipswich Town's European football match the same evening.

Ipswich is capable of producing volatile electoral behaviour. In the 1999 Euro elections Labour led by only 1.4 per cent, and in the 2000 local elections the Conservatives did particularly well. Surprises can never be ruled out in Ipswich, but for now it seems like a reliable Labour prospect.

SUFFOLK CENTRAL and IPSWICH NORTH

	2001		*1997*		*1992 notional*	
Electorate and turnout	74,200	63.5	70,388	75.0	*66,188*	*80.1*
Conservative	20,924	44.4	22,493	42.6	*29,610*	*55.8*
Labour	17,455	37.1	18,955	35.9	*10,980*	*20.7*
Lib Dem	7,593	16.1	10,886	20.6	*11,604*	*21.9*
Anti–EU	1,132	2.4	–	–	–	–
Others	–		489		*850*	
MP	Michael Lord (Con)		Michael Lord (Con)		Michael Lord (Con)	
					Suffolk Central	
Majority	3,469	7.4	3,538	6.7	*18,006*	*33.9*

The Central Suffolk portion, a bit over half the constituency, is deeply rural, agricultural and quite sparsely populated. There are a few market towns – Framlingham, Debenham, and Eye up in the north west of the seat. It, like Norfolk, has some remnants of the agricultural workers' unionised Labour vote. The Eye constituency produced a remarkable display of personal loyalty in the 1950s when former Liberal MP Edgar Granville transferred to Labour in 1955 and carried most of his voters with him. Now, however, the Conservatives lead in the area, although when Lib Dem and Labour voters unite they are capable of winning or running the Tories close in most of this area in county elections.

The north Ipswich portion of the seat, with 21,000 electors, returned a Labour majority in 2001. Two of the four wards, White House and Whitton, are safe Labour areas but had turnouts of approximately 50 per cent in 2001. The other two, Broom Hill and Castle Hill, were very marginal Labour wards in the county elections, in the latter case thanks to a Lib Dem failure to stand. In the local elections the north Ipswich portion provided a Labour lead of about 1,900. Another 10,000 or so electors are around Kesgrave, a growing area north east of Ipswich and effectively part of the town's built-up area; this seat was Liberal Democrat in the 2001 county elections.

In the general election, of course, there were no mutual withdrawals by Labour and Lib Dem, so the Conservatives prevailed against divided opposition. Labour, however, have been gathering strength here and achieved a very respectable showing in 2001 against Michael Lord, one of the more obscure but senior members of parliament.

SUFFOLK COASTAL

	2001		1997		1992 notional	
Electorate and turnout	76,823	65.6	74,219	75.8	70,061	81.8
Conservative	21,847	43.3	21,696	38.6	30,030	52.4
Labour	17,521	34.8	18,442	32.8	13,325	23.3
Lib Dem	9,192	18.2	12,036	21.4	13,008	22.7
Anti–EU	1,847	3.7	3,416	6.1	–	–
Others	–		666 (2)		921	
MP	John Gummer (Con)		John Gummer (Con)		John Gummer (Con)	
Majority	4,326	8.6	3,254	5.8	16,705	29.2

Suffolk is a rather mysterious county to many outsiders, and its countryside is mostly off the beaten track. The exception, however, is the coastal strip from Woodbridge up to Southwold, which has been 'discovered' by Londoners with enough money to afford weekend cottages and people looking for somewhere to retire. The towns are attractive little places, yachting havens and minor resorts of the kind that have not deteriorated in the way places like Great Yarmouth have done. The villages inland seem more carefully preserved than the muddy agricultural villages of central Suffolk. The town of Woodbridge is on the river Deben and within easy commuting distance of Ipswich. Aldeburgh is known to music buffs for its festival which has spilled over to Saxmundham, a little inland. To political historians Coastal is also the successor seat to the pre-1832 rotten borough of Dunwich, which fell into the sea because of coastal erosion but maintained its representation. Its freeholders met every election at a cliff top and cast their votes.

The main town of Suffolk Coastal is Felixstowe (19,000 electors), originally a resort town whose docks have grown considerably in recent decades – employers liked the fact that it was not part of the National Dock Labour Scheme. Parts of the town are Labour-voting, but overall it is surprisingly Conservative (perhaps reflecting its free market origins) – its three core wards in the 2001 local elections produced a 400-vote Tory lead. The smaller towns up the coast have a high Conservative vote, but in the 2001 locals the apparent Lib-Lab electoral pact enabled opposing parties to get quite close or even win everywhere except Southwold. Labour tried quite hard in the 2001 general election, thinking that they had the off-chance of gaining Coastal on the basis of national polls, but despite their gains the Conservatives picked up a little more and the seat is fairly safe. It seems appropriate that this attractive part of the world should be represented by an environmentally-aware Conservative, former Cabinet minister John Gummer.

SUFFOLK SOUTH

	2001		1997		1992 notional	
Electorate and turnout	68,456	66.2	67,335	77.2	65,382	80.6
Conservative	18,748	41.4	19,402	37.3	27,036	51.3
Labour	13,667	30.2	15,227	29.3	11,504	21.8
Lib Dem	11,296	24.9	14,395	27.7	13,828	26.3
Anti–EU	1,582	3.5	2,740	5.3	–	–
Others	–		211		319	
MP	Tim Yeo (Con)		Tim Yeo (Con)		Tim Yeo (Con)	
Majority	5,081	11.2	4,175	8.0	13,208	25.1

Suffolk South covers nearly all of the county's southern border, consisting of the north bank of the river Stour and territory to its north. It is, like several in Suffolk, predominantly rural. Sudbury, the largest settlement in Suffolk South, is an attractive little market town – the birthplace of Gainsborough – just north of the Essex border, although like many towns in eastern England it was swollen by overspill developments between the 1950s and 1970s. It has spawned a satellite town, Great Cornard, as well as its own estates. The Sudbury urban area, with over 15,000 electors, gave Labour a majority of a bit over 1,000 in the local elections. Labour lost its best area of the old Suffolk South in the boundary changes when Haverhill was transferred to the new Suffolk West seat.

The rest of the constituency is rural, except for the smaller town of Hadleigh. Some of it, around the Stour valley, is rather Conservative, but the Liberal Democrats are active in local elections in the area and have made recent progress, winning most of the county council wards in the constituency in 2001. It was also their best constituency in the general election in Suffolk, although they were still third; as in other areas Labour attracted a lot of the local Lib Dem vote. The Conservatives prevailed against disunited opposition with a rather low share of the vote; it is numerically their safest seat in Suffolk. Sudbury was one of Labour's more surprising gains in 1945 but they seem unlikely to repeat the performance.

SUFFOLK WEST

	2001		1997		1992 notional	
Electorate and turnout	70,129	60.5	68,638	71.5	67,074	78.8
Conservative	20,201	47.6	20,081	40.9	28,455	53.8
Labour	15,906	37.5	18,214	37.1	12,692	24.0
Lib Dem	5,017	11.8	6,892	14.0	11,283	21.4
Anti–EU	1,321	3.1	3,724	7.6	–	–
Others	–		171		419	
MP	Richard Spring (Con)		Richard Spring (Con)		Richard Spring (Con)	
					Bury St. Edmunds	
Majority	4,295	10.1	1,867	3.8	15,763	29.8

The largest town in Suffolk West is Haverhill, although it is an anomalous part of the constituency. In 1957 Haverhill was the first town to sign an agreement with London to accept 'overspill' and its population rose from around 4,000 to 14,000 by 1974 mainly through the construction of council estates. The local accent retains a strong trace of working class London and an eels, pie and mash shop sits proudly in the main street. Employment for the displaced Londoners came in the form of a large industrial estate including a plastic factory. Its growth did not fulfil its early projections (it is now around 20,000 in population) and some of Haverhill's estates are now unpleasant places by any comparison. Haverhill is the principal source of the Labour vote.

The rest of the constituency is a different matter. Haverhill's surroundings are attractive, and the other centre of the constituency is very different. Newmarket is a single-industry town based around horse racing, with most of the sport's central organisations including the National Stud and the Jockey Club found here; jockeys seem to be a significant proportion of the town's population. Newmarket votes Conservative, but not overwhelmingly, and the racing interest is an important Conservative-supporting element in local affairs. North east of Newmarket are several towns with a strong armed forces, particularly RAF, presence – Lakenheath and Mildenhall bases have residential areas for service people and support staff and formed a quite marginal ward in the 2001 local elections.

Labour did well to run the Conservatives close in the new seat in 1997, but the Tories managed a strong increase in their share of the vote in 2001 and it is now their 44th most marginal seat. It would take an election result considerably worse than 1997 or 2001 for them to lose it now.

WAVENEY

	2001		1997		1992 notional	
Electorate and turnout	77,613	60.8	75,420	74.6	74,320	81.2
Conservative	15,361	32.6	19,393	34.5	28,352	47.0
Labour	23,914	50.7	31,486	56.0	23,976	39.8
Lib Dem	5,370	11.4	5,054	9.0	7,728	12.8
Anti–EU	1,097	2.3	–	–	–	–
Others	1,425 (2)		318		265	
MP	Bob Blizzard (Lab)		Bob Blizzard (Lab)		David Porter (Con)	
Majority	8,553	18.1	12,093	21.5	4,376	7.3

Waveney is the constituency based on the town of Lowestoft (population 58,000), in the north east of Suffolk. It is not far from Great Yarmouth but seems in much better condition; there are deprived areas of Lowestoft, particularly in the town centre and the inner north, but nothing as grim as southern Yarmouth. Areas of Lowestoft are quite staid, Victorian villas such as Gunton. The town was originally primarily a fishing port, but it has other port functions and also a small resort area. The constituency goes inland along the river Waveney to the little towns of Beccles and Bungay and a small rural area. The Broads reach into the urban area at Oulton Broad. There are some safe Labour wards in Lowestoft, such as St. Margaret's and Normanston, but many of the wards are competitive in local elections when the party is not winning overwhelmingly.

The whole constituency is marginal, although it has tended to remain with the same party for quite long periods (Labour 1945-59, Conservative 1959-97) despite national swings of the pendulum. It was the base of Jim Prior's political career. Now it is the fiefdom of Bob Blizzard, who had previously led the local authority. He swept in with a very high share of the vote in 1997 which slipped back in 2001, but the seat is at best semi-marginal: it is Labour's 130th most vulnerable and if the party lost that much ground they would probably be the second party in a hung parliament.

Surrey

	Conservative		Labour		Liberal Democrat		Others	
	Share of vote	Seats	Share of vote	Seats	Share of vote	Seats	Share of vote	Seats
2001	47.6	10	21.8	0	27.0	1	3.6	0
1997	46.2	11	22.3	0	24.5	0	7.0	0
1992	59.9	11	13.6	0	25.5	0	1.0	0
1987	60.6	11	11.4	0	27.6	0	0.4	0
1983	59.4	11	11.0	0	28.6	0	1.0	0

Surrey lies just south of Greater London and the capital has a pervasive influence over life in the county. In the 1960s a large built-up part of Surrey became part of Greater London, including Kingston, Croydon and Richmond, and is dealt with in the chapter London – Outer South. The parts which remained were small town and rural areas, plus one or two fringe areas of London sprawl which managed to persuade the Macmillan government not to merge them with London. The current county of Surrey consists of some of the wealthiest parts of the country and overall it is very prosperous – 1998 average weekly earnings were £487, below only London and Berkshire. There are several exclusive little areas such as Virginia Water and St. George's Hill which are occupied by the very rich – successful entrepreneurs, directors of large companies, semi-retired rock stars, lottery winners and the like. More common, though, is ordinary wealth, from executives commuting to London from the classic 'stock-broker belt' and more modest small business success. There is some distinction between the east – more sparsely populated with some agriculture and population in smaller towns – and the bustling west around the A3 and M3, but it is the distinction between different kinds of affluence rather than a social divide. The east is more traditionally English and comfortable, while the west has some American features like brash consumer culture, high car ownership and strong evangelical churches.

Surrey is not entirely rural and suburban. It has several large towns, notably Guildford, Reigate and Woking, each with less affluent sides to them. However, these relatively working class areas are not poor as the term is understood in the inner cities and have been helped by the general buoyancy of Surrey's economy. There are some agricultural areas, particularly in the south and east of the county, but farming is but a minor element in the local economy. Most of the countryside comprises hills and woods – Surrey is the most wooded county in England. Surrey is the most Conservative county in England, with the highest Tory share of the vote in 2001 and the strongest history of Tory parliamentary representation. Labour won the Spelthorne constituency (then in Middlesex and containing part of what is now Hayes and Harlington) in 1945, but other than that this area has been exclusively Tory since Liberal gains in the 1906 landslide were reversed in January 1910. While Labour have had areas of strength in towns such as Reigate none of the towns is quite big enough for an entirely urban parliamentary constituency, and the Labour patches have never been enough to prevail over the very Conservative surrounding areas. The unbroken record of Conservative wins survived even the 1997 rout, but was destroyed in June 2001 with the victory of the Liberal Democrats in Guildford. Surrey South West (around Farnham) nearly went to the Liberal Democrats as well, while the Conservatives have also had to look over their shoulders at Spelthorne, where there is a substantial Labour vote. It is just about possible to imagine the Lib Dems moving up to challenge in Woking, but everywhere else in the county will probably be Conservative to the last ditch.

The UK Independence Party won 3.2 per cent in 2001 and the combined Eurosceptic parties won 5.6 per cent in 1997 in Surrey. These were surprisingly high votes for anti-European parties, considering that the county has no more pensioners than the national average; the over 60s are the core of the anti-EU vote. This indicates the presence of an ultra-conservative strand in Surrey politics, which was not a temporary response to the troubles of the 1992-97 government. Conservative attitudes are deep rooted, and part of the appeal of moving to Surrey is the ability, in parts of it, to look around and imagine that little has changed in old England for decades.

Local government
Surrey county council is back under secure Conservative control, after an unprecedented lapse in 1993-97. The Conservatives won 51 seats in 2001, to six Labour (two in Reigate, the others scattered), 13 Lib Dems (three Guildford, two Farnham, two Dorking, two near Surbiton and the rest scattered) and six others (mainly Residents from Epsom & Ewell).

The Conservatives now exercise control with large majorities in Spelthorne (the only authority where Labour can offer a serious challenge), Tandridge in east Surrey (where the Lib Dems could poll well during the 1990s), Runnymede (where there were, unusually, no Lib Dem councillors on the eve of the 2002 annual elections) and Reigate & Banstead where the Liberal Democrats have lost a lot of ground in local elections.

Waverley (south west Surrey) is, like the parliamentary constituency, hard fought between Conservatives and Lib Dems, with the former currently having the upper hand (31 seats, to 24 Lib Dems and 2 Labour in 2001). The Conservatives have nearly retaken Mole Valley (Dorking area) after a period in the mid 1990s when the Lib Dems were the leading party. Woking is a perennial hung council, with annual elections and areas of considerable strength for all three parties – both Tories and Lib Dems can hope to gain control in future elections. Guildford is also hung, with the Lib Dems the largest party – there was little actual change despite the Lib Dems losing their one-seat majority from the 1995 elections. There are two councils where Resident political parties are a strong force. They have run Epsom & Ewell since 1936 and have a large majority; in Elmbridge (the area around Esher, Walton and Weybridge) locally based resident parties are a more recently established presence. They gained an overall majority at the 2002 annual elections, having previously been in coalition with the Lib Dems.

Boundary review
There will be no change to six of the county's eleven seats and only very minor alterations to the rest – Guildford and Surrey SW are realigned with new ward boundaries, and one ward is moved from Epsom & Ewell to Reigate.

EPSOM and EWELL

	2001		1997		1992 notional	
Electorate and turnout	74,266	62.8	73,222	74.0	72,957	80.0
Conservative	22,430	48.1	24,717	45.6	35,621	61.1
Labour	12,350	26.5	13,192	24.3	8,789	15.1
Lib Dem	10,316	22.1	12,380	22.8	13,561	23.2
Anti–EU	1,547	3.3	2,899 (2)	5.4	–	–
Others	–		993 (2)		372	
MP	Chris Grayling (Con)		Archie Hamilton (Con)		Archie Hamilton (Con)	
Majority	10,080	21.6	11,525	21.3	22,060	37.8

The borough of Epsom and Ewell is run by a local coalition of Residents' Associations (registered as a political party), who have been in control since 1936. There are no local Conservative councillors as such, but a few Labour and Lib Dem representatives. But the RA is not a front for Conservatism – it regularly takes on and beats Conservative candidates in county elections, and people who vote Conservative in general elections are only slightly more inclined to vote RA locally than supporters of other parties.

Epsom and Ewell are both effectively suburbs of London and could well have ended up in Greater London. Epsom's famous well is incongruously sited on a little green in a housing estate. Most of the seat (including areas such as Stoneleigh) forms a continuous suburban area with the neighbouring London borough of Sutton and has similar social and architectural characteristics, although Sutton's adherence to Lib Dem voting has no echo south of the border. It is almost completely without a manual working class population. The constituency also includes some areas of the neighbouring authorities of Mole Valley (the Ashtead area between Epsom and Leatherhead) and Reigate and Banstead (Tattenham and the strangely named but very affluent Nork ward), which bolster the Conservative vote.

There are only 33 safer Tory seats. Voters in Epsom and Ewell gave strong support to balding right winger Chris Grayling in 2001, a sign that as far as people here are concerned there has been little wrong with the outcome of the last two Conservative leadership elections.

ESHER and WALTON

	2001		1997		1992 notional	
Electorate and turnout	73,541	61.9	72,236	74.3	71,598	76.5
Conservative	22,296	49.0	26,747	49.8	33,237	60.7
Labour	10,758	23.6	12,219	22.8	9,513	17.4
Lib Dem	10,241	22.5	10,937	20.4	12,013	21.9
Anti–EU	2,236	4.9	3,462 (2)	6.4	–	–
Others	–		302		–	
MP	Ian Taylor (Con)		Ian Taylor (Con)		Ian Taylor (Con)	
					Esher	
Majority	11,538	25.3	14,528	27.1	21,224	38.8

Esher and Walton is the most up-market constituency in Surrey, which is saying something. According to the 1991 census there was only one constituency in the country, Kensington & Chelsea, which had a higher proportion of its population in the highest socio-economic groups. Esher itself is an elite area, and the other elements of the seat strung along the south western railway lines out of Waterloo are not much less affluent – Hersham, Cobham and Stoke D'Abernon, plus Molesey just across from Hampton Court Palace. Walton-on-Thames is a bit more mixed. The anti-Tory vote is split down the middle in general elections. In county elections Labour can win the West Molesey ward and came near to winning Walton in the 2001 elections, while the Lib Dems' best areas are around Claygate and Thames Ditton just across the border from their Surbiton stronghold; Cobham, Oxshott and south Walton are, on the other hand, extremely Conservative. In Elmbridge district elections various residents' associations have recently become dominant.

There are only 16 seats with a larger Conservative percentage majority, and by any stretch of the imagination this is a Tory stronghold. The MP, Ian Taylor, is a strongly pro-European moderate who resigned from Hague's front bench over the Euro and supported Ken Clarke in 1997 and 2001. The UKIP vote was rather high for a Home Counties seat, which presumably reflected some hard-line Tory disaffection with Taylor. However, Taylor's personality and political ideas probably kept some voters loyal to him who would have otherwise voted Labour or Lib Dem.

GUILDFORD

	2001		1997		1992 notional	
Electorate and turnout	76,302	62.7	76,301	74.6	76,323	77.6
Conservative	19,820	41.4	24,230	42.5	32,820	55.4
Labour	6,558	13.7	9,945	17.5	6,732	11.4
Lib Dem	20,358	42.6	19,439	34.1	19,478	32.9
Anti–EU	736	1.5	3,050 (2)	5.4	–	–
Others	370		294		229	
MP	Sue Doughty (LD)		Nick St Aubyn (Con)		David Howell (Con)	
Majority	538	1.1	4,791	8.4	13,342	22.5

The loss of Guildford was a shattering personal experience for its inoffensive and relatively new MP Nick St Aubyn, but it was also one of the most startling results of an election where the usual pattern was for no change. Conservatives still shake their heads and wonder how they managed to lose Guildford.

Guildford is bustling and prosperous, and large enough and far enough from London not to be wholly dependent on commuting. The town houses many of the central features of Surrey –its largest shopping centre, its only cathedral and its university, but it is not yet the county town. Surrey County Council continues, anomalously, to meet in Kingston-upon-Thames but plans to move to Guildford soon. Less welcome is the prospect of an enormous incinerator near the town, which overshadowed the 2001 elections despite the major candidates both opposing it. The remainder of the constituency is of a different character. There are little commuter villages just outside Guildford, such as Worplesdon and Shalford (the base of the new MP Sue Doughty), and a stretch of dense woodland beyond which is the anonymous little town of Cranleigh and neighbouring Ewhurst.

The town area in Guildford is the weakest part of the constituency for the Conservatives; it voted 34 per cent Conservative, 22 per cent Labour (who won the West ward) and 44 per cent Lib Dem in the 2001 county elections. In the general election the Lib Dems were probably further ahead because of tactical voting. The section outside the town produces a Conservative lead in local elections, but it is of the order of 50-35 rather than being truly overwhelming.

The Conservatives were confident of winning in 2001, and were surprised to find that the decline in the anti-EU vote did not benefit them. On the other hand, Labour were squeezed and there were some Tory losses to the Lib Dems who increased their vote substantially. The Tories will be desperate to reverse their humiliation here, and need overturn only a 538 majority (the fifth most vulnerable Lib Dem seat). However, the Lib Dems now have the advantage of incumbency and a not negligible Labour base from which to seek tactical support. Guildford will be one of the key constituencies in the 2005/6 election.

MOLE VALLEY

	2001		1997		1992 notional	
Electorate and turnout	68,316	68.9	69,529	78.4	70,500	81.6
Conservative	23,790	50.5	26,178	48.0	35,313	61.4
Labour	7,837	16.6	8,057	14.8	5,386	9.4
Lib Dem	13,637	29.0	15,957	29.3	16,486	28.6
Anti–EU	1,333	2.8	2,859 (2)	5.2	–	–
Others	475		1,473 (2)		373	
MP	Paul Beresford (Con)		Paul Beresford (Con)		Kenneth Baker (Con)	
Majority	10,153	21.6	10,221	18.7	18,827	32.7

Mole Valley is the picturesque name for the largest constituency (in area) in Surrey. The largest towns are Dorking and Leatherhead, along the actual valley of the river Mole, but much of the acreage comprises the Surrey hills. It is a surprisingly rural seat with some remote corners and has the largest retired population of any of the Surrey seats. Dorking, an old fashioned coaching town, in particular has Liberal Democrat tendencies – they won 49 per cent of the county election vote here in 2001, but the Leatherhead area is more Conservative.

The parliamentary constituency also has some more traditional commuterland at Effingham and Send near Guildford, which formed the most Conservative element of the constituency in 2001 with the party's local election candidates winning around 60 per cent of the vote. Not all of the local Lib Dem vote came across in the general election, and – rather unusually – the Conservatives seemed to have gained slightly more than Labour from this factor in Mole Valley. This is a very safe Conservative seat – there are only 34 which are safer.

REIGATE

	2001		1997		1992 notional	
Electorate and turnout	65,618	60.2	64,759	74.4	64,307	78.8
Conservative	18,875	47.8	21,123	43.8	29,148	57.5
Labour	10,850	27.5	13,382	27.8	8,870	17.5
Lib Dem	8,330	21.1	9,615	20.0	12,208	24.1
Anti–EU	1,062	2.7	3,642 (2)	7.6	–	–
Others	357		412		441	
MP	Crispin Blunt (Con)		Crispin Blunt (Con)		George Gardiner (Con) (Ref)	
Majority	8,025	20.3	7,741	16.1	16,940	33.4

Reigate, with Redhill to the east, forms a significant urban centre in east Surrey with a population of over 50,000. It sits on the main line between Croydon and Gatwick just south of the North Downs. There is some internal variety in the Reigate constituency. The east side of Reigate is quite poor, for Surrey (although you wouldn't mistake it for an inner city slum), but there are some high-class areas in the north of the town. The town wards were 40 per cent Conservative to 30 per cent each for Labour and Lib Dem in 2001, a sign that there is some political diversity too.

The rest of the seat stretches up to the Greater London border across from Coulsdon and Sutton, and this is where the Conservative preponderance is to be found in wealthy villages like Banstead, Tadworth, Kingswood and Chipstead on their own eccentric little commuter branch line. The Banstead South county ward was over 60 per cent Conservative in 2001.

Labour's best chance to win Reigate was in 1997, when the deselected incumbent Sir George Gardiner stood for the Referendum Party. But despite the divided loyalties in the Conservative Association, Gardiner under his new label did not attract all that much more support than his fellow Referendum candidates elsewhere in Surrey. The 2001 election saw no significant change, except that most of Gardiner's vote returned to the Tories. Crispin Blunt, who commented that you could put up a donkey as the Conservative candidate in Reigate and still win, was revealed to have penetrating political judgement as far as the psephology of Reigate is concerned. There are only 43 safer Conservative seats.

RUNNYMEDE and WEYBRIDGE

	2001		1997		1992 notional	
Electorate and turnout	75,569	56.1	72,123	71.5	71,478	79.0
Conservative	20,646	48.7	25,051	48.6	34,645	61.4
Labour	12,286	29.0	15,176	29.4	9,004	16.0
Lib Dem	6,924	16.3	8,397	16.3	11,905	21.1
Anti–EU	1,332	3.1	2,775 (2)	5.4	–	–
Others	1,238		162		878	
MP	Philip Hammond (Con)		Philip Hammond (Con)		Geoffrey Pattie (Con)	
					Chertsey & Walton	
Majority	8,360	19.7	9,875	19.2	22,740	40.3

The borough of Runnymede is based around Chertsey and Egham. Although these are the largest towns the borough is known for its less populated areas – Runnymede meadows by the Thames, where the Magna Carta was signed and more recently a little square of territory given to the United States as a memorial for John Kennedy. Runnymede's most famous residential areas are the exclusive neighbourhoods of Virginia Water and Wentworth, home to General Pinochet during his arrest in Britain; it was said at the time that the General was a bit too much of a left winger to join the local golf club. Egham, across the Thames from Staines, can boast the gothic splendour of the Royal Holloway College building of the University of London.

Weybridge, from the Elmbridge district, is a suitable fit with the rest of the seat. It is an affluent commuter town between Woking and Esher with its own exclusive enclave of St. George's Hill and very low levels of social deprivation. Nowhere in the constituency, except a small part of Chertsey, could be described as poor; it is best described as thoroughly middle class with the occasional ultra-rich element.

This is a very safe Conservative seat, even for Surrey – the Tories led comfortably even in the disastrous 1995 local elections. Labour has some support in Chertsey in particular and are only completely negligible in Weybridge; the Lib Dems are not much of a force anywhere except Weybridge.

SPELTHORNE

	2001		1997		1992 actual	
Electorate and turnout	68,731	60.8	70,562	73.6	69,344	80.4
Conservative	18,851	45.1	23,306	44.9	32,627	58.5
Labour	15,589	37.3	19,833	38.2	12,784	22.9
Lib Dem	6,156	14.7	6,821	13.1	9,202	16.5
Anti–EU	1,198	2.9	1,957 (2)	3.8	–	–
Others	–		248		1,113 (3)	
MP	David Wilshire (Con)		David Wilshire (Con)		David Wilshire (Con)	
Majority	3,262	7.8	3,473	6.7	19,843	35.6

Spelthorne is the umbrella name for a number of towns and suburbs that have run together into an urbanised area which is not all that different to outer London neighbourhoods just across the border such as Feltham and Twickenham. It is on the north bank of the Thames, and until the 1960s was part of Middlesex. When Middlesex was abolished Spelthorne managed, rather illogically, to avoid incorporation into Greater London and ended up in Surrey instead. Staines is the largest town in Spelthorne but it also includes Ashford, Shepperton (known for its film studios and its resident author J.G. Ballard) and Sunbury at the start of the M3. Spelthorne is the southern hinterland of Heathrow and 13 per cent of its working population are employed there.

Staines has recently acquired fame as the fictional home of Ali G., who almost certainly doesn't vote. Spelthorne's ethnic minority population is only 3.4 per cent, although whether Ali G. would count is debatable. His West Staines is the more Conservative part of town, although it is marginal in a good Labour year, while east Staines is more consistently Labour. Labour's real strength in the seat is at council-built Stanwell, north of Staines jammed between Heathrow and some large reservoirs. Sunbury has some Liberal Democrats, a fair proportion of whom seem to vote Labour in general elections.

If Labour are ever going to get a seat in Surrey, it would be this one, but it is still a tough seat for them. Spelthorne voted Labour by only 0.5 per cent in the 1995 local elections and it is their 19th target from the Conservatives – it seems unlikely that the Conservatives will do badly enough to lose it.

SURREY EAST

	2001		1997		1992 notional	
Electorate and turnout	74,338	63.3	73,224	74.6	71,659	81.6
Conservative	24,706	52.5	27,389	50.1	35,676	61.1
Labour	8,994	19.1	11,573	21.2	6,135	10.5
Lib Dem	11,503	24.4	12,296	22.5	15,704	26.9
Anti–EU	1,846	3.9	3,225 (2)	5.9	–	–
Others	–		173		919	
MP	Peter Ainsworth (Con)		Peter Ainsworth (Con)		Peter Ainsworth (Con)	
Majority	13,203	28.1	15,093	27.6	19,972	34.2

The east of Surrey is much less bustling and built-up than the west, and supports two constituencies with a substantial genuinely rural element – Mole Valley and this seat. Surrey East has no single centre to it, but rather several small and rather sleepy commuter towns such as Caterham, Warlingham and Oxted set amid hilly countryside studded with little villages. The first two are effectively extensions of the suburbia of Croydon South, while Oxted is further out and a bit more independent. Sleepy is not a word that can be used to describe the other town in the seat, Horley – it sits right by Gatwick Airport. While there are no ultra-exclusive areas of the kind found in west Surrey, the entire constituency is bathed in a comfortable, secure prosperity.

As might be expected, Surrey East is very Conservative – after the 2001 election it was the ninth safest Tory seat in the land. In the 2001 county elections all its wards were Conservative with at least 45 per cent of the vote. On occasion, though, the Lib Dems can score well in local elections – in 1995 they even took a nine-point lead over the Conservatives – but there is no threat to the Tories in a general election.

SURREY HEATH

	2001		1997		1992 notional	
Electorate and turnout	75,858	59.5	73,813	74.1	71,492	78.4
Conservative	22,401	49.7	28,231	51.6	35,731	63.7
Labour	9,640	21.4	11,511	21.0	6,326	11.3
Lib Dem	11,582	25.7	11,944	21.8	12,977	23.1
Anti–EU	1,479	3.3	3,038 (2)	5.6	–	–
Others	–		–		1,035	
MP	Nick Hawkins (Con)		Nick Hawkins (Con)		Michael Grylls (Con) Surrey North West	
Majority	10,819	24.0	16,287	29.8	22,754	40.6

The largest town in Surrey Heath is Camberley, which has a population of 46,000. Camberley, with Frimley, Mytchett and Ash, is Surrey's part of the literal military-industrial complex running from Sandhurst in Berkshire to Aldershot in Hampshire. There are several army bases around the place – much of the heathland is off-limits as military land – and the Royal Military Academy is in the town. Farnborough's aviation complex is a couple of miles away. There are also a large number of commuters and employees of small firms, and a more vulgar variety of affluence than is on display in most of Surrey; a few overspill estates do not disturb the general tone. Surrey Heath has exceptionally low unemployment, which was at 0.5 per cent at the time of the 2001 election.

Further up the M3 towards London, across the bleak and sandy heathland which gives the constituency its name, lie several more classically Surrey stockbroker belt villages – Bagshot, Windlesham, Chobham and Bisley. Every county ward voted Conservative with around 50 per cent of the vote in 2001; what Labour support exists is concentrated in Camberley while the Lib Dems have some adherents in Frimley Green and Bagshot. Surrey Heath is an ironclad Conservative stronghold (their 23rd safest), and a safe haven for Nick Hawkins who managed a successful chicken run from his previous seat in Blackpool South in 1997.

SURREY SOUTH WEST

	2001		1997		1992 actual	
Electorate and turnout	70,570	70.3	72,841	77.5	72,312	82.7
Conservative	22,462	45.3	25,165	44.6	35,008	58.5
Labour	4,321	8.7	5,333	9.4	3,840	6.4
Lib Dem	21,601	43.6	22,471	39.8	20,033	33.5
Anti–EU	1,208	2.4	3,231 (2)	5.7	–	–
Others	–		258		955 (3)	
MP	Virginia Bottomley (Con)		Virginia Bottomley (Con)		Virginia Bottomley (Con)	
Majority	861	1.7	2,694	4.8	14,975	25.0

Surrey South West is the Conservative seat third most vulnerable to the Lib Dems, after Taunton and Orpington; the result in 2001 was extremely close and rather a relief for the Conservatives, who saw neighbouring Guildford go down and were afraid of seeing a large splodge of yellow appear in this corner of Surrey.

2001 was the closest shave the Tories have had here, but in 1997 and in the by-election in May 1984 when Virginia Bottomley was first elected their majority has fallen below 3,000. The source of the trouble for the Conservatives is the largest town, Farnham (36,000 population). It is an attractive 18th century town with a castle, and Waverley Abbey, and a slight air of intellectualism reminiscent of Winchester but rather unusual in businesslike Surrey. In the 2001 county elections, which came close to replicating the parliamentary vote, Farnham voted 49-42 for the Lib Dems. Godalming, the other town in the constituency (population 20,000) and itself a churchy, public school place (the home of Charterhouse) was similarly close fought although it has the only inkling of Labour support in local elections. The Conservatives led quite narrowly in Haslemere and the rural areas, making every element of the constituency a close fight.

Surrey SW is one of Labour's weakest seats in the country – only five seats, all Lib Dem, had lower Labour shares of the vote in 2001, and Labour has run third in every election since 1964. Extra tactical voting helped the Lib Dems to gain Guildford, but the Labour vote here had already been reduced to rock bottom here. The pitched electoral battle kept turnout over 70 per cent in 2001, the ninth highest in Britain, and the next general election will surely also see a hard fight for Surrey South West. The impact of Virginia Bottomley's decision to stand down remains to be seen.

WOKING

	2001		1997		1992 notional	
Electorate and turnout	71,254	60.2	70,053	72.7	69,318	79.9
Conservative	19,747	46.0	19,553	38.4	32,718	59.1
Labour	8,714	20.3	10,695	21.0	7,398	13.4
Lib Dem	12,988	30.3	13,875	27.3	14,987	27.1
Anti–EU	1,461	3.4	2,721 (2)	5.3	–	–
Ind Con	–	–	3,933	7.7	–	–
Others	–		137		257	
MP	Humfrey Malins (Con)		Humfrey Malins (Con)		Cranley Onslow (Con)	
Majority	6,759	15.8	5,678	11.2	17,731	32.0

Woking was a Victorian creation around the railways and the enormous cemetery at Brookwood to the south west of the town, where London's dead were exported. Living commuters still shuttle back and forward to London on the frequent trains to Waterloo. Woking also encompasses Byfleet, further in towards London, and spills a little westwards to Pirbright from the Guildford council area. Most of the constituency is built-up. It is not one of Surrey's most exclusive constituencies – the town of Woking contains a mix of areas including inner terraces with a substantial Asian population (Woking's mosque is the oldest established in Britain) and a council-built estate at Sheerwater (whose Labour-voting district ward is among the 20 per cent most deprived in England). However, the tone is set by the Victorian villas and rich suburbs either side of the narrow town centre squeezed between the canal and the railway line – Horsell, Mount Hermon and particularly West Byfleet which is the 11th least deprived out of 8,414 in England. In the 2001 county elections all the wards of Woking borough voted Conservative except for West (Lib Dem). Philip Gould, Labour's focus group guru, grew up in Woking and his political outlook was formed by exposure to the views of its people. However, even Gould and Blair have not been able to re-establish Labour in Woking enough to repeat the 31 per cent the party gained in 1966, Gould's first election as an activist.

The Conservative vote plummeted by nearly 21 percentage points in 1997; it was their worst result in the country excluding the exceptional cases of Tatton and North Down (and Gordon, where the 1992 boundary estimate may have been inaccurate). The reason was a split in their vote between the official candidate and an independent Conservative who polled 7.7 per cent; the end of the split in 2001 caused a substantial bounce-back in their vote (11th best nationally), although the real change in politics that election was possibly the inching forward of the Liberal Democrats, who are active in the town. Despite its elements of political and social pluralism, Woking is dominated by high-class commuterland, and therefore the Conservatives – although the Lib Dems must hope their Guildford achievement can spread here.

East Sussex including Brighton & Hove

	Conservative		Labour		Liberal Democrat		Others	
	Share of vote	Seats	Share of vote	Seats	Share of vote	Seats	Share of vote	Seats
2001	39.5	3	30.2	4	24.0	1	6.4	0
1997	39.4	3	29.2	4	24.0	1	7.4	0
1992	52.8	8	17.5	0	27.5	0	2.1	0
1987	57.8	8	15.2	0	26.3	0	0.7	0
1983	58.4	8	13.6	0	27.2	0	0.9	0

The county of East Sussex lies south of London, the other side of Surrey. It has a coastline of bustling resorts and gracious retirement villas, some attractive countryside around the Weald and the South Downs and some plush little commuter towns. It is a sign of how politics has changed that the place is not a Conservative stronghold any more.

Brighton is the key to this change. It is within daily commuting distance of London, and this has affected its social composition for years. As early as 1851 it was classified as 'a suburb of the metropolis'. Those who choose to commute from here are predominantly young, academic or professional people who still enjoy city life and are not fleeing it for the joys of a large house and a big garden, as the commuters of the inland towns and villages are. Brighton is, in terms of lifestyle and values, one of the most metropolitan parts of Britain: Kensington and Soho by sea. It has a considerable gay population, based initially in Kemptown but spread throughout the city, who influence the tone of the place. A further element is a large student population, drawn by two universities including the University of Sussex which has a radical reputation. Once highly Conservative, Brighton has moved a long way to the left in the last thirty years; now the Greens do well and have three members of the council. Labour have won all three seats from the Brighton-Hove conurbation in 1997 and 2001; the previous scorecard of non-Tory victories amounts to Labour wins in the Kemptown seat in 1964 and 1966 and a one-off Liberal win in 1906.

Part of the reason for this long-term political change has been social change wrought by the universities since they were established in the 1960s – students and academics tend to be hostile to the Tories. Part is the increasing confidence and political clout of the gay community in Brighton. Part is Labour's improved ability to attract support from non-manual, non-unionised workers who abound in industries like hotels and catering. But a lot is about social liberalism, and Brighton's pride rather than shame in its permissive, hedonistic reputation.

Most of East Sussex has relatively little in common with the exotic city by the coast; it is a staid, conservative place where little changes. The population of pension age in the county excluding Brighton & Hove is nearly 26 per cent compared to the national average of 18 per cent, and 19 per cent in the city.

Wealden is lush countryside and prosperous small towns; Eastbourne is a genteel and quiet retirement resort; Bexhill makes Eastbourne look almost raucous by comparison. These areas provide a solid Conservative vote which keeps the county total in the blue corner, although the very concentration of the Tory vote in Wealden and Bexhill & Battle means their vote is distributed inefficiently in the county as a whole. Lewes, closest constituency in to Brighton, was formerly also a safe-looking Conservative seat but has caught some of the city's dislike of the Tories and elected a Lib Dem MP with a large majority in 2001. Hastings, on the other hand, has some of Brighton's youth and dependence on tourism but has fallen on harder times (although it, too, has been an extraordinary growth area for Labour in recent years). Before recent results, neither seat had deviated from the Tories (discounting an Independent Tory in Hastings in 1922) since 1906 Liberal gains were wiped out in January 1910.

East Sussex presents a worrying picture for the Conservatives of the party's long run decline in its former strongholds in the south east of England. Its parliamentary delegation is half Labour, including three gains that came as a complete surprise to most observers (Hove, Brighton Kemptown and Hastings & Rye). The county continued to swing against the Tories in 2001. None of these seats is now on the political front line. A sign of how bad things have got is that Hove is the seat the Tories need to gain to get their parliamentary delegation up to 200 MPs, while Kemptown is just over the point at which their gains would wipe out Labour's majority. East Sussex is likely to be an important battleground in the next general election.

Local government

The unitary city authority of Brighton and Hove is under Labour control, with a majority of 14 following the last elections in 1999. Labour gained Brighton for the very first time in 1987, a signal of its leftward drift, and won Hove in 1995 for its final couple of years of independence. Labour control should be able to withstand the next set of local elections even if Labour have become unpopular in 2003; it would be a bad night for the party if it fell. Voters in Brighton & Hove decided, by a 62-38 margin, against an elected mayor in October 2001. The turnout in the postal referendum at 32 per cent was relatively high.

The truncated East Sussex county council is less of a Conservative stronghold than might be imagined. The former county, including Brighton, was an authority the Conservatives were shocked to lose for the first time in a century in 1985. However, their majority in the June 2001 county elections was only four, without Brighton and Hove. The Conservatives have strongholds in Wealden and the Bexhill area while Labour dominate Hastings and the Lib Dems have strength in Lewes.

Eastbourne, in local as in national politics, is a battleground between the Conservatives and Liberal Democrats, with a short-lived Conservative administration ejected in 2002 and the Lib Dems taking over. In Lewes the Lib Dems are also in control and have had power continuously since 1991; they survived the 1999 local elections well while the party endured setbacks elsewhere. Hastings was a Labour gain in 1998; during the 1990s the Conservatives were pushed out entirely and it was a battle between Labour and Lib Dem for control. More recently the Tories have recovered and on new ward boundaries in 2002 the general election pattern was repeated, with Labour keeping control and the Lib Dems nearly wiped out. Rother (Bexhill and Rye), was a Conservative gain in 1999 of a council they should never have lost; the Tory administration is controversial for its 'redevelopment' of the Art Deco masterpiece the De La Warr pavilion. Wealden, too, is Conservative controlled although there is a substantial Lib Dem group.

Boundary review

East Sussex will have an unchanged allocation of eight seats after the general election although it is likely that there will be some shuffling of wards. Wealden is too big and will probably have to donate some wards around Hailsham to Lewes, and Kemptown might stretch out a little further along the coast. Both changes would probably help the Tories a little. Even though Brighton & Hove is now a unitary city council, it might create too large a disparity in electorates between county and borough seats to give it three seats entirely to itself. If it was given independent consideration, the outcome would probably strengthen Labour in both Kemptown and Hove.

BEXHILL and BATTLE

	2001		1997		1992 notional	
Electorate and turnout	69,010	64.9	65,803	74.5	66,158	78.6
Conservative	21,555	48.1	23,570	48.1	31,347	60.3
Labour	8,702	19.4	8,866	18.1	4,877	9.4
Lib Dem	11,052	24.7	12,470	25.5	15,007	28.9
Anti–EU	3,474	7.8	4,088 (2)	8.3	–	–
Other	–		–		784 (2)	
MP	Gregory Barker (Con)		Charles Wardle (Con)		Charles Wardle (Con)	
Majority	10,503	23.5	11,100	22.7	16,340	31.4

Bexhill and Battle is a safe Conservative seat. Bexhill is a more genteel, elderly twin to Hastings (31.3 per cent of the population of the district council covering the area are of pension age). Battle, where the Battle of Hastings was fought in 1066, lies inland, but electoral conflict around here is hardly epic. The seat, dependent on retirement, tourism and agriculture, is Tory to the core although in the past Liberal Democrats have polled respectably in local elections. Battle voted for a Lib Dem county councillor in 2001, and Bexhill North voted Labour, so there is more variety in local politics than in the other Conservative stronghold in the county, Wealden. The other wards were all Conservative, with the party usually winning massive majorities against split opposition.

Another feature, correlated with its elderly population, is that Bexhill in particular is traditionalist and Eurosceptic. This was reflected in the high share of the vote for the fringe parties in 1997 and 2001; in 2001 the best UKIP showing in the country. In 2001, UKIP candidate Nigel Farage was supported by the outgoing Tory MP Charles Wardle, who had fallen out with his party over a variety of issues including his own relationship with Mohamed Fayed. However, Wardle's successor Greg Barker won without any difficulty and should have the seat for life.

BRIGHTON KEMPTOWN

	2001		1997		1992 notional	
Electorate and turnout	68,119	57.6	65,319	70.6	65,932	77.1
Conservative	13,823	35.3	17,945	38.9	26,828	52.8
Labour	18,745	47.8	21,479	46.6	16,571	32.6
Lib Dem	4,064	10.4	4,478	9.7	7,056	13.9
Anti–EU	543	1.4	1,526	3.3	–	–
Green	1,290	3.3	–	–	–	–
Other	738 (3)		704 (4)		371	
MP	Desmond Turner (Lab)		Desmond Turner (Lab)		Andrew Bowden (Con)	
Majority	4,922	12.6	3,534	7.7	10,257	20.2

Since Brighton was split into two seats in 1950, Kemptown has always been the more marginal of the two. Pavilion used to be safely Conservative, while Kemptown narrowly elected Labour MP Dennis Hobden in 1964 (by seven votes, against a Tory MP who spent most of his time looking for the Loch Ness Monster) and 1966. Kemptown is still marginal, but Pavilion has swung over to being a relatively safe Labour seat.

Kemptown is east Brighton, from the Palace Pier to the Marina and beyond along the sea front, and inland among the terraces and council estates around the racecourse and the downs. This constituency contains the poorer parts of Brighton – the worst areas for unemployment, drug addiction and insecure casual work; this is the Brighton of Greene's *Brighton Rock*. The seaside stretch has some grand buildings concealing considerable social problems, but Queen's Park is an ordinary working class area and Moulsecoomb a troubled peripheral estate with a reputation for poverty and crime. East Brighton is not all grim, of course – the gay community has made Kemp Town a quite attractive and upwardly mobile area, but they too tend to support Labour (or at least vote against the Conservatives).

Why, then, is Kemptown marginal? The answer is that the five solid Labour wards are balanced by the best part of four mainly Conservative areas. it includes some very Conservative smaller beach and retirement communities along the coast. Woodingdean (which Labour can win only in exceptional years like 1995) and Rottingdean are part of Brighton and the reason that the old seat was generally Tory. The seat now includes Peacehaven and Telscombe from Lewes district, below Roedean school and the cliffs. Peacehaven is not a complete desert for Labour – in the June 2001 county elections the party came a respectable second with 35 per cent, but they are very weak in Telscombe. Labour managed a substantial increase in its majority in 2001, probably because of increasing support in its weaker areas.

If the Conservatives are to recover, they should gain seats like this one. It is Labour's 84th most vulnerable seat; if Labour lose 83 then their majority disappears. It still remains to be seen whether, in its political orientation at least, the new Kemptown really does swing both ways.

BRIGHTON PAVILION

	2001		1997		1992 *notional*	
Electorate and turnout	69,568	58.5	66,720	73.4	*66,008*	*75.7*
Conservative	10,203	25.1	13,556	27.7	*22,619*	*45.3*
Labour	19,846	48.7	26,737	54.6	*20,089*	*40.2*
Lib Dem	5,348	13.1	4,644	9.5	*6,169*	*12.3*
Anti–EU	361	0.9	1,483 (2)	3.0	–	–
Green	3,806	9.3	1,249	2.6	*963*	*2.2*
Other	1,159 (3)		1,282 (3)		*135*	
MP	David Lepper (Lab)		David Lepper (Lab)		Derek Spencer (Con)	
Majority	9,643	23.7	13,181	26.9	*2,530*	*5.1*

Pavilion constituency contains the central and northern parts of Brighton, including the florid pleasure dome that the boundary commissioners, in a rare flash of poetry, have decided to name the seat after. It is a distinguished-looking constituency; the architecture is made up of Regency terraces and Victorian villas, and it has combined grandeur and the whiff of decadence since the Prince Regent put the place on the map two centuries ago.

The seaside, with its hotels, leisure and conference trade, is far from the only industry in Brighton Pavilion. The university buildings are out at Stanmer, but students and academics are dispersed throughout the town. The area around Brighton station has become desirable London commuter territory, as have the suburbs in the north around Preston Park. The inner wards all vote Labour, with the exception of St. Peters which was Green in 1999; Labour score quite well in the suburbs although Patcham, right by the downs, is still very Conservative.

Pavilion was formerly extremely Conservative, and never seemed under threat until Labour got within striking distance in 1992 and won nearly two to one against an incumbent Conservative MP in 1997. It is one of the most dramatic demonstrations of long-term political change in Britain.

Although now safely Labour, Pavilion was quite an interesting contest in 2001. Conservative candidate David Gold was openly gay when he was selected, a first for his party. Labour's vote dropped quite a bit, but the beneficiaries were the Greens and to a lesser extent the Lib Dems. Pavilion recorded the highest Green share anywhere in 2001, reflecting its young, radical population. It achieved the same honour in the 1999 Euro elections, with 19 per cent voting Green. Brighton Pavilion, like the parts of inner north London it now so resembles, contains a substantial number of people who consider the Blair government insufficiently radical.

EASTBOURNE

	2001		1997		1992 notional	
Electorate and turnout	75,170	59.6	72,347	72.8	70,602	81.6
Conservative	19,738	44.1	22,183	42.1	30,548	53.0
Labour	5,967	13.3	6,576	12.5	2,697	4.7
Lib Dem	17,584	39.3	20,189	38.3	23,739	41.2
Anti–EU	907	2.0	(2) 2,978	5.7	–	–
Other	574		741		643	
MP	Nigel Waterson (Con)		Nigel Waterson (Con)		Nigel Waterson (Con)	
Majority	2,154	4.8	1,994	3.8	6,809	11.8

Eastbourne is a large seaside resort and retirement town on the Sussex coast between Brighton and Hastings; its social make-up is dominated by its function as 'God's Waiting Room' for the many retired people who live in its elegant villas and its wide variety of old people's homes. 28 per cent of the borough's population was of pension age in 1991, and because of their greater willingness to vote, they may well have contributed towards 40 per cent of the vote cast in 2001. Unlike other retirement seats, however, Eastbourne is not completely dominated by the Conservatives and did not, at least in 2001, vote particularly enthusiastically for the UKIP.

Eastbourne has only fallen to the Liberal Democrats once – in a 1990 by-election (the previous Liberal victory was in 1906). The by-election was a damaging blow to Margaret Thatcher, who was forced out the following month, but the result reflected a classic letting-off of steam in a by-election and the continuing support of Eastbourne voters for Conservative government was asserted in the 1992 result. The Liberal Democrats failed to regain the seat in the elections of 1997 and 2001. This was a considerable disappointment for them, as more unlikely seats fell on both occasions. Eastbourne, narrowly, still clung to the Conservatives.

Even in June 2001, the county elections produced a narrow Lib Dem lead in the constituency, by something like 44–41 with 13 per cent for Labour. There seemed to be a small but crucial element of the electorate who were willing to vote for Lib Dem local councillors but chose a Tory MP – perhaps through political calculation, perhaps through support for incumbents. The Conservative Party lives on, hoping that its retirement is not permanent, in Eastbourne.

HASTINGS and RYE

	2001		*1997*		*1992 actual*	
Electorate and turnout	70,734	58.3	70,388	69.7	71,839	74.9
Conservative	15,094	36.6	14,307	29.2	25,573	47.6
Labour	19,402	47.1	16,867	34.4	8,458	15.7
Lib Dem	4,266	10.3	13,717	28.0	18,939	35.2
Anti–EU	911	2.2	2,983 (2)	6.1	–	–
Other	1,545 (4)		1,195 (2)		808 (2)	
MP	Michael Foster (Lab)		Michael Foster (Lab)		Jacqui Lait (Con)	
Majority	4,308	10.5	2,560	5.2	6,634	12.3

Hastings & Rye was Labour's best result in Britain in June 2001, in the sense that the party's share of the vote increased more here (12.7 percentage points) than anywhere else. It was also, curiously, the Conservatives' 13th best performance. Given these facts, it is not too surprising that it was the worst result nationally for the Liberal Democrats who found themselves caught in a tactical squeeze.

Hastings is a depressed town tucked in the far corner of East Sussex; unlike sedate Eastbourne it is not a retirement centre and it lacks the elegance and excitement of Brighton. Unemployment, particularly long term unemployment, is relatively high. Of the sixteen wards of Hastings, nine are among the thousand most deprived areas of England. The seat also contains, as its name might suggest, the bijou Cinque Port of Rye as well as Winchelsea, a pretty half-abandoned mediaeval new town, and some beach areas in the Rother district.

Labour are strongest in Hastings town centre and the eastern suburbs, polling over 50 per cent in many wards in the local elections, and have fairly solid support throughout the town. The Conservatives can only really fight back in the west St. Leonards area, a slightly more upmarket resort which is an integral part of Hastings, and a couple of comparatively well-off northern suburbs, and in the non-Hastings areas included (although Labour can win district council seats in Rye). The Lib Dem collapse in the 2001 general election was echoed in local election voting – they were crushed again by the main parties in 2002.

Hastings & Rye is still a marginal seat; although the Lib Dems have been eliminated the Tories still have potential as shown by their vote increase in 2001 and their recovery in local elections. But the main story here is of the astonishing near-trebling of the Labour vote since 1992 because of economic conditions and the reversal of tactical voting decisions.

HOVE

	2001		1997		1992 actual	
Electorate and turnout	71,320	58.9	69,178	69.6	67,566	74.1
Conservative	16,082	38.3	17,499	36.4	24,525	49.0
Labour	19,253	45.9	21,458	44.6	12,257	24.5
Lib Dem	3,823	9.1	4,645	9.7	9,709	19.4
Anti–EU	358	0.9	2,140 (2)	4.4	–	–
Ind Con	–	–	1,735	3.6	2,658	5.3
Green	1,369	3.3	644	1.3	814	1.6
Other	1,103 (4)		–		126	
MP	Ivor Caplin (Lab)		Ivor Caplin (Lab)		Tim Sainsbury (Con)	
Majority	3,171	7.6	3,959	8.2	12,268	24.5

When Labour won control of Hove borough council in 1995 it was regarded as an outlandish example of a mid–term result that could not possibly be repeated in a general election. John Prescott made a special trip to Hove to celebrate with the new council leaders. But in 1997 Tony Blair, in his plane, had to grapple with the idea of Labour Hove and assumed that someone was having a joke at his expense. In 2001 John O'Farrell commented that: '"Labour gain Hove" was surreal; "Labour hold Hove" is the world turned upside down.'

Hove's reputation as a staid, Conservative place depended in part on its oft-stressed distinction from seedy, sinful Brighton. In fact, the border between the two towns was never very apparent to the naked eye and they always shared a football club; now 'Hove, actually' is more than ever just a state of mind. Its borough council has been merged with Brighton. Much of Hove's property is cheaper than central Brighton's and it has been affected by the same social trends that have transformed the Brighton Pavilion constituency. It is still the more staid side of town, but in Brighton that is not saying a great deal. In the west of the seat is the Portslade area, some of which is industrial, but Labour now has a presence throughout quiet, residential Hove.

The 2001 result was even worse than it looks for the Conservatives, because they were not handicapped by an independent Conservative rival as they were in 1997 and 1992; the smaller parties in 2001 were mostly to the left rather than as before to the right. Ivor Caplin is a canny local politician and social change is still favouring Labour; it is still a seat the Tories must hope to take back but it might prove difficult.

LEWES

	2001		*1997*		*1992 notional*	
Electorate	66,332	68.5	64,340	76.4	*63,412*	*81.8*
Conservative	15,878	34.9	19,950	40.6	*26,638*	*51.3*
Labour	3,317	7.3	5,232	10.6	*4,270*	*8.2*
Lib Dem	25,588	56.3	21,250	43.2	*20,301*	*39.1*
Anti–EU	650	1.4	2,737 (2)	5.6	–	–
Other	–		–		*677*	
MP	Norman Baker (LD)		Norman Baker (LD)		Tim Rathbone (Con)	
Majority	9,710	21.4	1,300	2.6	*6,337*	*12.2*

Several of the 1997 intake facing their first election as an incumbent enjoyed startling victories – Martin Salter in Reading West, Edward Davey in Kingston & Surbiton, Jim Murphy in Eastwood – and Norman Baker in Lewes. Baker has had a high national profile as captain of the parliamentary awkward squad, whose questions undermined Peter Mandelson and upheld the traditions of parliamentary scrutiny of the executive.

Lewes is the county town of East Sussex – an attractive town set among the hills north of Brighton; it is to the brash seaside city as Bath is to Bristol, or Winchester to Southampton. Lewes town is too small to be a constituency by itself, so the seat also includes some surrounding countryside, the troubled ferry port of Newhaven, the resort town of Seaford (in fact the largest town in the seat), and even Polegate, a small town on the edge of Eastbourne. It seems improbable for such a place to have spurned the Conservatives, but the Liberal Democrats have a history of activism here and first won the local council in 1991. In the 2001 county elections there were no overwhelming strongholds for either Conservative or Lib Dem, although Newhaven and Lewes itself tend to the Lib Dems in local elections. Nearly half of the local Labour vote appears to have gone to Norman Baker, alongside some Tories who presumably saw voting Baker back in as the most effective way of annoying Tony Blair. The Labour candidate in 2001 was Paul Richards, who wrote a book called *How to Win an Election*, but even the best tactics could not win Lewes for Labour.

WEALDEN

	2001		1997		1992 notional	
Electorate and turnout	83,066	63.5	80,206	73.7	74,245	80.8
Conservative	26,279	49.8	29,417	49.8	37,256	61.7
Labour	10,705	20.3	10,185	17.2	5,578	9.2
Lib Dem	12,507	23.7	15,213	25.7	16,328	27.1
Anti–EU	1,539	2.9	4,096 (2)	6.9	–	–
Other	1,726 (2)		188		1,184 (2)	
MP	Charles Hendry (Con)		Geoffrey Johnson Smith (Con)		Geoffrey Johnson Smith (Con)	
Majority	13,772	26.1	14,204	24.0	20,928	34.7

Wealden is a large inland constituency north of Eastbourne and Brighton. Its name comes from its geographical position in the Sussex Weald, amid hills, forests and fields. The main towns of the constituency are Crowborough, Hailsham and Uckfield; Crowborough, the largest, provides only around 20,000 of the constituency's electorate. The towns are comfortable little places with a high proportion of commuters and the most prosperous retired people, and they are surrounded by many smaller villages.

All the county council wards of Wealden were Conservative in 2001, although this included three gains from the Lib Dems since 1997. The narrowest margin was in Hailsham. Labour's vote in Wealden is thinly but evenly spread, with between 13 per cent and 23 per cent in all the wards the party fought. The increase in the party's vote in 2001 was in line with trends in the most affluent and upper middle class areas in Sussex and elsewhere. The Liberal Democrats seem to be weakening here, and the Wealden seat is a fortress of Conservatism. The Tories led even in the 1995 local elections and currently have a majority on the district council. It is the 14th safest Conservative seat in the country.

West Sussex

	Conservative		Labour		Liberal Democrat		Others	
	Share of vote	Seats	Share of vote	Seats	Share of vote	Seats	Share of vote	Seats
2001	46.0	7	25.9	1	23.0	0	5.2	0
1997	44.7	7	24.3	1	25.6	0	5.5	0
1992	57.3	7	14.6	0	25.7	0	2.4	0
1987	60.0	7	11.8	0	27.6	0	0.6	0
1983	59.9	7	9.8	0	29.3	0	1.0	0

The county of West Sussex divides into four sections, defined by physical geography. There is a coastal strip composed mainly of a string of resorts and retirement centres, the largest of which is Worthing. Three constituencies – Worthing East & Shoreham, Worthing West and Bognor Regis & Littlehampton – are made up entirely of this sort of territory. The electorate of this area is quite elderly, with 26.8 per cent of the population of the borough of Worthing being of pension age and 24.9 per cent in neighbouring Adur. Worthing is seen as a centre for most of the area, although parts also look to Brighton.

To the west is a low-lying area, an extension of the inlets and harbours of the Portsmouth area in the south of the Chichester constituency. North of the coastal strip there is a hilly rural area along the South Downs which is sparsely populated – the constituency of Arundel & South Downs is composed entirely of this area and so is a fair proportion of Chichester. Its villages, although there is some agriculture, house a relatively high proportion of retired people and an admixture of some very affluent London commuters. North of the Downs is an area heavily under the influence of London, with commuter settlements along the rail line in Sussex Mid and in Horsham, and a New Town full of expatriate south Londoners at Crawley. The northern part of the county has a smaller proportion of retired people, although only in Crawley is it below the national average.

Although there are several different sorts of territory in West Sussex, with the exception of Crawley they are united by allegiance to the Conservative Party. Historically, West Sussex is a county of extreme Conservative strength. Labour had never won a seat in the county until 1997 and the Liberals and successors have been out for a duck since 1880, except for a one-off win in Chichester in 1923. It was only the implantation of New Town residents at Crawley that created the opportunity for a Labour victory in the county, and that took longer than expected to accomplish. In contrast to the position in other strongly Tory counties such as Buckinghamshire and Surrey, there were no other seats in which they were even run close in 1997 or 2001. With the possible exception of Worthing East & Shoreham none of the others seem all that worthy of any other party putting in an effort. The slight swing to Labour in 2001, also detectable in East Sussex, reflected a small accretion of support from well-off professionals who had not felt sufficiently sure about New Labour's intentions in 1997 to cast a vote for them. These people were satisfied in 2001 and alienated by the Hague brand of populism; some surprising Labour votes were cast on the way to the City trains on the morning of 7 June 2001.

In future the Conservatives must also look to the relatively high and resilient vote for the minor Eurosceptic parties (5.3 per cent in 1997, 3.7 per cent in 2001) as a source of additional support, but have to avoid further disaffection among professionals and pensioners. Whatever the national problems of the Conservative Party, West Sussex looks likely to provide a solid phalanx of Tory MPs for the foreseeable future. If they return to government, they might regain Crawley and once again exercise their traditional monopoly.

Local government

West Sussex county council has a Conservative majority, but it is less emphatic than might be imagined. There are 42 Tories to 18 Liberal Democrats (mainly from Horsham town, Worthing and the eastern edge of the county) and 11 Labour councillors (a bloc of seven from Crawley and scattered others). The Conservatives regained the council in 1997 after four years of no overall control.

Three of the more urban district councils in West Sussex have annual local elections although all-out elections on new boundaries are due in May 2003. Crawley is solidly Labour and has been continuously since 1973. Worthing has alternated between the Conservatives, who controlled it before 1994 and for a spell after 1999 and Lib Dems, who gained it in 2002. There are no Labour councillors. In contrast, Adur (Shoreham and Southwick) is perhaps the most interesting local authority in the county. From control of Adur district council from 1986 until 1999 (29 out of 39 councillors in 1995) the Lib Dems have crashed to third and Labour have come from nowhere to running a minority administration for a while after 1999 before a Conservative-Independent alliance (known locally as the CIA) staged a coup. The Conservatives gained control in 2002 while the Lib Dems, humiliatingly, fielded no candidates.

The other local authorities elect every four years. Arun is the largest, covering Bognor, Littlehampton, Rustington and Arundel. It is one of only a dozen or so Conservative councils to survive the 1995 rout albeit only with a majority of two seats; the Tories had a more comfortable margin after 1999 with opposition divided quite evenly between Lib Dems and Labour. The Conservatives actually lost Chichester in the 1995 elections when the Lib Dems won half the seats, but regained it in 1999 and it is normally a safely Tory authority. There was a very similar story in Horsham, except here the Lib Dems achieved majority control in 1995. Neither Chichester nor Horsham have any Labour councillors. Mid Sussex was another Conservative regain in 1999 of an authority they should never have lost in 1995 – the Lib Dems took an overall majority then and remain competitive in local elections.

Boundary review

West Sussex will retain its current allocation of eight seats and any boundary alterations will be minor. The current Horsham seat is oversized and growing, while Bognor Regis & Littlehampton is a bit small with a stable population, so there is a case for shuffling a few Chichester wards to Bognor in return for a rural area from Horsham. The partisan effects would be minimal.

ARUNDEL and SOUTH DOWNS

	2001		1997		1992 *notional*	
Electorate and turnout	70,956	64.7	68,010	75.5	65,056	81.7
Conservative	23,969	52.2	27,251	53.1	33,365	62.8
Labour	9,488	20.7	9,376	18.3	4,957	9.3
Lib Dem	10,265	22.4	13,216	25.7	13,349	25.1
Anti–EU	2,167	4.7	1,494	2.9	–	–
Others	–		–		1,464	2.8
MP	Howard Flight (Con)		Howard Flight (Con)		NEW SEAT	
Majority	13,704	29.9	14,035	27.3	20,016	37.7

Arundel and South Downs is a rural constituency lying just inland of the coastal strip of retirement seaside towns. As the name suggests, its geography is dominated by the South Downs, a chain of hills which punctuate the Sussex landscape and distinguish between the resorts and the commuter areas inland. It is a particularly diffuse constituency, with an irregular outline that suggests it was the least worst option for creating an extra seat in the county rather than having any great commonality of its own. It extends from a short stretch of the Brighton railway line in the east to areas inland of Bognor to the west. It has few towns of any size within it, excluding possibly Arundel itself – a feudal little place nestling around the Duke of Norfolk's castle and influenced by aristocratic Catholicism – and the downland town of Pulborough. Most of its component parts are very strongly Conservative, although the Liberal Democrats can win wards in local elections at the east end of the constituency.

Before 1832 this was an area rich in rotten boroughs and unusual results. As its new member Howard Flight commented in 1997:

> The great Wilberforce represented Bramber- although he did not know where it was at the time, because it was the third rottenest borough. I discovered that one John Major represented Steyning for about 20 years, until the Reform Act of 1832 abolished the "labour" vote that had sustained him.

The modern Arundel and South Downs is so loyally Conservative that it was one of only 45 constituencies that voted Tory in the local elections of 1995 – by nearly seven percentage points. It is a Tory banker (the seventh safest of their seats), and suitably enough Howard Flight is a Tory banker too.

BOGNOR REGIS and LITTLEHAMPTON

	2001		1997		1992 notional	
Electorate and turnout	66,903	58.2	66,736	69.6	65,567	76.0
Conservative	17,602	45.2	20,537	44.2	28,316	56.9
Labour	11,959	30.7	13,216	28.5	6,700	13.5
Lib Dem	6,846	17.6	11,153	24.0	13,309	26.7
Anti–EU	1,779	4.6	1,537	3.3	–	–
Others	782		–		1,474	
MP	Nick Gibb (Con)		Nick Gibb (Con)		Michael Marshall (Con) Arundel	
Majority	5,643	14.5	7,321	15.8	15,007	30.1

This, like its eastern neighbours, is a mainly urban coastal constituency. Its name describes its contents fairly accurately – the seaside resort of Bognor Regis plus Littlehampton and a stretch of coast in between including Middleton-on-Sea. Bognor added the 'Regis' in 1929 after King George V spent several months here convalescing; his opinion about the place uttered from his deathbed seems to have been less indulgent. As well as the resort centre there are affluent areas of the town at Aldwick and Felpham. Littlehampton (the 'little' was apparently to distinguish it from the larger port of Southampton along the coast) is also a resort, but it has port functions, a regatta and the headquarters of the Body Shop. The River ward of Littlehampton is the most deprived area of West Sussex, falling just outside the most deprived 10 per cent of England.

Starting from a low base, Labour have achieved an enormous cumulative swing in the last two elections. For Labour to have won over 30 per cent of the vote in Bognor Regis and Littlehampton is a strange phenomenon, particularly considering that the predecessor seat of Arundel returned a Labour vote of only 8 per cent in 1983. Labour's best area in the constituency is Littlehampton, where the party had a lead of around 400 votes in the 2001 county elections and possibly a little more in the general election. The town's district councillors divide six Labour to two Tories and one Lib Dem. Bognor, on the other hand, is a traditional Conservative seaside area. Labour came out narrowly on top in three-way fights in Bersted and Hotham county wards, but the Conservatives had comfortable leads in Bognor Regis itself and the Nyetimber ward (whose very name is redolent of retired bliss).

It is doubtful how much further Labour can get in this area, which surely has an inbuilt Conservative majority under any normal circumstances. However, the short history of the Bognor Regis & Littlehampton constituency indicates that the West Sussex coast is not without political variety or interest, even if the Conservatives are firmly in the lead.

CHICHESTER

	2001		1997		1992 notional	
Electorate and turnout	77,703	63.8	74,812	74.6	75,835	77.8
Conservative	23,320	47.0	25,895	46.4	34,971	59.3
Labour	10,627	21.4	9,605	17.2	6,703	11.4
Lib Dem	11,965	24.1	16,161	29.0	15,690	26.6
Anti–EU	2,380	4.8	4,118 (2)	7.4	–	–
Green	1,292	2.6	–	–	809	1.4
Others	–		–		816	
MP	Andrew Tyrie (Con)		Andrew Tyrie (Con)		Tony Nelson (Con)	
Majority	11,355	22.9	9,734	17.5	19,281	32.7

Chichester is the county town of West Sussex; a small cathedral city with a strong tradition of art and theatre. It is much too small for a constituency all of its own (the city makes up only about a quarter of the electorate), so the constituency takes in a large stretch of country to its north and a rather smaller hinterland to the south. The distance from north to south within the constituency is over 30 miles. In the far north it borders on commuterland seats such as Surrey South West and Hampshire North East but much of the rural area in the centre around Midhurst is less influenced by London. To the south, the coastal part of the constituency around Selsey is subject to severe erosion and floods; global warming is not an issue of purely academic importance here.

The Conservatives are comfortably ahead in all parts of the seat in general and recent local elections, although there is some Liberal Democrat activity in the city area in particular and a residual Labour vote in the south of Chichester. Even at the Conservatives' nadir in 1995 they were still five points ahead of the Lib Dems. Whatever hopes the Lib Dems have had lately have been dashed in general elections by the resilience of the Conservative vote and the upward creep in Labour's share which has made the battle for second place a serious issue for the first time in decades. Conservative MP Andrew Tyrie, who has taken a close interest in constitutional issues and supervision of the executive (a bit like his Sussex colleague Lib Dem Norman Baker), and was a prominent supporter of Kenneth Clarke, has the 29th safest Conservative seat in the land.

CRAWLEY

	2001		1997		1992 notional	
Electorate and turnout	71,629	55.2	69,194	72.9	66,707	77.5
Conservative	12,718	32.2	16,043	31.8	22,738	44.0
Labour	19,488	49.3	27,750	55.0	20,848	40.3
Lib Dem	5,009	12.7	4,141	8.2	7,492	14.5
Anti–EU	1,137	2.9	2,253 (2)	4.5	–	–
Others	1,175 (4)		230		645	
MP	Laura Moffatt (Lab)		Laura Moffatt (Lab)		Nicholas Soames (Con)	
Majority	6,770	17.1	11,707	23.2	1,890	3.7

Crawley is the only New Town south of London, first designated in the original programme in 1947 and home to a large population whose origins can be traced back mostly to south London. It has common features with other New Towns in its planned environment of self-contained neighbourhoods surrounding a new town centre, although unlike others it has always had convenient connections back to London because the main Brighton line passes through it at Three Bridges. The most notable local industry is Gatwick Airport, which has spawned other subsidiary industries as well as employing 32,000 workers.

Crawley was first designated a seat on its own in 1983, but it disappointed Labour hopes in its first three elections. Then it produced a very large swing to Labour in 1997, as did many New Towns, but in 2001 it had an above-average fall in the Labour vote. It was a target seat in 1997 and it seems apparent that Liberal Democrats voted tactically. In 2001, as a safe Labour seat, they stopped doing so. A lot of people who felt obliged to vote in 1997 apparently also wandered off in 2001 – the fall in turnout was particularly dramatic here and was the tenth worst in the country. Turnout in some Labour estates such as Bewbush and Broadfield fell well below 50 per cent.

Crawley is still growing, but the new growth is different from the New Town core. It is more upscale private development in the east of the town at Pound Hill and the Maidenbower district. Maidenbower has inflated the electorate of the Furnace Green ward and turned it into a Conservative area – the 2001 candidate Henry Smith won the seat from Labour in the county elections of 1997. On the whole, though, Crawley is now a reasonably reliable Labour seat which would only revert to the Conservatives if they were winning an election nationally.

HORSHAM

	2001		1997		1992 notional	
Electorate and turnout	79,604	63.8	75,899	75.3	71,982	79.8
Conservative	26,134	51.5	29,015	50.8	35,769	62.3
Labour	10,267	20.2	10,691	18.7	6,858	12.0
Lib Dem	12,468	24.6	14,153	24.8	13,078	22.8
Anti–EU	1,472	2.9	3,100 (2)	5.4	–	–
Others	429		206		1,704	
MP	Francis Maude (Con)		Francis Maude (Con)		Peter Hordern (Con)	
Majority	13,666	26.9	14,862	26.0	22,691	39.5

Horsham town is a comfortable and affluent place at the end of two commuter rail lines, and it is surrounded by some very wealthy commuter and retirement villages. The constituency boundaries step delicately around Crawley and include some areas to the east of the new town as well as Balcombe on the main railway line to the south. The constituency is such a concentrated area of wealth and comfort that 13 of its 22 wards are among the 10 per cent least deprived in England and the other nine are not that much worse off. The town itself has Liberal Democrat tendencies in local elections at least, with the three most heavily built-up county council wards in the town all returning Lib Dem councillors and giving the party a 2,000 vote lead in June 2001. In the constituency as a whole they polled considerably better in the 2001 county elections than they managed in the general election. They managed a five-point lead in the Conservative meltdown local elections of 1995, but pose no threat to the 11th safest Conservative seat. The slight, and rather futile, swing to Labour in 2001 was characteristic of many of the highest-income constituencies.

Before 1983 there was a more tightly drawn constituency called Horsham & Crawley, in which Labour came relatively close in October 1974, but paired with villages and little towns like Billingshurst, Horsham produces an extremely safe Conservative seat. Francis Maude enjoyed big majorities and over 50 per cent of the vote in both the disastrous elections of 1997 and 2001, a far cry from his ex-mining marginal of Warwickshire North which he represented from 1983 to 1992.

SUSSEX MID

	2001		1997		1992 notional	
Electorate and turnout	70,623	64.9	68,928	77.6	70,654	80.3
Conservative	21,150	46.2	23,231	43.5	33,415	58.9
Labour	8,693	19.0	9,969	18.6	6,034	10.6
Lib Dem	14,252	31.1	16,377	30.6	16,008	28.2
Anti–EU	1,126	2.5	3,752 (2)	7.0		
Others	601		134		1,271	
MP	Nicholas Soames (Con)		Nicholas Soames (Con)		Tim Renton (Con)	
Majority	6,898	15.1	6,854	12.8	17,407	30.7

Sussex Mid has some of the most affluent and highly favoured residential areas in the country. It consists of a roll-call of stations along the railway line between Brighton and Gatwick – Haywards Heath, Burgess Hill, plus East Grinstead and some smaller settlements like Cuckfield and Horsted Keynes. Despite the ambiguity of its name, it is on the eastern edge of West Sussex rather than the western edge of East Sussex (East Grinstead, to confuse matters, switched sides in the 1970s and had previously given its name to something very like the current Wealden seat in East Sussex). Trains into London are fast and frequent, if such a claim can be made about anywhere, and ferry a large commuting population to and fro every weekday.

This constituency is one of several safe Conservative seats in Sussex, but it has rather a different profile in local elections. If people had voted the same way as they did in the June 2001 county elections, the Liberal Democrats would have been breathing down the neck of Nicholas Soames, to conjure up an unappealing mental image. The commuter towns all have considerable Lib Dem support tucked away, with their support in the high 40s in the county elections in both Burgess Hill and East Grinstead. Labour have support only in parts of Haywards Heath. The Conservatives do better in the relatively small rural part of the constituency, and there is a certain amount of Lib Dem local support choosing Labour nationally, but there are a significant element who split tickets between Lib Dems and Tories. This used to be a relatively common phenomenon but it is rarer now the Conservative national, and Lib Dem local, polls have both declined from their peaks.

WORTHING EAST and SHOREHAM

	2001		1997		1992 notional	
Electorate and turnout	72,101	59.7	70,770	72.9	71,891	78.1
Conservative	18,608	43.2	20,864	40.5	28,824	51.4
Labour	12,469	29.0	12,335	23.9	7,476	13.3
Lib Dem	9,876	22.9	15,766	30.6	18,919	33.7
Anti–EU	1,195	2.8	2,604 (2)	5.0	–	–
Others	920		–		909	
MP	Tim Loughton (Con)		Tim Loughton (Con)		Michael Stephen (Con)	
					Shoreham	
Majority	6,139	14.3	5,098	9.9	9,905	17.6

The constituency of Worthing East & Shoreham is based mainly on the old port town of Shoreham and its surrounding small towns and suburbs like Southwick and Lancing, which comprise the Adur district council area. The two main monuments in the area are Lancing College and Shoreham's power station (the original was demolished in 1998 and replaced by a gas-powered station). Before 1997 Adur was paired with a small area to the west of Worthing and the resulting constituency was the shape of an arch, with Worthing in the middle. Now it is paired with four wards from Worthing, basically the suburban territory to the east of the A24 road, and seems a more sensible shape.

This constituency is the furthest east along the West Sussex coast, and some of Labour's increasing strength has spilled over from Brighton and Hove next door. Southwick, right by the border with Hove's Portslade, has been a Labour ward on the county council since 1997. Labour also polled quite well without winning in Sompting, home of parliamentary candidate Daniel Yates, in 2001 and are even the largest single party on the parish council there. In the Adur district the Conservatives led by 40 per cent, to 32 for Labour and 27 for the Lib Dems in the 2001 county elections. This is all very different from the previous history of the area. Shoreham used to be a Liberal Democrat centre but the party's chances here seem to have crashed out in local elections as well as national. In 2001 Worthing East and Shoreham produced the worst result of any Lib Dem target seat. Labour now pose the most plausible challenge to the continued Conservative minority hold on the seat, but are gravely handicapped by their weakness in the Worthing wards, one of which, Offington, is an exceptionally well-off retirement area. The Conservative lead in 2001 is almost certainly too large for Labour to overhaul in the next election even if the Lib Dems collapse even further.

WORTHING WEST

	2001		1997		1992 notional	
Electorate and turnout	72,419	59.7	71,639	71.8	71,764	78.5
Conservative	20,508	47.5	23,733	46.1	34,762	61.7
Labour	9,270	21.5	8,347	16.2	4,883	8.7
Lib Dem	11,471	26.5	16,020	31.1	15,483	27.5
Anti–EU	1,960	4.5	3,342 (2)	6.5	–	–
Others	–		–		1,175	
MP	Peter Bottomley (Con)		Peter Bottomley (Con)		Terence Higgins (Con)	
					Worthing	
Majority	9,037	20.9	7,713	15.0	19,279	34.2

Worthing West contains the bulk of the town of Worthing, including the town centre and the northern and western suburbs. The town started off life as a resort in 1798 when George III sent his daughter here to convalesce – it was close enough to Brighton for visits from her brother but it was deliberately far enough away not to be affected by his pleasure-seeking exploits. Gentility and respectability are hard-wired into Worthing's very identity; it describes itself as 'a gentle, welcoming resort and its main attraction is still the sea and all that goes with it.' The borough has a high proportion of the population, and an even higher proportion of votes cast, from retired people. Only the two inner wards of Central and Heene have even a trace of the poverty and shabbiness of less favoured seaside resorts (and they are not quite in the most deprived 20 per cent of England – compare Great Yarmouth and Hastings, for example). The Marine ward to the west of the centre is well-off by any standards. The constituency also includes an area of the Arun district to the west of Worthing, at Ferring and Rustington, which is of rather similar character.

When Tory MP Peter Bottomley relocated here from marginal Eltham in 1997 retirement was the last thing on his mind: his backbench career gained a new lease of life courtesy of Worthing's loyal Tories. Worthing West is the 40th safest Conservative seat in the country, although it has Liberal Democrat tendencies in local elections. The Lib Dems were two points ahead in 1995 and did much better than their parliamentary share in 2001. As in some other areas in Sussex, the local Lib Dem vote did not translate into national preferences and about a third of it flaked away to Labour and the Conservatives. Labour support in Worthing has grown considerably in recent years – from under 6 per cent in 1983 to the 2001 level of 21.5 per cent, but the party seems a long way short of winning a ward here, let alone challenging for the parliamentary seat. Even in the 1997 and 2001 elections the Conservatives prevailed comfortably, and surely will do so in future.

Tyne and Wear

	Conservative		Labour		Liberal Democrat		Others	
	Share of vote	Seats	Share of vote	Seats	Share of vote	Seats	Share of vote	Seats
2001	17.7	0	62.9	13	16.6	0	2.8	0
1997	17.3	0	67.1	13	11.8	0	3.8	0
1992	28.8	1	57.1	12	13.7	0	0.4	0
1987	27.6	1	53.6	12	18.6	0	0.3	0
1983	31.3	2	45.4	11	23.3	0	0.1	0

Tyne and Wear was a creation of the local government review of the 1970s. The county name has meant less since the abolition of the county council (with the other metropolitan counties) by Margaret Thatcher in 1986, though a number of quasi-governmental bodies still operate within its boundaries. Local government is now the preserve of five unitary metropolitan authorities, which in any case better reflect local communities and divides than does one 'super-council'. To the north of the Tyne, Newcastle is the most well-known of the region's towns and cities, a vibrant place which is in many ways the most clear-cut example of an English regional capital. The city has an influential council and currently provides the best part of three parliamentary seats, all held by Labour but with a significant opposition presence, formerly represented by the Conservatives (who had one parliamentary seat more or less continuously until 1987), though now as much by Liberal Democrats. Neighbouring North Tyneside is a mixture of traditional working class areas on the north bank of the Tyne (Wallsend, North Shields) and areas on the North Sea coast dominated by middle class professionals and the retired (Whitley Bay, Tynemouth); its parliamentary seats and local council both reflect this west–east division. Thus the Tyneside North parliamentary seat, currently held by cabinet minister, Stephen Byers, is safely Labour while the Tynemouth constituency was Conservative from 1950 until 1997; for the last ten of those years this was their only seat in Tyne and Wear.

To the south of the Tyne, Gateshead is a somewhat sprawling borough which is home to two of the north east's modern icons, the Metro Centre and 'Angel of the North' statue, which is dramatically situated next to both the main A1 and east coast railway line. Gateshead currently boasts only one whole parliamentary seat (Blaydon) but the largest part of two others (Tyne Bridge, Gateshead East & Washington West), although this is likely to change at the forthcoming boundary review (see below). South Tyneside is an uneasy marriage of South Shields and Jarrow, though just about the only thing which unites the two is loyal support for the Labour party, and finally Sunderland, whose population is actually the largest of the five areas, provides three more very safe Labour seats and these days the fastest counts anywhere on election night.

Politically the whole area is dominated by the Labour Party, who currently represent all 13 constituencies at Westminster and over 75 per cent of the 339 council seats. The Conservatives have no representation at all (aside from one regional MEP) in Gateshead, South Tyneside and Newcastle, but might retain long-term ambitions of regaining the Newcastle Central constituency, even though they have now fallen to third place here. Sunderland is one of very few urban areas in the north which retains something of a 'working class Tory' tradition, this resurfacing in 1999 when they narrowly won the ward of the sitting Labour council leader. Having said that, Labour still remain very much in the ascendancy and the prospect of a Tory MP in Sunderland, something which has existed as recently as 1964, seems a faintly ludicrous idea. The Tories will more likely pin their hopes on regaining Tynemouth, though they made little headway in 2001. The Liberal Democrats did rather better in Blaydon, which is now their top target in the region, and they will undoubtedly make another big push in 2005/6.

Local government

All five metropolitan authorities in Tyne and Wear are Labour controlled and have been for some time. Only North Tyneside presents a serious possibility of Labour losing their majority, since they face the challenge not only of a well-established Conservative group who represent the wards in the more affluent eastern section of the borough, but also a growing Lib Dem threat in their heartland wards around Wallsend. North Tyneside voted in favour of an elected mayor in a 2001 referendum and narrowly elected a Conservative mayor on the same day as the 2002 council elections returned a Labour council – an arrangement which will test the whole concept of elected mayors. Elsewhere local elections are a little less exciting, though South Tyneside (only ten non-Labour councillors out of sixty) is enlivened by internal Labour rivalries and Gateshead (where the Lib Dems provide the only opposition to Labour) held the most successful electoral pilot exercises in the country in May 2000 and May 2002, when all-postal ballots more than doubled the turnout. Sunderland has also experimented with a less successful week-long voting pilot exercise, though the newly designated city was more memorable in recent times for its Labour council leader being defeated in his ward by two votes; overall Labour still have a very large overall majority. Finally, one of the most striking patterns across the UK over recent decades has been the almost total collapse of the Conservatives in the urban north, and Newcastle council provides a textbook case. The former (pre-1973) council was actually controlled by the Tories following Labour's problems in the late 1960s, and even until 1984 the Tory group always exceeded twenty councillors, but their numbers gradually declined in the late 1980s and early 1990s until their last councillor was voted out of office in 1996. For a city the size of Newcastle upon Tyne to have no Conservative councillors at all, not even in prosperous neighbourhoods such as Gosforth or Jesmond, is a striking reminder of the serious problems the party must reverse if it is to again become a party of all England, never mind Scotland and Wales.

Boundary review

Tyne and Wear is destined to lose one of its thirteen constituencies when the boundary commissioners make their recommendations for the area. The most likely casualty is Tyne Bridge, an unloved 1980s creation which straddles the river to include wards from both Newcastle and Gateshead. Ten of the other twelve constituencies are under-sized (most by between 4,000 and 6,000 electors) and the process of bringing them up to the 69,000 average is bound to involve considerable upheaval. However, the boundary commission will be helped by the happy coincidence that the 21,000 shortfall of electors in constituencies to the north of the Tyne and 37,000 shortfall to the south almost exactly replicate the numbers which can be redistributed from each part of the Tyne Bridge seat.

BLAYDON

	2001		1997		1992 actual	
Electorate and turnout	64,574	57.4	64,699	71.0	66,044	77.7
Conservative	4,215	11.4	6,048	13.2	13,685	26.7
Labour	20,340	54.8	27,535	60.0	27,028	52.7
Lib Dem	12,531	33.8	10,930	23.8	10,602	20.7
Ind Labour	–	–	1,412	3.1	–	–
MP	John McWilliam (Lab)		John McWilliam (Lab)		John McWilliam (Lab)	
Majority	7,809	21.1	16,605	36.2	13,343	26.0

The constituency of Blaydon is entirely situated within the borough of Gateshead, though most lies well away from the centre of the town on the outside of the A1. Until 1973 this was part of County Durham, and as befits a Durham seat it has continually returned Labour Members of Parliament since 1935. One of the many communities which make up the seat, Chopwell, was affectionately known in the inter-war years as 'Little Moscow' because of its militancy: Karl Marx and Lenin appeared with Labour leader Keir Hardie on its colliery banner and the village still includes a Marx Terrace and a Lenin Terrace.

Now however Labour face potentially their greatest challenge yet in this part of the world, and one which comes not from the Conservatives (or Communists) but the Liberal Democrats. The Lib Dem strength, in local elections at least, is concentrated in some of the other small communities which make up the seat, such as Ryton, Crawcrook & Greenside, and Whickham. Their vote has been gradually building for a decade, most recently securing victory in Winlaton in the 2000 local elections, a ward where they picked up just 18 per cent of the vote in the mid 1990s. The council elections of 2000 saw the Lib Dems plus a couple of Liberals win six of the nine wards in the constituency and lead Labour overall by 52-40 per cent. Often this sort of advance has not translated into parliamentary votes, particularly in the urban north, but in 2001 some clearly did rub off in Blaydon. The 10 per cent Lib Dem advance was their 16th best performance in the country and their best in a Labour-held northern constituency, and came on top of a decent showing made in 1997. Whether they can go a stage further and actually gain the seat remains to be seen (there was a swing back to Labour in the 2002 locals), but in any event this now appears to represent the Liberal Democrats' best chance of defeating Labour in a seat they have not previously held in the north of England.

GATESHEAD EAST and WASHINGTON WEST

	2001		1997		1992 notional	
Electorate and turnout	64,041	52.5	64,114	67.2	67,822	71.7
Conservative	4,970	14.8	6,097	14.2	13,492	27.7
Labour	22,903	68.1	31,047	72.1	28,192	58.0
Lib Dem	4,999	14.9	4,622	10.7	6,963	14.3
Anti–EU	743	2.2	1,315	3.1	–	–
MP	Joyce Quin (Lab)		Joyce Quin (Lab)		Joyce Quin (Lab)	
					Gateshead East	
Majority	17,904	53.3	24,950	57.9	14,700	30.2

Gateshead East contains six wards to the south and east of the borough, together with two Washington wards which were added to the seat in the 1990s. Most of this is solid Labour territory, the party racking up no less than 77 per cent of the vote in the 2000 local elections in the Felling, Leam and High Fell wards, though in High Fell this marked a drop from the 89 per cent recorded in a three-way contest in 1995 when the Conservatives polled just 3.4 per cent. In the new town of Washington it is a similar story, though the turnout here in the 2000 council elections was particularly dismal, with fewer than one in six bothering to vote. The highest local election turnouts tend to come in Low Fell, which contains some of Gateshead's more affluent areas; here the Lib Dems win the council ward, and in the recent local polls they have also gained Pelaw & Heworth, a result which probably helped the party edge the Conservatives into third place in 2001. MP and former minister Joyce Quin (one of several North East MPs taking a close interest in the campaign for a regional assembly) will not be unduly concerned as despite a modest fall in the Labour vote, the parliamentary seat remains Labour's 22nd safest in the country.

HOUGHTON and WASHINGTON EAST

	2001		1997		1992 notional	
Electorate and turnout	67,946	49.5	67,343	62.1	66,678	69.4
Conservative	4,810	14.3	5,391	12.9	10,046	21.7
Labour	24,628	73.2	31,946	76.4	30,995	67.0
Lib Dem	4,203	12.5	3,209	7.7	5,221	11.3
Anti–EU	–	–	1,277	3.1	–	–
MP	Fraser Kemp (Lab)		Fraser Kemp (Lab)		Roland Boyes (Lab)	
Majority	19,818	58.9	26,555	63.5	20,949	45.3

The eastern half of the new town of Washington is linked with Houghton-le-Spring and a number of smaller communities such as Hetton-le-Hole, Ryhope, Penshaw and Shiney Row in what is essentially the borough of Sunderland's third constituency. This is a rock-solid Labour seat, currently their 8th safest in the UK, and has been held by former Labour party official and local lad Fraser Kemp since the retirement of Roland Boyes in 1997. Much of the constituency was at one time dominated by coal mining, but despite the industry's disappearance and consequent transformation of the landscape, the electoral geography has remained steadfast in its loyalty to Labour. In the 2000 local elections, the party's share of the vote exceeded 70 per cent in Hetton, Houghton, Ryhope and Shiney Row, while Washington North as usual went unopposed. Support for Labour is not quite as monolithic in the eastern estates of Washington, but this hardly matters when parliamentary majorities are in the order of 20,000. The area's most famous landmark, the temple-like Penshaw monument, seems likely to gaze over a Labour seat for many years to come.

JARROW

	2001		1997		1992 notional	
Electorate and turnout	62,631	55.1	63,963	68.7	65,577	73.2
Conservative	5,056	14.7	6,564	14.9	11,243	23.4
Labour	22,777	66.1	28,497	64.9	29,978	62.5
Lib Dem	5,182	15.0	4,865	11.1	6,749	14.1
Anti–EU	716	2.1	1,034	2.4	–	–
Ind Labour	391*	1.1	2,538	5.8	–	–
Others	357		444		–	
MP	Stephen Hepburn (Lab)		Stephen Hepburn (Lab)		Don Dixon (Lab)	
Majority	17,595	51.0	21,933	49.9	18,735	39.1

* the same candidate stood in 1997 and 2001, but title in 2001 was 'Independent'.

Jarrow is best known for mass unemployment (estimated at 68 per cent) in the 1930s and the resulting Jarrow Crusade when several hundred men marched in a dignified manner the length of the country to present a petition in London. What is less well known is that the parliamentary seat was actually won by the Conservatives in 1931, 'Red' Ellen Wilkinson regaining it for Labour by just 2,350 votes in 1935. This was not an unusual pattern (seats like Durham and Sedgefield were also lost during that four year period) but what it does clearly demonstrate is that the Conservatives attracted a large amount of working class support in the immediate pre-war years. This has more or less disappeared since 1945, and Jarrow is sometimes portrayed (for example by author John O'Farrell) as the totemic safe Labour seat, though in fact there are, as of 2001, twenty-nine which are even safer.

The constituency laps all the way around South Shields as far as the North Sea coast at Marsden Rock, and although most of the parliamentary seat is fertile territory for Labour, they poll less well in the wards farthest away from Jarrow itself, with villages such as Whitburn and Cleadon decidedly upmarket. Locally, the most serious threat to Labour comes from the Liberal Democrats, whose two South Tyneside wards (Cleadon & East Boldon and Hebburn Quay) both lie within the constituency. However in 2001 Labour's vote actually increased, almost certainly a result of changes in election law (the Registration of Political Parties Act) which would have prevented an 'Independent Labour' candidate who took 6 per cent of the vote in 1997 standing under the same label in 2001.

NEWCASTLE UPON TYNE CENTRAL

	2001		1997		1992 notional	
Electorate and turnout	67,970	51.3	69,926	65.9	69,376	70.5
Conservative	7,414	21.3	10,792	23.4	17,393	35.6
Labour	19,169	55.0	27,272	59.2	25,281	51.7
Lib Dem	7,564	21.7	6,911	15.0	6,208	12.7
Anti–EU	–	–	1,113	2.4	–	–
Others	723		–		–	
MP	Jim Cousins (Lab)		Jim Cousins (Lab)		Jim Cousins (Lab)	
Majority	11,605	33.3	16,480	35.8	7,888	16.1

It seems a long time since Newcastle Central was a Conservative-held seat and Piers Merchant was its MP, but this was the reality as recently as the mid-1980s. This misnamed seat (its centre of gravity being the large open space of the Town Moor rather than the city centre) was always felt to be a good Tory bet after the boundary revisions of the early 1980s as it included many of Newcastle's middle class neighbourhoods such as Jesmond, Kenton and South Gosforth. The majority of these areas were included in the former Newcastle North division, which was held by the Conservatives without interruption from creation in 1918 until abolition in 1983 and which somewhat confusingly was the main ancestral constituency to this one.

Tory strength here has ebbed rapidly since Merchant's defeat in 1987. Their vote has now fallen in four consecutive general elections, a period which has coincided with their wipe out on Newcastle council. Even in the 2000 local elections when they revived elsewhere, the Conservatives finished third in Jesmond and a distant second in Kenton, picking up less than 30 per cent of the vote in wards which they held until the mid 1990s. Consequently their fall to third place in the 2001 general election was no surprise, as the Liberal Democrats have long since taken over as the main opposition to Labour on Newcastle city council. This is all a stark reminder of just how far Conservative fortunes have fallen in the urban north, even in a mainly middle class constituency such as this.

NEWCASTLE UPON TYNE EAST and WALLSEND

	2001		1997		1992 notional	
Electorate and turnout	61,494	53.2	63,272	65.7	65,989	70.1
Conservative	3,873	11.8	5,796	13.9	10,421	22.5
Labour	20,642	63.1	29,607	71.2	26,466	57.2
Lib Dem	6,419	19.6	4,415	10.6	8,628	18.7
Anti–EU	–	–	966	2.3	–	–
Others	1,760(4)		805 (2)		744	
MP	Nick Brown (Lab)		Nick Brown (Lab)		Nick Brown (Lab)	
Majority	14,223	43.5	23,811	57.3	16,045	34.7

This constituency takes in the working class east end of Newcastle, including Walker, Byker and its (in)famous Byker Wall housing development, but also more residential areas around Heaton and some very upmarket territory neighbouring Jesmond Dene, where Labour polled less than 20 per cent in the 2000 local elections. Since the last boundary review the seat has extended eastwards into North Tyneside to include Wallsend, home of the Swan Hunter shipyard. The MP here for 18 years has been Nick Brown, formerly Labour's chief whip, who was unfortunate enough to be Minister for Agriculture at the time of the foot and mouth crisis.

Brown first gained election by a surprisingly wide margin, when in a titanic three-way battle in 1983, sitting MP Mike Thomas, an ex-Labour convert to the Social Democrats, finished in third place with just 27 per cent of the vote. The centre-party vote continued to disappoint until 2001, when there was a significant swing away from Labour towards the Liberal Democrats. Given that Newcastle East and Wallsend is an entirely urbanised seat, this was highly unlikely to have had much to do with the crisis in farming, but did reflect the advances made by the Lib Dems in recent council contests, particularly in Wallsend and the neighbouring North Tyneside ward of Northumberland. In the latter, Labour polled three-quarters of the vote in 1995, but by 2000 had lost all three council seats to the Lib Dems and were reduced to 30 per cent, a collapse in support which, as in nearby Blaydon, appears to have partly fed through into general election results. For now this leaves Labour's position in the constituency unaffected aside from a drop in the pecking order from 32nd safest seat in 1997 to 72nd after 2001; it seems a fair bet that for the moment at least Labour and Nick Brown will not be losing too much sleep over this having fought and won tougher battles in the past.

NEWCASTLE UPON TYNE NORTH

	2001		1997		1992 actual	
Electorate and turnout	63,208	57.5	65,385	69.2	66,187	76.8
Conservative	7,424	20.4	8,793	19.4	16,175	31.8
Labour	21,874	60.1	28,125	62.2	25,121	49.4
Lib Dem	7,070	19.4	6,578	14.5	9,542	18.8
Anti–EU	–	–	1,733	3.8	–	–
MP	Doug Henderson (Lab)		Doug Henderson (Lab)		Doug Henderson (Lab)	
Majority	14,450	39.7	19,332	42.7	8,946	17.6

Labour's result in Newcastle North in 2001 was one of their better outcomes in the north east region and appears strikingly at odds with their poor result in Newcastle East, all the more strange given that this is the one Newcastle constituency which includes a chunk of rural territory. Another oddity is the name of this constituency: a more accurate title would be Newcastle North West since many of the city's northern suburbs are in the present Central seat and bizarrely the old (pre-1983) Newcastle North provided no electors at all to the new version.

Much of this seat lies west of the city centre, beyond the A1, and a great deal of Labour's strength can be found in wards such as Lemington, Newburn and Denton. Indeed virtually the whole constituency is based on an outer tier of housing around the edges of the city, some such as Fawdon based on council estates and strongly Labour, and some, such as Grange and part of Westerhope more affluent and thus better for the opposition parties. The rural segment of the seat, which is all contained within Newcastle borough boundaries, includes Woolsington, Newcastle Airport and Dinnington, but its presence does not affect the political balance of the constituency, and Labour have been comfortable here since winning a tight three-way contest in 1983. Doug Henderson, North's MP since 1987, was briefly in the spotlight when he was made Minister for Europe immediately after Labour's 1997 election victory and despatched on a plane to Brussels, but since a short stint as Minister for the Armed Forces he has returned to the back-benches.

SOUTH SHIELDS

	2001		1997		1992 notional	
Electorate and turnout	61,285	49.7	62,324	62.5	65,863	69.7
Conservative	5,140	16.9	5,681	14.6	12,220	26.6
Labour	19,230	63.2	27,834	71.4	28,041	61.1
Lib Dem	5,127	16.8	3,429	8.8	5,626	12.3
Anti–EU	689	2.3	1,660	4.3	–	–
Others	262		374		–	
MP	David Miliband (Lab)		David Clark (Lab)		David Clark (Lab)	
Majority	14,090	46.3	22,153	56.8	15,821	34.5

South Shields is a surprisingly large town and occasional seaside resort guarding the south entrance to the River Tyne. It has a mainly working class character, though also includes a growing number of new housing developments and some more established affluent neighbourhoods close to the coastal attractions. Politically, this has been a safe Labour seat since 1935, when it was regained by the still largely unknown Home Secretary during the Attlee government, J.Chuter Ede. Ede's parliamentary career spanned forty-one years from his election in Mitcham in 1923 until standing down at the age of 82, a record that even surpasses recent incumbent David Clark, who stood down shortly before the 2001 election having also first been elected elsewhere (for Colne Valley) some thirty-one years previously. Few would bet against Clark's successor David Miliband, formerly the head of Tony Blair's policy unit, following his illustrious predecessors into the cabinet; certainly he should have few problems holding South Shields, though Labour here are not as monolithic in local contests as in some parts of the north east, with a respectable vote gained by both Conservative and 'Progressive' candidates in recent council elections in the wards near the coast.

SUNDERLAND NORTH

	2001		1997		1992 notional	
Electorate and turnout	60,846	49.0	64,711	59.1	65,400	68.4
Conservative	5,331	17.9	6,370	16.7	12,423	27.8
Labour	18,685	62.7	26,067	68.2	26,649	59.6
Lib Dem	3,599	12.1	3,973	10.4	4,895	11.0
Anti–EU	1,518	5.1	1,394	3.6	–	–
Others	687		409		747	
MP	Bill Etherington (Lab)		Bill Etherington (Lab)		Bill Etherington (Lab)	
Majority	13,354	44.8	19,697	51.5	14,226	31.8

Sunderland was for many years a heavily industrialised town including active shipyards and warehouses along the Wear and even its own coal mine at Wearmouth which was on a prominent site now occupied by the gleaming 'Stadium of Light' football ground. Such a heritage has left a lasting legacy of loyal support for the Labour party, even though the banks of the Wear have been transformed, now lined with modern industrial units, retail parks and a new University campus. Despite this change of appearance, large housing estates off the main roads such as Town End Farm and Castletown remain and continue to provide almost monolithic support for Labour. This does not mean Labour are without difficulties here: on the south bank of the Wear, Central ward produced a turnout of just 12 per cent in the 1999 local elections and an even more derisory figure in the following month's Euro poll. In 2002, Town End Farm produced a large minority vote (almost 30 per cent) for the BNP in the council elections. Meanwhile, a Southwick greengrocer has become nationally known as the 'Metric Martyr' after his prosecution for selling fruit and vegetables in imperial measures, which led to a great deal of publicity and a respectable vote for an anti-Euro Independent in 2001. Despite all this, and there being a reasonable Conservative vote up the coast in areas such as St Peter's, Roker, Seaburn and Fulwell, this remains and is likely to remain a very safe Labour seat.

SUNDERLAND SOUTH

	2001		1997		1992 notional	
Electorate and turnout	64,577	48.3	67,937	58.8	72,010	69.7
Conservative	6,254	20.1	7,536	18.9	14,706	29.3
Labour	19,921	63.9	27,174	68.1	28,829	57.5
Lib Dem	3,675	11.8	4,606	11.5	5,933	11.8
Anti–EU	470	1.5	609	1.5	–	–
Others	867 (2)		–		690	
MP	Chris Mullin (Lab)		Chris Mullin (Lab)		Chris Mullin (Lab)	
Majority	13,667	43.8	19,638	49.2	14,123	28.2

South was traditionally the more Tory of the Sunderland constituencies, though these days it is difficult to notice. Today the seat is memorable for producing record-breaking counts lasting less than an hour and the first declared result, which for a few minutes at least leaves novelist and former government minister Chris Mullin as the country's sole member of parliament. The result here gives the first clues to the national outcome, with the small 2 per cent swing to Labour in 1992 and much larger 10.5 per cent figure in 1997 providing a surprisingly accurate portent of things to come on both nights.

It is a surprise to many that this seat was represented by a Conservative from 1953 until 1964; even that year Labour only regained it by 1,500 votes. Some of the streets in wards like Thornholme still give an impression of faded grandeur, with names such as 'The Esplanade' and 'The Cloisters' suggesting a location in Harrogate or Cheltenham rather than Sunderland. In fact there was undoubtedly a great deal of wealth here in days gone by, much stemming from the busy port and shipbuilding industry, but as this has diminished in recent decades, there has been a significant political shift to the left. In recent council contests there seems to have been a revival by a group of voters previously assumed to have disappeared in urban seats such as this: the working class Tory. In 1999, the run down ward of Hendon, which is situated next to the docks, dramatically voted out Sunderland's council leader Bryn Sidaway, who had won by nearly 1,000 in 1995, the margin just two votes. A year later the Hendon voters proved that this was no flash in the pan by electing a second Conservative councillor, this time by a somewhat more comfortable margin. The Tories have thus been given great heart, and Labour a serious warning, by these results, though they will need to become even more dramatic if Sunderland South is to return to its former status as a marginal.

TYNE BRIDGE

	2001		1997		1992 notional	
Electorate and turnout	58,900	44.2	61,058	57.1	67,085	63.7
Conservative	3,456	13.3	3,861	11.1	9,443	22.1
Labour	18,345	70.5	26,767	76.8	28,520	66.8
Lib Dem	3,213	12.3	2,785	8.0	4,755	11.1
Anti–EU	–	–	919	2.6	–	–
Socialist	1,018 (2)	3.9	518	1.5	–	–
MP	David Clelland (Lab)		David Clelland (Lab)		David Clelland (Lab)	
Majority	14,889	57.2	22,906	65.7	19,077	44.7

The constituency of Tyne Bridge is alone in Tyne and Wear in bridging the famous river, but this relatively recent creation (1983) is unlikely to be mourned if, as expected, it is abolished in the forthcoming boundary review. The constituency includes inner-city wards of Gateshead such as Bensham and Saltwell, extending out to Dunston, which is best known for the large Federation Brewery and for producing the footballer Paul 'Gazza' Gascoigne. Much of the housing in the Gateshead section of Tyne Bridge consists of closely-packed terraced streets with the odd tower block and estate, all favourable territory for Labour, who recorded approximately 70 per cent of the vote in the 2000 local elections and over 80 per cent four years previously.

On the opposite bank, the four Newcastle wards in the seat cover the working class west end of the city: Scotswood, Benwell, Elswick and West City. All of these areas are now much harsher environments than the impression given out thirty years ago in *The Likely Lads*, often featuring in media reports as examples of inner-city deprivation. Elswick and West City include areas where the slums made way for ugly tower blocks in the late 1960s, and in a way these grim, fortress-like buildings sum up the problems here today, though it must be said that the terraced streets and even some new housing in Benwell reflect a certain sense of urban decay as well, one new estate facing demolition as nobody wanted to live there. Residents from Scotswood were in the forefront of opposition to recent Newcastle city council plans to knock down some of the housing in their ward; certainly no one could claim that this is an easy constituency to represent. That task has been performed since a 1985 by-election by David Clelland, who must contend with a very tough caseload, lower than average turnouts, but on the bright side very large majorities: after 2001 this was Labour's 11th safest seat in Britain.

TYNEMOUTH

	2001		1997		1992 notional	
Electorate and turnout	65,184	67.4	66,341	77.1	68,616	81.1
Conservative	14,686	33.5	17,045	33.3	27,056	48.6
Labour	23,364	53.2	28,318	55.4	23,527	42.3
Lib Dem	5,108	11.6	4,509	8.8	4,507	8.1
Anti–EU	745	1.7	1,281 (2)	2.5	–	–
Others	–		–		543	
MP	Alan Campbell (Lab)		Alan Campbell (Lab)		Neville Trotter (Con)	
Majority	8,678	19.8	11,273	22.0	3,529	6.3

Tynemouth can be categorised with a scattered group of seaside constituencies which were gained by Labour on above-average swings in 1997 to end lengthy periods of Conservative dominance. The swing here of 14 per cent was matched by that further down the east coast at Scarborough & Whitby, and exceeded by Hove on the south coast and by Crosby and Morecambe on the west. Four years on, all of these seats produced similar results for the second successive election. This time, the lack of any serious change reconfirmed the status of voters in traditional seaside resorts as a key, if somewhat unsung, section of the 'New Labour coalition'.

The great strides made by the Conservatives in local contests in Tynemouth since 1997 must have left the party bitterly disappointed not to have done better in 2001. Middle-class wards along the coast such as St. Marys, Whitley Bay, Cullercoats and Tynemouth itself were won by massive margins in 2000, despite the last three being won by Labour in the mid 1990s. Even though Labour remained very strong in Chirton, which includes the infamous Meadow Well estate, they lost North Shields as well, and overall the Tories won seven of nine wards in the constituency in 2000, leading Labour by more than 20 percentage points.

That Labour's local problems failed to feed through into the general election outcome at all is slightly mysterious, though one should note that the same pattern was repeated in both Morecambe and Scarborough. In Tynemouth Labour had the added advantage of the presence of their huge national call centre, whose success could be gauged by the announcement soon after the election that it would be replacing London's Millbank Tower as the party's permanent centre of operations. The move was widely trumpeted as a return to Labour's 'heartlands' and although this is a slight exaggeration (Tynemouth being held by the Conservatives from 1950 until 1997), party workers will hope that their relocation helps keep this seat, and as a result the whole of Tyne and Wear, in the red column on future election nights.

TYNESIDE NORTH

	2001		1997		1992 notional	
Electorate and turnout	64,914	57.7	66,449	67.9	68,368	73.8
Conservative	5,459	14.6	6,167	13.7	13,130	26.0
Labour	26,027	69.5	32,810	72.7	30,764	61.0
Lib Dem	4,649	12.4	4,762	10.6	6,580	13.0
Anti–EU	770	2.1	1,382	3.1	–	–
Socialist	564 (2)	1.5	–	–	–	–
MP	Stephen Byers (Lab)		Stephen Byers (Lab)		Stephen Byers (Lab)	
					Wallsend	
Majority	20,568	54.9	26,643	59.0	17,634	34.9

The western half of the North Tyneside council area forms the parliamentary seat confusingly known either as the same name as the borough or as Tyneside North. Like so many others in the region this is very strong territory for Labour, providing a secure berth since 1992 for former cabinet minister Stephen Byers. Most of the seat was previously part of the Wallsend constituency, which had been held by Labour throughout the post-war years, and which in an earlier period was represented by Britain's first woman cabinet minister, Margaret Bondfield, before like most of the Labour government she lost her seat in 1931. In the most recent boundary changes the town itself was linked up with Newcastle East, leaving a majority of electors behind and a need for a new name.

Whatever the title of the constituency, most of its neighbourhoods consist of a combination of terraced streets and council estates, extending from the Riverside ward (which includes the entrance to the Tyne Tunnel, international ferry terminal and Royal Quays retail development) in a north-westerly direction through Howdon and Battle Hill off the A19 and out to Longbenton and Killingworth, which are more or less a continuation of Newcastle and both Labour strongholds. The seat continues even further to include Dudley and the splendidly named Wide Open, which borders the A1 due north of Newcastle. The character of this far flung corner of the constituency is changing, with increasing numbers of Newcastle-bound commuters attracted by modern housing estates, but the growing Tory vote in local elections here seems to be doing little obvious damage to Labour's huge general election majority, this being their 15th safest seat in Britain after 2001.

Warwickshire

	Conservative		Labour		Liberal Democrat		Others	
	Share of vote	Seats	Share of vote	Seats	Share of vote	Seats	Share of vote	Seats
2001	39.4	1	42.4	4	15.6	0	2.5	0
1997	38.7	1	43.8	4	13.9	0	3.6	0
1992	49.6	3	33.4	2	16.0	0	1.0	0
1987	50.9	5	26.3	0	22.1	0	0.7	0
1983	49.2	5	24.3	0	26.0	0	0.5	0

Warwickshire was reduced in size by the formation of the West Midlands metropolitan county in the 1970s, which took the Solihull area out of it and left the remainder a peculiar boomerang shape stretching either side of Birmingham and Coventry. The constituencies in the current county are a bit of a patchwork, each having more to do with Birmingham or Coventry than they do with each other, but Warwickshire is a historic county with its own identity. The county, according to most opinion, gets more desirable as one progresses from north to south. Nuneaton and Bedworth are working class towns with mining heritage; Rugby is a mixture of railway and public school; Kenilworth, Warwick and Leamington are urbane and civilised and Stratford off to the south sits in deep rural territory. The county covers environments from Cotswold villages to tough midland industrial towns. The common impression of Warwickshire as an Old England heritage theme park – many visitors only see Stratford and possibly Warwick Castle – is belied by the reality of the industrial north.

The politics of the area has been similarly heterogeneous. The south has traditionally been a highly Conservative mixture of countryside and some cultured middle class towns, while the north was instinctively Labour-voting. Rugby in the middle swung from one side to the other, often according to its own particular opinions without paying a great deal of attention to the national movement of opinion. Recent political history in Warwickshire neatly illustrates the breakdown of the old certainties of politics. The Conservatives won Nuneaton in 1983, a seat which had been so safe for Labour in the 1960s that Harold Wilson trusted it to go to the polls four times in four years to facilitate the entry and exit of Frank Cousins from his Cabinet. They also carried Warwickshire North off for a clean sweep of the county in 1983 and 1987. The north Warwickshire midlands (ex) mining area joined similar areas in Leicestershire, Derbyshire and Nottinghamshire in voting Tory.

However, the Conservatives could only aspire to win all five constituencies in a landslide year; both Nuneaton and Warwickshire North would have been Labour in 1979 and they duly returned to Labour in 1992 when the Conservative majority was cut to 21. Neither is, in the short term, a realistic target for the Tories although over the long term the trends which have carried neighbouring Bosworth in Leicestershire into their column might work for them in North, and both seats had appreciable swings in their favour in 2001.

Unfortunately for the Conservatives, the Warwick & Leamington seat illustrates another trend – the 1990s collapse (continued in 2001) of the previously monolithic support the party enjoyed from affluent professionals, and the harmful effects on the local Conservative vote that flow from establishing an institution of higher learning. A similar lesson can be drawn from Rugby & Kenilworth – the formula of adding a marginal town to an exclusive wealthy enclave should be a recipe for a reliable Conservative seat. These two seats also illustrated the power of incumbency, at least in elections when voters do not perceive that they are making an important choice about the destiny of Britain. The Conservatives can only be relieved that the Lib Dems have not got very far with their activities in Stratford. With Warwick & Leamington probably slipping away from the Tories, with the aid of boundary changes, Rugby & Kenilworth is going to be the principal battleground in the next election or two. If the Conservatives do not snatch it back they are in big trouble.

Local government

Labour lost their casting vote control of Warwickshire county council in 2001 in a rather divided election in which the party lost support at both ends of the county but gained in the middle. The bulk of the Labour delegation of 28 (who form a minority administration) are from the towns of Nuneaton, Rugby and Warwick-Leamington. There are 20 Conservatives distributed from around the county, including better-off bits of the towns and rural areas, with a concentration in Stratford. The Liberal Democrats were the main gainers in the 2001 elections, rising from six to 13 scattered throughout the centre and south – the north is still bleak territory for them. There is a sole Whitnash Ratepayer, who continues to win elections despite the abolition of domestic rates in 1990.

Nuneaton & Bedworth borough council has been controlled by Labour since it was formed in 1973. The party has usually had a large majority, and continued to do so after all-out elections for new wards in 2002. It covers the most working class areas of the two constituencies in the north of the county. Neighbouring Rugby is a different matter, mixing urban and rural areas of entrenched party loyalties and consequently being under no overall control since 1973 except for a spell under the Conservatives in 1976-79. It usually elects annually, but all-out elections on new ward boundaries took place in 2002. The other council with annual elections is Stratford-on-Avon, which the Conservatives narrowly regained in 2000 after it had spent most of the 1990s under no overall control. It is the only district council in Warwickshire where the Liberal Democrats have much of a base. The other two councils are North Warwickshire (Polesworth, Arley, Atherstone) which has been under Labour control since 1973 except in 1976-79, although the Conservatives must hope to gain ground here after doing quite well in 2001, and Warwick (also covering Leamington and Kenilworth). Warwick council was Conservative from 1976 to 1995, but since then they have declined to being the third largest group on the council behind Labour and the Lib Dems.

Boundary review

The boundary changes promised in the next review will have radical implications in Warwickshire. It will gain a sixth seat and there will be knock-on alterations to the oversized constituencies in the south of the county. The provisional scheme created a new seat to be called Warwickshire Mid, based around

Kenilworth and a patch of countryside to its east around Southam, which will rival its near namesake Worcestershire Mid for the title of the safest Conservative seat in the midlands. Its creation will be marvellous for one Conservative's career, but a disaster for the Tories of the two marginal seats next to it – Warwick & Leamington and the renamed Rugby – which lose their best areas. Even if the Tories manage to regain one or both in the 2005 election it could prove a short term lease. Not surprisingly, there was a public inquiry but it had not reported at the time of going to press.

NUNEATON

	2001		1997		1992 actual	
Electorate and turnout	72,101	60.1	71,960	74.4	70,907	83.7
Conservative	15,042	34.7	16,540	30.9	25,526	43.0
Labour	22,577	52.1	30,080	56.2	27,157	45.8
Lib Dem	4,820	11.1	4,732	8.8	6,671	11.2
Anti–EU	873	2.0	1,771 (2)	3.3	–	–
Others	–		390		–	
MP	Bill Olner (Lab)		Bill Olner (Lab)		Bill Olner (Lab)	
Majority	7,535	17.4	13,540	25.3	1,631	2.8

Like Stratford, Nuneaton identifies strongly with a literary figure – in this case George Eliot, who set many of her novels in the area and after whose characters many of Nuneaton's schools and hospital wards are named. Her Nuneaton connections are arguably stronger than Shakespeare's with Stratford, but as she is a less internationally famous writer and there is less memorabilia to see, Nuneaton is not troubled by throngs of tourists. It is a working class, workaday town with a mining history, although its council takes great pride in its floral displays which would not disgrace a genteel spa.

Nuneaton has tended to vote Labour in all but the best Conservative years, although its allegiance was bolstered by the inclusion of Bedworth before 1983. Nuneaton is less of a monopoly than Bedworth; it is quite polarised, having some extremely safe Labour wards like Stockingford (74 per cent Labour in 2001) and Abbey (71 per cent). There are also middle class wards in the east of the town like Whitestone and Weddington where the Tories prevail more narrowly, plus the distinctly affluent St. Nicolas. The current boundaries take in an area from Rugby's rural surroundings which narrowly favours the Tories. The whole adds up to a seat that Labour could regain on a fairly large swing in 1992 and hold comfortably in the next two elections despite an adverse swing in 2001.

RUGBY and KENILWORTH

	2001		1997		1992 notional	
Electorate and turnout	79,764	67.4	79,406	77.1	78,639	83.0
Conservative	21,344	39.7	25,861	42.3	34,218	52.4
Labour	24,221	45.0	26,356	43.1	20,894	32.0
Lib Dem	7,444	13.8	8,737	14.3	9,971	15.3
Anti–EU	787	1.5	–	–	–	–
Others	–		251		202	
MP	Andy King (Lab)		Andy King (Lab)		James Pawsey (Con)	
Majority	2,877	5.3	495	0.8	13,324	20.4

Rugby is a town that seems to enjoy elections – it has consistently high turnout and showed a creditable commitment to parliamentary democracy in 2001. It also enjoys springing surprises and going its own way in elections, as in 1970 when it swung strongly to Labour and October 1974 when it moved towards the Tories. It has been influenced by MPs with strong personalities, such as W.J. Brown in the 1940s (who won as an Independent in 1945 against both Labour and Conservative) and Bill Price in 1966-79. Price managed to generate a considerable pro-Labour swing in 1970 despite the party's national defeat; observers at the time found it difficult to explain but it now appears an early demonstration of the impact an energetic candidate, who is hyperactive in the local media and good with casework, can achieve. More recently Rugby has reflected national trends but still surprised observers with its strong Labour showing in 1997 and 2001. It produced another demonstration of the strength of incumbency in 2001 with its endorsement of Andy King.

The current constituency links the town of Rugby with a small strip of rural territory leading to the wealthy small town of Kenilworth. Rugby is a railway town by tradition with an industrial, Labour presence particularly in the northern wards by the railway line and in the centre; it also has a noted public school and some middle class suburbs. Kenilworth is traditionally Conservative, although a sprinkling of its residents surely converted to New Labour in 2001 and 1997. Two of the three Kenilworth wards voted Lib Dem in the 2001 county elections, and although there must have been a Tory lead of some sort in the town in the general election the place has gone rather wobbly for them. The boundary changes will eventually remove Kenilworth, making the new Rugby seat a stronger bet for Labour – although with Rugby you can never be quite sure.

STRATFORD-ON-AVON

	2001		1997		1992 notional	
Electorate and turnout	84,219	65.2	81,542	76.2	77,443	80.1
Conservative	27,606	50.3	29,967	48.3	37,252	58.8
Labour	9,164	16.7	12,754	20.5	8,512	13.4
Lib Dem	15,804	28.8	15,861	25.5	16,247	25.7
Anti–EU	1,184	2.2	2,620 (2)	4.2	–	–
Green	1,156	2.1	–		–	–
Others	–		897 (3)		–	
MP	John Maples (Con)		John Maples (Con)		Alan Howarth (Con) (Lab)	
Majority	11,802	21.5	14,106	22.7	21,005	33.2

Stratford is, of course, known the world over as the birthplace of Shakespeare and reminders of this fact are everywhere in a town where tourism is the main industry. In summer it throngs with visitors from across the world, particularly the United States, but it also serves as a centre for a large rural area across the south of Warwickshire and has commuter trains to Birmingham. It is rather atypical of the constituency that bears its name, consisting of only about a third of the electorate and tending to prefer the Lib Dems to the Conservatives. The rest is in small towns like Alcester, Southam and a large number of villages, some of which are remote and agricultural and some rather charming and on the edge of the Cotswolds.

Stratford emerged as its own constituency in 1950 when it sent John Profumo to parliament; it has been Conservative since then with the exception of an interlude in 1995-97 when its sitting member, Alan Howarth, crossed the floor from Conservative to Labour. Like two other seats of exceptional Labour weakness, Leominster and Cornwall North, it has oddly had a period represented by a Labour MP. It predictably reverted to the Conservatives in 1997 when John Maples, defeated in Lewisham in 1992, won the seat back.

In a very good year the Liberal Democrats could think about challenging for Stratford. They led in local elections in 1991 and 1995 although their fortunes have faded in local government and the Conservatives have regained the council. Despite this waning base, the Lib Dems did manage a small swing in their favour in 2001. But the odds in Stratford are very heavily stacked towards the Conservatives. Other than Stratford town and Alcester, the Conservatives polled over 40 per cent in every ward in the county elections and over 60 per cent in two. It is their 36th safest seat in the country.

WARWICK and LEAMINGTON

	2001		1997		1992 notional	
Electorate and turnout	81,405	65.8	79,975	75.1	77,853	80.4
Conservative	20,155	37.6	23,349	38.9	31,028	49.6
Labour	26,108	48.8	26,747	44.5	19,564	31.2
Lib Dem	5,964	11.1	7,133	11.9	10,729	17.1
Anti–EU	648	1.2	1,790 (2)	3.0	–	–
Others	664		1,072 (3)		1,303	
MP	James Plaskitt (Lab)		James Plaskitt (Lab)		Dudley Smith (Con)	
Majority	5,953	11.1	3,398	5.7	11,464	18.3

Despite the ordering of the names, Leamington is a larger town than Warwick, although the two have grown together into a continuous urban area. Leamington is an attractive spa town, with gracious parks and Regency terraces in its centre, although there is some poverty behind the façade in wards such as Brunswick. It also has a considerable managerial and, increasingly, professional population commuting to Birmingham or Coventry, particularly the University of Warwick which lies between the town and Coventry. Many university workers and students prefer to live in Leamington than Coventry. There are some traditional working class areas, such as Brunswick and Willes wards (62 and 63 per cent Labour in 2001), as parts of the town are very much within the West Midland motor production network. Warwick is a smaller and older town. The constituency also includes a small rural element around the twin towns and a strip up to the west at the extremely affluent little town of Henley-in-Arden.

The constituency went Conservative in 1910 and for 87 years after that, and from 1923 to 1957 it was the constituency of Anthony Eden who served as Prime Minister in 1955-57. Even in 1945 Eden had a majority of over 17,000 although to be fair the constituency then included areas now part of Stratford. A more similar seat was still Tory by over 8,000 in 1966. Labour's gain in 1997 was an unprecedented triumph. Labour benefited not only from the national tide, but from demographic change.

New housing, often occupied by young and relatively liberal-minded professionals attracted by the architectural and cultural charms of the area, has sprouted in the area and the University of Warwick influence has been important. It was one of comparatively few places where the Conservatives did worse in the 1999 local elections than they did in 1995, and Labour followed up in 2001 with an even more emphatic victory.

In the boundary changes proposed by the commission, the Tory area of Henley-in-Arden and Tanworth is removed to the Stratford seat to compensate it for losses to the new Mid Warwickshire. The new version of this seat is so completely urban that it is designated a borough constituency, and it contains only one county ward where the Conservatives managed to win in 2001, namely Warwick South. With the Tories needing a 5.6 per cent swing to win already, with the demographic trend in the wrong direction for them and the prospective boundary changes on the way, we are a very long way from the days of Anthony Eden.

WARWICKSHIRE NORTH

	2001		1997		1992 notional	
Electorate and turnout	73,825	60.2	72,552	74.8	72,314	82.8
Conservative	14,384	32.4	16,902	31.2	26,124	43.6
Labour	24,023	54.1	31,669	58.4	27,577	46.1
Lib Dem	5,052	11.4	4,040	7.4	6,161	10.3
Anti–EU	950	2.1	1,450 (2)	2.7	–	–
Others	–		178		–	
MP	Mike O'Brien (Lab)		Mike O'Brien (Lab)		Mike O'Brien (Lab)	
Majority	9,639	21.7	14,767	27.2	1,453	2.4

Warwickshire North is a large semi-rural constituency just north of Birmingham and Coventry. It was brought together in 1983, when Bedworth was detached from Nuneaton and the remainder of the seat had to be disconnected from Meriden because of the metropolitan county boundary. Its political inclinations have been towards Labour in all but the best years for the Conservatives; although Francis Maude won it in its first two contests Mike O'Brien won with large majorities in 1997 and 2001.

Bedworth is the core Labour area in the constituency, a working class industrial town of 33,000 population lying between Nuneaton and Coventry which grew up because of coal seams lying close to the surface. Although mining has disappeared, its legacy is apparent. Its four wards varied between 55 per cent and 74 per cent Labour support in the 2001 county elections.

The rest of the constituency is in North Warwickshire borough, and consists of several little towns around the A5 (Roman Watling Street) and a rural former coalfield surrounding them. Atherstone, the headquarters of the council, has a population of only 8,600 and although mines and hats have gone (the last hat factory closed in 1999) it has distribution (TNT road haulage have their main depot here because of its strategic location) and manufacturing. In the south of this area, at Coleshill and Water Orton, the villages are convenient for Birmingham commuters and have been changing composition; Coleshill is comparable to Sutton Coldfield in some ways. The southern fringe is the only part which is regularly Conservative, although they also gained traditionally Labour Arley in 2001. Labour have some cause for concern after local election losses and a slightly above-average swing, but it is still a seat Labour are in little immediate danger of losing.

West Midlands – city of Birmingham

	Conservative		Labour		Liberal Democrat		Others	
	Share of vote	Seats	Share of vote	Seats	Share of vote	Seats	Share of vote	Seats
2001	26.4	1	51.6	10	15.6	0	6.4	0
1997	28.4	1	54.6	10	12.8	0	4.2	0
1992	40.3	3	45.9	9	13.0	0	0.8	0
1987	41.4	6	41.1	6	16.8	0	0.7	0
1983	41.4	6	39.1	6	18.8	0	0.7	0

Britain's second largest city, its population hovering slightly above one million, is Birmingham. It is a creation of the Industrial Revolution, having been fields and small villages in the 18th century, and despite its proud tradition of local government it was only designated a municipal borough in 1838. Manufacturing industry grew rapidly here throughout the Victorian period and Birmingham became the workshop of the world, producing a vast multiplicity of finished manufactured goods. In the 20th century it attracted the motor industry and is still sensitive to the fluctuations of that volatile trade.

Though dependent on manufacturing industry, Birmingham is far from being a single-class metropolis. Managerial and clerical workers were required to keep industry going, and Birmingham became a commercial and professional centre not just for its own trades but for the industries of the neighbouring Black Country region and the West Midlands more generally. Victorian Birmingham created not only smoky industrial slums but also grand villas and avenues in its suburbs and handsome civic and commercial buildings in the centre. The city centre was the work of the radical Liberal leader of Birmingham Joseph Chamberlain, who replanned it, municipalised services and established a powerful political machine in the 1870s which won all the city seats for the Liberals when it was divided in 1885. Then disaster struck the Liberals – Chamberlain fell out with Gladstone over Irish Home Rule and his machine worked in 1886 for the breakaway Liberal Unionists. From then on, Birmingham was solidly Unionist – the Liberal Unionists formally merged with the Tories in 1912. Their control was so total that they did not lose any seats even in the Liberal landslide of 1906.

Birmingham politics became a bit more plural with the rise of Labour in the 1920s, although it was not until 1924 that the party won its first Birmingham seat (King's Norton). In 1929, however, there was a short-lived Labour surge in the city, with Oswald Mosley playing an important part; but in 1931 and 1935 Labour lost everything again and Mosley abandoned reputable politics. Labour finally broke the hold of the Conservatives on Birmingham in 1945. The swing since 1935 was around 23 per cent, and over 30 per cent in some areas, making the national swing of 12 per cent look mild. Labour then won control of the city council in 1946. Birmingham's exceptional politics continued, as the prosperity of the 1950s held considerable attractions for Birmingham's working class voters and Labour did particularly badly in the city in 1959; when the economy seemed to be doing well under Wilson there was a big swing back to Labour in 1966. Since then, it has behaved more normally.

Birmingham's labour shortage in the 1950s and 1960s attracted large numbers of immigrants from Ireland (an Irish community had become established in the inter-war period) and further afield – the Indian subcontinent and the Caribbean. The inner city areas to the east (Small Heath and Sparkbrook) and west (Handsworth and Ladywood) of the city centre have become steadily more and more ethnic minority areas. At the time of the 1991 census the Asian population was 13.5 per cent of the city's total, with about 8 per cent in other ethnic minorities and 15 per cent (according to separate research) being Irish. The Asian proportion in particular will be considerably higher now.

These trends have had political consequences; as early as 1970 it was noticed that while the Conservatives achieved good swings in the white working class areas (like Northfield), they fared badly in more mixed areas (like Sparkbrook). Handsworth was a safe Tory seat in the 1950s but it fell to Labour in February 1974 and stayed comfortably Labour in 1979. Inner city north Birmingham even swung a little to Labour in 1983. Ethnic minority voters have now created rock-solid Labour seats, although in local elections many Muslim voters in particular have in recent years supported candidates with no major party affiliation.

Conservatism is still just about a going concern in Birmingham, unlike most of the other great cities. They hold Sutton Coldfield and can entertain hopes of recovering Edgbaston and Hall Green if they are fortunate in a future election, although Northfield and Selly Oak (which they won in the general elections of 1979, 1983 and 1987) now look very difficult. Since Chamberlain's defection Birmingham has been difficult ground for the Liberals and successors, although there was a brief flowering of municipal activism in the late 1960s which delivered them the Ladywood seat in a 1969 by-election. This victory was short lived and Yardley, their best hope, has frustrated them in 1997 and 2001.

Local government

Birmingham is a traditionally marginal city, which switched back and forward between Labour and the Conservatives seven times between 1966 and 1984. Labour have run the city since 1984, and enjoy a majority of 17 in 2002, which would withstand anything short of disastrous results in 2003. The Conservatives are secure in the Sutton Coldfield wards and have regained ground in the Edgbaston wards, and here and there in other areas like Northfield and Hodge Hill. In 2000 they overtook the Liberal Democrats to become the principal opposition party once again, although the Lib Dems also have solid areas in Yardley and some other scattered wards. No party other than Labour has a realistic chance of taking power on their own.

Boundary review

Birmingham wards, because of the size of the city, are very large, with electorates of around 17,000. This makes it difficult to assemble parliamentary constituencies, as with most seats three wards would produce a small seat and four wards a big one.

However, Birmingham is now only entitled to 10.2 seats, compared with its current allocation of 11. It is likely that the city will lose another constituency, having shed a seat at every redistribution since

1974. The eastern part of Birmingham has three small seats – Hall Green, Hodge Hill and Yardley – and it is likely that the most radical changes will be in this part of the city, but there are too many possible permutations to second-guess. There could even be a cross-borough seat with Walsall because of the low electorates in the northern Black Country seats.

BIRMINGHAM EDGBASTON

	2001		1997		1992 notional	
Electorate and turnout	67,405	56.0	70,310	68.9	70,873	71.8
Conservative	13,819	36.6	18,712	38.6	25,059	49.3
Labour	18,517	49.1	23,554	48.6	20,003	39.3
Lib Dem	4,528	12.0	4,691	9.7	5,158	10.1
Anti–EU	–	–	1,065	2.2	–	–
Others	885 (2)		443		643	
MP	Gisela Stuart (Lab)		Gisela Stuart (Lab)		Jill Knight (Con)	
Majority	4,698	12.4	4,842	10.0	5,056	9.9

Edgbaston is the constituency based on the west end of Birmingham, which like the west ends of other industrial cities (see Bristol, Sheffield and Glasgow) is the residential area favoured by the professional and intellectual middle class. Edgbaston ward has the oldest university in the city, the cricket ground and much high status housing, the latter trait shared with the neighbouring Harborne ward. But the old west end spills over into the Selly Oak seat and Edgbaston takes in some more ordinary suburban territory to the west in Quinton. The constituency and the traditional west end are not identical. The south-western side of Edgbaston is a rather different kind of area. Bartley Green ward has a certain notoriety among those who follow local elections for its wild electoral swings. It is a white, skilled working class and lower middle class area which can vote Labour from time to time but in a good Tory year like 2000 it is 70 per cent Conservative. Its deprivation statistics, however, are a little worse than safe Labour Birmingham wards like Stockland Green and in the worst 10 per cent in England.

In contrast to other cities the Conservatives are still strong in the west end of Birmingham and the Liberal Democrats do not feature. Labour only won Harborne ward in 1995 (and Edgbaston only in 1994, 1995 and 1998); Quinton is more inclined to the party and voted for them in 1998 ,1999 and 2002 as well as the peak years. The Conservatives have polled strongly in recent local elections here and led by 23 per cent in 2000, but were still trounced in the general election. Edgbaston was the first televised Labour gain on election night 1997 (see also Crosby) and an early declaration in 2001 also indicated that Labour was on course to hold on to nearly all its marginal seats. It is still sufficiently competitive that it is worth watching, and the Conservatives have not faded away here in local elections as in some other places; if they manage to win the parliamentary seat back Labour's overall majority will be nearly wiped out – it is the party's 82nd most vulnerable seat.

BIRMINGHAM ERDINGTON

	2001		1997		1992 *notional*	
Electorate and turnout	65,668	46.6	66,431	60.8	*74,434*	*68.1*
Conservative	7,413	24.2	11,107	27.5	*18,498*	*36.5*
Labour	17,375	56.8	23,764	58.8	*27,021*	*53.3*
Lib Dem	3,602	11.8	4,112	10.2	*5,187*	*10.2*
Anti–EU	521	1.7	1,424	3.5	–	–
Socialist	1,012 (2)	3.3	–	–	–	–
Others	681		–		–	
MP	Siôn Simon (Lab)		Robin Corbett (Lab)		Robin Corbett (Lab)	
Majority	9,962	32.6	12,657	31.3	*8,523*	*16.8*

Erdington is a mainly white working class constituency, with a strong Irish presence, in north east Birmingham. Its most famous landmarks are Spaghetti Junction, a complicated motorway interchange between the M6, A38 and local roads, and Fort Dunlop. Like West Bromwich East, it has seemed marginal in the past but has never fallen to the Tories since before 1945 – despite favourable boundary changes and Labour's weak campaign in 1983.

Kingsbury and Kingstanding are wards at opposite ends of the constituency, but they are similar in many ways – they are both mainly white and composed of inter-war and post-war council-built housing. Kingstanding has voted Labour solidly since 1970, as has Kingsbury since 1983. Stockland Green and Erdington wards have more mixed housing, and Erdington has even voted Conservative in better years for them in the past (although not since 1992). To the north, Erdington ward adjoins Sutton Coldfield but to the south Stockland Green and Kingsbury shade into the heavy industrial territory of Ladywood and Hodge Hill, and socially and politically the Erdington constituency stands somewhere between them. Robin Corbett stood down in 2001 and bequeathed a safe seat to his young successor, *Spectator* columnist Siôn Simon.

BIRMINGHAM HALL GREEN

	2001		1997		1992 *actual*	
Electorate and turnout	57,563	57.5	58,783	71.1	60,103	78.2
Conservative	11,401	34.5	13,952	33.4	21,649	46.1
Labour	18,049	54.6	22,372	53.5	17,984	38.3
Lib Dem	2,926	8.8	4,034	9.6	7,342	15.6
Anti–EU	708	2.1	1,461	3.5	–	–
MP	Stephen McCabe (Lab)		Stephen McCabe (Lab)		Andrew Hargreaves (Con)	
Majority	6,648	20.1	8,420	20.1	3,665	7.8

Hall Green is a suburban constituency to the south of Birmingham city centre, adjoining Solihull and although much less affluent it has some attractive and leafy areas. It was Conservative from its creation in 1950 until Labour captured it in 1997 on a very high swing.

Hall Green constituency is composed of three wards. Hall Green itself is a rather traditional inter-war suburb inhabited by white families and a habit of voting Liberal Democrat (it has done so since 1984, except for occasional Tory victories in 1992, 1998 and 2002). Billesley and Brandwood are both mixtures of privately built and rather superior council-built housing. Both have usually been Labour, with Billesley a little more loyal in the past; both voted Tory in the council elections of 2000 but Labour in 2002. Despite Hall Green ward's Lib Dem tendencies in local elections, the parliamentary constituency is a very weak one for the centre party and Labour currently has a strong lead and a high share of the vote. Hall Green is still, just about, a marginal. To win the next general election the Conservatives will need to reclaim Hall Green and then a few more on top, so it is one to watch if the party recovers well. The Tories still exist in local government here, and enjoyed a slight lead across the constituency in relatively poor local elections for them in 1998 and 1999.

BIRMINGHAM HODGE HILL

	2001		1997		1992 actual	
Electorate and turnout	55,254	47.9	56,082	60.9	57,581	70.9
Conservative	5,283	20.0	8,198	24.0	14,827	36.3
Labour	16,901	63.9	22,398	65.6	21,895	53.6
Lib Dem	2,147	8.1	2,891	8.5	3,740	9.2
Anti–EU	275	1.0	660	1.9	–	–
BNP/ NF*	889	3.4	–	–	370	0.9
PJP	561	2.1	–	–	–	–
Others	409 (2)		–		–	
MP	Terry Davis (Lab)		Terry Davis (Lab)		Terry Davis (Lab)	
Majority	11,618	43.9	14,200	41.6	7,068	17.3

* BNP vote 2001, NF vote 1992

Hodge Hill is a working class area of Birmingham stretching eastwards from the city centre. Labour has only lost the seat, which was previously called Stechford, once - in a 1977 by-election. Hodge Hill falls into two rather distinct parts. The outer wards, Shard End and Hodge Hill, are mainly white with a high proportion of council tenants – particularly in Shard End, a post-war council built area. The inner ward, Washwood Heath, is older owner-occupied housing which has been undergoing rapid demographic change as it becomes an increasingly Asian area, a northern extension to the Sparkbrook district.

While all component parts have voted Labour in the last couple of general elections, the main challenger in local elections is different in each section. Hodge Hill ward goes Tory in a relatively good year for them such as 1987, 1991 or 2000, but is generally Labour. Shard End is Labour except for a freak Tory win in 1992. Washwood Heath was solidly for Labour from 1969 to 1998, but in 1999 and 2000 Asian candidates standing under the 'Justice for Kashmir' label won.

Hodge Hill/Stechford has had, other than the 1977-79 Conservative interlude, only two MPs since it was split from Yardley in 1950. First was Roy Jenkins, and by the end of the current parliament Terry Davis will nearly have matched Jenkins's 27 years of service.

BIRMINGHAM LADYWOOD

	2001		1997		1992 *notional*	
Electorate and turnout	71,113	44.3	70,126	54.2	*71,943*	*58.5*
Conservative	3,551	11.3	5,052	13.3	*8,596*	*20.4*
Labour	21,694	68.9	28,134	74.1	*30,065*	*71.4*
Lib Dem	2,586	8.2	3,020	8.0	*3,447*	*8.2*
Anti–EU	283	0.9	1,086	2.9	–	–
PJP	2,112	6.7	–	–	–	–
Others	1,267 (3)		685		–	
MP	Clare Short (Lab)		Clare Short (Lab)		Clare Short (Lab)	
Majority	18,143	57.6	23,082	60.8	*21,469*	*51.0*

Ladywood is effectively Birmingham Central. The constituency, and indeed the Ladywood ward, includes the civic and shopping centres of the city as well as a stretch of inner city territory to its north and west in the wards of Nechells, Aston and Soho. Despite the imposing Victorian buildings of the city centre the Ladywood constituency suffers from severe poverty and deprivation. Ladywood had the highest unemployment of any constituency in the UK at the time of the 2001 election – 13 per cent in May 2001. Aston is the 27th most deprived ward in England, and the other elements of the constituency are not much better off.

It is also a 'majority-minority' seat in which Asian and black voters are the majority, and all parts of the seat are ethnically mixed. Soho is composed of older terraces, while Aston and Nechells have a lot of post-war council housing. Ladywood sends Clare Short to parliament and is an utterly safe Labour seat. In local elections there has not been the same challenge as in the eastern inner city from Justice For Kashmir (who polled only 18 votes in the Ladywood ward in 2000), but the Liberal Democrats won a surprising – possibly fluke – four-vote victory in Nechells in 2000.

BIRMINGHAM NORTHFIELD

	2001		1997		1992 *notional*	
Electorate and turnout	55,922	52.8	56,866	68.3	*54,594*	*74.4*
Conservative	8,730	29.6	10,873	28.0	*17,273*	*42.5*
Labour	16,528	56.0	22,316	57.4	*18,652*	*45.9*
Lib Dem	3,322	11.2	4,078	10.5	*4,692*	*11.6*
Anti–EU	550	1.9	1,243	3.2	–	–
Others	404 (3)		337		–	
MP	Richard Burden (Lab)		Richard Burden (Lab)		Richard Burden (Lab)	
Majority	7,798	26.4	11,443	29.5	*1,379*	*3.4*

Northfield is, despite its name, in the far south west of Birmingham, strung out along the A38 on the edge of the West Midland conurbation. Much of its housing was built in the interwar period, by the council and by private developers, to house the workers of the expanding car and engineering industries sited out here. The dominant presence is the troubled motor works at Longbridge, which came close to closure in 2000 and contributed to some poor local election results for Labour in the West Midlands.

The constituency is a white, working class marginal, which unlike Erdington did transfer allegiance to the Conservatives in the three Thatcher general elections. Labour regained it narrowly in 1992 and have held it comfortably since, only suffering a small adverse swing in 2001 after the Longbridge trouble.

Northfield itself is a ward which is Conservative in all but the best Labour years (1990, 1994-96) – it is mainly owner-occupied. Weoley, a sprawling area of council and private estates, is by contrast Labour in all but best Tory years (1983, 1987, 1991-92, 2000). Longbridge, a similar sort of area, voted similarly except in 2000 when Labour hung on despite a large swing to the Conservatives. Having weathered the Longbridge crisis, Labour can look forward to holding the seat with renewed confidence, although the party can never be complacent about Northfield. After all, it was the place that went Conservative in 1979 on a swing of over 10 per cent and reaffirmed its allegiance to the Tories in 1983 despite the industrial devastation of the early 1980s.

BIRMINGHAM PERRY BARR

	2001		1997		1992 notional	
Electorate and turnout	71,121	52.6	71,150	64.5	72,453	73.4
Conservative	8,662	23.1	9,964	21.7	19,867	37.4
Labour	17,415	46.5	28,921	63.0	27,596	51.9
Lib Dem	8,566	22.9	4,523	9.9	5,720	10.8
Anti–EU	352	0.9	843	1.8	–	–
Socialist	2,230 (3)	6.0	–	–	–	–
Others	192		1,636 (3)		–	
MP	Khalid Mahmood (Lab)		Jeff Rooker (Lab)		Jeff Rooker (Lab)	
Majority	8,753	23.4	18,957	41.3	7,729	14.5

Perry Barr, the north west section of Birmingham, is divided into two dissimilar pieces. The northern wards of Oscott (north of the M6) and Perry Barr are predominantly white, with Oscott being a council built estate and Perry Barr more mixed, and formed the core of the previously marginal Perry Barr constituency. The other half of the current seat belongs to the inner city – Handsworth and Sandwell wards. These were, back in the 1950s and 1960s, the core of a Conservative residential seat, but the streets and avenues of Handsworth and Sandwell have become majority non-white. The area gained a bad reputation in 1985 because of riots, although there are also some extremely pleasant districts.

The changing demography of the inner city part is reflected in politics. Labour gained Handsworth ward for the first time in 1971, and have never lost it since; Sandwell was first gained in 1981 and, other than a lapse in 1982, has been Labour since. The other two wards are less decisive. Oscott has been generally Labour, though the Conservatives made a surprise gain in 2002. Perry Barr has had phases of voting for all three parties, but is now mostly Lib Dem v Labour.

Perry Barr produced Labour's third worst result nationally in 2001, with a drop of 16.5 per cent in the party's share of the vote; only Wyre Forest and Shaun Woodward's St. Helens South seat saw a greater slide in Labour support.

Khalid Mahmood replaced popular Labour MP Jeff Rooker in 2001. It seems probable that some white voters in the north of the seat swung behind the Liberal Democrats, while Labour also suffered defections to left wing parties which polled 6 per cent. Mahmood should be able to recoup most of the losses in the next general election. Although safely Labour, Perry Barr still has interesting if rather unsavoury electoral features; it is hard to resist the conclusion that the scale of the desertion from Labour in 2001 had a lot to do with racism.

BIRMINGHAM SELLY OAK

	2001		1997		1992 actual	
Electorate and turnout	71,237	56.3	72,136	70.1	72,195	76.6
Conservative	10,676	26.6	14,033	27.8	23,370	42.3
Labour	21,015	52.4	28,121	55.6	25,430	46.0
Lib Dem	6,532	16.3	6,121	12.1	5,679	10.3
Anti–EU	568	1.4	1,520	3.0	–	–
Green	1,309	3.3	–	–	535	1.0
Others			755 (3)		262 (2)	
MP	Lynne Jones (Lab)		Lynne Jones (Lab)		Lynne Jones (Lab)	
Majority	10,339	25.8	14,088	27.9	2,060	3.7

Selly Oak is a sliver of territory from the southern edge of the city stretching inwards towards the city centre. Its four wards are an interesting mixture. Moseley is the inner ward, a Conservative area until the 1980s when demographic change tipped it over to Labour (Labour only won it once before 1988, and have only lost it once since).

Selly Oak ward was once a ward which Labour could aspire to only in the best years, like 1952 and 1981, but it has been Labour in good times and bad from 1994 until at least the time of writing. Kings Norton is a peripheral post-war council estate ward; parts of it are run down but for the most part it is a relatively good estate. Bournville is a model suburb constructed for workers at a chocolate factory; it is still governed by restrictive covenants that prohibit the sale of alcohol within the Bournville estate, but most of it is owner-occupied. The outer wards, Kings Norton and Bournville, can vote Conservative in a good year for that party like 2000 or 2002, but Labour are more resilient in the inner two wards. In a relatively even year like 1999 all the Selly Oak wards vote Labour.

Labour first won the parliamentary seat in October 1974, and the retrieval of the seat from the Conservatives in 1992 has an air of finality to it now. Selly Oak has just a trace of the post-Labour switch of educated progressives to the Lib Dems and others. The most serious threat is probably from the boundary review; Selly Oak borders two undersized seats and it is quite possible that it could be redistributed beyond recognition.

BIRMINGHAM SPARKBROOK and SMALL HEATH

	2001		*1997*		*1992 notional*	
Electorate and turnout	74,358	49.3	73,215	57.0	*72,745*	*67.7*
Conservative	3,948	10.8	7,315	17.5	*12,604*	*25.6*
Labour	21,087	57.5	26,841	64.3	*31,052*	*63.1*
Lib Dem	4,841	13.2	3,889	9.3	*3,916*	*8.0*
Anti–EU	634	1.7	737	1.8	–	–
PJP	4,770	13.0	–	–	–	–
Green	–	–	959	2.3	*1,657*	*3.4*
Others	1,367 (3)		2,024 (4)		–	
MP	Roger Godsiff (Lab)		Roger Godsiff (Lab)		Roy Hattersley (Lab)	
					B'ham Sparkbrook	
Majority	16,246	44.3	19,526	46.8	*18,448*	*37.5*

Sparkbrook and Small Heath is the south-eastern inner city constituency of Birmingham, a strongly Asian – particularly Muslim – area. The wards of this seat have taken to behaving strangely in local elections. The mainly white council estate ward of Fox Hollies resembles neighbouring Yardley in voting Lib Dem by over 55 per cent in local elections (except in a by-election in June 2001, when increased turnout led to a Labour win on a swing of over 20 per cent). This is no coincidence, as it seemed possible that the ward would move into Yardley at the last boundary review, but the activism has continued. Small Heath ward returned 'Justice for Kashmir' (JFK, aka PJP – People's Justice Party) councillors in all local elections during the 1997 parliament but returned to Labour in 2002. Sparkbrook ward, a wretchedly deprived area, is still Labour, although PJP is capable of a strong challenge, and Sparkhill is a confusing battle between Labour, Lib Dem and various fragments from Labour and PJP, where Labour won with under 25 per cent of the vote in 2000.

In contrast to this diversity and confusion at a local level, the parliamentary constituency is solidly Labour. Sparkbrook has voted Tory once since the war, in 1959, but in both parts of this seat the Tories disappeared from view by the 1980s as it became increasingly Asian. There was not much room for further growth in Labour support in the 1990s and Muslim voters in particular have become less solid in their allegiance. The People's Justice Party won 13 per cent of the vote in 2001 in the parliamentary election, a sign that there might be a future for religiously based parties in certain areas.

BIRMINGHAM YARDLEY

	2001		*1997*		*1992 actual*	
Electorate and turnout	52,444	57.2	53,151	71.1	54,755	78.0
Conservative	3,941	13.1	6,736	17.8	14,722	34.5
Labour	14,083	46.9	17,778	47.0	14,884	34.9
Lib Dem	11,507	38.3	12,463	33.0	12,899	30.2
Anti–EU	329	1.1	810 (2)	2.1	–	–
Others	151		–		192	
MP	Estelle Morris (Lab)		Estelle Morris (Lab)		Estelle Morris (Lab)	
Majority	2,576	8.6	5,315	14.1	162	0.4

Yardley is an incongruous place for a serious Lib Dem challenge. It lacks the social base of students and middle class professionals which has created their stronger areas in other big cities – Bristol West, Cardiff Central and north Leeds. Yardley is instead a white, working class area to the east of the city, which before 1992 produced surprisingly good results for the Conservatives in the elections they won. Now the Tories have been squeezed out of contention and the Liberal Democrats have made Yardley the most marginal seat in the city of Birmingham, and Estelle Morris the Cabinet minister most vulnerable to electoral defeat.

The story of local elections in Yardley has been of Liberal Democrat consolidation. Before the 2002 elections, Yardley ward itself had voted solidly for them since 1984, Sheldon since 1988 and Acocks Green since 1990. In local elections the Liberal Democrats grind out victories year after year with around 56–57 per cent of the vote across the constituency but in 2002 excelled themselves by gaining two-thirds of the votes cast. There are still comparatively few seats where there is a two-party battle involving only Labour and the Lib Dems, and Yardley is the front line. The Lib Dems thought they might have won it in 2001, particularly as their candidate John Hemming had won fame as the man who saved Longbridge, but Labour held on thanks to a burst of hard campaigning and the loyalty of the Labour vote. However, the Lib Dems could well win Yardley in an election when Labour are more vulnerable nationally than 2001.

SUTTON COLDFIELD

	2001		1997		1992 actual	
Electorate and turnout	71,856	60.5	71,918	72.9	71,444	79.5
Conservative	21,909	50.4	27,373	52.2	37,001	65.2
Labour	11,805	27.2	12,488	23.8	8,490	15.0
Lib Dem	8,268	19.0	10,139	19.3	10,965	19.3
Anti–EU	1,186	2.7	2,401	4.6	–	–
Others	284		–		324	
MP	Andrew Mitchell (Con)		Norman Fowler (Con)		Norman Fowler (Con)	
Majority	10,104	23.3	14,885	28.4	26,036	45.9

Sutton Coldfield sends, rather reluctantly, a delegation of councillors to Birmingham city hall although it has up to now resisted any idea of being described as 'Birmingham Sutton' or any such formulation for parliamentary purposes. The other middle class Birmingham Tory seats have succumbed to demographic and political change but Sutton remains safe for the party. It is a semi-independent, affluent township composed of wealthy suburban closes and avenues – Four Oaks, Vesey and New Hall are the three, all Conservative, wards of the seat. Its residents are the wealthiest members of the Birmingham middle class.

Sutton Coldfield is so loyally Conservative that its previous member, Norman Fowler, would occasionally be amused by projections on by-election results programmes in the 1980s and 1990s that he would be the sole survivor among Tory MPs. Even in the wipe out local elections of 1995 the Conservatives won only a shade below 50 per cent against evenly split opposition. The Conservatives have not even lost a local council election for any Sutton ward since a one-off Liberal win in April 1973. Despite a pick-up in the Labour share of the vote in 2001, typical for such a high-status area, Sutton Coldfield has only slid to the relative weakness of being the 28th safest Conservative seat in the land. Fowler passed the torch to Andrew Mitchell, former MP for Gedling, in 2001.

West Midlands – Black Country

(Comprising the boroughs of Dudley, Sandwell, Walsall and Wolverhampton)

	Conservative		Labour		Liberal Democrat		Others	
	Share of vote	Seats	Share of vote	Seats	Share of vote	Seats	Share of vote	Seats
2001	32.3	1	54.1	12	9.8	0	3.8	0
1997	29.5	1	51.0	11	9.1	0	10.4	1
1992	42.4	4	45.9	9	10.6	0	1.1	0
1987	43.1	5	40.4	8	16.6	0	0.0	0
1983	40.8	4	38.2	9	20.7	0	0.3	0

The Black Country is a sprawling conurbation to the west of Birmingham. It was not produced by growth around a big city but by the expansion of a lot of smaller industrial towns and villages in the early 19th Century. Its mines are all long-since worked out but there is still a good deal of manufacturing industry, based on medium-sized plants rather than big industrial combines. Towns became specialists in one area or another – locks in Willenhall, chains in Cradley Heath, glass-blowing in Wordsley. Except in Wolverhampton there has traditionally been little commerce or middle class employment in the area other than in a managerial capacity, with many professional services being conducted out of Birmingham. It is still a mainly working class area, a landscape of straggling and very parochial small industrial towns crisscrossed by railways and canals. An important factor in local politics and society is the enormous circulation of the local paper, the *Wolverhampton Express and Star*, which helps foster a distinct political culture.

The Black Country has a peculiar local political tradition of populist Conservatism. It was affected by Chamberlain's defection from the Liberals in 1886 and, although all seats were vulnerable to the Liberals in a good year for them like 1906, an even election like December 1910 saw the Conservatives dominate. Labour swept to victory in these areas in 1945 but the tide then ebbed in each election until 1966. It had never been as supportive of Labour as its working class demographics would have suggested, and in the 1960s in particular it had a reputation for working class racism. Now, however, the ethnic minority population has become well-integrated – young Asians talk with broad Black Country accents - and race relations tend to be good in the area with a few exceptions. There is little appetite for racist politics now except in a couple of wards; even in a low turnout by-election in West Bromwich West in November 2000 the BNP lost its deposit. The ethnic minority population is concentrated in the Warley constituency at Smethwick, south Walsall and the eastern and central parts of Wolverhampton.

A generation ago, things were very different. Enoch Powell, the MP for the anomalous (for this region) middle class seat of Wolverhampton South West, with his notorious Rivers of Blood speech in

1968, attracted instant support across the country but had a more significant effect on the politics of the region. In June 1970 the national swing was 4.7 per cent, but it reached 7 per cent here. Powell's advice to vote Labour in February 1974 was followed by a 7.5 per cent swing to Labour compared to 0.8 per cent nationally. In the 1980s, however, the Black Country was a zone of stability despite national political trends. The Alliance made no impact, there was no particular increase in working class Conservatism and Labour held on comparatively well except in Wolverhampton North East and the increasingly middle class seats of Dudley West and Aldridge Brownhills. Black Country seats all voted the same way in 1992 as they did in 1983 and 1979.

All the seats in the area voted Labour in 1997, on swings approximating the national trend, save two. One of the exceptions was technical, as Speaker Betty Boothroyd's seat at West Bromwich West was not contested by the main parties, but the other (Aldridge-Brownhills) was an impressive Conservative hold in a seat which had voted Labour in both 1974 elections.

In the period after 1997 it looked as if the Black Country would be one of the better areas for the Conservatives at the 2001 election. Local and European election results in the area had been encouraging in 1999 and 2000, and in the West Bromwich West by-election of November 2000 they achieved their best result of the parliament (the swing to Labour since the last party contest here in 1992 was only 2 per cent). It might have been expected that Black Country voters would respond favourably to Hague's populism and nationalism in the general election. In the event, the swing between 1997 and 2001 in the region (excluding non-comparable West Bromwich West) was only 1.1 per cent to the Conservatives, a desperately disappointing result that produced no gain in seats.

For the next election, the Conservatives must aspire to regain Wolverhampton South West and Stourbridge, although both seats require nearly a 5 per cent swing. The two Dudley seats and Halesowen & Rowley Regis are more distant targets, clustering around a required 9 per cent swing. New Labour had a firm grip on the loyalties of this peculiar region in the elections of 1997 and 2001 and it looks difficult for the Tories to recover – although nothing can be ruled out here. Dudley in particular has a tradition of extreme swings.

Local government

Before reorganisation in the 1960s and 1970s the Black Country was a confusing area administratively, with islands of Worcestershire such as Dudley town and even Oldbury marooned in a sea of Staffordshire. New county boroughs were created in 1966 and then some merged again when the West Midlands metropolitan county took over in 1974. Since its abolition in 1986 there have been four free-standing metropolitan boroughs.

Sandwell borough, covering Warley and West Bromwich, is the most solidly Labour local authority in the region. Labour still won over two thirds of the wards at stake in the 2000 local elections, so there appears to be no real challenge to the party's control. Dudley borough, which includes Stourbridge, was often Conservative before the 1990s and elected more Tory than Labour councillors in 2000, and Labour's majority fell to a precarious two in May 2002. This will be tested in subsequent rounds of elections. Wolverhampton, too, is marginal, with a Labour majority of eight; a Conservative challenge failed badly in 2002 and they must hope to do better over the next few years. Walsall has the most peculiar local politics of any of the West Midland boroughs. Labour have sometimes taken control, but never for very long, and often in controversial circumstances. The leadership of the council were expelled in the mid 1990s and carried on operating as dissident Labour councillors for a while. Walsall was the left wing exception to the generally stolid centre right Labour politics of the Black Country. Walsall now has a unique system of internal devolution, in which neighbourhood councillors are elected from 'patches' – an electoral unit smaller than a ward. Walsall is now a closely balanced hung council.

Boundary review

Sandwell and Dudley were paired in the 1997 boundary review and awarded seven seats, which will probably remain minimally disturbed. The problem is more in the northern two boroughs, both of which have three rather small seats. It would be possible to pair Walsall and Wolverhampton and for the pairing to lose a seat, to leave them untouched except for shifting one ward in Wolverhampton, or even to create seats crossing the Walsall borough boundary on both sides, with Birmingham and Wolverhampton. As in the rest of the West Midlands, we will not find out the boundary commission's proposals until near the end of the current review.

ALDRIDGE-BROWNHILLS

	2001		1997		1992 actual	
Electorate and turnout	62,361	60.6	62,441	74.3	63,404	82.6
Conservative	18,974	50.2	21,856	47.1	28,431	54.3
Labour	15,206	40.2	19,330	41.7	17,407	33.3
Lib Dem	3,251	8.6	5,184	11.2	6,503	12.4
Others	379		–		–	
MP	Richard Shepherd (Con)		Richard Shepherd (Con)		Richard Shepherd (Con)	
Majority	3,768	10.0	2,526	5.4	11,024	21.1

Aldridge-Brownhills, the eastern stretch of the borough of Walsall, has a peculiar electoral record – it is the only seat Labour won in 1974 but not before (under the guise of Walsall South) or since. Boundary changes in 1983 helped the Conservatives, but not decisively. The 1974 Labour victories probably owed something to Enoch Powell, but since then demographic change has carried the seat to the right as the towns have become increasingly suburban, inhabited by middle-aged white people. Another important factor is Conservative MP Richard Shepherd, a genuinely libertarian, sceptical voice on many issues with a significant personal vote. These factors helped the Tories to damp down the swing here to less than 8 per cent in 1997. The increase in their majority in 2001 has probably put the seat beyond Labour's reach.

Parts of Aldridge-Brownhills are highly Conservative, as are several other of the wards of this constituency – Aldridge Central & South over 80 per cent in 2000, with Streetly and Aldridge North & Walsall Wood not far behind. Streetly is in the bottom 10 per cent of wards in England for deprivation. It sits just across Sutton Park from Sutton Coldfield and is part of that bourgeois township for postal purposes. The other two Tory fortresses are only middling socially, but this area seems not to like its proximity to the sometimes chaotic Labour politics of Walsall. Hatherton-Rushall is a little less safe, and Pelsall is now Lib Dem, but in a good year like 2000 the Tories have a comfortable lead even in Brownhills, a small and traditionally working class place which is effectively part of the Cannock Chase scatter of industrial towns.

DUDLEY NORTH

	2001		1997		1992 notional	
Electorate and turnout	68,964	55.9	68,886	69.4	70,484	77.1
Conservative	13,295	34.5	15,014	31.4	23,776	43.8
Labour	20,095	52.1	24,471	51.2	24,730	45.5
Lib Dem	3,352	8.7	3,939	8.2	5,273	9.7
Anti–EU	–	–	1,201	2.5	–	–
Socialist	–	–	2,155	4.5	–	–
BNP/ NF *	1,822	4.7	1,028 (2)	2.2	565	1.0
MP	Ross Cranston (Lab)		Ross Cranston (Lab)		John Gilbert (Lab)	
					Dudley East	
Majority	6,800	17.6	9,457	19.8	954	1.8

* BNP vote 2001, combined NF and National Democrat vote 1997, NF 1992.

The north constituency covers the town centre of Dudley, including its castle and zoo. The centre of Dudley has a rather depressed air to it because of the construction of the shopping centre at Merry Hill in Dudley South, but Dudley is actually one of the better-off of the Black Country towns. Dudley North also includes the Black Country Museum which examines the area's industrial past. Despite being rather hilly terrain, the area is crisscrossed by canals. The town centre wards are generally Labour, although the Lib Dems managed to win the St. James ward in 2002 as an island in a generally weak area for them. The Castle & Priory ward gave the BNP 26 per cent in the 2002 election.

As well as Dudley town centre, Dudley North contains several semi-independent industrial villages and small towns. Precisely which towns are added determines the allegiance of the seat – the previous Dudley East was Labour even in 1983, while North is basically a marginal seat. Coseley is furthest north, towards Wolverhampton, and its East ward is consistently Labour while West (part of Sedgley and the suburb of Roseville) is marginal. Sedgley is a rather middle class and Conservative area on the very edge of the West Midland conurbation, looking out from its ridge over the plains of Shropshire, and Gornal to its south is a Conservative-inclined marginal which has seen large privately-built estates springing up in recent years. The latter areas came from the former Tory-inclined marginal seat of Dudley West rather than the Labour East seat. All the wards showed very large swings against Labour in the local elections of May 2000, giving the Conservatives a lead of 49 per cent to 38 per cent; the Tories led by 2 points in the 1999 Euro elections. However, the disgruntlement shown then had dissipated by the time of the general election and Ross Cranston had a very small swing against him. The rise of the BNP in 2001 – it was the extreme right party's best constituency in the West Midlands – casts a small cloud over the politics of the area. Dudley North is a seat the Conservatives must aspire to win if they intend to be the largest party in the next parliament, and Dudley South will probably ride in tandem.

DUDLEY SOUTH

	2001		1997		1992 notional	
Electorate and turnout	65,579	55.4	66,793	71.7	66,927	79.5
Conservative	11,292	31.1	14,097	29.4	22,296	41.9
Labour	18,109	49.8	27,124	56.6	25,025	47.0
Lib Dem	5,421	14.9	5,214	10.9	5,886	11.1
Anti–EU	859	2.4	1,467	3.1	–	–
Others	663		–		–	
MP	Ian Pearson (Lab)		Ian Pearson (Lab)		John Blackburn (Con) Dudley West**	
Majority	6,817	18.8	13,027	27.2	2,729*	5.1*

* Estimated Labour majority allowing for boundary changes
** Ian Pearson (Lab) elected for Dudley West at December 1994 by–election.

Dudley South consists of a number of small interconnected towns stretching west from the inner southern area of Dudley itself. To the west are the towns of Kingswinford and Wordsley, traditional mining and glass centres and to the east Netherton and Pensnett. In the centre is Brierley Hill, site of the Merry Hill shopping centre which is so enormous that it has its own small monorail system.

It is a seat with an interesting past. As Kingswinford it was one of Labour's first ever gains, a Conservative loss against the tide in 1918, and stayed loyal to Labour except for the 1931 wipe out. After 1950, under new boundaries as Brierley Hill, it was more marginal and went Conservative in 1959. The rapid growth of new suburban housing in the area, changing the social composition of what had previously been insular industrial and coal mining towns, tipped the constituency to the right and Labour failed to win it back even in 1966. Enoch Powell helped Labour recover it in 1974, this time in a new form as Dudley West, but it continued the drift to the Conservatives after they gained it in 1979. The death of MP John Blackburn in 1994 caused the first by-election of Blair's leadership, and a mammoth swing of 29 per cent showed that the new suburbanites had taken an instant positive view of New Labour. Yet more boundary changes in 1997 made the new South seat an even better bet for Labour (it lost the rather Tory Sedgley and Gornal and gained the Labour-inclined Netherton area) and despite its traditional marginality Ian Pearson had another crushing win in 1997.

Labour performed poorly in mid term in 1997-2001. The Conservatives had a wafer-thin lead in the 1999 Euro election, but Labour led in the 2000 local elections by 122 votes despite suffering a large hostile swing. The reason Labour could lead narrowly was the 30 per cent polled by the Lib Dems, who are a presence in Kingswinford in particular in local elections but do not show in national elections at the moment. South did produce quite a large swing against Labour in 2001, but much of this was because of the unwinding of the by-election factor which had inflated Labour's performance in 1997.

HALESOWEN and ROWLEY REGIS

	2001		*1997*		*1992 notional*	
Electorate and turnout	65,683	59.8	66,538	73.3	68,414	79.4
Conservative	13,445	34.2	16,029	32.9	24,306	44.7
Labour	20,804	53.0	26,366	54.1	24,181	44.5
Lib Dem	4,089	10.4	4,169	8.5	5,384	9.9
Anti–EU	936	2.4	1,244	2.6	–	–
Others	–		953 (2)		452	
MP	Sylvia Heal (Lab)		Sylvia Heal (Lab)		NEW SEAT	
Majority	7,359	18.7	10,337	21.2	125	0.2

Halesowen and Rowley Regis attracted some attention in the run-up to the 2001 election as the seat the Conservatives would need to gain to win an overall majority in the House of Commons. It was not surprising, given the national result, that the Conservatives were still well adrift when the votes were counted in June 2001. It is now Labour's 132nd most marginal constituency, and the 154th Conservative target. They could now win it while falling ten seats short of an overall majority, so it is still one of the key battlegrounds of the next election if the Conservatives are going to challenge for power.

57 per cent of the constituency is in the borough of Dudley, around the town of Halesowen. This area sits on the edge of the West Midland conurbation and has some affluent neighbourhoods – its Tory-voting South ward is the least deprived in the Black Country other than Streetly (in Aldridge-Brownhills); it is a continuation of the middle class residential belt of Birmingham Edgbaston. Halesowen's other three wards are less select, a mixture of estates, residential areas and a rather down-market town centre. Hayley Green is a Labour area, while Halesowen North and Belle Vue & Hasbury have usually been Labour lately but were Conservative gains on very high swings in 2000 and the latter ward was still Tory in 2002.

The minority of the constituency comes from the Sandwell borough, around the attractively named industrial town of Rowley Regis and including Cradley Heath and Blackheath. This part is solidly Labour and, despite large swings in 2000 the party retained all three wards. This area forms something of an anchor for the Labour vote in a rather volatile constituency.

STOURBRIDGE

	2001		1997		1992 notional	
Electorate and turnout	64,610	61.8	64,984	76.5	65,947	77.3
Conservative	15,011	37.6	17,807	35.8	24,907	48.8
Labour	18,823	47.1	23,452	47.2	19,519	38.3
Lib Dem	4,833	12.1	7,123	14.3	6,011	11.8
Anti–EU	763	1.9	1,319	2.7	–	–
Others	494		–		566	
MP	Debra Shipley (Lab)		Debra Shipley (Lab)		Warren Hawksley (Con) Halesowen & Stourbridge	
Majority	3,812	9.5	5,645	11.4	5,388	10.6

Stourbridge, unlike most of the rest of the Black Country, was formerly in Worcestershire rather than Staffordshire and preserves a certain distance from the conurbation. It has much less heavy industry and is for the most part a residential area with a distant history as a market town and a more recent tradition of glass manufacture. About half the constituency is the town and its outskirts, but about a third is more reminiscent of other Black Country seats in consisting of closely packed and interconnected small industrial towns at Quarry Bank, Cradley and Lye. The remainder is made up by Amblecote, which was formerly one of the faster growing parts of the old Dudley West constituency with new private housing estates. It is a mixed constituency and something of a microcosm of marginal England. It has voted Labour, but not overwhelmingly, in its first two contests since it was separated from Halesowen in 1997. There is a spectrum of different sorts of ward, from the safe suburban Conservative ward of Pedmore & Stourbridge East (containing the Junction station) to safe Labour industrial Quarry Bank & Cradley; there are two wards in the west of the constituency where the Lib Dems are locally active.

As in a lot of the region, Stourbridge can be volatile. Labour did badly in the 2000 local elections and four of the six wards changed hands. The Conservative lead of 18 points gave them hope that the seat would be winnable in 2001, but as it happened there was little change on 1997. It remains a key marginal (Labour's 53rd most vulnerable), although Labour could survive its loss with an overall majority of 50.

WALSALL NORTH

	2001		1997		1992 actual	
Electorate and turnout	65,981	49.0	67,587	64.1	69,605	75.0
Conservative	9,388	29.1	11,929	27.5	20,563	39.4
Labour	18,779	58.1	24,517	56.6	24,387	46.7
Lib Dem	2,923	9.0	4,050	9.4	6,629	12.7
Anti–EU	812	2.5	1,430	3.3	–	–
Ind Con	–	–	911	2.1	–	–
Others	410		465		614	
MP	David Winnick (Lab)		David Winnick (Lab)		David Winnick (Lab)	
Majority	9,391	29.1	12,588	29.1	3,824	7.3

Walsall North does include the north, and part of the centre of the town of Walsall, but the bulk of its electorate is in two separate small industrial towns which are part of the metropolitan borough of Walsall. Three wards of Walsall North are Bloxwich (including Blakenall), a severely deprived heavy industrial town north of Walsall itself. Blakenall is particularly badly off. Another two wards are Willenhall, one of the more depressed and down-at-heel of the Black Country towns (it was formerly a centre for making locks). The North seat contains some estates and inner city areas at Birchills-Leamore and part of the rather better-off Victorian town centre, which has a celebrated New Art Gallery. Walsall as a whole has been dominated by heavy metal-bashing industry and the production of leather goods (the football team are known as the Saddlers).

Despite all this, and an electorate dominated by working class voters, North has not been a safe Labour seat since a shock Conservative gain in a 1976 by-election (caused by the pending imprisonment of John Stonehouse and taking place during the IMF crisis). Though David Winnick regained the seat in 1979 the Conservatives remained competitive and fielded strong candidates in successive elections, and can do well in local elections even in pretty unprepossessing wards in Bloxwich. Labour did well in 2001 to repeat their 1997 percentage majority given the constituency's recent history and the reunion of the Conservative vote behind a populist campaign. Former council leader Dave Church stood for the Socialist Alliance but only attracted 1.3 per cent of the vote. While a peculiar seat, Walsall North has affected normality in the last couple of contests.

WALSALL SOUTH

	2001		1997		1992 actual	
Electorate and turnout	62,626	55.7	64,221	67.3	65,643	76.3
Conservative	10,643	30.5	13,712	31.7	20,955	41.9
Labour	20,574	59.0	25,024	57.9	24,133	48.2
Lib Dem	2,365	6.8	2,698	6.2	4,132	8.3
Anti–EU	974	2.8	1,662	3.8	–	–
Others	343		149		840 (2)	
MP	Bruce George (Lab)		Bruce George (Lab)		Bruce George (Lab)	
Majority	9,931	28.5	11,312	26.2	3,178	6.4

Before 1974 there was a Conservative constituency called Walsall South, but that included places now in Aldridge-Brownhills. Like West Bromwich East, the current Walsall South is a Labour constituency which the Conservatives have come close to winning in their best years 1983 and 1987 but never actually followed through.

Walsall South contains some middle class suburban areas, Paddock and Pheasey; the latter lies just across the border from the Oscott area of Birmingham Perry Barr, and Paddock in particular is almost as powerfully Conservative as places in Aldridge-Brownhills. Labour strike back in this divided constituency in the inner city, Asian areas such as Pleck, Palfrey and the town centre St. Matthews ward (although the Conservatives won the latter two in 2000), and most strongly in the distinct town of Darlaston in the west of the constituency.

Labour are capable of polling very poorly in mid term elections here, such as the 1999 European election when the Conservatives were ahead – it is the furthest seat south which Labour 'lost' then but had held in 1983 and 1987. The 2000 local elections were another terrible beating for Labour in wards which should, on the basis of their demographics, be utterly reliable. None of this, however, seems to make much difference in general elections and Bruce George had a small swing in his favour in 2001. Walsall seems to take pleasure in defying expectations.

WARLEY

	2001		1997		1992 notional	
Electorate and turnout	58,065	54.1	59,793	65.0	62,589	71.5
Conservative	7,157	22.8	9,362	24.1	15,334	34.3
Labour	19,007	60.5	24,813	63.8	23,743	53.1
Lib Dem	3,315	10.6	3,777	9.7	5,112	11.4
Anti–EU	–	–	941	2.4	–	–
Socialist	1,936	6.2	–	–	–	–
Others	–		–		561	
MP	John Spellar (Lab)		John Spellar (Lab)		Andrew Faulds (Lab)	
					Warley East	
Majority	11,850	37.7	15,451	39.7	8,409	18.8

'Warley' is an umbrella name for part of the patchwork of industrial and post-industrial towns and villages that makes up the Black Country. The best-known of these towns is Smethwick, which became famous in political circles for rejecting Labour's Patrick Gordon Walker in 1964 in a spasm of racist opinion but is now a place with a generally tolerant attitude and a large Asian population. It lies just west of the Ladywood area of Birmingham and is similarly dominated by the Labour Party even in bad years. The Soho and Victoria ward, comprising the north side of Smethwick, is among the 100 worst-off wards in England. Further south is Warley itself, across the city border from Edgbaston and having more suburban and Conservative characteristics than the other wards of the seat. To the west, Langley and Bristnall are a bit more volatile. The landscape of Warley is very industrial and its population, except in the Old Warley area, is working class and multiracial.

There is no threat to Labour's dominance in Warley in local or national politics, although it is notable for having given Arthur Scargill's Socialist Labour Party a saved deposit, with 6.2 per cent of the vote against right-wing Labour minister John Spellar.

WEST BROMWICH EAST

	2001		1997		1992 notional	
Electorate and turnout	61,180	53.4	63,432	65.4	67,232	73.8
Conservative	8,487	26.0	10,126	24.4	18,797	37.9
Labour	18,250	55.9	23,710	57.2	23,782	47.9
Lib Dem	4,507	13.8	6,179	14.9	6,591	13.3
Anti–EU	835	2.6	1,472	3.5	–	–
Others	585		–		477	
MP	Tom Watson (Lab)		Peter Snape (Lab)		Peter Snape (Lab)	
Majority	9,763	29.9	13,584	32.7	4,985	10.0

West Bromwich East is the north eastern part of the Black Country borough of Sandwell. It is where the M5 and M6 meet at a giant motorway intersection which is a visual (and audible) presence in many parts of the seat. East contains the centre of West Bromwich, a town with a fairly easy ethnic mix and a shopping centre that serves a considerable hinterland. To the east of the centre, hard by the Birmingham city limit, is The Hawthorns, the home of West Bromwich's football team. The constituency also extends to some estates and suburban areas around the town, such as Friar Park and the Jekyll-and-Hyde Charlemont area, a mixture of some leafy avenues and a gaunt tower block estate. Geographically distinct from the main part of the constituency are two wards which lie between Birmingham's Perry Barr district and the south of Walsall, namely Great Barr and Newton. These have a much more suburban quality than the rest of the constituency and indeed the borough – they are the best residential areas in the Sandwell borough except for the Old Warley area. The Liberal Democrats do surprisingly well in local elections, particularly in the Newton-Great Barr area and Charlemont and polling over 30 per cent in the constituency as a whole, but this is not apparent from their general election performance.

West Bromwich East has in the past seemed the most marginal constituency in Sandwell. Labour had a close shave in 1983 when Peter Snape survived by fewer than 300 votes, and his lead remained in three figures in 1987. But West Bromwich East has never actually tipped over into the Conservative column, and in the last two elections Labour's majority has been boosted into relatively safe levels. The party would have to be doing almost as badly as the Tories did in 1997 or 2001 to lose this seat.

WEST BROMWICH WEST

	2001		1997		1992 notional	
Electorate and turnout	66,765	47.7	67,513	54.4	68,115	69.4
Conservative	7,997	25.1	–	–	17,763	37.6
Labour	19,352	60.8	–	–	23,937	50.6
Lib Dem	2,168	6.8	–	–	5,577	11.8
Speaker	–	–	23,969	65.3	–	–
Anti–EU	499	1.6	–	–	–	–
Ind Lab	–	–	8,546	23.3	–	–
BNP/ ND*	1,428	4.5	4,181	11.4	–	–
Others	396		–		–	
MP	Adrian Bailey (Lab)		Betty Boothroyd (Speaker)		Betty Boothroyd (Lab) (Speaker)	
Majority	11,355	35.7	15,423	42.0	6,174	13.1

* BNP vote 2001, National Democrat vote 1997

Parliamentary by-election 23 November 2000: [Electorate 68,408 Turnout 27.6%]. Lab 9,640 (51.1), Con 6,408 (33.9%, LD 1,791 (9.5), BNP 794 (4.2), Anti–EU 246 (1.3). MP: Adrian Bailey (Lab) majority 3,232 (17.1).

As with some other seats this constituency's name is a simplification. East contains West Bromwich's town centre; West consists of outlying districts and small joined-up towns which would admit to being part of West Brom only if pushed. The largest centre is Wednesbury, where mining was replaced by heavy industry in the Victorian era. There are some poor and unpleasant council estates in the area, a dependence on declining heavy industry and an ethnically mixed population.

Oldbury, has a history of chemicals production; now it houses Sandwell borough's civic centre and is the site for new shopping development. Tipton has attracted some notoriety lately for political extremism. It gave the BNP 24 per cent in the 2000 local elections and is also home to some islamic extremists. However, the BNPvote in 2001 in the constituency was a lot less than the 16 per cent polled by the National Front (admittedly in the absence of a Liberal candidate to split the protest vote) when Betty Boothroyd was first elected in 1973. Labour prevail in most wards in a normal local election, although there are Conservatives in Wednesbury in particular.

Boothroyd's last contest in 1997 was as incumbent Speaker; the Lib Dems and Conservatives stood down and in some cases actively campaigned for her. When she resigned from parliament and normal party politics resumed, the Conservatives had some hope for the West Bromwich West by-election in November 2000. It came quite soon after the 'fuel crisis' had caused the only serious wobble in the first-term Labour government's popularity and the Black Country had been one of the better areas for the Conservatives in their good local elections of May 2000. While it was their best result in the parliament, Tory hopes were disappointed and they fell significantly short of their 1992 performance.

WOLVERHAMPTON NORTH EAST

	2001		1997		1992 notional	
Electorate and turnout	59,616	52.8	61,677	67.1	63,383	78.2
Conservative	9,019	28.6	11,547	27.9	20,528	41.4
Labour	18,984	60.3	24,534	59.3	24,275	49.0
Lib Dem	2,494	7.9	2,214	5.3	3,657	7.4
Anti–EU	997	3.2	1,192	2.9	–	–
Liberal	–	–	1,560	3.8	1,087	2.2
Others	–		356		–	
MP	Ken Purchase (Lab)		Ken Purchase (Lab)		Ken Purchase (Lab)	
Majority	9,965	31.6	12,987	31.4	3,747	7.6

Wolverhampton North East now seems like a solid Labour seat again, but it provided the party with the only loss it suffered outside London and the south east in the 1987 election. The Conservative gain in 1987 was truly historic – they had never won the seat or its predecessor Wolverhampton East before as it was Liberal from 1885 to 1945 and thereafter solidly Labour. It also proved to be an aberration which was quickly put to an end, with Labour's Ken Purchase recovering the seat thanks to a large increase in his vote in 1992. In 1997 and 2001 it turned in big Labour majorities and now seems out of danger.

North East is a mixture of several different sorts of heavily urban territory. In the north there are peripheral, mainly white estates at Oxley and Bushbury, while to the south are the severely deprived inner city areas of Low Hill and Heath Town. The Low Hill estate is officially the worst-off place in the city, while Heath Town is ethnically mixed and troubled. Further out are suburbs at Fallings Park, and the notionally separate community of Wednesfield. There is only one usually Conservative ward in North East, the rather low-status estate of Bushbury, but in a good year for them they can win both Wednesfield wards and Fallings Park. The Conservatives led Labour here by 44 per cent to 41 per cent in the 2000 local elections, winning four out of seven wards (and missing Oxley by six votes) compared to only one in 1999, so there is still the potential for serious two party competition in elections here. This potential has been dormant in recent general elections and the Conservatives can only hope to come back into contention if they are doing well nationally and can craft a special appeal to the white working class.

WOLVERHAMPTON SOUTH EAST

	2001		1997		1992 actual	
Electorate and turnout	53,243	51.3	54,329	64.1	56,170	72.9
Conservative	5,945	21.8	7,020	20.2	12,975	31.7
Labour	18,409	67.4	22,202	63.7	23,215	56.7
Lib Dem	2,389	8.8	3,292	9.4	3,881	9.5
Anti–EU	–	–	980	2.8	–	–
Others	554		1,336 (2)		850	
MP	Dennis Turner (Lab)		Dennis Turner (Lab)		Dennis Turner (Lab)	
Majority	12,464	45.7	15,182	43.6	10,240	25.0

Wolverhampton South East is the strongest Labour seat in the borough. The south eastern parts of the city of Wolverhampton include some very poor and deprived areas – East Park ward is a sad shadow of its western twin, Blakenhall is an ethnically mixed inner city area and Ettingshall is industrial; all three vote Labour even in bad local elections for the party. The balance of the seat is made up by Spring Vale, an estate that is the only Lib Dem voting area of Wolverhampton, and the town of Bilston which tends to vote Labour. Wolverhampton SE voted 51 per cent Labour, 27 per cent Conservative in the 2000 local elections when Labour generally did poorly. Blakenhall's Labour support exceeded 70 per cent even then. In all, the seat adds up to a gritty, industrial and loyal Labour constituency just outside the ranks of the fifty safest.

The electorate in this constituency is too small for it to remain undisturbed by the boundary review. In the absence of a more radical solution pairing the Black Country boroughs together, this might well involve the transfer of a ward from South West, but whichever is chosen will have little impact on the Labour stronghold of South East.

WOLVERHAMPTON SOUTH WEST

	2001		1997		1992 actual	
Electorate and turnout	65,909	62.1	67,553	72.4	67,368	78.2
Conservative	16,248	39.7	19,539	39.9	25,969	49.3
Labour	19,735	48.3	24,657	50.4	21,003	39.9
Lib Dem	3,425	8.4	4,012	8.2	4,470	8.5
Anti–EU	684	1.7	–	–	–	–
Liberal	–	–	713	1.5	1,237	2.3
Green	805	2.0	–	–	–	–
MP	Robert Marris (Lab)		Jenny Jones (Lab)		Nicholas Budgen (Con)	
Majority	3,487	8.5	5,118	10.5	4,966	9.4

Wolverhampton South West is one of several constituencies – Finchley and Huyton (until 1983) are others – which is indelibly associated with a single politician. In this case the politician is Enoch Powell, who represented the constituency from 1950 until his public repudiation of the Heath government in February 1974. Powell's successor Nick Budgen was rather in his mould – a Tory intellectual who was 'dry' economically but capable of hitting populist notes in campaigns for immigration control and against entanglements with the European Union.

At the high point of Powellism in 1970, and for a while in the 1980s, South West seemed a safe Conservative seat, but it should be noted that its predecessor had been Labour in 1945 and even 1929 and 1906. Labour's gain in 1997 was, however, surprisingly easy given the apparently ingrained Tory loyalties in the constituency. The Conservatives reasserted themselves quickly, with leads of 13 points in the 1999 local elections and 22 points in 2000, and it was a surprise that Labour held on relatively easily in 2001 despite the retirement after one term of Jenny Jones.

The South West seat includes Wolverhampton's city centre in the St. Peter's ward, and Graiseley to its south, which usually give Labour a healthy majority, but most of the constituency is affluent white middle class suburbia. Park ward is the old west end of Wolverhampton, and while the Conservatives usually win there is a respectable Labour vote. The outer four wards are heavily Conservative, with all of them voting more than 60 per cent for the Tories in 2000 (Tettenhall Wightwick was over 70 per cent for them even in 1998). It adds up to a seat Labour can probably win only in landslide years; fortunately for new candidate Robert Marris, 2001 was in this category.

South West's future might be affected by boundary changes. If Wolverhampton retains three seats, a ward could well be transferred to the South East seat. Much depends on whether it is Asian, working class Graiseley, or suburban Penn.

West Midlands – Coventry and Solihull

	Conservative		Labour		Liberal Democrat		Others	
	Share of vote	Seats	Share of vote	Seats	Share of vote	Seats	Share of vote	Seats
2001	34.3	2	44.5	3	15.6	0	5.6	0
1997	32.9	2	47.0	3	13.6	0	6.5	0
1992	44.6	3	36.3	3	13.5	0	5.6	0
1987	44.0	3	36.2	3	19.5	0	0.3	0
1983	44.3	3	32.4	3	22.9	0	0.4	0

The former West Midland metropolitan county extends eastwards from Birmingham across a small rural neck to the city of Coventry; this chapter deals with all of this territory. It forms a salient sticking into Warwickshire, which gives the truncated shire county a rather odd shape. The two boroughs covered in this section are rather different. Solihull is essentially a suburban area within the orbit of Birmingham and most of its population lives in areas that are part of the Birmingham built up area. To the south, at Solihull and Dorridge, these are well-heeled suburbs served by commuter trains to the centre of the city. To the east, there is an expanse of housing estates in the overspill township of Chelmsley Wood, then Birmingham airport and some open country around Meriden.

Coventry is by contrast a large (population 300,000) and rather working class city, the city boundaries drawn tightly around its urban core. It has some historic interest as the place where Lady Godiva made her famous ride around town, but it is for the most part an assertively modern place. The old trades of weaving, watchmaking and ribbons fell upon hard times in the 19th Century but were replaced by sewing machine and bicycle production, and after technological progress it became an important auto-motive and aviation manufacturing centre. Coventry boomed in the inter-war period; its population were attracted there from depressed areas of the north because of the ready availability of work. Disaster struck in November 1940 with a ferocious bombing raid in which 75 per cent of Coventry's factories were damaged, hundreds were killed and the mediaeval centre including the cathedral was completely destroyed. After the war, Coventry was rebuilt in concrete and glass and a new cathedral rose alongside the ruins of the old. The phoenix was added to the city's coat of arms. Coventry's industrial prosperity continued to increase, and the city was suffused with a culture of working class material well-being. In contrast to Essex, this was wrapped up with left-wing politics, trade unionism and municipal socialism. Only very gradually did the Conservatives make any headway – their only general election win between 1945 and 1979 was in 1959 in Coventry South.

The 1979-81 recession caused unaccustomed problems in Coventry as industrial closures bit deep. The Specials sang that Coventry had become a *Ghost Town*, and the council appointed a Lady Godiva (who is still in post) to cheer Coventry citizens up. Things have improved since, but Coventry still wrestles with the problems of deindustrialisation. It is still an engineering and car production centre, with Rolls Royce, BMW-Rover and Jaguar all having plants here. Courtaulds (now known as Acordis) has a large heavy engineering complex. Coventry also has two fairly recently founded universities, Warwick on its southern fringe and Coventry in the city centre, and quite a large student population to add to the mix.

Its strong labour movement is less apparent than in the post war period, although Coventry is still a very loyal Labour city and remained so when other skilled working class seats swung over to Thatcherite Conservatism. The Conservatives remained penned in to the South West constituency, the most middle class area of the city, and could not take North West even in favourable circumstances like a 1976 by-election, 1983 or 1987. In recent years Coventry's left wing nature has also been apparent in the support that non-Labour socialist candidates have received, most notably Dave Nellist's near victory in South East in 1992.

Local government
Coventry has been under Labour control since 1979, and for most of the period since the city has shown unusually strong loyalty to the party in local elections. Labour have only really done badly in 2000, when the party won 8 seats, to 8 Conservatives and 2 others, although their showing in 2002 was nothing to write home about and they must fight off a challenge to their overall majority in 2003. The Liberal Democrats are not a strong presence in the city, having only one ward (Upper Stoke) where they mount a serious challenge. There is a fourth force in Coventry politics on the independent left, where the split caused by the expulsion of Dave Nellist in 1991 has led to a continuing Socialist presence, particularly in the central St. Michael's ward where their candidates are capable of beating Labour.

Solihull is the most (and after 2002, only) Conservative metropolitan borough, although the party was surprisingly deprived of an overall majority for much of the 1990s. Solihull returned to Tory control in 2000 and, unless the Liberal Democrats can consolidate their advances, should remain so.

Boundary review
After the loss of a seat in the 1990s boundary review, this area is unlikely to see any major alterations although all its seats are a little large.

COVENTRY NORTH EAST

	2001		1997		1992 notional	
Electorate and turnout	74,017	50.3	74,173	64.8	77,680	72.8
Conservative	6,988	18.8	9,287	19.3	15,854	28.0
Labour	22,739	61.0	31,856	66.2	28,083	49.6
Lib Dem	4,163	11.2	3,866	8.0	5,948	10.5
Anti–EU	–	–	1,125	2.3	–	–
Socialist	2,638	7.1	597	1.2	2,645	4.7
Ind Lab	–	–	–	–	4,008	7.1
Others	737		1,354 (2)		43	
MP	Bob Ainsworth (Lab)		Bob Ainsworth (Lab)		Bob Ainsworth (Lab)	
Majority	15,751	42.3	22,569	46.9	12,229	21.6

Coventry North East is the Labour heartland of the city of Coventry, where the party polled 48 per cent even at its 1983 nadir and enjoys the thumping victories on low turnouts that characterises the very safest Labour seats now. North East is very similar to Coventry East, which was represented from 1945 to 1974 by Labour intellectual and 1964–70 Cabinet minister Richard Crossman.

The seat consists of a wedge of the city from the inner city Foleshill area, dominated by heavy industry and the main ethnic minority area in Coventry, to the edge. This side, however, is the unfavoured part of the city and there are depressing council-built estates in the Longford and Henley areas on the edge of the city. Foleshill is particularly badly off (the 182nd most deprived ward in England), but only Wyken is not in the bottom quarter of wards in England. Crossman described one estate in the area as being a new slum within a few years of it being put up. Four out of six wards were Labour even in 2000, and the party normally gets all six with large majorities (although *Focus* Lib Dems might dig in at Upper Stoke ward).

As in the other Coventry seats there have been splinters from the Labour vote in recent years. In 1992 deselected MP John Hughes stood as an independent, and in 1997 the former MP for South East, Dave Nellist, tried his hand here as a Socialist Alliance candidate. The challenges did no more than chip at the edge of Labour's massive lead here.

COVENTRY NORTH WEST

	2001		1997		1992 notional	
Electorate and turnout	76,673	55.5	76,845	70.7	79,194	76.6
Conservative	11,018	25.9	14,300	26.3	22,425	37.0
Labour	21,892	51.4	30,901	56.9	31,083	51.2
Lib Dem	5,832	13.7	5,690	10.5	7,152	11.8
Anti–EU	650	1.5	1,269	2.3	–	–
Socialist*	3,159	7.4	940	1.7	–	–
Others			1,222 (3)		–	
MP	Geoffrey Robinson (Lab)		Geoffrey Robinson (Lab)		Geoffrey Robinson (Lab)	
Majority	10,874	25.6	16,601	30.6	8,658	14.3

* 2001: 'Socialist' vote is Independent standing with Socialist Alliance support.

Bablake church on the west side of Coventry served as a prison in 1647 to confine royalist troops. The people of Coventry were so strongly committed to the parliamentary cause that they would not fraternise in any way with the royalists – hence the phrase 'sent to Coventry'. It was an early sign of Coventry's dogged commitment to the left. Coventry North West has ignored the Conservatives at all general elections since 1945 despite its relatively well off skilled working class and middle class population.

The constituency covers a slice of the city from inner city Radford to the more affluent western suburbs of Whoberley and Bablake, and the poorer Holford area in the north. Radford and Holford are strongly Labour, but the other wards are capable of volatile behaviour– Conservative in the 2000 local elections but backing Labour strongly in the 2001 general election.

The 2001 election confirmed North West's history of loyalty to Labour. It was felt that Geoffrey Robinson was in some difficulty because of his repeated appearances before the Standards and Privileges Committee and their condemnation of him for failing to make full disclosure of his business interests, not to mention his resignation in December 1998 over the Mandelson house loan. But there was little demand for the man in the white suit to ride into town, and the swing here turned out to be only just above the national average. Even this was accounted for by the candidature of former MEP Christine Oddy, who stood as an independent with backing from the Coventry socialists.

This was quite a surprising outcome, not only because of Robinson's troubles but also because Labour had done particularly badly here in mid term elections. In the Euro elections the Tories were just ahead, with ex-Labour MEP Christine Oddy taking nearly a quarter of the vote as an independent socialist, and in the 2000 local elections the Tories gained four out of six wards in the constituency, outpolling Labour 45-39. In 2002 the Conservatives also had a fractional lead. If Labour really disappoints in its second term, it seems possible that North West could swing a long way to the right despite its traditions and Robinson's impressive result in 2001.

COVENTRY SOUTH

	2001		1997		1992 notional	
Electorate and turnout	72,570	55.3	72,967	68.7	73,575	77.4
Conservative	11,846	29.5	14,558	29.0	22,674	39.8
Labour	20,125	50.2	25,511	50.9	19,770	34.7
Lib Dem	5,672	14.1	4,617	9.2	5,260	9.2
Anti–EU	–	–	943	1.9	–	–
Socialist	1,889 (2)	4.7	3,262	6.5	7,934	13.9
Others	564		1,233 (3)		1,295	
MP	Jim Cunningham (Lab)		Jim Cunningham (Lab)		TWO SEATS MERGE	
Majority	8,279	20.6	10,953	21.9	2,904	5.1

South was formed in 1997 from a merger of the largest elements of two seats. South West had provided the Conservatives with a marginal outpost in the city between 1979 and its abolition, and contained the most middle class areas of this working class city. South East included the city centre and some working class suburbs and was consistently Labour. Its MP from 1983 until 1992 was Dave Nellist, who was expelled in 1991 for his Militant connections. Nellist was a popular and hard working MP, who nearly managed to keep the seat when he stood without Labour Party backing in 1992.

Coventry South is the middle class seat in this working class city. Some of the suburban avenues in Wainbody ward are very grand indeed and the ward is solidly Conservative, even surviving the disastrous 1995 elections. The constituency also houses both the city's universities and therefore most of its student and professional populations. To the south east, however, it has the respectable working class area of Cheylesmore (with its manor house) and the rougher Binley-Willenhall district. The South seat also includes the city centre ward of St Michael's, where non-Labour socialists are strong enough to win local elections.

South is basically a Labour seat vulnerable to the Conservatives only in the best of years for them – it was Tory in 1959 and had it existed in current form would probably have put the Tories ahead in 1983 and 1987 (but not 1992 were it not for the split Labour vote). The Tories led more recently in the Euro elections and the 2000 and 2002 local elections, and by a whisker in 1999, and South remains their best target in Coventry. The Tories made miserably little progress here in 2001, with the main change being the rise in Lib Dem support – these trends are linked with the constituency's professional middle class element.

MERIDEN

	2001		1997		1992 actual	
Electorate and turnout	73,787	60.4	76,348	71.7	77,009	78.8
Conservative	21,246	47.7	22,997	42.0	33,462	55.1
Labour	17,462	39.2	22,415	41.0	18,763	30.9
Lib Dem	4,941	11.1	7,098	13.0	8,489	14.0
Anti–EU	910	2.0	2,208	4.0	–	–
MP	Caroline Spelman (Con)		Caroline Spelman (Con)		Iain Mills (Con)	
Majority	3,784	8.5	582	1.1	14,699	24.2

Unusually for a Tory seat in 1997, Labour have won the constituency called Meriden relatively frequently in the past (1955, 1964, 1966, 1974 twice), but in a sense the current seat was a new invention in 1983 when nearly half the old Meriden vanished into Warwickshire North. The current Meriden is a peculiarly drawn seat. Its core is an area of suburbs and overspill estates to the east of Birmingham around the M42 and M6 motorways and Birmingham airport. Chelmsley Wood, a Birmingham overspill area constructed in the late 1960s and 1970s, is the largest settlement in the area. It suffers from some of the problems common to overspill development; its four wards are among the 10 per cent most deprived wards in Britain.

The constituency spills eastwards towards Coventry, over a rural area which includes the village of Meriden (one of several claiming to be the geographical centre of England); the gap between Birmingham and Coventry is enforced by a strict Green Belt. The Meriden seat also throws out a salient to the west comprising territory with little in common with the rest of the seat – the very affluent large villages of Knowle, Dorridge and Packwood which are effectively southern suburbs of Solihull.

Meriden is a very divided seat. Labour are strong in Chelmsley Wood, but turnout here has been wretched in recent years. Three wards had turnout lower than 16 per cent in the 2000 local elections and it seems clear that differential turnout has been the key to Conservative success in holding the parliamentary constituency. The remainder of the constituency, except for volatile Bickenhill, is extremely Conservative with May 2000 shares of the vote of between 56 and 75 per cent – Castle Bromwich and Knowle are their best areas. The Conservatives did very well in the May 2000 local elections (a 60-22 lead over Labour) and the Euro elections, and Caroline Spelman's hold with an increased majority in 2001 was not unexpected. It now looks an unlikely seat for Labour to aspire to win, especially if future elections continue to see low turnout.

SOLIHULL

	2001		1997		1992 notional	
Electorate and turnout	76,298	63.3	78,943	74.6	78,171	80.5
Conservative	21,935	45.4	26,299	44.6	38,277	60.8
Labour	12,373	25.6	14,334	24.3	10,512	16.7
Lib Dem	12,528	26.0	14,902	25.3	13,202	21.0
Anti–EU	1,061	2.2	2,748	4.7	–	–
Others	374		623		925	1.5
MP	John Taylor (Con)		John Taylor (Con)		John Taylor (Con)	
Majority	9,407	19.5	11,397	19.3	25,075	39.9

Solihull lies south east of Birmingham and is the most desirable suburban area on the south side of the city, a mirror image of Sutton Coldfield to the north. Solihull, however, has not been incorporated into the city but (with Meriden) is a separate borough. Its quiet town centre stands, amid avenues and parks, just off the A41 road, although the constituency extends on either side – north east towards Elmdon and the airport, and west to Shirley, a suburb along the A34 south of Birmingham. Nowhere in the constituency can be described as poor; it is a fairly uniform tract of suburbia ranging from the comfortable to the opulent; St. Alphege ward is one of the hundred least deprived in England.

The Liberal Democrats have been active in some of the Solihull wards – Lyndon, Olton and Shirley East. This area forms the innermost suburban part of Solihull, just across the border from Birmingham. The Birmingham areas it adjoins are, perhaps not coincidentally, Liberal Democrat wards in Birmingham Yardley and their Fox Hollies outpost in Sparkbrook. Labour can win in a good year in neighbouring Elmdon. The Solihull wards are decidedly upmarket of Yardley, but there is some industrial employment such as the Land Rover plant. The rest of Solihull, however, is strongly Conservative in elections for all levels of government and on balance the constituency is a Conservative stronghold. There are only 47 safer Tory seats.

Wiltshire including Swindon

	Conservative		Labour		Liberal Democrat		Others	
	Share of vote	Seats	Share of vote	Seats	Share of vote	Seats	Share of vote	Seats
2001	42.1	4	29.0	2	25.0	0	3.9	0
1997	40.2	4	28.0	2	26.2	0	5.6	0
1992	50.9	5	18.3	0	28.7	0	2.1	0
1987	51.9	5	16.7	0	31.2	0	0.2	0
1983	50.3	5	14.9	0	34.2	0	0.6	0

Wiltshire is a diverse county that covers a large area. It lacks a unifying urban centre to serve as a county capital. The south east of the county looks to Salisbury or even Southampton; some of the south is inclined towards Dorset; the north west to Bath or Bristol, and the north east centres around Swindon and is influenced by London. The county council is run from Trowbridge, in the Westbury constituency. Swindon is now an independent unitary authority with county status.

Wiltshire's landscape is hilly, except in the very south of the county, and has a rather mysterious air with stone circles and prehistoric barrows such as Avebury, Stonehenge and West Kennet. The centre of the county is sparsely populated, rather beautiful chalk downland, with small towns along the Vale of Pewsey serving as market centres; the south is more productive country. The northern downs are more aristocratic and horsy places, similar to neighbouring areas of Berkshire and Gloucestershire. Although Salisbury is a mediaeval city of great distinction, its population is rather small and only Swindon of the Wiltshire towns has sufficient electorate to produce a parliamentary constituency dominated by a single urban area.

Swindon grew as a railway town but the works have now closed and been replaced by an outlet shopping mall. Swindon was not impoverished by the closure; the town has a diverse economic base and has grown rapidly in recent years – it is one of the fastest-growing towns (it aspires to be a city) in Europe and was awarded a second parliamentary seat in 1997. The only other town to gain a seat was Aberdeen. There are frequent reviews of ward boundaries (which make it difficult to compare local elections over a period of time). Swindon is a popular site for corporate headquarters (Nationwide Building Society, W.H. Smith), technological and large office employers; one of the latest organisations to move to Swindon is the National Trust. Despite this conservationist presence, Swindon is functional rather than beautiful. The town has recently become very popular among market researchers as a microcosm of modern Britain; product testing and focus group research are regularly conducted in Swindon. It is therefore a key location for the New Labour project.

The rest of Wiltshire's political inclinations are those of a transitional area between the south east and the south west. Historically, it was part of an arc of constituencies 70-90 miles out from London, beginning in Dorset, stretching via Northamptonshire and Cambridgeshire to Norfolk, in which Conservatism was relatively weak compared to its strongholds in the south east and west midlands. This weakness owed much to the strength of Nonconformist religious observance, traditionally associated with Liberalism, very late industrialisation with its concomitant lack of an organised working class, and parochialism. As late as 1955 the pattern was still faintly visible in election results, but since then much has changed. Growth of industry from the 1920s onward, the mechanisation of farming, the mass media and the increasing accessibility of the region through motorways from the 1950s have changed the central belt socially and politically, bringing it closer to London and eroding its distinct traditions. These changes have brought population growth, with Wiltshire being awarded an extra parliamentary constituency in the 1990s boundary review and another in the review that began in 2000.

The political consequences of Wiltshire's modernisation have tended to strengthen the Conservatives, as in other central band constituencies. It is in or around the central band where one finds most of the constituencies which Labour won in 1945 but not 1997. In Wiltshire, however, the Liberals have suffered. A century ago, the Liberals enjoyed a clean sweep in 1906 and were only a seat short in 1885. Even in 1923 only Swindon eluded their grasp, but they lost all their seats in 1924 and have not won one since. Even after 1997 and 2001 Wiltshire lacks a Liberal Democrat MP, a unique distinction for the south west and unusual in southern England. Their vote has flowed, and lately more usually ebbed, in several seats of the county since 1974 and although they have come close – formerly in Salisbury, now in North Wilts – they have never managed a win. The Lib Dems have not consolidated a strong position in local government as they did in Somerset or Devon, with weakness on the county council and firm control of only one local council, West Wilts.

Labour are not serious challengers in any of the rural Wiltshire seats, although there is a scattered vote for the party in some of the hilly towns of the north as well as Salisbury. This weakness is quite recent – in the 1960s Labour challenged strongly for Devizes and even came relatively close to the Conservatives in Salisbury. Labour interest is concentrated in Swindon. Christopher Addison won the seat for Labour in 1929, lost it in 1931 but held it again in 1934-35. From 1945 until 1983 it was Labour except for a short interlude in 1969-70. Swindon was then a Thatcherite, prosperous working class Tory seat until 1997, although Labour controlled the council continuously from 1978 to 2000. The town now provides a base for two Labour seats with respectable majorities in the 1997 and 2001 general elections.

Local government

The Conservatives control Wiltshire county council with a majority of 13 (42, to 18 Lib Dems and 11 Labour) after the June 2001 elections, an increase on their 1997 majority. Before the excision of Swindon in 1997 Wiltshire was frequently hung. Swindon (or Thamesdown as it used to be known) is generally Labour, although the party slipped a seat short of control in 2000 and it is currently ruled by a precarious Conservative minority administration; after the 2002 elections there were 29 Labour, 22 Conservative and 8 Lib Dem councillors. Labour will hope to recover control in future annual local elections. Moving to the district councils, Kennet (the Devizes area) is Conservative controlled, with a large Independent group. Salisbury is hung with the quaintly titled 'Conservative and Independent Group' just short of overall control, although the Liberal Democrats had a majority in 1995-99. In North Wiltshire the Lib Dems are just short of overall control in a traditional Con-LD battleground.

The Lib Dems control West Wiltshire outright, having swept away a Conservative council that was subject to allegations about financial mismanagement in 1991.

Boundary review

Recent population growth in Wiltshire has been in the north of the county, and this is where the extra seat will appear. The North Wiltshire seat will be split into two parts, North Wiltshire and Chippenham, each of which will acquire territory from neighbouring oversized seats. Its present marginal status will end; the new North Wilts will be safely Tory while the new Chippenham will be an extremely attractive seat from a Lib Dem point of view. There are smaller knock-on effects on other seats, tending to help the Conservatives in Devizes, Westbury and maybe Salisbury too.

DEVIZES

	2001		*1997*		*1992 notional*	
Electorate and turnout	82,925	64.2	80,383	74.7	*75,555*	*84.0*
Conservative	25,159	47.2	25,710	42.8	*33,603*	*53.0*
Labour	13,263	24.9	14,551	24.2	*7,613*	*12.0*
Lib Dem	11,756	22.1	15,928	26.5	*20,584*	*32.5*
Anti–EU	1,521	2.9	3,643 (2)	6.1	*–*	*–*
Others	1,550 (2)		204		*1,640 (2)*	
MP	Michael Ancram (Con)		Michael Ancram (Con)		Michael Ancram (Con)	
Majority	11,896	22.3	9,782	16.3	*13,019*	*20.5*

Devizes is a hilly rural division in mid–Wiltshire: its main towns are Devizes itself, Calne, Melksham and Marlborough. The Vale of Pewsey, along which the A4 runs, is the main artery of the constituency, linking the towns. Parts of Calne and Melksham are surprisingly rough and deprived, but in general the constituency is quietly prosperous. Labour nearly won the constituency in a by-election in 1964 but since then it has been safely Conservative, particularly when the Swindon suburbs were taken out of the seat in 1997. There is no basis for a big Labour vote now, although there are a few Labour wards in Devizes town, Melksham and Calne. The Liberal Democrats have slipped back in general elections and are not particularly active in local elections despite something of a base at Marlborough. Thanks to an evenly split anti-Tory vote and a reasonable recovery in 2001, Party Chairman Michael Ancram had a larger percentage majority than the area would have produced in 1992. Ancram made a doomed bid for the leadership in 2001 as the candidate of continuity. While this may be an attractive option for the Conservatives in Devizes, it failed to convince elsewhere.

Devizes was shorn of nearly half its Labour voters in the 1990s boundary review, when they were redistributed into Swindon North. It will become even more Conservative after the next review, when it loses more territory (Calne, Melksham) because of its persistent population growth.

SALISBURY

	2001		1997		1992 actual	
Electorate and turnout	80,527	65.3	79,099	73.6	75,917	79.9
Conservative	24,527	46.6	25,012	42.9	31,546	52.0
Labour	9,199	17.5	10,242	17.6	5,483	9.0
Lib Dem	15,824	30.1	18,736	32.2	22,573	37.2
Anti–EU	1,958	3.7	3,332	5.7	–	–
Others	1,095		917 (3)		1,052 (4)	
MP	Robert Key (Con)		Robert Key (Con)		Robert Key (Con)	
Majority	8,703	16.5	6,276	10.8	8,973	14.8

Salisbury is a well-known and historic city, but it is a small city which needs a substantial rural element to make up numbers for a parliamentary seat – the rules have changed since Old Sarum (presumably the scene of Edmund Blackadder's electoral triumph in the television series) was able to send two representatives to parliament despite losing all its population. The modern parliamentary seat of Salisbury covers a large tract of southern Wiltshire, including the adjacent town of Wilton, known for its carpets; Southampton-influenced areas like Whiteparish; and distant army camps and chilly villages on Salisbury Plain up towards Amesbury and Durrington.

The city area contributes 30,000 electors, who divided their favours 37 per cent Conservative, 32 per cent Lib Dem and 27 per cent Labour in the county elections (whose overall result replicated the parties' shares of the vote in the constituency in the general election). Labour are strongest in the north west of the city, where there are some council estates, and the Conservatives do best in the cathedral area and south at Harnham. However, the 50,000-strong rural area produces a sea of Conservative support with the odd island of Lib Dem activity such as Wilton and perhaps surprisingly the army areas at Bulford and Durrington. The rural hinterland has kept Salisbury Conservative since 1924.

Salisbury is a vague Liberal Democrat target which has never really looked like coming across despite their efforts. On current figures it is a safer Conservative seat in 2001 than it was in 1992, thanks to a slippage in the Lib Dem vote to the benefit of third-placed Labour.

SWINDON NORTH

	2001		1997		1992 notional	
Electorate and turnout	69,355	61.0	65,535	73.7	64,530	77.2
Conservative	14,266	33.7	16,341	33.9	20,391	40.9
Labour	22,371	52.9	24,029	49.8	21,273	42.7
Lib Dem	4,891	11.6	6,237	12.9	7,299	14.6
Anti–EU	800	1.9	1,533	3.2	–	–
Others	–		130		879	
MP	Michael Wills (Lab)		Michael Wills (Lab)		NEW SEAT	
Majority	8,105	19.1	7,688	15.9	882	1.8

Swindon North is the unglamorous side of a pretty unglamorous town. It is set for a population explosion with the construction of Abbey Meads, the largest new private housing estate in Europe, to the west. This should not alter the character of the seat much, as it is largely owner-occupied post-1965 sprawl anyway. Most of it is prosperous white working class and lower middle class territory but there are some islands of deprivation such as the Whitworth area in the inner north west.

Swindon North was created in 1997 from the north side of Swindon plus some territory formerly in Michael Ancram's Devizes constituency such as the towns of Blunsdon and Highworth, and the suburban sprawl of Stratton St. Margaret. Swindon is not technically a New Town, but as an Expanded Town it shares many of their characteristics. Curiously, most New Towns swung slightly to the Tories in 2001 while the Expanded Towns, Swindon included, continued their movement to Labour. This was a bit of a surprise in the light of the local and European elections here in 1999 and 2000, when the Conservatives were ahead. In previous general elections they would certainly have been ahead in 1987 and perhaps (contra the standard calculation) in 1992 as well. The low swing in 1997 and the mid-term results meant that Labour in Swindon did not suffer from complacency, and there were frequent visits during the 2001 campaign from Labour's leading figures.

Michael Wills now has a fairly large majority and the boundary review will eventually help by removing the Cricklade ward. However, it is an article of New Labour faith that the party can never relax in its pursuit of the materialistic, aspirational lower middle class voter found in such large numbers in Swindon North.

SWINDON SOUTH

	2001		1997		1992 notional	
Electorate and turnout	71,080	61.0	70,207	72.9	68,197	81.8
Conservative	14,919	34.4	18,298	35.8	27,312	48.9
Labour	22,260	51.3	23,943	46.8	17,209	30.8
Lib Dem	5,165	11.9	7,371	14.4	10,439	18.7
Anti–EU	713	1.6	1,273	2.5	–	–
Other	327		277 (2)		842	
MP	Julia Drown (Lab)		Julia Drown (Lab)		Simon Coombs (Con)	
					Swindon	
Majority	7,341	16.9	5,645	11.0	10,103	18.1

When Swindon was split, the town's Tory MP Simon Coombs had what looked like a relatively safe seat, after three elections of precarious survival. His gain in 1983 was the first general election since 1935 when the Tories won Swindon and he did well to hold on despite the depressed condition of the town in 1992. The South seat contained the more pleasant districts of the old town plus the more affluent suburban growth zones such as Freshbrook, and a strip of rural territory around Wroughton and Chiseldon which had previously been in Devizes. However, the New Labour tide of 1997 ran particularly strongly in areas like this and continued to flow in during the election of 2001 to the extent that Swindon South looks almost safe for Julia Drown.

There is greater internal variation in voting patterns and demographics than in the North seat. The Lawns area of Swindon old town is very attractive, affluent and Conservative; the rural part has seen the Liberal Democrats challenging the Tories in recent years, and there are strong Labour elements in some of the old railway workers' areas and council-built estates such as Park ward. If the Conservatives are ever going to revive in urban England, they should be challenging strongly in seats such as Swindon South. Their very bad result in 2001 was most disappointing for the party in general, and Simon Coombs, who attempted to recover the seat from Drown, in particular.

WESTBURY

	2001		1997		1992 notional	
Electorate and turnout	76,056	66.6	74,457	76.2	74,489	81.8
Conservative	21,299	42.1	23,037	40.6	31,821	52.3
Labour	10,847	21.4	11,969	21.1	6,457	10.6
Lib Dem	16,005	31.6	16,949	29.9	20,668	33.9
Anti–EU	1,261	2.5	(2) 2,680	4.8	–	–
Liberal	–	–	1,956	3.4	1,217	2.0
Others	1,216		140		740	
MP	Andrew Murrison (Con)		David Faber (Con)		David Faber (Con)	
Majority	5,294	10.5	6,088	10.7	11,153	18.3

Westbury is an admirably concise name for a constituency that includes several towns in west Wiltshire: if the Boundary Commission had followed the policy applied in other areas this would risk being called 'Trowbridge, Warminster and Bradford-on-Avon'. The constituency is mainly composed of small, formerly quite industrial towns by the Avon, set in hilly countryside. Trowbridge, Wiltshire's county town, is the largest settlement but it only contributes 20,000 electors who incline to favour the Liberal Democrats (51 per cent to 31 per cent for the Conservatives in the 2001 county elections). Of the smaller towns Warminster, which has a distinct Salisbury Plain military flavour, is more Conservative while in the north pretty Bradford-on-Avon and its surroundings also tend to the Lib Dems and have high turnout. Bradford is rather an extension of Bath – most of the constituency is under the influence of Bath and more distantly Bristol. To the south, the Conservative majority stacks up in the little villages of the Wylye Valley and the downlands reaching to Mere by the Dorset border.

The Liberal Democrats are locally active and control the council, but have been unable to translate this success into national politics despite trimming down the Conservative majority in the last couple of general elections. They have been frustrated by the rise in the Labour vote, and have puzzlingly failed to make their case for tactical voting despite the lack of Labour strength on the ground. There are no Labour councillors from the areas within the Westbury seat, and the relatively strong Labour vote in the general election should in theory be squeezable. Westbury is worth cultivation from the Lib Dem point of view, but the Tories remain ahead at the moment.

WILTSHIRE NORTH

	2001		1997		1992 notional	
Electorate and turnout	78,624	67.3	77,440	74.9	71,312	83.9
Conservative	24,090	45.5	25,390	43.8	33,626	56.2
Labour	7,556	14.3	8,261	14.2	6,087	10.2
Lib Dem	20,212	38.2	21,915	37.8	18,866	31.5
Anti–EU	1,090	2.1	2,184 (2)	3.8	–	–
Others	–		263		1,287	
MP	James Gray (Con)		James Gray (Con)		Richard Needham (Con)	
Majority	3,878	7.3	3,475	6.0	14,760	24.7

Wiltshire North has been a consistent disappointment to Liberals for forty years, since a by-election near miss in 1962. There were close calls for the Tories in several subsequent elections. It was a serious prospect of a gain in 2001, but unlike some other seats in this category it produced a virtual standstill result on 1997 with a fractional increase in the Conservative majority. The Lib Dem candidate was Hugh Pym, formerly a senior ITN political journalist. Chippenham is the largest town in the seat, with a bit short of 30,000 electors, and is a Lib Dem centre. The rest of the constituency is predominantly rural, with the next largest settlement being the market town of Wootton Bassett near RAF Lyneham (which tends to the Conservatives) and far to the north little Malmesbury, marginal between Lib Dems and Tories. The Conservatives managed to gain rural support by campaigning on hunting and foot and mouth disease and James Gray won again. North Wiltshire will remain a Lib Dem target, but perhaps Westbury is now more likely to come off – at least until the forthcoming boundary review is implemented.

Wiltshire's population growth has given it another seat, and the current North Wiltshire is effectively being split. The revised North Wiltshire will include Calne from Devizes and Cricklade from Swindon North, plus most of the current seat except the towns of Chippenham and Corsham to its south. A new seat of Chippenham will be created, and will take in Bradford-on-Avon from the current Westbury seat and Melksham from Devizes. We can be fairly precise about the political complexion of the new seats, as the county council vote in June 2001 replicated the general election performance in this area. The new North Wiltshire is a Tory stronghold, which voted 50 per cent Conservative, 35 per cent Lib Dem and 13 per cent Labour. The new Chippenham is a beast of a different stripe – it voted 35 per cent Tory, 41 per cent Lib Dem and a squeezable 21 per cent Labour. After forty years of frustration, the boundary review may have finally delivered Chippenham into Liberal hands.

North Yorkshire including York

	Conservative		Labour		Liberal Democrat		Others	
	Share of vote	Seats	Share of vote	Seats	Share of vote	Seats	Share of vote	Seats
2001	43.6	4	29.6	3	23.5	1	3.4	0
1997	40.0	4	32.8	3	23.0	1	4.2	0
1992	52.8	6	23.6	1	22.9	0	0.7	0
1987	53.1	7	19.0	0	27.5	0	0.4	0
1983	56.1	7	16.3	0	27.4	0	0.2	0

North Yorkshire is an extremely large county which stretches most of the way across northern England, and all of the way over the Pennines from Ingleton in the west as far as the North Sea coast at Filey and Scarborough. The western areas are sparsely populated, but draw in plenty of day-trippers to the unspoilt Dales, while most of its towns are either in the central plain (close to the main A1 road) or along the east coast, which is also a major tourist destination. Of the few urban areas, the most populous is York (about 150,000), particularly after it became a unitary authority in the 1990s local government review and expanded to take in former villages (in reality now suburbs) previously just outside the old city boundaries. The next biggest towns are Harrogate and then Scarborough. No other settlement can really be described as 'large', though there are several of 5,000-10,000 inhabitants such as Northallerton, Richmond, Selby, Skipton, Whitby, Filey, Knaresborough, Thirsk and Ripon, which all have a prosperous and pleasant air. Some of these places boast castles and other historic buildings, of which the county has more than its fair share. Many other local communities are based around large open town or village squares, and this can certainly seem a relaxed, conservative area. Indeed, whether one is looking for stately homes (Castle Howard), ruined abbeys (Rievaulx, Fountains, Whitby), national parks (Yorkshire Dales, North York Moors) or racecourses (Catterick, Ripon, Thirsk, York), North Yorkshire is surprisingly well-endowed.

Ever since the decline of religious non-conformity and its link with Liberal politics just before the first world war, North Yorkshire has presented the largest obstacle to simple theories of a 'north-south divide' in British politics. As in neighbouring rural seats in East Yorkshire, Cumbria and Lancashire, Conservative allegiances have become very deep-rooted, and this area (which contains some of England's largest constituencies) often produces a huge unbroken strip of blue territory on election nights. The Conservatives won all the seats in North Yorkshire in 1983 and 1987, and also enjoyed a period of unbroken dominance in the areas which now make up the county between 1950 and 1966. In between these times, their sole losses were the city of York, held by Labour's Alex Lyon between 1966 and 1983, and the former seat of Ripon, which was gained for a single year by the Liberals in a 1973 by-election.

All has not been well for the Conservatives in North Yorkshire in recent times. Early signs of trouble were demonstrated in two by-elections in normally safe seats in the mid and late 1980s. In Ryedale, Liberal Elizabeth Shields won a famous by-election victory in 1986, though this was one of several instances of the third party winning a by-election during the Thatcher years only to lose it again at the following general election. In Richmond, a new Conservative aspirant called William Hague held on in 1989 thanks to the presence of two centre-party candidates (continuing SDP and newly merged 'Social and Liberal Democrats') who split the 54 per cent centre-party vote and gave the Conservatives victory despite their share of the vote dropping from 61 per cent in 1987 to 37 per cent in 1989.

Such fortune was in short supply in subsequent national contests. In 1992, Labour regained York after their vote advanced by almost 8 per cent (one of their best results that year) and at the next general election the Conservatives recorded their worst set of results in the North Yorkshire area since 1906, losing both Selby and Scarborough & Whitby to Labour, and Harrogate to the Liberal Democrats. The Tory vote in the county dropped by 13 per cent, even more than the national average, though they did win the newly created Vale of York constituency. In 2001, very little changed despite one of the larger county-wide swings from Labour to Conservative: it is possible that we could call this a 'Hague effect' (though the foot and mouth crisis may have been as important) given that Richmond rose through the rankings from the Tories' 25th best seat to their safest, and neighbouring Vale of York also moved up from 41st to 17th. Unfortunately for the Conservative leader, this success did not even extend to all parts of the county, never mind the rest of the country. Labour held on to their newly-gained and extremely marginal seats of Selby and Scarborough in reasonable comfort, and the Liberal Democrat majority in Harrogate increased further, making the recovery task of the Tories next time all the more difficult.

Local government

The pattern of local council control in North Yorkshire is more complex than a simple divide between rural Conservative areas and Labour or Lib Dem towns. There are a large number of local Independents who survive in district like Richmondshire, while the Lib Dems also have a good scattering of councillors across the whole county. As a result, many authorities are currently hung, including Richmondshire, Craven (Skipton and the west of the county) and Ryedale. In the past, Hambleton (which includes Northallerton and Thirsk) has also been controlled by Independents, but is now heavily Conservative. For many years, Labour have run York (though the Tories were the biggest group on the old district council until 1984), but they lost overall control of the new unitary authority in a by-election in 2000. Nevertheless, they retained power as a minority administration at the time of writing (early 2002) and there is bound to be a major battle here in 2003. After many years of Tory control or balance, Labour gained their first ever majority on Selby in 1995, and though they lost it in 1999, remain the largest party on the council. Labour were also the biggest party on perennially hung Scarborough between 1995 and 1999, but then fell back to their customary third place behind Conservatives and Independents. Harrogate was run by the Conservatives from 1973 until 1990, but the following year the Lib Dems became the largest group and after taking control they continued to strengthen. In 1999, the Lib Dems could boast 41 out of 59 councillors, a figure which then began to fall (along with Craven, Harrogate has annual elections). In 2002, all-out elections saw the Lib Dems lose 12 seats and control of the council after a strong campaign by the Conservatives. Finally, North Yorkshire county council has a small but comfortable Conservative majority, with around 40 Tory councillors as against 17 Lib Dems (most from Harrogate wards), 12 Labour (almost all from Selby or Scarborough) and a few Independents.

Boundary review

North Yorkshire remains entitled to eight constituencies in the current review, but matters are complicated by the new wider boundaries of York unitary authority, now entitled to two seats of its own as against six for the rest of the county. The impact of this will fall most on Vale of York, which will be abolished after a very short life, and Selby, which will lose the wards around Heslington (the York university campus). The most likely addition to Selby is a large rural area around Marston Moor (part of Harrogate district) which is currently part of the Vale of York, and which will almost certainly bring to an end Selby's brief period in the Labour column. The commission propose to disperse bits of Vale of York to six constituencies – a radical piece of butchery. As well as Selby, Richmond, Ryedale Harrogate & Knaresborough and Skipton & Ripon benefit, as does a strange new creation called 'York Outer'. This suburban seat would completely surround the city, and probably be a battle between Lib Dems and Tories. In the jargon of boundary determination a compact urban seat is a 'doughnut' – York may become an unprecedented 'ring doughnut'. There will be a public inquiry.

HARROGATE and KNARESBOROUGH

	2001		1997		1992 notional	
Electorate and turnout	65,243	64.6	65,394	72.9	65,257	76.7
Conservative	14,600	34.6	18,322	38.5	25,909	51.8
Labour	3,101	7.4	4,151	8.7	6,777	13.5
Lib Dem	23,445	55.6	24,558	51.5	16,698	33.4
Anti–EU	761	1.8	–	–	–	–
Others	272		614		658	
MP	Phil Willis (LD)		Phil Willis (LD)		Robert Banks (Con)	
Majority	8,845	21.0	6,236	13.1	9,211	18.4

The affluent town of Harrogate had for some time seemed a possible Liberal Democrat target. They became the largest party on the council in 1991, proceeded to win the similar 'spa' towns of Bath and Cheltenham in 1992, and irrespective of their national revival, Labour remained extremely weak here. Then in 1997 the Tory MP for 23 years, Robert Banks, stood down and was replaced by former Chancellor of the Exchequer Norman Lamont, whose own seat of Kingston-upon-Thames had been effectively abolished by the boundary commission. It was not a happy move for Lamont. His Liberal Democrat opponent Phil Willis had been leader of Harrogate borough council for some years and Lamont's candidature allowed the Lib Dems to campaign on their strongest trump card: local knowledge. In the event the swing away from the Conservatives here was almost 16 per cent, with Willis able to rake up a majority of over 6,000.

It always seemed a likely scenario that Willis would follow Don Foster in Bath and Nigel Jones in Cheltenham by building up a reasonably secure parliamentary base here, and so it has proved. In 2001, the Lib Dem majority increased significantly, both in terms of percentage share and real votes, suggesting that maybe Lamont was not such a bad candidate after all, though much of this improvement could be put down to an initial incumbency effect, which is often larger for third party MPs than representatives of the major parties. Whatever the cause, Harrogate & Knaresborough is now the Lib Dems' 13th safest of their 52 seats. Locally, the Lib Dems built up in a strong position; they originally gained control of the council in the early 1990s and with the help of regular *Focus* newsletters had a very strong majority until 2002. Then, however, they lost several seats in all-out elections, the Conservatives finally making a recovery on the issue of the perceived threat to the 'character' of the town. Whether they can consolidate and go on to seriously challenge Willis at the next election remains to be seen.

RICHMOND

	2001		1997		1992 notional	
Electorate and turnout	65,360	67.4	65,058	73.4	64,287	78.1
Conservative	25,951	58.9	23,326	48.9	30,333	60.4
Labour	9,632	21.9	13,275	27.8	5,797	11.6
Lib Dem	7,890	17.9	8,773	18.4	13,626	27.1
Anti–EU	–	–	2,367	5.0	–	–
Others	561		–		445	
MP	William Hague (Con)		William Hague (Con)		William Hague (Con)	
Majority	16,319	37.1	10,051	21.1	16,707	33.3

Richmond has long been a Tory stronghold. In 1945, Labour polled just 6,000 votes here, and though that total increased slightly in the 1950s and 1960s, the Conservative majority in general elections never fell below 13,000 between 1950 and 1997. In 1989, they even managed to hold the seat in a by-election (an extreme rarity in those times) when 27-year old William Hague took advantage of two candidates fighting over the centre party vote. Within nine years of his initial victory, Hague had become the youngest leader of his party in modern times following their 1997 defeat. Four years on, a second successive drubbing at the polls led to his immediate resignation, though it should be pointed out that in Richmond, the Conservatives had managed to add no less than 10 per cent to their share of the vote, their fourth best showing nationally. As a result no Tory seat in the land is currently safer, whether in percentage terms or numerical majority.

The small town of Richmond itself is typical for North Yorkshire – full of delightful stone cottages and small shops around its large main square. Smaller places in 'Richmondshire' such as Leyburn, Middleham and Reeth are miniature versions, while to the west the valleys of Wensleydale, Swaledale and the even more wild and unknown Arkengarthdale are perhaps the most beautiful of all the Yorkshire Dales. The favourite spot for Hague (and many others) is the far end of Swaledale about twenty miles west of Richmond and a short distance from the windswept Tan Hill Inn on the Yorkshire/Durham/Cumbria border. The constituency extends almost as far to the east of Richmond as it does to the west, taking in the army bases around Catterick, the prosperous town of Northallerton (home of North Yorkshire County Council) and extending as far as Great Ayton, early home of the explorer Captain Cook.

Politically, most of this area is fairly Conservative, though much of Richmondshire is represented by Independent councillors, and a few Lib Dems get elected as well. Labour put up few candidates locally and have little support. In the North Yorks county council elections in 2001, the Conservatives were well ahead in most seats, including those covering Northallerton, Catterick and Richmond, though the Lib Dems continued to enjoy a fair amount of support in Richmond itself. Many of their county council voters must have switched to Labour in the general election, scuppering the possibility of an effective Lib Dem challenge. With Labour as their main opponent in general elections, the Conservative position appears all the more secure.

RYEDALE

	2001		1997		1992 notional	
Electorate and turnout	66,849	65.7	65,215	74.8	63,182	81.0
Conservative	20,711	47.2	21,351	43.8	28,338	55.4
Labour	6,470	14.7	8,762	18.0	7,497	14.7
Lib Dem	15,836	36.1	16,293	33.4	15,340	30.0
Anti–EU	882	2.0	2,377 (2)	4.9	–	–
MP	John Greenway (Con)		John Greenway (Con)		John Greenway (Con)	
Majority	4,875	11.1	5,058	10.4	12,998	25.4

Ryedale had its fifteen minutes of fame when the Liberals won a by-election in 1986, a result which ended a hundred years of continuous Conservative representation in the area. The seat was known as Thirsk and Malton until 1983, and although the Liberals moved into second place in 1974, they hardly appeared threatening, as the Tory majority still exceeded 20,000 in 1979. This figure was to fall to 16,000 after the loss of Thirsk in the boundary changes of the early 1980s, but even so, Elizabeth Shields needed a large swing for the Liberals to emerge triumphant in May 1986. Her tenure was to last just a year, as John Greenway regained the constituency by almost 10,000 votes in 1987. The Lib Dems have not really looked like repeating their triumph in the relatively normal conditions, even in 1997, of a general election and Greenway looks reasonably secure.

The district of Ryedale covers much of the North York Moors national park, with the towns of Pickering, Malton and Norton to the south. It also takes in famous landmarks such as Rievaulx Abbey near Helmsley, Castle Howard (where *Brideshead Revisited* was filmed) and the famous Catholic public school at Ampleforth. The largest Liberal Democrat vote can be found in the towns (Shields is still elected in local council contests with the aid of a large personal vote in Norton), but the Conservatives hit back in many of the surrounding villages. The constituency also takes in a couple of wards from Scarborough district including the small North Sea resort of Filey, where almost four in ten of the population are over sixty, and which regularly returns Conservative councillors.

SCARBOROUGH and WHITBY

	2001		1997		1992 actual	
Electorate and turnout	75,213	63.2	75,862	71.6	76,364	77.2
Conservative	18,841	39.6	19,667	36.2	29,334	49.8
Labour	22,426	47.2	24,791	45.6	17,600	29.9
Lib Dem	3,977	8.4	7,672	14.1	11,133	18.9
Anti–EU	970	2.0	2,191	4.0	–	–
Green	1,049	2.2	–	–	876	1.5
Others	260		–		–	
MP	Lawrie Quinn (Lab)		Lawrie Quinn (Lab)		John Sykes (Con) Scarborough	
Majority	3,585	7.5	5,124	9.4	11,734	19.9

Scarborough and Whitby was one of many coastal constituencies up and down the country which fell to Labour on a bigger than average swing in 1997. As with places like Morecambe, Hove and Hastings, this was a completely unanticipated gain (Labour were third in 1987), yet Lawrie Quinn was able to accumulate a majority of over 5,000. The Conservatives sensed that he might last just a single parliament, and former MP John Sykes (who himself was defeated after one term), stood again in 2001. In the event, although the Tory vote increased percentage-wise, so too did Labour's, and Quinn won again by 3,500. This is still Labour's 33rd most marginal seat and a third successive major battle in 2005/6 seems inevitable.

Scarborough remains one of Britain's most popular seaside resorts, while Whitby is a bustling and picturesque fishing port dominated by its Abbey, but all this masks pockets of deprivation which are not found anywhere else in North Yorkshire. Castle and Eastfields are the county's only two wards in the most deprived 10 per cent nationally, and although in the past seats such as this voted Conservative much more heavily than they should have given their socio-economic breakdown, this pattern seemed to come to a decisive end in 1997. Labour held on in the 2001 general election despite poor local election results in 1999 (at which they returned to third place, behind the Conservatives and Independents), again an outcome which was repeated in many other seaside constituencies. It will be fascinating to see if this unheralded part of the 'New Labour coalition' (about a dozen of Labour's 80 most marginal seats are similar to this one) can hold good for a third successive election next time.

SELBY

	2001		1997		1992 notional	
Electorate and turnout	77,391	65.0	75,373	74.7	72,159	80.5
Conservative	20,514	40.8	22,002	39.1	29,739	51.2
Labour	22,652	45.1	25,838	45.9	20,752	35.7
Lib Dem	5,569	11.1	6,778	12.0	7,595	13.1
Anti–EU	635	1.3	1,698 (2)	3.1	–	–
Green	902	1.8	–	–	–	–
MP	John Grogan (Lab)		John Grogan (Lab)		Michael Alison (Con)	
Majority	2,138	4.3	3,836	6.8	8,987	15.5

The Selby constituency covers the southernmost part of North Yorkshire, an area roughly bordered by the M62 motorway to the south, A1 to the west, River Derwent to the east and York to the north. It includes some 29 local government wards, and shares roughly similar boundaries with the district of the same name (though some wards are now part of the expanded York unitary authority). Only the towns of Selby and Tadcaster contain a significant number of electors, with a large number of smaller settlements, scattered from the outskirts of Castleford in the south west of the constituency as far as York, providing the bulk of the electorate. This would appear to make Selby an unlikely Labour constituency, and until the 1980s it formed a large part of Barkston Ash, which was won by the Conservatives at all general elections from 1885 onwards. At its inaugural contest in 1983, Selby was won easily by Michael Alison (MP for Barkston Ash since 1964) for the Tories, the margin 16,000 votes over the Liberals, with Labour in third place. Then however the area became probably the last in Britain to be exploited for coal, a huge new mine opening up to the south east of Selby itself. In the following two elections, the Labour vote advanced at twice the rate of their national recovery, John Grogan adding 6 per cent in 1987 and 8 per cent in 1992. Five years later, Grogan finally won the seat with a third successive above-average swing.

The county council results of 2001 suggest that Labour attract surprisingly high levels of support all over the constituency (they won six seats to the Conservatives' four), though they probably do best of all in Selby itself (63 per cent of the vote in Selby North). The constituency also takes in the York university campus at Heslington, which has certainly provided a good source of support for Labour in the past, though not necessarily in 2001. The brewery town of Tadcaster is the strongest Conservative area, but their votes were not enough to topple Grogan in 2001, a reduced majority of 2,138 leaving this as Labour's 15th most vulnerable seat nationally.

SKIPTON and RIPON

	2001		1997		1992 *notional*	
Electorate and turnout	74,326	66.1	72,784	74.7	*70,154*	*81.2*
Conservative	25,736	52.4	25,294	46.5	*32,944*	*57.9*
Labour	8,543	17.4	12,171	22.4	*8,442*	*14.8*
Lib Dem	12,806	26.1	13,674	25.2	*15,547*	*27.3*
Anti–EU	2,041	4.2	3,212	5.9	–	–
MP	David Curry (Con)		David Curry (Con)		David Curry (Con)	
Majority	12,930	26.3	11,620	21.4	*17,397*	*30.6*

Skipton and Ripon is another very large constituency, which covers the entire district of Craven to the north and west of Skipton itself, together with the western section of Harrogate district. This area includes Pateley Bridge, Ripon and Masham (known for the Theakston brewery) as well as the splendours of Fountains Abbey, while Craven takes in the southern part of the Yorkshire Dales, including Bolton Priory, Wharfedale, Malham and the famous three peaks. Politically, the Conservatives are on top in most parts, though there are several areas of Liberal Democrat strength locally. Indeed Skipton was a Liberal seat before the first world war, and they managed to cut the Tory majority to 590 in October 1974. In the separate constituency of Ripon, the Liberals went a stage further by gaining the seat in a July 1973 by-election, but their MP David Austick lasted just seven months in Parliament before Keith Hampson defeated him by 4,335 in February 1974. After the two seats merged in 1983, Hampson moved with the town of Otley down to Leeds North West, while Skipton and Ripon was won easily by another Conservative, John Watson. He was replaced by local old boy and old style Tory, David Curry in 1987, though neither this nor the strong anti-EU vote in recent contests has made any difference to the outcome here, as the Lib Dems have completely failed to put in a strong parliamentary challenge to match earlier successes.

Locally, the areas of Lib Dem strength include Ripon itself (where they narrowly won both county council seats in 2001), Pateley Bridge and, many miles distant at the opposite end of the constituency, Bentham and Settle. Most of the council seats in Skipton are held by the Conservatives, and they accumulate even larger majorities in the nearby villages of Embsay (77 per cent against the Lib Dems in 1999) and Grassington (85 per cent in 2000), where four out of every ten residents are sixty years old or over.

VALE OF YORK

	2001		1997		1992 notional	
Electorate and turnout	73,335	66.1	70,128	76.0	65,009	80.8
Conservative	25,033	51.6	23,815	44.7	31,854	60.6
Labour	12,516	25.8	14,094	26.5	5,837	11.1
Lib Dem	9,799	20.2	12,656	23.8	14,626	27.8
Anti–EU	1,142	2.4	2,503	4.7	–	–
Others	–		197		247	
MP	Anne McIntosh (Con)		Anne McIntosh (Con)		NEW SEAT	
Majority	12,517	25.8	9,721	18.3	17,228	32.8

Vale of York was a new seat created at the last boundary review, taking in the flat expanse between York and Harrogate and northwards. The constituency covers the eastern parts of Harrogate district (including the civil war battle site of Marston Moor), southern part of Hambleton, and northern fringes of York, some of which was affected by serious flooding in late 2000. The towns included are Easingwold, Thirsk, Boroughbridge, Bedale and Leeming up the A1 as well as a large and growing number of electors on the edge of York (but within its new unitary authority boundaries) such as Clifton Without, Rawcliffe and Haxby.

As it sounds, much of this territory is strongly Conservative, particularly the wards within Hambleton district, but also many of the rural Harrogate wards as well. For example, the Tories polled about 60 per cent in Boroughbridge ward in the county elections in 2001, 65 per cent in Bedale and 76 per cent in Thornton (a rural ward just south of Northallerton), and all of these were three-way contests. The Liberal Democrats enjoy a major area of support in council elections in the York segment: the five wards of Clifton Without, Haxby, Huntingdon & New Earswick, Rawcliffe & Skelton and Wigginton provided over 7,000 votes (as against 1,900 each for the Conservatives and Labour) and all ten councillors in 1999. Even though they have only isolated pockets elsewhere, it would seem that many of these local Lib Dem voters must have deserted to Labour in the 1997 and 2001 general elections, since apart from recent successes in Thirsk, Labour are extremely weak in local elections all over the constituency. This ticket splitting will not worry Anne McIntosh, who (partly as a result of foot and mouth) added 7 per cent to her share in 2001. McIntosh was one of the few candidates of any party who actually polled more votes numerically in 2001 than 1997, as Vale of York jumped from the 41st to 17th safest Conservative seat in Britain.

YORK

	2001		1997		1992 actual	
Electorate and turnout	81,354	59.0	79,710	73.2	79,242	81.0
Conservative	11,293	23.5	14,433	24.7	25,183	39.3
Labour	25,072	52.3	34,956	59.9	31,525	49.1
Lib Dem	8,519	17.8	6,537	11.2	6,811	10.6
Green	1,465	3.1	880	1.5	594	0.9
Anti–EU	576	1.2	1,402 (2)	2.4	–	–
Others	1,055 (2)		137		54	
MP	Hugh Bayley (Lab)		Hugh Bayley (Lab)		Hugh Bayley (Lab)	
Majority	13,779	28.7	20,523	35.2	6,342	9.9

Before 1970, York was only ever won by Labour in years of national triumph (1929, 1945 and 1966), with the historic city represented by Conservative MPs for all but seven of the forty-eight years between the end of the first world war and 1966. In this context, Labour's victory here by 2,197 votes in 1970 marked a major turning point, even though the Tories were to briefly win the seat back in 1983. Four years later, they held on by just 147 votes, but after narrowly missing out on that occasion, Hugh Bayley comfortably won the rematch with Conal Gregory next time around, the 5 per cent swing well above average for 1992. A majority of 6,000 was, however, next to nothing compared with the extraordinary lead of over 20,000 accumulated in 1997; even in a landslide year that was some achievement in a city as generally prosperous as this. Although the Labour vote was inevitably to fall from this historic highpoint in the 2001 general election, the fact that the Tory vote fell even further from its historic low hardly suggests an imminent reversal of fortunes. Indeed, they now find themselves less than 3,000 ahead of the Lib Dems, with a share of the vote which has dropped by 30 percentage points over the last fifty years, as compared with 18 points nationally.

York is quite a diverse place, including famous old buildings such as the huge Minster, terraced streets just outside the centre and leafy suburbs beyond that. It is well known as a railway centre, still housing the National Rail Museum, but its university (actually sited within the Selby constituency) may help explain the leftward political drift, as the same has happened in other seats full of students such as Leeds North West and Cambridge. Labour are also undoubtedly helped by the fact that many of the affluent suburbs to which the professional classes have moved are in the next door Vale of York seat, although even in the suburbs the Liberal Democrats win council elections at the moment rather than the Conservatives. Indeed the Tories won just three seats out of a total of fifty-three in 1999 and it is a little difficult at the moment to see where any recovery might come from.

South Yorkshire

	Conservative		Labour		Liberal Democrat		Others	
	Share of vote	Seats	Share of vote	Seats	Share of vote	Seats	Share of vote	Seats
2001	18.8	0	58.9	14	18.0	1	4.2	0
1997	16.7	0	62.3	14	16.6	1	4.4	0
1992	25.8	1	57.9	14	15.7	0	0.6	0
1987	24.9	1	56.0	14	18.9	0	0.2	0
1983	28.0	1	48.8	14	23.0	0	0.2	0

South Yorkshire, which comprises the city of Sheffield together with the boroughs of Barnsley, Doncaster and Rotherham, is a highly industrialised and well-populated area, even after the closure of much of its large coalfield. Prior to the 1990s, mining dominated Barnsley in particular and the small towns and villages which surrounded it; this was the heart of Arthur Scargill's NUM power base in the 1980s. Most of the industry has now disappeared (there are a few mines left to the north of Doncaster and one or two elsewhere), although it has left its mark on the landscape, as well as a lasting pall of depression in many former pit villages. Rotherham and Sheffield were both noted for their steel and cutlery (Sheffield United football club are still known as 'The Blades'), but much of this former industry that once dominated the bleak areas along the River Don between the M1 and respective town and city centres is now gone. In its place can be found the large Meadowhall shopping complex, as well as the odd industrial park, many newer employers attracted by a favourable strategic location at the heart of Britain's motorway network. Sheffield can also boast a 'Supertram' system and new stadium constructed for the World Student Games (the city somewhat hopefully describes itself as the 'National City of Sport'), but these developments rebounded badly against the Labour-run council in the 1990s, contributing to a severe financial crisis. This fate was at least less severe than that suffered by the city in two recent disaster movies. For some reason, both *Threads* (the classic 1980s film about a nuclear holocaust) and a more recent series about the aftermath of a meteor hitting the Earth, were set in the ruins of Sheffield, though on a somewhat lighter note, the city was also the setting for *The Full Monty*.

Traditionally, South Yorkshire (the county was only established in the 1970s having previously been a part of the West Riding of Yorkshire) has been very strong 'heartland' territory for the Labour Party. In the post-war period, they have always held all constituencies except for three, many with enormous majorities. Thus in February 1974 for example, Labour candidates could poll 48,737 votes in Don Valley and 52,532 in Rother Valley, both of which were mining seats. The Conservatives had an enclave in Sheffield, holding both Hallam and Heeley for long periods, and between 1951 and 1964 they also won Doncaster. By the 1970s, they were reduced to just Hallam, and as a result, even in their disastrous year of 1983, Labour won all but one of South Yorkshire's fifteen constituencies. In those days, Arthur

Scargill and the NUM were a major influence, the left wing leader of Sheffield city council was a certain David Blunkett and the county council promoted cheap public transport; the label 'Socialist Republic of South Yorkshire' seemed highly appropriate.

Despite the decline of the coal-mining industry since the year-long strike of 1984-85, Labour's vote has in fact subsequently increased in South Yorkshire as everywhere else. The only difference has been that, here, there were no more seats for the party to gain. The only change has come in Sheffield Hallam, where the Conservatives finally lost their only remaining seat to the Liberal Democrats in 1997 after a huge swing exceeding 18 per cent. In 2001, it was comfortably retained with an increased majority. Indeed, the fact that Tory leader William Hague went to school in Wath-upon-Dearne (just about the geographical centre of South Yorkshire) appeared to make very little difference to his party's fortunes, though given the size of Labour's leads outside of Sheffield Hallam, that was perhaps hardly surprising. Out of fourteen Labour-held constituencies, only in one (Don Valley) was their 2001 majority below 34 per cent, with all the others included on the list of Labour's 150 safest seats nationally.

Local government

What interest there has been in South Yorkshire politics over recent years has concentrated on local government. Following the financial problems of the 1990s, Labour spectacularly lost control of Sheffield city council to the Liberal Democrats in 1999; seven years earlier Labour had 67 councillors and the Lib Dems only nine. The capture of the council marked one of the Lib Dems' greatest triumphs in a traditionally Labour area, which one could place alongside their rise to power in Liverpool. The dramatic change took place over a number of elections in the mid and late 1990s (all metropolitan councils outside London elect annually), and it seems likely that it will take Labour some time to recover. In the 2000 council elections, they did at least steady their decline, holding onto two wards which had been lost a year earlier, and then in 2002 they mounted a stronger recovery, falling just short of regaining control. The council was balanced after 2002 but is on a knifedge – both Labour and Lib Dems will look to regain a majority in 2003 and 2004.

It is rarely pointed out that the Labour share of the vote in the other three South Yorkshire boroughs fell by even more over the 1995-1999 period than in Sheffield. Labour were in such a dominant position to start with that even a 20 per cent drop in support in Doncaster from the mid to late 1990s left the party still in comfortable control of the council with 40 or so councillors out of 63. This period included the 'Donnygate' scandal over councillors' expenses, which severely embarrassed the Labour Party and led to the suspension of a number of leading councillors. The opposition are now split four ways (including Independents and a 'Community Group') and this division helped Labour win the first mayoral poll in 2002 (on a minority vote) after 65 per cent had supported the concept in a referendum. Compared with Sheffield and Doncaster, the other two metropolitan authorities remain rather uninteresting; in Barnsley Labour still boasted 49 councillors out of 66 in 2002, and in Rotherham 58 out of 66. Each of these councils has a smattering of Conservatives and 'others' and very few Lib Dems.

Boundary review

South Yorkshire is now only entitled to 13.8 seats rather than the current total of 15, and will thus lose one at the forthcoming boundary review. Barnsley and Sheffield are both too small for their current number of constituencies, and one possibility is a seat which links the two. There are many permutations, though in any event it seems likely that one Sheffield seat will be abolished in its present form and be merged with an existing seat outside the city.

BARNSLEY CENTRAL

	2001		1997		1992 notional	
Electorate and turnout	60,086	45.8	61,160	59.7	64,092	70.2
Conservative	3,608	13.1	3,589	9.8	8,340	18.5
Labour	19,181	69.6	28,090	77.0	31,844	70.8
Lib Dem	4,051	14.7	3,481	9.5	4,823	10.7
Anti–EU	–	–	1,325	3.6	–	–
Socialist	703	2.6	–	–	–	–
MP	Eric Illsley (Lab)		Eric Illsley (Lab)		Eric Illsley (Lab)	
Majority	15,130	54.9	24,501	67.2	23,504	52.2

In many ways Barnsley is the epicentre of working-class, industrial Yorkshire: it is the birthplace of many well-known Yorkshiremen such as television presenter Michael Parkinson and cricket umpire Dickie Bird, while another famous cricketer Geoff Boycott was born and still lives nearby. A famous Barnsley political name was Roy Mason, the Labour MP for the area for 34 years between 1953 and 1987, who then moved across to the House of Lords.

Electorally, the Barnsley constituencies together with their neighbours are about as solidly Labour as it is possible to find: Barnsley Central (the successor to the old Barnsley constituency) has been held by the party continually since 1935. It was the 6th safest seat in the country after 1997, though it fell back to 14th after a higher than average swing to the Conservatives in 2001. It should be noted that Barnsley is one of very few places never to have elected a Conservative MP; it was represented by Liberals between 1885 and 1922 and again from 1931 to 1935.

Barnsley's staunch loyalty to Labour over the post-second world war period owes much to strong coal-mining traditions. The town has been the headquarters of Arthur Scargill's National Union of Mineworkers (NUM) for many years and was previously at the centre of a rich coalfield which prompted the growth of virtually all of the surrounding villages. As in areas such as County Durham and West Cumbria, support for the Labour party appears to have survived intact despite the end of coal-mining here. The result is that Labour (and Mason's successor Eric Illsley, a former NUM official) still record huge majorities without the need for glitzy campaigning, and all that the opposition parties can do is worry about who finishes second.

BARNSLEY EAST and MEXBOROUGH

	2001		1997		1992 notional	
Electorate and turnout	65,655	49.5	68,105	63.6	69,088	72.2
Conservative	4,024	12.4	4,936	11.4	8,654	17.4
Labour	21,945	67.5	31,699	73.1	36,375	72.9
Lib Dem	5,156	15.9	4,489	10.4	4,864	9.8
Anti–EU	662	2.0	797	1.8	–	–
Socialist	722	2.2	1,213	2.8	–	–
Others	–		201		–	
MP	Jeff Ennis (Lab)		Jeff Ennis (Lab)		Terry Patchett (Lab)* Barnsley East	
Majority	16,789	51.6	26,763	61.8	27,721	55.6

* Jeff Ennis (Lab) elected at December 1996 by–election.

Barnsley now has three constituencies bearing its name, but this seat is based on the smaller towns and villages to the east such as Wombwell, Darfield, Bolton-upon-Dearne and Mexborough, which is in the borough of Doncaster. This is unremitting working-class, Labour voting territory typified by former pit villages such as Grimethorpe (immortalised as 'Grimley' in the film *Brassed Off*) and Goldthorpe. Housing generally falls into two types: council estates and ageing terraces, and as in Barnsley Central, aside from the race to finish second, general elections are not really contests at all. This has been true now for many decades: indeed until 1983, many of these areas were included in the Hemsworth constituency (see West Yorkshire), well-known as a seat dominated by coal-mining in which Labour recorded over 40,000 votes (and an 80 per cent share) at all general elections between 1950 and February 1974. The end of mining in these parts has prompted a slight shift away from Labour in the last three decades, though it is hardly apparent from the huge majorities still being piled up by present incumbent Jeff Ennis.

BARNSLEY WEST and PENISTONE

	2001		1997		1992 actual	
Electorate and turnout	65,291	52.9	64,912	65.0	63,391	75.7
Conservative	7,892	22.8	7,750	18.4	13,461	28.0
Labour	20,244	58.6	25,017	59.3	27,965	58.3
Lib Dem	6,428	18.6	7,613	18.0	5,610	11.7
Anti–EU	–	–	1,828	4.3	–	–
Green	–	–	–	–	970	2.0
MP	Mick Clapham (Lab)		Mick Clapham (Lab)		Mick Clapham (Lab)	
Majority	12,352	35.7	17,267	40.9	14,504	30.2

Barnsley's third seat extends all the way from Worsbrough and Hoyland to the south of Barnsley itself westwards beyond the small town of Penistone and into the foothills of the Peak District. On paper this is the least safe of the Barnsley constituencies, but that is not to give the opposition parties much hope since Labour won by over 10,000 votes even in 1983. In fact there are Conservative voters in Penistone: the party won one local ward in the 1999 local elections and two in 2000, their only councillors elected across the entire Barnsley district. In general elections however, this part of the constituency makes up only one in four of the electorate, and is easily outvoted by more working class wards in Barnsley like Worsbrough and Dodworth on either side of the M1 motorway.

The former Penistone constituency was a little more marginal than this one, though even that was Labour from 1935 until 1978, with the party surviving a 1978 by-election (following the death of its MP, John Mendelson) by 5,000 votes. In 1983, about half of the old seat was transferred to Sheffield Hillsborough, what was left being supplemented by three wards from the old Barnsley seat. The last boundary review did not produce any changes, but the next probably will, as the current electorate is on the small side and Barnsley is now entitled to only 2.4 seats. The current MP here (since 1992) is another former NUM official, Mick Clapham.

DONCASTER CENTRAL

	2001		1997		1992 actual	
Electorate and turnout	65,690	51.6	67,965	63.9	68,890	74.2
Conservative	8,035	23.7	9,105	21.0	17,113	33.5
Labour	20,034	59.1	26,961	62.1	27,795	54.3
Lib Dem	4,390	12.9	4,091	9.4	6,057	11.8
Anti–EU	926	2.7	1,735 (2)	4.0	–	–
Socialist	517	1.5	854	2.0	–	–
Others	–		694		184	
MP	Rosie Winterton (Lab)		Rosie Winterton (Lab)		Harold Walker (Lab)	
Majority	11,999	35.4	17,856	41.1	10,682	20.9

This constituency includes most of the town of Doncaster together with the mining village of Armthorpe and more upmarket suburbs towards the M18 motorway. Central (which, as in Barnsley, more or less succeeded the single former constituency bearing the town's name) was represented for more than thirty years by Harold Walker, who difficult as it is to believe now, actually gained Doncaster from the Conservatives in 1964. The current incumbent is Rosie Winterton, who formerly worked for John Prescott, and is one of two women MPs currently representing Doncaster seats.

Despite what one might think from the constituency name, this is a long way from the 'super-safe' Labour territory one finds towards Barnsley. There are prosperous neighbourhoods on either side of the racecourse, notably Bessacarr out to the south east, where Labour finish third in council elections. As recently as the 1983 general election, while they retained a majority of nearly 13,000 in Doncaster North, Labour held on by just 2,500 votes in Central on a 42 per cent share of the vote, and despite much improved showings since then, the party got back into difficulties with the Donnygate affair, which erupted in the 1990s involving unfeasibly large expenses being claimed by a number of leading councillors. In the event, the publicity surrounding the case appeared to have little effect on general election outcomes in 1997 or 2001, with this seat following national movements of opinion and Rosie Winterton safely returned with five-figure majorities on each occasion.

DONCASTER NORTH

	2001		1997		1992 notional	
Electorate and turnout	62,124	50.5	63,019	63.3	63,972	71.0
Conservative	4,601	14.7	5,906	14.8	10,131	22.3
Labour	19,788	63.1	27,843	69.8	29,272	64.4
Lib Dem	3,323	10.6	3,369	8.4	6,022	13.3
Independent	2,926	9.3	1,181	3.0	–	–
Anti–EU	725	2.3	1,589	4.0	–	–
MP	Kevin Hughes (Lab)		Kevin Hughes (Lab)		Kevin Hughes (Lab)	
Majority	15,187	48.4	21,937	55.0	19,141	42.1

Doncaster's safest Labour seat does not include the centre of the town, but starts at Bentley on the other side of the River Don, taking in Adwick-le-Street, Carcroft and Askern before looping around to the north east to include the small town of Thorne, previously part of the old Goole seat. This is a constituency built on coal-mining, and needless to say is strongly pro-Labour. Even in the local elections of 2000 (after Donnygate) Labour held all the local council seats here, though their vote had dropped a little from 1995 when they recorded an almost monolithic 92.7 per cent of the vote in Bentley Central, and over 85 per cent in Bentley North Road and Adwick. They currently face opposition from the 'Community group' who won Thorne in 2002 and enabled the Conservatives to win Hatfield on a split vote.

In recent general elections, the party has easily withstood an Independent challenge resulting from the Donnygate affair, and this remains one of Labour's fifty safest seats. Kevin Hughes has been MP here since 1992 and was a government whip in Labour's first term, though probably gained greater notoriety with his more recent comments dismissing critics of the government as the 'yoghurt and muesli-eating, *Guardian* reading fraternity'. Given that the *Guardian* probably sells few copies in Doncaster North, such remarks are unlikely to do Hughes too much damage.

DON VALLEY

	2001		1997		1992 notional	
Electorate and turnout	66,787	54.8	65,643	66.4	65,391	78.7
Conservative	10,489	28.6	10,717	24.6	18,927	36.8
Labour	20,009	54.6	25,376	58.3	26,046	50.6
Lib Dem	4,089	11.2	4,238	9.7	5,718	11.1
Anti–EU	777	2.1	1,379	3.2	–	–
Socialist	466	1.3	1,024	2.4	–	–
Others	800		823 (2)		803	
MP	Caroline Flint (Lab)		Caroline Flint (Lab)		Martin Redmond (Lab)	
Majority	9,520	26.0	14,659	33.7	7,119	13.8

Don Valley includes the remainder of the borough of Doncaster, taking in heavily pro-Labour areas immediately to the south of the town such as Conisbrough (an otherwise bleak town notable for its striking castle and more recent 'Earth Centre' attraction), Edlington and New Rossington, but also more marginal territory along the county boundary to the south and east. Here, small towns such as Bawtry and Tickhill seem almost out of place in South Yorkshire, and there is significant support for the Conservatives. The Tories picked up 55 per cent of the vote in the South East and Southern Parks wards in the 1999 local elections and over 60 per cent in 2000; as a result, a significant proportion of their total number of councillors in South Yorkshire (only 17 at the time of going to press) represent this small bit of one constituency.

In the 1999 Euro elections, these voters were enough to tip Don Valley into the Tory column because of the appallingly low turnout (18 per cent). Such an outcome was never in any serious danger of being repeated in 2001 as long as Labour voters in working class wards elsewhere in the constituency came out to the polls. Though there was a small swing away from Labour, Caroline Flint was comfortably re-elected with a majority just under 10,000.

ROTHERHAM

	2001		1997		1992 actual	
Electorate and turnout	57,931	50.7	59,942	62.8	60,937	71.7
Conservative	5,682	19.4	5,383	14.3	10,372	23.7
Labour	18,759	63.9	26,852	71.3	27,933	63.9
Lib Dem	3,117	10.6	3,919	10.4	5,375	12.3
Anti–EU	730	2.5	1,132	3.0		
Others	1,066 (3)		364		–	–
MP	Dennis MacShane (Lab)		Dennis MacShane (Lab)		James Boyce (Lab)*	
Majority	13,077	44.5	21,469	57.0	17,561	40.2

* Dennis MacShane (Lab) elected at May 1994 by–election.

Rotherham is a town of just under 100,000 inhabitants on the other side of the M1 motorway from Sheffield. It is another industrial and working class town, though much of its former industry, whether coal or steel, has now gone. Three of the constituency's eight local government wards are in the most deprived 200 nationally, though there are new business parks and industrial estates springing up, and also the Magna science adventure centre on part of the huge former steelworks site.

The parliamentary seat was won by all three parties around the time of the first world war, but has become rather more predictable since then. Thus Rotherham was Liberal from 1885 until 1918, Conservative from 1918 to 1923 (and again between 1931 and 1933) and Labour from 1923 to 1931. From 1933 onwards it became a very safe Labour seat, with five-figure majorities recorded by the party at all sixteen general elections from 1945 until the present day.

Closer contests have occurred in two by-elections, with Labour holding the seat by 4,500 in 1976 and just under 7,000 in 1994, when the Liberal Democrats recorded a strong second place (and Lord Sutch managed over a thousand votes, almost saving his deposit). The Lib Dem vote receded in 1997 and 2001, though they did win the Thorpe Hesley ward in the 2000 council elections. The Conservatives also won Broom to the south east of the centre in that contest, but Labour remain very strong in Greasborough (70 per cent in 2000), Herringthorpe and the Central ward, which is the 108th most deprived in the country and contains most of the town's ethnic minority population. The seat should remain utterly safe for the very 'New Labour' Dennis MacShane.

ROTHER VALLEY

	2001		1997		1992 actual	
Electorate and turnout	69,174	53.2	68,693	67.2	68,304	75.0
Conservative	7,969	21.7	7,699	16.7	13,755	26.9
Labour	22,851	62.1	31,184	67.6	30,977	60.5
Lib Dem	4,603	12.5	5,342	11.6	6,483	12.7
Anti–EU	1,380	3.7	1,932	4.2	–	–
MP	Kevin Barron (Lab)		Kevin Barron (Lab)		Kevin Barron (Lab)	
Majority	14,882	40.4	23,485	50.9	17,222	33.6

Rother Valley takes in a number of towns and small villages, such as Maltby, Kiveton Park and Dinnington, in the far south-east corner of Yorkshire on the fringes of Sheffield and Rotherham. It is a semi-rural landscape, but the communities here almost all had some connection with coal-mining, most notably Orgreave, the scene of a famous confrontation in the 1984-85 miners strike at which NUM leader Arthur Scargill was arrested. These days, most of the pits have gone (the works at Orgreave have been completely obliterated on maps), but the associated political traditions have proved more long-lasting in terms of loyal support for the Labour party, who have tended to be represented by former miners such as present incumbent Kevin Barron.

In previous elections, Labour piled up the votes here, their majority even exceeding 10,000 in 1931, when the party was reduced to 52 seats nationally. Between 1945 and 1979, they recorded more than 40,000 votes at all general elections bar one. The huge figures of the past were to come to an end when the seat was cut down to size by the creation of Wentworth in 1983, and Labour's vote dropped to about half its previous total in 2001. Swings away from the government were not necessarily unusual for former mining seats in the most recent general election (see also Nottinghamshire), but Barron remains very safe here. In the 2000 local elections, Labour comfortably held all the wards in the constituency, though Thurcroft and Whiston (which includes the M1/M18 junction) elected a Liberal Democrat councillor in 1999.

SHEFFIELD ATTERCLIFFE

	2001		1997		1992 actual	
Electorate and turnout	67,697	52.9	68,548	64.7	69,177	71.8
Conservative	5,443	15.2	7,119	16.1	13,083	26.3
Labour	24,287	67.8	28,937	65.3	28,563	57.5
Lib Dem	5,092	14.2	6,973	15.7	7,283	14.7
Anti–EU	1,002	2.8	1,289	2.9	–	–
Green	–	–	–	–	751	1.5
MP	Clive Betts (Lab)		Clive Betts (Lab)		Clive Betts (Lab)	
Majority	18,844	52.6	21,818	49.2	15,480	31.2

Sheffield contains two former industrial seats in the east of the city which have been Labour strongholds for many years, matching anything to be found in the surrounding mining areas. Attercliffe first went Labour in 1909, and was thereafter only lost in 1918 and 1931, on the second occasion by just 165 votes. Since 1945, Labour have racked up huge leads here, usually recording about 70 per cent of the vote until the 1970s, though slightly less since then. Its MP since 1992 has been Clive Betts, who led the city council for five years after David Blunkett's election to parliament in 1987.

The constituency covers the south east of the city off the A57 and A616 roads, reaching almost as far as the M1 motorway at Mosborough. The innermost wards contain terraced housing and a number of council estates - as of the 1991 census, a third of homes in Attercliffe were rented from the council, though this figure will almost certainly have declined by 2001. Mosborough, the furthest out ward in the constituency, is completely different, containing an area of what seems like endless new housing, which has increased its electorate to more than 25,000, nearly double that in the other three wards. Despite this, it has continued to return Labour councillors. At the other end of the seat, Darnall is very different, still containing stark industrial scenes as well as the new Don Valley stadium; it is one of a large number of Sheffield wards to feature in the most deprived ten per cent nationally. Darnall was also one of many which produced a dramatic Liberal Democrat advance in council elections in the 1990s, culminating in victory in one of its three seats in 1999, though Labour made a significant recovery to win in 2000 and 2002. This pattern was repeated in Birley, though the fourth ward in the seat, Handsworth, has remained strongly Labour throughout. In 2001, Labour put their local council difficulties firmly behind them to increase both their percentage vote and majority and this is currently their 25th safest seat in the country.

SHEFFIELD BRIGHTSIDE

	2001		1997		1992 actual	
Electorate and turnout	54,134	47.2	58,930	57.5	63,810	66.3
Conservative	2,601	10.2	2,850	8.4	7,090	16.8
Labour	19,650	76.9	24,901	73.5	29,771	70.4
Lib Dem	2,238	8.8	4,947	14.6	5,273	12.5
Anti–EU	348	1.4	624	1.8	–	–
Socialist	715 (2)	2.8	482	1.4	–	–
Others	–		61		150	
MP	David Blunkett (Lab)		David Blunkett (Lab)		David Blunkett (Lab)	
Majority	17,049	66.7	19,954	58.9	22,681	53.6

The other constituency in the east of Sheffield is Brightside, which covers the hilly area to the north of the River Don. Like Attercliffe it is a very safe Labour seat, and also saw a significant swing to the party in 2001; although this seems to have partly made up for a below average swing in 1997, Brightside can now boast Labour's second largest percentage majority in the country. Its MP is former council leader David Blunkett, who succeeded Joan Maynard in 1987, entered the cabinet as Education and Employment Secretary in 1997 and became Home Secretary after 2001. It is not beyond the bounds of imagination that he might one day become Britain's first blind Prime Minister.

Blunkett's constituency is very working class and traditional, which is sometimes reflected in his approach to politics. In 1991, over half of homes in Brightside were rented from the local authority, while more recent figures reveal that all five wards in the seat are in the most deprived 10 per cent in the country. Highest (or lowest) on this list is Southey Green (43rd out of 8,000 or so in England) whose council estates overlook Sheffield Wednesday's football ground. Labour were still recording vote shares of 70 per cent here at the height of the Lib Dem surge in 1999; it was their best ward in the city in both 1999 and 2000. Neighbouring Firth Park has a similar character, and overall Labour held all the council seats in the constituency in both 1999 and 2000, the only constituency in Sheffield in which this was the case.

SHEFFIELD CENTRAL

	2001		1997		1992 notional	
Electorate and turnout	60,765	49.5	68,667	53.0	71,980	59.3
Conservative	3,289	10.9	4,341	11.9	7,983	18.7
Labour	18,477	61.4	23,179	63.6	25,448	59.6
Lib Dem	5,933	19.7	6,273	17.2	8,068	18.9
Anti–EU	257	0.9	863	2.4	–	–
Socialist	1,043 (2)	3.5	466	1.3	–	–
Green	1,008	3.4	954	2.6	840	2.3
Others	62		343 (2)		341	
MP	Richard Caborn (Lab)		Richard Caborn (Lab)		Richard Caborn (Lab)	
Majority	12,544	41.7	16,906	46.4	17,380	40.7

Sheffield Central was resurrected as a parliamentary constituency in 1983, thirty-three years after the original seat was abolished in the first major post-war boundary review. In the meantime, much of its territory was included in Park, which was also overwhelmingly Labour and held by Fred Mulley from 1950 until 1983. As one would expect, Central takes in many of the residential tower blocks in and around the centre of the city, most of Sheffield's Asian community, and a large number of university students. Also included are the railway station, Crucible Theatre (well known for its snooker championships) and Sheffield United football ground. This is highly appropriate, since the MP since 1983 has been Richard Caborn, a United supporter who became Minister of Sport after 2001, following previous stints as Minister for the Regions at the DETR and then a Trade Minister.

The Labour majority in Central was over forty percentage points even in 1983, when it ranked as Labour's 13th safest seat. By 1992 that margin had increased to more than fifty points, but then its boundaries expanded to take in a ward from Hallam, which notionally cut the Labour vote by almost ten per cent, not that the boundary change particularly threatened the overall outcome. In general elections the only point of note since then has been the Liberal Democrats moving into second place, reflecting their local victories in Nether Edge and Netherthorpe wards. Labour have continued to win the other wards relatively comfortably in council elections and will surely continue to win the parliamentary seat as well for the foreseeable future.

SHEFFIELD HALLAM

	2001		1997		1992 notional	
Electorate and turnout	58,982	64.8	62,834	72.4	61,133	73.1
Conservative	11,856	31.0	15,074	33.1	22,180	49.6
Labour	4,758	12.4	6,147	13.5	8,246	18.4
Lib Dem	21,203	55.4	23,345	51.3	13,740	30.7
Anti–EU	429	1.1	788	1.7	–	–
Others	–		125		546	
MP	Richard Allan (LD)		Richard Allan (LD)		Irvine Patnick (Con)	
Majority	9,347	24.4	8,271	18.2	8,440	18.9

Considering that it had been won by the Conservatives at all the previous twenty-nine general elections, the Liberal Democrats' gain of Sheffield Hallam was one of their biggest triumphs of the 1997 election. The size of the swing between the two parties (over 18 per cent) was equally impressive as they over-turned a previous (notional) Conservative majority of over 8,000 and replaced it with a similar lead of their own. Labour's vote actually fell here by five per cent, a very similar pattern to that in Harrogate, the other seat in Yorkshire gained by the Lib Dems. The party's run of success in Sheffield then continued with the gain of the council from Labour in 1999, when they won all the constituency's four wards and increased their share of the vote to almost sixty per cent, though this figure slipped back a little the following year. In 2001, the Lib Dem majority increased further at the expense of both other parties (as in Harrogate) and this is now their sixth safest seat in Britain; one can certainly envisage them holding it in the future even in the event of a significant Conservative recovery nationally.

Hallam itself is not the sort of inner city urban constituency one might expect to find in the north of England. It includes affluent suburbs such as Dore to the south of the centre along the railway line as well as neighbouring Ecclesall, which reverses the pattern in much of the rest of the city by its inclusion in the list of 500 least deprived wards in the country. In view of this, it is perhaps unsurprising that the seat had been safely held by the Conservatives at all general elections since 1885, though there was a peculiar two-year Liberal interlude from 1916-18 when H. Fisher was allowed to take the seat unopposed in a wartime by-election and thus join the coalition government. In more normal times the seat was rarely threatened (the smallest majority was just under 3,000 in 1945) until the Liberals started to come within striking distance from 1987. Since then the Labour vote has been squeezed in classic style and the Conservatives have lost their hold on yet another northern suburban seat.

SHEFFIELD HEELEY

	2001		1997		1992 actual	
Electorate and turnout	61,949	55.1	66,599	65.0	70,953	70.9
Conservative	4,864	14.2	6,767	15.6	13,051	25.9
Labour	19,452	57.0	26,274	60.7	28,005	55.7
Lib Dem	7,748	22.7	9,196	21.3	9,247	18.4
Anti–EU	634	1.9	1,029	2.4	–	–
Green	774	2.3	–	–	–	–
Socialist	667	2.0	–	–	–	–
MP	Meg Munn (Lab)		Bill Michie (Lab)		Bill Michie (Lab)	
Majority	11,704	34.3	17,078	39.5	14,954	29.7

Heeley lies to the south of the city centre between Hallam and Attercliffe. It provided a second Conservative seat in Sheffield in the 1950s, and was even regained in 1970, before being lost to Labour again in 1974. Since then, boundary changes and the general swing away from the Tories in the urban north have both contributed to the party's vote almost disappearing altogether. They were reduced to third place in 1997; their 2001 candidate Carolyn Abbott had hardly any help in her campaign as Conservatives were encouraged to go to Hallam, but their vote in both seats was to drop even further.

Just south of the centre, Heeley comprises terraced streets off the A61 Chesterfield Road of the sort that would once have been described as desirable, though probably no longer, while further out there are a number of newer council estates right on the edge of the city such as Gleadless, which includes a number of tower blocks. In general elections this mix has proved fertile territory for Labour in recent contests, the party's majority steadily climbing (like some of the streets here) to reach a plateau of 17,000 votes in 1997. But in council elections it has been a different matter entirely, as the Liberal Democrats moved beyond early gains in wards like Beauchief to win all the other wards in the seat as well. In 1999 and 2000, they polled over half of the vote in Heeley, their performances even better here than in neighbouring Hallam. Despite such success locally, national votes have been much harder to come by, and although they moved into second place, the 2001 result must have been extremely disappointing given that Labour MP Bill Michie was retiring after 18 years to be replaced by a new candidate, Meg Munn. The Liberal Democrats will need to start translating local election support into general election votes in places like this if they are to seriously challenge Labour in their northern heartlands, but they did not have a good start in 2002 when Labour regained a number of council seats.

SHEFFIELD HILLSBOROUGH

	2001		*1997*		*1992 actual*	
Electorate and turnout	74,180	57.3	74,642	71.0	77,343	77.2
Conservative	7,801	18.3	7,707	14.5	11,640	19.5
Labour	24,170	56.8	30,150	56.9	27,563	46.2
Lib Dem	9,601	22.6	13,699	25.8	20,500	34.3
Anti–EU	964	2.3	1,468	2.8	–	–
MP	Helen Jackson (Lab)		Helen Jackson (Lab)		Helen Jackson (Lab)	
Majority	14,569	34.3	16,451	31.0	7,063	11.8

Sheffield Hillsborough was a rare Labour-Liberal marginal in the 1980s and early 1990s, but in the reverse of the local council pattern (and that in Chesterfield), it has been Labour who have since pulled away, increasing their majority further in 2001.

The constituency covers the terraced streets in the northern part of Sheffield (behind Sheffield Wednesday football ground) as well as smaller towns to the north (but still within the city boundaries) such as Chapeltown and Stocksbridge. These latter areas were previously in the old Penistone seat, and their inclusion from 1983 turned Hillsborough from a strong Labour seat (held by the party since 1935) into something potentially more difficult. In Labour's disastrous year of 1983, Martin Flannery's majority was cut to just 1,500 votes by a Liberal who had contested Penistone four times over the previous ten years. Thus Hillsborough became a rare South Yorkshire marginal, though as things turned out, it would take another fourteen years for the third party to gain a seat in the area, and it would not be this one. Labour's majority increased to the rather more comfortable margin of 3,000 in 1987, and then doubled again at Helen Jackson's first contest in 1992. Five years later, while storming to victory in Hallam, the Liberal Democrats seemed to lose their way completely in Hillsborough, and the seat finally returned to its previous safe Labour status.

The Lib Dems have not completely disappeared here; in local council elections they still attract a good vote, winning all five wards and polling approximately 55 per cent across the constituency in 2000 (although losing ground in 2002). As in Heeley, this seems to have made little or no difference to the results of general elections, with a growing number of voters (as in Liverpool) appearing to be dividing their loyalties between Liberal Democrats locally and Labour nationally.

WENTWORTH

	2001		1997		1992 actual	
Electorate And turnout	64,033	52.8	63,951	65.3	64,915	74.0
Conservative	6,349	18.8	6,266	15.0	10,490	21.8
Labour	22,798	67.5	30,225	72.3	32,939	68.5
Lib Dem	3,652	10.8	3,867	9.3	4,629	9.6
Anti–EU	979	2.9	1,423	3.4	–	–
MP	John Healey (Lab)		John Healey (Lab)		Peter Hardy (Lab)	
Majority	16,449	48.7	23,959	57.3	22,449	46.7

A new constituency (re) created in 1983, Wentworth is named after the historic house and gardens which provide the seat with few electors and a totally misleading guide to its character. In fact this is yet another South Yorkshire seat dominated by its coal-mining past. The seat extends northwards from Rotherham to include Rawmarsh, Swinton and Wath-upon-Dearne, once home to a teenage William Hague, whose claims of 14-pints a day beer drinking exploits in these years met with the same general incredulity in these parts as elsewhere.

The triangle of land between Barnsley, Doncaster and Rotherham has for many years (even when Hague was growing up here) been as safe a Labour area as one will find anywhere in the country. The extent of Labour dominance can be gauged from recent council elections: over 70 per cent of the vote in Swinton, Wath and the two Rawmarsh wards in 1999 and 67 per cent in Brampton, site of the former Cortonwood colliery. Even these shares were significantly lower than the 85-95 per cent achieved four years previously (Rawmarsh East produced a 95.3 per cent Labour vote against a Conservative), and although Labour and its MP John Healey are unlikely to be too concerned as yet, there are signs, as elsewhere, that former mining areas are inching away from their previously monolithic political character. The Conservatives can put their efforts into the Bramley ward to the east of Rotherham, which they won by 16 votes in 2000, though at the moment at least they have little realistic hope in other wards or indeed in general election contests throughout most of South Yorkshire.

West Yorkshire

	Conservative		Labour		LiberalDemocrat		Others	
	Share of vote	Seats	Share of vote	Seats	Share of vote	Seats	Share of vote	Seats
2001	30.0	0	51.5	23	14.0	0	4.5	0
1997	28.8	0	54.0	23	12.9	0	4.2	0
1992	38.2	9	45.5	14	15.0	0	1.3	0
1987	37.9	9	41.0	14	20.8	0	0.4	0
1983	37.3	11	35.7	10	26.0	2	0.9	0

West Yorkshire includes the major cities of Leeds and Bradford, a number of large towns including Halifax, Huddersfield, and Wakefield and plenty of smaller ones as well like Keighley, Dewsbury, Castleford and Pontefract. As this suggests, it is a heavily built-up area, but aside from the former mining area to the south east of Leeds, it has never been a complete Labour stronghold. Many of the smaller towns, particularly to the north and west of Leeds-Bradford, have always had a large Conservative vote, and the Tories were dominant in the two northern Leeds seats for many years as well. In 1959 for example there was an almost perfect north-south divide within what is now West Yorkshire (the old West Riding also included the current South Yorkshire and some parts of North). The Conservatives held a belt of nine seats from Halifax in the west across the north of Bradford and Leeds as far as the oversized Barkston Ash (now Elmet and Selby) in the east - these seats of course adjoined other Tory strongholds farther north. Labour held everything to the south of this line (sixteen seats in total) with the exception of Huddersfield West, which was Liberal partly as a result of the Conservatives not fielding a candidate there.

The overall pattern in the 1950s was remarkably similar to that in 1987 and 1992. The only differences are that by that stage three non-Tory seats had been abolished (one each in Bradford, Leeds and Huddersfield), the Conservatives had lost Halifax, Bradford North and Bradford West and compensated by picking up Calder Valley, Batley & Spen and Colne Valley. This latter group of constituencies are of a fairly similar type, consisting of a band of small towns and surrounding semi-rural areas to the south of Halifax/Bradford/Leeds. They all had traditional manufacturing industry of their own (notably woollens) in years gone by, which for many years formed the basis of a large Labour vote, but in the 1970s and 1980s things were to change dramatically. The change came about for two main reasons. First, much of the small-town industry began to shut down, and second, there was a simultaneous influx of affluent middle class commuters, who worked in places like the increasingly prosperous Leeds (which claims to be the commercial capital of the north). The main factor behind this migration and resultant social change (which has taken place in many parts of the country) was undoubtedly the spread of car ownership in the 1970s. The following decade in particular was to see a trend for those who could afford it to move out of densely populated urban areas, and buy up old stone cottages in the surrounding rural villages, from which they could easily commute into work on a daily basis. The political effect in West Yorkshire was exemplified by Colne Valley (based around Holmfirth), which elected a Conservative MP for the first time in its one hundred-year history in 1987.

In the big towns and cities, another development was sharpening the urban-rural divide. Bradford in particular, but also towns like Batley, Dewsbury, Halifax and Huddersfield, were attracting a large number of immigrants from Asia, who moved in to many of the areas being vacated by people moving out. This was also to have profound political implications, because non-whites, and particular those of Asian origin, have tended to support Labour in very heavy numbers. This could best be seen in Bradford West, a Conservative seat in the 1950s but safely Labour from 1974 onwards. Indeed the Tories have only won a single parliamentary election in Bradford since 1974, whereas not long before they could boast two constituencies in the city. By 1991, the non-white population was over 36 per cent in West (it is almost certainly now much larger), but the last few years have seen another political twist, with the Conservatives starting to select candidates from the large Pakistani community, including their parliamentary candidate in 1997 and 2001. This seems to be having the desired effect of breaking old automatic Labour-voting habits and in 1997, the Conservatives enjoyed one of only two positive swings in the country here. A number of local breakthroughs followed the selection for council seats of non-white Conservative candidates in overwhelmingly non-white wards, and three years later the Tories gained minority control of Bradford council. Unsurprisingly, local parties are now starting to repeat the same selection policy elsewhere in West Yorkshire.

Aside from the political effects of changes in social and ethnic composition, very little changed in West Yorkshire in the 1980s and early 1990s. The Conservatives briefly regained Bradford North and Halifax in 1983, also picking up Dewsbury, but lost them all again in 1987. Their gain of Colne Valley (from the Liberals) in 1987 was held in 1992, and their overall vote remained very stable, while Labour slowly recovered ground lost to the Alliance in 1983, including the regain of Leeds West. Labour were finding it very difficult to make further progress at the Conservatives' expense, failing to gain any of several key marginals in 1992 including Batley & Spen, Calder Valley, Colne Valley and Keighley. In all these seats the Tory vote was actually creeping upwards as a result of the social changes mentioned above, and they all appeared such tough nuts to crack that Labour included them in a special 'Pennine belt' group of constituencies prior to the 1997 election which it was assumed would be difficult if not impossible to gain.

In the event, they need not have worried. The Conservatives were completely wiped out in West Yorkshire in 1997, losing all their nine seats to Labour, including the likes of Leeds North West and Pudsey which Labour had never won, and indeed had been in third place in recent elections. The non-targeted constituencies which were gained in the landslide included Shipley, where the most senior Conservative back-bench MP in the country was unceremoniously dumped out of office by an unknown 24 year old. Labour's achievement of a full house - 23 seats out of 23 - was repeated in 2001, when only Shipley came close to being lost. Percentage majorities were even increased in the two north Leeds seats, where social change seems to be acting against the Conservatives. That being said, there is no question that the Conservatives will have to start regaining a number of these constituencies if they are to have any chance of returning to power in the future, and West Yorkshire will again be a major battleground in 2005/6.

Local government

The five metropolitan authorities in West Yorkshire were all held by Labour in the early-mid 1990s, but since then they have lost control of Calderdale, Kirklees and Bradford. Only Wakefield (which includes the former mining area to its east) has been held continually since 1973, with the Conservatives reduced to three councillors by 1987, few Liberal Democrats elected and usually an enormous Labour majority (still 54 seats against just nine opposition members after 2002). Leeds was run by the Conservatives for a period in the late 1970s (Labour's local election vote went into meltdown in 1976 and 1977), but Labour have held control of this large authority since 1980, during which time a number of council members (and even their political assistant) have become MPs in the region. Having said that, Labour's majority here is not as comfortable as in many other urban councils; the Conservatives have always had a reasonably sized group and the Liberal Democrats are growing again after previous periods of strength in the 1970s and early 1980s. Bradford hit the headlines with the 2001 race riots and a later report came to the (hardly earth-shattering) conclusion that racial segregation in the city was a major factor. Both of the main parties would have to take any blame for council policies, since although Labour were in control for most of the 1990s, there have also been spells of Conservative rule in the 1970s and 1980s. Currently the city is being run by a Tory-Liberal Democrat administration after Labour lost power in 2000. Kirklees (which includes Huddersfield, Dewsbury and the many small towns in between) was lost by Labour in 1999. Since 2000, the Liberal Democrats have been the largest party on the finely balanced council, though there is also a reasonably sized Tory group and a handful of Greens. Calderdale (Halifax and the Calder Valley) has also seen a few changes in control, with the Conservatives in charge in the late 1970s and again from 2000 until 2002. Labour were in charge in the early 1990s, but have now been reduced to third party status behind the Lib Dems.

Boundary review

Unusually for a metropolitan county, West Yorkshire retained all its parliamentary seats in the last boundary review, but is now on the cusp of losing one in the current round. It is theoretically entitled to 22.5 seats, and the boundary commission could leave things as they are (which, for mathematical reasons, would leave the mean constituency size closer to the 69,932 quota, and cause less disruption) or reduce the overall number from 23 to 22. If this happens, then clearly Labour will be the initial losers, given that they presently hold all of the seats. Whatever changes are proposed (and we will not know until the very end of the present review), they are likely to prove politically contentious given the highly marginal nature of the west, centre and north of the county.

BATLEY and SPEN

	2001		1997		1992 notional	
Electorate and turnout	63,665	60.5	64,202	73.2	64,754	78.4
Conservative	14,160	36.7	17,072	36.4	22,676	44.7
Labour	19,224	49.9	23,213	49.4	21,831	43.0
Lib Dem	3,989	10.3	4,133	8.8	5,757	11.3
Anti–EU	574	1.5	1,691	3.6	–	–
Green	595	1.5	384	0.8	520	1.0
BNP	–	–	472	1.0	–	–
MP	Mike Wood (Lab)		Mike Wood (Lab)		Elizabeth Peacock (Con)	
Majority	5,064	13.1	6,141	13.1	845	1.7

Batley and Spen is one of a number of crucial marginal constituencies which lie in small town West Yorkshire along with near-neighbours Calder Valley, Colne Valley, Elmet and others. It has proved an extremely tough seat for Labour to crack: Conservative Elizabeth Peacock won by only 1,362 votes in 1987, then actually increased her majority (despite a national swing to Labour) in 1992, before finally being defeated by Mike Wood in 1997 on a swing of 7.4 per cent, which was far lower than the national average. In 2001, almost nothing changed, further underlining the area's reputation for fixed political loyalties.

Batley itself is home to a substantial Asian population in the centre and east of the town, but the area becomes almost exclusively white as one moves westwards into the other small towns in this constituency, and the key to success is winning votes from both sides of the seat. However, in local elections prior to 2001, Birstall & Birkenshaw and Spen wards elected Conservatives while Cleckheaton and Batley West plumped for the Liberal Democrats. Of the five council wards in the constituency, Labour were reduced from winning four wards in 1995 to just Batley East in 2000, a result which if repeated would have left them extremely vulnerable in 2001. When the crunch came, voters demonstrated that they were quite happy to return a Labour government nationally whatever they did locally, thus dashing any hopes Elizabeth Peacock might have had for a quick return to Parliament. Labour's success continued in 2002 when they narrowly regained Batley West and also won Spen Ward to add to Batley East.

BRADFORD NORTH

	2001		*1997*		*1992 actual*	
Electorate and turnout	66,443	52.7	66,228	63.3	66,711	73.4
Conservative	8,450	24.1	10,723	25.6	15,756	32.2
Labour	17,419	49.7	23,493	56.1	23,420	47.8
Lib Dem	6,924	19.8	6,083	14.5	9,133	18.7
BNP	1,613	4.6	–	–	–	–
Anti–EU	–	–	1,227	2.9	–	–
Others	611		369		654 (2)	
MP	Terry Rooney (Lab)		Terry Rooney (Lab)		Terry Rooney (Lab)	
Majority	8,969	25.6	12,770	30.5	7,664	15.7

Bradford North covers the wards in the east and north east of the city, off the Harrogate and Leeds roads. It is a very mixed area, starting with the residential, village-like Idle at the north end of the seat, which is still a favoured location for the white middle classes. Moving south, Eccleshill and Undercliffe wards have a mix of housing, including areas of terraced streets and the odd council estate, and immediately east of the centre can be found the largely Asian wards of Bowling and Bradford Moor (the constituency was 20 per cent non-white in 1991). Politically, it is these areas where Labour traditionally do best, though they did lose Bradford Moor in 1999 to a Conservative from the Asian community, one of three Hussains to gain council seats in the city that year. In the northern part of the constituency, three wards are now won by Liberal Democrats in local elections, while Undercliffe was Labour in 1999 and Conservative the year after. The 2000 local elections produced almost a three-way split in votes overall, with Labour slightly ahead, but when it comes to general elections the Lib Dem vote tends to subside.

The constituency was held by the Conservatives between 1950 and 1964, and they briefly regained it in 1983 after the de-selection of Labour MP Ben Ford, and his replacement by the left wing Pat Wall. Ford opted to stand as an Independent Labour candidate, picking up 4,000 votes, and as a result the Tories won with just 34 per cent. Normality and a Labour victory returned in 1987, but Wall's triumph was short-lived as he died in 1990. The resulting by-election saw the first victory for a Mormon, Terry Rooney, a campaign boycott by local left-wing Labour party members and the Lib Dems move into second place at the Tories' expense. Unlike in Chesterfield, they failed to build on this position at the following contest, though they did advance in 2001 while the Conservative share slightly fell. This division in the opposition vote will probably ensure continued Labour victories in Bradford North even if there is a significant swing against the government next time.

BRADFORD SOUTH

	2001		1997		1992 actual	
Electorate and turnout	68,441	51.3	68,391	65.9	69,930	75.6
Conservative	9,941	28.3	12,622	28.0	20,283	38.4
Labour	19,603	55.8	25,558	56.7	25,185	47.6
Lib Dem	3,717	10.6	5,093	11.3	7,243	13.7
Anti–EU	783	2.2	1,785	4.0	–	–
Socialist	873 (2)	2.5	–	–	–	–
Others	220		–		156	
MP	Gerry Sutcliffe (Lab)		Gerry Sutcliffe (Lab)		Bob Cryer (Lab)*	
Majority	9,662	27.5	12,936	28.7	4,902	9.3

* Gerry Sutcliffe (Lab) elected at June 1994 by–election.

Bradford South is the white working class seat in the city, with the Asian population just 6 per cent in 1991. It covers a thin sliver of territory running across the south of the city, starting from the village of Tong at its south east extremity. Heading west, the constituency takes in the rugby league stadium at Odsal, nearby Wibsey village, the Buttershaw estate and finally Queensbury on the way to Halifax, a sort of terraced Basildon where the Conservatives win local elections despite a skilled working class population. In the 2000 council poll, the Conservatives led across the constituency by 7,150 votes to 6,560 for Labour and just 2,200 for the Liberal Democrats, who finished third in all six wards. However in general elections Labour has won here since 1945, and their majority remained a comfortable near-10,000 in 2001.

Labour only looked like losing a national contest here in the mid 1980s, with the Conservatives just 110 votes adrift in 1983 and 309 short in 1987. Bob Cryer then increased his majority to almost 5,000 in 1992, but he was killed in a car crash in 1994, causing a by-election in which Labour's share of the vote increased to 55 per cent. Cryer's replacement was Gerry Sutcliffe, a former Bradford council leader and more recently captain of the parliamentary football team.

BRADFORD WEST

	2001		1997		1992 actual	
Electorate and turnout	71,611	53.6	71,961	63.3	70,017	69.9
Conservative	14,236	37.1	15,055	33.0	16,544	33.8
Labour	18,401	48.0	18,932	41.5	26,046	53.2
Lib Dem	2,437	6.4	6,737	14.8	5,150	10.5
Anti–EU	427	1.1	1,348	3.0	–	–
Green	2,672	7.0	861	1.9	735	1.5
Socialist	–	–	1,796 (2)	3.9	–	–
Others	197		839		471	
MP	Marsha Singh (Lab)		Marsha Singh (Lab)		Max Madden (Lab)	
Majority	4,165	10.9	3,877	8.5	9,502	19.4

Bradford West has seen some fascinating political swings in its relatively short history since it was created in 1955. At first it appeared to be the best Conservative seat in Bradford, with a 5,000–plus majority in 1959, and even after it was lost to Labour in 1966 it was quickly regained at the following contest. From 1970 until 1992 however, its political character was to change, a pattern surely connected with the influx of Asians (mainly from Pakistan) who made up a third of the population by 1991. Over this period there was a swing from Conservative to Labour of over 11 per cent, compared with about 5 per cent in Bradford North, less than 2 per cent in Bradford South and a swing to the Conservatives across the country as a whole. Thus Max Madden was able to bequeathe a majority of over 9,500 in 1992, a larger lead than in the two neighbouring constituencies.

Just as it looked like Bradford West would become a totally safe Labour seat (which it would have done with anything like the national swing), there was another, this time abrupt, change in political character in 1997. Conservative candidate Mohammed Riaz managed to reduce the Labour majority by more than half, a result which went totally against the national pattern and was shared only in Bethnal Green & Bow, another seat with a volatile ethnic mix. Unquestionably Riaz was able to attract support from the dominant Muslim community, particularly since his Labour opponent Marsha Singh was a Sikh. This same pattern was to repeat itself in the 1999 council elections when the Conservatives dramatically gained the University ward with an enormous swing since 1995. Labour's problems here are serious, since it is their best wards which are now under threat. To the west, the white middle class suburbs such as Thornton are already overwhelmingly Conservative, and there seems a danger of Labour suffering a 'double whammy' from both ends of the seat.

In 2001 both the Conservatives and Labour added to their vote share, at the expense of the Liberal Democrats and others. That result will have been a relief to Singh, but the battle is by no means over, and Bradford West is now officially Labour's 64th most vulnerable seat, easier to gain for the Tories than Enfield Southgate, Harrow West or either of the Reading constituencies.

CALDER VALLEY

	2001		1997		1992 actual	
Electorate and turnout	75,298	63.0	74,901	75.4	74,418	82.1
Conservative	17,150	36.2	19,795	35.1	27,753	45.4
Labour	20,244	42.7	26,050	46.1	22,875	37.4
Lib Dem	7,596	16.0	8,322	14.7	9,842	16.1
Anti–EU	729	1.5	1,380	2.4	–	–
Green	1,034	2.2	488	0.9	622	1.0
Others	672		431		–	
MP	Christine McCafferty (Lab)		Christine McCafferty (Lab)		Donald Thompson (Con)	
Majority	3,094	6.5	6,255	11.1	4,878	8.0

Calder Valley was the focus of Pete Davies' *This England*, an account of the 1997 election campaign. The constituency runs along the eponymous river from Brighouse as far as the Lancashire border, taking in the town of Elland to the south of Halifax, hippified Hebden Bridge and the closely-packed terraced streets of Todmorden on the way. This is one of several seats in the 'Pennine belt' area which Labour have found difficult in recent times. Donald Thompson, who initially won in 1979, was the first Conservative to win the seat (under its previous name of Sowerby) in the post-war period, but he held on fairly comfortably against a divided opposition in 1983 and strong Labour challenges in 1987 and 1992. There was nothing he could do in 1997 however, as the national landslide swept him away and replaced him with local councillor Christine McCafferty, the swing only fractionally below the national average.

Labour were behind in the constituency in all contests between 1997 and 2001, their local election vote halving from 1995 to 1999. The Liberal Democrats continue to do well here in local polls, and were just about ahead across the constituency in both 1998 and 1999. The Conservatives then took a narrow lead in May 2000, pushing Labour into third place. The Tories were also well ahead at the Euro elections (a lead of 12.5 per cent), but all that was to count for nothing in June 2001, when Labour won again, albeit with a much reduced majority. Whether they can hold the seat again remains to be seen - it is now the 27th most marginal Labour seat and very winnable for the Conservatives.

COLNE VALLEY

	2001		1997		1992 actual	
Electorate and turnout	74,192	63.3	73,347	76.9	72,029	82.0
Conservative	14,328	30.5	18,445	32.7	24,804	42.0
Labour	18,967	40.4	23,285	41.3	17,579	29.8
Lib Dem	11,694	24.9	12,755	22.6	15,953	27.0
Anti–EU	917	2.0	478	0.8	–	–
Green	1,081	2.3	493	0.9	443	0.8
Others	–		955 (2)		277 (3)	
MP	Kali Mountford (Lab)		Kali Mountford (Lab)		Graham Riddick (Con)	
Majority	4,639	9.9	4,840	8.6	7,225	12.2

Colne Valley includes the western section of Huddersfield as well as a number of traditional towns and villages which formed the core of this historic constituency: Marsden, Slaithwaite, Meltham and Holmfirth. This is truly *Last of the Summer Wine* country with strong and entrenched support for each of the three main parties, which makes general election contests extremely competitive and fascinating. The unpredictability of Colne Valley was amply demonstrated during the 2001 campaign, when the Conservatives attempted to squeeze the Liberal Democrat vote in order to narrow the gap with Labour, but far from succeeding, as they have elsewhere in similar situations, saw their vote fall and that of the Lib Dems increase. Such bizarre behaviour is nothing new: Labour lost the seat for the first time in the post-war period while sweeping to a national triumph in 1966, then promptly won it back again four years later despite being ejected from office.

At that time Colne Valley was a rare Labour-Liberal marginal, and it was Richard Wainwright and the Liberals who won again in 1974, but when they were defeated in 1987 after yet another close battle, it was the Conservatives who came out on top for the first time. Their sudden emergence had a lot to do with social changes in rural areas like this, a growing number of commuters, allied to the loss of some of the small industry which provided the towns with their independence, prompting the seat towards more 'normal' political behaviour. This was again apparent in 1997 when Colne Valley closely followed the national pattern, a 10.4 per cent swing being enough for Kali Mountford to secure a reasonably comfortable win. Labour held on easily in 2001 despite not winning a single local council election here in 1999 or 2000, and it now appears that Colne Valley's political fortunes are following national patterns, though with the odd quirk remaining.

DEWSBURY

	2001		1997		1992 notional	
Electorate and turnout	62,345	58.8	61,519	70.0	61,210	80.1
Conservative	11,075	30.2	12,963	30.1	19,637	40.0
Labour	18,524	50.5	21,286	49.4	23,186	47.3
Lib Dem	4,382	12.0	4,422	10.3	4,835	9.9
BNP	1,632	4.5	2,232	5.2	660	1.3
Anti–EU	478	1.3	1,019	2.4	–	–
Green	560	1.5	383	0.9	579	1.2
Ind Labour	–	–	770	1.8	146	0.3
MP	Ann Taylor (Lab)		Ann Taylor (Lab)		Ann Taylor (Lab)	
Majority	7,449	20.3	8,323	19.3	3,549	7.2

Dewsbury has been held by Labour's Ann Taylor since 1987, prior to which it was held by the Conservatives for a single parliamentary term. Labour's loss of the seat in 1983 was partly caused by its MP since 1959, David Ginsburg, defecting and standing for the SDP, splitting the non-Tory vote. However, extremely low swings in both 1992 and 1997 have resulted in the constituency never quite shaking off its marginal status. The seat borders Batley and Spen, which has been similarly resistant to the strong Labour advances made elsewhere. As in Batley, there is an Asian population in Dewsbury itself, and the suspicion that recent voting behaviour here reflects some sort of ethnic polarization is reinforced by the strong showing for the extreme-right British National Party in both 1997 and 2001.

Unlike most other West Yorkshire marginals, Labour managed to stay ahead across Dewsbury constituency at all local elections between 1997 and 2001. In May 1998, their lead was 7.5 per cent; it then increased to 15 per cent in 1999 before dropping to 3.5 per cent in 2000. Even in the Euro elections, the Conservatives only out-polled Labour by a mere 11 votes, which suggested that Labour would do much better here than in other seats when it came to the general election, and so it was to prove in 2001, when Taylor managed to slightly increase her majority in percentage terms. There is still a large Tory vote in Mirfield and Thornhill and the constituency is still just about a marginal (Labour's 145th most vulnerable) but it would take a very large Tory advance for them to win it back in one go.

ELMET

	2001		1997		1992 actual	
Electorate and turnout	70,041	65.6	70,423	76.8	70,711	82.4
Conservative	17,867	38.9	19,569	36.2	27,677	47.5
Labour	22,038	48.0	28,348	52.4	24,416	41.9
Lib Dem	5,001	10.9	4,691	8.7	6,144	10.5
Anti–EU	1,031	2.2	1,487	2.7	–	–
MP	Colin Burgon (Lab)		Colin Burgon (Lab)		Spencer Batiste (Con)	
Majority	4,171	9.1	8,779	16.2	3,261	5.6

Elmet constituency is made up of the eastern wards of the metropolitan borough of Leeds, which largely comprises territory outside of the city itself. Before 1983 the constituency (together with what is now Selby) formed the oversized division of Barkston Ash, which was held by the Conservatives by 116 votes in 1945 and more comfortably after that, their majority almost reaching 20,000 in 1979. Elmet should always have been a better bet for Labour than the old seat, but it was won by Spencer Batiste for the Conservatives from creation in 1983 until 1997. His 1992 lead was just over 3,000, and this was a seat officially targeted by Labour in 1997.

The constituency includes one ward on the outer edge of the city of Leeds, the occasionally rough council estates of Whinmoor, where Labour are traditionally strong. It also takes in the town of Garforth just off the new M1 link, along with the smaller Swillington, Barwick and Kippax to the south which are all generally Labour-inclined. However, Elmet also includes the comfortable and strongly Conservative town of Wetherby a few miles to the north, which in character seems like part of North Yorkshire rather than metropolitan West and is enough to swing the balance in all but the best Labour years.

Labour's vote in Elmet has gradually been falling since the mid 1990s: from almost 60 per cent in the 1995 local elections, their share fell to 52 per cent in the 1997 general election (still enough to win by 9,000 votes), 50% in the 1998 local elections, 47% the year after and 40% in May 2000, when the Conservatives led by 6 percentage points. On this last occasion the voters of Wetherby succeeded in out-polling all the other wards of the constituency, which is the nightmare scenario for Labour MP Colin Burgon. In 2001 he held on with 48 per cent of the vote and a reduced majority, but like many other seats in the county (Calder Valley, Keighley, Shipley) this is somewhere the Conservatives will know they have to win if they are to become a party of power again.

HALIFAX

	2001		1997		1992 actual	
Electorate and turnout	69,870	57.8	71,701	70.5	73,402	78.7
Conservative	13,671	33.8	16,253	32.1	24,637	42.7
Labour	19,800	49.0	27,465	54.3	25,115	43.5
Lib Dem	5,878	14.6	6,059	12.0	7,364	12.7
Anti–EU	1,041	2.6	779	1.5	–	–
Others	–		–		649	
MP	Alice Mahon (Lab)		Alice Mahon (Lab)		Alice Mahon (Lab)	
Majority	6,129	15.2	11,212	22.2	478	0.8

The terraced streets of Halifax seem to have had permanent marginal status; regularly oscillating between Labour and the Conservatives (changing hands in 1928, 1931, 1945 and 1955) even before Dr Shirley Summerskill gained it for Labour in 1964 by about a thousand votes. She was to hold on in 1970 by the rather tighter margin of 198, before becoming a government minister during the 1974–79 period, but could not survive the 1983 landslide when Conservative Roy Galley won by about 1,800. Labour hit back in 1987, when another female candidate Alice Mahon regained the seat by just over 1,200 votes following another tight battle.

As a result of a slight swing back to the Conservatives in 1992, Labour remained worried about Halifax in 1997, when it was designated a rare Labour-held 'key seat'. It is still not entirely safe, and after Labour's vote fell by 5 percentage points in 2001 it remains their 112th most marginal constituency. That result followed some poor displays in local council elections, with the Conservatives ahead by 48-34 per cent in 1998, 45-38 per cent in 1999 and 55-31 per cent in 2000. Indeed, Labour won just one of the nine wards in the constituency in May 2000 (Ovenden) while losing three others to the Tories. One element that may, for the moment, be protecting Labour's position in general elections is the presence in the centre of the town of a significant Asian population. As in Bradford however, the Conservatives have started to select ethnic candidates in local elections, increasing their vote in St. John's for example from 15 per cent in 1995 to a winning 44 per cent in 2000. If this vote can be tapped in national contests while retaining existing supporters in surrounding villages like Northowram & Shelf, then the Conservatives will have found a general election-winning formula here.

HEMSWORTH

	2001		1997		1992 notional	
Electorate and turnout	67,946	51.8	66,967	67.9	68,411	76.1
Conservative	7,400	21.0	8,096	17.8	13,428	25.8
Labour	23,036	65.4	32,088	70.6	33,229	63.8
Lib Dem	3,990	11.3	4,033	8.9	5,424	10.4
Anti–EU	–	–	1,260	2.8	–	–
Socialist	801	2.3	–	–	–	–
MP	Jon Trickett (Lab)		Jon Trickett (Lab)		Derek Enright (Lab)*	
Majority	15,636	44.4	23,992	52.8	19,801	38.0

* Jon Trickett (Lab) elected at February 1996 by–election.

Hemsworth is the classic mining seat where Labour regularly polled 40,000 votes in previous general elections – the peak was an incredible 47,934 in 1950. From 1945 until 1974, Labour always recorded vote shares exceeding 80 per cent, but in 1983 the constituency was split in two following the earlier division of West Riding into West and South Yorkshire. Approximately 33,000 electors were transferred to Barnsley East, and although some territory was gained around Featherstone, the days of 'weighing the vote' were at an end. There has undoubtedly also been a slight swing away from Labour here, so that after 2001, this was 'only' their 64th safest seat.

The main towns in Hemsworth are neighbouring South Kirkby and South Elmsall, along with Hemsworth itself, Ackworth and Featherstone, with the Wakefield South ward also included. Much of this territory remains scarred by coal-mining, though the mines have closed, causing a pall of depression which has not yet lifted, despite the odd bits of industry and distribution depots near the A1. Three of the constituency's six wards are in the country's most deprived 10 per cent, and South Elmsall, which includes the closed Frickley colliery, once featured in a television programme about car crime. Politically, Labour usually win all the wards except Wakefield South, which as a rugby-union (rather than league) playing, Conservative voting area is a total anomaly in this seat. Its inclusion at the last set of boundary changes partially explains Labour's weakening position here – the estimate was that it caused the Labour vote to fall (and the Tory share to rise) by 7 per cent – though this still hardly means Labour are seriously threatened here.

HUDDERSFIELD

	2001		1997		1992 *actual*	
Electorate and turnout	64,350	55.0	65,837	67.7	67,574	72.4
Conservative	8,794	24.9	9,323	20.9	16,574	33.9
Labour	18,840	53.2	25,171	56.5	23,832	48.7
Lib Dem	5,300	15.0	7,642	17.2	7,777	15.9
Anti–EU	613	1.7	1,480	3.3	–	–
Green	1,254	3.5	938	2.1	576	1.2
Others	582 (2)		–		135	
MP	Barry Sheerman (Lab)		Barry Sheerman (Lab)		Barry Sheerman (Lab)	
Majority	10,046	28.4	15,848	35.6	7,258	14.8

Huddersfield has been a Labour seat since the second world war, represented by just two MPs: Joseph Mallalieu from 1945 until 1979 and Barry Sheerman since then. In fact the town had two constituencies before 1983, but a large portion of the old Huddersfield West (won by the Liberals from 1950-64 as a result of the Tories not fielding candidates) was transferred to Colne Valley; the present seat is very much based on the old East.

As elsewhere the Lib Dems do well in local elections here, amassing 66 per cent in Almondbury ward in 2002 and winning a second ward to the east of the centre, Dalton. An even more striking series of victories have been won by Greens in Newsome ward. They polled as many as 2,400 votes in 2000, something which may well be connected with the large number of university students here. Labour still win Birkby where there is a high concentration of Asians to the north of the centre, but are being challenged strongly by the Lib Dems in Paddock and Deighton, which is the most deprived ward in Kirklees borough. Overall the Lib Dems polled 31 per cent in the 2000 locals, but their vote subsided in the general election and Labour's majority remained a very comfortable 10,000.

KEIGHLEY

	2001		1997		1992 actual	
Electorate and turnout	68,330	63.4	67,231	76.6	66,379	82.6
Conservative	16,883	39.0	18,907	36.7	25,983	47.4
Labour	20,888	48.2	26,039	50.6	22,387	40.8
Lib Dem	4,722	10.9	5,064	9.8	5,793	10.6
Anti–EU	840	1.9	1,470	2.9	–	–
Green	–	–	–	–	642	1.2
MP	Ann Cryer (Lab)		Ann Cryer (Lab)		Gary Waller (Con)	
Majority	4,005	9.2	7,132	13.9	3,596	6.6

Keighley has changed hands on six occasions since the second world war, held by the party that won nationally in 13 of the 16 post-war general elections. If anything it was slightly inclined to Labour in the past, staying with the party in 1951, 1955 and 1979 despite national defeats, though the addition of Conservative Ilkley in 1983 probably makes it a more accurate bellwether seat these days. Keighley was a Labour target in both 1987 and 1992, but as elsewhere the party had to wait until May 1997 before ultimately tasting victory. A nationally average 10 per cent swing saw Gary Waller defeated by Ann Cryer, wife of the late Labour MP for Bradford South, Bob Cryer and mother of another new Labour MP, Hornchurch's John Cryer.

The constituency includes not only the town of Keighley itself, but also its up-market neighbour of Ilkley (a sort of mini Harrogate), on the other side of the famous moor to the north. In the 2000 locals, the Conservatives led Labour here (who were in third place) by the massive margin of 2,000 votes, despite a turnout of only 36 per cent. The Tories also win, though less easily, the rural Worth Valley ward to the south of Keighley, which is connected to the town by a steam railway. This part of the seat includes the village of Haworth, home of the Bronte sisters. The political complexion of the constituency means that Labour need to win Keighley itself by a distance to win overall. This they have generally done since 1997, though Labour did lose a council seat in the North ward to the Conservatives in 2000.

In 2001, a modest swing from Labour to the Conservatives again mirrored the national pattern, but left the Tories some distance from victory. It is currently Labour's 50th most marginal seat, which could theoretically mean them losing it while still retaining an overall majority, but in all likelihood Keighley and Labour's majority will either both fall in 2005/6, or neither will.

LEEDS CENTRAL

	2001		1997		1992 notional	
Electorate and turnout	65,497	41.7	68,309	54.2	73,780	62.3
Conservative	3,896	14.3	5,077	13.7	10,281	22.4
Labour	18,277	66.9	25,766	69.6	29,273	63.7
Lib Dem	3,607	13.2	4,164	11.3	6,416	14.0
Anti–EU	775	2.8	1,042	2.8	–	–
Socialist	751	2.8	960 (2)	2.6	–	–
MP	Hilary Benn (Lab)		Derek Fatchett (Lab)		Derek Fatchett (Lab)	
Majority	14,381	52.7	20,689	55.9	18,992	41.3

Parliamentary by-election 10 June 1999: Labour 6,361 (48.2), Lib Dem 4,068 (30.8), Conservative 1,618 (12.3), Green 478 (3.6), Anti-EU 353 (2.7), 2 Others 309. Electorate 67,280, Turnout 19.6%. MP: Hilary Benn (Lab), Majority 2,293 (17.4).

Leeds Central produced one of the worst turnouts in history in 1999, when only about one in six bothered to vote at a by-election caused by the sudden death of minister Derek Fatchett. The constituency was only saved from the stigma of lowest ever by wartime contests, but nonetheless it was to prove an early indicator of the collapse in turnout across the country in 2001. The by-election also marked the emergence of Hilary Benn, who became the latest generation of Benns in parliament and allowed his father, Tony, to retire in 2001 having witnessed his son make his maiden speech.

The Central seat is a bit of a misnomer as it contains large parts of the old Leeds South East and Leeds South seats, the latter held by Hugh Gaitskell until his death in 1963 and thereafter by Labour Home Secretary, Merlyn Rees – both of whose names are now commemorated by schools in the constituency. In fact those two schools are close to some extremely run-down and depressing housing estates in Beeston and Belle Isle (just south of Hunslet), while Richmond Hill east of the city centre is barely any better. This is undoubtedly a very poor constituency – in 1991 it was in the bottom 50 for owner occupation, while it was ranked 27th for numbers of unskilled manual workers; the bottom of the social scale. However the seat does include the University and much of the thriving city centre, which includes a number of new office blocks and developments like the Canal Wharf behind the railway station. To add to its variety, Leeds Central also includes a heavily Asian neighbourhood around Beeston Hill and the football ground at Elland Road. Perhaps the only thing which unites these very different areas is support for Labour in both local and general elections (it is currently their 24th safest seat), though low turnout (only one of the five council wards exceeded 20 per cent in 2000) now sadly seems another shared feature.

LEEDS EAST

	2001		1997		1992 actual	
Electorate and turnout	56,400	51.5	57,023	62.8	61,720	70.0
Conservative	5,647	19.4	6,685	18.7	12,232	28.3
Labour	18,290	62.9	24,151	67.5	24,929	57.7
Lib Dem	3,923	13.5	3,689	10.3	6,040	14.0
Anti–EU	634	2.2	1,267	3.5	–	–
Others	561 (2)		–		–	
MP	George Mudie (Lab)		George Mudie (Lab)		George Mudie (Lab)	
Majority	12,643	43.5	17,466	48.8	12,697	29.4

Leeds East was for many years associated with Denis Healey, Labour Chancellor of the Exchequer in the 1970s. Healey was a tough and unforgiving operator who had to contend with being shouted down at the annual party conference and the winter of discontent. Nevertheless he was the right's standard bearer in the 1980 leadership contest; had he won, Labour's 1983 meltdown probably never would have happened. On retirement from the Commons in 1992, he was replaced by current incumbent George Mudie, bequeathing to the former Leeds city council leader a very strong Labour seat. When Healey won his first general election in Leeds East in the 1950s, Labour only out polled the Conservatives by about 5,000 votes, but the majority was about double that in Healey's last contest, 1987. Since then the national tide of opinion has left the constituency looking even safer, not quite on a par with Central, but still in the national top hundred.

Most wards included in East are full of terraced streets and council estates, and it seems hardly surprising that the place returns Labour representatives. The two most heavily Labour wards are Burmantofts nearest in to the city centre and Seacroft, which is farthest out on the outer ring road. Labour polled 78 per cent of the vote in this largely council estate ward in 1999 and only marginally less in 2000. Harehills, which is 30 per cent non-white, is competitive between Labour and the Lib Dems in local council elections, while the altogether different Halton ward, which includes Temple Newsam Country Park, is largely middle class and actually elected a Conservative in 2000. This area, which has been boosted by the new M1 extension to its east, is seeing plenty of new development at the moment, though it seems unlikely that this will have any effect on future political outcomes.

LEEDS NORTH EAST

	2001		1997		1992 actual	
Electorate and turnout	64,123	62.0	63,399	71.8	64,607	76.6
Conservative	12,451	31.3	15,409	33.9	22,462	45.4
Labour	19,540	49.1	22,368	49.2	18,218	36.8
Lib Dem	6,325	15.9	6,318	13.9	8,274	16.7
Anti–EU	382	1.0	946	2.1	–	–
Others	1,075 (3)		468		546	
MP	Fabian Hamilton (Lab)		Fabian Hamilton (Lab)		Timothy Kirkhope (Con)	
Majority	7,089	17.8	6,959	15.3	4,244	8.6

Leeds North East was the constituency where Labour left winger Liz Davies was first selected and then promptly deselected before the 1997 general election. These internal ructions appeared to have little impact when the electors of the seat finally had their say; Fabian Hamilton (who had contested the constituency in 1992, adding over 11 percentage points to the Labour vote) gained the seat with an above average swing of 12 per cent and a majority of almost 7,000.

This is certainly a constituency of contrasts, including the ethnically mixed inner-city area of Chapeltown, but also wealthy neighbourhoods in North Leeds such as Roundhay and Moortown, home to the second largest Jewish population outside London. For over thirty years the seat was represented by right-wing Conservative MP Keith Joseph, whose majority was 11,500 at his first general election in 1959 and just under 10,000 at his last in 1983. In that contest, it was the SDP who finished in second place, and a Labour victory here would have seemed unlikely to say the least. Yet suburban constituencies such as this have been slowly but surely turning from the Conservatives to Labour in recent years, and the Labour share of the vote surged upwards from 25 per cent in 1987 (when they were still third) to 37 per cent in 1992 and 49 per cent in 1997. It was notable that Labour were still ahead here locally by 7 per cent in the council elections of 1999, when clearly behind in many of their other 1997 gains up and down the country. Sure enough, in 2001, Hamilton notched up another impressive result, the Tory vote dropping for a fourth successive general election. It is now just about conceivable that Labour could hold Leeds North East even if they lost nationally, which shows just how far it has swung over recent decades.

LEEDS NORTH WEST

	2001		*1997*		*1992 actual*	
Electorate and turnout	72,945	58.2	70,833	69.7	69,733	72.5
Conservative	12,558	29.6	15,850	32.1	21,750	43.0
Labour	17,794	41.9	19,694	39.9	13,782	27.3
Lib Dem	11,431	26.9	11,689	23.7	14,079	27.8
Anti–EU	668	1.6	1,325	2.7	–	–
Others	–		818 (3)		946 (2)	
MP	Harold Best (Lab)		Harold Best (Lab)		Keith Hampson (Con)	
Majority	5,236	12.3	3,844	7.8	7,671	15.2

One of Labour's most impressive gains in 1997 came in Leeds North West, where they started the campaign in third place, a position they had been in for the last three elections. Despite this handicap, and feeble Liberal Democrat attempts to claim it was they who were best placed to defeat the Conservatives, the 12 per cent swing to Labour was almost identical to that in neighbouring Leeds North East. The result was a majority of almost 4,000 for left- winger Harold Best, the first time Labour had ever won this seat.

The North West constituency takes in the Yorkshire cricket ground at Headingley, the nearby Leeds Metropolitan University campus and surrounding residential areas, and also the small town of Otley, which is some miles to the north west. Little of this is traditional Labour territory (the constituency could boast the 23rd highest proportion of professionals in Britain according to the 1991 census), and the Liberal Democrats still do very well in local council contests. In the 2000 local elections, the Lib Dems and Conservatives shared out the council seats between them, the Tories winning Cookridge, to the north of the ring road, and Otley & Wharfedale, which has been won by all the main parties in recent years. The Liberal Democrats won student-dominated Headingley and Weetwood, and they had high hopes of making up for their 1997 disappointment in 2001, particularly given the large proportion of university students in the constituency. These aspirations were to be dashed, and although the Lib Dem vote did increase (a notably different pattern to other seats where they were reduced to third place in 1997 such as Hastings and Shrewsbury), so did Labour's. Indeed Harold Best was one of very few Labour MPs who could boast a numerically larger majority after 2001 than before, and although the seat is still his party's 81st most marginal, one can certainly envisage them again holding it next time around.

LEEDS WEST

	2001		1997		1992 actual	
Electorate and turnout	64,218	50.0	64,194	62.7	67,074	71.2
Conservative	5,008	15.6	7,048	17.5	12,482	26.2
Labour	19,943	62.1	26,819	66.7	26,310	55.1
Lib Dem	3,350	10.4	3,622	9.0	4,252	8.9
Anti–EU	758	2.4	1,210	3.0	–	–
Green	2,573	8.0	896	2.2	569	1.2
Liberal	462	1.4	625	1.6	3,980	8.3
Others	–		–		132	
MP	John Battle (Lab)		John Battle (Lab)		John Battle (Lab)	
Majority	14,935	46.5	19,771	49.2	13,828	29.0

Leeds West has an interesting recent history, having been gained for the then Liberal-Alliance by Michael Meadowcroft in 1983, an election when large numbers of notionally Alliance-held seats (most by former Labour MPs) were being lost. The Liberal period here did not last long, with Labour's John Battle regaining what traditionally had always been a Labour seat in 1987, and increasing his majority to safety at the following two contests. He was helped in this by Meadowcoft's refusal to join the newly merged Liberal Democrats, opting instead to continue with an Independent Liberal Party, and polling nearly 4,000 votes in 1992. Although the Liberals limp on here (their current standard-bearer Noel Nowosielski once carried the slogan 'the name to remember'), the relative success for minor party candidates in Leeds West appears to have now passed on to the Greens, who recorded their second best result anywhere in Britain in 2001 with 8 per cent.

Leeds West runs along either side of the A647 Stanningley Road, including the wards of Armley, Wortley, Kirkstall and Bramley. Labour out-poll the Conservatives heavily in all of them, but their main opposition locally is provided by the Liberal Democrats, who can win Bramley, and the Greens, who won Wortley with 2,700 votes in 1999, 2000 and 2002. In this as well as the recent historical context, John Battle's majorities in 1997 and especially 2001 are quite impressive - the seat is officially Labour's 51st safest at present. This is a very different outcome from that in the Alliance's other 1983 gains (Ross, Cromarty & Skye and Yeovil), which remain Liberal Democrat strongholds, as well as the bases of their present and former leader.

MORLEY and ROTHWELL

	2001		1997		1992 notional	
Electorate and turnout	71,815	53.5	68,434	67.1	66,804	75.1
Conservative	9,829	25.6	12,086	26.3	18,523	36.9
Labour	21,919	57.0	26,836	58.5	24,843	49.5
Lib Dem	5,446	14.2	5,087	11.1	6,506	13.0
Anti–EU	1,248	3.2	1,359	3.0	–	–
Others	–		529 (2)		327	
MP	Colin Challen (Lab)		John Gunnell (Lab)		John Gunnell (Lab)	
					Leeds Sth & Morley	
Majority	12,090	31.4	14,750	32.1	6,320	12.6

Morley and Rothwell is, like Pudsey and Elmet, entirely within the metropolitan borough of Leeds, which brings the total number of parliamentary seats within the city boundaries to eight. As well as the two towns named in the constituency title, the ward of Middleton is also included, which was previously a part of the old Leeds South seat held by Hugh Gaitskell and Merlyn Rees in days gone by. Rees continued for two elections after the constituency became 'Leeds South and Morley' in 1983, and in 1992 was succeeded by 58-year old John Gunnell (not the oldest new MP that year as Piara Khabra in Ealing Southall was 67). Gunnell lasted two terms before in turn being replaced by Labour Party organiser Colin Challen in 2001.

The Conservatives still poll strongly in Morley, which adjoins the M62 motorway and likes to see itself as slightly distinct from Leeds. Rothwell, which was in the Normanton seat until 1997, is some miles to the east, and was won comfortably by Labour in the 1990s, but by the Liberal Democrats in 2000. Middleton is the only really safe Labour ward, as befits the fact that its neighbouring ward of Hunslet is part of the Leeds Central seat. Overall, Challen enjoyed a majority of 12,000 in 2001, without suffering an adverse swing as in several nearby constituencies. Although not as much a stronghold as many of the Labour seats to its south, it should remain safely in their column for the foreseeable future.

NORMANTON

	2001		*1997*		*1992 notional*	
Electorate and turnout	65,935	52.2	62,983	68.3	*61,873*	*74.8*
Conservative	9,215	27.0	10,153	23.6	*16,467*	*35.6*
Labour	19,152	56.1	26,046	60.6	*23,659*	*51.1*
Lib Dem	4,990	14.6	5,347	12.4	*6,155*	*13.3*
Anti–EU	–	–	1,458	3.4	–	–
Socialist	798	2.3	–	–	–	–
MP	Bill O'Brien (Lab)		Bill O'Brien (Lab)		Bill O'Brien (Lab)	
Majority	9,937	29.1	15,893	37.0	*7,192*	*15.5*

Normanton can just about lay claim to the distinction of having had the longest continuous representation by Labour MPs. From 1885 until 1906, it was won by 'Lib–Lab' candidates, with their sitting member in 1909, Fred Hall, officially joining the Labour party once the Miners' Federation of Great Britain finally decided to affiliate. Labour have never looked in any real danger ever since - Hall was returned unopposed in both 1918 and 1924 when many of his colleagues were being defeated, and even in 1931 Labour won here by nearly 13,000 votes while being decimated elsewhere.

This remains predominantly a working class seat, which includes small towns near the M1-M62 junction like Horbury, Ossett, Normanton itself, Stanley, Altofts and Wrenthorpe. These places surround the city of Wakefield on three sides, and as in many other parts of Yorkshire were formerly safer territory for Labour than the major centre of population itself - the reverse urban-rural divide to that found most commonly today. Thus while Wakefield has often had rather more modest majorities, Labour recorded vote shares in Normanton of more than 70 per cent in the 1950s and 1960s. These figures dropped away somewhat in the 1970s, and then following boundary changes which brought in Ossett, Labour's majority was cut to just 4,000 in 1983, the first election contested by former miner and current incumbent Bill O'Brien. That margin has increased since then, though another boundary change in the 1990s (the loss of Rothwell and replacement by Horbury) further weakened Labour's position.

Local election results confirm the east-west divide in Normanton. The traditional mining parts of the seat in the east return Labour councillors, while of the newer additions to the west of the M1, Ossett voted Lib Dem in 2000 and 2002 and Horbury Conservative. There is no doubt that the motorway seems to form some sort of divide in these parts, with areas to its west seen as more desirable and those to the east (with the exception of some parts of Wakefield) less so. The political impact is equally clear, with Labour doing much better in the east, whether in Morley & Rothwell to the north, Normanton or indeed Wakefield and Barnsley West & Penistone to the south.

PONTEFRACT and CASTLEFORD

	2001		*1997*		*1992 actual*	
Electorate and turnout	63,183	49.7	62,397	66.3	64,655	74.3
Conservative	5,512	17.6	5,614	13.6	10,051	20.9
Labour	21,890	69.7	31,339	75.7	33,546	69.9
Lib Dem	2,315	7.4	3,042	7.3	4,410	9.2
Anti–EU	739	2.4	1,401	3.4	–	–
Socialist	935 (2)	3.0	–	–	–	–
MP	Yvette Cooper (Lab)		Yvette Cooper (Lab)		Geoffrey Lofthouse (Lab)	
Majority	16,378	52.2	25,725	62.1	23,495	48.9

Pontefract and Castleford are two moderately sized towns on either side of the M62 motorway to the east of Leeds. This is very much former coal-mining country – indeed there are still actually a few working mines in the area – and has been strongly Labour for a long time. 'Cas', bordered to the north by the River Aire and to the south by the motorway, is actually the larger of the two towns and probably best known for rugby league. It is staunchly Labour, with the party picking up no less than 89 per cent of the vote in the Whitwood ward in 1999, and 82 per cent in a three-cornered contest in Glasshoughton. On the other side of the M62, Pontefract is notable, in no particular order, for its castle, racecourse and liquorice 'cakes'. Its northern ward is also heavily Labour, though the Conservatives boast their only reasonable vote to the south of the centre. The third town in the constituency is Knottingley, beyond the huge power station at Ferrybridge and nearby M62/A1 services. Even here, there is no respite for the opposition parties as Labour could poll 82 per cent in 1999.

Unsurprisingly in view of all this, Labour has held the parliamentary seat since it was created in 1950. Following the late retirement of Geoffrey Lofthouse (MP since 1978) in 1997, 28-year old Yvette Cooper won a hastily arranged selection contest and then the general election by over 25,000 votes. It was Labour's 2nd safest seat in Yorkshire (after Barnsley Central) in 1997 and 14th safest nationally, though dropped down to 27th after a five-point swing away from the party in 2001.

PUDSEY

	2001		1997		1992 actual	
Electorate and turnout	71,405	63.3	71,009	74.3	70,996	80.8
Conservative	16,091	35.6	19,163	36.3	25,067	43.7
Labour	21,717	48.1	25,370	48.1	16,695	29.1
Lib Dem	6,423	14.2	7,375	14.0	15,153	26.4
Anti–EU	944	2.1	823	1.6	–	–
Green	–	–	–	–	466	0.8
MP	Paul Truswell (Lab)		Paul Truswell (Lab)		Giles Shaw (Con)	
Majority	5,626	12.5	6,207	11.8	8,372	14.6

Pudsey is squeezed between Leeds and Bradford, with the parliamentary seat extending north through residential Horsforth and into the towns of Rawdon, Yeadon and Guiseley, which is famous for the original Harry Ramsden's fish and chip restaurant. The constituency had never been won by Labour before 1997, and for a time in the 1980s it seemed as if the Liberals were more likely to provide any serious challenge to the Conservatives. But Labour's Paul Truswell achieved one of his party's best results in the country at the 1997 election, a 19 per cent increase in the Labour vote ending an unbroken period of Conservative domination which had lasted for three-quarters of a century.

Most of the areas which make up the Pudsey seat are affluent and middle class and few, if any, are safely Labour. Aireborough, covering the three small towns in the north, was won at a local (and presumably national) level during the 1990s, though its council seat was won by the Conservatives in 2000 and 2002. Horsforth (the least deprived ward in Leeds according to official figures) is in council elections a Tory-Lib Dem marginal, with Labour in third place. Pudsey North is the strongest Conservative area of all, where they could poll as many as 4,000 votes in 2000. Pudsey South is the one ward which consistently votes Labour, though only narrowly. Overall, the Conservatives were slightly ahead in the 1999 local council elections and then 17.5 per cent clear of Labour in 2000. However all this seemed to make little difference in 2001, when Truswell's share of the vote was unchanged from four years previously, and the Tory vote even fell further. Clearly this is an area which is quite happy at the moment to vote Labour nationally, whatever it does locally, and the fact that it is only Labour's 83rd most marginal seat shows just how big a trough the Conservatives are currently in.

SHIPLEY

	2001		1997		1992 actual	
Electorate and turnout	69,564	66.2	69,281	76.3	68,827	82.1
Conservative	18,815	40.9	19,966	37.8	28,463	50.4
Labour	20,243	44.0	22,962	43.4	16,081	28.5
Lib Dem	4,996	10.9	7,984	15.1	11,288	20.0
Anti–EU	580	1.3	1,960	3.7	–	–
Green	1,386	3.0	–	–	680	1.2
MP	Chris Leslie (Lab)		Chris Leslie (Lab)		Marcus Fox (Con)	
Majority	1,428	3.1	2,996	5.7	12,382	21.9

Perhaps no single result better encapsulated the unpredictable nature of general elections, and the power of national tides of opinion, than the 1997 defeat of eminent back-bench Tory MP, Sir Marcus Fox, by an unknown 24-year old, Chris Leslie. As he mentioned in his first speech in the Commons, when Fox was first elected in 1970, Leslie had not even been born. The result in Shipley provided a stark reminder of the absence of any significant incumbency factor in parliamentary elections: voters had simply decided it was time for a change, whether or not Fox had been a hard-working MP for 27 years. The 'For Sale' notice that appeared outside the local Conservative Club soon after only emphasised the rather abrupt nature of British politics.

Shipley is the northern part of Bradford, and home to many of its middle class residents. In particular people have been moving out to Baildon, just north of Shipley itself, for years. The constituency also includes the model village and mill at Saltaire (now a popular art gallery) and the town of Bingley, just up the road. It is not exactly natural Labour territory, though there are clearly elements of the electorate who have been shifting leftwards in recent years. However in local government elections, Labour are well behind. In 2000 they polled just 11 per cent to finish a distant third in Baildon, while the Conservatives win the rural wards of Rombalds (which extends all the way over the moor to Burley in Wharfedale) and Bingley Rural, by miles. Labour's only reliable ward is Shipley East, and although Leslie himself had won Bingley in the recent past, that too was lost in 1999 and 2000. Meanwhile Shipley West was won by a Green in 2000 and 2002, Labour coming third here too.

Overall Labour polled just over 25 per cent of the vote here in 2000 compared with the Conservatives' 48 per cent, but as in many cases elsewhere, voters clearly returned to the party in 2001 (and are in any case increasingly distinguishing between different sorts of election). Leslie held on with a reduced majority of 1,428, dashing the hopes of Conservative David Senior for a straightforward regain. As this is now Labour's 10th most marginal seat (down from 25th after 1997), Leslie will be very lucky indeed if his government remains popular enough for him to win again next time.

WAKEFIELD

	2001		1997		1992 *notional*	
Electorate and turnout	75,750	54.5	73,236	68.9	*71,951*	*75.5*
Conservative	12,638	30.6	14,373	28.5	*21,983*	*40.5*
Labour	20,592	49.9	28,977	57.4	*26,207*	*48.3*
Lib Dem	5,097	12.4	5,656	11.2	*6,128*	*11.3*
Anti–EU	677	1.6	1,480	2.9	–	–
Green	1,075	2.6	–	–	–	–
Socialist	1,175 (2)	2.8	–	–	–	–
MP	David Hinchliffe (Lab)		David Hinchliffe (Lab)		David Hinchliffe (Lab)	
Majority	7,954	19.3	14,604	28.9	*4,224*	*7.8*

Although held by the party since 1932, Wakefield is a far less safe seat for Labour than some of its neighbours, and is now just about vulnerable to a national Conservative recovery after a 7.5 per cent drop in the Labour vote in 2001. The constituency has become larger geographically, and a slightly better bet for the Tories electorally since the last set of boundary changes, when Denby Dale and Kirkburton wards (west of the M1 motorway in the metropolitan borough of Kirklees) were transferred into the constituency from Dewsbury. Although the old bits of the seat which moved out - Horbury (now in Normanton) and Wakefield South (now in Hemsworth) - were always fairly Tory, the well-heeled villages around Kirkburton are even more so. Thus in the 2000 local elections, the Conservatives led Labour here by 47-26 per cent, and also narrowly won Denby Dale. The overall estimate was that the effect of the new rural parts of the seat replacing the old was worth a 2 per cent swing from Labour to Conservatives, which just may become important in future contests.

Wakefield itself was the administrative centre of West Yorkshire until the county council was abolished in 1986, was briefly considered as a new home for Yorkshire cricket club, and is still noted for its two railway stations (Westgate and Kirkgate). It retains the appearance of a reasonably bustling place, and was highly marginal in the 1980s, particularly when Labour held on by just 360 votes in 1983. That was to prove the last election for the former deputy Chief whip, Walter Harrison, who was replaced by Wakefield councillor David Hinchliffe in 1987. Hinchliffe has built up a respectable majority in subsequent contests, and now has a fairly high-profile role as chairman of the Commons Select Committee on Health. He will be hoping that his government manages to deliver on this crucial issue in their second term, as Wakefield (which was narrowly 'won' by the Conservatives in the 1999 Euro elections - their first victory since 1931) will probably just about be considered a marginal at the next general election.

Scotland

By Mark Stuart

In terms of seats changing hands at recent elections, Scotland is probably the dullest country in the United Kingdom. At the Scottish parliamentary elections in May 1999 only three seats changed hands as the Liberal Democrats gained Aberdeen South, Dennis Canavan gained Falkirk West and the SNP gained Inverness East, Nairn and Lochaber all from Labour. In 2001, the Tory gain of Galloway and Upper Nithsdale provided the only change of seat on election night. Even the turnout in 2001 was almost unchanged on its 1999 level of 58 per cent, leaving psephologists to speculate whether the next Scottish elections in 2003 will produce a similar turnout, or a drastically lower one. Granted, the 2001 turnout was significantly down on the 1997 Westminster election, but the trend was repeated across Great Britain; it was only slightly lower than in England. The main reason for the apparently dull electoral scene is Labour's continued dominance north of the border.

In 2001, the Scottish Labour party outperformed their English counterpart by 2.5 per cent in terms of the national share of the vote. The party lost no seats in Scotland on their 1997 performance despite the fact that their vote fell by 1.7 per cent. Labour's only worry is that a growing gap will begin to emerge between their performance at Westminster elections and at Scottish elections. Any further erosion in Labour's 39 per cent constituency vote enjoyed in 1999 could see the SNP make constituency gains at the next Scottish General Election in 2003.

The best that could be said about the Conservatives is that their support bottomed out in 2001, standing at exactly the same level as it had in the Scottish parliamentary elections in 1999, but almost unbelievably, nearly 2 per cent down on Labour's landslide year of 1997. Even the Tories in both England and Wales had increased their share of the vote by 1.5 percentage points on their 1997 performance. More worryingly, across many of the Scottish seats that the Conservatives used to hold in the early 1980s, their vote share has virtually halved since 1992. In Labour and Liberal Democrat seats where the Tories were in second place, their vote share either stagnated or dropped on its 1997 performance, with the exception of Malcolm Rifkind's performance in Edinburgh Pentlands where his vote rose by a modest 4 per cent. In Eastwood (now a Labour seat), the Tory vote fell by nearly 5 percentage points; in Aberdeenshire West and Kincardine (now a Liberal Democrat seat), it fell by 4 points.

The only ray of sunshine on the morning of 8 June 2001 was the fact that the Tories could now boast one Westminster seat to match their only constituency seat in the Scottish Parliament, gained by John Scott at the Ayr by-election in March 2000. But even Peter Duncan's win (by only 74 votes) in Galloway and Upper Nithsdale only involved a 3.3 per cent increase in the Tory vote on its 1997 performance. This may have been partly due to the fact that the area was badly affected by the foot and mouth outbreak in early 2001. After all, in the 1991 census, Galloway and Upper Nithsdale had the highest proportion of workers engaged in agriculture in the United Kingdom (approximately one in six). But while this factor may partly explain the modest rise in the Tory share of the vote, there was no anti-Government effect in the constituency; Labour's share of the vote actually rose by nearly 4 per cent. Any explanation for the narrow Tory victory must include the 10-point drop in the SNP's share of the vote. A similar phenomenon was repeated in Perth where the SNP's share of the vote fell by almost 7 percentage points, the Tory share of the vote hardly changed, yet their candidate Elizabeth Smith came within 48 votes of winning a second Scottish seat. In Perth, apart from the restrictions on the movement of cattle, there was no direct foot and mouth effect to help the Tories. In other words, there was no Tory revival in Scotland, only a sharp decline in the SNP share of the vote.

So, the only logical explanation for these two close results must rest with the decision of both sitting SNP Westminster MPs (Alasdair Morgan in Galloway and Upper Nithsdale and Roseanna Cunninghame in Perth) to stand down in 1999 to devote all their time to the Scottish Parliament. This decision, taken by five of the six SNP Westminster MPs sent the wrong signal to Scottish electors, and SNP supporters in particular, that the Westminster elections counted for less than the Scottish elections. It was a logical conclusion for SNP voters to make; their party is, after all, a party of independence. With the establishment of the Scottish Parliament now seen as the first step on the road to independence, why should they bother anymore about Westminster? The SNP campaign in 2001 tried to emphasise that the real decisions over Scotland's share of the national cake were still made in London (through the Barnett Formula), but the point was lost on their supporters. As a result, not only was the SNP's national share of the vote 8.5 per cent down on 1999, it was also lower than that recorded in the 1997 Westminster elections.

Another constituency example can be cited using Moray, where Margaret Ewing's successor Angus Roberston held on, but his vote share fell by over 11 per cent, reducing the SNP's majority from over 5,500 in 1997 to around 1,750 in 2001. Again, the SNP's poor showing did not benefit the Tories – Labour leapfrogged the Conservatives into second place. By contrast, in neighbouring Banff and Buchan, Alex Salmond's decision to serve in the Westminster parliament was vindicated - while his vote share may have fallen by a tiny proportion, his percentage majority increased on 1997 as the second place Tory vote fell by nearly four points. In the other two SNP Westminster seats, Angus and Tayside North, the SNP vote fell by 13 and 5 percentage points respectively, and the two new MPs, Michael Weir and Peter Wishart, were only saved by the fact that the Labour and Liberal Democrat share of the vote rose, rather than the second place Tories. There was therefore no deep desire among former Tory voters in SNP-Tory marginals to see the Tories re-elected, suggesting that a Conservative revival in Scotland remains a long way off. Meanwhile, the SNP only has itself to blame for its poor performance in 2001.

Given their disastrous performance in 2001, the SNP must focus all of their efforts in gaining more constituency seats from Labour at the next Scottish parliamentary elections in 2003. Of the measly seven constituency seats they won in 1999, only one – Inverness East, Nairn and Lochaber, was an SNP gain on their 1997 result. The SNP advance in terms of the share of the vote – from 22.1 per cent in 1997 to 28.7 per cent in 1999 - together with the 28 regional top-up seats gained as a result, signalled their emergence as a truly national party for the first time, and one that was in clear second place to Labour. Contrary to press coverage at the time, the SNP did not fail to win more seats because of their pledge to increase income tax by a penny or because of Alex Salmond's opposition to the NATO bombing of Kosovo. It failed to do better because a narrow majority of voters placed their trust in the dominant forces behind the Scottish devolution settlement, Labour and the Liberal Democrats. Arguing in favour of full independence was not a realistic option for the SNP or for the Scottish voters in 1999, because of the SNP's decision to join the Scotland Forward umbrella campaign in favour of the devolution settlement in the referendum of September 1997.

While the SNP licked their wounds in June 2001, the Liberal Democrats celebrated as they replaced the Tories as the third party in Scotland in terms of percentage share of the vote. There had been fears that the Liberal Democrats' position as Labour's coalition partner in the Scottish Parliament might damage their prospects. Instead, the junior partner of the coalition was the only party in Scotland to increase its share of the vote from 13 per cent in 1997 to 16.4 per cent in 2001. However, the Liberal Democrats merely held onto their ten existing Westminster seats. The main threat to the Liberal Democrat seats in the future comes, not from the Tories, but from Labour who occupied second place in five seats in 1997, and now six, having pushed the Tories into third place in Edinburgh West in 2001. The main obstacle to any further advance by the Liberal Democrats is their continued poor showing in Glasgow and the West of Scotland. With the exception of mini-revivals of old support in Glasgow Kelvin and Greenock and Inverclyde, the Liberal Democrats have yet to appeal to the disaffected Scottish working class.

That group of voters is increasingly turning to the Scottish Socialist Party (SSP), led by Tommy Sheridan. At the 1999 Scottish parliamentary elections, the SSP polled 7.3 per cent of the vote across the list vote in the city of Glasgow, more than the Liberal Democrats and only around half a point behind the Conservatives. This strong show of support enabled Tommy Sheridan to become the party's first list MSP. In both the Ayr (March 2000) and Glasgow Anniesland (November 2000) Scottish parliamentary by-elections, the SSP demonstrated their power as a protest party by finishing in fourth place ahead of the Liberal Democrats. Moreover, in the Hamilton South Westminster by-election held in September 1999, they finished third with a vote share of 9.5 per cent. In 2001, the SSP's progress was limited by the first-past-the-post system, but it managed to win third place ahead of the Liberal Democrats and the Tories in Pollok and Shettleston, and it became the fourth party in Baillieston (ahead of the Lib Dems) and Maryhill (ahead of the Tories). However, even including Glasgow Springburn (home of the Speaker, Michael Martin where the Tories and the Liberal Democrats chose not to stand), the SSP is still the fifth party in Glasgow, behind the Liberal Democrats who beat the Tories into fourth place by six votes. In West of Scotland, the SSP polled around 3.5 per cent of the vote, but its grandiose claims to have emerged as Scotland's fifth party need to be qualified somewhat because in areas like the North East of Scotland its support is much lower.

Local government

In 1995, the Conservative government imposed a unitary system of local government on both Scotland and Wales. In Scotland, 32 all-purpose unitary authorities replaced the former two-tier system comprising nine upper tier regions, 53 lower tier districts and three all-purpose island councils. All the new authorities have single member wards, and elections, which are held every four years involve electing all councillors at one time. On 6 May 1999, the Scottish local elections were held on the same day as the Scottish parliamentary elections, giving a much-needed boost to the turnout. Since then, all matters relating to local government have become the responsibility of the Scottish Parliament, including the electoral system, which is currently first-past-the-post, but may shift to a form of proportional representation if the Liberal Democrats and the SNP have their way, though not in time for the next local elections in 2003.

Boundary review

The Boundary Commission review begun in February 2002 will be the most controversial that Scotland has ever seen. The creation of a Scottish Parliament has re-awakened Tam Dalyell's 'West Lothian' question, which asks, Why should Scottish Westminster MPs vote on English matters when English MPs cannot vote on Scottish matters? One way of alleviating potential tensions between Scotland and England (but not solving the West Lothian question because Scottish MPs would still be allowed to vote on English matters) is to reduce Scottish over-representation at Westminster. At present, the average Scottish seat represents only 55,000 electors, compared with around 70,000 voters in England. Given that the power over education, health and housing has been devolved to Scotland, it is surely sensible to reduce Scottish representation at Westminster. But two controversial questions arise as a consequence: who decides Scotland's representation, Holyrood or Westminster? Second, does any reduction in Scotland representation at Westminster automatically reduce the number of seats in the Scottish Parliament? The Scotland Act 1998 has a clear answer to both these questions: Westminster retains the reserved power over the Boundary Commission and at present, any reduction in Scottish Westminster seats would lead to an automatic reduction in the number of seats at Holyrood. One of the fears expressed about the Scottish Assembly proposed in 1979 was that it would be Central Belt dominated and would not adequately represent the wishes of all of the people of Scotland. The proportional Additional Member System, the toleration of small seats in the Highlands, including separate representation for Orkney and Shetland, ensure that all corners of Scotland are fully represented at Holyrood. Moreover, the Scottish Parliament is heavily reliant on a strong committee system. Large numbers of MSPs are required to staff these committees. Cut the number of MSPs then (so the argument runs) several of these committees will have to be merged together. In the next few years, there is likely to be a growing demand inside Scotland for the current law to be changed to allow the Scottish Parliament to decide its own level of representation.

Section 86 of the Scotland Act 1998 changed the schedule 2 rules of the Parliamentary Constituencies Act 1986 in three important ways. First, the guarantee giving Scotland a minimum of 71 Westminster seats was removed. Second, the Boundary Commission was obliged to use the electoral quota for England (69,934) to determine the number of Scottish seats at Westminster. Third, the 1998 Act stated that Orkney and Shetland could not be combined with any other local authority area to form a constituency broadly in line with the quota. The Commission must also now attempt where possible to align the new constituencies with local authority boundaries (which have been in existence since 1995). At present, local authority boundaries have very little relationship with Scottish Westminster constituencies. Operating within this remit, the Boundary Commission published its provisional recommendations for the redrawing of Scottish Westminster seats on 7 February 2002.

The Commission recognised that operating strictly under the English quota rules would produce a theoretical cut in the number of Scottish seats of 15. However, it has opted for a reduction of 13 seats from the present 72 to 59. The two-seat gap between the theory and the practice can be explained by the Commission's decision to make generous allowances for the remote nature of the Highlands region. Beyond the statutory obligation to maintain the Orkney and Shetland seat, the Commission felt that although the Western Isles' (henceforth to be known by its Gaelic name, Comhairle nan Eilean Siar) electorate (21,884) fell well short of the English electoral quota, because the islands were detached from the mainland and were already governed by a Western Isles Council, they should be given a single constituency. Elsewhere in the Highlands, although the local Council region is entitled to only 2.3 seats based on the English electoral quota, the Commission took into consideration other factors such as 'the geography, topography, settlement patterns and communication links' and left the Highland Council area with three seats. Apart from a bit of tinkering, there are no major changes in the Highland region, leaving the bulk of the cuts to fall further south.

In the rest of Scotland, prominent figures in the Scottish Labour party could be involved in bitter reselection battles if the proposals are accepted. Hamilton North and Bellshill might disappear, leaving the Northern Ireland Secretary, John Reid to look for a new seat. Dunfermline East, the seat of the Chancellor, Gordon Brown is also set to disappear. In Ayrshire, Carrick, Cumnock and Doon Valley is likely to be dismembered, leaving George Foulkes, Minister of State at the Scotland Office, in search of a seat.

The city of Glasgow has borne the brunt of the cutbacks, losing three of its ten seats. The Commission has left no room for sentiment either, renaming the constituencies Central, East, North, North East, North West, South and South West. The number of Edinburgh city seats will be reduced from six to five, with, like Glasgow, a no frills approach being adopted to the new names: North East, North West, South, South East and West. In the North-East of Scotland, Dundee would keep its two seats under the proposals, but Aberdeen would lose one of its three seats (Aberdeen Central), with the area around the city reverting roughly to the position that existed before the 1995 boundary changes.

In the West of Scotland, the two Paisley seats and the other local seat of Renfrewshire West may be merged into two constituencies. Clydebank and Milngavie may be broken up, with Milngavie going in with Bearsden, while Clydebank joins West Dunbartonshire. In Central Scotland, Falkirk East will disappear into the expanded Livingston and Linlithgow constituencies, leaving the town of Falkirk with only one seat. In Mid Scotland and Fife, Tayside north is likely to be absorbed into an expanded Angus and a new Perth and Atholl constituency. The South of Scotland sees the most controversial changes. The County of Dumfriesshire will move into an enormous new seat of Peebles, Clydesdale and Annandale, while the town of Dumfries will be linked with Kirkcudbrightshire and Wigtownshire, taking territory from Tory-held Galloway and Upper Nithsdale to form Dumfries and Galloway. Berwickshire, Roxburgh and Selkirk will be the only remaining Liberal Democrat seat in the region.

Despite the publication of the Boundary Commission's provisional recommendations, the proposals may not be finalised until 2006, meaning that the 2003 Scottish parliamentary elections and the next Westminster election in Scotland will probably be fought on the basis of existing constituencies. Meanwhile, the public and the political parties were given an opportunity to lodge objections to the Commission's plans, and assuming 100 or more objections were received, then a host of local inquiries were due to be established to take evidence from interested bodies. Much blood is likely to be spilt before agreement is finally reached in time for the third set of Scottish elections in 2007.

Central Scotland

	Conservative		Labour		Liberal Democrat		SNP		Others	
	Share of vote	Seats	Share of vote	Seats	Share of vote	Seats	Share of vote	Seats	Share of vote	Seats
2001	8.4	0	56.6	10	8.3	0	21.6	0	5.1	0
1997	10.4	0	59.4	10	5.2	0	23.4	0	1.6	0
1992	16.7	0	53.4	10	6.6	0	23.3	0	0	0
1999 C	9.6	0	46.5	9	6.6	0	29.9	0	7.4	1
1999 R	9.2	1	39.3	0	6.2	1	27.8	5	17.6	0

NOTE: 1999C=Scottish Parliamentary Elections Constituency vote; 1999R=Scottish Parliamentary Elections Regional top-up vote (7 seats available)

Central Scotland covers ten parliamentary constituencies stretching from the SNP-Labour marginal seat of Kilmarnock and Loudoun in the southwest, around the southeast of the city of Glasgow and up north through Lanarkshire as far as Falkirk. Despite the wide area covered, Labour dominates here, and won all ten Westminster seats in 1992, 1997 and 2001, peaking at nearly 60 per cent of the vote in 1997. Six Labour seats – Airdrie and Shotts, Coatbridge and Chryston, Hamilton North and Bellshill, Hamilton South, Motherwell and Wishaw and East Kilbride – are likely to remain firmly in Labour's hands in the future.

By contrast, this region provides few pickings for the Liberal Democrats and the Conservatives. In 2001, they could only poll about 8 per cent each, making it the worst region for the Liberal Democrats and the second worst region for the Conservatives (next to Glasgow) in terms of vote share. The SNP performs better in this region than the national average, and polled nearly 30 per cent of the constituency votes in the 1999 Scottish parliamentary elections. The SNP needed an 8 per cent swing to take Kilmarnock and Loudoun, their seventh target seat, but could only manage 4 per cent. The party also normally polls above the national average in Cumbernauld & Kilsyth, Falkirk East and Falkirk West. However, in 1999, Falkirk West provided the biggest upset in Scotland when Dennis Canavan, who had failed to pass Labour's new candidate selection process, stood and won as the 'Falkirk West' candidate in the Scottish parliamentary elections. His margin of victory over Labour's Ross Martin - 12,000 - was truly massive, and Canavan polled so well on the regional vote (amassing 27,500 votes) that it accounted for nearly half (8.4%) of the 17.6% polled by the 'other' candidates. Labour won the other nine constituency seats comfortably, but the seven regional 'top-up' seats (granted to each of Scotland's eight European regions) went predominantly to the SNP, who won five (Linda Fabiani, Alex Neil, Michael Matheson, Gil Paterson and Andrew Wilson). The Conservatives (Lyndsay McIntosh) and the Liberal Democrats (Donald Gorrie) gained one each.

Local government

Central Scotland comprises three large local authorities: North Lanarkshire (containing Motherwell, Airdrie, Cumbernauld and Coatbridge), South Lanarkshire (including Rutherglen, Hamilton and Bellshill) and Falkirk (both the town and the area around it including Grangemouth). It also contains that portion of East Ayrshire council that belongs to the Kilmarnock and Loudoun constituency. In 1999, Labour held onto 56 of North Lanarkshire's 70 council seats, despite running up a £5m deficit in its Direct Labour Organisation (DLO). Donald Dewar, then the Scottish First Minister, intervened by threatening to issue a closure notice to the council, which responded by contracting out much of its work to the private sector. Despite the bad publicity, Labour lost only three seats and gained two. The explanation for Labour avoiding electoral disaster may lie in the fact that an Accounts Commission report blamed mismanagement by officials rather than ineptitude by councillors, and that eight officials were eventually sacked. However, in East Ayrshire, where a similar crisis occurred with a DLO, the Labour party saw its 21-9 majority over the SNP shrink to only three seats, as council leader David Sneller lost his seat. Local council employees were said to be unhappy about the way Labour had handled the crisis. In Falkirk, Labour lost overall control, suffering from bad publicity surrounding the failure to select Dennis Canavan as the Labour candidate for Falkirk West. Labour lost five seats as the SNP moved up to 9 seats to Labour's 15, and an Independent also gained a seat. Finally, in South Lanarkshire, Labour lost six seats in 1999 but still retained overall control of the council by the massive margin of 54 to its nearest rival the SNP on 10.

AIRDRIE and SHOTTS

	2001		1997		1992 notional	
Electorate and turnout	58,349	54.4	57,673	71.4	59,264	74.7
Conservative	1,960	6.2	3,660	8.9	6,588	14.9
Labour	18,478	58.2	25,460	61.8	27,678	62.5
Lib Dem	2,376	7.5	1,719	4.2	1,997	4.5
SNP	6,138	19.3	10,048	24.4	8,023	18.1
Scot Unionist	1,439	4.5	–	–	–	–
Others	1,345 (2)		294		–	
MP	Helen Liddell (Lab)		Helen Liddell (Lab)		John Smith (Lab) *Monklands East	
Majority	12,340	38.9	15,412	37.4	19,655	44.4

* Helen Liddell (Lab) elected for Monklands East at May 1994 by–election.

Scottish Parliament Election 1999: Labour 18,338 (55.2), SNP 9,353 (28.2), Conservative 3,177 (9.6), Lib Dem 2,345 (7.1). Electorate 58,481, Turnout 56.8%.. MSP: Karen Whitefield (Lab), Majority 8,985 (27.1).

Two thirds of this constituency was formerly known as Monklands East, centring on the town of Airdrie and was home to John Smith, Labour leader from 1992 until his untimely death in 1994. Helen Liddell, former Scottish Secretary of the Labour party, held the seat in the subsequent by-election by 1,640 votes from the SNP. A classic Scottish Labour machine politician, Liddell was promoted to the post of the Secretary of State for Scotland in June 2001, after increasing her majority over the SNP.

Airdrie and Shotts was created in 1995, after 7,000 voters in the Calder council estate area were ceded to Coatbridge and Chryston. In return, the small industrial areas of Shotts, Stane, Dykehead, Newmains, Cleland and Bonkle were added to the town of Airdrie. Basically, Airdrie is overwhelmingly a Protestant town, and its people believe that neighbouring (and largely Catholic) Coatbridge has discriminated against it on the local council. Despite the typical religious-based feuding characteristic of this part of Scotland, both towns are filled with council house tenants (Airdrie has the highest proportion of council house tenants (62.5 per cent) of any British constituency, slightly more so than Coatbridge, which is tenth on 56 per cent) and both continue to vote Labour with regularity. In the Scottish Parliamentary elections in May 1999, Labour's Karen Whitefield easily held the seat, although the SNP vote rose by 4 per cent on 1997. In 2001, as Liddell increased her percentage majority by another 1.5 points, the SNP slipped back, and the Liberal Democrats nudged the Tories into fourth place, just ahead of Mary Dempsey, a Scottish Unionist candidate.

COATBRIDGE and CHRYSTON

	2001		1997		1992 notional	
Electorate and turnout	52,178	58.1	52,024	72.3	52,830	76.1
Conservative	2,171	7.2	3,216	8.6	6,241	15.5
Labour	19,807	65.3	25,694	68.3	24,843	61.8
Lib Dem	2,293	7.6	2,048	5.4	2,388	5.9
SNP	4,493	14.8	6,402	17.0	6,743	16.8
SSP	1,547	5.1	–	–	–	–
Others	–		249		–	
MP	Tom Clarke (Lab)		Tom Clarke (Lab)		Tom Clarke (Lab)	
					Monklands West	
Majority	15,314	50.5	19,292	51.3	18,100	45.0

Scottish Parliament Election 1999: Labour 17,923 (59.4), SNP 7,519 (24.9), Conservative 2,867 (9.5), Lib Dem 1,889 (6.3). Electorate 52,178, Turnout 57.9%. MSP: Elaine Smith (Lab), Majority 10,404 (34.5).

Formerly known as Monklands West, this seat still centres on the mainly Catholic town of Coatbridge, which has been in continual conflict with mainly Protestant Airdrie at a local level. An internal Labour inquiry has tried and failed to discover whether the Labour councillors of Coatbridge have taken all the best jobs in the council that they share uneasily with their neighbours in Airdrie.

In 1995, 7,000 voters were gained from the Calder council estate area of Monklands East (now Airdrie and Shotts), but it lost nearly as many electors from the area north of the River Kelvin, which was sensibly added to Strathkelvin and Bearsden. Whatever the boundary changes, Tom Clarke has held this seat for Labour since 1983, and in 1997 amassed over two thirds of the popular vote. Even his sacking as the Minister with responsibility for Films and Tourism in July 1998 could not prevent his percentage majority staying above 50 points in 2001. As with so much of urban Scotland, the Tory vote here has halved since 1992, and the Liberal Democrats pushed the Tories into fourth place in 2001. The SNP achieved a respectable quarter of the vote in the Scottish parliamentary elections, but Labour's Elaine Smith still won by over 10,000 votes. In 2001, however, the SNP's share of the vote slipped back to 15 per cent.

CUMBERNAULD and KILSYTH

	2001		*1997*		*1992 actual*	
Electorate and turnout	49,739	59.7	48,032	75.0	*46,515*	*79.0*
Conservative	1,460	4.9	2,441	6.8	*4,143*	*11.3*
Labour	16,144	54.4	21,141	58.7	*19,855*	*54.0*
Lib Dem	1,934	6.5	1,368	3.8	*2,118*	*5.8*
SNP	8,624	29.0	10,013	27.8	*10,640*	*28.9*
SSP	1,287	4.3	345	1.0	–	–
Others	250		716 (2)		–	–
MP	Rosemary McKenna (Lab)		Rosemary McKenna (Lab)		Norman Hogg (Lab)	
Majority	7,520	25.3	11,128	30.9	*9,215*	*25.1*

Scottish Parliament Election 1999: Labour 15,182 (49.6), SNP 10,923 (35.7), Lib Dem 2,029 (6.6), Conservative 1,362 (4.5), SSP 1,116 (3.7). Electorate 49,395, Turnout 62.0%. MSP: Cathy Craigie (Lab), Majority 4,259 (13.9).

The New Town of Cumbernauld, situated along the A80 road to the north east of Glasgow and the older town of Kilsyth north of the River Kelvin make up this safe Labour seat. While Mrs Thatcher's policy of council house sales persuaded residents of New Towns in England such as Milton Keynes to vote Conservative in the 1980s, the people of Cumbernauld have bought their houses in vast numbers, but have stayed resolutely with Labour.

Politically, little has changed in Cumbernauld and Kilsyth. Even the 1995 Boundary Commission largely left it alone. In 1997, Rosemary McKenna, a long-serving local councillor, replaced Norman Hogg, MP for Dunbartonshire East since 1979. In 1999, the fabulously named David McGlashan polled over 35 per cent for the SNP, but Labour's Cathy Craigie still won by over 4,000 votes. At the local elections held the same day, Labour lost overall control of East Dunbartonshire council as the SNP gained two seats. In 2001, however, the SNP fell back to 29 per cent, while the Tories struggled to maintain fourth place ahead of the Scottish Socialist Party.

EAST KILBRIDE

	2001		1997		1992 notional	
Electorate and turnout	66,572	62.6	65,229	74.8	63,525	79.1
Conservative	4,238	10.2	5,863	12.0	9,365	18.6
Labour	22,205	53.3	27,584	56.5	23,795	47.4
Lib Dem	4,278	10.3	3,527	7.2	5,221	10.4
SNP	9,450	22.7	10,200	20.9	11,855	23.6
SSP	1,519	3.6	–	–	–	–
Others	–		1,622 (3)		–	
MP	Adam Ingram (Lab)		Adam Ingram (Lab)		Adam Ingram (Lab)	
Majority	12,755	30.6	17,384	35.6	11,940	23.8

Scottish Parliament Election 1999: Labour 19,987 (48.4), SNP 13,488 (32.7), Conservative 4,665 (10.8), Lib Dem 3,373 (8.2). Electorate 66,111, Turnout 62.5%. MSP: Andy Kerr (Lab), Majority 6,499 (15.7).

The construction of the New Town of East Kilbride and its surrounding hinterland resulted in the creation of a new constituency in February 1974. In the seat's first contest, the Labour candidate Dr Maurice Miller held off a strong challenge from the SNP, and from the SDP-Liberal Alliance in 1983. However, since then, the seat has been safe for Labour.

Adam Ingram, a former Northern Ireland minister, and now Minister of State for Defence, has held the seat since 1987, and increased his margin of victory over the SNP in 1997 to over 35 per cent. The 1,170 votes polled by the Pro-Life (anti-abortion) candidate was the only other point of note in that year. East Kilbride is now notable as the home of Andy Kerr, Jack McConnell's choice to replace Angus MacKay (Edinburgh South) as Minister for Finance and Public Services in the Scottish Executive. It is also another example of a Holyrood seat that saw the SNP poll a third of the vote in the Scottish Parliamentary elections in 1999, only to fall back to nearer a quarter in 2001. If this were a New Town in England, the Tories would have a presence here; over six out of ten of its electors are owner-occupiers. Instead, in 2001, East Kilbride provided yet another example of a Scottish Central Belt seat where the Liberal Democrats just edged the Tories into a dismal fourth place.

FALKIRK EAST

	2001		1997		1992 notional	
Electorate and turnout	58,201	57.9	56,792	73.2	56,737	76.6
Conservative	3,252	9.6	5,813	14.0	8,771	20.2
Labour	18,536	55.0	23,344	56.1	19,183	44.2
Lib Dem	2,992	8.9	2,153	5.2	3,159	7.3
SNP	7,824	23.2	9,959	23.9	12,327	28.4
SSP	725	2.2	–	–	–	–
Others	373		325		–	
MP	Michael Connarty(Lab)		Michael Connarty(Lab)		Michael Connarty(Lab)	
Majority	10,712	31.8	13,385	32.2	6,856	15.8

Scottish Parliament Election 1999: Labour 15,721 (44.7), SNP 11,582 (32.9), Conservative 3,399 (9.7), Lib Dem 2,509 (7.1), Socialist Lab 1,643 (4.7), Others 358 (1.0). Electorate 57,345, Turnout 61.4%. MSP: Cathy Peattie (Lab), Majority 4,139 (11.8).

In 1983, Stirling, Falkirk and Grangemouth was divided up, and the eastern half of the town of Falkirk was combined with the expanding oil refining areas of Grangemouth and Bo'ness (formerly in West Lothian) to form Falkirk East. In 1995, the whole of the town of Falkirk was transferred to Falkirk West, and in return Falkirk East gained parts of Clackmannan (which became Ochil), and the town of Stenhousemuir.

The seat contains nearly as many council house tenants as homeowners, and suffers from high levels of unemployment. British Petroleum's announcement that they were sacking 600 workers at Grangemouth (as a consequence of BP's merger with Amoco) was the major issue at the 1999 Scottish Parliamentary elections. (A further 1,000 job losses were announced at the Grangemouth refinery in November 2001). At council level, the Labour administration was criticised by the SNP opposition for entertaining the prospect of Private Finance Initiatives (PFI) for local schools. Constituents also feared that Falkirk Royal Infirmary might lose out in services to the new unified trust at Stirling. The SNP were able to tap into these concerns at the Scottish elections, eating substantially into Labour's lead. At the local elections held on the same day, Labour lost overall control of the council thanks to another strong showing from the SNP. However, at the 2001 Westminster election, Michael Connarty, briefly PPS to Tom Clarke, the Film and Tourism Minister until Clarke's sacking in July 1998, again gained a convincing majority over the SNP. As with so much of urban Scotland, the Conservative vote has fallen by half here since 1992, despite some prosperous areas in the Park area of Grangemouth and at Polmont, near the Linlithgow Bridge. The party locally is now barely able to push the Liberal Democrats into fourth place.

FALKIRK WEST

	2001		1997		1992 *notional*	
Electorate and turnout	54,100	57.1	52,850	72.6	*53,947*	*75.9*
Conservative	2,321	7.5	4,639	12.1	*7,719*	*18.9*
Labour	16,022	51.9	22,772	59.3	*21,065*	*51.5*
Lib Dem	2,203	7.1	1,970	5.1	*2,522*	*6.2*
SNP	7,490	24.2	8,989	23.4	*9,635*	*23.5*
Independent	1,464	4.7	–	–	–	–
Others	1,391 (3)		–		–	
MP	Eric Joyce (Lab)		Dennis Canavan(Lab) (Ind)		Dennis Canavan (Lab)	
Majority	8,532	27.6	13,783	35.9	*11,430*	*27.9*

Scottish Parliament Election 1999: 'MP for Falkirk West' 18,511 (55.0), Labour 6,319 (18.8), SNP 5,986 (17.8), Conservative 1,897 (5.6), Lib Dem 954 (2.8). Electorate 53,404, Turnout 63.0%. MSP: Dennis Canavan (FW), Majority 12,192, (36.2).

Parliamentary by-election 21 December 2000: Labour 8,492 (43.5), SNP 7,787 (39.9), Conservative 1,621 (8.3), SSP 989 (5.1), Lib Dem 615 (3.2). Electorate 53,851, Turnout 36.2%. MP: Eric Joyce (Lab), Majority 705 (3.6).

Following the 1995 boundary changes, Falkirk West now comprises the whole of the town of Falkirk, and is natural Labour territory. Smaller towns in the constituency such as Bonnybridge, Denny, Dunipace and Larbert are also solidly Labour, although the SNP has managed to poll just under a quarter of the vote since 1992. Falkirk relies heavily on manufacturing industry, with distilling, engineering and heavy vehicle assembly featuring. However, with manufacturing industry suffering, the unemployment rate is over 5 per cent, well above the Scottish average. In February 1999, the Wrangler factory closed with the loss of 400 jobs.

Falkirk West provided most of the headlines in the Scottish Parliamentary elections in 1999 when Dennis Canavan, considered unsuitable by Labour's controversial candidate selection process because of his rebellious record at Westminster, chose instead to stand as the 'Falkirk West' candidate. Canavan's decision to stand was vindicated when he won an emphatic victory, polling 55 per cent of the popular vote, giving him a thumping 12,000 majority, trouncing Labour's candidate, Ross Martin who could only poll 19 per cent. Canavan's decision to stand for the Scottish Parliament meant that he lost the Labour whip. Relations between Canavan and New Labour broke down to such an extent that Canavan resigned his Westminster seat in November 2000. In the resulting by-election, Labour's Eric Joyce sneaked home by 705 votes over the SNP. By the time of the General Election in 2001, normal service was resumed and Joyce, while not managing to match Canavan's massive majorities of 1992 and 1997, still won by a comfortable 8,500 votes over the SNP.

HAMILTON NORTH and BELLSHILL

	2001		1997		1992 notional	
Electorate and turnout	53,539	56.8	53,607	70.9	52,793	76.1
Conservative	2,649	8.7	3,944	10.4	6,115	15.2
Labour	18,786	61.8	24,322	64.0	23,422	58.3
Lib Dem	2,360	7.8	1,924	5.1	2,715	6.8
SNP	5,225	17.2	7,255	19.1	7,932	19.7
SSP	1,189	3.9	–	–	–	–
Others	195		554		–	
MP	John Reid (Lab)		John Reid (Lab)		John Reid (Lab)	
					Motherwell North	
Majority	13,561	44.6	17,067	44.9	15,490	38.6

Scottish Parliament Election 1999: Labour 15,227 (48.8), SNP 9,621 (30.8), Conservative 3,199 (10.3), Lib Dem 2,105 (6.7), Socialist Lab 1,064 (3.4). Electorate 53,992, Turnout 57.8%. MSP: Michael McMahon (Lab), Majority 5,606 (18.0).

Despite its new name, the working-class town of Hamilton forms only a very small part of this constituency, which is located to the southeast of Glasgow astride both banks of the River Clyde. And just to complicate matters, the seat is largely based on the old Motherwell North, which did not include the town of Motherwell either. The 40,000 voters taken from Motherwell North generally live in Bellshill as well as a string of smaller working-class council housing on the east bank of the Clyde, such as in the wards of Birkenshaw, Mossend, Newarthill, Orbiston and Viewpark. Only Tannochside provides a high proportion of owner-occupiers. The old industries of coalmining and steel making, particularly around the famous Ravenscraig steel works (actually located in Motherwell and Wishaw) have long since disappeared, and nothing much has replaced them in recent years. On the west bank of the Clyde is situated the Hamilton North portion, which actually comprises around 15,000 voters from the towns of Bothwell and Uddingston. On this owner-occupied side of the river, local elections are a little more competitive, but at the national level, Labour still dominates.

John Reid, Secretary of State for Scotland from 1999 to 2001, and Northern Ireland Secretary since 2001, has held this seat for Labour since 1987 with huge majorities ever since then; in 1997 Labour's share of the vote nearly topped 65 per cent. In 1999 and 2001, Hamilton North and Bellshill behaved like a typical West of Scotland seat. The SNP vote rose from just under 20 per cent in 1997 to just over 30 per cent in 1999, cutting Labour's majority in the new Scottish Parliamentary seat, only for the SNP vote to fall back below 20 per cent in 2001. The dismal performance of the Conservatives and the Liberal Democrats is also typical: the Tory vote has halved here since 1992, and the Liberal Democrats have failed to gain a foothold.

HAMILTON SOUTH

	2001		1997		1992 notional	
Electorate and turnout	46,665	57.3	46,562	71.1	46,860	74.3
Conservative	1,876	7.0	2,858	8.6	5,596	16.1
Labour	15,965	59.7	21,709	65.6	19,816	57.0
Lib Dem	2,388	8.9	1,693	5.1	2,308	6.6
SNP	5,190	19.4	5,831	17.6	7,074	20.3
SSP	1,187	4.4	–	–	–	–
Others	151		1,000 (2)		–	
MP	Bill Tynan (Lab)		George Robertson (Lab)		George Robertson (Lab) Hamilton	
Majority	10,775	40.3	15,878	48.0	12,742	36.6

Scottish Parliament Election 1999: Labour 14,098 (54.4), SNP 6,922 (26.7), Conservative 2,918 (11.3), Lib Dem 1,982 (7.7). Electorate 46,765, Turnout 55.4%. MSP: Tom McCabe (Lab), Majority 7,176 (27.7).

Parliamentary by-election 23 September 1999: Labour 7,172 (36.9), SNP 6,616 (34.0), SSP 1,847 (9.5), Conservative 1,406 (7.2), Hamilton Accies 1,075 (5.5), Lib Dem 634 (3.3), 6 Others 704. Electorate 47,081, Turnout 41.3%. MP: Bill Tynan (Lab), Majority 556 (2.9).

Unlike its extremely confusing northern neighbour, this constituency covers exactly what it says on the tin. Hamilton South includes almost all of Hamilton's electors, and most of the former seat of Hamilton, as well as the area north west of the town as far as Blantyre. The small towns of Bothwell and Uddingston were lost to Hamilton North and Bellshill in the 1995 boundary changes.

Remarkably, this constituency has been the scene of three by-elections in the last 35 years. In 1967, Winnie Ewing won the SNP's first seat in over 20 years. Then, in 1978, Labour's George Robertson held off the challenge of Margo Macdonald, herself a by-election victor in Govan in 1973. Robertson rose to Secretary of State for Defence in the first Blair Government, before accepting a peerage together with the post of Secretary-General of NATO in August 1999. At the resulting by-election the following month, Annabelle Ewing, daughter of Winnie Ewing, came within 556 votes of pulling off another family triumph (in 2001, the latest of the Ewing clan did squeak home by 48 votes in Perth). The biggest shock of the night was the performance of the Scottish Socialist Party, who polled 9.5 per cent to finish ahead of the Tories in third place. Meanwhile, the Liberal Democrats suffered the embarrassment of being dumped into sixth place by the Hamilton Accies candidate (Accies being the nickname of Hamilton Academicals Football Club). At a Scottish parliamentary level in 1999, the SNP rallied to just over a quarter of the vote, but Labour's Tom McCabe, who briefly served as Labour's business manager in the Scottish Parliament under Donald Dewar and Henry McLeish before being dropped by Jack McConnell, won with nearly 55 per cent. In the 2001 Westminster election, Labour's Bill Tynan polled 60 per cent of the vote as the SNP fell back to less than 20 per cent.

KILMARNOCK and LOUDOUN

	2001		1997		1992 actual	
Electorate and turnout	61,048	61.7	61,466	77.1	62,043	79.9
Conservative	3,943	10.5	5,125	10.8	9,438	19.0
Labour	19,926	52.9	23,621	49.8	22,210	44.8
Lib Dem	3,177	8.4	1,891	4.0	2,722	5.5
SNP	9,592	25.5	16,365	34.5	15,231	30.7
SSP	1,027	2.7	–	–	–	–
Others	–		407 (2)		–	–
MP	Desmond Browne(Lab)		Desmond Browne(Lab)		William McKelvey(Lab)	
Majority	10,334	27.4	7,256	15.3	6,979	14.1

Scottish Parliament Election 1999: Labour 17,345 (44.1), SNP 14,585 (37.1), Conservative 4,589 (11.7), Lib Dem 2,830 (7.2). Electorate 61,454, Turnout 64.0%. MSP: Margaret Jamieson (Lab), Majority 2,760 (7.0).

This seat comprises Kilmarnock, as well as the smaller textile towns in the upper Irvine Valley, including Darvel, Galston and Newmilns. The area is also famous for distilling Johnnie Walker Scotch whisky, but the decline of textiles has led to an unemployment rate above the Scottish average.

From 1979 to 1997, Kilmarnock and Loudoun was held by Labour's William McKelvey, the left-wing former union official. Its current incumbent, Desmond Browne, an advocate specialising in family law, held the seat for Labour in 1997 with an increased majority. The constituency was seventh on the SNP's target list in the 1999 Scottish parliamentary elections, and one of only three industrial seats (the other two being Ochil and Glasgow Govan) that they stood a realistic chance of taking from Labour. However, Alex Neil, who had contested this seat since 1992, fell some way short of the 8 per cent swing required to take the seat from Labour's Margaret Jamieson. Although Neil was defeated, he became a list MSP for Central Scotland, and unsuccessfully stood for the SNP leadership against John Swinney in September 2000. In 2001, the SNP vote fell back to around 25 per cent, 9 points down on 1997, and 12 points down on 1999. As a consequence, Desmond Browne's Westminster majority increased by 3,000 on his 1997 performance to over 10,000. Browne is now Parliamentary Under-Secretary of State at the Northern Ireland Office.

MOTHERWELL and WISHAW

	2001		1997		1992 notional	
Electorate and turnout	52,418	56.6	52,252	70.1	53,282	75.3
Conservative	3,155	10.6	4,024	11.0	6,264	15.6
Labour	16,681	56.2	21,020	57.4	22,691	56.5
Lib Dem	2,791	9.4	2,331	6.4	2,433	6.1
SNP	5,725	19.3	8,229	22.5	8,601	21.4
SSP	1,260	4.2	–	–	–	–
Others	61		1,015 (2)		146	
MP	Frank Roy (Lab)		Frank Roy (Lab)		Jeremy Bray (Lab) Motherwell South	
Majority	10,956	36.9	12,791	34.9	14,090	35.1

Scottish Parliament Election 1999: Labour 13,955 (46.0), SNP 8,879 (29.2), Conservative 3,694 (12.2), Socialist Lab 1,941 (6.4), Lib Dem 1,895 (6.2). Electorate 52,613, Turnout 57.7%.MSP: Jack McConnell (Lab), Majority 5,076 (16.7).

Until the 1990s boundary changes, this seat was known as Motherwell South, and despite the change of name, little has changed except the addition of 2,600 voters from the old Motherwell North. The vast derelict site of the former Ravenscraig steelworks still dominates the landscape. The electors of Motherwell and Wishaw are very set in their ways, generally live in council houses, and apart from the residential wards of Ladywell and Cambusnethan, the Tories are not welcome here.

Motherwell and Wishaw, despite being an overwhelmingly Scottish seat (according to the 1991 census, 96 per cent of its electors were born in Scotland) was held for Labour by English-born Dr Jeremy Bray (who was first elected in the Middlesbrough West by-election in 1962, before being defeated in 1970) from October 1974 (the constituency was renamed Motherwell South in 1983 before reverting back to Motherwell and Wishaw by the time of Bray's retirement in 1987). His successor, Frank Roy, a former steelworker at Ravenscraig nearly maintained Bray's old majority in the Labour landslide of 1997, and very little changed in 2001. The only other interesting fact about this constituency in electoral terms is that it is now the power base of Jack McConnell, the former Minister for Finance under Donald Dewar, and Education Minister under Henry McLeish, who became Scotland's First Minister in November 2001 on the resignation of McLeish. McConnell, who co-ordinated Labour's 'Yes Yes' devolution referendum campaign in 1997, enjoys a Holyrood majority only half that of Frank Roy at Westminster. This is due to the typical pattern of the SNP's vote having peaked at around 30 per cent in 1999, only to fall back either to 25 per cent or in this case, below 20 per cent in 2001. The Tory vote here has bottomed out at just over 10 per cent, while the Liberal Democrats were thoroughly embarrassed in 1999 by being beaten into fifth place by a Socialist Labour candidate.

Glasgow

	Conservative		Labour		Liberal Democrat		SNP		Others	
	Share of vote	Seats	Share of vote	Seats	Share of vote	Seats	Share of vote	Seats	Share of vote	Seats
2001	7.7	0	50.9	9	9.6	0	17.2	0	14.6	1
1997	8.5	0	60.4	10	7.3	0	19.2	0	4.6	0
1992	14.1	0	54.9	11	8.4	0	20.2	0	2.5	0
1999 C	7.7	0	49.3	10	8.1	0	27.9	0	7.0	0
1999 R	7.9	1	43.9	0	7.2	1	25.5	4	15.5	1

NOTE: 1999C=Scottish Parliamentary Elections Constituency vote; 1999R=Scottish Parliamentary Elections Regional top-up vote (7 seats available)

This is one of the few European electoral regions in Scotland that makes any geographical sense, covering the city of Glasgow. The 1990s boundary changes radically reshaped Glasgow, and as a consequence of its declining population, the city lost one of its 11 Westminster seats - Glasgow Central. Whatever the boundaries, Labour are dominant here, winning all ten Westminster seats in 1997, and polling 60 per cent of the vote.

The above table appears to suggest that Labour's vote collapsed by ten percentage points in 2001. In fact, this is explained by the Labour vote share for June 2001 excluding Glasgow Springburn, home to Michael Martin, the new Speaker of the House of Commons. Of the other three main parties in Scotland, only the SNP chose to contest the seat. It has been listed under 'other' for the purposes of this book, causing that category (with the aid of the Scottish Socialist Party) to jump to 14.6 per cent. Other than the unique position of Springburn, Labour held onto all their Glasgow seats in 2001.

In the Scottish parliamentary elections in May 1999, the main point of interest was the election of Tommy Sheridan as a list MSP. The former anti-poll tax campaigner and now the National Convenor of the Scottish Socialist Party saw his new party (formed out of the Scottish Socialist Alliance) out-poll the Liberal Democrats in the regional top-up vote with just over 7 per cent, finishing narrowly behind the Conservatives. By contrast, the Greens could only manage 4 per cent of the list vote, missing out on a list MSP. Because Labour won all the constituency seats, they were denied any list seats. These were divided between the SNP, who won four (Dorothy-Grace Elder, Kenneth Gibson, Nicola Sturgeon and Sandra White), with the Liberal Democrats and the Conservatives gaining one each (Robert Brown and Bill Aitken, respectively) along with Tommy Sheridan for the SSP.

In 2001, the SSP proved that they had emerged as the fifth party in Glasgow (if not the rest of Scotland) by polling 6.8 per cent of the vote (if Springburn is included), finishing just behind the

Conservatives, who were dumped into fourth place by the Liberal Democrats. Although the Liberal Democrats have emerged as the third party in Glasgow, they have no real presence in the city: in only four of the nine constituencies they contested did they poll more than a tenth of the vote, and their highest vote share was only 18 per cent in Glasgow Kelvin, formerly part of Hillhead, won famously by Roy Jenkins in a 1982 by-election. The highest the Conservatives managed to poll was 13 per cent in Cathcart, a seat they held until 1979. The Tories were even beaten into fifth place in Maryhill, Pollok and Shettleston.

Meanwhile, the main problem in Glasgow for the SNP is that they have become expert at finishing in a distant second place to Labour: in 2001 only in Kelvin did the Liberal Democrats edge the SNP into third place. And although the SNP polled nearly 30 per cent of the vote across Glasgow in 1999 and finished in second place to Labour in all ten constituencies, they still lost by an average of 21.5 per cent of the vote. Even in Govan, Labour's second most marginal seat in Scotland, the SNP failed to win by 1,756 votes. More depressingly for the party, in 2001 Mohammed Sarwar doubled his Westminster majority in Govan, as the SNP vote fell back to 17 per cent across Glasgow. The SNP has also suffered from the emergence of the SSP in Glasgow, which has given disaffected working-class council tenants who can be bothered to vote (the turnout in Glasgow was only 47 per cent in 2001), an extra option if they want to register a protest vote against Labour.

Local government

Not all of the ten parliamentary constituencies that currently make up the European electoral region of Glasgow lie within the City of Glasgow authority. For instance, Rutherglen is located within South Lanarkshire. However, this is still by far the largest local authority in terms of population (around 611,000) in Scotland. In May 1999, Labour took over 50 per cent of the vote and won an astonishing 74 out of the 79 seats (up three on 1995). Thanks to the first-past-the-post electoral system, the SNP polled around 35 per cent of the vote (achieving a swing of around eight per cent from Labour), but ended up with just two seats (three less than 1995), with the Tories, the Liberal Democrats and the Scottish Socialist Party on only one seat each. Ironically, the strong performance of Tommy Sheridan's SSP in at least eight Glasgow wards may have handed victory to Labour.

GLASGOW ANNIESLAND

	2001		1997		1992 notional	
Electorate and turnout	53,290	50.1	53,112	63.8	53,667	70.2
Conservative	2,651	9.9	3,881	11.5	5,895	15.6
Labour	15,102	56.5	20,951	61.8	20,000	53.1
Lib Dem	3,244	12.1	2,453	7.2	5,166	13.7
SNP	4,048	15.1	5,797	17.1	6,411	17.0
SSP	1,486	5.6	229	0.7	–	–
Others	191		564 (4)		213	
MP	John Roberston (Lab)		Donald Dewar (Lab)		Donald Dewar (Lab)	
					Glasgow Garscadden	
Majority	11,054	41.4	15,154	44.7	13,589	36.1

Scottish Parliament Election 1999: Labour 16,749 (58.8), SNP 5,756 (20.2), Conservative 3,032 (10.7), Lib Dem 1,804 (6.3), SSP 1,000 (3.5), Others 139 (0.5). Electorate 54,378, Turnout 52.4%. MSP: Donald Dewar (Lab), Majority 10,993 (38.6).

Scottish Parliament by-election 23 November 2000: Labour 9,838 (48.7), SNP 4,462 (22.1), Conservative 2,148 (10.6), SSP 1,429 (7.1), Lib Dem 1,384 (6.8), Others 960 (4.7). Electorate 52,609, Turnout 38.4%. MSP: Bill Butler (Lab), Majority 5,376 (26.6).

Parliamentary by-election 23 November 2000: Labour 10,539 (52.1), SNP 4,202 (20.8), Conservative 2,188 (10.8), Lib Dem 1,630 (8.1), SSP 1,441 (7.1), Other 212. Electorate 52,609, Turnout 38.4%. MP: John Robertson (Lab), Majority 6,337 (31.4)

Anniesland used to be called Glasgow Garscadden before the Boundary Commission radically re-shaped Glasgow in 1995. Garscadden was home to the many of the post-war council estates built in the north west of Glasgow when its inner city slums were torn down in the inter-war years and after the Second World War. Unfortunately, the newer housing failed to improve the living conditions of the people. Drumchapel, in particular became synonymous with post-war squalor. De-population meant that Garscadden desperately needed more than its 41,000 voters, and nearly 12,000 electors were added from the Kelvindale ward, which had previously belonged to the old Glasgow Hillhead constituency. By contrast with the architectural failures of Drumchapel, Kelvindale includes part of the west end of Glasgow's best housing stock. However, the fine nineteenth century terraces have failed to attract any significant number of Tory voters.

Until recently, the re-shaped Anniesland was the personal fiefdom of the much-liked Scottish First Minister, Donald Dewar. He had begun his political career by unexpectedly seizing Aberdeen South from Lady Tweedsmuir in the Labour landslide of 1966, the first time Labour had ever won the seat. Despite losing in 1970, Dewar returned to Parliament as MP for Glasgow Garscadden in the April 1978 by-election. As Labour's Shadow Secretary of State for Scotland, he became a key architect of devolution in the dark days of the 1980s, before steering the Scotland Bill through Parliament as Secretary of State for

Scotland. On 6 May 1999, Scotland's new First Minister polled nearly 60 per cent of the popular vote in his constituency and then watched Labour hold off the challenge of the SNP across Scotland.

Dewar's death in October 2000 was a great loss to the Scottish Parliament. In more mundane electoral terms, it led to the first occasion in Scotland in which two by-elections were held simultaneously for the same constituency, one for the vacancy in the Scottish Parliament, the other for Dewar's seat at Westminster. As if in respect for the memory of Dewar, Labour's John Robertson polled 52 per cent of the vote in the Westminster contest, and Bill Butler, a left-wing Glasgow city councillor, polled a similar 49 per cent to inherit the Scottish parliamentary seat. As with the Ayr by-election held earlier in the year (in March 2000), the SSP illustrated its growing power as a party of protest when it ousted the Liberal Democrats into fifth place in the Scottish parliamentary vote. The combined turnout of 38 per cent represented a post-war low for a Scottish by-election, though it was relieved of this distinction by Falkirk West four weeks later.

GLASGOW BAILLIESTON

	2001		1997		1992 notional	
Electorate and turnout	49,268	47.2	51,185	62.2	52,207	66.7
Conservative	1,580	6.8	2,468	7.7	3,448	9.9
Labour	14,200	61.1	20,925	65.7	22,030	63.2
Lib Dem	1,551	6.7	1,217	3.8	1,505	4.3
SNP	4,361	18.7	6,085	19.1	7,865	22.6
SSP	1,569	6.7	970	3.0	–	–
Others	–	–	188		–	–
MP	James Wray (Lab)		James Wray (Lab)		NEW SEAT	
Majority	9,839	42.3	14,840	46.6	14,165	40.7

Scottish Parliament Election 1999: Labour 11,289 (47.6), SNP 8,217 (34.7), SSP 1,864 (7.9), Conservative 1,526 (6.4), Lib Dem 813 (3.4). Electorate 49,068, Turnout 48.3%. MSP: Margaret Curran (Lab), Majority 3,072 (13.0).

Glasgow Baillieston is another creation of the 1995 Boundary Commission's gutting of Glasgow. Its predecessor, Glasgow Provan had the highest rate of council housing of any constituency in the United Kingdom and the highest rate of unemployment in Scotland. It also had one of the most rapidly declining populations in Britain, falling to only 36,500 electors in 1992. The new seat comprises the 'outer east' of Glasgow, keeping Barlanark, Easterhouse, Gartloch and Queenslie from the old Provan, but also taking Baillieston, Carntyne and Mount Vernon from Glasgow Shettleston. Baillieston and Mount Vernon have a high number of owner-occupiers compared with the troubled housing estate in places like Easterhouse, but regardless of living conditions, people here vote Labour.

Labour's Jimmy Wray, MP for Provan since 1987, is a typical Scottish Labour MP, coming from a Catholic background, and being rewarded with a seat after a long period of service in local government. Even in the days of his predecessor, Hugh Brown, a Scottish Office Minister, Labour polled over 60 per cent of the vote. In 1999, the SNP's Dorothy Elder polled an impressive 35 per cent of the vote, cutting the Labour majority to around 3,000. However, Margaret Curran, Deputy Minister for Social Justice in the Scottish Executive since October 2000, still polled nearly half of the vote. The Scottish Socialist Party's success in finishing third, pushing the Tories and the Liberal Democrats into fourth and fifth places, illustrates that they are emerging as a credible alternative to Labour for council house tenants living in and around Glasgow, if not outside the West of Scotland. Even in the Westminster elections in 2001, the SSP finished ahead of the Liberal Democrats in Baillieston, and only just behind the Tories. Meanwhile, the SNP's vote fell back below 20 per cent, leaving Jimmy Wray over 40 points ahead. More worrying for democracy is the fact that turnout here fell below the 50 per cent mark in both 1999 and 2001, a trend repeated across much of Glasgow.

GLASGOW CATHCART

	2001		1997		1992 notional	
Electorate and turnout	52,094	52.6	49,416	67.6	51,940	73.0
Conservative	3,662	13.4	4,248	12.7	8,167	21.5
Labour	14,902	54.4	19,158	57.4	18,719	49.4
Lib Dem	3,006	11.0	2,302	6.9	2,732	7.2
SNP	4,086	14.9	6,193	18.5	7,244	19.1
SSP	1,730	6.3	458	1.4	–	–
Others	–		1,031 (2)		1,072	2.8
MP	Tom Harris (Lab)		John Maxton (Lab)		John Maxton (Lab)	
Majority	10,816	39.5	12,965	38.8	10,552	27.8

Scottish Parliament Election 1999: Labour 12,966 (48.1), SNP 7,592 (28.1), Conservative 3,311 (12.3), Lib Dem 2,187 (8.1), SWP 920 (3.4). Electorate 51,338, Turnout 52.6%. MSP: Mike Watson (Lab), Majority 5,374 (19.9).

It is hard to believe today that the eccentric Tory Teddy Taylor held this seat continuously from 1964 to 1979. Indeed, in the days of religious-based voting, the mainly Protestant Cathcart was a safe Tory seat; in 1955, the Conservative majority was nearly 16,000. In 1979, despite the national election result, the Euro-sceptic Teddy Taylor lost this former Glasgow Tory stronghold to John Maxton, nephew of the famous Clydesider Jimmy Maxton (MP for Glasgow Bridgeton, 1922-1946). The constituency had become increasingly marginal due to the continued growth of the massive Castlemilk council estate, swamping the Tory-voting residential areas of Cathcart, King's Park, Mount Florida and Newlands. More recently, Castlemilk has haemorrhaged people, but despite this, Maxton increased his lead over the SNP in 1997, its vote stubbornly refusing to rise above 20 per cent.

When Maxton announced his intention to retire from politics, he left two vacancies. His decision not to serve in the Scottish Parliament left the way open for Mike Watson (now Lord Watson of Invergowrie) to walk into a safe Labour seat after Watson's old Glasgow Central seat disappeared in the 1995 boundary changes, and he had lost a bitter Westminster selection battle in Glasgow Govan to Mohammad Sarwar. In 1999, Watson saw Maxton's 1997 majority over the SNP cut in half as the Nationalists polled 28 per cent of the vote, though the winning margin still exceeded 5,000 votes. In late 2001, Jack McConnell, the new Scottish First Minister, appointed Watson Minister for Tourism, Culture and Sport in the Scottish Executive. In June 2001, Tom Harris, a former press officer with the Scottish Labour party, inherited the Westminster seat, and actually further increased Maxton's old majority as the SNP's share of the vote slipped below 15 per cent.

GLASGOW GOVAN

	2001		1997		1992 *notional*	
Electorate and turnout	54,068	46.8	49,978	64.5	*50,351*	*72.3*
Conservative	2,167	8.6	2,839	8.8	*7,165*	*19.7*
Labour	12,464	49.3	14,216	44.1	*15,665*	*43.0*
Lib Dem	2,815	11.1	1,918	5.9	*2,033*	*5.6*
SNP	6,064	24.0	11,302	35.1	*10,056*	*27.6*
SSP	1,531	6.1	755	2.3	–	–
Others	243 (2)		1,215 (5)		*1,475*	*4.1*
MP	Mohammad Sarwar (Lab)		Mohammad Sarwar (Lab)		NEW SEAT	
Majority	6,400	25.3	2,914	9.0	*5,609*	*15.4*

Scottish Parliament Election 1999: Labour 11,421 (43.3), SNP 9,665 (36.7), Conservative 2,343 (8.8), Lib Dem 1,429 (5.6), SSP 1,275 (4.8), Others 190 (0.7). Electorate 53,257, Turnout 49.5%. MSP: Gordon Jackson (Lab), Majority 1,756 (6.7).

In the last thirty years, Govan has provided psephologists with more by-election excitement than any other Scottish constituency, but it has proved fairly dull at general elections because Labour have always won back the seat. Margo Macdonald dramatically won the seat for the SNP in November 1973, but she was defeated at the general election four months later. By 1988, Jim Sillars, former Labour MP for Ayrshire South, and a co-founder of the breakaway 'Scottish Labour Party' in 1976, had become the SNP candidate. The nomination of Bruce Millan, Secretary of State for Scotland from 1976 to 1979, as an EEC Commissioner, caused another by-election in which Sillars won the seat for the SNP from Labour, only to see it lost to Labour's Ian Davidson in 1992.

In the 1995 boundary changes, Davidson chose to fight the seat of Glasgow Pollok, which was re-shaped to include around half of his old Govan seat. In return, the new Govan seat gained the middle-class Shawlands area and Pollokshields, one third of whose electors are non-white, and mainly from the Pakistani community. Pakistan-born Mohammad Sarwar emerged from his powerbase in Pollokshields to challenge Labour's Mike Watson, who was casting round for a seat on the disappearance of his old Glasgow Central seat. The selection battle in Govan was particularly bitter, even by West of Scotland standards. In a hotly disputed first ballot, Watson won by only one vote. However, in the second ballot, Sarwar emerged victorious, and despite the internal Labour wrangling won the 1997 election by nearly 3,000 votes over the SNP's rising star Nicola Sturgeon. Following the election, Sarwar was accused of paying off a rival Pakistani candidate, and was suspended by the Labour party in June 1997, pending a court case. In March 1999, Sarwar was acquitted of all charges, and had the Labour whip restored to him by the end of that month. In May 1999, with the controversy over Sarwar, and Kvaerner's decision to put the Govan shipyard up for sale, it looked as if 28-year old Nicola Sturgeon (now a regional list MSP and the SNP's Health spokesperson) might gain Labour's second most marginal seat in Scotland. However, the Labour candidate Gordon

Jackson clung on by 1,750 votes. In 2001, Sarwar even doubled his majority, as he increased his vote share on 1997 by 5 per cent, while the SNP's share slumped by 11 points.

GLASGOW KELVIN

	2001		1997		1992 notional	
Electorate and turnout	61,534	43.6	58,198	56.1	53,680	67.5
Conservative	2,388	8.9	3,539	10.8	4,765	13.2
Labour	12,014	44.8	16,643	51.0	16,971	46.9
Lib Dem	4,754	17.7	4,629	14.2	6,848	18.9
SNP	4,513	16.8	6,978	21.4	6,982	19.3
SSP	1,847	6.9	386	1.2	–	–
Green	1,286	4.8	–	–	518	1.4
Others	–		479 (3)		131	
MP	George Galloway (Lab)		George Galloway (Lab)		George Galloway(Lab) Hillhead	
Majority	7,260	27.1	9,665	29.6	9,989	27.6

Scottish Parliament Election 1999: Labour 12,711 (44.8), SNP 8,303 (29.3), Lib Dem 3,720 (13.1), Conservative 2,253 (7.9), SSP 1,375 (4.9). Electorate 61,207, Turnout 46.3%.MSP: Pauline McNeill (Lab), Majority 4,408 (15.5).

Formerly known as Glasgow Hillhead, this is one of only three Glasgow constituencies to survive relatively unscathed as a result of the 1995 boundary changes. Only 6,000 electors were gained from the defunct Glasgow Central seat, and a couple of thousand from Maryhill. Most of the constituency is middle-class, including almost the whole of the city centre of Glasgow, especially George Square. The recently refurbished city centre contrasts with the working-class areas of Partick and Scotstoun. The constituency is also incredibly well educated. Not only does the seat contain Glasgow University, it also has more adults with university degrees than any other seat in Scotland.

When it was still known as Hillhead, the constituency was the scene of Roy Jenkins's dramatic by-election victory over the Tories for the fledgling SDP-Liberal Alliance in March 1982. In 1983, the SDP's first leader held onto the seat, which had been expanded to include the southern half of the old Kelvingrove. However, in 1987 Jenkins lost to George Galloway, and the outspoken opponent of Anglo-American military action in the Middle East has held onto the seat ever since. In 1997 and 1999, the SNP emerged as the clear challengers to Labour, but by 2001, as the Tory vote fell yet again to just 9 per cent, the Liberal Democrats re-lived some of their former glories in the seat by edging the SNP into second place.

GLASGOW MARYHILL

	2001		1997		1992 notional	
Electorate and turnout	55,431	40.1	52,693	56.4	52,291	64.3
Conservative	1,162	5.2	1,747	5.9	3,241	9.6
Labour	13,420	60.4	19,301	64.9	21,042	62.6
Lib Dem	2,372	10.7	2,119	7.1	2,238	6.7
SNP	3,532	15.9	5,037	16.9	6,530	19.4
SSP	1,745	7.8	409	1.4	–	–
Others	–		1,108 (4)		560	
MP	Ann McKeckin (Lab)		Maria Fyfe (Lab)		Maria Fyfe (Lab)	
Majority	9,888	44.5	14,264	48.0	14,512	43.2

Scottish Parliament Election 1999: Labour 11,455 (49.8), SNP 7,129 (31.0), Lib Dem 1,793 (7.8), SSP 1,439 (6.3), Conservative 1,194 (5.2). Electorate 56,469, Turnout 40.8%. MSP: Patricia Ferguson (Lab), Majority 4,326 (18.8).

The Maryhill constituency is situated in the north of Glasgow, and is mainly working class in character. As well as the long-established area of Maryhill, it includes the council house estates of Milton, Possil and Summerston, together with the outskirts of the city's west end at Woodside and North Kelvinside, the latter containing the largest number of Chinese electors in Scotland (albeit only one in every hundred voters). Unsurprisingly, Labour has never lost this seat in the post-war period.

In true West of Scotland Labour tradition, former councillor Jim Craigen handed over to another former city councillor, Maria Fyfe, in 1987. By 1997, Fyfe had increased Labour's vote share to nearly 65 per cent. In May 1999, the SNP gained just over 30 per cent of the vote, as Michael Fry, the Tory candidate, and a journalist for the Herald newspaper, finished fifth behind the Scottish Socialist Party candidate. The winning Labour candidate, Patricia Ferguson, was made Minister for Parliamentary Business in the Scottish Executive in late 2001, replacing Tom McCabe (Hamilton South). In June 2001, Labour's Ann McKechin kept her party's share of the vote at Westminster above 60 per cent, as the SNP slipped back to 16 per cent. Once again, the Tories finished fifth behind the SSP. Depressingly, in both 1999 and 2001, the turnout in Maryhill only managed to creep over four in ten.

GLASGOW POLLOK

	2001		1997		1992 notional	
Electorate and turnout	49,201	51.4	49,328	66.5	52,678	72.1
Conservative	1,417	5.6	1,979	6.0	3,107	8.2
Labour	15,497	61.3	19,653	59.9	18,945	49.9
Lib Dem	1,612	6.4	1,137	3.5	1,648	4.3
SNP	4,229	16.7	5,862	17.9	9,492	25.0
SSP*	2,522	10.0	3,639	11.1	4,811	12.7
Others	–	–	532 (2)		–	
MP	Ian Davidson (Lab)		Ian Davidson (Lab)		Jimmy Dunnachie (Lab)	
Majority	11,268	44.6	13,791	42.0	9,453	24.9

* Scottish Militant Labour in 1992

Scottish Parliament Election 1999: Labour 11,405 (43.7), SNP 6,763 (25.9), SSP 5,611 (21.5), Conservative 1,370 (5.3), Lib Dem 931 (3.6). Electorate 47,970, Turnout 54.4%. MSP: Johann Lamont (Lab), Majority 4,642 (17.8).

Pollok was radically re-shaped in the 1995 boundary changes. Almost half of Govan was added, leading to Ian Davidson's (Govan's MP from 1992 to 1997) decision to go with the electors of Cardonald, Hillington, Mosspark and Penilee (all formerly part of Craigton which disappeared in the 1983 boundary changes) into a seat made vacant by the retirement of Jimmy Dunnachie. In the fifty-fifty swap with Govan, Pollok lost Shawlands and Pollokshields. The rest of the present constituency comes from the pre-1990s Pollok seat, encompassing the vast council house estates of Arden, Cowglen, Nitshill and Pollok itself.

The main point of electoral interest in recent years has been the popularity of Tommy Sheridan. Formerly belonging to Scottish Militant Labour, Sheridan was a leading campaigner against the Poll Tax, and his opposition to warrant sales led to his imprisonment in 1992. Not to be undone, Sheridan stood for Pollok at the 1992 General Election from behind bars, and finished in second place behind Labour with over 6,000 votes. In 1997, Sheridan, by this time having formed the Scottish Socialist Alliance, a loose collection of left-wing organisations, was forced into third place by the SNP. However, the Scottish Parliamentary elections provided the ideal platform for Sheridan's new Scottish Socialist Party. As well as polling over 20 per cent of the vote in Pollok (and cementing third place), the 7.2 per cent share gained by the SSP across Glasgow on the list vote ensured that Sheridan was elected as a list MSP. Meanwhile, in 1999, the SNP advanced to over a quarter of the vote in Pollok, cutting Labour's Westminster majority by nearly two-thirds. In 2001, normal service was resumed as Ian Davidson polled over 60 per cent of the vote, with the SNP dropping back to 17 per cent and Keith Baldassara, the SSP candidate, managing only 10 per cent.

GLASGOW RUTHERGLEN

	2001		1997		1992 notional	
Electorate and turnout	51,855	56.3	50,673	70.1	52,265	74.3
Conservative	3,301	11.3	3,288	9.3	7,443	19.2
Labour	16,760	57.4	20,430	57.5	20,742	53.4
Lib Dem	3,689	12.6	5,167	14.5	4,529	11.7
SNP	4,135	14.2	5,423	15.3	6,052	15.6
SSP	1,328	4.5	251	0.7	–	–
Others	–		962 (2)		92	
MP	Thomas McAvoy (Lab)		Thomas McAvoy (Lab)		Thomas McAvoy (Lab)	
Majority	12,625	43.2	15,007	42.3	13,299	34.2

Scottish Parliament Election 1999: Labour 13,442 (46.3), SNP 6,155 (21.2), Lib Dem 5,798 (20.0), Conservative 2,315 (8.0), SSP 832 (2.9), Others 481 (1.7). Electorate 51,012, Turnout 56.9%. MSP: Janis Hughes (Lab), Majority 7,287 (25.1).

The ancient burgh of Rutherglen was finally incorporated into the City of Glasgow in the local government reorganisation of the 1970s. Labour's Gregor Mackenzie captured the seat from the Tories in the May 1964 by-election. Mackenzie was Parliamentary Private Secretary to James Callaghan from 1965 to 1970, before going on to serve as a Minister of State at the Scottish Office in Callaghan's government. All three major parties have occupied second place to Labour since 1979. From 1979 to 1987, Mackenzie's main challengers were the Liberals and then the SDP-Liberal Alliance, surprisingly because, with the fleeting exception of Glasgow Hillhead from 1982 to 1987, the Liberals have lacked a significant support base in the City of Glasgow. During the 1980s, the Alliance also won local council seats. Mackenzie eventually handed over to Tommy McAvoy in 1987, and by 1992, the Tories had re-occupied second place, only to be overtaken by the SNP in 1997. In 1999, the SNP held off the Liberal Democrats by a few hundred votes in the tussle for second place, a feat the party repeated in 2001. Tommy McAvoy, who has built up a fearsome reputation as a Labour whip, can sit back and relax while the other political parties battle it out for second spot; in 2001 his percentage majority actually increased slightly from 1997.

GLASGOW SHETTLESTON

	2001		1997		1992 notional	
Electorate and turnout	51,557	39.7	48,104	55.7	49,358	64.2
Conservative	1,082	5.3	1,484	5.5	3,876	12.2
Labour	13,235	64.7	19,616	73.2	20,767	65.5
Lib Dem	1,105	5.4	1,061	4.0	1,939	6.1
SNP	3,417	16.7	3,748	14.0	5,123	16.2
SSP	1,396	6.8	482	1.8	–	–
Others	230	1.1	422 (3)		–	–
MP	David Marshall (Lab)		David Marshall (Lab)		NEW SEAT	
Majority	9,818	48.0	15,868	59.2	15,644	49.3

Scottish Parliament Election 1999: Labour 11,078 (54.0), SNP 5,611 (27.3), SSP 1,640 (8.0), Conservative 1,260 (6.1), Lib Dem 943 (4.6). Electorate 50,592, Turnout 40.6%. MSP: Frank McAveety (Lab), Majority 5,467 (26.6).

The name of Glasgow Shettleston may have survived the 1990s boundary changes, but the nature of the seat has changed completely since then. More than half of the old seat, including Mount Vernon and Baillieston, was lost to Glasgow Baillieston, while the new seat gained nearly half of Glasgow Central, which disappeared completely as a result of the changes. As a consequence, the seat had moved from the east of Glasgow to the south and west as far as Crosshill and Queen's Park.

Whichever way the seat has been drawn and re-drawn in the past, this is rock-solid Labour territory, filled with large council house estates, and containing very few owner-occupiers (25 per cent in 1991). David Marshall, the MP since 1979, polled very nearly three-quarters of the vote in 1997. Although the SNP nearly doubled its share of the vote in 1999 on its 1997 performance, there is no prospect of this seat turning a different colour in the immediate future. Despite no longer being Deputy Minister for Communities with responsibility for Local Government in the Scottish Executive (having been dropped by Henry McLeish in October 2000), Labour's Frank McAveety's hold over Shettleston is also secure. The only party to see significant growth in 1999 and 2001 has been the SSP, who have pushed the Tories and the Liberal Democrats into fourth and fifth places in both elections. In 2001, Shettleston had the unenviable distinction of providing the lowest turnout of any constituency in Scotland, standing at a miserable 39.7 per cent.

GLASGOW SPRINGBURN

	2001		*1997*		*1992 notional*	
Electorate and turnout	55,192	43.7	53,576	58.9	*54,822*	*65.6*
Conservative	–	–	1,893	6.0	*3,909*	*10.9*
Labour	–	–	22,534	71.4	*23,347*	*64.9*
Lib Dem	–	–	1,349	4.3	*1,559*	*4.3*
SNP	4,675	19.4	5,208	16.5	*7,150*	*19.9*
SSP	1,879	7.8	407	1.3	–	–
Speaker	16,053	66.6	–	–	–	–
Others	1,497 (2)		186			–
MP	Michael Martin(Speaker)		Michael Martin (Lab)		Michael Martin (Lab)	
Majority	11,378	47.2	17,326	54.9	*16,197*	*45.0*

Scottish Parliament Election 1999: Labour 14,268 (58.6), SNP 6,375 (26.2), Conservative 1,293 (5.3), Lib Dem 1,288 (5.3), SSP 1,141 (4.7). Electorate 55,670, Turnout 43.8%. MSP: Paul Martin (Lab), Majority 7,893 (32.4).

Springburn is one of Glasgow's poorest constituencies, lying to the north of the city centre. In the 1995 boundary changes, it lost Keppochhill's 5,000 electors to its western neighbour Maryhill, but gained around 11,000 voters from Provan in the east in the form of Riddrie and Lethamhill. Unemployment levels are now the highest in the city, partly due the rapid decline of the Cowlairs railyard. At the heart of the constituency lies Dennistoun, which does have some owner-occupiers, but much of it comprises large tower blocks, especially in the Balornock and Barmulloch estates. In August 2001, the wisdom of the government's policy of dispersing asylum seekers was called into question when a 22 year-old Kurdish man from Turkey was stabbed to death in the Sighthill area of Springburn, which was acting as a temporary home to around 1,500 asylum seekers.

Labour's Michael Martin has been firmly ensconced here since 1979, polling over 70 per cent of the vote in 1997. The SNP managed to poll a quarter of the vote in 1999, but Labour's share of the vote was more than double that figure. In October 2000, the profile of Springburn and Martin was dramatically increased when he was elected Speaker of the House of Commons on the retirement of Betty Boothroyd. In 2001, the Conservatives and the Liberal Democrats followed their normal practice and chose not to stand candidates against the new Commons Speaker, wisely as it turned out; Martin won nearly two-thirds of the popular vote. Even with the other two main parties absent, the SNP only increased its share of the vote by about 4 per cent, while the SSP finished comfortably ahead of a Scottish Unionist candidate.

Highlands and Islands

	Conservative		Labour		Liberal Democrat		SNP		Others	
	Share of vote	Seats	Share of vote	Seats	Share of vote	Seats	Share of vote	Seats	Share of vote	Seats
2001	15.7	0	27.0	2	30.3	4	22.9	1	4.1	0
1997	16.2	0	27.0	2	27.7	4	26.7	1	2.4	0
1992	25.0	0	19.3	1	28.7	5	26.1	1	0.9	0
1999 C	14.3	0	27.4	1	28.3	5	28.5	2	1.6	0
1999 R	14.9	2	25.5	3	21.4	0	27.7	2	10.4	0

NOTE: 1999C=Scottish Parliamentary Elections Constituency vote; 1999R=Scottish Parliamentary Elections Regional top-up vote (7 seats available)

The Highlands and Islands region makes reasonable geographic sense, except that Moray has been taken from the old Grampian region and Argyll and Bute from the old Strathclyde region. It is also the most keenly contested electoral region in Scotland. In 1997, only 1.7 percentage points separated the Liberal Democrats from Labour in third place, with the SNP nestled in the middle. In 2001, the Liberal Democrats pushed into a clear lead on 30 per cent as Labour stagnated on 27 per cent and the SNP slipped back to 23 per cent, but the area remains hotly contested between the three parties.

The Highlands and Islands is the best region for the Liberal Democrats both in terms of seats and vote share. In 2001, the party held onto all four of its Westminster seats in the region – Argyll and Bute, Caithness, Sutherland and Easter Ross, Orkney and Shetland and Ross, Skye and Inverness West. Labour were their main challengers in all four seats. It came closest to winning in Argyll and Bute, where the retirement (and elevation to the House of Lords) of long-serving Liberal Democrat Ray Michie and her replacement by Alan Reid saw the Liberal Democrat majority fall by two-thirds. Jim Wallace's replacement in Orkney and Shetland, Alistair Carmichael also fought off a strong challenge from Labour as his majority was halved on the 1997 result. However, Viscount Thurso, the first hereditary peer to sit in the House of Commons bucked the trend by outperforming Robert Maclennan's 1997 result by 4 per cent. The most impressive result of the night occurred in Ross, Skye and Inverness West where Liberal Democrat leader, Charles Kennedy more than trebled his majority over Labour to over 12,000. During the election campaign, there had been press stories that Kennedy might lose his seat, claims which now appear ridiculous.

In 1999, the number of constituencies was expanded from seven to eight so that Orkney and Shetland could be represented separately in the Scottish parliament. Schedule 1, Clause 81 of the Scotland Act 1998 guarantees the islands' separate representation, regardless of future boundary commission attempts to cut Scotland's representation. Both seats were won by the Liberal Democrats, with Jim Wallace gaining a massive 67 per cent of the vote in Orkney. The Liberal Democrats easily held onto their three other seats, while the SNP held Moray with a slightly reduced majority, owing to a strong showing by Labour. Alex Salmond's opposition to the war in Kosovo during the election campaign was widely blamed for the SNP's failure to win more seats in Scotland, but in actual fact the only seat where the issue made a difference was in Moray where Labour surged into second place against the Tories, thanks to the presence of two RAF bases at Lossiemouth and Kinloss. The only constituency seat in the region to change hands in 1999 (based on the 1997 Westminster results) was Inverness East, Nairn and Lochaber. A Labour gain in 1997 from the Liberal Democrats in a four-way contest, it was a three-way marginal in 1999, being number one on the SNP's target list, and number two on the Liberal Democrats'. In the end, the SNP's Fergus Ewing achieved a modest swing of 3 per cent to take the seat by only 441 votes from Labour. Meanwhile, Labour won their only seat in the region in the Western Isles.

Despite their dismal performance in 1999, the Tories were rewarded with two top-up seats, currently represented by Jamie MacGrigor and Mary Scanlon. Because the Liberal Democrats had held onto all five of their constituencies, they were denied any list MSPs in the region. By contrast, Labour, who could only win the Western Isles, were compensated with three top-up seats (for Rhoda Grant, Maureen Macmillan and Peter Peacock), the party's only regional list seats in Scotland. Meanwhile, the SNP who marginally out-performed both the Liberal Democrats and Labour in terms of share of the vote in 1999, were rewarded with the remaining two top-up seats, one of which went to Winnie Ewing, the party's President and previously the Highlands and Islands MEP and the other to Duncan Hamilton (both of whom have chosen not to stand again in 2003).

Local government

The Highlands region contains six local authorities: Argyll and Bute, Highland (a vast area comprising Ross, Skye and Inverness West, Inverness East, Nairn and Lochaber, and Caithness, Sutherland and Easter Ross), Moray, Orkney, Shetland and the Western Isles. By the end of the local elections in 1999, all but Moray remained in the control of Independents in a region where people still vote for the individual rather than the party. Despite this, the Liberal Democrats gained two seats in Argyll and Bute, four seats in Highland, and five seats in Shetland, while Labour gained four seats in Highland and one in the Western Isles. The SNP lost overall control of Moray (part of which lies in Aberdeenshire and therefore in North East Scotland) as Labour made three gains, although Independent councillors now form the main 'opposition' in this council. The only bright spots for the SNP were three gains in the Western Isles and one in Highland. Meanwhile, the Tories only have four councillors across the whole of the region, three in Argyll and Bute and one in Moray. The huge Highland authority has created deep resentment among voters in Caithness, Sutherland and Skye who feel that decisions are made in Inverness without any real input at a local level.

ARGYLL and BUTE

	2001		1997		1992 actual	
Electorate and turnout	49,175	63.0	48,983	72.9	47,921	76.1
Conservative	6,436	20.8	6,774	19.0	10,117	27.7
Labour	7,592	24.5	5,596	15.7	4,946	13.6
Lib Dem	9,245	29.9	14,359	40.2	12,739	34.9
SNP	6,433	20.8	8,278	23.2	8,689	23.8
SSP	1,251	4.0	–	–	–	–
Anti–EU	–	–	713	2.0	–	–
MP	Alan Reid (LD)		Ray Michie (LD)		Ray Michie (LD)	
Majority	1,653	5.3	6,081	17.0	2,622	7.2

Scottish Parliament Election 1999: Lib Dem 11,226 (34.9), SNP 9,169 (28.5), Labour 6,470 (20.1), Conservative 5,312 (16.5). Electorate 49,609, Turnout 64.9%. MSP: George Lyon (LD), Majority 2,057 (6.4).

Argyll and Bute covers a huge area of 2,500 square miles, making it the fourth largest constituency in the United Kingdom. The constituency has dozens of islands within it, including Mull, Jura, Islay, Coll, Tiree, Colonsay and (since 1983), the island of Bute centring on the tourist town of Rothesay. The mainland part of the seat comprises the Kintyre Peninsula and the rugged moors of Argyll, featuring only two towns of any great size, Oban in the north, and Dunoon in the south.

Despite its inaccessibility, the seat has provided much excitement at general elections in the last thirty years, returning MPs from all the major parties in Scotland except Labour. In February 1974, the SNP's Iain MacCormick surprisingly captured what was then regarded as a safe Tory seat on the retirement of Michael Noble. In 1979, John MacKay recaptured the seat for the Tories, and held it in 1983. In 1987, the Liberal Democrat Ray Michie defeated Mackay (who subsequently became Lord Mackay of Arbrecknish, sadly dying in February 2001). Michie held the seat with ever increasing majorities until standing down in 2001. (She was subsequently elevated to the peerage as Baroness Michie of Gallanach). The 1999 Scottish Parliamentary elections produced a three-cornered contest, in which the Liberal Democrat, George Lyon, a farmer from Bute and former President of the Scottish National Farmers Union, edged out Duncan Hamilton, a rising star of the SNP, with Labour pushed into third. In 2001, Liberal Democrat newcomer Alan Reid held on, but Michie's old majority was cut by over two-thirds. Labour jumped from third to second place, with the SNP falling back to fourth, and the Tories finishing in third spot, making this seat a genuine four-way marginal. Despite the party battles at parliamentary elections, Argyll and Bute council remains in Independent hands after the 1999 local elections.

CAITHNESS, SUTHERLAND and EASTER ROSS

	2001		1997		1992 notional	
Electorate and turnout	41,315	60.2	41,652	70.0	41,318	71.7
Conservative	3,513	14.1	3,148	10.8	6,391	21.6
Labour	6,297	25.3	8,122	27.8	4,629	15.6
Lib Dem	9,041	36.4	10,381	35.6	13,150	44.4
SNP	5,273	21.2	6,710	23.0	5,440	18.4
SSP	544	2.2	–	–	–	–
Others	199		811 (3)		–	
MP	John Thurso (LD)		Robert Maclennan (LD)		Robert Maclennan (LD)	
Majority	2,744	11.0	2,259	7.8	6,759	22.8

Scottish Parliament Election 1999: Lib Dem 10,691 (41.1), Labour 6,300 (24.2), SNP 6,035 (23.2), Conservative 2,167 (8.3), Independent 554 (2.1), Others 282 (1.1). Electorate 41,581, Turnout 62.6%. MSP: Jamie Stone (LD), Majority 4,391 (16.9).

This far-flung constituency covers all the land mass north of Inverness, west across to Lochinver, north up to Cape Wrath, along the very tip of Scotland past the town of Thurso to John O'Groats, down the east coast and the port of Wick, as far as the Dornoch Firth. The 1995 boundary changes added 10,000 voters from Charles Kennedy's Ross and Cromarty seat, the segment of Easter Ross around Dornoch and Tain on the east coast. The people of Dornoch, Thurso and Wick were unhappy about the centralisation of decision-making in Inverness caused by the introduction of unitary authorities across Scotland in 1995. The general feeling within the constituency is that the abolition of smaller Highland councils into one all-purpose council in the Highland capital has led to the abandonment of autonomous decision-making, and its replacement with toothless local committees. Jobs are hard to come by, especially since the scaling down of the Dounreay nuclear reprocessing plant and the crisis in the farming industry. The recent slump in oil prices is also a worry to those workers who service oil platforms on the Moray Firth at Nigg. The only bright spots are in the hi-tech telecommunications industry, with British Telecom's new call centre in Thurso, which employs nearly 600 people. A new factory producing batteries nearby also employs several hundred people.

There is still a tradition here of voting for individuals rather than parties, illustrated by two interesting facts. By the 1980s, it had been represented by three of the four major parties, and also Independents, in the period since 1945. Secondly, the MP from 1966 to 1997, the relentless Robert Maclennan, was elected four times as a Labour MP, re-elected twice for the SDP in 1983 and 1987, and subsequently held onto the seat for the Liberal Democrats by an impressive 6,750 in 1992. Since then, Labour and the SNP have strengthened their challenge, while the Tories have gone from second to fourth place, making this seat a three-way marginal. In 1997, Maclennan survived a 12 per cent surge in the Labour vote. However, local Liberal Democrat councillor Jamie Stone won the Scottish Parliament seat with some margin to spare in 1999. And in 2001, on Maclennan's retirement, Viscount John Thurso became the first hereditary peer from the half-reformed House of Lords be elected to the House of Commons, slightly increasing the Liberal Democrat majority over Labour.

INVERNESS EAST, NAIRN and LOCHABER

	2001		1997		1992 notional	
Electorate and turnout	66,452	63.9	65,701	72.7	63,321	72.5
Conservative	5,653	13.3	8,355	17.5	10,777	23.5
Labour	15,605	36.8	16,187	33.9	10,633	23.2
Lib Dem	9,420	22.2	8,364	17.5	12,249	26.7
SNP	10,889	25.6	13,848	29.0	11,513	25.1
SSP	892	2.1	–	–	–	–
Others	–		1,014 (3)		720	
MP	David Stewart (Lab)		David Stewart (Lab)		Russell Johnston(LD)	
					Inverness, Nairn and Lochaber	
Majority	4,716	11.1	2,339	4.9	736	1.6

Scottish Parliament Election 1999: SNP 13,825 (33.1), Labour 13,384 (32.0), Lib Dem 8,508 (20.3), Conservative 6,107 (14.6). Electorate 66,285, Turnout 63.1%. MSP: Fergus Ewing (SNP), Majority 441 (1.1).

This vast constituency, covering over 3,400 square miles, is the second largest in the United Kingdom. It is also a seat full of contrasts. Most of the new City of Inverness lies within this seat. The city is rapidly expanding, and has large council house estates that form Labour's main base, together with the nearby town of Nairn. Inland to the west, the seat includes the Great Glen and Loch Ness, as well as the ghastly resort town of Aviemore and huge Highland 'hunting and fishing' estates that provide hope for the Tories. In the west, one encounters impossibly beautiful places like Kinlochleven and the bleak surroundings of historic Glencoe. On the coast is the holiday town of Fort William, while the beautiful village of Arisaig and the larger fishing port of Mallaig look out onto the islands of Rum, Eigg and Muck.

In 1992, only 1,741 votes separated the four parties in this exciting four-way marginal. In the end, Sir Russell Johnston, the Liberal incumbent since 1964, won by only 458 votes from Labour (although after boundary changes his notional majority was 736). With the retirement of Sir Russell in 1997, it looked as if the seat was turning into a straight SNP-Labour contest. Labour's David Stewart won the Westminster electoral contest in 1997, while Fergus Ewing, husband of Margaret Ewing and son of Winnie Ewing, won by only 441 votes in the Scottish Parliamentary elections in May 1999. The election of the Ewing clan's newest recruit meant that, for 1999 at least, this constituency shared with Aberdeen South and Falkirk West the distinction of being the only three seats in Scotland where the MSP sent to Holyrood was of a different political affiliation from the MP elected to Westminster (since then, the Tory victory in the Ayr the Scottish Parliament's first by-election in 2000, and Tory Peter Duncan's victory over the SNP in Galloway and Upper Nithsdale in 2001 have added to the list). In 2001, David Stewart doubled his majority, as the SNP's share of the vote fell by 3.5 per cent, and the Liberal Democrat vote went up by more than 4.5 per cent to turn this seat back into a three-way marginal.

MORAY

	2001		1997		1992 *notional*	
Electorate and turnout	57,898	57.4	58,302	68.2	*57,743*	*71.6*
Conservative	7,677	23.1	10,963	27.6	*15,517*	*37.5*
Labour	8,332	25.1	7,886	19.8	*4,913*	*11.9*
Lib Dem	5,224	15.7	3,548	8.4	*2,466*	*6.0*
SNP	10,076	30.3	16,529	41.6	*18,444*	*44.6*
SSP	821	2.5		–		–
–		–				
Others	1,093 (2)		840			–
MP	Angus Robertson (SNP)		Margaret Ewing (SNP)		Margaret Ewing (SNP)	
Majority	1,744	5.2	5,566	14.0	*2,927*	*7.1*

Scottish Parliament Election 1999: SNP 13,207 (38.8), Labour 8,898 (26.5), Conservative 8,595 (25.6), Lib Dem 3,056 (9.1). Electorate 58,388, Turnout 57.5%. MSP: Margaret Ewing (SNP), Majority 4,129 (12.3).

Believe it or not but one of the Ewings dominates this seat, and one of its smaller settlements is known as Dallas. But this is not oil-rich Texas, but rural Moray, which, like neighbouring Banff and Buchan, has its fair share of burghs and towns along the north coast, including Buckie (a bastion of the SNP) and Lossiemouth, birthplace of Ramsay MacDonald. However, this is not traditional Labour territory, though the party finds some comfort in the cathedral town of Elgin, the largest town in the seat. Through the heart of the constituency runs the River Spey, famous for its fishing and Scotch whisky distilleries, which produce such delights as Glenlivet and Glenfiddich. The seat also contains two RAF airbases at Kinloss and Lossiemouth.

Margaret Ewing, the daughter-in-law of Winnie Ewing (who became known as 'Madame Ecosse' for her defence of Scottish issues in the European Parliament) has held this seat since capturing it from Tory Alexander Pollock in 1987. Before her marriage into the Ewing dynasty, as Margaret Bain, she won East Dunbartonshire for the SNP in October 1974, before losing it in 1979. Margaret Ewing chose to devote all her energies to the Scottish parliament in 1999, and won comfortably despite a near doubling of Labour's share of the vote since 1992 (widely blamed on Alex Salmond's opposition to the war in Kosovo, and a backlash from service personnel in and around the two RAF bases), which edged the Tories narrowly into third place. The local election results held the same day as the Scottish parliamentary elections provided a warning to the SNP of Labour's growing strength in the constituency. The SNP lost overall control of Moray Council as Labour gained three seats. In 2001, a dramatic 10 per cent fall in the SNP vote combined with a strong performance from Labour (again finishing second place) served to reduce the SNP majority of the relatively unknown Angus Robertson by two-thirds.

ORKNEY and SHETLAND

	2001		1997		1992 actual	
Electorate and turnout	31,909	52.4	32,325	63.9	31,472	65.5
Conservative	3,121	18.7	2,527	12.2	4,542	22.0
Labour	3,444	20.6	3,775	18.3	4,093	19.8
Lib Dem	6,919	41.3	10,743	52.0	9,575	46.4
SNP	2,473	14.8	2,624	12.7	2,301	11.2
SSP	776	4.6	–	–	–	–
Anti–EU	–	–	820	4.0	–	–
Others	–		176 (2)		115	
MP	Alistair Carmichael (LD)		Jim Wallace (LD)		Jim Wallace (LD)	
Majority	3,475	20.8	6,968	33.7	5,033	24.4

Scottish Parliament Election 1999 (Orkney): Lib Dem 6,010 (67.4), Conservative 1,391 (15.6), SNP 917 (10.3), Labour 600 (6.7). Electorate 15,644, Turnout 57.0%. MSP: Jim Wallace (LD), Majority 4,619 (51.8).

Scottish Parliament Election 1999 (Shetland): Lib Dem 5,435 (54.5), Labour 2,241 (22.5), SNP 1,430 (14.3), Conservative 872 (8.7). Electorate 16,988, Turnout 58.7%. MSP: Tavish Scott (LD), Majority 3,194 (32.0).

The Orkney and Shetland Islands are one electoral entity for Westminster elections, but two separate constituencies for Scottish parliamentary elections. The Scotland Act 1998 addressed the fears in the two northern most islands of the United Kingdom that their concerns would be ignored in far-off Edinburgh by guaranteeing the existence of two separate seats for the Scottish Parliament. In the 1997 referendum, while both islands voted yes to the first question – Do you want a Scottish Parliament? - Orcadians voted narrowly against the tax-varying power (the only local authority area to do so apart from Dumfries and Galloway), while only 52 per cent of Shetlanders voted to vary income tax up or down by three pence in the pound.

Separated or cobbled together, since the 1950s the seats have produced the same outcome –Liberal and now Liberal Democrat victories. Jo Grimond, the Liberal leader from 1956 to 1967, held this seat ten times in a row from February 1950 until his retirement in 1983. His 28-year old successor, Jim Wallace steadily increased his majority from around 4,000 in 1983 to nearly 7,000 in 1997. In 1999, Wallace decided to concentrate on the Scottish parliament, becoming Deputy First Minister and Minister for Justice in the Labour-Liberal Democrat coalition. Wallace chose Orkney rather than Shetland, and won a staggering 67 per cent of the popular vote. His Liberal Democrat colleague, Tavish Scott, a farmer on the Shetland Island of Bressay, won a mere 55 per cent of the vote. In October 2000, Scott replaced Iain Smith (MSP for North East Fife) as Deputy Minister for Parliament (Liberal Democrat whip) in the Labour-Liberal Democrat coalition, before resigning from the post on 9 March 2001 over the Scottish Executive's fisheries policy. In June 2001, bereft of Wallace's personal vote,

Alistair Carmichael held the combined Westminster seat for the Liberal Democrats, but his majority was cut in half, after a stronger showing from both Labour and the Conservatives (at least on their dismal 1997 performance).

ROSS, SKYE and INVERNESS WEST

	2001		1997		1992 notional	
Electorate and turnout	55,915	62.3	55,780	71.6	52,810	73.2
Conservative	3,096	8.9	4,368	10.9	8,452	21.9
Labour	5,880	16.9	11,453	28.7	7,296	18.9
Lib Dem	18,832	54.1	15,472	38.7	14,957	38.7
SNP	4,901	14.1	7,821	19.6	7,276	18.8
Others	2,103 (4)		841 (2)		688	
MP	Charles Kennedy (LD)		Charles Kennedy (LD)		Charles Kennedy (LD) Ross, Cromarty and Skye	
Majority	12,952	37.2	4,019	10.1	6,505	16.8

Scottish Parliament Election 1999: Lib Dem 11,652 (32.9), Labour 10,113 (28.6), SNP 7,997 (22.6), Conservative 3,351 (9.5), Independent 2,302 (6.5). Electorate 55,845, Turnout 63.4%. MSP: John Farquhar Munro (LD), Majority 1,539 (4.4).

In 1983, when the seat was still known as Ross, Cromarty and Skye, a 23-year old Glasgow University graduate by the name of Charles Kennedy became the youngest MP elected that year, and the only SDP candidate to win a seat in the United Kingdom that did not already belong to a defecting Labour MP. The 1995 boundary changes saw Kennedy lose 10,000 voters in Easter Ross to Caithness and Sutherland, but gain a third of the expanding town of Inverness. Despite these alternations, this constituency is the largest in the United Kingdom, stretching through the southern half of Easter Ross, through rugged Wester Ross, and since 1983, including the island of Skye. The perennial political issues relate mainly to transport, especially high petrol prices, the status of ferry services run by Caledonian MacBrayne, and the high bridge tolls across the Skye Bridge.

In 2001, there were widespread reports in the media that Charles Kennedy might lose his seat to Labour. In retrospect, these claims seem laughable, but they were based on the close 1999 Scottish Parliamentary result when the Labour candidate, Donnie Munro, the former Runrig singer, came within 1,500 votes of unseating the posh-named Liberal Democrat Highland councillor and crofter, John Farquhar Munro. (The Independent candidate, Douglas Briggs also contributed to the close result by polling a respectable 6.5 per cent.). Instead, Kennedy amassed a huge personal vote in 2001, more than trebling his majority from 4, 000 in 1997 to nearly 13,000.

WESTERN ISLES

	2001		1997		1992 actual	
Electorate and turnout	21,706	60.6	22,983	70.1	22,785	70.4
Conservative	1,250	9.5	1,071	6.6	1,362	8.5
Labour	5,924	45.0	8,955	55.6	7,664	47.8
Lib Dem	849	6.5	495	3.1	552	3.4
SNP	4,850	36.9	5,379	33.4	5,961	37.2
Others	286		206		491	
MP	Calum MacDonald (Lab)		Calum MacDonald (Lab)		Calum MacDonald(Lab)	
Majority	1,074	8.2	3,576	22.2	1,703	10.6

Scottish Parliament Election 1999: Labour 7,248 (51.9), SNP 5,155 (36.9), Conservative 1,095 (7.9), Lib Dem 456 (3.3). Electorate 22,412, Turnout 62.3%. MSP: Alasdair Morrison (Lab), Majority 2,093 (15.0).

This 130-mile long constituency stretches from the northerly Butt of Lewis, down through the islands of Harris, Benbecula, North and South Uist as far as the islands of Barra and Vatersay. Despite its large geographical size, this constituency has the smallest electorate in the United Kingdom (if Orkney and Shetland are not counted separately, as happens in the Scottish parliamentary elections), numbering only 21,807. The seat is also unusual because 68 per cent of its population still speak Gaelic, while the same percentage live in detached housing (the highest percentage in the United Kingdom, but in wee crofts, not mansions) and almost everyone in the islands still observes the Sabbath. De-population remains the major issue in the islands, caused by the shortage of employment opportunities. Traditional industries such as fishing, whisky, farming and Harris Tweed are in decline. In 1999, major redundancies at oil fabrication yard, Lewis Offshore, the biggest private employer in the Western Isles, only exacerbated the problem.

In the post-war period, the Western Isles constituency has involved a straight fight between Labour and the SNP. From 1935 to 1970, the crofters of the island elected the Labour MP, Malcolm Macmillan. In 1970, Donald Stewart was the only SNP MP to be elected that year, and he served until 1987. In that year, the SNP vote collapsed, and Labour's Calum MacDonald was elected. MacDonald polled over 55 per cent of the popular vote in Labour's high tide of 1997, but he was sacked as a junior Scottish Office minister in July 1999. By 2001, his majority was halved in the face of a renewed challenge from the SNP. Labour's Alasdair Morrison held off the SNP's Alasdair Nicholson at the Scottish parliamentary elections in 1999. Morrison went on to become Deputy Minister for Enterprise and Lifelong Learning with responsibility for the Highlands and Islands and Gaelic, but he failed to survive Jack McConnell's reshuffle in late November 2001.

Lothians

| | Conservative | | Labour | | Liberal Democrat | | SNP | | Others | |
	Share of vote	Seats	Share of vote	Seats	Share of vote	Seats	Share of vote	Seats	Share of vote	Seats
2001	16.5	0	44.6	8	18.8	1	16.1	0	3.9	0
1997	19.2	0	45.9	8	14.9	1	18.4	0	1.5	0
1992	27.1	2	38.3	7	13.8	0	19.0	0	1.9	0
1999 C	15.9	0	40.2	8	15.7	1	26.9	0	1.4	0
1999 R	15.8	2	30.2	0	14.4	1	25.7	3	13.9	1

NOTE: 1999C=Scottish Parliamentary Elections Constituency vote; 1999R=Scottish Parliamentary Elections Regional top-up vote (7 seats available)

The Lothians region is nothing of the sort, because it does not include East Lothian, which now belongs to the South of Scotland region as a result of boundary changes. Six of the nine Westminster seats in the area are located within the city of Edinburgh. Livingston and Linlithgow lie to the west of the capital, while Midlothian lies to the south. By 1997, Labour held eight of the nine constituencies in the area, having gained Edinburgh Pentlands from the then Conservative Foreign Secretary, Malcolm Rifkind. In that year, the Tories also lost control of Edinburgh West to the Liberal Democrats, and have not won it back since. If this were England (and let's face it, Edinburgh is as close in character to England as Scotland ever gets) there should be a Conservative presence in the largely residential south and west of the city, but instead Scotland's middle-class electors engaged in a wholesale rejection of Thatcherism in the 1980s and 1990s. For example, in 1987, the Tories lost both Edinburgh Central and Edinburgh South, and they now poll only one in six of the vote in each case.

Traditionally, the SNP has not done well within the confines of Edinburgh. However, in 1999, the party dramatically improved their performance in the three seats to the south and west of the city (Pentlands, South and West) from 11.6 per cent in 1997 to an average of 20.8 per cent. In Edinburgh Central, East & Musselburgh and North & Leith, the SNP managed to increase their vote from only 18.3% in 1997 to an average of 26.5% in 1999. Outside the city, the party polled over 30 per cent in Midlothian, and over 36 per cent in both Livingston and Linlithgow, cutting Labour's 1997 majorities by two-thirds in both cases. Although the SNP gained no constituency seats, the party's strong perform-ance across the region ensured that they won three of the region's seven top-up seats (Fiona Hyslop, Kenny MacAskill and Margo Macdonald, the former MP for Govan). The other parties' list MSPs are also eminent. The two Tories are their leader David McLetchie and former Edinburgh West MP Lord James Douglas-Hamilton who served in three different legislative chambers in a bit over two years, while the sole Liberal Democrat is the former Liberal Leader and presiding officer of the parliament, David Steel. The other talking point in the Lothians was the election of Robin Harper, the Green candidate as the remaining list MSP. Harper polled 6.9 per cent, accounting for half of the 'other' votes cast in the list votes in the region. While Glasgow had elected a radical SSP politician, its Edinburgh rival had to be seen to be different by electing a nice, safe Green candidate.

In 2001, the SNP share of the vote in the region fell by nearly 11 percentage points on their 1999 performance as old voting trends reasserted themselves. In Edinburgh Pentlands, Sir Malcolm Rifkind increased his share of the vote by 4 per cent, but Labour held onto the seat with a reduced majority of 1,742. In Edinburgh West, John Barrett, the successor to Donald Gorrie, increased the Liberal Democrat majority by 4 per cent on 1997, a pattern repeated across the region as a whole. Indeed, the picture for the Liberal Democrats is even more encouraging if Edinburgh's six constituencies are analysed as a whole. In 2001, the Liberal Democrats polled 22.5% of the vote (as against 18.8% in the Lothians as a whole), compared to 19.9% for the Conservatives and 12.9% for the SNP (who admittedly polled better in the three seats outside the city). It appears that the Liberal Democrats are emerging as the preferred choice of Edinburgh's middle class voters, replacing the Conservatives. At Westminster elections, they are the clear challenger to Labour in the former Tory seats of Central and South, as well as North & Leith. However, the overall picture is of continued Labour dominance in the region: in 2001 they held onto their eight Westminster seats, polling only 1.3 per cent less than they had in 1997.

Local government

After the 1999 local elections, Edinburgh remains in Labour's hands, despite three Liberal Democrat gains. Labour has 31 councillors, with the Conservatives and the Liberal Democrats on 13 each and the SNP, who have never had a strong presence in the city, back on only one seat. Outside the city, Labour made gains from the SNP to reinforce its grip on West Lothian and Midlothian. The former authority contains the parliamentary constituencies of Linlithgow and Livingston, while the latter authority includes the town of Penicuik, which is actually located within the South of Scotland region.

EDINBURGH CENTRAL

	2001		1997		1992 notional	
Electorate and turnout	66,089	52.0	63,695	67.1	60,023	68.2
Conservative	5,643	16.4	9,055	21.2	12,013	29.4
Labour	14,495	42.1	20,125	47.1	15,770	38.5
Lib Dem	6,353	18.5	5,605	13.1	6,073	14.8
SNP	4,832	14.1	6,750	15.8	6,232	15.2
Green	1,809	5.3	607	1.4	610	1.5
Others	1,258		593 (2)		227	
MP	Alistair Darling (Lab)		Alistair Darling (Lab)		Alistair Darling (Lab)	
Majority	8,142	23.7	11,070	25.9	3,757	9.2

Scottish Parliament Election 1999: Labour 14,224 (38.0), SNP 9,598 (25.7), Lib Dem 6,187 (16.5), Conservative 6,018 (16.1), SSP 830 (2.2), Others 555 (1.5). Electorate 65,945, Turnout 56.7%. MSP: Sarah Boyack (Lab), Majority 4,626 (12.4).

Difficult as it now is to believe, prior to 1987, this seat was held by a Conservative, the late Sir Alex Fletcher, but Labour captured the seat in that year, and have held it ever since. As a result of the 1983 boundary changes, the city of Edinburgh lost one of its seven seats. The outcome was the creation of one of the most scenic urban constituencies in Britain. The historic Old Town, including Edinburgh Castle, the Royal Mile, Princes Street and Edinburgh University, was combined with the resplendent eighteenth century houses of the New Town to its north. However, the outcome of the 1995 Boundary Commission benefited Labour by removing the Tory-voting New Town (which was paired with Leith) plus the Stockbridge area, and replacing them with Moat and Stenhouse from Edinburgh West. The loss of the New Town combined with the acquisition of the solidly Labour-voting council estate of Stenhouse ensured that Alistair Darling, now the Secretary of State for Transport, nearly trebled his majority from 1992 to 1997.

Darling chose not to stand for the Scottish Parliament in the seat that includes both its temporary home (in the Church of Scotland headquarters) and the about-to-be-completed permanent Holyrood Parliament building. In May 1999, Sarah Boyack held the seat for Labour with a reduced majority as the SNP vote share rose to just above 25 per cent. Boyack served as the Minister for Transport and Environment before being dropped by Jack McConnell in late November 2001. Meanwhile, at the 2001 Westminster elections, the SNP vote share plummeted from over 25 per cent to 14 per cent as the Liberal Democrats pushed the Tories into third place for the first time. Because of the competition for second place between the other three major parties, Darling's percentage majority was only 2 per cent less than in 1997.

EDINBURGH EAST and MUSSELBURGH

	2001		1997		1992 notional	
Electorate and turnout	59,241	58.2	59,648	70.6	59,153	74.4
Conservative	3,906	11.3	6,483	15.4	10,568	24.0
Labour	18,124	52.6	22,564	53.6	19,669	44.7
Lib Dem	4,981	14.5	4,511	10.7	5,075	11.5
SNP	5,956	17.3	8,034	19.1	7,890	17.9
SSP	1,487	4.3	–	–	–	–
Others	–		526		801	
MP	Gavin Strang (Lab)		Gavin Strang (Lab)		Gavin Strang(Lab) Edinburgh East	
Majority	12,168	35.3	14,530	34.5	9,101	20.7

Scottish Parliament Election 1999: Labour 17,086 (46.2), SNP 10,372 (28.0), Conservative 4,600 (12.4), Lib Dem 4,100 (11.1), SSP 697 (1.9), Others 134 (0.4). Electorate: 60,167, Turnout 61.5%. MSP: Susan Deacon (Lab), Majority 6,714 (18.2).

This safe Labour seat comprises the area to the east and south of Arthur's Seat, as far as residential Portobello along the east coast, but also inland to include the run-down council schemes of Craigmillar and Niddrie. The 1995 Boundary Commission returned the town of Musselburgh to the confines of the city of Edinburgh, while the areas of Calton and Lochend to the north of the seat were ceded to Edinburgh North and Leith. The loss of Musselburgh during the period 1983 to 1992 proved no impediment to Dr Gavin Strang, who increased his hold over the area. Strang's sacking as Minister of Transport in July 1998 has also done nothing to dent his large majority over the SNP. Susan Deacon, the only person to win an appeal against Scottish Labour's controversial candidate selection process, faced a somewhat stronger challenge from the SNP in the Scottish Parliamentary Elections in 1999. However, Deacon won comfortably by 18 per cent of the vote, and served as Minister for Health and Community Care, before losing her job to her former deputy, Malcolm Chisholm in Jack McConnell's major reshuffle of November 2001 (Deacon was reported as having been offered the post of Social Justice Minister by McConnell, but refused and is now a backbencher).

EDINBURGH NORTH and LEITH

	2001		1997		1992 notional	
Electorate and turnout	62,731	53.0	61,617	66.5	60,235	71.4
Conservative	4,626	13.9	7,312	17.9	10,685	24.8
Labour	15,271	45.9	19,209	46.9	15,019	34.9
Lib Dem	6,454	19.4	5,335	13.0	5,038	11.7
SNP	5,290	15.9	8,231	20.1	8,749	20.3
SSP	1,334	4.0	–	–	–	–
Ind Labour	–	–	–	–	3,367	7.8
Others	259		858 (3)		162	
MP	Mark Lazarowicz(Lab)		Malcolm Chisholm(Lab)		Malcolm Chisholm(Lab) Edinburgh Leith	
Majority	8,817	26.5	10,978	26.8	4,334	10.1

Scottish Parliament Election 1999: Labour 17,203 (46.9), SNP 9,467 (25.8), Conservative 5,030 (13.7), Lib Dem 4,039 (11.0), SSP 907 (2.5). Electorate 62,976, Turnout 58.2%. MSP: Malcolm Chisholm (Lab), Majority 7,736 (21.1).

Originally to be re-named 'Edinburgh Inverleith', this constituency comprises the old seat of Edinburgh Leith, but since 1995 has gained the New Town and Stockbridge wards from Edinburgh Central, Calton and Lochend from Edinburgh East, while losing Muirhouse to Edinburgh West. Given the recent rejuvenation of the port of Leith, and the addition of the traditionally Tory-voting New Town, a challenge from the Conservatives might have been expected, but instead the Tory vote here, as in so much of Scotland, seems to be in terminal decline. The poverty of this seat is all too apparent in the slum area of Pilton, and even spruced up Leith remains essentially an old industrial area, despite the posh cafés and restaurants dotted along the quayside.

It is easy to forget the turbulent days of the left-wing maverick Ron Brown, hurler of the House of Commons mace, who was de-selected in 1990, and polled 4,000 votes as an Independent Labour candidate in 1992. His replacement, Malcolm Chisholm, a Campaign Group member, also proved controversial, resigning as a junior Scottish Executive minister in December 1997 over the cut in lone parent benefit. Chisholm has chosen to concentrate on his role as an MSP, and was surprisingly promoted to the Scottish Office as Deputy Minister for Health and Community Care by Henry McLeish in October 2000, before ousting his boss, Susan Deacon as Health Minister in the Jack McConnell reshuffle of November 2001. Chisholm's replacement at Westminster is Mark Lazarowicz, a well-known Edinburgh figure who previously chaired the Labour group on the city council. After polling a creditable 26 per cent in 1999, the SNP vote plummeted by 10 points in 2001, leaving Labour's percentage majority at Westminster virtually unchanged on its 1997 result.

EDINBURGH PENTLANDS

	2001		1997		1992 notional	
Electorate and turnout	60,484	64.4	59,635	76.7	59,432	77.3
Conservative	14,055	36.1	14,813	32.4	18,474	40.2
Labour	15,797	40.6	19,675	43.0	14,326	31.2
Lib Dem	4,210	10.8	4,575	10.0	5,828	12.7
SNP	4,210	10.8	5,952	13.0	7,203	15.7
SSP	555	1.4	–	–	–	–
Others	105		727 (3)		127	
MP	Lynda Clark (Lab)		Lynda Clark (Lab)		Malcolm Rifkind (Con)	
Majority	1,742	4.5	4,862	10.6	4,148	9.0

Scottish Parliament Election 1999: Labour 14,343 (36.2), Conservative 11,458 (28.9), SNP 8,770 (22.2), Lib Dem 5,029 (12.7). Electorate 60,029, Turnout 66.0%. MSP: Iain Gray (Lab), Majority 2,885 (7.3).

This is a seat of huge contrasts. The middle-class Tory-voting strongholds of the south west of Edinburgh include the residential areas of Colinton and Fairmilehead, as well as the new professional and managerial types in the affluent new housing along the A70 road south to Lanark. But venture into the Wester Hailes, Oxgangs or Sighthill council estates, and you encounter a world more characteristic of Irvine Welsh's *Trainspotting*.

Malcolm Rifkind, then Foreign Secretary, lost his 23-year tenure of the seat in 1997 when all the Scottish seats were shot down in one night. The victorious Labour candidate, Lynda Clark, a fellow barrister, became Advocate-General for Scotland in 1999. Despite Rifkind's promise to take the seat back in 2001, Labour's leasehold on the constituency remains, even if the former Foreign Secretary succeeded in cutting Clark's majority in half on a swing of 3 per cent, some way short of the 5.3 per cent required. The Scottish Parliament seat was also won by Labour, after Scottish Oxfam organiser Iain Gray comfortably beat off the challenge of David McLetchie, the leader of the Scottish Conservatives (McLetchie, however, became a list MSP for the Lothian region). Gray was recently promoted from Deputy Minister for Social Justice to Minister for Social Justice, after the sacking of Jackie Baillie (Dumbarton) in the McConnell reshuffle of late 2001.

EDINBURGH SOUTH

	2001		1997		1992 notional	
Electorate and turnout	64,437	57.7	62,467	71.8	61,638	72.0
Conservative	6,172	16.6	9,541	21.3	14,270	32.2
Labour	15,671	42.2	20,993	46.8	18,426	41.5
Lib Dem	10,172	27.4	7,911	17.6	5,855	13.2
SNP	3,683	9.9	5,791	12.9	5,719	12.9
SSP	933	2.5	–	–	–	–
Others	535		602 (2)		108	
MP	Nigel Griffiths (Lab)		Nigel Griffiths (Lab)		Nigel Griffiths (Lab)	
Majority	5,499	14.8	11,452	25.5	4,156	9.4

Scottish Parliament Election 1999: Labour 14,869 (37.1), SNP 9,445 (23.5), Lib Dem 8,961 (22.3), Conservative 6,378 (15.9), Others 482 (1.2). Electorate 64,100, Turnout 62.6%. MSP: Angus MacKay (Lab), Majority 5,424 (13.5).

In 1987, it seemed remarkable that Labour had gained this seat from the Conservative, Michael Ancram. The victor, Nigel Griffiths, now Under-Secretary of State at the Department of Trade and Industry, could marvel at his triumph in a constituency that included the affluent residential areas of Newington, Merchiston and large parts of Morningside. His new constituency contained one of the highest proportions (47.6) of professional and managerial workers in Scotland, many of them civil servants. Not even the presence of 20 per cent non-Scottish (mainly English) residents, the highest proportion in Scotland, was sufficient to halt the Tory decline in this seat.

Labour's Angus MacKay won the Scottish parliamentary elections in May 1999. MacKay, who served as Minister for Finance and Local Government under Henry McLeish, before being sacked from the Scottish Executive by Jack McConnell in November 2001, finished well ahead of the SNP. Despite this creditable second place, Edinburgh South is not natural territory for the SNP. Even in 1999, the party only polled 23.5 per cent, well below their national average of 28.7 per cent. Indeed, in 2001 the SNP vote share plummeted to less than one in ten as they finished fourth behind the Conservatives. Meanwhile, the Liberal Democrats replaced the Conservatives as the clear alternative to Labour at a Westminster level.

EDINBURGH WEST

	2001		1997		1992 notional	
Electorate and turnout	62,503	63.2	61,133	77.9	*61,995*	*83.2*
Conservative	8,894	22.5	13,325	28.0	*19,715*	*38.2*
Labour	9,130	23.1	8,948	18.8	*8,961*	*17.4*
Lib Dem	16,719	42.4	20,578	43.2	*15,424*	*29.9*
SNP	4,047	10.3	4,210	8.8	*6,471*	*12.5*
SSP	688	1.7	–	–	*–*	*–*
Others	–		570 (3)		*1,027*	
MP	John Barrett (LD)		Donald Gorrie (LD)		James Douglas-Hamilton (Con)	
Majority	7,589	19.2	7,253	15.2	*4,291*	*8.3*

Scottish Parliament Election 1999: Lib Dem 15,161 (36.5), Conservative 10,578 (25.4), Labour 8,860 (21.3), SNP 6,984 (16.8). Electorate 61,747, Turnout 67.3%. MSP: Margaret Smith (LD), Majority 4,583 (11.0).

The Edinburgh West constituency represents the home of the educated Edinburgh elite, including the catchment area of Edinburgh High School, one of the best comprehensive schools in Scotland. The close proximity of this sought after school has helped to push up property values in the already prosperous Cramond, Barton, Blackhall and Corstorphine residential areas. The 1995 boundary review expanded the seat much further to the west, taking Queensferry from Linlithgow and Kirkliston from Livingston.

The constituency is now safely in Liberal Democrat hands. Finally ousted in 1997, the Conservative MP, Lord James Douglas-Hamilton, the Conservative Scottish Office Minister, had clung onto the seat in a series of close contests in the period from 1983 to 1992. He scraped home with a majority of 498 in 1983, by 1,234 votes in 1987, and by only 879 in 1992 (though his notional majority after boundary changes was much higher at 4,291). After unsuccessfully contesting the seat on four occasions from 1970 Donald Gorrie, an Edinburgh councillor in Corstorphine, aged 64, finally triumphed in 1997 with a resounding majority of over 7,000 over Douglas-Hamilton. Indeed, between 1992 and 1997, the Conservative share of the vote fell by over 10 per cent. In 1999, Edinburgh city councillor Margaret Smith defeated Lord James Douglas-Hamilton (now known as Lord Selkirk) at the Scottish parliamentary elections, having first beaten Gorrie in a battle for the Liberal Democrat nomination. (However, both Gorrie and Douglas-Hamilton lived on to fight another day – Gorrie was subsequently elected as a list MSP in the Central Region, while Douglas-Hamilton was elected on the Lothian list). In the 2001 Westminster election, John Barrett increased the Liberal Democrat majority by 4 per cent. Labour and Conservative now vie with each other for second place, a remarkable turn around from 1992 when Labour finished a distant third.

LINLITHGOW

	2001		1997		1992 notional	
Electorate and turnout	54,603	58.0	53,706	73.8	53,066	77.1
Conservative	2,836	9.0	4,964	12.5	5,613	13.7
Labour	17,207	54.4	21,469	54.1	20,137	49.2
Lib Dem	2,628	8.3	2,331	5.9	2,843	7.0
SNP	8,078	25.5	10,631	26.8	12,340	30.2
SSP	695	2.2	–	–	–	–
Others	211		259		–	
MP	Tam Dalyell (Lab)		Tam Dalyell (Lab)		Tam Dalyell (Lab)	
Majority	9,129	28.8	10,838	27.3	7,797	19.1

Scottish Parliament Election 1999: Labour 15,247 (45.1), SNP 12,319 (36.5), Conservative 3,158 (9.4), Lib Dem 2,643 (7.8), Others 415 (1.2). Electorate 54,262, Turnout 62.3%. MSP: Mary Mulligan (Lab), Majority 2,928 (8.7).

Previously known as West Lothian, this seat has been home to Tam Dalyell, currently 'Father of the House', since his victory in a by-election in 1962. Dalyell's opposition to devolution based on the West Lothian question not only bears the name of his old constituency, it has meant that at every general election since 1962, the Labour MP has faced a determined challenge from the SNP, but on twelve successive occasions he has emerged the victor.

The 1983 Boundary Commission reduced the rapidly expanding electorate of West Lothian by removing Livingston and making the ancient burgh of Linlithgow the focal point of the constituency. Outside the main town, the seat follows the path of the M8 motorway between Glasgow and Edinburgh, characterised by the disfigured slag heaps from the era of shale-mining around the villages of Armadale, Bathgate (home of the former British Leyland car plant, and scene of 3,100 job losses after Motorola closed its mobile phone factory in 2001), Blackburn and Whitburn. These former mining and manufacturing areas have provided the main battleground between Labour and the SNP at council elections in recent years. The West Lothian Council elections in 1999 ended up with Labour winning 20 seats to the SNP's 11.

At the 1999 Scottish Parliamentary Elections, facing a strong challenge from the SNP, and without the personal following of Tam Dalyell, Mary Mulligan, former Edinburgh City Council housing convenor, saw Labour's majority reduced to around 3,000. Mulligan is now Deputy Minister for Health and Community Care in the Scottish Executive, following Jack McConnell's reshuffle of November 2001. The eventual retirement of Dalyell should also make the Labour-SNP contest at Westminster a great deal closer in the future.

LIVINGSTON

	2001		1997		1992 notional	
Electorate and turnout	64,852	55.6	60,296	71.0	58,068	73.1
Conservative	2,995	8.3	4,028	9.4	7,689	18.1
Labour	19,108	53.0	23,510	54.9	19,461	45.9
Lib Dem	3,969	11.0	2,876	6.7	3,857	9.1
SNP	8,492	23.6	11,763	27.5	11,013	26.0
SSP	1,110	3.1	–	–	–	–
Others	359		657 (2)		425	
MP	Robin Cook (Lab)		Robin Cook (Lab)		Robin Cook (Lab)	
Majority	10,616	29.5	11,747	27.4	8,448	19.9

Scottish Parliament Election 1999: Labour 17,313 (47.3), SNP 13,409 (36.7), Conservative 3,014 (8.2), Lib Dem 2,834 (7.8). Electorate 62,060, Turnout 58.9%. MSP: Bristow Muldoon (Lab), Majority 3,904 (10.7).

Lothian region's only New Town formed the basis for this new seat in 1983, when large chunks of Midlothian and West Lothian were welded together. Robin Cook, MP for Edinburgh Central since February 1974, had seen his constituency disappear into Edinburgh North and a new Edinburgh Central. Cook has survived, by only 5,000 votes in Labour's 1983 nadir, but very comfortably over the SNP since then. The former Foreign Secretary and now Leader of the House even increased his majority by 2 per cent in 2001, as the SNP's share of the vote fell by 4 per cent.

The town of Livingston provides the best hunting ground for the SNP, but Labour retains a strong presence in the Calders, and in the ex-mining villages of Broxburn and Uphall. Cook's decision to stay at Westminster meant a much harder battle with the SNP at the Scottish Parliament elections in 1999. Bristow Muldoon's majority was roughly a third of Cook's, and the SNP vote went up by nearly 9 percentage points on its 1997 performance. In 2001, the Liberal Democrats pushed the Conservatives into fourth place, although neither party has any real presence here.

MIDLOTHIAN

	2001		1997		1992 notional	
Electorate and turnout	48,625	59.1	47,600	74.1	47,952	74.1
Conservative	2,748	9.6	3,842	10.9	6,242	17.6
Labour	15,145	52.7	18,861	53.5	17,120	48.2
Lib Dem	3,686	12.8	3,235	9.2	3,552	10.0
SNP	6,131	21.3	8,991	25.5	8,256	23.2
SSP	837	2.9	–	–	–	–
Others	177		320		377	
MP	David Hamilton (Lab)		Eric Clarke (Lab)		Eric Clarke (Lab)	
Majority	9,014	31.4	9,870	28.0	8,864	24.9

Scottish Parliament Election 1999: Labour 14,467 (48.6), SNP 8,942 (30.1), Lib Dem 3,184 (10.7), Conservative 2,544 (8.6), Others 618 (2.1). Electorate 48,374, Turnout 61.5%. MSP: Rhona Brankin (Lab), Majority 5,525 (18.6).

The Midlothian seat situated south of Edinburgh is mainly working class in character, with a high number of council house tenants (41.5 per cent) by Lothian standards. Former mining communities such as Bonnyrigg, Dalkeith, Easthouses and Newtongrange dominate the constituency make up. The 1983 boundary changes saw the removal of the prosperous Edinburgh commuter belt areas of Currie and Balerno, strengthening Labour's hold over the area. In 1995, Midlothian lost Penicuik's 13,000 voters to Tweeddale, Ettrick and Lauderdale.

In 2001, Eric Clarke, a former coalminer, and MP since 1992, stood down in favour of another former miner, David Hamilton. The SNP vote in the seat had risen dramatically from 10% in 1987 to 22% in 1992, rose again to 25% in 1997, and peaked at 30% in the Scottish parliament elections, before falling back to only 21% in 2001. At the Scottish parliamentary elections, Rhona Brankin, a former chair of the Scottish Labour party, held onto the seat by just over 5,000 votes from the SNP. Brankin initially served as Deputy Minister for Culture and Sport under Donald Dewar, before being shifted to Rural Development by Henry McLeish. Jack McConnell, the new First Minister eventually sacked her in November 2001. Labour also dominate local politics in Midlothian. In the 1999 council elections, 17 of the 18 seats fell to Labour, including the only one previously held by the SNP.

Mid Scotland and Fife

	Conservative		Labour		Liberal Democrat		SNP		Others	
	Share of vote	Seats	Share of vote	Seats	Share of vote	Seats	Share of vote	Seats	Share of vote	Seats
2001	18.4	0	39.4	6	15.6	1	23.4	2	3.2	0
1997	21.1	0	40.0	6	12.6	1	25.3	2	1.0	0
1992	30.2	3	33.4	5	13.1	1	23.1	0	0.2	0
1999 C	18.6	0	36.4	6	12.8	1	31.4	2	0.8	0
1999 R	18.6	3	33.4	0	12.7	1	28.7	3	6.7	0

NOTE: 1999C=Scottish Parliamentary Elections Constituency vote; 1999R=Scottish Parliamentary Elections Regional top-up vote (7 seats available)

Mid Scotland and Fife is an odd collection of nine parliamentary constituencies, covering the whole of Fife, plus four large constituencies to the west and north – Ochil, Perth, Stirling and Tayside North. The southern part of the old Kingdom of Fife is resolutely Labour, with the party enjoying huge Westminster majorities over the SNP in the working-class areas of Fife Central, Dunfermline East and West and Kirkcaldy. However, go elsewhere in the region, and the political mosaic becomes multi-coloured. Ever since 1987, Menzies Campbell, the Liberal Democrats' Foreign Affairs Spokesman, has held middle-class Fife North East, centred on the historic golfing and university town of St Andrews. At Holyrood, Iain Smith also holds the seat for the Liberal Democrats. To the west lies the Labour-SNP marginal seat of Ochil, created by the 1995 Boundary Commission, largely out of the old Clackmannan seat. Labour has always comfortably held the seat at Westminster elections, but George Reid came within 1,303 votes of gaining the SNP's third target seat at the Scottish parliamentary elections in 1999. To the north of Ochil lies Perth, won by the SNP in a by-election in 1995, and held by the party ever since. However, in 2001, the SNP vote share fell by 7 per cent, and Annabelle Ewing, the latest member of the Ewing clan, won by only 48 votes from the Tory candidate, Elizabeth Smith. Ewing was only saved because the Tory vote share failed to improve on its 1997 performance, while Labour competed strongly for second place. To the west of Perth lies Stirling, where Michael Forsyth, the Secretary of State for Scotland held on in 1992, only to be swept away in the Labour landslide of 1997. Since then, Labour have increased their hold over the seat. Finally, Tayside North, once a safe Tory seat held by the Euro-sceptic Bill Walker, was one of the SNP's two gains from the Conservatives in 1997 (the other being Galloway and Upper Nithsdale). Since then, the SNP has had no problem in holding onto either the Holyrood seat, held by its new leader John Swinney or the Westminster seat, held by newcomer Peter Wishart.

In 1999, the Mid Scotland and Fife region was characterised by a very strong performance by the SNP. The party's 31.4 per cent constituency vote share was well above the national average of 28.7 per cent, and included an impressive 31 per cent share of the vote in Kirkcaldy, halving Labour's 1997 majority. Although the SNP failed to win Ochil, it held onto Perth and Tayside North, and gained three of the area's top-up seats, the same as the Tories who failed to win a single constituency seat, despite having held three of the seats in the area as recently as 1992. The SNP members are Bruce Crawford, Tricia Marwick and George Reid, while the Conservatives are Keith Harding, Murdo Fraser (Nick Johnson having stood down as a regional list MSP in August 2001) and Brian Monteith. Apart from their stronghold in Fife North East, this region is not natural territory for the Liberal Democrats. Despite this, they managed to gain one top-up seat in 1999, which went to the former Conservative MP for Delyn in north Wales, Keith Raffan.

Local government

Clackmannanshire local authority is comprised mostly of the Ochil parliamentary constituency, including the towns of Alloa and Clackmannan. However, its neighbouring authority, Stirling still controls Bridge of Allan, which belongs to Ochil at a parliamentary level. Perth and Kinross are combined for the purposes of local council elections, but separated for parliamentary purposes with Kinross belonging to Ochil. To complicate matters further, large chunks of Perth and Kinross council also belong to Tayside North at a parliamentary level. Fife makes more geographical sense, comprising the old Kingdom of Fife, including the towns of Kirkcaldy, Dunfermline, Glenrothes and St Andrews. In Clackmannanshire, Labour lost overall control as the SNP gained six seats to move one ahead of Labour by a margin of nine to eight. The lone Tory now holds the balance of power on the council. In Stirling, the loss of a single seat to the Tories also meant that Labour lost overall control. Labour now has 11 councillors to nine held by the Tories, with the SNP holding the balance of power on two seats. However, the region did not provide unbridled good news for the SNP. The party lost overall control of Perth and Kinross, as the Conservatives gained nine seats. The SNP now have 16 councillors, with the Tories on 11, and Labour and the Liberal Democrats on six each. Finally, in Fife, Labour stayed in overall charge holding 43 seats, with the Liberal Democrats occupying second place on 21, and the SNP on nine. After winning no seats in Fife in 1995, the Tories gained one in 1999.

DUNFERMLINE EAST

	2001		1997		1992 notional	
Electorate and turnout	52,811	57.0	52,133	70.2	50,674	75.2
Conservative	2,838	9.4	3,656	10.0	6,211	16.3
Labour	19,487	64.8	24,441	66.8	23,966	62.9
Lib Dem	2,281	7.6	2,164	5.9	2,329	6.1
SNP	4,424	14.7	5,690	15.6	5,619	14.7
SSP	770	2.6	–	–	–	–
Others	286		632		–	
MP	Gordon Brown (Lab)		Gordon Brown (Lab)		Gordon Brown (Lab)	
Majority	15,063	50.1	18,751	51.3	17,755	46.6

Scottish Parliament Election 1999: Labour 16,576 (55.9), SNP 7,877 (26.6), Conservative 2,931 (9.9), Lib Dem 2,275 (7.7). Electorate 52,087, Turnout 56.9%. MSP: Helen Eadie (Lab), Majority 8,699 (29.3).

Dunfermline East has been the personal fiefdom of Gordon Brown since 1983, and the Chancellor of the Exchequer's seat is one of the safest for Labour in the United Kingdom. Despite its name, the constituency does not include any of the town of Dunfermline, most of which went to Dunfermline West in the 1983 boundary changes, nor does it have any real link with Dunfermline. The heart of the seat lies in the former mining areas in Fife around the towns of Cowdenbeath and Lochgelly. The politically sensitive Rosyth Royal Navy Dockyard still clings for survival decommissioning nuclear submarines, but the area felt betrayed in 1993 when the Tory Government awarded the key contract to refit Britain's fleet of nuclear submarines to its rival Devonport. In February 2002, Intelligent Finance (IF) brought some hope to the area by announcing that it was locating its new administration and call centre in Cowdenbeath.

The seat, known in the inter-war years as Fife West, was home to the Communist MP, Willie Gallagher, and Communist regional councillors were elected in the area as recently as 1990. However, the fall of the Berlin Wall led to the collapse of the Communists and their disappearance from local politics, leaving Gordon Brown to poll over 60 per cent of the popular vote, with the SNP trailing a distant second on around 15 per cent. Labour's Helen Eadie, a well-known local councillor, also holds a commanding majority in the Scottish parliament, although the SNP share of the vote rose by 11 per cent on its 1997 performance.

DUNFERMLINE WEST

	2001		1997		1992 notional	
Electorate and turnout	54,293	57.1	52,538	69.3	51,187	75.9
Conservative	3,166	10.2	4,606	12.6	8,948	23.0
Labour	16,370	52.8	19,338	53.1	16,132	41.5
Lib Dem	4,832	15.6	4,963	13.6	6,066	15.6
SNP	5,390	17.4	6,984	19.2	7,703	19.8
SSP	746	2.4	–	–	–	–
Others	471		543		–	
MP	Rachel Squire (Lab)		Rachel Squire (Lab)		Rachel Squire (Lab)	
Majority	10,980	35.4	12,354	33.9	7,184	18.5

Scottish Parliament Election 1999: Labour 13,560 (44.2), SNP 8,539 (27.8), Lib Dem 5,591 (18.2), Conservative 2,981 (9.7). Electorate 53,112, Turnout 57.8%. MSP: Scott Barrie (Lab), Majority 5,021 (16.4).

This constituency is mainly formed around Dunfermline, the former capital city of Scotland, and burial place of Scottish kings and queens, including Robert the Bruce in the town's ancient abbey. The town is strongly Labour, as are the industrial towns of Culross, Kincardine and Torryburn that stretch west along the north bank of the River Forth. Even with nearly two-thirds of its electors being owner-occupiers and 30 per cent working in professional or managerial jobs, this seat is thoroughly safe for Labour.

English-born Rachel Squire has been the town's Labour MP since 1992, and the opposition vote has been split fairly evenly between her three rivals, but the SNP emerged as the clear challenger in the Scottish Parliamentary elections. Even in 1999 however, Labour's candidate Scott Barrie still finished over 5,000 votes ahead of the SNP. By 2001, the SNP vote share had fallen back to around 17.5 per cent, and Squire was able to increase her percentage majority by around 1.5 per cent. In 1997, the Tory performance was truly dismal as the party fell from second to fourth place, and there they stayed in 2001. As elsewhere in Scotland, the Liberal Democrats have been the main beneficiaries of the Tory slump, but even in 2001, their vote only returned to its 1992 level.

FIFE CENTRAL

	2001		*1997*		*1992 notional*	
Electorate and turnout	59,597	54.6	58,394	69.8	*57,702*	*73.9*
Conservative	2,351	7.2	3,669	9.0	*7,440*	*17.5*
Labour	18,310	56.3	23,912	58.7	*21,627*	*50.7*
Lib Dem	2,775	8.5	2,610	6.4	*2,937*	*6.9*
SNP	8,235	25.3	10,199	25.0	*10,636*	*24.9*
SSP	841	2.6	–	–	–	–
Others	–		375		–	
MP	John MacDougall (Lab)		Henry McLeish (Lab)		Henry McLeish (Lab)	
Majority	10,075	31.0	13,713	33.6	*10,991*	*25.8*

Scottish Parliament Election 1999: Labour 18,828 (57.3), SNP 10,153 (30.9), Lib Dem 1,953 (5.9), Conservative 1,918 (5.8). Electorate 58,850, Turnout 55.8%. MSP: Henry McLeish (Lab), Majority 8,675 (26.4).

Fife Central used to contain the ex-coal mining communities of Fife, but as a result of the 1983 boundary changes, these were ceded to Dunfermline East. The constituency now revolves around the New Town of Glenrothes, which is solidly Labour, as are the industrial towns of Buckhaven, Methil and Leven along the east coast.

The republican Willie Hamilton served as Labour MP for Fife West from 1950 until February 1974, and for Fife Central until his retirement in 1987, after surviving a bruising re-selection battle against Henry McLeish, then a local councillor for the Kennoway and Windygates wards in the constituency. On Hamilton's retirement in 1987 (he died in January 2000), McLeish took over the seat, and held onto it with more than half of the popular vote in both 1992 and 1997. In 1999, the SNP share of the vote rose to over 30 per cent, but at Westminster elections it remains stubbornly at 25 per cent, as with so many SNP-Labour contests in urban Scotland.

From 1997, McLeish was Minister of State for Scotland, and responsible for assisting the passage of the Scotland Bill through Parliament from 1997 to 1998. From May 1999, he served in the Scottish Executive, and was made the Minister for Enterprise and Lifelong Learning before taking over as Scottish First Minister after the premature death of Donald Dewar in October 2000. McLeish's Westminster seat was handed to John MacDougall, the former Fife councillor and boilermaker. The departure of McLeish from Westminster did nothing to dent Labour's 2001 majority, which remained over 10,000. The Tory vote has collapsed here, with the Liberal Democrats now occupying a distant third place behind the SNP. McLeish now contemplates life without ministerial office after being forced to step down as Scottish First Minister in November 2001 over the £36,000 in expenses claimed from sub-letting his constituency office while he was a Westminster MP.

FIFE NORTH EAST

	2001		1997		1992 notional	
Electorate and turnout	61,900	56.1	58,794	71.2	54,244	77.2
Conservative	8,190	23.6	11,076	26.5	16,129	38.5
Labour	3,950	11.4	4,301	10.3	2,337	5.6
Lib Dem	17,926	51.7	21,432	51.2	19,432	46.4
SNP	3,596	10.4	4,545	10.9	3,598	8.6
SSP	610	1.8	–	–	–	–
Others	420		485		379	
MP	Menzies Campbell (LD)		Menzies Campbell (LD)		Menzies Campbell (LD)	
Majority	9,736	28.1	10,356	24.8	3,303	7.9

Scottish Parliament Election 1999: Lib Dem 13,590 (37.8), Conservative 8,526 (23.7), SNP 6,373 (17.7), Labour 5,175 (14.4), Independent 1,540 (4.3), Others 737 (2.1). Electorate 60,886, Turnout 59.0%. MSP: Iain Smith (LD), Majority 5,064 (14.1).

Situated in the land between the firths of the Tay and the Forth, Fife North East is overwhelmingly middle-class in contrast to the rest of Fife. The constituency contains the historic east coast town of St Andrews, home of golf, and temporarily Prince William, along with several thousand other students at the town's ancient university. The rest of the seat is peppered with small towns like the fabulously-named Auchtermuchty, Cupar, Newport on Tay, Kilrenny, Crail and Tayport, which are full of middle-class residents, nearly 65 per cent of whom own their own homes. Good farming land, tourist areas (especially the visitor attraction of Falkland Palace) and golf courses fill the gaps between the communities that have changed little in recent years.

Unlike the rest of Fife, this seat has proved fertile territory for the Liberal Democrats. In 1987, Menzies (but known as 'Ming') Campbell won the seat in 1987 at his third attempt from the Conservative, Barry Henderson. 'Ming' resisted the temptation to sit in the Scottish Parliament, and the new Liberal Democrat candidate Iain Smith had no problem in defeating his Tory challenger into a distant second place. Smith was Deputy Minister for Parliamentary Business (Liberal Democrat whip) in the Scottish Executive before being dropped in the McLeish reshuffle of October 2000. At Westminster, the Lib Dems now poll over 50 per cent of the popular vote, while the Tory vote has fallen by 15 points since 1992. Meanwhile, Labour's vote had doubled, but only to 11 per cent, just ahead of the SNP.

KIRKCALDY

	2001		1997		1992 notional	
Electorate and turnout	51,559	54.6	52,266	66.9	50,837	74.4
Conservative	3,013	10.7	4,779	13.7	8,361	22.1
Labour	15,227	54.1	18,730	53.6	17,246	45.6
Lib Dem	2,849	10.1	3,031	8.7	3,671	9.7
SNP	6,264	22.2	8,020	22.9	8,561	22.6
SSP	804	2.9	–	–	–	–
Others	–		413		–	
MP	Lewis Moonie (Lab)		Lewis Moonie (Lab)		Lewis Moonie (Lab)	
Majority	8,963	31.8	10,710	30.6	8,685	23.0

Scottish Parliament Election 1999: Labour 13,645 (48.1), SNP 9,170 (32.4), Conservative 2,907 (10.3), Lib Dem 2,620 (9.2). Electorate 51,640, Turnout 54.9%. MSP: Marilyn Livingstone (Lab), Majority 4,475 (15.8).

Kirkcaldy is situated on the south east coast of Fife, more or less north of Edinburgh across the Firth of Forth. Home of Raith Rovers football club, the town is also birthplace of the architect Robert Adam and the philosopher Adam Smith. However, the free market ideas of Smith have no appeal at present in this industrial town; it is yet another Labour stronghold in Fife. The coastal towns of Burntisland and Kinghorn also vote Labour. The constituency lost the port of Methil in the 1983 boundary changes, but was left almost untouched in 1995.

Dr Lewis Moonie, a former consultant with Fife Health Board, was first elected in 1987, and has held the seat with massive majorities ever since. The SNP managed to halve Labour's majority at the 1999 Scottish Parliamentary elections polling nearly a third of the vote, but Marilyn Livingstone's tenure of the Holyrood seat still looks safe for 2003. At the 2001 Westminster election, Moonie, Under-Secretary of State for Defence since 2000, actually managed to increase his vote share on the 1997 result. Yet again, the pattern for urban Scotland is established at Westminster elections with the SNP struggling to reach 25 per cent, the Tory vote having halved since 1992, and the Liberals challenging them for third place.

OCHIL

	2001		1997		1992 notional	
Electorate and turnout	57,554	61.3	56,572	77.4	55,483	77.9
Conservative	4,235	12.0	6,383	14.6	10,367	24.0
Labour	16,004	45.3	19,707	45.0	18,620	43.1
Lib Dem	3,253	9.2	2,262	5.2	2,984	6.9
SNP	10,655	30.2	15,055	34.4	11,270	26.1
SSP	751	2.1	–	–	–	–
Others	405		379 (3)		–	
MP	Martin O'Neill (Lab)		Martin O'Neill (Lab)		Martin O'Neill (Lab) Clackmannan	
Majority	5,349	15.2	4,652	10.6	7,350	17.0

Scottish Parliament Election 1999: Labour 15,385 (41.7), SNP 14,082 (38.2), Conservative 4,151 (11.3), Lib Dem 3,249 (8.8). Electorate 57,083, Turnout 64.6%. MSP: Richard Simpson (Lab), Majority 1,303 (3.5).

The constituency is named after the scenic hills that form the backdrop to the New Zealand-like terrain in east central Scotland between Perth and Stirling. Ochil was formerly known as Clackmannan, but, following the 1995 boundary changes, it no longer contains any voters from Carron and Stenhousemuir, which now belong to Falkirk East. The industrial towns of Clackmannan, Alloa and Dollar did not constitute a large enough seat, so Ochil's boundary was extended eastward to include Kinross by the shores of Loch Leven, formerly in Perth and Kinross, and also westward to take in the Tory-voting Airthrey area from Stirling, including the picturesque village of Bridge of Allan.

The area has suffered heavily with the contraction of the textile industry in recent years. In February 1998, the Hodgsons knitwear company in Alva shed 145 jobs, while, shortly before the Scottish Parliamentary elections, Coats Viyella announced it would close its Alloa plant with the loss of a further 200 jobs, a double blow to the town after the closure of the Alloa Brewery by drinks giant Carlsberg Tetley in 1998.

Regardless of its name, the constituency has always been a battleground between Labour and the SNP. In February 1974, when the seat was known as Clackmannan and East Stirlingshire, George Reid, then a journalist and broadcaster, won the seat for the SNP before the present incumbent Martin O'Neill won it back in 1979, and he has held it comfortably ever since. O'Neill's decision to stay at Westminster gave George Reid another chance to wrest back the seat for the SNP, and he came within 1,303 votes of defeating Labour's Richard Simpson. Reid may have gained some comfort by becoming a list MSP for Mid Scotland and Fife, but the failure to take Ochil, the SNP' third target seat in 1999, signalled the end of the party's hopes of making any gains against Labour in its industrial heartland in that election. Meanwhile, Simpson is now Deputy Minister for Justice in the Scottish Executive, following Jack McConnell's reshuffle of November 2001.

In the May 1999 local elections (held on the same day as the Scottish elections), dissatisfaction with Clackmannan council saw Labour lose overall control, with the SNP gaining six seats, becoming the largest party with nine councillors to Labour's eight, and the single Tory holding the balance of power. By 2001, O'Neill was sent back to Westminster with a swing from Labour to the SNP of just over 2 per cent.

PERTH

	2001		1997		1992 notional	
Electorate and turnout	61,497	61.5	60,313	73.9	58,515	76.7
Conservative	11,189	29.6	13,068	29.3	18,159	40.5
Labour	9,638	25.5	11,036	24.8	5,922	13.2
Lib Dem	4,853	12.8	3,583	8.0	5,366	12.0
SNP	11,237	29.7	16,209	36.4	15,433	34.4
SSP	899	2.4	–	–	–	–
Others	–		655 (2)		–	
MP	Annabelle Ewing (SNP)		Roseanna Cunningham(SNP)		Nicholas Fairbairn (Con) Perth and Kinross*	
Majority	48	0.1	3,141	7.1	2,726	6.1

* Roseanna Cunningham (SNP) elected for Perth & Kinross at May 1995 by–election

Scottish Parliament Election 1999: SNP 13,570 (36.3), Conservative 11,543 (30.9), Labour 8,725 (23.3), Lib Dem 3,558 (9.5). Electorate 61,034, Turnout 61.3%. MSP: Roseanna Cunningham (SNP), Majority 2,027 (5.4).

Since the loss of Kinross to Ochil in 1995, the seat has become simply known as Perth. The prosperous and rapidly expanding town dominates the constituency, but the seat also includes some of the most fertile farmland in Scotland, not only for those who grow delicious strawberries and raspberries, but also for the Scottish Conservatives. Beautiful villages such as Glencarse and Bridge of Earn combine with small towns such as Auchterarder and the tourist haven of Crieff.

Traditionally, the Conservatives and the SNP have vied for control of this seat. In October 1974, the larger-than-life Nicholas Fairbairn won the seat by only 53 votes, but he defied the pundits (and his liver) by holding onto the seat until his death in 1995, when Roseanna Cunningham captured it for the SNP. In 1997, the former advocate consolidated her hold over the constituency by achieving a majority of over 3,000. In 1999, Cunningham, now the SNP's deputy leader, chose to stand down from her Westminster seat to become an MSP, and won Perth comfortably with a majority of just over 2,000. However, the warning signs came for the SNP at the local elections held the same day when the Tories gained nine seats, meaning that the SNP lost overall control of Perth and Kinross council.

Annabelle Ewing, daughter of Winnie Ewing, sister of Fergus and sister-in-law to Margaret, all of whom became MSPs in 1999, was handed the much more difficult task of defending Perth for the SNP at the 2001 General Election against a determined challenge from the Tory candidate, Elizabeth Smith. The most junior of the Ewing clan had already gained a good grounding in fighting elections having stood for the SNP in Stirling in the Scottish Elections in May 1999, and having come within 556 votes of winning the Hamilton South by-election in September 1999. The main issue during the 2001 campaign was the proposed closure of the maternity and paediatric departments at Perth Royal Infirmary. June 7 ended up being a long night in Perth Town Hall, before the latest of the Ewing family emerged as the victor by only 48 votes. The Tory candidate nearly won her party's third target seat, not from an increase in her own vote, but because of a 6 per cent drop in that of the SNP. Almost unnoticed, because of the drama of the SNP-Conservative contest, has been the dramatic rise in the Labour vote, which has almost doubled since 1992. The party have been able to exploit their support in the working class areas of Perth, including western Letham and Tulloch and now stand at around 25 per cent, transforming this seat into a three-way marginal.

STIRLING

	2001		1997		1992 notional	
Electorate and turnout	53,097	67.7	52,491	81.8	51,902	81.7
Conservative	8,901	24.8	13,971	32.5	16,607	39.2
Labour	15,175	42.2	20,382	47.4	16,371	38.6
Lib Dem	4,208	11.7	2,675	6.2	2,854	6.7
SNP	5,877	16.4	5,752	13.4	6,145	14.5
SSP	1,012	2.8	–	–	–	–
Others	757		178 (2)		410	
MP	Anne McGuire (Lab)		Anne McGuire (Lab)		Michael Forsyth (Con)	
Majority	6,274	17.5	6,411	14.9	236	0.6

Scottish Parliament Election 1999: Labour 13,533 (37.8), SNP 9,552 (26.7), Conservative 9,158 (25.6), Lib Dem 3,407 (9.5), Others 155 (0.4). Electorate 52,904, Turnout 67.7%. MSP: Sylvia Jackson (Lab), Majority 3,981 (11.1).

The town of Stirling itself is natural Labour territory, apart from the Tory-voting Viewforth district, but the constituency extends north and west into the tourist areas of the Trossachs, which have traditionally voted Conservative. The controversial Michael Forsyth won this seat for the Tories in 1983, and clung on by 548 votes in 1987 and by 703 votes in 1992. However, his hopes in 1997 were hampered two years earlier by the decision of the Boundary Commission to cede the Tory-voting Airthrey ward to Ochil, reducing his majority to an estimated 236. In the Tory rout of 1997, Labour's Anne McGuire defeated the Secretary of State for Scotland by a whopping 6,500 votes, and she even increased her percentage majority by nearly 2.5 per cent in 2001.

Although the local economy is thriving as a result of Scottish Amicable and the Bank of Bermuda locating to the area and the construction of the new £90 million Forthside shopping complex, the local Labour council managed to lose £800,000 from its accounts in 1998, closed two primary schools, and failed to do much about the shortage of parking spaces, not to mention the incomprehensible one-way system in the centre of the town. These local factors may have been responsible for Labour losing overall control of Stirling Council at the 1999 elections, as the Tories gained one seat from Labour, leaving the SNP to control the balance of power, something which was once determined here on the cut of a deck of cards. However, in the 1999 Scottish parliamentary elections held the same day, there was bad news for the Tories when their candidate Brian Monteith, a leading player in the Scottish Referendum 'No' campaign (known as 'Think Twice') was pushed into third place by the SNP, after a strong campaign by Annabelle Ewing, now MP for Perth. Sylvia Jackson, an Edinburgh University lecturer won the seat for Labour with a majority of nearly 4,000.

TAYSIDE NORTH

	2001		1997		1992 notional	
Electorate and turnout	61,645	62.5	61,398	74.3	59,626	76.1
Conservative	12,158	31.6	16,287	35.7	21,036	46.4
Labour	5,715	14.8	5,141	11.3	3,156	7.0
Lib Dem	4,365	11.3	3,716	8.2	3,579	7.9
SNP	15,441	40.1	20,447	44.8	17,597	38.8
SSP	620	1.6	–	–	–	–
Others	220		–		–	
MP	Peter Wishart (SNP)		John Swinney (SNP)		Bill Walker (Con)	
Majority	3,283	8.5	4,160	9.1	3,439	7.6

Scottish Parliament Election 1999: SNP 16,786 (44.1), Conservative 12,594 (33.1), Labour 5,727 (15.1), Lib Dem 2,948 (7.8). Electorate 61,795, Turnout 61.6%. MSP: John Swinney (SNP), Majority 4,192 (11.0).

Much of this large rural constituency comprises the historic counties of Perthshire and Angus, which formed the power base of Sir Alec Douglas-Home's Kinross & West Perthshire constituency from November 1963 when the new Prime Minister finally found a suitable by-election (thanks to George Younger, later Secretary of State for Scotland who vacated the seat) to befit his new status. In the 1983 boundary revisions, the names of the two constituencies in this area were changed to Perth & Kinross and Tayside North. In the 1990s changes, little was added to the latter seat, except the small cathedral city of Brechin, and the smaller town of Edzell, which were both ceded from Angus East. Although a predominantly rural seat, the town of Forfar dominates the eastern end, while further to'the west, there are a host of smaller towns such as Kirriemuir, Blairgowrie, Couper Angus, Dunkeld and Aberfeldy. The far western edge of the constituency borders on the Grampians, and is filled with lochs and forests. At the heart of the constituency lies the knitwear town of Pitlochry, as well as nearby Killiecrankie and Blair Atholl Castle. The skiing area of Glenshee, the historic town of Scone, once home of the Scottish kings, and Glamis Castle are all located within this extremely beautiful constituency.

This seat should be natural Conservative territory, and when it was fought first by Bill Walker (MP for Perth and East Perthshire from 1979 to 1983) in 1983, he won with a majority of just over 10,000. However, the Tory Euro-sceptic's majority over the SNP gradually dwindled. In 1997, John Swinney, who was later elected SNP leader after Alex Salmond's retirement in July 2000, gained the seat from Walker by a whopping majority of over 4,000. In 1999, Swinney chose to stand down from Westminster to devote all his time to the new Scottish Parliament. He held on easily at the Scottish elections, and unlike in neighbouring Perth, his successor at Westminster, Peter Wishart, a musician with the former Scottish rock band Runrig had no problems holding off the Tory challenge from rising star, Murdo Fraser. Although Wishart's own vote fell by over 4.5 per cent, the Tory vote fell by a similar amount.

North East Scotland

	Conservative		Labour		Liberal Democrat		SNP		Others	
	Share of vote	Seats	Share of vote	Seats	Share of vote	Seats	Share of vote	Seats	Share of vote	Seats
2001	18.8	0	31.0	5	22.3	2	25.8	2	2.1	0
1997	22.4	0	30.9	5	18.9	2	26.1	2	1.7	0
1992	32.1	2	25.2	3	16.5	1	25.6	2	0.5	0
1999 C	17.8	0	26.2	4	21.2	3	33.1	2	1.7	0
1999 R	18.3	3	25.5	0	17.5	0	32.4	4	6.5	0

NOTE: 1999C=Scottish Parliamentary Elections Constituency vote; 1999R=Scottish Parliamentary Elections Regional top-up vote (7 seats available)

The North East region covers Aberdeen and Dundee, together with the rural areas surrounding both cities. To the north of Aberdeen lies the rapidly expanding seat of Gordon and the farming and fishing area of Banff and Buchan. To the south and west of the Granite City lies the rich farming land of Aberdeenshire West and Kincardine. Around the city of Dundee (which has two constituencies to Aberdeen's three) lies Angus, centring on the old east coast fishing towns of Arbroath and Montrose.

At Westminster elections, Labour are all-powerful in both cities, although they have traditionally faced a stronger challenge from the SNP in Dundee than in Aberdeen. Gordon Wilson, the SNP's leader from 1974 until 1987, was MP for Dundee East. Neighbouring Angus has been an SNP seat ever since 1987 when Andrew Welsh gained it from the Conservatives. The city of Aberdeen technically gained an extra seat in the 1995 boundary changes, but the new electors were mostly pinched from surrounding Gordon and Aberdeenshire West and Kincardine, both of which have rapidly expanded as commuters from oil rich Aberdeen moved out of the city. Only the new seat of Aberdeen Central is wholly within the city's boundaries. Labour won all three Aberdeen seats in 1997, including the radically redrawn Aberdeen South, which was gained from the Tories.

In 1992, Malcolm Bruce, the Liberal Democrat MP for Gordon since 1983, survived by only 274 votes in the Tory mini-revival of that year, which saw the Conservatives win the highest share of the votes in the region, together with two gains - Aberdeen South from Labour and Kincardine and Deeside from the Liberal Democrats (who had won it at a by-election in 1991). In 1997, Bruce survived the radical redrawing of Gordon (in which he lost Liberal Democrat Bridge of Don and gained Tory Turriff), which appeared to give the Tories a notional majority of nearly 8,500. Bruce wisely ignored the psephologists and won by nearly 7,000 votes. Further north in Banff and Buchan, the SNP have consolidated their hold since Alex Salmond won the seat from the Tories in 1987. Salmond's decision in 2001 to stay on as a Westminster MP was vindicated when he polled nearly 55 per cent of the vote. His retirement from the Scottish Parliament also provoked a Scottish parliamentary election on the night of the Westminster election in which Salmond's replacement, Stewart Stevenson, easily held the seat for the SNP. To the west and south of Aberdeen, the redrawn Aberdeenshire West and Kincardine, regained by the Tories in 1992 after they had lost it at a by-election the previous year, was won back by the Liberal Democrats' Sir Robert Smith in 1997 and held again in 2001.

Aberdeen South was the only seat in the region to change hands in the 1999 Scottish parliamentary elections. Nicol Stephen, formerly a winner of the Kincardine and Deeside by-election for the Liberal Democrats in 1991, gained the seat from Labour by 1,760 votes as the Tories were pushed from second into third place. However, the Liberal Democrat gain masked a very strong showing from the SNP who polled a third of the vote across the region. The SNP performed strongly in the other two Aberdeen constituencies, causing Labour's majority fall to only 398 in North and 2,696 in Central. The party also did well in Dundee, but not quite in the way that they had expected. In Dundee East, where the SNP felt they had the best chance of taking a seat, they cut Labour's majority to less than 3,000, but in Dundee West, they came within 121 votes of winning. The Scottish parliamentary elections therefore created another two marginal seats for the SNP in addition to Aberdeen North and Dundee East. The party's failure to take these constituencies was compensated by the fact that it won four of the region's seven to-up seats (Brian Adam, Richard Lochhead, Irene McGugan and Shona Robison). If the SNP are to make further progress in 2003, then they must make these four constituency gains from Labour in the North East of Scotland. On the flip side, if Labour are to hold on to these seats in 2003, then they need to improve on a 26 per cent vote share, the party's lowest in any Scottish region in 1999. Meanwhile, the Tories made up for their failure to win any constituency seats in 1999 by gaining the region's three remaining top-up seats (David Davidson, Alex Johnstone and Ben Wallace). The Tory performance is particularly dreadful when one considers that as recently as 1983, they held five of the eight seats in the region (now increased to nine as a result of the 1995 boundary changes).

No Westminster seats changed hands in the region in 2001. While the SNP and Labour share of the vote remained virtually constant compared with 1997, the main beneficiaries were the Liberal Democrats who increased their vote by nearly 3.5 per cent at the expense of the Conservatives, whose vote share fell by roughly the same amount. Both sitting Liberal Democrat MPs – Malcolm Bruce in Gordon and Sir Robert Smith in Aberdeenshire West and Kincardine – increased their majorities over the second placed Conservatives.

Local government

This region roughly speaking comprises four local authorities: the city councils of Aberdeen and Dundee and the rural authorities of Aberdeenshire (mostly Gordon, Banff and Buchan and Aberdeenshire West and Kincardine combined), and Angus, the area around Dundee. In Aberdeen City, Labour held on to overall control of the council in 1999 by a single seat, despite losing seven councillors. The Liberal Democrats are now the main challengers boasting twelve councillors to Labour's twenty two. In Dundee, Labour lost overall control, as the SNP made sweeping gains. Labour have fourteen seats to the SNP's ten, with the four Tories and one Independent holding the balance of power. In Aberdeenshire, the council remains in no overall control with the SNP and the Liberal Democrats vying for supremacy at the expense of the Conservatives. In Angus (which includes the town of Brechin, part of Tayside North and therefore Mid Scotland and Fife), the SNP easily kept control of the council, holding onto 21 out of the 28 wards available.

ABERDEEN CENTRAL

	2001		1997		1992 notional	
Electorate and turnout	50,190	52.7	54,390	65.5	55,882	67.6
Conservative	3,761	14.2	6,944	19.5	10,872	28.8
Labour	12,025	45.5	17,745	49.8	16,269	43.1
Lib Dem	4,547	17.2	4,714	13.2	3,985	10.6
SNP	5,379	20.4	5,767	16.2	6,636	17.6
Others	717		446		–	
MP	Frank Doran (Lab)		Frank Doran (Lab)		NEW SEAT	
Majority	6,646	25.1	10,801	30.3	5,397	14.3

Scottish Parliament Election 1999: Labour 10,305 (38.9), SNP 7,609 (28.7), Lib Dem 4,403 (16.6), Conservative 3,655 (13.8), SSP 523 (2.0). Electorate 52,715, Turnout 50.3%. MSP: Lewis MacDonald (Lab), Majority 2,696 (10.2).

Central is the safest of Labour's three seats in Aberdeen, and it is now the only one which is a true city seat. Almost all the population growth associated with the oil industry has been on the outskirts of the city in Aberdeenshire West & Kincardine and Gordon which surround Aberdeen, and the radically reshaped North and South constituencies contain very little of the city itself. Created in the 1995 boundary changes, the coastal part of Central includes the hallowed turf of Pittodrie Stadium, home of Aberdeen FC, and the seat stretches along the Beach Esplanade from Seaton in the north to Footdee (pronounced 'Fittie') in the south. Inland, the constituency includes St Machar Cathedral and that part of the University of Aberdeen situated in Old Aberdeen at King's College. Working-class Seaton, Linksfield and Balgownie on the coast, run-down Tillydrone and slightly more diverse Hilton-Clifton area further to the west, were all taken from Aberdeen North in 1995 turning this seat into safe Labour territory. The Tories should have had a significant presence here, however, since the constituency includes the well-off wards of Rosemount, Queen's Cross, Harlaw and Rubislaw, which were taken from Aberdeen South.

When the boundary changes were announced, Labour's Frank Doran, a former solicitor vanquished by Tory Raymond Robertson in Aberdeen South in 1992, fought a bitter selection battle for control of Aberdeen Central with Bob Hughes, who had been MP for Aberdeen North since 1979. Doran emerged victorious by only one vote, and went on to poll nearly 50 per cent of the popular vote in 1997. In the 1999 Scottish parliamentary elections, Lewis MacDonald, a parliamentary researcher for Doran, fought off a strong challenge from the SNP as the Liberal Democrats pushed the Tories into fourth place. MacDonald is now Deputy Minister for Enterprise, Transport and Lifelong Learning in the Scottish Executive. In June 2001, at the Westminster election, the Tory vote showed no signs of recovery, while the SNP established themselves as the clear alternative to Labour, but way behind on 20 per cent.

ABERDEEN NORTH

	2001		1997		1992 notional	
Electorate and turnout	52,876	57.4	54,331	70.7	53,944	69.7
Conservative	3,047	10.0	5,763	15.0	7,002	18.6
Labour	13,157	43.3	18,389	47.9	13,189	35.1
Lib Dem	4,991	16.4	5,421	14.1	8,952	23.8
SNP	8,708	28.7	8,379	21.8	8,443	22.5
Others	454		463		–	
MP	Malcolm Savidge (Lab)		Malcolm Savidge (Lab)		Bob Hughes (Lab)	
Majority	4,449	14.7	10,010	26.1	4,237	11.3

Scottish Parliament Election 1999: Labour 10,340 (37.2), SNP 9,942 (35.7), Lib Dem 4,767 (17.1), Conservative 2,772 (10.0). Electorate 54,553, Turnout 51.0%. MSP: Elaine Thomson (Lab), Majority 398 (1.4).

Only the solidly Labour council estates of Mastrick (definitely not the Dutch town made famous by the European Treaty signed there) and Northfield lie within the city of Aberdeen. The bulk of the new Aberdeen North is a consequence of the population growth brought by the rapid expansion of the North Sea oil industry in the 1980s. Vast numbers of private houses sprang up in the 1980s in the Bridge of Don, Danestone, Persley, Bucksburn and Kingswells areas outside Aberdeen. In 1995, Malcolm Bruce, MP for Gordon lost 20,000 voters to Aberdeen North mostly from the Bridge of Don and the area around Dyce, Aberdeen's airport, which serves the offshore oil industry. It was assumed that without his supposed power base in the Bridge of Don Bruce would lose Gordon in 1997. Instead, the Liberal Democrat MP increased his majority, while his former supporters deserted to Labour and the SNP in Aberdeen North.

Labour's Malcolm Savidge won the massively altered seat by a comfortable 10,000 votes in 1997, but Elaine Thomson, the Aberdeen campaign co-ordinator for Scotland Forward (the 'Yes' campaign umbrella group in the 1997 referendum) was in for a shock in the 1999 Scottish parliamentary elections. Brian Adam, an Aberdeen councillor for eleven years, and a senior hospital biochemist, came within 398 votes of winning the seat for the SNP. In 2001, Labour's majority was halved as the SNP's vote increased by 7 per cent. The Liberal Democrats succeeded in pushing the Tories into fourth place, repeating their feat of 1999. In the local council elections held the same day, they also gained a seat, while Labour lost seven, but not enough to shift the council from Labour's hands to no overall control.

ABERDEEN SOUTH

	2001		1997		1992 notional	
Electorate and turnout	59,025	62.5	60,566	72.8	60,352	73.1
Conservative	7,098	19.2	11,621	26.4	16,487	37.4
Labour	14,696	39.8	15,541	35.3	10,545	23.9
Lib Dem	10,308	27.9	12,176	27.6	11,762	26.7
SNP	4,293	11.6	4,299	9.8	5,336	12.1
Others	495		425		–	
MP	Anne Begg (Lab)		Anne Begg (Lab)		Raymond Robertson (Con)	
Majority	4,388	11.9	3,365	7.6	4,725	10.7

Scottish Parliament Election 1999: Lib Dem 11,300 (32.6), Labour 9,540 (27.5), Conservative 6,993 (20.2), SNP 6,651 (19.2), Others 206 (0.6). Electorate 60,579, Turnout 57.3%. MSP: Nicol Stephen (LD), Majority 1,760 (5.1).

The seat of this name was won by Raymond Robertson over Frank Doran in 1992, the only Conservative gain from Labour in that election that had not previously been a by-election loss. However, just under half of the old Aberdeen South was subsumed into Aberdeen Central in the 1990s boundary changes. All that remains is working-class and Labour-voting Torry situated south across the River Dee, windswept Cove, the marginal Ferryhill ward around the beautiful roses at the Duthie Park, and over-whelmingly Tory Hazlehead (also next to another rose-covered park). The old Kincardine and Deeside (now Aberdeenshire West and Kincardine) lost 45 per cent of its territory to Aberdeen South, including the working class areas of Kincorth and Nigg, and Liberal Democrat voting Cults, Bieldside and Peterculter, and most of the area west into Deeside as far as the village of Blackhall.

In 1997, the reshaped Aberdeen South produced a three-way marginal in which Labour's Anne Begg, a schoolteacher confined to a wheelchair with brittle bone disease, emerged victorious ahead of the Liberal Democrat Nicol Stephen. The vanquished Tory MP Raymond Robertson was pushed into a humiliating third place. More drama occurred at the 1999 Scottish parliamentary elections when Nicol Stephen, briefly the Liberal Democrat MP for Kincardine and Deeside when he won the by-election in 1991 (but lost it to the Tories a year later), took Aberdeen South in one of the few seats to change hands on the night. Shortly before the contest, the Liberal Democrats had dramatically won the Garthdee by-election on a swing of 23 per cent, indicating that a much smaller swing of 4 per cent might be achieved on 6 May. Stephen is now Deputy Minister for Education and Young People in the Labour-Liberal Democrat coalition at Holyrood. In June 2001, Anne Begg increased her share of the vote by 4.5 per cent and her majority by 1,000 as the Liberal Democrats stood still on their 1997 performance and the Tory vote dropped by 7 points. However, this seat is set to remain a three-way marginal in the future.

ABERDEENSHIRE WEST and KINCARDINE

	2001		1997		1992 notional	
Electorate and turnout	61,391	61.8	59,123	73.1	55,093	76.9
Conservative	11,686	30.8	15,080	34.9	19,123	45.2
Labour	4,669	12.3	3,923	9.1	2,886	6.8
Lib Dem	16,507	43.5	17,742	41.1	14,686	34.7
SNP	4,634	12.2	5,649	13.1	5,280	12.5
Others	418		808		381	
MP	Robert Smith (LD)		Robert Smith (LD)		George Kynoch (Con) Kincardine & Deeside	
Majority	4,821	12.7	2,662	6.2	4,437	10.5

Scottish Parliament Election 1999: Lib Dem 12,838 (35.9), Conservative 10,549 (29.5), SNP 7,699 (21.5), Labour 4,650 (13.0). Electorate 60,702, Turnout 58.9%. MSP: Mike Rumbles (LD), Majority 2,289 (6.4).

This is yet another seat on the outskirts of Aberdeen that has been radically altered by the 1990s boundary changes. The new constituency has effectively been pushed out of the city of Aberdeen, and in return, large parts of West Aberdeenshire have been transferred in from Gordon, including the rapidly expanding residential area of Westhill near Dyce Airport, and the towns of Kemnay and Alford in the countryside to the south and west of Inverurie. The old constituency, from 1983 until 1992, was known as Kincardine and Deeside. The Kincardine component largely survives, encompassing the ugly commuter belt of Portlethen south of Aberdeen, the scenic seaside resort of Stonehaven, and the farmland of the Mearns, setting for the famous Scottish trilogy by Lewis Grassic Gibbon. The Deeside part was butchered with the loss of Bieldside, Cults and Peterculter to Aberdeen South. However, the well-heeled (and sometimes snooty) communities of Royal Deeside such as Aboyne, Banchory, Ballater and Braemar are still included in this seat.

From 1983, the MP for Kincardine and Deeside was Alick Buchanan-Smith, who had represented the old Angus North and Mearns since 1964. The death of the centrist Tory in 1991 provoked a by-election in which Nicol Stephen emerged victorious for the Liberal Democrats. However, his tenure at Westminster was short-lived as George Kynoch overturned the result for the Tories in their minor recovery north of the border in April 1992. In 1997, Sir Robert Smith, a local landowner whose grand-father, Sir William Smith was Tory MP for Central Kincardineshire between 1924 and 1945, won the new seat for the Liberal Democrats. Although Smith nearly doubled his majority in 2001, the seat will probably remain a Liberal-Conservative marginal in the future, though the SNP substantially increased its share of the vote in the 1999 Scottish Parliamentary elections, leaving the Liberal Democrat Mike Rumbles just over 2,000 votes ahead of the Tory 'outsider' from Perth, Ben Wallace.

ANGUS

	2001		1997		1992 notional	
Electorate and turnout	59,004	59.3	59,708	72.1	58,883	74.9
Conservative	8,736	25.0	10,603	24.6	16,801	38.1
Labour	8,183	23.4	6,733	15.6	5,708	12.9
Lib Dem	5,015	14.3	4,065	9.4	3,878	8.8
SNP	12,347	35.3	20,792	48.3	17,274	39.2
SSP	732	2.1	–	–	–	–
Others	–		833		449	
MP	Michael Weir (SNP)		Andrew Welsh (SNP)		Andrew Welsh (SNP)	
					Angus East	
Majority	3,611	10.3	10,189	23.7	473	1.1

Scottish Parliament Election 1999: SNP 16,055 (46.5), Conservative 7,154 (20.7), Labour 6,914 (20.0), Lib Dem 4,413 (12.8). Electorate 59,891, Turnout 57.7%. MSP: Andrew Welsh (SNP), Majority 8,901 (25.8).

The Angus seat covers many east coast towns, including the fishing ports of Arbroath and Montrose. Unemployment throughout the constituency matches the Scottish average (as of early 2002), but Arbroath has suffered from the decline of the fishing industry, while Montrose up the A92 coast road has survived by exploiting the oil industry. In July 1999, for the first time since 1976, Carnoustie hosted the Open Golf Championship, expanding tourist opportunities in the area. Inland, the constituency is dominated by a large expanse of farming land, but also includes two prosperous commuter villages outside Dundee, Monifieth to the north of the city, and rapidly expanding Longforgan to the south. Local politics is dominated by the issue of roads, particularly the demand for the removal of right-hand exits off the A90 and their replacement with flyovers, and whether to make the A92 road from Arbroath to Dundee into a dual carriageway. Electors are also worried about possible hospital closures (particularly at Arbroath Infirmary).

The history of this seat from the 1970s onwards was a lively one, with Andrew Welsh gaining (what was then) South Angus from the Conservatives in October 1974. Peter Fraser (now Lord Fraser of Carmyllie) wrested back control of the seat for the Conservatives in 1979. In the 1983 boundary changes, the seat became Angus East, and was held by Fraser until Andrew Welsh won it back in 1987, just holding on in the Scottish Tory recovery of 1992. In the 1990s boundary changes, Angus East was renamed Angus, losing Brechin and Edzell to Tayside North, but gaining Invergowrie and Longforgan.

Prior to 2001, this was the SNP's second safest seat in Scotland, the incumbent Andrew Welsh having increased his majority from 473 in 1992 to a whopping 10,189 in 1997. Welsh's decision to devote all his time to the Scottish Parliament may have paid off for the high-profile former SNP Chief Whip with a comfortable majority in the 1999 elections, but it stored up trouble for the relatively unknown Michael Weir, his successor at Westminster. The SNP majority fell by two thirds in 2001. Luckily for Weir, the Tory vote stagnated, as electors switched to Labour and the Liberal Democrats.

BANFF and BUCHAN

	2001		1997		1992 notional	
Electorate and turnout	56,669	54.4	58,493	68.7	58,015	70.3
Conservative	6,207	20.1	9,564	23.8	14,156	34.7
Labour	4,363	14.2	4,747	11.8	3,501	8.6
Lib Dem	2,769	9.0	2,398	6.0	2,387	5.9
SNP	16,710	54.2	22,409	55.8	20,724	50.8
Anti–EU	–	–	1,060	2.6	–	–
Others	757 (2)		–		–	
MP	Alex Salmond (SNP)		Alex Salmond (SNP)		Alex Salmond (SNP)	
Majority	10,503	34.1	12,845	32.0	6,568	16.1

Scottish Parliament Election 1999: SNP 16,695 (52.6), Conservative 5,403 (17.0), Lib Dem 5,315 (16.8), Labour 4,321 (13.6). Electorate 57,639, Turnout 55.1%. MSP: Alex Salmond (SNP), Majority 11,292 (35.6).

Scottish Parliament by-election June 2001: SNP 15,386 (50.1), Conservative 6,819 (22.2), Labour 4,597 (15.0), Lib Dem 3,231 (10.5), SSP 682 (2.2). Electorate 56,669, Turnout 54.4%. MSP: Stewart Stevenson (SNP), Majority 8,567 (27.9).

This constituency is dominated by two traditional industries, farming and fishing, and by the more recent arrival of a third, North Sea oil, which has greatly expanded the size of its two main towns, Fraserburgh and Peterhead. Non-conformism is as strong as the clipped speech of the locals along the north coast in the burghs of Rosehearty, Macduff, Banff and Portsoy. Along with neighbouring Moray, it survived the carnage of the 1995 boundary changes relatively unscathed, except for the loss of the Tory stronghold of Turriff to Gordon, which pleased sitting SNP MP, Alex Salmond.

Formerly known as Aberdeenshire East, this seat was held by the colourful Conservative Robert Boothby from 1924 until 1958 and by Patrick Wolrige-Gordon after that. In February 1974, the seat fell to the SNP's Douglas Henderson, but it was won back by Albert McQuarrie for the Conservatives in 1979. The independently minded McQuarrie grimly held off Henderson by just 937 votes when the seat was re-named Banff and Buchan in 1983, but he finally succumbed to 32-year old Alex Salmond in 1987. Salmond's percentage majority has grown ever since, especially in his strongholds of Fraserburgh and Peterhead as the Tory vote has declined.

The SNP's leader decision to stand down in July 2000 after ten years in the job stunned his party, and left the relatively unknown John Swinney in charge of the 2001 General Election campaign. Salmond was the only sitting SNP Westminster MP initially to declare his intention to stay on both at Holyrood and Westminster (exercising a 'dual mandate') under clauses 14 and 15 of the Scotland Act 1998. In the 1999 Scottish elections, he gained a very impressive majority over the Conservatives. On 15 January 2001,

Salmond announced his intention to devote all this energies to being a Westminster MP, despite being technically allowed to serve in both Parliaments. In 2001, the former SNP leader's decision sparked a Scottish parliamentary by-election on election night in which Stewart Stevenson easily won the seat for the SNP.

DUNDEE EAST

	2001		1997		1992 notional	
Electorate and turnout	56,535	57.3	58,487	69.3	61,286	73.4
Conservative	3,900	12.0	6,397	15.8	8,297	18.4
Labour	14,635	45.2	20,718	51.1	19,954	44.3
Lib Dem	2,784	8.6	1,677	4.1	1,939	4.3
SNP	10,169	31.4	10,757	26.5	14,437	32.1
SSP	879	2.7	–	–	–	–
Others	–		979 (3)		372	
MP	Iain Luke (Lab)		John McAllion (Lab)		John McAllion (Lab)	
Majority	4,466	13.8	9,961	24.6	5,517	12.3

Scottish Parliament Election 1999: Labour 13,703 (43.3), SNP 10,849 (34.3), Conservative 4,428 (14.0), Lib Dem 2,153 (6.8), SSP 530 (1.7). Electorate 57,222, Turnout 55.3%. MSP: John McAllion (Lab), Majority 2,854 (9.0).

The constituency includes all the area of Dundee City to the east of the A90 road to Aberdeen, along the Firth of Tay, and towards the middle-class residential areas of Broughty Ferry and Balgillo. However, Dundee East has as many council house tenants as owner-occupiers, as can be evidenced by the huge council house estates including Douglas and Angus, Fintry and Whitfield. The city also suffers from persistently high levels of unemployment, although in recent years manufacturing industries have moved into the outskirts of the city. For example, around four fifths of the UK's auto-teller machines are now produced in Dundee.

From February 1974, Dundee East was the SNP's only industrial seat in Scotland, and the bastion of its leader, Gordon Wilson. As his fellow SNP MPs lost their seats in 1979, Wilson doggedly clung on until 1987 thanks to a huge personal vote. Wilson eventually lost to Labour's John McAllion, a former schoolteacher, who was able to increase his majority from 1,000 in 1987 to over 5,500 in 1992. By 1997, McAllion's 10,000 lead over the SNP seemed impregnable. However, McAllion decision to spend all of his time in the Scottish Parliament reawakened SNP sentiment in the constituency. In 1999, the Nationalists increased their share of the vote by nearly 8 per cent on 1997, but it was not enough to prevent McAllion becoming an MSP with a reduced majority. Bereft of McAllion's undoubted personal vote, his Westminster successor Iain Luke faced a strong challenge from the SNP in 2001, but in the event he held the seat comfortably by nearly 4,500 votes.

DUNDEE WEST

	2001		1997		1992 notional	
Electorate and turnout	53,760	54.4	57,434	67.6	60,352	67.9
Conservative	2,656	9.1	5,105	13.2	7,717	18.8
Labour	14,787	50.6	20,875	53.8	19,520	47.7
Lib Dem	2,620	9.0	2,972	7.7	3,071	7.5
SNP	7,987	27.3	9,016	23.2	10,056	24.6
SSP	1,192	4.1	–	–	–	–
Others	–		839 (2)		591	
MP	Ernie Ross (Lab)		Ernie Ross (Lab)		Ernie Ross (Lab)	
Majority	6,800	23.3	11,859	30.6	9,464	23.1

Scottish Parliament Election 1999: Labour 10,925 (37.6), SNP 10,804 (37.2), Conservative 3,345 (11.5), Lib Dem 2,998 (10.3), SSP 1,010 (3.5). Electorate 55,725, Turnout 52.2%. MSP: Kate MacLean (Lab), Majority 121 (0.4).

This is a classic working-class industrial seat, and until recently, it has typified Labour's traditional areas of strength in Scotland. The demise of the jute industry has left persistently high levels of unemployment, and a growing drug problem, though new manufacturing jobs have come to the area. The city's port does service the offshore oil industry, though to a far lesser extent than Aberdeen. Nearly 10 per cent more of Dundee West's constituents rent council houses than own their own homes, but apart from the vast tower-block developments on the slopes of Dundee, there are some more leafy residential areas in the old 'West End', and the Riverside ward down on the banks of the Tay. However, the Tory vote has halved here since 1992, and the party now regularly vies with the Liberal Democrats for third place.

Unlike its neighbouring constituency, Labour has had, until recently, no problems dealing with a challenge from the SNP. Ernie Ross has held the seat with comfortable majorities since he first won it in 1979, and indeed increased his majority to nearly 12,000 in 1997. However, in 1999, Ross chose to stay on a Westminster MP, leaving the field clear for Kate MacLean, leader of Dundee City Council for seven years. McLean was in for a shock as the SNP's Calum Cashley came within 121 votes of taking Dundee West, rather than the party's main target of Dundee East. In 2001, Ernie Ross, despite being suspended briefly from the House of Commons in July 1999 for leaking the Foreign Affairs Select Committee Report into the Arms to Sierra Leone affair, held onto the seat with a comfortable majority of nearly 7,000.

GORDON

	2001		1997		1992 notional	
Electorate and turnout	60,059	58.3	58,762	71.9	56,716	72.0
Conservative	8,049	23.0	11,002	26.0	19,596	48.0
Labour	4,730	13.5	4,350	10.3	2,561	6.3
Lib Dem	15,928	45.5	17,999	42.6	11,110	27.2
SNP	5,760	16.5	8,435	20.0	7,593	18.6
Others	534		459		–	
MP	Malcolm Bruce (LD)		Malcolm Bruce (LD)		Malcolm Bruce (LD)	
Majority	7,879	22.5	6,997	16.6	8,486*	20.8*

* Estimated Conservative majority allowing for boundary changes.

Scottish Parliament Election 1999: Lib Dem 12,353 (36.7), SNP 8,158 (24.3), Conservative 6,602 (19.6), Lab 3,950 (11.8), Independent 2,559 (7.6). Electorate 59,497, Turnout 56.5%. MSP: Nora Radcliffe (LD), Majority 4,195 (12.5).

Gordon was the most rapidly expanding constituency in Scotland in the 1980s due to the expansion of the commuter belt around oil-rich Aberdeen. Towns such as Ellon and Inverurie grew out of all recognition to their original size. By 1992, it had expanded to over 80,000 constituents, and bore little relation to its predecessor seat (the old West Aberdeenshire), which was based on farming in the mart towns of Huntly and Keith. Despite the oil, farming remains an important part of the constituency, centring on Aberdeen and Northern Marts' Thainstone Agricultural Centre, one of the most modern agricultural auction marts in Europe.

In 1992, Malcolm Bruce, the Liberal Democrat MP since 1983, suffered a massive backlash from Unionist voters hostile to the idea of a Scottish Parliament, but he survived by just 274 votes, after a strong challenge from local man John Porter. Because of its enormous size, Gordon was a major victim of the 1995 boundary changes in the Grampian area. The constituency lost the towns of Kemnay and Alford to the new Aberdeenshire West and Kincardine seat. It seemed that Bruce was finally doomed when he lost his strongholds of the Bridge of Don and Dyce to Aberdeen North. As if to make matters worse, Bruce was given the Tory stronghold of Turriff (famous for its annual agricultural show) from Banff and Buchan. The notional results for the re-drawn parliamentary seat compiled by psephologists showed a Conservative majority of 8,486, making it the second safest Tory seat in Scotland (next to Eastwood). If this was right then Bruce achieved a remarkable 17 per cent swing in his favour in 1997, as his majority leapt to nearly 7,000.

At the Scottish parliamentary elections in 1999, the constituency also remained in Liberal Democrat hands, after Nora Radcliffe, Grampian Health Board official and former Inverurie councillor, held off a strong challenge from the SNP. The Tories slipped into third place, due to a strong showing from Independent candidate Hamish Watt, a well-known former councillor and columnist with the *Aberdeen*

Press and Journal. In 2001, Malcolm Bruce increased his personal vote even further as the Tories won back second place from the SNP.

South of Scotland

	Conservative		Labour		Liberal Democrat		SNP		Others	
	Share of vote	Seats	Share of vote	Seats	Share of vote	Seats	Share of vote	Seats	Share of vote	Seats
2001	22.3	1	41.0	6	16.9	2	17.0	0	2.9	0
1997	22.6	0	43.4	6	13.4	2	19.1	1	1.6	0
1992	31.7	3	35.1	4	14.5	2	18.3	0	0.3	0
1999 C	22.9	0	37.2	6	14.1	2	25.7	1	0	0
1999 R	21.6	4	31.0	0	12.0	0	25.2	3	10.2	0

NOTE: 1999C=Scottish Parliamentary Elections Constituency vote; 1999R=Scottish Parliamentary Elections Regional top-up vote (7 seats available)

The South of Scotland includes, logically enough, the three borders seats of Tweeddale, Ettrick and Lauderdale, Roxburgh and Berwickshire, and Dumfries. The other recognisably 'southern' constituency, Galloway and Upper Nithsdale, is also included, but less logical is the inclusion of Ayr, Cunninghame South, Clydesdale and Carrick, Cumnock and Doon Valley, from the old Strathclyde region. And positively barmy is the inclusion of East Lothian from the old Lothian region. If you look from far enough away (presumably in Brussels), then the whole region lies within the south of Scotland, but the drawing of the region defies all electoral geography.

Given the hotchpotch of constituencies within the region, it is unsurprising that it contains some crumbs of comfort for all the four major parties in Scotland. Labour can look to its strongholds in Carrick, Cumnock and Doon Valley, Clydesdale, Cunninghame South and East Lothian. It can also wonder over how Dumfries, once a safe Tory seat held by Sir Hector Monro until his retirement in 1997, can now be a safe Labour seat with a majority of almost 9,000 in 2001. At a Westminster level, Labour can also admire the view from Ayr, where the Tories were finally vanquished in 1997, and where Labour held off the Tory challenge in 2001. The Liberal Democrats, despite polling poorly in terms of share of the vote, still hold two seats – Tweeddale, Ettrick and Lauderdale and Roxburgh and Berwickshire. In fact, both sitting MPs, Michael Moore (who succeeded David Steel in 1997) and Archy Kirkwood (MP since 1983), increased their percentage majorities in 2001. Up until June 2001, the SNP could reflect on the gain of Galloway and Upper Nithsdale from Conservatives in 1997, which also saw the political demise of the then Trade Minister, Ian Lang. In 1999, the party held onto the seat and polled over 30 per cent of the vote in Clydesdale and just under that figure in Cunninghame South. In the share out of regional top-up seats, the SNP gained three of the seven available (Christine Grahame – elected as Christine Creech – Adam Ingram and Michael Russell).

Despite losing three Westminster seats here in 1997 (and their MEP in 1994), this has still been the Conservatives' best region in Scotland in terms of share of the vote over recent elections. In 1999, the Tories made up for the failure to retake any of their 1997 losses by gaining four of the seven top-up seats (for Alex Fergusson, Phil Gallie, David Mundell and Murray Tosh). Moreover, in the last two years, the area has provided the first fragile signs of a modest Tory revival north of the border. On 17 March 2000, John Scott seized Ayr for the Conservatives in a by-election caused by the withdrawal from politics of Labour's Ian Welsh. Scott's victory gave the Tories their first constituency MSP in the Scottish Parliament. Just over a year later, the Conservatives had a matching pair, when Peter Duncan won Galloway and Upper Nithsdale in the General Election from the SNP by only 74 votes. This constituency is currently (as of 2002) the only Conservative seat at Westminster in either Scotland or Wales.

Local government

This vast region not only makes no geographical sense, there is also only a tenuous link between the local authorities and the regional boundaries. It comprises the Scottish Borders, Dumfries and Galloway, East Lothian, the town of Penicuik within Midlothian council (most of which lies in the Lothian region) South Ayrshire (mainly the town of Ayr), those parts of East Ayrshire authority (which is not even in East Ayrshire!) around Dalmellington, and those parts of North Ayrshire within the parliamentary constituency of Cunninghame South (including Irvine and Kilwinning). In the Scottish Borders, the council remained under no overall control after the 1999 elections, with the Liberal Democrats and Independents both having 14 councillors each. Across to the west in Dumfries and Galloway, the council is also hung. Labour, despite having lost seven seats is still the second largest party to the Independents. However, the Conservatives gained six seats, a big improvement on their poor showing of 1995. In East Lothian, Labour remained firmly in control after winning 17 of the 23 seats available. In South Ayrshire, by contrast, Labour clung on to control of the council by a margin of four, despite the Conservatives gaining eight seats. In North Ayrshire, Labour remained utterly dominant, but faced a stronger challenge from the SNP in East Ayrshire (mainly located within the Central Scotland region).

AYR

	2001		1997		1992 notional	
Electorate and turnout	55,630	69.3	55,925	80.0	55,307	81.9
Conservative	14,256	37.0	15,136	33.8	17,417	38.5
Labour	16,801	43.6	21,679	48.4	19,312	42.6
Lib Dem	2,089	5.4	2,116	4.7	3,382	7.5
SNP	4,621	12.0	5,625	12.6	5,057	11.2
Others	793 (2)		200		132	
MP	Sandra Osborne (Lab)		Sandra Osborne (Lab)		Phil Gallie (Con)	
Majority	2,545	6.6	6,543	14.6	1,895*	4.2*

* Estimated Labour majority allowing for boundary changes.

Scottish Parliament Election 1999: Labour 14,263 (38.1), Conservative 14,238 (38.0), SNP 7,291 (19.5), Lib Dem 1,662 (4.4). Electorate 56,338, Turnout 66.5%. MSP: Ian Welsh (Lab), Majority 25 (0.1).

Scottish Parliament by-election, 17 March 2000: Conservative 12,580 (39.4), SNP 9,236 (29.0), Labour 7,054 (22.1), SSP 1,345 (4.2), Lib Dem 800 (2.5), Others 885 (2.8). Electorate 55,965, Turnout 57%. MSP: John Scott (Con), Majority 3,344 (10.4).

As they say after Scottish football matches, Ayr is a constituency of two halves. Parts of the town are filled with working class council estates like Braehead and Whitletts, which vote solidly Labour, while the coastal areas of the seat are much better known to tourists, including the town's seaside resort, as well as the neighbouring attractions of Prestwick and Troon.

This tale of two halves has produced an ultra marginal seat, which has hosted many of the most exciting electoral contests in the last 15 years. In 1987, George Younger, Defence Secretary, and formerly Secretary of State for Scotland clung by 182 votes to the seat he had held since 1964. On Younger's retirement in 1992 (he became a life peer in 1992 as Baron Younger of Prestwick and succeeded his father as Viscount Younger of Leckie in 1997), all the pundits predicted that his successor, Phil Gallie would lose the Tory's most vulnerable Scottish seat. Instead, Gallie contributed to the Tory's mini Scottish revival in 1992, holding on by only 85 votes.

The 1995 boundary changes ended Gallie's chances of pulling off another Houdini act when 10,000 voters from the mostly Tory wards of Alloway, Forehil and Holmston were ceded to Carrick, Cumnock and Doon Valley. Given the loss of these key Tory areas, especially rock-solid Alloway, it was unsurprising that Sandra Osborne, now Parliamentary Private Secretary to Scottish Office minister George Foulkes, won by a convincing 6,500 votes in 1997, seizing the seat for Labour for the first time.

However, in May 1999 the seat provided more drama in the Scottish parliamentary elections when Phil Gallie came within 25 votes of winning Ayr again. Gallie was forced to content himself with a regional list seat in the South of Scotland, but amazingly, he was handed another possible chance to win the seat in December 1999 when Ian Welsh, chief executive of Kilmarnock FC, and a former leader of South Ayrshire Council, quit as an MSP, citing family reasons. Gallie was in a dilemma. Did he risk standing down as a list MSP to fight a seat that he might lose? Or would he gamble on the chance to become the first Tory constituency MSP in the Scottish Parliament? Labour threatened to mount a legal challenge to the assumption that Gallie's list seat would automatically fall to Alasdair Hutton, the former Tory MEP, and the next Tory on the South of Scotland list. They argued that 'gifting' the Tories a list seat in this way would breach the proportionality principle inherent in the Additional Member System. In the event Phil Gallie announced on 5 January 2000 that he was not going to stand, and Labour's legal action was never brought. The Tories chose John Scott, who had previously been the Scottish parliamentary candidate in the neighbouring seat of Carrick, Cumnock and Doon Valley. On 17 March 2000, Scott won the by-election. The Scottish Labour party humiliated as the SNP were second place. A strong showing from the Scottish Socialist Party candidate meant that the Liberal Democrats were placed in an ignominious fifth spot. In 2001, Sandra Osborne held onto Ayr for Labour, though her 1997 majority was more than halved as the Tory vote went up by three per cent, and the SNP finished a distant third.

CARRICK, CUMNOCK and DOON VALLEY

	2001		1997		1992 *notional*	
Electorate and turnout	64,919	61.8	65,593	75.0	*67,001*	*77.2*
Conservative	7,318	18.2	8,336	17.0	*13,271*	*25.7*
Labour	22,174	55.3	29,398	59.8	*27,957*	*54.1*
Lib Dem	2,932	7.3	2,613	5.3	*2,690*	*5.2*
SNP	6,258	15.6	8,190	16.7	*7,802*	*15.1*
SSP	1,058	2.6	–	–	–	–
Others	367		634		–	
MP	George Foulkes (Lab)		George Foulkes (Lab)		George Foulkes (Lab)	
Majority	14,856	37.0	21,062	42.8	*14,686*	*28.4*

Scottish Parliament Election 1999: Labour 19,667 (47.9), SNP 10,864 (26.4), Conservative 8,123 (19.8), Lib Dem 2,441 (5.9). Electorate 65,580, Turnout 62.7%. MSP: Cathy Jamieson (Lab), Majority 8,803 (21.4).

Carrick on the coast is mainly Tory, but the Cumnock and Doon Valley areas are solidly Labour, situated in the former South Ayrshire coalfield area. Grim former mining communities like Dalmellington and New Cumnock provide Labour with a secure base.

The former name of this seat was Ayrshire South, won by Labour's Jim Sillars in October 1974, before he resigned the whip in 1976 to form the breakaway 'Scottish Labour Party'. In 1979, Sillars came within 1,500 votes of retaining the seat from the official Labour candidate, George Foulkes, who went onto hold the renamed Carrick, Cumnock and Doon Valley seat from 1983 onwards. Even the injection of 10,000 voters from neighbouring Ayr, many of them from strongly Tory Alloway, have made little difference to the political make up of this seat. Formerly International Development minister, and then Minister of State at the Scotland Office, Foulkes's majority fell marginally in 2001, but the two per cent rise in the Tory vote was extremely disappointing. Indeed, at the Scottish parliamentary elections in 1999, the SNP pushed the Tories into third place, as Labour's Cathy Jamieson gained a convincing majority of over 20 per cent. In November 2001, Jack McConnell promoted Jamieson to the post of Minister for Education and Young People in the Scottish Executive.

CLYDESDALE

	2001		1997		1992 actual	
Electorate and turnout	64,423	59.3	63,428	71.6	61,914	77.6
Conservative	5,034	13.2	7,396	16.3	11,231	23.4
Labour	17,822	46.6	23,859	52.5	21,418	44.6
Lib Dem	4,111	10.8	3,796	8.4	3,957	8.2
SNP	10,028	26.2	10,050	22.1	11,084	23.1
SSP	974	2.6	–	–	–	–
Others	253		311		342	
MP	Jimmy Hood (Lab)		Jimmy Hood (Lab)		Jimmy Hood (Lab)	
Majority	7,794	20.4	13,809	30.4	10,187	21.2

Scottish Parliament Election 1999: Labour 16,755 (43.0), SNP 12,875 (33.1), Conservative 5,814 (14.9), Lib Dem 3,503 (9.0). Electorate 64,262, Turnout 60.6%. MSP: Karen Turnbull (Lab), Majority 3,880 (10.0).

Clydesdale is another large Scottish seat, taking in much of the barren hill country either side of the M74 motorway on its way south to England. Labour does well in the industrial towns of Carluke and Stonehouse, both just south of Hamilton, as well as in the ex-mining communities of Coalburn, Douglas and Lesmahagow around the town of Lanark. East of Lanark lies the railway junction at Carstairs and the SNP stronghold of Biggar.

This seat was formerly known as Lanark, and was held by former Labour Cabinet Minister Judith Hart from 1959 until her retirement in 1987. Hart suffered a few scares along the way, narrowly edging out the Tories in February 1974, and the SNP in October of that year. From 1979 onwards, however, her majority over the Conservatives steadily increased. Jimmy Hood, the former miner and incumbent since 1987, has seen the SNP take over second place once more from the Tories, but neither party has troubled him greatly; in the Labour landslide of 1997, his majority was nearly 14,000. In 1999, the SNP's Ann Winning out-performed her party's national average by polling a third of the vote, cutting Karen Turnbull's majority to less than 4,000. In 2001, in contrast to much of the rest of Scotland, the SNP vote held up well, although Hood's majority was still nearly 8,000.

CUNNINGHAME SOUTH

	2001		1997		1992 actual	
Electorate and turnout	49,982	56.2	49,543	71.5	49,025	75.9
Conservative	2,782	9.9	3,571	10.1	6,070	16.3
Labour	16,424	58.4	22,233	62.7	19,687	52.9
Lib Dem	2,094	7.4	1,604	4.5	2,299	6.2
SNP	5,194	18.5	7,364	20.8	9,007	24.2
SSP	1,233	4.4	–	–	–	–
Others	382		672 (2)		128	
MP	Brian Donohoe (Lab)		Brian Donohoe (Lab)		Brian Donohoe (Lab)	
Majority	11,230	40.0	14,869	42.0	10,680	28.7

Scottish Parliament Election 1999: Labour 14,936 (52.8), SNP 8,395 (29.7), Conservative 3,229 (11.4), Lib Dem 1,717 (6.1). Electorate 50,443, Turnout 56.1%. MSP: Irene Oldfather (Lab), Majority 6,541 (23.1).

Formerly known as Central Ayrshire, this seat was re-named in 1983, and comprises the New Town of Irvine, with its 30,000 residents. Despite the existence of a Finnish-owned paper mill in the constituency, the town suffers from higher than average unemployment. Cunninghame South also includes the older towns of Stevenston and Kilwinning, the latter being the proud home of the oldest Masonic Lodge in Scotland. Whatever their religious affiliation, however, a majority of Cunninghame South's electors vote Labour.

From 1970 to 1992, they voted for Labour backbencher David Lambie. Since Lambie's retirement in 1992, they have voted for Brian Donohoe, another backbencher, who polled over 60 per cent of the vote in Labour's landslide of 1997. In the 1999 Scottish parliamentary elections, the SNP managed to poll nearly 30 per cent, cutting Labour's Westminster majority in half. However, in 2001 the SNP vote, as with so much of Scotland, slipped back by more than ten points. Neither the Liberal Democrats nor the Conservatives have been able to make significant inroads into this seat in recent years. In 2001, the SSP polled a respectable 4.4 per cent.

DUMFRIES

	2001		1997		1992 *notional*	
Electorate and turnout	63,571	67.0	62,759	78.9	*63,268*	*79.2*
Conservative	11,996	28.2	13,885	28.0	*21,597*	*43.1*
Labour	20,830	48.9	23,528	47.5	*14,831*	*29.6*
Lib Dem	4,955	11.6	5,487	11.1	*5,854*	*11.7*
SNP	4,103	9.6	5,977	12.1	*7,411*	*14.8*
Others	702		650 (2)		*419*	*0.8*
MP	Russell Brown (Lab)		Russell Brown (Lab)		Hector Monro (Con)	
Majority	8,834	20.7	9,643	19.5	*6,766*	*13.5*

Scottish Parliament Election 1999: Labour 14,101 (36.6), Conservative 10,447 (27.2), SNP 7,625 (19.8), Lib Dem 6,309 (16.4). Electorate 63,162, Turnout 60.9%.

MSP: Elaine Murray (Lab), Majority 3,654 (9.5).

This constituency is dominated by the town of Dumfries, the largest town in the south west of Scotland. Although Labour had no success in the seat until 1997, the working-class council estate of Terregles provided a core of support. The seat also includes a number of smaller towns such as Annan and Annandale, Lockerbie, Ecclefechan and Gretna Green on the border with England.

Dumfries used to be the bastion of Sir Hector Monro, the former Scottish Office minister, and due to his enormous personal vote, he held the seat by large margins from 1964 until his retirement in 1997, when the seat fell to Labour's Russell Brown by a staggering margin of over 9,500. The result can be attributed both to the departure of the highly respected Monro, his replacement by the non-local Struan Stevenson, and anti-Tory tactical voting in favour of Labour, who were clearly in second place after 1992. Brown chose to stay at Westminster, and his colleague Elaine Murray held on in 1999 with a reduced majority, which was caused by a near- doubling of the SNP vote, rather than any revival in Tory support. In the November 2001 reshuffle instigated by Jack McConnell, she was made Deputy Minister for Tourism, Culture and Sport in the Scottish Executive. In June 2001, at the Westminster elections, Brown again won easily, as the Tory vote continued to stagnate, despite the area around Lockerbie being badly affected by the foot and mouth outbreak.

EAST LOTHIAN

	2001		1997		1992 notional	
Electorate and turnout	58,987	62.5	57,489	75.5	56,283	82.6
Conservative	6,577	17.8	8,660	19.9	14,024	30.2
Labour	17,407	47.2	22,881	52.7	21,123	45.5
Lib Dem	6,506	17.7	4,575	10.5	5,147	11.1
SNP	5,381	14.6	6,825	15.7	6,171	13.3
SSP	624	1.7	–	–	–	–
Others	376		491		–	
MP	Anne Picking (Lab)		John Home Robertson(Lab)		John Home Robertson(Lab)	
Majority	10,830	29.4	14,221	32.7	7,099	15.3

Scottish Parliament Election 1999: Labour 19,220 (54.0), SNP 8,274 (23.3), Conservative 5,941 (16.7), Lib Dem 2,147 (6.0). Electorate 58,579, Turnout 60.7%. MSP: John Home Robertson (Lab), Majority: 10,946 (30.8).

At the eastern end of the Southern Upland Way, this now safe Labour seat covers an area of about 270 square miles, stretching east from the city of Edinburgh. It comprises both the ex-mining communities of Prestonpans and Ormiston in the west, and more Conservative farming and tourist areas nearer its 43 miles of North Sea coast, like Haddington, North Berwick and Dunbar. With the demise of the mining industry, only opencast mining remains and the area's principal sources of employment are in modern industries such as electronics, chemical research and printing. Other major employers include the Torness nuclear power station and the Belhaven Brewery at Dunbar. In 1998, the area suffered a blow when Mitsubishi closed its Haddington plant, resulting in over 500 job losses.

The seat has not always been safe for Labour. Before 1983, it was paired with Conservative Berwickshire, and John Mackintosh lost control in February 1974 before winning it back eight months later. On Mackintosh's unexpected death in 1978, the seat was held for Labour at the resulting by-election by John Home Robertson, who retained it until 2001, before stepping down to devote all his energies to the Scottish Parliament. He went on to serve briefly in the Scottish Executive as Deputy Minister for Rural Affairs, before being dropped by Henry McLeish in October 2000.

Home Robertson's long-term tenure of East Lothian was secured first when the 1983 Boundary Commission gave Berwickshire to a Borders seat, and second, in 1995, when the commission back-tracked on an original recommendation to hand back Berwickshire. The Labour town of Musselburgh was lost to Edinburgh East in the 1990s changes, but the Berwickshire proposals were dropped. Home Robertson now hands over the safe seat to Anne Picking, one of very few Labour women entrants of 2001. Labour also dominate local politics here. In the local council elections of 1999, the SNP gained only one seat while the Conservatives finished with five, Labour way ahead on seventeen.

GALLOWAY and UPPER NITHSDALE

	2001		1997		1992 notional	
Electorate and turnout	53,254	67.4	52,751	79.7	53,482	80.9
Conservative	12,222	34.0	12,825	30.5	18,173	42.0
Labour	7,258	20.2	6,861	16.3	5,609	13.0
Lib Dem	3,698	10.3	2,700	6.4	3,721	8.6
SNP	12,148	33.8	18,449	43.9	15,773	36.5
Others	588		1,183 (3)		–	
MP	Peter Duncan (Con)		Alasdair Morgan (SNP)		Ian Lang (Con)	
Majority	74	0.2	5,624	13.4	2,400	5.5

Scottish Parliament Election 1999: SNP 13,873 (39.3), Conservative 10,672 (30.2), Labour 7,209 (20.4), 3,562 (10.1). Electorate 53,057, Turnout 66.6%. MSP: Alasdair Morgan (SNP), Majority 3,201 (9.1).

In 1997, the SNP pulled off one of its two gains here (the other being in Tayside North), when Alasdair Morgan defeated the ever-dapper Ian Lang, Trade Secretary and former Secretary of State for Scotland. In 1999, the SNP's National Secretary chose to devote all his energies to the Scottish Parliament, and won the seat comfortably as the Tory vote stagnated.

This large constituency is located in the far southwest corner of Scotland, covering the old Scottish counties of Kirkcudbright and Wigtown. Stranraer is both a tourist town and a major ferry port. The Labour party draws some support in Upper Nithsdale from the ex-mining towns of Sanquhar and Kirkconnel, but the seat is overwhelmingly rural, and contains the highest proportion of people employed in farming, fishing and forestry in the United Kingdom. The area was badly affected by the foot and mouth outbreak in early 2001, and this may explain the four per cent rise in the Conservative vote, which led to Peter Duncan becoming the only Conservative MP in Scotland by the tiny margin of 74 votes. However, as with the close result in Perth, there was a substantial increase in the Labour share of the vote, also four percentage points, a phenomenon that does not fit the foot and mouth theory, while the SNP share of the vote collapsed by 10 per cent. The SNP's decision to stand down five of its six MPs to devote all their energies to the Scottish electorate sent the wrong signal to voters in SNP-held seats, that the Westminster elections counted for less than the Scottish elections. The relatively unknown Malcolm Fleming, the SNP candidate, paid the penalty for Morgan's decision to step down from Westminster in 2001.

ROXBURGH and BERWICKSHIRE

	2001		1997		1992 notional	
Electorate and turnout	47,515	60.6	47,288	73.9	47,068	76.9
Conservative	6,533	22.7	8,337	23.9	12,354	34.2
Labour	4,498	15.6	5,226	15.0	3,167	8.8
Lib Dem	14,044	48.8	16,243	46.5	16,807	46.5
SNP	2,806	9.7	3,959	11.3	3,844	10.6
Others	916 (2)		1,166 (3)		–	
MP	Archy Kirkwood (LD)		Archy Kirkwood (LD)		Archy Kirkwood (LD)	
Majority	7,511	26.1	7,906	22.6	4,453	12.3

Scottish Parliament Election 1999: Lib Dem 11,320 (40.6), Conservative 7,735 (27.8), SNP 4,719 (16.9), Labour 4,102 (14.7). Electorate 47,639, Turnout 58.5%. MSP: Euan Robson (LD), Majority 3,585 (12.9).

This seat was created in 1983 out of the division of David Steel's Roxburgh, Selkirk and Peebles constituency. Steel chose the western half (Tweeddale, Ettrick and Lauderdale), while Archy Kirkwood stood for the eastern side. So confident of victory was the sitting Conservative MP for Aberdeen South, Iain Sproat, that he would win the new seat, that he packed his bags for the Borders. Sproat famously lost Roxburgh and Berwickshire while Gerry Malone easily held Aberdeen South.

Roxburgh and Berwickshire includes the Borders towns of Hawick, Jedburgh and Kelso, all famous for their rugby union teams. Traditional industries such as farming and knitwear cling for survival as the tourists flock in to visit the ancient abbeys and fish in the swirling rivers. The local people still tend to vote for local, independent candidates at council elections, though their numbers continued to fall in the 1999 local contests.

Roxburgh and Berwickshire is now a safe seat for the Liberal Democrats, with the Tories more than 22 per cent behind in 1997, and 26 per cent behind in 2001. The catastrophic decline in the Tory vote has seen Kirkwood's majority nearly double since 1992. In 1999, Euan Robson was comfortably elected as the Liberal Democrat MSP, and he is now Deputy Minister for Parliamentary Business (Liberal Democrat Whip) in the Scottish Executive.

TWEEDDALE, ETTRICK and LAUDERDALE

	2001		1997		1992 notional	
Electorate and turnout	52,430	63.4	51,114	76.3	50,228	79.3
Conservative	5,118	15.4	8,623	22.1	12,218	30.7
Labour	8,878	26.7	10,689	27.4	6,538	16.4
Lib Dem	14,035	42.3	12,178	31.2	13,953	35.0
SNP	4,108	12.4	6,671	17.1	6,835	17.2
SSP	695	2.1	–	–	–	–
Others	383		840 (3)		276	
MP	Michael Moore (LD)		Michael Moore (LD)		David Steel (LD)	
Majority	5,157	15.5	1,489	3.8	1,735	4.4

Scottish Parliament Election 1999: Lib Dem 12,078 (35.8), SNP 7,600 (22.5), Labour 7,546 (22.4), Conservative 6,491 (19.3). Electorate 51,577, Turnout 65.4%. MSP: Ian Jenkins (LD), Majority 4,478 (13.3).

This is the western half of David Steel's original seat of Roxburgh, Selkirk and Peebles, created in 1983 by the Boundary Commission. Steel chose to remain here, believing it to be safe, but the Liberal Democrats have seen their vote crumble by eight per cent in 1987, another ten points in 1992, and a further four in 1997. The position of Steel's Liberal Democrat successor, Michael Moore was not helped by the 1995 Boundary Commission decision to uproot the 13,000 voters of Penicuik from Midlothian, and plonk them in a constituency of farms, villages and market towns such as Lauder, Peebles and Selkirk. The addition of Penicuik contributed to a dramatic rise in the Labour vote to 27 per cent in 1997, cutting Moore's majority to 1,489. By 1999, the seat had effectively become a three-way marginal between the Liberal Democrats, Labour and the SNP.

In the 1999 Scottish parliament elections, Tweeddale was Labour's top target seat and the SNP's fifth target. In the end neither party prevailed. Ian Jenkins held on for the Liberal Democrats, with the SNP jumping to second spot, closely followed by Labour and the Tories trailing in a truly dismal fourth place. In 2001, Michael Moore's position was greatly strengthened when he more than trebled his majority, while the Tory vote collapsed (now only half its 1992 size), the SNP flopped and the Labour vote stagnated. Meanwhile, Lord Steel of Aikwood revived his political career in 1999 by being elected as a list MSP in the Lothians region, and by becoming the first Presiding Officer of the Scottish Parliament.

West of Scotland

	Conservative		Labour		Liberal Democrat		SNP		Others	
	Share of vote	Seats	Share of vote	Seats	Share of vote	Seats	Share of vote	Seats	Share of vote	Seats
2001	15.7	0	50.0	9	13.2	0	17.5	0	3.6	0
1997	18.2	0	51.3	9	9.2	0	19.9	0	1.3	0
1992	28.2	1	43.5	8	9.9	0	18.1	0	0.3	0
1999 C	16.4	0	43.5	9	11.3	0	26.9	0	2.0	0
1999 R	15.7	2	38.6	0	11.0	1	25.9	4	8.9	0

NOTE: 1999C=Scottish Parliamentary Elections Constituency vote; 1999R=Scottish Parliamentary Elections Regional top-up vote (7 seats available)

The West of Scotland comprises all those bits of the old Strathclyde region outside of Glasgow that were not ceded to Highlands and Islands, Central Scotland or the South of Scotland. Labour held all nine of the parliamentary constituencies in 1997 and again in 2001, as the party polled over 50 per cent of the vote. If one were to go as far back as 1983, then the Tories held Renfrewshire West, Strathkelvin and Bearsden and Eastwood. But by 1992, only Eastwood was left, and even it fell on a massive swing to Labour of 14 per cent in 1997. The SNP were given some cause for optimism after the November 1997 by-election in Paisley South (caused by the suicide of Gordon McMaster), in which the party failed to take the seat, but managed a swing from Labour of 11 per cent. However, Labour comfortably held both Paisley North and Paisley South in 1999, although the SNP share of the vote rose above 30 per cent in both constituencies. The SNP also failed to win Renfrewshire West, their ninth target seat in 1999, although the party's vote share went up to 29 per cent. Dumbarton is also the kind of seat that the SNP must win if it is to form a government in Scotland. The party's 30 per cent vote share in 1999 is at least a launch pad for 2003. Elsewhere, the SNP made progress in Cunninghame North and Clydebank and Milngavie, where its vote share rose to 29 per cent and 31 per cent respectively. These strong performances resulted in the SNP being rewarded with four of the region's seven top-up seats (Colin Campbell, Fiona McLeod, Lloyd Quinan and Kay Ullrich).

The Tories' only ray of hope in 1999 was a tiny swing in their favour in Eastwood, which cut Labour's majority to 2,125. This second place in Eastwood (on 32.7%), together with fairly disastrous third places in former Tory seats of Renfrewshire West (21%) and Strathkelvin and Bearsden (16.3%), ensured that the Conservatives gained two of the region's seven top-up seats (Annabel Goldie and John Young). As in Glasgow, the Liberal Democrats have always struggled here, and in 1999 could only point to a creditable second place (on 26%) in Greenock and Inverclyde. The party's 11 per cent share, however, was enough to gain them one top-up seat (for Ross Finnie).

Strathkelvin and Bearsden provided the only drama of 2001 when a Scottish parliamentary by-election provoked by the retirement of Sam Galbraith, the former Education Minister (and latterly Environment Minister) in the Scottish Executive, saw Jean Turner, a former GP, worried about cuts to acute services at the local Stobhill hospital in the constituency, poll over 7,500 votes, beating all the other three main parties. Despite the fright for Scottish Labour, its candidate Brian Fitzpatrick emerged as the eventual winner. In the Westminster election, the main talking point was the extraordinary increase in Labour's majority in Eastwood, a Conservative seat from 1945 until 1997. Jim Murphy's shock gain of 1997 was consolidated when he trebled his majority, the Tory vote dropping by a further five points.

Local government
East Renfrewshire comprises Clarkston, Newton Mearns, Barrhead and Neilston. After the 1999 local elections, the authority remained in no overall control with Labour gaining one seat from the Conservatives to move ahead of the Tories by nine councillors to eight. Renfrewshire includes all of Paisley as well as Johnstone, Erskine, Bridge of Weir and Bishopton. Labour actually gained control of the council from no overall control by winning one seat, the party's only council gain of 1999 in Scotland. The party now stands at 21 councillors with the SNP narrowly behind on fifteen. West Dunbartonshire comprises mainly Clydebank and Dumbarton, while East Dunbartonshire includes Milngavie and Bearsden. Labour gained a ward in West Dunbartonshire to remain in overall charge from the SNP by a margin of 14 to seven. However, in East Dunbartonshire, the party lost overall control of the council. The Liberal Democrats are now the largest single party with ten councillors, followed by Labour with nine, the Tories on three and the SNP holding two wards. The West of Scotland also includes the Cunninghame North part of North Ayrshire, mainly Saltcoats, Ardrossan and Largs. Labour won 25 of the 30 seats in the council as a whole, even though they lost two seats, one to the SNP and the other to the Conservatives.

CLYDEBANK and MILNGAVIE

	2001		1997		1992 notional	
Electorate and turnout	51,979	62.5	52,092	75.0	51,276	77.3
Conservative	3,514	10.8	4,885	12.5	8,503	21.5
Labour	17,249	53.1	21,583	55.2	19,923	50.3
Lib Dem	3,909	12.0	4,086	10.5	3,778	9.5
SNP	6,525	20.1	8,263	21.1	7,319	18.5
SSP	1,294	4.0	–	–	–	–
Others	–		269		117	
MP	Tony Worthington(Lab)		Tony Worthington(Lab)		Tony Worthington(Lab)	
Majority	10,724	33.0	13,320	34.1	11,420	28.8

Scottish Parliament Election 1999: Labour 15,105 (45.3), SNP 10,395 (31.2), Lib Dem 4,149 (12.5), Conservative 3,688 (11.1). Electorate 52,461, Turnout 63.6%. MSP: Des McNulty (Lab), Majority 4,710 (14.1).

The former shipbuilding town of Clydebank dominates this Central Dunbartonshire seat, and is largely barren territory for the Tories. Most of its working class residents rent their homes from the council, and vote Labour with monotonous regularity. The exception was in February 1974 when the Communist Jimmy Reid polled nearly 6,000 votes in the wake of the sit-in during the Upper Clyde Shipbuilders (UCS) dispute. Well-off and residential Milngavie (pronounced 'Milguy') should be natural Conservative territory, (and there are still small pockets of Tory support), but this is Scotland, so its middle-class electors prefer the Liberal Democrats, especially at local elections. In 1995, nearly 3,500 voters were added from the residential Kilmardinny ward of Strathkelvin and Bearsden, but this had not blunted Clydebank's (and therefore Labour's) controlling influence over this constituency.

English-born Tony Worthington was elected to this seat in 1987, and has held it with massive majorities ever since. In 1999, the SNP out-performed their national share of the vote by polling over 30 per cent, leaving Des McNulty's Holyrood majority at half the level of support enjoyed by Worthington at Westminster. Worthington was sacked as a junior minister in the Northern Ireland Office in 1998, but despite his lower profile, the SNP stagnated in 2001, and they failed to make any inroads into Labour's enormous majority. Meanwhile, the Tories slipped into fourth place behind the Liberal Democrats.

CUNNINGHAME NORTH

	2001		1997		1992 actual	
Electorate and turnout	54,993	61.5	55,526	74.1	54,856	78.1
Conservative	6,666	19.7	9,647	23.5	14,625	34.1
Labour	15,571	46.1	20,686	50.3	17,564	41.0
Lib Dem	3,060	9.0	2,271	5.5	2,864	6.7
SNP	7,173	21.2	7,584	18.4	7,813	18.2
SSP	964	2.9	–	–	–	–
Others	382		941		–	
MP	Brian Wilson (Lab)		Brian Wilson (Lab)		Brian Wilson (Lab)	
Majority	8,398	24.8	11,039	26.8	2,939	6.9

Scottish Parliament Election 1999: Labour 14,369 (42.9), SNP 9,573 (28.6), Conservative 6,649 (19.9), Lib Dem 2,900 (8.7). Electorate 55,867, Turnout 60.0%. MSP: Allan Wilson (Lab), Majority 4,796 (14.3).

Cunninghame North is a creation of the 1983 Boundary Commission. It comprises most of North Ayrshire and Bute, an old Tory seat held by John Corrie, minus Bute, which was lost to Argyll. The constituency contains a number of islands in the Firth of Clyde, most notably Arran. The coastal resort of Largs garners votes for the Tories, but further down the coast, Labour is dominant in the towns of Ardrossan and Saltcoats. Inland, the former mining communities of Beith, Dalry and Kilbirnie can also be relied upon to vote Labour.

Brian Wilson, MP here since 1987, saw his majority cut to less than 3,000 in the Tory mini revival of 1992, but since then, Labour has won easily, and the SNP have replaced the Tories in second place. Unsurprisingly, given that he had run the 1979 'Labour Vote No' campaign in the Scottish devolution referendum, Wilson chose to stay on at Westminster rather than stand in the Scottish parliamentary elections. At these elections, Allan Wilson (no relation of Brian), former Labour leader of Cumbernauld and Kilsyth District Council, held off a strong challenge from the SNP. In October 2000, Henry McLeish, the new Scottish First Minister, promoted Allan Wilson to Deputy Minister for Sport and Culture in the Scottish Executive. Then, in the major Jack McConnell reshuffle of November 2001, he was moved to a junior post in Environment and Rural Development. In June 2001, Brian Wilson, the former Minister of State at the Scotland Office, and now Minster for Industry and Energy, secured a 25 per cent majority over the SNP, with the Tories finishing a close third.

DUMBARTON

	2001		1997		1992 actual	
Electorate and turnout	55,643	61.1	56,229	73.4	57,252	77.1
Conservative	4,648	13.7	7,283	17.7	13,126	29.7
Labour	16,151	47.5	20,470	49.6	19,255	43.6
Lib Dem	5,265	15.5	3,144	7.6	3,425	7.8
SNP	6,576	19.3	9,587	23.2	8,127	18.4
SSP	1,354	4.0	–	–	–	–
Others	–		780		192	
MP	John McFall (Lab)		John McFall (Lab)		John McFall (Lab)	
Majority	9,575	28.2	10,883	26.4	6,129	13.9

Scottish Parliament Election 1999: Labour 15,181 (43.8), SNP 10,423 (30.0), Conservative 5,060 (14.6), Lib Dem 4,035 (11.6). Electorate 56,090, Turnout 61.9%. MSP: Jackie Baillie (Lab), Majority 4,758 (13.7).

Dumbarton is another one of those polarised Scottish seats. Dumbarton town's 18,000 voters make up a third of the constituency, and they have traditionally been relied upon to vote Labour. By contrast, the scenic town of Helensburgh, situated on the Firth of Clyde can normally be relied upon to deliver votes to the Conservatives. However, the final third of this seat – the Vale of Leven – is barren territory for the Tories. The former textile communities of Alexandria, Bonhill, Jamestown and Renton guarantee that Labour wins by wide margins here.

In 1997, John McFall, Labour MP since 1987, polled almost 50 per cent of the popular vote, with the SNP way behind on 23 per cent. But as with so many other seats of this kind, at the Scottish parliamentary elections in 1999, the SNP's vote rose to 30 per cent, leaving Jackie Baillie's Holyrood majority at half the level of that enjoyed by John McFall at Westminster. Neither does Baillie have the comfort of a job in the Scottish Executive, having been sacked by McConnell as Minister for Social Justice in November 2001. In June 2001, the SNP slipped back to under 20 per cent, as the Lib Dem vote nearly doubled on its 1997 performance, dumping the Tories into fourth place.

EASTWOOD

	2001		1997		1992 notional	
Electorate and turnout	68,297	70.8	66,769	78.3	65,846	79.9
Conservative	13,895	28.7	17,530	33.5	24,544	46.6
Labour	23,036	47.6	20,766	39.7	12,706	24.1
Lib Dem	6,239	12.9	6,110	11.7	8,651	16.4
SNP	4,137	8.6	6,826	13.1	6,589	12.5
Others	1,061 (2)		1,020 (3)		146	
MP	Jim Murphy (Lab)		Jim Murphy (Lab)		Allan Stewart (Con)	
Majority	9,141	18.9	3,236	6.2	11,838	22.5

Scottish Parliament Election 1999: Labour 16,970 (37.4), Conservative 14,845 (32.7), SNP 8,760 (19.3), Lib Dem 4,472 (9.9), Others 349 (0.8). Electorate 67,248, Turnout 67.5%. MSP: Kenneth Macintosh (Lab), Majority 2,125 (4.7).

If this middle-class suburban commuter seat south west of Glasgow were situated in England, it would be rock-solid Conservative. Nearly 80 per cent of its electors own their own homes, and three-quarters work in non-manual jobs. The Labour-voting town of Barrhead used to be an exception when pitted against plush suburban areas like Clarkston, Giffnock and Newton Mearns.

However, just before the 1997 election, Allan Stewart, the man with the amazing sideburns, and the Conservative MP for East Renfrewshire since 1979, and this seat since 1983, announced his intention to step down after a series of scandals and personal problems. Then, Michael Hirst, former Tory party chairman in Scotland, was forced to pull out from the race to succeed Stewart when a sexual scandal threatened to appear in the newspapers. Paul Cullen, the Solicitor-General for Scotland, eventually became the candidate, but too late to stop the Tories' safest Scottish seat from falling to Labour on a swing of over 14 per cent.

The Conservatives put up a better performance in the Scottish parliamentary elections in 1999, thanks to efforts of the 66-year old veteran Glasgow councillor, John Young. However, in 2001, Jim Murphy, a former President of the National Union of Students, trebled his 1997 majority against Raymond Robertson, the Scottish Tory chairman and victor in Aberdeen South in 1992. Robertson undoubtedly suffered from tactical voting against him. The SNP vote here collapsed by 4.5 per cent and Labour's shot up by nearly eight per cent. The Tory vote also dropped further (as it did in a number of seats like this south of the border), though any future Conservative recovery in Scotland (if one is ever to come) must surely include the party recapturing this seat.

GREENOCK and INVERCLYDE

	2001		1997		1992 notional	
Electorate and turnout	47,884	59.3	48,971	70.8	51,442	74.5
Conservative	3,000	10.6	3,976	11.5	8,081	21.1
Labour	14,929	52.5	19,480	56.2	18,319	47.8
Lib Dem	5,039	17.7	4,791	13.8	5,324	13.9
SNP	4,248	14.9	6,440	18.6	6,621	17.3
SSP	1,203	4.2	–	–	–	–
MP	David Cairns (Lab)		Norman Godman (Lab)		Norman Godman(Lab) Greenock and Port Glasgow	
Majority	9,890	34.8	13,040	37.6	10,238	26.7

Scottish Parliament Election 1999: Labour 11,817 (41.3), Lib Dem 7,504 (26.2), SNP 6,762 (23.6), Conservative 1,699 (5.9), SSP 857 (3.0). Electorate 48,584, Turnout 59.0%. MSP: Duncan McNeil (Lab), Majority 4,313 (15.1).

The old seat of Greenock and Port Glasgow was dismembered in 1995 when it lost the former ship-building town of Port Glasgow to Renfrewshire West. In return, Greenock gained the Inverclyde area, including the towns of Gourock and Wemyss (pronounced 'Weems') Bay. The old industries that sustained the working-class town of Greenock have been replaced in recent years by computer and electronics factories, but the town still votes Labour. The English-born Dr Norman Godman served as the MP here from 1983 until his retirement in 2001.

Like Glasgow Kelvin, this seat was once a rare Scottish example of Labour-Liberal competition. In 1970, Labour won the seat by only 3,000 votes from the Liberals, and local elections regularly resulted in the election of Liberal councillors. In October 1981, the sitting Labour MP Dr Dickson Mabon defected to the SDP, but the Liberals in Greenock would not let him stand as the SDP-Liberal Alliance candidate in 1983, so he stood unsuccessfully in neighbouring Renfrew West and Inverclyde. Even without Mabon, the local Liberal candidate still polled 36 per cent of the vote. The Tories briefly occupied second place in 1992, before the SNP emerged as the nearest challengers to Labour in 1997. Recent electoral results in 1999 and 2001, however, suggest that the Liberal Democrats have re-emerged in second place behind Labour, although the Scottish parliamentary contest developed into a three-way marginal between Labour, the Liberal Democrats and the SNP. Given all this keen competition for second place, the position of David Cairns, former Roman Catholic priest and successor to Godman, looks very secure without the need to resort to prayer to ensure his re-election.

PAISLEY NORTH

	2001		1997		1992 notional	
Electorate and turnout	47,994	56.6	49,725	68.6	49,702	73.9
Conservative	2,404	8.9	3,267	9.6	5,757	15.7
Labour	15,058	55.5	20,295	59.5	19,043	51.9
Lib Dem	2,709	10.0	2,365	6.9	2,828	7.7
SNP	5,737	21.1	7,481	21.9	8,629	23.5
SSP	982	3.6	–	–	–	–
Others	263		727 (2)		456	
MP	Irene Adams (Lab)		Irene Adams (Lab)		Irene Adams (Lab)	
Majority	9,321	34.3	12,814	37.5	10,414	28.4

Scottish Parliament Election 1999: Labour 13,492 (48.6), SNP 8,876 (32.0), Conservative 2,242 (8.1), Lib Dem 2,133 (7.7), SSP 1,007 (3.6). Electorate 49,020, Turnout 56.6%. MSP: Wendy Alexander (Lab), Majority 4,616 (16.6).

Paisley was once home to Golden Shred marmalade and several cotton mills that produced the town's famous Paisley pattern (now reduced to just one), but it still boasts St Mirren Football Club, who have won the Scottish Cup on three occasions. Until 1983, Scotland's fifth largest urban centre consisted of only one parliamentary constituency, and was briefly held by the Liberal leader and former Prime Minister Herbert Asquith from 1920 until he lost to Labour in October 1924. In 1983, the town was split in half, with Paisley North gaining the nearby town of Renfrew, and in 1997 it took in the former car plant town of Linwood from Renfrewshire West. Both towns are solidly Labour. The only prospects for the Tories in Paisley lie in the town's middle-class Ralston area. The seat also contains the notorious Ferguslie Park estate (known as 'Feegie' by the locals), whose tenement dwellers lived in some of the worst council housing in Scotland. Fortunately, much of this estate has now been demolished but the social problems in Paisley, particularly those associated with drugs, still remain.

By tragic coincidence, both of Paisley's MPs (Allen Adams and Norman Buchan) died in the same month (November 1990), and both by-elections were held on the same day. Labour's Irene Adams was selected to succeed her late husband, Allen Adams (MP for Paisley from 1979, and for re-drawn Paisley North from 1983) at the by-election, which was overshadowed by the Tory leadership contest of that month. Both Mrs Adams and Gordon McMaster in Paisley South easily held off the challenge of the SNP. Freed from any serious challenger, the local Labour party adopted the favourite Scottish tradition of engaging in internal feuding. In 1997, Adams spoke out against Tommy Graham, her neighbouring MP in Renfrewshire West, who was accused of mounting a whispering campaign against Gordon McMaster in Paisley South. It was alleged that Graham's behaviour had contributed to the suicide of McMaster in July 1997. Despite the local feuding, Labour remains impregnable here. At the Scottish parliamentary elections in May 1999, Labour's Wendy Alexander, who became Minister for

Communities in the First Scottish Executive under Donald Dewar, finished with a percentage majority roughly half that of that enjoyed by Adams at Westminster (still a majority of almost 5,000), as the SNP polled 32 per cent. Alexander survived McConnell's reshuffle in late 2001 to remain as Minister for Enterprise, Transport and Lifelong Learning (a job she held under Henry McLeish) though she resigned in 2002. As with so much of urban Scotland, the SNP fell back to around 20 per cent at the Westminster elections in 2001.

PAISLEY SOUTH

	2001		1997		1992 *notional*	
Electorate and turnout	53,351	57.2	54,040	69.1	*53,800*	*74.2*
Conservative	2,301	7.5	3,237	8.7	*6,129*	*15.4*
Labour	17,830	58.4	21,482	57.5	*20,268*	*50.8*
Lib Dem	3,178	10.4	3,500	9.4	*3,548*	*8.9*
SNP	5,920	19.4	8,732	23.4	*9,799*	*24.6*
SSP	835	2.7	–	–	–	–
Others	472 (2)		400 (2)		*150*	
MP	Douglas Alexander(Lab)		Gordon McMaster(Lab)		Gordon McMaster(Lab)	
Majority	11,910	39.0	12,750	34.1	*10,469*	*26.2*

Scottish Parliament Election 1999: Labour 13,899 (45.3), SNP 9,404 (30.7), Lib Dem 2,974 (9.7), Conservative 2,433 (7.9), Independent 1,273 (4.2), SWP (2.2). Electorate 53,637, Turnout 57.2%. MSP: Hugh Henry (Lab), Majority 4,495 (14.7).

Parliamentary by-election 6 November 1997: Labour 10,346 (44.1), SNP 7,615 (32.5), Lib Dem 2,582 (11.0), Conservative 1,643 (7.0), 5 Others 1,249. Electorate 54,386, Turnout 43.1%. MP: Douglas Alexander (Lab), Majority 2,731 (11.7).

Since the 1983 boundary changes, the southern half of Paisley has included the smaller town of Johnstone. But despite the 1983 split of Paisley, the town's southern half votes very similarly to its northern half, providing secure Labour majorities.

As previously mentioned, Paisley South saw one of two by-elections held in the town on 29 November 1990, after the death of Norman Buchan, MP for Renfrewshire West from 1964 to 1983, and for the re-drawn seat of Paisley South until 1990. As with Irene Adams in Paisley North, Labour's Gordon McMaster comfortably held off the SNP, and increased his majority in 1992 and 1997. However, his suicide in July 1997 provoked a second by-election in the constituency. In November 1997, Douglas Alexander, brother of Paisley North MSP Wendy Alexander, and a former researcher to the Chancellor, Gordon Brown, saw his party's 1997 majority over the SNP cut by nearly 10,000 votes to just over 2,700. Then, in the 1999 Scottish parliamentary elections, Hugh Henry, Labour's candidate and a former leader of Renfrewshire Council held the seat despite the SNP polling over 30 per cent of the vote. Henry was promoted to the Scottish Executive as the Deputy Minister for Health and Community Care as a result of the McConnell reshuffle of November 2001. In June 2001, Douglas Alexander, who played a key role in Labour's overall election campaign, was returned to Westminster by a much more comfort-able margin, increasing McMaster's majority over the SNP by five per cent.

RENFREWSHIRE WEST

	2001		1997		1992 notional	
Electorate and turnout	52,889	63.3	52,348	76.0	51,833	77.3
Conservative	5,522	16.5	7,387	18.6	11,128	27.8
Labour	15,720	46.9	18,525	46.6	17,174	42.9
Lib Dem	4,185	12.5	3,045	7.7	3,375	8.4
SNP	7,145	21.3	10,546	26.5	8,258	20.6
SSP	925	2.8	–	–	–	–
Others	–		283		129	
MP	James Sheridan (Lab)		Thomas Graham(Lab)		Thomas Graham(Lab)	
			(Ind Lab)		Renfrew West and Inverclyde	
Majority	8,575	25.6	7,979	20.1	6,046	15.1

Scottish Parliament Election 1999: Labour 12,708 (37.3), SNP 9,815 (28.8), Conservative 7,243 (21.3), Lib Dem 2,659 (7.8), Independent 1,136 (3.3), Others 476 (1.4). Electorate 52,452, Turnout 64.9%. MSP: Patricia Godman (Lab), Majority 2,893 (8.5).

Renfrew West and Inverclyde was a creation of the 1983 Boundary Commission, and, believe it or not, a Tory seat held by Anna McCurley until 1987. Since then, both the political affiliation of the former Tory MP and the colour of the constituency have changed. By the 1999 Scottish parliamentary elections, McCurley had changed party, and stood as the Liberal Democrat candidate in Eastwood. In 1987, Labour's Tommy Graham took the seat for Labour, but struggled to hold it from the Tories in the mini-Conservative revival of 1992 when Annabel Goldie, the local Tory candidate from Bishopton came within 1,744 votes of recapturing the seat.

Then, in 1995, the Boundary Commission came to the aid of Labour when it ceded the mostly Tory seaside towns of Gourock and Wemyss Bay in the Inverclyde area to form the new seat of Greenock and Inverclyde. Not only that, but Labour gained the former shipbuilding town of Port Glasgow from Greenock, a pretty good deal for Labour by any standards. Despite these losses, the Tories could still look to the fact that 60 per cent of the new constituency's electors were owner-occupiers. The well-heeled towns of Bishopton, Bridge of Weir, Houston and Kilmacolm could be counted upon as Tory areas, although Labour could also boast its old stronghold in the New Town of Erskine. But the 1995 Boundary Commission's actions meant that Labour's majority here in 1997 rose to almost 8,000.

In July 1997, the Renfrewshire area was rocked by the suicide of Gordon McMaster, Labour MP in the neighbouring Paisley South. Tommy Graham was accused of conducting a smear campaign against his colleague, and was suspended, and later expelled from the Labour party.

Patricia Godman, a Glasgow city councillor and wife of Norman Godman, the MP for Greenock and Inverclyde from 1983 to 2001, won the Scottish parliamentary seat after a closely fought battle with the SNP's Colin Campbell. Both Campbell and the third place Tory Annabel Goldie were elected as regional list MSPs for the West of Scotland. The journalist and Liberal Democrat candidate, Neal Ascherson could only poll 2,659 votes. Former local football hero and Greenock Morton manager, Allan McGraw, endorsed by the expelled Tommy Graham, who chose not to stand in the Scottish parliament elections on health grounds, polled a respectable 1,136 votes. In 2001, Graham's replacement, James Sheridan increased Labour's majority by over 5 per cent, as the SNP slipped back to 21 per cent. Charles Cormack, son of the Staffordshire South MP, Sir Patrick Cormack, finished in third place ahead of the Liberal Democrats.

STRATHKELVIN and BEARSDEN

	2001		1997		1992 notional	
Electorate and turnout	62,869	66.0	63,056	78.8	63,483	80.8
Conservative	6,635	16.0	9,986	20.1	16,710	32.6
Labour	19,250	46.4	26,278	52.9	23,658	46.1
Lib Dem	7,533	18.2	4,843	9.7	4,252	8.3
SNP	6,675	16.1	8,111	16.3	6,621	12.9
SSP	1,393	3.4	–	–	–	–
Others	–		494 (2)		85	
MP	John Lyons (Lab)		Sam Galbraith (Lab)		Sam Galbraith (Lab)	
Majority	11,717	28.2	16,292	32.8	6,948	13.5

Scottish Parliament Election 1999: Labour 21,505 (50.7), SNP 9,384 (22.1), Conservative 6,934 (16.4), Lib Dem 4,144 (9.8), Others 423 (1.0). Electorate 63,111, Turnout 67.2%. MSP: Sam Galbraith (Lab), Majority 12,121 (28.6).

Scottish Parliament by-election June 2001: Labour 15,401 (37.0), Independent 7,572 (18.2), Lib Dem 7,147 (17.2), SNP 6,457 (15.5), Conservative 5,037 (12.1). Electorate 62,869, Turnout 66.2%. MSP: Brian Fitzpatrick (Lab), Majority 7,829 (18.8).

Just as Eastwood would be a safe Tory seat if it were located in England, so would Strathkelvin and Bearsden. The seat as a whole had an owner-occupancy rate of 75 per cent in the 1991 census, with the Bearsden area reaching 90 per cent. Over 40 out of ten of this constituency's electors have professional or managerial jobs, while only a third work in manual trades. Admittedly, Strathkelvin comprises the mainly Labour towns of Bishopbriggs and Kirkintilloch, but the houses in Bearsden are among the best of the suburbs situated to the north of the City of Glasgow. And yet, in 1987, Labour's Sam Galbraith, a consultant neurosurgeon, took this seat from the Conservative Michael Hirst. Galbraith, a Scottish Office minister since 1997, stood down in 1999 to devote all his energies as a minister in the Scottish Executive. Although Galbraith had no trouble beating the SNP into second place (with the Tories finishing a distant and dismal third), he had much more difficulty as Minister for Education during the summer of 2000 when many Scottish pupils were given the wrong exam results. In October 2000, Galbraith was shunted sideways as Environment Minister before choosing to retire in 2001. In June 2001, the Liberal Democrats jumped from fourth to second in the Westminster elections, pushing the Tories into an unbelievable fourth place, as Galbraith's successor John Lyons ran home the easy winner. On the same day, Galbraith's decision to retire from Holyrood provoked a by-election in which Labour's Brian Fitzpatrick held on, despite a strong challenge from Jean Turner, a retired local GP, who stood as an Independent candidate in order to protest at changes to acute services at the local Stobhill Hospital. Turner finished in second place with over 7,500 votes, half of whom appear to have supported Labour in the general election.

Wales

By Russell Deacon, University of Wales Institute, Cardiff

Since the Liberals lost their control of Welsh politics in the early part of the twentieth century, Wales has been a Labour Party fiefdom. At Westminster level Labour have dominated to an even greater extent over the last two elections than ever before. In 1997 and 2001 they won 34 of the 40 Welsh seats, many with substantial majorities. The 2001 general election, as in many places in the United Kingdom, was something of a non-event in Wales. Although ten new MPs were elected, only two resulted from seats changing hands and the overall political score sheet remained unchanged from 1997. The two gains (Plaid Cymru's Adam Price gaining Carmarthen East & Dinefwr from Labour, and Labour's Albert Owen gaining Ynys Mon from Plaid) constituted the least change at an election in Wales since October 1974. The most prominent feature of the general election was the failure of any new women to gain election to Wales. The closest was the Liberal Democrat Jenny Willott in Cardiff Central. Wales has an appalling record in electing women to Westminster; since Ann Clwyd was elected for the Cynon Valley in 1984, there has not been a single woman elected to Westminster without the help of all-women short lists.

Wales has been important to Labour in the past because it has provided seats for two of their Prime Ministers: Ramsay MacDonald and James Callaghan; and three leaders who never became Prime Minister: Keir Hardie, Michael Foot and Neil Kinnock. Of these, only Kinnock was actually Welsh. It has provided them with statesmen and Cabinet members: Aneurin Bevan, Jim Griffiths, Cledwyn Hughes and George Thomas to name but a few. Much of industrial Wales has always remained loyal to Labour, even when their cause looked hopeless as in the 1980s. Since Kinnock's departure from British politics in 1995 there have, however, been few prominent Welsh Labour politicians. Outside of the now 'toothless' position of Welsh Secretary there have been no MPs representing Welsh constituencies in the Cabinet of any party, let alone Labour, since 1979. Alun Michael and Peter Hain remain the strongest Welsh MPs within the government, though Wales normally has four or so other MPs with junior Ministerial posts. The Wales Labour Party has therefore lost much of the influence it once had over the national Labour Party. Under Rhodri Morgan, however, it has recovered much of its internal Welsh strength.

At the time of writing (early 2002), Labour remain pre-eminent in Welsh politics: dominant at Westminster, the largest party in Welsh local government, the largest group in the National Assembly for Wales (Welsh Assembly) and equal with Plaid Cymru in their number of MEPs (two). A number of Welsh Labour MPs are sitting on some of their party's safest majorities in the United Kingdom. Many of the constituencies they represent also lack any significant organised opposition, which makes it a formidable task for anyone challenging Labour. Currently at Westminster, Labour represent every constituency on the North Wales coast and every constituency on the South Wales coast, though they control nothing in between. Their weakness lies only in rural Wales.

The last time Labour seriously wobbled at a Westminster level was in 1983, when a strong intervention by the Liberal / SDP Alliance reduced the Labour vote enough to enable the Conservatives to gain 14 seats in Wales. For the first time ever it was possible to travel from the tip of North Wales to the bottom of East Wales without leaving Conservative-held territory. Their fortunes have since been reversed, and for the past two elections have not been able to win a single seat in Wales, the country remaining a 'Tory-free zone' (unlike Scotland) in 2001. With the Conservatives being wiped out in 1997 after forty years as the second party of Wales, Plaid Cymru took this position by default, without gaining another seat but managing to hold their existing four.

The Conservatives in Wales appear to be in terminal decline. They have suffered wide-scale defections and voter apathy. They no longer have councillors on half of Welsh local authorities, having a lower number in total than any other major political party in Wales. Their failure to secure a single Westminster seat in 2001 has also damaged their credibility. Although the party remains firmly against proportional representation for elections, it remains their only salvation. Their one MEP and 8 out of 9 Assembly Members (AM's) are only there because of PR elections. Nearly all of the Assembly Members, including the party's leader Nick Bourne, were supporters of Kenneth Clarke in the leadership contest, which means they may not sit too comfortably in Iain Duncan Smith's Conservative Party. The party's Assembly elections under the leadership of Nick Bourne in 2003 will represent the first chance for the Conservatives to prove that they are still a living force to be reckoned with. They have a lot of work to do electorally.

Plaid Cymru, now the second party of Wales, were responsible for Labour's second wobble in recent history. That was in the 1999 Assembly and county councils elections, when Plaid gained no fewer than 17 of the 60 seats, and came within a whisker of depriving Labour of six more. At the same time they took control of two of Labour's heartland councils (Caerphilly and Rhondda Cynon Taff), making them the second party of local government as well. Plaid Cymru's success shocked and stunned much of the Wales Labour Party and seats long taken for granted by them (Islwyn, Rhondda) were lost. Since then, however, Plaid Cymru have suffered a number of serious misfortunes. Dafydd Wigley, the charismatic leader of the party stepped down in the summer of 2000 and was replaced by the much weaker Ieuan Wyn Jones. Since then the party's fortunes have declined, and although they increased their share of vote in the general election of 2001 and gained one seat, Carmarthen East & Dinefwr, at the same time they lost their leader's former seat, Ynys Mon (Anglesey), to Labour. In January 2002, three of Plaid Cymru's most prominent politicians announced that they would not stand again for the Welsh Assembly (former leader Dafydd Wigley, former MP and head of policy Cynog Dafis, and Professor Phil Williams). Plaid Cymru has also been suffering defections to the Conservatives and the Independent Wales Party. Whilst the party is by no means finished, it is no longer as healthy as it was in 1999. There is a lot of work to be done before they can effectively challenge a Labour Party still riding the success of its 2001 general election results.

The Liberal Democrats remain the fourth party of Welsh politics at the Welsh Assembly and in Europe, but the third party at Westminster and in local government. At election times, they are often written off but nevertheless they have managed to hang on and now form part of the Welsh Assembly's ruling coalition. Electorally they have a habit of winning new seats only to lose an old one. This could happen again, with them gaining Cardiff Central for example, whilst losing Brecon and Radnorshire. They remain slow movers electorally, and only increase their percentage of the vote incrementally. The biggest threat they hold to the other political parties is in taking votes off them when challenging Labour for a seat. Under their new leader Mike German they have become more effective at targeting and the 2003 Assembly elections may see them increase their number of list Assembly Members by one or two, probably at the expense of Plaid Cymru.

Local government

Since 1995, Welsh local government has been structured under 22 unitary authorities. In the first elections to the new bodies, Labour won control (either outright or through coalitions) of 17 of them, but this did not last and in 1999 they lost a number of authorities, particularly in South Wales. Plaid Cymru are now the second party of local government, controlling three councils outright (Caerphilly, Gwynedd and Rhondda Cynon Taff) and having an influence on a number of other council cabinets including Carmarthenshire, Conwy, Denbighshire and the Vale of Glamorgan. The Conservatives control no councils outright but are the lead party in two authorities (Monmouthshire and the Vale of Glamorgan). The Liberal Democrats only have council coalition representation on two authorities (Ceredigion and Conwy) but are not the largest group in any Welsh council. The Independents reasserted themselves in the 1999 elections and today lead some six councils and are in coalition or the main opposition in around eight more.

In the autumn of 2001, the National Assembly set up the Sunderland Commission to review the future method of elections to Welsh local authorities. Its chair is Professor Eric Sunderland, chair of the Welsh Local Government Boundary Commission. The Sunderland Commission is examining a number of electoral systems including the current 'First Past The Post' system, Single Transferable Vote and the Additional Member System, currently used in the Assembly elections. The existing system suffers from two main problems; first, the high number of unopposed councillors, over 50 per cent in some authorities. Second, the electoral system encourages the skewing of votes and the subsequent rise of one party states with no or little opposition and the consequent problems over accountability that this involves. The Sunderland Commission will seek to find solutions to these concerns.

The Welsh Assembly has determined that the Welsh local government elections will be in 2004 and not 2003 as was originally intended. Officially this is because they do not want them to clash with the Assembly elections so that one body undermines the elections to the other. Unofficially Labour AMs blame their party's poor performance in 1999 on the fact that a number of the unpopular Labour councils had helped Plaid Cymru persuade voters to support them at both the Assembly and council elections. Thus the 2004 elections should be undertaken without the confusion of any other elections occurring on the same day. Depending on the conclusions of the Sunderland Commission, however, and whether these are endorsed by the Welsh Assembly and Westminster, they could also be the last council elections under First Past The Post or the first under a new electoral system.

Boundary review

The Boundary Commission for Wales' review of Parliamentary and Assembly constituencies is currently timetabled to commence in 2002 and report in the summer of 2005. Therefore there will be no changes to the existing Parliamentary and Assembly constituencies for Wales (for example in the Assembly elections in 2003) until after the next rounds of Assembly and Westminster elections. Unlike Scotland, it is not expected that Wales will lose seats in the forthcoming review because the Welsh Assembly is not a law-making parliament and all primary legislation remains at Westminster.

North Wales

	Conservative		Labour		Liberal Democrat		Plaid Cymru		Others	
	Share of vote	Seats	Share of vote	Seats	Share of vote	Seats	Share of vote	Seats	Share of vote	Seats
2001	25.7	0	45.2	8	12.0	0	15.3	1	1.7	0
1997	24.2	0	46.9	7	11.7	0	14.1	2	3.0	0
1992	36.2	2	37.7	5	12.8	0	12.7	2	0.6	0
1999 C	19.0	0	35.5	6	10.1	0	32.3	3	3.0	0
1999 R	19.4	2	34.2	0	10.3	1	32.3	1	3.9	0

NOTE: 1999C=Welsh Assembly Elections Constituency vote; 1999R=Welsh Assembly Elections Regional top-up vote (4 seats available)

The North Wales electoral region covers nine constituencies from Caernarfon in the west to Wrexham on the border with England. The majority of these seats stretch along the A55 or A5 North Wales roads, which is about the only thing they all have in common. Like Mid and West Wales the region contains some of the highest and lowest percentages of Welsh speakers in Wales. At a Parliamentary level the region has traditionally been the stronghold of both Welsh Conservatism and Nationalism with Labour recording its least successful electoral performances in this region. From 1997 onwards, however, constituencies have been divided between Plaid Cymru and the Labour Party with the Conservatives and Liberal Democrats having to make do with the odd Assembly list seat. Nationally, the Tories must regain Clwyd West if they are to improve their position at all; an overall majority would probably require Conwy and Vale of Clwyd as well.

In total, the region now includes nine parliamentary constituencies, six unitary authorities, nine Assembly constituencies and four regional list members (currently Peter Rogers, Conservative; Rod Richards, Independent Conservative; Eleanor Burnham, Liberal Democrat and Janet Ryder, Plaid Cymru). With the exception of Ieuan Wyn Jones, Plaid Cymru's leader, there is an absence of senior political figures in the region. All of the Assembly Cabinet Ministers, for instance, are based in the South of Wales. This factor only adds to the feeling that North Wales is excluded from much of the political power in both Wales and Westminster.

Local government
There are six unitary councils in North Wales (though Gwynedd is split with Mid and West Wales and will be dealt with under that section). Two are controlled by Independents, three by Labour or Labour-

led coalitions, and one by Plaid Cymru. As elsewhere in Wales, the councils are often the political training ground for future MPs and AMs. Unlike elsewhere in Wales, however, most councils are pluralistic in nature with none of the appearance of one party states that occur in the South. The Independent tradition is prominent in all of them, and they make up at least 20 per cent of members on each authority.

The former district councils of Aberconwy and Colwyn were joined together to make Conwy county borough council in 1995. Bearing in mind recent electoral history, it should have been the Liberal Democrats who were the majority party on the new council, as they had the largest number of councillors on the two former councils. In the event, Labour gained the largest share of councillors (18), with the Lib Dems coming a close second (17 councillors) and the other parties also enjoying representation together with Independents. The 1999 elections saw a slight decline in Liberal Democrat and Conservative fortunes and a rise in those of Plaid Cymru and the Independents. Not that politics is a reason for exclusion in Conwy. Though Labour have held the leadership, every group has a post in the cabinet and posts are shared out in accordance with the number of council seats held. Denbighshire county council existed for a century before being abolished prior to the local government reorganisation of 1974. It then came back again some twenty-one years later as part of the Conservatives reorganisation of Welsh local government. It is another of those authorities which Independent councillors tend to dominate. The Independents have gained the largest number of council seats at both the 1995 and 1999 elections (19 and then 17). Although always short of a majority (47 seats overall in 1999) the Independents have continued to control the council through a coalition with Plaid Cymru. Flintshire county council also has historic roots that date back centuries. Unlike Denbighshire, however, it a strongly Labour county. Up until 1999 the council leader was Tom Middlehurst now Labour AM for Alyn and Deeside. Labour have had little trouble in the last two council elections in gaining over half of the seats. Their nearest political opponents, the Liberal Democrats have languished on 7 seats for the last two elections compared to Labour's 42 in 1995 and 40 in 1999. The Independents have some 15 seats, and the other political parties just a handful. Flintshire is also currently unique in having Wales' only elected Green councillor.

The only thing that changes in Anglesey county council is the name, alternating between Ynys Mon and Anglesey, depending on the mood of the council. Whatever it is called, it has been controlled by Independents at a borough and then county council level for as long as anyone can remember. At times Plaid Cymru, Labour and the Conservatives have managed to secure a handful of councillors; currently Plaid Cymru have eight and Labour four against the Independents' 28. Over recent years the council has been the subject of a number of critical reviews concerning the Independent run authority. Despite widespread local anger concerning this mismanagement, there has not been an effective challenge to the status quo with the political parties being unable to secure anywhere near enough candidates to take on the Independents. Finally, Wrexham county borough council is made up of the former Wrexham Maelor district council and the southern part of Glyndwr district council. Wrexham Maelor was always a strongly held Labour council, with Glyndwr controlled by Independents. When this was translated into the new authority in 1995, it resulted in a Labour controlled council with a large group of Independents. The Liberal Democrats, whose power base is the town of Wrexham itself, remain the strongest political party outside of Labour but with only around a quarter of Labour's councillors. The Conservatives also have a significant number of councillors, although they now go under the designation of 'Independent

Conservatives'. Labour lost overall control in 1999 but remain in power with the help of coalition allies. The next elections therefore could see the emergence of a rainbow coalition that would take control of the council off Labour, or Labour's return to full control. Either way, there seems likely to be fierce competition for all seats within the council.

ALYN and DEESIDE

	2001		1997		1992 *notional*	
Electorate and turnout	60,478	58.6	58,091	72.2	*57,815*	*78.7*
Conservative	9,303	26.3	9,552	22.8	*16,770*	*36.9*
Labour	18,525	52.3	25,955	61.9	*23,157*	*50.9*
Lib Dem	4,585	12.9	4,076	9.7	*4,431*	*9.7*
Plaid Cymru	1,182	3.3	738	1.8	*517*	*1.1*
Anti–EU	481	1.4	1,627	3.9	–	–
Others	1,345 (3)		–		*633*	
MP	Mark Tami (Lab)		Barry Jones (Lab)		Barry Jones (Lab)	
Majority	9,222	26.0	16,403	39.1	*6,387*	*14.0*

Welsh Assembly Election 1999: Labour 9,772 (51.4), Conservative 3,413 (17.9), Plaid Cymru 2,304 (12.1), Lib Dem 1,879 (9.9), 2 Others 1,662. Electorate 59,386, Turnout 32.0%. AM: Tom Middlehurst (Lab), Majority 6,359 (33.4).

The heavily industrial area of Alyn and Deeside is the Welsh hinterland of Chester and Merseyside. The seat is mainly industrial and the home of European Airbus' wing construction, which is based at Broughton. The people of Alyn and Deeside have more affinity with England and Liverpool than with Wales and Cardiff and therefore their politics closely reflect that area at a Westminster level. While Barry Jones was MP from 1970-2001, (the seat was known as East Flint until 1983), the constituency has been solidly Labour in its preferences. Although he served in the Wilson/Callaghan government (1974-1979), Jones never rose above the rank of Parliamentary Private Secretary. Nevertheless he was Shadow Welsh Secretary and Welsh Affairs Spokesman between 1983-87 under former leader Neil Kinnock. Kinnock's demise also saw the fall of Jones who left the Shadow Cabinet and was never called to join the Blair government. In 2001, Jones decided to resign at the last minute in response to being offered a peerage and the seat was filled by Labour's Mark Tami, Welsh University educated and Head of Policy at the Amalgamated and Electrical Engineering Union. Tami has the reputation of something of a rising star and may succeed in gaining that elusive post in government denied to his predecessor.

The Conservative vote increased to 26.6 per cent in the 2001 general election, though in 1983 (the first year that the seat was established) they came within 1,368 (3.1%) of winning. Since that date, however, the Labour majority has never been less than 13.6% (1987). This is also one of Plaid Cymru's weakest Westminster seats with them failing to have every retained their deposit here. In the current political climate, this seat looks set to stay firmly in Labour's grasp.

Assembly seat
In the 1997 Assembly Referendum, some six out of ten of the forty percent who bothered to turn out

voted against having a Welsh Assembly. This gave Alyn and Deeside (within the county of Flintshire) the third highest 'No' vote of Wales' 22 counties. Therefore it was perhaps unsurprising that the seat had the worst electoral turnout in Wales at the Assembly elections, just 32 per cent. Tom Middlehurst, former Leader of Flintshire County Council and Chair of the Welsh Local Government Association, was elected for Labour with a massive 33.5 per cent majority, one of the highest in Wales for Labour. Middlehurst resigned from the Cabinet in October 2000 in opposition to the formation of a coalition government with the Liberal Democrats. Although many saw this as a case of resigning before being pushed, his backbench status is unlikely to impact much on his seat's majority. The size of the Labour majority reflects the fact that it is resistant to the Nationalist pressures that plague similarly structured industrial seats in the South of Wales. The main threat is from the Conservatives, but this remains very distant.

CAERNARFON

	2001		1997		1992 actual	
Electorate and turnout	46,850	62.0	46,815	73.7	45,348	80.1
Conservative	4,403	15.2	4,230	12.3	6,963	19.2
Labour	9,383	32.3	10,167	29.5	5,641	15.5
Lib Dem	1,823	6.3	1,686	4.9	2,101	5.8
Plaid Cymru	12,894	44.4	17,616	51.0	21,439	59.0
Anti–EU	550	1.9	811	2.4	–	–
Others	–		–		173	
MP	Hywel Williams (PC)		Dafydd Wigley (PC)		Dafydd Wigley (PC)	
Majority	3,511	12.1	7,449	21.6	14,476	39.9

Welsh Assembly Election 1999: Plaid Cymru 18,748 (65.8), Labour 6,475 (22.7), Conservative 2,464 (8.7), Lib Dem 791 (2.8). Electorate 47,213, Turnout 60.3%. AM: Dafydd Wigley (PC), Majority: 12,273 (43.1)

Caernarfon covers the Lleyn Peninsula and sections of the Snowdonia National Park. As the name suggests it also covers the town of Caernarfon, in whose castle Prince Charles was crowned Prince of Wales in 1969. Ironically, this is perhaps the most nationalist and hence republican of any Welsh constituency. Between 1945 and 2001 there were only two MPs for the seat; Goronwy Roberts, Labour's pro-nationalist Welsh Office Minister (1945-1974), and the even more Nationalist former leader of Plaid Cymru, Dafydd Wigley (1974-2001). Wigley developed into one of the best orators his party has produced and gathered up a massive personal vote in his seat and for his party in general. Until ill health forced him to resign as President of his party in the summer of 2000, he was widely regarded as one the most formidable politicians in Wales.

Wigley was a hard act to follow when he announced he was to resign his Westminster seat at the 2001 election. His successor Hywel Williams was elected with a greatly reduced majority and Labour came into serious contention for the seat for the first time since October 1974. Caernarfon is now the tenth most marginal constituency in Wales. Williams will have to work hard to match the success of his predecessor and the next general election will be a fierce Plaid Cymru – Labour battle. An interesting seat to watch.

Assembly Seat

Dafydd Wigley achieved the highest majority for both himself and Plaid Cymru during the 1999 Assembly elections, a massive 43.1 per cent over his Labour rival. It is perhaps a fitting tribute to the way that Wigley worked the seat as a constituency MP, combined with his leadership of Plaid Cymru, that such a massive majority was accumulated. At these elections Wigley was able to take Plaid Cymru closer to power than anyone but the most faithful nationalist had deemed possible. In January 2002, however, Wigley announced he was to leave the Welsh Assembly at the 2003 elections. Statistically Plaid Cymru should comfortably be able to hold onto the seat, but without the Wigley factor, the situation may alter radically. Added to the problems of Wigley's departure will be the contesting of the seat by the Independent Wales Party (IWP). The IWP are committed to an independent Welsh republic, something which Plaid Cymru are not, but it is a notion that many of the their members and supporters believe in. The IWP's share of the vote may weaken Plaid Cymru's position enough to allow a strong challenger some hope of victory. If the Westminster elections are anything to go by, Labour will be putting considerable resources into trying to win this prize trophy off Plaid Cymru, in revenge for their own losses in 1999.

CLWYD SOUTH

	2001		1997		1992 notional	
Electorate and turnout	53,680	62.4	53,495	73.6	53,963	79.0
Conservative	8,319	24.8	9,091	23.1	12,897	30.3
Labour	17,217	51.4	22,901	58.1	21,229	49.8
Lib Dem	3,426	10.2	3,684	9.4	4,727	11.1
Plaid Cymru	3,982	11.9	2,500	6.3	3,394	8.0
Anti–EU	552	1.6	1,207	3.1	–	–
Others	–		–		390	
MP	Martyn Jones (Lab)		Martyn Jones (Lab)		Martyn Jones (Lab)	
					Clwyd South West	
Majority	8,898	26.6	13,810	35.1	8,332	19.5

Welsh Assembly Election 1999: Labour 9,196 (42.2), Plaid Cymru 5,511 (25.3), Conservative 4,167 (19.1), Lib Dem 2,432 (11.1), 1 Other 508. Electorate 53,843, Turnout 40.5%. AM: Karen Sinclair (Lab), Majority 3,685 (16.9).

Clwyd South was created in 1997 from the former seat of Clwyd South West and parts of Wrexham thrown in for good measure. The constituency's main employment is in the agricultural, service, and light industrial manufacturing areas; it thus lacks the heavy engineering and mining background of some of its neighbours. Former microbiologist Martyn Jones won the new seat, having been MP for the old Clwyd South West from 1987-1997. Jones is prominent for his chairing of the Welsh Affairs Select Committee, which has a key role is scrutinising all aspects of government policy affecting Wales.

Prior to Jones' victory in 1987, the Conservatives had held the former constituency of Denbigh, part of which went to make up the new constituency, and Clwyd South is another one of the North Wales seats where the Conservatives have polled a respectable second place in the past. In 1997, the colourful figure of Boris Johnson, now MP for Henley, became one of the Conservative alumni who have contested the seat and its predecessors. Clwyd South also has a sizeable Welsh speaking population, around 23 per cent, which has helped boost the Plaid Cymru vote in recent elections.

Assembly seat

Labour's victor in the 1999 Assembly election for Clwyd South had trod the well travelled path to winning a constituency seat. Karen Sinclair had been a local district and county councillor for some years, an active member of the 'Yes' campaign in the Welsh referendum and importantly a key member of UNISON. At the Welsh Assembly she holds the position of Welsh Whip which is an apt profession for someone whose preferred pastime is horse riding. Sinclair secured a 16.9 per cent majority over Plaid Cymru, and it was the Nationalists best ever showing in the seat. Although the result was less good for

Labour than that in recent general elections, Sinclair is still in a commanding position. The Conservatives failed to make the same challenge that they do at Westminster, and Clwyd South looks set to remain in the Labour camp baring another massive surge to Plaid Cymru.

CLWYD WEST

	2001		1997		1992 notional	
Electorate and turnout	53,962	64.1	53,467	75.3	53,827	77.2
Conservative	12,311	35.6	13,070	32.5	20,132	48.5
Labour	13,426	38.8	14,918	37.1	12,819	30.9
Lib Dem	3,934	11.4	5,151	12.8	6,526	15.7
Plaid Cymru	4,453	12.9	5,421	13.5	1,906	4.6
Anti–EU	476	1.4	1,114	2.8	–	–
Others	–		583		151	
MP	Gareth Thomas (Lab)		Gareth Thomas (Lab)		Rod Richards (Con)	
					Clwyd North West	
Majority	1,115	3.2	1,848	4.6	7,313	17.6

Welsh Assembly Election 1999: Labour 7,824 (31.0), Conservative 7,064 (28.0), Plaid Cymru 6,886 (27.3), Lib Dem 3,462 (13.7). Electorate 53,952, Turnout 46.8%. AM: Alan Pugh (Lab), Majority: 760 (3.0).

Clwyd West was formed from the former Clwyd North West seat in 1997. At its top is the urban area which surrounds the coastal resort of Colwyn Bay, but the remainder of the constituency is largely rural. Traditionally the seat has been home to a large number of English migrants which has boosted Conservative strength. Clwyd North West was one of the Conservatives' strongest seats in Wales, and from 1970 until 1992 it was the seat of Sir Anthony Meyer, who became a controversial figure when he put himself up as a 'stalking horse' in the leadership election against Margaret Thatcher in late 1989. After Meyer's departure the seat was held by an even more controversial figure in the shape of Rod Richards. Richards, a Welsh speaker, became a Welsh Office Minister who publicly described Labour councillors as 'short, fat, slimy and fundamentally corrupt'. This was just one incident in a controversial career that involved resigning his Ministerial post due to the public revelations of an extra marital affair, later on there was a court case over alleged assault (for which he was acquitted) and an incident concerning being found drunk on a park bench. During this period Richards was elected as Welsh Conservative Party leader and became a fierce opponent in the Welsh Assembly. He once described the consensus politics within the Assembly as being nothing more that a 'poodles parlour'. Richards, stood down as leader while his court case, concerning the alleged assault, was being processed. He was later expelled from the Conservative group for 'a poor voting record'. He now sits as an Independent Welsh Conservative but has ambitions of returning as the Welsh Assembly candidate for the mainstream Conservative Party.

The Labour MP for Clwyd West, Gareth Thomas, who took the seat off Richards, is a former barrister. A keen supporter of the Welsh Assembly he failed to get the nomination for the Assembly seat in 1999 and has been at Westminster since. The seat is a Labour-Conservative marginal, the fifth most marginal in Wales. It was widely predicted that the Conservatives would gain this seat at the 2001 election, but in the event Gareth Thomas's majority was only slightly reduced. Clwyd West remains one of the key seats the Conservatives must win in order to gain a Westminster presence in Wales again.

Assembly seat

The Conservatives were keen to take Clwyd West in 1999, having lost it in the general election in 1997. They didn't, and their candidate Rod Richards, instead became a Conservative Assembly list member for North Wales. The seat was won by Labour's Alun Pugh, born and educated in South Wales, but who had taken a job in education as an Assistant Principal in West Cheshire, closer to the constituency for which he was to become Assembly Member. He has since become a junior Minister in the Welsh Assembly. Although Pugh won the seat in 1999, it became a three way marginal, with Plaid Cymru's Eilian Williams finishing a close third. There are less than a thousand votes between Labour, Conservatives and Plaid Cymru, and as a result this is one of the most competitive Welsh seats and one which may go any of three ways in 2003.

CONWY

	2001		1997		1992 actual	
Electorate and turnout	54,637	62.9	55,092	75.4	53,668	78.7
Conservative	8,147	23.7	10,085	24.3	14,250	33.7
Labour	14,366	41.8	14,561	35.0	10,883	25.8
Lib Dem	5,800	16.9	12,965	31.2	13,255	31.4
Plaid Cymru	5,665	16.5	2,844	6.8	3,108	7.4
Anti–EU	388	1.1	760	1.8	–	–
Others	–		345		751	
MP	Betty Williams (Lab)		Betty Williams (Lab)		Wyn Roberts (Con)	
Majority	6,219	18.1	1,596	3.8	995	2.4

Welsh Assembly Election 1999: Plaid Cymru 8,285 (30.6), Labour 8,171 (30.1), Conservative 5,006 (18.5), Lib Dem 4,480 (16.5), 1 Other 1,160. Electorate 55,189, Turnout 49.1%. AM: Gareth Jones (PC), Majority 114 (0.4).

Conwy is centred around the seaside resort of Llandudno and the University town of Bangor. There is a mix of Welsh and English in a seat which also has a large number of retired people within it. For much of the post war period it was a Conservative seat, held by former Welsh Secretary Peter Thomas (1951-1966) and then by Sir Wyn Roberts between 1970 and 1997. Sir Wyn went on to become the longest serving Conservative Minister in one post, serving at the Welsh Office between 1979 and 1994.

Between 1979 and 1992 the seat became a battleground between the two Roberts'. In the blue Conservative corner was Sir Wyn, while in the yellow corner was Roger Roberts for the Liberal Democrats. Eventually Conwy became one of the closest Conservative-Lib Dem marginals in the United Kingdom, just 2.4 per cent separating them in 1992. It was Labour's Betty Williams, however, who took the seat off the Conservatives in 1997, after Sir Wyn had retired. Roger Roberts ran her a close second making this one of Wales' most marginal seats. Welsh speaking Reverend Roberts was successful in gaining much of the Plaid Cymru vote. His successor Vicky MacDonald was not, and gained only a fraction of his vote in 2001. The Conservatives have now regained the number two slot, but (thanks partly to a completely divided opposition) Conwy appears to be no longer a marginal seat and Labour look to have a firm grip on it. Any of the three other parties who have challenged for control, or even gained it in the past, look set to have a tough fight in doing so again.

Assembly Seat

Conwy is the most marginal Welsh Assembly seat, with Plaid Cymru's Gareth Jones winning by just 114 votes from his Labour rival. Jones had taken his party from a poor fourth position at the general election two years previously to first in 1999, though he was the Assembly Member elected with the lowest percentage of the vote in Wales (30.6%). The Conservatives and Liberal Democrats, the normal challengers or possessors of the seat, were reduced to the role of passive spectators in 1999. The Lib Dem standard-bearer Christine Humphreys did at least have the consolation of being elected as her party's one list member for North Wales.

This seat is one which Plaid Cymru will need to hold if they are to have any chance of gaining control of the Assembly. At the same time it is one Labour must win in order to become the government in their own right. The Conservatives and Liberal Democrats are also seeking to make an impact here, as they have done in the past at a Westminster level. All this will result in what could be a fierce four-way contest at the next election.

DELYN

	2001		1997		1992 notional	
Electorate and turnout	54,732	63.3	53,693	75.9	54,713	80.4
Conservative	9,220	26.6	10,607	26.0	17,428	39.6
Labour	17,825	51.5	23,300	57.2	20,606	46.9
Lib Dem	5,329	15.4	4,160	10.2	4,822	11.0
Plaid Cymru	2,262	6.5	1,558	3.8	1,116	2.5
Anti–EU	–	–	1,117	2.7	–	–
MP	David Hanson (Lab)		David Hanson (Lab)		David Hanson (Lab)	
Majority	8,605	24.8	12,693	31.2	3,178	7.2

Welsh Assembly Election 1999: Labour 10,672 (44.7), Conservative 5,255 (22.0), Plaid Cymru 4,837 (20.3), Lib Dem 3,089 (13.0). Electorate 54,047, Turnout 44.1%. AM: Alison Halford (Lab), Majority 5,417 (22.7).

Delyn was created in 1983, covering the west side of the Dee Estuary, including the towns of Flint, Holywell and Mold. For the first two terms of its existence, it was a Conservative-held seat under Keith Raffan. He later left the Conservatives and went on an extraordinary political journey. First he became an HTV political question-master before leaving journalism to go back to his native roots in Scotland, joining the Liberal Democrats and is now sitting as a Member of the Scottish Parliament. Raffan's departure, as well as boundary changes which moved the more Conservative supporting areas into the new Vale of Clwyd constituency, spelled the end of Tory chances in this seat. The sitting Labour MP, David Hanson now has a 25 per cent majority. Hanson is firmly part of New Labour, serving as a junior Minister at the Welsh Office.

Although the Conservatives still gain a sizeable number of votes and remain in second position, they are no longer an effective challenger. The 2001 general election saw a swing to the Liberal Democrats but they still remain far in the distance politically. The seat is unlikely to provide much serious competition to Labour in the near future.

Assembly seat

Alison Halford gained the Delyn seat for Labour with a majority of 22.7 per cent, having polled almost twice the vote of her Conservative rival. The contest in 1999 was unusual in that the seat was one of the few which was contested solely by women. This is certainly an indication that Welsh Assembly elections are different from those at Westminster: the 2001 general election in Delyn was contested solely by men! The Liberal Democrat candidate who came fourth, Eleanor Burnham, subsequently replaced Christine Humphreys as the list Member in the spring of 2001.

Halford was a former Assistant Chief Constable in the Merseyside Police Authority who fought a public battle with the Police Authority over sexual discrimination. She became a Flintshire county councillor before going into the Welsh Assembly were she injected her own personality and humour into the Chamber's debates. Halford has announced that she is not contesting the seat in 2003, which means that the real contest will probably be within the Labour Party over her successor. The constituency appears to be in no real danger of falling to the opposition parties.

VALE OF CLWYD

	2001		1997		1992 notional	
Electorate and turnout	50,842	63.6	52,426	74.6	53,013	82.4
Conservative	10,418	32.2	11,662	29.8	19,118	43.7
Labour	16,179	50.0	20,617	52.7	16,941	38.8
Lib Dem	3,058	9.5	3,425	8.8	5,435	12.4
Plaid Cymru	2,300	7.1	2,301	5.9	2,095	4.8
Anti–EU	391	1.2	1,127 (2)	2.8	–	–
Others	–		–		123	
MP	Chris Ruane (Lab)		Chris Ruane (Lab)		NEW SEAT	
Majority	5,761	17.8	8,955	22.9	2,177	5.0

Welsh Assembly Election 1999: Labour 8,359 (37.7), Conservative 5,018 (22.6), Plaid Cymru 4,295 (19.3), Democratic Alliance 1,908 (8.6), Lib Dem 1,376 (6.2), 2 Others 1,247. Electorate 51,124, Turnout 43.4%. AM: Ann Jones (Lab), Majority 3,341 (15.1).

The Vale of Clwyd is one of Wales' newest seats, having been created in 1997 from parts of the former Conservative held Clwyd North West and the Labour-Conservative marginal of Delyn. The constituency is centred around Rhyl and Prestatyn on the North Wales coast, with an additional rural hinterland. Although notionally a Conservative win in 1992, it saw a substantial majority for Labour's Chris Ruane (22.9 per cent) five years later. Rhyl and Prestatyn have some of the most deprived wards in Wales, their support for Labour cancelling out (and exceeding) the Conservative rural vote. The new MP Ruane was a former teacher who developed his political background through chairing the West Clwyd NUT and town council politics. Since entering parliament he has remained outside of government but joined the appropriate Parliamentary committees and groups.

Although on its establishment it was expected that the Vale of Clwyd would become a marginal between the Conservatives and Labour, this has not yet occurred. Despite the furore surrounding the infamous 'Prescott punch' (which took place in Rhyl), the Conservatives were only able to slightly reduce Labour's majority in 2001 and they still have a mountain to climb if they are to win next time around. This is currently Labour's 126th most vulnerable seat and it may well remain in Labour's control, at least in the near future.

Assembly seat

The Vale of Clwyd Constituency Labour party didn't have far to go to get their candidate for the 1999 Assembly election; Ann Jones, who was Chris Ruane MP's constituency agent, filled the vacancy. The Conservatives' normally strong position in the constituency weakened, and many of their supporters may have backed Plaid Cymru instead. Consequently Plaid achieved their best ever result in the constituency. Jones was Chair of the Assembly Labour Group at the time of Alun Michael's resignation, but aside from this has had a low profile in the Assembly. She enjoys, however, a substantial 15 per cent majority, which is only likely to be threatened if a clear challenger (either the Conservatives or Plaid Cymu) emerges.

WREXHAM

	2001		1997		1992 *notional*	
Electorate and turnout	50,465	59.5	50,741	71.8	*51,318*	*78.8*
Conservative	6,746	22.5	8,688	23.9	*13,101*	*32.4*
Labour	15,934	53.0	20,450	56.1	*20,191*	*50.0*
Lib Dem	5,153	17.1	4,833	13.3	*6,054*	*15.0*
Plaid Cymru	1,783	5.9	1,170	3.2	*1,075*	*2.7*
Anti–EU	432	1.4	1,195	3.3	–	–
Others	–		86		–	
MP	Ian Lucas (Lab)		John Marek (Lab)		John Marek (Lab)	
Majority	9,188	30.6	11,762	32.3	*7,090*	*17.5*

Welsh Assembly Election 1999: Labour 9,239 (53.1), Lib Dem 2,767 (15.9), Conservative 2,747 (15.8), Plaid Cymru 2,659 (15.3). Electorate 50,932, Turnout 34.2%. AM: John Marek (Lab), Majority 6,472 (37.2).

Wrexham, as the name indicates, is centred on the town of Wrexham itself. Traditionally a mining and heavy industrial area it is now the centre of light manufacturing and Japanese inward investment companies. The seat was traditionally Labour, but the defection of the sitting MP Tom Ellis to the SDP and his subsequent challenge for the seat in 1983, brought the Conservatives to within 424 votes of defeating Labour's new candidate, Dr John Marek. Marek was English born and educated, but worked as a lecturer in applied Mathematics between 1966 and 1983 at the University of Wales, Aberystwyth. It was whilst at Aberystwyth that he started on the political road to Westminster, serving on both Ceredigion district council and Dyfed county council. Despite his English background, Marek became one of the strongest and most active supporters for a Welsh Parliament, a key member of the campaign group. In 1996 he introduced a Bill at Westminster with the specific aim of creating a law-making and tax raising Parliament for Wales. Marek remained at a minor level whilst at Westminster, but his support for the Welsh Assembly led him to resign his Westminster seat in 2001 and put all of his efforts into being a Member of the Welsh Assembly.

Marek's replacement was English born and Oxford educated Ian Lucas, whose connection with Wrexham was that he had previously lived there for seven years. He looks to be in a firm position for the time being. The Conservatives still hold the number two slot at Westminster elections, but the Liberal Democrats are gaining ground fast. At a local level the Liberal Democrats are also now the second party to Labour in terms of councillors. The signs indicate that, after their fortunes in Conwy have seen a dramatic decline, the Lib Dems will now make this their top North Wales target, but they still have a long way to go before they make this seat a truly two-way contest.

Assembly seat

Marek was only selected as a prospective Assembly Member at the last minute after the lists were reopened to allow Alun Michael to contest the Labour party's Welsh leadership election. Marek was a keen supporter of the Welsh Assembly and therefore his interest in contesting a seat for this new institution was welcomed by many observers. Although his vote was significantly down on his Westminster figure it was still more than three times that secured by his nearest opponent. The three opposition parties all came within a whisker of each other at around 15 per cent of the vote, with the Liberal Democrats' second place their best result in the seat since 1974. Although Plaid Cymru candidate Janet Ryder (Sunderland born) came last she was still elected as a regional list Member.

Marek is a much respected political figure, one of Labour's strongest supporters of devolution, and was elected Deputy Presiding Officer in 2001. It is difficult to see such a popular local Assembly Member being seriously challenged whilst he remains the incumbent. The challenge in the next Assembly election is likely to be for second place, and whether they can break away from the others. Indications at the moment, through local council by-elections and their increased vote Westminster, are that it will be the Liberal Democrats.

YNYS MON

	2001		1997		1992 actual	
Electorate and turnout	53,398	63.7	53,294	74.9	53,412	80.6
Conservative	7,653	22.5	8,569	21.5	14,878	34.6
Labour	11,906	35.0	13,275	33.2	10,126	23.5
Lib Dem	2,772	8.1	1,537	3.8	1,891	4.4
Plaid Cymru	11,106	32.6	15,756	39.5	15,894	37.1
Anti–EU	359	1.1	793	2.0	–	–
Others	222		–		182	
MP		Albert Owen (Lab)		Ieuan Wyn Jones(PC)		Ieuan Wyn Jones(PC)
Majority	800	2.4	2,481	6.2	1,106	2.6

Welsh Assembly Election 1999: Plaid Cymru 16,469 (52.6), Labour 7,181 (22.9), Conservative 6,031 (19.3), Lib Dem 1,630 (5.2). Electorate 52,571, Turnout 59.6%. AM: Ieuan Wyn Jones, Majority 9,288 (29.7).

Ynys Mon is the constituency covering (and the Welsh name for) the Island of Anglesey. The constituency is connected to the mainland by the famous Menai Bridge, and also the newer Britannia Bridge. At its western side is the ferry port of Holyhead, and at its east the town of Beaumaris. The seat has the fourth highest Welsh speaking population in Wales, just over 60 per cent.

Ynys Mon is the only constituency in Wales to have been held by all four political parties since 1945. Between 1929 and 1951 it was held for the Liberals by Lady Megan Lloyd George, daughter of the former Prime Minister. She was defeated by Labour's Cledwyn Hughes, a pro nationalist who went on to become, amongst other things, Welsh Secretary, Agriculture Secretary and Labour Leader in the House of Lords. When he stood down in 1979, there was a shock in store for Labour when the Conservative Keith Best overturned a substantial Labour majority (17.8 per cent) to win the seat. Although Best learnt Welsh and held the seat at the next general election, he was forced to resign following a financial scandal concerning the purchase of BT shares. When Best stepped down in 1987, there was another change of party, Ieuan Wyn Jones taking the seat for Plaid Cymru with a substantial 10 per cent majority. Despite being a high profile Plaid Cymru figure Jones was unable to consolidate this majority and the seat became a Plaid Cymru-Conservative marginal in 1992, moving over to a Plaid Cymru-Labour marginal in 1997.

Ieuan Wyn Jones was elected to the Welsh Assembly in 1999, became President of Plaid Cymru in the summer of 2000 and announced that he was to stand down from the Westminster seat in 2001. His successor, Holyhead solicitor Eilian Williams, looked set to take over the seat for Plaid Cymru once more. This was not to be the case, however, and Labour's former Assembly candidate, Albert Owen, a former merchant seaman, gained the seat in 2001. It was the only seat that Labour gained in Wales and one of only two across Britain. It was a tremendous morale boast to Labour and body blow to Plaid

Cymru. No departing incumbent has succeeded in handing the seat on to a member of the same party since 1929. Owen's victory enabled Labour to win the seats in all four corners of Wales for the first time since 1970. The seat remains a marginal, which Plaid will be desperate to bring back into their fold at future elections. Labour will be fighting just as hard to keep it out of Plaid Cymru's hands.

Assembly seat

In the landslide that gave Plaid Cymru almost a third of the North Wales vote in 1999, it was not surprising that Ieuan Wyn Jones won the seat with a massive majority of almost 30 per cent. Labour and the Conservatives came a poor second and third, and seem to have little chance of winning the assembly seat in the near future. The 2001 Westminster result, however, seems to have given the opposition parties, especially Labour, renewed hope.

Ieuan Wyn Jones was elected President of Plaid Cymru in the summer of 2000 and also became leader of his party in the Welsh Assembly. His leadership has seen an increase in Plaid Cymru's share of the Westminster vote, but not a rise in the number of Westminster MPs. His position as President depends on him delivering even better results in seats like his constituency of Ynys Mon, than the party achieved in 1999. However, indications from the general election and council by-elections are that Plaid Cymru are becoming weaker in this seat and others. The spectre of the Independent Wales Party taking his party's votes may also weaken him considerably in this seat. Nevertheless it would a political disaster for Plaid Cymru if the leader were to lose his base in 2003. For that reason, Ynys Mon is likely to have as intense competition between Plaid Cymru and Labour as will occur in many of the South Wales contests.

Mid and West Wales

	Conservative		Labour		Liberal Democrat		Plaid Cymru		Others	
	Share of vote	Seats	Share of vote	Seats	Share of vote	Seats	Share of vote	Seats	Share of vote	Seats
2001	23.4	0	30.8	3	19.4	2	24.4	3	2.0	0
1997	20.7	0	37.8	4	18.4	2	20.1	2	3.0	0
1992	28.9	1	32.6	3	20.3	2	17.7	2	0.6	0
1999 C	15.3	0	26.3	2	17.7	2	35.7	4	5.0	0
1999 R	16.7	2	24.5	1	13.4	0	38.5	1	6.9	0

NOTE: 1999C=Welsh Assembly Elections Constituency vote; 1999R=Welsh Assembly Elections Regional top-up vote (4 seats available)

The Mid and West Wales electoral region covers around 60 per cent of the land area of Wales. It is also the most sparsely populated of all of the Welsh regions. The region contains some of the highest and lowest percentages of Welsh speakers. It is the centre of Welsh agriculture and is predominately rural in nature; at a local government level it continues with the tradition of Independent councillor representation.

The region consists of eight parliamentary constituencies and five unitary authorities. It also has eight Assembly constituencies and four regional list members. Currently (2002), the Welsh Conservative leader Nick Bourne has his list seat in this region, and it was also the list seat of former First Minister and Welsh Labour leader, Alun Michael; after he resigned Delyth Evans took his place as Labour list member. Cynog Dafis, former MP for Ceredigion, is Plaid Cymru's list member, and Glyn Davies completes the quartet as a second Conservative list AM.

Mid and West Wales is different to other regions in Wales in that it is the weakest area politically for the Labour Party, which otherwise dominates Wales. Labour have only three of the eight Parliamentary seats, and just two of the eight Assembly seats. It is traditionally the strongest area politically for both Plaid Cymru and the Liberal Democrats, with Plaid gaining a third seat (Carmarthen East & Dinefwr) in 2001. A number of seats are marginal, notably Brecon & Radnorshire, which the Conservatives will hope to regain in 2005/6.

Local government
There are five unitary authorities in Mid and West Wales. It is the only region in which none are controlled by the Labour Party. The region has a long tradition of Independent run councils, and also

of a large number of seats remaining unopposed at council election time. Indeed, this is one of the last strongholds of the Independent councillor in the United Kingdom.

Carmarthenshire county council consists of the former Districts of Carmarthen , Dinefwr and Llanelli under the previous Dyfed county council. Until 1999, it was run by the Labour Party, and they remain the largest political party (28 seats). The 1999 elections saw Plaid Cymru increase its representation from 8 to 15 seats, with the Independents claiming 29 and Independent Labour having 2. The number of council seats was also reduced from 81 to 74, and the result of this and the reduction in Labour seats was the formation of an Independent – Plaid Cymru coalition to run the council. Labour have the potential to regain outright control with just another 8 seats needed to gain a majority. Ceredigion is one of the few councils in Wales whose area also forms the Parliamentary seat. Its origins come from the old county of Cardiganshire abolished in 1974 to make way for Ceredigion district council and Dyfed county council. The Liberal and then Liberal Democrats were always the largest political party on the former district council with Plaid Cymru only having a handful of seats and the council having the fewest number of Labour councillors in Wales from 1973-1995. The Independents always had the majority of the seats until 1999 and ran the council. Then two things changed, Plaid Cymru became the largest political party, with 13 seats, against the Liberal Democrats 7, and the Independents lost overall control. The council is now run as an Independent/Liberal Democrat coalition.

Gwynedd council was constructed in 1995 from the district councils of Arfon, Dwyfor and Meirionnydd, which were under the previous county council also named Gwynedd. The new council established in 1995 was originally titled by the Welsh Office 'Caernarfonshire and Merionethshire', historic county names which go back to the 16th Century. The name of Gwynedd, goes back even further, however, and the Plaid Cymru controlled council consequently soon changed the name back again to Gwynedd. The council has the highest proportion of Welsh speakers of any council in Wales (72.7 per cent), and also the highest number of unopposed returns at election time of any council in the UK. In 1999 there were 42 unopposed councillors, over half the total number of seats. Despite Plaid Cymru's success at a Parliamentary level in Gwynedd, they never managed to translate this into controlling of any of its district councils. In 1995, however, they were successful in getting many nationalist Independents to show their true political colours and stand for the party. The result was Plaid winning some 47 out of a possible 83 seats. The nearest political opposition was Labour with 12, although Independents still won 20. This was Plaid's first overall victory at council level since they gained control of Merthyr Tydfil in 1976. The 1999 elections saw them lose four seats to Labour and the Liberal Democrats but retain control. They are now just two seats away from losing overall control of their flagship council, and the 2004 elections will be an interesting test of Plaid Cymru's ability to retain power in the same council for a third time, something that they have never managed before.

The people of Pembrokeshire never really forgave the Conservative government for abolishing the county in 1974. Neither did the Pembrokeshire Conservatives who acted as a powerful lobby group in getting the county restored to its former status. Although the county is controlled by Labour at both a parliamentary level and Assembly level it is the Independents who control the council, and with 41 seats out of 60 they enjoy a substantial majority. In 1999 all four political parties were also represented on the council with Labour being the largest group, but subsequently the Conservatives lost all four of their councillors when three joined the Independent ruling coalition and the remaining councillor defected to the Lib Dems. Political parties find it difficult to make a break through in this largely rural council and the most unusual thing about politics within the county is to see the three political parties frequently unite to oppose the Independents, one of the few occasions political parties come together in Wales for any reason. Powys County Council is the only authority in Wales to remain largely unchanged from the 1995 local government reforms. It took over from the former Powys county council and contains the former district councils of Brecknock, Montgomeryshire and Radnor. It is the only council in Wales to have less political representation on it now than in 1973 when the council was first established. Every other county has become more political, Powys less so. Independents hold four fifths of the county's seats and consequently control the county itself.

BRECON and RADNORSHIRE

	2001		1997		1992 actual	
Electorate and turnout	53,247	70.5	52,142	82.2	51,564	85.9
Conservative	13,073	34.8	12,419	29.0	15,977	36.1
Labour	8,024	21.4	11,424	26.6	11,634	26.3
Lib Dem	13,824	36.8	17,516	40.8	15,847	35.8
Plaid Cymru	1,301	3.5	622	1.5	418	0.9
Anti–EU	452	1.2	900	2.1	–	–
Others	842 (2)		–		393	
MP	Roger Williams (LD)		Richard Livsey (LD)		Jonathan Evans (Con)	
					Brecon and Radnor	
Majority	751	2.0	5,097	11.9	130	0.3

Welsh Assembly Election 1999: Lib Dem 13,022 (44.6), Conservative 7,170 (24.5), Labour 5,165 (17.7), Plaid Cymru 2,356 (8.1), Independent 1,502 (5.1). Electorate 51,166, Turnout 57.1% . AM: Kirsty Williams (LD), Majority 5,852 (20.0).

Brecon and Radnor is, in area, one of the largest Parliamentary constituencies in the United Kingdom, though substantial boundary changes in 1983 removed much of the Labour-supporting Valleys population that had made the seat theirs between 1938 and 1979. Brecon and Radnor is now mainly a farming seat, based around the market towns of Brecon, Builth Wells and Radnor, and the spa town of Llandrindod Wells, though it retains a substantial Labour supporting area around the valleys town of Ystradgynlais.

Tom Hooson took the seat for the Conservatives in 1979 general election and in 1983 increased his majority to 8,784 (23.2 per cent). Brecon and Radnor was beginning to look like a safe Conservative seat. In 1985 however, Hooson died, and the subsequent by-election was to change the course of political history here. In 1970, Geraint Howells (later Liberal MP for Ceredigion), had become the first Liberal to contest Brecon and Radnor in fifteen years, finishing third with fewer than one in five votes. At subsequent elections, the Liberals also remained in third position. Yet in 1985 Richard Livsey managed to gain the seat the seat for the Alliance with a slim majority over Labour of 559. He won again in the 1987 general election with a majority of just 56 votes, this time over the Conservatives' Jonathan Evans. Brecon and Radnor had become one of the most marginal seats in the United Kingdom, a status which was to continue in 1992 when the seat swung back to the Conservatives under Evans, this time by the tender margin of just 130 votes. In 1997, Livsey reclaimed the constituency with a majority of over 5,000. At last, the Liberal Democrats thought that they had secured Brecon and Radnorshire (it was renamed in 1997 to include the extra 'shire') with rather more than the see saw political margins of the past.

In 1999, Jonathan Evans was elected a Welsh Conservative MEP, while Richard Livsey's decision to step down from the seat in 2001 has thrown it back to being marginal. His successor Roger Williams held the seat by the much reduced majority of 751 votes over his Conservative opponent Felix Aubel. Whilst by Brecon and Radnor standards this is quite a high majority, it does mean that the seat has once again become a hyper-marginal. If either Labour or Plaid Cymru are able to increase their vote at the expense of the Liberal Democrats this seat could once again fall to the Conservatives. Competition here is likely to remain fierce.

Assembly seat

When the 'Yes' campaign sought to sell the Welsh Assembly to the Welsh electorate in the 1997 referendum they made it clear that the Assembly's membership would be different from Westminster or Welsh local government. It would be more inclusive of the whole Welsh population, not just representing the political class (who mainly consist of party officials and councillors). In the event, very few Assembly Members trod a path any different to that of their Westminster colleagues when they arrived there, namely serving their time in the local council or in the party machine. The winning candidate for Brecon and Radnorshire, Liberal Democrat, Kirsty Williams was the rare exception to this: female, under thirty, and with no previous council experience or full-time service in the party machine. When they selected such a relatively inexperienced candidate, the Lib Dem constituency party of Brecon and Radnorshire made a gamble. It was to pay off and Williams secured the highest majority over her Conservative rival, future Welsh Conservative leader Nick Bourne, her party had ever achieved in the seat. Williams soon established herself in a prominent position in the Assembly as chair of the Health Committee. As one of the few young female faces in Welsh politics she has also enjoyed a prominent media profile, and is unlikely to be defeated at the next Assembly election.

CARMARTHEN EAST and DINEFWR

	2001		1997		1992 notional	
Electorate and turnout	54,035	70.4	53,121	78.6	53,256	82.8
Conservative	4,912	12.9	5,022	12.0	8,953	20.3
Labour	13,540	35.6	17,907	42.9	18,305	41.5
Lib Dem	2,815	7.4	3,150	7.5	4,023	9.1
Plaid Cymru	16,130	42.4	14,457	34.6	12,815	29.1
Anti–EU	656	1.7	1,196	2.9	–	–
MP	Adam Price (PC)		Alan Williams (Lab)		Alan Williams (Lab) Carmarthen	
Majority	2,590	6.8	3,450	8.3	5,490	12.5

Welsh Assembly Election 1999: Plaid Cymru 17,328 (53.1), Labour 10,348 (31.7), Conservative 2,776 (8.5), Lib Dem 2,202 (6.7). Electorate 53,634, Turnout 60.9%. AM: Rhodri Glyn Thomas (PC), Majority 6,980 (21.4).

Carmarthen East and Dinefwr was created from the former parliamentary seat of Carmarthen in 1997. The new seat does not actually contain the town of Carmarthen, which is in the neighbouring seat of Carmarthen West and South Pembrokeshire. Instead it consists of the rural Welsh speaking heartlands of West Wales. The former seat of Carmarthen had great significance in terms of Welsh political history. In 1966 the Labour MP for Carmarthen, Megan Lloyd George (daughter of Liberal Prime Minister David Lloyd George and herself formerly a Liberal MP in Anglesey) died, and in the subsequent by-election Plaid Cymru's Gwynfor Evans went from third to first and won Plaid Cymru's first ever Westminster seat. Although Evans lost to Labour in 1970 he took it back again in October 1974. Plaid Cymru's success was to remain short-lived; Labour's Dr Roger Thomas regained the seat in 1979 and Dr Alan Williams reinforced this success when he too was victorious from 1987.

Despite the continued Labour success, Carmarthen remained top of Plaid Cymru's wish list for two decades. It was not until 2001, however, that 32-year old Plaid Cymru candidate Adam Price was able to become their first MP for the area since Gwynfor Evans. Price enjoys a respectable majority of 2,590. With Labour knocking at the door, however, the seat remains relatively marginal in Welsh terms and a continued hard fought contest between Labour and Plaid Cymru is guaranteed.

Assembly Seat

Plaid Cymru's Rhodri Glyn Thomas' failure to win the Westminster seat in 1997 was compensated somewhat by his substantial victory over Labour in the 1999 Assembly elections. Thomas secured a majority of 6,980 over Labour, and on paper this remains one of Plaid Cymru's strongest Assembly seats, with the party having secured over half of the vote. Thomas has since become chair of the

Assembly's Agriculture and Rural Development Committee, a position of some importance in a rural constituency such as this. The next Assembly election will test Plaid's strength, but the indications at the 2001 general election appear to indicate that unless disaster strikes, they are likely to retain this seat.

CARMARTHEN WEST and SOUTH PEMBROKESHIRE

	2001		1997		1992 notional	
Electorate and turnout	56,518	65.3	55,724	76.5	55,393	77.7
Conservative	10,811	29.3	11,335	26.6	15,278	35.5
Labour	15,349	41.6	20,956	49.1	16,588	38.6
Lib Dem	3,248	8.8	3,516	8.2	4,672	10.9
Plaid Cymru	6,893	18.7	5,402	12.7	6,497	15.1
Anti–EU	537	1.5	1,432	3.4	–	–
Others	78		–		–	
MP	Nick Ainger (Lab)		Nick Ainger (Lab)		NEW SEAT	
Majority	4,538	12.3	9,621	22.6	1,310	3.1

Welsh Assembly Election 1999: Labour 9,891(35.1), Plaid Cymru 8,399 (29.8), Conservative 5,079 (18.0), Independent 2,090 (7.4), Lib Dem 1,875 (6.7), 1 Other 815. Electorate 55,655, Turnout 50.6%. AM: Christine Gwyther (Lab), Majority: 1,492 (5.3).

The constituency of Carmarthen West and South Pembrokeshire has the distinction of having the longest constituency name in the UK. This apart, the seat remains very much on the political margins of Welsh political life. It was constituted from parts of the former Pembroke and Carmarthen seats in 1997. Pembroke had been Conservative from 1970 until 1992, being the seat of the former Welsh Secretary Nicholas Edwards for all but five years of that period. The area transferred to this constituency includes the English speaking territory that surrounds the towns of Tenby and Pembroke Dock. Meanwhile, Carmarthen was a Labour-Plaid Cymru marginal, and the town itself along with some Welsh-speaking areas around it are included in this constituency.

At a Westminster level, the anglicised population that populates a lot of the area have tended to avoid voting for Plaid Cymru. Pembroke had been a battleground between Labour and Conservatives, and could also have been called the seat of the 'Nicks', because Labour's Nick Ainger won the seat off the Conservatives Nick Bennett (1987-1992) who had in turn succeeded Nick Edwards. The latest Nick (Ainger) still enjoys a substantial majority over the Conservatives although they are clearly closing the gap. Plaid Cymru are also increasing their share of the vote, although nowhere near their 1999 Assembly success here. In the current political climate the seat looks safely Labour although it is one that the Conservatives must hope to win if they ever wish to regain a majority at Westminster.

Assembly seat

It was Plaid Cymru knocking on Labour's door at the Welsh Assembly elections rather than the Conservatives. In the event, Christine Gwyther won with the slender majority of 1,492 (5.3 per cent). Gwyther was then appointed Agriculture Secretary by Alun Michael in the new Assembly Cabinet, something of a poisoned chalice for a vegetarian who was charged with promoting Welsh livestock during a farming crisis. She became the first Minister to be censured by the Welsh Assembly in November 1999. Despite this, she did not resign and was finally sacked by Rhodri Morgan on the eve of the Royal Welsh Show in July 2000. Such a history cannot have been the best start for an Assembly Member in a relatively marginal constituency. Nevertheless she has had the time to develop the seat and the 2003 Assembly elections will test whether her constituents are more supportive than her Assembly colleagues.

CEREDIGION

	2001		1997		1992 *notional*	
Electorate and turnout	56,125	61.7	54,378	73.9	*54,467*	*77.9*
Conservative	6,730	19.4	5,983	14.9	*10,178*	*24.0*
Labour	5,338	15.4	9,767	24.3	*7,889*	*18.6*
Lib Dem	9,267	26.9	6,616	16.5	*11,251*	*26.5*
Plaid Cymru	13,241	38.3	16,728	41.6	*13,144*	*31.0*
Anti–EU	–	–	1,092	2.7	–	–
MP	Simon Thomas (PC)		Cynog Dafis (PC)		Cynog Dafis (PC)	
					Ceredigion & Pembroke North	
Majority	3,944	11.4	6,961	17.3	*1,893*	*4.5*

Welsh Assembly Election 1999: Plaid Cymru 15,258 (47.8), Labour 5,009 (15.7), Independent 4,114 (12.9), Lib Dem 3,571 (11.2), Conservative 2,944 (9.2), Green 1,002 (3.1). Electorate 55,311, Turnout 57.7%. AM: Elin Jones (PC), Majority 10,249 (32.1).

Parliamentary by-election 3 February 2000: Plaid Cymru 10,716 (42.8), Lib Dem 5,768 (23.0), Conservative 4,138 (16.5), Labour 3,612 (14.4), Anti-EU 487 (1.9), 2 Others 344. Electorate 55,025, Turnout 45.6%. MP: Simon Thomas (PC), Majority 4,948 (19.7).

Ceredigion was created from the old Ceredigion and Pembroke North seat in 1997. The constituency is rural in nature with the largest population being based around the University towns of Aberystwyth and Lampeter and the county town of Cardigan. It also has a large Welsh speaking population of around 60 per cent according to the 1991 census. For most of the twentieth century it was a Liberal and then a Liberal Democrat seat. Although Labour held it between 1966 and 1974, it then remained firmly in Liberal hands up until 1992, when Cynog Dafis (who had contested the seat twice before) took Plaid Cymru from fourth to first, thus removing the sitting Liberal Democrat MP Geraint Howells. Both Howells and Dafis traded off their ability to relate closely with the local population in what is normally a highly localised contest. Dafis, a fluent Welsh speaker and Plaid Cymru's Director of Policy, built up the seat into something of a Plaid Cymru stronghold. He reduced his former Liberal Democrat rivals to a poor third in the 1997 general election, with Labour advancing to second place.

In 1999, Dafis was placed in a personal political dilemma. He had put himself on the Plaid Cymru regional Assembly list in order to attract additional support from his Ceredigion base, but they were to do so well in Mid and West Wales that he unexpectedly found himself elected. He then had to choose between Westminster and Cardiff. A year later he stood down from the Westminster seat in order to allow another Plaid Cymru MP to strengthen their Westminster team (three of the four Plaid MPs were now in Cardiff as well as Westminster). In the subsequent by-election the Liberal Democrat candidate Mark Williams put his party back into second position, although Plaid Cymru's Simon Thomas still won with a handsome 4,948 majority (19.7 per cent). The 2001 general election saw a further increase in the

Liberal Democrat vote and a decline in the Plaid Cymru vote. Thomas still enjoys a substantial majority of 3,974 (11.4 per cent) but the seat is no longer as safe for them as it once was. If the Liberal Democrats are able to harness the student vote, whilst squeezing that of Labour and the Conservatives, they may regain their old seat once more. It is the ninth most marginal seat in Wales and the only one where Plaid Cymru are in serious competition with the Liberal Democrats.

Assembly seat

Whereas the Westminster seat has become more competitive over the last decade, there was little sign of this in the 1999 Assembly election. Here Elin Jones secured the seat with a massive majority of 10,249 votes (32.1 per cent) over Labour's Maria Battle. In this deeply Welsh-speaking area, Plaid Cymru will surely have little difficulty in a Welsh Assembly election in securing another victory. Certainly they cannot hope to form the Executive at the National Assembly without being able to secure another win in Ceredigion. The only real challenge to Plaid Cymru may come from the Liberal Democrats, testing their strength for the following Westminster election. They have, however, a Welsh mountain to climb first, coming fourth behind an Independent in the 1999 Assembly contest.

LLANELLI

	2001		1997		1992 *notional*	
Electorate and turnout	58,148	62.3	58,293	70.7	*59,729*	*77.2*
Conservative	3,442	9.5	5,003	12.1	*7,851*	*17.0*
Labour	17,568	48.6	23,851	57.9	*25,122*	*54.5*
Lib Dem	3,065	8.5	3,788	9.2	*5,884*	*12.8*
Plaid Cymru	11,183	30.9	7,812	19.0	*7,253*	*15.7*
Others	922 (2)		757		–	
MP	Denzil Davies (Lab)		Denzil Davies (Lab)		Denzil Davies (Lab)	
Majority	6,403	17.7	16,039	38.9	*17,271*	*37.5*

Welsh Assembly Election 1999: Plaid Cymru 11,973 (42.2), Labour 11,285 (39.8), Lib Dem 2,920 (10.3), Conservative 1,864 (6.6), 1 Other 345. Electorate 58,371, Turnout 48.6%. AM: Helen Mary Jones (PC), Majority 688 (2.4).

The industrial seat of Llanelli has long been a Labour stronghold. From 1935 until 1970 it was held by the popular pro-devolution MP, James Griffiths. Griffiths was Deputy Leader of the Labour party, the man who brought the Welsh Office to Wales and the first Welsh Secretary from 1964-66. He was replaced by anti-devolution, Euro-sceptic MP Denzil Davies. Davies was seen as one of the brightest Labour MPs during the 1970s, a former Oxford educated barrister and law lecturer at the University of Chicago. He was a Minister of State at the Treasury from 1975-79. Since then, however, his star has faded somewhat and despite obtaining massive majorities within the constituency, his public profile is relatively low across Wales and nationally. He was briefly prominent during the Assembly Referendum campaign and the passage of the Government of Wales Bill 1998, on the 'anti' side.

The 2001 general election saw a significant rise in the Plaid Cymru vote, rising to its highest level ever. At the same time the Labour vote fell below 50 per cent, although they still enjoy a large majority. Liberal Democrat and Conservatives votes have been effectively squeezed in the seat and any future contest looks set to be between Plaid Cymru and Labour. The next significant battle in the seat at a Westminster seat will occur if Denzil Davies steps down. He will be 68, if the general election is held in 2006. A contest will then be an opportunity to test the constituency fully without Davies' long held personal presence and vote being felt.

Assembly Seat

The winning Assembly Member for Llanelli was born in Colchester in 1960 and educated at Colchester County High School for Girls. She was not representing Labour, however, but Plaid Cymru. Helen Mary Jones was not expecting to win Llanelli and overturn Labour's previous massive majority. Nevertheless that is exactly what happened and on a night which saw a number of solid Labour seats tumble to Plaid Cymru, Llanelli became another tally on their scoresheet. Jones' victory was marginal

(688 votes, 2.5 per cent) but enough to put Plaid Cymru's mark on the town. Labour's support may well have been damaged by the well known anti-Assembly views held by the town's MP, in a Welsh speaking constituency (48.7 per cent according to the 1991 census figures) that had overwhelmingly backed the new Assembly in the 1997 referendum.

Jones has had a high public profile since her election in 1999. She contested the Plaid Cymru leadership elections in August 2000, though without gathering significant support. She is the chair of the Plaid Cymru group in the National Assembly. Jones will need all of her political skills if she is to retain Llanelli, and it is a seat that both Labour and Plaid Cymru will need to win if either wishes to form the future Welsh Executive in their own right.

MEIRIONNYDD NANT CONWY

	2001		1997		1992 *actual*	
Electorate and turnout	32,969	63.9	32,345	76.0	32,413	81.5
Conservative	3,962	18.8	3,922	16.0	6,995	26.5
Labour	4,775	22.7	5,660	23.0	4,978	18.8
Lib Dem	1,872	8.9	1,719	7.0	2,358	8.9
Plaid Cymru	10,459	49.6	12,465	50.7	11,608	44.0
Anti–EU	–	–	809	3.3	–	–
Others	–		–		471	
MP	Elfyn Llwyd	(PC)	Elfyn Llwyd	(PC)	Elfyn Llwyd (PC)	
Majority	5,684	27.0	6,805	27.7	4,613	17.5

Welsh Assembly Election 1999: Plaid Cymru 12,034 (63.8), Labour 3,292 (17.4), Conservative 2,170 (11.5), Lib Dem 1,378 (7.3). Electorate 32,922, Turnout 57.3%. AM: Lord Dafydd Elis-Thomas (PC), Majority 8,742 (46.3).

Meirionnydd Nant Conwy is the constituency which has Wales's highest mountain within its bounds. As well as the Snowdonia National Park, there is Blaenau Ffestiniog and the slate quarries that surround it and dominate the landscape. The constituency has Wales' smallest electorate of just under 33,000 and is one of Plaid Cymru's strongest constituencies. Since Dafydd Elis-Thomas gained the seat from Labour's Will Edwards in February 1974, it has been in the party's firm control. The current Plaid Cymru MP, Elfyn Llwyd, easily secured the seat for Plaid Cymru with a majority of 5,684 in 2001. The Conservatives were the most serious challengers to the seat in the mid-1980s, but since then they have fallen back considerably and Labour now hold the number two slot.

Elfyn Llwyd is now Plaid Cymru's leader in the House of Commons and the only MP they have there with significant Parliamentary experience. This therefore gives him a higher public profile than his newer Plaid Cymru colleagues. The largely Welsh speaking seat looks likely to remain firmly in the hands of Plaid and the only real threat may be from the intervention of another Welsh political party such as the Independent Wales Party. This may split Plaid Cymru's vote enough to allow in another political party, either Labour or Conservatives, to gain the seat.

Assembly seat

In February 1974, Dafydd Elis-Thomas won the seat then known as Merioneth from Labour. This, together with the win in Caernarfon, was the first time Plaid Cymru had won a parliamentary seat in Wales at a general election. Thomas went on to become the President of Plaid Cymru between 1984-91. He stood down from the seat in 1992 and was ennobled as Lord Elis-Thomas of Nant Conwy the same year. Elis-Thomas became Plaid Cymru's first and only Peer, the party having decided later on never to have another member ennobled. Elis-Thomas went on to chair the Welsh Language Board between 1993-1999 and took an active part in the 'Yes' Campaign in the Welsh Assembly referendum. Having won the referendum, Elis-Thomas was keen to become a member of the new Assembly and it was in his old seat of Meirionnydd Nant Conwy that he set about doing so.

Elis-Thomas secured Plaid Cymru's highest ever percentage of the vote in the seat, with nearly four times the vote of his nearest opponent (Labour). The problems of having a former Plaid Cymru leader in the new Assembly with a current leader, then Dafydd Wigley, posed a dilemma for the party. Luckily this was soon resolved when he was appointed the Presiding Officer (Speaker) of the National Assembly for Wales at its opening session, 12 May 1999. Since then Elis-Thomas has been fighting hard to establish the Assembly as an independent body from Westminster and Whitehall. His role as a Plaid Cymru AM has been limited because of the neutrality of the Presiding Officer's role. Whether this will dent the massive majority Plaid Cymru enjoys in the seat remains to be seen.

MONTGOMERYSHIRE

	2001		1997		1992 actual	
Electorate and turnout	44,243	65.5	42,753	74.7	41,386	79.9
Conservative	8,085	27.9	8,344	26.1	10,822	32.7
Labour	3,443	11.9	6,109	19.1	4,115	12.4
Lib Dem	14,319	49.4	14,647	45.9	16,031	48.5
Plaid Cymru	1,969	6.8	1,608	5.0	1,581	4.8
Anti–EU	786	2.7	879	2.8	–	–
Others	381 (2)		338		508	
MP	Lembit Öpik (LD)		Lembit Öpik (LD)		Alex Carlile (LD)	
Majority	6,234	21.5	6,303	19.7	5,209	15.8

Welsh Assembly Election 1999: Lib Dem 10,374 (48.4), Conservative 4,870 (22.7), Plaid Cymru 3,554 (16.6), Labour 2,638 (12.3). Electorate 43,386, Turnout 49.4%. AM: Mick Bates (LD), Majority 5,504 (25.7%).

Montgomeryshire is the only seat in Wales that has never had a Labour MP. For all but four years over the last century this has been a Liberal seat, with MPs including the former leader of the Liberals, Clement Davies (1945-1962), and two Liberal QCs, Emlyn Hooson (1962-1979) and Alex Carlile (1983 to 1997). For the intervening four years it was held by the Conservative, Delwyn Williams. The rural seat of Montgomeryshire, with the towns of Welshpool and Newtown at its heart, was the first seat in what is now referred to as the 'Liberal quintet', which runs along Wales and the Marches (the five seats being Brecon & Radnorshire, Hereford, Ludlow, Montgomeryshire and, following the defection of its MP, Shrewsbury & Atcham). It is the bastion of Welsh Liberal Democrat power at a Westminster level. The Conservatives remain the main challengers and although their chances of winning the seat are always written up by political pundits as an election comes nearer, they still remain a long way off seriously threatening victory here.

The present Liberal Democrat MP is Lembit Opik. Opik is of Estonian parents, but hails from Northern Ireland and gained his political experience as a city councillor in Newcastle upon Tyne. Opik is something of a rising star within the Liberal Democrats federally. He is the Northern Ireland spokesman, the party's Youth Affairs Spokesman and Leader of the Welsh Liberal Democrats. He also makes frequent appearances on TV shows, ranging from *Have I Got News For You?* to *Ready, Steady, Cook*. His regular appearances on TV and development as a first division politician have only enhanced still further the Liberal Democrat grip on the seat.

Assembly seat
Safe as the Parliamentary seat appears to be for the Liberal Democrats, the Assembly seat appears to be

safer still. Mick Bates, farmer and former NFU activist, gained nearly twice the vote of his Conservative opponent Glyn Davies in 1999. Yet due to Davies winning a regional list, both still face each other on a day to day basis in the Assembly. The 1999 election also saw Plaid Cymru gain its strongest ever share of the vote in Montgomeryshire (16.6 per cent), where they had normally lost their deposit. Given the current state of the Conservative party and the traditional strength of the Liberals in this seat it is very unlikely that they will lose this seat in the 2003 elections.

PRESELI PEMBROKESHIRE

	2001		1997		1992 notional	
Electorate and turnout	54,283	67.8	54,150	78.3	54,295	80.5
Conservative	12,260	33.3	11,741	27.7	17,270	39.5
Labour	15,206	41.3	20,477	48.3	16,667	38.1
Lib Dem	3,882	10.6	5,527	13.0	5,379	12.3
Plaid Cymru	4,658	12.7	2,683	6.3	3,773	8.6
Anti–EU	319	0.9	1,574	3.7	–	–
Others	452		401		642	
MP	Jackie Lawrence (Lab)		Jackie Lawrence (Lab)		Nick Ainger (Lab) Pembroke	
Majority	2,946	8.0	8,736	20.6	603	1.4

Welsh Assembly Election 1999: Labour 9,977 (34.3), Plaid Cymru 7,239 (24.9) Conservative 6,585 (22.6), Lib Dem 3,338 (11.5), Independent 1,944 (6.7). Electorate 54,225, Turnout 53.6%. AM: Richard Edwards (Lab), Majority 2,738 (9.4).

Preseli Pembrokeshire was created as a new seat in 1997. It was based on the former district council of the same name. The seat was made up of sections of the old Ceredigion & Pembroke North and Pembroke seats. This means that parts of the constituency have been represented by MPs from all four Welsh political parties over the last decade. The rural areas within the constituency have traditionally supported the Conservatives whilst the urban areas of Milford Haven and Haverfordwest have backed Labour. The seat was notionally a Conservative win in 1992, but the 1997 general election saw them gain just over half of Labour's winning vote. The Labour victor in that election was Jackie Lawrence, who owes her place in part to the all-women short lists in operation by Labour at the time.

Lawrence's majority over her Conservative opponents has decreased from over twenty per cent in 1997 to just eight per cent in 2001. This is now the Conservatives' fifth target seat in Wales and the seventh most marginal seat in Wales. It is one which the Conservatives need to win if they are to become a national government again. They still have some way to go but the gap is narrowing.

Assembly seat

When Richard Edwards won the Preseli Pembrokeshire Assembly Seat, he had a majority of 2,738 (9.4 per cent). The runner-up was not the Conservatives, however, but Plaid Cymru, as Preseli Pembrokeshire became one of a number of seats where Plaid either challenged or overtook the Tories for second place. The seat has become a three-horse race, with all three parties now seemingly capable of gaining it. It is possible that the Conservatives' and Plaid Cymru's strength will cancel each other out, allowing the Labour hardcore vote to keep the seat in their hands. If either Plaid Cymru or the

Conservatives can attract the other's votes in significant numbers, it is possible that they may win the seat. Otherwise it is likely to remain Labour, even though the present incumbent Richard Edwards is leaving the seat for a new Labour contender to fight in 2003.

South Wales East

	Conservative		Labour		Liberal Democrat		Plaid Cymru		Others	
	Share of vote	Seats	Share of vote	Seats	Share of vote	Seats	Share of vote	Seats	Share of vote	Seats
2001	18.7	0	57.5	8	11.0	0	10.0	0	2.9	0
1997	16.7	0	66.1	8	9.4	0	4.2	0	3.6	0
1992	24.1	1	62.2	7	9.7	0	3.9	0	0.1	0
1999 C	16.3	1	44.4	6	11.6	0	21.1	1	6.5	0
1999 R	16.8	1	41.5	0	12.2	1	24.3	2	5.2	0

NOTE: 1999C=Welsh Assembly Elections Constituency vote; 1999R=Welsh Assembly Elections Regional top-up vote (4 seats available)

South Wales East consists of eight parliamentary constituencies and six unitary authorities. It also has eight Assembly constituencies and four regional list members: currently (2002) two Plaid Cymru (Phil Williams and Jocelyn Davies), one Conservative (William Graham) and one Liberal Democrat (Michael German). The whole region, with the exception of Monmouthshire, is traditional Labour territory. From time to time there have been political upheavals in which Labour is overthrown or humbled for a period, but they always come back and reassert themselves. The last such period was the 1999 Assembly elections when they lost two constituencies they hold at Westminster, Islwyn and Monmouth. They held all of their 1997 general election constituencies, however, at the 2001 general election which indicated that this rot had not spread to Westminster elections. The next period of political interest for this region therefore will be the Assembly elections, in which there will be a chance to see if Labour domination is breaking up at an Assembly level or returning to the type of dominance seen at general elections. Interest at the general election will again focus on Monmouth, the best chance of a Conservative gain in Wales. All the other seats are rock-solid Labour and likely to remain so.

Local government

There are six unitary authorities in the South Wales East area, and until 1999 all were run by the Labour party. The situation since then has become somewhat different with Caerphilly in the hands of Plaid Cymru, Monmouthshire now controlled by the Conservatives and Independents and Merthyr Tydfil (at the time of writing) controlled by Labour with a majority of one.

Since the inception of Blaenau Gwent in 1973, Labour have never failed to have anything but a substantial majority on first the borough council (1973-1995) and then the unitary authority (1995 to date). If anything, their stranglehold on power has got even stronger with opposition numbers dwindling to a mere handful. Even corruption allegations that resulted in the expulsion of a number of prominent Labour councillors before the 1999 unitary authority elections failed to dent their majority when elections were held. The Lib Dems provide the only party political opposition on the council with just two seats, with Labour having thirty-three and the other six opposition councillors Independents. The unitary authority of Caerphilly is a combination of two former borough councils, Rhymney Valley, part of the old Mid Glamorgan and Islwyn, which was in the former county of Gwent. Rhymney Valley briefly had a Plaid Cymru majority between 1976 and 1979; otherwise the authority had been solidly Labour. Islwyn was always strongly Labour. When the two authorities merged in 1995, Labour secured some 55 seats out of a total of 68. Unlike a number of Labour controlled authorities in South Wales, the administration under Labour leader Graham Court ran the authority well, with a lack of 'scandals' of any sort. It was therefore something of shock for Labour in the 1999 council elections when their 55 seats were reduced to 28, with Plaid Cymru increasing from 10 to 38. The Lib Dems also gained four seats, making this their strongest Welsh Valleys council group. By-elections since 1999 indicate that Labour are regaining their dominant position and surprisingly it is now the Lib Dems who are their main opposition at by-elections rather than Plaid Cymru. The 2004 unitary authority elections are likely to see a very fierce contest in Caerphilly between Labour and Plaid Cymru, with the Liberal Democrats snapping at the rear.

The county borough of Merthyr Tydfil is the smallest of all the Welsh unitary authorities in terms of population. For much of its history it has been firmly in the hands of the Labour party. On occasion, however, there has been a political revolution and Labour have lost power. One of these occasions was in 1976 when Plaid Cymru gained control of the council (their first ever) and knocked Labour down to 8 seats from 25. This did not last long and by 1983 Plaid Cymru had lost every seat they had held. It was 1999 before they gained a significant presence on the council again, with four seats. There was significant anti-Labour feeling running up to the 1999 council elections, but it was mainly Independents who benefited, gaining 10 seats. They would have gained control of the council if one their number had not defected back to the Labour party from where he had just come. With the narrowest of Labour majorities, control of Merthyr Tydfil remains on a political knife edge with the first council by-election literally deciding the future control of the council.

Just like the Assembly and Westminster constituency of Monmouth, the county of Monmouthshire covers one of the most prosperous areas of Wales. Between 1973 and 1995 the Conservatives controlled the council with a substantial majority of seats. In 1995, however, they lost control to the Labour Party in a landslide which saw them reduced to small rump of 11 councillors out of 42. In 1999, in combination with the Assembly elections the Conservatives were able to come back as the largest party, with 19 seats to Labour's 18, and control the council with the help of the 4 Independent councillors. Between 1995 and 1999, Newport county borough council had the distinction of being the best example of a one party state in Wales, with Labour holding 46 seats to the Conservatives' one. This meant that the council had no official opposition at all, as one member cannot form a group. Things had been different in the late 1970s when the Conservatives were in control, and things have become a little more balanced recently as they now have five seats, the Liberal Democrats one and others two. Torfaen has always been controlled by the Labour Party. Until the mid 1990s, there were always a substantial number of Independent councillors in opposition to the Labour party, but even they faded away to the extent that by 2001, just five of the 44 councillors did not represent Labour. Apart from some minor success by the Liberal Democrats at the start of the 1990s the council has remained firmly in Labour hands and is likely to remain so for the foreseeable future.

BLAENAU GWENT

	2001		1997		1992 actual	
Electorate and turnout	53,353	59.5	54,815	72.3	55,643	78.1
Conservative	2,383	7.5	2,607	6.6	4,266	9.8
Labour	22,855	72.0	31,493	79.5	34,333	79.0
Lib Dem	2,945	9.3	3,458	8.7	2,774	6.4
Plaid Cymru	3,542	11.2	2,072	5.2	2,099	4.8
Others	–	–	–	–	–	–
MP	Llew Smith (Lab)		Llew Smith (Lab)		Llew Smith (Lab)	
Majority	19,313	60.9	28,035	70.7	30,067	69.2

Welsh Assembly Election 1999: Labour 16,069 (61.8), Plaid Cymru 5,501 (21.2), Lib Dem 2,980 (11.5), Conservative 1,444 (5.6). Electorate 53,919, Turnout 48.2%. AM: Peter Law (Lab), Majority 10,568 (40.7).

The industrial constituency of Blaenau Gwent was built upon coal and steel. Even today it remains very much a working class seat with nearly half of all employment being in manufacturing. At its heart lies the town of Ebbw Vale which was famous for its now closed steel works, and for being the last place in Wales to hold a garden festival (aimed at rejuvenating industrial areas) in 1992. Other major towns in Blaenau Gwent are Tredegar, Brynmawr, Blaina and Abertillery. The constituency was created in 1983 from parts of the former Abertillery, Brecon and Radnor and Ebbw Vale seats.

The MPs who have represented both Blaenau Gwent and its predecessors have always been on the left of the Labour party and today would be described as 'Old Labour'. From 1929-60 the seat was held by Aneurin Bevan, the founder of the National Health Service. His successor was Michael Foot, leader of the Labour Party during one of the worst periods in its history (1980–83). When Foot retired from Parliament in 1992 he was replaced by the strongly socialist Llew Smith. Smith, a former MEP, has never shirked away from the ideals of 'Old Labour' and during the 1997 devolution referendum he was a fervent campaigner for the 'No' campaign. Since then he has remained firmly in the rebel camp of Labour MPs in Westminster voting against the government on a number of occasions.

Blaenau Gwent remains one the safest Labour seats in the United Kingdom, and although the 2001 election saw a fall in turnout, Smith still enjoys a massive majority. In percentage terms, the constituency remains the safest Labour seat in Wales and the sixth safest overall. The only real purpose of opposition candidates standing in this seat is to test their resolve for further political battles, something that Jonathan Evans (Welsh Conservative MEP and former MP for Brecon and Radnor) and David Melding (Conservative AM for South Wales Central) have done in the past.

Assembly Seat

The Assembly seat is very similar in electoral terms to the parliamentary one. The only real difference here is that Plaid Cymru candidate Professor Phil Williams, who came second in the 1999 election, was elected to the National Assembly on his party's regional list. The current Assembly Member Peter Law was initially the Secretary for the Environment in the Cabinet but was dropped when the coalition with the Liberal Democrats was formed in October 2000. Law was a former Mayor and councillor on Bleanau Gwent council, which means his roots are firmly planted in the constituency he now represents. This seat is unlikely to provide any surprises in the 2003 Assembly election. Even in the massive swing to Plaid Cymru that occurred in 1999 the party could only manage 21.2 per cent of the vote, against Labour's 61.8 per cent. There is nothing to indicate that Plaid Cymru's fortunes have increased in the constituency since then and the seat looks set to remain firmly in Labour hands.

CAERPHILLY

	2001		1997		1992 actual	
Electorate and turnout	67,300	57.7	64,621	70.1	64,555	77.2
Conservative	4,415	11.4	4,858	10.7	9,041	18.1
Labour	22,597	58.2	30,697	67.8	31,713	63.7
Lib Dem	3,649	9.4	3,724	8.2	4,247	8.5
Plaid Cymru	8,172	21.0	4,383	9.7	4,821	9.7
Anti–EU	–	–	1,337	3.0	–	–
Others	–		270		–	
MP	Wayne David (Lab)		Ron Davies (Lab)		Ron Davies (Lab)	
Majority	14,425	37.1	25,839	57.1	22,672	45.5

Welsh Assembly Election 1999: Labour 12,602 (44.2), Plaid Cymru 9,741 (34.2), Lib Dem 3,543 (12.4), Conservative 2,213 (7.8), 1 Other 412. Electorate 65,997, Turnout 43.2%. AM: Ron Davies (Lab), Majority 2,861 (10.0).

The town and constituency of Caerphilly are famous for three things, their cheese, their castle and their politicians. Sometimes all three are combined, notably in the town's 'Big Cheese' festival each summer. The constituency was dominated until the mid-1980s by the coal mining industry. Today employment in the town of Caerphilly itself and the surrounding area is dominated by a number of manufacturing and retail servicing operations including the massive General Electrics aero engine plant at Nantgarw, and Peters Pies at Bedwas. Caerphilly is also increasingly serving as a part of the commuter belt to nearby Cardiff. The name of Labour's political heroes are dominant throughout the constituency; for example there is a housing estate called Lansbury Park (after George Lansbury, Leader of the Labour Party 1932-35), its streets including Attlee Court and Snowdon Court (Philip Snowdon was the pre-war Labour Chancellor). There was until recently a Harold Wilson Industrial Estate, and there is the Morgan Jones Park and council ward, named after the constituency's former Labour MP. The signs of Labour's past are literally everywhere in Caerphilly.

Since the mid-1960s, there has been intense political rivalry and at times open political warfare between Plaid Cymru and the Labour party in the Caerphilly constituency, whatever level of political contest is being fought. In 1968, Plaid Cymru's Dr Phil Williams came within a few thousand votes of winning the seat at a by-election resulting from the death of Ness Edwards. Some 31 years later Professor Phil Williams won a list seat in the Welsh Assembly for the eight constituencies that represent South Wales East, including Caerphilly. Williams' success in getting elected typifies the gradual progress of Plaid Cymru in the Caerphilly constituency, which has seen numerous peaks and troughs.

Ronald Davies, later known to the world as Ron Davies, brought the focus of media attention to Caerphilly as never before. Davies was elected for Caerphilly in 1983 and served as Shadow Agriculture and later Shadow Welsh Secretary, before becoming Welsh Secretary after the 1997 general election. He led the devolution campaign for a 'Yes' vote and consequently became known as the 'father of devolution' amongst Welsh nationalist circles. He was also elected for short time as leader of the Wales Labour Party, beating Rhodri Morgan in the contest. It was Davies' resignation as Welsh Secretary and Labour's Welsh leader after a 'moment of madness' on Clapham Common that brought both national and international attention to Caerphilly. Davies, however, hung on as MP and AM and was able to hand the first of these jobs over to the former Labour Euro MP Wayne David in 2001. Although Plaid Cymru doubled their vote in the 2001 general election, their three time candidate Lindsay Whittle was still nowhere nearer gaining the seat that his party had been thirty years before.

Assembly seat

The Assembly seat in 1999 saw a much closer contest between Labour and Plaid Cymru than any of the recent Westminster elections. In the constituency vote, Plaid were just ten per cent behind Ron Davies, but in the list vote, they actually out-polled Labour. Caerphilly was one of the first constituencies to declare and at the time it was thought that high Plaid Cymru vote was something to do with a backlash against Davies over his 'moment of madness' and the subsequent scandal. As the results came in across Wales, however, it was evident that this was not the case and that there had been a genuine surge of support for Plaid Cymru within this and nearby constituencies. The other notable fact about the Assembly election in Caerphilly was that this was also the seat in which Michael German, the Liberal Democrat leader and future deputy first minister, stood. Despite coming third, German still secured his party's number one position on the regional list and entered the Assembly.

The 2001 general election result and subsequent council by-election results indicate that Plaid Cymru's strength may have peaked. Davies' pro devolution sympathies also tend to attract some of the soft nationalist vote. In addition, the 2003 Assembly election will not be held on the same day as the county council elections, which undoubtedly benefited Plaid Cymru last time.

ISLWYN

	2001		1997		1992 actual	
Electorate and turnout	51,230	61.9	50,540	72.0	51,082	81.4
Conservative	2,543	8.0	2,864	7.9	6,180	14.9
Labour	19,505	61.5	26,995	74.2	30,908	74.3
Lib Dem	4,196	13.2	3,064	8.4	2,352	5.7
Plaid Cymru	3,767	11.9	2,272	6.2	1,606	3.9
Anti–EU	–	–	1,209	3.3	–	–
Others	1,680 (2)		–		547	
MP	Don Touhig (Lab)		Don Touhig (Lab)		Neil Kinnock (Lab)*	
Majority	15,309	48.3	23,931	65.7	24,728	59.5

* Don Touhig (Lab) elected at Feb 1995 by–election.

Welsh Assembly Election 1999: Plaid Cymru 10,042 (42.0), Labour 9,438 (39.4), Lib Dem 2,351 (9.8), Conservative 1,621 (6.8), 1 Other 475. Electorate 50,600, Turnout 47.3%. AM: Brian Hancock (PC), Majority 604 (2.5).

In 1983 the parliamentary constituency of Bedwellty was restructured and renamed Islwyn. For twenty-five years (1970-1995), this coal mining and industrial seat, centred on the town of Blackwood, was represented by Neil Kinnock. He became the leader of the Labour Party after the national defeat in 1983 and was famous for pushing his party down the path to electability. Kinnock left the seat in 1995 to become a European Commissioner. His wife, Glenys Kinnock, also represented Islwyn when she became the MEP for South Wales East (1995-1999) and later on Wales (1999 – present). In a by-election in 1995, Labour Gwent county councillor Don Touhig replaced Neil Kinnock as MP for Islwyn. Touhig was the Parliamentary Private Secretary to Gordon Brown at the Treasury before being appointed as the Welsh Party Whip.

Like many of the surrounding seats, the constituency has been controlled for most of its recent history by the Labour party, although the population are far more likely to change their allegiances to Plaid Cymru or the Liberal Democrats if the occasion dictates than elsewhere. Plaid Cymru have not made the same breakthrough in this seat at a Westminster level that they have at Assembly and unitary authority elections, however. In the 2001 general election they were beaten into third place by a popular local Liberal Democrat councillor Kevin Etheridge. This was the only seat in the South Wales valleys where Plaid came third. It is likely that if Etheridge or any other strong third party candidate stands at future elections it will split the anti- Labour vote and the seat will continue to be a Labour parliamentary bastion.

Assembly seat

One of the shocks of the 1999 Welsh Assembly elections was the news that one of Labour's safest Westminster seats had fallen to Plaid Cymru. Brian Hancock beat Labour's Shane Williams to secure the seat for Plaid Cymru. Plaid were undoubtedly helped by having the unitary authority elections on the same day, in which they swept the board as well. Nevertheless it was a remarkable achievement considering that in the Parliamentary election in 1997 they had secured just 6.2 per cent of the vote and finished fourth. Since the 1999 election, Plaid Cymru have performed poorly in local council by-elections and at the 2001 general election. The next Assembly election will therefore be an interesting one for Islwyn, to see whether the voters will continue clearly distinguishing between who they want to represent them in Cardiff as opposed to Westminster.

MERTHYR TYDFIL and RHYMNEY

	2001		1997		1992 actual	
Electorate and turnout	54,919	57.7	56,507	69.3	58,430	75.8
Conservative	2,272	7.2	2,508	6.4	4,904	11.1
Labour	19,574	61.8	30,012	76.7	31,710	71.6
Lib Dem	2,385	7.5	2,926	7.5	4,997	11.3
Plaid Cymru	4,651	14.7	2,344	6.0	2,704	6.1
Anti–EU	–	–	660	1.7	–	–
Independent	1,936	6.1	–	–	–	–
Others	866 (2)		691		–	
MP	Dai Havard (Lab)		Ted Rowlands (Lab)		Ted Rowlands (Lab)	
Majority	14,923	47.1	27,086	69.2	26,713	60.3

Welsh Assembly Election 1999: Labour 11,024 (43.9), Plaid Cymru 6,810 (27.1), Independent 3,746 (14.9), Lib Dem 1,682 (6.7), Conservative 1,246 (5.0), 1 Other 580. Electorate 55,858, Turnout 44.9%. AM: Huw Lewis (Lab), Majority 4,214 (16.8).

Merthyr Tydfil is as steeped in the history and development of the Labour Party as anywhere that surrounds it. The town was once the cradle of the industrial revolution in Wales and its coal and steel helped build and run the ships that ran the British Empire. It was the seat of the founder of the Labour Party, Keir Hardie, who was one of two MPs elected for the new party in 1900. Between 1934 and 1972 it was represented by fervent Labour devolutionist S.O. Davies who was finally returned as an Independent Labour MP from 1970 until his death in 1972. It was then that Ted Rowlands, a former Welsh Office Minister who had lost his Cardiff seat at the 1970 general election was elected, against a strong Plaid Cymru showing. Rowlands held the seat, increasing his already strong majority at every election, although after his appearance as a Foreign Office Minister during the Callaghan Government he remained very much on the back benches.

For some time the Liberal Democrats remained second to Labour in the constituency although a long way behind and often only a few hundred votes ahead of the other political parties. When the Welsh Secretary of the MSF union, Dai Havard, inherited the seat for Labour in 2001, Plaid Cymru rose to second position, although still some 14,923 votes short of taking the seat. In addition, the voters of Merthyr Tydfil have a record of supporting strong independent candidates at parliamentary, Assembly or council elections (an Independent was third in 1999 and another polled well in 2001), but nonetheless the seat looks like remaining firmly in the hands of the Labour party.

Assembly seat
In 1999, Huw Lewis gained the Assembly seat for Labour with a minority of the total vote for Labour

(43.9 per cent). He is also married to Lynne Neagle the Labour Assembly Member for Torfaen. Plaid Cymru polled well with 27 per cent of the vote, and an Independent candidate, Tony Rogers, came third, well ahead of the other political parties. On paper, Merthyr Tydfil remains a seat that could be won by Plaid Cymru. Although eleven of its wards are in the Labour-run Merthyr Tydfil unitary authority, eight are in the Caerphilly unitary authority, which is run by Plaid Cymru. This goes some way to explaining their strength in the Assembly election as opposed to the parliamentary, since in 1999 elections for the council were held on the same day as the Assembly, helping to boost Plaid's vote. This will not be the case in 2003, which may provide a truer test of whether or not Plaid Cymru have become the serious challenger they looked in 1999.

MONMOUTH

	2001		1997		1992 *actual*	
Electorate and turnout	62,200	71.5	60,873	80.5	59,148	86.1
Conservative	18,637	41.9	19,226	39.2	24,059	47.3
Labour	19,021	42.8	23,404	47.7	20,855	41.0
Lib Dem	5,080	11.4	4,689	9.6	5,562	10.9
Plaid Cymru	1,068	2.4	516	1.1	431	0.8
Anti–EU	656	1.5	1,190	2.4	–	–
MP	Huw Edwards (Lab)		Huw Edwards (Lab)		Roger Evans (Con)	
Majority	384	0.9	4,178	8.5	3,204	6.3

Welsh Assembly Election 1999: Conservative 12,950 (40.9), Labour 10,238 (32.3), Lib Dem 4,639 (14.6), Plaid Cymru 1,964 (6.2), 1 Other 1,911. Electorate 61,999, Turnout 51.1%. AM: David Davies (Con), Majority 2,712 (8.5).

Monmouth is different in structure and social make-up from the areas that surround it in Wales. The constituency is rural in nature and one of the most prosperous areas in Wales. It is centred around the towns of Abergavenny, Monmouth, Usk, Raglan and Chepstow, each with their own castle reflecting the troubled nature of this borderland. Until the mid-1970s, Monmouthshire was not technically part of Wales, with the description always being given of 'Wales and Monmouthshire'. It acted as a buffer county between Wales and England. It was perhaps for these reasons that the seat shared the Conservative politics of the English border counties of Herefordshire and Shropshire. Monmouth was for decades as predictably Conservative as much of the rest of South Wales was Labour. From 1918 until 1966 the seat was true blue; from 1950-1966 it was the seat of former Conservative Chancellor and Defence Secretary Peter Thorneycroft. He was one of only two post-war Conservative MPs for Welsh seats to be in the Cabinet (Nicholas Edwards, the Welsh Secretary in 1979-87, being the other).

Thorneycroft was defeated in 1966 by Labour's Donald Anderson (who later became the MP for Swansea East). The seat then returned to the Conservatives under Sir John Stradling Thomas in 1970, who held it until he died in 1991 when Huw Edwards took the seat for Labour in the subsequent by-election from his Conservative opponent Roger Evans. Evans regained the seat in the 1992 general election, only for Edwards to take it back again for Labour in 1997. The two fought it out yet again in the 2001 general election and Edwards' majority of over 4,000 was reduced to just 384, making it the most marginal seat in Wales. If the Conservatives are ever to gain control of the Westminster government again, then they must win Monmouth, and consequently this will remain a tightly fought seat.

Assembly seat
Owing to the fact that Labour lost so many seats to Plaid Cymru in 1999, the gain by the Conservatives of Monmouth slipped by almost unnoticed. David Davies easily secured the seat for the Conservatives

with a majority of 2,712. The Labour candidate, Cherry Short, was a black Cardiff councillor who was seen to a great extent as being imposed on the seat as part of the Labour twining exercise. This factor, together with Davies' fierce campaigning style and a general upturn in Conservatives fortunes in what is traditionally one of their best seats, gave them their only constituency victory in Wales (all the other Conservative Assembly Members are regional list members). Davies has since become one of the more lively Assembly Members; a keen supporter of Iain Duncan Smith, he is very much at home under the current right wing Conservative Party.

At the 2003 election a number of factors will therefore determine whether the Conservatives hold onto the seat. The choice of Labour's candidate is clearly one. Another is what will happen to the Plaid Cymu and Liberal Democrat vote in the constituency. If either party could squeeze these quite substantial votes (Lib Dems 14.6 per cent and Plaid Cymru 6.1 per cent) then they will probably win the seat. The final factor is the turnout of Conservative Party supporters to vote for an institution that many did not want and appear no happier to have now. If this sceptical group does not come out, then the seat may well fall back to Labour.

NEWPORT EAST

	2001		1997		1992 *actual*	
Electorate and turnout	57,219	54.7	50,676	73.5	51,602	81.2
Conservative	7,246	23.2	7,958	21.4	13,151	31.4
Labour	17,120	54.7	21,481	57.7	23,050	55.0
Lib Dem	4,394	14.0	3,880	10.4	4,991	11.9
Plaid Cymru	1,519	4.9	721	1.9	716	1.7
Anti–EU	410	1.3	1,267	3.4	–	–
Socialist	420	1.3	1,951	5.2	–	–
Others	173		–		–	
MP	Alan Howarth (Lab)		Alan Howarth (Lab)		Roy Hughes (Lab)	
Majority	9,874	31.6	13,523	36.3	9,899	23.6

Welsh Assembly Election 1999: Labour 9,497 (49.4), Conservative 4,386 (22.8), Lib Dem 2,684 (14.0), Plaid Cymru 2,647 (13.8). Electorate 54,196, Turnout 35.5%. AM: John Griffiths (Lab), Majority 5,111 (26.6).

The constituency of Newport was broken up into Newport East and Newport West in 1983. East Newport was traditionally the safest area for Labour containing the working class neighbourhoods that surround Llanwern steelworks. Perhaps the most famous of the previous MPs for Newport was Sir Frank Soskice (1955-1966), who was Harold Wilson's first Home Secretary. His successor was Roy Hughes who went on to represent Newport and then Newport East from 1966-1997. Hughes stayed very much on the backbenches although briefly taking up the position of Chairman of the Welsh Grand Committee in 1990. He possibly became more famous for giving up his seat shortly before the 1997 general election in order to be catapulted into the House of Lords as Lord Islwyn of Casnewydd. This act helpfully ensured that Conservative defector Alan Howarth (formerly MP for Stratford upon Avon) was given a safe seat. Despite vigorous protests at the time from party members about having a former vice chair of the Conservatives thrust upon them, this made little impact with the Labour voters and Howarth increased the massive majority of his predecessor.

Howarth subsequently held the seat in 2001, and although the Conservatives increased their share of the vote they are still a long way off being a serious threat to Labour. Unless a political earthquake occurs, this seat is likely to stay solidly Labour.

Assembly seat

John Griffith, the Labour Assembly Member for Newport East, has a background that makes him the exact opposite of its Westminster MP, Alan Howarth. Griffiths was born in Newport and has spent his whole political career there as a Gwent County Councillor, Newport County Borough Councillor and now Assembly Member. Griffiths is on the left of the party and a devout anti-monarchist. In the 1999 Assembly elections the only real surprises were that Labour secured less than half of the vote and that Plaid Cymru gained 13.8 per cent in a seat where they normally lose their deposit. These two factors apart, this seat remains, like the Westminster constituency, a traditionally solid Labour seat, with the Conservatives remaining firmly in second place.

NEWPORT WEST

	2001		1997		1992 *actual*	
Electorate and turnout	59,345	59.1	53,914	74.6	54,872	82.8
Conservative	9,185	26.2	9,794	24.4	16,360	36.0
Labour	18,489	52.7	24,331	60.5	24,139	53.1
Lib Dem	4,095	11.7	3,907	9.7	4,296	9.5
Plaid Cymru	2,510	7.2	648	1.6	653	1.4
Anti–EU	506	1.4	1,522 (2)	3.8	–	–
Others	278		–		–	
MP	Paul Flynn (Lab)		Paul Flynn (Lab)		Paul Flynn (Lab)	
Majority	9,304	26.5	14,537	36.2	7,779	17.1

Welsh Assembly Election 1999: Labour 11,538 (47.6), Conservative 6,828 (28.2), Plaid Cymru 3,053 (12.6), Lib Dem 2,820 (11.6). Electorate 57,243, Turnout 42.3%. AM: Rosemary Butler (Lab), Majority 4,710 (19.4%).

Unlike its sister seat, Newport West started its life being won by the Conservatives, if only by a small majority of 581 for Mark Robinson. West contains the more wealthy wards of Allt-yr-Yn and Graig, as well as the towns of Caerleon and Rogerstone and much of the resident population of University of Wales College, Newport, all areas that traditionally supported the Conservatives. Although Robinson became a Minister at the Welsh Office, which projected his public profile, the seat was still won for Labour by former Newport Borough Councillor Paul Flynn in 1987 with a 2,708 majority.

Flynn has become one of Wales's best-known MPs and in 1996 was voted joint-winner of the *Spectator* Backbencher of the Year Award. Flynn has established himself as a hard working constituency MP and on occasion party rebel. His 1999 book *Dragons led by Poodles*, for instance, gave a damning indictment of Labour's 1999 Assembly leadership election. Flynn has also been a frequent campaigner for the legalisation of cannabis. It is with this background that he has built up a substantial majority over his Conservative opponents, which makes the seat only slightly less safe now that its neighbour Newport East.

Assembly seat

The Conservatives, Plaid Cymru and the Liberal Democrats all increased their share of the vote in the 1999 Assembly election in Newport West from the general election two years earlier. It was still, however, not enough to seriously dent Labour's control of the seat. Rosemary Butler won the seat with a substantial majority, 4,710. Butler became Cabinet Secretary for pre-16 Education but returned to the backbenches after the formation of the Labour-Lib Dem coalition in October 2000. This seat was also of interest because it was fought by the Conservatives' number one on their regional list, William

Graham, who was subsequently elected both as a county councillor and to the Assembly. The interest in this seat next time, if Graham stands, will be to see if his presence in the Assembly and on the local council enhances his percentage of the vote against his Labour opponent. If the Plaid Cymru or Liberal Democrat vote can be squeezed in his favour this could become one of the closer political competitions in South Wales East.

TORFAEN

	2001		1997		1992 actual	
Electorate and turnout	61,115	57.7	60,343	71.7	61,103	77.5
Conservative	5,603	15.9	5,327	12.3	9,598	20.3
Labour	21,883	62.1	29,863	69.1	30,352	64.1
Lib Dem	3,936	11.2	5,249	12.1	6,178	13.1
Plaid Cymru	2,720	7.7	1,042	2.4	1,210	2.6
Anti–EU	657	1.9	1,245	2.9	–	–
Others	443		519		–	
MP	Paul Murphy (Lab)		Paul Murphy (Lab)		Paul Murphy (Lab)	
Majority	16,280	46.2	24,536	56.7	20,754	43.8

Welsh Assembly Election 1999: Labour 9,080 (38.0), Ind Labour 3,795 (15.9), Independent 2,828 (11.8), Lib Dem 2,614 (10.9), Plaid Cymru 2,614 (10.9), Conservative 2,152 (9.0), 1 Other 839. Electorate 61,037, Turnout 39.2%. AM: Lynne Neagle (Lab), Majority 5,285 (22.1).

Torfaen is centred on the New Town of Cwmbran at the south of the constituency, with Pontypool in the middle and the World (industrial) Heritage Site of Blaenavon located in the north. The seat was previously known as Pontypool and served by the Labour MP, Leo Abse (1958-1983), who distinguished himself as a backbencher, social reformer and author of some note. This is another solid Labour seat, almost as firm at Westminster and council level as its neighbour Blaenau Gwent, which is to the constituency's west. Perhaps the most notable fact about the Torfaen Constituency is that it is the seat of Welsh Secretary Paul Murphy. Despite his Irish surname and term as a Minister at the Northern Ireland Office, Murphy was both brought up and served as a county councillor in the constituency he now represents. Having a Cabinet Minister allows the political spotlight to shine upon a seat which, due to its substantial Labour majority, is normally ignored by political commentators. This point aside the Westminster seat offers little prospect of being anything but a foregone victory for whoever stands for Labour.

Assembly Seat

Torfaen voted 'No' in the Welsh Assembly referendum (50.3 per cent to 49.7 per cent). This provides some indication as to why Labour recorded one of its lowest percentages at an Assembly election whilst still winning the seat (38 per cent). The majority of the voters in Torfaen voted for a party other than Labour, something that has only happened at Westminster elections in the meltdown year of 1983. An Independent Labour candidate (Michael Gough) came in second place (16 per cent) to Labour's Lynne Neagle (husband of the Assembly Member for Merthyr Tydfil and Rhymney). Another Independent

Ingrid Nutt came in third with 11.8 per cent. This suggests that there is a substantial anti-Labour vote in Torfaen waiting to be garnered by the right candidate. The problem in 1999 was that with six opposition candidates fighting Labour, there were just too many candidates trying to tap the same anti-Labour seam. The secret to winning Torfaen from the Labour Party lies in gaining the independent vote and squeezing that of the remaining political parties. If this occurs then Torfaen might possibly elect a non-Labour Assembly Member.

South Wales Central

	Conservative		Labour		Liberal Democrat		Plaid Cymru		Others	
	Share of vote	Seats	Share of vote	Seats	Share of vote	Seats	Share of vote	Seats	Share of vote	Seats
2001	20.1	0	53.5	8	14.4	0	10.1	0	1.9	0
1997	20.3	0	58.1	8	11.8	0	5.6	0	4.2	0
1992	29.5	2	54.3	6	10.4	0	5.1	0	0.6	0
1999 C	16.5	0	41.5	6	14.8	1	25.9	1	1.3	0
1999 R	16.2	2	36.9	0	14.3	0	27	2	5.6	0

NOTE: 1999C=Welsh Assembly Elections Constituency vote; 1999R=Welsh Assembly Elections Regional top-up vote (4 seats available)

The South Wales Central region consists of eight parliamentary constituencies and three unitary authorities. It also has eight Assembly constituencies and four regional list members: currently (2002) two Plaid Cymru (Pauline Jarman and Owen John Thomas), and two Conservatives (David Melding and Jonathan Morgan). The region is the heart of the Welsh political scene because it contains the nation's capital, Cardiff, and within that the National Assembly for Wales and the associated administration.

For the last two general elections, South Wales Central has returned eight Labour MPs, but as recently as 1987 the region had four Conservative and four Labour MPs. Since their 1997 wipeout, however, the Conservatives have failed to regain their strength at either a Westminster or Welsh Assembly level. In the Assembly, the Labour Party hold six constituency seats, Plaid Cymru one and the Liberal Democrats one. Labour's vote took a battering in 1999, and it is clear that the strength of the Labour Party in the area has weakened over recent years, though like elsewhere in the industrial south of Wales it still remains the dominant force and ever present. At the next general election, interest will focus on two Cardiff seats, Central and North. Central is now a tight Labour–Liberal Democrat battle, while in North the Conservatives have declined from their previously dominant position – but this is a seat they must regain if they are seriously challenging for power.

Local government

There are only three unitary authorities in the South Wales Central area and from 1995 until 1999, all were run by the Labour party. All four Welsh political parties play a key role in at least one of the councils of South Wales Central. The Labour Party still run Cardiff with a substantial majority, with their opposition being the Liberal Democrats. Meanwhile, the councils to the north and south of Cardiff are run either by Plaid Cymru or a Conservative-Plaid Cymru coalition. Each of these councils has been rocked by political or corruption scandals or other controversies over recent years making local government in the area far from sedate.

Despite previous periods of Conservative rule in Cardiff, Labour swept the board at the 1995 elections taking 56 of the 67 seats. The Conservatives won just one seat, and the Liberal Democrats became the official opposition more by default rather than by any success of their own, retaining their previous nine city council seats. Plaid Cymru also gained just one seat, although this was a minor triumph as it was their first council seat in the capital. The 1999 elections saw the number of councillors in Cardiff rise to 75 of which Labour took 50, the Liberal Democrats 18, the Conservatives 5 and Plaid Cymru and the Independents one each. Since then, Labour leader Russell Goodway has become the highest paid council leader in the United Kingdom and despite the best efforts of the Welsh Assembly to reduce this amount he remains the highest paid leader in Wales. The *South Wales Echo* has dubbed him Russell 'Goodwage'. Local government remains an essential credential to gaining political office at all tiers of government in Cardiff; every MP and AM in the city has served some time on either the old city or present unitary council.

Rhondda Cynon Taff county borough council (RCT) is one of the poorest and the second most populous of all Welsh local authorities, comprising four previous councils. Only one of them, Taff Ely (centred around Pontypridd), had been controlled by a party other than Labour. In the early 1990s it was run by a rainbow coalition of Plaid Cymru, Lib Dems, Conservatives and Independents, led by Janet Davies who went on to become a Plaid Cymru AM. The other authorities were staunchly Labour, with occasional pockets of Plaid Cymru support; indeed the Rhondda and Cynon valleys had no history of backing anyone else other than Labour. When the 1995 council elections came, Labour took 56 of the 75 seats, leaving a small Plaid Cymru opposition of 14. Over the next four years, however, RCT suffered from a series of leadership coups, political infighting between rival Labour groups, a reluctance to endorse the Welsh Assembly 'Yes' vote (with Labour members openly supporting the No campaign), critical auditors reports and the running up of a severe budget deficit. The council earned itself such a poor reputation than in the 1999 council elections, Labour's 56 seats were reduced to 26, whilst Plaid Cymru's 14 rose to 42. Since then, the new administration has also been bedevilled by infighting and defections. The former chairman of the council, Graham Beard, left the Plaid Cymru group in the spring of 2001 with three other members to form a Democratic Alliance Group with Liberal Democrats and Independents. It seems that RCT is a troubled authority no matter who runs it. It is however an important showpiece council for Plaid Cymru, and both they and Labour will battle hard for its control in 2004.

The Vale of Glamorgan has been one of the strongholds of the Conservatives in Wales. In 1995 however, Labour gained 35 seats on the new unitary council to the Conservatives' 7 and Plaid Cymru's 5. Running the Vale of Glamorgan council proved no bed of roses for Labour. Their leader was involved in a financial scandal and lost office. The Labour administration was then involved in a number of mismanagement issues and when the 1999 elections came, the Conservatives became the largest council group again. However they did not have an overall majority and so went into a coalition with Plaid Cymru, the only 'blue-green alliance' in Wales. Plaid are strong around the town of Dinas Powys, and have developed the same pavement politics favoured by the Lib Dems. Their local government vote is often double or triple that achieved at Westminster, but they are still very much the third party in number of council seats. The coalition seems built on the foundation that 'my enemy's enemy is my friend' and it was something both parties were keen to brush under the carpet only a few miles up the road in the Welsh Assembly, where the two continued to state that they would never work together at a national level.

CARDIFF CENTRAL

	2001		1997		1992 actual	
Electorate and turnout	59,785	58.3	60,393	70.0	57,780	74.3
Conservative	5,537	15.9	8,470	20.0	14,549	33.9
Labour	13,451	38.6	18,464	43.7	18,014	42.0
Lib Dem	12,792	36.7	10,541	24.9	9,170	21.4
Plaid Cymru	1,680	4.8	1,504	3.6	748	1.7
Anti–EU	221	0.6	760	1.8	–	–
Socialist	283	0.8	2,230	5.3	–	–
Others	878 (2)		284 (2)		435 (2)	
MP	Jon Owen Jones(Lab)		Jon Owen Jones(Lab)		Jon Owen Jones(Lab)	
Majority	659	1.9	7,923	18.8	3,465	8.1

Welsh Assembly Election 1999: Lib Dem 10,937 (42.3), Labour 7,769 (30.0), Plaid Cymru 3,795 (14.7), Conservative 3,034 (11.7), 1 Other 338. Electorate 57,815, Turnout 44.8%. AM: Jenny Randerson, Majority 3,168 (12.2).

In 1992, former Conservative Welsh Office Minister Ian Grist, who had been dropped from his Ministerial post in 1990 after John Major won the leadership election, lost his seat to Labour's Jon Owen Jones. Owen Jones was a Cardiff city councillor who had previously been chairman of the Parliament for Wales Campaign. From its creation in 1983 until 1992, Cardiff Central had been a three way marginal between Labour, Conservatives and Liberal Democrats. When Labour took the seat in 1992, they did so by squeezing the Lib Dem vote. Central, however, is a university seat with a massive student population which provides it one of the youngest electorates in Wales, if not the UK. The key to the seat is winning the student vote.

In the 1997 general election the Conservative vote slipped back significantly and Owen Jones enjoyed a majority of 7,923 (18.8 per cent), making this on paper appear a very safe Labour seat. The Liberal Democrats, however, are well entrenched locally, holding nearly all of the constituencies' council seats. In the 1999 council elections, the Lib Dems established a firmer grip on the constituency by removing all but a handful of Labour councillors, and at the same time they took the Assembly seat. The 2001 general election was held at a time when most of the students had left the constituency for the summer. This meant that the election was fought out mainly within the indigenous population. An opinion poll by HTV indicated that Owen Jones was set to take the seat by another huge majority. In the event, his Liberal Democrat opponent, 27 year-old Jenny Willott, in the event reduced the majority to a mere 659. This was one of the best results for the party in the United Kingdom in a Labour-held seat. The contest was even more interesting because only two miles down the road in the Assembly, Labour and the Liberal Democrats were in coalition, running Wales together. This closeness at a Welsh level appears to have made little impact on Westminster politics, though with the exception of Conwy, Cardiff Central is the only Welsh constituency where there has been a serious battle between the Liberal Democrats and the Labour Party in the last three decades. The contest looks set to continue.

Assembly seat

With Plaid Cymru taking Labour heartland seats throughout Wales in the May 1999 Assembly election, the Lib Dems gain of Cardiff Central was not registered by many observers. Yet for the Liberal Democrats, it represented a major political breakthrough. This was their first presence in an urban or a South Wales seat since the 1920s. Jenny Randerson, twice Westminster candidate for the Liberal Democrats (1992 and 1997), took the seat with a 3,168 (12.3 per cent) majority over Labour. Randerson was clearly helped by being a well-known local councillor and by the fact the council elections were held on the same day, since the Liberal Democrats win most of the constituencies wards. The 2003 Assembly elections are not being held on the same day as the council elections, and Randerson is now in the Cabinet, making joint decisions with her former Labour opponents. Both of these factors will have to be taken into account by the electorate. The seat, as at Westminster, will remain a two-horse race between the Liberal Democrats and Labour.

CARDIFF NORTH

	2001		1997		1992 *actual*	
Electorate and turnout	62,634	69.0	60,468	80.2	56,757	84.1
Conservative	13,680	31.6	16,334	33.7	21,547	45.1
Labour	19,845	45.9	24,460	50.4	18,578	38.9
Lib Dem	6,631	15.3	5,294	10.9	6,487	13.6
Plaid Cymru	2,471	5.7	1,201	2.5	916	1.9
Anti–EU	613	1.4	1,199	2.5	–	–
Others	–		–		207 (2)	
MP	Julie Morgan (Lab)		Julie Morgan (Lab)		Gwilym Jones (Con)	
Majority	6,165	14.3	8,126	16.8	2,969	6.2

Welsh Assembly Election 1999: Labour 12,198 (38.7), Conservatives 9,894 (31.4), Lib Dem 5,088 (16.1), Plaid Cymru 4,337 (13.8). Electorate 61,398, Turnout 51.3%. AM: Sue Essex (Lab), Majority 2,304 (7.3).

Cardiff North was created in 1983 and consists of some of the wealthiest of the city's suburbs. Previously, the areas covered by the seat were in Cardiff North West, and produced substantial Conservative majorities. This was to continue for another decade in the new constituency. In the 1983 general election, the Liberal-SDP Alliance provided the strongest challenge in the seat, and in 1987 they were still only about a hundred votes short of coming second. Unlike in Cardiff Central, however, the Lib Dems did not retain their strong position and by 1992 the seat had become a Conservative - Labour marginal, with the Labour Party successfully squeezing the Liberal vote. The Conservative Welsh Office Minister and former city councillor, Gwilym Jones, held the seat from 1983 to 1997 with ever decreasing majorities.

Jones' Labour challenger was Julie Morgan, a Cardiff city councillor and wife of Rhodri Morgan, MP for neighbouring Cardiff West. Thus when she was elected in 1997, Wales had its first husband and wife MPs, sitting for adjoining seats. Morgan's victory in 1997 drove the last Conservative MP out of the capital of Wales. The 2001 general election did not see their return or in fact anything close to it. Whilst Labour's percentage of the vote dropped, so did that of the Conservatives, and it was the Liberal Democrats and Plaid Cymru who saw a rise in their vote. Cardiff North now looks reasonably safe for Labour with the Conservatives remaining as the challengers. The Conservatives are likely to continue to target the seat, partly because they have so few others in Wales which are now worth targeting.

Assembly seat

The main question at the 1999 Assembly elections was whether Cardiff North would return to the Conservative fold after the pressure of the 1997 general election was over. In the red corner stood Sue

Essex, the former leader of Cardiff city council and university academic. In the blue corner was 24 year-old Conservative, Jonathan Morgan, pro European and on the left wing of the party. The contest was intense in Cardiff North but there was to be no breakthrough for the Conservatives. Morgan had to be satisfied with second place and a seat in the Assembly via the regional list system. Although the result was closer than at the Westminster level in 1997 (or 2001) it is by no means one of Labour most marginal seats. An increase in both the Liberal Democrat and Plaid Cymru vote undoubtedly did not help Morgan. The key to this seat at the next Assembly elections therefore is what happens to these third party votes. If they can be weakened and squeezed, then the seat could once again fall to the Conservatives; otherwise Labour may hold on again.

CARDIFF SOUTH and PENARTH

	2001		1997		1992 actual	
Electorate and turnout	62,627	57.1	61,138	68.3	61,490	77.2
Conservative	7,807	21.8	8,786	20.7	15,958	33.6
Labour	20,094	56.2	22,647	53.4	26,383	55.5
Lib Dem	4,572	12.8	3,964	9.3	3,707	7.8
Plaid Cymru	1,983	5.5	1,356	3.2	766	1.6
Anti–EU	501	1.4	1,211	2.9	–	–
Ind Labour	–	–	3,942	9.3	–	–
Others	794 (2)		514 (2)		676	
MP	Alun Michael (Lab)		Alun Michael (Lab)		Alun Michael (Lab)	
Majority	12,287	34.4	13,861	32.7	10,425	22.0

Welsh Assembly Election 1999: Labour 11,057 (48.0), Conservative 4,254 (18.5), Plaid Cymru 3,931 (17.1), Lib Dem 2,890 (12.6), 3 Others 904. Electorate 61,149, Turnout 37.7%. AM: Lorraine Barrett (Lab), Majority 6,803 (29.5).

Cardiff South and Penarth was established in 1983 and was formerly known as Cardiff South East. The constituency name was well known throughout the country because it was held by James Callaghan for 37 years between 1950 and 1987 including a stint as Prime Minister from 1976 until 1979. His successor was Rhodri Morgan's political rival for the Labour Party leadership and his predecessor as First Minister at the Welsh Assembly, Alun Michael. Michael was Tony Blair's number two when they shadowed the Home Office together in the mid-1990s. He was Blair's first choice as Welsh Secretary and Welsh Leader when Ron Davies fell from office in 1998. Although it was evident that Michael was happier at Westminster, he still went to the Welsh Assembly, but this was to last less than a year before he was forced to resign just before a vote of no confidence. The events that surrounded Michael's departure as First Minister in 2000 made little impact on his Westminster fortunes. Michael remains a close ally of Tony Blair, perhaps his closest Wales. This has ensured that, even after his days at the Assembly were finished, he has remained at the heart of government, resuming his ministerial career in 2001.

The constituency is divided between two county councils, Cardiff and the Vale of Glamorgan. Those wards contained in Cardiff are traditional Labour supporting inner city wards, whilst those contained in the Vale comprise mainly middle class wards which on a number of occasions have been Conservative strongholds. In 1983, the Conservatives came within a few thousand votes of taking the seat off Labour. In 1987 Jenny Randerson, now the Assembly Member for Cardiff Central, contested the seat for the Liberals but made little progress. Generally, the seat has remained very secure for Callaghan and now Michael. There is little reason to see this changing.

Assembly seat

Although Alun Michael resigned from the Assembly in May 2000, he was not the Assembly Member for Cardiff South and Penarth. He was the Assembly Member for the Mid and West Wales regional list seat. It was his former secretary and former county councillor, Lorraine Barrett, who took the seat for Labour in 1999. Barrett remained loyal to Michael throughout his troubles at the Assembly and as a result is one of the Labour AMs who have condemned the coalition between Labour and the Liberal Democrats. The 1999 Assembly election nearly saw Plaid Cymru take second place from the Conservatives, but did not, however, see the Labour majority seriously threatened. Cardiff South and Penarth looks set to remain firmly in Labour's hands at the next Assembly elections.

CARDIFF WEST

	2001		1997		1992 notional	
Electorate and turnout	58,348	58.4	58,244	69.2	59,470	76.9
Conservative	7,273	21.3	8,669	21.5	15,028	32.9
Labour	18,594	54.6	24,297	60.3	24,319	53.2
Lib Dem	4,458	13.1	4,366	10.8	5,005	11.0
Plaid Cymru	3,296	9.7	1,949	4.8	1,178	2.6
Anti–EU	462	1.4	996	2.5	–	–
Others	–		–		184	
MP	Kevin Brennan (Lab)		Rhodri Morgan (Lab)		Rhodri Morgan (Lab)	
Majority	11,321	33.2	15,628	38.8	9,291	20.3

Welsh Assembly Election 1999: Labour 14,305 (61.6), Conservative 3,446 (14.8), Plaid Cymru 3,402 (14.7), Lib Dems 2,063 (8.9). Electorate 57,717, Turnout 40.2%. AM: Rhodri Morgan (Lab), Majority 10,859 (46.8).

Since 1945, Cardiff West has been held by the Labour Party for all but four years, 1983–87, when it was held by the Conservative Stefan Terlezki. The seat is a mixture of middle class and inner city wards, which has made its politics unpredictable at certain times. The former Welsh Secretary and Commons Speaker, George Thomas, held Cardiff West between 1945 and 1983. Thomas was a fierce pro-unionist and anti devolutionist; it was therefore with some irony that the seat was inherited by Rhodri Morgan, who was Thomas's exact political opposite in terms of devolution. Morgan had the reputation of something of a rebel and a man for the Labour activists, despite his Oxford and Harvard education. He was a shadow front bench spokesman on Welsh Affairs prior to the 1997 general election. Upon Labour's victory, however, Tony Blair informed him not only was there no place for him in the Welsh Office as a Minister at that time, but there never would be a place for him. He was deemed to be 'too old' for government.

Morgan did not, however, deem himself too old for the leadership of the Welsh Labour Party. In both elections for the party leadership, first against Ron Davies (1998) and then Alun Michael (1999), he took the majority of the Labour membership vote but lost out on trade union block votes. After having lost two elections, however, Morgan was installed as the Welsh Labour Leader and subsequently First Minister upon the resignation of Alun Michael in February 2000. A man whom the Prime Minister had not deemed fit to serve in government was now the leader of his party in Wales. There was genuine delight across the political establishment at Morgan's victory, which was recognition for his years of hard pro–devolution work. All of this, however, meant that Morgan would be leaving Westminster at the 2001 election. His successor was Kevin Brennan, a Cardiff councillor and Morgan's right-hand man for the previous decade. Brennan, a former president of the Oxford Union and a contemporary of William Hague, had worked the seat closely with Morgan and his selection as replacement was widely anticipated. Although there was a slight drop in the Labour vote, Brennan held on easily against his Conservative opponents. This seat remains firmly in Labour hands.

Assembly seat

Rhodri Morgan was the only Labour Assembly Member to see an increase in his share of the vote in the 1999 Assembly elections on the general election two years before. His popularity, both with his own party and the local populace, combined with his huge public profile, meant that the seat was never in danger of falling to anyone else. The most interesting point concerning the election in Cardiff West, apart from the rise in Labour vote, was the fact that Plaid Cymru almost pushed the Conservatives into third place in a constituency they had held just twelve years before.

Morgan's position as First Minister and his genuine popularity amongst the voters in the constituency mean that he is likely to represent Cardiff West until he decides to step down. It will only be then that the opposition may stand a better chance of prising the seat off Labour.

CYNON VALLEY

	2001		1997		1992 actual	
Electorate and turnout	48,639	55.4	48,286	69.2	49,696	76.5
Conservative	2,045	7.6	2,260	6.8	4,890	12.9
Labour	17,685	65.6	23,307	69.7	26,254	69.1
Lib Dem	2,541	9.4	3,459	10.3	2,667	7.0
Plaid Cymru	4,687	17.4	3,552	10.6	4,186	11.0
Anti–EU	–	–	844	2.5	–	–
MP	Ann Clwyd (Lab)		Ann Clwyd (Lab)		Ann Clwyd (Lab)	
Majority	12,998	48.2	19,755	59.1	21,364	56.2

Welsh Assembly Election 1999: Labour 9,883 (45.6), Plaid Cymru 9,206 (42.5), Lib Dem 1,531 (7.1), Conservative 1,046 (4.8). Electorate 47,619, Turnout 45.5%. AM: Christine Chapman (Lab), Majority 677 (3.1).

The former coal mining area of the Cynon Valley contains (at the time of writing) the only deep coal mine still in operation in South Wales, Tower Colliery at Hirwaun. The whole valley is deeply working class in nature and its politics has traditionally been Labour. Ioan Evans held the seat from 1974–1984 (it changed its name from Aberdare to Cynon Valley in 1983). Upon his death, it was won by Labour's Ann Clwyd, then the MEP for Mid and West Wales. The by-election was also significant for the fact that the SDP-Alliance candidate, Felix Aubel, defected to the Conservatives. Some 17 years later, Aubel was defeated by a whisker when he took on the Liberal Democrat candidate in Brecon and Radnorshire, some posthumous revenge for the Alliance!

For thirteen years, Clwyd remained the only female MP in Wales. She held various positions in the Shadow Cabinet until the fall out concerning her inability to return for a three line whip in 1994 led to her being sent to the backbenches. Since then she has been a campaigner on a number of issues and on some occasions a Labour rebel.

Plaid Cymru represent the only serious challenge to Labour in the Cynon Valley. Even they, however, have failed to gain over 20 per cent at Westminster elections. The seat remains one of Labour's strongest parliamentary seats in Wales; their fifth safest in 2001(up from ninth in 1997).

Assembly Seat

The Welsh Assembly seat in 1999 proved to be nowhere near as safe as the Parliamentary seat. The Plaid Cymru tide that was sweeping the country almost engulfed the Cynon Valley, with Phil Richards just 677 votes short (3.1 per cent) of depriving Labour's Christine Chapman of victory. The Cynon Valley had never seen such a close contest before. Richards was helped by the county council elections being held on the same day, in which there was a voter backlash against a deeply unpopular Labour-run council. Nevertheless, the rise in the Plaid Cymru vote was quite a shock to the Labour establishment in the Cynon Valley.

Chapman, a former county councillor, is an academic expert on women within the Labour Party, and chair of the powerful Objective 1 European Funding Monitoring Group. She has spent the last few years bedding down in the constituency and seeking to ensure that Plaid Cymru do not improve on their 1999 performance. The 2003 elections were still set, however to be a contest between Labour and Plaid Cymru and with the closeness of the competition last time everything is still to play for.

PONTYPRIDD

	2001		1997		1992 actual	
Electorate and turnout	71,768	53.4	64,185	71.4	61,685	79.3
Conservative	5,096	13.3	5,910	12.9	9,925	20.3
Labour	22,963	59.9	29,290	63.9	29,722	60.8
Lib Dem	4,152	10.8	6,161	13.4	4,180	8.5
Plaid Cymru	5,279	13.8	2,977	6.5	4,448	9.1
Anti–EU	603	1.6	874	1.9	–	–
Others	216		643 (3)		615	
MP	Kim Howells (Lab)		Kim Howells (Lab)		Kim Howells (Lab)	
Majority	17,684	46.2	23,129	50.4	19,797	40.5

Welsh Assembly Election 1999: Labour 11,330 (38.6), Plaid Cymru 9,755 (33.3), Lib Dem 5,040 (17.2), Conservative 2,485 (8.5), 2 Others 716. Electorate 64,597, Turnout 45.4%. AM: Jane Davidson (Lab), Majority 1,575 (5.4).

The constituency of Pontypridd had its boundaries altered substantially in 1983. At one time it contained a lot of the prosperous areas now contained in the Vale of Glamorgan seat. The revisions in 1983 focused the constituency around the industrial towns of Pontypridd and Llantrisant. Until 1989, the seat was held by Labour's Brynmor John (1970-1989), but his death in that year caused a by-election at which Plaid Cymru's vote soared to a quarter of the total; nevertheless Labour's Dr Kim Howells still won the seat by over 10,000 votes. Howells was the former full-time official of the South Wales National Union of Mineworkers. He became a fervent anti-nationalist and anti devolutionist, although the pressures of being in the Labour government as a Minister stopped him campaigning against the Welsh Assembly; indeed, he even did some minor campaigning in favour of it. Howells remains a constant critic of anything he deems to pander too much to the Welsh Nationalist cause.

Until 1997, the Conservatives always came second in general elections. A deeper examination however reveals that at a local level the Conservatives have not held a county council or town council seat in Pontypridd itself for decades. In fact the constituency is atypical of many of the other South Wales Valley seats owing to the fact that there has been a long established Liberal presence. For example the town council had a Liberal Democrat Mayor as recently as 2001-2002. This presence means that opposition to Labour remains divided. In Westminster elections it remains most unlikely that Labour will be in for any serious competition.

Assembly seat

The caveat that applies to Liberal Democrat support at general and council elections became fully clear during the 1999 Assembly elections. Their candidate Gianni Orsi polled a substantial 17.2 per cent of the vote, which was enough to ensure that Plaid Cymru's Bleddyn Hancock remained five percent behind Labour's Jane Davidson. Although Labour had attracted less than 40 per cent of the vote in the seat for the first time since it was established, the split in the opposition ensured Davidson's victory.

Davidson is a firm member of the Rhodri Morgan camp having been his office manager for five years. After spending a brief period as Deputy Speaker, Morgan appointed her as Education and Lifelong Learning Minister in October 2000, a position with some relevance as Pontypridd is also a university seat (University of Glamorgan) with some 8,000 students living within the constituency. The student vote apart, the next Assembly election result is likely to depend on whether Labour or Plaid Cymru can squeeze the Lib Dem vote.

RHONDDA

	2001		1997		1992 actual	
Electorate and turnout	56,121	60.6	57,105	71.5	59,955	76.6
Conservative	1,557	4.6	1,551	3.8	3,588	7.8
Labour	23,230	68.3	30,381	74.5	34,243	74.5
Lib Dem	1,525	4.5	2,307	5.7	2,431	5.3
Plaid Cymru	7,183	21.1	5,450	13.4	5,427	11.8
Anti–EU	–	–	658	1.6	–	–
Others	507		460		245	
MP	Chris Bryant (Lab)		Allan Rogers (Lab)		Allan Rogers (Lab)	
Majority	16,047	47.2	24,931	61.1	28,816	62.7

Welsh Assembly Election 1999: Plaid Cymru 13,558 (48.7), Labour 11,273 (40.5), Lib Dem 1,303 (4.7), Independent 913 (3.3), Conservative 774 (2.8) Electorate 55,398, Turnout 50.2%. AM: Geraint Davies (PC), Majority 2,285 (8.2).

For the first half of the twentieth century, the miners of the Rhondda supplied the coal that ran the British Empire. The whole valley was a stanch working class Labour stronghold, though in 1967, at the Rhondda West by-election, Plaid Cymru almost gained the seat. This sent shock waves through the Labour establishment and from this date onwards Plaid Cymru were seen as the number one political enemy to Labour in the Rhondda. Yet in the decades that followed, the combined seat of Rhondda East and West remained firmly under Labour's control, first under Alec Jones (1967-1983) and then Allan Rogers (1983-2001). Although Rogers was a front bench spokesman he was not appointed to the government upon Labour's victory in 1997. He remained on the backbenches and was one of the least active Labour MPs, only making his presence felt when expressing anti devolution opinions during the passage of the Government of Wales Bill 1998.

Rogers retired from the Commons in 2001 on the grounds of ill health. Labour chose as his replacement an openly gay candidate who was a former Conservative Party member, Chris Bryant. Plaid Cymru's candidate Leanne Wood, who had previously contested the seat in the 1997 general election, thought that this was the stroke of luck that she needed in order to repeat her party's Assembly victory. This however, was not to be. Bryant had worked hard within the constituency and had motivated his supporters to campaign for victory, something that had previously been a rarity for Labour in the Rhondda. In June 2001, despite Plaid Cymru returning its best ever general election result of 21.1 per cent, this was still nowhere near Labour's huge share of the vote. In a seat where the Conservatives and the Liberal Democrats regularly lose their deposits, there is little opposition vote to squeeze. Plaid Cymru's success at the Assembly elections can only be repeated at Westminster contests by turning Labour supporters to Plaid Cymru, something that has proved very difficult in the past.

Assembly seat

The loss of the Rhondda constituency to Plaid Cymru in 1999 marked one of Labour's worst ever defeats in Wales. In the 1997 general election, although they came second, Plaid Cymru had secured just 13.4 per cent of the vote. Labour had, not unusually, polled almost three-quarters of the vote (74.5%) or three out of every four votes cast. Yet two years later Geraint Davies gained 48.7 per cent of the vote against Wayne David's 40.5 per cent. Labour had been beaten in the Rhondda by its traditional political foe Plaid Cymru for the first time. The news dominated the papers the following day and the shock waves paralysed the Labour Party.

Plaid Cymru had been aided by a number of factors, foremost of which was the that the elections were held on the same day as the council elections in which Rhondda voters removed the unpopular Labour-run Rhondda Cynon Taff council. When this was combined with the fallout over the botched Labour leadership election in Wales, and the general swing to Plaid Cymru, the scene was set for a historic Plaid victory. The question for the 2003 Assembly elections is whether Plaid Cymru can retain the seat without the combination of these factors. They may be helped by an incumbent AM, but this will be a very hard fought battle.

VALE OF GLAMORGAN

	2001		1997		1992 notional	
Electorate and turnout	67,774	66.7	67,413	80.0	67,152	81.3
Conservative	15,824	35.0	18,522	34.4	24,207	44.3
Labour	20,524	45.4	29,054	53.9	24,188	44.3
Lib Dem	5,521	12.2	4,945	9.2	5,042	9.2
Plaid Cymru	2,867	6.3	1,393	2.6	1,159	2.1
Anti–EU	448	1.0	–	–	–	–
MP	John Smith (Lab)		John Smith (Lab)		Walter Sweeney (Con)	
Majority	4,700	10.4	10,532	19.5	19	0.0

Welsh Assembly Election 1999: Labour 11,448 (35.0), Conservative 10,522 (32.1), Plaid Cymru 7,848 (24.0), Lib Dem 2,938 (9.0). Electorate 67,804, Turnout 48.3%. AM: Jane Hutt (Lab), Majority 926 (2.8).

The Vale of Glamorgan is one of the most prosperous constituencies in Wales. Its rolling hills and small farms make it more like a leafy English county than part of the Welsh Valleys to its north. The seat also contains the port and seaside resort of Barry, which is a working class stronghold in an otherwise Conservative Welsh heartland.

For most of the last century, the Vale of Glamorgan (before 1983 known as Barry) returned Conservative MPs. From 1951 until his death, ironically whilst campaigning during the 1989 Pontypridd by-election, Sir Raymond Gower represented the seat. In the by-election that followed his death the seat was won for Labour by John Smith, a local councillor. Smith gained the seat with a majority of over six thousand votes over the Conservative candidate Rod Richards (Richards then won the seat of Clwyd North West in 1992). At the general election three years later, Smith lost the seat to the Conservative Walter Sweeney. Sweeney only had a majority of 19, which was the smallest majority in the United Kingdom between 1992-1997.

Despite sterling efforts to hold the seat, Sweeney was washed away in Labour's 1997 landslide by a massive 10,532 votes, the victor once again John Smith. From 1997 onwards the Conservatives targeted the Vale of Glamorgan as one of their key seats in Wales. In 2001, Susan Inkin improved on her party's 1997 performance, reducing Smith's majority down to 10 per cent (about half that of 1997), but there is still a long way to go. Although this still remains a two-horse race between Labour and the Conservatives, Smith still enjoys a reasonable lead, which will take some battling to be reduced. The constituency is the eighth most marginal in Wales.

Assembly seat
Having seen what had traditionally been a Conservative seat fall to Labour at the 1997 general election,

the Conservatives were determined to ensure that this was a mere flash in the pan. Their candidate David Melding took on Labour's Jane Hutt knowing that it was important to the future of his party to show that their heartland could be regained. On election day, however, the Conservative share of the vote remained static, and although Labour's vote fell sharply, it was in the direction of Plaid Cymru, whose support had risen to almost a quarter of the total vote in a seat in which they had always previously lost their deposit. It was this factor rather than anything achieved by the Conservatives which saw Hutt scrape in with a majority of less than a thousand votes. If the 2003 Assembly elections see a further inroad into Labour's vote by Plaid Cymru, the Vale of Glamorgan could fall to the Conservatives by default. There is nothing as yet to indicate that without this assistance, Conservative fortunes can rise enough to overturn Labour's majority.

South Wales West

	Conservative		Labour		Liberal Democrat		Plaid Cymru		Others	
	Share of vote	Seats	Share of vote	Seats	Share of vote	Seats	Share of vote	Seats	Share of vote	Seats
2001	16.3	0	56.7	7	12.2	0	11.6	0	3.2	0
1997	15.0	0	65.6	7	10.7	0	5.7	0	3.0	0
1992	23.7	0	61.3	7	9.2	0	5.1	0	0.6	0
1999 C	11.4	0	42.2	7	13.0	0	26.2	0	7.2	0
1999 R	12.6	1	42.2	0	11.1	1	30.4	2	3.7	0

NOTE: 1999C=Welsh Assembly Elections Constituency vote; 1999R=Welsh Assembly Elections Regional top-up vote (4 seats available)

South Wales West consists of seven parliamentary and Assembly constituencies and three unitary authorities. It also has seven Assembly constituencies and four regional list members: currently (2002) two Plaid Cymru (Janet Davies and Dai Lloyd), one Conservative (Alun Cairns) and one Liberal Democrat (Peter Black). The whole region normally supports Labour at both Westminster elections and the Welsh Assembly. Although many of the Labour Assembly Members in this region, including some of the their Cabinet members, only gained between 30 and 40 per cent of the vote, it was enough to enable them to retain the seven seats. Unlike all of the other regions in Wales, there are no real marginals here at either Assembly or Westminster level. The voting is skewed heavily in Labour's favour and although in 2001 they achieved just over half of the vote, they gained 100 per cent of the seats. Similarly Labour controls the three county councils. The leadership of the Wales Labour Party subsequently acknowledged the fact that there is a substantial power base here by giving the region three of their seven Cabinet posts.

Of the other political parties, the Conservatives are second but Plaid Cymru have been gaining ground in the region and are now close to overtaking the Liberal Democrats for the third position at Westminster elections. Plaid are already second at the Assembly elections, and they are likely to pose the greatest threat to Labour, although even they seem set to remain well behind.

Local government

There are just three unitary authorities in South Wales West, and since their creation in 1995, all have been run by Labour. Bridgend county borough frequently has the largest number of uncontested wards in South Wales at council elections. In 1995, 16 of the 44 Labour councillors were returned unopposed, and in 1999 this figure remained 12 of 40. The fact that the opposition is weak on the council, particularly in the Ogmore Vale and Gawr Valley areas, means that Labour remain in a very solid position. Between 1995 and 1998 there was no official opposition on the council at all. Although Labour have suffered severe internal squabbles, this has not dented their hold over the county. The Liberal Democrat leader Cheryl Green leads an opposition group of some 14 councillors; the Conservatives have been all but wiped out.

There was tremendous opposition from both Neath and Port Talbot about being merged into one unitary authority in 1995, with both areas claiming they had little in common with each other. To the outsider, however, there is little to tell them apart. Both have a history of backing Labour with no other political party being able to mount a serious challenge. The 1999 elections did see, however, a significant advance by Plaid Cymru, increasing their strength from three to ten seats. Currently, Labour enjoy a majority of 16 over the combined opposition. The next elections could see this further eroded and Labour may for the first time face a serious challenge to their continued control.

In 1976, Labour were virtually wiped out in Swansea when after a serious of political and corruption scandals, Independents took 32 of the 51 seats and reduced Labour from 30 seats to just 7. Three years later, the Independents were extinguished and Labour once more regained control; they have remained in charge ever since. Currently, Labour hold 47 of the new unitary council's 72 seats, down from the 56 they held in 1995. The Labour controlled council has sought hard to exert itself as Wales's number two city and even challenged Cardiff for the home of the Welsh Assembly. Until 1995, the Conservatives were always the main opposition, with between 8 and 16 seats. However, they lost all but one of them in 1995, and their remaining member then defected to the Liberal Democrats, the new official opposition, who now have eleven seats.

ABERAVON

	2001		1997		1992 actual	
Electorate and turnout	49,524	61.0	50,031	71.9	51,655	77.6
Conservative	2,296	7.6	2,835	7.9	5,567	13.9
Labour	19,063	63.1	25,650	71.3	26,877	67.1
Lib Dem	2,933	9.7	4,079	11.3	4,999	12.5
Plaid Cymru	2,955	9.8	2,088	5.8	1,919	4.8
Anti–EU	–	–	970	2.7	–	–
Others	2,943 (3)		341		707	
MP	Hywel Francis (Lab)		John Morris (Lab)		John Morris (Lab)	
Majority	16,108	53.4	21,571	60.0	21,310	53.2

Welsh Assembly Election 1999: Labour 11,941 (51.3), Plaid Cymru 5,198 (22.3), Lib Dem 3,165 (13.6), Conservative 1,624 (7.0), 2 Others 1,366. Electorate 49,786, Turnout 46.8%. AM: Brian Gibbons (Lab), Majority 6,743 (29.0).

Aberavon remains very much an industrial seat, with a huge steel works based at its centre. In the 2001 general election, the constituency moved from being the eighth safest Labour seat in Wales up to third (21st nationally). The constituency was held by Labour's first Prime Minister, Ramsay MacDonald, in the 1920s, though Aberavon has remained more solidly Labour than MacDonald did thereafter. The constituency also launched the political career of Geoffrey Howe, who stood here for the Conservatives here in 1955 and 1959. Howe subsequently acknowledged this and his Welsh roots by being ennobled as Lord Howe of Aberavon.

There have only been four Labour MPs in the seat since 1922. As well as MacDonald, Sir John Morris QC (1959-2001) also served in a Labour Cabinet. He served as Welsh Secretary under Wilson and Callaghan in 1974-1979 and as Attorney General under Blair in 1997-99. He was the only Labour Cabinet Minister from the 1970s to serve again in the 1990s. Morris was Welsh Secretary during the first failed attempt to bring an Assembly to Wales. After the referendum result was known, he made the memorable comment: 'when you see an elephant on your doorstep you know you have lost'.

The present Labour MP is Professor Hywel Francis, formerly of Swansea University. Francis was one of the key campaigners during the 1997 Assembly referendum campaign but was unable to secure a seat for the Assembly itself. He then became a political adviser to Welsh Secretary Paul Murphy, before gaining the nomination for a local constituency. Bearing in mind the political history of this seat Francis will remain its MP for as long as he and the local Labour Party desire.

Assembly Seat

It was no great surprise that Labour won the Aberavon constituency in 1999. They had traditionally enjoyed loyal support from the citizens of this parliamentary seat, and once again there was no serious challenge. The newly elected Labour Assembly Member was Irish born GP Brian Gibbons, whose still strong Irish accent reminds Assembly Members and the Welsh public that Wales has close links with its Irish neighbour. The other noteworthy point about the Assembly election was that Janet Davies, former Plaid Cymru leader of Taff Ely borough council, who finished second in Aberavon, was elected as one of her party's list members. As with the parliamentary constituency, the Assembly seat is one of Labour's strongest. Therefore in 2003, the other parties will be seeking to maximise their list vote in the seat rather than seriously tackling the constituency themselves.

BRIDGEND

	2001		1997		1992 actual	
Electorate and turnout	61,496	60.2	59,826	72.3	58,518	80.5
Conservative	9,377	25.3	9,867	22.8	16,817	35.7
Labour	19,423	52.5	25,115	58.1	24,143	51.3
Lib Dem	5,330	14.4	4,968	11.5	4,827	10.3
Plaid Cymru	2,653	7.2	1,649	3.8	1,301	2.8
Anti–EU	–	–	1,662	3.8	–	–
Others	223		–		–	
MP	Win Griffiths (Lab)		Win Griffiths (Lab)		Win Griffiths (Lab)	
Majority	10,046	27.1	15,248	35.2	7,326	15.6

Welsh Assembly Election 1999: Labour 9,321 (37.2), Conservative 5,063 (20.2), Plaid Cymru 4,919 (19.7), Lib Dem 3,910 (15.6), Independent 1,819 (7.3). Electorate 60,234, Turnout 41.6%. AM: Carwyn Jones (Lab), Majority 4,258 (17.0).

The Bridgend seat was created in 1983 after boundary changes gave Wales an extra two seats. The constituency is split between a rural area, the seaside resort of Porthcawl and the county town of Bridgend. It has a heavy industrial base as well, with Ford's main UK engine plant based at Pencoed. Bridgend is atypical of all of the other seats in South Wales West in that it is the only one recently held by a party other than Labour. Between 1983 and 1987 it was held by Peter Hubbard Miles for the Conservatives, and since then they have returned some of their best results in the region here, though without threatening to return the seat to marginal status.

The former Labour MEP Win Griffiths took the seat off the Conservatives in 1987 and has held it ever since. Griffiths served as a front bench spokesman on Welsh Affairs together with Ron Davies and Rhodri Morgan. He did not, however, gain the favour of Blair and was the first Welsh Labour Minister to be sent to the backbenches in July 1998, where he has remained ever since. Today, this is one of Labour's weakest seats in South Wales West but even here they retain a commanding lead. Griffiths has built up a substantial majority over the Conservatives and they would need to benefit from a massive reversal in fortunes to win the seat back again. This seems unlikely and at local government level they presently hold just one council seat.

Assembly seat

Bridgend was most notable for being the only Assembly seat in South Wales West where Plaid Cymru did not finish second. This privilege fell instead to the Conservatives, who gained a respectable 20.2 per cent of the vote, but were still some 4,258 votes short of beating Labour's Carwyn Jones. Nevertheless, the Conservative runner-up Alun Cairns got the consolation prize of a regional list seat.

Jones is a former barrister who took over the poisoned chalice of Secretary for Agriculture and Rural Development following the sacking of Christine Gwyther in July 2000. He weathered the impact of foot and mouth in Wales, and in a poll in December 2001 was deemed the most trusted UK Government Minister by Welsh farmers. If the Conservatives were able to effectively squeeze the Plaid Cymru or Liberal Democrat Assembly vote then they may be able to make a serious attempt at gaining the seat in 2003. At the last Assembly elections, however, Plaid Cymru stood almost as good a chance of winning the seat as the perennial Conservative favourites. It is likely that both parties will continue to cancel each other out and Labour will remain comfortably ahead.

GOWER

	2001		1997		1992 actual	
Electorate and turnout	58,935	63.4	57,707	75.1	57,229	81.9
Conservative	10,281	27.5	10,306	23.8	16,437	35.1
Labour	17,676	47.3	23,313	53.8	23,485	50.1
Lib Dem	4,507	12.1	5,624	13.0	4,655	9.9
Plaid Cymru	3,865	10.3	2,226	5.1	1,639	3.5
Anti–EU	–	–	1,745	4.0	–	–
Others	1,024 (2)		122		636 (3)	
MP	Martin Caton (Lab)		Martin Caton (Lab)		Gareth Wardell (Lab)	
Majority	7,395	19.8	13,007	30.0	7,048	15.0

Welsh Assembly Election 1999: Labour 9,813 (35.4), Plaid Cymru 6,653 (24.0), Conservative 3,912 (14.1), Lib Dem 3,260 (11.8), Independent 2,307 (8.3), Other 1,755. Electorate 58,523, Turnout 47.3%. AM: Edwina Hart (Lab), Majority 3,160 (11.4).

In 1983 the Conservatives came within 1,205 votes of winning the newly created Gower seat. That was the closest this seat has come to real political excitement. For the rest of its history (and that of the areas the seat covered before) there has always been a substantial Labour dominance. Although the constituency covers some of Swansea's wealthiest suburbs and the beautiful Gower peninsula, it also encompasses the industrial areas of the Lliw Valley, which helps explain the considerable Labour vote here.

Gareth Wardell held the seat from a 1982 by-election until 1997. Wardell was chair of the Welsh Affairs Select Committee in 1984-1997 when he established it as a formidable investigative machine. He was replaced in 1997 by Martin Caton, who has since maintained a low profile outside his constituency, though he voted against the government on changes to invalidity benefit in November 1999.

Although the Conservatives do quite well in this seat, they have not made any significant progress to threaten a breakthrough over the last decade. Barring a massive Conservative revival the seat looks set to stay within Labour's grip.

Assembly seat

Whereas the MP for Gower remains relatively unknown in Wales, the same cannot be said of its Assembly Member. Edwina Hart, former chair of the Wales TUC, is a formidable politician. Since May 1999 she has been the Assembly Finance Secretary and is highly regarded by many both inside and outside of her party. With her strong socialist credentials, Hart is seen as a popular successor to Rhodri Morgan as the next Welsh Labour leader. In the 1999 Assembly election, Plaid Cymru made a very strong challenge and secured a good second place. Although the seat became a lot more marginal than it has been, there still appears to be little serious threat of Labour losing the seat. The next election is likely to be interesting only as an indicator of the extent to which Hart has been able to build up her own personal vote and whether the Conservatives can regain the number two slot.

NEATH

	2001		1997		1992 actual	
Electorate and turnout	56,001	62.5	55,541	74.3	56,355	80.6
Conservative	3,310	9.5	3,583	8.7	6,928	15.2
Labour	21,253	60.7	30,324	73.5	30,903	68.0
Lib Dem	3,335	9.5	2,597	6.3	2,467	5.4
Plaid Cymru	6,437	18.4	3,344	8.1	5,145	11.3
Anti–EU	–	–	975	2.4	–	–
Others	685 (2)		420		–	
MP	Peter Hain (Lab)		Peter Hain (Lab)		Peter Hain (Lab)	
Majority	14,816	42.3	26,741	64.8	23,975	52.8

Welsh Assembly Election 1999: Labour 12,234 (45.5), Plaid Cymru 9,616 (35.8), Lib Dem 2,631 (9.8), Conservative 1,895 (7.1), Other 519. Electorate 56,085, Turnout 48.0%. AM: Gwenda Thomas (Lab), Majority 2,618 (9.7).

Its MP Peter Hain has put the constituency of Neath firmly on the Westminster map. Based around the town of Neath and the Upper Swansea Valley, the seat has always been solidly Labour. Hain, as Minister for Europe, has enjoyed more publicity than most Cabinet Ministers and is perhaps the best known Welsh MP since Neil Kinnock stood down in 1995.

Hain won the seat in a by election in 1991 after the death of Donald Coleman (1964-1991). South African born and educated, he first achieved national prominence for his work in the anti-apartheid movement with his attempt to stop the Springboks tour in 1970. After that he became chair of the Young Liberals between 1971 and 1973. The Young Liberals, however, were always well to the left of their party leadership and Hain saw the rising Labour left as more in tune with his ideals; he thus joined Labour in 1977. In recent years Hain has proved himself as a Blair loyalist. He played a key part in the 1997 Assembly Referendum, acted as the campaign manager for Alun Michael during the 1998-9 Welsh Labour leadership elections and is currently a key public figure behind the Yes campaign in the Euro referendum. Hain's public profile brings media attention to a seat that otherwise would be just another Labour valleys stronghold.

Neath has always been a strong Labour seat. It has a significant number of Welsh speakers, which perhaps indicates why Plaid Cymru tend to do quite well here. Plaid have been gaining strength in recent elections, but still remain a long way off being a serious threat to Labour.

Assembly seat

Plaid Cymru did a lot better in the 1999 Assembly election in Neath than they have ever done at a Westminster election. Their efforts did not prevent the election of Labour's Gwenda Thomas, but left her as Assembly Member for one of the most marginal seats in the region. Since her election, Thomas has stayed on the Assembly's backbenches, though she does chair the Local Government and Housing Committee. This is a factor that could aid Plaid Cymru in securing its first constituency win in South Wales West. They would first, however, need to make further inroads into the Labour vote, or squeeze the Liberal Democrat and Conservative vote dry. Neath is a seat Plaid Cymru need to win if they were to gain overall control of the Welsh Assembly. Similarly it is one which Labour must hold. This is therefore an interesting seat to watch in the next Assembly elections.

OGMORE

	2001		1997		1992 *actual*	
Electorate and Turnout	52,185	58.2	52,193	72.9	52,196	80.6
Conservative	3,383	11.2	3,716	9.8	6,359	15.1
Labour	18,833	62.0	28,163	74.0	30,186	71.7
Lib Dem	3,878	12.8	3,510	9.2	2,868	6.8
Plaid Cymru	4,259	14.0	2,679	7.0	2,667	6.3
MP	Ray Powell (Lab)*		Ray Powell (Lab)		Ray Powell (Lab)	
Majority	14,574	48.0	24,447	64.2	23,827	56.6

Welsh Assembly Election 1999: Labour 10,407 (48.2), Plaid Cymru 5,842 (27.1), Independent 2,439 (11.3), Lib Dem 1,496 (6.9), Conservative 1,415 (6.6). Electorate 51,998, Turnout 41.5%. AM: Janice Gregory (Lab), Majority 4,565 (21.1).

Parliamentary by-election 14 February 2002: Labour 9,548 (52.0), Plaid Cymru 3,827 (20.8), Lib Dem 1,608 (8.8), Conservative 1,377 (7.5), 2 Socialists 1,357 (7.4), 4 Others 659. Electorate 51,325, Turnout 35.8%. MP: Huw Irranca-Davies (Lab), Majority 5,721 (31.2).

Ogmore, whose boundaries were altered in 1983, is based around the Ogmore Valley (though no longer Ogmore by Sea), thus the name of the constituency. The seat is very industrial and hence, as is usually the case in Wales, very Labour. The late Sir Ray Powell, who held the seat from 1979 until his death in December 2001, used to say 'you don't count the Labour votes here, you weigh them'; there has never been any serious organised opposition to Labour. Sir Ray was an MP of the Old Welsh Labour unionist school. Rising through the ranks as a councillor and agent before becoming MP, he was anti devolution and anti PR. Attempts to shift him in 1997 in order to bring in a Tory defector by offering him a peerage came to nothing when he publicly rejected the offer. Sir Ray ended up falling out with most of the New Labour establishment by the time of his death.

The Labour selection contest for the February 2002 by-election was more exciting than the poll itself, with no fewer than forty prospective candidates entering the race to succeed Powell. Mark Seddon, editor of *Tribune*, failed to reach the short list, Cardiff's well-remunerated Russell Goodway also lost out and the final stage was eventually won by a tourism lecturer at Swansea Institute, Huw Irranca-Davies, who had been the Labour candidate for Brecon and Radnorshire in 2001. The strongest challenge to Davies came from Plaid Cymru, who selected Bleddyn Hancock, the former candidate for Pontypridd, but in the event Labour comfortably held the seat with a majority exceeding 30 per cent. The other notable feature of the result was that the Socialist Labour Party polled 6 per cent of the vote and retained their deposit, the first time they have done so in Wales.

Assembly seat

Although Sir Ray Powell is dead, his political legacy goes on in the shape of his daughter Janice Gregory. Gregory won the seat for Labour in 1999 with a much smaller majority than her father, but still substantial compared to many other Labour Assembly seats. Gregory was a key Alun Michael loyalist right up to the latter's defeat. She resigned her position as a Labour whip after Michael's fall, claiming that other members had plotted to oust him. Although she is very unlikely to feature in a Labour Cabinet under Rhodri Morgan, the seat looks set to stay firmly in Labour hands in 2003.

SWANSEA EAST

	2001		1997		1992 actual	
Electorate and turnout	57,520	52.3	57,371	67.4	59,187	75.6
Conservative	3,026	10.1	3,582	9.3	7,697	17.2
Labour	19,612	65.2	29,151	75.4	31,179	69.7
Lib Dem	3,064	10.2	3,440	8.9	4,248	9.5
Plaid Cymru	3,464	11.5	1,308	3.4	1,607	3.6
Anti–EU	443	1.5	904	2.3	–	–
Others	463		289		–	
MP	Donald Anderson (Lab)		Donald Anderson (Lab)		Donald Anderson (Lab)	
Majority	16,148	53.7	25,569	66.1	23,482	52.5

Welsh Assembly Election 1999: Labour 9,495 (45.6), Plaid Cymru 5,714 (27.4), Lib Dem 3,963 (19.0), Conservative 1,663 (8.0). Electorate 57,766, Turnout 36.1%. AM: Val Feld (Lab), Majority 3,781 (18.2).

Welsh Assembly by-election 27 September 2001: Labour 7,484 (58.1), Plaid Cymru 2,465 (19.1), Lib Dem 1,592 (12.4), Conservative 675 (5.2), Anti–EU 243 (1.9), 3 Others 416. Electorate 56,970, Turnout 22.6%. AM: Val Lloyd (Lab), Majority 5,019 (39.0).

Swansea East is based upon the city of Swansea and covers mainly industrial areas with a number of large council estates. Once again it is a seat which provides large Labour majorities for its MPs. There have only been three since 1945, D.L. Mort (1945-1963), Neil McBride (1963-1974) and since then Donald Anderson. Anderson, a former barrister and diplomat, was the MP for Monmouth between 1966-1970, when he lost the seat. Four years later, he ended up in Swansea where he had been a school and University student and university lecturer. Anderson has moulded himself well in the role of a distinguished and well-respected Parliamentary figure. He chairs the Foreign Affairs Select Committee with such competence and respect from fellow MPs that he survived an attempted Blairite coup in autumn 2001, when there was an attempt to oust him and fellow select committee chairs.

The seat remains firmly in Labour's grasp at Westminster elections. Although Plaid Cymru have been making steady progress, neither they nor any other political party are able to gain more than one in ten votes against Labour's six or seven out of ten. Labour will have to suffer a severe drop in fortunes for this seat to be taken by anyone else.

Assembly seat
One of the shining lights of the female cause in politics and particularly the Labour Party in Wales was the late Val Feld, who won the Swansea East seat in 1999 with a fairly substantial 18 per cent majority.

Feld was one of the architects of Welsh devolution and had tried on various occasions to become a MP in Wales, failing as so many females had before her to effectively beat the male domination of Welsh politics. With the arrival of the Welsh Assembly she was finally able to gain a place in national politics. Sadly, however, it was only for a short time before her death in the spring of 2001. She was replaced as Assembly Member by another Val, Val Lloyd in the Assembly's first by-election (the other two Assembly Members to be replaced, Alun Michael and Christine Humphreys, had been Assembly list members which meant no election was required as the list member beneath them simply took their place). Swansea East was also the seat where Peter Black, the Liberal Democrats regional list member, stood. Black gained 19 per cent of the vote, which was the best result of any of the three Liberal Democrat list members.

The Swansea East by-election was notable for two things, first an appallingly low turnout of just over one in five, and second the opportunity it gave to test Plaid Cymru's strength in Assembly elections post 1999. In the event, Labour's majority increased and Plaid Cymru and the other political parties fell back on their May 1999 performance. The indications therefore are that this seat will stay firmly in Labour's hands in 2003.

SWANSEA WEST

	2001		1997		1992 actual	
Electorate and turnout	57,493	55.8	59,849	67.6	59,791	73.3
Conservative	6,094	19.0	8,289	20.5	13,760	31.4
Labour	15,644	48.7	22,748	56.2	23,238	53.0
Lib Dem	5,313	16.6	5,872	14.5	4,620	10.5
Plaid Cymru	3,404	10.6	2,675	6.6	1,668	3.8
Anti–EU	653	2.0	–	–	–	–
Others	992 (2)		885		564	
MP	Alan Williams (Lab)		Alan Williams (Lab)		Alan Williams (Lab)	
Majority	9,550	29.8	14,459	35.7	9,478	21.6

Welsh Assembly Election 1999: Labour 8,217 (34.6), Plaid Cymru 6,291 (26.5), Conservative 3,643 (15.4), Lib Dem 3,543 (14.9), 3 Others 2,033. Electorate 59,369, Turnout 40.0%. AM: Andrew Davies (Lab), Majority 1,926 (8.1).

Alan Williams took Swansea West from the Conservatives in 1964 and has been the Labour MP there ever since. He is Wales' longest serving MP, having been in the House of Commons before a number of his Welsh colleagues were even born. After holding a number of Shadow posts, Williams did not make it into the new Labour government and has remained as an experienced hand on the backbenches.

The seat contains much of the student population for the University of Swansea and Swansea Institute. Until the boundary changes in 1983, which removed many of the Conservative supporting areas to the Gower constituency, the seat was a Labour-Conservative marginal. In 1979, the Conservatives came within 401 votes of winning the seat, but today the competition is nothing like as fierce. Although the Conservatives still finish in second, they are within a whisker of losing this position to the Liberal Democrats, who have considerable support amongst the student population. At the Westminster level, the seat looks set to remain firmly in the Labour camp.

Assembly Seat

Andrew Davies, Labour's former political 'wheeler and dealer' behind the Welsh Assembly Referendum, became the Assembly Member for Swansea East. This victory was based on one of Labour's lowest percentage shares of the vote in the 1999 elections and Plaid Cymru now represent a serious threat in this seat, replacing the Conservatives in the number two slot. The Plaid Cymru candidate, Dai Lloyd, became a list member in the region. In a seat where Labour normally achieve only around 50 per cent of the vote at the Westminster elections, Swansea West is somewhere Plaid Cymru will need to gain from Labour if they are to take control of the Assembly in 2003. Davies remains one of the key figures in the Assembly Cabinet, as the Assembly's Business Secretary (the equivalent of the Leader of the House in the Commons). His high public profile will undoubtedly help him in a seat that could be a tight contest next time.

Northern Ireland

By Sydney Elliott, Queen's University Belfast

	UUP		DUP		Other Unionist		Conservative	
	Share of vote	Seats	Share of vote	Seats	Share of vote	Seats	Share of vote	Seats
2001	26.8	6	22.5	5	3.3	0	0.3	0
1997	32.7	10	13.6	2	3.0	1	1.2	0
1992	34.5	9	13.1	3	2.5	1	5.7	0
1998	21.3	28	18.1	20	10.9	10	0.2	0
1996	24.2	30	18.8	24	9.4	7	0.5	0

1998: NI Assembly elections (6 seats per constituency), 1996 - NI Forum elections

	SDLP		SF		Alliance		Others	
	Share of vote	Seats	Share of vote	Seats	Share of vote	Seats	Share of vote	Seats
2001	21.0	3	21.7	4	3.6	0	0.9	0
1997	24.1	3	16.1	2	8.0	0	1.4	0
1992	23.5	4	10.0	0	8.7	0	2.0	0
1998	22.0	24	17.6	18	6.4	6	3.5	2
1996	21.4	21	15.5	17	6.5	7	3.7	4

1998: NI Assembly elections (6 seats per constituency), 1996 - NI Forum elections

Although the 2001 general election aroused little interest in Britain, it was a different matter in Northern Ireland. Turnout was much higher, passions were aroused and seven out of eighteen seats changed hands. The political context was very different. While the election date had been anticipated, the announcement by David Trimble that he would resign as First Minister with effect from 1 July was not expected. It was a reminder that June 2001 had been the date set a year earlier by the two governments for the completion of decommissioning of illegal weapons. In effect, the British and Irish governments considered that they had parked the issue until after the elections and that since the remit of the de Chastelain commission had been extended to February the previous date could be pushed back without telling the parties. The post dated resignation letter brought an added focus to the electoral competition within unionism and nationalism as well as between traditional rivals. The Democratic Unionists had been plotting the electoral downfall of the UUP for the best part of a year and had withdrawn Peter Robinson and Nigel Dodds from the Northern Ireland Executive in July 2000 to lead that campaign. The first fruits of the campaign had been the victory in the South Antrim by election in September when Rev William McCrea (DUP) defeated David Burnside (UUP) in the second safest UUP seat. Thereafter the notion of a 'meltdown' in UUP support was played hard by the DUP but when the UUP did not replace David Trimble as leader then the contest over who 'spoke for unionism' had to be decided at the general and local government elections.

The UUP could not avoid the appearance of disunity for six of its nine members of parliament were opposed to the Belfast Agreement. The re-selection of candidates pointed up disunity in circumstances where the party leadership was powerless to intervene. In North Belfast the long serving pro-Agreement MP Cecil Walker, who had decided to retire, was persuaded to stay on. In North Down there was a long running dispute over the selection of Peter Weir (anti Agreement) as the parliamentary candidate which was in and out of the courts until the eve of nominations.

The Democratic Unionists nominated in 13 constituencies, their largest number since 1983, with North Belfast and Strangford (the former seat of the deputy leader of UUP John Taylor) as specific targets. They had prepared for a candidate in Fermanagh & South Tyrone, Maurice Morrow, but weighed in behind the candidacy of Jim Dixon, a Victims campaigner who had been seriously injured by the Enniskillen bombing in 1987. Some anti-Agreement UUP candidates were contested as in the case of Willie Ross in East Londonderry who was opposed by Gregory Campbell. There had even been a suggestion that the issue between pro and anti Agreement Unionists be decided in a head to head contest between David Trimble and Rev Ian Paisley in Upper Bann. The contest in that personalised sense did not come about but there was a great deal of personalities and name calling in the campaign. The Alliance party suffered criticism because of their decision to withdraw candidates in a number of constituencies to boost the chances of pro-Agreement UUP candidates. However, the UUP did not agree to stand down in East Belfast in favour of the Alliance candidate.

There was considerable rivalry between the SDLP and SF electoral organisations. Earlier suggestions by SF of an electoral pact against unionist held seats in the west was rejected by SDLP as being too one sided. The decision of the SDLP to transfer Brid Rodgers from Upper Bann to West Tyrone, one of Sinn Fein's target seats, was regarded as a hostile act. The high profile Minister for Agriculture was pitted against Pat Doherty (SF) who had been cultivating the seat for three years. The contest in North Belfast between Alban Maginness (SDLP) and Gerry Kelly (SF) was another where no holds were barred between the rival parties. Sinn Fein's aim of 'greening the west' meant that Fermanagh & South Tyrone was also targeted but success depended on the split in the unionist vote. In general Sinn Fein aimed at a further increase in its share of the vote which had increased at each election since 1993.

Although there were fewer candidates than in the 1997 election interest in the election was high and the two simultaneous elections did ensure an improved turnout for the district councils. Turnout was the highest in the UK at 68 per cent and the electoral competition did result in considerable change. The UUP lost four seats, two to SF (Tyrone West and Fermanagh & South Tyrone) and two to the DUP (Belfast North and Strangford). They also won back the Antrim South constituency from the

DUP and also gained Down North from Bob McCartney (UKUP). The UUP remained the largest party with 26.8 per cent of the vote. The DUP moved up to second party position with five seats and 22.5 per cent of the vote. In the immediate aftermath of the election the role of DUP in the outcome of the Fermanagh & South Tyrone result was highlighted but as time moved on the focus became electoral irregularities and an election petition challenging the 53-vote majority for Michelle Gildernew (SF). In the competition for leadership among nationalist and republican voters Sinn Fein came out on top. By adding two constituencies they had four seats to the SDLP's three and with 21.7 per cent of the vote against 21.0 per cent they had achieved a position of leadership 20 years after the Hunger Strike by-elections had paved the way for a political path. The seats held by Seamus Mallon and John Hume have begun to look increasingly vulnerable to SF at the next election. The Alliance vote shrunk to 3.6 per cent and to 28,999 votes partly as a result of their stepping aside in favour of pro-Agreement candidates from other parties.

Despite the poor election results for the UUP there was no attempt to challenge David Trimble as party leader at the postponed UUP Council meeting on 23 June 2001, but there was a suggestion of a policy review in the autumn. Prime Minister Tony Blair and Taoiseach Bertie Ahern began intensive talks on the outstanding issues of the Good Friday Agreement on 28 June but there was no progress on decommissioning before the end of the month and Trimble resigned as First Minister. However, he appointed an alternate, Sir Reginald Empey, and the other UUP ministers remained in place. The effects were not as catastrophic as first thought but the two offices of FM and DFM ceased to exist and the Assembly had to find replacements within six weeks, that is by 12 August 2001.

Local government

When the current system of 26 district councils was created in 1973 the main services of education, health and personal social services, housing, planning and roads, water and sewerage were centralised on government departments. The objective was to increase the uniformity and level of professional service delivery and to increase the level of political accountability. The failure of the power sharing Assembly and Executive in 1974 meant that for most of the past 26 years the level of accountability for local services was deficient. There was accountability through a direct rule minister to Parliament but not to the people for whom the services were provided – the essence of local government. This 'Macrory gap' as it was called (after the chairman of the committee which had recommended the changes in local government) was frequently commented upon. The obvious success in the professionalism and delivery of local services rarely attracted comment.

There are 26 District Councils in Northern Ireland with direct responsibility for a narrow range of minor environmental functions, in addition to leisure, local community relations, tourism and more recently local economic development. Elected by PR (STV) only two local authorities are controlled by a single party - one UUP and one SDLP. Some 16 councils, including Belfast, operate on a power-sharing basis. However, their total spending of around £300 million is very small in comparison to the total of £9.9 billion public spending carried out in the province.

The main services carried out by local government, such as education, health and personal social services, are administered by boards on behalf of the respective government departments. There are five Education and Library Boards and four Health and Social Services Boards. Housing is the responsibility of the Housing Executive for the Department of the Environment. Roads, water and sewage, planning are administered through agencies and divisional offices with the emphasis on the professional delivery of services.

The system of devolution could produce a marked change in the source of accountability and the structure of the services. One of the early tasks of the Assembly may be to revise the entire system of service delivery and the number and powers of District Councils. A review will begin in the spring of 2002.

In Northern Ireland parliamentary and local elections had never coincided before and there was a further complication because different methods of election were used for each body. The parliamentary elections used simple plurality in single member constituencies and the district councils used the single transferable vote in multi member constituencies. The DUP were critical of the decision to hold the two elections on the same day and portrayed it as an attempt by the Secretary of State to assist their rivals, the pro-Agreement UUP.

The decision to hold the District Council elections on the same day as the parliamentary elections produced a turnout of 68 per cent an increase of 14 per cent. The count did not begin until Monday, 11 June and there was speculation over whether electors would vote in the same way as in the parliamentary election since they had the freedom of the preferential ballot. With PR (STV) tactical voting is less of a consideration than with the X vote and voters can clearly indicate their party of first choice. Broadly speaking the change in the parliamentary election was reflected in the district council results. UUP remained the largest party with 154 seats, a loss of 31 since 1997, and polled 23.0 per cent of the vote. DUP came second with 131 seats, a gain of 40, and 21.5 per cent of the vote. SDLP managed to hold 117 seats a loss of only three, and SF won 108, a gain of 34 seats. However, as at the general election SF with 20.7 per cent overtook SDLP's 19.4 per cent. The Alliance party vote of 5.1 per cent was as normal but with 28 seats it had lost 13 since 1997. It did hold the balance of power in Belfast City Council. One of the biggest changes was the reduction in the representation of small parties and independents from 70 in 1997 to 43 in 2001. In part this was a product of the targeting of seats by the larger parties. For example, many of the DUP gains were at the expense of independent unionists and smaller parties. One of the initial concerns after the election was the impact on existing power sharing arrangements. These had been mainly between SDLP and UUP but gains by SF and DUP could produce pressure for more majoritarian arrangements.

The District Council Election Results of 7 June 2001

Party	1st Pref. Votes	(1997)	% 1st Pref.	(1997)	Seats	(1997)
Ulster Unionist	181,336	(176,239)	22.95	(29.7)	154	(185)
Democratic Unionist	169,477	(98,686)	21.45	(15.6)	131	(91)
SDLP	153,424	(130,417)	19.4	(20.6)	117	(120)
Sinn Fein	163,269	(106,938)	20.67	(16.9)	108	(74)
Alliance	40,443	(41,421)	5.1	(6.6)	28	(41)
Progressive Unionists	12,261	(13,774)	1.55	(2.2)	–	-
UK Unionist	4763	(2975)	0.6	(0.5)	2	(4)
UU Assembly party	2648	0.3	2	–	-	-
C	1985	(2634)	0.3	(0.4)	0	(3)
NI Unionist	1818	0.2	–	–	-	–
Workers Party	1421	(2348)	0.2	(0.4)	0	(0)
Others	57,223	(53415)	7.2	(8.4)	44	(71)
Total	790,068	(632,197)	100.0	(100.0)	582	(582)

ANTRIM EAST

	2001		1997		1992 notional	
Electorate and turnout	60,897	59.1	59,032	58.2	56,732	62.5
UUP	13,101	36.4	13,318	38.8	15,465	43.6
DUP	12,973	36.0	6,682	19.5	8,046	22.7
PUP	–	–	1,751	5.1	–	–
SDLP	2,641	7.3	1,576	4.6	–	–
SF	903	2.5	543	1.6	–	–
Alliance	4,483	12.5	6,929	20.2	8,919	25.2
Conservative	807	2.2	2,334	6.8	2,788	7.9
Others	1,092		1,214 (2)		250	
MP	Roy Beggs (UUP)		Roy Beggs (UUP)		Roy Beggs (UUP)	
Majority	128	0.4	6,389	18.6	6,546	18.5

Assembly election 1998 first preferences: UUP 10,547 (29.6), DUP 7,889 (22.2), Alliance 7,168 (20.1), UKUP 2,866 (8.0), SDLP 2,106 (5.9), PUP/UDP 2,028 (5.7), Ind Unionist 1,571 (4.4), SF 746 (2.1), 3 Others 689. Electorate 59,313, Turnout 60.1%. MLAs: Roy Beggs (UUP), Sean Neeson (Alliance), David Hilditch (DUP), Ken Robinson (UUP), Roger Hutchinson (Ind Unionist, originally UKUP), Danny O'Connor (SDLP).

Antrim East was created in 1983 as one of Northern Ireland's five new constituencies and had been part of the old North Antrim held by Rev Ian Paisley. The constituency is formed from the district councils of Larne and Carrickfergus, along with four wards from Newtownabbey. To the north are villages at the head of rural glens and sheep or mixed farms – an area of outstanding natural beauty. The port of Larne lies in the constituency with links to Stranraer and Cairnryan in Scotand. Antrim East also has a tradition of heavy industry, such as a power station at Ballylumford and undersea power links to Scotland. Carrickfergus was hit by the closure of ICI and Courtaulds in the 1980s, but has recovered and developed a tourist industry through hotels and a marina and the historic Norman castle where William of Orange landed in 1690 on his way to the Battle of the Boyne. It has also become a popular dormitory town for Belfast.

At its inaugural contest the Ulster Unionist, Roy Beggs beat the DUP by less than 400 votes. Beggs was not opposed by the DUP in the mid 1980s and thus won easily in both the 1986 by-election and 1987, and even when seriously challenged by a strong DUP candidate in 1992, Nigel Dodds, then Lord Mayor of Belfast, he had a 7,000 majority.

Beggs voted against the Belfast Agreement but by 2001 he had accepted the decision of the referendum and canvassed with David Trimble. His DUP opponent was another Lord Mayor of Belfast, Sammy Wilson, who was strongly anti-agreement and it was said that the DUP position on the RUC had support from a significant number of police officers living in the constituency. Beggs had also been embarrassed by criticism from the parliamentary standards committee for not declaring an interest in a landfill site in the constituency. An Independent candidate, Robert L. Mason, who was also a councillor from Larne, campaigned on the landfill issue. The SDLP candidate was Danny O'Connor, who represented the constituency in the Northern Ireland assembly. The Alliance Party, which had run second in 1997, selected John Mathews as candidate ahead of the party leader and 1997 candidate, Sean Neeson.

The result proved tighter than Beggs, or even his rival Wilson, expected – Beggs held on by 128 votes while the DUP made a massive gain of 16.5 percentage points. There was a swing of 9.5 per cent between the two unionist parties, while the Alliance were squeezed out.

ANTRIM NORTH

	2001		1997		1992 actual	
Electorate and turnout	74,451	66.1	72,491	63.7	69,114	65.8
UUP	10,315	21.0	10,921	23.6	8,216	18.1
DUP	24,539	49.9	21,495	46.5	23,152	50.9
SDLP	8,283	16.8	7,333	15.9	6,512	14.3
SF	4,822	9.8	2,896	6.3	1,916	4.2
Alliance	1,258	2.6	2,845	6.2	3,442	7.6
Others	–		696 (2)		2,263	
MP	Ian Paisley (DUP)		Ian Paisley (DUP)		Ian Paisley (DUP)	
Majority	14,224	28.9	10,574	22.9	14,936	32.8

Assembly election 1998 first preferences: DUP 18,687 (37.6), UUP 11,064 (22.3), SDLP 8,415 (16.9), SF 4,045 (8.1), Ind Unionist 3,297 (6.6), Alliance 2,282 (4.6), PUP/UDP 1,041 (2.1), 4 Others 866. Electorate 73,247, Turnout 69.0%. MLAs: Ian Paisley (DUP), Ian Paisley Jnr (DUP), Sean Farren (SDLP), Robert Coulter (UUP), Gardiner Kane (DUP), James Leslie (UUP).

The largely rural Antrim North constituency includes the towns of Ballymena, Ballycastle and Ballymoney and comprises three complete District Council areas: Ballymena, Ballymoney and Moyle. It also includes the world heritage site of the Giants Causeway, and nearby beaches. Away from the tourist attractions, there is some industry, both of an agriculturally based kind and of more modern types: Gallahers cigarette plant in Ballymena has suffered cutbacks in recent years but Old Bushmills Distillery has been making whiskey since 1608.

The North Antrim constituency has been represented by Rev. Dr. Ian Paisley since 1970; he founded the Democratic Unionist Party in 1970 and remains its sole leader. Even radical boundary changes in 1983 did not affect Paisley's large majorities. When the UUP decided to contest the seat in 1992, after a period of agreed candidates, Paisley obtained a 15,000 majority and an absolute majority of the vote. The constituency was the only one left unchanged in Northern Ireland in the pre-1997 boundary changes. In 1997 a new UUP candidate reduced Paisley's majority to 10,574 but he still had twice as many votes as his closest challenger in a field of seven. In June 2001 there were five candidates, three of them members of the Northern Ireland Assembly and the two others were Ballymena councillors. Ian Paisley again won with a large majority and will surely continue to do so until he retires – although even then Paisley victories could continue under Ian Paisley Jnr who represents the area in the Northern Ireland Assembly.

ANTRIM SOUTH

	2001		1997		1992 notional	
Electorate and turnout	70,651	62.5	69,512	57.8	67,045	59.5
UUP	16,366	37.1	23,108	57.5	28,447	71.4
DUP	15,355	34.8	–	–	–	–
PUP	–	–	3,490	8.7	–	–
SDLP	5,336	12.1	6,497	16.2	5,397	13.5
SF	4,160	9.4	2,229	5.5	1,220	3.1
Alliance	1,969	4.5	4,668	11.6	4,362	10.9
Others	972		203		442	
MP	David Burnside (UUP)		Clifford Forsythe (UUP)		Clifford Forsythe (UUP)	
Majority	1,011	2.3	16,611	41.3	23,050	57.8

Assembly election 1998 first preferences: UUP 13,175 (29.9), DUP 8,850 (20.1), SDLP 7,783 (17.7), UKUP 4,360 (9.9), Alliance 3,778 (8.6), SF 3,226 (7.3), PUP 1,546 (3.5), NIWC 1,108 (2.5), 2 Others 165. Electorate 69,426, Turnout 64.2%. MLAs: Jim Wilson (UUP), Wilson Clyde (DUP), Norman Boyd (NI Unionist Party, originally UKUP), Donovan McClelland (SDLP), Duncan Shipley-Dalton (UUP), David Ford (Alliance).

Parliamentary by-election 21 September 2000: DUP 11,601 (38.0), UUP 10,779 (35.3), SDLP 3,496 (11.4), SF 2,611 (8.5), Alliance 2,031 (6.6), 1 Other 49. Electorate 71,047, Turnout 43.0%. MP: William McCrea (DUP), Majority 822 (2.7)

South Antrim includes the entire Antrim district council area and 16 wards from Newtownabbey. The seat is mainly rural with an important agricultural sector not to mention an eel fishing industry. It also includes Northern Ireland's principle airport at Aldergrove, near the shore of Lough Neagh.

The name South Antrim, as a parliamentary constituency dates back to 1950 and until 1983 held the record as the largest constituency not only in Northern Ireland, but also the United Kingdom, with 132,000 electors. In its earlier form the constituency regularly produced enormous majorities: over 50,000 in 1959, and almost 40,000 for Ulster Unionist James Molyneaux in 1979 The smaller seat created after the 1983 boundary changes contained less than half of the original as parts were hived off to Lagan Valley, where Molyneaux chose to stand, East Antrim and North Belfast. The boundary review of 1995 made only small changes. In 1992 Clifford Forsythe, the MP since 1983, had a 24,500 majority over SDLP and he still had a strong lead in 1997.

The death of Forsythe resulted in a September 2000 by-election at which William McCrea (DUP) defeated David Burnside (UUP) by a majority of 822. With a 43 per cent turnout on a very wet day, McCrea polled 38 per cent of the valid vote to 35.3 per cent for Burnside. The assumption was that many more Ulster Unionist voters simply stayed at home while DUP organizers got the vote out. This result, in the second safest unionist seat in Northern Ireland, was used by the DUP as a signal of the awaited 'meltdown' of the UUP vote. Burnside was re-selected for the general election and discussions took place with Alliance to persuade them to stand down to enhance the chances of the larger pro-Agreement party. However, the Alliance party candidate, David Ford, was not convinced about the views of David Burnside and remained in the field. Altogether six candidates sought the seat – three brands of unionism, one alliance, one SDLP and one SF. The increased interest in the contest resulted in a turnout of 62.5 per cent, 20 per cent higher than in the by-election, and the second reversal of fortune in less than a year. The success of David Burnside with a majority of 1,011 over William McCrea provided one of two gains for the UUP in the election.

BELFAST EAST

	2001		1997		1992 notional	
Electorate and turnout	58,455	63.0	61,837	63.1	63,881	65.0
UUP	8,550	23.2	9,886	25.3	–	–
DUP	15,667	42.5	16,640	42.6	22,635	54.5
PUP	3,669	10.0	–	–	–	–
SDLP	880	2.4	629	1.6	–	–
SF	1,237	3.4	810	2.1	686	1.7
Alliance	5,832	15.8	9,288	23.8	11,337	27.3
Conservative	800	2.2	928	2.4	4,170	10.0
Others	194 (2)		848 (3)		2,723	
MP	Peter Robinson (DUP)		Peter Robinson (DUP)		Peter Robinson (DUP)	
Majority	7,117	19.3	6,754	17.3	11,298	27.2

Assembly election 1998 first preferences: DUP 12,225 (30.9), UUP 9,620 (24.3), Alliance 7,144 (18.0), PUP/UDP 5,901 (14.9), UKUP 1,362 (3.4), SDLP 1,025 (2.6), SF 917 (2.3), NIWC 711 (1.8), 5 Others 688. Electorate 60,562, Turnout 66.6%. MLAs: Peter Robinson (DUP), John Alderdice (Alliance), David Ervine (PUP), Reg Empey (UUP), Sammy Wilson (DUP), Ian Adamson (UUP).

Belfast has traditionally been divided into four geographically-based constituencies since 1885 (except for an anomalous interval of nine seats in 1918-22). The establishment of a Northern Ireland Boundary Commission in 1944 continued the tradition because they had little discretion on the number of seats and merely adjusted the electorates as best they could. By the time of the award of five extra seats in 1982 Belfast's population had declined too far for a fifth city seat. The most recent Boundary Commission in 1995 considered the number of seats for Belfast and its provisional recommendation was for the removal of one seat, South Belfast, and the confinement of Belfast constituencies to the boundary of Belfast City Council. However, the knock on effects for other constituencies, especially South Down, and the weight of representations meant that the final report left Belfast with four seats with their boundaries extending into neighbouring local authorities.

Belfast East comprises eleven wards from Belfast City Council and nine from Castlereagh borough council. It lies east of the river Lagan and is surrounded by South Belfast, Strangford and North Down. When last revised before the 1997 election the constituency had 63,881 voters but the numbers continue to fall. East Belfast has strong historical claims to be the heartland of unionism. Within it sits the Stormont estate with Parliament Buildings, which once housed the Northern Ireland Parliament but is now home to the Northern Ireland Assembly, and Stormont Castle, once the base of Direct Rule ministers and a number of civil service buildings. In recent times the estate has also hosted music concerts and international cross-country running events. The other very visible feature is the two massive shipyard cranes named Samson and Goliath. There is still quite a lot of inner city industrial terrace housing close to the shipyard but elsewhere there is redevelopment and rehabilitation and luxury apartments as well as the tree lined areas of Knock and Belmont.

The old East Belfast was solidly unionist but with a significant Northern Ireland Labour Party vote until the 1970s. In 1979 Peter Robinson, the deputy leader of the Democratic Unionist party, defeated William Craig, the Official Unionist candidate, by just 64 votes. Oliver Napier of the Alliance Party, was also just a few hundred votes behind. Robinson won the first contest on the new boundaries of 1983 without major unionist opposition and again in 1987 in a pact with the UUP, in opposition to the Alliance. UUP did not run in opposition to DUP in 1992 even though there were growing signs of differences on the political way ahead. The middle class areas continued to provide significant backing for the Alliance party. In 1992 the Alliance leader, John Alderdice, received 30 per cent of the vote. The Conservatives also did better than in most seats in their first General Election in Northern Ireland, achieving a 9 per cent share.

The new boundaries in 1997 seemed to spur political competition and nine candidates sought the seat. Robinson's majority fell to 6,754 but he was still 17 points ahead of his UUP rival, Reg Empey. Robinson is one of the most active DUP campaigners in their attempt to overhaul the UUP as the main Unionist Party, and locally has a strong lead over divided opposition. Empey was fully committed to the Assembly and Executive at the time of the 2001 and the UUP stood Tim Lemon, a local businessman with no previous political experience. There was some talk about the UUP dropping out in favour of David Alderdice of the Alliance, a former Lord Mayor of Belfast, in exchange for a clear UUP run in North Down, but nothing came of it. Robinson held the seat with an improved majority as the Alliance and UUP fell back; David Ervine of the PUP polled a fairly strong 10 per cent of the vote.

BELFAST NORTH

	2001		1997		1992 notional	
Electorate and turnout	60,941	67.2	64,645	64.1	67,989	63.3
UUP	4,904	12.0	21,478	51.8	22,259	51.7
DUP	16,718	40.8	–	–	–	–
SDLP	8,592	21.0	8,454	20.4	7,867	18.3
SF	10,331	25.2	8,375	20.2	4,882	11.3
Alliance	–	–	2,221	5.4	3,321	7.7
Conservative	–	–	–	–	2,678	6.2
Others	387 (2)		924 (3)		2,041 (3)	
MP	Nigel Dodds (DUP)		Cecil Walker (UUP)		Cecil Walker (UUP)	
Majority	6,387	15.6	13,024	31.4	14,392	33.4

Assembly election 1998 first preferences: SF 8,775 (21.3), DUP 8,764 (21.3), SDLP 8,661 (21.1), PUP/UDP 4,662 (11.3), UUP 4,480 (10.9), Ind Unionist 2,976 (7.2), Alliance 1,267 (3.1), UKUP 748 (1.8), 5 Others 793. Electorate 62,541, Turnout 67.3%. MLAs: Nigel Dodds (DUP), Alban Maginness (SDLP), Gerry Kelly (SF), Billy Hutchinson (PUP), Fraser Agnew (Ind Unionist), Fred Cobain (UUP).

The Belfast North constituency comprises fourteen Belfast electoral wards and five from the neighbouring borough of Newtownabbey. The wards lie along part of the north shore of Belfast Lough, north of the river Lagan and up into the hills overlooking the city. The population continues to decline with movement out to the boroughs of Antrim and Newtownabbey and internally as the Catholic sector increases.

Reciting the neighbourhoods of this constituency is like recounting a history of the Troubles over the past thirty years. It is a constituency with many interfaces and where riots still occur and local peace lines are being extended or raised. Ardoyne, New Lodge, Crumlin, and Woodvale have been synonymous with security and public order problems but they have been joined by Duncairn and other more localized trouble spots. The pernicious dispute over access to Holy Cross Primary School since June 2001 was affected by a local challenge to a thirty year understanding about the siting and access to the school. The parliamentary representation of the constituency has normally been unionist but the nationalist vote has been rising. Until 2001 North Belfast was held by Cecil Walker (UUP) from the 1983 election [North Belfast was held by Cecil Walker (UUP) from the 1983 election until 2001]. In the boundary changes before the 1997 election the constituency gained five wards and 11,000 electors from the adjacent borough of Newtownabbey. At the first test of the new boundaries in 1997 Cecil Walker had a majority of 13,024 over opposition nearly evenly divided between SDLP and SF.

Six candidates contested the election in 2001. Two, Rainbow Weiss (Vote 4 Yourself) who was also a candidate in the other Belfast constituencies, and Marcella Delaney (WP) were rank outsiders. The other four encapsulated the competition between unionism and nationalism/republicanism, with each other and within the two blocks: UUP and DUP on the one hand and SDLP and SF on the other. Walker, aged 76, had hoped to retire but found that he was required to stand one more time. His DUP opponent, Nigel Dodds, had topped the poll in the Assembly election and he had a high profile as Minister for Social Development in the Northern Ireland Executive before being withdrawn by his party, along with Peter Robinson, in July 2000 to plot the electoral downfall of the UUP. Dodds had been Lord Mayor of the city on two occasions and there was no rising UUP candidate of similar quality. The choice for nationalist and republican voters was between two high profile candidates, Gerry Kelly (SF) and Alban Maginness (SDLP), who had been the first nationalist Lord Mayor of Belfast in 1997. In the 1998 Assembly election, SF had overtaken SDLP for the first time but only by 114 votes.

If the UUP had hoped for loyalty to Cecil Walker to prevail for one last time it was blown away by a disastrous election programme on Ulster Television in which Walker appeared stumbling in his answers to audience questions and afterwards confessed to problems with the batteries of his hearing aid. In addition, Billy Hutchinson (PUP) who had earlier withdrawn from the contest, declined to advise his supporters to vote for Walker. The outgoing MP crashed to defeat with only 12 per cent support as the DUP won a decisive victory in the intra-unionist battle and in the seat as a whole. In the nationalist sideshow, SF edged ahead of the SDLP.

BELFAST SOUTH

	2001		1997		1992 notional	
Electorate and turnout	59,436	63.9	63,633	62.0	64,491	68.5
UUP	17,008	44.8	14,201	36.0	23,258	52.7
DUP	–	–	–	–	–	–
PUP	1,112	2.9	5,687	14.4	–	–
SDLP	11,609	30.6	9,601	24.3	6,266	14.2
SF	2,894	7.6	2,019	5.1	1,116	2.5
Alliance	2,042	5.4	5,112	12.9	6,921	15.7
Conservative	–	–	962	2.4	5,154	11.7
NIWC	2,968	7.8	–	–	–	–
Others	319 (2)		1,902 (4)		1,437 (3)	
MP	Martin Smyth (UUP)		Martin Smyth (UUP)		Martin Smyth (UUP)	
Majority	5,399	14.2	4,600	11.7	16,337	37.0

Assembly election 1998 first preferences: UUP 9,533 (23.4), SDLP 8,838 (21.7), DUP 5,321 (13.1), Alliance 4,086 (10.0), NIWC 3,912 (9.6), PUP/UDP 3,857 (9.5), SF 2,605 (6.4), UKUP 1,496 (3.7), 6 Others 1,076. Electorate 61,209, Turnout 67.4%. MLAs: Michael McGimpsey (UUP), Alasdair McDonnell (SDLP), Esmond Birnie (UUP), Mark Robinson (DUP), Monica McWilliams (NIWC), Carmel Hanna (SDLP).

This constituency is bounded by East Belfast on one side and West Belfast on the other and to the south by Lagan Valley and Strangford. South Belfast contains many of the most desirable and valuable residential areas in the city, it is the home of Queen's University, the City Hospital and several schools of high academic reputation. It does have working class loyalist areas and pressure on space has seen the destruction of large houses and gardens for the construction of luxury apartments. It also houses a considerable student population from Queen's University and University of Ulster as well as nurses and other young professionals.

South Belfast may have escaped the riots associated with the Troubles but it has experienced sectarian and political assassination. The representation of the constituency was traditionally unionist and in 1981, its MP, Rev Robert Bradford, was shot dead in one of his advice centers. The by-election was won by Rev Martin Smyth (UUP), Grand Master of the Orange Order of Ireland who continues to hold the seat. The closest challengers have usually been the SDLP, despite the unionist majority in the seat, but the Alliance vote has also been at a significant level. In recent times there have been accounts of significant inward movement of middle class Catholics in retreat from West Belfast. The Boundary Commission originally suggested the abolition of Belfast South, but in the end the constituency gained about 12,000 electors from Strangford around Newtownbreda, Beechill and Minnowbum whose modern development is contiguous with the Belfast city wards of Upper Malone, Stranmillis and Rosetta.

Smyth won on a minority vote in 1997.

As a prominent anti-Agreement unionist Smyth had no opposition from the DUP in 2001. However, there were seven other candidates of which only one, Dawn Purvis (PUP), was ostensibly unionist. Alasdair McDonnell (SDLP) had gradually built his support among a growing middle class electorate in the constituency. There was some pre-election pressure on other pro-Agreement candidates to give way in favour of a straight fight with Smyth but it came to nothing. In the end Smyth held the seat again; both he and McDonnell increased their shares of the vote, at the expense of the PUP and the Alliance. Monica McWilliams (NIWC), one of the seat's representatives in the Northern Ireland assembly, came third.

BELFAST WEST

	2001		1997		1992 notional	
Electorate and turnout	59,617	68.7	61,920	74.1	62,940	72.0
UUP	2,541	6.2	1,556	3.4	5,275	11.6
DUP	2,641	6.4	–	–	–	–
SDLP	7,754	18.9	17,753	38.7	20,045	44.2
SF	27,096	66.1	25,662	55.9	19,027	42.0
Alliance	–	–	–	–	–	–
Others	950 (3)		914 (3)		975	
MP	Gerry Adams (SF)		Gerry Adams (SF)		Joe Hendron (SDLP)	
Majority	19,342	47.2	7,909	17.2	1,018	2.3

Assembly election 1998 first preferences: SF 24,650 (59.0), SDLP 10,420 (24.9), PUP 2,180 (5.2), UUP 1,640 (3.9), DUP 1,345 (3.2), UKUP 666 (1.6), 4 Others 893. Electorate 60,699, Turnout 70.5%. MLAs: Gerry Adams (SF), Joe Hendron (SDLP), Sue Ramsey (SF), Barbre De Brun (SF), Alex Maskey (SF), Alex Attwood (SDLP).

West Belfast comprises thirteen wards from Belfast City council and four wards from Lisburn. It is bounded to the west by the hills above Belfast and by the South Antrim and Lagan Valley constituencies; to the north lies the constituency of North Belfast and to the east South Belfast. The constituency is now overwhelmingly Catholic in religion and nationalist and republican in politics. There used to be a sizeable protestant population but outward movement and the establishment of new sectarian boundaries has radically changed the nature of political competition.

The historic West Belfast constituency saw Joe Devlin (Nationalist) fighting some big elections against unionist candidates. After 1945 the contest was usually between a local Labour candidate and a unionist. From 1966 to 1983 the seat was represented by Gerry Fitt, first as 'Republican Labour' and then SDLP and finally Independent Socialist after he resigned from SDLP in 1979. The modern political representation of West Belfast was set in 1983 when Fitt stood as an Independent but was opposed by a former SDLP colleague, Joe Hendron and Gerry Adams of Sinn Fein. The SDLP split gave Adams the seat and Sinn Fein a great coup. Despite not attending Westminster, Adams held it against Hendron four years later. In 1992, though, Hendron beat Adams by less than 600 votes, probably as a result of unionist tactical votes. Next time the situation was rather different. The boundary changes before the 1997 election brought four wards and 9500 electors from Lisburn borough – Poleglass, Twinbrook, Kilwee and Collin Glen – which were thought to be favourable towards Sinn Fein, and with the general rise in the SF vote Adams won relatively easily. The sole unionist polled only 3.4 per cent.

Since decisively re-taking the constituency in 1997, Gerry Adams and Sinn Fein have made a succession of electoral gains. The Assembly election in 1998 returned four SF to two SDLP with a vote share of 59 to 25 per cent. With only 12-13 per cent unionist votes cast in 1998 and the slippage in the SDLP share, there was no longer any point in a tactical vote by unionists to the SDLP in 2001. Although the new SDLP candidate, Alex Attwood, had a high profile as party chairman and member of the Northern Ireland Assembly, the voters considered the result a foregone conclusion and five per cent fewer went to the polls. Adams won the largest majority in Northern Ireland – almost 20,000.

DOWN NORTH

	2001		1997		1992 notional	
Electorate and turnout	63,212	58.8	63,101	57.9	61,745	60.9
UUP	20,833	56.0	11,368	31.1	–	–
DUP	–	–	–	–	3,153	8.4
UKUP	13,509	36.3	12,817	35.1	–	–
UPUP	–	–	–	–	15,298	40.7
SDLP	1,275	3.4	1,602	4.4	–	–
SF	313	0.8	–	–	–	–
Alliance	–	–	7,554	20.7	5,894	15.7
Conservative	815	2.2	1,810	5.0	13,033	34.6
Others	444		1,405 (3)		255	
MP	Sylvia Hermon (UUP)		Robert McCartney (UKUP)		James Kilfedder (UPUP)*	
Majority	7,324	19.7	1,449	4.0	2,265	6.0

* Robert McCartney (UKUP) elected at June 1995 by–election.

Assembly election 1998 first preferences: UUP 12,147 (32.6), UKUP 8,188 (22.4), Alliance 5,368 (14.4), DUP 2,571 (6.9), SDLP 2,048 (5.5), NIWC 1,808 (4.8), PUP/UDP 1,641 (4.4), Ind Unionist 1,382 (3.7), Independent 1,327 (3.6), 4 Others 660. Electorate 62,942, Turnout 60.2%. MLAs: Robert McCartney (UKUP), John Gorman (UUP), Alan McFarland (UUP), Eileen Bell (Alliance), Jane Morrice (NIWC), Peter Weir (UUP).

North Down comprises the land on the southern side and entrance to Belfast Lough – from Holywood, through Bangor, to Donaghadee and Millisle. It comprises all of North Down borough council and three coastal wards from neighbouring Ards borough council. The constituency was created in this current form from 1983 and the last commission before the 1997 election removed parts of Castlereagh to Strangford and in return Donaghadee and Millisle were added to North Down.

The area has a history of supporting unionist candidates with a distinctly independent disposition. James Kilfedder won the seat in 1983 under a Popular Unionist label after holding the previous North Down seat from 1974 as an Ulster Unionist until he resigned from the party in 1979. He held the seat in 1987 and 1992 against a strong challenge from Robert McCartney (Real Unionist) and Laurence Kennedy (Conservative). After Kilfedder's death, the by-election was won by McCartney as a UK Unionist in the face of UUP competition and retained at the 1997 general election. The 1998 Assembly elections were ominous for McCartney – although he was elected on an anti-Agreement platform pro-agreement parties dominated the area's assembly representation. The UUP had a lead over the combined anti-Agreement unionists, but were divided in the run-up to the 2001 election; their original candidate Peter Weir MLA was deselected but contested the legality of the decision. Weir opposed the

Agreement, unlike his successor Lady Sylvia Hermon. Hermon was helped by the decision of the Alliance to stand down in her favour and she won a comfortable majority over McCartney.

DOWN SOUTH

	2001		1997		1992 notional	
Electorate and turnout	73,519	70.8	69,977	70.7	67,516	77.6
UUP	9,173	17.6	16,248	32.8	18,531	35.4
DUP	7,802	15.0	–	–	–	–
SDLP	24,136	46.3	26,181	52.9	29,408	56.2
SF	10,278	19.7	5,127	10.4	1,860	3.6
Alliance	685	1.3	1,711	3.5	1,308	2.5
Others	–		219		1,262	
MP	Eddie McGrady (SDLP)		Eddie McGrady (SDLP)		Eddie McGrady (SDLP)	
Majority	13,858	26.6	9,933	20.1	10,877	20.8

Assembly election 1998 first preferences: SDLP 23,257 (45.3), SF 7,771 (15.1), UUP 7,419 (14.4), DUP 4,826 (9.4), UKUP 2,576 (5.0), NIWC 1,658 (3.2), Ind Unionist 1,562 (3.0), Alliance 1,502 (2.9), 4 Others 782. Electorate 71,000, Turnout 73.7%. MLAs: Eddie McGrady (SDLP), Mick Murphy (SF), Dermot Nesbitt (UUP), PJ Bradley (SDLP), Jim Wells (DUP), Eamon O'Neill (SDLP).

A constituency which comprises most of the coastline and rural areas of county Down south of the Strangford constituency and Lagan Valley, it lies east of Newry & Armagh and Upper Bann and includes the Mourne Muntains, Downpatrick and Newcastle, extending down the coast to Carlingford Lough and Warrenpoint. The modern South Down was created in 1983 and comprised all the Down district council with thirteen wards from Newry and Mourne and eight from Banbridge. In the boundary changes before the 1997 election the constituency lost a few wards from Down (around Saintfield) to Strangford and four wards from Banbridge to Lagan Valley. The provisional recommendations of the Commission had been very contentious as a consequence of the decision to have only three Belfast constituencies and ninety per cent of submissions to the review concerned South Down, including Irish government backed submissions.

Since winning the seat from Enoch Powell in 1987 Eddie McGrady (SDLP) has made the seat his own with increased majorities of 6,000 in 1992 and 9,933 on the even more favourable new boundaries in 1997. The changes were also evident in the falling unionist share of the vote. In 1997 the single UUP candidate, Dermot Nesbitt, polled just under 33 per cent and SF 10.4 per cent. In 2001 the UUP candidate was challenged to within 1,400 votes by the DUP and pushed into third position behind SF. Although SF gained ground they were still well behind the SDLP.

FERMANAGH and SOUTH TYRONE

	2001		1997		1992 notional	
Electorate and turnout	66,640	78.0	64,740	74.6	63,090	75.9
UUP	17,686	34.0	24,862	51.5	25,071	52.4
DUP	–	–	–	–	–	–
Ind Unionist	6,843	13.2	–	–	–	–
SDLP	9,706	18.7	11,060	22.9	10,982	22.9
SF	17,739	34.1	11,174	23.1	9,143	19.1
Alliance	–	–	977	2.0	830	1.7
Others	–		217		1,841	
MP	Michelle Gildernew (SF)		Ken Maginnis (UUP)		Ken Maginnis (UUP)	
Majority	53	0.1	13,688	28.3	14,089	29.4

Assembly election 1998 first preferences: SF 13,714 (26.9), UUP 12,572 (24.6), SDLP 11,007 (21.6), DUP 7,082 (13.9), UKUP 4,262 (8.3), NIWC 1,729 (3.4), Alliance 614 (1.2), 1 Other 63. Electorate 65,383, Turnout 79.4%. MLAs: Tommy Gallagher (SDLP), Sam Foster (UUP), Gerry McHugh (SF), Michelle Gildernew (SF), Joan Carson (UUP), Maurice Morrow (DUP).

The constituency occupies the most south westerly corner of Northern Ireland and approximately half the border with its southern neighbour runs around Fermanagh. It comprises all the Fermanagh District Council and fifteen wards from Dungannon. It is rural and agricultural but with tourism around the Erne lakes and southern links to the Shannon waterway system. The District Council has struggled to maintain the St Angelo airport to facilitate tourism. The main urban centre is Enniskillen, site of the cenotaph bombing in 1987 and the county has the distinction of having more unresolved murders than any other. A number of smaller market towns are scattered about this rural seat. At the other end of the constituency Dungannon is the main town and has a number of industries based on agriculture and quarrying.

The two counties of Fermanagh and Tyrone were linked as a two member constituency after 1920 and nationalists usually demonstrated their local majority in elections but often adopted abstentionism to show their preference for a united Ireland. The two counties were partially split after 1945 with the creation of Fermanagh and South Tyrone and Mid Ulster. Since then, the history of this constituency has been as bitter as anywhere in the United Kingdom. Cahir Healy (Nationalist) won the seat in 1950 but in 1955 nationalist voters elected Philip Clarke (SF). As a convicted felon Clarke was removed by election petition and unionists held the seat in 1964 and 1966. Frank McManus (Unity) won the seat for the nationalists in 1970 but lost it to the Unionist Party in February 1974. Frank Maguire, an independent Republican pub owner restored nationalist unity in October 1974 and held on in 1979. His death in 1981 occurred ata tense time in Northern Ireland. The April by-election was won by H-Block hunger-striker Bobby Sands, who died the next month. Sands' election agent Owen Carron retained the seat in the August by-election. He did not take his seat at Westminster. SDLP had contested neither of the two by-elections in 1981 but they split the Nationalist vote in 1983 and enabled Ken Maginnis (UUP) to hold the seat until his resignation early in 2001. Boundary changes involving the removal of the nationalist town of Coalisland helped Maginnis achieve a majority of over 13,000 in 1997.

Maginnis's retirement, announced early in 2001, resulted in the selection of James Cooper, a local solicitor, vice chairman of the UUP executive and close ally of David Trimble. Only the SDLP retained its 1997 candidate, namely, Tommy Gallagher who had topped the poll in the Assembly election. The DUP selected Maurice Morrow as its candidate but he eventually withdrew when an Independent Unionist, Jim Dixon, decided to stand. Dixon had formerly stood under the UKUP label and had been seriously injured in the Enniskillen bombing of 1987 and was a prominent member of a victims' organization. At one stage he had withdrawn alleging 'dirty tricks' but in coming back into the contest he removed the need for 'official' opposition from a DUP candidate. With 7,000 votes cast for DUP in 1998 and 4,262 for the UKUP, Dixon's candidacy had the potential to be a major influence on the result, especially if there was some tactical voting from SDLP to SF.

There was intense interest in the contest, especially between the two unionist candidates. Indeed, SF may have played down its expectations in the lakeland constituency in favour of the contest in West Tyrone in order not to panic the unionists into supporting a single candidate. In the event their candidate Michelle Gildernew won the seat by 53 votes and helped in the 'greening of the west'. Cooper would undoubtedly have won had it not been for Dixon's intervention, and alleged that there had been other factors as well when he contested the election result in an election petition to the High Court. The basis of the case was that the polling place at Garrison had been forced to re-open after 10.00pm and that more than the 53-vote difference was cast illegally. Although further irregularities came to light after the date of for lodging the petition the issue was decided on the number of votes likely to have been cast in the period after 10.00pm. Although the judge was highly critical of the intimidation and electoral abuse exercised by SF the result was allowed to stand. Whatever the electoral abuse, the presence of the second unionist candidate was the direct cause of the loss of the seat to unionism. The outcome was the product of the determination of DUP to inflict damage on the UUP and the 'softly, softly don't frighten the unionists' tactics of SF.

FOYLE

	2001		1997		1992 notional	
Electorate and turnout	70,943	68.9	67,905	70.4	64,199	67.2
UUP	3,360	6.9	–	–	–	–
DUP	7,414	15.2	10,290	21.5	10,809	25.1
SDLP	24,538	50.2	25,109	52.5	23,291	54.0
SF	12,988	26.6	11,445	23.9	7,475	17.3
Alliance	579	1.2	817	1.7	866	2.0
Others	–		154		709	
MP	John Hume (SDLP)		John Hume (SDLP)		John Hume (SDLP)	
Majority	11,550	23.6	13,664	28.6	12,482	28.9

Assembly election 1998 first preferences: SDLP 23,342 (47.8), SF 12,696 (26.0), DUP 6,112 (12.5), UUP 4,669 (9.6), Alliance 1,058 (2.2), 4 Others 917. Electorate 68,888, Turnout 72.0%. MLAs: Mitchel McLaughlin (SF), Mark Durkan (SDLP), John Tierney (SDLP), William Hay (DUP), Mary Nelis (SF); John Hume (SDLP) resigned December 2000, replaced by Annie Courtney (SDLP).

The traditional unit for parliamentary representation in this area was the county of Londonderry and so long as it remained, it was represented by a Unionist. The county was divided in the 1983 boundary review. The constituency of Foyle comprised Derry City Council and seven wards from Strabane. The constituency is bounded to the west by the river Foyle and beyond by Donegal, to the north by Lough Foyle and to the east by the Sperrin mountains. It is a compact unit whose politics is dominated by those of Derry; more than 70 per cent of its population is catholic in faith and nationalist in politics.

John Hume has represented Foyle since it was created in 1983. The most recent boundary commission confined the constituency to the boundaries of Derry City Council, a SDLP stronghold, and moved the wards from Strabane district council to the new constituency of West Tyrone. Hume's main electoral opponent in the last two general elections has been Mitchel McLaughlin, national chairman of Sinn Fein and the leading figure of two SF MLAs for the constituency. There are fewer than 25 per cent of electors who support the unionists, but they were given a choice in 2001 between William Hay of the DUP and Andrew Donaldson, a pro-Agreement liberal from the UUP. There was a slight swing from the SDLP to SF, but it was much smaller than the shift in other seats. Hume had resigned his Assembly seat in December 2000 and it was anticipated that 2001 might be his last Westminster contest. So long as he remains a candidate Hume is likely to retain the seat for SDLP, with McLaughlin making little headway, but much might change when he retires from electoral politics.

LAGAN VALLEY

	2001		1997		1992 notional	
Electorate and turnout	72,671	63.2	71,341	62.1	67,551	68.5
UUP	25,966	56.5	24,560	55.4	30,957	66.9
DUP	6,164	13.4	6,005	13.6	–	–
SDLP	3,462	7.5	3,436	7.8	4,192	9.1
SF	2,725	5.9	1,110	2.5	956	2.1
Alliance	7,624	16.6	7,635	17.2	5,453	11.8
Conservative	–	–	1,212	2.7	4,170	9.0
Others	–		352 (2)		542	
MP	Jeffrey Donaldson (UUP)		Jeffrey Donaldson (UUP)		James Molyneaux (UUP)	
Majority	18,342	39.9	16,925	38.2	25,504	55.1

Assembly election 1998 first preferences: UUP 14,339 (30.8), DUP 8,350 (18.0), Alliance 6,788 (14.6), UKUP 5,361 (11.5), SDLP 4,039 (8.7), PUP 3,725 (8.0), SF 2,000 (4.3), NIWC 955 (2.1), 3 Others 953. Electorate 71,661, Turnout 65.7%. MLAs: Seamus Close (Alliance), Billy Bell (UUP), Edwin Poots (DUP), Ivan Davis (UUP), Patrick Roche (NI Unionist Party, originally UKUP), Patricia Lewsley (SDLP).

This constituency is located to the south-west of Belfast and is based on the borough of Lisburn. The council area is second only to Belfast in population – ahead of Derry, and is one of the fastest growing constituencies in Northern Ireland. Lagan Valley takes its name from the river which rises in the Mournes and flows through Belfast. The constituency is divided by the M1 motorway and this has encouraged the development of Moira, Hillsborough and Glenavy as commuters move out of Belfast. The constituency is also the junction for road traffic south to Dublin on the A2. The constituency is predominantly unionist and mainly Ulster Unionist.

The seat was created in 1983 and the Ulster Unionist leader, James Molyneaux, chose it rather than the much-reduced Antrim South. He had DUP opposition only in the inaugural contest but he was regularly opposed by Alliance who were usually over 20,000 votes behind in second place. When he retired before the 1997 general election he bequeathed a very safe seat to his successor, Jeffrey Donaldson. The boundary commission removed four wards Twinbrook and 9,500 mainly nationalist electors to West Belfast but in compensation Lagan Valley gained 6,400 electors around Dromore from Banbridge district council.

In June 2001, Donaldson was defending the largest majority in Northern Ireland – 16,925 - against candidates from the four other main political parties. Since the Belfast Agreement and the Assembly elections he had become one of the main critics of the leadership of his party leader, David Trimble. His criticism of the Belfast Agreement probably limited the damage which Edwin Poots (DUP), a member of the Northern Ireland Assembly and local Lisburn councilor, hoped to inflict on the UUP. However, the strongest pro-Agreement party was the Alliance and their candidate Seamus Close hoped to gain from pro-Agreement Unionist voters disaffected at the attempt to deselect district councillors who supported the party leadership.

The party competition helped turnout increase by 1.1 per cent but there was no change in the result. Indeed, Donaldson increased his majority slightly as neither Alliance nor DUP made any headway.

LONDONDERRY EAST

	2001		1997		1992 *notional*	
Electorate and turnout	60,215	66.2	58,938	64.6	*57,023*	*63.0*
UUP	10,912	27.4	13,558	35.6	*23,287*	*64.9*
DUP	12,813	32.1	9,764	25.6	*–*	*–*
SDLP	8,298	20.8	8,273	21.7	*7,134*	*19.9*
SF	6,221	15.6	3,463	9.1	*1,261*	*3.5*
Alliance	1,625	4.1	2,427	6.4	*2,634*	*7.3*
Others	–		617 (3)		*1,589*	
MP	Gregory Campbell (DUP)		Willie Ross (UUP)		Willie Ross (UUP)	
Majority	1,901	4.8	3,794	10.0	*16,153*	*45.0*

Assembly election 1998 first preferences: UUP 9,954 (25.2), DUP 9,379 (23.7), SDLP 9,366 (23.7), SF 3,860 (9.8), Ind Unionist 3,811 (9.6), Alliance 2,395 (6.1), PUP/UDP 753 (1.9), 1 Other 46. Electorate 59,370, Turnout 67.7%. MLAs: Gregory Campbell (DUP), David McClarty (UUP), John Dallat (SDLP), Arthur Doherty (SDLP), Pauline Armitage (UUP), Boyd Douglas (Ind Unionist).

The Londonderry East constituency is mainly the rural remainder of the old county Londonderry constituency left over after Foyle was created in 1983. It comprises two district council areas, Limavady and Coleraine, and until 1997 it contained twelve wards from Magherafelt district council. The main towns are Coleraine and Limavady; Coleraine includes the campus of the University of Ulster. The constituency also includes a stretch of coast around Portrush. Londonderry East is predominantly unionist but about one third of its electors support SDLP or SF, with the former clearly ahead.

Willie Ross (UUP) had represented the old county seat since 1974 and won the new East Londonderry seat in 1983. Without DUP opposition Ross had a majority of 18,527 in 1992 (pre-boundary changes) and the SDLP were in second place with 22.5 per cent. In 1997 the DUP intervened, running Gregory Campbell and hoping to exploit dissension within the local UUP, and his good showing in 1997 – and the weakness of the UUP in the 1998 elections when Campbell topped the poll – gave the DUP grounds for optimism in 2001.

Ross had a record as a strong opponent of the Belfast Agreement, who had been heavily engaged in opposition to David Trimble in Ulster Unionist Council meetings and was seen as leader of the traditionalists in the UUP. He might have expected to be free from opposition from other unionist candidates in June 2001. In South Belfast Rev Martin Smyth (UUP) was not opposed by the DUP, in part because he was anti-Agreement. However, Ross was not so fortunate. Campbell, now Minister for Regional Development in the Northern Ireland Executive, was not going to give up his strong base. The UUP leadership attempted to mobilize the vote by visiting the constituency but Ross did not join Trimble on a canvass covered by the media. The SDLP was stronger than SF in the area and their combined vote was around 33 per cent in the Assembly election, but the contest was essentially one for the unionist parties to decide; a side bet on whether DUP or UUP would speak for unionists west of the Bann. The outcome was a narrow victory in a divided poll for Gregory Campbell and the DUP.

NEWRY and ARMAGH

	2001		1997		1992 *notional*	
Electorate and turnout	72,466	76.8	70,807	75.2	*68,656*	*76.0*
UUP	6,833	12.3	18,015	33.8	*18,930*	*36.3*
DUP	10,795	19.4	–	–	–	–
SDLP	20,784	37.4	22,904	43.0	*25,740*	*49.3*
SF	17,209	30.9	11,218	21.1	*6,530*	*12.5*
Alliance	–	–	1,015	1.9	*972*	*1.9*
Others	–		123		–	
MP	Seamus Mallon (SDLP)		Seamus Mallon (SDLP)		Seamus Mallon (SDLP)	
Majority	3,575	6.4	4,889	9.2	*6,810*	*13.1*

Assembly election 1998 first preferences: SDLP 18,953 (35.0), SF 14,052 (26.0), UUP 9,819 (18.1), DUP 7,214 (13.3), Independent 1,227 (2.3), NIWC 1,138 (2.1), 3 Others 1,733. Electorate 71,553, Turnout 77.3%. MLAs: Seamus Mallon (SDLP), Paul Berry (DUP), Danny Kennedy (UUP), Pat McNamee (SF), Conor Murphy (SF), John Fee (SDLP).

The Newry & Armagh constituency forms the eastern part of the border with the Republic of Ireland. It comprises all the district council of Armagh and seventeen wards from Newry and Mourne district council. Around two thirds of the electorate support nationalist parties. The constituency is very scenic and mainly agricultural in occupation except for Newry with its port and other facilities. The village of Meigh was one of the centres where foot and mouth disease was detected in Northern Ireland. The northern part of the constituency has Armagh city and its cathedrals. Despite the scenic qualities of the constituency, the hill top forts and the regular helicopter traffic out of security bases could not hide the deadly struggle between the security forces and the IRA over the period of the Troubles in an area described as 'bandit country'.

The constituency was created in 1983 as one of five new seats for Northern Ireland and approximately two-thirds of electors were nationalist in politics. Jim Nicholson (UUP) won the seat in 1983 owing to the split between the SDLP and SF. An early opportunity to re-test opinion occurred with the unionists' decision to resign their seats in opposition to the Anglo-Irish Agreement and seek endorsement in a series of by-elections in January 1986. However, Seamus Mallon (SDLP) defeated Nicholson and subsequently built up his position until he achieved a 7,000 majority in 1992; radical proposed boundary changes were dropped before 1997 and Mallon won again despite a united Unionist candidate and some slippage in the nationalist vote to Sinn Fein.

In June 2001 Seamus Mallon indicated that it was probably his last defense. The Good Friday Agreement and the creation of devolved institutions meant that Mallon, as Deputy First Minister, was heavily committed and had a very high profile in Northern Ireland. Unlike John Hume, who had divested himself of his Assembly seat, Mallon did not have the luxury of such a choice. In 2001 the contest was a test of unionism versus nationalism but more so of the rival tendencies within each sector. Sinn Fein had ambitions for the constituency and had reduced the SDLP 43-21 per cent lead in 1997 to 35-26 in the Assembly elections. They replaced their previous candidate with Conor Murphy who was a rising star. In 1997 the single unionist candidate, Danny Kennedy, had been in second place with 33.8 per cent but his election and commitment to the Northern Ireland Assembly meant that the UUP had to seek a new candidate. Sylvia McRoberts, an Armagh councilor, was eventually selected in a process interrupted by restrictions on population movement imposed due to foot and mouth disease in the area. The Democratic Unionists nominated Paul Berry, who represented the area in the Northern Ireland Assembly, and was also felt to be a rising spokesman for border protestants.

Mallon was returned again but behind him the ground was moving. The DUP outpolled the UUP, but more importantly SF moved up to a good second place and put down a clear marker of its interest in the succession stakes in the constituency.

STRANGFORD

	2001		1997		1992 *notional*	
Electorate and turnout	72,192	59.9	70,073	59.4	*66,420*	*62.8*
UUP	17,422	40.3	18,431	44.3	*20,473*	*49.0*
DUP	18,532	42.8	12,579	30.2	*8,295*	*19.9*
SDLP	2,646	6.1	2,775	6.7	–	–
SF	930	2.2	503	1.2	–	–
Alliance	2,902	6.7	5,467	13.1	*6,736*	*16.1*
Conservative	–	–	1,743	4.2	*5,945*	*14.2*
Others	822		121		*295*	
MP	Iris Robinson (DUP)		John Taylor (UUP)		John Taylor (UUP)	
Majority	1,110	2.6	5,852	14.1	*12,178*	*29.2*

Assembly election 1998 first preferences: UUP 12,514 (29.2), DUP 11,901 (27.7), Alliance 5,216 (12.2), SDLP 3,865 (9.0), UKUP 3,078 (7.2), Ind Unionist 2,247 (5.2), PUP/UDP 1,664 (3.9), Ind Unionist 951 (2.2), SF 614 (1.4), 5 Others 872. Electorate 70,868, Turnout 61.6%. MLAs: Iris Robinson (DUP), John Taylor (UUP), Kieran McCarthy (Alliance), Cedric Wilson (NI Unionist Party, originally UKUP), Jim Shannon (DUP), Tom Benson (UUP) died December 2000, replaced by Tom Hamilton (UUP).

Strangford comprises the territory surrounding the lough of the same name: the Ards peninsula to the east minus Donaghadee and Millisle which were included in North Down by the last Boundary Commission; and to the west as far south as Killyleagh. It also includes suburban areas, from Dundonald to Carryduff, fringing Belfast but forming part of Castlereagh borough council.

The constituency was created from the old North Down constituency in 1983 as one of the five new seats awarded by the boundary commission. The seat was held by John Taylor (UUP) from 1983 until his retirement before the 2001 general election, but there was always a DUP vote in the constituency which was apparent in 1992. The DUP groomed Iris Robinson after her election for the constituency in 1996 to the Northern Ireland Forum and she reduced Taylor's majority in the 1997 election. The normal personality and party clashes were intensified in 1998 with the Belfast Agreement and the division of unionism into pro and anti camps. Robinson topped the poll by 276 votes in the 1998 Assembly elections and the overall UUP margin over the DUP was only 29.2 to 27.7 per cent. However, other anti Belfast Agreement parties polled well to give anti-agreement unionists 18,177 votes to 14,178 for pro Agreement unionists, a majority of 3,999. The constituency was targeted by the DUP as part of their electoral strategy designed to show that they, and not the UUP, represented a majority of unionists in Northern Ireland.

The sudden decision of John Taylor to stand down as candidate in February left his party little time to find a successor. The constituency association chose David McNarry, a successful businessman and

Orangeman who had sought a resolution to the Drumcree dispute. With limited support in the constituency for pro Agreement loyalist parties the campaign turned on whether Alliance or SDLP voters would be prepared to vote tactically for McNarry. The Alliance would not agree to stand down, as they had done in North Down, and there was no chance of support from NIUP voters. In a poll of 60 per cent Iris Robinson won the seat by a majority of 1,110 on a swing of 8 per cent, to the delight of the DUP's electoral strategists.

TYRONE WEST

	2001		1997		1992 notional	
Electorate and turnout	60,739	79.9	58,428	79.2	56,970	71.3
UUP	14,774	30.4	16,003	34.6	–	–
DUP	–	–	–	–	15,738	38.8
SDLP	13,942	28.7	14,842	32.1	12,590	31.0
SF	19,814	40.8	14,280	30.9	8,102	20.0
Alliance	–	–	829	1.8	1,900	4.7
Others	–	–	321 (2)		2,282	
MP	Pat Doherty (SF)		William Thompson (UUP)		NEW SEAT	
Majority	5,040	10.4	1,161	2.5	3,148	7.8

Assembly election 1998 first preferences: SF 15,666 (34.1), SDLP 11,815 (25.7), DUP 8,015 (17.4), UUP 7,237 (15.7), Independent 1,269 (2.8), Alliance 1,011 (2.2), 4 Others 938. Electorate 59,081, Turnout 79.4%. MLAs: Oliver Gibson (DUP), Pat Doherty (SF), Joe Byrne (SDLP), Derek Hussey (UUP), Eugene McMenamin (SDLP), Barry McElduff (SF).

The West Tyrone constituency was created after the most recent boundary commission recommendations and were effective from the 1997 election. It became the eighteenth constituency in Northern Ireland. It comprises two local government districts, Omagh and Strabane. Most of the new constituency had been in Mid Ulster previously but Strabane town had been in Foyle. Around two-thirds of the electorate is nationalist or republican.

William Thompson (UUP) won this new constituency in 1997 with a vote share of only 34.6 per cent. This outcome depended upon an even split in the nationalist and republican vote with the SDLP polling 32.1 per cent and SF 30.9 per cent. The Democratic Unionist Party decided not to oppose Thompson in 2001, in part because of his opposition to the Belfast Agreement, even though they had polled more votes than the UUP in the Assembly election in 1998. Despite the UUP win in 1997, Pat Doherty, vice President of SF, started as favourite and his party's 34.1 per cent in the Assembly elections was more than the combined unionist share. The strength of Doherty, who had been elected on the first count to the Assembly, had a consequence for the tactics of the SDLP. Joe Byrne, who had been in second place in 1997, was replaced by Brid Rodgers, who was Minister for Agriculture in the Northern Ireland Executive, and had been acclaimed for her actions in dealing with the foot and mouth crisis.

The contest to mobilise the unionist and nationalist electorate was intense. The constituency produced the second highest turnout in the UK and a decisive win for Sinn Fein. The fact that the most high profile SDLP candidate was now in third place spoke volumes of the fortunes of SF and SDLP. The outgoing MP, William Thompson, was in second place with 30.4 per cent, the realistic future position for unionists, with fewer than one-third of the votes.

ULSTER MID

	2001		1997		1992 notional	
Electorate and turnout	61,390	81.3	59,086	85.8	56,935	82.5
UUP	–	–	–	–	–	–
DUP	15,549	31.1	18,411	36.3	19,274	41.0
SDLP	8,376	16.8	11,205	22.1	14,360	30.6
SF	25,502	51.1	20,294	40.1	11,340	24.1
Alliance	–	–	460	0.9	1,229	2.6
Others	509		299 (2)		779	
MP	Martin McGuinness (SF)		Martin McGuinness (SF)		NEW SEAT	
Majority	9,953	19.9	1,883	3.7	4,914	10.5

Assembly election 1998 first preferences: SF 20,305 (40.8), SDLP 11,076 (22.2), DUP 10,646 (21.4), UUP 6,938 (13.9), Alliance 497 (1.0), 3 Others 336. Electorate 59,991, Turnout 84.4%. MLAs: William McCrea (DUP), Martin McGuinness (SF), Billy Armstrong (UUP), Francie Molloy (SF), Denis Haughey (SDLP), John Kelly (SF).

The modern Mid Ulster is a west central constituency which takes in the west shore of Lough Neagh and an area west of the Lower Bann river. It comprises the Cookstown and Magherafelt district councils and six wards from Dungannon. The constituency is rural and scenic and includes part of the Sperrins. It is mainly agricultural with some associated industry.

The historic Mid Ulster created in the 1940s had a dramatic electoral history. Like, Fermanagh and South Tyrone, it had a nationalist majority but elections were affected by abstentionism, disqualification and fear of vote splitting by both unionist and nationalist. The nationalist electorate united behind Tom Mitchell (SF) in 1955 but when he was disqualified as a convicted felon, the nationalist vote split and George Forrest (UU) was elected. On his death the seat was won by a 21 year old student Bernadette Devlin (Unity) at a 1969 by-election. She lost it to the Ulster Unionist John Dunlop on another split vote in February 1974 and he held the seat until it was revised in 1983. Rev William McCrea won the seat by 78 votes in 1983 over Danny Morrison (SF) and held it in 1987 and 1992 when the nationalist vote was fairly evenly divided.

In the mid 1990s, the boundaries were comprehensively changed as a consequence of the decision to create a new seat called West Tyrone. This constituency lost Omagh district but gained the remainder of Magherafelt and six wards around Coalisland from Dungannon. The constituency was probably even more nationalist but only an agreed candidate or a degree of tactical voting between SF and SDLP could to remove McCrea as MP. Tactical voting took place in 1997 when Martin McGuinness won the seat for Sinn Fein on a very high turnout of 85.8 per cent. The SDLP vote had fallen back in a 'remove the unionist' vote.

In June 2001 Martin McGuinness was defending a small majority. However, the 1997 victory was a breakthrough for SF in that it not only defeated the DUP member but it also swept SDLP aside from a position of equality to being almost 2:1 ahead in vote share. Since then McGuinness had been elected to the Northern Ireland Assembly and as Minister for Education in the Northern Ireland Executive he was in charge of one of the highest spending departments. None of his former rival candidates for the constituency remained. McCrea was defending South Antrim after a by-election victory there in September 2000.

Turnout was down 4.5 per cent but at 81.3 per cent was still the highest in the UK in June 2001. McGuinness was re-elected with a massively increased majority and over 50 per cent of the vote as the SDLP continued to crumble and the DUP vote fell away somewhat.

UPPER BANN

	2001		1997		1992 notional	
Electorate and turnout	72,574	70.3	70,503	67.8	69,079	65.8
UUP	17,095	33.5	20,836	43.6	26,824	59.0
DUP	15,037	29.5	5,482	11.5	–	–
SDLP	7,607	14.9	11,584	24.2	10,661	23.4
SF	10,771	21.1	5,773	12.1	2,777	6.1
Alliance	–	–	3,017	6.3	2,541	5.6
Others	527		1,095 (3)		2,676 (2)	
MP	David Trimble (UUP)		David Trimble (UUP)		David Trimble (UUP)	
Majority	2,058	4.0	9,252	19.4	16,163	35.5

Assembly election 1998 first preferences: UUP 14,559 (28.9), SDLP 11,947 (23.7), DUP 7,812 (15.5), SF 7,216 (14.3), Ind Unionist 4,855 (9.6), Alliance 1,556 (3.1), UKUP 1,405 (2.8), 5 Others 1,049. Electorate 70,852, Turnout 72.3%. MLAs: David Trimble (UUP), Brid Rogers (SDLP), Dara O'Hagan (SF), Mervyn Carrick (DUP), Denis Watson (Ind Unionist), George Savage (UUP).

Upper Bann lies to the south of Lough Neagh and is mainly the northern and eastern part of the old county Armagh seat. It is named after the river Bann which rises in the Mournes and flows into the lough. The constituency comprises the Craigavon borough council area and nine ward from Banbridge district. The seat is mainly rural with a strong dependence on agriculture, but it also contains. Lurgan and Portadown, the two towns which were the basis for the new city of Craigavon (whose growth has not fulfilled the expectations of 1960s planners). The constituency also includes the town of Banbridge and a section of the M1 motorway.

The constituency was created in 1983 and the former MP for the county seat, Harold McCusker (UUP), won it easily. Traditionally the constituency is a stronghold of Ulster Unionism. McCusker easily won the 1986 by-election protest at the Anglo Irish Agreement. However, his sudden death at 50 in 1990 produced the vacancy which resulted in the election of the current MP, David Trimble, who was elected leader of the UUP in succession to James Molyneaux in 1995. The Drumcree dispute meant that the MP had a very high profile during the marching season. The constituency was largely unchanged in the boundary review before the 1997 general election.

Trimble's position is not completely dominant. There are nationalist voters in the area, who elected Brid Rogers (SDLP) to the Assembly, and a DUP presence. The division in unionist opinion over the Belfast Agreement as expressed in the Assembly election showed the UUP only a few hundred votes ahead of anti-Agreement unionists. The general election in June 2001 was very keenly fought. The DUP promoted David Simpson, virtually unknown outside the constituency, but as a businessman, gospel singer and Orangeman he had appeal for anti-Agreement voters. In their electoral strategy this was the seat where a victory for DUP would cut the head off the pro-Agreement campaign among unionists. In was a very bitter contest where the MP and his wife had to be given tight police protection on entering the counting centre. Trimble had a majority of 2,058, though the returning officer was intimidated into giving a recount. His vote share per cent was down ten per cent while that of Simpson (DUP) was up eighteen per cent. It may have been fortunate for Trimble that the Alliance party had not run their usual candidate. A hostile crowd jostled the newly elected MP and his wife despite the close attention of personal security officers. The competition between the nationalist parties showed SF ahead for the first time.

Index of Constituencies

Constituency	Party	Maj 2001	(%)	Chapter	Page
Battersea	Lab	5,053	13.7	London–Inner South	110
Beaconsfield	Con	13,065	31.0	Buckinghamshire	202
Beckenham	Con	4,959	10.9	London–Outer South East	125
Bedford	Lab	6,157	15.2	Bedfordshire	182
Bedfordshire Mid	Con	8,066	17.3	Bedfordshire	183
Bedfordshire North East	Con	8,577	19.0	Bedfordshire	184
Bedfordshire South West	Con	776	1.8	Bedfordshire	185
Belfast East	DUP	7,117	19.3	Northern Ireland	968
Belfast North	DUP	6,387	15.6	Northern Ireland	970
Belfast South	UUP	5,399	14.2	Northern Ireland	972
Belfast West	SF	19,342	47.2	Northern Ireland	974
Berwick-upon-Tweed	LD	8,458	23.3	Northumberland	530
Bethnal Green & Bow	Lab	10,057	26.2	London–East	92
Beverley & Holderness	Con	781	1.7	Humberside	416
Bexhill & Battle	Con	10,503	23.5	East Sussex	612
Bexleyheath & Crayford	Lab	1,472	3.6	London–Outer South East	126
Billericay	Con	5,013	11.0	Essex	311
Birkenhead	Lab	15,591	53.8	Merseyside	493
Birmingham Edgbaston	Lab	4,698	12.4	West Mids–Birmingham	657
Birmingham Erdington	Lab	9,962	32.6	West Mids–Birmingham	658
Birmingham Hall Green	Lab	6,648	20.1	West Mids–Birmingham	659
Birmingham Hodge Hill	Lab	11,618	43.9	West Mids–Birmingham	660
Birmingham Ladywood	Lab	18,143	57.6	West Mids–Birmingham	661
Birmingham Northfield	Lab	7,798	26.4	West Mids–Birmingham	662
Birmingham Perry Barr	Lab	8,753	23.4	West Mids–Birmingham	663
Birmingham Selly Oak	Lab	10,339	25.8	West Mids–Birmingham	664
Birmingham Sparkbrook & Small Heath	Lab	16,246	44.3	West Mids–Birmingham	665
Birmingham Yardley	Lab	2,576	8.6	West Mids–Birmingham	666
Bishop Auckland	Lab	13,926	36.1	County Durham	299
Blaby	Con	6,209	13.0	Leicestershire	469
Blackburn	Lab	9,249	23.0	Lancashire	451
Blackpool North & Fleetwood	Lab	5,721	13.4	Lancashire	452
Blackpool South	Lab	8,262	21.3	Lancashire	453
Blaenau Gwent	Lab	19,313	60.9	South Wales East	908
Blaydon	Lab	7,809	21.1	Tyne & Wear	633
Blyth Valley	Lab	12,188	35.3	Northumberland	531
Bognor Regis & Littlehampton	Con	5,643	14.5	West Sussex	623
Bolsover	Lab	18,777	49.1	Derbyshire	260
Bolton North East	Lab	8,422	21.6	Greater Manchester	341
Bolton South East	Lab	12,871	37.7	Greater Manchester	342
Bolton West	Lab	5,518	13.4	Greater Manchester	343

Constituency	Party	Maj 2001	(%)	Chapter	Page
Dorset South	Lab	153	0.3	Dorset	293
Dorset West	Con	1,414	2.9	Dorset	294
Dover	Lab	5,199	11.6	Kent	435
Down North	UUP	7,324	19.7	Northern Ireland	976
Down South	SDLP	13,858	26.6	Northern Ireland	978
Dudley North	Lab	6,800	17.6	West Mids-Black Country	672
Dudley South	Lab	6,817	18.8	West Mids-Black Country	673
Dulwich & West Norwood	Lab	12,310	32.2	London-Inner South	113
Dumbarton	Lab	9,575	28.2	West of Scotland	853
Dumfries	Lab	8,834	20.7	South of Scotland	844
Dundee East	Lab	4,466	13.8	North East Scotland	833
Dundee West	Lab	6,800	23.3	North East Scotland	834
Dunfermline East	Lab	15,063	50.1	Mid Scotland & Fife	811
Dunfermline West	Lab	10,980	35.4	Mid Scotland & Fife	812
Durham North	Lab	18,683	48.4	County Durham	302
Durham North West	Lab	16,333	41.6	County Durham	303
Ealing Acton & Shepherd's Bush	Lab	10,789	29.0	London-West	156
Ealing North	Lab	11,837	26.3	London-West	157
Ealing Southall	Lab	13,683	29.2	London-West	158
Easington	Lab	21,949	66.5	County Durham	304
East Ham	Lab	21,032	56.4	London-East	95
East Kilbride	Lab	12,755	30.6	Central Scotland	765
East Lothian	Lab	10,830	29.4	South of Scotland	845
Eastbourne	Con	2,154	4.8	East Sussex	615
Eastleigh	LD	3,058	6.4	Hampshire	372
Eastwood	Lab	9,141	18.9	West of Scotland	854
Eccles	Lab	14,528	43.8	Greater Manchester	348
Eddisbury	Con	4,568	10.3	Cheshire	224
Edinburgh Central	Lab	8,142	23.7	Lothians	800
Edinburgh East & Musselburgh	Lab	12,168	35.3	Lothians	801
Edinburgh North & Leith	Lab	8,817	26.5	Lothians	802
Edinburgh Pentlands	Lab	1,742	4.5	Lothians	803
Edinburgh South	Lab	5,499	14.8	Lothians	804
Edinburgh West	LD	7,589	19.2	Lothians	805
Edmonton	Lab	9,772	28.1	London-North	75
Ellesmere Port & Neston	Lab	10,861	26.2	Cheshire	225
Elmet	Lab	4,171	9.1	West Yorkshire	739
Eltham	Lab	6,996	20.7	London-Outer South East	128
Enfield North	Lab	2,291	6.0	London-North	76
Enfield Southgate	Lab	5,546	13.2	London-North	77
Epping Forest	Con	8,426	19.9	Essex	317

Constituency	Party	Maj 2001	(%)	Chapter	Page
Great Grimsby	Lab	11,484	34.8	Humberside	419
Great Yarmouth	Lab	4,564	11.3	Norfolk	511
Greenock & Inverclyde	Lab	9,890	34.8	West of Scotland	855
Greenwich & Woolwich	Lab	13,433	41.3	London-Outer South East	130
Guildford	LD	538	1.1	Surrey	600
Hackney North & Stoke Newington	Lab	13,651	46.1	London-East	96
Hackney South & Shoreditch	Lab	15,049	49.6	London-East	97
Halesowen & Rowley Regis	Lab	7,359	18.7	West Mids–Black Country	674
Halifax	Lab	6,129	15.2	West Yorkshire	740
Haltemprice & Howden	Con	1,903	4.3	Humberside	420
Halton	Lab	17,428	50.6	Cheshire	226
Hamilton North & Bellshill	Lab	13,561	44.6	Central Scotland	768
Hamilton South	Lab	10,775	40.3	Central Scotland	769
Hammersmith & Fulham	Lab	2,015	4.5	London–West	160
Hampshire East	Con	8,890	17.7	Hampshire	375
Hampshire North East	Con	13,257	30.2	Hampshire	376
Hampshire North West	Con	12,009	24.7	Hampshire	377
Hampstead & Highgate	Lab	7,876	22.2	London–North	79
Harborough	Con	5,252	11.3	Leicestershire	472
Harlow	Lab	5,228	13.0	Essex	319
Harrogate & Knaresborough	LD	8,845	21.0	North Yorkshire	703
Harrow East	Lab	11,124	23.1	London–West	161
Harrow West	Lab	6,156	13.2	London–West	162
Hartlepool	Lab	14,571	38.3	Cleveland	234
Harwich	Lab	2,596	5.4	Essex	320
Hastings & Rye	Lab	4,308	10.5	East Sussex	616
Havant	Con	4,207	10.4	Hampshire	378
Hayes & Harlington	Lab	13,466	41.6	London–West	163
Hazel Grove	LD	8,435	21.9	Greater Manchester	349
Hemel Hempstead	Lab	3,742	8.2	Hertfordshire	403
Hemsworth	Lab	15,636	44.4	West Yorkshire	741
Hendon	Lab	7,417	18.2	London–North	80
Henley	Con	8,458	19.0	Oxfordshire	552
Hereford	LD	968	2.2	Hereford & Worcester	391
Hertford & Stortford	Con	5,603	11.9	Hertfordshire	404
Hertfordshire North East	Con	3,444	7.7	Hertfordshire	405
Hertfordshire South West	Con	8,181	17.3	Hertfordshire	406
Hertsmere	Con	4,902	11.8	Hertfordshire	407
Hexham	Con	2,529	6.0	Northumberland	532
Heywood & Middleton	Lab	11,670	30.1	Greater Manchester	350
High Peak	Lab	4,489	9.3	Derbyshire	269

Constituency	Party	Maj 2001	(%)	Chapter	Page
Leicester West	Lab	9,639	29.0	Leicestershire	476
Leicestershire North West	Lab	8,157	18.1	Leicestershire	477
Leigh	Lab	16,362	46.4	Greater Manchester	351
Leominster	Con	10,367	22.2	Hereford & Worcester	392
Lewes	LD	9,710	21.4	East Sussex	618
Lewisham Deptford	Lab	15,293	52.5	London-Inner South	114
Lewisham East	Lab	9,003	29.9	London-Inner South	115
Lewisham West	Lab	11,920	38.7	London-Inner South	116
Leyton & Wanstead	Lab	12,904	38.3	London-East	101
Lichfield	Con	4,426	10.6	Staffordshire	577
Lincoln	Lab	8,420	22.7	Lincolnshire	486
Linlithgow	Lab	9,129	28.8	Lothians	806
Liverpool Garston	Lab	12,494	38.3	Merseyside	498
Liverpool Riverside	Lab	13,950	54.7	Merseyside	499
Liverpool Walton	Lab	17,996	63.2	Merseyside	500
Liverpool Wavertree	Lab	12,319	38.3	Merseyside	501
Liverpool West Derby	Lab	15,853	51.3	Merseyside	502
Livingston	Lab	10,616	29.5	Lothians	807
Llanelli	Lab	6,403	17.7	Mid & West Wales	898
Londonderry East	DUP	1,901	4.8	Northern Ireland	984
Loughborough	Lab	6,378	14.4	Leicestershire	478
Louth & Horncastle	Con	7,554	17.0	Lincolnshire	487
Ludlow	LD	1,630	3.8	Shropshire	560
Luton North	Lab	9,977	25.5	Bedfordshire	186
Luton South	Lab	10,133	25.8	Bedfordshire	187
Macclesfield	Con	7,200	15.8	Cheshire	227
Maidenhead	Con	3,284	7.6	Berkshire	191
Maidstone & The Weald	Con	10,318	22.6	Kent	440
Makerfield	Lab	17,750	50.9	Greater Manchester	352
Maldon & Chelmsford East	Con	8,462	19.2	Essex	321
Manchester Blackley	Lab	14,464	54.5	Greater Manchester	353
Manchester Central	Lab	13,742	53.0	Greater Manchester	354
Manchester Gorton	Lab	11,304	41.5	Greater Manchester	355
Manchester Withington	Lab	11,524	32.9	Greater Manchester	356
Mansfield	Lab	11,038	30.0	Nottinghamshire	541
Medway	Lab	3,780	9.8	Kent	441
Meirionnydd Nant Conwy	PC	5,684	27.0	Mid & West Wales	900
Meriden	Con	3,784	8.5	West Mids-Coventry & S	689
Merthyr Tydfil & Rhymney	Lab	14,923	47.1	South Wales East	914
Middlesbrough	Lab	16,330	48.4	Cleveland	235
Middlesbrough South and East Cleveland	Lab	9,351	21.3	Cleveland	236

Constituency	Party	Maj 2001	(%)	Chapter	Page
Oldham East & Saddleworth	Lab	2,726	6.0	Greater Manchester	357
Oldham West & Royton	Lab	13,365	33.4	Greater Manchester	358
Orkney & Shetland	LD	3,475	20.8	Highlands & Islands	794
Orpington	Con	269	0.5	London–Outer South East	131
Oxford East	Lab	10,344	26.0	Oxfordshire	553
Oxford West & Abingdon	LD	9,185	17.8	Oxfordshire	554
Paisley North	Lab	9,321	34.3	West of Scotland	856
Paisley South	Lab	11,910	39.0	West of Scotland	858
Pendle	Lab	4,275	10.8	Lancashire	461
Penrith & the Border	Con	14,677	33.2	Cumbria	253
Perth	SNP	48	0.1	Mid Scotland & Fife	818
Peterborough	Lab	2,854	7.2	Cambridgeshire	217
Plymouth Devonport	Lab	13,033	31.2	Devon	279
Plymouth Sutton	Lab	7,517	19.2	Devon	280
Pontefract & Castleford	Lab	16,378	52.2	West Yorkshire	751
Pontypridd	Lab	17,684	46.2	South Wales Central	936
Poole	Con	7,166	18.3	Dorset	295
Poplar & Canning Town	Lab	14,108	41.4	London–East	102
Portsmouth North	Lab	5,134	13.9	Hampshire	381
Portsmouth South	LD	6,093	15.5	Hampshire	382
Preseli Pembrokeshire	Lab	2,946	8.0	Mid & West Wales	904
Preston	Lab	12,268	34.0	Lancashire	462
Pudsey	Lab	5,626	12.5	West Yorkshire	752
Putney	Lab	2,771	8.1	London–Inner South	117
Rayleigh	Con	8,290	19.4	Essex	322
Reading East	Lab	5,595	12.8	Berkshire	193
Reading West	Lab	8,849	21.1	Berkshire	194
Redcar	Lab	13,443	35.2	Cleveland	237
Redditch	Lab	2,484	6.7	Hereford & Worcester	393
Regent's Park & Kensington North	Lab	10,266	27.7	London–West	165
Reigate	Con	8,025	20.3	Surrey	602
Renfrewshire West	Lab	8,575	25.6	West of Scotland	859
Rhondda	Lab	16,047	47.2	South Wales Central	938
Ribble Valley	Con	11,238	22.9	Lancashire	463
Richmond	Con	16,319	37.1	North Yorkshire	704
Richmond Park	LD	4,964	10.1	London–Outer South	142
Rochdale	Lab	5,655	14.3	Greater Manchester	359
Rochford & Southend East	Con	7,034	18.8	Essex	323
Romford	Con	5,977	16.7	London–East	102
Romsey	LD	2,370	4.9	Hampshire	383
Ross, Skye & Inverness West	LD	12,952	37.2	Highlands & Islands	796

Constituency	Party	Maj 2001	(%)	Chapter	Page
Southampton Itchen	Lab	11,223	27.1	Hampshire	384
Southampton Test	Lab	11,207	27.0	Hampshire	385
Southend West	Con	7,941	21.2	Essex	325
Southport	LD	3,007	7.3	Merseyside	505
Southwark North & Bermondsey	LD	9,632	26.1	London–Inner South	118
Spelthorne	Con	3,262	7.8	Surrey	604
Stafford	Lab	5,032	11.3	Staffordshire	579
Staffordshire Moorlands	Lab	5,838	13.7	Staffordshire	580
Staffordshire South	Con	6,881	16.3	Staffordshire	581
Stalybridge & Hyde	Lab	8,859	27.6	Greater Manchester	361
Stevenage	Lab	8,566	20.2	Hertfordshire	410
Stirling	Lab	6,274	17.5	Mid Scotland & Fife	820
Stockport	Lab	11,569	32.7	Greater Manchester	362
Stockton North	Lab	14,647	41.3	Cleveland	238
Stockton South	Lab	9,086	20.6	Cleveland	239
Stoke-on-Trent Central	Lab	11,818	41.7	Staffordshire	582
Stoke-on-Trent North	Lab	11,784	39.1	Staffordshire	583
Stoke-on-Trent South	Lab	10,489	29.1	Staffordshire	584
Stone	Con	6,036	13.2	Staffordshire	585
Stourbridge	Lab	3,812	9.5	West Mids–Black Country	675
Strangford	DUP	1,110	2.6	Northern Ireland	988
Stratford-on-Avon	Con	11,802	21.5	Warwickshire	651
Strathkelvin & Bearsden	Lab	11,717	28.2	West of Scotland	861
Streatham	Lab	14,630	39.2	London–Inner South	119
Stretford & Urmston	Lab	13,271	34.0	Greater Manchester	363
Stroud	Lab	5,039	9.1	Gloucestershire	333
Suffolk Central & Ipswich North	Con	3,469	7.4	Suffolk	591
Suffolk Coastal	Con	4,326	8.6	Suffolk	592
Suffolk South	Con	5,081	11.2	Suffolk	593
Suffolk West	Con	4,295	10.1	Suffolk	594
Sunderland North	Lab	13,354	44.8	Tyne & Wear	641
Sunderland South	Lab	13,667	43.8	Tyne & Wear	642
Surrey East	Con	13,203	28.1	Surrey	606
Surrey Heath	Con	10,819	24.0	Surrey	606
Surrey South West	Con	861	1.7	Surrey	607
Sussex Mid	Con	6,898	15.1	West Sussex	627
Sutton & Cheam	LD	4,304	10.8	London–Outer South	143
Sutton Coldfield	Con	10,104	23.3	West Mids–Birmingham	667
Swansea East	Lab	16,148	53.7	South Wales West	954
Swansea West	Lab	9,550	29.8	South Wales West	956
Swindon North	Lab	8,105	19.1	Wiltshire	696

Constituency	Party	Maj 2001	(%)	Chapter	Page
Wantage	Con	5,600	11.4	Oxfordshire	555
Warley	Lab	11,850	37.7	West Mids-Black Country	678
Warrington North	Lab	15,156	39.0	Cheshire	229
Warrington South	Lab	7,397	16.3	Cheshire	230
Warwick & Leamington	Lab	5,953	11.1	Warwickshire	652
Warwickshire North	Lab	9,639	21.7	Warwickshire	653
Watford	Lab	5,555	12.0	Hertfordshire	411
Waveney	Lab	8,553	18.1	Suffolk	595
Wealden	Con	13,772	26.1	East Sussex	619
Weaver Vale	Lab	9,637	24.5	Cheshire	231
Wellingborough	Lab	2,355	4.6	Northamptonshire	527
Wells	Con	2,796	5.4	Somerset	570
Welwyn Hatfield	Lab	1,196	2.8	Hertfordshire	412
Wentworth	Lab	16,449	48.7	South Yorkshire	728
West Bromwich East	Lab	9,763	29.9	West Mids-Black Country	679
West Bromwich West	Lab	11,355	35.7	West Mids-Black Country	680
West Ham	Lab	15,645	53.4	London-East	106
Westbury	Con	5,294	10.5	Wiltshire	698
Western Isles	Lab	1,074	8.2	Highlands & Islands	797
Westmorland & Lonsdale	Con	3,147	6.6	Cumbria	254
Weston-super-Mare	LD	338	0.7	Avon	178
Wigan	Lab	13,743	40.9	Greater Manchester	364
Wiltshire North	Con	3,878	7.3	Wiltshire	699
Wimbledon	Lab	3,744	9.1	London-Outer South	145
Winchester	LD	9,634	16.3	Hampshire	386
Windsor	Con	8,889	21.1	Berkshire	196
Wirral South	Lab	5,049	12.7	Merseyside	507
Wirral West	Lab	4,035	10.0	Merseyside	508
Witney	Con	7,973	16.2	Oxfordshire	556
Woking	Con	6,759	15.8	Surrey	608
Wokingham	Con	5,994	13.7	Berkshire	197
Wolverhampton North East	Lab	9,965	31.6	West Mids-Black Country	681
Wolverhampton South East	Lab	12,464	45.7	West Mids-Black Country	682
Wolverhampton South West	Lab	3,487	8.5	West Mids-Black Country	683
Woodspring	Con	8,798	18.0	Avon	179
Worcester	Lab	5,766	13.0	Hereford & Worcester	394
Worcestershire Mid	Con	10,627	23.7	Hereford & Worcester	395
Worcestershire West	Con	5,374	12.0	Hereford & Worcester	396
Workington	Lab	10,850	25.9	Cumbria	255
Worsley	Lab	11,787	33.3	Greater Manchester	365
Worthing East & Shoreham	Con	6,139	14.3	West Sussex	628

*Labour MP in Shrewsbury & Atcham has now joined the Liberal Democrats